EUROSTAT YEARBOOK 2001

The statistical guide to Europe

Data 1989-99

eurostat

Published by

*Office for Official Publications
of the European Communities
Luxembourg, 2001*

Sixth edition

Edited and produced by
Eurostat

Directorate C: Information and dissemination
C1   *Chr. Bellersen, C. Botto, M. Copers, C. Kormann*

*with the assistance and support of the
following Eurostat directorates:*

Directorate A: Statistical information system, research and data analysis; technical cooperation with Phare and Tacis countries
A4   *Research and development, methods and
      data analysis (F. Foyn, I. Laafia)*
A5   *Technical cooperation with Phare and Tacis
      countries (J. Erbe, A. Krüger)*

Directorate B: Economic statistics and economic and monetary convergence
B2   *Economic accounts and international
      markets: production and analysis
      (J.-Ph. Arnotte, J. Heuschling, C. Hublart,
      F. Lefort)*
B3   *Price comparisons, correction coefficients
      (M. Hussain, P. Klees, C. Olsson)*
B4   *Accounts and financial indicators, statistics
      for the excessive deficits procedure
      (O. Delobbe)*
B5   *International trade in services, direct
      investments, balance of payments
      (S. Pantazidis, P. Passerini, S. Villaume)*

Directorate C: Information and dissemination; transport, technical cooperation with non-member countries (except Phare and Tacis countries); external and intra-community trade statistics
C2   *Transport (H. Strelow)*
C4   *Methodology, nomenclature and statistics
      of external and intra-Community trade
      (T. Allen, C. Corsini)*

Directorate D: Business statistics
D0   *J. Pleyte*
D1   *Special sectors (R. Deiss, J. Migge,
      H.-W. Schmidt, D. Tornaboni)*
D2   *Structural business statistics
      (I. Maquet, N. Navet, P. Sneijers)*
D3   *Production. Short-term business statistics
      (D. Amil)*

Directorate E: Social and regional statistics and geographical information system
E0   *G. Thomas*
E1   *Labour market (B. Delville, A. Franco,
      A. Nobre)*
E2   *Living conditions (C. Mottet, C. Wirtz)*
E3   *Education, health and other social fields
      (M. Beck, D. Dupré, L. Freysson, E. Kailis,
      A. Montserrat, P. Whitten)*
E4   *Regional indicators and accounts,
      population and geographical information
      system (F.-C. Bovagnet, T. Chrissanthaki,
      A. Laihonen, A. Lööf)*

Directorate F: Agricultural, environmental and energy statistics
F1   *Economic and structural statistics for
      agriculture (including forestry)
      (U. Eidmann, G. Mahon, E. Mikkola, J. Selenius)*
F2   *Agricultural products and fisheries
      (D. Cross, S. Ribaille, F. Weiler, F. Zampogna)*
F3   *Environment (D. Heal)*
F4   *Energy (A. Gikas)*

EFTA *(A. Ottestad)*

Maps
      Directorate E, Unit E4: GISCO (C. de Diego Díez)

Translation
      *Translation Service of the European
      Commission, Luxembourg*

Cataloguing data can be found at the end of this publication.

*A great deal of additional information on
Eurostat is available on the Internet:
http://europa.eu.int/eurostat
http://www.europa.eu.int/comm/eurostat/*

*Office for Official Publications of
the European Communities, 2001
ISBN 92-894-0462-0 (printed version, Danish)
ISBN 92-894-0464-7 (printed version, English)
ISBN 92-894-0465-5 (printed version, French)
ISBN 92-894-0463-9 (printed version, German)
ISBN 92-828-8653-0 (electronic version: 1 CD-ROM
contains all 11 official languages of the European
Union)*

One way of better understanding our neighbours is simply by comparing them with us. That is what international statistics are all about. They are an important and down-to-earth way of making these comparisons and a means of measuring how we are doing in our daily lives.

That is why Eurostat, the Statistical Office of the European Communities, produces this yearbook on Europe and Europeans. It compares significant features of each country of the European Union and, in turn, of other European countries, those in EFTA, and the United States of America, Canada and Japan.

Moreover, the yearbook presents all the relevant statistics on the situation of the national economies, thus giving a unique means of analysis of economic capacities of the countries that make up the European Union.

Europe evolves, the yearbook evolves too. The enlargement process is going on and the information society takes on a growing importance. For this edition, a special effort was made to present new data on candidate countries and on the information society.

For ease of comparison, all statistics in this publication are either compiled in the same way or harmonised by Eurostat or accepted by them as offering sensible comparisons. But even when statistics are compiled in the same way, one has to be careful to allow for people's varied backgrounds, be they cultural, economic, or even climatic.

For the European Union to work — to really work — we must continually grow in our understanding of each other. If this yearbook can add — however modestly — to such growth, then truly it has served its purpose.

I invite you to read it, to make comparisons and to get to know your European neighbours just a little better.

Yves Franchet
Director-General

The people   **9**

Age and sex, past, present and future	15
Life and life risk	32
Health and safety	38
Family life	75
International migration	87
Non-national citizens	97
Education	103
People in the labour market	116
Earnings	145
Consumption, spending and housing	151
Income	170

The land and the environment   **175**

Key features	179
Emissions and pollutants	187
Fertilisers, pesticides	192
Waste and recycling	195

National income and expenditure   **197**

Economic growth	203
Contribution to output by industry	208
Consumption and spending	214
Factor incomes	220
Government receipts and spending	224
Social protection	234
Consumer prices and interest rates	246
Balance of payments	249
Trade in services	264
Trade in goods	270
Key figures on the labour market	284
Research and development	290

Enterprises and activities in Europe   **303**

Agriculture	309
Forestry	334
Fisheries	337
Key figures on businesses	344
Industry and construction	350
Distributive trades	366
Services including financial sector	371
Credit institutions	375
Insurance services	377
Information society	379
Energy	384
Tourism	402
Transport	412

The European Union   **421**

Consumer prices, interest and exchange rates	425
EU budget	434
Internal economy	436
The European market	454

The candidate countries   **479**

Population, education	483
Gross domestic product	490
Interest rates, consumer prices	493
Imports, exports, balance of payments	495
Unemployment, labour cost	500
Research and development	507
Industry and agriculture	508
Information society	512
Transport	516

Annexes   **517**

Glossary	518
Geographical nomenclature	530
Classification of economic activities, NACE Rev. 1	532

1

2

3

4

5

6

eurostat

How can I use the Eurostat Yearbook? What kind of information is available in the Yearbook?

The aim has been to give statistics from the point of view of the user rather than the producer. Eurostat figures have therefore been supplemented by statistics published by other international producers of statistics. In such cases the source is mentioned. Otherwise the source is Eurostat.

This publication comes from Eurostat, the Statistical Office of the European Communities. The choice and presentation of data do not necessarily reflect the official opinions of the European Commission.

As far as possible the data are in time series covering 1989–99. This enables the reader to compare the present situation of Member States and other countries as well as their recent development.

However, not all statistics used for this sixth edition lend themselves to such treatment. For example, some statistics are produced with higher priority given to reflecting the present situation rather than to comparing them with data published 10 years ago. Other statistics are produced with emphasis on detailed rather than rapid publication. And as all statistics originate from national sources, different priorities have influenced data availability, comparability and timeliness. This is reflected in this publication by some subjects being better covered than others.

This year, a new theme was integrated in chapter 4: information society. Chapter 6, dedicated to candidate countries contains a lot of new series.

The publication includes data on the EU-15 (total of Member States of the EU), EUR-11 (countries participating in the euro zone) and as far as possible the EFTA countries, the United States, Canada and Japan.

Germany is included in three different ways. Some tables and graphs include Germany as constituted prior to the unification of 3 October 1990 (D-W), while D-E constitutes the new *Länder* and East Berlin. Many tables now deliver data for the whole of Germany.

All data from Eurostat were extracted on 15 September 2000.

How can I find something in the Yearbook?

The yearbook was prepared to be a useful and user-friendly guide.

Main tools available at the beginning of the publication:
– a short table of contents
– list of main abbreviations
Chapters:
– there are six chapters, each of them containing themes

– a colour bar at the right-hand side of each chapter has been introduced to aid users looking for a particular chapter.
– a complete list of tables, graphs and maps is available at the beginning of each chapter

Main tools available at the end of the publication:
– glossary
– nomenclatures

Where can I find other information?

Most tables contain suggested further reading. The publications recommended are available through Eurostat Data Shops, national sales and subscription agencies. A list is included at the end of the publication.

A complete list of Eurostat publications can also be downloaded on Eurostat web site:
www.europa.eu.int/comm/eurostat/
or
http://europa.eu.int/comm/eurostat/

The data available in the yearbook is a very small selection of our databases. You may need more detailed data, or longer historical series: for each theme we indicate the domain in the database New Cronos, where this data is available. This data can be ordered from the Data Shop network.

We are interested in your reactions, please fill in the questionnaire and send it back to Eurostat in Luxembourg.

Symbols

-	Nil
0	Less than half the final digit shown
.	Not applicable
..	Confidential data. Data not conclusive or withheld owing to non-disclosure practice
:	Data not available
★	Provisional or estimated figures
#	Rebased, adjusted or recalculated by Eurostat
|	Break in series, because data on each side of the bar are not fully comparable

Maps

Non-coloured regions on maps represent either 'data not available' or 'confidential data'.

NUTS: Nomenclature of territorial units for statistics, 1999.
The number after NUTS indicates the level of regional breakdown.

Figures appearing in the legends of maps should be interpreted as follows:
e.g.   8–   above 8;
       5–8   above 5 and up to 8;
       –5   5 or below.

Abbreviations

EU–15	The 15 Member States of the European Union (B, DK, D, EL, E, F, IRL, I, L, NL, A, P, FIN, S, UK)
EUR–11	The euro zone with 11 countries participating (B, D, E, F, IRL, I, L, NL, A, P, FIN)
B	Belgium
DK	Denmark
D	Germany
D-E	territory of former East Germany
D-W	territory of former West Germany
EL	Greece
E	Spain
F	France
IRL	Ireland
I	Italy
L	Luxembourg
NL	Netherlands
A	Austria
P	Portugal
FIN	Finland
S	Sweden
UK	United Kingdom
BG	Bulgaria
CA	Canada
CH	Switzerland
CY	Cyprus
CZ	Czech Republic
EE	Estonia
HU	Hungary
IS	Iceland
JP	Japan
LI	Liechtenstein
LV	Latvia
LT	Lithuania
MT	Malta
NO	Norway
PL	Poland
RO	Romania
SK	Slovakia
SI	Slovenia
TR	Turkey
US	United States of America
EEA	European Economic Area (EU + EFTA countries without Switzerland)
EFTA	European Free Trade Association
ECSC	European Coal and Steel Community
EAGGF	European Agricultural Guidance and Guarantee Fund
ERDF	European Regional Development Fund
ESF	European Social Fund

EMS	European Monetary System
PPS	purchasing power standard
PPP	purchasing power parities
VAT	value added tax
GDP	gross domestic product
GNP	gross national product
GVA	gross value added
cif	costs, insurance and freight
fob	free on board
n.e.s.	not elsewhere specified
sq km/km²	square kilometre
m³	cubic metre
kg	kilogram
hl	hectolitre
ha	hectare
kWh	kilowatt hour
kgoe	kilogram of oil equivalent
GWh	gigawatt hour (10^6 kWh)
t	tonne (metric ton)
GT	gross tonnage
tkm	tonne-km
toe	tonne of oil equivalent
GBAORD	Government budget appropriation outlays for research and development

Money

ECU	European currency unit
EUR	euro – European currency as from 1.1.1999
ECU/EUR	data up to 31.12.1998 in ecu, from 1.1.1999 in euro
ATS	Austrian schilling
BEF	Belgian franc
DEM	German mark
DKK	Danish crown (krone)
ESP	Spanish peseta
FIM	Finnish markka
FRF	French franc
GBP	Pound sterling
GRD	Greek drachma
IEP	Irish pound
ITL	Italian lira
LUF	Luxembourg franc
NLG	Dutch guilder
PTE	Portuguese escudo
SEK	Swedish crown (krona)
CAD	Canadian dollar
JPY	Japanese yen
USD	US dollar

the people

1

Age and sex, past, present and future 15
Total population at 1 January. 1 000s 16
Population projections by different organisations. 1 000s: 16
Eurostat, low estimate 16
Eurostat, baseline estimate 16
Eurostat, high estimate 16
National statistical institutes 16
United Nations 16
Total population. EU-15. Millions 17
World population 17
Population increase . 1989 = 100 18
Population increase per 1 000 people 18
Crude rate of total population change. Average 1995–97 19
Natural population increase per 1 000 inhabitants 20
Net migration including corrections per 1 000 people 20
Natural population increase and net migration, including corrections, per 1 000 inhabitants. EU-15 21
Population by age. 1999 22
People aged under 15 as % of total population 24
People aged 15 to 24 as % of total population 24
People aged under 15. EU-15. Millions 25
People aged 15 to 24. EU-15. Millions 25
People aged 25 to 49 as % of total population 26
People aged 50 to 64 as % of total population 26
People aged 25 to 49. EU-15. Millions 27
People aged 50 to 64. EU-15. Millions 27
People aged 65 to 79 as % of total population 28
People aged 80 or over as % of total population 28
People aged 65 to 79. EU-15. Millions 29
People aged 80 or over. EU-15. Millions 29
Women per 100 men 30
Women per 100 men of their total age group 30
Women per 100 men at different ages. EU-15. 1999 31
Women per 100 men 31

Life and life risks 32
Life expectancy at birth: girls 32
Life expectancy at birth: boys 32
Life expectancy at birth: difference between girls and boys. 1999 33
Life expectancy at birth: boys and girls. EU-15 33
Life expectancy at birth for 1997: girls 34
Life expectancy at 65: women 35
Life expectancy at 65: men 35
Life expectancy at 65: difference between women and men. 1998 36
Life expectancy at 65: women and men. EU-15 36
Infant mortality, per 1 000 live births 37
Perinatal mortality, per 1 000 live births 37

Health and safety 38
Self-perception of a person's own health (16 + years), % (non-standardised). 1996 38
Hampered in daily activities because of chronic conditions (16 + years), % (non-standardised). 1996 38
Self-perception of a person's own health (16 + years), % (non-standardised). 1996 39
Hampered in daily activities because of chronic conditions (16 + years), % (non-standardised). 1996 39
Body mass index (BMI), % of population. 1996 40

Participation in some physical activities by age group (%). 1997 40
Percentage of total energy available from fat 41
Average number of calories per person/day. kcal 41
Average amount of pure alcohol available on the market per person (older than 15) per year. Litres 42
Average number of cigarettes available on the market per person per year 42
Percentage of population (age over 15), who are daily cigarette smokers, by sex and age groups. 1995 43
Some characteristics of persons treated for drug problems 44
AIDS incidence rates per million population by year of diagnosis, with adjustments for reporting delays 45
Cumulative AIDS cases by transmission group. People aged 13 or over, reported by 31 December 1999. % 45
Incidence of type of cancer in 1996. Age standardised rate per 100 000 males using a standard world population 46
Incidence of type of cancer in 1996. Age standardised rate per 100 000 females using a standard world population 46
Incidence of type of cancer in 1996. Age standardised rate per 100 000 males using a standard world population 47
Incidence of type of cancer in 1996. Age standardised rate per 100 000 females using a standard world population 47
Incidence of tuberculosis, total per 100 000 persons 48
Incidence of diseases preventable by recommended immunisation, total per 100 000 persons. 1996–98 49
Prevalence rate (per 10 000 births, per year) of some congenital anomalies. EU-15. 1980–96 50
Estimated cases (per 1 000) of all dementia and Alzheimer's disease over population aged more than 65 years. 1997 50
Main causes of death (% of total causes) (EU-15). 1997 51
Standard death rates by 65, causes per 100 000 men. EU-15. 1997 52
Standard death rates by 65, causes per 100 000 women. EU 15. 1997 54
Death (SDR) from ischaemic heart diseases: women per 100 000 women 56
Death (SDR) from ischaemic heart diseases: men per 100 000 men 56
Death (SDR) from cerebrovascular diseases: women per 100 000 women 57
Death (SDR) from cerebrovascular diseases: men per 100 000 men 57
Death (SDR) from cancer: women per 100 000 women 58
Death (SDR) from cancer: men per 100 000 men 58
Death (CDR) from cancer. 1996 59
Death (SDR) by suicide: women per 100 000 women 60
Death (SDR) by suicide: men per 100 000 men 60
Deaths (SDR) in motor-vehicle traffic accidents: women per 100 000 women 61
Deaths (SDR) in motor-vehicle traffic accidents: men per 100 000 men 61
Deaths (CDR) in motor-vehicle traffic accidents. 1996 62
Leisure and home accidents by place of accident (in % of total). EU-15. 1997–98 63
Number of accidents at work with more than three days' absence by main branches and high-risk sectors. EU-15 64
Number of fatal accidents at work by main branches and high-risk sectors. EU-15 64

CONTENTS

Rate of accidents at work with more than three days' absence per 100 000 workers by main branch of activity. EU-15 — 65

Rate of fatal accidents at work per 100 000 workers by main branch of activity. EU-15 — 65

Rate of accidents at work with more than three days' absence per 100 000 workers. 1996 — 66

Rate of fatal accidents at work per 100 000 workers. 1996 — 66

Rate of accidents at work with more than three days' absence per 100 000 workers by age group. EU-15. 1997 — 66

Number of recognised cases of occupational diseases by group of diagnosis and age. EU-15. 1995 — 67

Total health expenditure per head of population in PPS — 68

Total health expenditure as a proportion of GDP — 68

Consultations to a general practitioner, medical specialist or dentist during the last 12 months. 1996 — 69

Total number of physicians per 100 000 inhabitants — 70

Total number of dentists per 100 000 inhabitants — 70

Hospital beds per 100 000 inhabitants — 71

Psychiatric hospital beds per 100 000 inhabitants — 71

Discharged hospital patients by main group of diagnosis (patients admitted for night and day). 1998 — 72

Hospitalisation during the last 12 months (16 + years). 1996 (% non-standardised) — 73

Average length of stay in hospital, all causes (in days) — 73

Solid organ transplants in Europe per million population — 74

Family life — 75

Marriages per 1 000 people — 75

Divorces per 1 000 people — 75

Mean age at first marriage: women and men. 1998 — 76

Marriages and divorces per 1 000 people. EU-15 — 76

Total fertility — 77

Completed fertility by generation — 77

Total fertility and completed fertility. EU-15 — 79

Mean age of women at childbearing — 80

Live births outside marriage as % of all live births — 80

Total fertility rate in 1997 — 81

Fertility by age. 1998 — 82

Average number of persons per household — 84

Proportion of persons living in private households by type of household. 1996 — 84

Percentage of dependent children living in lone-parent families — 85

Percentage of couples living in a consensual union. 1996 — 85

International migration — 87

Immigration from other EEA countries. 1 000s — 87

Immigration from non-EEA countries. 1 000s — 87

Immigration by country of citizenship. 1998. 1 000s — 88

Immigration of nationals as percentage of total immigration — 90

Immigration, total. 1 000s — 90

Emigration to other EEA countries. 1 000s — 91

Emigration to non-EEA countries. 1 000s — 91

Emigration by country of citizenship. 1998. 1 000s — 92

Emigration of nationals as percentage of total emigration — 94

Emigration, total. 1 000s — 94

Asylum applications. 1 000s — 95

Refugee status granted according to the Geneva Convention. 1 000s — 95

Asylum applications by country of citizenship. 1999 — 96

Non-national citizens — 97

Non-national EEA citizens. 1 000s — 97

Non-EEA citizens. 1 000s — 97

Population by country of citizenship. 1.1.1998. 1 000s — 98

Population by country of citizenship. 1.1.1998. 1 000s — 99

Non-EEA citizens living in EU regions as percentage of total population. 1998 — 100

Acquisition of citizenship — 101

Acquisition of citizenship as percentage of non-national population — 101

Non-national EEA citizens living in EU regions as percentage of total population. 1998 — 102

Education — 103

Pupils and students (primary, secondary and tertiary education). 1 000s — 104

Enrolment in education by level. 1997/98. 1 000s — 105

Basic data on education. 1997/98: — 105

Participation rate in pre-primary education. % — 105

Duration of compulsory schooling (age) — 105

Pupils/teachers ratio in primary education. 1997/98 — 106

Average number of foreign languages learnt per pupil in primary and secondary general education. 1997/98 — 106

Percentage of pupils in upper secondary education learning English, French and German as a foreign language. 1997/98. % — 107

Percentage of pupils in upper secondary education enrolled in vocational stream, by gender. 1997/98 — 107

Participation rates in education at all levels by age. 1997/98. % — 108

Participation rate in education for 18- to 24-year-olds, by level. 1997/98. % — 108

Students in tertiary education. 1989/99. 1 000s — 109

Median age in tertiary education. 1997/98 — 110

Women among students in tertiary education. 1997/98. % — 110

Non-national students in tertiary education. 1997/98 — 111

Fields of education chosen by students in tertiary education, by gender. EU-15. 1997/98. % — 112

Women among students in some fields of study in tertiary education, 1997/98. % — 112

Public expenditure on education by level of education as % of GDP. 1997 — 113

Expenditure per pupil/student in public intitutions by level of education (in PPS). 1997 — 113

Percentage of the population aged 25 to 59 having completed at least upper secondary education, women and men. 1999 — 114

Percentage of the total population aged 25 to 59 having completed at least upper secondary education, women. 1999 — 114

Unemployment rates for men and women aged 25 to 59 by educational level. %. 1999 — 115

Unemployment rates by age and educational level. EU-15. 1999 — 115

People in the labour market — 116

Labour force by age group (men and women). 1 000s — 116

Labour force by age group, men. 1 000s — 116

EU-15 population, labour force, persons economically inactive. 1 000s. 1999 — 117

Labour force by age group, women. 1 000s — 117

Activity rate of men and women by age group — 118
Activity rate of men by age group — 118
Activity rate of women by age group — 119
Activity rate of men. 1999 — 120
Activity rate of women. 1999 — 121
Persons in employment: men and women. 1 000s — 122
Persons in employment: men. 1 000s — 122
Persons in employment: women. 1 000s — 123
Employment rates of men and women (15-64). 1999 — 124
Employment rate of men and women by age group — 125
Employment rate of men by age group — 125
Employment rate by age group and sex. EU-15. 1999 — 126
Employment rate of women by age group — 126
Share of industry in employment. 1999 — 127
Share of services in employment. 1999 — 128
Men and women employed part-time as % of total employment — 129
Men employed part-time as % of all employed men — 129
Women employed part-time as % of all employed women — 130
Percentage of involuntary part-time employed — 130
Number of hours usually worked per week — 131
Percentage of persons usually working on Saturday, Sunday, at night or doing shiftwork — 131
Percentage of employees with contract of limited duration. 1999 — 132
Percentage of employed population with a second job. 1999 — 132
Unemployment: men and women. 1 000s — 133
Unemployment: men. 1 000s — 133
Unemployment: women. 1 000s — 134
Unemployment: aged less than 25 years. 1 000s — 134
Unemployment rate of men and women — 135
Unemployment rate of men — 135
Unemployment rate of women — 136
Unemployment rate of population aged less than 25 years — 136
Unemployment rate of women. 1999 — 137
Unemployment rate of men. 1999 — 138
Long-term unemployed (12 months or more), as % of all unemployed — 139
Long-term unemployed women (12 months or more), as % of all unemployed women — 139
Long-term unemployed as % of all unemployed. 1999 — 140
Long-term unemployed men (12 months or more), as % of all unemployed men — 140
Percentage of population not in the labour force: men and women aged 15 years and over — 141
Percentage of men aged 15 years and over not in the labour force — 141
Percentage of population not in the labour force by age and sex. 1999. EU-15 — 142
Percentage of women aged 15 years and over not in the labour force — 142
Long-term unemployment rate in % of total unemployment. 1999 — 143
Unemployment rate of people aged less than 25. 1999 — 144

Earnings — 145
Average gross hourly earnings of manual workers in industry. ECU — 145
Average gross monthly earnings of non-manual workers in industry. ECU — 146

Average gross monthly earnings of employees in industry and services (sections C to K of NACE Rev. 1). Women. ECU — 147
Average gross monthly earnings of employees in industry and services (sections C to K of NACE Rev. 1). Men. ECU — 147
Average gross monthly earnings of employees in industry and services (sections C to K of NACE Rev. 1). Total. ECU — 148
Earnings of women as percentage of men, 1998. Industry and services (sections C to K of NACE Rev. 1) — 148
Monthly net earnings of a couple: manual workers with two average salaries and no children. Manufacturing industries. ECU — 149
Monthly net earnings of a couple: one manual worker's salary with two children. Manufacturing industries. ECU — 149
Social security as % of gross earnings of a single male manual worker's average salary in manufacturing industry — 150
Income tax as % of gross earnings of a single male manual worker's average salary in manufacturing industry — 150

Consumption, spending and housing — 151
Consumption of meat. Volume indices. 1990 = 100 — 152
Consumption of fish. Volume indices. 1990 = 100 — 153
Consumption of fruits and vegetables. Volume indices. 1990 = 100 — 153
Consumption of milk, cheese and eggs. Volume indices. 1990 = 100 — 154
Consumption of potatoes, manioc and other tubers. Volume indices. 1990 = 100 — 154
Consumption of sugar. Volume indices. 1990 = 100 — 155
Consumption of oils and fats. Volume indices. 1990 = 100 — 155
Consumption of coffee, tea and cocoa. Volume indices. 1990 = 100 — 156
Consumption of non-alcoholic beverages. Volume indices. 1990 = 100 — 156
Consumption of alcoholic drinks and tobacco at current prices as % of total consumption — 157
Consumption expenditure in restaurants, cafés and hotels. Volume indices. 1990 = 100 — 157
Consumption of alcoholic beverages. Volume indices. 1990 = 100 — 158
Consumption of tobacco. Volume indices. 1990 = 100 — 158
Consumption of gross rent and water charges. Volume indices. 1990 = 100 — 159
Consumption of fuel and power. Volume indices. 1990 = 100 — 159
Consumption of gross rent, fuel and power at current prices as % of total consumption — 160
Consumption of gross rent, fuel and power. Volume indices. 1990 = 100 — 160
Consumption of clothing and footwear. Volume indices. 1990 = 100 — 161
Consumption of clothing and footwear in current prices as % of total consumption — 161
Consumption of furniture, furnishings and household equipment, including repairs, current operations and domestic services. Volume indices. 1990 = 100 — 162
Consumption of furniture, furnishings and household equipment; including repairs, current operations and domestic services at current prices as % of total consumption — 162
Consumption of personal transport equipment and its operations. Volume indices. 1990 = 100 — 163

1

Consumption of purchased transport and communications. Volume indices. 1990 = 100 ... 163

Consumption of transport and communications at current prices as % of total consumption ... 164

Consumption of transport and communications. Volume indices 1990 = 100 ... 164

Consumption of medical care. Volume indices. 1990 = 100 ... 165

Consumption of medical care at current prices as % of total consumption ... 165

Consumption of education, books and newspapers. Volume indices. 1990 = 100 ... 166

Consumption of education, books and newspapers at current prices as % of total consumption ... 166

Consumption of entertainment, recreational and cultural services, excluding hotels and restaurants. Volume indices. 1990 = 100 ... 167

Consumption of entertainment, recreational and cultural services, excluding hotels, restaurants and cafés, at current prices as % of total consumption ... 167

Percentage of households living in houses. 1996 ... 168

Percentage of households owning their accommodation. 1996 ... 168

Percentage of the population that is living in overcrowded conditions, i.e. more than one person per room. 1996 ... 169

Percentage of households lacking at least one of three basic amenities. 1996 ... 169

Income ... 170

Mean equivalised net income per person ... 170

Equivalised income components. % ... 170

Percentage of persons in households that receive social transfers ... 171

Share ratio S80/S20 — measuring inequality in the income distribution ... 171

Percentage of persons living in low-income households ... 172

Percentage of children (aged under 16) in low-income households ... 172

Percentage of persons living in low-income households by household type. 1996 ... 173

Percentage of persons living in low-income households by household type. 1996 ... 173

eurostat

The EU share of world population is falling fast

With almost 376.5 million inhabitants on 1 January 2000, the European Union ranked third in world population, well behind China (1 253 million) and India (1 009 million).

The EU population rose slightly in 1999, with an increase of about 997 000 inhabitants. In the last 35 years, however, population growth has slowed down. In 1960 the growth rate for EU-15 was just under 8 per 1 000 inhabitants; by 1999 it was only 2.6, ranging from 0.8 in Sweden to 15 in Luxembourg.

In the near future, the total EU population should reach equilibrium or even decline. If current trends for fertility, mortality and international migration continue (Eurostat basic forecast, see graphs on population), the population will peak around 2025 and revert more or less to the current level by 2050.

While the world population increased by approximately 80 million in 1999, the EU accounted for only 1.3 % of this increase, whereas China accounted for 14.6 % and India 20.8 %. At the same time, the United States recorded population growth that was almost three times as high as the EU figure. In most other developed regions, however — such as Japan and Russia — population growth is below the EU level.

The EU share of total world population is thus declining. EU-15 accounted for 12 % of people on the planet in 1950, but the figure has now dropped to 6.2 %. If current population and migration trends continue, by 2050 the figure will have dropped to just 4 %.

More data on this in Eurostat's database

This domain covers the main demographic indicators and gives detailed figures on population, fertility, mortality and nuptiality.

➤ ➤ ➤ **DOMAIN DEMO IN DATABASE NEW CRONOS**

1

Total population at 1 January. 1 000s

	1990	1991	1992	1993	1994	1995	1996	1997	1998	1999	2000	
EU-15	363 763	365 435	367 073	368 994	370 433	371 590	372 670	373 717	374 584 *	375 458 *	376 455 *	**EU-15**
B	9 948	9 987	10 022	10 068	10 101	10 131	10 143	10 170	10 192	10 214	10 236 *	**B**
DK	5 135	5 147	5 162	5 181	5 197	5 216	5 251	5 275	5 295	5 314	5 330	**DK**
D	79 113	79 753	80 275	80 975	81 338	81 539	81 818	82 012	82 057	82 037	82 164 *	**D**
EL	10 121	10 200	10 295	10 349	10 410	10 443	10 465	10 487	10 511	10 522	10 546 *	**EL**
E	38 826	38 875	38 965	39 051	39 121	39 177	39 242	39 299	39 348	39 394	39 442 *	**E**
F	56 577	56 893	57 218	57 530	57 779	58 020	58 258	58 492	58 728 *	58 973 *	59 296 *	**F**
IRL	3 507	3 521	3 548	3 569	3 583	3 598	3 620	3 652	3 694 *	3 735	3 777 *	**IRL**
I	56 694	56 744	56 757	56 960	57 139	57 269	57 333	57 461	57 563 *	57 613	57 680	**I**
L	379	384	390	395	401	407	413	418	424	429	436	**L**
NL	14 893	15 010	15 129	15 239	15 342	15 424	15 494	15 567	15 654	15 760	15 864	**NL**
A	7 690	7 769	7 868	7 962	8 015	8 040	8 055	8 068	8 075	8 083	8 103 *	**A**
P	9 920	9 878	9 865	9 869	9 892	9 912	9 921	9 934	9 957	9 980	9 998 *	**P**
FIN	4 974	4 999	5 029	5 055	5 078	5 099	5 117	5 132	5 147	5 160	5 171	**FIN**
S	8 527	8 591	8 644	8 692	8 745	8 816	8 838	8 845	8 848	8 854	8 861	**S**
UK	57 459	57 685	57 907	58 099	58 293	58 500	58 704	58 905	59 090 *	59 391 *	59 623 *	**UK**
IS	254	256	260	262	265	267	268	270	272	276	279	**IS**
NO	4 233	4 250	4 274	4 299	4 325	4 348	4 370	4 393	4 418	4 445	4 479	**NO**
EEA	368 279	369 969	371 635	373 586	375 053	376 236	377 339	378 410	379 305 *	380 100 *	381 235 *	**EEA**
CH	6 674	6 751	6 843	6 908	6 969	7 019	7 062	7 081	7 097	7 124	7 164 *	**CH**
US	248 143	250 660	253 589	256 537	259 159	261 687	264 162	266 490	269 106 *	271 465	274 035	**US**
CA	27 567	27 952	28 322	28 723	29 077	29 437	29 789	30 111	30 425	:	:	**CA**
JP	123 611	124 043	124 452	124 764	125 034	125 570	125 504	124 645	126 110	126 057	126 299	**JP**

1F2AA

Further reading: European social statistics. Demography. Edition 2000. Eurostat.   D: includes in all years data on the former GDR. JP: 1 October.

Population projections by different organisations. 1 000s

	Eurostat, low estimate		Eurostat, baseline estimate		Eurostat, high estimate		National statistical institutes		United Nations		
	2010	**2020**	**2010**	**2020**	**2010**	**2020**	**2010**	**2020**	**2010**	**2020**	
EU-15	372 082	363 784	385 382	388 233	401 142	416 383	:	:	375 693	371 123	**EU-15**
B	10 089	9 898	10 484	10 658	10 824	11 270	10 328	10 338	10 136	10 017	**B**
DK	5 215	5 075	5 452	5 526	5 679	5 950	5 496	5 568	5 327	5 283	**DK**
D	81 722	79 074	84 854	84 670	88 779	91 559	81 036	78 445	82 032	80 996	**D**
EL	10 614	10 450	11 079	11 269	11 422	11 900	:	:	10 554	10 141	**EL**
E	38 981	37 809	40 372	40 307	42 198	43 504	39 800	39 331	39 089	37 627	**E**
F	59 614	59 307	61 387	62 831	63 626	66 896	61 721	63 453	60 597	61 500	**F**
IRL	3 626	3 652	3 760	3 909	3 939	4 248	3 832	3 947	4 016	4 302	**IRL**
I	55 443	52 753	57 633	56 543	59 820	60 334	57 495	55 939	55 782	52 913	**I**
L	442	445	471	501	501	555	459	488	457	464	**L**
NL	15 900	15 819	16 659	17 204	17 231	18 319	16 470	16 898	15 973	15 876	**NL**
A	8 018	7 882	8 326	8 443	8 749	9 231	8 283	8 354	8 348	8 279	**A**
P	9 927	9 808	10 293	10 513	10 738	11 265	:	:	9 777	9 515	**P**
FIN	5 103	5 008	5 290	5 350	5 519	5 777	5 233	5 222	5 235	5 266	**FIN**
S	8 818	8 792	9 176	9 470	9 609	10 248	9 043	9 222	9 039	9 099	**S**
UK	58 569	58 013	60 146	61 038	62 508	65 326	60 352	61 082	59 331	59 845	**UK**
IS	288	294	297	311	305	326	298	312	304	321	**IS**
NO	4 476	4 494	4 663	4 851	4 819	5 156	4 656	4 831	4 648	4 777	**NO**
EEA	376 878	368 604	390 376	393 429	406 302	421 902	:	:	380 682	376 261	**EEA**
CH	:	:	:	:	:	:	7 443	7 553	7 603	7 624	**CH**
US	:	:	:	:	:	:	:	:	297 989	317 124	**US**
CA	:	:	:	:	:	:	:	:	33 929	36 641	**CA**
JP	:	:	:	:	:	:	:	:	127 315	123 893	**JP**

1F2AE

1F2AK

1F2AF

1F2AG

1F2AH

Further reading: World population prospects: the 1998 revision. United Nations. European social statistics. Demography. Edition 2000. Eurostat. Beyond the predictable: demographic changes in the EU up to 2050; Statistics in focus, population and social conditions, 1997/7. Eurostat.   D: includes in all years data on the former GDR.

1

Three types of population projections can be distinguished: forecasts that aim to provide 'best guesses' for the next 10 to 15 years; uncertainty variants that describe, in addition to a forecast, a plausible range of short- and medium-term developments; and scenarios that attempt to sketch the possible medium- and long-term future. Various institutes produce national population projections and most national statistical institutes frequently compile forecasts, together with at least two uncertainty variants.

Total population. EU-15. Millions

1F2AI

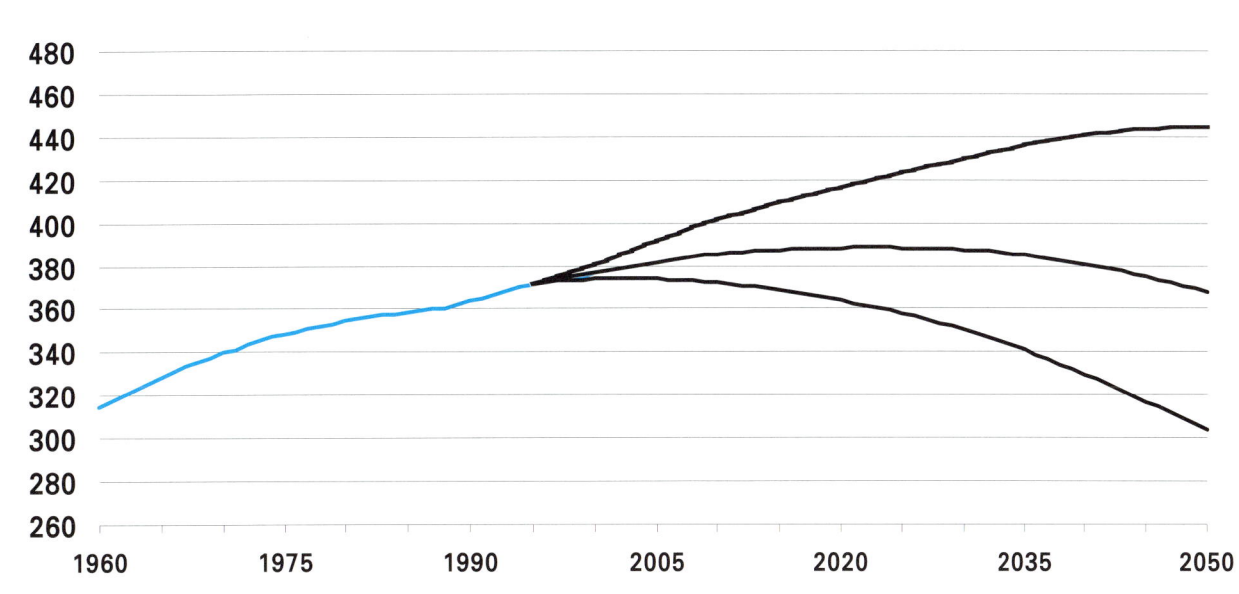

Black: low and high + baseline scenario; colour: observed.

Further reading: Beyond the predictable: demographic changes in the EU up to 2050;
Statistics in focus, population and social conditions, 1997/7. Eurostat.

World population

1F2AJ

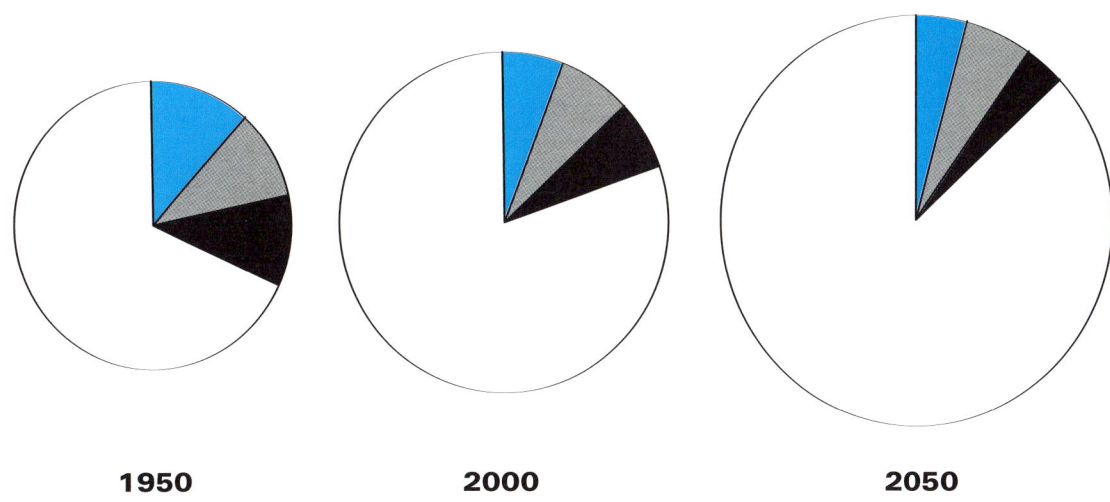

1950   2000   2050

Black: other developed countries; colour: EU-15; white: less developed countries; grey: US, CA, JP.

Further reading: European social statistics. Demography. Edition 2000. Eurostat.

1

Population increase. 1989 = 100

	1989	1990	1991	1992	1993	1994	1995	1996	1997	1998	1999	
EU-15	100,0	100,5	100,9	101,4	101,9	102,3	102,6	102,9	103,2	103,4	103,7	EU-15
B	100,0	100,2	100,6	101,0	101,4	101,7	102,0	102,2	102,4	102,7	102,9	B
DK	100,0	100,1	100,3	100,6	101,0	101,3	101,7	102,4	102,8	103,2	103,6	DK
D	100,0	100,9	101,7	102,4	103,3	103,8	104,0	104,4	104,6	104,7	104,7	D
EL	100,0	100,6	101,4	102,4	102,9	103,5	103,8	104,0	104,3	104,5	104,6	EL
E	100,0	100,2	100,3	100,5	100,8	100,9	101,1	101,3	101,4	101,5	101,6	E
F	100,0	100,5	101,1	101,7	102,2	102,7	103,1	103,5	103,9	104,4	104,8	F
IRL	100,0	99,8	100,2	100,9	101,5	101,9	102,3	103,0	103,9	105,1	106,3	IRL
I	100,0	100,1	100,2	100,2	100,5	100,9	101,1	101,2	101,4	101,6	101,7	I
L	100,0	101,2	102,5	104,0	105,4	106,9	108,5	110,1	111,6	113,0	114,5	L
NL	100,0	100,6	101,4	102,2	102,9	103,6	104,2	104,7	105,1	105,7	106,5	NL
A	100,0	100,8	101,8	103,1	104,4	105,1	105,4	105,6	105,8	105,9	106,0	A
P	100,0	99,6	99,2	99,1	99,1	99,4	99,6	99,7	99,8	100,0	100,2	P
FIN	100,0	100,4	100,9	101,5	102,0	102,5	102,9	103,3	103,6	103,9	104,1	FIN
S	100,0	100,8	101,6	102,2	102,8	103,4	104,2	104,5	104,6	104,6	104,7	S
UK	100,0	100,4	100,7	101,1	101,5	101,8	102,2	102,5	102,9	103,2	103,7	UK
IS	100,0	100,4	100,9	101,4	101,9	102,3	102,6	102,9	103,2	103,5	103,7	IS
NO	100,0	100,7	101,6	103,1	104,2	105,2	106,0	106,4	107,1	108,1	109,4	NO
EEA	100,0	100,3	100,7	101,3	101,9	102,5	103,0	103,5	104,1	104,7	105,3	EEA
CH	100,0	100,8	102,0	103,4	104,4	105,3	106,0	106,7	107,0	107,2	107,6	CH
US	100,0	100,9	101,9	103,0	104,2	105,4	106,4	107,5	108,5	109,5	110,5	US
CA	100,0	101,6	103,2	104,7	106,0	107,5	108,9	110,2	111,5	112,7	113,9	CA
JP	100,0	100,4	100,7	101,1	101,4	101,6	101,9	102,3	102,5	102,7	102,7	JP

Further reading: European social statistics. Demography. Edition 2000. Eurostat.   D: includes in all years data on the former GDR.

1F2BA

Population increase per 1 000 people

	1989	1990	1991	1992	1993	1994	1995	1996	1997	1998	1999	
EU-15	4,5	4,6	4,5	5,2	3,9	3,1	2,9	2,8	2,3 *	2,3 *	2,6 *	EU-15
B	2,0	3,9	3,5	4,6	3,2	3,0	1,2	2,7	2,2	2,1	2,5 *	B
DK	1,1	2,2	3,0	3,6	3,1	3,7	6,8	4,6	3,7	3,5	3,0	DK
D	9,2	8,1	6,5	8,7	4,5	2,5	3,4	2,4	0,6	- 0,2 *	1,6 *	D
EL	6,2	7,8	9,2	5,3	5,8	3,2	2,1	2,1	2,3	1,0	2,3 *	EL
E	1,8	1,2	2,3	2,2	1,8	1,4	1,6	1,4	1,3	1,2 *	1,2 *	E
F	5,4	5,6	5,7	5,4	4,3	4,2	4,1	4,0	4,0 *	4,2 *	4,3 *	F
IRL	-2,3	4,0	7,5	6,2	3,9	4,0	6,2	8,9	11,4 *	11,0 *	10,7 *	IRL
I	0,8	0,9	0,2	3,6	3,1	2,3	1,1	2,2	1,8	0,9	1,17	I
L	11,7	13,4	13,9	13,8	14,3	14,1	15,1	13,2	12,8	12,9	15,0	L
NL	5,9	7,9	7,9	7,2	6,7	5,4	4,5	4,7	5,6	6,7	6,5	NL
A	8,0	10,3	12,7	11,9	6,6	3,1	1,9	1,6	0,9	1,0	1,1 *	A
P	-3,6	-4,3	-1,3	0,4	2,3	2,0	0,9	1,3	2,3	2,2	1,8 *	P
FIN	4,0	4,8	6,1	5,2	4,5	4,1	3,5	3,0	2,9	2,4	2,2	FIN
S	8,0	7,4	6,2	5,5	6,1	8,1	2,4	0,8	0,4	0,8	0,8	S
UK	3,5	3,9	3,9	3,3	3,3	3,6	3,5	3,4	3,1 *	5,1 *	3,9 *	UK
IS	7,4	8,2	15,0	10,2	10,2	7,2	3,7	7,1	9,3	12,2	12,0 *	IS
NO	2,9	3,9	5,6	6,0	5,9	5,4	4,9	5,2	5,6	6,3	7,4 *	NO
EEA	4,5	4,6	4,5	5,2	3,9	3,1	2,9	2,8	2,4 *	2,4 *	2,7 *	EEA
CH	8,1	11,4	13,6	9,5	8,7	7,2	6,2	2,7	2,1	3,8 *	5,2 *	CH
US	:	:	:	:	:	:	:	:	:	9,5	9,4	US
CA	:	:	:	:	:	:	:	:	:	:	:	CA
JP	:	:	:	:	:	:	-0,5	-6,8	11,6	2,0	1,9	JP

Further reading: European social statistics. Demography. Edition 2000. Eurostat.   D: includes in all years data on the former GDR.

1F2BB

1F2BC

Crude rate of total population change. Average 1995–97

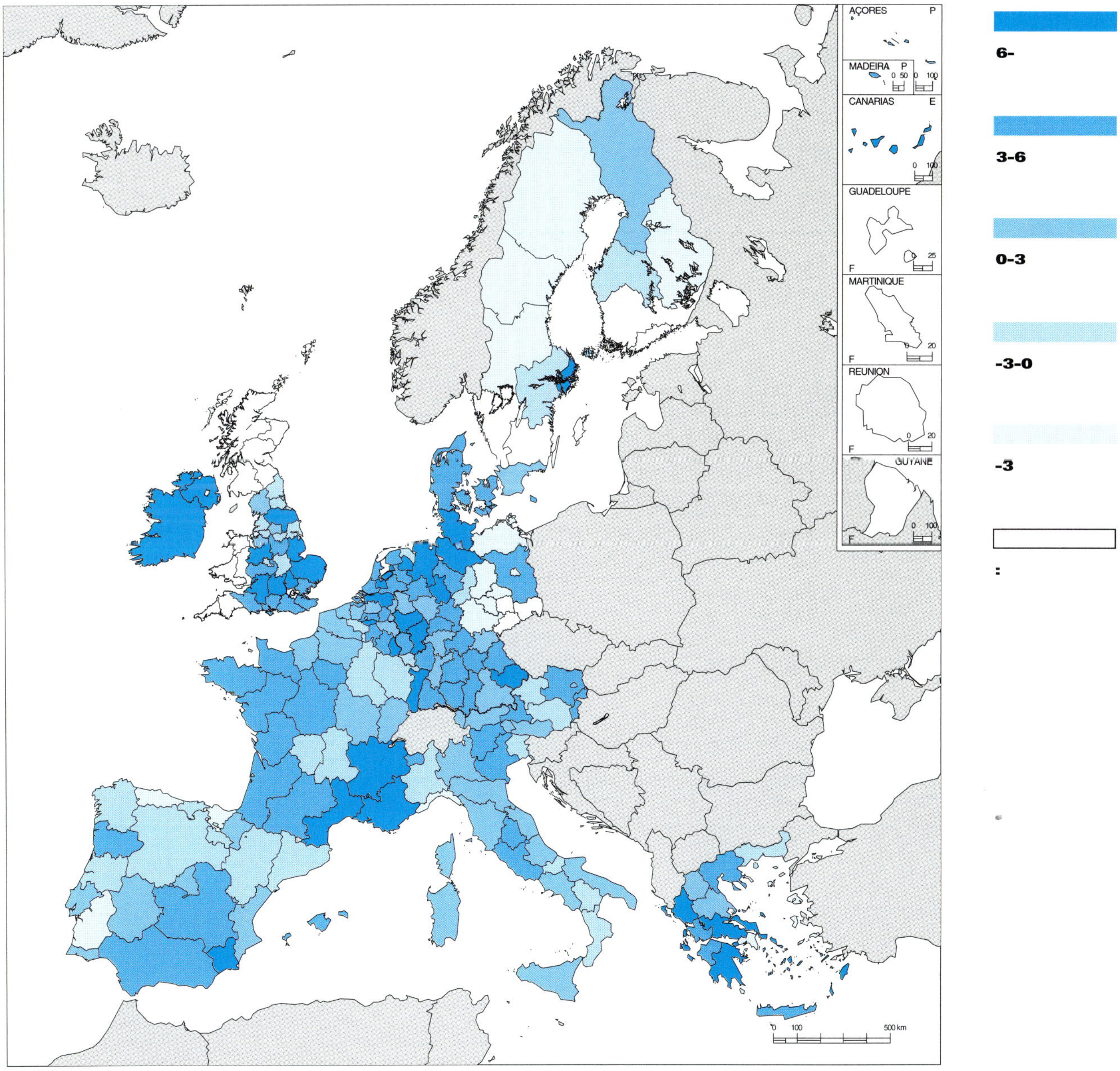

AÇORES	P
MADEIRA	P
	0 50 0 100
CANARIAS	E
	0 100
GUADELOUPE	
F	0 25
MARTINIQUE	
F	0 20
REUNION	
F	0 20
GUYANE	
F	0 100

6-

3-6

0-3

-3-0

-3

:

500 km
0 100

Further reading: Demographic statistics, 2000. Eurostat. Regions, statistical yearbook, 2000. Eurostat.

NUTS 2. NUTS 1: IRL.

1

Natural population increase per 1 000 inhabitants

	1989	1990	1991	1992	1993	1994	1995	1996	1997	1998	1999	
EU-15	1,7	1,8	1,5	1,6	1,0 *	1,0 *	0,7 *	0,8 *	1,0 *	0,8 *	0,7 *	EU-15
B	1,4	2,0	2,2	2,0	1,3 *	1,1 *	0,9 *	1,1 *	1,2 *	1,0	0,9 *	B
DK	0,4	0,5	0,9	1,3	0,9	1,6	1,3	1,3	1,5	1,5	1,3	DK
D	-0,3	-0,2	- 1,0	-0,9	-1,2	-1,4	-1,5	-1,1	-0,6	-0,8	- 0,9 *	D
EL	0,9	0,8	0,7	0,6	0,4	0,6	0,1	0,0	0,2	-0,2	- 0,1 *	EL
E	2,2	1,8	1,5	1,7	1,2	0,8	0,4	0,3	0,5 *	0,1 *	0,2 *	E
F	4,2	4,2	4,1	3,9	3,1	3,3	3,4	3,4	3,4 *	3,4 *	3,4 *	F
IRL	5,7	6,2	6,1	5,7	4,8	4,8	4,6	5,2 *	5,7 *	6,0	5,8 *	IRL
I	0,5	0,5	0,2	0,4	-0,1	-0,4	-0,5	-0,5	- 0,4 *	-0,8	- 0,5	I
L	1,8	3,0	3,2	2,9	3,6	4,1	4,0	4,3	3,7	3,5	4,1	L
NL	4,0	4,6	4,6	4,4	3,8	4,0	3,5	3,3	3,6	3,9	3,7	NL
A	0,7	1,0	1,4	1,5	1,6	1,5	0,9	1,0	0,6	0,4	0,0 *	A
P	2,2	1,3	1,2	1,4	0,8	1,0	0,3	0,3	0,8	0,7	0,7 *	P
FIN	2,9	3,1	3,2	3,3	2,7	3,4	2,7	2,3	2,0	1,5	1,5	FIN
S	2,8	3,4	3,3	3,2	2,4	2,3	1,1	0,1	-0,3	-0,5	- 0,7	S
UK	2,1	2,7	2,5	2,5	1,8	2,1	1,5	1,7	1,6 *	1,5	1,2 *	UK
IS	11,3	12,0	10,6	11,1	10,9	10,2	8,8	9,1	8,5	8,6	7,9 *	IS
NO	3,3	3,5	3,7	3,6	3,0	3,7	3,5	3,9	3,5	3,2	3,2 *	NO
EEA	1,7	1,8	1,6	1,6	1,1 *	1,0 *	0,8 *	0,9 *	1,0 *	0,8 *	0,8 *	EEA
CH	3,1	3,0	3,5	3,6	3,1	3,0	2,7	2,9	2,5	2,3	2,0 *	CH
US	:	:	:	:	:	:	:	:	:	5,9	5,8	US
CA	:	:	:	:	:	:	:	:	:	:	:	CA
JP	:	:	:	:	:	:	2,1	2,5	2,3	2,0	1,9	JP

Further reading: European social statistics. Demography. Edition 2000. Eurostat.   D: includes in all years data on the former GDR.

1F2CA

Net migration including corrections per 1 000 people

	1989	1990	1991	1992	1993	1994	1995	1996	1997	1998	1999	
EU-15	2,8	2,8	2,9	3,7	2,9 *	2,1 *	2,2 *	2,0 *	1,4 *	1,5 *	1,9 *	EU-15
B	0,7	2,0	1,3	2,6	1,9 *	1,8 *	0,4 *	1,6 *	0,9 *	1,1	1,6 *	B
DK	0,7	1,7	2,1	2,2	2,2	2,0	5,5	3,3	2,3	2,1	1,7	DK
D	9,5	8,3	7,5	9,6	5,7	3,9	4,9	3,4	1,1	0,6	2,5 *	D
EL	5,3	7,0	8,5	4,7	5,4	2,6	2,0	2,1	2,1	1,2 *	2,4 *	EL
E	-0,4	-0,5	0,8	0,5	0,6	0,6	1,2	1,2	0,8 *	1,1 *	1,0 *	E
F	1,3	1,4	1,6	1,6	1,2	0,9	0,7	0,6	0,7 *	0,8 *	0,8 *	F
IRL	- 8,0	-2,2	1,4	0,5	-0,9	-0,8	1,6	3,6 *	5,8 *	5,0 *	4,9 *	IRL
I	0,3	0,4	0,1	3,2	3,2	2,7	1,7	2,7	2,2 *	1,6	1,7	I
L	9,9	10,3	10,7	10,9	10,7	10,0	11,2	8,9	9,1	9,4	10,8	L
NL	1,8	3,3	3,3	2,8	2,9	1,3	1,0	1,4	1,9	2,8	2,8	NL
A	7,3	9,3	11,2	10,4	5,0	1,6	0,9	0,6	0,4	0,6	1,1 *	A
P	-5,8	-5,6	-2,5	- 1,0	1,6	1,0	0,5	1,0	1,5	1,5	1,1 *	P
FIN	1,2	1,7	2,9	1,8	1,8	0,7	0,8	0,8	0,9	0,9	0,6	FIN
S	5,2	4,1	2,9	2,3	3,7	5,8	1,3	0,7	0,7	1,2	1,5	S
UK	1,4	1,2	1,3	0,8	1,5	1,4	2,0	1,8	1,5 *	3,6	2,7 *	UK
IS	-3,9	-3,9	4,4	-0,9	-0,7	- 3,0	-5,1	- 2,0	0,7	3,6	4,1 *	IS
NO	-0,4	0,4	1,9	2,4	2,9	1,7	1,5	1,3	2,2	3,0	4,3 *	NO
EEA	2,8	2,7	2,9	3,7	2,9 *	2,1 *	2,2 *	2,0 *	1,4 *	1,6 *	1,9	EEA
CH	5,1	8,4	10,1	5,9	5,7	4,2	3,5	-0,2	-0,4	1,5	3,1 *	CH
US	:	:	:	:	:	:	:	:	:	3,6	3,5	US
CA	:	:	:	:	:	:	:	:	:	:	:	CA
JP	:	:	:	:	:	:	-2,6	-9,3	9,4	-0,4	0,0	JP

Further reading: European social statistics. Demography. Edition 2000. Eurostat.   D: includes in all years data on the former GDR.

1F2CB

eurostat

1F2CC

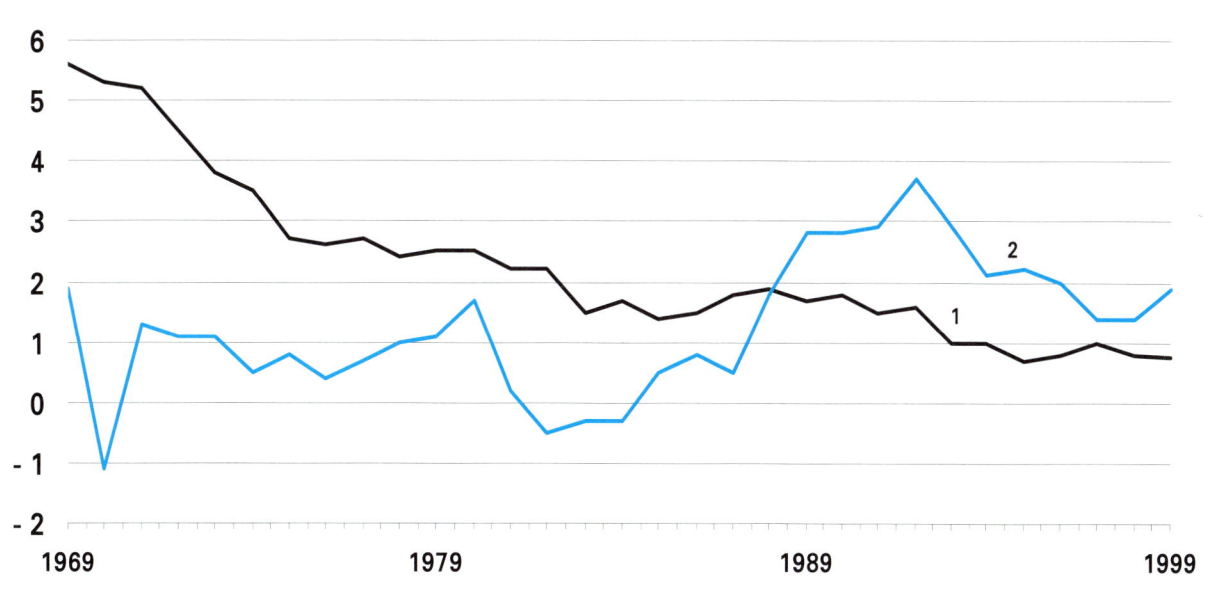

Natural population increase and net migration, including corrections, per 1 000 inhabitants. EU-15

1: natural population increase; 2: net migration.

Further reading: European social statistics. Demography. Edition 2000. Eurostat.

Population by age. 1999

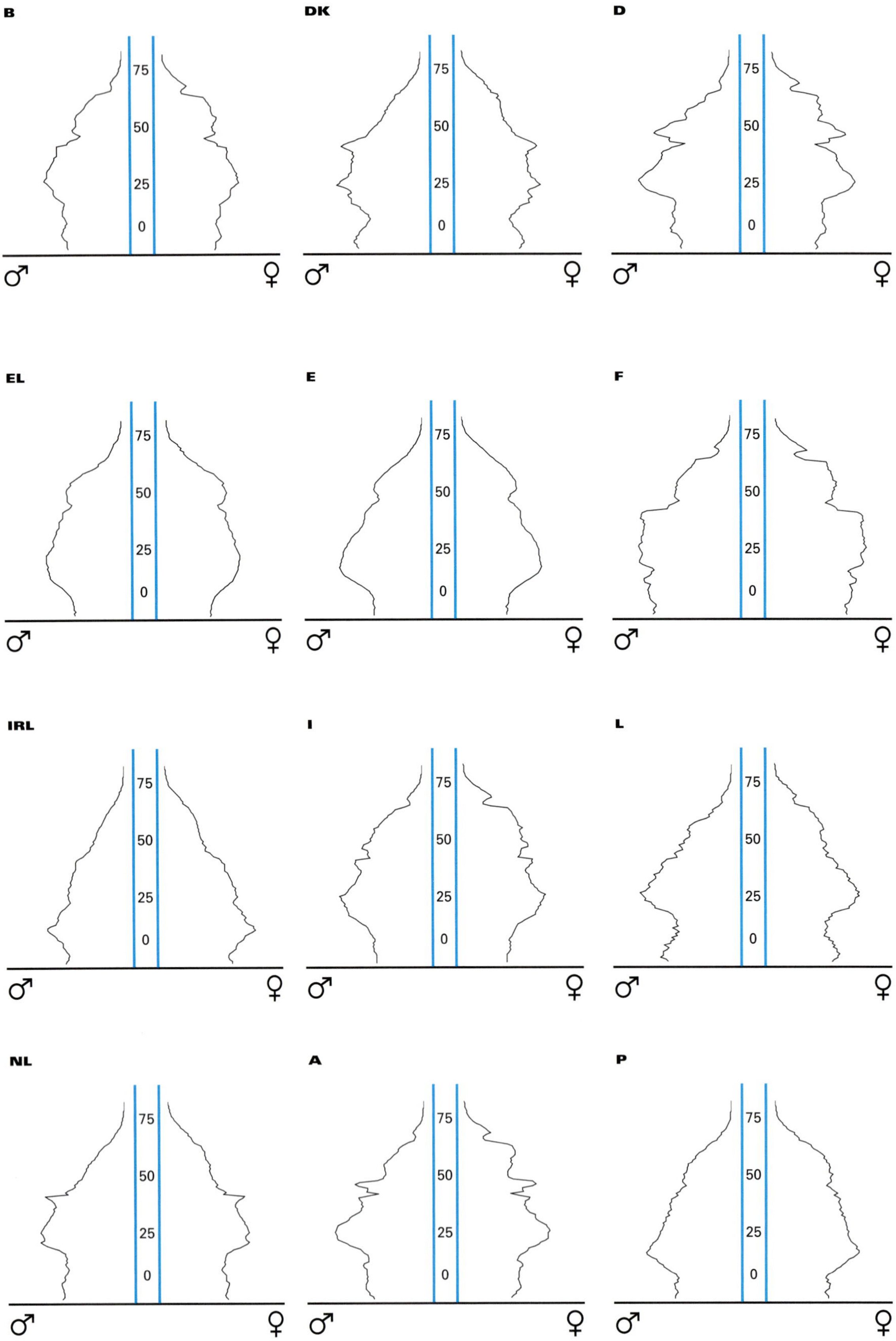

B

DK

D

1E2AA

♂ ♀ ♂ ♀ ♂ ♀

EL

E

F

♂ ♀ ♂ ♀ ♂ ♀

IRL

I

L

♂ ♀ ♂ ♀ ♂ ♀

NL

A

P

♂ ♀ ♂ ♀ ♂ ♀

Vertical axis: age; horizontal axis: %; left: males; right: females.

Further reading: European social statistics. Demography. Edition 2000. Eurostat.

Population by age. 1999

1E2AB

FIN

S

UK

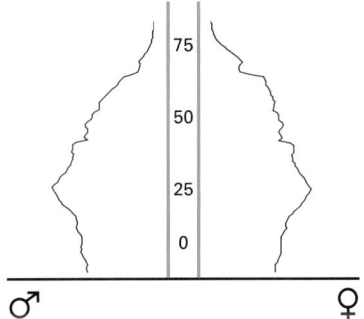

EU-15

LI

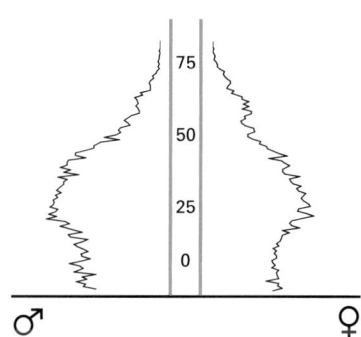

IS

NO

CH

Vertical axis: age; horizontal axis: %; left: males; right: females.

Further reading: European social statistics. Demography. Edition 2000. Eurostat.

1

People aged under 15 as % of total population

	1989	1990	1991	1992	1993	1994	1995	1996	1997	1998	1999	
EU-15	19	18	18	18	18	18	18	17	17	17	:	EU-15
B	18	18	18	18	18	18	18	18	18	18	18	B
DK	17	17	17	17	17	17	17	18	18	18	18	DK
D	16	16	16	16	16	16	16	16	16	16	16	D
EL	20	20	19	19	18	18	17	17	16	16	15	EL
E	21	20	20	19	18	18	17	16	16	16	15	E
F	20	20	20	20	20	20	20	19	19	19	19	F
IRL	28	27	27	26	26	25	25	24	23	23	22	IRL
I	17	17	16	16	16	15	15	15	15	15	:	I
L	17	17	18	18	18	18	18	19	19	19	19	L
NL	18	18	18	18	18	18	18	18	18	18	19	NL
A	18	18	17	18	18	18	18	18	17	17	17	A
P	22	21	20	19	19	18	18	18	17	17	:	P
FIN	19	19	19	19	19	19	19	19	19	19	18	FIN
S	18	18	18	18	19	19	19	19	19	19	:	S
UK	19	19	19	19	19	19	19	19	19	19	19	UK
IS	25	25	25	25	25	25	25	24	24	24	:	IS
NO	19	19	19	19	19	19	19	20	20	20	20	NO
EEA	19	18	18	18	18	18	18	17	17	17	:	EEA
CH	17	17	17	17	17	18	18	18	18	18	18	CH
US	22	22	22	22	22	22	22	22	22	:	:	US
CA	21	21	21	21	21	20	20	20	20	:	:	CA
JP	19	18	18	17	17	16	16	16	15	:	:	JP

Further reading: European social statistics. Demography. Edition 2000. Eurostat.   D: includes in all years data on the former GDR.

1E1AA

People aged 15 to 24 as % of total population

	1989	1990	1991	1992	1993	1994	1995	1996	1997	1998	1999	
EU-15	16	15	15	15	14	14	14	13	13	13	:	EU-15
B	15	14	14	14	13	13	13	13	13	12	12	B
DK	15	15	15	14	14	14	14	13	13	12	12	DK
D	15	14	13	13	12	12	11	11	11	11	11	D
EL	15	15	15	15	15	15	15	15	15	15	14	EL
E	17	17	17	17	17	17	17	16	16	16	15	E
F	15	15	15	15	14	14	14	14	14	13	13	F
IRL	17	17	17	17	17	17	17	17	18	18	18	IRL
I	16	16	16	15	15	15	14	14	13	13	:	I
L	14	13	13	13	12	12	12	12	12	11	11	L
NL	16	16	15	15	15	14	13	13	13	12	12	NL
A	16	15	15	15	14	13	13	13	12	12	12	A
P	16	16	16	17	17	17	17	16	16	16	:	P
FIN	14	13	13	13	13	12	12	12	12	13	13	FIN
S	14	14	14	13	13	13	12	12	12	12	:	S
UK	16	15	15	14	14	13	13	13	12	12	12	UK
IS	17	17	16	16	16	16	16	16	16	16	:	IS
NO	16	16	15	15	15	14	14	13	13	13	12	NO
EEA	16	15	15	15	14	14	14	13	13	13	:	EEA
CH	15	14	14	13	13	13	12	12	12	12	12	CH
US	15	15	15	14	14	14	14	14	14	:	:	US
CA	15	15	15	14	14	14	14	14	13	:	:	CA
JP	15	15	16	15	15	15	15	15	14	:	:	JP

Further reading: European social statistics. Demography. Edition 2000. Eurostat.   D: includes in all years data on the former GDR.

1E1AB

People aged under 15. EU-15. Millions

1E1AC

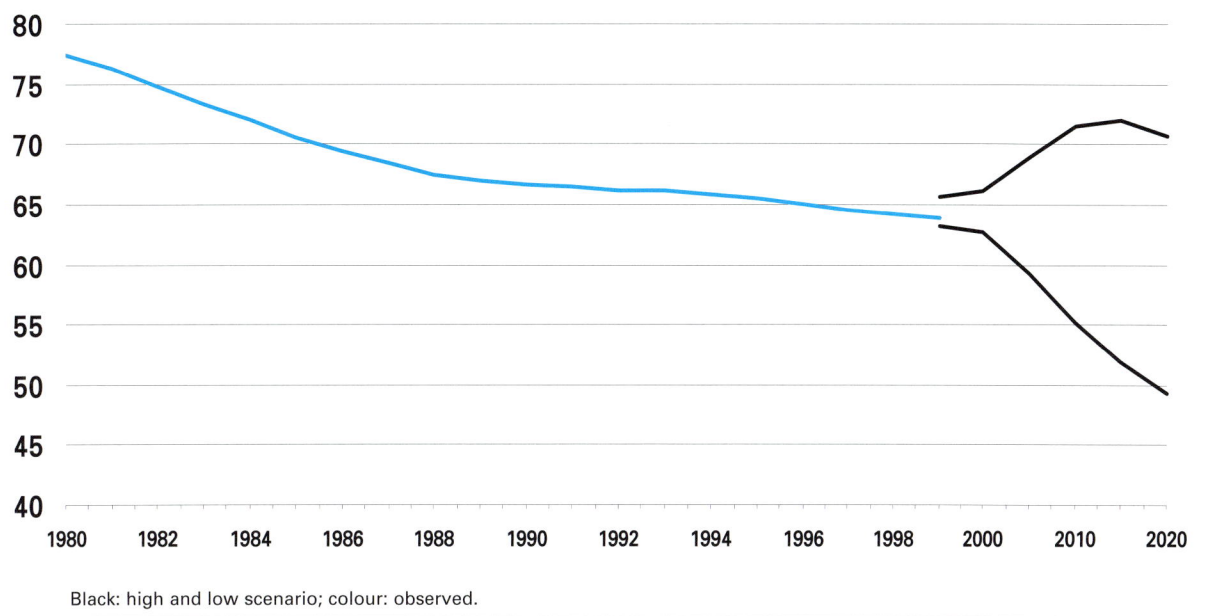

Black: high and low scenario; colour: observed.

Further reading: European social statistics. Demography. Edition 2000. Eurostat. Beyond
the predictable: demographic changes in the EU up to 2050; Statistics
in focus, population and social conditions, 1997/7. Eurostat.

People aged 15 to 24. EU-15. Millions

1E1AD

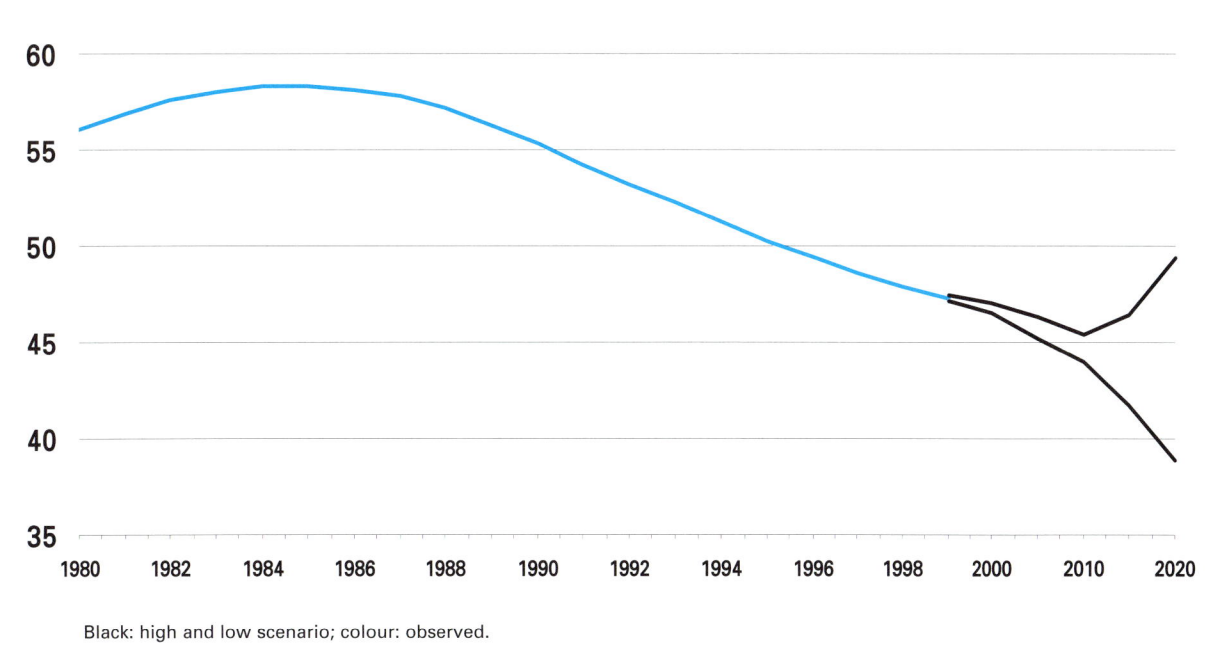

Black: high and low scenario; colour: observed.

Further reading: European social statistics. Demography. Edition 2000. Eurostat. Beyond
the predictable: demographic changes in the EU up to 2050; statistics
in focus, population and social conditions, 1997/7. Eurostat.

People aged 25 to 49 as % of total population

	1989	1990	1991	1992	1993	1994	1995	1996	1997	1998	1999	
EU-15	35	35	35	36	36	37	37	37	37	37	:	EU-15
B	35	36	36	37	37	37	37	37	37	37	37	B
DK	37	37	37	38	38	38	38	37	37	37	37	DK
D	36	36	36	37	37	37	38	38	38	38	38	D
EL	33	33	33	34	34	34	35	35	35	36	36	EL
E	33	33	34	34	35	35	36	36	36	37	37	E
F	35	35	36	36	36	37	37	37	37	37	37	F
IRL	32	32	32	33	33	33	34	34	34	35	35	IRL
I	34	35	35	35	36	36	36	37	37	37	:	I
L	38	39	39	39	39	39	40	40	40	40	39	L
NL	38	38	39	39	39	40	40	40	40	40	39	NL
A	36	36	37	37	37	38	38	39	39	39	39	A
P	33	33	33	34	34	34	35	35	35	36	:	P
FIN	38	38	39	39	39	39	39	38	38	37	36	FIN
S	35	35	36	36	36	35	35	35	35	34	:	S
UK	34	35	35	36	36	36	37	37	37	37	36	UK
IS	35	36	36	36	36	37	37	36	36	36	:	IS
NO	35	36	36	36	37	37	37	37	37	37	37	NO
EEA	35	35	35	36	36	37	37	37	37	37	:	EEA
CH	38	38	38	39	39	39	39	39	39	39	38	CH
US	38	38	38	38	38	38	38	39	38	:	:	US
CA	39	40	40	40	40	40	40	40	40	:	:	CA
JP	36	36	36	35	35	35	35	36	36	:	:	JP

1E1BA

Further reading: European social statistics. Demography. Edition 2000. Eurostat.   D: includes in all years data on the former GDR.

People aged 50 to 64 as % of total population

	1989	1990	1991	1992	1993	1994	1995	1996	1997	1998	1999	
EU-15	17	17	17	17	17	17	17	17	17	17	:	EU-15
B	17	17	17	17	16	16	16	16	16	16	17	B
DK	15	15	15	15	16	16	16	17	18	18	18	DK
D	18	19	19	19	19	19	19	19	19	19	19	D
EL	19	19	19	19	18	18	18	18	18	18	18	EL
E	17	16	16	16	16	16	16	16	16	16	16	E
F	16	16	15	15	15	15	15	15	15	15	16	F
IRL	12	12	12	12	13	13	13	13	13	14	14	IRL
I	18	18	18	18	18	18	18	18	18	18	:	I
L	18	18	17	17	17	17	16	16	16	16	16	L
NL	15	15	15	15	15	15	15	15	16	16	17	NL
A	16	16	16	16	16	16	17	16	16	17	17	A
P	17	17	17	17	17	17	17	17	17	17	:	P
FIN	16	16	16	16	16	16	16	16	17	17	18	FIN
S	15	15	15	15	15	16	16	17	17	18	:	S
UK	16	16	15	15	15	15	16	16	16	16	17	UK
IS	12	12	12	12	12	12	12	12	13	13	:	IS
NO	14	14	14	14	14	14	14	14	15	15	16	NO
EEA	17	17	17	17	17	17	17	17	17	17	:	EEA
CH	16	16	16	16	16	16	17	17	17	17	18	CH
US	13	13	13	13	13	13	13	13	14	:	:	US
CA	14	13	13	13	14	14	14	14	14	:	:	CA
JP	18	18	19	19	19	19	19	19	20	:	:	JP

1E1BB

Further reading: European social statistics. Demography. Edition 2000. Eurostat.   D: includes in all years data on the former GDR.

People aged 25 to 49. EU-15. Millions

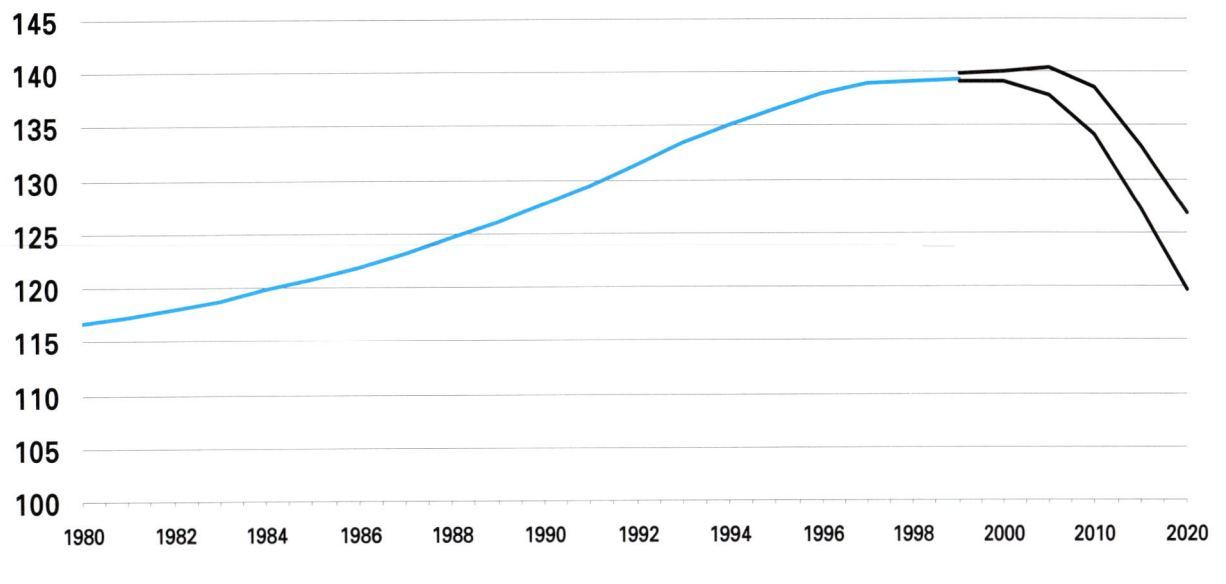

Black: high and low scenario; colour: observed.

Further reading: European social statistics. Demography. Edition 2000. Eurostat. Beyond
the predictable: demographic changes in the EU up to 2050; statistics
in focus, population and social conditions, 1997/7. Eurostat.

People aged 50 to 64. EU-15. Millions

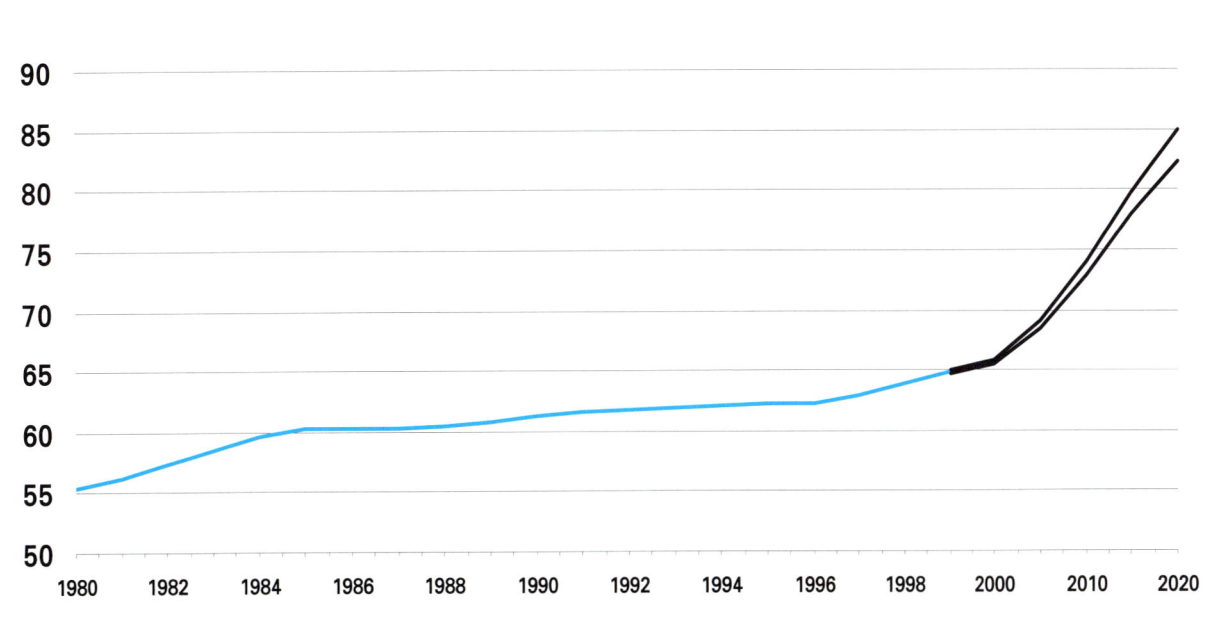

Black: high and low scenario; colour: observed.

Further reading: European social statistics. Demography. Edition 2000. Eurostat. Beyond
the predictable: demographic changes in the EU up to 2050; Statistics
in focus, population and social conditions, 1997/7. Eurostat.

Where is your nearest Data Shop? Addresses at the end of the book

EUROSTAT YEARBOOK 2001

27

People aged 65 to 79 as % of total population

	1989	1990	1991	1992	1993	1994	1995	1996	1997	1998	1999	
EU-15	11	11	11	11	11	11	12	12	12	12	:	**EU-15**
B	11	11	12	12	12	12	12	12	13	13	13	**B**
DK	12	12	12	12	12	12	11	11	11	11	11	**DK**
D	11	11	11	11	11	11	11	12	12	12	12	**D**
EL	11	11	11	11	11	12	12	12	13	13	13	**EL**
E	10	11	11	11	11	12	12	12	12	13	13	**E**
F	10	10	10	11	11	11	11	11	12	12	12	**F**
IRL	9	9	9	9	9	9	9	9	9	9	9	**IRL**
I	11	12	12	12	12	12	12	13	13	13	:	**I**
L	11	10	10	10	10	11	11	11	11	11	11	**L**
NL	10	10	10	10	10	10	10	10	10	10	10	**NL**
A	11	11	11	11	11	11	11	11	12	12	12	**A**
P	11	11	11	11	11	12	12	12	12	12	:	**P**
FIN	11	11	11	11	11	11	11	11	11	11	11	**FIN**
S	14	14	14	13	13	13	13	13	13	13	:	**S**
UK	12	12	12	12	12	12	12	12	12	12	12	**UK**
IS	8	8	8	8	8	8	9	9	9	9	:	**IS**
NO	13	13	13	13	12	12	12	12	12	12	11	**NO**
EEA	11	11	11	11	11	11	12	12	12	12	:	**EEA**
CH	11	11	11	11	11	11	11	11	11	11	11	**CH**
US	10	10	10	10	10	10	10	10	10	:	:	**US**
CA	9	9	9	9	9	9	9	9	9	:	:	**CA**
JP	9	10	10	11	11	11	11	12	12	:	:	**JP**

Further reading: European social statistics. Demography. Edition 2000. Eurostat.   D: includes in all years data on the former GDR.

1E1CB

People aged 80 or over as % of total population

	1989	1990	1991	1992	1993	1994	1995	1996	1997	1998	1999	
EU-15	3,3	3,4	3,5	3,6	3,7	3,8	3,9	3,9	3,8	3,7	:	**EU-15**
B	3,4	3,5	3,5	3,6	3,7	3,7	3,8	3,8	3,7	3,6	3,5	**B**
DK	3,6	3,7	3,7	3,8	3,9	3,9	3,9	3,9	3,9	3,9	3,9	**DK**
D	3,6	3,7	3,8	3,8	3,9	4,0	4,1	4,0	3,9	3,7	3,5	**D**
EL	2,9	3,0	3,1	3,2	3,3	3,4	3,4	3,5	3,5	3,5	3,5	**EL**
E	2,7	2,8	3,0	3,0	3,1	3,2	3,3	3,4	3,4	3,5	3,6	**E**
F	3,6	3,7	3,8	3,9	4,0	4,1	4,2	4,1	3,9	3,7	3,6	**F**
IRL	2,1	2,1	2,2	2,3	2,4	2,4	2,5	2,5	2,5	2,5	2,5	**IRL**
I	3,0	3,1	3,3	3,5	3,7	3,9	4,0	4,1	4,1	4,0	:	**I**
L	2,9	3,1	3,1	3,2	3,3	3,3	3,4	3,4	3,3	3,2	3,1	**L**
NL	2,8	2,9	2,9	2,9	3,0	3,0	3,1	3,1	3,1	3,2	3,1	**NL**
A	3,5	3,5	3,6	3,7	3,7	3,8	3,9	3,8	3,7	3,5	3,4	**A**
P	2,3	2,5	2,6	2,7	2,7	2,8	2,8	2,8	2,8	2,8	:	**P**
FIN	2,7	2,8	2,9	3,0	3,1	3,1	3,2	3,2	3,2	3,3	3,3	**FIN**
S	4,1	4,2	4,3	4,4	4,5	4,5	4,6	4,7	4,8	4,8	:	**S**
UK	3,5	3,6	3,7	3,8	3,9	3,9	4,0	4,0	4,0	4,0	3,9	**UK**
IS	2,5	2,5	2,5	2,5	2,5	2,6	2,6	2,6	2,6	2,7	:	**IS**
NO	3,6	3,7	3,8	3,8	3,9	3,9	4,0	4,0	4,1	4,2	4,2	**NO**
EEA	3,3	3,4	3,5	3,6	3,7	3,8	3,9	3,9	3,8	3,7	:	**EEA**
CH	3,6	3,7	3,7	3,8	3,8	3,9	4,0	4,0	4,0	4,0	4,0	**CH**
US	2,7	2,8	2,8	2,9	3,0	3,0	3,1	3,1	3,2	:	:	**US**
CA	2,2	2,3	2,3	2,4	2,5	2,6	2,7	2,7	2,8	:	:	**CA**
JP	2,3	2,4	2,5	2,6	2,7	3,0	3,2	3,2	3,3	:	:	**JP**

Further reading: European social statistics. Demography. Edition 2000. Eurostat.   D: includes in all years data on the former GDR.

1E1CC

People aged 65 to 79. EU-15. Millions

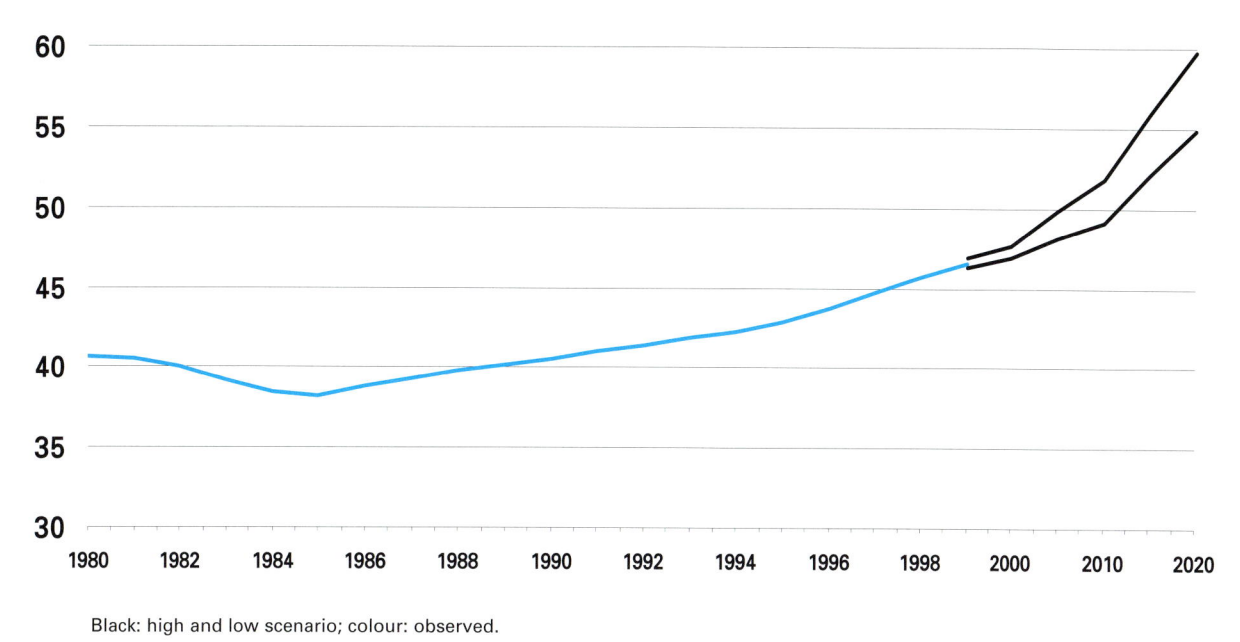

Black: high and low scenario; colour: observed.

Further reading: European social statistics. Demography. Edition 2000. Eurostat. Beyond
the predictable: demographic changes in the EU up to 2050; Statistics
in focus, population and social conditions, 1997/7. Eurostat.

People aged 80 or over. EU-15. Millions

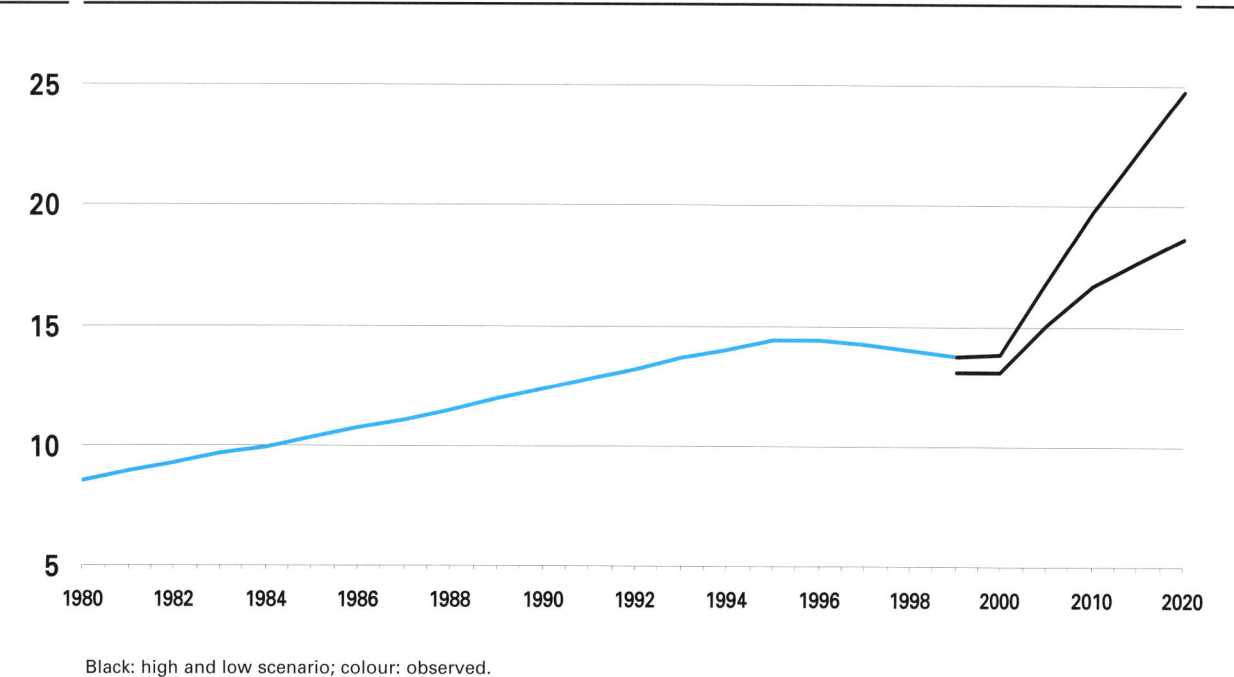

Black: high and low scenario; colour: observed.

Further reading: European social statistics. Demography. Edition 2000. Eurostat. Beyond
the predictable: demographic changes in the EU up to 2050; Statistics
in focus, population and social conditions, 1997/7. Eurostat.

Women per 100 men

	1989	1990	1991	1992	1993	1994	1995	1996	1997	1998	1999	
EU-15	106	106	105	105	105	105	105	105	105	105	105	**EU-15**
B	105	105	105	105	105	105	105	105	105	105	105	**B**
DK	103	103	103	103	103	103	103	103	103	102	102	**DK**
D	108	108	107	107	106	106	106	105	105	105	105	**D**
EL	103	103	103	103	103	103	103	103	103	103	103	**EL**
E	104	104	104	104	104	104	104	104	104	105	105	**E**
F	105	105	105	105	105	105	105	105	105	105	105	**F**
IRL	101	101	101	101	101	101	101	101	101	102	101	**IRL**
I	106	106	106	106	106	106	106	106	106	106	106	**I**
L	105	105	104	104	104	104	104	104	104	104	103	**L**
NL	102	102	102	102	102	102	102	102	102	102	102	**NL**
A	109	109	108	107	107	107	106	106	106	106	106	**A**
P	107	107	107	108	108	108	108	108	108	108	108	**P**
FIN	106	106	106	106	106	106	106	105	105	105	105	**FIN**
S	103	102	102	102	102	102	102	102	102	102	102	**S**
UK	105	105	105	105	104	104	104	104	104	104	103	**UK**
IS	99	99	99	99	99	99	99	100	100	100	100	**IS**
NO	102	102	102	102	102	102	102	102	102	102	102	**NO**
EEA	106	106	105	105	105	105	105	105	105	105	105	**EEA**
CH	105	105	105	105	105	105	105	105	105	105	105	**CH**
US	105	105	105	105	105	105	105	105	105	105	:	**US**
CA	102	102	102	102	102	102	102	102	102	:	:	**CA**
JP	104	104	104	104	104	104	104	104	104	104	:	**JP**

Further reading: European social statistics. Demography. Edition 2000. Eurostat.   D: includes in all years data on the former GDR.

Women per 100 men of their total age group

	Aged 65 to 79					Aged 80 or over					
	1985	1990	1995	2000	2020	1985	1990	1995	2000	2020	
EU-15	147	144	136	131	118	223	223	221	224	177	**EU-15**
B	142	136	131	129	113	223	235	236	235	181	**B**
DK	128	128	126	125	110	196	204	204	202	167	**DK**
D	182	182	160	142	117	241	255	269	287	172	**D**
EL	124	123	121	120	115	147	139	140	146	144	**EL**
E	139	135	129	127	124	190	191	194	200	190	**E**
F	142	136	131	130	118	233	226	218	221	184	**F**
IRL	118	121	124	121	113	169	183	179	185	167	**IRL**
I	136	135	132	130	120	205	200	194	204	177	**I**
L	146	156	145	136	110	216	239	238	240	170	**L**
NL	137	135	132	127	111	201	224	231	229	179	**NL**
A	173	175	159	146	120	248	249	249	261	182	**A**
P	137	132	133	136	132	212	203	193	195	200	**P**
FIN	171	167	154	142	119	264	264	264	264	185	**FIN**
S	122	122	122	121	109	184	188	187	185	162	**S**
UK	138	133	128	124	114	255	243	229	222	174	**UK**
IS	117	116	113	113	107	153	157	161	158	152	**IS**
NO	128	127	126	123	109	189	198	200	200	167	**NO**
EEA	147	144	136	131	117	223	223	221	224	177	**EEA**
CH	137	135	134	:	:	213	213	214	:	:	**CH**
US	136	134	130	127	114	214	216	208	198	165	**US**
CA	127	128	125	:	:	189	192	191	:	:	**CA**
JP	138	141	132	:	:	178	185	193	:	:	**JP**

Further reading: European social statistics. Demography. Edition 2000. Eurostat. Beyond the predictable: demographic changes in the EU up to 2050; Statistics in focus, population and social conditions, 1997/7. Eurostat.

D: includes in all years data on the former GDR. Data for 2000 and 2020: Eurostat projections.

Women per 100 men at different ages. EU-15. 1999

1E1DC

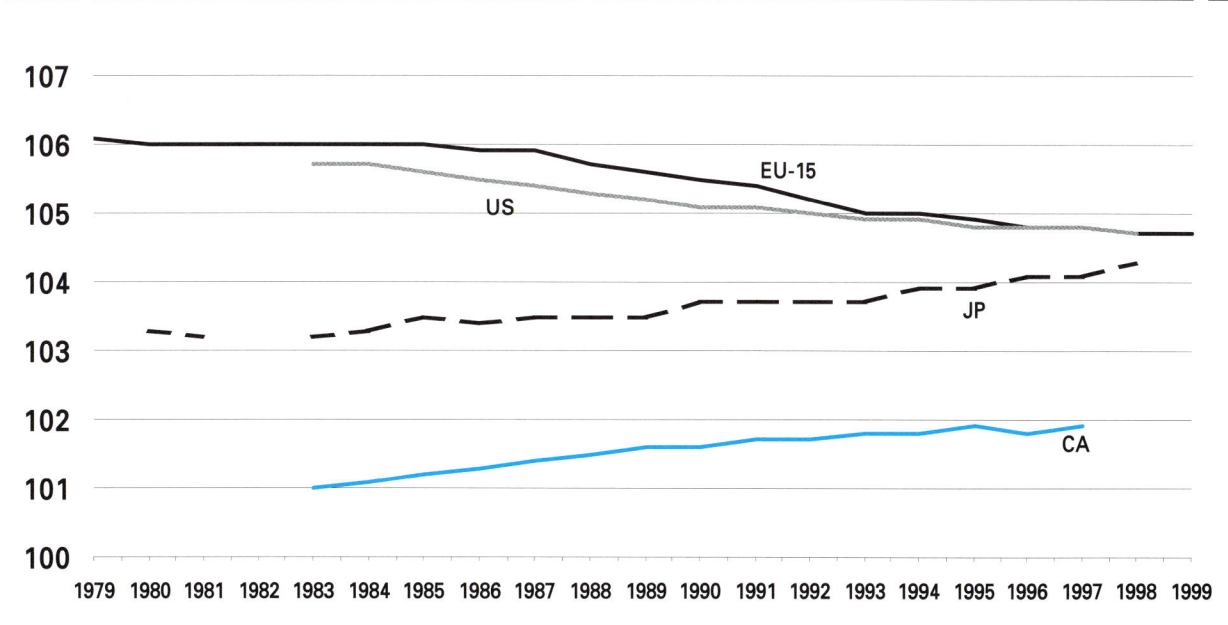

Further reading: European social statistics. Demography. Edition 2000. Eurostat.

Women per 100 men

1E1DD

Further reading: European social statistics. Demography. Edition 2000. Eurostat.

eurostat

Life expectancy at birth: girls

	1989	1990	1991	1992	1993	1994	1995	1996	1997	1998	1999	
EU-15	79,2	79,4	79,6	79,9	79,9 *	80,3 *	80,4 *	80,6 *	80,9 *	80,9 *	:	EU-15
B	79,0	79,4	79,6	79,8	79,9 *	80,1 *	80,2 *	80,5 *	80,6 *	80,5	:	B
DK	77,7	77,7	78,0	78,0	77,8	78,1	77,8	78,2	78,4	78,8	:	DK
D	78,5	78,4	78,7	79,2	79,2	79,6	79,7	79,9	80,3	80,6 *	:	D
EL	79,4	79,5	79,7	79,6	79,9	80,2	80,3	80,4	80,8	80,6 *	:	EL
E	80,3	80,4	80,6	81,1	81,1	81,4	81,5	81,7	81,9	82,4	:	E
F	80,6	80,9	81,1	81,4	81,4	81,9	81,9	82,0	82,2 *	82,3 *	:	F
IRL	77,2	77,6	77,8	78,2	78,1	78,6	78,4	78,6 *	78,6 *	79,1	:	IRL
I	80,0	80,1	80,2	80,6	80,7	81,0	81,3	81,4	81,3 *	81,8 *	:	I
L	78,3	78,5	79,1	78,5	79,4	79,7	80,2	79,9	79,8	80,5	:	L
NL	79,9	80,9	80,1	80,3	80,0	80,3	80,4	80,3	80,5	80,6 *	:	NL
A	78,7	78,9	79,0	79,2	79,4	79,7	80,1	80,2	80,6	80,9 *	:	A
P	77,7	77,4	77,4	78,0	77,9	78,6	78,6	78,6	78,8	78,9	:	P
FIN	78,9	78,9	79,3	79,4	79,5	80,1	80,2	80,5	80,5	80,8	:	FIN
S	80,6	80,4	80,5	80,8	80,8	81,4	81,4	81,5	81,8	81,9	:	S
UK	78,1	78,5	78,7	79,0	78,8	79,3	79,2	79,5	79,6 *	79,7 *	:	UK
IS	80,1	80,5	81,1	80,7	80,8	81,2	80,0	81,2	81,5	81,5 *	:	IS
NO	79,8	79,8	80,1	80,3	80,2	80,6	80,8	81,0	81,0	81,3	:	NO
EEA	79,3	79,4	79,6	79,9	79,9 *	80,3 *	80,4 *	80,6 *	80,9 *	80,9 *	:	EEA
CH	80,9	80,7	81,1	81,3	81,4	81,7	81,7	82,0	82,1	82,4 *	:	CH
US	78,5	78,8	78,9	79,1	78,8	79,0	78,9	79,4	79,5	:	:	US
CA	80,8	81,0	80,4	81,1	81,0	81,1	81,3	81,4	:	:	:	CA
JP	81,8	81,9	82,1	82,2	82,5	83,0	83,0	83,3	83,2	:	:	JP

1A1AB

Further reading: European social statistics. Demography. Edition 2000. Eurostat.   D: includes in all years data on the former GDR.

Life expectancy at birth: boys

	1989	1990	1991	1992	1993	1994	1995	1996	1997	1998	1999	
EU-15	72,7	72,8	72,9	73,3	73,4 *	73,8 *	73,9 *	74,2 *	74,6 *	74,6 *	:	EU-15
B	72,4	72,7	72,9	73,1	73,0 *	73,4 *	73,4 *	73,8 *	74,1 *	74,3	:	B
DK	72,0	72,0	72,5	72,6	72,6	72,7	72,7	73,1	73,6	73,9	:	DK
D	72,1	72,0	72,2	72,6	72,7	73,1	73,3	73,6	74,0	74,5 *	:	D
EL	74,5	74,6	74,7	74,7	75,0	75,2	75,0	75,1	75,6	75,5 *	:	EL
E	73,3	73,3	73,4	73,8	73,9	74,2	74,3	74,4	74,9	75,1	:	E
F	72,5	72,7	72,9	73,2	73,3	73,8	73,9	74,1	74,6 *	74,6 *	:	F
IRL	71,7	72,1	72,3	72,7	72,6	73,0	72,9	73,1 *	73,4 *	73,5	:	IRL
I	73,6	73,6	73,6	74,0	74,4	74,6	74,9	75,3	74,9 *	75,5 *	:	I
L	71,2	72,3	72,0	71,9	72,2	73,2	73,0	73,3	74,1	73,7	:	L
NL	73,7	73,8	74,0	74,3	74,0	74,6	74,6	74,7	75,2	75,2 *	:	NL
A	72,0	72,4	72,4	72,7	73,0	73,4	73,6	73,9	74,3	74,7 *	:	A
P	70,7	70,4	70,2	70,7	70,6	71,6	71,2	71,1	71,6	71,7	:	P
FIN	70,9	70,9	71,3	71,7	72,1	72,8	72,8	73,0	73,4	73,5	:	FIN
S	74,8	74,8	74,9	75,4	75,5	76,1	76,2	76,5	76,7	76,9	:	S
UK	72,6	72,9	73,1	73,6	73,5	74,1	74,0	74,3	74,7 *	74,8 *	:	UK
IS	76,1	75,4	74,8	76,7	77,0	77,1	75,9	76,5	76,3	77,7 *	:	IS
NO	73,3	73,4	74,0	74,2	74,2	74,9	74,8	75,4	75,5	75,6	:	NO
EEA	72,7	72,8	73,0	73,3	73,4 *	73,9 *	73,9 *	74,2 *	74,6 *	74,6 *	:	EEA
CH	74,1	74,0	74,1	74,5	74,9	75,2	75,3	75,9	76,3	76,3 *	:	CH
US	71,7	71,8	72,0	72,3	72,2	72,4	72,5	72,7	72,8	:	:	US
CA	74,0	74,6	74,8	74,9	74,9	76,1	75,3	75,7	:	:	:	CA
JP	75,9	75,9	76,1	76,1	76,3	76,6	76,6	77,0	76,8	:	:	JP

1A1AA

Further reading: European social statistics. Demography. Edition 2000. Eurostat.   D: includes in all years data on the former GDR.

Life expectancy at birth is the average number of years a person would live if age-specific mortality rates observed for a certain calendar year or period were to continue.

1A1AE

Life expectancy at birth: difference between girls and boys. 1999

Further reading: European social statistics. Demography. Edition 2000. Eurostat.

EU–15, B, D, I, L, A, P, UK, NO, EEA, CA: 1998.

1A1AH

Life expectancy at birth: boys and girls. EU-15

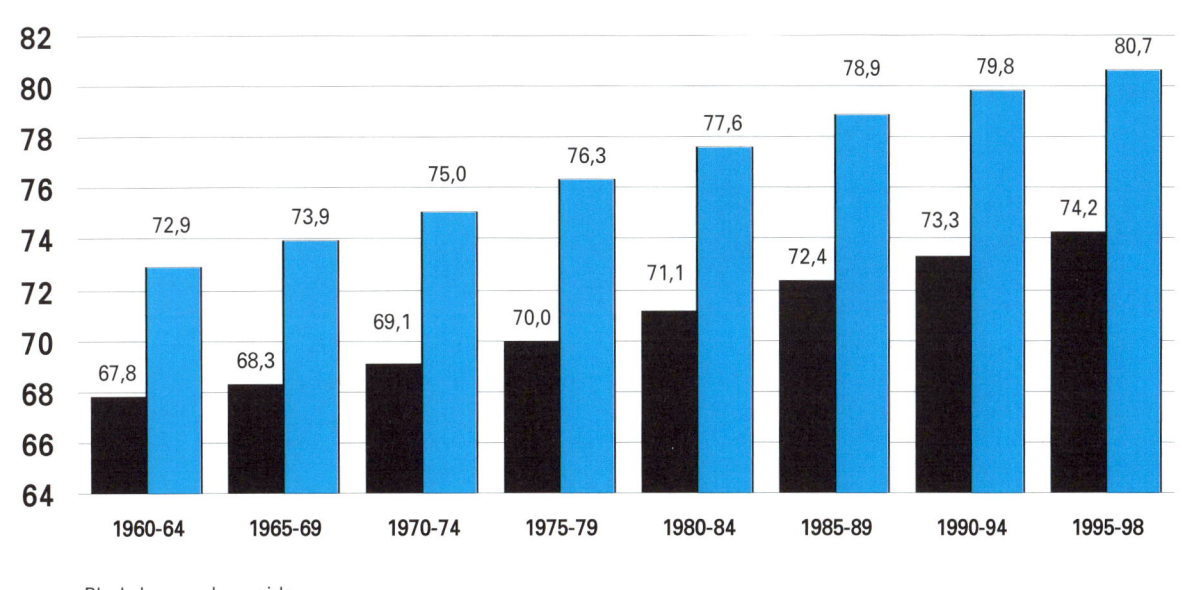

Black: boys; colour: girls.

Further reading: European social statistics. Demography. Edition 2000. Eurostat.

1

Life expectancy at birth for 1997: girls

Number of expected years at birth

1A1AJ

82,5-

81-82,5

80-81

-80

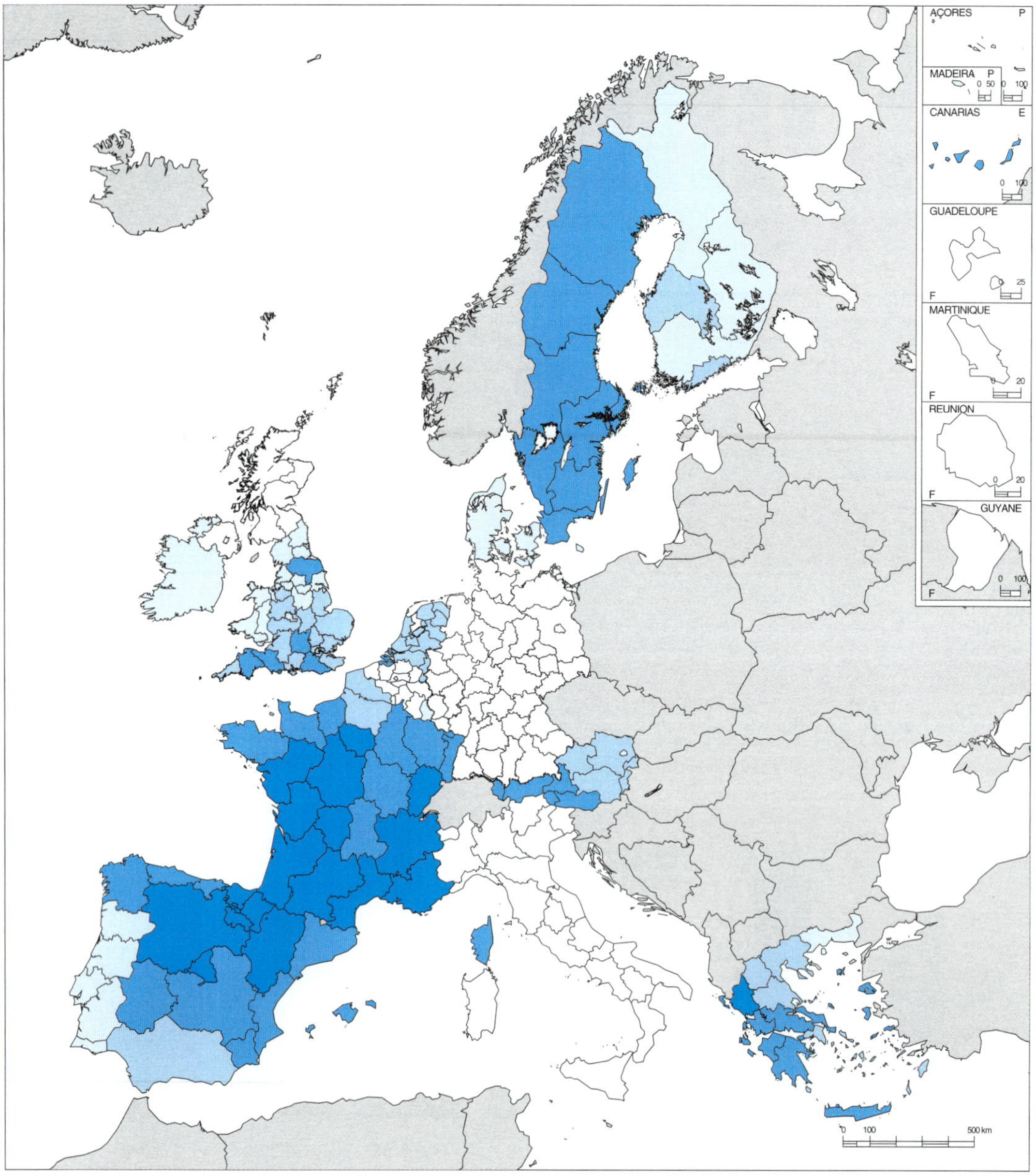

:

Further reading: Demographic statistics, 2000. Eurostat. Regions, statistical yearbook, 2000. Eurostat.

NUTS 2: B, DK, D, EL, E, F, I, L, NL, A, P, FIN, S, UK. NUTS 1: B, IRL, I: 1995.

1A1DB

Life expectancy at 65: women

	1989	1990	1991	1992	1993	1994	1995	1996	1997	1998	1999	
EU-15	18,3	18,4	18,5	18,8	18,7	19,0	19,1	19,2	19,4	:	:	EU-15
B	18,2	18,5	18,6	18,8	18,7	19,1	19,1	19,2	19,4	19,3	:	B
DK	17,9	17,8	17,9	17,8	17,5	17,7	17,5	17,8	17,9	18,1	:	DK
D	17,6	17,6	17,8	18,1	18,2	18,4	18,5	18,6	18,9	19,0	:	D
EL	17,9	18,0	18,0	18,0	18,3	18,4	18,4	18,6	18,9	18,7	:	EL
E	19,0	19,1	19,2	19,6	19,5	19,8	19,8	19,9	20,0	:	:	E
F	19,7	19,9	20,1	20,3	20,3	20,6	20,6	20,6	20,8	20,8	:	F
IRL	16,4	16,9	16,9	17,2	17,0	17,3	17,3	17,3	17,5	17,7	:	IRL
I	18,7	18,8	18,9	19,2	19,3	19,4	19,6	19,8	:	:	:	I
L	17,6	18,2	18,6	18,1	18,5	18,7	19,2	19,2	19,0	19,2	:	L
NL	18,9	18,9	18,9	19,1	18,8	19,0	19,0	19,0	19,2	19,2	:	NL
A	17,8	18,0	18,0	18,1	18,4	18,5	18,7	18,8	19,1	19,3	:	A
P	17,5	17,0	17,2	17,5	17,3	17,9	17,7	17,7	17,9	17,9	:	P
FIN	17,7	17,7	18,0	18,1	17,9	18,6	18,6	18,7	18,9	19,1	:	FIN
S	19,1	19,0	19,2	19,2	19,1	19,7	19,6	19,7	19,9	19,9	:	S
UK	17,6	17,9	17,9	18,1	17,9	18,3	18,2	18,3	18,4	18,5	:	UK
IS	19,0	19,5	19,7	19,1	19,0	19,7	19,0	19,2	19,9	19,7	:	IS
NO	18,7	18,5	18,8	19,0	18,7	19,2	19,1	19,4	19,4	19,6	:	NO
EEA	18,3	18,4	18,5	18,8	18,7	19,0	19,1	19,2	19,4	:	:	EEA
CH	19,7	19,4	19,7	19,9	20,0	20,2	20,2	20,3	20,4	20,5	:	CH
US	18,8	18,9	19,1	19,3	:	19,0	18,9	:	:	:	:	US
CA	:	:	20,0	20,0	20,1	20,1	20,1	20,2	:	:	:	CA
JP	20,0	20,0	20,2	20,3	20,6	21,0	:	:	:	:	:	JP

Further reading: European social statistics. Demography. Edition 2000. Eurostat. D: includes in all years data on the former GDR.

1A1DA

Life expectancy at 65: men

	1989	1990	1991	1992	1993	1994	1995	1996	1997	1998	1999	
EU-15	14,6	14,6	14,8	15,0	15,0	15,3	15,3	15,4	15,6	:	:	EU-15
B	14,0	14,3	14,4	14,6	14,4	14,8	14,8	15,0	15,2	15,2	:	B
DK	14,2	14,0	14,3	14,2	14,0	14,3	14,1	14,4	14,6	14,8	:	DK
D	14,0	14,0	14,2	14,5	14,4	14,7	14,7	14,9	15,2	15,3	:	D
EL	15,7	15,7	15,8	15,7	15,9	16,1	16,1	16,1	16,5	16,4	:	EL
E	15,5	15,4	15,6	15,8	15,8	16,0	16,0	16,0	16,1	:	:	E
F	15,4	15,6	15,7	15,9	15,9	16,2	16,1	16,1	16,3	16,3	:	F
IRL	13,1	13,3	13,5	13,5	13,4	13,8	13,6	13,9	14,1	14,2	:	IRL
I	15,0	15,1	15,1	15,4	15,5	15,6	15,8	16,0	:	:	:	I
L	13,7	14,2	14,6	14,0	14,2	14,6	14,7	14,8	14,8	15,1	:	L
NL	14,3	14,4	14,5	14,7	14,4	14,8	14,7	14,8	15,0	15,1	:	NL
A	14,3	14,4	14,5	14,7	14,8	15,1	15,1	15,3	15,4	15,6	:	A
P	14,2	13,9	14,0	14,2	13,9	14,4	14,3	14,2	14,4	14,3	:	P
FIN	13,8	13,7	14,0	13,9	14,0	14,6	14,5	14,6	15,0	14,9	:	FIN
S	15,4	15,3	15,4	15,6	15,5	16,0	16,0	16,1	16,2	16,3	:	S
UK	13,8	14,0	14,1	14,3	14,2	14,6	14,6	14,8	15,1	15,2	:	UK
IS	16,0	16,2	15,5	16,7	16,7	16,8	16,2	16,2	16,3	16,6	:	IS
NO	14,7	14,6	14,9	15,0	14,8	15,2	15,1	15,5	15,5	15,7	:	NO
EEA	14,6	14,6	14,8	15,0	15,0	15,3	15,3	15,4	15,6	:	:	EEA
CH	15,4	15,3	15,5	15,7	15,8	16,1	16,1	16,3	16,5	16,6	:	CH
US	15,2	15,1	15,3	15,4	:	15,5	15,6	:	:	:	:	US
CA	:	:	15,8	15,9	16,0	16,1	16,2	16,3	:	:	:	CA
JP	16,2	16,2	16,3	16,3	16,4	16,7	:	:	:	:	:	JP

Further reading: European social statistics. Demography. Edition 2000. Eurostat. D: includes in all years data on the former GDR.

Need access to Eurostat's databases? Ask your Data Shop

Life expectancy at 65 is the average number of years a person aged 65 would live if age-specific mortality rates for people aged 65 and over observed for a certain calendar year or period were to continue.

Life expectancy at 65: difference between women and men. 1998

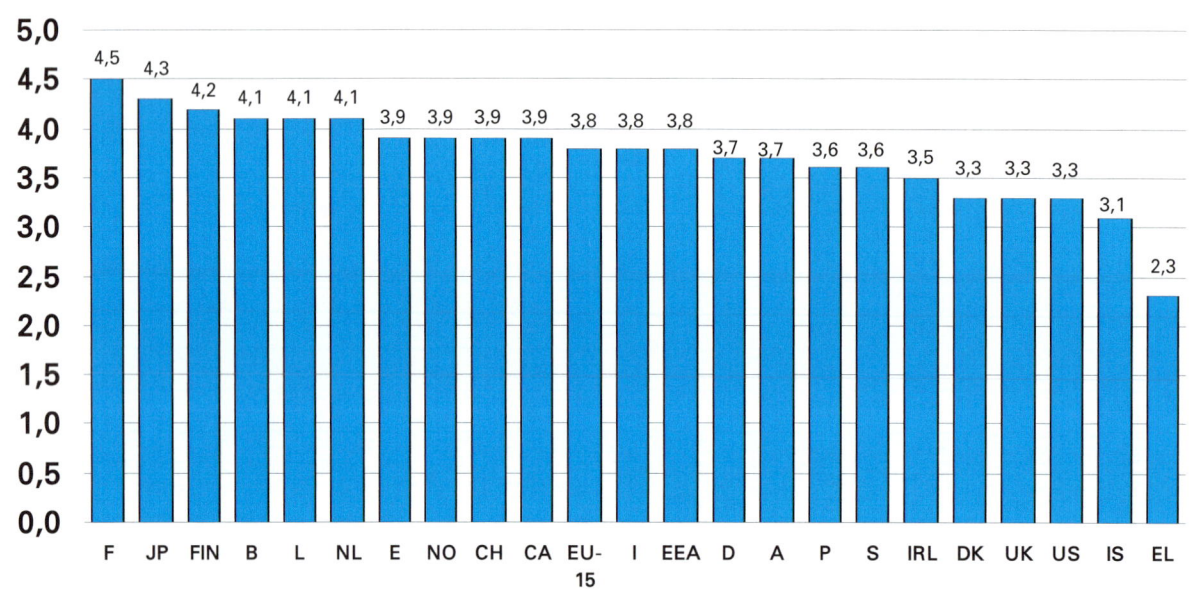

1A1DC

Further reading: European social statistics. Demography. Edition 2000. Eurostat.   E: 1997; I: 1996.

Life expectancy at 65: women and men. EU-15

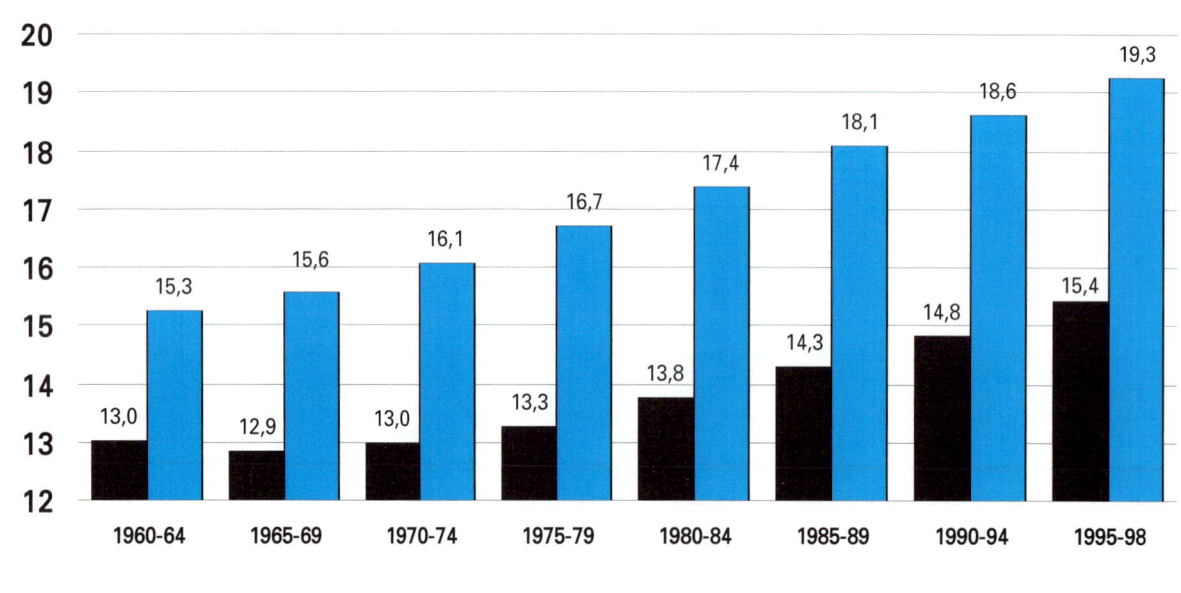

Black: men; colour: women.

1A1DF

Further reading: European social statistics. Demography. Edition 2000. Eurostat.   1998: estimates.

Infant mortality, per 1 000 live births

1A2BC

	1989	1990	1991	1992	1993	1994	1995	1996	1997	1998	1999	
EU-15	8,0	7,6	7,4	6,9	6,5 *	6,1 *	5,6 *	5,5 *	5,2 *	5,2 *	5,0 *	**EU-15**
B	8,7	8,0	8,4	9,6	8,0 *	7,6 *	6,1 *	5,6 *	6,1 *	5,6	5,3 *	**B**
DK	8,0	7,5	7,3	6,6	5,4	5,5	5,1	5,6	5,2	4,7	4,2	**DK**
D	7,5	7,0	6,9	6,2	5,8	5,6	5,3	5,0	4,9	4,7 *	4,6 *	**D**
EL	9,7	9,7	9,0	8,4	8,5	7,9	8,1	7,2	6,4	5,7 *	5,9 *	**EL**
E	7,8	7,6	7,2	7,1	6,7	6,0	5,5	5,5	5,0	5,7 *	4,9 *	**E**
F	7,5	7,3	7,3	6,8	6,5	5,9	4,9	4,8	4,8 *	5,2 *	4,8 *	**F**
IRL	8,1	8,2	7,6	6,5	6,1	5,7	6,3	5,5	6,2 *	6,2 *	5,5 *	**IRL**
I	8,7	8,2	8,1	7,9	7,1	6,6	6,2	5,9	5,5 *	5,3 *	5,1 *	**I**
L	9,9	7,3	9,2	8,5	6,0	5,3	5,5	4,9	4,2	5,0	4,7	**L**
NL	6,8	7,1	6,5	6,3	6,3	5,6	5,5	5,7	5,0	5,2	5,2 *	**NL**
A	8,3	7,8	7,5	7,5	6,5	6,3	5,4	5,1	4,7	4,9	4,4	**A**
P	12,2	11,0	10,8	9,3	8,7	8,1	7,5	6,9	6,4	6,0	5,4 *	**P**
FIN	6,0	5,6	5,9	5,2	4,4	4,7	3,9	4,0	3,9	4,2	3,6	**FIN**
S	5,8	6,0	6,2	5,3	4,8	4,4	4,1	4,0	3,6	3,5	2,9	**S**
UK	8,4	7,9	7,4	6,6	6,3	6,2	6,2	6,1	5,9	5,7 *	5,8 *	**UK**
IS	5,5	5,9	5,5	4,8	4,8	3,2	6,1	3,7	5,5	2,6	2,4 *	**IS**
NO	7,9	7,0	6,4	5,9	5,1	5,2	4,0	4,0	4,1	4,0	:	**NO**
EEA	8,0	7,6	7,4	6,9	6,5 *	6,1 *	5,6 *	5,4 *	5,2 *	5,2 *	5,0 *	**EEA**
CH	7,3	6,8	6,2	6,4	5,6	5,1	5,0	4,7	4,8	4,8	4,6 *	**CH**
US	9,8	9,2	8,9	8,5	8,4	8,0	7,6	7,2	6,6	7,2	6,9	**US**
CA	7,1	6,8	6,4	6,1	6,3	6,3	6,1	5,6	5,2	5,2	5,1	**CA**
JP	4,6	4,6	4,4	4,5	4,3	4,2	4,3	3,8	4,0	4,0	4,0	**JP**

Further reading: European social statistics. Demography. Edition 2000. Eurostat.   D: includes in all years data on the former GDR.

Perinatal mortality, per 1 000 live births

1A2AC

	1989	1990	1991	1992	1993	1994	1995	1996	1997	1998	1999	
EU-15	8,8	8,3	8,0	7,6	:	:	:	:	:	:	:	**EU-15**
B	9,1	8,9	8,3	8,4	:	:	:	:	:	:	:	**B**
DK	9,1	8,3	7,9	8,1	7,4	7,8	7,5	8,0	:	.	:	**DK**
D	6,8	6,3	5,8	5,8	5,4	6,4	6,8	6,8	6,5	:	:	**D**
EL	12,1	11,9	11,1	10,0	10,9	9,7	10,4	9,5	9,5	8,9	:	**EL**
E	8,2	7,6	7,2	7,3	6,6	6,5	6,0	6,4	:	:	:	**E**
F	8,9	8,3	8,2	7,7	7,2	7,4	7,4	8,2	:	:	:	**F**
IRL	10,3	10,1	9,4	9,3	9,1	9,3	10,2	:	:	:	:	**IRL**
I	11,0	10,5	9,8	8,8	8,3	:	7,1	:	:	:	:	**I**
L	9,0	6,9	9,6	7,7	6,3	6,2	7,0	:	6,9	:	:	**L**
NL	9,6	9,6	9,1	9,1	9,1	8,6	8,0	8,4	7,9	7,9	:	**NL**
A	7,6	6,9	6,5	6,8	6,1	6,2	6,8	7,1	6,4	6,6	:	**A**
P	16,3	14,2	13,7	11,9	10,2	9,3	9,1	8,6	7,2	6,7	:	**P**
FIN	6,4	6,2	6,8	5,9	5,1	5,4	4,9	4,9	5,9	:	:	**FIN**
S	6,6	6,5	6,6	5,8	5,9	5,4	5,5	:	5,4	:	:	**S**
UK	8,3	8,1	8,1	7,7	9,1	8,9	:	8,7	:	:	:	**UK**
IS	4,2	6,3	4,6	6,7	4,1	4,5	6,3	7,4	:	:	:	**IS**
NO	7,6	7,5	7,4	7,4	6,9	7,5	6,1	6,5	:	:	:	**NO**
EEA	8,8	8,3	8,0	7,6	:	:	:	:	:	:	:	**EEA**
CH	7,8	7,7	7,1	7,0	6,8	6,1	7,0	6,3	6,9	:	:	**CH**
US	9,6	9,1	8,7	8,5	:	:	:	:	:	:	:	**US**
CA	7,6	7,6	6,8	7,1	7,1	7,0	6,9	:	:	:	:	**CA**
JP	6,0	5,7	5,3	5,2	5,0	5,0	:	:	:	:	:	**JP**

Further reading: European social statistics. Demography. Edition 2000. Eurostat.   D: includes in all years data on the former GDR.

The ECHP (European Community household panel) is a longitudinal, multi-subject survey covering many aspects of daily life, particularly employment and income, but also demographic characteristics, environment, education and health. The health section of the ECHP survey contains questions on perceived health, being hampered in daily activities because of chronic conditions, temporary reduction of activity because of health problems, hospitalisation in the 12 months preceding the interview and consultations to health professionals.

Self-perception of a person's own health (16 + years),% (non-standardised). 1996

		EU-15	B	DK	D	EL	E	F	IRL
Male	Very good or good								
	All ages	68	76	77	69	78	70	64	83
	16–24	89	91	96	91	:	94	84	92
	25–49	79	85	84	82	93	82	72	88
	50–64	57	69	70	55	74	53	54	75
	+ 65	39	52	54	44	37	35	34	62
	Bad or very bad								
	All ages	8	5	6	7	8	9	7	3
	16–24	1	0	1	1	:	1	2	0
	25–49	4	3	2	3	3	3	4	2
	50–64	12	7	7	12	9	16	9	5
	+ 65	20	8	19	17	24	26	16	9
Female	Very good or good								
	All ages	61	68	72	64	74	63	56	78
	16–24	86	89	90	89	99	93	78	94
	25–49	76	78	81	81	92	82	67	86
	50–64	50	63	53	53	66	44	48	73
	+ 65	32	43	36	36	32	25	27	47
	Bad or very bad								
	All ages	11	7	9	9	9	14	9	4
	16–24	2	1	1	1	1	1	2	1
	25–49	4	4	4	3	2	4	5	2
	50–64	13	5	10	10	11	20	11	5
	+ 65	25	16	26	20	28	36	19	11
Total	Very good or good								
	All ages	65	72	75	66	76	67	60	80
	16–24	88	90	93	90	98	94	81	93
	25–49	78	81	85	81	93	82	70	87
	50–64	53	66	64	54	70	49	51	74
	+ 65	35	47	48	39	34	29	30	54
	Bad or very bad								
	All ages	9	6	8	8	9	12	8	4
	16–24	2	1	1	1	1	1	2	1
	25–49	4	4	3	3	2	4	5	2
	50–64	12	6	9	11	10	18	10	5
	+ 65	23	13	23	19	26	32	18	10

5A1AZ

Further reading: European Community household panel, 1996. Eurostat. Key data on health, 2000. Eurostat.

EU-15: data for S not available.

Hampered in daily activities because of chronic conditions (16 + years), % (non-standardised). 1996

	EU-15	B	DK	D	EL	E	F	IRL
Male								
Yes, severely	7	7	7	7	6	5	9	3
Yes, to some extent	12	10	12	15	8	9	12	10
No	81	83	81	78	86	86	79	87
Female								
Yes, severely	8	8	9	7	6	6	10	4
Yes, to some extent	14	10	18	16	9	12	14	12
No	78	82	74	77	85	82	76	84
Total								
Yes, severely	7	7	8	7	6	6	10	4
Yes, to some extent	13	10	15	15	8	10	13	11
No	80	82	77	77	86	84	77	85

5A1BB

Further reading: European Community household panel, 1996. Eurostat. Key data on health, 2000. Eurostat.

EU-15: data for S not available.

According to 1996 results, two out of three Europeans perceive their own health as very good or good. One out of ten reports a bad or very bad health status and a quarter perceive their own health as fair. Almost 13 % report temporary reduction of activity because of physical or mental health problems.

Self-perception of a person's own health (16 + years), % (non-standardised). 1996

I	L	NL	A	P	FIN	S	UK		
								Male	Very good or good
62	70	77	75	53	55	:	72		All ages
92	91	94	94	85	70	:	:		16–24
76	84	85	86	67	70	:	79		25–49
51	53	64	56	33	33	:	66		50–64
24	37	50	45	12	18	:	55		+ 65
									Bad or very bad
11	7	3	7	19	8	:	7		All ages
2	0	2	1	3	1	:	:		16–24
4	3	2	3	9	3	:	5		25–49
13	9	4	12	26	13	:	12		50–64
32	18	8	22	51	24	:	11		+ 65
								Female	Very good or good
52	64	70	69	41	57	:	67		All ages
88	91	86	96	83	77	:	:		16–24
72	77	79	86	53	77	:	76		25–49
37	52	62	55	19	35	:	62		50–64
17	30	44	34	7	18	:	48		+ 65
									Bad or very bad
15	8	6	9	28	9	:	8		All ages
2	2	1	0	5	2	:	:		16–24
3	4	4	3	12	3	:	5		25–49
19	11	7	11	42	13	:	9		50–64
38	16	12	25	62	23	:	15		+ 65
								Total	Very good or good
57	67	73	72	47	56	:	69		All ages
90	91	90	95	84	73	:	:		16–24
74	81	82	86	60	74	:	78		25–49
44	52	63	55	25	34	:	64		50–64
20	33	46	38	9	18	:	51		+ 65
									Bad or very bad
13	7	5	8	24	8	:	10		All ages
2	1	2	1	4	2	:	:		10–24
3	4	3	3	11	3	:	5		25–49
16	10	6	11	35	13	:	10		50–64
35	17	10	24	57	23	:	13		+ 65

5A1BA

Further reading: European Community household panel, 1996. Eurostat. Key data on health, 2000. Eurostat.

Hampered in daily activities because of chronic conditions (16 + years), % (non-standardised). 1996

I	L	NL	A	P	FIN	S	UK	
								Male
5	6	6	5	10	10	:	8	Yes, severely
8	14	13	12	13	17	:	15	Yes, to some extent
88	79	81	83	78	72	:	77	No
								Female
6	6	9	7	12	11	:	8	Yes, severely
9	16	16	13	15	20	:	18	Yes, to some extent
85	78	75	81	73	69	:	74	No
								Total
5	6	8	6	11	10	:	8	Yes, severely
8	15	14	12	14	19	:	17	Yes, to some extent
86	79	78	82	75	71	:	75	No

5A1BC

Further reading: European Community household panel, 1996. Eurostat. Key data on health, 2000. Eurostat.

eurostat

EUROSTAT YEARBOOK 2001

Need more data on this topic? Ask your Data Shop

1

The European Commission conducts the Eurobarometer survey every year in order to gather information on the attitudes of the population towards the EU and its policy. Each year, additional questions about specific subjects are appended. In 1996 it was concerning height and weight of Europeans. The body mass index (BMI) is a measure of a person's weight relative to his or her height that correlates fairly well with body fat content in adults and is accepted by experts as the most useful measure of obesity. BMI is calculated as the result of dividing body weight (in kg) by body height (in m) squared. If the result is between 18 and 20 the person is underweight, and is severely underweight when below 18. A person with a BMI between 27 and 30 is overweight, and severely overweight with a BMI of 30 or more. Generally speaking, most Europeans have a correct BMI (between 20 and 26); that is the case for 69.5 % of men and 64.6 % of women. However, 19.6 % of men have problems of obesity and 6.1 % are overweight. For women 14.4 % are obese and 6.9 % are overweight. To be underweight is relevant in the case of women (3.1 %) and not so relevant in the case of men (0.9 %). A survey on attitudes to physical activity/exercise, body weight and health, the Health and Fitness Survey, was developed, with the support of the European Commission's Employment and Social Affairs DG, by the Institute of European Food Studies in Dublin in 1997. From a list of 28 options the most popular physical activities in the EU are walking, gardening, cycling and swimming.

Body mass index (BMI), % of population. 1996

	Severely underweight		Underweight		Normal body mass index		Obesity		Severe obesity		
	< 18		18-19		20-26		27-30		30 +		
	Male	Female	Male	Female	Male	Female	Male	Female	Male	Female	
EU-15	0,9	3,0	4,0	11,6	69,5	64,6	19,5	14,4	6,1	6,9	**EU-15**
B	1,9	4,8	6,2	10,8	69,2	66,3	16,1	9,8	6,5	8,3	**B**
DK	0,4	2,8	2,7	15,3	74,6	65,5	16,9	9,5	5,4	6,8	**DK**
D	0,4	1,9	1,8	8,9	69,1	71,1	23,2	15,1	5,4	3,8	**D**
EL	0,6	1,9	3,0	10,4	61,0	55,7	26,7	17,8	8,7	13,0	**EL**
E	0,9	3,4	4,0	12,3	63,0	62,1	24,2	15,7	7,8	6,2	**E**
F	0,6	4,6	5,4	20,5	72,9	59,7	16,5	10,4	4,6	4,4	**F**
IRL	0,4	3,1	5,1	11,3	74,5	69,3	15,6	10,5	4,4	6,0	**IRL**
I	0,4	4,6	4,5	15,2	75,3	61,8	15,4	13,4	4,3	5,4	**I**
L	1,1	5,4	5,2	16,8	62,6	58,9	22,6	12,2	8,5	7,1	**L**
NL	0,8	2,7	6,9	8,9	74,9	68,2	14,4	14,4	2,9	6,8	**NL**
A	1,3	2,7	2,6	11,4	69,8	66,0	20,4	15,6	5,9	6,0	**A**
P	1,2	2,4	3,4	9,2	70,7	61,7	16,7	21,2	7,9	9,4	**P**
FIN	0,4	3,2	4,4	8,2	68,3	64,2	18,3	17,6	8,6	8,2	**FIN**
S	0,6	2,3	4,3	11,1	68,1	68,7	22,2	13,8	4,9	3,8	**S**
UK	2,1	2,3	2,8	9,8	65,6	62,0	21,4	17,8	8,1	10,1	**UK**

5A1BI

Further reading: Eurobarometer 44.3. 1996. Key data on health, 2000. Eurostat.

Participation in some physical activities by age group (%). 1997

	Cycling			Gardening			Swimming			Walking			
	15-34	35-54	+ 55	15-34	35-54	+ 55	15-34	35-54	+ 55	15-34	35-54	+ 55	
EU-15	18	18	14	8	21	27	12	10	7	25	30	40	**EU-15**
B	22	17	18	9	19	17	16	8	4	22	27	32	**B**
DK	32	27	24	17	43	41	11	12	7	22	32	35	**DK**
D	29	28	26	12	25	33	14	13	10	14	19	35	**D**
EL	3	2	1	2	11	19	4	4	5	19	24	33	**EL**
E	11	7	3	1	4	4	7	7	4	24	37	50	**E**
F	14	13	11	8	20	26	11	11	9	26	28	43	**F**
IRL	22	9	12	15	32	37	19	10	5	49	62	56	**IRL**
I	8	8	5	5	14	20	9	4	2	18	25	34	**I**
L	18	15	18	13	32	41	24	17	12	29	46	57	**L**
NL	53	52	54	19	37	44	20	16	13	21	25	26	**NL**
A	40	45	29	17	41	50	22	22	14	35	44	43	**A**
P	6	2	1	4	2	3	9	1	1	16	19	24	**P**
FIN	27	30	27	3	11	19	14	15	14	60	69	76	**FIN**
S	38	44	34	9	29	45	15	11	12	45	67	74	**S**
UK	12	12	5	9	26	36	15	14	5	45	43	41	**UK**

5A3BJ

Further reading: Health and fitness survey, Institute of European Food Studies, Dublin (supported by European Commission).

The recommended dietary allowances (RDA) for most EU countries are about 2 900 kcal in certain maximal cases (for males in the 25–50 years age bracket, about 176 cm and 79 kg) or 2 200 kcal for women (for women in the 25–50 years age bracket, about 163 cm and 63 kg); these RDA can, however, differ among individuals according to certain characteristics. In the case of average number of calories per person/day (expressed in kcal), all the EU countries (except Finland) consume on average more than 3 000 kcal/day and the trend is not decreasing anywhere. A similar trend of unhealthy overconsumption can be observed in the fat intake that should not exceed approximately 30–33 % of total energy intake according to recommendations from some food administrations (especially the International Union of Nutrition Sciences).

Percentage of total energy available from fat

	1989	1990	1991	1992	1993	1994	1995	1996	1997	1998	1999	
EU-15	38	38	39	39	39	39	39	39	39	:	:	EU-15
B	40	40	40	39	40	40	41	40	40	:	:	B
DK	38	38	36	38	37	36	37	36	35	:	:	DK
D	37	38	38	38	38	38	38	39	38	:	:	D
EL	36	36	37	37	36	37	37	39	38	:	:	EL
E	37	38	39	39	39	39	40	39	39	:	:	E
F	42	41	42	42	42	42	42	42	42	:	:	F
IRL	35	34	34	33	33	33	33	32	34	:	:	IRL
I	38	38	38	37	38	38	38	38	38	:	:	I
L	40	40	40	39	40	40	41	40	40	:	:	L
NL	38	39	37	37	39	39	41	39	39	:	:	NL
A	40	40	40	41	41	41	40	40	41	:	:	A
P	30	32	32	32	32	32	32	32	32	:	:	P
FIN	36	36	36	37	37	36	37	37	37	38	:	FIN
S	37	37	37	36	37	37	38	37	38	:	:	S
UK	38	38	38	40	39	39	39	39	39	:	:	UK
IS	36	37	35	35	35	35	35	34	35	:	:	IS
NO	37	37	37	37	37	37	37	37	36	:	:	NO
CH	41	41	41	40	40	41	41	40	40	:	:	CH

Further reading: Faostat database, Food and Agriculture Organisation. Key data on health, 2000. Eurostat.

Average number of calories per person/day. kcal

	1989	1990	1991	1992	1993	1994	1995	1996	1997	1998	1999	
EU-15	3 395	3 372	3 416	3 443	3 378	3 368	3 373	3 406	3 423	3 437	:	EU-15
B/L	3 523	3 533	3 568	3 658	3 589	3 597	3 578	3 599	3 649	3 606	:	B/L
DK	3 188	3 153	3 234	3 310	3 288	3 267	3 319	3 303	3 387	3 433	:	DK
D	3 457	3 315	3 414	3 477	3 323	3 341	3 394	3 404	3 394	3 402	:	D
EL	3 608	3 506	3 520	3 605	3 523	3 623	3 577	3 528	3 606	3 630	:	EL
E	3 211	3 244	3 315	3 399	3 296	3 267	3 237	3 348	3 324	3 348	:	E
F	3 559	3 506	3 538	3 547	3 536	3 522	3 539	3 513	3 529	3 541	:	F
IRL	3 624	3 656	3 643	3 666	3 646	3 588	3 546	3 543	3 588	3 622	:	IRL
I	3 540	3 573	3 629	3 529	3 461	3 456	3 485	3 523	3 553	3 608	:	I
L	:	:	:	:	:	:	:	:	:	:	:	L
NL	3 185	3 282	3 345	3 409	3 318	3 115	3 198	3 298	3 269	3 282	:	NL
A	3 468	3 496	3 543	3 532	3 511	3 398	3 548	3 542	3 540	3 531	:	A
P	3 397	3 505	3 533	3 511	3 573	3 614	3 615	3 647	3 657	3 691	:	P
FIN	3 215	3 146	3 120	3 185	3 040	2 973	3 068	3 021	3 099	3 180	:	FIN
S	2 978	2 974	2 951	3 065	3 138	3 163	3 092	3 100	3 086	3 114	:	S
UK	3 197	3 220	3 188	3 274	3 233	3 219	3 135	3 223	3 281	3 257	:	UK
IS	3 148	3 056	3 128	3 102	3 085	3 073	3 110	3 009	3 174	3 222	:	IS
NO	3 175	3 147	3 214	3 235	3 249	3 280	3 262	3 334	3 376	3 425	:	NO
EEA	:	:	:	:	:	:	:	:	:	:	:	EEA
CH	3 329	3 345	3 254	3 329	3 286	3 268	3 249	3 292	3 257	3 222	:	CH
US	3 422	3 483	3 514	3 554	3 608	3 681	3 631	3 647	3 720	3 757	:	US
CA	3 009	2 999	3 007	3 058	3 009	3 136	3 084	3 068	3 118	3 167	:	CA
JP	2 906	2 895	2 894	2 886	2 884	2 903	2 915	2 929	2 900	2 874	:	JP

Further reading: Faostat database, Food and Agriculture Organisation. Key data on health, 2000. Eurostat.

5A3LK

5A4GH

Average amount of pure alcohol available on the market per person (older than 15) per year. Litres

	1989	1990	1991	1992	1993	1994	1995	1996	1997	1998	1999	
EU-15	11,7	11,5	11,4	11,2	11,1	:	:	:	:	:	:	EU-15
B	12,0	12,4	11,8	12,0	12,0	:	:	:	:	:	:	B
DK	11,6	11,7	11,6	11,9	11,7	12,0	12,1	12,2	12,2	11,6	:	DK
D	13,8	13,8	12,0	11,8	11,3	11,4	11,1	10,9	10,9	:	:	D
EL	10,5	10,6	10,5	10,4	11,2	10,8	:	:	:	:	:	EL
E	13,8	13,5	13,2	12,5	12,0	11,7	11,4	11,1	:	:	:	E
F	16,8	16,6	16,2	16,0	16,2	15,8	15,7	15,6	:	:	:	F
IRL	12,0	10,5	10,6	11,0	11,1	11,4	12,1	11,9	:	:	:	IRL
I	11,1	10,9	10,7	10,6	10,2	10,3	10,4	10,5	:	:	:	I
L	15,1	14,7	15,2	15,1	15,3	15,3	:	:	:	:	:	L
NL	9,9	9,9	10,0	10,0	9,7	9,7	9,8	9,9	10,0	9,9	:	NL
A	12,5	12,6	12,8	12,1	12,3	11,9	11,9	11,8	11,5	11,4	11,4	A
P	10,4	10,1	11,6	10,7	10,4	10,8	11,0	11,2	:	:	:	P
FIN	9,4	9,5	9,2	8,9	8,4	8,2	8,3	8,2	8,5	8,6	8,7	FIN
S	6,5	6,4	6,3	6,3	6,2	6,3	6,2	6,0	5,9	5,8	:	S
UK	9,7	9,7	9,4	9,2	9,2	9,5	9,2	9,6	9,8	9,7	:	UK
IS	5,5	5,2	5,1	4,7	4,5	4,6	4,8	4,9	5,1	5,6	:	IS
NO	5,1	5,0	4,9	4,7	4,6	4,7	4,8	5,0	5,4	:	:	NO
EEA	10,9	10,8	10,7	10,5	10,4	:	:	:	:	:	:	EEA
CH	13,1	12,9	12,9	12,3	12,1	11,8	11,4	11,3	11,2	11,2	:	CH
US	9,3	9,5	8,9	8,9	8,6	8,6	8,4	8,5	8,5	8,3	:	US
CA	9,6	9,2	8,8	7,5	7,5	7,4	7,4	7,2	:	:	:	CA
JP	8,6	8,9	8,9	9,0	8,8	8,7	8,6	8,5	8,8	:	:	JP

Further reading: World drink trends, NL. Health for all database, 2000, WHO. Key data on health, 2000. Eurostat.

1A4AA

Average number of cigarettes available on the market per person per year

	1989	1990	1991	1992	1993	1994	1995	1996	1997	1998	1999	
EU-15	1 777	1 816	1 773	1 757	1 743	1 747	1 713	1 641	1 646	:	:	EU-15
B	1 532	1 534	1 678	1 815	2 246	1 526	1 585	1 573	1 568	:	:	B
DK	1 560	1 566	1 560	1 609	1 540	1 558	1 702	1 800	1 791	:	:	DK
D	1 943	2 025	1 796	1 894	1 795	1 840	1 859	1 835	1 841	:	:	D
EL	2 865	2 864	2 946	2 911	3 016	3 012	2 937	2 959	3 020	:	:	EL
E	2 049	2 122	2 241	2 132	1 971	2 119	1 989	1 902	1 929	:	:	E
F	1 690	1 689	1 702	1 679	1 624	1 556	1 519	1 476	1 443	:	:	F
IRL	1 764	1 770	1 759	1 747	1 736	1 729	1 723	1 751	1 784	:	:	IRL
I	1 753	1 662	1 602	1 552	1 619	1 688	1 531	1 516	1 541	:	:	I
L	:	1 671	1 808	1 936	2 276	2 140	:	:	:	:	:	L
NL	1 429	1 555	1 606	1 718	1 803	1 685	2 322	1 216	1 245	:	:	NL
A	1 848	1 791	1 943	1 699	1 681	1 784	1 568	1 578	1 685	:	:	A
P	1 409	1 569	1 617	1 694	1 724	1 777	1 638	1 627	1 681	:	:	P
FIN	1 557	1 436	1 390	1 369	1 089	1 055	1 019	882	817	:	:	FIN
S	1 317	1 254	1 254	1 256	998	992	920	933	893	:	:	S
UK	1 561	1 710	1 651	1 531	1 629	1 621	1 552	1 531	1 515	:	:	UK
IS	:	2 159	2 132	2 106	2 085	2 068	2 058	2 232	2 190	:	:	IS
NO	694	695	707	626	654	597	609	621	619	:	:	NO
EEA	:	:	:	:	:	:	:	:	:	:	:	EEA
CH	2 393	2 489	2 433	2 323	2 492	2 322	2 199	2 139	2 061	:	:	CH

Further reading: Tobacco Journal International (D). Health for all database, 2000, WHO. Key data on health, 2000. Eurostat.

1A4AB

The average of pure alcohol sold per capita in a country is defined as the total amount of pure ethanol in spirits, wine and beer sold/consumed in the country during the calendar year or calculated from official statistics on local production, import and export taking into account stocks and home production, whenever available. This amount is divided by the average-year population and tends to underestimate or overestimate actual consumption.

The average number of cigarettes per person/year available on the market in a country is defined by WHO (the World Health Organisation) as the result of dividing the cigarette production plus the cigarette imports, minus the cigarette exports, by the population of 15 years of age and over. As it does not include consumption of privately imported (or exported) quantities, it tends to underestimate and overestimate actual consumption.

In 1995, the Eurobarometer Survey 44.3 estimated the daily smoker population of 15 years and over.

The daily smoker population of 15 years and over was 29.0 % in 1995, with higher percentages in the younger age group (15–24 years) and 25–34 years. However, and based on national health surveys, the general trend in smoking prevalence is downwards in a majority of Member States, even if smoking among women is not decreasing with the same intensity as for men (especially in southern Europe).

Percentage of population (age over 15), who are daily cigarette smokers, by sex and age groups. 1995

	Total			15-24			25-34			35-44			
	Male	Female	All	Male	Female	All	Male	Female	All	Male	Female	All	
EU-15	33	25	29	37	33	35	44	33	38	38	29	33	EU-15
B	34	28	31	36	28	32	43	41	42	27	41	34	B
DK	39	37	38	50	45	47	55	36	44	30	47	38	DK
D (W)	30	21	25	39	35	37	33	25	29	30	22	26	D (W)
EL	49	29	39	46	36	41	56	47	52	60	39	50	EL
E	39	23	31	33	26	30	49	56	52	58	33	45	E
F	39	31	35	51	58	54	57	38	47	41	37	39	F
IRL	31	28	29	31	31	31	37	29	33	39	31	35	IRL
I	33	24	38	29	22	25	28	39	33	49	34	41	I
L	28	28	28	28	34	31	37	34	36	30	20	25	L
NL	37	31	34	57	40	48	44	33	38	34	36	35	NL
A	37	13	24	49	27	37	58	37	48	45	11	27	A
P	35	21	28	42	33	38	53	25	37	37	20	28	P
FIN	22	18	20	27	13	19	35	28	32	35	25	29	FIN
S	18	25	22	18	25	22	14	18	16	27	33	30	S
UK	29	26	27	28	30	29	32	37	34	32	26	29	UK

Further reading: Eurobarometer 43.0 European Commission. Key data on health, 2000. Eurostat.

Percentage of population (age over 15), who are daily cigarette smokers, by sex and age groups. 1995

	45-54			55-64			65 +			
	Male	Female	All	Male	Female	All	Male	Female	All	
EU-15	34	23	29	27	16	21	16	11	13	EU-15
B	44	44	44	30	12	20	22	9	14	B
DK	34	29	32	40	37	39	28	26	27	DK
D (W)	31	25	28	24	15	20	17	5	10	D (W)
EL	65	27	44	40	11	25	28	7	17	EL
E	32	20	26	37	3	19	22	-	8	E
F	37	20	28	17	15	16	15	10	12	F
IRL	26	21	23	27	29	28	2	22	21	IRL
I	35	27	31	36	21	28	21	7	13	I
L	29	27	28	26	36	31	18	21	19	L
NL	34	24	28	45	33	38	13	18	16	NL
A	32	6	16	30	-	12	11	-	5	A
P	37	31	34	20	10	15	15	9	12	P
FIN	35	21	27	13	10	12	3	-	2	FIN
S	20	24	22	17	24	20	11	33	21	S
UK	33	26	29	31	23	27	17	15	16	UK

Further reading: Eurobarometer 43.0 European Commission. Key data on health, 2000. Eurostat.

Need longer time series? Ask your Data Shop

According to the EMCDDA (European Monitoring Centre for Drugs and Drug Addiction), since 1990 the majority of EU countries have mounted nationwide surveys of illegal drug use in the general population, asking a representative cross-section of the population whether they have used drugs. As applied to drug use, the method suffers important limitations and comparison is also hampered by different sampling and data collection methods. Cannabis is the most used illegal drug throughout the EU countries with significant lifetime prevalence (10–31 %) on the population between 18 and 69 years of age. Amphetamines appear as the second (2–9 %). Many countries reported that ecstasy and LSD are becoming more popular among young people. Cocaine ranges from 1 to 3 % and only 1 % of adults have ever tried heroin. Illegal drug use has increased among schoolchildren and young people almost everywhere.

Some characteristics of persons treated for drug problems

		B(1)	B(2)	B(3)	DK	D	EL	E	F	IRL
Mean age		30,0	26,6	27,4	32,5	28,1	31,6	29,6	29,8	24,3
Age distribution										
under 25		21,0	52,0	37,4	20,0	41,0	21,0	24,8	21,0	60,5
over 35		17,0	18,5	14,1	40,0	22,0	35,1	18,9	21,5	8,2
Sex distribution										
Male		78,0	75,0	74,0	73,0	77,0	84,0	84,0	76,0	69,0
Female		22,0	25,0	26,0	27,0	23,0	16,0	16,0	24,0	31,0
% of intravenous		:	:	24,0	27,0	37,1	77,5	27,3	63,0	49,2
Distribution of main drugs in %										
Opiates	Total	77,1	39,5	67,7	84,6	64,6	91,9	84,9	78,6	79,8
	from which IV (%)	:	:	34,0	53,0	49,0	84,0	31,0	73,0	65,0
Cocaine	Total	7,2	7,1	3,8	0,7	7,1	0,7	8,9	3,1	0,9
	from which IV (%)			35,0	:	38,0	0,0	6,0	47,0	10,0
Amphetamines	Total	:	18,7	0,7	2,0	3,2	0,0	0,6	0,5	1,0
	from which IV (%)			0,0		13,0	0,0	2,0	56,0	0,0
Ecstasy		:	1,2	2,5	:	:	0,0	0,5	0,7	5,0
Hallucinogens		0,1	4,9	0,1	:	1,2	0,0	0,2	0,4	0,5
Cannabis		6,6	22,0	13,2	10,5	18,0	5,7	4,2	11,0	10,6
Others		8,6	5,5	11,9	0,6	5,9	1,7	0,7	5,7	2,1

1P8ML

Further reading: European Monitoring Centre for Drugs and Drug Addiction, Lisbon, 1999. Key data on health, 2000. Eurostat.

In some countries amphetamines includes ecstasy. B (1): Brussels; B (2): Flanders; B (3): Wallonia. B, DK, E, F, IRL: 1997. D, EL: 1998. E, D, I, L: IV = intravenous. D, I, L: intravenous refers to heroin. F, NL: Data refers to specialised centres only.

Some characteristics of persons treated for drug problems

		I	L	NL	A	P	FIN	S	UK
Mean age		30,5	28,5	30,8	:	28,2	:	33,0	:
Age distribution									
under 25		19,5	27,0	23,2	:	29,1	37,2	17,0	42,0
over 35		25,0	15,0	30,4	:	16,0	22,7	42,0	15,0
Sex distribution									
Male		86,0	81,0	81,0	:	80,0	72,0	72,0	74,0
Female		14,0	19,0	19,0	:	20,0	28,0	28,0	26,0
% of intravenous		:	79,0	9,8	:	41,9	:	:	40,0
Distribution of main drugs in %									
Opiates	Total	86,4	81,0	65,1	:	96,9	27,2	39,0	71,0
	from which IV (%)	74,0	88,0	13,6	:	:	:	:	58,0
Cocaine	Total	3,2	15,0	17,5	:	1,2	0,6	0,9	4,0
	from which IV (%)	23,6	80,0	2,6	:	:	:	:	5,0
Amphetamines	Total	0,2	1,0	3,0	:	:	47,9	20,0	9,0
	from which IV (%)	6,8	:	8,7	:	:	:	:	44,0
Ecstasy		0,7	1,0	1,1	:	:	:	:	:
Hallucinogens		0,2	:	0,2	:	:	6,4	0,9	0,0
Cannabis		67,5	4,0	10,9	:	1,9	17,9	7,0	8,0
Others		1,7	:	2,0	:	1,5	:	33,0	7,0

1P7MM

Further reading: European Monitoring Centre for Drugs and Drug Addiction, Lisbon, 1999. Key data on health, 2000. Eurostat.

I, NL: 1998. L, P, FIN, UK: 1997. S: 1996.

A IDS is surveyed by the European Centre for the Epidemiological Monitoring of AIDS (supported by the European Commission). Cases are recorded according to the AIDS-case definition of 1982 and later revisions. Because of reporting delays (time between diagnosis on an AIDS case and report to national level) the incidence trends being best assessed by examining data by year of diagnosis with adjustment for reporting delay rather than by year of report. After some years since the start of the epidemic of AIDS, the annual number of cases reported continues to decrease (last increase was in 1995). Annual AIDS incidence per million (adjusted for reporting delays) is estimated at 24.8 in 1998 with a cumulative total of cases in the EU of 207 933. Injecting drug users (40.1 % of total cases) and homo/bisexual males (34.5 %) remain the major risk groups of transmission.

AIDS incidence rates per million population by year of diagnosis, with adjustments for reporting delays

	1989	1990	1991	1992	1993	1994	1995	1996	1997	1998	1999	
EU-15	37,2	43,1	49,1	53,7	58,4	66,1	63,7	54,6	37,2	28,5	:	**EU-15**
B	16,7	20,6	25,7	24,8	25,2	25,3	24,2	19,7	12,4	13,8	:	**B**
DK	33,9	38,4	40,8	40,4	46,1	45,3	41,0	30,2	20,4	14,0	13,2	**DK**
D	20,0	19,0	21,3	22,7	23,6	23,6	20,9	16,9	10,3	7,9	6,1	**D**
EL	10,5	14,1	18,0	18,4	16,3	20,6	20,3	22,1	16,0	11,1	11,6	**EL**
E	80,6	99,7	116,4	127,0	137,4	184,2	176,1	161,4	116,6	86,6	71,1	**E**
F	67,6	76,3	81,8	88,1	93,3	96,7	88,1	66,5	37,6	30,2	:	**F**
IRL	16,2	19,4	20,4	20,4	21,1	20,9	14,7	15,1	8,1	5,2	10,5	**IRL**
I	43,8	55,3	67,4	74,6	84,1	96,4	98,7	87,6	58,2	41,7	36,0	**I**
L	29,3	23,7	31,2	30,8	50,5	32,4	36,9	31,6	24,0	21,6	11,8	**L**
NL	26,4	28,1	29,7	33,7	31,2	31,4	34,5	28,6	21,5	14,5	8,2	**NL**
A	18,9	21,3	25,6	24,4	29,6	20,8	25,4	17,0	11,5	11,8	11,0	**A**
P	20,0	25,4	30,1	41,1	55,3	66,1	75,7	87,7	87,2	90,1	88,3	**P**
FIN	3,8	3,0	5,2	4,2	4,9	8,5	7,8	4,7	3,7	3,0	2,1	**FIN**
S	15,5	15,5	16,1	14,7	20,9	21,4	22,1	15,1	8,6	6,7	7,7	**S**
UK	18,9	21,6	24,1	27,2	30,7	31,6	30,0	23,9	18,1	13,4	11,9	**UK**
IS	11,9	11,8	31,3	11,5	26,6	22,6	14,9	11,1	3,7	7,3	0,0	**IS**
NO	10,2	13,7	13,9	11,9	14,9	17,1	15,4	12,8	7,8	7,9	6,7	**NO**
EEA	89,7	91,7	88,1	102,3	94,8	95,8	83,8	68,7	46,7	32,9	40,6	**EEA**
CH	:	:	:	:	:	:	:	:	:	:	:	**CH**
US	136,0	167,0	173,0	180,0	397,0	297,0	269,0	250,0	217,0	171,0	:	**US**
CA	50,5	51,2	55,1	60,2	60,6	58,4	52,9	34,2	20,5	14,9	:	**CA**
JP	0,2	0,3	0,3	0,4	0,7	1,1	1,4	2,0	2,1	1,9	2,4	**JP**

Further reading: Surveillance in Europe, quarterly reports on AIDS. European Centre for the Epidemiological Monitoring of AIDS, Paris. Key data on health, 2000. Eurostat.

Cumulative AIDS cases by transmission group. People aged 13 or over, reported by 31 December 1999. %

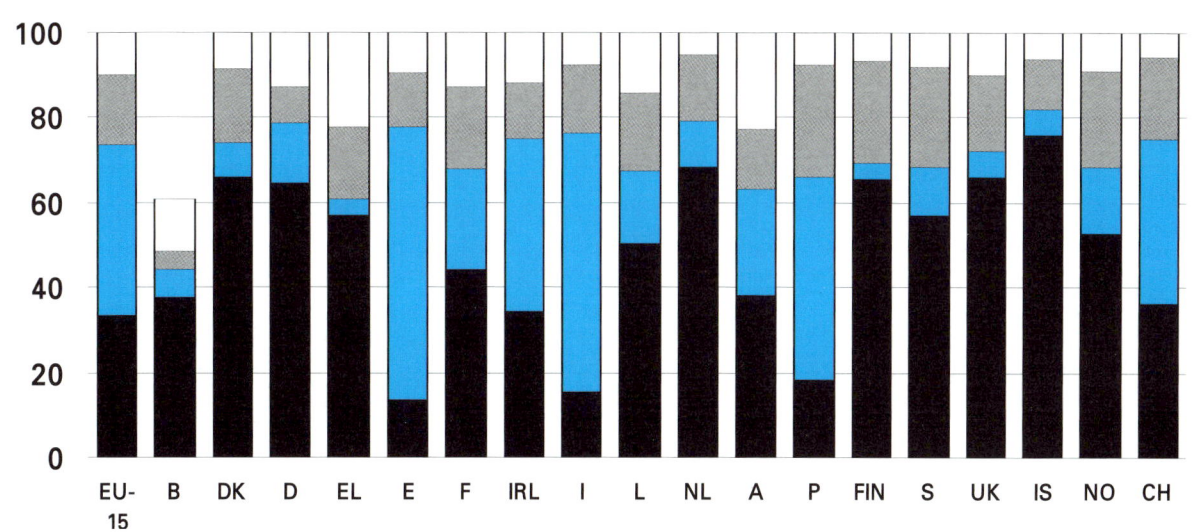

Black: homo/bisexual male; colour: heterosexual contact; grey: injecting drug user; white: other and undetermined.

Further reading: Surveillance in Europe, quarterly reports on AIDS. European Centre for the Epidemiological Monitoring of AIDS, Paris. Key data on health, 2000. Eurostat.

Incidence of type of cancer in 1996. Age standardised rate per 100 000 males using a standard world population

Malignant neoplasm (cancer) of	EU-15	B	DK	D	EL	E	F	IRL
All sites but skin	278,7	297,1	272,5	282,3	219,2	272,9	300,5	260,3
Bronchus/lung	54,1	81,5	48,7	54,0	56,4	53,8	47,6	41,4
Colon/rectum	34,0	29,9	37,8	37,2	16,3	29,4	37,8	40,9
Breast	-	-	-	-	-	-	-	-
Prostate	34,1	42,7	26,7	41,4	14,2	20,4	40,6	43,1
Stomach	15,4	10,6	8,4	16,2	11,7	17,5	10,9	12,3
Oesophagus	6,6	4,7	5,4	5,5	1,4	6,2	12,1	7,6
Bladder	21,9	20,6	26,6	18,0	24,2	30,0	19,2	14,0
Larynx	8,3	9,9	5,7	5,9	7,0	14,1	10,3	4,6
Testis	5,5	4,0	10,3	8,2	3,0	3,9	5,0	4,6
Cervix uteri	-	-	-	-	-	-	-	-
Ovary	-	-	-	-	-	-	-	-
Corpus uteri	-	-	-	-	-	-	-	-
Leukaemias	8,1	7,9	8,3	7,8	8,2	7,7	7,9	9,0
Liver	6,7	3,3	3,2	4,8	11,5	7,1	8,5	1,9
Non Hodgkins lymphoma	9,9	7,5	9,2	8,4	4,9	8,4	11,6	9,6
Hodgkin's disease	2,1	1,4	2,1	1,9	3,6	1,9	1,4	1,9
Pancreas	6,8	7,3	7,0	8,2	6,0	5,5	5,0	6,0
Lip, oral cavity, pharynx	15,1	10,1	11,7	14,1	4,8	22,8	31,6	9,8
Kidney	9,5	8,0	9,5	11,9	6,6	6,9	9,5	6,5
Melanoma of skin	5,3	4,9	10,1	6,0	1,8	2,8	5,3	5,9
Myeloma multiple	2,8	2,7	3,4	2,5	2,0	1,7	2,4	3,9
Brain, nervous system	6,9	9,3	11,3	7,1	11,6	7,6	5,3	8,4
Thyroid	1,5	0,5	0,5	2,0	0,8	1,3	1,4	0,8

5A1BK

Further reading: International agency on research on cancer. Lyon. Key data on health, 2000. Eurostat.

Incidence of type of cancer in 1996. Age standardised rate per 100 000 females using a standard world population

Malignant neoplasm (cancer) of	EU-15	B	DK	D	EL	E	F	IRL
All sites but skin	202,6	202,1	272,4	206,0	149,4	154,8	194,0	223,1
Bronchus/lung	11,0	10,8	30,2	10,6	7,8	3,7	5,4	17,2
Colon/rectum	23,2	21,8	28,6	26,0	12,8	19,0	24,6	27,3
Breast	65,1	70,7	77,7	63,4	46,5	45,4	76,6	67,7
Prostate	-	-	-	-	-	-	-	-
Stomach	7,2	5,4	3,5	8,6	5,7	7,5	4,4	5,7
Oesophagus	1,4	1,2	1,7	1,0	0,4	0,5	1,2	4,2
Bladder	4,3	4,8	7,7	4,1	3,9	3,5	2,9	3,7
Larynx	0,6	1,2	1,0	0,5	0,5	0,2	0,5	0,7
Testis	-	-	-	-	-	-	-	-
Cervix uteri	9,9	8,0	13,2	12,1	7,3	6,9	10,0	7,7
Ovary	10,1	11,3	13,4	10,8	7,2	8,4	8,9	13,0
Corpus uteri	10,9	11,0	13,6	8,5	6,5	11,1	10,0	9,6
Leukaemias	5,0	5,1	5,4	4,7	5,2	5,1	4,4	4,2
Liver	2,1	1,8	1,3	1,9	4,3	2,3	1,3	0,5
Non Hodgkins lymphoma	6,2	5,3	6,0	5,3	2,3	4,9	7,2	7,3
Hodgkin's disease	1,6	0,6	1,3	1,7	1,9	1,1	1,2	1,6
Pancreas	4,4	4,5	5,8	5,4	3,5	3,2	2,5	4,8
Lip, oral cavity, pharynx	2,7	2,6	3,3	3,0	1,1	2,4	3,4	2,9
Kidney	4,2	3,8	6,0	5,2	2,5	2,8	3,8	3,8
Melanoma of skin	6,2	4,8	13,6	6,4	1,8	4,0	6,3	10,6
Myeloma multiple	1,9	1,6	1,8	1,8	1,3	1,0	1,7	2,5
Brain, nervous system	4,9	5,8	11,5	5,1	6,8	5,0	3,4	5,9
Thyroid	3,1	1,0	1,9	4,2	2,7	2,7	2,4	1,8

5A1BM

Further reading: International agency on research on cancer. Lyon. Key data on health, 2000. Eurostat.

Incidence of type of cancer in 1996. Age standardised rate per 100 000 males using a standard world population

	I	L	NL	A	P	FIN	S	UK	Malignant neoplasm (cancer) of
	302,8	290,0	295,4	260,0	249,4	260,8	235,8	254,9	All sites but skin
	63,8	65,0	66,5	47,2	33,0	42,6	21,1	53,2	Bronchus/lung
	33,6	33,2	37,2	38,4	36,0	26,5	29,4	32,7	Colon/rectum
	-	-	-	-	-	-	-	-	Breast
	24,3	38,6	54,5	40,8	24,2	62,0	60,7	30,6	Prostate
	21,1	11,0	13,5	16,5	30,0	13,2	8,1	12,9	Stomach
	4,4	6,6	6,2	3,9	5,9	3,2	2,8	8,6	Oesophagus
	32,5	15,8	14,1	13,4	18,5	16,0	15,3	18,9	Bladder
	11,6	4,8	5,8	7,0	12,9	2,9	1,9	4,2	Larynx
	4,1	4,0	4,3	6,1	4,6	3,1	4,9	5,7	Testis
	-	-	-	-	-	-	-	-	Cervix uteri
	-	-	-	-	-	-	-	-	Ovary
	-	-	-	-	-	-	-	-	Corpus uteri
	9,3	5,6	8,3	6,2	6,7	7,4	7,8	8,0	Leukaemias
	13,9	4,5	1,6	7,0	4,8	3,6	3,6	2,3	Liver
	12,5	9,8	10,8	6,3	9,1	8,5	10,4	10,9	Non Hodgkins lymphoma
	2,4	2,6	2,0	2,8	2,3	2,5	1,8	2,4	Hodgkin's disease
	7,6	6,6	6,0	9,1	6,1	8,7	5,9	6,6	Pancreas
	11,8	15,9	8,6	13,0	15,7	8,4	6,2	6,2	Lip, oral cavity, pharynx
	11,4	6,7	9,8	9,7	5,8	11,1	8,6	7,1	Kidney
	4,2	4,0	7,6	7,7	1,9	7,5	11,1	5,9	Melanoma of skin
	3,4	1,6	3,3	2,4	2,5	2,7	3,5	3,4	Myeloma multiple
	6,9	6,6	6,0	6,1	7,2	10,2	8,2	5,9	Brain, nervous system
	1,7	0,8	0,9	1,8	1,3	2,8	1,2	1,2	Thyroid

5A1BL

Further reading: International agency on research on cancer. Lyon. Key data on health, 2000. Eurostat.

Incidence of type of cancer in 1996. Age standardised rate per 100 000 females using a standard world population

	I	L	NL	A	P	FIN	S	UK	Malignant neoplasm (cancer) of
	212,4	191,7	238,0	194,3	179,8	224,4	238,6	221,1	All sites but skin
	8,8	9,9	15,3	11,7	5,3	8,5	12,9	23,2	Bronchus/lung
	22,3	22,0	28,0	22,2	22,2	19,2	22,9	22,2	Colon/rectum
	63,1	67,1	87,3	60,1	52,2	76,7	76,1	67,4	Breast
	-	-	-	-	-	-	-	-	Prostate
	10,1	5,3	5,6	8,9	14,0	7,2	4,4	5,2	Stomach
	0,7	0,8	2,1	0,5	0,9	1,5	0,8	3,8	Oesophagus
	5,3	2,9	3,0	3,5	4,2	3,6	4,3	5,7	Bladder
	0,7	0,4	0,9	0,5	0,6	0,3	0,2	0,8	Larynx
	-	-	-	-	-	-	-	-	Testis
	9,0	2,7	6,3	12,2	14,7	4,4	7,3	10,7	Cervix uteri
	8,5	8,4	11,8	10,2	6,2	14,4	15,2	11,7	Ovary
	16,8	13,7	11,1	10,4	12,3	13,7	13,2	9,1	Corpus uteri
	6,0	2,5	5,3	3,8	4,8	4,2	6,3	4,9	Leukaemias
	4,5	1,0	0,7	2,2	1,6	1,4	2,0	1,0	Liver
	7,6	4,1	6,8	4,0	5,8	6,5	7,0	6,9	Non Hodgkins lymphoma
	1,8	1,8	1,6	2,4	1,7	1,6	1,2	2,1	Hodgkin's disease
	4,9	3,9	4,4	6,1	3,3	5,9	5,1	4,9	Pancreas
	2,1	1,6	3,6	2,4	2,0	4,1	3,0	2,5	Lip, oral cavity, pharynx
	4,4	2,4	5,4	4,7	2,5	6,8	5,3	3,5	Kidney
	4,2	3,5	10,6	8,6	2,7	6,4	11,4	7,7	Melanoma of skin
	2,3	0,8	2,2	1,9	1,7	2,4	2,3	2,4	Myeloma multiple
	4,7	4,1	4,1	4,4	4,8	11,3	8,5	3,9	Brain, nervous system
	4,3	4,7	2,0	1,9	2,6	8,0	3,9	1,9	Thyroid

5A1BN

Further reading: International agency on research on cancer. Lyon. Key data on health, 2000. Eurostat.

EUROSTAT YEARBOOK 2001

47

Cases of cancer are collected by the European Network of Cancer Registries and the International Agency for Research on Cancer (IARC)/WHO, with the support of the Europe Against Cancer programme from the European Union. The information on the incidence of cancer for 1996 was reported from 29 centres in Europe. Both incidence and mortality rates were higher in males than females in all countries. Even if fewer men have been dying of lung cancer since the 1980s, in 1996 it was this type of cancer which was the most common amongst men. Amongst women, it was breast cancer which occurred most frequently in 1996. Pancreas, liver and lung cancer have the lowest five-year age-standardised relative survival.

Data on incidence of tuberculosis and for the other communicable diseases are collected by WHO (via the EuroTB network for tuberculosis). The incidence rate is the number of new cases per year based on data on hospital discharge diagnoses in countries' reports on communicable diseases. The EU average incidence for tuberculosis remains at 13.7 despite a significant decrease since 1975 and a certain increase in some countries in the 1980s due to the strong influence of co-infection by HIV and tuberculosis. In terms of incidence per 100 000 persons, some of the communicable diseases preventable by immunisation can be considered practically eradicated in the EU (tetanus, poliomyelitis and diphtheria). Mumps, rubella, pertussis and measles remain a health problem in some Member States.

Incidence of tuberculosis, total per 100 000 persons

	1989	1990	1991	1992	1993	1994	1995	1996	1997	1998	1999	
EU-15	:	15,1	14,8	15,4	15,5	15,3	14,6	13,9	13,7	:	:	**EU-15**
B	16,6	15,8	14,6	13,3	14,9	15,0	13,6	13,3	12,4	11,9	:	**B**
DK	6,4	6,8	6,5	6,9	7,9	9,5	8,6	9,3	10,6	10,0	:	**DK**
D	:	18,5	16,9	17,5	17,4	15,9	15,0	14,4	13,6	:	:	**D**
EL	10,6	8,6	7,4	8,9	9,6	8,8	9,0	9,0	7,2	10,9	:	**EL**
E	20,7	19,5	23,1	24,9	24,1	24,1	22,1	21,0	23,5	22,5	:	**E**
F	16,1	15,9	14,9	15,0	16,6	15,7	14,7	12,8	11,4	:	:	**F**
IRL	19,1	17,8	18,1	17,0	16,7	14,6	12,9	12,2	11,6	11,5	:	**IRL**
I	6,9	7,4	6,5	8,2	8,3	10,2	9,1	9,0	9,0	:	:	**I**
L	11,9	12,6	12,4	6,4	9,6	10,6	8,3	9,1	10,2	9,0	:	**L**
NL	8,9	9,2	8,9	9,7	10,4	11,8	10,4	10,8	9,4	8,6	:	**NL**
A	17,4	19,7	18,2	17,1	15,9	15,7	17,4	18,0	17,0	16,1	:	**A**
P	67,1	62,8	60,6	60,1	55,2	56,8	56,8	53,5	52,0	53,3	:	**P**
FIN	19,5	15,5	15,4	13,9	10,7	10,9	13,0	12,6	11,1	12,2	:	**FIN**
S	7,0	6,5	6,1	7,1	7,1	6,1	6,4	5,6	5,1	5,0	:	**S**
UK	10,6	10,3	10,5	11,1	11,1	10,6	10,6	10,7	10,8	10,5	:	**UK**
IS	7,1	7,1	5,8	6,1	4,2	6,8	4,5	4,1	3,6	6,2	:	**IS**
NO	6,0	6,7	6,8	6,7	5,9	5,6	5,4	5,0	4,6	5,5	:	**NO**
EEA	:	:	:	:	:	:	:	:	:	:	:	**EEA**
CH	16,6	19,0	16,7	14,4	13,4	13,2	11,5	10,5	10,1	10,3	:	**CH**
US	:	10,3	10,4	10,5	9,8	9,4	8,7	8,0	7,4	:	:	**US**
CA	:	:	:	:	7,0	7,1	6,5	6,2	3,0	:	:	**CA**
JP	:	:	:	39,3	38,0	35,7	34,3	33,7	33,9	:	:	**JP**

1A5IA

Further reading: Health for all database, WHO, 2000. Surveillance of tuberculosis in Europe: report of tuberculosis cases notified in 1998. Euro TB and the national coordinators for tuberculosis surveillance in the WHO European Region, 2000. Key data on health, 2000. Eurostat.

CH: Includes Liechtenstein.

 eurostat

Incidence of diseases preventable by recommended immunisation, total per 100 000 persons. 1996–98

6T2BV

	Tetanus			Rubella			Acute poliomyelitis			Pertussis			
	1996	1997	1998	1996	1997	1998	1996	1997	1998	1996	1997	1998	
EU-15	0,1	0,1	0,1	24,0	20,3	:	.	.	.	10,4	7,9	6,5	EU-15
B	0,0	0,0	.	:	8,4	:	.	.	.	0,1	0,1	0,1	B
DK	.	0,0	0,0	0,2	0,0	.	.	.	.	1,7	3,8	2,4	DK
D	0,0	0,0	0,0	.	.	.	.	.	.	:	:	:	D
EL	0,1	0,0	0,0	1,4	0,7	0,5	0,0	.	0,0	0,9	1,0	2,1	EL
E	0,1	0,1	0,1	42,7	9,6	2,2	.	.	.	9,0	2,8	0,8	E
F	0,1	0,1	.	:	:	:	.	.	.	0,8	:	:	F
IRL	0,1	.	0,0	16,6	3,1	2,2	.	.	.	7,2	12,5	6,7	IRL
I	0,2	0,2	0,2	38,1	60,8	5,8	.	.	.	6,8	5,9	12,1	I
L	0,2	.	.	:	2,4	:	.	.	.	0,2	.	.	L
NL	0,0	0,0	.	0,3	0,1	0,1	.	.	.	17,9	22,4	14,3	NL
A	.	.	.	.	.	.	.	.	.	1,2	1,5	1,4	A
P	0,2	0,2	0,2	2,8	2,7	0,8	.	.	.	0,2	0,1	0,1	P
FIN	0,0	.	0,0	0,0	0,0	0,0	.	.	.	11,4	11,8	16,1	FIN
S	0,0	0,0	0,0	0,1	0,0	.	.	.	.	95,8	28,2	14,7	S
UK	0,0	0,0	:	19,9	7,1	.	.	.	.	4,6	6,2	:	UK
IS	.	.	.	:	11,4	2,2	.	.	.	37,2	17,4	4,4	IS
NO	0,0	0,1	0,0	0,4	.	0,1	.	.	.	2,1	41,7	52,8	NO
CH	0,0	0,0	0,0	41,1	50,8	26,4	.	.	.	162,8	183,6	183,2	CH
US	0,1	0,2	:	0,1	0,1	:	0,0	0,0	.	2,9	2,5	:	US
CA	:	:	:	1,9	13,2	:	.	.	.	17,8	14,6	:	CA
JP	0,0	0,0	:	:	:	:	.	.	.	0,2	0,0	:	JP

Further reading: Health for all database, WHO, 2000. Key data on health, 2000. Eurostat.

Incidence of diseases preventable by recommended immunisation, total per 100 000 persons. 1996–98

6T2BX

	Mumps			Measles			Diphtheria			
	1996	1997	1998	1996	1997	1998	1996	1997	1998	
EU-15	54,4	36,6	:	44,5	48,6	:	.	.	.	EU-15
B	94,1	50,0	:	71,1	38,0	:	.	.	.	B
DK	0,8	0,6	0,4	2,3	1,2	0,5	.	.	0,0	DK
D	:	:	:	1,0	:	:	.	.	.	D
EL	1,4	1,4	0,5	0,9	1,0	0,8	.	.	.	EL
E	37,3	17,6	7,2	12,6	4,6	1,1	.	.	.	E
F	86,9	68,2	:	113,0	136,0	:	.	.	.	F
IRL	11,6	7,8	1,5	6,3	5,1	5,5	.	.	:	IRL
I	112,8	51,6	25,6	56,8	71,8	7,1	.	.	.	I
L	:	0,5	:	6,0	0,2	.	.	.	.	L
NL	0,2	0,3	0,2	0,4	0,1	0,1	.	0,0	.	NL
A	:	:	:	:	.	:	.	.	.	A
P	113,6	195,2	28,4	1,1	1,3	1,0	.	.	.	P
FIN	0,0	0,0	0,0	.	.	0,0	0,1	.	.	FIN
S	0,1	0,2	:	0,5	0,7	0,1	.	0,0	:	S
UK	3,7	3,8	:	11,7	8,2	:	0,0	:	:	UK
IS	13,4	8,1	4,3	0,4	0,4	.	.	.	.	IS
NO	0,4	0,1	0,2	0,6	0,3	0,0	.	.	.	NO
CH	181,2	77,7	112,7	28,3	84,7	28,2	.	.	.	CH
US	0,3	0,3		1,9	0,5	:	0,0	0,0	:	US
CA	28,3	30,1		1,1	1,9	:	.	.	:	CA
JP	:	:	:	1,3	0,7	:	.	.	:	JP

Further reading: Health for all database, WHO, 2000. Key data on health, 2000. Eurostat.

Eurocat registries, coordinated since 1992 at the Scientific Institute of Public Health — Louis Pasteur in Brussels, aim to cover all foetal deaths from 20 weeks' gestation. This low limit eliminates any artificial distinction between live births and stillbirths of low gestational age. This is especially important for malformed babies considered not to be viable (such as those with anencephaly), since whether they are considered live born or stillborn may be influenced by medical customs or social or welfare considerations. The total prevalence rate for major congenital anomalies based is 23.6 per 1 000 births. The most frequent anomalies according to the group of anomalies are limb defects and cardiac defects.

Data for cognitive and behavioural disorders on elderly people comes from various sources (Alzheimer associations, experts, scientific publications) presenting strong problems of comparison. Estimative rates are calculated on the basis of Eurostat data on population and should be used with a lot of caution.

Prevalence rate (per 10 000 births, per year) of some congenital anomalies. EU-15. 1980–96

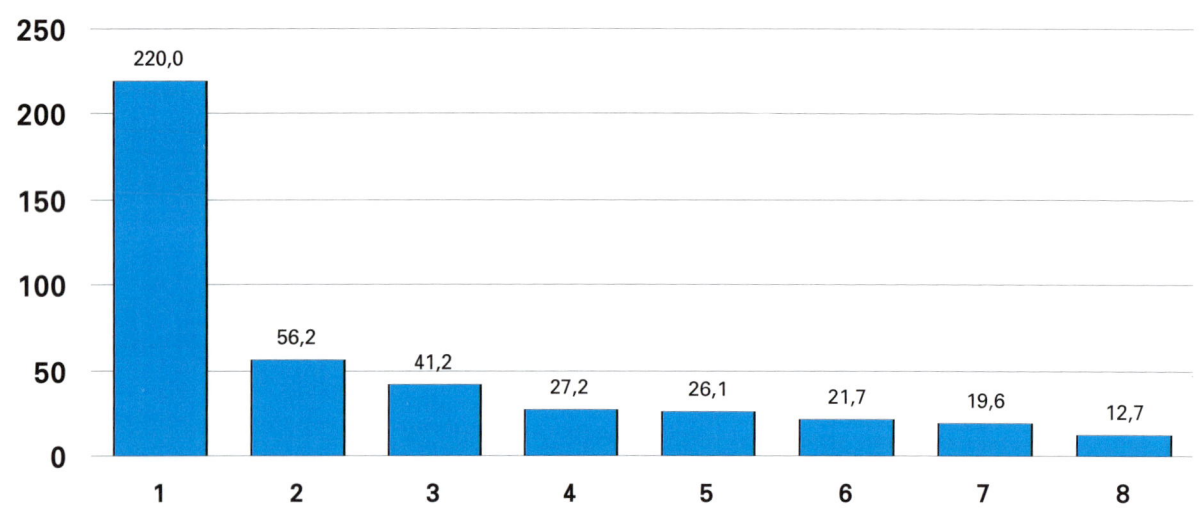

1: Total congenital anomalies; 2: Congenital heart disease; 3: Anomalies of limbs; 4: Total chromosomal anomalies; 5: Anomalies of the internal urogenital system; 6: Total musculoskeletal and connective tissue anomalies; 7: Nervous system anomalies; 8: Anomalies of external genital organs.

Further reading: Eurocat (European registration of congenital anomalies) supported by the European Commission. Key data on health, 2000. Eurostat.

Estimated cases (per 1 000) of all dementia and Alzheimer's disease over population aged more than 65 years. 1997

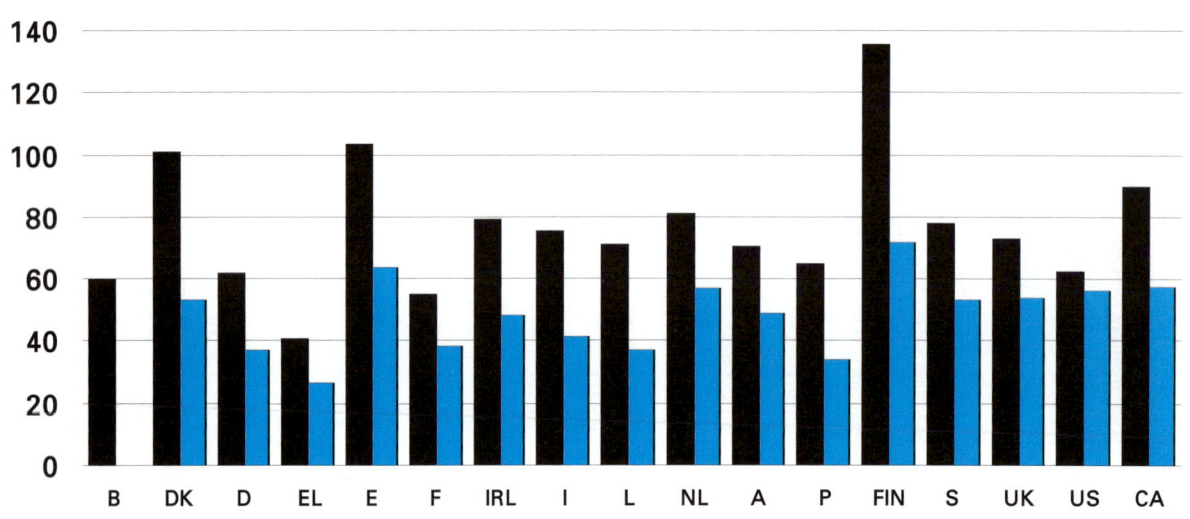

Black: All dementia; colour: Alzheimer's disease.

Further reading: Alzheimer Europe (Luxembourg) and national Alzheimer's associations. Calculation by Eurostat. Key data on health, 2000. Eurostat.

A: 1996; B: 1997, Alzheimer non-available; DK: April 1997; FIN: February 1996; F: March 1997; D: 1997 (only moderate and severe cases); EL: April 1997 (> 70 years old); IRL: April 1997; I: 1990/98; L: 1992; NL: 1997; P: 1994; E: April 1997; S: 1995; UK: 1997.

Analysis of causes of death is based on the underlying cause as indicated in Section B of the death certificate. Causes of death are defined on the basis of the WHO international classification of diseases, adopted by most countries. Although definitions are harmonised, the statistics might not be fully comparable as classifications may vary when cause of death is multiple or difficult to evaluate and because of different notification procedures. On the 3.370 million deaths that occurred in 1997, the mortality patterns are dominated by four main groups: circulatory diseases, cancer, respiratory diseases and external causes (including accidents and suicides). Deaths per cause are calculated as a standard death rate (SDR); this is the death rate of a population of a standard age distribution. As most causes of death vary significantly with people's age and sex, use of standard death rates improves comparability over time and between countries, as they aim at measuring death rates independently of different age structures of populations. Standard death rates used here are calculated by WHO on the basis of a standard European population. Ischaemic heart disease is the most important single cause. Causes of death vary greatly depending on age, sex and region. Standard death rates are normally higher for men than for women.

More data on this in Eurostat's database

Eurostat presents here, in the framework of the theme health and safety, a systematic and, as far as possible, harmonised set of regular and official statistics which are directly relevant to Community actions in the field of health. The domain is divided into two main items: public health, and health and safety at work.

The field public health has been divided into four chapters: lifestyles (which will include tables on anthropometric characteristics, smoking, drinking, etc.), health status (which will include mainly tables on disabilities and some specific diseases such as AIDS, cancer and others), healthcare (tables on human resources on health, hospital beds and treatments) and causes of death.

The field health and safety at work is divided into two chapters: occupational diseases and accidents at work.

➤ ➤ ➤ **DOMAIN HEALTH IN DATABASE NEW CRONOS**

Main causes of death (% of total causes) (EU-15). 1997

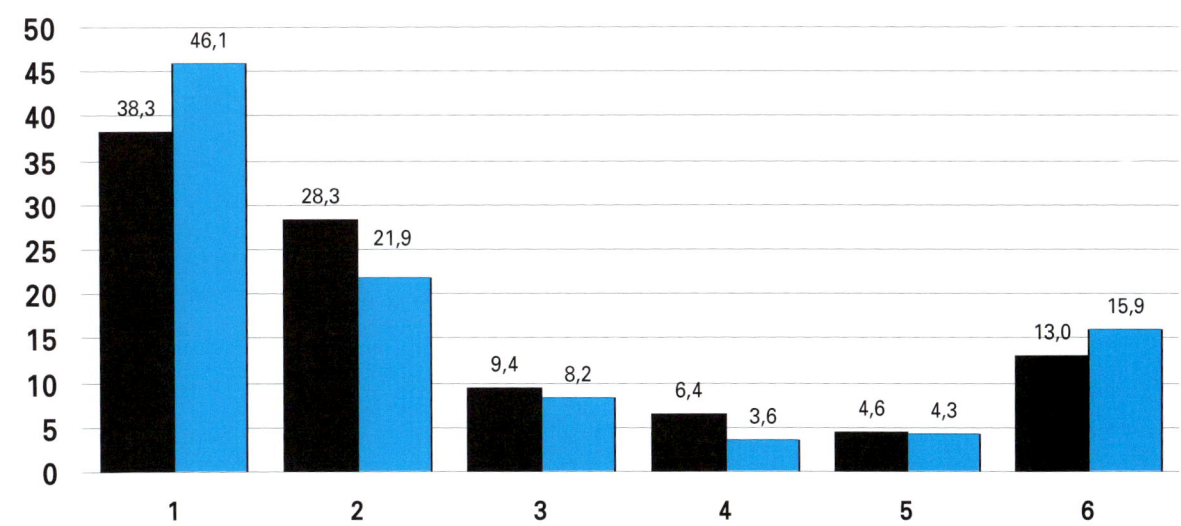

Black: Men; colour: Women. 1. Circulatory diseases; 2. Malignant neoplasms; 3. Respiratory diseases; 4. External causes; 5. Digestive system diseases; 6. Others.

Further reading: Causes of death statistics. Eurostat. Key data on health, 2000. Eurostat.

Standard death rates by 65, causes per 100 000 men. EU-15. 1997

	EU-15	B	DK	D	EL	E	F	IRL	I
All causes of death	908,5	1 041,0	1 049,0	961,7	818,7	874,0	881,9	1 064,7	851,0
Infectious and parasitic diseases	12,3	13,5	11,6	9,2	6,2	22,0	14,7	4,8	15,9
Tuberculosis	1,5	1,8	1,2	1,2	0,9	2,0	1,9	1,5	1,4
Meningococcal infection	0,2	0,2	0,1	0,1	0,3	0,3	0,0	0,2	0,1
AIDS (HIV disease)	4,6	2,7	5,2	1,5	0,5	11,3	3,5	1,6	11,3
Viral hepatitis	0,7	0,9	0,5	0,5	0,5	1,9	0,5	0,1	1,1
Neoplasms	262,1	307,3	275,3	260,4	219,2	266,9	291,6	257,3	271,0
Malignant neoplasms	256,3	305,4	269,0	254,5	219,1	260,4	285,0	255,8	261,2
lip, oral cavity, pharynx	8,2	8,4	6,7	8,9	2,9	9,8	15,1	6,8	7,1
œsophagus	8,6	8,2	9,2	7,5	2,6	7,7	12,3	12,3	5,1
stomach	16,1	14,1	10,7	17,5	12,4	18,4	11,0	15,1	21,2
colon	19,0	20,8	22,2	21,6	11,3	19,3	19,9	23,1	17,8
rectum and anus	8,5	7,6	12,7	10,9	1,7	7,2	7,0	8,9	7,6
liver and the intrahepatic bile ducts	10,8	6,4	5,2	6,8	18,3	12,9	16,8	4,6	19,5
pancreas	11,0	11,0	11,1	12,5	9,5	9,3	11,7	10,4	11,0
larynx and trachea/bronchus/lung	74,3	113,6	76,8	69,8	77,9	79,6	76,4	65,0	83,2
skin	2,2	1,6	4,0	2,5	0,7	1,5	2,1	1,8	2,1
breast	0,3	0,4	0,4	0,3	0,1	0,3	0,4	0,5	0,3
prostate	26,6	34,7	33,9	28,0	16,5	24,7	28,6	33,0	19,5
kidney	5,9	5,8	5,9	7,2	4,1	4,4	6,5	5,3	5,6
bladder	10,7	12,7	14,8	10,2	10,1	14,2	10,9	7,2	11,8
lymph/haematopoietic tissue	18,3	20,7	20,0	18,4	14,7	16,3	19,3	20,6	19,3
Diseases of the blood (-forming organs), immunological disorders	3,0	4,7	2,1	1,8	1,5	4,0	4,3	4,1	3,2
Endocrine, nutritional and metabolic diseases	18,3	15,7	14,8	21,8	6,9	18,6	16,7	18,5	24,0
Diabetes mellitus	14,5	11,0	10,8	18,9	5,2	15,1	8,8	15,3	20,7
Mental and behavioural disorders	14,7	18,2	15,2	16,7	1,1	17,5	17,3	12,2	10,3
Alcohol abuse (including alcoholic psychosis)	4,6	3,6	8,5	10,7	0,5	1,2	6,5	3,2	0,6
Drug dependence, toxicomania	1,8	0,7	0,4	2,6	:	0,3	1,0	2,4	3,4
Diseases of the nervous system and the sense organs	16,5	24,2	13,2	17,4	8,8	14,9	19,8	19,2	16,0
Meningitis (other than meningococcal infection)	0,4	0,4	1,0	0,3	0,4	0,4	0,4	0,4	0,3
Diseases of the circulatory system	343,9	350,6	374,3	416,9	371,4	279,9	245,8	464,5	323,6
Ischaemic heart diseases	156,5	132,3	200,4	203,6	129,5	104,1	80,2	284,7	120,9
Other heart diseases	62,4	98,1	54,6	74,7	102,1	60,8	65,4	60,9	71,0
Cerebrovascular diseases	77,3	76,9	76,9	82,4	112,8	71,9	54,9	77,2	80,5
Diseases of the respiratory system	83,4	118,7	90,1	65,9	44,1	98,2	68,7	151,0	56,9
Influenza	0,7	1,6	2,0	0,2	0,0	0,7	0,9	0,3	0,9
Pneumonia	29,3	25,9	30,6	18,8	6,7	18,3	25,3	64,5	9,8
Chronic lower respiratory diseases	40,4	69,8	50,3	39,5	10,5	54,6	29,8	70,4	34,6
of which asthma	2,9	3,5	3,4	5,9	0,6	1,5	2,7	3,0	2,4
Diseases of the digestive system	42,4	37,6	43,2	50,1	22,2	48,7	46,0	28,1	41,9
Ulcer of stomach, duodenum and jejunum	3,7	3,9	8,2	3,6	2,0	2,5	2,3	5,7	3,2
Chronic liver diseases	20,7	14,2	18,2	28,7	7,0	21,7	23,0	3,7	23,5
Diseases of the skin and subcutaneous tissue	1,0	2,2	0,4	0,3	0,2	1,1	2,2	2,0	0,6
Diseases of the musculoskeletal system/connective tissue	2,2	2,8	2,7	1,3	0,9	3,8	2,7	4,0	1,6
Rheumatoid arthritis and osteoarthrosis	0,5	0,7	1,0	0,4	0,0	0,3	0,4	2,1	0,5
Diseases of the genitourinary system	11,6	13,6	10,3	9,8	12,4	17,1	11,1	21,4	10,9
Diseases of the kidney and ureter	8,8	11,2	7,1	7,7	11,8	13,5	8,2	16,5	9,4
Certain conditions originating in the perinatal period	4,2	5,1	4,6	3,7	5,3	3,6	3,7	4,1	5,6
Congenital malformations and chromosomal abnormalities	4,0	4,6	6,0	3,8	5,1	4,5	3,2	5,1	4,1
Congenital malformations of the nervous system	0,4	0,6	0,7	0,4	0,6	0,4	0,4	0,8	0,4
Congenital malformations of the circulatory system	1,8	1,5	2,5	1,6	2,8	2,0	1,6	1,6	1,8
Symptoms, signs, abnormal findings, ill-defined causes	27,6	36,4	113,0	25,9	53,4	14,7	45,9	6,5	11,4
Sudden infant death syndrome	1,0	3,9	0,7	1,6	0,3	0,4	1,0	1,3	0,2
Unknown and unspecified causes	17,6	21,9	99,2	19,2	36,4	3,6	30,6	1,8	5,7
External causes of injury and poisoning	61,0	85,8	72,0	56,9	59,9	58,5	88,3	60,3	53,9
Accidents	38,4	48,2	43,5	32,0	51,7	44,2	53,3	39,0	39,2
transport accidents	17,7	25,9	15,3	15,9	33,1	22,7	19,8	18,9	19,5
accidental falls	8,9	11,6	17,1	9,2	3,9	4,9	11,3	6,6	12,1
accidental poisoning	1,9	2,4	4,2	0,4	4,5	4,1	0,9	3,3	0,8
Suicide and intentional self-harm	17,4	30,1	23,0	20,7	5,7	12,2	27,4	19,6	11,2
Homicide, assault	1,4	2,2	1,3	1,1	2,5	1,2	1,2	1,1	2,2
Events of undetermined intent	3,4	3,5	3,8	3,0	0,9	0,5	5,1	0,6	1,3

Further reading: Causes of death 1995–97 statistics. Eurostat 2000. Key data on health, 2000. Eurostat.   B: 1993; IS: 1995; DK, I, IRL, S, NO, CH: 1996.

2W2CV

 eurostat

2W2CV

Standard death rates by 65, causes per 100 000 men. EU-15. 1997

L	NL	A	P	FIN	S	UK	IS	NO	CH	
861,4	919,8	941,1	1 139,5	1 004,3	810,4	924,9	809,8	886,0	814,2	All causes of death
4,7	9,8	4,3	32,8	6,6	7,4	6,6	8,6	9,2	14,1	Infectious and parasitic diseases
1,1	0,9	1,2	7,1	2,4	0,9	0,9	0,7	1,3	0,9	Tuberculosis
0,6	0,4	0,1	0,2	0,0	0,2	0,5	0,7	0,3	0,1	Meningococcal infection
1,4	1,9	1,2	16,1	0,2	1,3	0,8	2,3	2,1	8,3	AIDS (HIV-disease)
0,4	0,3	0,3	1,9	0,1	0,3	0,5	:	0,1	0,4	Viral hepatitis
228,4	282,4	248,8	246,5	216,9	196,0	248,5	200,9	234,5	230,9	Neoplasms
227,3	275,6	244,0	241,7	212,7	191,4	245,4	200,1	228,9	225,0	Malignant neoplasms
7,8	4,1	7,6	10,2	2,8	3,0	4,1	1,6	4,4	7,1	lip, oral cavity, pharynx
6,1	9,4	5,5	8,2	4,2	4,5	12,9	11,6	3,8	7,1	œsophagus
12,1	14,2	18,3	31,4	14,7	10,1	13,8	15,7	14,3	10,4	stomach
22,0	22,3	22,9	20,0	10,5	13,8	17,8	17,3	18,0	15,5	colon
5,1	6,8	10,4	10,0	7,5	8,3	9,7	0,9	11,9	7,5	rectum and anus
6,3	3,3	11,5	7,2	5,7	6,0	4,1	5,3	2,1	8,5	liver and the intrahepatic bile ducts
8,6	10,4	13,8	9,7	13,4	12,5	9,8	10,9	11,5	10,8	pancreas
76,4	92,5	63,2	52,1	60,2	33,5	69,7	43,5	48,4	56,5	larynx and trachea/bronchus/lung
1,2	3,1	4,0	1,3	2,9	3,5	2,5	2,6	4,9	4,4	skin
:	0,5	0,2	0,6	0,2	0,1	0,2	0,0	0,3	0,2	breast
23,2	33,0	29,7	34,0	30,8	37,4	27,8	25,3	43,8	32,9	prostate
3,7	6,7	6,0	3,1	7,8	6,5	5,5	9,6	6,1	5,9	kidney
9,9	9,8	8,4	8,1	6,1	6,5	10,1	8,7	9,7	7,7	bladder
18,3	20,0	16,8	16,1	19,9	19,0	18,2	24,5	20,4	19,2	lymph/haematopoietic tissue
7,3	1,9	0,9	2,1	0,9	3,4	3,2	0,7	1,8	1,7	Diseases of the blood (-forming organs), immunological disorders
18,4	19,9	16,4	29,2	11,0	16,4	11,8	5,1	13,1	24,1	Endocrine, nutritional and metabolic diseases
12,8	16,2	15,8	25,1	9,1	13,6	9,4	4,4	10,2	21,1	Diabetes mellitus
30,9	17,6	6,9	3,7	38,9	20,6	13,0	0,9	23,0	27,5	Mental and behavioural disorders
12,9	2,1	5,6	1,1	7,3	5,0	1,5	:	8,0	4,9	Alcohol abuse (including alcoholic psychosis)
1,8	:	1,1	0,1	0,6	2,3	2,7	:	7,0	6,8	Drug dependence, toxicomania
15,7	16,7	13,3	12,9	24,7	12,4	16,3	18,5	17,6	22,7	Diseases of the nervous system and the sense organs
:	0,4	0,3	0,8	0,4	0,4	0,5	:	0,4	0,2	Meningitis (other than meningococcal infection)
326,9	332,4	456,6	396,2	428,2	379,6	378,8	370,5	377,1	299,8	Diseases of the circulatory system
126,9	149,4	211,3	100,3	273,3	216,3	233,3	221,9	202,9	146,9	Ischaemic heart diseases
85,7	73,2	100,1	57,5	31,0	41,7	24,1	29,8	53,9	60,7	Other heart diseases
73,0	65,5	92,2	197,5	84,3	68,2	74,6	84,8	15,1	49,7	Cerebrovascular diseases
70,9	99,6	46,1	111,0	93,3	64,4	139,5	79,0	72,5	53,8	Diseases of the respiratory system
:	1,7	1,0	0,9	1,1	2,2	0,4	3,3	0,6	1,7	Influenza
13,2	35,6	12,4	46,5	50,4	34,5	74,5	45,9	32,1	12,5	Pneumonia
39,0	55,9	28,8	36,7	35,3	21,7	51,1	21,6	34,2	33,0	Chronic lower respiratory diseases
4,1	0,3	3,0	2,7	1,4	2,2	1,9	1,7	5,9	3,5	of which asthma
41,2	29,2	50,4	58,4	42,4	26,0	32,5	13,0	26,7	28,1	Diseases of the digestive system
1,3	2,3	3,6	4,7	5,7	4,1	6,1	2,8	4,9	3,1	Ulcer of stomach, duodenum and jejunum
22,8	6,0	35,6	32,2	17,8	7,0	10,3	0,9	8,0	13,0	Chronic liver diseases
0,2	1,5	0,2	1,5	0,2	0,9	0,9	0,0	0,8	0,5	Diseases of the skin and subcutaneous tissue
0,2	3,5	0,8	1,4	2,8	2,3	2,8	3,3	3,8	3,5	Diseases of the musculoskeletal system/connective tissue
:	0,7	0,3	0,2	1,5	0,6	0,8	:	1,3	1,5	Rheumatoid arthritis and osteoarthrosis
9,8	14,7	8,0	15,4	8,5	10,3	10,7	8,4	11,0	7,3	Diseases of the genitourinary system
9,8	8,7	7,2	14,2	5,1	6,6	6,5	6,0	7,0	4,7	Diseases of the kidney and ureter
										Certain conditions originating in the perinatal period
2,8	3,9	2,9	4,3	2,6	1,8	5,1	6,2	3,6	4,0	Congenital malformations and chromosomal abnormalities
1,5	5,2	3,6	4,5	4,2	3,6	3,9	7,8	4,4	5,0	Congenital malformations of the nervous system
0,4	0,5	0,5	0,3	0,5	0,3	0,4	0,8	0,6	0,4	Congenital malformations of the circulatory system
0,6	1,6	1,6	2,1	1,8	1,4	1,9	1,6	1,5	1,7	Symptoms, signs, abnormal findings, ill-defined causes
31,3	41,7	7,0	137,9	4,5	10,4	10,7	4,4	29,1	28,4	Sudden infant death syndrome
1,1	0,3	1,1	0,1	0,6	0,4	1,1	0,7	1,1	1,0	Unknown and unspecified causes
15,9	31,6	0,5	96,3	3,4	4,6	2,3	2,8	22,3	21,8	
71,2	39,6	74,8	81,7	118,6	54,8	40,6	80,2	57,9	62,8	External causes of injury and poisoning
39,9	23,7	44,4	49,8	70,5	28,2	23,7	55,5	38,8	32,2	Accidents
20,7	10,8	20,4	32,6	15,8	8,5	9,6	20,7	11,8	13,1	transport accidents
6,3	3,7	11,8	6,4	22,1	9,5	5,6	5,7	14,7	11,3	accidental falls
3,7	0,9	2,0	1,7	15,4	2,3	2,8	5,1	2,2	0,3	accidental poisoning
28,0	13,1	28,7	9,6	40,1	18,8	10,6	17,1	17,3	27,8	Suicide and intentional self-harm
0,8	1,8	0,8	1,9	3,9	1,6	1,0	:	1,1	1,3	Homicide, assault
2,5	0,4	0,9	20,2	2,3	6,1	5,2	7,7	0,5	0,7	Events of undetermined intent

Further reading: Causes of death 1995–97 statistics. Eurostat 2000. Key data on health, 2000. Eurostat.

B: 1993; IS: 1995; DK, I, IRL, S, NO, CH: 1996.

Standard death rates by 65, causes per 100 000 women. EU-15. 1997

	EU-15	B	DK	D	EL	E	F	IRL	I
All causes of death	537,8	588,4	682,9	569,8	549,1	484,1	463,1	666,2	502,5
Infectious and parasitic diseases	6,0	7,6	5,0	5,3	4,4	8,9	7,5	3,7	6,2
Tuberculosis	0,6	0,5	0,3	0,4	0,4	0,7	0,9	0,9	0,5
Meningococcal infection	0,2	0,1	0,4	0,1	0,1	0,4	0,0	0,5	0,0
AIDS (HIV disease)	1,2	0,6	0,8	0,3	0,1	2,4	0,8	0,3	3,5
Viral hepatitis	0,4	0,6	-	0,3	0,3	1,1	0,3	0,2	0,8
Neoplasms	146,7	154,6	207,1	155,4	116,0	119,4	131,5	173,8	143,0
Malignant neoplasms	142,8	153,0	201,4	151,4	115,9	115,2	127,2	172,6	137,1
lip, oral cavity, pharynx	1,6	2,0	2,5	1,7	0,8	1,3	1,8	1,8	1,6
œsophagus	2,0	1,7	2,6	1,4	0,5	0,8	1,6	5,4	1,0
stomach	7,6	6,3	4,7	9,1	6,7	8,1	4,2	7,7	10,2
colon	12,8	14,7	17,5	15,4	8,5	12,2	11,7	15,2	11,3
rectum and anus	4,6	4,0	7,2	5,9	1,2	3,7	3,6	3,5	4,4
liver and the intrahepatic bile ducts	3,8	2,7	3,3	2,7	8,2	4,8	3,3	2,0	7,3
pancreas	7,3	7,5	9,2	8,3	5,7	5,4	6,7	8,5	7,2
larynx and trachea/bronchus/lung	15,5	13,8	40,0	14,7	10,8	6,4	10,0	25,9	12,3
skin	1,6	1,6	2,2	1,6	0,7	1,2	1,5	1,7	1,4
breast	29,2	35,0	39,4	30,4	21,6	22,8	28,3	35,7	28,2
cervix uteri	2,8	3,4	5,1	3,7	1,5	2,5	2,1	4,9	1,1
other parts of the uterus	4,4	5,0	4,5	4,4	3,2	4,1	5,1	3,3	5,6
ovary	8,7	9,9	14,5	9,9	5,5	6,0	8,1	11,5	6,5
kidney	2,6	3,0	3,7	3,2	1,6	1,7	2,5	2,6	2,1
bladder	2,4	2,8	4,4	2,8	1,9	1,9	2,0	2,1	1,8
lymph/haematopoietic tissue	11,6	12,9	12,0	11,3	9,4	10,4	11,9	12,2	12,3
Diseases of the blood (-forming organs), immunological disorders	2,1	3,2	1,9	1,3	1,3	2,6	2,7	3,2	2,4
Endocrine, nutritional and metabolic diseases	16,4	17,2	10,6	19,4	7,2	18,4	13,9	11,6	23,3
Diabetes mellitus	13,0	12,6	7,1	16,8	5,9	15,2	6,8	8,3	20,2
Mental and behavioural disorders	10,3	14,0	7,9	6,5	0,7	17,8	12,6	7,9	6,9
Alcohol abuse (including alcoholic psychosis)	1,1	1,0	2,2	2,7	0,0	0,2	1,5	0,9	0,1
Drug dependence, toxicomania	0,4	0,4	0,2	0,6	:	0,0	0,2	0,5	0,4
Diseases of the nervous system and the sense organs	11,9	18,9	10,4	11,1	6,0	11,7	14,0	14,1	12,1
Meningitis (other than meningococcal infection)	0,3	0,2	0,6	0,3	0,2	0,3	0,2	0,3	0,2
Diseases of the circulatory system	217,9	221,3	220,7	264,8	289,1	191,5	140,8	278,9	214,2
Ischaemic heart diseases	75,6	60,4	99,2	103,9	56,9	46,2	32,4	134,7	57,8
Other heart diseases	45,5	69,8	31,8	53,7	98,8	53,0	41,6	43,2	52,4
Cerebrovascular diseases	62,3	61,8	60,3	64,3	114,4	59,1	38,6	69,6	65,0
Diseases of the respiratory system	40,6	40,1	64,9	26,8	28,8	36,7	32,2	97,3	21,2
Influenza	0,6	1,5	2,1	0,1	0,0	0,7	0,9	0,4	0,7
Pneumonia	18,8	14,0	21,8	10,2	4,6	9,2	13,4	48,9	5,4
Chronic lower respiratory diseases	14,5	16,7	37,2	12,8	3,5	12,6	12,0	34,1	10,1
of which asthma	2,2	2,7	4,5	3,1	0,3	2,0	2,4	3,2	1,3
Diseases of the digestive system	24,3	25,8	27,7	26,9	12,0	24,6	24,0	22,2	23,8
Ulcer of stomach, duodenum and jejunum	2,2	2,1	6,5	2,2	1,3	1,2	1,2	2,8	1,6
Chronic liver diseases	8,7	7,5	7,7	11,4	2,2	7,3	9,1	3,1	11,3
Diseases of the skin and subcutaneous tissue	1,3	3,1	0,7	0,5	0,5	1,4	2,6	1,9	0,8
Diseases of the musculoskeletal system/connective tissue	3,3	4,5	3,1	1,9	1,0	5,5	2,9	5,2	2,9
Rheumatoid arthritis and osteoarthrosis	1,0	1,0	0,9	0,8	0,0	0,8	0,7	3,1	1,1
Diseases of the genitourinary system	7,0	9,0	6,2	5,9	9,0	10,2	5,8	12,0	6,3
Diseases of the kidney and ureter	5,4	7,8	4,6	4,9	8,5	7,9	4,4	9,1	5,9
Complications of pregnancy, childbirth and puerperium	0,1	0,1	0,2	0,1	:	0,0	0,2	0,2	0,1
Certain conditions originating in the perinatal period	3,5	3,8	3,2	2,8	5,0	3,0	2,8	3,8	5,0
Congenital malformations and chromosomal abnormalities	3,5	3,4	5,1	3,4	4,4	3,9	2,8	4,6	3,6
Congenital malformations of the nervous system	0,4	0,7	0,7	0,4	0,5	0,4	0,4	0,8	0,4
Congenital malformations of the circulatory system	1,5	1,1	2,3	1,4	2,5	1,9	1,4	1,6	1,5
Symptoms, signs, abnormal findings, ill-defined causes	18,8	25,6	73,8	15,5	46,1	11,2	29,4	5,8	7,6
Sudden infant death syndrome	0,7	2,5	0,5	1,1	0,1	0,3	0,7	0,9	0,1
Unknown and unspecified causes	8,9	14,3	56,8	9,1	29,3	1,8	15,8	1,4	2,4
External causes of injury and poisoning	24,0	36,1	34,4	22,2	17,7	17,5	37,4	19,8	23,2
Accidents	16,3	21,9	22,3	13,7	16,3	13,0	24,7	15,2	18,7
transport accidents	5,4	8,1	5,0	5,1	9,8	6,2	6,4	5,8	5,4
accidental falls	6,5	8,2	13,2	6,0	2,1	2,2	8,8	5,3	10,7
accidental poisoning	0,6	1,3	1,6	0,2	0,9	0,8	0,6	1,2	0,4
Suicide and intentional self-harm	5,6	10,2	8,7	6,6	0,9	3,6	9,4	3,6	3,5
Homicide, assault	0,6	1,5	0,8	0,7	0,6	0,4	0,7	0,8	0,6
Events of undetermined intent	1,3	1,4	2,4	1,1	0,1	0,1	1,8	0,1	0,5

Further reading: Causes of death 1995–97 statistics. Eurostat 2000. Key data on health, 2000. Eurostat.

B: 1993; IS: 1995; DK, I, IRL, S, NO, CH: 1996.

3W3CV

3W3CV

Standard death rates by 65, causes per 100 000 women. EU-15. 1997

L	NL	A	P	FIN	S	UK	IS	NO	CH	
521,9	560,6	555,6	670,3	564,7	511,1	604,4	576,7	537,9	482,0	All causes of death
2,8	5,9	1,5	8,9	4,7	4,7	4,4	4,1	5,1	7,0	Infectious and parasitic diseases
0,4	0,3	0,4	1,1	1,5	0,6	0,5	0,5	0,5	0,5	Tuberculosis
:	0,2	0,1	0,2	:	0,1	0,5	0,0	0,3	0,2	Meningococcal infection
:	0,3	0,2	3,0	0,0	0,3	0,2	0,0	0,2	3,1	AIDS (HIV disease)
0,5	0,1	0,1	0,6	0,1	0,2	0,1	:	0,0	0,2	Viral hepatitis
149,2	166,4	149,3	127,4	134,4	145,2	171,9	175,2	163,0	132,2	Neoplasms
148,8	162,7	145,9	124,3	130,6	141,0	169,3	173,5	159,0	127,7	Malignant neoplasms
2,9	1,6	1,6	1,3	1,7	1,3	1,7	0,7	2,0	1,8	lip, oral cavity, pharynx
1,8	3,1	0,8	1,1	2,1	1,4	5,3	3,5	1,1	1,5	œsophagus
7,7	6,1	10,0	14,7	7,6	5,2	5,9	7,5	6,3	4,9	stomach
15,2	15,2	12,0	12,3	8,3	11,2	12,3	15,3	15,9	9,3	colon
6,2	3,7	5,9	4,4	4,8	4,8	4,9	2,5	6,9	4,3	rectum and anus
3,6	2,0	3,7	3,1	4,3	3,7	2,2	0,9	1,0	2,5	liver and the intrahepatic bile ducts
7,4	8,9	9,7	5,5	10,4	9,9	7,2	7,9	9,0	7,2	pancreas
18,9	21,6	16,3	7,1	10,8	18,6	30,3	31,0	21,0	12,6	larynx and trachea/bronchus/lung
2,2	2,2	2,4	1,1	2,0	1,9	1,9	0,0	3,2	2,3	skin
24,7	37,1	28,8	25,2	23,4	23,9	33,6	51,7	28,6	29,3	breast
1,0	2,5	3,3	3,3	2,1	2,4	3,8	2,7	4,8	2,5	cervix uteri
7,3	3,3	5,6	5,8	3,7	3,8	3,2	3,9	3,5	4,0	other parts of the uterus
9,5	9,8	9,2	5,3	9,2	9,8	11,5	11,2	11,6	8,0	ovary
4,0	3,3	3,3	1,2	3,5	4,0	2,8	2,1	3,0	2,4	kidney
1,7	2,7	2,2	2,2	1,2	1,9	3,2	3,1	2,8	2,7	bladder
11,0	13,2	12,0	10,3	13,3	12,4	11,9	9,1	12,6	11,6	lymph/haematopoietic tissue
1,7	1,7	0,8	1,7	0,8	2,2	2,1	1,8	1,5	1,5	Diseases of the blood (-forming organs), immunological disorders
7,4	20,5	12,8	27,2	9,1	10,9	8,6	5,3	9,5	19,7	Endocrine, nutritional and metabolic diseases
6,2	15,5	12,1	24,1	7,3	8,6	6,4	3,0	6,4	16,7	Diabetes mellitus
22,0	20,4	1,7	3,2	38,4	17,7	10,8	1,4	13,0	18,4	Mental and behavioural disorders
4,2	0,4	1,2	0,2	1,1	1,2	0,6	:	1,9	1,2	Alcohol abuse (including alcoholic psychosis)
:	0,0	0,3	:	0,2	0,6	0,6	:	1,2	1,3	Drug dependence, toxicomania
10,3	14,0	9,4	7,5	19,9	9,0	11,8	17,1	12,8	18,2	Diseases of the nervous system and the sense organs
:	0,4	0,4	0,3	0,3	0,3	0,3	:	0,4	0,2	Meningitis (other than meningococcal infection)
210,4	191,8	290,6	289,5	236,7	218,9	227,6	205,6	209,9	184,7	Diseases of the circulatory system
55,3	64,8	104,4	53,4	123,8	99,0	109,9	96,4	85,8	71,3	Ischaemic heart diseases
56,1	46,8	70,7	47,1	18,2	28,1	19,3	21,3	40,7	41,4	Other heart diseases
58,2	54,5	73,4	154,1	68,5	56,0	66,1	60,5	11,6	39,8	Cerebrovascular diseases
31,1	44,4	20,9	49,1	39,2	37,4	90,7	85,3	45,0	23,0	Diseases of the respiratory system
0,1	0,8	0,9	0,6	0,9	1,7	0,4	3,7	0,6	1,8	Influenza
9,2	22,3	8,3	23,2	27,4	19,6	55,7	56,0	24,3	8,0	Pneumonia
13,6	18,3	9,7	11,2	8,1	12,6	26,2	22,1	17,5	10,0	Chronic lower respiratory diseases
3,6	0,4	1,5	1,4	1,7	2,1	2,2	1,3	3,9	1,9	of which asthma
27,8	22,7	23,4	24,4	22,5	16,1	25,4	15,9	15,4	18,4	Diseases of the digestive system
1,6	1,8	2,3	2,0	3,0	2,3	4,0	0,6	2,6	2,0	Ulcer of stomach, duodenum and jejunum
8,9	3,7	11,4	10,2	6,5	2,8	5,8	2,0	2,6	5,1	Chronic liver diseases
0,2	2,6	0,4	1,4	0,3	0,9	1,3	0,7	0,4	0,7	Diseases of the skin and subcutaneous tissue
1,5	4,6	1,4	2,0	5,0	3,2	5,0	0,8	5,2	4,8	Diseases of the musculoskeletal system/connective tissue
0,7	1,4	0,7	0,6	3,3	1,3	1,8	:	2,7	2,2	Rheumatoid arthritis and osteoarthrosis
5,2	10,9	5,7	8,6	7,6	5,7	7,2	9,8	5,8	4,9	Diseases of the genitourinary system
4,9	5,8	5,3	8,0	5,8	3,8	4,2	7,5	3,6	3,6	Diseases of the kidney and ureter
:	0,2	0,0	0,1	0,1	0,1	0,1	:	0,0	0,1	Complications of pregnancy, childbirth and puerperium
3,5	2,9	3,5	3,7	2,0	2,0	4,3	3,6	2,2	2,7	Certain conditions originating in the perinatal period
1,2	4,7	3,3	3,7	4,3	2,9	3,3	8,6	3,6	4,6	Congenital malformations and chromosomal abnormalities
:	0,8	0,5	0,4	0,4	0,3	0,4	0,7	0,2	0,4	Congenital malformations of the nervous system
0,6	1,4	0,9	1,8	1,6	0,9	1,5	0,7	1,5	1,3	Congenital malformations of the circulatory system
21,7	26,8	5,9	87,4	2,5	10,2	13,2	3,7	19,0	14,9	Symptoms, signs, abnormal findings, ill-defined causes
0,6	0,2	0,7	0,2	0,4	0,5	0,7	0,0	0,9	0,4	Sudden infant death syndrome
10,9	15,7	0,3	44,1	1,6	2,1	1,0	2,4	11,1	10,1	Unknown and unspecified causes
26,0	20,0	25,0	24,4	37,1	23,9	16,7	37,9	26,4	26,3	External causes of injury and poisoning
16,5	12,5	15,0	15,2	24,3	12,4	11,1	34,4	19,3	14,3	Accidents
6,9	4,1	6,0	8,5	5,7	3,6	3,1	8,3	4,3	4,2	transport accidents
6,1	2,6	5,7	3,1	10,5	5,3	4,5	5,3	9,7	7,0	accidental falls
2,3	0,2	0,6	0,3	4,3	0,6	1,0	1,7	1,1	0,3	accidental poisoning
9,0	6,2	8,6	2,4	10,3	7,7	3,0	3,5	5,9	10,4	Suicide and intentional self-harm
:	0,7	1,0	0,6	1,4	0,8	0,4	:	1,0	0,8	Homicide, assault
0,4	0,2	0,4	6,1	0,6	2,9	2,2	0,0	0,3	0,5	Events of undetermined intent

Further reading: Causes of death 1995–97 statistics. Eurostat 2000. Key data on health, 2000. Eurostat.

B: 1993; IS: 1995; DK, I, IRL, S, NO, CH: 1996.

Death (SDR) from ischaemic heart diseases: women per 100 000 women

	1989	1990	1991	1992	1993	1994	1995	1996	1997	1998	1999	
EU-15	87	86	87	84	85	80	79	77	:	:	:	**EU-15**
B	59	55	56	52	60	58	:	:	:	:	:	**B**
DK	147	148	136	130	135	114	116	99			:	**DK**
D		107	112	110	112	108	108	106	103	102	:	**D**
EL	59	61	57	60	57	56	57	57	56	:	:	**EL**
E	47	48	48	47	47	45	47	:	:	:	:	**E**
F	41	40	39	37	37	34	33	33	31	:	:	**F**
IRL	175	157	149	146	149	146	145	137	:	:	:	**IRL**
I	64	63	63	60	60	60	59	57	:	:	:	**I**
L	81	68	63	62	69	67	55	57	60	:	:	**L**
NL	83	82	80	76	78	73	71	69	64	:	:	**NL**
A	104	109	114	110	110	107	108	107	104	106	:	**A**
P	55	59	58	56	59	54	53	53	53	52	:	**P**
FIN	160	158	152	150	154	142	141	129	:	:	:	**FIN**
S	121	120	117	115	114	102	102	98	:	:	:	**S**
UK	151	145	144	139	137	126	122	116	110		:	**UK**
IS	129	118	120	119	116	112	97	:	:	:	:	**IS**
NO	116	116	111	106	103	96	94	:	:	:	:	**NO**
EEA	:	:	:	:	:	:	:	:	:	:	:	**EEA**
CH	70	71	68	70	68	68	:	:	:	:	:	**CH**
US	:	:	:	:	:	:	:	:	:	:	:	**US**
CA	:	:	:	:	:	:	:	:	:	:	:	**CA**
JP	:	:	:	:	:	:	:	:	:	:	:	**JP**

1A5DB

Further reading: Health for all database, WHO, 2000. Key data on health, 2000. Eurostat.   SDR: standard death rate.

Death (SDR) from ischaemic heart diseases: men per 100 000 men

	1989	1990	1991	1992	1993	1994	1995	1996	1997	1998	1999	
EU-15	189	186	186	180	180	169	168	162	:	:	:	**EU-15**
B	133	129	123	121	133	123	:	:	:	:	:	**B**
DK	302	293	277	271	260	233	227	200	:	:	:	**DK**
D	:	225	231	226	229	219	217	209	201	197	:	**D**
EL	137	136	132	134	129	123	128	130	128	:	:	**EL**
E	106	106	108	106	105	102	103	105	:	:	:	**E**
F	95	91	91	87	86	81	81	80	76	:	:	**F**
IRL	351	339	329	309	319	306	307	288	:	:	:	**IRL**
I	139	135	136	129	128	125	124	119	:	:	:	**I**
L	187	163	151	161	160	150	142	162	138	:	:	**L**
NL	205	194	185	175	181	166	164	156	148	:	:	**NL**
A	224	221	224	220	215	211	212	207	209	206	:	**A**
P	111	115	114	111	120	104	103	105	100	105	:	**P**
FIN	363	359	340	346	326	299	304	285	:	:	:	**FIN**
S	270	270	261	249	247	229	230	215	:	:	:	**S**
UK	317	306	304	292	290	265	259	247	232	:	:	**UK**
IS	264	233	266	246	233	240	225	:	:	:	:	**IS**
NO	276	278	260	250	237	221	224	:	:	:	:	**NO**
EEA	:	:	:	:	:	:	:	:	:	:	:	**EEA**
CH	163	163	161	156	153	145	:	:	:	:	:	**CH**
US	:	144	:	:	:	127	124	119	114	:	:	**US**
CA	:	:	:	:	:	:	:	:	:	:	:	**CA**
JP	:	:	:	:	:	:	:	:	:	:	:	**JP**

1A5DA

Further reading: Health for all database, WHO, 2000. Key data on health, 2000. Eurostat.   SDR: standard death rate.

1A5EB

Death (SDR) from cerebrovascular diseases: women per 100 000 women

	1989	1990	1991	1992	1993	1994	1995	1996	1997	1998	1999	
EU-15	81	80	80	75	74	70	68	65	:	:	:	EU-15
B	67	66	62	60	62	58	:	:	:	:	:	B
DK	62	66	65	65	68	61	61	60	:	:	:	DK
D	:	80	83	79	77	75	71	68	64	61	:	D
EL	138	137	138	131	124	124	124	114	113	:	:	EL
E	86	83	82	75	72	70	65	62	:	:	:	E
F	51	48	47	44	43	39	38	38	37	:	:	F
IRL	84	80	81	77	77	75	72	71	:	:	:	IRL
I	84	82	81	78	77	75	68	64	:	:	:	I
L	128	117	104	102	91	79	79	70	63	:	:	L
NL	62	62	62	63	61	58	58	53	54	:	:	NL
A	94	89	91	82	79	77	74	77	73	70	:	A
P	181	190	188	176	180	166	168	166	153	152	:	P
FIN	93	89	87	83	89	78	83	70	:	:	:	FIN
S	62	64	63	61	60	57	55	56	:	:	:	S
UK	87	84	83	80	75	71	71	69	66		:	UK
IS	56	59	55	46	56	58	61	:	:	:	:	IS
NO	78	77	72	71	72	66	63	:	:	:	:	NO
EEA	:	:	:	:	:	:	:	:	:	:	:	EEA
CH	53	51	48	47	45	44	:	:	:	:	:	CH
US	:	:	:	67	69	70	:	:	:	:	:	US
CA	:	:	:	:	61	60	60	:	:	:	:	CA
JP	:	103	:	:	:	102	121	116	114	113	:	JP

Further reading: Health for all database, WHO, 2000. Key data on health, 2000. Eurostat.   SDR: standard death rate.

Death (SDR) from cerebrovascular diseases: men per 100 000 men

1A5EA

	1989	1990	1991	1992	1993	1994	1995	1996	1997	1998	1999	
EU-15	100	97	98	93	90	86	83	80	:	:	:	EU-15
B	80	79	76	77	77	72	:	:	:	:	:	B
DK	78	82	80	81	83	75	78	77	:	:	:	DK
D	:	100	104	99	97	94	91	87	82	78	:	D
EL	130	130	129	125	116	121	120	113	112	:	:	EL
E	102	97	97	90	86	82	80	75	:	:	:	E
F	71	66	65	61	60	55	55	53	52	:	:	F
IRL	96	91	84	86	90	80	80	79	:	:	:	IRL
I	110	105	105	98	97	92	84	79	:	:	:	I
L	151	137	122	112	117	99	101	100	79	:	:	L
NL	77	75	76	74	73	71	68	65	65	:	:	NL
A	120	114	107	107	98	94	92	94	91	86	:	A
P	235	242	243	232	240	216	213	213	197	196	:	P
FIN	104	112	112	104	107	99	102	84	:	:	:	FIN
S	72	76	77	74	73	69	69	68	:	:	:	S
UK	97	93	96	91	83	79	78	77	74		:	UK
IS	63	78	78	59	66	69	86	:	:	:	:	IS
NO	92	95	87	89	91	80	80	:	:	:	:	NO
EEA	:	:	:	:	:	:	:	:	:	:	:	EEA
CH	:	:	:	:	:	:	:	:	:	:	:	CH
US	:	:	:	46	47	47	:	:	:	:	:	US
CA	:	:	:	:	45	:	:	:	:	:	:	CA
JP	:	96	:	:	:	91	114	109	108	107	:	JP

Further reading: Health for all database, WHO, 2000. Key data on health, 2000. Eurostat.   SDR: standard death rate.

Death (SDR) from cancer: women per 100 000 women

	1989	1990	1991	1992	1993	1994	1995	1996	1997	1998	1999	
EU-15	154	153	150	151	150	150	148	145	144	:	:	EU-15
B	160	155	155	156	153	154	:	:	:	:	:	B
DK	206	201	206	204	204	207	209	201	:	:	:	DK
D	:	160	164	162	162	159	156	155	151	151	:	D
EL	116	113	113	115	116	116	115	117	115	:	:	EL
E	118	118	119	117	118	119	118	115	:	:	:	E
F	132	129	129	129	129	126	126	126	123	:	:	F
IRL	196	182	185	188	181	183	178	173	:	:	:	IRL
I	146	145	146	144	144	143	136	136	:	:	:	I
L	166	170	159	160	158	154	147	141	161	:	:	L
NL	164	162	162	160	162	162	159	160	162	:	:	NL
A	162	161	158	159	158	155	153	147	145	140	:	A
P	125	127	127	126	128	123	126	124	124	123	:	P
FIN	137	137	132	135	135	126	130	123	:	:	:	FIN
S	144	144	144	143	144	138	142	141	:	:	:	S
UK	188	189	185	183	182	179	177	174	172	169	:	UK
IS	168	177	157	163	186	171	173	:	:	:	:	IS
NO	150	150	145	144	150	154	152	:	:	:	:	NO
EEA	:	:	:	:	:	:	:	:	:	:	:	EEA
CH	144	147	146	145	142	139	:	:	:	:	:	CH
US	:	:	:	:	:	:	:	:	:	:	:	US
CA	:	:	:	:	:	:	:	:	:	:	:	CA
JP	137	139	142	147	148	153	163	167	170	175	:	JP

Further reading: Health for all database, WHO, 2000. Key data on health, 2000. Eurostat.   SDR: standard death rate.

1A5AB

Death (SDR) from cancer: men per 100 000 men

	1989	1990	1991	1992	1993	1994	1995	1996	1997	1998	1999	
EU-15	275	273	273	272	270	266	262	259	:	:	:	EU-15
B	312	307	303	303	307	301	:	:	:	:	:	B
DK	273	279	265	272	278	280	275	268	:	:	:	DK
D	:	269	272	273	272	266	263	259	252	250	:	D
EL	214	215	217	217	219	219	221	218	217	:	:	EL
E	251	253	255	258	258	261	262	257	:	:	:	E
F	303	298	297	295	293	284	282	280	273	:	:	F
IRL	266	268	266	272	274	263	267	257	:	:	:	IRL
I	286	285	284	278	276	275	261	258	:	:	:	I
L	298	301	285	303	304	268	302	281	250	:	:	L
NL	304	296	295	295	292	286	282	280	273	:	:	NL
A	268	268	269	263	265	251	250	245	242	238	:	A
P	216	219	215	222	229	229	235	239	241	243	:	P
FIN	241	238	229	232	230	222	221	224	:	:	:	FIN
S	197	199	200	197	195	192	191	190	:	:	:	S
UK	278	276	276	275	267	262	258	252	244	:	:	UK
IS	226	227	234	204	182	190	202	:	:	:	:	IS
NO	226	223	225	225	230	229	227	:	:	:	:	NO
EEA	:	:	:	:	:	:	:	:	:	:	:	EEA
CH	267	263	263	259	254	248	:	:	:	:	:	CH
US	:	:	:	221	222	221	:	:	:	:	:	US
CA	:	:	:	:	212	214	214	:	:	:	:	CA
JP	211	216	223	231	234	242	262	270	273	281	:	JP

Further reading: Health for all database, WHO, 2000. Key data on health, 2000. Eurostat.   SDR: standard death rate.

1A5AA

The crude death rate (CDR) is a weighted average of the age-specific mortality rates. The weighting factor is the age distribution of the population whose mortality experience is being observed. To compare the CDR from two or more populations (at the NUTS 2 level in this publication) is a comparison of a combination of different age-specific death rates and different population structures not reflecting the 'real' mortality differences but including also the effect of the population structure on the total number of deaths and on the crude death rates.

Death (CDR) from cancer. 1996

1A5AC

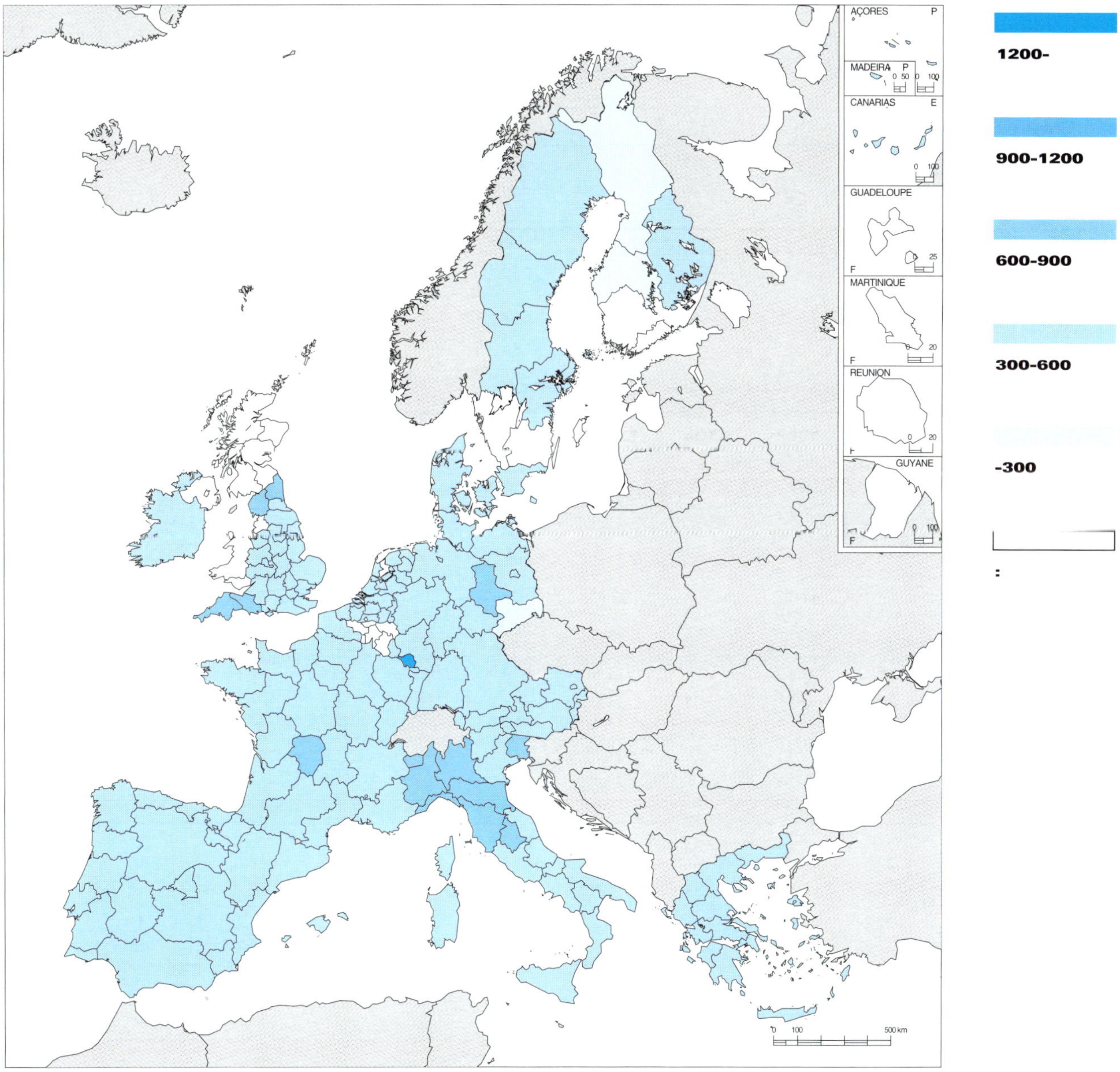

	1200-
	900-1200
	600-900
	300-600
	-300

AÇORES   P

MADEIRA   P
0 50 100

CANARIAS   E
0 100

GUADELOUPE
F   25

MARTINIQUE
F   20

REUNION
F   20

GUYANE
F   100

0   100   500 km

Further reading: Regions, statistical yearbook, 1999. Eurostat. Causes of death 1995–97 Statistics, Eurostat, 2000. Key data on health, 2000. Eurostat.

NUTS 2. NUTS 95. NUTS 1: D, UK9 (Wales), UKA (Scotland). CDR: crude death rate.

Death (SDR) by suicide: women per 100 000 women

	1989	1990	1991	1992	1993	1994	1995	1996	1997	1998	1999	
EU-15	6,9	6,6	6,5	6,2	6,1	5,8	5,8	5,7	:	:	:	EU-15
B	10,5	10,5	9,4	9,9	10,3	10,3	:	:	:	:	:	B
DK	18,6	14,8	13,6	13,7	13,8	10,2	9,7	8,7	:	:	:	DK
D	:	8,6	8,5	8,0	7,3	7,0	7,1	6,8	6,6	6,0	:	D
EL	1,9	1,4	1,5	1,2	1,8	1,2	1,1	1,0	0,9	:	:	EL
E	3,5	3,6	3,4	3,0	3,3	3,2	3,3	3,8	:	:	:	E
F	10,8	10,2	10,3	10,0	10,5	9,8	9,8	9,5	9,2	:	:	F
IRL	4,2	5,3	4,1	3,7	4,2	5,5	4,9	3,6	:	:	:	IRL
I	3,6	3,6	3,6	3,5	3,4	3,2	3,2	3,5	:	:	:	I
L	9,2	9,7	10,8	14,3	7,3	6,4	8,0	8,8	9,4	:	:	L
NL	7,4	6,8	7,1	6,7	6,4	6,1	6,1	6,3	6,2	:	:	NL
A	12,5	11,6	10,1	10,4	9,7	10,4	9,2	8,9	8,5	7,9	:	A
P	3,5	4,0	4,2	4,2	3,4	2,9	3,9	2,7	2,4	2,2	:	P
FIN	11,1	11,9	11,2	11,0	10,9	11,4	11,4	10,3	:	:	:	FIN
S	9,8	9,7	9,5	8,9	8,9	7,9	8,4	7,7	:	:	:	S
UK	3,6	3,6	3,3	3,4	3,2	3,1	3,0	3,1	3,0	:	:	UK
IS	5,2	4,9	7,0	4,6	6,4	2,9	3,5	:	:	:	:	IS
NO	8,1	7,8	8,0	7,5	6,1	6,8	6,1	:	:	:	:	NO
EEA	:	:	:	:	:	:	:	:	:	:	:	EEA
CH	12,0	11,5	10,5	9,7	10,3	10,9	:	:	:	:	:	CH
US	:	:	:	4,6	4,6	4,5	:	:	:	:	:	US
CA	:	:	:	:	5,4	5,3	5,4	:	:	:	:	CA
JP	:	12,4	:	:	:	10,9	11,3	11,5	11,9	14,7	:	JP

Further reading: Health for all database, WHO, 2000. Key data on health, 2000. Eurostat.   SDR: standard death rate.

1A5GB

Death (SDR) by suicide: men per 100 000 men

	1989	1990	1991	1992	1993	1994	1995	1996	1997	1998	1999	
EU-15	19,1	18,7	18,7	18,5	18,5	18,5	18,1	17,4	:	:	:	EU-15
B	26,6	25,8	25,0	25,5	30,2	29,9	:	:	:	:	:	B
DK	33,0	30,7	28,6	27,7	27,6	24,9	22,9	22,9	:	:	:	DK
D	:	23,6	23,7	22,6	21,6	21,8	21,8	20,5	20,6	20,0	:	D
EL	5,4	5,1	5,6	5,2	5,7	5,1	5,5	5,2	5,7	:	:	EL
E	11,8	11,2	11,0	10,8	11,6	12,1	11,8	11,9	:	:	:	E
F	29,9	29,1	28,9	29,4	30,4	30,2	28,8	27,3	26,8	:	:	F
IRL	13,4	16,1	17,2	18,4	15,5	17,9	18,4	19,4		:	:	IRL
I	10,8	10,7	10,8	11,2	11,6	11,1	11,1	11,1		:	:	I
L	28,0	24,4	27,5	14,3	23,9	30,6	21,4	25,0	28,5	:	:	L
NL	12,9	12,1	13,7	13,5	13,1	13,9	12,5	13,0	13,0	:	:	NL
A	35,5	33,9	33,5	32,9	31,4	32,2	32,9	33,0	28,6	28,9	:	A
P	11,9	13,6	14,9	13,3	12,2	12,2	11,9	9,9	9,6	8,3	:	P
FIN	45,7	47,9	47,5	45,5	43,5	42,3	41,8	37,0	:	:	:	FIN
S	25,4	22,5	23,0	20,4	20,9	19,9	20,3	18,8	:	:	:	S
UK	11,3	12,2	12,1	12,2	11,8	11,4	11,3	10,6	10,6	:	:	UK
IS	13,1	27,2	23,0	18,1	15,1	16,4	17,1	:	:	:	:	IS
NO	22,5	22,6	23,2	20,5	20,3	17,4	18,5	:	:	:	:	NO
EEA	:	:	:	:	:	:	:	:	:	:	:	EEA
CH	31,0	29,9	32,3	29,5	28,3	29,6	:	:	:	:	:	CH
US	:	:	:	19,6	22,1	21,9	:	:	:	:	:	US
CA	:	:	:	:	21,0	20,5	21,5	:	:	:	:	CA
JP	:	20,4	:	:	:	23,1	23,4	24,3	26,0	36,5	:	JP

Further reading: Health for all database, WHO, 2000. Key data on health, 2000. Eurostat.   SDR: standard death rate.

1A5GA

Deaths (SDR) in motor-vehicle traffic accidents: women per 100 000 women

	1989	1990	1991	1992	1993	1994	1995	1996	1997	1998	1999	
EU-15	6,8	7,0	6,7	6,4	5,9	5,7	5,7	5,4	:	:	:	EU-15
B	9,1	8,5	8,3	7,9	7,8	8,5	:	:	:	:	:	B
DK	6,1	6,6	5,5	5,1	5,3	5,4	6,2	4,8	:	:	:	DK
D	:	6,7	6,4	6,2	5,7	5,4	5,5	5,1	4,8	4,5	:	D
EL	8,9	9,9	9,3	9,1	7,6	9,1	9,8	10,6	9,4	:	:	EL
E	9,1	8,5	8,1	7,3	6,6	6,0	6,2	6,0	:	:	:	E
F	9,0	8,7	7,9	7,5	7,6	7,3	7,1	6,8	6,2	:	:	F
IRL	6,8	6,6	6,6	6,0	6,0	5,7	5,8	5,6	:	:	:	IRL
I	5,7	6,3	6,5	6,8	5,7	5,9	5,7	5,3	:	:	:	I
L	6,5	8,9	11,8	11,4	12,5	7,3	8,9	6,8	6,9	:	:	L
NL	5,4	4,8	4,1	4,6	3,9	4,1	4,0	3,8	3,9	:	:	NL
A	7,8	7,6	7,4	7,0	6,7	6,3	6,0	5,5	5,6	5,0	:	A
P	10,5	11,0	11,4	10,6	10,0	9,4	9,8	9,4	7,9	7,4	:	P
FIN	8,0	7,4	7,1	6,8	5,0	5,0	3,8	3,7			:	FIN
S	5,3	5,2	4,4	4,3	4,0	3,2	3,3	3,2			:	S
UK	4,8	4,7	4,5	4,1	3,5	3,3	3,1	3,0	3,0		:	UK
IS	8,4	6,7	6,4	5,8	1,4	1,6	7,5	:	:	:	:	IS
NO	4,5	3,5	4,5	3,7	3,5	3,6	3,9	:	:	:	:	NO
EEA	:	:	:	:	:	:	:	:	:	:	:	EEA
CH	5,8	5,9	5,3	5,0	4,2	4,4	:	:	:	:	:	CH
US	:	:	:	9,8	9,9	10,2	:	:	:	:	:	US
CA	:	:	:	:	7,6	6,3	6,6	:	:	:	:	CA
JP	:	7,0	:	:	:	6,8	6,9	6,6	6,5	6,1	:	JP

1A5HB

Further reading: Health for all database, WHO, 2000. Key data on health, 2000. Eurostat.   SDR: standard death rate.

Deaths (SDR) in motor-vehicle traffic accidents: men per 100 000 men

	1989	1990	1991	1992	1993	1994	1995	1996	1997	1998	1999	
EU-15	21,7	21,8	21,5	20,1	18,5	17,8	17,6	16,7	:	:	:	EU-15
B	26,1	26,2	25,3	23,2	24,8	26,4	:	:	:	:	:	B
DK	17,3	15,5	15,9	15,5	14,5	13,2	14,4	13,6	·	:	:	DK
D	:	18,4	19,5	18,2	17,2	16,9	16,0	14,9	14,8	13,0	:	D
EL	30,7	32,3	32,4	32,2	28,5	30,7	33,6	34,0	31,9	:	:	EL
E	31,9	30,7	29,4	25,2	23,3	21,0	21,3	20,8	:	:	:	E
F	26,0	25,4	23,8	22,0	21,5	20,0	19,5	18,6	18,6	:	:	F
IRL	19,5	20,0	17,4	14,8	16,6	16,6	17,1	17,5	:	:	:	IRL
I	22,6	23,2	24,5	24,3	21,4	20,9	20,1	18,7	:	:	:	I
L	28,6	26,1	30,7	24,7	26,2	26,4	22,2	25,6	19,8	:	:	L
NL	12,8	11,8	11,9	11,5	11,2	11,1	10,9	10,7	10,0	:	:	NL
A	28,2	26,4	25,1	21,2	21,6	23,1	20,3	16,8	18,5	14,8	:	A
P	45,7	44,2	46,0	44,0	37,7	33,5	37,9	34,1	31,1	29,2	:	P
FIN	21,1	18,1	16,2	15,4	11,9	12,6	11,8	10,4	:	:	:	FIN
S	13,5	11,2	10,6	10,5	8,7	7,2	7,4	7,0	:	:	:	S
UK	13,2	13,6	12,1	11,1	9,3	8,9	8,6	8,8	8,9	:	:	UK
IS	8,2	13,0	16,4	9,3	14,4	5,8	12,2	:	:	:	:	IS
NO	12,6	11,6	9,5	9,9	8,5	9,1	9,4	:	:	:	:	NO
EEA	:	:	:	:	:	:	:	:	:	:	:	EEA
CH	20,6	20,1	18,4	15,6	14,6	12,8	:	:	:	:	:	CH
US	:	:	:	:	:	:	:	:	:	:	:	US
CA	:	:	:	:	:	:	:	:	:	:	:	CA
JP	:	19,1	:	:	:	17,4	17,7	16,6	16,0	15,6	:	JP

1A5HA

Further reading: Health for all database, WHO, 2000. Key data on health, 2000. Eurostat.   SDR: standard death rate.

1

Deaths in road accidents are people killed outright or who die within 30 days. Between 1989 and 1997 the number of deaths due to road accidents declined by nearly 14 % on average. However, 45 179 people lost their lives on the roads of the EU in 1997. The most deadly regions in road accidents per million inhabitants were the Alentejo (P), Algarve (P), the Luxembourg region in Belgium (B), Centro (P), Brandenburg (D), Sterea Ellada (EL), Dytiki Ellada (EL), Kriti (EL), Bourgogne (F), Castilla-La Mancha (E), Mecklenburg-Vorpommern (D), Baleares (E), Castilla-León (E) and Peloponnissos (EL).

Deaths (CDR) in motor-vehicle traffic accidents. 1996

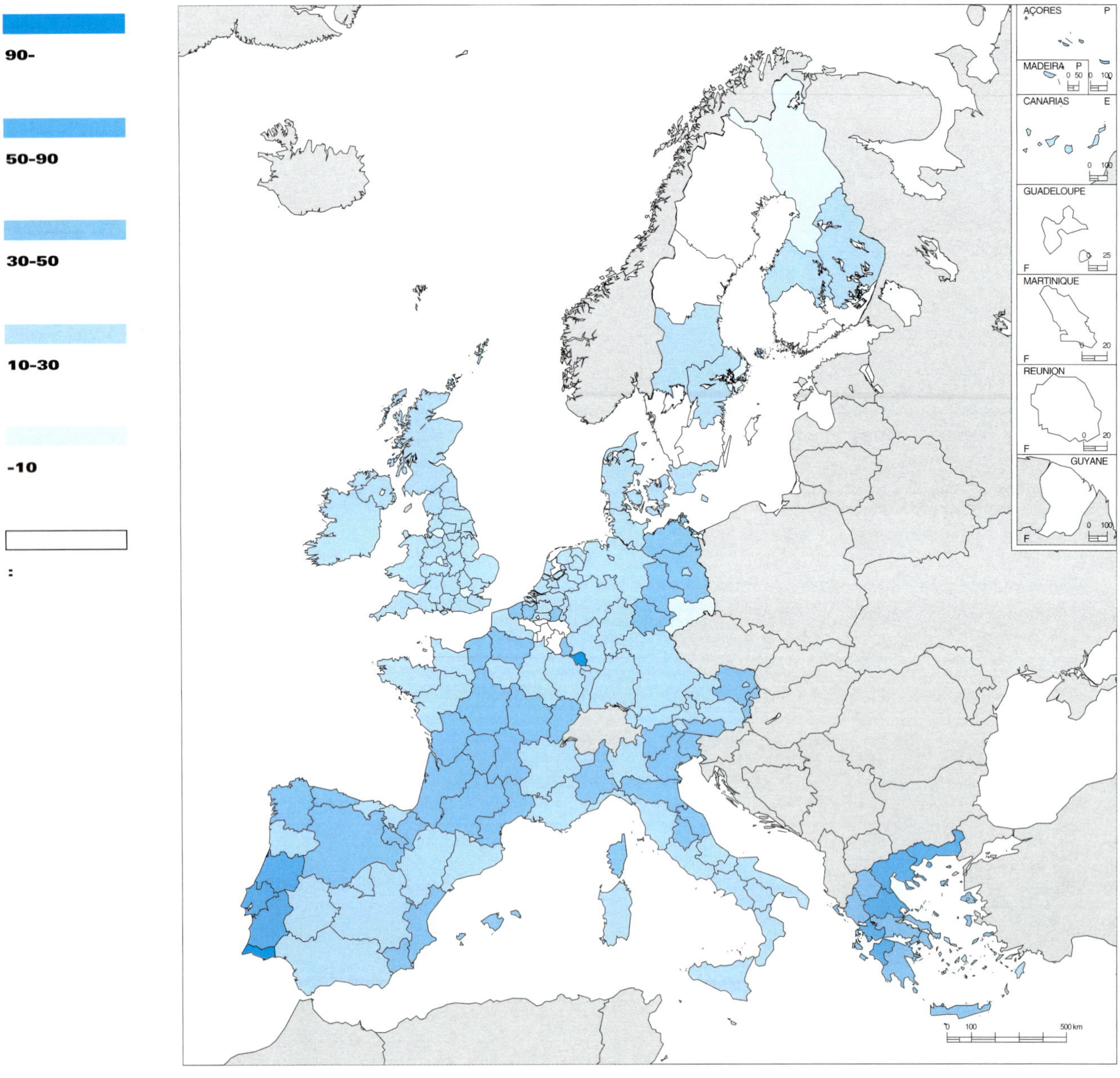

90-

50-90

30-50

10-30

-10

:

1A5HC

AÇORES   P

MADEIRA   P

CANARIAS   E

GUADELOUPE

MARTINIQUE

REUNION

GUYANE

Further reading: Regions, statistical yearbook, 1999. Eurostat. Causes of death 1995–97 Statistics, Eurostat, 2000. Key data on health, 2000. Eurostat.

NUTS 2. NUTS 95. NUTS 1: D, UK9 (Wales), UKA (Scotland). CDR: crude death rate.

The data from Ehlass (European home and leisure accident surveillance system), supported by the European Union, are obtained from the casualty departments of hospitals selected by the Member States and by means of household surveys.

The home and leisure accidents exclude road traffic accidents, occupational accidents, sudden illness, suicides and cases of violence (except children's brawls) and include school accidents and cases due to animals (bites, stings, etc.).

Leisure and home accidents by place of accident (in % of total). EU-15. 1997–98

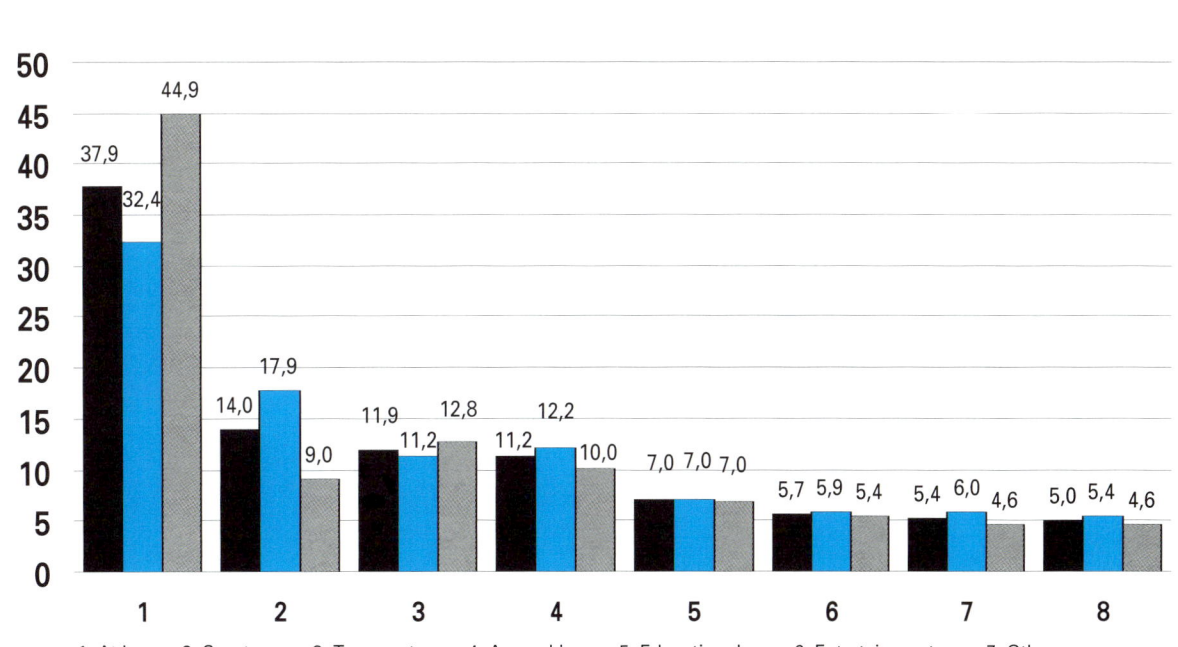

1. At home; 2. Sports area; 3. Transport area; 4. Around home; 5. Educational area; 6. Entertainment area; 7. Other areas; 8. Unknown. Black: total; Colour: men; Grey: women.

Further reading: European home and leisure accidents surveillance system, European Commission. Key data on health, 2000. Eurostat.

EUROSTAT YEARBOOK 2001

63

1

European statistics on accidents at work cover accidents at work resulting in more than three days' absence and fatalities, on the basis of harmonised definitions. They cover almost 90 % of the persons in employment in the European Union and Norway (for some Member States self-employers, family workers, civil servants, or other specific groups are not included in the statistics). For seven countries, Denmark, Greece, Ireland, the Netherlands, Norway, Sweden, and the UK the accidents with more than three days' absence are partly reported to the authorities and only an estimation of the number of accidents occurred is available. The nine other Member States, in which it is compulsory to report accidents at work in order to qualify for treatment under the social security or insurance schemes, record all accidents (except for the Italian craft sector). Then the figures are not fully comparable between these two groups of countries.

Number of accidents at work with more than three days' absence by main branches and high-risk sectors. EU-15

	1993	1994	1995	1996	1997	1998
Agriculture	:	348 309	331 252	361 186	364 578 *	350 779 *
Manufacturing including:	1 555 621	1 515 556	1 451 752	1 357 022	1 377 579 *	1 406 412 *
Food and beverages	224 142	215 798	295 219	283 446	287 740 *	293 762 *
Wood and wood products	124 094	105 051	93 573	89 909	91 271 *	93 181 *
Glass, ceramics, construction products	76 917	72 155	75 369	69 578	70 632 *	72 110 *
Basic metals and metal products	376 493	365 537	388 864	357 066	362 475 *	370 062 *
Electricity, gas, water	:	:	19 964	19 734	19 750 *	19 254 *
Construction	892 802	858 129	867 837	831 000	823 672 *	827 274 *
Wholesale, trade, repairs	476 699	487 656	507 607	491 424	514 820 *	540 716 *
Hotels, restaurants	169 288	179 489	177 572	176 472	184 874 *	194 173 *
Transport including:	:	421 133	412 293	438 973	444 012 *	461 044 *
Land transport	152 220	168 468	160 212	188 231	190 392 *	197 696 *
Auxiliary transport activities	223 303	200 060	198 488	181 145	183 224 *	190 253 *
Financial intermediation, renting, business	203 414	225 828	242 214	240 411	247 392 *	268 823 *
Total all branches	:	4 918 066	4 820 451	4 757 611	4 700 668 *	4 819 929 *

5H1DD

Further reading: Statistics in focus: population and social conditions, 2000. Eurostat. Key data on health, 2000. Eurostat.   1997, 1998: estimations.

Number of fatal accidents at work by main branches and high-risk sectors. EU-15

	1993	1994	1995	1996	1997	1998
Agriculture	:	770	768	676	701 *	728 *
Manufacturing including:	1 513	1 330	1 221	1 128	1 105 *	1 077 *
Food and beverages	262	257	203	191	187 *	182 *
Wood and wood products	69	56	85	69	68 *	66 *
Glass, ceramics, construction products	125	99	77	83	81 *	79 *
Basic metals and metal products	344	259	336	325	318 *	310 *
Electricity, gas, water	:	:	55	67	70 *	48 *
Construction	1 452	1 457	1 491	1 349	1 257 *	1 253 *
Wholesale, trade, repairs	598	519	561	486	453 *	461 *
Hotels, restaurants	95	82	84	53	49 *	50 *
Transport including:	:	917	959	841	834 *	843 *
Land transport	632	661	668	608	603 *	609 *
Auxiliary transport activities	228	179	224	167	166 *	168 *
Financial intermediation, renting, business	287	298	282	258	244 *	260 *
Total all branches	:	6 423	6 229	5 549	5 346 *	5 228 *

5H2DD

Further reading: Statistics in focus: population and social conditions, 2000. Eurostat. Key data on health, 2000. Eurostat.   Including road traffic accidents and transport accidents (except IRL and UK) in the course of work. 1997, 1998: estimations.

Rate of accidents at work with more than three days' absence per 100 000 workers by main branch of activity. EU-15

5A1EZ

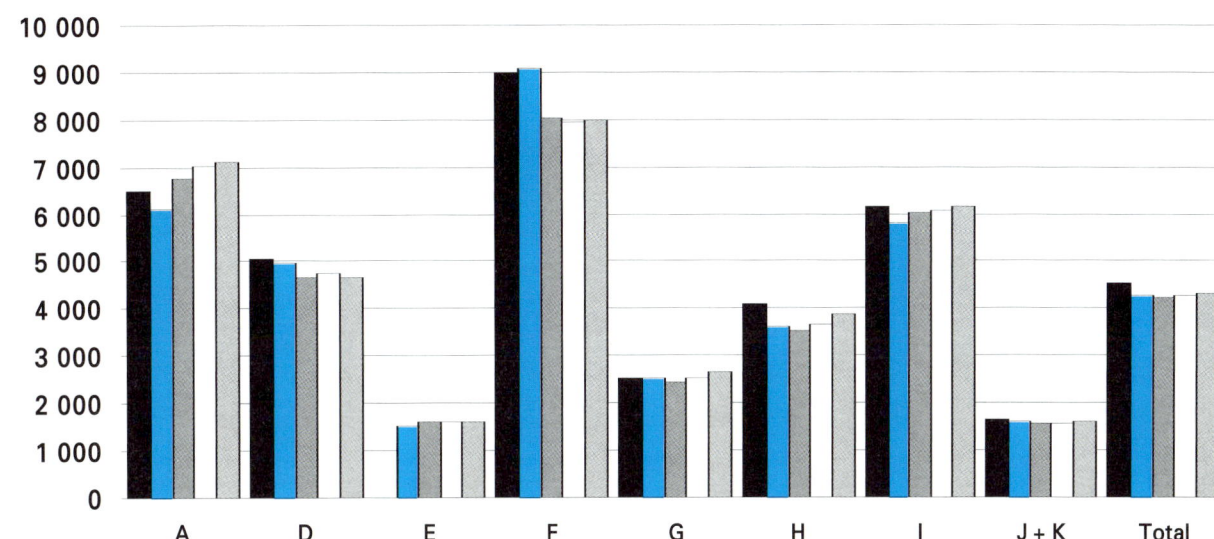

Black: 1994; colour: 1995; grey: 1996; white: 1997, light grey: 1998. Main branches from NACE: A: agriculture, hunting and forestry; D: manufacturing; E: electricity, gas and water supply; F: construction; G: wholesale and retail trade and repairs; H: hotels and restaurants; I: transport and communication; J: financial intermediation; K: real estate, renting and business activities. Total: A, D to K: total nine branches.

Further reading: Statistics in focus: population and social conditions, 2000. Eurostat. Key data on health, 2000. Eurostat.

Employment figures are based on the Eurostat labour force survey. Data for NACE E is not available for 1994. 1997, 1998: estimations.

Rate of fatal accidents at work per 100 000 workers by main branch of activity. EU-15

5A1FA

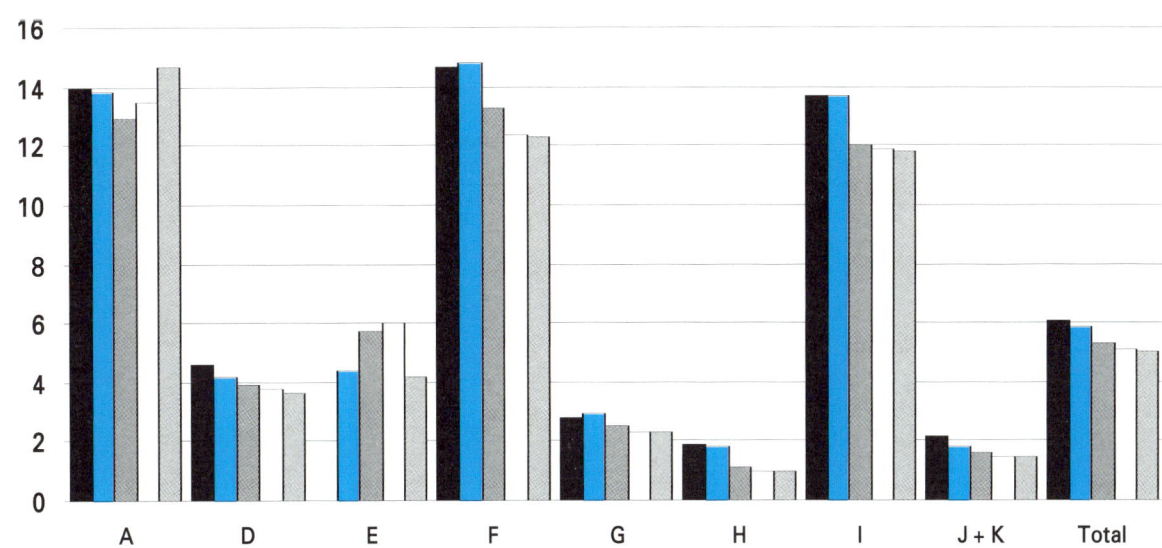

Black: 1994; colour: 1995; grey: 1996; white: 1997, light grey: 1998. Main branches from NACE: A: agriculture, hunting and forestry; D: manufacturing; E: electricity, gas and water supply; F: construction; G: wholesale and retail trade and repairs; H: hotels and restaurants; I: transport and communication; J: financial intermediation; K: real estate, renting and business activities. Total: A, D to K: total nine branches.

Further reading: Statistics in focus: population and social conditions, 2000. Eurostat. Key data on health, 2000. Eurostat.

Employment figures are based on the Eurostat labour force survey. Including road traffic accidents and transport accidents (except IRL and UK) in the course of work. Data for NACE E is not available for 1994. 1997, 1998: estimations.

eurostat

1

Rate of accidents at work with more than three days' absence per 100 000 workers. 1996

5A1FB

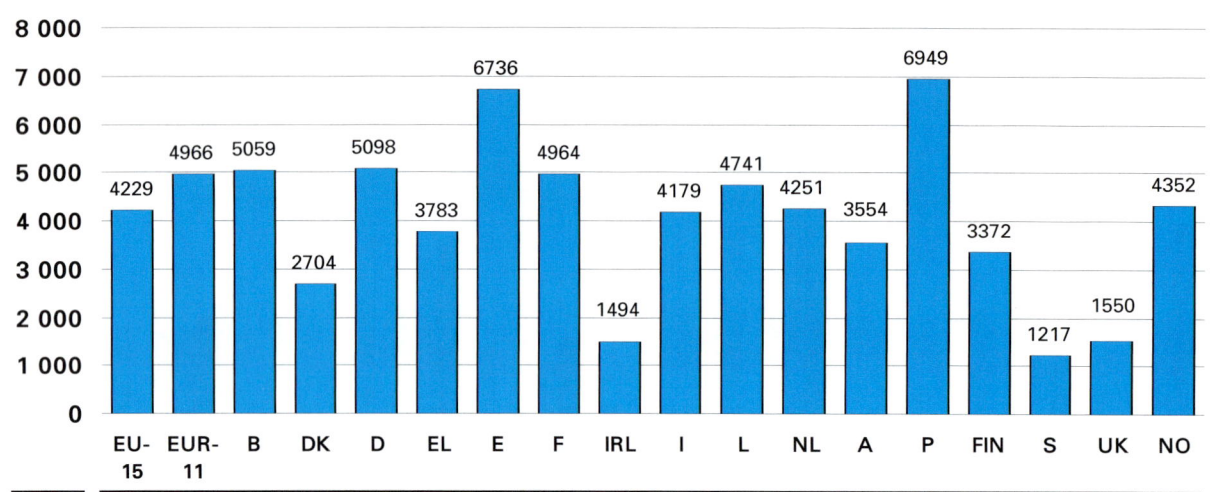

Further reading: Statistics in focus: population and social conditions, 2000. Eurostat.
Key data on health, 2000. Eurostat.

Employment figures are based on the Eurostat labour force survey.

Rate of fatal accidents at work per 100 000 workers. 1996

5A1FC

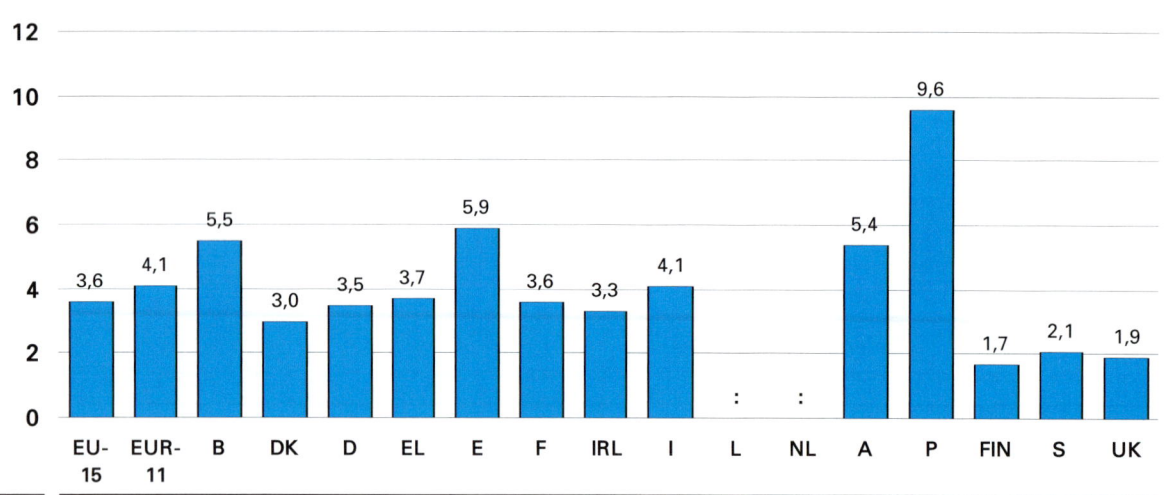

Further reading: Statistics in focus: population and social conditions, 2000. Eurostat.
Key data on health, 2000. Eurostat.

Employment figures are based on the Eurostat labour force survey.
Excluding road traffic accidents and transport accidents in the course
of work.

Rate of accidents at work with more than three days' absence per 100 000 workers by age group. EU-15. 1997

5H7DD

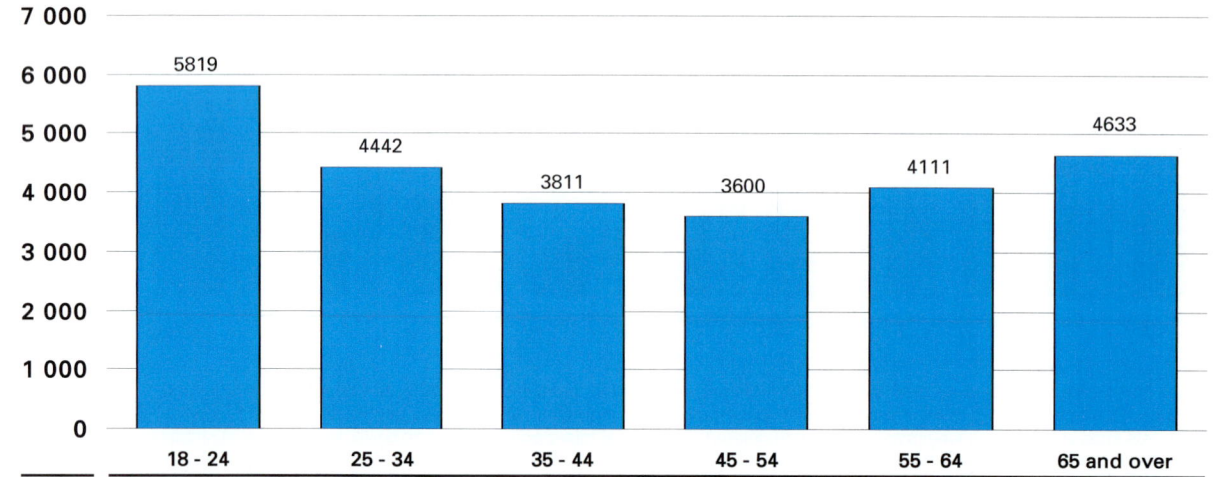

Further reading: Statistics in focus: population and social conditions, 2000. Eurostat.
Key data on health, 2000. Eurostat.

Employment figures are based on the Eurostat labour force survey.
Estimations.

Eurostat collected data on recognised occupational diseases in the 15 Member States for 31 selected items of the European Schedule of Occupational Disease for the year 1995. The recognition criteria of the compensation systems are not harmonised between the Member States. Consequently, the data on recognised occupational diseases does not only reflect the occurrence of such diseases. However, data on recognised cases of occupational disease represent a high degree of causality between the exposure and the diagnosis. They also provide detailed information on exposure and on medical and social consequences. Finally, the 31 diseases included in the data collection were selected because they were covered in all Member States on about 85 % of the persons in employment in the European Union. On the opposite, cases recognised in the national recognition system for other occupational diseases as well as for some Member States self-employed, family workers or civil servants were not covered.

Number of recognised cases of occupational diseases by group of diagnosis and age.
EU-15. 1995

	Total	Less than 36	36–55	56 and over	Unknown
Allergic effects	5 429	2 517	2 208	642	62
Cancer	2 144	11	317	1 756	60
Cardiovascular disorders	263	22	130	111	0
Eye disorders	50	10	36	4	0
Gastrointestinal disorders	26	10	13	3	0
Haematological disorders	112	30	50	32	0
Hearing disorders	17 207	477	7 236	9 240	254
Hepatic disorders	82	17	50	14	1
Irritant effects of the skin or mucous membranes	3 713	1 783	1 459	403	68
Neurological disorders	3 049	753	1 952	342	2
Pulmonary disorders	9 653	1 136	1 784	6 527	206
Musculoskeletal disorders	4 090	810	2 232	995	53
Infectious diseases	1 911	831	867	198	15
Other not elsewhere mentioned	274	53	118	86	17
Unspecified	9 411	1 352	3 577	4 115	367
Total	57 414	9 812	22 029	24 468	1 105

5H8DD

Further reading: Working paper: population and social conditions. European statistics on occupational diseases. Evaluation of the 1995 pilot data. Key data on health, 2000. Eurostat.

Data on cases recognised in 1995 for 31 items of the European schedule of occupational diseases.

1

Total health expenditure per head of population in PPS

	1989	1990	1991	1992	1993	1994	1995	1996	1997	1998	1999	
EU-15	1 097	1 199	1 274	1 386	1 438	1 492	1 613	1 685	1 708	1 768	:	EU-15
B	1 159	1 246	1 367	1 519	1 605	1 642	1 793	1 911	1 973	2 081	:	B
DK	1 386	1 442	1 509	1 575	1 715	1 803	1 887	2 006	2 032	2 133	2 186	DK
D	1 496	1 602	1 600	1 829	1 839	1 973	2 178	2 288	2 325	2 424	2 476	D
EL	664	706	777	887	919	979	1 059	1 114	1 157	1 167	:	EL
E	715	811	903	973	1 009	1 017	1 068	1 119	1 154	1 218	:	E
F	1 420	1 545	1 666	1 788	1 850	1 886	2 014	2 019	2 003	2 077	:	F
IRL	658	796	897	1 061	1 103	1 225	1 314	1 333	1 432	1 436	1 508	IRL
I	1 168	1 321	1 449	1 541	1 532	1 581	1 608	1 691	1 754	1 783	1 839	I
L	1 337	1 485	1 563	1 734	1 878	1 944	2 113	2 181	2 147	2 215	:	L
NL	1 300	1 403	1 490	1 607	1 675	1 728	1 889	1 937	2 004	2 070	:	NL
A	1 130	1 209	1 267	1 425	1 541	1 616	1 875	1 967	1 886	1 968	2 039	A
P	563	614	731	804	874	942	1 051	1 090	1 151	1 237	:	P
FIN	1 150	1 292	1 412	1 386	1 332	1 297	1 421	1 486	1 491	1 502	:	FIN
S	1 422	1 548	1 460	1 501	1 508	1 507	1 622	1 716	1 712	1 746	:	S
UK	894	964	1 013	1 165	1 189	1 246	1 301	1 410	1 406	1 461	1 583	UK
IS	1 403	1 377	1 455	1 504	1 556	1 581	1 829	1 915	1 919	2 103	2 284	IS
NO	1 270	1 365	1 513	1 680	1 724	1 746	1 864	2 042	2 154	2 425	:	NO
EEA	1 126	1 219	1 298	1 411	1 462	1 513	1 640	1 719	1 747	1 826	:	EEA
CH	1 672	1 782	1 958	2 136	2 214	2 294	2 477	2 549	2 697	2 794	:	CH
US	2 475	2 755	2 990	3 225	3 430	3 580	3 716	3 855	3 998	4 178	4 390	US
CA	1 565	1 702	1 840	1 929	1 990	2 027	2 154	2 141	2 185	2 312	2 411	CA
JP	1 013	1 083	1 165	1 275	1 366	1 459	1 631	1 699	1 809	1 822	:	JP

6J1AA

Further reading: Ecosanté database, 2000. OECD. Key data on health, 2000. Eurostat.

Total health expenditure as a proportion of GDP

	1989	1990	1991	1992	1993	1994	1995	1996	1997	1998	1999	
EU-15	7,5	7,6	7,9	8,2	8,3	8,2	8,1	8,2	8,0	8,0	:	EU-15
B	7,4	7,4	7,8	7,9	8,1	7,9	8,2	8,6	8,6	8,8	:	B
DK	8,6	8,4	8,3	8,4	8,7	8,5	8,2	8,3	8,2	8,3	8,3	DK
D	8,8	8,7	9,1	9,7	9,7	9,8	10,2	10,6	10,5	10,6	10,5	D
EL	7,5	7,6	7,9	8,3	8,3	8,3	8,3	8,3	8,5	8,3	:	EL
E	6,5	6,9	7,0	7,4	7,6	7,4	7,0	7,1	7,0	7,1	:	E
F	8,5	8,8	9,0	9,2	9,7	9,6	9,8	9,7	9,6	9,6	:	F
IRL	6,6	7,0	7,4	7,8	7,8	7,7	7,4	7,2	7,0	6,4	6,1	IRL
I	7,7	8,1	8,4	8,5	8,6	8,4	8,0	8,1	8,4	8,4	8,4	I
L	6,2	6,6	6,5	6,6	6,7	6,5	6,3	6,4	6,0	5,9	:	L
NL	8,8	8,8	9,0	9,2	9,4	9,2	8,9	8,8	8,6	8,6	:	NL
A	7,3	7,2	7,2	7,6	8,1	8,1	8,9	8,9	8,2	8,2	8,3	A
P	6,4	6,4	7,0	7,2	7,5	7,5	7,7	7,7	7,6	7,8	:	P
FIN	7,2	7,9	9,0	9,1	8,3	7,8	7,5	7,7	7,3	6,9	:	FIN
S	8,8	8,8	8,7	8,8	8,9	8,6	8,4	8,7	8,5	8,4	:	S
UK	5,9	6,0	6,4	6,9	6,9	7,0	7,0	7,0	6,7	6,7	7,0	UK
IS	8,5	8,0	8,1	8,2	8,3	8,1	8,2	8,1	7,9	8,3	8,4	IS
NO	7,7	7,8	8,1	8,2	8,1	8,0	8,0	8,0	8,1	8,9	:	NO
EEA	7,6	7,7	7,9	8,2	8,3	8,1	8,1	8,2	8,0	8,1	:	EEA
CH	8,3	8,3	8,9	9,3	9,4	9,5	9,6	10,1	10,3	10,4	:	CH
US	11,6	12,4	13,2	13,6	13,9	13,9	13,9	13,8	13,6	13,6	13,7	US
CA	8,7	9,2	9,9	10,2	10,1	9,8	9,5	9,4	9,3	9,5	9,5	CA
JP	6,2	6,1	6,1	6,3	6,6	6,9	7,2	7,1	7,4	7,6	:	JP

6J1AB

Further reading: Ecosanté database, 2000. OECD. Key data on health, 2000. Eurostat.

The Member States of the European Union base their statistics on manpower in the field of health care on different concepts, sometimes the number of physicians means the number of active practitioners and sometimes it means only practitioners 'entitled to practice', which includes practitioners who are unemployed or work without directly practising medicine. In the United Kingdom and Ireland, only the public sector is covered. Similar methodological differences can be observed in the case of dentists and medical specialists.

The number of beds is given as an annual average. Changes in the number of beds are accounted for pro rata temporis. Bed-counts include only beds used for full in-patient accommodation. Not necessarily included are beds in hospitals available for nursing day care, medical children's homes, nurseries for toddlers under medical supervision and institutions for the sensorially handicapped. The average length of stay is defined as the number of bed-days in hospitals divided by the number of admissions or discharges. A reduction in the number of hospital beds per capita could be observed virtually everywhere. This reduction is more marked for the psychiatric beds. This reduction of beds can be explained by developments in medical technologies which have made it possible to reduce the average length of hospitalisation. Another reason is the financial constraints of the 1980s, which led to rationalisation of the health services.

Consultations to a general practitioner, medical specialist or dentist during the last 12 months. 1996

	EU-15	B	DK	D	EL	E	F	IRL
Mean number of times having consulted a								
general practitioner	4	5	3	5	2	4	:	4
medical specialist	2	2	1	3	2	2	:	1
dentist	1	1	2	2	1	1	:	1
Percentage of persons having consulted a doctor, dentist or optician during the last 12 months								
1 or 2 times	16	17	25	13	21	23	:	28
3 to 5 times	22	28	35	26	23	22	:	23
6 to 9 times	16	20	19	23	12	13	:	12
more than 10 times	21	29	15	35	15	20	:	16
Never	25	6	6	3	29	22	:	21

Further reading: European Community household panel, 1996. Eurostat. Key data on health, 2000. Eurostat.

EU-15: available countries.

Consultations to a general practitioner, medical specialist or dentist during the last 12 months. 1996

	I	L	NL	A	P	FIN	S	UK
Mean number of times having consulted a								
general practitioner	5	3	3	5	4	2	:	4
medical specialist	1	2	2	:	1	1	:	1
dentist	1	2	2	2	1	1	:	1
Percentage of persons having consulted a doctor, dentist or optician during the last 12 months								
1 or 2 times	20	14	26	:	19	22	:	22
3 to 5 times	25	31	32	:	24	31	:	30
6 to 9 times	16	28	18	:	18	18	:	20
more than 10 times	23	24	18	:	19	12	:	20
Never	16	3	6	:	20	17	:	8

Further reading: European Community household panel, 1996. Eurostat. Key data on health, 2000. Eurostat.

EU-15: available countries.

eurostat

1

Total number of physicians per 100 000 inhabitants

	1989	1990	1991	1992	1993	1994	1995	1996	1997	1998	1999	
EU-15	:	305 |	313 |	:	:	:	:	:	:	:	:	EU-15
B	337	345	353	361	366	374	379	382	386	395	:	B
DK	:	278	285	:	:	291	:	:	:	:	:	DK
D	292	301 |	306	314	321	329	336	341	345	349	:	D
EL	330	339	365	376	388	389	393	397	410	:	:	EL
E	371	383	394	401	408	414	415	422	428	436	:	E
F	262	269	275	280	284	285	300	303	307	299	300	F
IRL	149	155	170 |	200	203	200	210	211	214	219	226	IRL
I	451	470	488	502	550	559	566	571	578	583	:	I
L	199	202	203	209	215	228	229	236	245	250	255	L
NL	243	252	260	:	:	:	:	:	:	295	311	NL
A	277	282	287	290	292	294	296	301	306	312	:	A
P	158	160	161	163	164	165	170	175	:	:	:	P
FIN	292	303	309	321	328	339	347	353	361	:	:	FIN
S	239	243	247	257	264	270	277	285	296	300	306	S
UK	284	286	287	297	297	301	303	313	328	:	:	UK
IS	:	:	261	266	271	279	296	306	308	:	:	IS
NO	286	260	270	274	275	281	279	280	278	:	:	NO
EEA	:	:	:	:	:	:	:	:	:	:	:	EEA
CH	294	300	305	303	307	313	317	322	:	:	:	CH
US	:	227	237	240	244	242	256	264	:	:	:	US
CA	214	213	213	214	215	213	211	208	206	210	:	CA
JP	:	165	:	170	:	177	:	184	:	189	:	JP

6J1AC

Further reading: Key data on health, 2000. Eurostat.

B, DK, EL, F, A, S, UK, IS, NO, CH, US, CA: in activity. E, I, NL, P, FIN: entitled to practise. D, JP: practising doctors. IRL, UK: NHS only.

Total number of dentists per 100 000 inhabitants

	1989	1990	1991	1992	1993	1994	1995	1996	1997	1998	1999	
EU-15	50	:	:	:	56	:	:	:	:	:	:	EU-15
B	71	72	71	70	69	70	70	71	72	70	:	B
DK	90	89	89	89	89	88	89	:	:	:	:	DK
D	68	:	69	70	72	73	74	75	76	76	:	D
EL	96	99	101	101	104	104	102	109	111	:	:	EL
E	24	27	29	30	31	34	36	38	39	41	:	E
F	68	69	69	69	69	70	70	70	69	:	:	F
IRL	35	37	38	40	40	42	44	45	46	46	48	IRL
I	15	24	35	40	43	46	49	52	53	55	:	I
L	51	52	52	53	51	50	56	57	60	62	63	L
NL	53	53	:	:	48	:	48	47	47	:	:	NL
A	43	43	43	43	44	45	42	44	45	45	48	A
P	16	17	17	18	21	23	26	28	30	33	:	P
FIN	88	90	91	92	91	92	93	94	94	94	94	FIN
S	107	101	104	103 |	97	95	:	86	85	81	:	S
UK	39	39	38	38	39	41	41	42	43	44	45	UK
IS	87	91	94	99	101	103	101	103	105	:	:	IS
NO	:	:	:	:	88	84	:	85	84	:	:	NO
EEA	:	:	:	:	:	:	:	:	:	:	:	EEA
CH	49	49	48	49	48	50	49		:	:	:	CH
US	:	59	63	60	60	60	:	60	:	:	:	US
CA	52	52	52	52	52	52	53	53	54	55	:	CA
JP	:	58	:	61	:	63	:	66	:	68	:	JP

8A1AJ

Further reading: Key data on health, 2000. Eurostat.

B, DK, EL, F, A, S, UK, IS, NO, CH, US, CA: in activity. E, I, NL, P, FIN: entitled to practise. D, JP: practising doctors. IRL, UK: NHS only.

Hospital beds per 100 000 inhabitants

	1989	1990	1991	1992	1993	1994	1995	1996	1997	1998	1999	
EU-15	:	747	724 |	699	669	:	:	:	:	:	:	**EU-15**
B	823	810	795	777	772	764	744	734	:	:	:	**B**
DK	589	567	546	519	510	504	494	475	465	455	:	**DK**
D	:	850	835	806	776	760	747	726	708	697	:	**D**
EL	512	507	503	500	497	498	500	503	500		:	**EL**
E	435	428	423	415	407	403	395	391	:	:	:	**E**
F	1 018	1 003	986	970	952	931	915	897	:	:	:	**F**
IRL	633	619	609	590	565	549	539	525	507	495	484	**IRL**
I	688	723	680	686	668	654	622	650	582	:		**I**
L	1 238	1 182	1 155	1 136	1 154	1 108	:	:	:	:	:	**L**
NL	603	583	573	565	555	535	523	517	514	504	:	**NL**
A	1 058	1 031	997	979	949	938	931	920	909	:	:	**A**
P	440	433	426	424	416	411	409	414	391	401	:	**P**
FIN	1 300	1 255	1 131	1 101	1 006	:	928 |	811	789	773	:	**FIN**
S	1 298	1 249	1 189 |	764	705	654	609	560	522	:	:	**S**
UK	623	590	559	532	502	482	465	420	:	:	:	**UK**
IS	1 065	1 052	1 011	982	973	937	911	:	:	:	:	**IS**
NO	480	465	442	430	420	407	406	401	398	398	390	**NO**
EEA	:	738	716	691	669	:	:	:	:	:	:	**EEA**
CH	:	:	2 092	:	:	:	:	:	1 828	1 815	:	**CH**
US	496	486	476	461	451	433	411	400	388	:	:	**US**
CA	:	:	:	:	:	:	:	:	:	:	:	**CA**
JP	:	1 366	:	:	:	:	1 343	1 335	1 329	:	:	**JP**

Further reading: Key data on health, 2000. Eurostat.

D, NL, P, IS: Nursing homes and day-care beds not included.
E: Nursing homes and day-care beds partially included. EL, I: Beds in military hospitals not included. IRL, S, UK: Only beds in public hospitals are included. UK: Eurostat estimation.

Psychiatric hospital beds per 100 000 inhabitants

	1989	1990	1991	1992	1993	1994	1995	1996	1997	1998	1999	
EU-15	:	135	127	118	109	:	97	:	:	:	:	**EU-15**
B	209	195	192	179	178	170	169	164	:	:	:	**B**
DK	102	96	93	85	83	83	81	81	80	79	:	**DK**
D	:	121	116	103	91	87	84	79	76	74	:	**D**
EL	123	117	114	112	111	102	110	107	107	:	:	**EL**
E	77	71	68	64	62	62	60	49	:	:	:	**E**
F	182	174	167	158	149	143	138	132	126	:	:	**F**
IRL	273	228	217	195	181	171	162	150	137	130	123	**IRL**
I	84	84	75	73	70	68	48	54	39	:	:	**I**
L	267	225	207	204	186	98	102	:	:	:	:	**L**
NL	:	178	177	175	175	174	171	172	171	166	:	**NL**
A	87	85	81	76	74	70	67	61	58	:	:	**A**
P	88	89	86	74	72	72	73	74	72	70	:	**P**
FIN	251	234	217	198	152	:	130	122 |	114	109	:	**FIN**
S	184	170	151	137	125	112	95	82	71	:	:	**S**
UK	204	189	173	158	137	127	119	86	84	81		**UK**
IS	153	151	143	144	132	131	118	:	:	:	:	**IS**
NO	89	86	82	77	78	73	72	71	71	72	71	**NO**
EEA	:	133	126	117	108	:	96	:	:	:	:	**EEA**
CH	162	178	175	166	142	136	128	125	120	119	:	**CH**
US	:	109	:	106	:	97	:	:	:	:	:	**US**
CA	:	:	:	:	:	:	:	:	:	:	:	**CA**
JP	:	293	:	:	:	291	:	:	:	:	:	**JP**

Further reading: Key data on health, 2000. Eurostat.

5A1BP

5H3AM

eurostat

Need access to Eurostat's databases? Ask your Data Shop

EUROSTAT YEARBOOK 2001

71

The frequency of admission (discharges from hospitals) is divided into 17 main groups following the international classification of diseases (Version 9). Comparisons of diagnosis between various geographic areas are difficult and contain a number of potential sources of error which may be differences in classifications, quality of the registers, use of different codes for the same type of diagnosis and variations from one country to another in the way of counting diagnosis in hospitals.

Discharged hospital patients by main group of diagnosis (patients admitted for night and day). 1998

Diagnosis	EU-15	B	DK	D	EL	E	F	IRL	I	L	NL
Infectious and parasitic diseases	333	378	447	347	383	196	467	446	316	:	122
Neoplasms	1 391	975	1 664	1 640	1 461	615	1 244	669	1 074	:	799
Endoc., nutrit. and metabolic diseases and immunity disorders	396	379	431	545	336	190	569	198	355	:	187
Diseases of blood and bloodforming organs	158	116	191	112	475	79	183	135	128	:	91
Mental disorders	545	:	252	950	333	268	483	115	489	:	142
Diseases of the nervous system and sense organs	1 171	886	779	1 127	801	627	1 998	591	1 184	:	473
Diseases of the circulatory system	2 314	2 288	2 501	3 070	1 927	1 238	2 299	1 476	2 610	:	1 528
Diseases of the respiratory system	1 252	1 371	1 563	1 217	1 103	987	1 491	1 559	1 221	:	719
Diseases of the digestive system	1 912	1 738	1 623	1 787	1 495	1 284	3 008	1 329	1 857	:	859
Diseases of the genitourinary system	1 176	1 051	1 036	1 296	1 163	763	1 466	832	1 157	:	516
Deliveries and complicat. of pregnancy, childbirth and puer.	1 520	1 374	1 766	1 349	1 200	1 239	1 970	1 060	1 350	:	848
Diseases of the skin and subcutaneous tissue	285	173	264	270	230	136	397	252	259	:	103
Diseases of the musculoskeletal system and connective tis.	1 119	1 350	1 018	1 262	589	618	1 563	537	961	:	739
Congenital anomalies	152	130	200	141	118	86	217	126	154	:	93
Certain conditions originating in the perinatal period	208	69	171	139	160	131	228	111	261	:	404
Symptoms, signs and ill-defined conditions	1 126	599	1 136	655	903	806	1 495	1 088	881	:	634
Injury and poisoning	1 631	1 699	1 847	1 981	1 250	827	2 257	1 705	1 674	:	758
Special admissions (including live births in hospitals)	1 514	1 580	:	:	:	912	3 636	468	811	:	846

Further reading: Ecosanté database, 2000. OECD. Key data on health, 2000. Eurostat.

Figures are for discharges, not for concluded treatment of patients in wards. EL: 1993; B, E, F: 1997.

6D3HW

Discharged hospital patients by main group of diagnosis (patients admitted for night and day). 1998

Diagnosis	A	P	FIN	S	UK	IS	NO	CH	US	CA	JP
Infectious and parasitic diseases	661	215	687	458	240	:	363	:	320	157	428
Neoplasms	2 393	540	2 372	1 441	2 164	:	1 533	:	489	720	:
Endoc., nutrit. and metabolic diseases and immunity disorders	848	189	501	372	242	:	234	:	487	215	340
Diseases of blood and bloodforming organs	170	70	219	125	259	:	95	:	140	81	58
Mental disorders	1 444	116	969	1 051	411	:	164	:	736	592	284
Diseases of the nervous system and sense organs	1 855	390	2 277	740	1 162	:	647	:	208	245	:
Diseases of the circulatory system	3 811	1 102	3 849	2 983	1 788	:	2 403	:	2 285	1 545	1 345
Diseases of the respiratory system	1 898	691	2 512	1 193	1 280	:	1 291	:	1 302	696	940
Diseases of the digestive system	2 255	1 010	1 861	1 330	2 141	:	1 102	:	1 124	1 114	1 122
Diseases of the genitourinary system	1 649	510	1 358	833	1 339	:	805	:	635	632	504
Deliveries and complicat. of pregnancy, childbirth and puer.	1 587	1 259	1 669	1 279	2 000	:	1 598	:	187	2 851	1 055
Diseases of the skin and subcutaneous tissue	427	139	337	125	427	:	151	:	170	117	97
Diseases of the musculoskeletal system and connective tis.	2 353	296	2 309	895	1 077	:	973	:	562	453	453
Congenital anomalies	198	87	250	145	167	:	234	:	58	59	78
Certain conditions originating in the perinatal period	168	29	136	151	321	:	172	:	52	54	164
Symptoms, signs and ill-defined conditions	737	172	1 724	1 598	2 229	:	1 142	:	103	591	292
Injury and poisoning	2 762	786	2 181	1 631	1 237	:	1 698	:	945	849	967
Special admissions (including live births in hospitals)	905	1 443	631	12 581	1 797	:	843	:	167	434	584

Further reading: Ecosanté database, 2000. OECD. Key data on health, 2000. Eurostat.

Figures are for discharges, not for concluded treatment of patients in wards. CA: 1997/98; A, US: 1997; JP: 1996; UK: finished consultant episodes in NHS hospitals for the period 1 April 1998 to 31 March 1999.

6D3HX

The ECHP also contains questions on hospitalisation in the 12 months preceding the interview and on consultation to health professionals. Figures for hospitalisation from surveys such as the ECHP have some limitations, i.e. the fact that persons living in institutions are not included in this survey. This leads to small underestimations. According to 1996 results of the ECHP, 10.2 % of Europeans have experienced hospitalisation during the last 12 months. The differences between countries may partly reflect differences in organisation of healthcare services. In 1996, for EU-15 (without Sweden) the average number of nights spent in a hospital during the last 12 months was 14 nights. The average length of stay is identical for men and women. The percentage of persons having consulted a doctor, a dentist or an optician during the last 12 months of 1995 was 88 % for the EU.

Hospitalisation during the last 12 months (16 + years). 1996 (% non standardised)

| | Total | | Yes, by age | | | | Yes, by sex | | |
	Yes	No	16–24	25–49	50–64	65 and over	Males	Females	
EU-15	10	90	7	8	11	18	10	11	**EU-15**
B	12	88	8	9	13	20	11	12	**B**
DK	10	90	10	10	15	20	10	11	**DK**
D	13	87	3	3	7	14	13	14	**D**
EL	6	94	3	6	9	13	6	6	**E**
E	7	93	6	8	10	20	8	7	**EL**
F	10	90	5	8	11	20	10	11	**F**
IRL	10	90	5	6	9	18	9	11	**IRL**
I	9	91	14	8	14	27	9	9	**I**
L	13	87	14	8	14	27	13	14	**L**
NL	8	82	3	6	8	15	7	9	**NL**
A	14	86	9	10	16	23	12	15	**A**
P	6	94	3	5	8	10	7	6	**P**
FIN	14	86	11	10	15	27	13	15	**FIN**
S	:	:	:	:	:	:	:	:	**S**
UK	11	89	:	8	12	16	10	12	**UK**

Further reading: European Community household panel, 1996. Eurostat. Key data on health, 2000. Eurostat.

Persons that spent one night or more in a hospital, excluding hospitalisation for childbirth.

Average length of stay in hospital, all causes (in days)

	1989	1990	1991	1992	1993	1994	1995	1996	1997	1998	1999	
EU-15	15,0	14,8	14,3	13,2	:	12,2	11,9	11,7			:	**EU-15**
B	14,4	13,8	13,0	12,3	12,0	11,7	11,5	11,3	:	:	:	**B**
DK	8,5	8,2	8,0	7,8	7,6	7,5	7,3	7,2	7,1		:	**DK**
D	15,7	17,2	16,2	15,6	:	14,7	14,2	13,6	12,5	12,0	:	**D**
EL	9,8	9,9	9,9	9,2	8,8	8,5	8,2	8,2	:	:	:	**EL**
E	12,6	12,2	11,9	11,5	11,5	11,3	11,2	10,0	:	:	:	**E**
F	13,4	13,3	11,9	11,7	11,7	11,7	11,2	11,2	10,8	:	:	**F**
IRL	8,0	7,9	7,8	7,7	7,6	7,4	7,2	7,0	:	:	:	**IRL**
I	11,7	11,7	11,6	11,2	11,1	10,8	10,1	9,4	8,1	:	:	**I**
L	17,4	17,6	17,6	16,5	15,7	15,5	15,3	15,3	:	:	:	**L**
NL	34,3	34,1	33,8	33,5	33,3	32,7	32,8	32,5	31,7	33,7	:	**NL**
A	12,9	13,0	12,4	12,0	11,5	11,2	10,9	10,5	9,7	9,3	:	**A**
P	11,2	10,8	10,5	10,1	9,9	9,5	9,8	9,8	9,3	9,0	:	**P**
FIN	19,2	18,2	18,8	16,6	14,8	13,1	11,8	11,6	11,1	10,9	:	**FIN**
S	18,6	18,0	16,8	10,1	9,4	8,1	7,8	7,5	:	:	:	**S**
UK	18,0	15,6	14,1	12,4	10,2	10,0	9,9	9,8	:	:	:	**UK**
IS	18,5	18,3	17,8	16,8	:	:	:	:	:	:	:	**IS**
NO	9,1	:	:	:	:	10,1	10,0	9,9	:	:	:	**NO**
EEA	15,3	:	:	:	:	:	:	:	:	:	:	**EEA**
CH	:	:	:	:	:	:	:	:	14,7	13,7	:	**CH**
US	9,2	9,1	9,0	8,8	8,6	8,2	7,8	7,5	7,3	7,1	:	**US**
CA	13,9	13,0	12,7	12,6	:	:	10,7	10,7	8,4	:	:	**CA**
JP	51,4	50,5	49,3	47,9	46,4	45,5	44,2	43,7	42,5	40,8	:	**JP**

Further reading: Ecosanté database, 2000. OECD. Key data on health, 2000. Eurostat.

5H4AM

5A1BQ

Eurostat collects this information on the basis of results disseminated from different specialised national and international organisations. The Council of Europe has in the past developed the ethical principles governing organ transplantation. Kidney transplants remain the most frequent type of transplants. On average, for every one million Europeans, there are 30 kidney transplants, slightly more than 6 heart transplants, almost 11 liver transplants and between 1 and 2 lung transplants. Spain, Austria and Belgium/Luxembourg have the highest transplantation rates for all organs in the EU. Greece has the lowest rates.

Solid organ transplants in Europe per million population

		EU-15	B/L	DK	D	EL	E	F	I	NL
Kidney	1992	:	:	35,8	26,1	:	38,3	:	:	32,5
	1993	:	:	36,3	26,7	:	38,1	:	:	28,9
	1994	:	:	34,1	24,2	:	41,7	26,2	:	25,4
	1995	29,1	33,2	29,5	26,1	12,5	45,9	27,0	20,1	31,8
	1996	28,9	42,0	32,0	24,6	10,1	43,4	28,1	21,6	32,6
	1997	30,3	40,5	30,3	27,4	12,8	47,4	28,9	22,8	32,8
	1998	31,2	36,5	38,2	28,5	16,1	50,7	32,1	21,6	30,9
	1999	31,2	43,1	31,6	27,7	14,6	51,4	31,2	23,6	30,3
Heart	1992	:	:	5,0	6,4	:	6,5	:	:	2,9
	1993	:	:	6,8	6,2	:	7,3	:	:	3,6
	1994	:	:	5,2	5,9	:	7,5	6,9	:	3,9
	1995	6,0	9,6	5,8	5,8	1,0	7,1	7,0	6,8	3,1
	1996	5,8	10,1	6,1	6,0	0,7	7,2	6,8	6,0	3,9
	1997	6,4	11,7	6,3	7,1	0,8	8,1	7,2	6,5	3,4
	1998	5,8	9,0	5,1	6,4	1,2	8,7	6,3	5,8	2,6
	1999	5,7	8,6	4,9	6,1	0,7	8,5	5,9	5,8	2,9
Liver	1992	:	:	5,8	6,3	:	12,0	:	:	4,3
	1993	:	:	9,5	7,3	:	12,7	:	:	4,3
	1994	:	:	10,4	7,2	:	15,7	9,8	:	4,9
	1995	9,7	13,1	6,9	7,2	0,7	17,8	11,3	7,1	6,4
	1996	10,0	13,9	7,8	8,5	1,0	17,8	11,2	7,4	4,9
	1997	10,8	13,1	7,4	9,3	1,7	20,1	10,7	8,2	5,7
	1998	11,3	13,1	6,4	8,5	1,7	22,8	11,8	9,5	6,4
	1999	12,1	15,9	5,8	9,2	1,1	24,4	11,9	11,8	6,0
Lung	1992	:	:	:	:	:	0	:	:	:
	1993	:	:	:	:	:	1	:	:	:
	1994	:	:	:	:	:	0,9	:	:	:
	1995	1,2	1,5	3,5	0,7	0,1	1,1	1,4	0,7	1,3
	1996	1,4	1,8	5,3	1,1	0,3	1,9	1,2	1,0	1,3
	1997	1,5	2,5	4,2	1,1	0,1	2,7	1,1	1,3	0,6
	1998	1,8	3,0	6,8	1,4	-	3,3	1,5	1,1	1,1
	1999	2,1	2,6	8,7	1,8	-	3,4	1,7	1,7	1,2

Further reading: Key data on health, 2000. Eurostat.　　　　Kidney: cadaveric and living donors.

Solid organ transplants in Europe per million population

		A	P	FIN	S	UK/IRL	NO	CH	US	CA
Kidney	1992	:	:	:	:	:	:	29,8	37,9	26,2
	1993	:	:	:	:	:	:	34,5	39,9	30,7
	1994	:	34,5	:	:	:	:	33,3	40,4	31,2
	1995	37,8	36,4	32,6	31,3	30,7	43,5	28,4	41,6	31,8
	1996	45,3	40,5	34,8	34,9	27,1	42,6	29,6	42,1	31,4
	1997	41,4	38,8	28,1	37,8	28,5	41,0	33,3	43,0	32,0
	1998	46,2	31,0	36,3	40,3	28,1	46,0	36,8	45,1	32,8
	1999	51,6	36,8	31,6	34,0	27,0	45,9	34,6	46,8	33,8
Heart	1992	:	:	:	:	:	:	5,4	8,5	4,3
	1993	:	:	:	:	:	:	6,8	8,8	5,9
	1994	:	0,8	:	:	:	:	7,0	8,9	5,8
	1995	13,4	0,8	5,1	2,4	5,4	5,1	6,1	8,9	6,1
	1996	12,8	0,9	5,7	2,5	4,5	5,0	5,8	8,7	5,5
	1997	11,4	0,6	3,9	4,5	5,1	5,5	4,9	8,5	5,3
	1998	11,6	0,8	3,5	4,1	4,5	7,5	6,2	8,6	5,1
	1999	11,8	1,2	2,9	4,2	4,6	7,2	6,6	8,2	5,7
Liver	1992	:	:	:	:	:	:	6,6	11,7	7,6
	1993	:	:	:	:	:	:	7,4	13,0	10,0
	1994	:	3,4	:	:	:	:	8,6	13,6	10,3
	1995	13,7	6,8	6,1	9,9	11,1	4,4	6,7	14,5	10,7
	1996	16,4	12,8	5,7	8,5	10,2	4,6	9,5	14,7	11,6
	1997	16,2	14,5	5,5	10,4	11,1	4,1	7,8	15,0	11,2
	1998	16,5	13,4	7,6	11,9	11,0	5,7	10,9	16,3	11,2
	1999	17,3	15,9	5,8	10,5	11,2	6,5	10,8	17,6	12,6
Lung	1992	:	:	:	:	:	:	0,1	2,1	1,8
	1993	:	:	:	:	:	:	2,2	2,6	2,0
	1994	:	:	:	:	:	:	3,4	2,8	2,2
	1995	3,6	-	0,8	1,8	1,8	3,2	2,6	3,3	2,4
	1996	3,6	-	1,0	2,6	1,9	1,6	4,4	3,0	2,4
	1997	3,7	0,1	0,6	1,9	1,8	3,0	2,3	3,5	2,8
	1998	7,6	-	0,2	3,7	1,3	2,0	4,2	3,2	:
	1999	8,7	-	-	2,9	1,7	2,5	4,5	3,3	3,0

Further reading: Key data on health, 2000. Eurostat.　　　　Kidney: cadaveric and living donors.

1

1B3AD

Marriages per 1 000 people

	1989	1990	1991	1992	1993	1994	1995	1996	1997	1998	1999	
EU-15	6,2	6,0	5,6	5,5	5,3	5,2	5,1	5,1	5,1 *	5,0 *	5,1 *	EU-15
B	6,4	6,5	6,1	5,8	5,4	5,1	5,1	5,0	4,7	4,4	4,3 *	B
DK	6,0	6,1	6,0	6,2	6,1	6,8	6,6	6,8	6,5	6,5	6,6	DK
D	6,7	6,5	5,7	5,6	5,5	5,4	5,3	5,2	5,2	5,1	5,2 *	D
EL	6,1	5,8	6,4	4,7	6,0	5,4	6,1	4,3	5,8	5,3	5,9 *	EL
E	5,7	5,7	5,6	5,6	5,2	5,1	5,1	4,9	5,0	5,1 *	5,2 *	E
F	5,0	5,1	4,9	4,7	4,4	4,4	4,4	4,8	4,9	4,8 *	4,9 *	F
IRL	5,2	5,1	4,9	4,7	4,7	4,6	4,3	5,0	4,3	4,5	4,9 *	IRL
I	5,7	5,6	5,5	5,5	5,3	5,1	5,1	4,9	4,7 *	4,8 *	4,8 *	I
L	5,8	6,1	6,7	6,4	6,0	5,8	5,1	5,1	4,8	4,8	4,8	L
NL	6,1	6,4	6,3	6,2	5,8	5,4	5,3	5,5	5,4	5,5	5,7	NL
A	5,6	5,8	5,6	5,8	5,6	5,4	5,3	5,2	5,1	4,7	4,9 *	A
P	7,4	7,2	7,3	7,1	6,9	6,7	6,6	6,4	6,6	6,9	6,8 *	P
FIN	4,9	5,0	4,9	4,7	4,9	4,9	4,6	4,8	4,6	4,7	4,7	FIN
S	12,8	4,7	4,3	4,3	3,9	3,9	3,8	3,8	3,7	3,6	4,0	S
UK	6,8	6,5	6,1	6,1	5,9	5,7	5,5	5,3	5,3 *	5,1 *	:	UK
IS	4,7	4,5	4,8	4,8	4,6	4,9	4,6	5,0	5,5	5,6	5,6	IS
NO	4,9	5,2	4,7	4,5	4,5	4,8	5,0	5,3	5,4	5,3	:	NO
EEA	6,2	5,9	5,6	5,5	5,3	5,2	5,1	5,1	5,1 *	5,0 *	5,1 *	EEA
CH	6,8	6,9	7,0	6,6	6,2	6,1	5,8	5,7	5,5	5,4	5,8 *	CH
US	:	:	:	:	:	:	:	:	:	8,4	8,4	US
CA	:	:	:	:	:	:	:	:	:	:	:	CA
JP	:	:	:	:	:	:	:	:	:	:	:	JP

Further reading: European social statistics. Demography. Edition 2000. Eurostat.   D: includes in all years data on the former GDR.

'B3BB

Divorces per 1 000 people

	1989	1990	1991	1992	1993	1994	1995	1996	1997	1998	1999	
EU-15	1,7	1,7	1,6	1,6	1,7	1,8	1,8	1,8	1,8	1,8 *	:	EU-15
B	2,0	2,0	2,1	2,2	2,1	2,2	3,5	2,8	2,6	2,6	2,6 *	B
DK	3,0	2,7	2,5	2,5	2,5	2,6	2,5	2,4	2,4	2,5	2,5 *	DK
D	2,2	2,0	1,7	1,7	1,9	2,0	2,1	2,1	2,3	2,3	:	D
EL	0,6	0,6	0,6	0,6	0,7	0,7	1,1	0,9	0,9	0,8	0,9 *	EL
E	0,6	0,6	0,7	0,7	0,7	0,8	0,8	0,8	0,9	0,9 *	:	E
F	1,9	1,9	1,9	1,9	1,9	2,0	2,1	2,0	2,0	2,0 *	:	F
IRL	:	:	:	:	:	:	:	:	:	:	:	IRL
I	0,5	0,5	0,5	0,5	0,4	0,5	0,5	0,6	0,6	0,6 *	:	I
L	2,3	2,0	2,0	1,8	1,9	1,7	1,8	2,0	2,4	2,4	2,4	L
NL	1,9	1,9	1,9	2,0	2,0	2,4	2,2	2,2	2,2	2,1	2,1	NL
A	2,0	2,1	2,1	2,1	2,0	2,1	2,3	2,2	2,2	2,2	:	A
P	1,0	0,9	1,1	1,3	1,2	1,4	1,2	1,4	1,4	1,5	1,8 *	P
FIN	2,9	2,6	2,6	2,6	2,5	2,7	2,7	2,7	2,6	2,7	2,7 *	FIN
S	2,2	2,3	2,3	2,5	2,5	2,5	2,6	2,4	2,4	2,3	2,4	S
UK	2,9	2,9	3,0	3,0	3,1	3,0	2,9	2,9	2,7	2,7 *	:	UK
IS	2,1	1,9	2,1	2,0	2,0	1,8	1,8	2,0	1,9	1,8 *	1,7 *	IS
NO	2,2	2,4	2,4	2,4	2,5	2,5	2,4	2,3	2,3	2,1	:	NO
EEA	1,7	1,7	1,7	1,7	1,7	1,8	1,8	1,8	1,8	1,8 *	:	EEA
CH	1,9	2,0	2,0	2,1	2,2	2,2	2,2	2,3	2,4	2,5 *	2,9 *	CH
US	:	:	:	:	:	:	:	:	:	4,3	4,2 *	US
CA	:	:	:	:	:	:	:	:	:	:	:	CA
JP	:	:	:	:	:	1,6	1,6	:	:	:	:	JP

Further reading: European social statistics. Demography. Edition 2000. Eurostat.   D: includes in all years data on the former GDR. IRL: divorce was
                                                                                        not allowed before 1996.

1

Mean age at first marriage: women and men. 1998

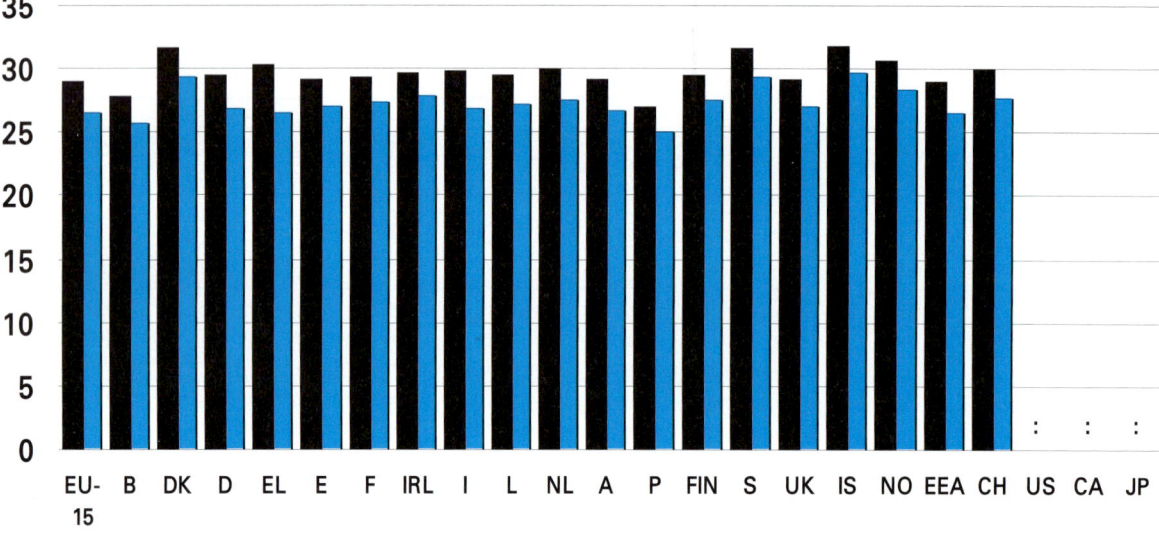

Black: men; colour: women.

Further reading: European social statistics. Demography. Edition 2000. Eurostat.   EU-15, IRL, EEA: 1995. E, F, I, UK: 1996.

Marriages and divorces per 1 000 people. EU-15

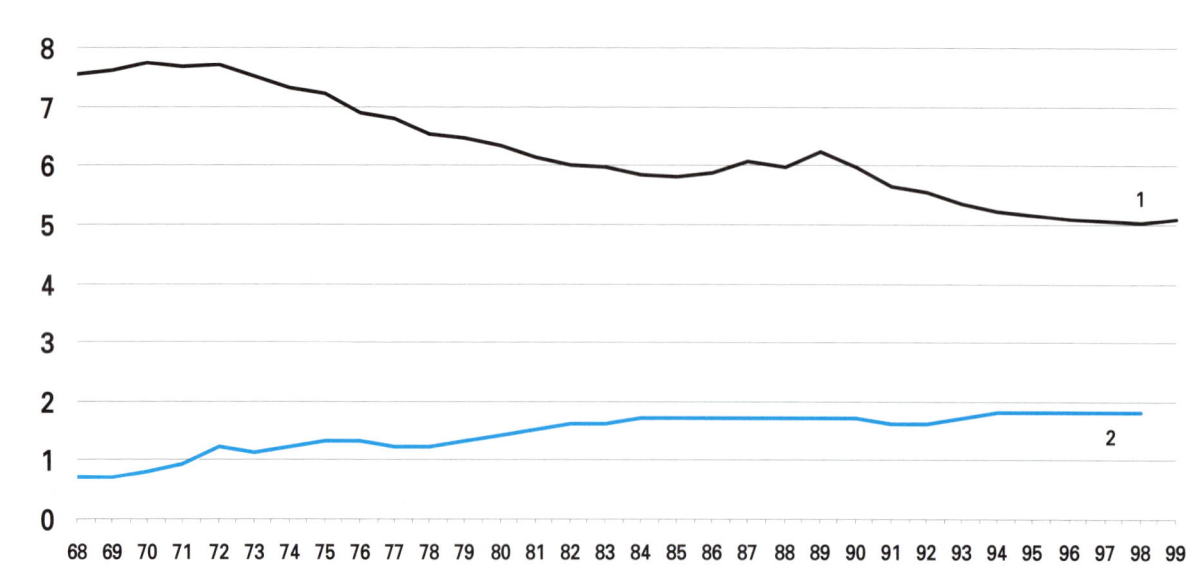

1: marriages; 2: divorces.

Further reading: European social statistics. Demography. Edition 2000. Eurostat.

Total fertility

1B4AB

	1989	1990	1991	1992	1993	1994	1995	1996	1997	1998	1999	
EU-15	1,56	1,57	1,53	1,51	1,47	1,44	1,42	1,44	1,45	1,45 *	1,45 *	**EU-15**
B	1,58	1,62	1,66	1,65	1,61	1,56	1,55	1,55	1,55	1,53	1,54 *	**B**
DK	1,62	1,67	1,68	1,76	1,75	1,81	1,80	1,75	1,75	1,72	1,74	**DK**
D	1,42	1,45	1,33	1,30	1,28	1,24	1,25	1,32	1,37	1,36	1,37	**D**
EL	1,40	1,39	1,38	1,38	1,34	1,35	1,32	1,30	1,31	1,29	1,30 *	**EL**
E	1,40	1,36	1,33	1,32	1,27	1,21	1,18	1,17	1,19	1,15	1,19 *	**E**
F	1,79	1,78	1,77	1,73	1,65	1,66	1,70	1,72	1,71	1,75 *	1,77 *	**F**
IRL	2,08	2,11	2,08	1,99	1,90	1,85	1,84	1,89	1,92	1,93 *	1,89 *	**IRL**
I	1,33	1,33	1,31	1,31	1,25	1,21	1,18	1,20	1,22	1,20 *	1,21 *	**I**
L	1,52	1,61	1,60	1,64	1,70	1,72	1,69	1,76	1,71	1,68	1,73	**L**
NL	1,55	1,62	1,61	1,59	1,57	1,57	1,53	1,53	1,56	1,63	1,64 *	**NL**
A	1,44	1,45	1,49	1,49	1,48	1,44	1,40	1,42	1,37	1,34	1,30 *	**A**
P	1,58	1,57	1,57	1,54	1,52	1,44	1,40	1,43	1,46	1,46	1,48 *	**P**
FIN	1,71	1,78	1,79	1,85	1,81	1,85	1,81	1,76	1,75	1,70	1,74	**FIN**
S	2,01	2,13	2,11	2,09	1,99	1,88	1,73	1,60	1,52	1,50	1,50	**S**
UK	1,79	1,83	1,81	1,79	1,75	1,74	1,71	1,72	1,72	1,72	1,70 *	**UK**
IS	2,19	2,30	2,18	2,21	2,22	2,14	2,08	2,12	2,04	2,05	1,99 *	**IS**
NO	1,89	1,93	1,92	1,88	1,86	1,86	1,87	1,89	1,86	1,81	1,84 *	**NO**
EEA	1,56	1,58	1,54	1,52	1,47	1,44	1,43	1,45	1,46	1,45	1,45 *	**EEA**
CH	1,56	1,59	1,60	1,58	1,51	1,49	1,48	1,50	1,51	1,47	1,50 *	**CH**
US	2,01	2,08	2,07	2,07	2,05	2,04	2,02	2,04	2,06	2,07	2,05	**US**
CA	1,66	1,71	1,70	1,69	1,66	1,62	1,62	1,62	:	:	:	**CA**
JP	1,57	1,54	1,53	1,50	1,46	1,50	1,42	1,44	1,44	1,40	1,40	**JP**

Further reading: European social statistics. Demography. Edition 2000. Eurostat.   D: includes in all years data on the former GDR.

Completed fertility by generation

1B4AE

	1930	1935	1940	1945	1950	1955	1959	1960	1961	1964	
EU-15	2,42	2,39	2,23	2,08	1,97	1,90	1,83	1,81	1,77	:	**EU-15**
B	2,30	2,27	2,17	1,93	1,84	1,83	1,84	1,85	1,81	1,75	**B**
DK	2,36	2,38	2,24	2,06	1,90	1,84	1,88	1,89	1,90	1,91	**DK**
D	2,17	2,16	1,98	1,79	1,72	1,67	1,66	1,65	1,62	1,54	**D**
EL	2,21	2,02	2,01	2,00	2,07	2,03	1,94	1,95	1,88	1,75	**EL**
E	2,59	2,67	2,59	2,43	2,19	1,90	1,79	1,75	1,68	1,59	**E**
F	2,64	2,58	2,41	2,22	2,11	2,13	2,11	2,10	2,08	2,00	**F**
IRL	3,50	3,44	3,27	3,27	3,00	2,67	2,44	2,41	2,34	2,19	**IRL**
I	2,29	2,29	2,14	2,06	1,90	1,79	1,68	1,65	1,60	1,49	**I**
L	1,97	2,00	1,92	1,82	1,72	1,68	1,71	1,71	1,70	1,67	**L**
NL	2,65	2,50	2,21	1,99	1,90	1,87	1,85	1,86	1,82	1,75	**NL**
A	2,32	2,45	2,13	1,93	1,86	1,77	1,71	1,68	1,65	1,61	**A**
P	2,95	2,85	2,61	2,31	2,12	1,97	1,91	1,88	1,86	1,81	**P**
FIN	2,51	2,30	2,03	1,87	1,85	1,89	1,95	1,95	1,95	1,90	**FIN**
S	2,11	2,14	2,05	1,96	2,00	2,03	2,04	2,05	2,01	1,97	**S**
UK	2,35	2,41	2,36	2,17	2,03	2,01	1,97	1,96	1,94	1,88	**UK**
IS	3,50	:	3,15	2,87	2,67	2,47	2,46	2,48	2,47	2,40	**IS**
NO	2,49	2,57	2,45	2,21	2,09	2,05	2,08	2,09	2,09	2,06	**NO**
EEA	2,44	2,41	2,26	2,09	1,98	1,90	1,84	1,82	1,77	:	**EEA**
CH	2,18	2,20	2,07	1,85	1,79	1,75	1,76	1,77	1,74	1,64	**CH**
US	3,16	3,16	2,78	2,29	2,03	:	:	:	:	:	**US**
CA	:	:	:	:	:	:	:	:	:	:	**CA**
JP	:	:	:	:	2,00	1,97	2,03	2,10	:	:	**JP**

Further reading: European social statistics. Demography. Edition 2000. Eurostat.   D: includes in all years data on the former GDR.

Ageing refers to the change in the balance in the population age structure towards older age groups. Though the timing and extent vary across the EU, all Member States are experiencing this phenomenon. Three factors govern ageing in the EU: fertility, population structure and longevity.

Lowering of the number of births as a result of the decline in fertility, even to below replacement levels, has led to the dejuvenation of the population (the percentage of the population under 20 fell from 32 % in 1970 to 23 % in 1998). With the halting of the decline in fertility at the end of the 1990s, the process of dejuvenation now seems to have ended.

The entrance of the baby-boom generation born in the 1940s into the retirement age group (60 +) will increase the speed of ageing somewhat in the beginning of the next millennium. The most numerous generations in the EU age pyramid, however, are located around age 30–35. Therefore the working age population will age first. It is only after this bulge passes the age of 60 that the greying of the population will reach its peak. The share of the age group 60 + increased from 19.8 % in 1990, to 21.2 % in 1998 and will further increase to 24 % in 2010, 27 % in 2020 and is expected to reach a maximum of around one third of the total population in the mid-2040s.

Improvements in life expectancy are now mainly gained at higher ages which means that people spend a longer part of their life in old age, the third contribution to ageing. The share of the oldest (80 +) is increasing, from 17 % of 60 + in 1990 to 18 % in 1998 and to 20 % in 2010. Greater longevity of females compared with males means, in addition, that most of the oldest are women (70 %).

More data on this in Eurostat's database

This domain covers the main demographic indicators and gives detailed figures on population, fertility, mortality and nuptiality.

➤ ➤ ➤ **DOMAIN DEMO IN DATABASE NEW CRONOS**

Total fertility of a certain calendar year is the average number of children that would be born alive to a woman during her lifetime if she were to experience during her childbearing years the age-specific fertility rates of the respective calendar year or period. Completed fertility is the ultimate average number of children born alive to women born in a particular year. Average age of all mothers giving birth is based on age-specific fertility rates.

Total fertility and completed fertility. EU-15

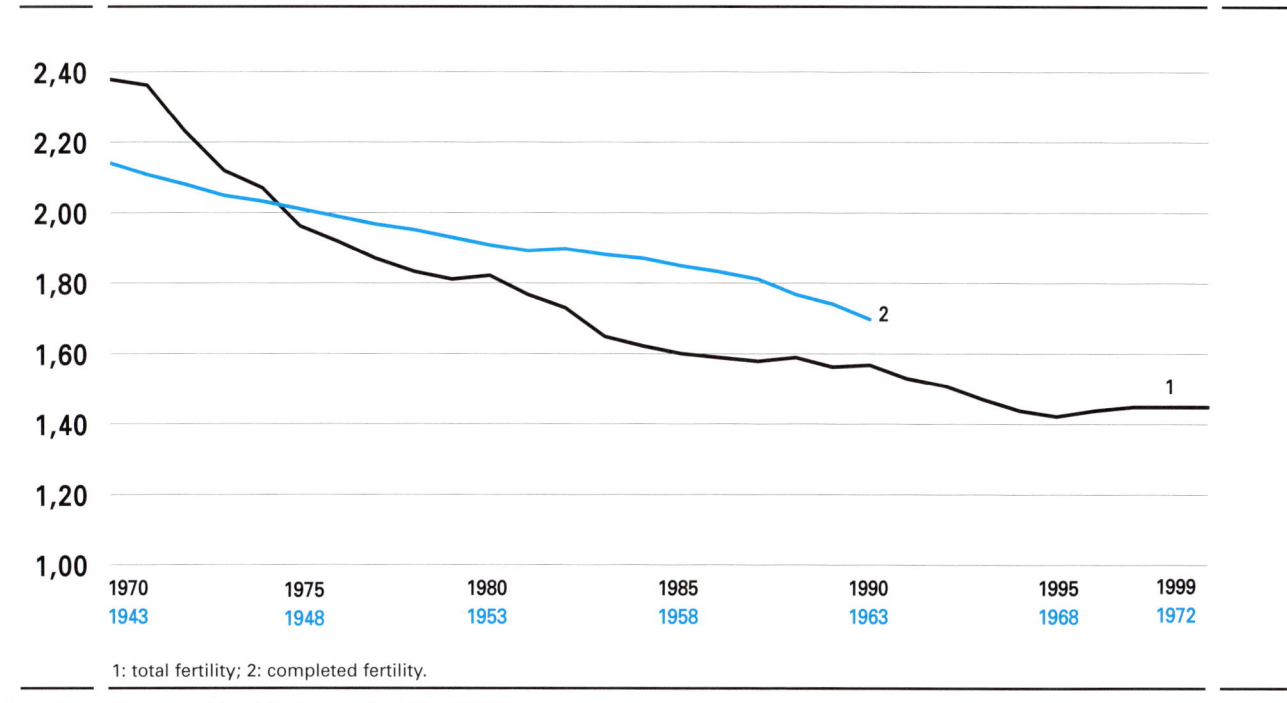

1: total fertility; 2: completed fertility.

Further reading: European social statistics. Demography. Edition 2000. Eurostat.

Need longer time series? Ask your Data Shop

EUROSTAT YEARBOOK 2001

79

1

Mean age of women at childbearing

	1989	1990	1991	1992	1993	1994	1995	1996	1997	1998	1999	
EU-15	28,1	28,2	28,3	28,5	28,6	28,7	28,9	29,0	:	:	:	**EU-15**
B	27,8	27,9	28,0	28,1	28,2	28,3	28,5	:	:	:	:	**B**
DK	28,3	28,5	28,6	28,8	28,9	29,1	29,2	29,3	29,4	:	:	**DK**
D	27,6	27,6	27,8	27,9	28,1	28,2	28,3	28,4	28,5	28,6	:	**D**
EL	27,0	27,2	27,4	27,5	27,9	28,0	28,2	28,4	28,6	28,7	:	**EL**
E	28,7	28,9	29,0	29,3	29,5	29,7	30,0	30,2	30,4	:	:	**E**
F	28,2	28,3	28,4	28,6	28,7	28,8	29,0	29,1	29,2	29,3	:	**F**
IRL	29,9	29,9	29,9	30,0	30,0	30,1	30,2	30,2	30,4	30,4	:	**IRL**
I	28,7	28,9	29,0	29,2	29,3	29,5	29,7	30,0	:	:	:	**I**
L	28,2	27,9	28,4	28,6	28,6	28,8	28,9	29,2	29,2	29,3	:	**L**
NL	29,2	29,3	29,5	29,7	29,8	29,9	30,0	30,2	30,2	30,3	:	**NL**
A	27,1	27,2	27,2	27,3	27,3	27,5	27,7	27,8	27,9	28,0	:	**A**
P	27,2	27,3	27,5	27,6	27,7	27,9	28,1	28,2	28,3	28,5	:	**P**
FIN	28,8	28,9	28,9	28,9	29,0	29,1	29,3	29,3	29,4	29,5	:	**FIN**
S	28,6	28,6	28,7	28,9	29,0	29,2	29,2	29,4	29,5	29,7	:	**S**
UK	27,6	27,7	27,7	27,8	27,9	28,1	28,2	28,2	28,3	28,3	:	**UK**
IS	27,5	27,6	28,0	28,5	28,6	28,6	28,7	28,8	28,6	28,8	:	**IS**
NO	28,0	28,1	28,3	28,4	28,6	28,7	28,9	29,0	29,1	29,2	:	**NO**
EEA	28,1	28,2	28,3	28,5	28,6	28,7	28,9	29,0	:	:	:	**EEA**
CH	28,9	28,9	29,0	29,1	29,2	29,4	29,4	29,5	28,5	29,7	:	**CH**
US	26,8	26,9	27,0	:	:	:	:	:	:	:	:	**US**
CA	28,0	28,1	28,2	28,4	28,5	28,7	28,8	29,0	:	:	:	**CA**
JP	28,9	28,9	28,9	28,9	29,0	29,0	:	:	:	:	:	**JP**

Further reading: European social statistics. Demography. Edition 2000. Eurostat.   D: includes in all years data on the former GDR.

1B4BA

Live births outside marriage as % of all live births

	1989	1990	1991	1992	1993	1994	1995	1996	1997	1998	1999	
EU-15	19	20	21	21	22	23	23	25	25	26 *	:	**EU-15**
B	11	12	13	14	15	16	17	18	19	:	:	**B**
DK	46	46	47	46	47	47	46	46	45	45	45	**DK**
D	16	15	15	15	15	15	16	17	18	20	22 *	**D**
EL	2	2	2	3	3	3	3	3	3	4	4 *	**EL**
E	9	10	10	11	11	11	11	12	13	:	:	**E**
F	28	30	32	33	35	36	38	39	40	41 *	41 *	**F**
IRL	13	15	17	18	20	21	22	75	27	28	31	**IRL**
I	6	6	7	7	7	8	8	8	9	9 *	:	**I**
L	12	13	12	13	13	13	13	15	17	18	19	**L**
NL	11	11	12	12	13	14	16	17	19	21	23 *	**NL**
A	23	24	25	25	26	27	27	28	29	30	31	**A**
P	15	15	16	16	17	18	19	19	20	20 *	:	**P**
FIN	23	25	27	29	30	31	33	35	37	37	39	**FIN**
S	52	47	48	49	50	52	53	54	54	55	55	**S**
UK	27	28	30	31	32	32	34	36	37	38	39 *	**UK**
IS	53	55	56	57	58	60	61	61	65	64	63 *	**IS**
NO	36	39	41	43	44	46	48	48	49	49	:	**NO**
EEA	19	20	21	21	22	23	24	25	26	26	:	**EEA**
CH	6	6	7	6	6	6	7	7	8	9	10 *	**CH**
US	27	28	30	30	31	:	32	32	:	:	:	**US**
CA	23	25	27	28	29	30	30	31	:	:	:	**CA**
JP	1	1	1	1	1	1	:	:	:	:	:	**JP**

Further reading: European social statistics. Demography. Edition 2000. Eurostat.   D: includes in all years data on the former GDR.

1B4BB

1

1B4CE

Total fertility rate in 1997

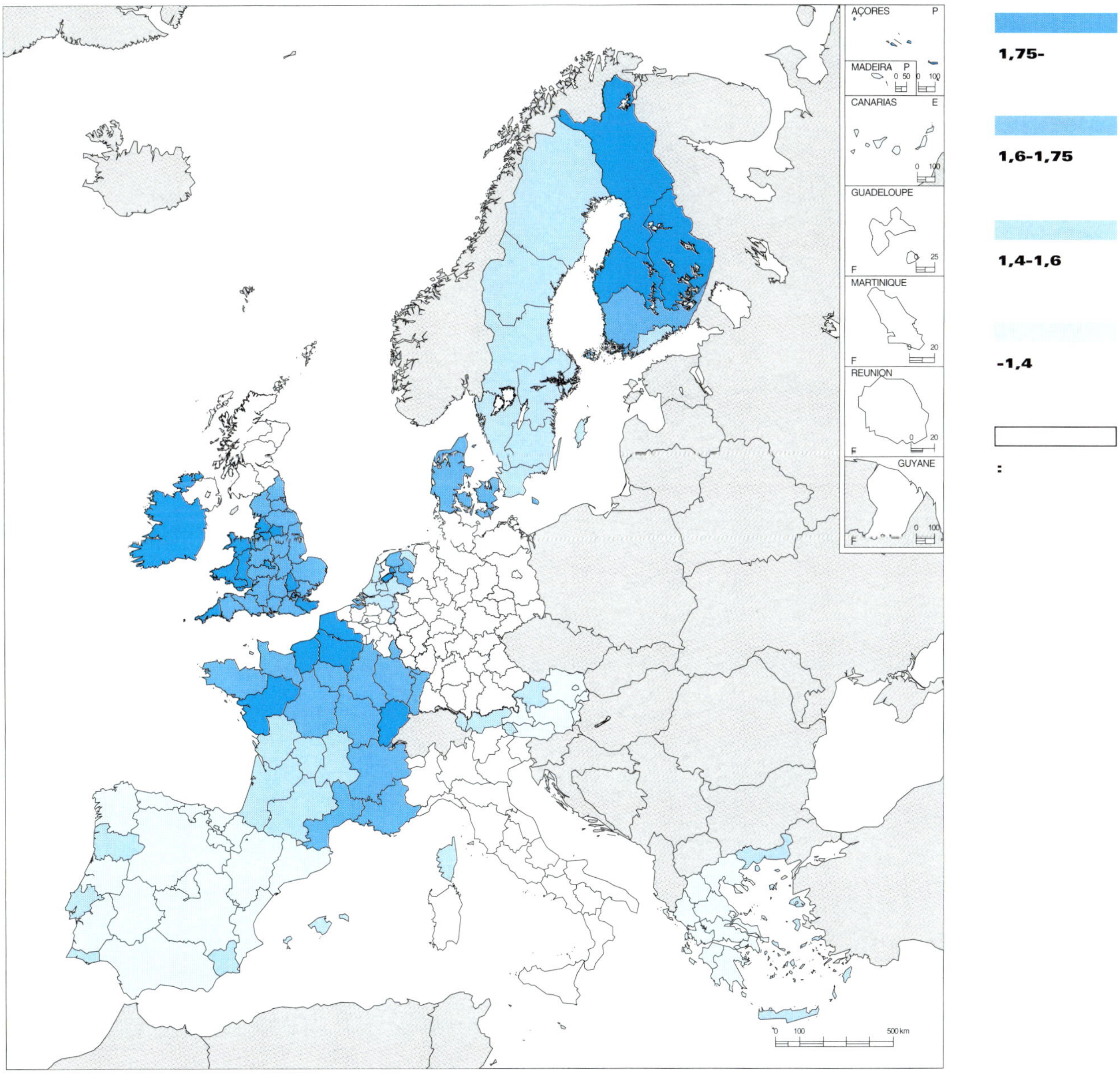

AÇORES · P

MADEIRA P
0 50 100

CANARIAS E
0 100

GUADELOUPE
F 25

MARTINIQUE
F 20

REUNION
F 20

GUYANE
F 0 100

1,75-

1,6-1,75

1,4-1,6

-1,4

:

0 100   500 km

Further reading: Demographic statistics, 2000. Eurostat. Regions, statistical yearbook,   NUTS 2. NUTS 1: IRL.
2000. Eurostat.

1

Fertility by age. 1998

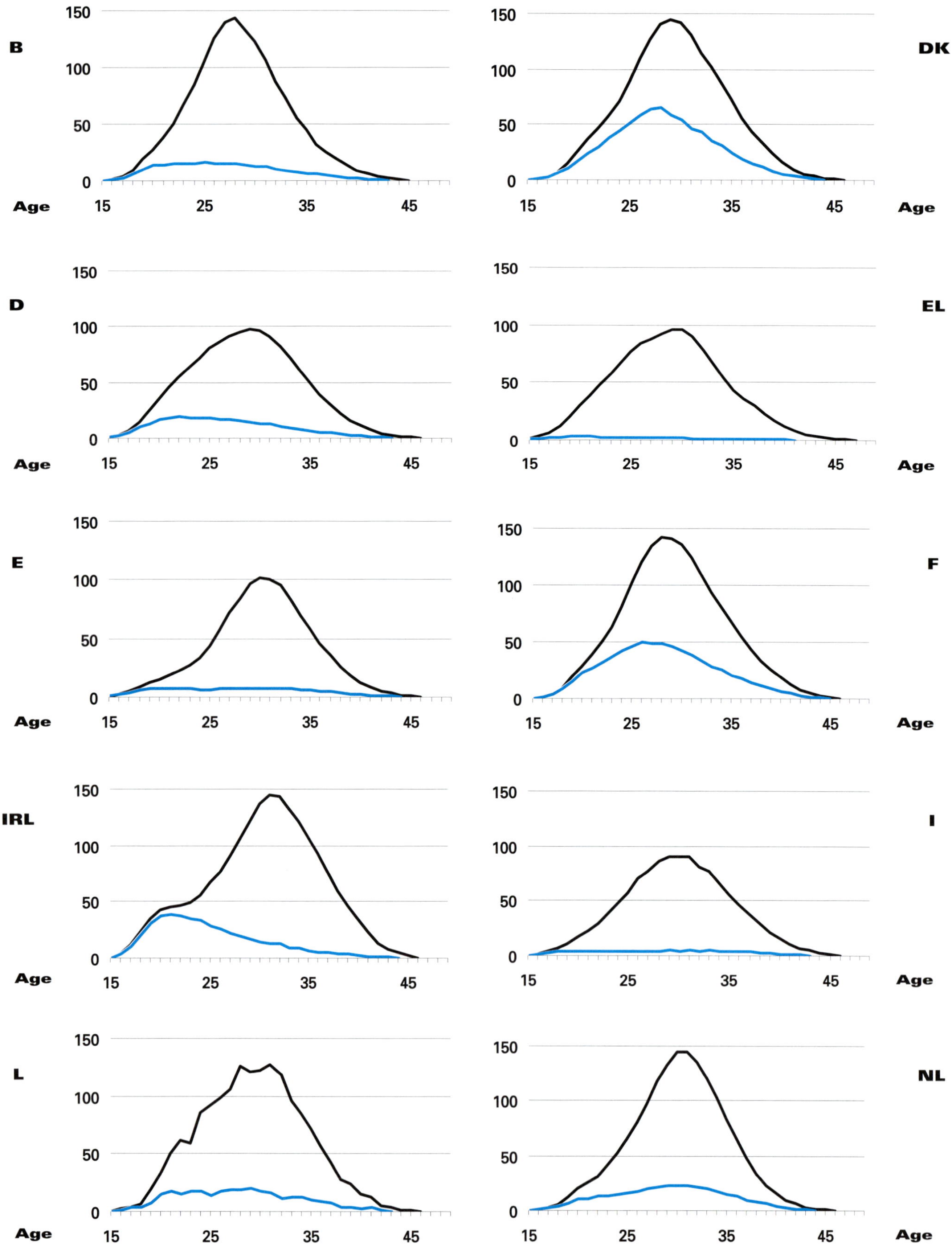

B

DK

1B4CF

D

EL

E

F

IRL

I

L

NL

Vertical axis: children per 1 000 women; horizontal axis: age. Black: total fertility; colour: children born out of wedlock.

Further reading: European social statistics. Demography. Edition 2000. Eurostat.   B: 1995; I: 1996; E, F: 1997.

Fertility by age. 1998

1B4CG

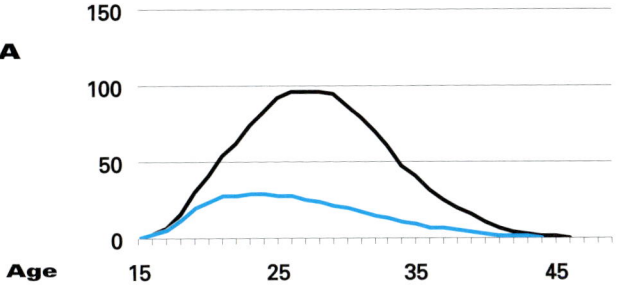
A

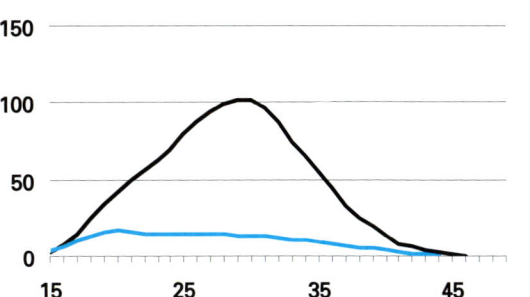
P

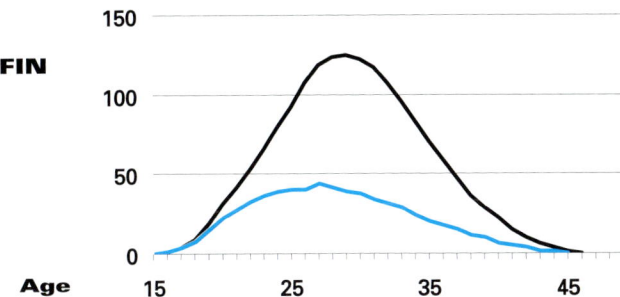
FIN

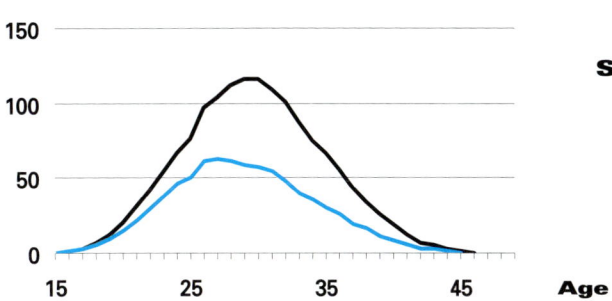
S

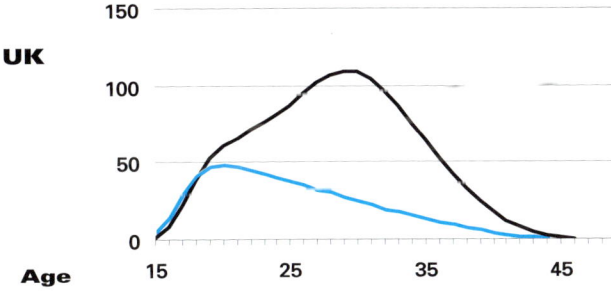
UK

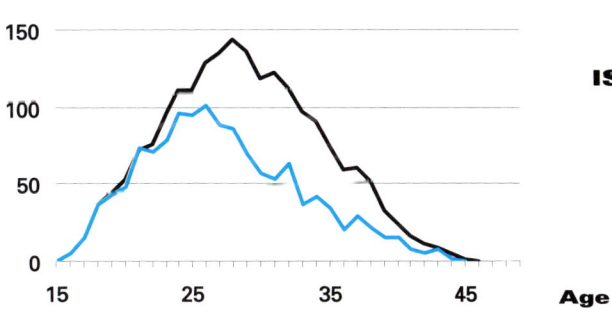
IS

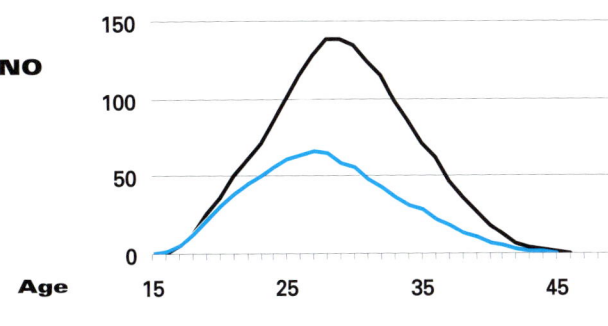
NO

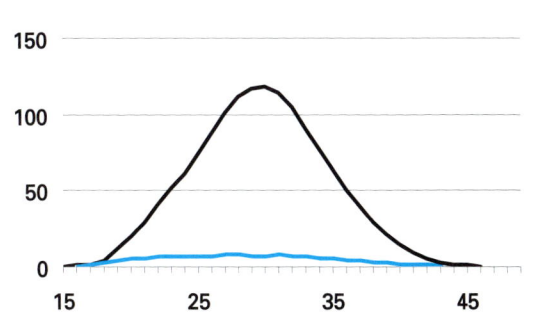
CH

Vertical axis: children per 1 000 women; horizontal axis: age. Black: total fertility; colour: children born out of wedlock.

Further reading: European social statistics. Demography. Edition 2000. Eurostat.

eurostat

Need an update for this indicator? Ask your Data Shop

EUROSTAT YEARBOOK 2001

83

Average number of persons per household

	1981/82	1998	
EU-15	2,8	2,5	EU-15
B	2,7	2,4	B
DK	2,4	2,2	DK
D	2,5	2,2	D
EL	3,1	2,7	EL
E	3,6	3,1	E
F	2,7	2,4	F
IRL	3,6	3,0	IRL
I	3,0	2,7	I
L	2,8	2,6	L
NL	2,8	2,3	NL
A	2,7	2,5	A
P	3,3	3,0	P
FIN	2,6	2,1	FIN
S	2,3	2,3	S
UK	2,7	2,3	UK

1F1AA

Further reading: The social situation in the European Union 2000, European Commission.

Source: 1981–82 data from census, 1998 data from labour force survey.

Proportion of persons living in private households by type of household. 1996

	Total	1 adult living alone	lone-parent with dependent children	2 adults with dependent children	3 or more adults with dependent children	2 or more adults without dependent children	
EU-15	100	11	4	37	11	37	EU-15
B	100	13	5	42	8	33	B
DK	100	17	3	36	7	36	DK
D	100	16	3	34	7	40	D
EL	100	7	2	38	16	38	EL
E	100	4	1	36	23	36	E
F	100	13	4	43	8	32	F
IRL	100	8	3	40	22	27	IRL
I	100	8	2	36	16	38	I
L	100	11	2	41	11	34	L
NL	100	14	2	38	7	38	NL
A	100	10	3	34	18	34	A
P	100	5	3	37	23	33	P
FIN	100	16	6	41	4	32	FIN
S	:	:	:	:	:	:	S
UK	100	12	7	35	7	39	UK

1F1BB

Further reading: The social situation in the European Union 2000, European Commission.

Source: European Community household panel.

1F1CC

Percentage of dependent children living in lone-parent families

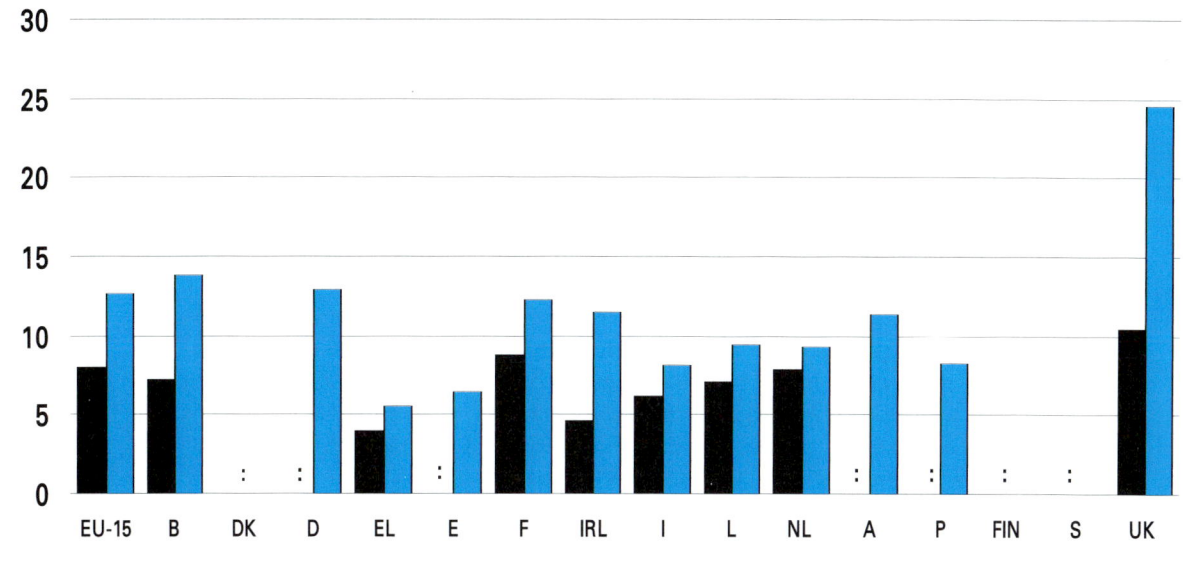

Black: 1983; colour: 1998.

Further reading: The social situation in the European Union 2000, European Commission.

Source: labour force survey.

1F1DD

Percentage of couples living in a consensual union. 1996

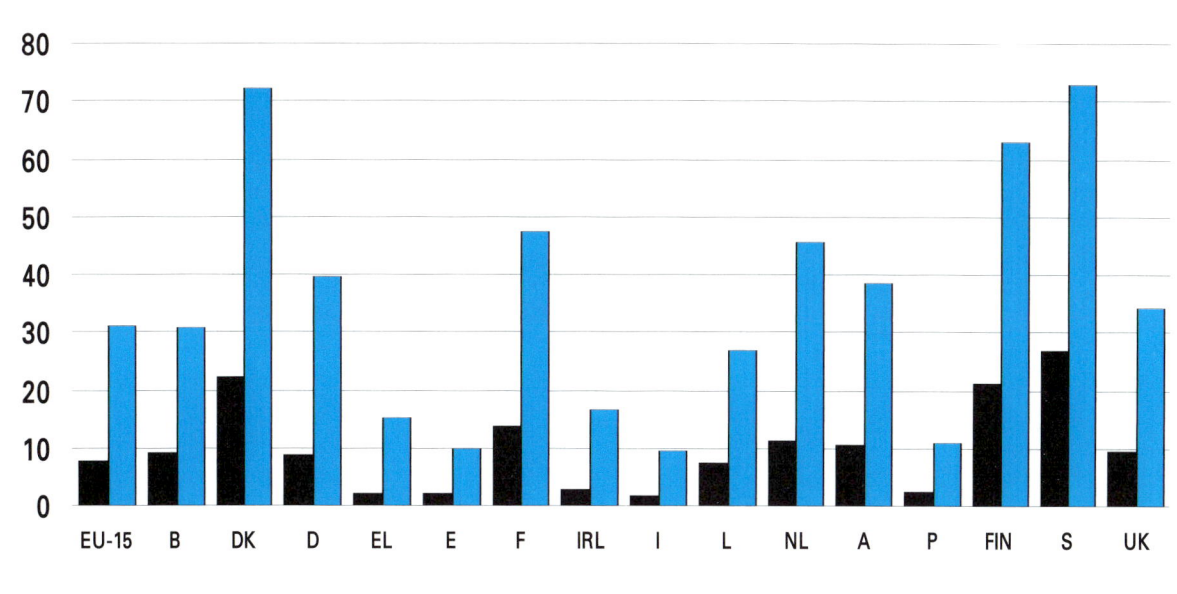

Black: total population; colour: age group 16–29.

Further reading: The social situation in the European Union 2000, European Commission.

Source: European Community household panel.

eurostat

Due to the overall economic changes and the transition in central Europe and the former Soviet Union, the migration pattern of EU Member States has radically changed recently. In northern EU countries the inflows of non-nationals and their presence has been consolidated — but mainly because of family reunification and second generations increase — while southern Member States became immigration countries.

Migration flows today include new types, such as highly qualified persons, temporary migration and study reasons. There is also illegal migration, making the EU a kind of 'frontier zone'. As a consequence, the phenomenon, which may remain underestimated, has gained the attention of public opinion and policy-makers.

Since 1989 net migration (the difference between immigration and emigration) represents the main component of population change of the EU, ensuring for some countries — Germany, Italy and Sweden, based on 1999 provisional data — the increase of the total population. Nevertheless, the mass exodus to the western and northern Europe after the events of the beginning of the 1990s did not materialise: net migration reached 1.3 million in 1992 and is now around 700 000.

In 1997 about 50 % of immigrants to the EU were from the CEECs (mostly former Yugoslavia), the former Soviet Union and Turkey, while remaining people were mainly from the Maghreb countries (17 %). Their composition by sex is now roughly equal, women representing in some instances more than half of the total.

Also, the number of asylum seekers in the 1990s showed a very high increase, from 400 000 applications in 1990 to 672 000 in 1992, that is + 168 % in two years. After this peak, the number fell to 517 000 in 1993 and to slightly more than 330 000 in 1999. Germany is still receiving 30 % of all applications (it was over 60 % in 1992–93), as well as almost 60 % together with the Netherlands and the UK from 1994 on.

The estimated foreign nationals in the EU on 1 January 1998 are about 19 million, which represent 5 % of total population and 70 % of those (over 13 million) are non-EU citizens, the highest part being represented in Austria (8 %) and Germany (7 %). In terms of EU non-nationals, they are mainly recorded in Belgium (6 %) and in Luxembourg (31 %).

More data on this in Eurostat's database

The data refer to asylum applications by citizenship, acquisition of citizenship, immigration and emigration by sex, citizenship, age group, country of previous residence and next residence.

➤ ➤ ➤ **DOMAIN MIGRAT IN DATABASE NEW CRONOS**

Immigration from other EEA countries. 1 000s

1C1FC

	1989	1990	1991	1992	1993	1994	1995	1996	1997	1998	1999	
B	10	27	28	:	:	:	:	:	:	:	:	B
DK	12	13	14	14	16	21	21	22	21	21	:	DK
D	168		167	175	160	165	188	206	203	182	169	:	D
EL	8	6	3	4	4	5	5	5	4	3	:	EL
E	15	13	9	12	11	12	12	10	22	31	:	E
F	:	:	:	:	:	:	:	:	:	:	:	F
IRL	18	23	23	29	24	21	22	25	28	32	:	IRL
I	28	27	23	21	18	22	23	21	:	:	:	I
L	:	:	:	:	:	:	:	:	:	:	:	L
NL	28	33	34	36	33	28	30	33	34	36	:	NL
A	:	:	:	:	:	:	:	16	18	19	:	A
P	:	:	:	2	2	2	3	2	2	3	:	P
FIN	8	8	7	5	4	4	6	6	6	7	:	FIN
S	27	23	14	13	13	15	16	16	15	18	:	S
UK	57	70	75	70	52	78	71	81	93	100	:	UK
IS	2	2	2	2	1	2	2	3	3	3	:	IS
NO	10	12	12	12	12	12	16	14	17	20	:	NO
CH	:	:	:	:	:	:	:	:	:	:	:	CH

Further reading: European social statistics — Migration, 2000. Eurostat.

Data exclude unrecorded migration. P: only non-nationals. UK: international passenger survey. IRL: labour force survey. EL: only non-nationals from 1994 on.

Immigration from non-EEA countries. 1 000s

1C1FD

	1989	1990	1991	1992	1993	1994	1995	1996	1997	1998	1999	
B	45	35	40	:	:	:	:	:	:	:	:	B
DK	26	28	30	29	28	24	42	33	29	30	:	DK
D	1 354		1 485	1 024	1 342	1 112	895	890	757	659	634	:	D
EL	31	36	21	28	23	13	16	17	18	10	:	EL
E	19	21	16	27	23	22	24	20	36	50	:	E
F	:	:	:	:	:	:	:	:	:	:	:	F
IRL	9	11	10	12	11	9	9	14	16	16	:	IRL
I	54	140	104	93	82	78	74	152	:	:	:	I
L	:	:	:	:	:	:	:	:	:	:	:	L
NL	71	85	86	81	86	64	67	76	76	86	:	NL
A	:	:	:	:	:	:	:	54	52	54	:	A
P	:	:	:	12	8	4	3	1	1	3	:	P
FIN	3	6	12	10	10	7	7	7	8	8	:	FIN
S	39	37	35	33	49	69	30	24	30	31	:	S
UK	193	197	192	146	157	175	174	178	192	233	:	UK
IS	1	2	2	1	1	1	1	1	1	1	:	IS
NO	16	14	14	15	20	15	9	13	15	17	:	NO
CH	:	:	:	:	:	:	:	:	:	:	:	CH

Further reading: European social statistics — Migration, 2000. Eurostat.

Data exclude unrecorded migration. P: only non-nationals. UK: international passenger survey. IRL: labour force survey. EL: only non-nationals from 1994 on.

Immigration by country of citizenship. 1998. 1 000s

	EU-15	B	DK	D	EL	E	F	IRL	I	L
Total	:	:	51,4	802,5	:	81,2	:	47,5	:	:
Nationals	:	:	22,5	197,0	:	24,0	:	25,9	:	:
Non-nationals	:	:	28,8	605,5	12,6	57,2	100,0	21,6	:	:
Europe	:	:	38,8	641,8	:	49,8	18,3	:	:	:
EU-15	:	:	30,5	332,9	:	47,2	:	:	:	:
B	:	:	0,2	1,9	0,1	1,3	0,4	:	:	:
DK	:	:	22,5	2,4	0,1	0,3	0,1	:	:	:
D	:	:	1,7	197,0	0,8	7,1	0,7	:	:	:
EL	:	:	0,1	16,0	:	0,1	0,1	:	:	:
E	:	:	0,5	7,5	0,0	24,0	0,6	:	:	:
F	:	:	0,8	14,3	0,4	2,7	:	:	:	:
IRL	:	:	0,1	3,1	0,0	0,2	0,1	25,9	:	:
I	:	:	0,5	35,6	0,3	2,0	0,8	:	:	:
L	:	:	0,0	0,6	0,0	0,0	0,0	:	:	:
NL	:	:	0,6	6,5	0,2	1,1	0,2	:	:	:
A	:	:	0,2	11,1	0,1	0,3	0,1	:	:	:
P	:	:	0,1	18,8	0,0	1,4	2,0	:	:	:
FIN	:	:	0,4	2,8	0,1	0,7	0,1	:	:	:
S	:	:	1,5	3,4	0,2	0,5	0,2	:	:	:
UK	:	:	1,3	11,9	0,6	4,5	0,9	7,9	:	:
IS	:	:	1,2	:	0,0	0,0	0,0	:	:	:
NO	:	:	1,6	:	0,1	0,3	0,0	:	:	:
CH	:	:	0,1	3,1	0,1	0,6	0,5	:	:	:
CEEC	:	:	4,1	253,7	5,5	2,5	5,4	:	:	:
PL	:	:	0,7	66,3	0,2	0,4	1,1	:	:	:
RO	:	:	0,2	17,0	0,7	0,5	0,6	:	:	:
fSU	:	:	1,8	51,0	2,4	1,4	1,1	:	:	:
fYUG	:	:	1,2	85,6	0,4	0,3	2,1	:	:	:
Other Europe	:	:	1,3	52,1	0,2	0,1	6,2	:	:	:
TR	:	:	1,3	49,2	0,1	0,0	6,0	:	:	:
Africa	:	:	2,8	36,6	1,4	13,1	61,0	:	:	:
MA	:	:	0,3	4,5	0,0	10,6	13,9	:	:	:
DZ	:	:	0,1	:	0,0	0,7	15,3	:	:	:
TN	:	:	0,0	2,3	0,0	0,0	4,9	:	:	:
America	:	:	2,4	31,5	0,9	15,5	6,0	:	:	:
US	:	:	1,4	16,0	0,6	0,6	1,6	2,5	:	:
CA	:	:	0,3	2,1	0,1	0,1	0,6	:	:	:
BR	:	:	0,2	4,2	0,0	0,9	0,4	:	:	:
Asia	:	:	6,7	91,7	1,5	2,7	14,3	:	:	:
IN	:	:	0,3	4,7	0,0	0,2	0,7	:	:	:
IR	:	:	0,5	5,6	0,0	0,1	0,3	:	:	:
PK	:	:	0,4	2,9	0,1	0,3	0,6	:	:	:
Oceania	:	:	0,4	2,4	0,1	0,1	0,2	:	:	:
AU	:	:	0,3	:	0,1	0,0	0,1	:	:	:
NZ	:	:	0,1	:	0,0	0,0	0,0	:	:	:

CEEC: Countries of central and eastern Europe; PL: Poland; RO: Romania; fSU: former Soviet Union; fYUG: former Yugoslavia; TR: Turkey; MA: Morocco; DZ: Algeria; TN: Tunisia; BR: Brazil; IN: India; IR: Iran; PK: Pakistan; AU: Australia; NZ: New Zealand.

Further reading: European social statistics — Migration, 2000. Eurostat.

Data exclude unrecorded migration. UK: international passenger survey. IRL: labour force survey.

1C1FG

Immigration by country of citizenship. 1998. 1 000s

1C1FH

NL	A	P	FIN	S	UK	IS	NO	EEA	CH	
122,4	72,7	:	14,2	49,4	332,4	4,6	36,7	:	96,0	Total
40,7	13,5	:	5,9	137,7	11,3	2,8	10,0	:	23,8	Nationals
81,7	59,2	6,5	8,3	35,7	221,1	1,8	26,7	:	72,2	Non-nationals
72,3	62,4	:	11,4	31,9	:	4,1	27,3	:	72,8	Europe
60,6	25,5	:	7,4	22,0	182,1	0,6	13,3	:	32,6	EU-15
1,9	0,2	0,1	0,0	0,1	:	0,0	0,1	:	0,6	B
0,4	0,2	0,0	0,1	1,1	:	0,2	2,1	:	0,5	DK
4,7	6,3	0,6	0,2	1,1	:	0,1	1,1	:	9,0	D
0,7	0,5	0,0	0,0	0,2	:	0,0	0,1	:	0,2	EL
1,2	0,3	0,5	0,0	0,3	:	0,0	0,1	:	1,4	E
2,1	0,6	0,5	0,1	0,6	:	0,0	0,4	:	5,3	F
0,5	0,1	0,0	0,0	0,1	:	0,0	0,0	:	0,3	IRL
1,4	1,2	0,2	0,1	0,3	:	0,0	0,2	:	4,4	I
0,0	0,0	0,0	0,0	0,0	:	0,0	0,0	:	0,1	L
40,7	0,5	0,2	0,0	0,3	:	0,0	0,4	:	1,0	NL
0,4	13,5	0,0	0,0	0,1	:	0,0	0,1	:	1,2	A
0,7	0,4	:	0,0	0,1	:	0,0	0,1	:	4,7	P
0,5	0,3	0,0	5,9	3,0	:	0,0	1,4	:	0,4	FIN
0,7	0,4	0,1	0,8	13,7	:	0,1	6,0	:	0,8	S
4,7	0,9	0,5	0,2	1,0	:	0,0	1,3	:	2,7	UK
0,1	0,0	0,0	0,0	0,3	:	2,8	0,9	:	0,0	IS
0,3	0,1	0,0	0,1	1,6	:	0,1	10,0	:	0,3	NO
0,2	0,4	0,1	0,0	0,1	:	0,0	0,1	:	23,8	CH
5,9	30,4	0,2	3,7	7,1	:	0,7	2,6	:	13,8	CEEC
1,5	4,9	0,0	0,0	0,6	:	0,4	0,2	:	0,4	PL
0,4	1,5	0,0	0,0	0,3	:	0,0	0,2	:	0,4	RO
1,8	1,2	0,1	3,4	1,5	:	0,1	0,9	:	1,8	fSU
1,2	17,0	0,0	0,2	4,3	:	0,1	1,0	:	9,9	fYUG
5,1	5,9	0,0	0,1	0,8	:	0,0	0,5	:	2,2	Other Europe
5,1	5,9	0,0	0,1	0,8	:	0,0	0,5	:	2,2	TR
10,9	2,5	1,7	0,7	2,5	:	0,1	2,4	:	4,4	Africa
5,3	0,1	0,0	0,0	0,2	:	0,0	0,2	:	0,7	MA
0,2	0,2	0,0	0,0	0,1	:	0,0	0,1	:	0,3	DZ
0,2	0,1	0,0	0,0	0,1	:	0,0	0,0	:	0,5	TN
9,9	2,3	1,3	0,4	2,7	:	0,2	1,8	:	8,2	America
3,3	1,2	0,3	0,2	1,0	:	0,1	1,0	:	2,9	US
0,6	0,2	0,0	0,1	0,2	:	0,0	0,2	:	1,0	CA
0,7	0,3	0,7	0,0	0,2	:	0,0	0,1	:	1,4	BR
11,3	5,1	0,3	1,6	11,5	:	0,2	5,0	:	9,8	Asia
0,9	0,7	0,0	0,1	0,3	:	0,0	0,3	:	1,0	IN
0,3	0,7	0,0	0,2	1,5	:	0,0	0,7	:	0,2	IR
0,4	0,2	0,0	0,0	0,1	:	0,0	0,6	:	0,2	PK
0,8	0,3	0,0	0,1	0,4	:	0,0	0,2	:	0,6	Oceania
0,6	0,2	0,0	0,1	0,3	:	0,0	0,1	:	0,5	AU
0,2	0,0	0,0	0,0	0,1	:	0,0	0,0	:	0,2	NZ

CEEC: Countries of central and eastern Europe; PL: Poland; RO: Romania; fSU: former Soviet Union; fYUG: former Yugoslavia;
TR: Turkey; MA: Morocco; DZ: Algeria; TN: Tunisia; BR: Brazil; IN: India; IR: Iran; PK: Pakistan; AU: Australia; NZ: New Zealand.

Further reading: European social statistics — Migration, 2000. Eurostat.

Data exclude unrecorded migration. UK: international passenger survey. IRL: labour force survey.

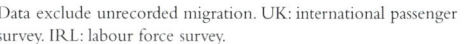

The definition of an immigrant varies between reporting countries. Some countries, such as the United Kingdom, record nationals and non-nationals who arrive from abroad with the intention of residing in the country for a certain period. Others record the de facto situation. The qualifying period varies from one month for a Dutch person returning to the Netherlands to 12 months for any person entering the United Kingdom. Not all EU countries collect data, and in those that do, collection varies. For example, the UK does not record flows between its territory and Ireland; France has no statistics on immigration of nationals. Data are therefore not fully comparable.

Immigration of nationals as percentage of total immigration

	1989	1990	1991	1992	1993	1994	1995	1996	1997	1998	1999	
B	20	20	20	18	17	15	16	16	16	17	:	B
DK	50	52	49	51	53	53	38	42	45	44	:	DK
D	49	49	23	19	23	28	28	26	27	25	:	D
EL	27	41	45	54	40	:	:	:	:	:	:	EL
E	58	60	57	53	54	46	46	44	38	30	:	E
F	:	:	:	:	:	:	:	:	:	:	:	F
IRL	:	:	68	63	57	55	56	45	47	53	:	IRL
I	66	42	44	48	49	47	29	17	:	:	:	I
L	9	9	9	8	9	9	7	8	9	10	:	L
NL	34	31	30	29	27	28	30	29	30	33	:	NL
A	:	:	:	:	:	:	:	:	19	19	:	A
P	:	:	:	:	:	:	:	:	:	:	:	P
FIN	63	52	30	29	27	34	40	43	40	41	:	FIN
S	11	11	12	13	11	11	21	27	25	28	:	S
UK	42	40	44	48	44	47	37	38	34	:	:	UK
IS	63	65	57	67	65	67	67	66	65	61	:	IS
NO	29	38	39	36	30	34	36	35	31	27	:	NO
CH	24	20	19	16	15	17	20	24	24	25	:	CH

1C1FE

Further reading: European social statistics — Migration, 2000. Eurostat.

Data exclude unrecorded migration. UK: international passenger survey. IRL: labour force survey.

Immigration, total. 1 000s

	1989	1990	1991	1992	1993	1994	1995	1996	1997	1998	1999	
B	54	63	68	67	64	66	63	62	59	62	68	B
DK	38	41	44	43	43	45	63	54	50	51	50	DK
D	1 522	1 652	1 199	1 502	1 277	1 083	1 096	960	841	802	874	D
EL	39	42	24	32	28	18	21	22	22	:	:	EL
E	34	34	24	39	33	34	36	30	58	81	:	E
F	105	97	102	111	94	64	50	47	66	100	:	F
IRL	27	33	33	41	35	30	31	39	44	44	47	IRL
I	81	167	127	114	100	99	97	172	:	166	190	I
L	9	10	11	11	10	10	10	10	10	12	13	L
NL	99	117	120	117	119	92	96	109	110	122	120	NL
A	:	:	:	:	:	95	:	70	70	70	73	A
P	:	:	:	14	10	6	5	4	3	6	:	P
FIN	11	14	19	15	15	12	12	13	14	14	15	FIN
S	66	60	50	45	62	84	46	40	45	49	50	S
UK	250	267	267	216	210	253	246	258	285	402	:	UK
IS	3	3	4	3	3	3	3	4	4	5	5	IS
NO	26	26	26	27	32	27	26	26	32	37	:	NO
CH	130	154	165	157	145	130	114	74	92	96	:	CH

1C1FF

Further reading: European social statistics — Migration, 2000. Eurostat.

Data exclude unrecorded migration. F and P: only non-nationals. UK: international passenger survey. IRL: labour force survey. EL: only non-nationals from 1994 on.

Emigrants generally are nationals and non-nationals travelling abroad with the intention of residing there for a certain minimum period. For example, 12 months for Dutch emigrants leaving the Netherlands. There are many exceptions; Germans are considered emigrants when they leave their occupied residence; Britons are emigrants when intending to live abroad for more than 12 months after being resident in the UK for the previous 12 months; the Irish are emigrants when already resident abroad after being resident in Ireland for one previous year.

Emigration to other EEA countries. 1 000s

1C1GC

	1989	1990	1991	1992	1993	1994	1995	1996	1997	1998	1999	
B	22	21	21	:	:	:	:	:	:	:	:	**B**
DK	14	14	14	14	15	18	17	18	19	20	:	**DK**
D	117 |	114	126	124	132	173	179	193	200	189	:	**D**
EL	:	:	:	:	:	:	:	:	:	:	:	**EL**
E	:	:	:	:	:	:	:	:	:	:	:	**E**
F	:	:	:	:	:	:	:	:	:	:	:	**F**
IRL	52	41	26	24	24	20	18	19	17	15	:	**IRL**
I	42	29	30	29	30	66	23	24	:	:	:	**I**
L	:	:	:	:	:	:	:	:	:	:	:	**L**
NL	28	27	27	27	27	26	30	33	30	30	:	**NL**
A	:	:	:	:	:	:	:	12	19	19	:	**A**
P	:	:	:	12	12	:	5	8	7	4	:	**P**
FIN	6	6	5	5	5	6	7	7	8	8	:	**FIN**
S	17	20	19	17	17	17	19	20	23	24	:	**S**
UK	46	60	74	60	64	55	57	73	72	62	:	**UK**
IS	2	2	2	2	2	3	4	4	3	3	:	**IS**
NO	20	16	10	9	9	10	:	11	12	13	:	**NO**
CH	:	:	:	:	:	:	:	:	:	:	:	**CH**

Further reading: European social statistics — Migration, 2000. Eurostat.

Data exclude unrecorded migration. IRL: labour force survey. UK: international passenger survey.

Emigration to non-EEA countries. 1 000s

1C1GD

	1989	1990	1991	1992	1993	1994	1995	1996	1997	1998	1999	
B	12	11	13	:	:	:	:	:	:	:	:	**B**
DK	21	19	19	18	18	17	17	19	20	20	:	**DK**
D	429 |	497	471	596	683	567	519	485	547	566	:	**D**
EL	:	:	:	:	:	:	:	:	:	:	:	**EL**
E	:	:	:	:	:	:	:	:	:	:	:	**E**
F	:	:	:	:	:	:	:	:	:	:	:	**F**
IRL	18	15	9	9	11	15	15	12	12	14	:	**IRL**
I	23	27	28	28	32		20	23	:	:	:	**I**
L	:	:	:	:	:	:	:	:	:	:	:	**L**
NL	32	31	31	32	32	28	33	33	32	30	:	**NL**
A	:	:	:	:	:	:	:	54	50	45	:	**A**
P	:	:	:	11	11	:	3	3	2	4	:	**P**
FIN	1	1	1	1	2	2	2	4	2	2	:	**FIN**
S	5	5	5	8	12	16	15	14	16	15	:	**S**
UK	159	171	165	167	149	136	135	139	153	137	:	**UK**
IS	2	2	1	2	1	1	1	1	1	1	:	**IS**
NO	7	8	8	8	10	9	:	10	10	10	:	**NO**
CH	:	:	:	:	:	:	:	:	:	:	:	**CH**

Further reading: European social statistics — Migration, 2000. Eurostat.

Data exclude unrecorded migration. IRL: labour force survey; UK: international passenger survey.

Emigration by country of citizenship. 1998. 1 000s

	EU-15	B	DK	D	EL	E	F	IRL	I	L
Total	:	:	40,3	755,4	:	:	:	29,0	:	7,6
Nationals	:	:	24,7	116,4	:	:	:	:	:	0,9
Non-nationals	:	:	15,6	639,0	:	:	:	:	:	6,7
Europe	:	:	35,5	627,7	:	:	:	:	:	6,9
EU-15	:	:	30,5	263,0	:	:	:	:	:	6,3
B	:	:	0,1	1,8	:	:	:	:	:	0,7
DK	:	:	24,7	2,8	:	:	:	:	:	0,2
D	:	:	1,0	116,4	:	:	:	:	:	0,5
EL	:	:	0,1	20,3	:	:	:	:	:	0,1
E	:	:	0,4	8,4	:	:	:	:	:	0,1
F	:	:	0,5	12,9	:	:	:	:	:	1,1
IRL	:	:	0,1	3,8	:	:	:	:	:	0,1
I	:	:	0,5	37,9	:	:	:	:	:	0,4
L	:	:	0,0	0,4	:	:	:	:	:	0,9
NL	:	:	0,4	6,6	:	:	:	:	:	0,2
A	:	:	0,1	9,7	:	:	:	:	:	0,0
P	:	:	0,1	22,1	:	:	:	:	:	1,5
FIN	:	:	0,4	2,9	:	:	:	:	:	0,1
S	:	:	1,0	3,3	:	:	:	:	:	0,1
UK	:	:	1,2	13,8	:	:	:	:	:	0,4
IS	:	:	1,3	:	:	:	:	:	:	0,0
NO	:	:	1,2	:	:	:	:	:	:	0,0
CH	:	:	0,1	2,7	:	:	:	:	:	0,1
CEEC	:	:	2,2	:	:	:	:	:	:	0,4
PL	:	:	0,4	60,8	:	:	:	:	:	0,0
RO	:	:	0,1	13,5	:	:	:	:	:	0,0
fSU	:	:	1,1	22,3	:	:	:	:	:	0,1
fYUG	:	:	0,4	184,4	:	:	:	:	:	0,1
Other Europe	:	:	0,3	:	:	:	:	:	:	0,0
TR	:	:	0,3	47,2	:	:	:	:	:	0,0
Africa	:	:	1,2	28,0	:	:	:	:	:	0,1
MA	:	:	0,0	2,8	:	:	:	:	:	0,0
DZ	:	:	0,0	:	:	:	:	:	:	0,0
TN	:	:	0,0	1,6	:	:	:	:	:	0,0
America	:	:	1,8	26,0	:	:	:	:	:	0,4
US	:	:	1,3	15,7	:	:	:	:	:	0,3
CA	:	:	0,2	1,9	:	:	:	:	:	0,0
BR	:	:	0,1	2,8	:	:	:	:	:	0,0
Asia	:	:	1,5	67,9	:	:	:	:	:	0,2
IN	:	:	0,1	5,0	:	:	:	:	:	0,0
IR	:	:	0,1	4,3	:	:	:	:	:	0,0
PK	:	:	0,2	2,9	:	:	:	:	:	0,0
Oceania	:	:	0,3	1,9	:	:	:	:	:	0,0
AU	:	:	0,2	:	:	:	:	:	:	0,0
NZ	:	:	0,1	:	:	:	:	:	:	0,0

CEEC: Countries of central and eastern Europe; PL: Poland; RO: Romania; fSU: former Soviet Union; fYUG: former ugoslavia; TR: Turkey; MA: Morocco; DZ: Algeria; TN: Tunisia; BR: Brazil; IN: India; IR: Iran; PK: Pakistan; AU: Australia; NZ: New Zealand.

Further reading: European social statistics — Migration, 2000. Eurostat.

Data exclude unrecorded migration. UK: international passenger survey. IRL: labour force survey.

1C1GG

Emigration by country of citizenship. 1998. 1 000s

NL	A	P	FIN	S	UK	IS	NO	EEA	CH	
60,4	64,3	:	10,8	38,5	198,9	3,7	22,9	:	94,8	Total
39,2	19,4	:	9,1	24,4	111,2	3,0	10,9	:	30,8	Nationals
21,3	44,9	:	1,7	14,1	87,7	0,7	12,0	:	64,0	Non-nationals
52,1	57,5	:	10,4	34,6	:	3,6	19,5	:	80,6	Europe
49,5	27,2	:	9,9	30,7	138,3	0,4	6,9	:	39,1	EU-15
1,0	0,1	:	0,0	0,0	:	0,0	0,1	:	0,4	B
0,2	0,1	:	0,1	1,2	:	0,2	1,4	:	0,4	DK
3,0	3,8	:	0,1	0,5	:	0,0	0,4	:	5,7	D
0,3	0,3	:	0,0	0,3	:	0,0	0,0	:	0,3	EL
0,6	0,2	:	0,0	0,2	:	0,0	0,1	:	5,4	E
0,8	0,4	:	0,0	0,2	:	0,0	0,3	:	3,6	F
0,3	0,1	:	0,0	0,1	:	0,0	0,0	:	0,3	IRL
0,6	0,9	:	0,0	0,1	:	0,0	0,1	:	9,1	I
0,0	0,0	:	0,0	0,0	:	0,0	0,0	:	0,1	L
39,2	0,4	:	0,0	0,2	:	0,0	0,2	:	1,2	NL
0,1	19,4	:	0,0	0,0	:	0,0	0,0	:	1,1	A
0,2	0,3	:	0,0	0,1	:	0,0	0,0	:	7,8	P
0,2	0,2	:	9,1	2,9	:	0,0	0,6	:	0,4	FIN
0,3	0,3	:	0,4	24,4	:	0,1	2,7	:	0,8	S
2,6	0,6	:	0,1	0,6	:	0,0	0,8	:	2,3	UK
0,0	0,0	:	0,0	0,5	:	3,0	0,5	:	0,0	IS
0,2	0,1	:	0,1	1,8	:	0,1	10,9	:	0,3	NO
0,1	0,3	:	0,0	0,1	:	0,0	0,1	:	30,8	CH
1,3	25,9	:	0,4	1,4	:	0,1	1,0	:	8,3	CEEC
0,4	4,7	:	0,0	0,2	:	0,1	0,1	:	0,3	PL
0,0	1,2	:	0,0	0,1	:	0,0	0,0	:	0,2	RO
0,4	0,9	:	0,3	0,2	:	0,0	0,3	:	1,0	fSU
0,3	14,3	:	0,0	0,9	:	0,0	0,5	:	6,3	fYUG
0,9	4,0	:	0,0	0,2	:	0,0	0,1	:	2,0	Other Europe
0,9	4,0	:	0,0	0,2	:	0,0	0,1	:	2,0	TR
1,7	1,6	:	0,1	0,5	:	0,0	0,7	:	2,0	Africa
0,6	0,1	:	0,0	0,0	:	0,0	0,0	:	0,2	MA
0,0	0,1	:	0,0	0,0	:	0,0	0,0	:	0,1	DZ
0,1	0,1	:	0,0	0,0	:	0,0	0,0	:	0,1	TN
2,9	1,7	:	0,2	1,5	:	0,1	1,3	:	5,6	America
1,8	1,1	:	0,1	0,8	:	0,1	0,9	:	2,7	US
0,3	0,1	:	0,0	0,1	:	0,0	0,1	:	0,8	CA
0,2	0,2	:	0,0	0,1	:	0,0	0,1	:	0,6	BR
3,1	3,1	:	0,1	1,5	:	0,0	1,3	:	6,0	Asia
0,2	0,4	:	0,0	0,0	:	0,0	0,1	:	0,8	IN
0,1	0,5	:	0,0	0,4	:	0,0	0,1	:	0,1	IR
0,1	0,1	:	0,0	0,0	:	0,0	0,2	:	0,1	PK
0,3	0,2	:	0,0	0,2	:	0,0	0,1	:	0,5	Oceania
0,2	0,2	:	0,0	0,2	:	0,0	0,1	:	0,4	AU
0,1	0,0	:	0,0	0,0	:	0,0	0,0	:	0,1	NZ

CEEC: Countries of central and eastern Europe; PL: Poland; RO: Romania; fSU: former Soviet Union; fYUG: former Yugoslavia; TR: Turkey; MA: Morocco; DZ: Algeria; TN: Tunisia; BR: Brazil; IN: India; IR: Iran; PK: Pakistan; AU: Australia; NZ: New Zealand.

Further reading: European social statistics — Migration, 2000. Eurostat.

Data exclude unrecorded migration. UK: international passenger survey. IRL: labour force survey.

1C1GH

1

Emigration of nationals as percentage of total emigration

	1989	1990	1991	1992	1993	1994	1995	1996	1997	1998	1999	
B	42	42	39	38	30	38	40	40	40	33	:	**B**
DK	73	73	68	71	69	69	68	65	63	61	:	**DK**
D	20	24	17	15	13	18	19	18	15	15	:	**D**
EL	:	:	:	:	:	:	:	:	:	:	:	**EL**
E	:	:	:	:	:	:	:	:	:	:	:	**E**
F	:	:	:	:	:	:	:	:	:	:	:	**F**
IRL	:	:	:	:	:	:	:	:	:	:	:	**IRL**
I	91	87	89	88	90	91	82	82	:	:	:	**I**
L	:	13	13	13	14	14	14	12	12	11	:	**L**
NL	64	64	63	61	63	67	66	66	65	65	:	**NL**
A	:	:	:	:	:	:	:	:	27	30	:	**A**
P	:	:	:	95	95	:	100	98	:	:	:	**P**
FIN	88	86	81	76	76	82	83	72	84	84	:	**FIN**
S	39	36	39	49	50	52	55	57	60	63	:	**S**
UK	60	59	57	60	59	57	62	65	58	:	:	**UK**
IS	75	73	67	55	70	77	83	84	81	85	:	**IS**
NO	61	59	54	52	45	51	53	51	53	48	:	**NO**
CH	31	33	29	26	26	30	30	30	31	32	:	**CH**

1C1GE

Further reading: European social statistics — Migration, 2000. Eurostat.

Data exclude unrecorded migration. IRL: labour force survey. UK: international passenger survey.

Emigration, total. 1 000s

	1989	1990	1991	1992	1993	1994	1995	1996	1997	1998	1999	
B	34	33	34	34	45	37	36	37	39	49	41	**B**
DK	35	32	33	32	32	35	35	37	38	40	41	**DK**
D	545	611	597	720	815	768	698	678	747	755	672	**D**
EL	:	:	:	:	:	:	:	:	:	:	:	**EL**
E	:	:	:	:	:	:	:	:	:	:	:	**E**
F	:	:	:	:	:	:	:	:	:	:	:	**F**
IRL	71	56	35	33	35	35	33	31	29	21	29	**IRL**
I	66	56	58	57	61	66	43	48	:	57	76	**I**
L	:	6	7	6	7	6	6	6	7	8	8	**L**
NL	60	57	57	59	59	54	63	65	62	60	59	**NL**
A	:	:	:	:	:	:	:	66	69	64	:	**A**
P	:	:	:	22	22	8	7	10	10	8	:	**P**
FIN	7	7	6	6	6	9	9	11	10	11	12	**FIN**
S	22	25	25	26	30	33	34	34	39	39	36	**S**
UK	205	231	239	227	213	191	192	212	225	224	:	**UK**
IS	4	4	3	3	3	3	4	4	4	4	37	**IS**
NO	27	24	18	17	19	20	19	21	21	23	:	**NO**
CH	97	98	103	117	105	99	100	103	99	95	:	**CH**

1C1GF

Further reading: European social statistics — Migration, 2000. Eurostat.

Data exclude unrecorded migration. IRL: labour force survey. UK: international passenger survey.

Asylum applications. 1 000s

1C2AB

	1989	1990	1991	1992	1993	1994	1995	1996	1997	1998	1999	
EU-15	292	397	511	672	517	300	264	227	241	289	342 *	**EU-15**
B	8	13	15	18	27	14	11	12	12	22	33	**B**
DK	5	5	5	14	14	7	5	6	5	6	6	**DK**
D	121	193	256	438	323	127	128	116	104	99	95	**D**
EL	7	4	3	2	1	1	1	2	4	2	2	**EL**
E	4	9	8	12	13	12	6	5	5	7	8	**E**
F	61	55	47	29	28	26	20	17	21	22	30	**F**
IRL	0	0	0	0	0	0	0	1	2	5	8	**IRL**
I	2	4	24	3	1	2	2	1	2	7	12 *	**I**
L	0	0	0	0	0	0	0	0	0	0	3	**L**
NL	14	21	22	20	35	53	29	23	34	45	39	**NL**
A	22	23	27	16	5	5	6	7	7	14	20	**A**
P	0	0	0	1	2	1	0	0	0	0	0	**P**
FIN	0	3	2	4	2	1	1	1	1	1	3	**FIN**
S	30	29	27	84	38	19	9	6	10	13	12	**S**
UK	17	38	73	32	29	33	44	30	33	46	70	**UK**
IS	0	0	0	0	:	:	:	:	:	:	0 *	**IS**
NO	4	4	5	5	13	3	1	2	2	8	9 *	**NO**
EEA	296	401	516	678	530	304 *	265 *	229 *	243 *	297 *	351 *	**EEA**
CH	24	36	42	18	25	16	17	18	24	41	61 *	**CH**

Further reading: European social statistics — Migration, 2000. Eurostat.

B, I: excluding dependent children. DK: excluding applications outside Denmark and rejected applications at the border. D: including dependent children if the parents requested asylum for them. EL: figures for 1989–92 are the sum of the applications registered with the Greek authorities and those registered with UNHCR (United Nations High Commission for Refugees). E, UK: excluding dependents. F: excluding children and some accompanying adults. A: excluding displaced persons from fYUG who benefit from exceptional leave to stay. CH: partly excluding rejected persons at the border (especially those lacking proper identity papers).

Refugee status granted according to the Geneva Convention. 1 000s

1C2AK

	1989	1990	1991	1992	1993	1994	1995	1996	1997	1998	1999	
EU-15	:	:	:	:	:	:	:	:	:	:	:	**EU-15**
B	1	1	1	1	0	:	:	2	2	1	:	**B**
DK	1	1	1	1	1	3	5	1	5	:	:	**DK**
D	6	7	12	9	16	26	:	14	8	11	:	**D**
EL	:	0	:	0	0	0	0	0	0	0	:	**EL**
E	:	:	:	:	:	0	:	0	0	0	:	**E**
F	9	13	15	10	10	7	5	4	4	:	:	**F**
IRL	:	:	:	0	0	:	:	0	0	0	:	**IRL**
I	0	1	1	0	0	0	0	0	0	1	:	**I**
L	:	0	0	0	0	:	:	0	:	:	:	**L**
NL	1	1	1	5	10	7	2	9	6	2	:	**NL**
A	3	1	2	2	1	1	1	1	1	:	:	**A**
P	0	0	0	:	:	:	:	0	0	0	:	**P**
FIN	0	0	0	0	0	1	0	0	0	0	:	**FIN**
S	3	2	1	1	1	1	:	:	1	1	:	**S**
UK	2	1	1	1	2	1	1	2	4	5	:	**UK**
IS	-	-	-	-	-	0	:	0	:	0	:	**IS**
NO	0	0	0	0	0	0	:	:	0	0	:	**NO**
EEA	:	:	:	:	:	:	:	:	:	:	:	**EEA**
CH	1	1	1	1	4	3	:	:	3	2	:	**CH**

Further reading: European social statistics — Migration, 2000. Eurostat.

Asylum applications by country of citizenship. 1999

1C2AL

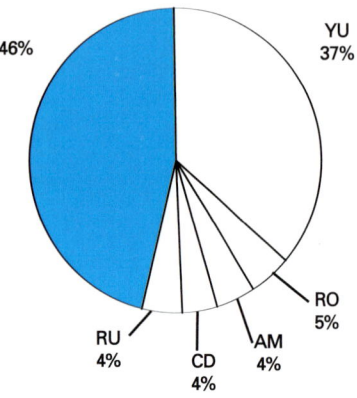

B

YU 37%
46%
RO 5%
RU 4%
CD 4%
AM 4%

D

YU 33%
39%
TR 10%
IR 4%
AF 5%
IQ 9%

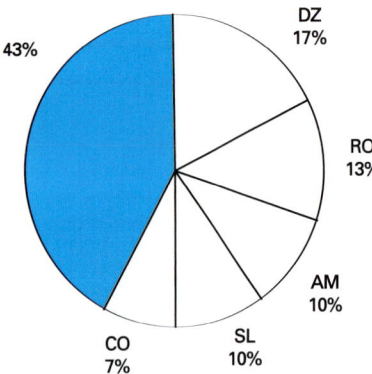

E

DZ 17%
43%
RO 13%
AM 10%
SL 10%
CO 7%

F

CN 17%
54%
YU 8%
CD 8%
TR 7%
LK 6%

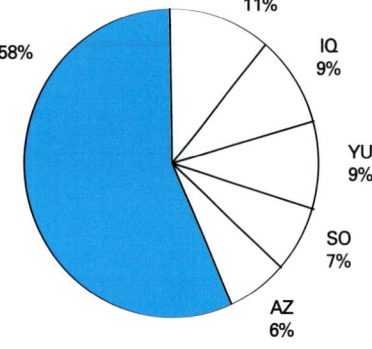

NL

AF 11%
58%
IQ 9%
YU 9%
SO 7%
AZ 6%

S

37%
IQ 34%
YU 13%
IR 8%
BA 4%
RU 4%

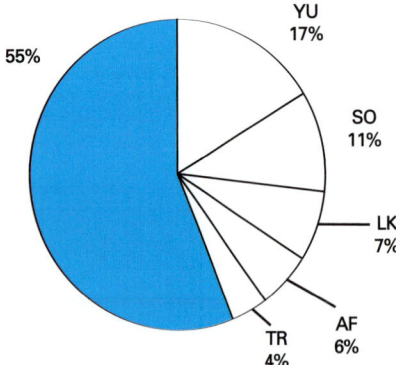

UK

YU 17%
55%
SO 11%
LK 7%
AF 6%
TR 4%

A

YU 34%
24%
IR 17%
AF 11%
IQ 10%
IN 4%

Colour: other countries. AF: Afghanistan; AM: Armenia; AZ: Azerbaijan; BA: Bosnia and Herzegovina; CD: Democratic Republic of the Congo (Kinshasa); CN: China; CO: Columbia; DZ: Algeria; IN: India; IQ: Iraq; IR: Iran; LK: Sri Lanka; PL: Poland; RO: Romania; RU: Russian Federation; SL: Sierra Leone; SO: Somalia; TR: Turkey; YU: Yugoslavia.

Further reading: European social statistics — Migration, 2000. Eurostat.

Non-national EEA citizens. 1 000s

1D1ED

	1989	1990	1991	1992	1993	1994	1995	1996	1997	1998	1999	
B	540	545	556	560	543	549	553	556	561	563	:	**B**
DK	50	51	52	53	54	56	59	62	66	69	:	**DK**
D	1 450	1 517	1 645	1 699	1 727	1 759	1 789	1 821	1 849	1 859	:	**D**
EL	51	55	60	63	66	43	44	45	46	:	:	**EL**
E	225	249	259	294	184	203	223	239	255	264	:	**E**
F	:	1 324	:	:	:	:	:	:	:	:	:	**F**
IRL	:	:	69	73	:	:	73	:	81 *	85 *	:	**IRL**
I	:	:	165	162	162	121	125	:	134	134	:	**I**
L	93	96	104	108	111	116	120	124	128	131	:	**L**
NL	165	169	176	184	190	196	195	193	190	192	:	**NL**
A	:	:	80	:	:	:	:	:	:	94 *	:	**A**
P	26	28	30	32	33	37	39	42	44	46	:	**P**
FIN	10	11	12	13	13	13	14	14	15	16	:	**FIN**
S	232	238	239	232	227	221	218	216	215	212	:	**S**
UK	961	919	814	827	775	823	912	826	814	:	:	**UK**
IS	:	:	3	3	3	3	3	3	3	3	:	**IS**
NO	62	59	58	58	60	61	63	64	67	:	:	**NO**
CH	773	784	807	824	829	832	837	838	829	820	:	**CH**

Further reading: European social statistics — Migration, 2000. Eurostat.

Non-EEA citizens. 1 000s

1D1EE

	1989	1990	1991	1992	1993	1994	1995	1996	1997	1998	1999	
B	328	336	348	362	367	371	369	354	330	340	:	**B**
DK	92	100	109	117	126	133	138	160	172	181	:	**DK**
D	3 039	3 329	3 698	4 184	4 768	5 119	5 201	5 353	5 465	5 506	:	**D**
EL	172	171	169	191	197	106	109	110	116	:	:	**EL**
E	135	149	148	190	209	227	238	260	295	345	:	**E**
F	:	2 273	:	:	:	:	:	:	:	:	:	**F**
IRL	:	:	19	22	:	:	23	:	33 *	26 *	:	**IRL**
I	:	:	616	418	762	503	558	:	750	:	:	**I**
L	12	13	9	10	12	12	13	14	15	16	:	**L**
NL	459	474	517	549	567	584	562	533	490	486	:	**NL**
A	:	:	437	:	:	:	:	:	:	640 *	:	**A**
P	68	73	78	79	89	100	118	126	129	129	:	**P**
FIN	8	10	14	25	33	43	49	54	58	65	:	**FIN**
S	189	218	245	262	272	286	319	316	312	310	:	**S**
UK	1 012	976	991	1 200	1 245	1 207	1 184	1 166	1 307	:	:	**UK**
IS	:	:	2	2	2	2	2	2	2	3	:	**IS**
NO	74	81	85	89	94	101	101	96	90	:	:	**NO**
CH	258	282	320	366	414	460	495	526	541	555	:	**CH**

Further reading: European social statistics — Migration, 2000. Eurostat.

1

Population by country of citizenship. 1.1.1998. 1 000s

1D1DA

	EU-15	B	DK	D	EL	E	F	IRL	I	L
Total	374 582,8 *	10 192,3	5 294,9	82 057,4	10 486,6	39 347,9	56 652,0	3 704,9	57 461,0	423,7
Nationals	355 500,0 *	9 289,1	5 045,2	74 691,5	10 325,4	38 738,1	53 055,4	3 593,8	56 576,4	276,0
Non-nationals	19 100,0 *	903,1	249,6	7 365,8	161,1	609,8	3 596,6	111,1	884,6	147,7
Europe	:	9 952,5	5 198,4	80 696,2	10 422,9	39 027,4	54 716,8	3 690,2 *	56 921,6	:
EU-15	361 500,0 *	9 851,2	5 096,5	76 541,6	10 370,5	38 998,7	54 376,9	3 679,1	56 709,9	407,4
B	:	9 289,1	0,5	23,3	1,2	10,5	56,1	:	4,8	13,2
DK	:	3,3	5 045,2	20,5	1,3	5,2	3,5	:	2,0	2,0
D	:	33,3	11,9	74 691,5	9,4	49,9	52,7	:	32,8	10,0
EL	:	19,2	0,7	363,2	10 325,4	0,7	6,1	:	11,4	1,3
E	:	47,4	1,6	131,6	0,7	38 738,1	216,0	:	12,3	2,9
F	:	103,6	3,0	103,9	5,1	34,3	53 055,4	:	25,3	16,5
IRL	:	3,3	1,1	16,0	0,5	2,9	3,5	3 593,8	2,0	0,9
I	:	205,8	2,6	607,9	5,6	22,6	252,8	:	56 576,4	19,9
L	:	4,5	0,0	5,6	0,0	0,2	3,0	:	0,2	276,0
NL	:	82,3	3,8	112,8	2,7	14,5	17,9	:	6,5	3,8
A	:	1,7	0,7	185,1	1,4	2,8	3,3	:	5,6	0,5
P	:	25,3	0,5	132,3	0,2	38,2	649,7	:	4,2	54,5
FIN	:	2,3	2,1	15,1	1,0	3,6	1,6	:	1,2	0,6
S	:	3,9	10,0	17,5	1,8	7,0	4,8	:	2,7	0,9
UK	:	26,1	12,8	115,2	14,1	68,3	50,4	66,2	22,7	4,4
IS	:	:	5,9	1,6	0,0	0,1	0,2	:	0,1	:
NO	:	1,2	11,9	7,6	0,6	3,6	1,9	:	0,7	:
CH	:	2,2	1,2	36,8	1,1	7,1	22,1	:	11,6	:
CEEC	:	14,9 *	45,4	1 999,4	47,3	16,7	115,5 *	:	191,4	:
PL	:	6,0	5,5	283,3	5,0	5,5	47,1	:	16,6	:
RO	:	2,2	1,1	95,2	5,6	2,4	5,1	:	17,9	:
fSU	:	2,9	4,4	254,0	19,8	3,5	4,7	:	7,4	:
fYUG	:	1,3	33,9	1 269,6	5,9	2,6	52,5	:	85,0	:
Other Europe	:	82,9 *	37,6	2 109,0	3,4	1,1	200,2 *	:	7,8	:
TR	:	73,8	37,5	2 107,4	3,2	0,4	197,7	:	4,2	:
Africa	:	171,1	22,1	305,6	13,2	142,8	1 633,1	:	296,3	:
MA	:	132,8	3,6	83,9	0,4	111,1	572,7	:	117,5	:
DZ	:	8,9	0,4	17,5	0,2	5,8	614,2	:	6,3	:
TN	:	4,7	0,5	25,4	0,3	0,5	206,3	:	44,2	:
America	:	22,0	9,6	194,4	20,0	127,0	72,8	:	88,4	:
US	:	12,6	5,2	110,1	15,2	13,4	24,2	10,0	17,6	:
CA	:	2,1	1,1	11,1	1,0	1,2	6,8	:	2,6	:
BR	:	1,5	0,8	19,6	0,7	6,3	6,3	:	13,9	:
Asia	:	25,7	53,8	781,0	27,9	49,3	227,0	:	151,3	:
IN	:	3,1	1,1	35,6	1,5	6,8	4,6	:	14,2	:
IR	:	1,1	6,8	113,8	1,3	1,7	15,2	:	8,4	:
PK	:	1,9	6,9	38,5	1,7	3,4	9,8	:	7,1	:
Oceania	:	0,7	1,1	9,6	1,2	0,9	2,3	:	2,9	:
AU	:	0,5	0,8	7,2	1,0	0,7	1,7	:	2,6	:
NZ	:	:	0,3	1,3	0,2	0,1	:	:	0,2	:

CEEC: Countries of central and eastern Europe; PL: Poland; RO: Romania; fSU: former Soviet Union; fYUG: former Yugoslavia; TR: Turkey; MA: Morocco; DZ: Algeria; TN: Tunisia; BR: Brazil; IN: India; IR: Iran; PK: Pakistan; AU: Australia; NZ: New Zealand.

Further reading: European social statistics — Migration, 2000. Eurostat. European social statistics demography 2000 edition.

F: 1990 Census results, metropolitan France; IRL and UK: labour force survey, Spring 1998; A: 1991 Census results; IS: data refer to 1.12.1997.

Population by country of citizenship. 1.1.1998. 1 000s

1D1DH

NL	A	P	FIN	S	UK	IS	NO	EEA	CH	
15 654,3	7 795,8	9 957,3	5 147,3	8 847,6	58 185,0	272,4	4 392,7	379 304,1 *	7 096,5	Total
14 976,1	7 278,1	9 782,0	5 066,7	8 325,6	56 058,0	266,7	4 235,2	360 000,0 *	5 721,3	Nationals
678,2	517,7	175,3	79,9	522,0	2 121,0	5,6	157,1	19 300,0 *	1 375,2	Non-nationals
15 328,5 *	7 745,1	9 831,7	5 120,4	8 687,3	57 046,0	270,7	4 330,7	:	6 962,1	Europe
15 166,3	7 357,5	9 828,1	5 081,7	8 502,4	56 863,0	2,4	64,1	366 100,0 *	817,4	EU-15
24,4	0,5	1,7	0,1	0,5	5,0	0,0	0,4	:	6,9	B
2,2	0,4	0,7	0,5	25,4	13,0	0,9	18,1	:	2,8	DK
53,9	57,3	8,3	2,0	14,5	62,0	0,3	5,1	:	95,7	D
5,3	1,0	0,1	0,3	4,4	21,0	0,0	0,2	:	6,7	EL
16,6	0,7	9,8	0,4	3,0	34,0	0,1	0,9	:	94,9	E
11,2	2,2	5,4	0,6	3,7	59,0	0,1	1,9	:	56,8	F
4,0	0,2	0,4	0,2	0,9	443,0	0,0	0,4	:	1,3	IRL
17,4	8,6	2,2	0,6	4,1	82,0	0,0	0,9	:	344,6	I
0,3	0,3	0,1	0,0	0,0	:	:	0,0	:	0,8	L
14 976,1	2,6	3,1	0,5	3,1	29,0	0,1	3,1	:	14,2	NL
3,1	7 278,1	0,4	0,2	2,7	9,0	0,0	0,5	:	28,3	A
8,7	0,2	9 782,0	0,1	1,4	26,0	0,1	0,5	:	137,1	P
1,5	0,5	0,4	5 066,7	101,3	4,0	0,1	3,9	:	2,2	FIN
2,5	1,4	1,1	7,5	8 325,6	18,0	0,3	17,3	:	5,2	S
39,2	3,4	12,3	1,9	11,7	56 058,0	0,3	10,9	:	19,8	UK
0,3	0,1	0,0	0,1	4,5	:	266,7	3,2	:	0,1	IS
1,7	0,3	0,4	0,5	31,0	9,0	0,3	4 235,2	:	1,4	NO
1,9	4,9	1,2	0,3	2,3	8,0	0,0	0,8	:	5 721,3	CH
43,5 *	263,2	2,0	36,1	128,6	84,0	1,2	23,4	:	339,7	CEEC
5,7	18,3	0,2	0,7	15,8	25,0	0,7	2,3	:	4,3	PL
1,1	18,5	0,1	0,4	3,2	3,0	0,0	0,5	:	2,3	RO
6,3 *	2,1	0,8	30,2	8,3	23,0	0,2	2,2	:	6,4	fSU
28,4	197,9	0,4	4,3	95,9	17,0	0,2	17,8	:	316,6	fYUG
114,7 *	118,7	0,1	1,7	18,6	82,0	0,0	4,0	:	80,6	Other Europe
114,7	118,6	0,1	1,7	18,4	59,0	0,0	3,9	:	80,3	TR
175,5	8,5	81,7	8,5	27,9	277,0	0,1	10,0	:	31,3	Africa
135,7	0,2	0,3	0,6	1,4	8,0	0,0	1,4	:	4,7	MA
1,1	0,1	0,1	0,2	0,4	5,0	0,0	0,2	:	2,9	DZ
1,5	0,8	0,0	0,2	0,9	:	0,0	0,2	:	3,6	TN
37,1	9,5	35,8	3,3	33,0	252,0	0,8	15,2	:	42,3	America
13,0	5,8	8,4	1,9	9,4	110,0	0,6	8,7	:	13,0	US
2,7	0,8	2,2	0,5	1,5	40,0	0,1	1,2	:	3,7	CA
2,4	0,6	20,0	0,1	1,4	6,0	0,0	0,5	:	6,2	BR
70,0 *	25,7	7,2	12,5	84,7	493,0	0,7	34,9	:	58,4	Asia
2,8	3,0	1,1	0,5	1,5	121,0	0,0	2,4	:	5,0	IN
7,8	5,7	0,6	1,7	26,2	22,0	0,0	3,8	:	3,4	IR
3,2	0,9	0,9	0,2	0,8	70,0	0,0	8,6	:	1,6	PK
2,5	0,7	0,5	0,4	2,0	87,0	0,1	0,8	:	2,1	Oceania
2,0	0,6	0,4	0,4	1,5	58,0	0,0	0,6	:	1,6	AU
0,5	0,1	0,0	0,0	0,4	29,0	0,0	0,2	:	0,4	NZ

CEEC: Countries of central and eastern Europe; PL: Poland; RO: Romania; fSU: former Soviet Union; fYUG: former Yugoslavia; TR: Turkey; MA: Morocco; DZ: Algeria; TN: Tunisia; BR: Brazil; IN: India; IR: Iran; PK: Pakistan; AU: Australia; NZ: New Zealand.

Further reading: European social statistics — Migration, 2000. Eurostat. European social statistics demography 2000 edition.

F: 1990 Census results, metropolitan France; IRL and UK: labour force survey, Spring 1998; IS: data refer to 1.12.1997.

Where is your nearest Data Shop? Addresses at the end of the book

EUROSTAT YEARBOOK 2001
99

NON-NATIONAL CITIZENS

Non-nationals are citizens of a country other than the one in which they live. Data on non-nationals are collected in cooperation with national statistical institutes, whose statistical practices can vary. Figures should be interpreted with care. If no data are indicated, this might mean either data not collected or not transmitted to Eurostat or that their magnitude is insignificant.

Non-EEA citizens living in EU regions as percentage of total population. 1998

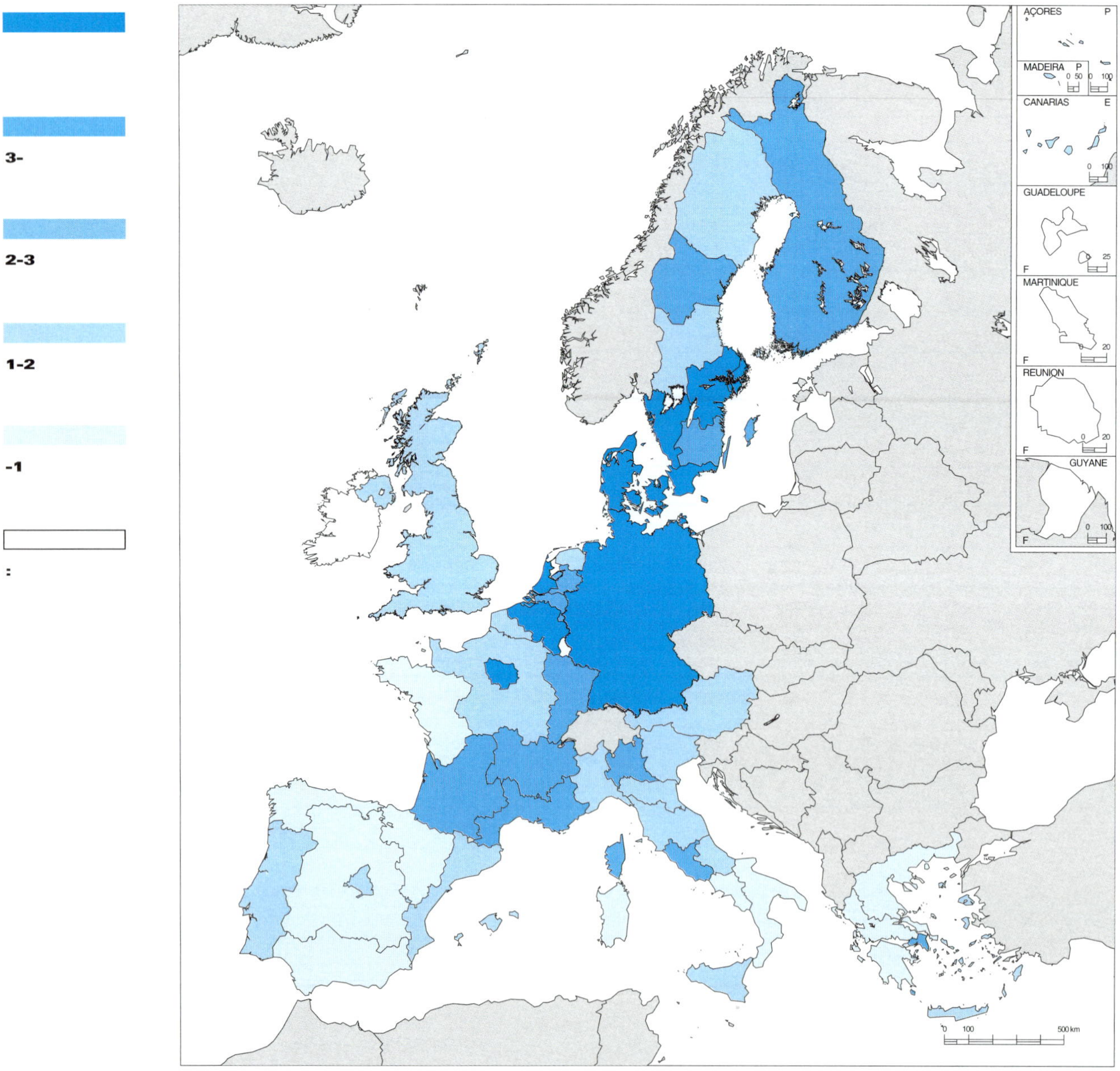

3-

2-3

1-2

-1

:

1D2AA

NUTS 1. NUTS 0: B, D, A, P, UK. NUTS 2: S. F: 1990 Census results, metropolitan France. IRL and UK: labour force survey. L: estimate. A: 1991 Census results.

Acquisition of citizenship

1D1FA

	1989	1990	1991	1992	1993	1994	1995	1996	1997	1998	1999	
EU-15	264 038	197 392	238 749	280 086	290 491	329 946	288 198	:	:	:	:	**EU-15**
B	8 797	8 658	8 470	46 485	16 379	25 808	26 149	24 581	:	34 034	:	**B**
DK	3 258	3 028	5 484	5 104	5 037	5 736	5 260	7 283	5 482	10 262	:	**DK**
D	17 573	20 078	27 162	37 000	45 016	61 625	31 797	86 356	83 027	106 790	:	**D**
EL	1 217	1 090	886	1 204	1 803	383	1 258	716	930	807	:	**EL**
E	5 919	7 033	3 752	5 226	8 348	7 802	6 756	8 433	9 801	12 550	:	**E**
F	49 330	54 366	59 684	59 252	60 013	77 515	49 843	63 055	83 676	81 449	:	**F**
IRL	299	179	188	150	133	175	355	226	294	1 474	:	**IRL**
I	4 238	5 256	4 542	4 408	6 469	5 993	7 442	:	:	:	:	**I**
L	780	893	748	739	800	293	270	305	761	631	:	**L**
NL	28 730	12 794	29 112	36 237	43 069	49 448	71 445	82 690	59 831	59 173	:	**NL**
A	7 305	8 980	11 137	11 656	14 131	15 275	14 366	15 627	15 792	17 786	:	**A**
P	210	97	43	117	2	144	80	1 154	1 364	799	:	**P**
FIN	1 501	899	1 236	876	839	651	668	981	1 439	4 017	:	**FIN**
S	17 752	16 770	27 663	29 389	42 659	35 065	31 993	25 549	28 875	46 090	:	**S**
UK	117 129	57 271	58 642	42 243	45 793	44 033	40 516	43 069	37 010	53 934	:	**UK**
IS	127	105	165	155	177	205	229	308	289	352	:	**IS**
NO	4 622	4 757	5 055	5 132	5 538	8 778	11 778	12 237	12 037	9 244	:	**NO**
EEA	268 873	202 336	244 033	285 428	296 271	338 998	300 274	:	:	:	:	**EEA**
CH	10 342	8 658	8 757	11 133	12 880	13 739	16 790	19 159	19 169	21 277	:	**CH**

Further reading: European social statistics — Migration, 2000. Eurostat.

Acquisition of citizenship as percentage of non-national population

1D1FB

	1989	1990	1991	1992	1993	1994	1995	1996	1997	1998	1999	
EU-15	2	1	2	2	2	2	2	:	:	:	:	**EU-15**
B	1	1	1	5	2	3	3	3	:	4	:	**B**
DK	2	2	3	3	3	3	3	3	2	4	:	**DK**
D	0	0	1	1	1	1	0	1	1	1	:	**D**
EL	1	0	0	0	1	0	1	0	1	0	:	**EL**
E	2	2	1	1	2	2	1	2	2	2	:	**E**
F	:	2	:	:	:	:	:	:	:	:	:	**F**
IRL	0	0	0	0	0	0	0	0	0	1	:	**IRL**
I	:	:	1	1	1	1	1	:	:	:	:	**I**
L	1	1	1	1	1	0	0	0	1	0	:	**L**
NL	5	2	4	5	6	6	9	11	9	9	:	**NL**
A	:	:	2	:	:	2	2	2	2	2	:	**A**
P	0	0	0	0	0	0	0	1	1	0	:	**P**
FIN	8	4	5	2	2	1	1	1	2	5	:	**FIN**
S	4	4	6	6	9	7	6	5	5	9	:	**S**
UK	5	2	2	2	2	2	2	2	2	3	:	**UK**
IS	3	2	3	3	4	4	5	6	6	6	:	**IS**
NO	3	3	4	3	4	5	7	8	8	6	:	**NO**
EEA	2	1	2	2	2	2	2	:	:	:	:	**EEA**
CH	1	1	1	1	1	1	1	1	1	2	:	**CH**

Further reading: European social statistics — Migration, 2000. Eurostat.

Non-national EEA citizens living in EU regions as percentage of total population. 1998

2-

1-2

0,3-1

-0,3

:

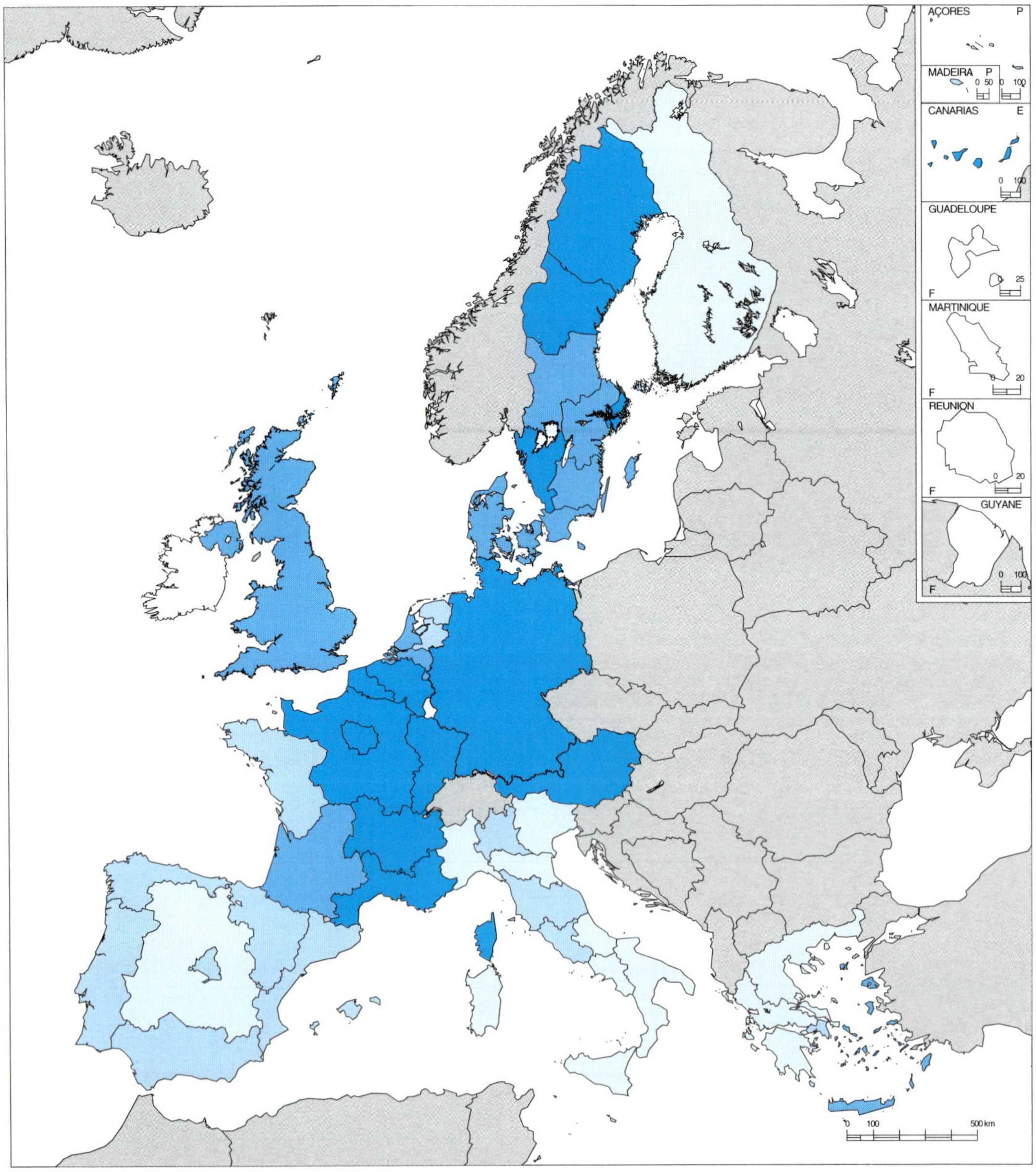

1D2AB

AÇORES   P

MADEIRA   P   0 50   0   100

CANARIAS   E   0   100

GUADELOUPE   0   25

MARTINIQUE   F   0   20

REUNION   F   0   20

GUYANE   F   0   100

0   100   500 km

NUTS 1. NUTS 0: B, D, A, P, UK. NUTS 2: S. F: 1990 Census
results, metropolitan France. IRL and UK: labour force survey.
L: estimate. A: 1991 Census results.

The main source of data presented in this chapter is the joint Unesco/OECD/Eurostat questionnaires which constitute the core database on education. The data, which are collected annually, relate to various educational fields, including enrolment, graduates, educational personnel and educational expenditures. An additional Eurostat questionnaire provides information on the study of foreign languages. Data on educational attainment of population come from the Community labour force survey.

The new classification of levels of education, ISCED 97, has been implemented for the first time using data from the school year 1997/98. Change in ISCED classification has had some consequences on the data. The most relevant difference for this publication is the introduction of a new level — level 4: post-secondary non-tertiary education. This change affects the comparability of chronological series, especially for level 3 (upper secondary education) and for level 5 (tertiary education).

New classification ISCED 97 distinguishes six levels of education:

– level 0: pre-primary education;
– level 1: primary education
– level 2: lower secondary education;
– level 3: upper secondary education;
– level 4: post-secondary non-tertiary education;
– level 5: tertiary education, first stage;
– level 6: tertiary education, second stage (leading to an advanced research qualification).

The data cover full- and part-time-students in public and private establishments. They cover school-based general education and vocational education/training (including combined school- and work-based programmes such as dual system apprenticeship).

Pre-primary education refers to the education-oriented institutions which obligatorily recruit staff with specialised qualification in education. In principle, these institutions are designed to meet the educational and development needs of children of at least 3 years of age.

The participation rate in education is the number of pupils/students enrolled as a percentage of the total population of a given age group. In the vast majority of countries, the reference age of students is their age as of 31 December/1 January of the school year.

The pupils-teacher ratio shows the number of pupils per teacher (both expressed in full-time equivalents) at a given level of education. Only the category of classroom teachers was taken into account in this calculation (excluding teacher aides and head teachers also involved in administrative tasks).

The average number of foreign languages learnt by pupils is obtained by dividing the number of pupils studying modern languages by the total number of pupils enrolled at a given level of education. The provided data refer to the considered school year, not to the whole schooling time of the given level. This aggregated indicator takes into account all foreign languages studied in each country, not only the most widespread. When a national language is taught in schools where it is not the teaching language, it is not considered as a foreign language.

One table shows the percentage of pupils learning three of the most widespread, at EU-level, languages: English, French and German.

1

Pupils and students (primary, secondary and tertiary education). 1 000s

	1989	1990	1991	1992	1993	1994	1995	1996	1997	1998	1999	
EU-15	67 771	67 516 |	70 242	70 917 |	72 354 *	73 014 *	73 027	73 380	73 296	72 987 *	:	**EU-15**
B	2 072	2 072	2 056	2 033	2 087	2 113	2 153	2 160	2 168	:	:	**B**
DK	974	960	948	933	938	942	943	942	955	973	:	**DK**
D	10 569	10 484 |	13 218	13 338	13 629	13 858	14 035	14 210	14 441	14 568	:	**D**
EL	1 895	1 878	1 865	1 860 |	1 892	1 889	1 850	1 840	1 833	1 904	:	**EL**
E	9 098	8 860	8 830	8 773	8 813	8 778	8 637	8 509	8 239	8 087	:	**E**
F	11 618	11 711	11 800	11 911	11 998	12 145	12 148	12 137	12 131	12 092	:	**F**
IRL	867	870	875	886 |	892	897	893	885	886	1 000	:	**IRL**
I	9 892	9 798	9 632	9 553	9 467	9 572	9 099	9 300	9 306	9 202	:	**I**
L	50	49	49	49	:	:	54	57	60	62	:	**L**
NL	3 538	3 529	3 550	3 534	3 539	3 241	3 201	3 179	3 116	3 136	:	**NL**
A	1 317	1 321	1 323	1 352	1 372	1 387	1 402	1 412	1 416	1 426	:	**A**
P	1 967	1 974 |	1 970	2 024	2 099	2 145	2 166	2 134	2 085	2 076	:	**P**
FIN	943	960	980	1 007	1 025	1 044	1 047	1 059	1 077	1 101	:	**FIN**
S	1 376	1 361	1 359	1 377 |	1 623	1 656	1 698	1 753	1 814	1 962	:	**S**
UK	11 594	11 688	11 786	12 289	12 931	13 298	13 700	13 802	13 232	13 238	:	**UK**
IS	:	:	61	62	:	:	67	67	68	71	:	**IS**
NO	:	:	843	850 |	:	895	858	865	884	958	:	**NO**
EEA	:	: |	71 146	71 829 |	:	:	73 951	74 312	74 253	74 016 *	:	**EEA**
US	54 224	55 096	54 769	56 564	57 979	58 573	59 225	59 781	60 622	61 816	:	**US**
CA	6 357	6 422	6 563	6 681	7 434	7 519	6 666	6 717	6 670	6 530	:	**CA**
JP	24 170	23 833	:	:	:	22 842	22 408	22 346	:	21 368	:	**JP**

1H1AA

Further reading: Education across Europe: statistics and indicators, 1999. Eurostat. Key
data on education in Europe, 1999/2000. European Commission.

Enrolment in education by level. 1997/98. 1 000s

	Total	Pre-primary	Primary	Lower secondary	Upper secondary	Post-secondary not tertiary	Tertiary	
EU-15	83 655 *	10 667 *	23 815 *	17 157 *	18 506 *	1 023 *	12 333 *	**EU-15**
B	2 589	421	751	353	703	.	361	**B**
DK	1 216	243	361	208	216	5	183	**DK**
D	16 851	2 283	3 866	5 463	2 618	453	2,098	**D**
EL	2 045	141	649	392	406	83	374	**EL**
E	9 212	1 125	2 634	1 056	2 333	318	1 746	**E**
F	14 495	2 403	3 979	3 324	2 652	25	2 027	**F**
IRL	1 003	3	465	195	159	38	143	**IRL**
I	10 795	1 592	2 818	1 803	2 688	25	1 869	**I**
L	72	10	29	15	15	1	2	**L**
NL	3 526	390	1 254	765	632	23	461	**NL**
A	1 653	227	385	379	363	52	247	**A**
P	2 286	210	833	455	437	.	352	**P**
FIN	1 220	119	381	207	263	.	250	**FIN**
S	2 309	347	746	336	599	:	281	**S**
UK	14 383	1 152	4 664	2 206	4 422	.	1 938	**UK**
IS	86	14	30	13	20	0	8	**IS**
NO	1 092	134	402	155	214	4	183	**NO**
EEA	84 833	10 815	24 247	17 325	18 741	1 027	12 524	**EEA**
US	68 916	7 100	24 691	12 124	10 115	1 601	13 284	**US**
CA	7 058	528	2 402	1 213	1 433	303	1 179	**CA**
JP	24 306	2 939	7 884	4 502	4 672	13	3 964	**JP**

2E1EB

Further reading: Education across Europe: statistics and indicators, 1999. Eurostat. Key data on education in Europe, 1999/2000. European Commission. B: 1996/97.

Basic data on education. 1997/98

	Participation rate in pre-primary education. %			Duration of compulsory schooling (age)		
	3-year-olds	4-year-olds	5-year-olds	From	To	
EU-15	66 *	90 *	92 *	:	:	**EU-15**
B	99	100	100	6	18	**B**
DK	71	89	94	7	16	**DK**
D	62	84	86	6	18	**D**
EL	0	54	83	6	15	**EL**
E	72	99	100	6	16	**E**
F	100	100	100	6	16	**F**
IRL	3	.	.	6	15	**IRL**
I	96	97	97	6	14	**I**
L	:	:	:	4	15	**L**
NL	0	98	98	5	17	**NL**
A	33	73	91	6	15	**A**
P	52	62	70	6	15	**P**
FIN	33	38	42	7	16	**FIN**
S	62	67	71	7	16	**S**
UK	51	94	.	5	16	**UK**
IS	84	89	89	6	16	**IS**
NO	67	74	78	6	16	**NO**

2E2EB

2E3EB

Further reading: Education across Europe: statistics and indicators, 1999. Eurostat. Key data on education in Europe, 1999/2000. European Commission. B, D, NL: 1996/97 part-time included. Northern Ireland: 4–16.

Pupils/teachers ratio in primary education. 1997/98

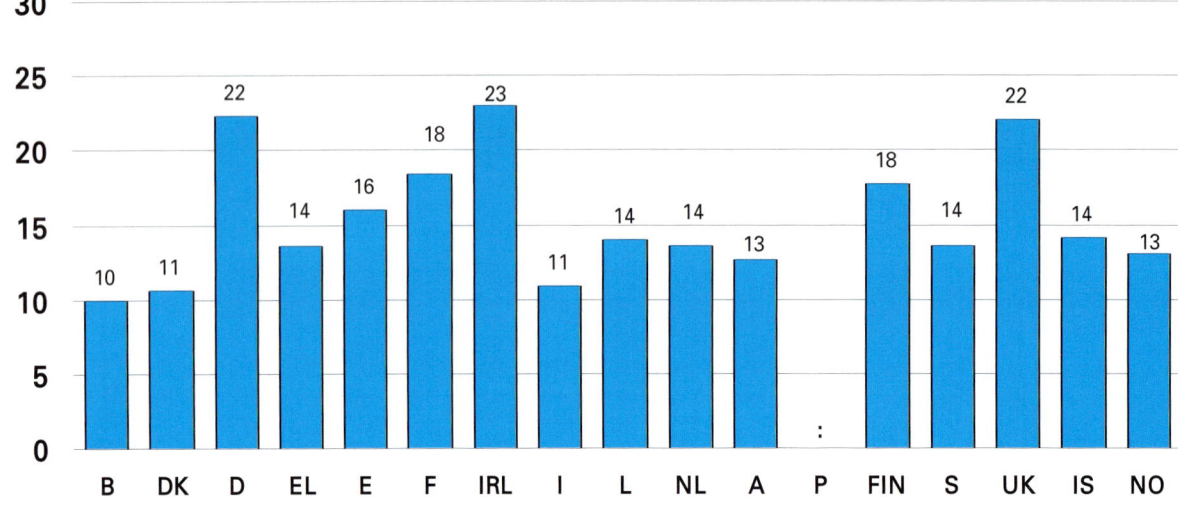

2E4EB

B: 1996/97.

Average number of foreign languages learnt per pupil in primary and secondary general education. 1997/98

	B (F)	B (VL)	DK	D	EL	E	F	IRL	I
Primary	0,4	0,3	0,3	0,1	0,5	0,7	0,4	:	0,5
Lower secondary general	0,9	1,4	1,7	1,2	1,8	1,6	1,5	1,1	1,2
Upper secondary general	1,9	2,5	2,4	1,4	1,2	1,1	1,9	1,0	1,1

6H1AB

Further reading: Education across Europe: statistics and indicators, 1999. Eurostat. Key data on education in Europe, 1999/2000. European Commission.

B (F) = French-speaking community (includes small German-speaking community). B (VL) = Flemish-speaking community. B, EL: 1996/97.

Average number of foreign languages learnt per pupil in primary and secondary general education. 1997/98

	L	NL	A	P	FIN	S	UK	IS	NO
Primary	1,8	:	0,6	:	0,8	0,7	:	0,4	1,0
Lower secondary general	:	:	1,0	:	2,3	1,7	:	2,1	1,5
Upper secondary general	2,9	:	1,7	:	2,8	:	:	1,4	:

Further reading: Education across Europe: statistics and indicators, 1999. Eurostat. Key data on education in Europe, 1999/2000. European Commission.

B (F) = French-speaking community (includes small German-speaking community). B (VL) = Flemish-speaking community. B, EL: 1996/97.

6H1AT

Percentage of pupils in upper secondary education learning English, French and German as a foreign language. 1997/98. %

	B (F)	B (VL)	DK	D	EL	E	F	IRL	I
English	92	100	100	90	70	96	99	.	78
French	.	100	34	33	43	15	.	69	21
German	8	54	83	.	4	1	36	22	7

Further reading: Education across Europe: statistics and indicators, 1999. Eurostat. Key data on education in Europe, 1999/2000. European Commission.

B, EL: 1996/97.
B (F): French-speaking community. B (VL): Dutch speaking community.

Percentage of pupils in upper secondary education learning English, French and German as a foreign language. 1997/98. %

	L	NL	A	P	FIN	S	UK	IS	NO
English	77	:	99	.	99	:	:	:	:
French	98	:	47	:	21	:	:	:	:
German	98	:	.	:	44	:	:	:	:

Further reading: Education across Europe: statistics and indicators, 1999. Eurostat. Key data on education in Europe, 1999/2000. European Commission.

B, EL: 1996/97.

1B5MB

Percentage of pupils in upper secondary education enrolled in vocational stream, by gender. 1997/98

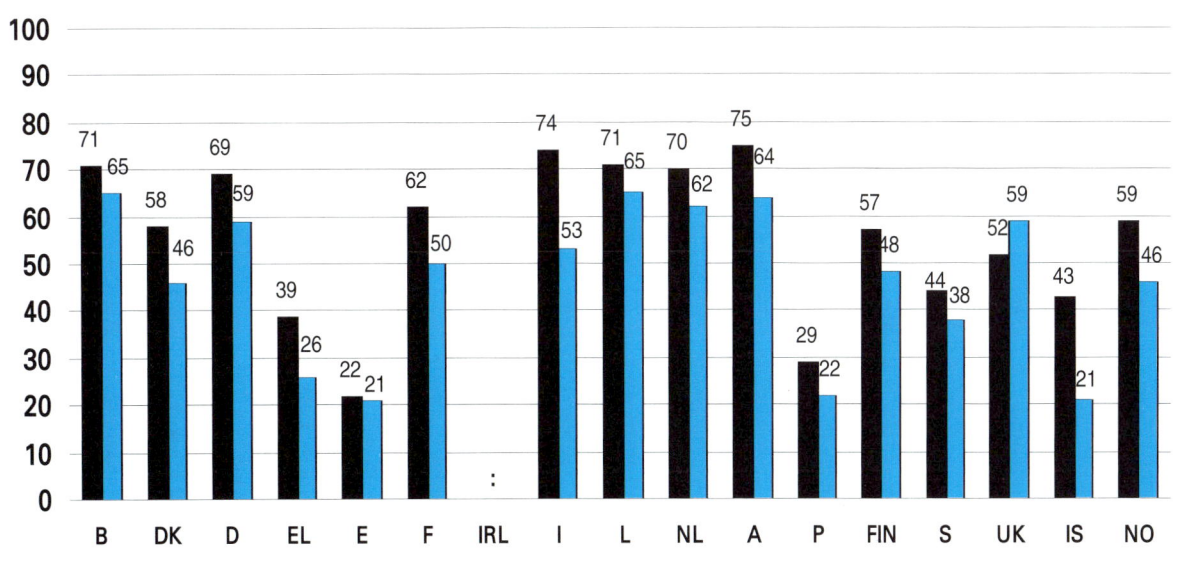

Black: boys; colour: girls.

Further reading: Education across Europe: statistics and indicators, 1999. Eurostat. Key data on education in Europe, 1999/2000. European Commission.

B: 1996/97.

Need access to Eurostat's databases? Ask your Data Shop

Participation rates in education at all levels by age. 1997/98. %

	16 years	18 years	20 years	22 years	24 years	18–24 years	
EU-15	90	72	48	34	19	42	**EU-15**
B	99	86	63	38	20	50	**B**
DK	93	75	40	38	33	45	**DK**
D	97	86	48	45	19	46	**D**
EL	90	71	59	24	13	42	**EL**
E	88	66	55	40	23	45	**E**
F	96	82	57	34	15	46	**F**
IRL	92	72	42	21	9	35	**IRL**
I	79	68	38	26	20	35	**I**
L	80	72	46	:	:	:	**L**
NL	97	79	58	38	27	48	**NL**
A	89	68	29	23	19	32	**A**
P	85	66	40	27	19	37	**P**
FIN	89	85	45	48	38	51	**FIN**
S	98	96	42	41	32	47	**S**
UK	82	49	43	23	16	32	**UK**
IS	89	67	48	42	33	48	**IS**
NO	94	88	48	41	31	48	**NO**

1B6MB

Further reading: Education across Europe: statistics and indicators, 1999. Eurostat. Key data on education in Europe, 1999/2000. European Commission.

B: 1996/97. Horizontal axis: age of students in years.

Participation rate in education for 18- to 24-year-olds, by level. 1997/98. %

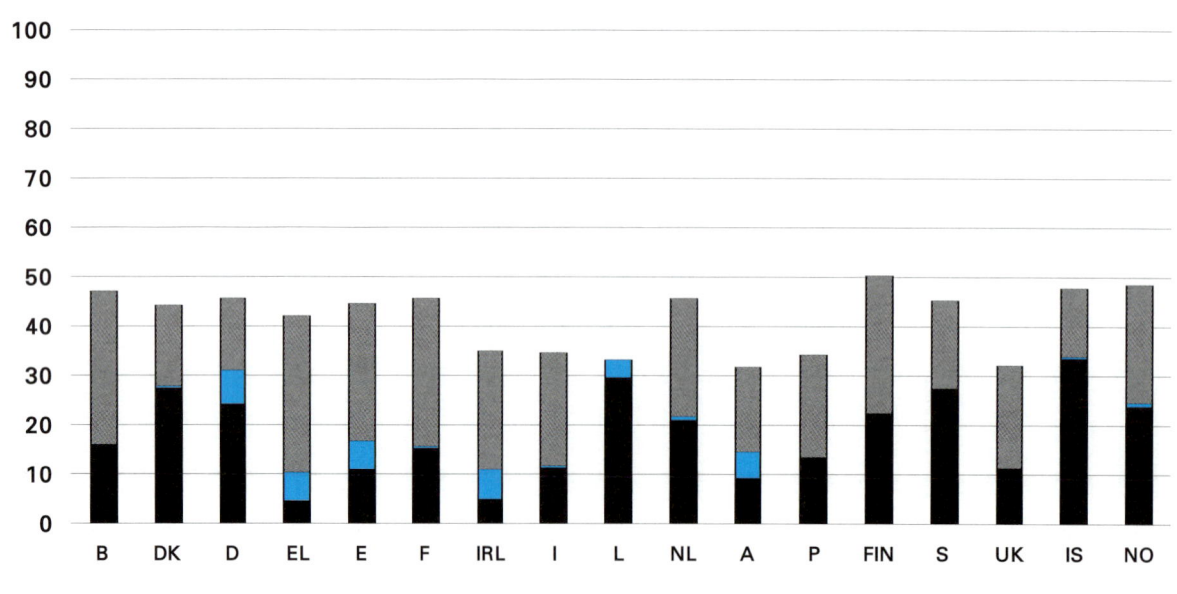

Black: upper secondary; colour: post-secondary non-tertiary; grey: tertiary.

1H1BS

Further reading: Education across Europe: statistics and indicators, 1999. Eurostat. Key data on education in Europe, 1999/2000. European Commission.

B: 1996/97.

Students in tertiary education. 1989/99. 1 000s

1B7MB

	1989	1990	1991	1992	1993	1994	1995	1996	1997	1998	1999	
EU-15	8 415	8 816 |	9 614	10 114 |	10 845 *	11 528 *	11 790 *	11 931 *	12 266 *	12 333 *	:	**EU-15**
B	261	271	276	286	307	322	353	358	361	:	:	**B**
DK	127	135	143	150	164	170	170	167	180	183	:	**DK**
D	1 687	1 720 |	2 049	2 034	2 113	2 148	2 156	2 144	2 132	2 098	.	**D**
EL	188	194	195	200 |	299	314	296	329	363	374	:	**EL**
E	1 101	1 166	1 222	1 302	1 371	1 469	1 527	1 592	1 684	1 746	:	**E**
F	1 477	1 585	1 699	1 840	1 952	2 083	2 073	2 092	2 063	2 027	:	**F**
IRL	81	85	90	101	108	118	122	128	135	143	:	**IRL**
I	1 306	1 373	1 452	1 533	1 615	1 770	1 792	1 775	1 893	1 869	:	**I**
L	1	1	1	1	:	:	:	:	2	2	:	**L**
NL	416	437	479	494	507	532	503	492	469	461	:	**NL**
A	193	200	206	217	221	227	234	239	241	248	:	**A**
P	130	131 |	186	191	248	276	301	320	351	352	:	**P**
FIN	147	155	166	174	188	197	205	214	226	250	:	**FIN**
S	187	185	193	207	223	234	246	261	275	281	:	**S**
UK	1 113	1 178	1 258	1 385	1 528	1 664	1 813	1 821	1 891	1 938	:	**UK**
IS	:	:	5	6	:	:	7	7	8	8	:	**IS**
NO	:	:	142	154	:	177	173	180	185	183	:	**NO**
EEA	:	: |	9 761	10 274 |	:	:	:	12 119 *	7 739	7 762	:	**EEA**
CH	:	:	137	143	146	149	148	148		:		**CH**
US	13 055	13 539	13 065	14 359	14 486	14 305	14 279	14 262	14 300	13 284	:	**US**
CA	1 791	1 822	1 898	1 943	2 633	2 662	1 784	1 763	1 717	1 179	:	**CA**
JP	2 588	2 683	:	:	:	3 841	3 918	3 945	:	3 964	:	**JP**

Further reading: Education across Europe: statistics and indicators, 1999. Eurostat. Key
data on education in Europe, 1999/2000. European Commission.

Median age in tertiary education. 1997/98

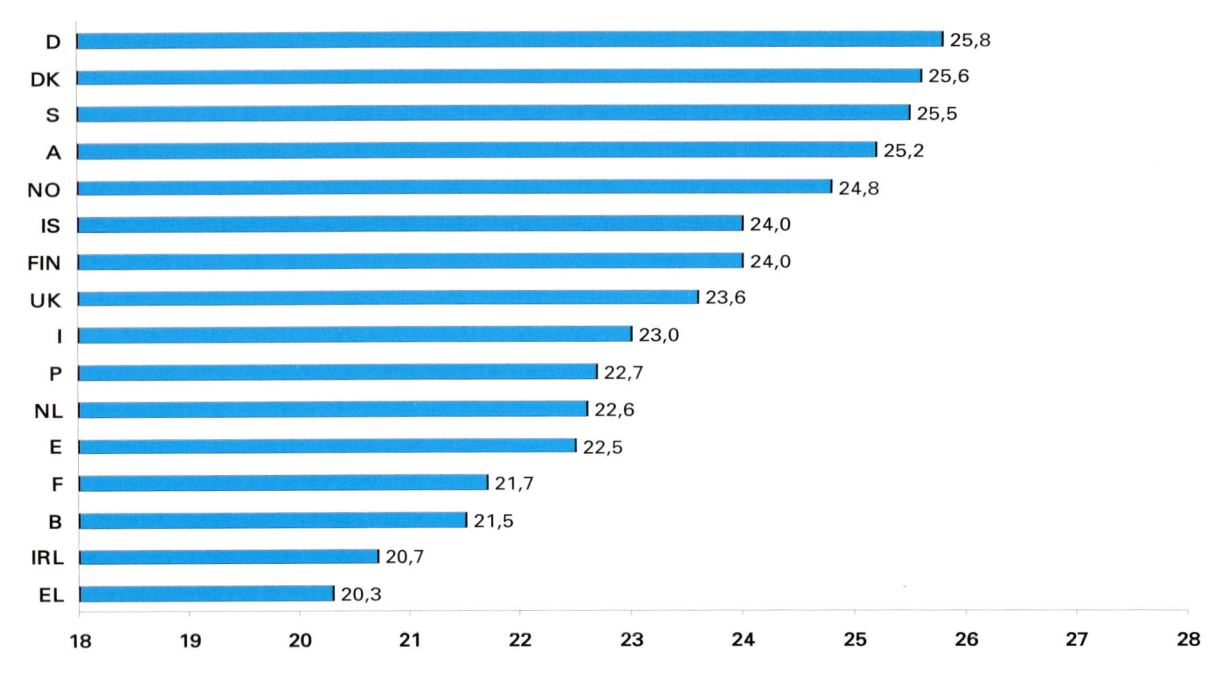

1B8MB

Further reading: Education across Europe: statistics and indicators, 1999. Eurostat. Key data on education in Europe, 1999/2000. European Commission.

B: 1996/97.

Women among students in tertiary education. 1997/98. %

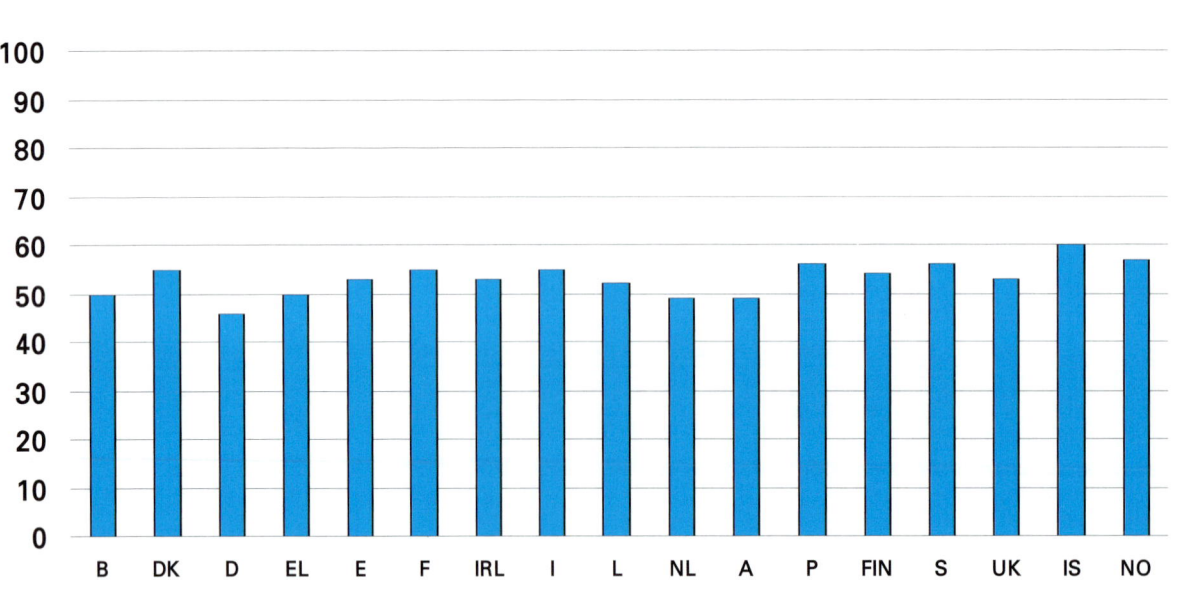

1B9MB

Further reading: Education across Europe: statistics and indicators, 1999. Eurostat. Key data on education in Europe, 1999/2000. European Commission.

B: 1996/97.

6H1AQ

Non-national students in tertiary education. 1997/98

From:	Total	EU-15	B	DK	D	EL	E	F	IRL	I	L	
EU-15	:	:	:	:	:	:	:	:	:	:	:	EU-15
B	35 468	14 540	.	52	531	863	1 464	5 972	63	3 913	1 682	B
DK	11 022	926	20	.	583	24	67	115	41	75	1	DK
D	171 151	30 469	997	651	.	8 491	5 223	6 341	646	6 818	1 302	D
EL	:	:	:	:	:	.	:	:	:	:	:	EL
E	29 000	11 750	927	289	3 221	258	.	3 894	262	2 886	13	E
F	126 389	18 702	1 796	312	5 187	2 716	3 408	.	578	3 608	1 097	F
IRL	6 904	1 466	64	22	524	31	231	479	.	101	14	IRL
I	23 206	13 419	102	57	1 022	11 392	200	612	16	.	17	I
L	559	356	63	0	18	3	10	215	0	47	.	L
NL	:	:	:	.	:	:	:	:	:	:	:	NL
A	28 447	13 551	91	64	5 420	348	286	381	43	6 621	297	A
P	:	:	:	:	:	:	:	:	:	:	:	P
FIN	4 331	402	14	37	174	20	23	62	23	49	:	FIN
S	12 579	2 085	21	658	695	164	116	227	49	153	2	S
UK	209 513	83 525	2 125	1 734	12 915	25 267	6 852	12 574	16 359	5 196	503	UK
IS	194	60	0	30	14	1	5	5	2	3	0	IS
NO	5 750	1 142	20	630	296	14	44	86	15	36	1	NO
US	430 786	25 800	774	951	8 332	2 743	3 912	5 363	888	2 766	69	US
CA	32 890	5 036	137	94	757	123	134	3 534	86	162	9	CA
JP	55 751	551	34	13	195	21	52	141	14	78	3	JP

Further reading: Education across Europe: statistics and indicators, 1999. Eurostat. Key data on education in Europe, 1999/2000. European Commission.   B: 1996/97.

Non-national students in tertiary education. 1997/98

From:	NL	A	P	FIN	S	UK	Non-EU	IS	NO	US	CA	JP	
EU-15	:	:	:	:	:	:	:	:	:	:	.	.	EU-15
B	3 127	43	569	49	52	287	16 801	6	34	:	:	:	B
DK	97	30	20	90	432	369	9 058	626	1 153	235	50	33	DK
D	2 345	6 776	1 675	1 124	1 049	2 820	124 893	264	1 113	4 044	452	1 802	D
EL	:	:	:	:	:	:	:	:	:	:	:	:	EL
E	793	492	760	240	403	2 347	12 215	19	206	526	47	80	E
F	585	356	3 468	289	825	3 411	98 753	49	343	2 283	972	1 198	F
IRL	45	41	12	81	62	1 735	3 462	4	61	1 261	78	38	IRL
I	86	94	30	63	104	204	9 205	3	5	196	47	155	I
L	1	0	110	0	0	3	89	0	0	0	0	0	L
NL	.	:	:	:	:	:	:	:	:	:	:	:	NL
A	100	.	42	183	263	206	14 102	22	87	423	58	294	A
P	.	:	.	:	:	:	:	:	:	:	:	:	P
FIN	34	24	19	.	371	114	3 367	38	41	152	65	51	FIN
S	156	130	37	2 357	.	433	7 381	341	988	444	62	66	S
UK	2 533	1 045	1 985	2 433	2 982	.	115 010	205	3 656	9 717	2 893	5 350	UK
IS	1	2	1	16	18	4	92	.	25	16	4	3	IS
NO	100	24	18	137	569	375	3 385	194	.	304	57	23	NO
US	1 735	856	764	874	3 949	6 744	390 065	492	2 073	.	19 737	42 134	US
CA	155	78	77	100	248	1 065	26 131	34	146	3 305	.	1 308	CA
JP	50	29	18	15	41	259	54 788	7	12	1 055	178	.	JP

Further reading: Education across Europe: statistics and indicators, 1999. Eurostat. Key data on education in Europe, 1999/2000. European Commission.   B: 1996/97.

eurostat

Need more data on this topic? Ask your Data Shop

EUROSTAT YEARBOOK 2001
111

Fields of education chosen by students in tertiary education, by gender. EU-15. 1997/98. %

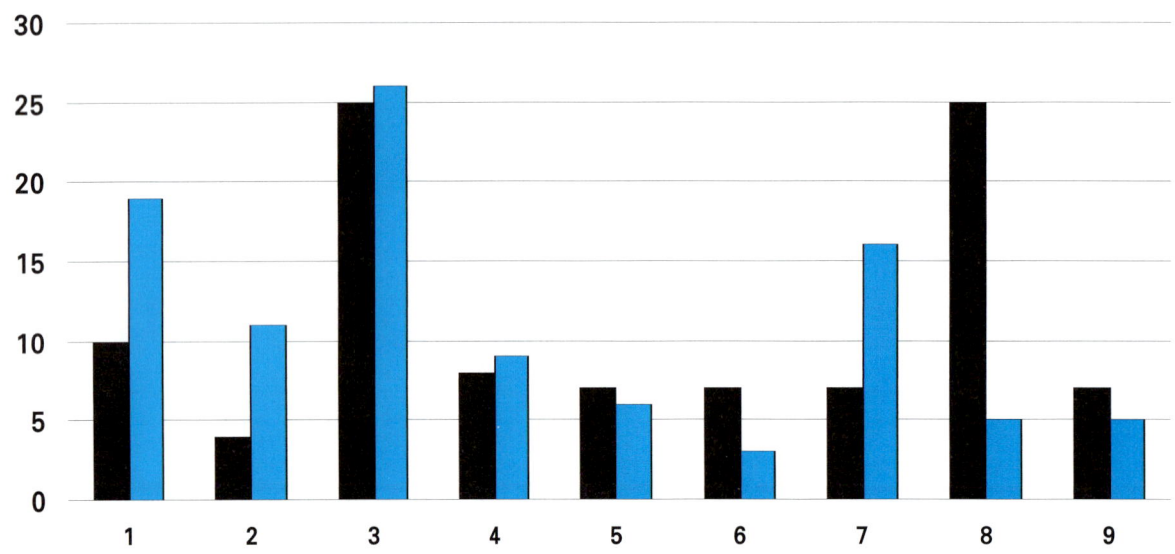

Black: men; colour: women. 1. Humanities and arts; 2. Education science; 3. Social science; 4. Law; 5. Natural science; 6. Mathematics, computer science; 7. Medical science; 8. Engineering, architecture; 9. Others.

Further reading: Education across Europe: statistics and indicators, 1999. Eurostat. Key data on education in Europe, 1999/2000. European Commission.

Women among students in some fields of study in tertiary education. 1997/98. %

	Humanities and arts	Education science	Medical science	Mathematics and computer science	Engineering and architecture	
EU-15	67	74	70	28	20	**EU-15**
B	56	70	67	18	20	**B**
DK	66	69	80	22	35	**DK**
D	61	74	69	22	17	**D**
EL	:	:	:	:	:	**EL**
E	63	76	73	29	25	**E**
F	:	:	:	:	:	**F**
IRL	66	76	69	33	16	**IRL**
I	77	81	57	45	25	**I**
L	:	:	:	:	:	**L**
NL	58	69	74	14	12	**NL**
A	64	75	61	20	17	**A**
P	68	78	74	38	29	**P**
FIN	71	79	84	30	17	**FIN**
S	65	75	78	35	25	**S**
UK	61	71	77	25	15	**UK**

Further reading: Education across Europe: statistics and indicators, 1999. Eurostat. Key data on education in Europe, 1999/2000. European Commission.   B, UK: 1996/97.

8B2BM

Public expenditure on education by level of education as % of GDP. 1997

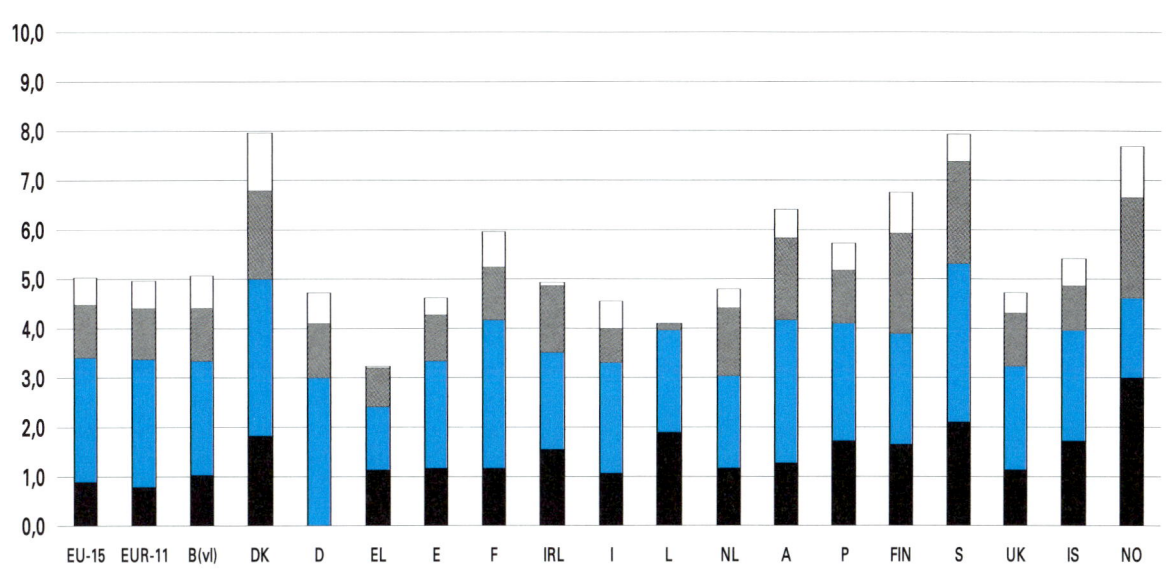

Black: primary (ISCED 1); colour: secondary (ISCED 2, 3, 4); grey: tertiary (ISCED 5,6); white: others.

Further reading: Statistics in focus: population and social conditions, 8/2000. Eurostat.

Information comes from the UOE (Unesco, OECD, Eurostat) questionnaire on education finance and from New Cronos for GDP.
B(VL): Flemish community; D: ISCED 1, 2, 3, 4; NO: ISCED 1, 2.

Expenditure per pupil/student in public institutions by level of education (in PPS). 1997

8B3BM

	Primary (ISCED 1)	Secondary (ISCED 2, 3, 4)	Tertiary (ISCED 5,6)	
EU-15	3 533	4 940	7 075	EU-15
EUR-11	3 575	5 125	7 012	EUR-11
B(VL)	3 516	6 078	7 224	B(VL)
DK	6 349	6 699	6 699	DK
D	3 253	4 196	9 044	D
EL	2 549	2 150	2 881	EL
E	3 277	4 549	4 910	E
F	3 415	6 501	6 452	F
IRL	2 421	3 637	7 694	IRL
I	4 560	5 694	5 368	I
L	3 222	10 009	:	L
NL	3 198	4 678	11 247	NL
A	5 859	7 676	10 435	A
P	3 104	4 310	6 179	P
FIN	4 278	4 614	6 624	FIN
S	5 110	5 025	11 834	S
UK	3 060	4 398	7 795	UK
IS	:	4 527	5 464	IS
NO	5 936	6 767	8 790	NO

Further reading: Statistics in focus: population and social conditions, 8/2000. Eurostat.

Information comes from the UOE (Unesco, OECD, Eurostat) questionnaire on education finance and from New Cronos for GDP.
B (VL): Flemish community; B (VL), NL, UK: Public and government dependent institutions; IS: ISCED 1, 2, 3, 4; NO: ISCED 1, 2.

1

Attainment levels of the population have improved significantly over the last 30 years. By comparing between different age groups, it is possible to monitor the trends over a long time-period.

In 1999, 48 % of persons aged 55–59 in EU-15 had completed at least upper secondary education. This proportion had risen to 71 % among the younger age group 25–29.

Percentage of the population aged 25 to 59 having completed at least upper secondary education, women and men. 1999

ISCED 3–7	25–59	25–29	30–34	35–39	40–44	45–49	50–54	55–59	
EU-15	61,8	71,4	68,6	65,7	62,7	58,5	52,3	48,4	**EU-15**
B	60,2	77,5	71,2	64,9	58,1	54,1	46,7	40,4	**B**
DK	81,1	89,4	85,2	79,8	79,5	79,8	78,0	74,8	**DK**
D	81,6	83,3	84,6	83,5	83,2	81,6	78,3	75,0	**D**
EL	53,9	74,4	68,1	61,8	54,7	47,3	37,6	27,6	**EL**
E	37,7	58,3	50,5	43,9	37,0	28,4	21,1	15,8	**E**
F	63,4	77,7	73,6	67,0	61,5	57,7	53,3	45,2	**F**
IRL	51,3	68,9	62,3	57,4	49,7	38,9	35,9	31,5	**IRL**
I	45,8	59,6	52,7	51,1	49,1	41,6	32,7	25,4	**I**
L	64,0	67,7	68,9	67,3	66,1	60,2	59,4	51,3	**L**
NL	66,2	75,6	73,3	70,3	67,1	61,2	57,4	52,0	**NL**
A	76,8	85,0	83,3	81,3	76,8	71,0	70,5	64,4	**A**
P	22,0	35,1	25,4	21,8	20,6	16,6	13,9	11,4	**P**
FIN	74,5	84,5	86,5	84,5	79,0	72,3	61,1	51,3	**FIN**
S	78,8	87,3	87,5	82,9	78,8	76,9	71,4	65,6	**S**
UK	63,5	69,3	65,5	64,8	65,5	64,4	59,0	51,9	**UK**
IS	63,8	69,4	63,4	63,8	67,4	64,6	59,3	53,8	**IS**
NO	86,3	93,9	92,9	90,9	88,1	82,5	78,6	71,4	**NO**
CH	83,0	91,1	87,1	84,4	83,2	79,8	78,3	74,6	**CH**

6H1AP

Further reading: Education across the European Union: statistics and indicators, 1998. Eurostat.
Living conditions in Europe — Statistical pocketbook, 2000 Edition (Chapter 3), Eurostat.

Source: European Union labour force survey.
IRL: 1997 data. UK: GSCE, O level have been considered as lower secondary education qualification.
IS: ISCED 3c shorter than three years are included.

Percentage of the total population aged 25 to 59 having completed at least upper secondary education, women. 1999

ISCED 3–7	25–59	25–29	30–34	35–39	40–44	45–49	50–54	55–59	
EU-15	58,7	72,0	68,0	63,8	59,1	53,7	46,2	41,2	**EU-15**
B	61,0	82,3	75,1	68,5	58,2	53,0	42,5	37,9	**B**
DK	78,5	88,0	85,5	77,7	79,9	76,6	71,3	67,7	**DK**
D	77,6	82,2	82,9	81,0	79,9	76,5	71,5	66,7	**D**
EL	52,3	77,9	68,6	62,0	53,0	43,2	33,1	22,3	**EL**
E	36,5	62,8	52,5	44,3	34,0	24,8	16,2	11,3	**E**
F	60,7	78,8	73,0	65,6	58,1	53,1	48,4	39,0	**F**
IRL	55,0	73,1	67,3	61,4	52,1	42,2	39,3	33,9	**IRL**
I	45,4	62,1	55,5	52,5	48,1	38,9	29,0	21,7	**I**
L	59,4	66,3	69,2	63,0	63,3	52,9	51,7	37,7	**L**
NL	62,5	76,6	74,4	69,2	64,4	55,3	48,3	39,6	**NL**
A	69,9	81,5	78,4	75,5	69,3	62,8	62,0	53,6	**A**
P	23,5	38,7	28,3	24,4	20,5	16,2	12,8	11,5	**P**
FIN	76,1	86,2	88,3	87,3	81,4	73,8	61,0	52,3	**FIN**
S	80,6	86,8	89,4	84,2	81,1	80,2	73,7	67,6	**S**
UK	54,7	65,6	59,6	57,5	55,6	53,8	46,5	37,9	**UK**
IS	55,7	71,2	58,5	53,5	61,3	53,0	47,9	34,0	**IS**
NO	85,8	94,6	93,2	92,7	87,3	80,0	76,8	69,4	**NO**
CH	78,6	88,8	83,4	81,9	80,0	75,5	71,5	64,8	**CH**

6H1AH

Further reading: Education across the European Union: statistics and indicators, 1998. Eurostat.
Living conditions in Europe — statistical pocketbook, 2000 Edition (Chapter 3), Eurostat.

Source: European Union labour force survey.
IRL: 1997 data. UK: GSCE, O level have been considered as lower secondary education qualification.
IS: ISCED 3c shorter than three years are included.

In general, higher education qualifications seem to reduce, albeit to different degrees, the chances of unemployment. In 1999, the unemployment rate of persons with a tertiary education qualification in EU-15 stood at 5.2 % compared with 7.7 % for persons who had completed at best upper secondary education and 11.6 % among those who had not gone beyond compulsory schooling.

Unemployment rates for men and women aged 25 to 59 by educational level. %. 1999

| | ISCED 0–2 | | | ISCED 3–4 | | | ISCED 5–6 | | | |
	Men	Women	Men and women	Men	Women	Men and women	Men	Women	Men and women	
EU-15	10,0	13,8	11,6	6,5	9,3	7,7	4,3	6,3	5,2	**EU-15**
B	9,9	16,3	12,2	5,2	8,7	6,7	2,4	3,9	3,1	**B**
DK	7,0	7,4	7,2	3,4	5,1	4,1	2,6	3,6	3,1	**DK**
D	17,1	14,6	15,8	8,2	9,5	8,8	4,5	5,8	5,0	**D**
EL	5,8	14,9	9,1	6,6	17,3	10,9	5,3	10,3	7,5	**EL**
E	10,4	23,4	15,0	7,7	20,8	13,3	6,9	15,5	10,9	**E**
F	14,0	17,0	15,4	7,1	12,3	9,4	5,3	7,1	6,2	**F**
IRL	14,6	16,0	15,0	5,5	7,8	6,6	3,0	4,0	3,5	**IRL**
I	7,6	16,6	10,5	5,8	11,2	8,2	5,0	9,5	7,1	**I**
L	2,9	5,0	3,7	.	.	1,2	.	.	.	**L**
NL	3,6	6,9	5,0	1,4	3,5	2,3	1,5	2,1	1,7	**NL**
A	9,6	6,6	7,9	4,0	4,2	4,1	2,0	1,8	1,9	**A**
P	3,8	4,6	4,2	4,2	6,3	5,2	.	.	2,5	**P**
FIN	12,4	14,9	13,5	9,3	9,8	9,5	3,2	6,0	4,7	**FIN**
S	9,4	10,5	9,9	7,8	6,1	7,0	5,1	2,9	4,0	**S**
UK	9,6	6,0	7,6	4,8	3,6	4,4	2,9	2,4	2,7	**UK**
IS	.	.	.	.	.	.	.	.	.	**IS**
NO	1,9	1,6	1,8	1,8	2,2	2,0	1,6	1,3	1,5	**NO**
CH	3,6	5,9	4,8	2,2	2,4	2,3	1,4	2,9	1,8	**CH**

Further reading: Labour force survey, results 1998, Eurostat. Living conditions in Europe — statistical pocketbook, 2000 Edition (Chapter 4), Eurostat.

Source: European Union labour force survey.
IRL: 1997 data. UK: GCSE, O level have been considered as lower secondary education qualification.
ISCED 0–2: pre-primary, primary and lower secondary education;
ISCED 3–4: upper secondary and post-secondary education, ISCED 5–6: higher education.

Unemployment rates by age and educational level. EU-15. 1999

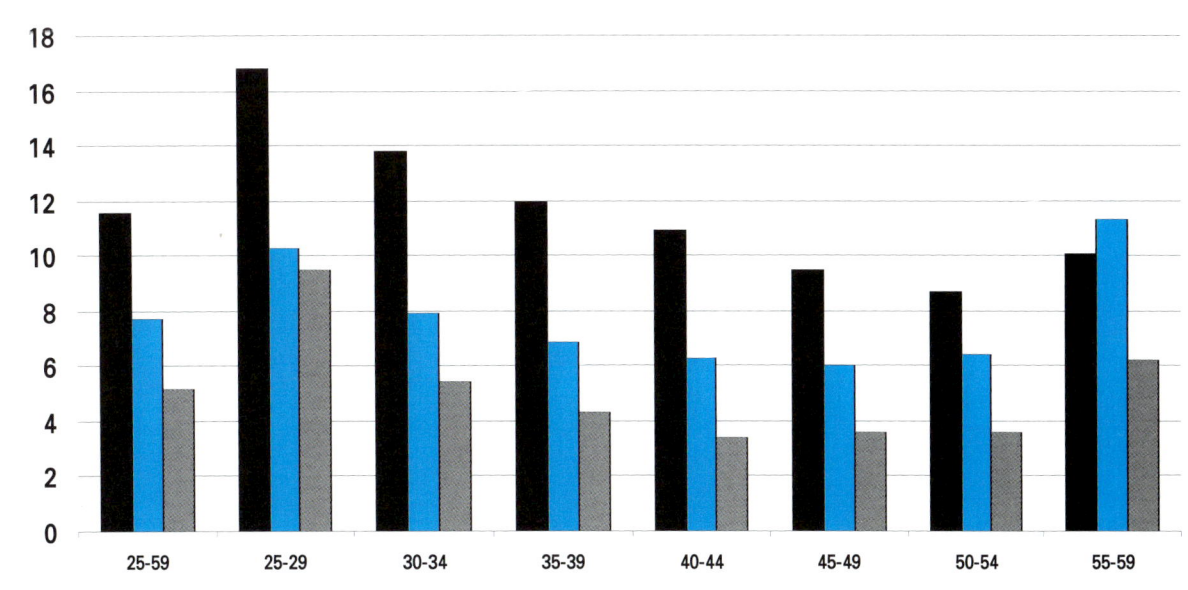

Black: ISCED 0–2; colour: ISCED 3–4; grey: ISCED 5–6.

Further reading: Labour force survey, results 1998, Eurostat. Living conditions in Europe — statistical pocketbook, 2000 Edition (Chapter 4), Eurostat.

Source: European Union labour force survey.
IRL: 1997 data. UK: GCSE, O level have been considered as lower secondary education qualification.
ISCED 0–2: pre-primary, primary and lower secondary education;
ISCED 3–4: upper secondary and post-secondary education, ISCED 5–6: higher education.

eurostat

Need longer time series? Ask your Data Shop

Labour force by age group (men and women). 1 000s

	15–64			15–24			25–49			50–64			
	1989	1994	1999	1989	1994	1999	1989	1994	1999	1989	1994	1999	
EU-15	:	:	169 702	:	:	21 694	:	:	113 501	:	:	34 507	EU-15
EUR-11	:	:	129 522	:	:	15 925	:	:	88 174	:	:	25 423	EUR-11
B	3 895	4 127	4 332	511	461	410	2 806	3 099	3 231	578	568	691	B
DK	2 811	2 741	2 839	577	484	445	1 733	1 710	1 725	500	546	669	DK
D	28 811	38 949	39 244	5 062	4 952	4 454	17 510	24 954	25 931	6 240	9 043	8 860	D
EL	3 855	4 027	4 357	535	518	553	2 361	2 592	2 857	958	917	947	EL
E	14 591	15 356	16 223	3 052	2 760	2 492	8 438	9 712	10 599	3 101	2 884	3 132	E
F	23 882	24 737	25 787	3 423	2 729	2 614	16 291	18 086	18 486	4 169	3 922	4 688	F
IRL	1 269	1 381	1 655	300	279	334	768	880	1 037	201	221	284	IRL
I	22 991	22 266	23 012	4 047	3 200	2 650	14 531	14 995	16 199	4 413	4 072	4 162	I
L	155	169	180	27	22	16	105	123	137	23	25	27	L
NL	6 535	7 164	7 837	1 341	1 264	1 267	4 301	4 908	5 209	892	992	1 362	NL
A	:	:	3 825	:	:	534	:	:	2 654	:	:	636	A
P	4 596	4 562	4 798	959	752	751	2 650	2 849	3 050	987	961	998	P
FIN	:	:	2 627	:	:	402	:	:	1 641	:	:	584	FIN
S	:	:	4 331	:	:	432	:	:	2 651	:	:	1 247	S
UK	28 188	27 956	28 654	6 205	4 751	4 339	16 507	17 690	18 094	5 476	5 515	6 221	UK
IS	:	:	147	:	:	26	:	:	89	:	:	32	IS
NO	:	:	2 294	:	:	331	:	:	1 440	:	:	522	NO
CH	:	:	3 884	:	:	567	:	:	2 439	:	:	877	CH

Further reading: Labour force survey, results 1999. Eurostat.   D: only West Germany in 1989.

114DD

Labour force by age group, men. 1 000s

	15–64			15–24			25–49			50–64			
	1989	1994	1999	1989	1994	1999	1989	1994	1999	1989	1994	1999	
EU-15	:	:	96 404	:	:	11 677	:	:	63 834	:	:	20 894	EU-15
EUR-11	:	:	74 119	:	:	8 591	:	:	49 843	:	:	15 685	EUR-11
B	2 382	2 426	2 468	271	249	225	1 679	1 782	1 793	432	395	450	B
DK	1 513	1 470	1 519	306	263	227	920	891	920	288	316	372	DK
D	17 351	22 294	22 057	2 627	2 610	2 363	10 609	14 125	14 441	4 115	5 560	5 253	D
EL	2 422	2 515	2 592	286	278	284	1 474	1 596	1 670	661	641	637	EL
E	9 553	9 602	9 782	1 675	1 526	1 381	5 568	5 990	6 219	2 310	2 086	2 182	E
F	13 421	13 542	13 986	1 741	1 411	1 420	9 253	9 914	9 988	2 427	2 217	2 577	F
IRL	845	860	980	164	151	182	523	545	603	157	163	194	IRL
I	14 527	13 988	14 159	2 159	1 789	1 469	9 106	9 267	9 815	3 262	2 931	2 875	I
L	101	107	109	14	12	9	69	77	82	18	18	18	L
NL	4 018	4 210	4 455	674	645	640	2 709	2 898	2 931	635	667	883	NL
A	:	:	2 144	:	:	284	:	:	1 462	:	:	398	A
P	2 622	2 495	2 615	523	406	411	1 476	1 508	1 639	623	581	566	P
FIN	:	:	1 364	:	:	207	:	:	868	:	:	289	FIN
S	:	:	2 268	:	:	225	:	:	1 391	:	:	651	S
UK	16 053	15 702	15 907	3 360	2 603	2 349	9 407	9 913	10 009	3 286	3 186	3 548	UK
IS	:	:	78	:	:	13	:	:	47	:	:	17	IS
NO	:	:	1 217	:	:	169	:	:	767	:	:	281	NO
CH	:	:	2 156	:	:	287	:	:	1 368	:	:	502	CH

Further reading: Labour force survey, results 1999. Eurostat.   D: only West Germany in 1989.

5A1EL

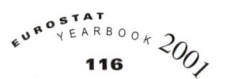

The Community labour force survey (LFS) is the main source of internationally comparable EU labour market statistics. Data presented here corresponds to spring. It covers the entire population living in private households and excludes those in collective households such as boarding houses, halls of residence and hospitals. Definitions used are common to all EU countries and based on international recommendations by the International Labour Office (ILO).

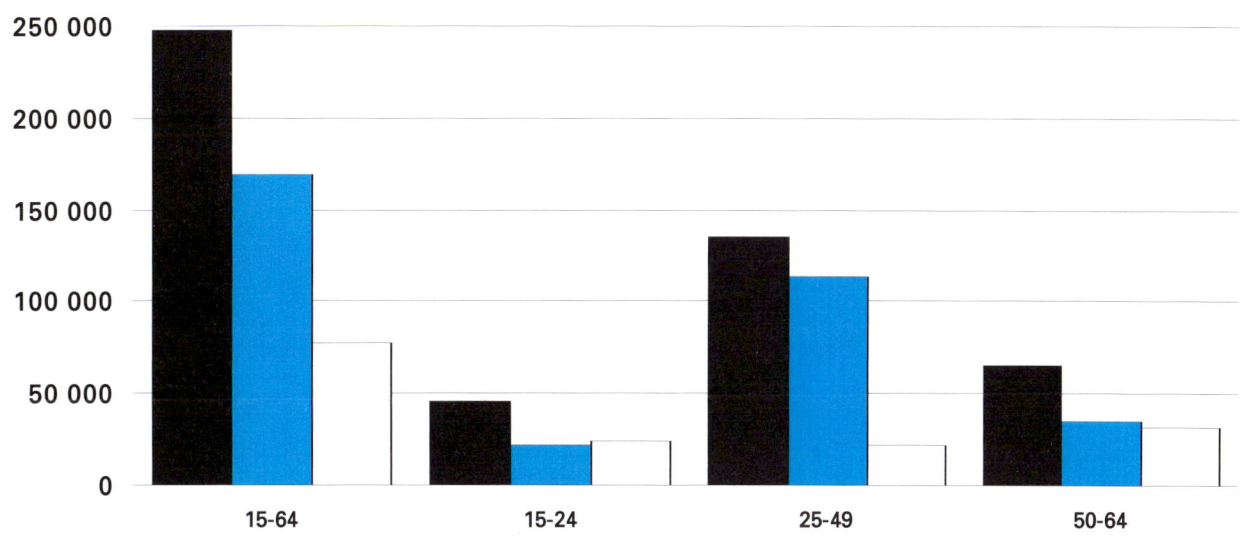

EU-15 population, labour force, persons economically inactive. 1 000s. 1999

5A1EJ

Black: population; colour: labour force; white: economically inactive.

Further reading: Labour force survey, results 1999. Eurostat.

Labour force by age group, women. 1 000s

	15–64			15–24			25–49			50–64		
	1989	1994	1999	1989	1994	1999	1989	1994	1999	1989	1994	1999	
EU-15	:	:	73 298	:	:	10 017	:	:	49 667	:	:	13 613	EU-15
EUR-11	:	:	55 403	:	:	7 333	:	:	38 331	:	:	9 738	EUR-11
B	1 512	1 701	1 864	240	212	185	1 127	1 317	1 438	145	172	241	B
DK	1 297	1 271	1 320	272	222	219	813	819	805	213	230	297	DK
D	11 461	16 654	17 188	2 435	2 342	2 091	6 901	10 829	11 490	2 125	3 484	3 607	D
EL	1 433	1 512	1 765	249	240	269	886	996	1 187	298	276	310	EL
E	5 038	5 754	6 441	1 378	1 234	1 111	2 870	3 722	4 379	791	797	950	E
F	10 461	11 195	11 801	1 683	1 319	1 194	7 038	8 173	8 497	1 741	1 704	2 110	F
IRL	425	521	675	136	128	152	245	335	434	44	58	90	IRL
I	8 464	8 279	8 853	1 888	1 411	1 181	5 425	5 727	6 385	1 151	1 140	1 287	I
L	54	63	71	13	11	8	36	45	54	6	7	9	L
NL	2 517	2 954	3 383	668	619	627	1 592	2 010	2 278	258	325	478	NL
A	:	:	1 681	:	:	250	:	:	1 192	:	:	238	A
P	1 973	2 067	2 183	435	346	340	1 174	1 341	1 411	364	380	432	P
FIN	:	:	1 263	:	:	196	:	:	773	:	:	295	FIN
S	:	:	2 062	:	:	207	:	:	1 260	:	:	596	S
UK	12 135	12 254	12 747	2 845	2 148	1 990	7 100	7 776	8 084	2 190	2 330	2 673	UK
IS	:	:	69	:	:	13	:	:	41	:	:	15	IS
NO	:	:	1 077	:	:	163	:	:	673	:	:	241	NO
CH	:	:	1 727	:	:	281	:	:	1 071	:	:	375	CH

5A1EK

Further reading: Labour force survey, results 1999. Eurostat.   D: only West Germany in 1989.

eurostat

1

Activity rate of men and women by age group

	15–64			15–24			25–49			50–64			
	1989	1994	1999	1989	1994	1999	1989	1994	1999	1989	1994	1999	
EU-15	:	:	68,6	:	:	47,3	:	:	83,6	:	:	52,6	EU-15
EUR-11	:	:	67,1	:	:	44,3	:	:	83,3	:	:	49,6	EUR-11
B	58,7	61,7	64,6	36,0	35,2	32,9	80,2	82,9	85,7	33,6	34,6	40,8	B
DK	82,0	78,8	80,6	75,3	69,1	73,3	91,6	87,9	89,0	65,2	65,7	68,5	DK
D	68,1	70,9	71,2	59,5	54,9	50,8	79,0	84,3	85,9	53,4	55,4	54,7	D
EL	59,8	59,5	62,9	39,9	36,9	39,3	74,5	75,5	80,2	49,5	47,4	48,5	EL
E	58,2	59,6	62,1	47,6	43,0	41,4	71,1	75,7	78,4	45,7	44,3	47,7	E
F	67,3	67,4	68,8	45,2	36,7	36,1	84,9	86,9	87,4	47,7	46,6	51,4	F
IRL	60,3	61,8	66,4	50,8	46,4	50,8	70,0	74,3	79,3	47,9	49,3	53,8	IRL
I	60,0	57,5	59,6	48,6	39,1	38,1	75,4	73,9	76,4	41,1	39,6	39,8	I
L	60,2	62,3	63,1	52,5	46,5	34,0	74,2	77,7	80,0	35,7	37,1	40,4	L
NL	64,8	68,7	73,6	57,5	60,6	67,7	76,7	81,0	85,1	41,5	43,5	51,4	NL
A	:	:	71,6	:	:	58,4	:	:	86,4	:	:	46,9	A
P	68,8	67,6	70,9	59,5	45,2	47,6	82,2	84,8	85,9	53,5	55,6	60,6	P
FIN	:	:	76,4	:	:	63,0	:	:	88,7	:	:	61,5	FIN
S	:	:	76,4	:	:	42,3	:	:	87,6	:	:	77,2	S
UK	76,2	75,0	75,2	72,6	64,6	63,2	84,3	84,2	84,8	61,8	61,7	62,9	UK
IS	:	:	87,2	:	:	71,8	:	:	91,9	:	:	89,9	IS
NO	:	:	80,5	:	:	64,7	:	:	88,6	:	:	73,5	NO
CH	:	:	81,0	:	:	69,0	:	:	88,0	:	:	73,0	CH

5A1DV

Further reading: Labour force survey, results 1999. Eurostat.   D: only West Germany in 1989.

Activity rate of men by age group

	15–64			15–24			25–49			50–64			
	1989	1994	1999	1989	1994	1999	1989	1994	1999	1989	1994	1999	
EU-15	:	:	78,1	:	:	50,9	:	:	93,6	:	:	64,6	EU-15
EUR-11	:	:	77,0	:	:	47,9	:	:	93,8	:	:	62,3	EUR-11
B	71,7	72,0	73,0	38,2	37,3	35,5	94,5	93,8	93,9	51,7	49,3	53,8	B
DK	87,6	83,7	85,0	79,3	72,1	76,7	95,1	91,7	93,3	76,7	75,3	73,7	DK
D	81,5	80,2	79,3	61,3	56,9	53,9	94,1	93,9	94,1	72,0	68,0	64,9	D
EL	77,8	77,0	76,9	45,2	41,8	41,3	96,0	95,6	95,9	70,0	68,7	67,6	EL
E	77,2	75,3	76,2	51,8	47,2	45,8	94,8	93,6	93,4	70,8	66,8	69,2	E
F	77,1	75,0	75,5	48,0	38,7	39,8	96,8	95,9	95,3	57,5	54,4	57,5	F
IRL	79,3	76,7	78,3	54,6	49,3	54,5	94,6	92,6	92,7	74,7	72,5	73,1	IRL
I	77,1	73,1	73,7	52,4	44,1	42,4	95,3	91,7	92,2	63,2	59,0	56,4	I
L	77,9	77,3	75,7	54,5	47,9	36,0	96,1	95,8	95,1	55,5	53,5	54,2	L
NL	78,9	79,8	82,6	57,8	61,6	67,4	94,5	93,7	94,3	60,1	58,6	66,1	NL
A	:	:	80,5	:	:	62,6	:	:	94,6	:	:	59,9	A
P	81,9	77,2	79,1	65,8	48,9	51,8	95,5	94,8	93,9	72,4	71,5	73,7	P
FIN	:	:	78,9	:	:	65,1	:	:	91,7	:	:	62,2	FIN
S	:	:	78,8	:	:	43,1	:	:	90,1	:	:	80,2	S
UK	86,8	83,8	82,9	77,4	69,0	67,1	95,9	93,8	92,7	75,7	72,3	72,6	UK
IS	:	:	90,7	:	:	68,9	:	:	97,4	:	:	95,1	IS
NO	:	:	84,4	:	:	66,5	:	:	92,4	:	:	78,7	NO
CH	:	:	89,7	:	:	68,5	:	:	97,5	:	:	86,2	CH

112AA

Further reading: Labour force survey, results 1999. Eurostat.   D: only West Germany in 1989.

More data on this in Eurostat's database

This is a household survey which provides data on population (persons living in private households), the working population and the non-national population. The main emphasis is on employment, unemployment and inactivity. The information available on these topics includes patterns of work, working time, occupations, economic activities, length of unemployment and methods of job search.

➤ ➤ ➤ **DOMAIN LFS IN DATABASE NEW CRONOS**

Activity rate of women by age group

	15–64			15–24			25–49			50–64		
	1989	1994	1999	1989	1994	1999	1989	1994	1999	1989	1994	1999	
EU-15	:	:	59,2	:	:	43,7	:	:	73,5	:	:	40,9	**EU-15**
EUR-11	:	:	57,2	:	:	40,7	:	:	72,6	:	:	37,4	**EUR-11**
B	45,6	51,2	56,0	33,8	33,0	30,1	65,5	71,6	77,3	16,4	20,6	28,2	**B**
DK	76,4	73,8	76,1	71,3	65,9	70,1	87,9	84,1	84,6	54,2	55,9	63,0	**DK**
D	54,4	61,4	62,9	57,7	52,9	47,6	63,4	74,5	77,4	35,7	42,7	44,6	**D**
EL	43,0	43,2	49,7	35,2	32,6	37,4	54,3	56,5	65,1	30,0	27,6	30,7	**EL**
E	39,7	44,2	48,5	43,3	38,7	37,0	47,9	57,8	63,9	22,4	23,6	27,8	**E**
F	57,9	60,1	62,2	42,7	34,7	32,5	73,2	78,0	79,7	38,5	39,2	45,6	**F**
IRL	40,8	46,7	54,4	47,0	43,3	46,9	45,0	56,2	66,1	21,0	25,9	34,3	**IRL**
I	43,4	42,2	45,6	45,0	34,3	33,8	55,8	56,2	60,4	20,6	21,5	24,0	**I**
L	42,4	47,0	50,2	50,5	45,0	31,9	51,6	58,8	64,6	16,8	20,9	27,0	**L**
NL	50,4	57,4	64,4	57,2	59,6	68,0	58,2	67,7	75,5	23,6	28,4	36,4	**NL**
A	:	:	62,7	:	:	54,2	:	:	78,1	:	:	34,4	**A**
P	56,7	58,8	63,0	53,3	41,6	43,3	69,9	75,9	78,3	37,0	41,5	49,2	**P**
FIN	:	:	73,9	:	:	60,9	:	:	85,5	:	:	60,7	**FIN**
S	:	:	74,0	:	:	41,4	:	:	85,0	:	:	74,1	**S**
UK	65,6	66,1	67,4	67,7	60,0	59,1	72,7	74,5	76,6	48,4	51,4	53,5	**UK**
IS	:	:	83,5	:	:	74,9	:	:	86,3	:	:	84,6	**IS**
NO	:	:	76,5	:	:	63,0	:	:	84,6	:	:	68,3	**NO**
CH	:	:	72,2	:	:	69,4	:	:	78,3	:	:	60,6	**CH**

Further reading: Labour force survey, results 1999. Eurostat.   D: only West Germany in 1989.

1l2AB

eurostat

Need an update for this indicator? Ask your Data Shop

1

Activity rate of men. 1999

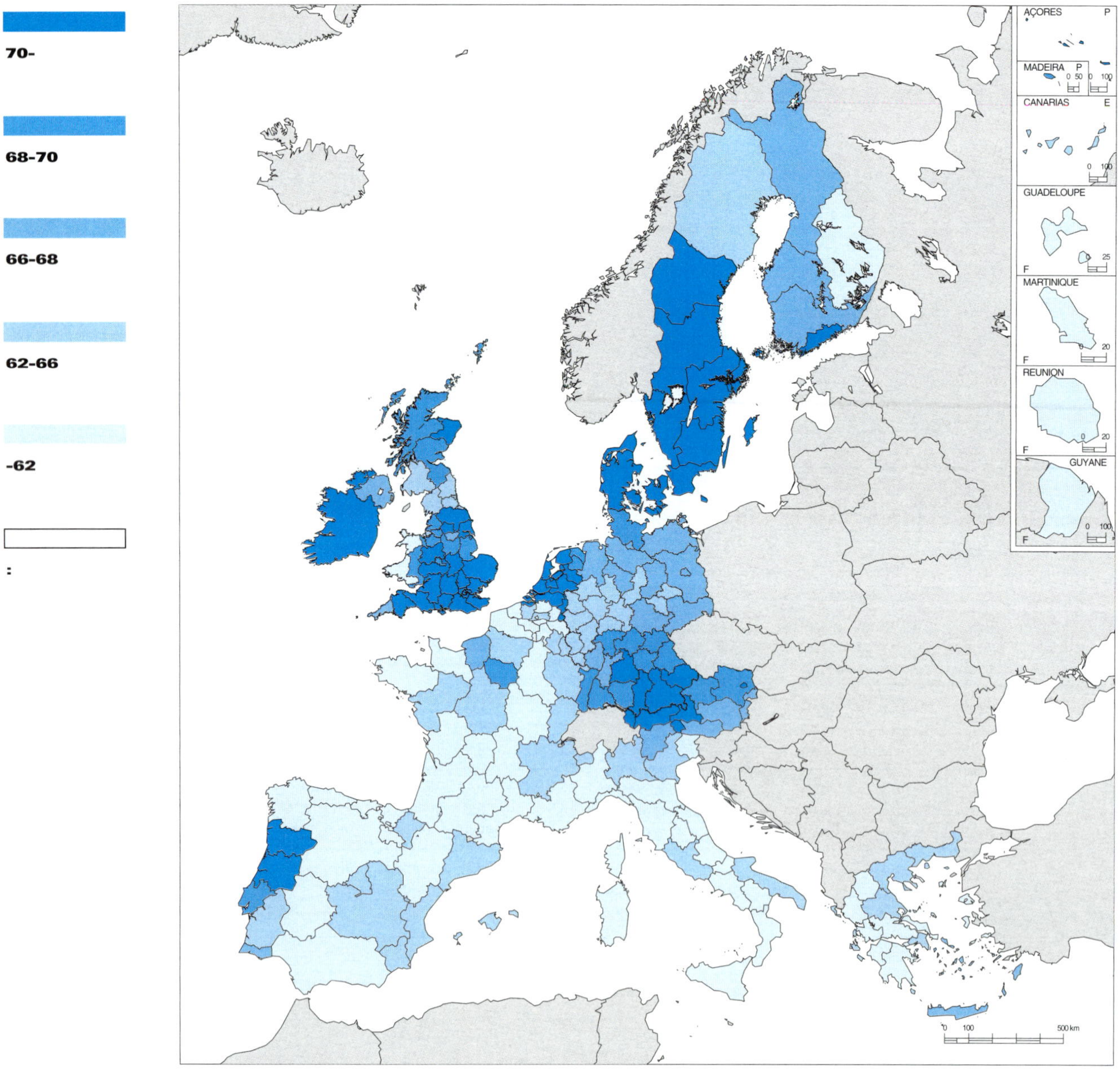

70-

68-70

66-68

62-66

-62

:

7R1B

AÇORES   P

MADEIRA   P
        0 50 0 100

CANARIAS   E
                0 100

GUADELOUPE

MARTINIQUE

REUNION

GUYANE

Further reading: Regions, statistical yearbook, 2000. Eurostat.   NUTS 2. NUTS 1: DED (D Saxony); IRL.

More data on this in Eurostat's database

REGIO is the domain of New Cronos relating to the main aspects of economic life in the European Union at regional level. Created in 1975, REGIO is subdivided into eight statistical domains: demography; economic accounts; unemployment; labour force sample survey; energy statistics; transport; agriculture; and statistics concerning research and development. The regions are classified in line with a specific system called NUTS (nomenclature of territorial units for statistics).

➤ ➤ ➤ **DOMAIN REGIO IN DATABASE NEW CRONOS**

Activity rate of women. 1999

7R1IC

60-

50-60

40-50

30-40

-30

:

AÇORES P
MADEIRA P
CANARIAS E
GUADELOUPE F
MARTINIQUE F
REUNION F
GUYANE F

500 km

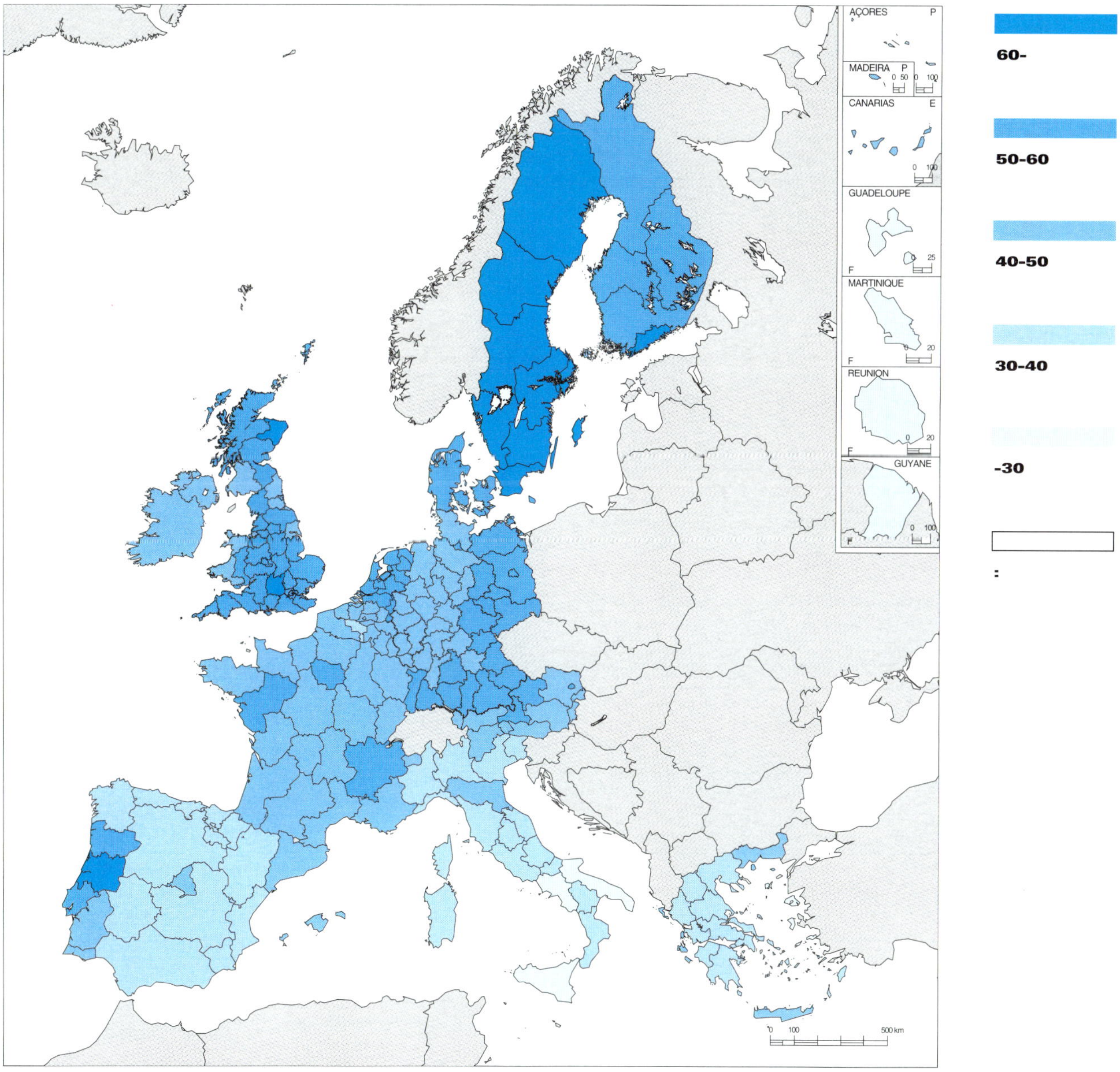

Further reading: Regions, statistical yearbook, 2000. Eurostat.   NUTS 2. NUTS 1: DED (D Saxony); IRL.

eurostat

The broad sectoral shifts in EU employment over the long term are well known: a decreasing share of agricultural and industrial employment and a strong increase in the number of jobs in the service sector. These movements — driven by changes in demand as well as in technology and productivity — have been associated with growth of employment in services, for example healthcare provision, tourism and environmental protection. These areas have become among the most important sources of new jobs.

Persons in employment: men and women. 1 000

	Agriculture			Industry			Services			
	1989	**1994**	**1999**	**1989**	**1994**	**1999**	**1989**	**1994**	**1999**	
EU-15	:	:	6 898	:	:	45 400	:	:	102 690	**EU-15**
EUR-11	:	:	5 594	:	:	35 661	:	:	75 762	**EUR-11**
B	120	108	95	1 127	1 082	1 028	2 340	2 557	2 864	**B**
DK	149	127	90	715	670	726	1 748	1 728	1 882	**DK**
D	1 056	1 171	1 034	11 006	13 261	12 210	15 344	21 408	22 845	**D**
EL	930	788	669	945	894	902	1 795	2 104	2 369	**EL**
E	1 605	1 164	1 020	3 985	3 530	4 215	6 605	7 034	8 538	**E**
F	1 503	1 128	968	6 552	5 830	5 991	13 574	14 750	15 789	**F**
IRL	169	151	136	314	335	451	609	716	996	**IRL**
I	1 912	1 550	1 118	6 659	6 429	6 675	12 238	12 045	12 825	**I**
L	6	5	3	45	44	39	103	114	133	**L**
NL	286	262	231	1 603	1 532	1 610	4 116	4 769	5 368	**NL**
A	:	:	229	:	:	1 094	:	:	2 354	**A**
P	881	522	611	1 580	1 442	1 704	2 099	2 476	2 516	**P**
FIN	:	:	148	:	:	645	:	:	1 532	**FIN**
S	:	:	121	:	:	1 013	:	:	2 917	**S**
UK	593	534	424	8 607	7 087	7 098	17 190	17 890	19 760	**UK**
IS	:	:	13	:	:	35	:	:	102	**IS**
NO	:	:	104	:	:	501	:	:	1 647	**NO**
CH	:	:	178	:	:	918	:	:	2 622	**CH**

Further reading: Labour force survey, results 1999. Eurostat.   D: only West Germany in 1989.

114DA

Persons in employment: men. 1 000

	Agriculture			Industry			Services			
	1989	**1994**	**1999**	**1989**	**1994**	**1999**	**1989**	**1994**	**1999**	
EU-15	:	:	4 601	:	:	35 130	:	:	49 692	**EU-15**
EUR-11	:	:	3 721	:	:	27 529	:	:	37 080	**EUR-11**
B	88	76	62	913	870	835	1 265	1 307	1 408	**B**
DK	115	97	72	527	494	535	784	776	849	**DK**
D	583	552	500	8 346	8 237	7 638	7 774	8 324	8 647	**D**
EL	515	456	385	723	705	715	1 147	1 289	1 366	**EL**
E	1 176	850	755	3 338	2 957	3 538	3 869	3 936	4 486	**E**
F	978	747	662	4 957	4 368	4 523	6 535	6 990	7 388	**F**
IRL	153	135	120	244	258	352	336	363	471	**IRL**
I	1 257	995	779	5 013	4 891	5 096	7 452	7 074	7 244	**I**
L	4	3	2	40	39	34	56	61	71	**L**
NL	216	195	163	1 353	1 280	1 320	2 210	2 436	2 716	**NL**
A	:	:	117	:	:	867	:	:	1 079	**A**
P	449	265	296	1 097	970	1 178	1 113	1 230	1 177	**P**
FIN	:	:	100	:	:	488	:	:	632	**FIN**
S	:	:	92	:	:	791	:	:	1 239	**S**
UK	478	401	331	6 599	5 456	5 561	7 933	8 199	9 157	**UK**
IS	:	:	10	:	:	26	:	:	44	**IS**
NO	:	:	77	:	:	400	:	:	717	**NO**
CH	:	:	118	:	:	712	:	:	1 253	**CH**

Further reading: Labour force survey, results 1999. Eurostat.   D: only West Germany in 1989.

5A1EG

An extensive concept of employment is used in international guidelines on labour statistics. All people with at least an hour's paid work in the reference period are counted as employed.

In 1999, the level of the employment rate in the EU is low (62 %) compared with around 75 % in Japan and the US. If the European Union had the same employment rate as those two countries, around 30 million more people would have a job which is almost twice the number of the unemployed recorded in the same year. Nevertheless, in 1999 all countries except Greece present an increase in the employment rate compared with 1998.

Persons in employment: women, 1 000s

	Agriculture			Industry			Services			
	1989	1994	1999	1989	1994	1999	1989	1994	1999	
EU-15	:	:	2 297	:	:	10 269	:	:	52 999	**EU-15**
EUR-11	:	:	1 873	:	:	8 131	:	:	38 682	**EUR-11**
B	32	32	34	213	212	192	1 075	1 251	1 456	**B**
DK	35	30	18	188	175	192	963	952	1 033	**DK**
D	473	467	370	2 660	3 176	2 910	7 570	11 400	12 437	**D**
EL	415	332	284	222	189	187	648	816	1 003	**EL**
E	428	314	265	647	573	677	2 736	3 097	4 052	**E**
F	525	381	306	1 595	1 462	1 468	7 039	7 760	8 401	**F**
IRL	16	17	16	70	77	99	273	353	525	**IRL**
I	655	555	339	1 646	1 538	1 579	4 786	4 972	5 581	**I**
L	2	2	:	5	5	5	47	54	63	**L**
NL	70	67	68	250	253	290	1 906	2 333	2 652	**NL**
A	:	:	112	:	:	227	:	:	1 275	**A**
P	433	257	314	483	472	526	986	1 246	1 339	**P**
FIN	:	:	49	:	:	157	:	:	900	**FIN**
S	:	:	29	:	:	222	:	:	1 678	**S**
UK	115	132	93	2 008	1 631	1 538	9 258	9 691	10 603	**UK**
IS	:	:	:	:	:	9	:	:	58	**IS**
NO	:	:	26	:	:	101	:	:	929	**NO**
CH	:	:	60	:	:	206	:	:	1 369	**CH**

5A1EF

Further reading: Labour force survey, results 1999. Eurostat.   D: only West Germany in 1989.

Employment rate of men and women (15–64). 1999

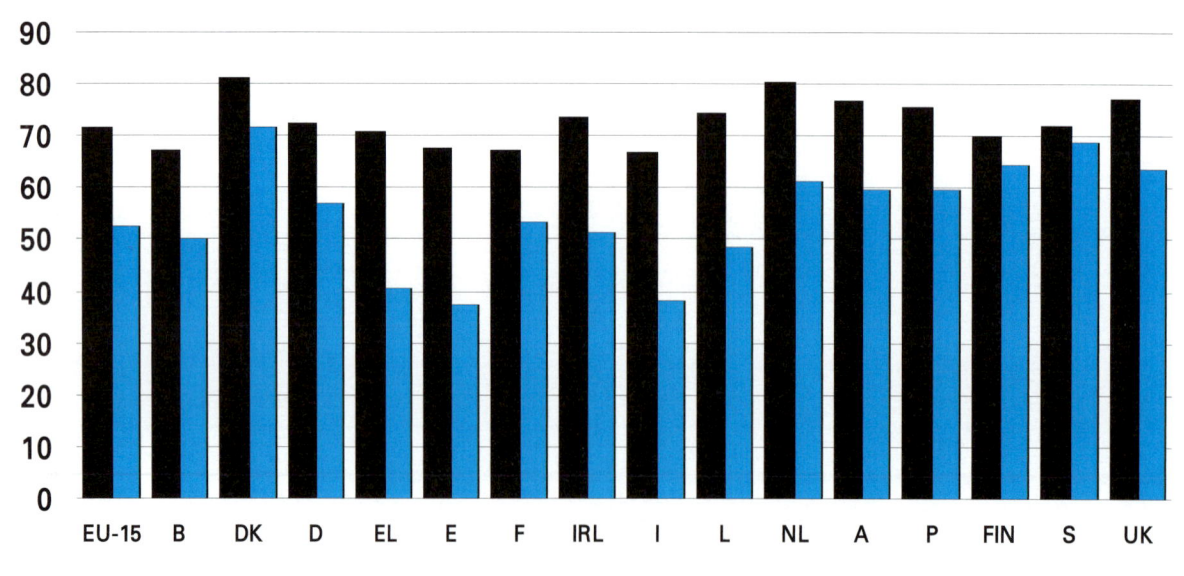

Black: men; colour: women.

Further reading: Labour force survey, results 1999. Eurostat.

113BE

Employment rate of men and women by age group

	15–64			15–24			25–49			50–64			
	1989	1994	1999	1989	1994	1999	1989	1994	1999	1989	1994	1999	
EU-15	:	:	62,1	:	:	38,7	:	:	76,5	:	:	48,6	EU-15
EUR-11	:	:	60,1	:	:	35,6	:	:	75,6	:	:	45,4	EUR-11
B	53,8	55,7	58,9	30,4	27,5	25,5	74,0	75,8	79,2	32,0	32,7	38,5	B
DK	75,3	72,4	76,5	66,7	62,1	66,0	84,6	81,0	85,3	60,7	61,1	65,5	DK
D	64,1	64,7	64,8	56,2	50,0	46,2	74,7	77,3	79,1	49,9	49,8	48,2	D
EL	55,2	54,1	55,4	30,0	26,7	26,8	70,0	70,0	71,8	48,5	45,7	46,0	EL
E	48,0	45,0	52,3	31,3	23,6	29,2	60,8	59,1	67,1	41,6	38,4	43,1	E
F	60,8	58,9	60,4	36,4	26,1	26,5	77,9	77,0	77,8	44,3	42,9	47,0	F
IRL	50,3	52,6	62,5	39,7	35,7	46,5	59,1	64,3	75,1	42,3	44,4	51,3	IRL
I	53,3	50,9	52,5	33,2	26,8	25,5	69,4	67,1	68,6	40,0	38,0	37,9	I
L	59,3	60,2	61,6	50,8	42,8	31,7	73,2	75,3	78,4	35,5	36,6	40,0	L
NL	59,1	63,8	70,9	50,0	53,7	62,7	70,5	75,5	82,5	39,1	41,7	50,0	NL
A	:	:	68,2	:	:	54,9	:	:	82,6	:	:	44,5	A
P	65,1	62,9	67,4	52,5	38,7	43,3	78,7	79,7	82,3	52,4	53,5	58,4	P
FIN	:	:	67,4	:	:	45,0	:	:	80,9	:	:	56,3	FIN
S	:	:	70,6	:	:	35,4	:	:	81,4	:	:	72,6	S
UK	70,6	67,7	70,6	65,1	54,1	55,3	78,9	77,2	80,4	57,4	56,4	60,0	UK
IS	:	:	85,4	:	:	68,7	:	:	90,2	:	:	89,1	IS
NO	:	:	77,9	:	:	56,8	:	:	86,7	:	:	72,9	NO
CH	:	:	78,4	:	:	64,7	:	:	85,6	:	:	71,2	CH

5A1DZ

Further reading: Labour force survey, results 1999. Eurostat.   D: only West Germany in 1989.

Employment rate of men by age group

	15–64			15–24			25–49			50–64			
	1989	1994	1999	1989	1994	1999	1989	1994	1999	1989	1994	1999	
EU-15	:	:	71,6	:	:	42,2	:	:	87,0	:	:	59,9	EU-15
EUR-11	:	:	70,3	:	:	39,3	:	:	86,9	:	:	57,4	EUR-11
B	67,9	66,5	67,5	33,9	29,7	27,5	90,1	87,7	88,0	49,7	46,9	51,1	B
DK	80,9	77,6	81,2	70,8	64,8	69,5	88,2	85,6	89,9	72,2	70,3	71,1	DK
D	77,8	74,1	72,4	58,1	51,5	48,6	90,1	87,4	87,1	68,2	62,3	57,5	D
EL	74,1	72,2	70,9	37,5	33,5	31,8	92,6	90,9	89,6	68,6	66,4	64,9	EL
E	67,0	60,1	67,8	37,6	27,6	35,2	84,7	77,6	84,7	64,3	57,9	63,4	E
F	71,4	66,6	67,5	40,2	28,2	29,9	91,0	86,6	86,7	53,8	50,2	52,7	F
IRL	66,4	65,3	73,6	41,7	36,9	49,8	79,9	80,1	87,5	66,1	65,2	69,5	IRL
I	71,4	66,5	67,1	38,8	31,4	30,3	90,6	85,4	85,3	61,7	56,8	54,1	I
L	77,0	74,9	74,4	52,9	43,8	33,7	95,2	93,4	93,8	55,1	52,6	53,7	L
NL	73,5	74,5	80,3	50,6	53,2	62,9	88,9	88,2	92,3	57,1	56,7	65,1	NL
A	:	:	76,7	:	:	59,2	:	:	90,5	:	:	56,7	A
P	78,9	72,5	75,7	60,4	42,8	47,9	92,9	90,1	90,5	71,0	68,3	70,6	P
FIN	:	:	70,2	:	:	47,2	:	:	84,5	:	:	56,7	FIN
S	:	:	72,1	:	:	35,8	:	:	83,2	:	:	74,6	S
UK	80,2	74,1	77,2	68,7	55,7	57,5	89,9	84,7	87,6	69,7	64,4	68,5	UK
IS	:	:	89,3	:	:	66,5	:	:	96,4	:	:	93,9	IS
NO	:	:	81,7	:	:	57,8	:	:	90,5	:	:	77,9	NO
CH	:	:	87,2	:	:	64,1	:	:	95,4	:	:	84,1	CH

5A1DY

Further reading: Labour force survey, results 1999. Eurostat.   D: only West Germany in 1989.

Employment rate by age group and sex. EU-15. 1999

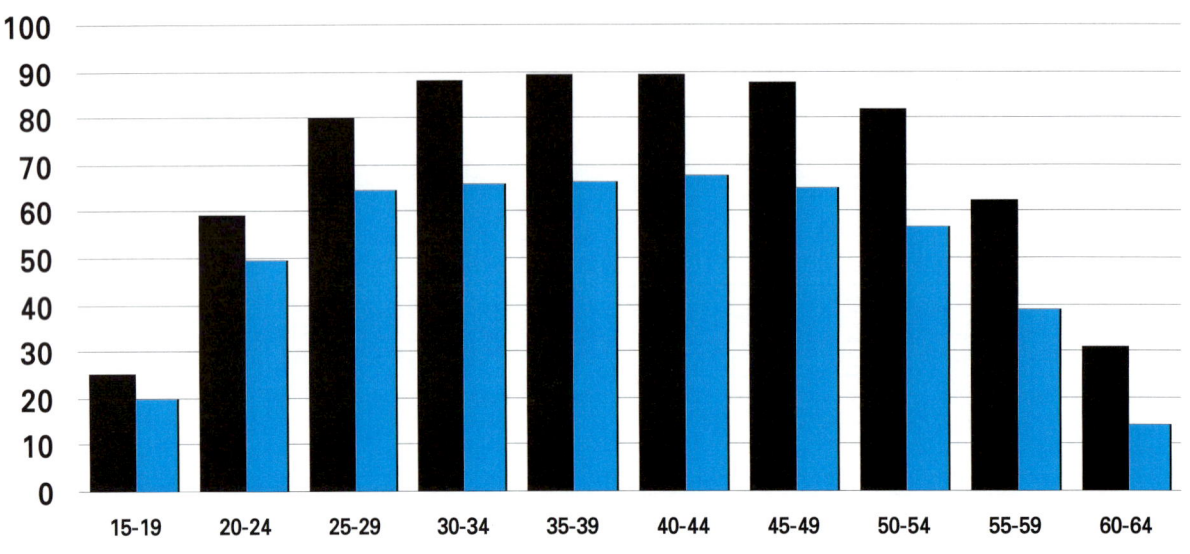

Black: men; colour: women.

Further reading: Labour force survey, results 1999. Eurostat.

5A1EA

Employment rate of women by age group

	15–64			15–24			25–49			50–64			
	1989	1994	1999	1989	1994	1999	1989	1994	1999	1989	1994	1999	
EU-15	:	:	52,6	:	:	35,2	:	:	65,9	:	:	37,6	EU-15
EUR-11	:	:	50,0	:	:	31,9	:	:	64,3	:	:	33,8	EUR-11
B	39,7	44,8	50,2	27,0	25,3	23,4	57,4	63,5	70,1	15,2	19,1	26,2	B
DK	69,5	67,1	71,6	62,5	59,1	62,8	80,8	76,4	80,5	49,8	51,7	59,5	DK
D	50,3	55,0	57,1	54,3	48,4	43,9	58,6	66,9	70,8	32,3	37,4	38,9	D
EL	37,6	37,1	40,7	23,2	20,6	22,1	48,8	50,2	54,8	29,3	26,5	28,4	EL
E	29,5	30,2	37,3	24,9	19,5	23,1	37,3	40,7	50,0	20,5	20,5	24,3	E
F	50,6	51,3	53,5	32,9	24,1	23,3	64,9	67,6	69,1	35,4	36,0	41,5	F
IRL	33,9	39,8	51,4	37,8	34,4	43,0	37,9	48,7	62,9	18,5	23,4	32,8	IRL
I	35,8	35,6	38,1	27,6	22,1	20,8	48,5	48,9	51,7	19,9	20,4	22,5	I
L	41,3	44,9	48,5	48,6	41,8	29,5	50,4	56,3	62,6	16,7	20,7	26,6	L
NL	44,4	52,7	61,3	49,3	54,3	62,5	51,3	62,2	72,4	21,8	26,7	34,8	NL
A	:	:	59,7	:	:	50,7	:	:	74,6	:	:	32,9	A
P	52,4	54,1	59,6	44,9	34,5	38,5	65,5	70,3	74,5	36,3	40,4	47,8	P
FIN	:	:	64,6	:	:	42,8	:	:	77,1	:	:	55,9	FIN
S	:	:	68,9	:	:	35,0	:	:	79,5	:	:	70,6	S
UK	60,9	61,1	63,9	61,4	52,3	52,9	67,8	69,6	73,1	45,6	48,6	51,7	UK
IS	:	:	81,3	:	:	71,0	:	:	83,9	:	:	84,2	IS
NO	:	:	74,0	:	:	55,8	:	:	82,7	:	:	67,8	NO
CH	:	:	69,6	:	:	65,4	:	:	75,6	:	:	59,2	CH

Further reading: Labour force survey, results 1999. Eurostat.   D: only West Germany in 1989.

1I4AB

5A1EW

Share of industry in employment. 1999

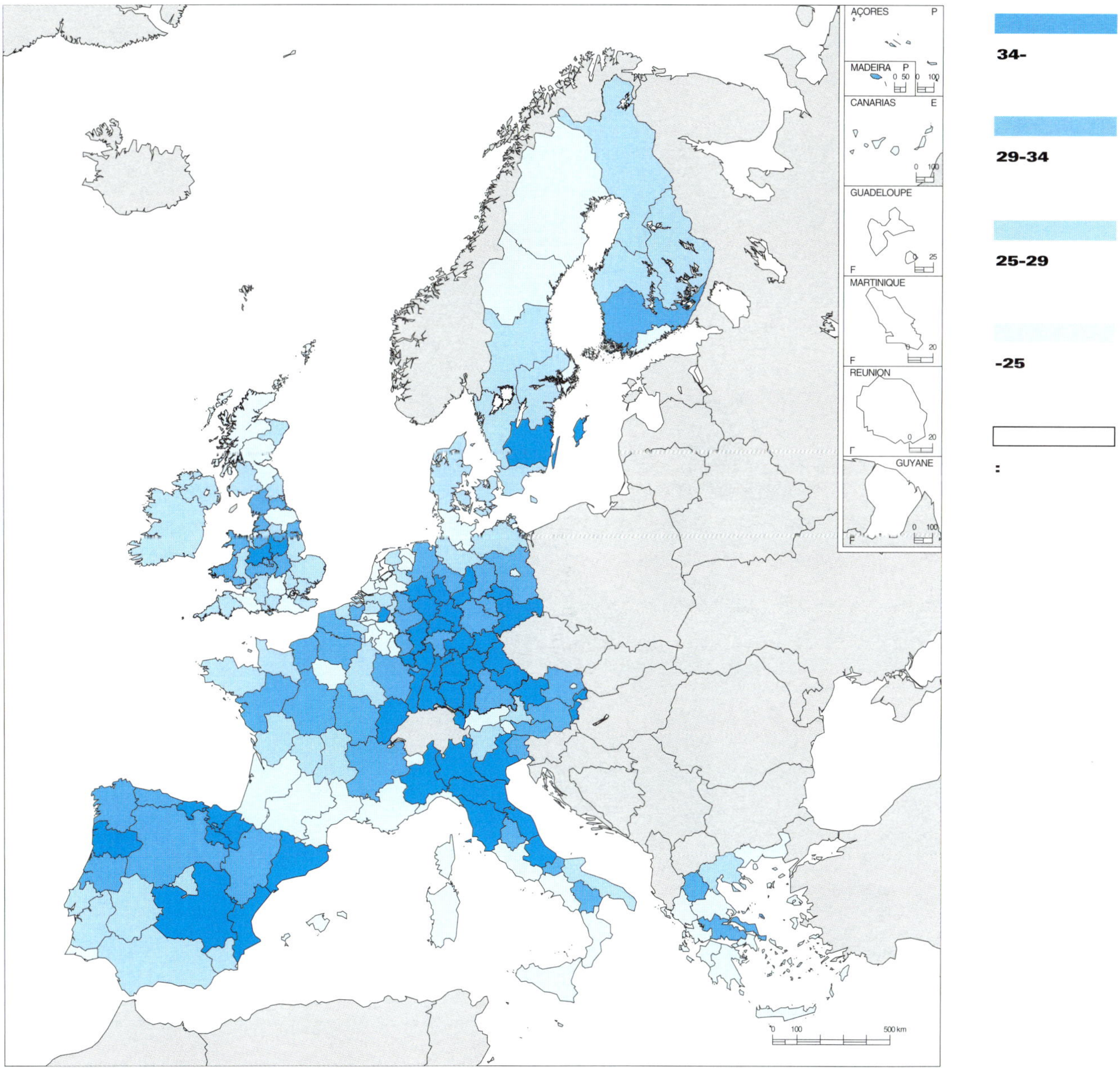

Legend:
- 34-
- 29-34
- 25-29
- -25
- :

Inset maps: AÇORES P, MADEIRA P, CANARIAS E, GUADELOUPE F, MARTINIQUE F, REUNION F, GUYANE F

Further reading: Labour force survey, results 1999. Eurostat.   NUTS 2. NUTS 1: DED (D Saxony), IRL.

eurostat

160 million data in New Cronos, Eurostat's reference database

1

Share of services in employment. 1999

68-

64-68

61-64

-61

:

5A1EV

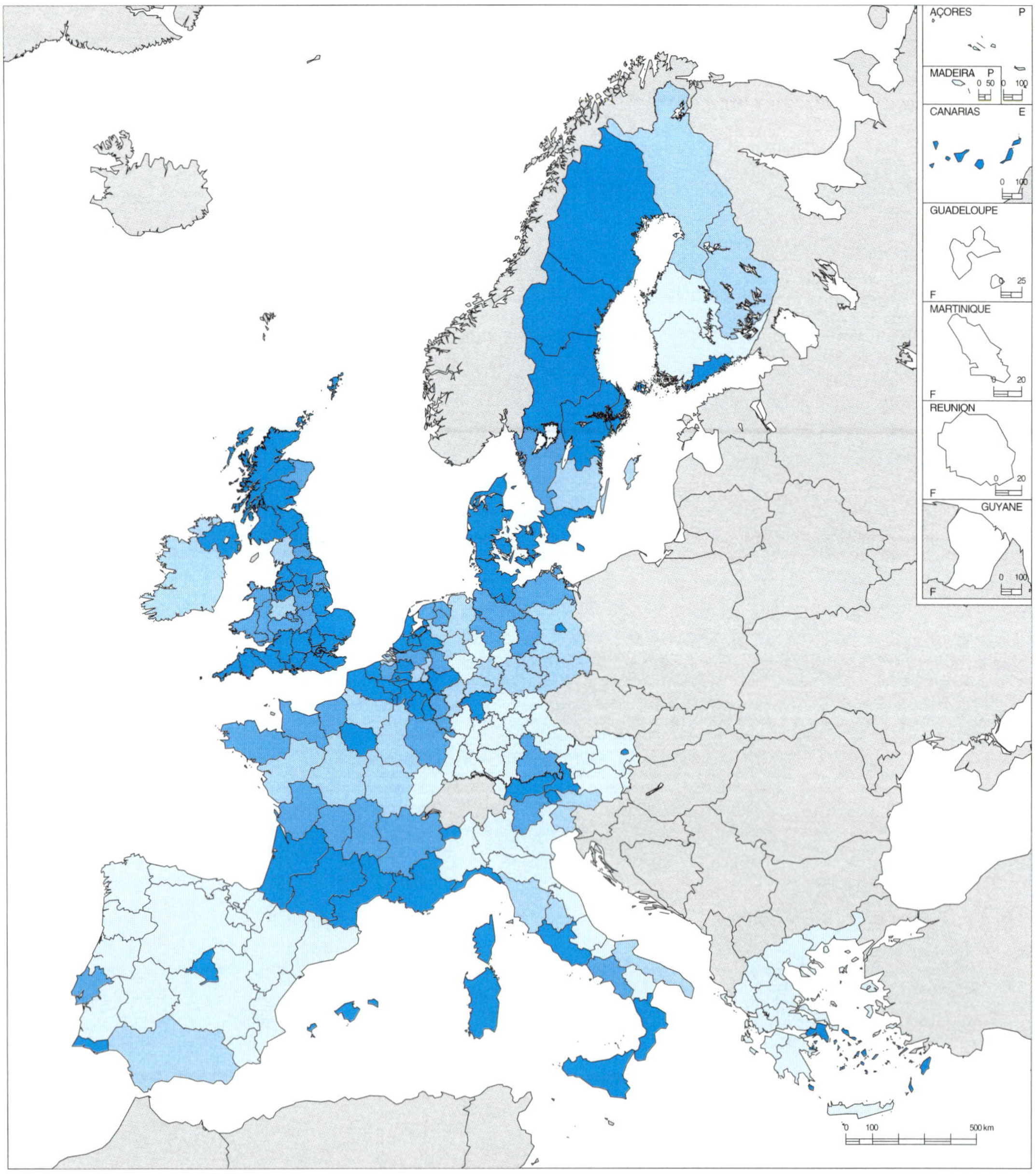

Further reading: Labour force survey, results 1999. Eurostat.   NUTS 2. NUTS 1: DED (D Saxony), IRL.

Men and women employed part-time as % of total employment

	1989	1990	1991	1992	1993	1994	1995	1996	1997	1998	1999	
EU-15	:	:	:	:	:	:	:	16,4	16,9	17,4	17,7	**EU-15**
EUR-11	:	:	:	:	:	:	14,1	14,4	15,1	15,7	16,2	**EUR-11**
B	10,2	10,9	11,8	12,4	12,8	12,8	13,6	14,0	14,7	15,7	19,8	**B**
DK	23,4	23,3	23,1	22,5	23,3	21,2	21,6	21,5	22,3	22,3	20,8	**DK**
D	13,4	15,2	14,1	14,4	15,1	15,8	16,3	16,5	17,5	18,3	19,0	**D**
EL	4,4	4,1	3,8	4,8	4,3	4,8	4,8	5,3	4,6	6,0	6,1	**EL**
E	4,8	4,9	4,7	5,8	6,6	6,9	7,5	8,0	8,2	8,1	8,3	**E**
F	12,1	11,9	12,1	12,7	13,9	14,9	15,6	16,0	16,8	17,3	17,2	**F**
IRL	7,5	8,1	8,4	9,1	10,8	11,3	12,1	11,6	12,3	16,7	16,7	**IRL**
I	5,7	4,9	5,5	5,8	5,4	6,2	6,4	6,6	7,1	7,4	7,9	**I**
L	6,9	6,9	7,4	6,9	7,3	8,0	7,9	7,7	8,2	9,5	10,7	**L**
NL	31,6	31,7	32,5	34,5	35,0	36,4	37,3	38,1	38,0	38,8	39,4	**NL**
A	:	:	:	:	:	:	13,9	14,9	14,9	15,8	16,8	**A**
P	5,9	5,9	7,0	7,3	7,4	8,0	7,5	8,7	9,9	11,1	11,0	**P**
FIN	:	:	:	:	:	:	11,8	11,6	11,4	11,7	12,2	**FIN**
S	:	:	:	:	:	:	:	24,5	24,5	23,9	23,8	**S**
UK	21,7	21,7	22,2	23,0	23,4	23,8	24,1	24,6	24,9	24,9	24,8	**UK**
IS	:	:	:	:	:	:	:	28,1	28,9	29,9	28,5	**IS**
NO	:	:	:	:	:	:	27,7	26,7	27,2	26,7	26,5	**NO**
CH	:	:	:	:	:	:	:	28,1	29,3	29,6	30,3	**CH**

Further reading: Labour force survey, results 1999. Eurostat.   D: only West Germany in 1989 and 1990.

Men employed part-time as % of all employed men

	1989	1990	1991	1992	1993	1994	1995	1996	1997	1998	1999	
EU-15	:	:	:	:	:	:	:	5,5	5,8	6,1	6,2	**EU-15**
EUR-11	:	:	:	:	:	:	4,5	4,8	5,0	5,4	5,5	**EUR-11**
B	1,7	2,0	2,0	2,1	2,3	2,5	2,8	3,0	3,3	3,5	4,7	**B**
DK	9,4	10,4	10,5	10,1	11,0	10,0	10,4	10,8	12,1	10,9	9,6	**DK**
D	2,3	2,6	2,4	2,6	2,9	3,2	3,6	3,8	4,2	4,7	4,9	**D**
EL	2,4	2,2	2,1	2,8	2,6	3,1	2,8	3,3	2,6	3,3	3,6	**EL**
E	1,6	1,6	1,6	2,0	2,4	2,6	2,7	3,1	3,2	3,0	3,0	**E**
F	3,5	3,3	3,4	3,6	4,1	4,6	5,1	5,2	5,5	5,7	5,6	**F**
IRL	3,1	3,4	3,6	3,9	4,8	5,1	5,4	5,0	5,4	7,8	7,4	**IRL**
I	3,1	2,4	2,9	2,8	2,5	2,8	2,9	3,1	3,3	3,5	3,4	**I**
L	1,9	1,9	1,5	:	:	:	:	1,5	:	1,8	1,8	**L**
NL	14,9	14,9	15,6	15,4	15,3	16,1	16,7	17,0	17,0	18,1	17,9	**NL**
A	:	:	:	:	:	:	4,0	4,2	4,0	4,4	4,4	**A**
P	3,1	3,4	4,0	4,1	4,5	4,7	4,2	5,1	5,7	6,2	6,3	**P**
FIN	:	:	:	:	:	:	8,0	7,9	7,6	6,9	7,9	**FIN**
S	:	:	:	:	:	:	:	8,9	9,3	9,2	9,4	**S**
UK	5,0	5,3	5,5	6,3	6,6	7,1	7,7	8,1	8,8	8,8	8,9	**UK**
IS	:	:	:	:	:	:	:	10,4	11,4	11,5	10,9	**IS**
NO	:	:	:	:	:	:	10,0	10,3	10,4	10,4	10,7	**NO**
CH	:	:	:	:	:	:	:	8,7	9,2	9,3	9,9	**CH**

Further reading: Labour force survey, results 1999. Eurostat.   D: only West Germany in 1989 and 1990.

5A1EC

1I4BB

1

The distinction between full-time and part-time work is made on the basis of a spontaneous answer given by the respondent. It is impossible to establish a more exact distinction between part-time and full-time work, due to variations in working hours between Member States and also between branches of industry. In the EU, 18 % of the population in employment works part-time, 80 % of these part-time workers being women. The Netherlands is the country showing the highest percentage of part-time employment but also the lowest percentage of involuntary part-time workers.

Women employed part-time as % of all employed women

	1989	1990	1991	1992	1993	1994	1995	1996	1997	1998	1999	
EU-15	:	:	:	:	:	:	:	31,6	32,4	33,1	33,5	EU-15
EUR-11	:	:	:	:	:	:	28,1	28,4	29,5	30,4	31,2	EUR-11
B	25,0	25,9	27,4	28,1	28,5	28,3	29,8	30,5	31,4	33,3	39,9	B
DK	40,1	38,4	37,8	36,7	37,4	34,4	35,5	34,5	34,5	35,8	33,9	DK
D	30,7	33,8	30,1	30,7	32,0	33,1	33,8	33,6	35,1	36,4	37,2	D
EL	8,0	7,6	7,2	8,4	7,7	8,0	8,4	9,0	8,1	10,5	10,2	EL
E	11,9	12,1	11,2	13,7	14,8	15,2	16,6	17,0	17,4	17,2	17,6	E
F	23,8	23,6	23,5	24,5	26,3	27,8	28,9	29,5	30,9	31,6	31,7	F
IRL	16,5	17,6	17,8	18,6	21,3	21,7	23,1	22,1	23,2	30,1	30,6	IRL
I	10,9	9,6	10,4	11,5	11,0	12,4	12,7	12,7	13,7	14,4	15,7	I
L	16,4	16,5	18,2	16,6	18,3	19,5	20,3	18,4	20,2	22,5	24,6	L
NL	60,1	59,5	59,8	63,8	64,5	66,0	67,3	68,5	67,9	67,9	68,6	NL
A	:	:	:	:	:	:	26,9	28,8	29,0	30,3	32,5	A
P	9,9	9,4	11,0	11,3	11,1	12,1	11,6	13,0	15,0	17,2	16,7	P
FIN	:	:	:	:	:	:	15,8	15,6	15,6	17,0	17,0	FIN
S	:	:	:	:	:	:	:	41,8	41,4	40,7	40,0	S
UK	43,6	43,2	43,7	43,9	43,9	44,4	44,3	44,8	44,9	44,8	44,4	UK
IS	:	:	:	:	:	:	:	48,5	49,2	51,3	48,8	IS
NO	:	:	:	:	:	:	48,0	45,8	46,6	45,3	44,5	NO
CH	:	:	:	:	:	:	:	53,5	55,2	55,4	56,2	CH

Further reading: Labour force survey, results 1999. Eurostat. D: only West Germany in 1989 and 1990.

114BA

Percentage of involuntary part-time employed

	1989	1990	1991	1992	1993	1994	1995	1996	1997	1998	1999	
EU-15	:	:	:	:	:	:	:	19,1	19,7	18,0	16,8	EU-15
EUR-11	:	:	:	:	:	:	20,1	21,0	21,8	19,6	18,3	EUR-11
B	26,8	29,4	27,2	30,0	29,3	28,4	27,7	26,5	26,0	26,2	20,3	B
DK	12,0	11,7	14,1	16,0	17,1	18,2	17,1	14,5	13,6	13,6	15,3	DK
D	5,9	4,5	5,4	5,4	6,8	9,4	9,8	11,9	13,3	13,6	13,0	D
EL	29,4	28,6	29,1	34,9	38,0	40,6	37,2	39,6	41,0	44,8	43,8	EL
E	25,7	25,7	21,9	15,6	14,6	18,6	20,9	22,5	24,3	24,7	25,1	E
F	:	:	:	30,5	34,8	39,0	39,4	39,6	41,3	29,7	27,5	F
IRL	31,2	29,4	30,6	31,2	33,7	32,9	32,5	29,9	25,2	24,4	12,7	IRL
I	36,0	37,2	35,2	33,7	33,2	36,9	36,9	37,6	37,9	36,8	36,4	I
L	:	:	:	:	:	:	:	:	:	:	9,8	L
NL	20,3	18,3	17,6	4,7	5,1	6,0	7,2	6,2	5,5	5,5	4,3	NL
A	:	:	:	:	:	:	7,3	9,3	8,4	15,2	11,3	A
P	24,8	23,2	20,3	19,4	20,4	19,2	23,1	21,5	21,6	23,7	23,7	P
FIN	:	:	:	:	:	:	43,7	40,9	37,6	33,4	37,9	FIN
S	:	:	:	:	:	:	:	29,5	32,0	30,1	29,6	S
UK	7,2	6,3	8,0	11,1	13,3	13,8	13,4	12,6	12,2	11,5	10,3	UK
IS	:	:	:	:	:	:	:	15,0	12,0	:	:	IS
NO	:	:	:	:	:	:	14,2	13,0	12,7	10,3	10,0	NO
CH	:	:	:	:	:	:	:	5,6	7,0	6,8	5,5	CH

Further reading: Labour force survey, results 1999. Eurostat. D: only West Germany in 1989 and 1990.

5A1EB

118AA

Number of hours usually worked per week

	Full-time				Part-time			
	1993	1996	1999		1993	1996	1999	
EU-15	:	42,1	41,9		:	19,7	19,5	**EU-15**
EUR-11	:	:	41,3		:	:	19,8	**EUR-11**
B	40,1	40,5	38,4		20,8	21,3	21,7	**B**
DK	40,1	40,1	40,0		18,8	19,1	19,6	**DK**
D	:	41,6	41,8		:	18,5	17,7	**D**
EL	44,9	44,6	44,7		24,1	24,8	21,3	**EL**
E	42,3	42,2	42,2		18,8	18,2	18,2	**E**
F	41,4	41,2	40,9		22,4	22,7	22,9	**F**
IRL	44,0	43,9	42,1		18,7	18,9	18,6	**IRL**
I	40,3	40,6	40,5		25,1	24,5	23,4	**I**
L	41,6	40,6	40,6		21,0	20,9	21,1	**L**
NL	41,3	41,5	41,0		17,7	18,4	18,7	**NL**
A	:	41,8	41,9		:	22,2	22,0	**A**
P	43,8	43,7	42,4		25,5	26,2	20,4	**P**
FIN	:	40,5	41,0		:	20,3	20,8	**FIN**
S	:	41,4	41,3		:	23,4	23,5	**S**
UK	44,5	44,8	44,4		17,1	17,5	18,0	**UK**
IS	:	:	50,0		:	:	21,8	**IS**
NO	:	39,7	39,5		:	21,9	22,3	**NO**
CH	:	:	43,0		:	:	19,6	**CH**

Further reading: Labour force survey, results 1999. Eurostat.

118BA

Percentage of persons usually working on Saturday, Sunday, at night or doing shiftwork

	Sunday			Saturday			Night			Shiftwork			
	1993	1996	1999	1993	1996	1999	1993	1996	1999	1993	1996	1999	
EU-15	:	11,9	:	:	28,4	:	:	5,4	:	:	10,9	:	**EU-15**
EUR-11	:	11,2	:	:	28,8	:	:	5,1	:	:	9,9	:	**EUR-11**
B	9,3	9,6	4,7	18,3	18,5	9,6	5,2	5,1	2,7	13,1	13,0	8,8	**B**
DK	19,9	19,1	18,9	27,1	26,1	24,3	8,0	7,1	7,9	7,6	7,4	7,2	**DK**
D	10,9	11,4	:	22,2	22,8	:	7,4	6,9	:	9,7	10,1	:	**D**
EL	15,1	14,1	15,0	44,4	43,4	42,3	4,8	3,9	4,4	7,6	8,6	13,3	**EL**
E	14,8	15,6	:	38,6	38,2	:	4,3	4,8	:	4,7	5,6	:	**E**
F	8,6	8,3	8,5	25,5	24,2	24,0	3,6	3,6	3,9	7,2	7,7	9,4	**F**
IRL	18,0	17,7	:	31,5	30,1	:	5,1	6,7	:	9,0	10,3	:	**IRL**
I	8,1	8,0	8,3	41,6	41,2	38,5	4,6	4,9	5,2	13,8	13,9	18,9	**I**
L	9,7	7,8	:	20,2	19,7	:	5,3	3,2	:	14,7	9,0	:	**L**
NL	13,6	14,7	15,2	25,7	27,3	27,1	2,2	2,1	2,3	7,3	7,3	8,5	**NL**
A	:	14,3	15,2	:	25,1	26,5	:	8,4	9,5	:	15,7	16,1	**A**
P	12,0	13,7	12,0	28,9	32,6	29,4	0,8	0,8	8,9	6,5	5,9	7,9	**P**
FIN	:	20,5	17,9	:	29,2	25,2	:	9,4	8,7	:	22,4	23,1	**FIN**
S	:	17,0	18,0	:	19,5	19,8	:	7,1	7,6	:	26,4	25,0	**S**
UK	12,4	13,2	14,5	25,1	25,7	28,3	6,4	6,6	12,6	12,9	14,2	11,2	**UK**
IS	:	18,1	16,2	:	25,6	25,6	:	7,4	5,7	:	16,2	21,4	**IS**
NO	:	14,1	14,2	:	24,4	23,4	:	5,5	5,3	:	23,5	21,1	**NO**
CH	:	10,1	9,6	:	24,3	22,9	:	1,4	1,7	:	4,6	6,8	**CH**

Further reading: Labour force survey, results 1999. Eurostat.

Percentage of employees with contract of limited duration. 1999

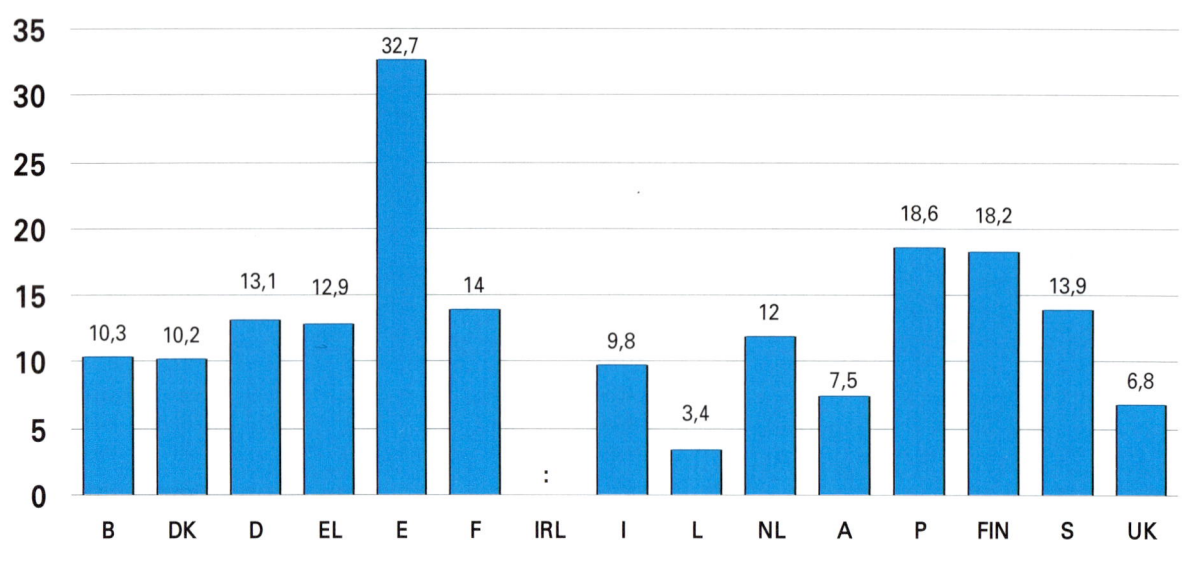

5A1EU

Further reading: Labour force survey, results 1999. Eurostat.

Percentage of employed population with a second job. 1999

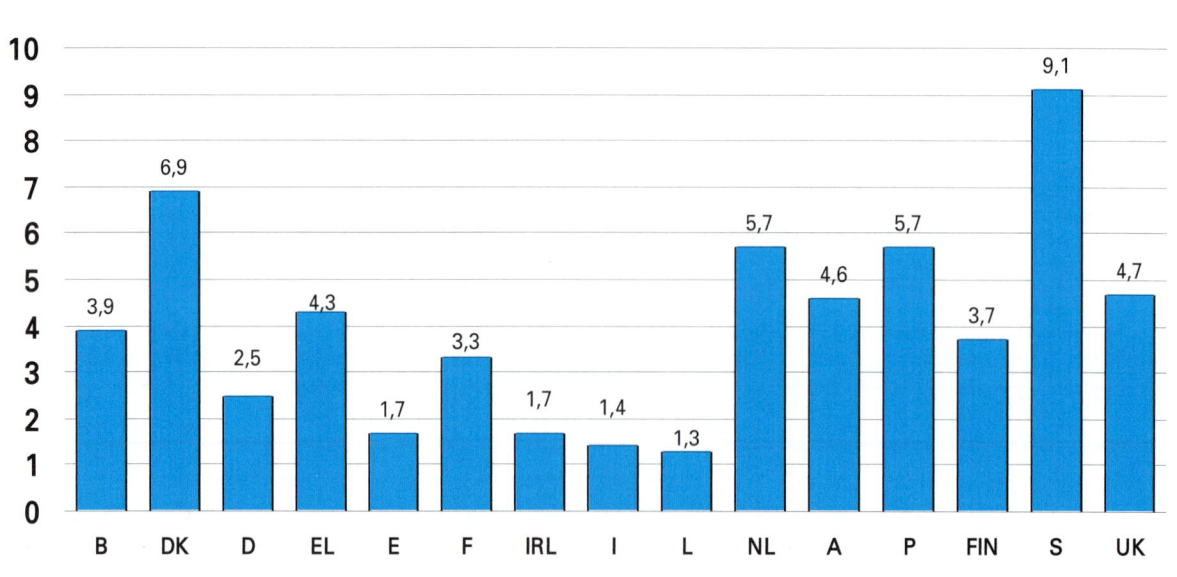

5A1ET

Further reading: Labour force survey, results 1999. Eurostat.

Unemployment: men and women. 1 000s

	1989	1990	1991	1992	1993	1994	1995	1996	1997	1998	1999	
EU-15	:	:	13 568	15 241	17 674	18 409	17 788	18 086	17 851	16 909	15 763	EU-15
EUR-11	:	:	10 370	11 522	13 647	14 655	14 311	14 713	14 808	14 080	12 997	EUR-11
B	293 *	261 *	262 *	294	362	416	416	409	399	408	396	B
DK	208 *	220 *	242 *	265 *	291	229	203	192	159	148	149	DK
D	:	:	2 182	2 563	3 074	3 306	3 186	3 462	3 870	3 692	3 461	D
EL	262 *	255 *	276 *	318	352	370	386	411	421	483	521	EL
E	2 553	2 439	2 469	2 789	3 477	3 734	3 579	3 535	3 351	3 058	2 607	E
F	2 259	2 169	2 312	2 553	2 901	3 058	2 921	3 126	3 126	3 019	2 887	F
IRL	190 *	176 *	197 *	209	216	203	178	174	153	124	96	IRL
I	2 300 *	2 113 *	2 052 *	2 084 *	2 328	2 532	2 641	2 663	2 690	2 746	2 649	I
L	3	3	3	4	5	6	5	5	5	5	4	L
NL	452 *	414 *	397 *	393 *	464	517	508	468	395	312	263	NL
A	:	:	:	:	151	147	149	165	167	171	146	A
P	240	224	201	202	267	331	346	349	331	258	228	P
FIN	80	82	169	292	405	408	382	363	314	285	261	FIN
S	71	80	143	252	401	412	391	426	437	368	319	S
UK	2 081	2 021	2 537	2 866	2 990	2 737	2 493	2 346	2 026	1 830	1 766	UK

5A1EM

Annual averages.

More data on this in Eurostat's database

This domain contains harmonised statistics on unemployment according to the ILO definition.

It also includes unemployment by duration, and numbers of persons registered at employment offices.

➤ ➤ ➤ **DOMAIN UNEMPLOY IN DATABASE NEW CRONOS**

Unemployment: men. 1 000s

	1989	1990	1991	1992	1993	1994	1995	1996	1997	1998	1999	
EU-15	:	:	6 697	7 736	9 264	9 566	9 023	9 232	8 982	8 357	7 746	EU-15
EUR-11	:	:	4 781	5 402	6 745	7 238	6 922	7 226	7 241	6 780	6 218	EUR-11
B	112 *	98 *	103 *	126	165	194	191	186	183	193	195	B
DK	102 *	108 *	115 *	127 *	146	110	89	85	71	62	69	DK
D	:	:	1 027	1 156	1 476	1 613	1 571	1 816	2 051	1 967	1 854	D
EL	102 *	99 *	111 *	127	146	157	161	159	166	190	201	EL
E	1 256	1 165	1 194	1 386	1 836	1 911	1 753	1 723	1 580	1 364	1 106	E
F	953	914	996	1 128	1 359	1 424	1 325	1 450	1 466	1 390	1 331	F
IRL	123 *	112 *	124 *	132	134	126	109	106	93	77	59	IRL
I	1 047 *	954 *	932 *	962 *	1 112	1 243	1 282	1 296	1 294	1 313	1 260	I
L	1	1	1	2	2	3	2	2	2	2	2	L
NL	195 *	176 *	169 *	179 *	235	268	246	214	170	138	103	NL
A	:	:	:	:	67	64	66	78	78	81	70	A
P	93	87	76	95	124	160	170	170	162	113	108	P
FIN	43	49	106	178	235	235	204	186	160	143	130	FIN
S	37	42	83	157	247	248	225	236	238	199	169	S
UK	1 214	1 207	1 608	1 910	1 985	1 800	1 619	1 530	1 263	1 128	1 082	UK

5A1EN

Annual averages.

Unemployment: women. 1 000s

	1989	1990	1991	1992	1993	1994	1995	1996	1997	1998	1999	
EU-15	:	:	6 872	7 504	8 410	8 843	8 765	8 855	8 869	8 552	8 018	EU-15
EUR-11	:	:	5 589	6 120	6 902	7 417	7 388	7 487	7 566	7 300	6 779	EUR-11
B	180 *	163 *	159 *	168	198	222	225	223	215	215	201	B
DK	106 *	112 *	127 *	138 *	145	119	114	108	89	87	80	DK
D	:	:	1 155	1 407	1 598	1 693	1 615	1 646	1 819	1 725	1 607	D
EL	160 *	156 *	166 *	191	205	213	225	252	254	293	320	EL
E	1 297	1 275	1 275	1 403	1 641	1 823	1 826	1 812	1 771	1 693	1 502	E
F	1 307	1 255	1 316	1 425	1 542	1 634	1 595	1 676	1 660	1 629	1 555	F
IRL	67 *	64 *	73 *	78	81	77	68	68	60	47	38	IRL
I	1 253 *	1 159 *	1 120 *	1 122 *	1 216	1 289	1 359	1 367	1 396	1 433	1 389	I
L	2	1	1	2	2	3	3	3	3	3	2	L
NL	256 *	238 *	228 *	214 *	229	249	262	254	225	174	160	NL
A	:	:	:	:	84	83	83	87	89	91	77	A
P	147	137	125	108	143	171	176	179	169	146	120	P
FIN	38	33	62	114	170	174	178	176	154	142	131	FIN
S	35	38	61	95	154	164	166	190	199	168	150	S
UK	868	814	930	957	1 005	936	874	816	763	701	683	UK

Annual averages.

5A1EO

Unemployment: aged less than 25 years. 1 000s

	1989	1990	1991	1992	1993	1994	1995	1996	1997	1998	1999	
EU-15	:	:	4 418	4 689	5 257	5 211	4 896	4 875	4 616	4 282	3 898	EU-15
EUR-11	:	:	3 373	3 512	4 011	4 070	3 844	3 839	3 670	3 380	3 023	EUR-11
B	84 *	76 *	73 *	78	102	114	108	100	96	98	105	B
DK	64 *	63 *	63 *	65 *	69	55	54	53	41	37	44	DK
D	:	:	348	354	416	430	400	435	468	436	412	D
EL	119 *	116 *	122 *	133	142	143	145	157	155	169	175	EL
E	1 061	979	921	992	1 221	1 248	1 150	1 128	1 033	919	749	E
F	698	650	674	709	798	803	728	763	733	663	611	F
IRL	61 *	57 *	66 *	69	71	64	54	51	45	36	28	IRL
I	1 144 *	1 032 *	1 006 *	994 *	1 027	1 029	1 027	999	958	942	865	I
L	1	1	1	1	1	2	2	2	2	1	1	L
NL	129 *	114 *	110 *	112 *	142	145	151	142	116	99	90	NL
A	:	:	:	:	39	35	33	35	36	34	27	A
P	112	100	81	83	97	112	116	116	106	81	67	P
FIN	33	35	56	82	96	91	78	73	72	70	70	FIN
S	28	32	52	82	121	117	99	102	99	78	62	S
UK	637	638	809	894	920	823	752	725	653	617	588	UK

Annual averages.

5A1EP

Unemployment rate of men and women

	1989	1990	1991	1992	1993	1994	1995	1996	1997	1998	1999	
EU-15	:	:	8,2	9,2	10,7	11,1	10,7	10,8	10,6	9,9	9,2	**EU-15**
EUR-11	:	:	8,2	9,2	10,8	11,6	11,3	11,5	11,5	10,9	10,0	**EUR-11**
B	7,5 *	6,7 *	6,6 *	7,2	8,8	10,0	9,9	9,7	9,4	9,5	9,1	**B**
DK	7,3 *	7,7 *	8,4 *	9,2 *	10,2	8,2	7,2	6,8	5,6	5,2	5,2	**DK**
D	:	:	5,6	6,6	7,8	8,4	8,2	8,9	9,9	9,4	8,8	**D**
EL	6,7 *	6,4 *	7,0 *	7,9	8,6	8,9	9,2	9,6	9,8	10,9	11,7	**EL**
E	17,2	16,2	16,4	18,4	22,7	24,1	22,9	22,2	20,8	18,8	15,9	**E**
F	9,4	9,0	9,5	10,4	11,7	12,3	11,7	12,4	12,3	11,8	11,3	**F**
IRL	14,7 *	13,4 *	14,7 *	15,4	15,6	14,3	12,3	11,7	9,9	7,6	5,7	**IRL**
I	9,8 *	9,0 *	8,6 *	8,8 *	10,2	11,1	11,6	11,7	11,7	11,8	11,3	**I**
L	1,8	1,7	1,7	2,1	2,6	3,2	2,9	3,0	2,7	2,7	2,3	**L**
NL	6,9 *	6,2 *	5,8 *	5,6 *	6,5	7,1	6,9	6,3	5,2	4,0	3,3	**NL**
A	:	:	:	:	4,0	3,8	3,9	4,3	4,4	4,5	3,8	**A**
P	5,2	4,8	4,2	4,3	5,7	6,9	7,3	7,3	6,8	5,2	4,5	**P**
FIN	3,1	3,2	6,6	11,7	16,3	16,6	15,4	14,6	12,7	11,4	10,2	**FIN**
S	1,6	1,7	3,1	5,6	9,1	9,4	8,8	9,6	9,9	8,3	7,2	**S**
UK	7,3	7,0	8,8	10,0	10,5	9,6	8,7	8,2	7,0	6,3	6,1	**UK**

5A1DX

Unemployment rate of men

	1989	1990	1991	1992	1993	1994	1995	1996	1997	1998	1999	
EU-15	:	:	6,9	8,0	9,6	9,9	9,4	9,6	9,3	8,6	7,9	**EU-15**
EUR-11	:	:	6,4	7,3	9,1	9,8	9,4	9,8	9,8	9,1	8,3	**EUR-11**
B	4,7 *	4,1 *	4,3 *	5,2	6,8	7,9	7,7	7,6	7,4	7,8	7,8	**B**
DK	6,6 *	7,0 *	7,5 *	8,3 *	9,6	7,4	5,8	5,5	4,6	4,1	4,5	**DK**
D	:	:	4,6	5,2	6,6	7,2	7,1	8,2	9,2	8,9	8,3	**D**
EL	4,1 *	3,9 *	4,4 *	5,0	5,7	6,0	6,2	6,1	6,4	7,1	7,5	**EL**
E	12,9	12,0	12,3	14,3	19,0	19,8	18,2	17,6	16,0	13,8	11,2	**E**
F	7,1	6,8	7,3	8,3	10,0	10,5	9,7	10,5	10,6	10,0	9,6	**F**
IRL	14,3 *	12,9 *	14,2 *	15,1	15,4	14,2	12,2	11,5	9,9	7,8	5,8	**IRL**
I	7,0 *	6,3 *	6,1 *	6,4 *	7,6	8,6	8,9	9,0	9,0	9,1	8,7	**I**
L	1,3	1,2	1,3	1,7	2,2	2,7	2,1	2,2	2,0	1,9	1,7	**L**
NL	4,9 *	4,3 *	4,1 *	4,3 *	5,6	6,3	5,8	4,9	3,9	3,1	2,3	**NL**
A	:	:	:	:	3,1	3,0	3,1	3,7	3,7	3,8	3,3	**A**
P	3,5	3,3	2,8	3,6	4,8	6,1	6,5	6,5	6,1	4,1	3,9	**P**
FIN	3,2	3,6	8,0	13,6	18,1	18,1	15,7	14,3	12,3	10,9	9,8	**FIN**
S	1,5	1,7	3,4	6,6	10,7	10,8	9,7	10,1	10,2	8,6	7,2	**S**
UK	7,4	7,4	9,9	11,8	12,4	11,2	10,1	9,5	7,9	7,0	6,7	**UK**

112AC

Where is your nearest Data Shop? Addresses at the end of the book

135

Youth unemployment has been the focus of extensive and intensive action. The rate of youth unemployment in the EU has decreased since 1996. Approximately half of the unemployed aged less than 25 years are looking for a first job.

Unemployment rate of women

112AD

	1989	1990	1991	1992	1993	1994	1995	1996	1997	1998	1999	
EU-15	:	:	10,0	10,9	12,1	12,7	12,5	12,4	12,3	11,7	10,9	**EU-15**
EUR-11	:	:	10,9	11,9	13,3	14,2	14,0	14,0	14,0	13,3	12,2	**EUR-11**
B	12,0 *	10,7 *	10,0 *	10,2	11,7	12,9	12,9	12,7	12,1	11,8	10,7	**B**
DK	8,1 *	8,4 *	9,4 *	10,1 *	10,8	9,3	8,9	8,3	6,8	6,6	6,0	**DK**
D	:	:	6,9	8,5	9,6	10,1	9,6	9,8	10,7	10,1	9,3	**D**
EL	11,1 *	10,8 *	11,8 *	13,0	13,6	13,7	14,1	15,2	15,2	16,7	17,8	**EL**
E	25,4	24,2	23,8	25,5	29,2	31,4	30,5	29,5	28,3	26,6	23,0	**E**
F	12,4	11,9	12,1	13,0	13,8	14,5	14,0	14,5	14,4	13,9	13,3	**F**
IRL	15,6 *	14,6 *	15,8 *	16,0	16,0	14,6	12,5	11,8	9,9	7,3	5,5	**IRL**
I	15,0 *	13,7 *	13,0 *	13,1 *	14,7	15,6	16,2	16,1	16,3	16,3	15,6	**I**
L	2,7	2,5	2,3	2,8	3,4	4,1	4,4	4,3	4,0	4,0	3,3	**L**
NL	10,2 *	9,1 *	8,4 *	7,6 *	7,9	8,3	8,6	8,1	7,0	5,3	4,7	**NL**
A	:	:	:	:	5,0	4,9	5,0	5,2	5,4	5,4	4,5	**A**
P	7,5	6,8	5,9	5,2	6,8	8,0	8,2	8,3	7,7	6,4	5,2	**P**
FIN	3,0	2,7	5,1	9,6	14,4	14,8	15,1	14,9	13,0	12,0	10,7	**FIN**
S	1,6	1,7	2,8	4,4	7,3	7,8	7,8	9,0	9,5	8,1	7,1	**S**
UK	7,1	6,6	7,5	7,7	8,1	7,5	7,0	6,5	6,0	5,5	5,3	**UK**

Unemployment rate of population aged less than 25 years

5A1DW

	1989	1990	1991	1992	1993	1994	1995	1996	1997	1998	1999	
EU-15	:	:	16,2	18,0	21,3	22,0	21,5	21,9	21,1	19,5	17,9	**EU-15**
EUR-11	:	:	16,9	18,5	22,2	23,6	23,3	23,9	23,2	21,3	19,1	**EUR-11**
B	16,3 *	15,3 *	14,9 *	16,1	21,7	24,2	23,9	23,2	23,1	23,2	24,9	**B**
DK	11,1 *	11,4 *	11,6 *	12,7 *	13,9	11,1	10,6	10,6	8,4	8,0	9,8	**DK**
D	:	:	5,9	6,4	8,0	8,8	8,8	10,0	10,8	9,9	9,2	**D**
EL	22,5 *	21,5 *	22,9 *	25,1	26,8	27,7	28,5	31,0	30,8	30,1	31,6	**EL**
E	34,4	32,3	31,1	34,5	43,2	45,1	42,5	41,9	38,9	35,4	29,5	**E**
F	20,2	19,5	21,3	23,3	27,3	29,2	27,5	29,1	29,2	26,5	24,2	**F**
IRL	20,5 *	19,4 *	22,4 *	24,4	25,3	23,0	19,5	18,2	15,4	11,3	8,3	**IRL**
I	29,2 *	27,2 *	25,9 *	27,0 *	30,5	32,3	33,7	34,0	33,8	33,8	32,7	**I**
L	4,2	3,9	3,2	4,0	5,3	7,3	7,4	8,5	8,1	7,2	6,8	**L**
NL	9,9 *	8,6 *	8,3 *	8,5 *	11,0	11,5	12,1	11,7	9,5	8,0	7,2	**NL**
A	:	:	:	:	6,3	5,7	5,5	6,2	6,7	6,4	5,1	**A**
P	11,9	10,8	9,5	10,4	12,8	15,0	16,6	16,8	15,1	10,6	9,0	**P**
FIN	8,6	9,3	16,3	26,4	33,6	34,0	29,7	28,0	25,2	23,5	21,4	**FIN**
S	3,7	4,4	7,6	13,2	22,0	22,0	19,1	20,5	20,6	16,6	13,6	**S**
UK	10,4	10,8	14,4	16,7	18,1	17,0	15,9	15,5	14,2	13,6	13,0	**UK**

The Community labour force survey applies the internationally accepted definition of unemployment. According to this, the unemployed are those out of work, available to start work within two weeks and actively seeking a job. Only such harmonised unemployment estimates are comparable between EU countries.

113GD

Unemployment rate of women. 1999

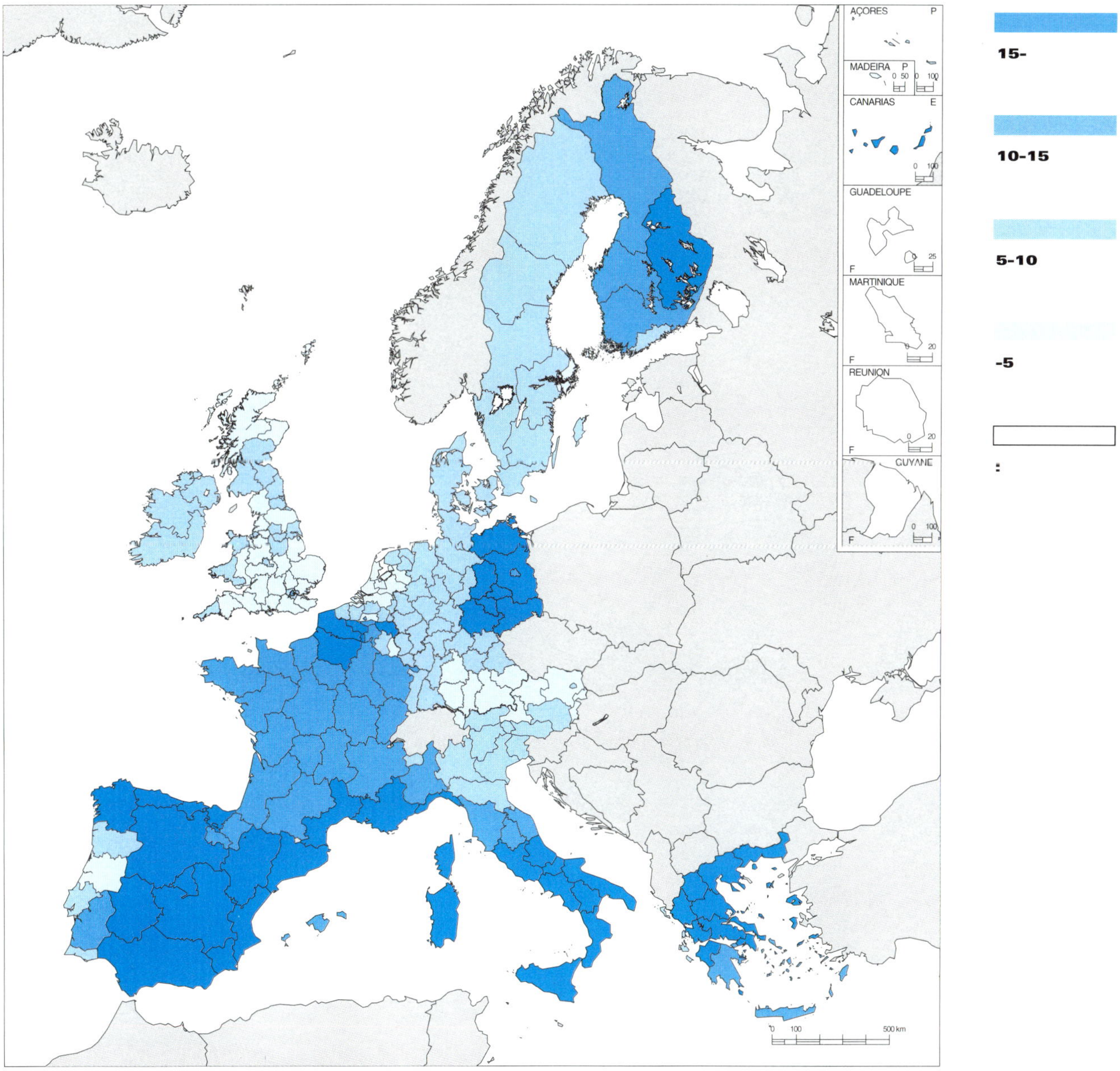

AÇORES — P

MADEIRA — P
0 50 100

CANARIAS — E
0 100

GUADELOUPE
F   25

MARTINIQUE
F   20

REUNION
F   20

GUYANE
F   0 100

15-

10-15

5-10

-5

:

0 100 500 km

Further reading: Regions, statistical yearbook, 2000. Eurostat. Statistics in focus — Regions, 2000. Eurostat.

NUTS 2. NUTS 1: DED (D Saxony).

1

Unemployment rate of men. 1999

15-

10-15

5-10

-5

:

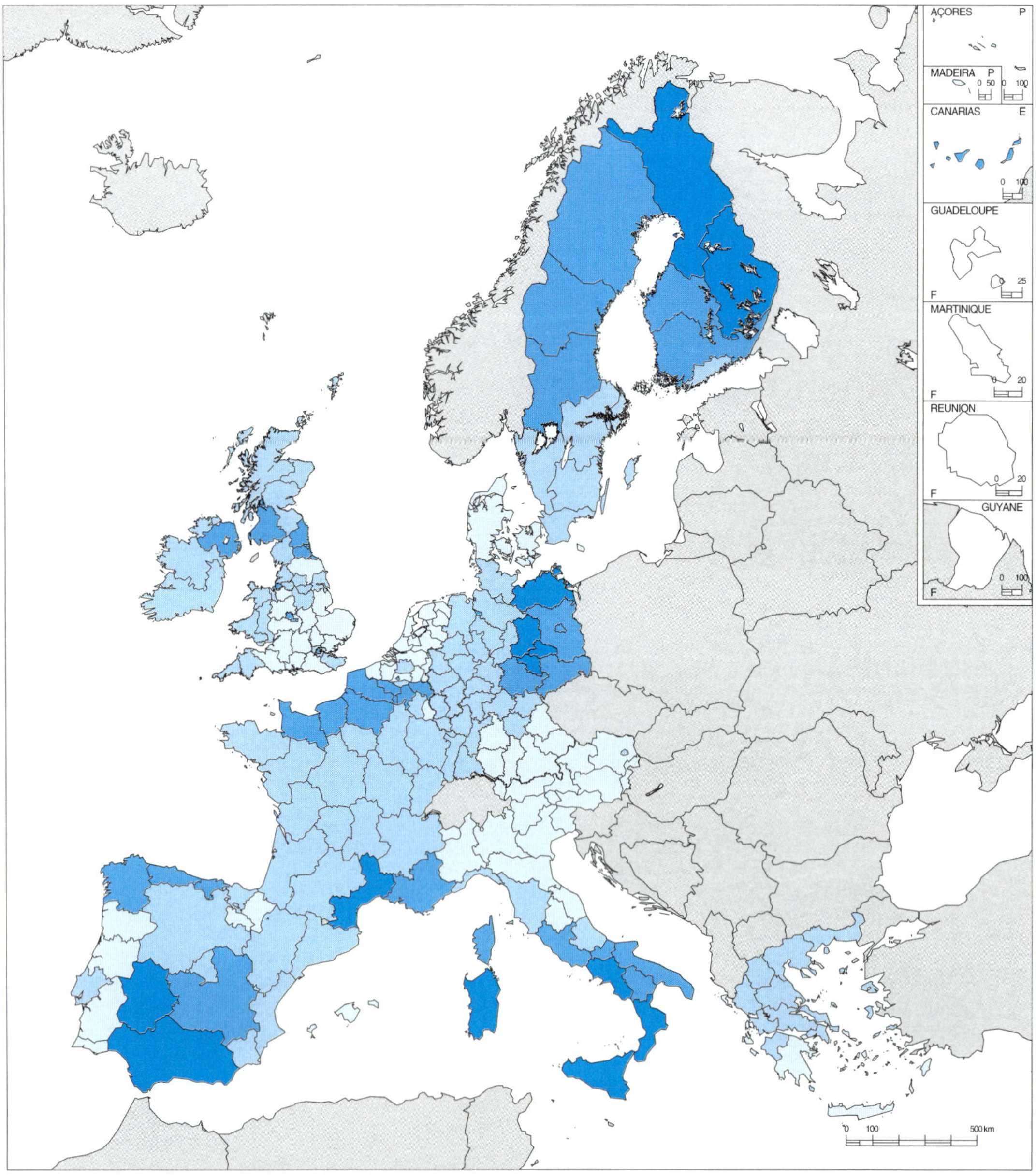

1l3AB

AÇORES   P

MADEIRA   P   0 50 0   100

CANARIAS   E

GUADELOUPE

MARTINIQUE

REUNION

GUYANE

Further reading: Regions, statistical yearbook, 2000. Eurostat. Statistics in focus —   NUTS 2. NUTS 1: DED (D Saxony).
Regions, 2000. Eurostat.

1

112BC

Long-term unemployed (12 months or more), as % of all unemployed

	1989	1990	1991	1992	1993	1994	1995	1996	1997	1998	1999	
EU-15	:	:	:	:	:	:	:	48,2	49,0	47,9	46,0	EU-15
EUR-11	:	:	:	:	:	:	51,0	50,4	50,9	50,1	48,5	EUR-11
B	75,0	66,8	61,6	59,0	53,0	58,3	62,4	61,3	60,5	61,7	60,5	B
DK	20,9	28,8	31,2	27,0	25,2	32,1	28,1	26,5	27,2	26,9	20,5	DK
D	48,4	45,9	30,8	33,5	40,3	44,3	48,7	47,8	50,1	52,6	51,7	D
EL	50,1	49,5	47,1	49,7	50,2	50,5	51,2	56,7	55,7	54,9	55,3	EL
E	56,1	51,1	49,1	44,0	46,2	52,7	54,6	52,9	51,8	49,9	46,3	E
F	43,7	39,7	38,7	34,6	33,3	37,5	40,2	38,2	39,6	41,6	38,7	F
IRL	65,0	64,8	60,3	58,9	59,1	64,3	61,4	59,5	57,0	:	:	IRL
I	68,6	69,0	67,2	57,0	58,2	61,5	63,6	65,6	66,3	59,6	61,4	I
L	34,2 *	34,2 *	28,3 *	17,5 *	30,4 *	29,6	23,2 *	27,6	34,6	31,3	32,3 *	L
NL	45,7	46,6	43,2	44,0	52,4	49,4	46,8	50,0	49,1	47,9	43,5	NL
A	:	:	:	:	:	:	27,5	25,6	28,7	29,2	31,7	A
P	45,1	44,3	38,3	31,1	37,8	43,4	50,9	53,1	55,6	44,7	41,2	P
FIN	:	:	:	:	:	:	37,0	35,9	29,8	28,1	22,7	FIN
S	:	:	:	:	:	:	:	19,1	34,2	37,8	29,5	S
UK	38,1	33,5	28,1	35,7	43,0	45,4	43,6	39,8	38,6	32,7	29,6	UK
IS	:	:	:	:	:	:	:	:	:	:	:	IS
NO	:	:	:	:	:	:	39,3	20,6	17,2	13,9	12,6	NO
CH	:	:	:	:	:	:	:	24,6	25,6	28,0	35,8	CH

Further reading: Labour force survey, results 1999. Eurostat.   D: only West Germany in 1989 and 1990.

112CC

Long-term unemployed women (12 months or more), as % of all unemployed women

	1989	1990	1991	1992	1993	1994	1995	1996	1997	1998	1999	
EU-15	:	:	:	:	:	:	:	50,2	50,7	49,2	47,3	EU-15
EUR-11	:	:	:	:	:	:	53,0	53,3	53,3	51,6	50,0	EUR-11
B	76,0	68,3	64,3	61,0	59,0	62,6	63,2	63,3	61,5	63,5	60,9	B
DK	24,0	30,8	34,2	28,5	27,0	32,4	25,0	25,3	27,9	29,0	20,1	DK
D	45,8	43,7	26,8	30,6	43,5	47,2	51,3	51,7	53,6	55,6	54,0	D
EL	56,5	55,6	53,8	57,2	56,8	57,2	57,8	62,5	62,2	61,5	59,5	EL
E	63,4	58,4	57,3	52,7	55,5	59,4	60,0	59,6	57,3	54,5	50,7	E
F	45,9	41,9	40,9	36,7	35,2	38,1	41,1	39,8	41,0	41,8	39,5	F
IRL	56,2	55,3	52,1	51,3	52,5	57,4	52,3	51,2	46,9	:	:	IRL
I	70,0	70,0	68,4	56,9	60,4	63,3	64,4	67,1	66,2	58,8	60,7	I
L	:	:	:	:	30,3 *	24,6 *	21,0 *	25,3 *	36,1 *	26,3 *	27,2 *	L
NL	40,6	42,1	36,9	41,6	52,0	48,7	42,0	46,1	48,5	45,2	40,4	NL
A	:	:	:	:	:	:	30,6	28,8	28,4	32,5	36,1	A
P	47,9	48,9	41,4	36,5	40,0	44,3	53,4	54,4	57,7	45,6	42,9	P
FIN	:	:	:	:	:	:	31,5	31,0	27,0	23,2	21,3	FIN
S	:	:	:	:	:	:	:	15,9	32,5	33,3	24,3	S
UK	27,1	22,9	21,1	27,8	33,9	33,9	32,3	28,0	27,8	24,0	21,5	UK
IS	:	:	:	:	:	:	:	:	:	:	:	IS
NO	:	:	:	:	:	:	39,2	18,5	15,0	12,1	10,2 *	NO
CH	:	:	:	:	:	:	:	30,8	31,5	27,0	38,0	CH

Further reading: Labour force survey, results 1999. Eurostat.   D: only West Germany in 1989 and 1990.

1

Long-term unemployed as % of all unemployed. 1999

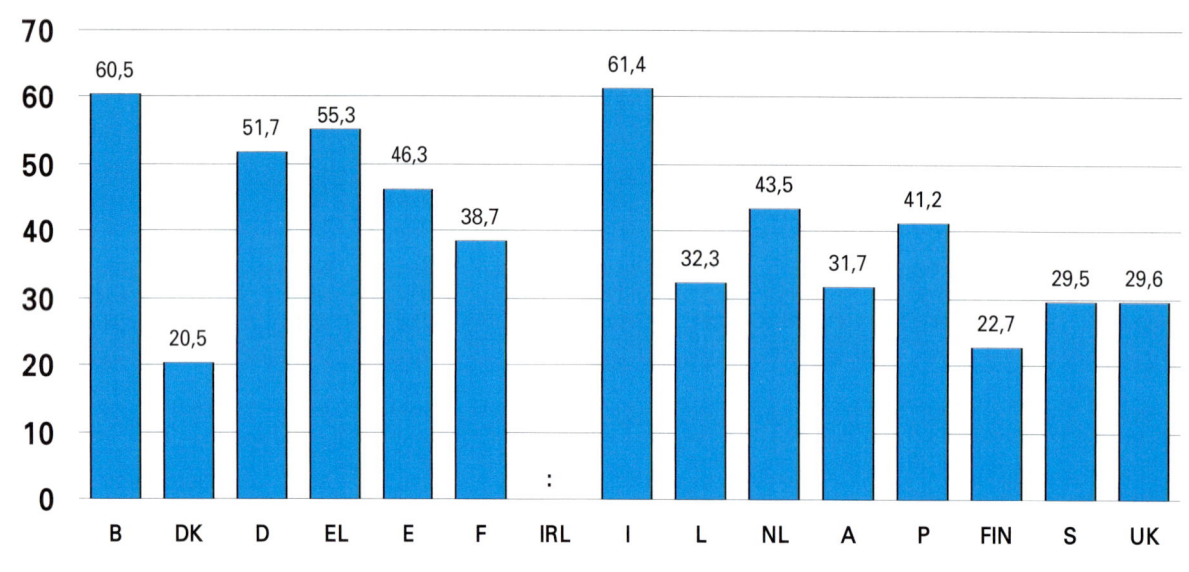

Further reading: Labour force survey, results 1999. Eurostat.

5A1ES

Long-term unemployed men (12 months or more), as % of all unemployed men

	1989	1990	1991	1992	1993	1994	1995	1996	1997	1998	1999	
EU-15	:	:	:	:	:	:	:	46,3	47,5	46,6	44,7	EU-15
EUR-11	:	:	:	:	:	:	48,8	47,5	48,6	48,4	46,9	EUR-11
B	73,3	64,3	57,4	56,3	45,6	53,4	61,4	58,9	59,4	59,5	60,1	B
DK	17,8	26,7	27,9	25,3	23,5	31,9	31,9	28,1	26,3	23,9	20,9	DK
D	51,2	48,2	35,2	37,0	36,9	41,2	45,9	44,5	47,1	49,9	49,9	D
EL	39,9	39,5	37,2	38,2	41,0	41,3	42,3	47,3	45,8	44,7	48,6	EL
E	48,6	43,1	40,5	34,9	37,8	46,3	49,0	45,9	45,8	44,3	40,2	E
F	40,7	36,8	35,7	32,0	31,2	36,8	39,1	36,4	38,0	41,3	37,6	F
IRL	69,4	70,0	64,9	63,1	63,0	68,5	66,8	64,6	63,3	:	:	IRL
I	66,7	67,6	65,6	57,2	55,7	59,6	62,7	64,1	66,5	60,4	62,1	I
L	:	:	:	:	30,6 *	33,8 *	26,0 *	30,1 *	32,7 *	38,0 *	38,6 '	L
NL	51,2	52,1	50,6	47,0	52,7	50,0	51,6	54,3	49,9	51,3	47,7	NL
A	:	:	:	:	:	:	24,6	23,2	28,9	26,6	28,1	A
P	40,9	37,3	33,0	25,0	35,3	42,3	48,4	51,7	53,4	43,6	39,5	P
FIN	:	:	:	:	:	:	42,0	40,5	32,3	32,8	24,2	FIN
S	:	:	:	:	:	:	:	21,5	35,6	41,0	33,3	S
UK	45,8	40,7	32,2	39,6	47,4	51,2	49,6	45,9	44,9	38,0	34,5	UK
IS	:	:	:	:	:	:	:	:	:	:	:	IS
NO	:	:	:	:	:	:	39,3	22,7	19,4	15,8	14,8	NO
CH	:	:	:	:	:	:	:	18,9	21,4	28,9	33,5	CH

5A1ED

Further reading: Labour force survey, results 1999. Eurostat.   D: only West Germany in 1989 and 1990.

Percentage of population not in the labour force: men and women aged 15 years and over

	1989	1990	1991	1992	1993	1994	1995	1996	1997	1998	1999	
EU-15	:	:	:	:	:	:	:	44,7	44,6	44,4	44,1	EU-15
EUR-11	:	:	:	:	:	:	46,3	46,1	46,0	45,8	45,4	EUR-11
B	51,6	51,7	50,7	50,4	50,3	49,7	49,5	49,6	49,5	49,1	48,1	B
DK	32,3	31,9	32,2	:	:	:	35,4	34,8	34,6	34,8	34,2	DK
D	43,9	42,0	40,6	41,3	41,7	41,8	42,3	42,4	42,3	42,3	42,1	D
EL	49,4	50,1	51,7	51,4	51,3	50,9	50,8	50,3	51,1	49,0	49,3	EL
E	51,8	51,4	51,8	51,9	51,9	51,6	51,8	51,2	50,9	50,7	50,6	E
F	43,8	44,1	44,6	44,5	44,5	44,5	44,6	44,2	44,6	44,5	44,2	F
IRL	47,3	47,0	46,8	47,4	46,7	46,1	46,1	45,1	44,6	43,5	42,1	IRL
I	50,1	50,3	49,3	51,6	52,1	52,6	52,6	52,3	52,3	52,2	51,9	I
L	48,9	49,9	48,2	46,4	47,3	47,3	49,2	49,0	48,8	48,6	47,6	L
NL	44,0	42,9	42,3	42,0	41,8	41,1	40,8	40,3	39,1	38,3	37,5	NL
A	:	:	:	:	:	:	40,6	41,2	41,6	41,2	41,0	A
P	41,1	41,1	39,5	40,6	41,2	41,5	41,9	42,3	42,3	39,1	38,7	P
FIN	:	:	:	:	:	:	38,9	40,6	39,9	39,7	37,0	FIN
S	:	:	:	:	:	:	:	38,7	39,2	39,8	39,1	S
UK	37,1	37,0	37,3	37,6	38,1	38,3	38,5	38,4	38,2	38,4	37,9	UK
IS	:	:	:	:	:	:	:	18,8	19,9	18,7	17,3	IS
NO	:	:	:	:	:	:	30,6	28,9	27,3	26,1	26,5	NO
CH	:	:	:	:	:	:	:	32,4	32,5	32,0	32,1	CH

Further reading: Labour force survey, results 1999. Eurostat.   D: only West Germany in 1989 and 1990.

5A1EE

Percentage of men aged 15 years and over not in the labour force

	1989	1990	1991	1992	1993	1994	1995	1996	1997	1998	1999	
EU-15	:	:	:	:	:	:	:	34,0	34,1	34,1	34,0	EU-15
EUR-11	:	:	:	:	:	:	34,9	35,0	35,1	35,0	35,0	EUR-11
B	38,5	39,0	38,6	38,8	39,4	38,8	38,8	39,1	39,3	39,4	38,8	B
DK	24,8	24,9	25,7	:	:	:	27,9	28,1	27,9	28,9	28,2	DK
D	28,9	28,0	28,1	29,4	30,1	30,6	31,4	31,8	32,1	32,4	32,6	D
EL	33,2	34,2	35,3	35,6	35,8	35,5	35,6	35,8	37,1	36,0	36,8	EL
E	34,2	33,9	34,7	35,9	36,6	37,2	38,1	37,7	37,7	37,6	37,7	E
F	33,4	34,1	35,3	35,4	35,9	36,3	36,6	36,3	36,7	37,0	36,7	F
IRL	28,9	29,3	29,4	31,3	31,5	31,1	31,6	31,5	31,5	30,7	29,7	IRL
I	34,1	34,3	33,3	36,0	36,6	37,6	38,1	38,1	38,2	38,0	38,2	I
L	31,3	32,3	31,2	31,3	31,4	32,3	33,6	34,6	35,3	35,4	35,7	L
NL	29,8	29,2	29,0	29,7	29,9	29,6	29,6	29,6	28,5	27,8	27,8	NL
A	:	:	:	:	:	:	29,5	30,2	30,9	30,7	30,6	A
P	27,7	28,3	27,4	29,2	30,6	31,5	32,2	32,9	32,9	29,5	29,5	P
FIN	:	:	:	:	:	:	33,6	35,5	34,1	34,1	31,8	FIN
S	:	:	:	:	:	:	:	34,6	34,7	34,4	34,5	S
UK	25,5	25,6	26,2	27,0	28,1	28,5	28,8	29,1	29,2	29,5	29,2	UK
IS	:	:	:	:	:	:	:	13,5	14,3	13,4	12,9	IS
NO	:	:	:	:	:	:	25,7	24,0	22,3	21,5	22,2	NO
CH	:	:	:	:	:	:	:	21,0	21,2	21,5	21,8	CH

Further reading: Labour force survey, results 1999. Eurostat.   D: only West Germany in 1989 and 1990.

117CB

1

People not in the labour market (i.e. not in the labour force) are usually referred to as 'inactive'. These are people neither employed nor unemployed. Apart from the retired and disabled they include young people still in education and those working without income, even those doing housework or charity work.

Percentage of population not in the labour force by age and sex. 1999. EU-15

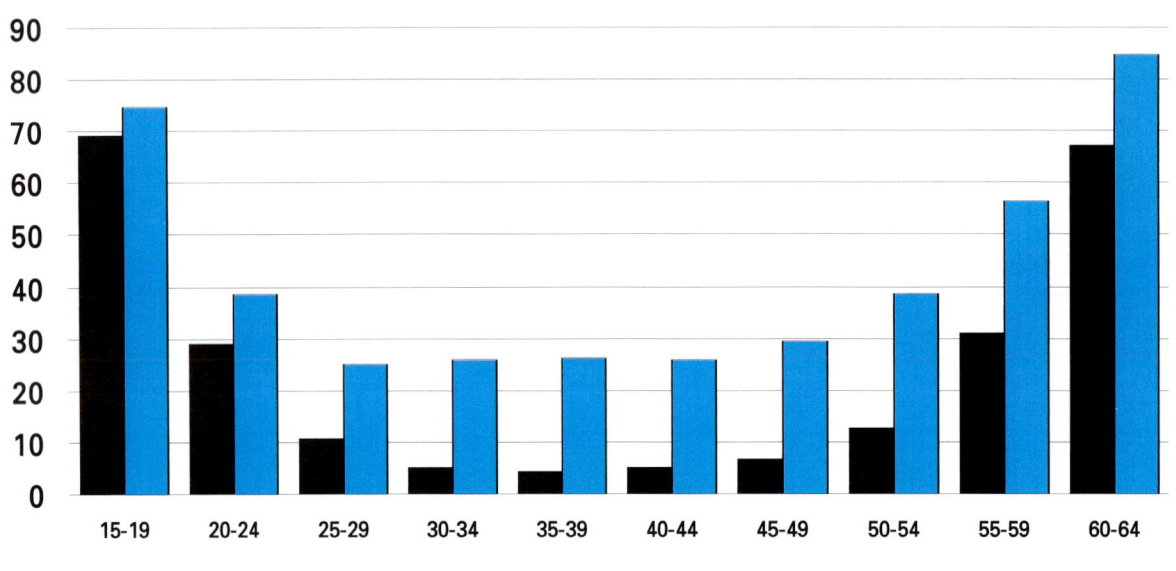

Black: men; colour: women.

5A1ER

Further reading: Labour force survey, results 1999. Eurostat.

Percentage of women aged 15 years and over not in the labour force

	1989	1990	1991	1992	1993	1994	1995	1996	1997	1998	1999	
EU-15	:	:	:	:	:	:	:	54,7	54,4	54,1	53,4	**EU-15**
EUR-11	:	:	:	:	:	:	56,7	56,4	56,1	55,8	55,1	**EUR-11**
B	63,8	63,4	62,0	61,1	60,4	59,8	59,5	59,4	59,0	58,3	56,8	**B**
DK	39,5	38,5	38,3	:	:	:	42,5	41,3	41,0	40,5	40,0	**DK**
D	57,5	54,6	51,9	52,1	52,4	52,2	52,3	52,2	51,8	51,6	51,0	**D**
EL	64,3	64,6	66,9	65,8	65,5	65,0	64,5	63,4	63,8	61,1	60,8	**EL**
E	68,0	67,4	67,4	66,6	66,2	65,0	64,6	63,8	63,3	62,9	62,5	**E**
F	53,2	53,3	53,1	52,7	52,3	52,1	51,8	51,4	51,8	51,4	51,1	**F**
IRL	65,4	64,6	64,0	63,2	61,4	60,5	60,1	58,4	57,3	56,0	54,0	**IRL**
I	64,9	65,0	64,0	65,9	66,4	66,3	66,1	65,4	65,2	65,3	64,6	**I**
L	65,5	66,4	64,1	60,9	62,4	61,6	64,1	63,0	61,9	61,5	59,3	**L**
NL	57,7	56,1	55,2	53,9	53,4	52,3	51,7	50,7	49,4	48,5	47,0	**NL**
A	:	:	:	:	:	:	50,6	51,2	51,3	50,7	50,5	**A**
P	52,8	52,5	50,1	50,5	50,5	50,4	50,5	50,7	50,6	47,8	47,1	**P**
FIN	:	:	:	:	:	:	43,7	45,4	45,1	44,9	41,9	**FIN**
S	:	:	:	:	:	:	:	42,6	43,5	45,0	43,6	**S**
UK	47,9	47,5	47,7	47,6	47,5	47,5	47,6	47,2	46,8	46,8	46,2	**UK**
IS	:	:	:	:	:	:	:	24,3	25,6	24,0	21,7	**IS**
NO	:	:	:	:	:	:	35,5	33,9	32,2	30,8	30,8	**NO**
CH	:	:	:	:	:	:	:	43,0	43,0	41,8	41,8	**CH**

117BC

Further reading: Labour force survey, results 1999. Eurostat.   D: only West Germany in 1989 and 1990.

1

Long-term unemployment rate in % of total unemployment. 1999

8A1AN

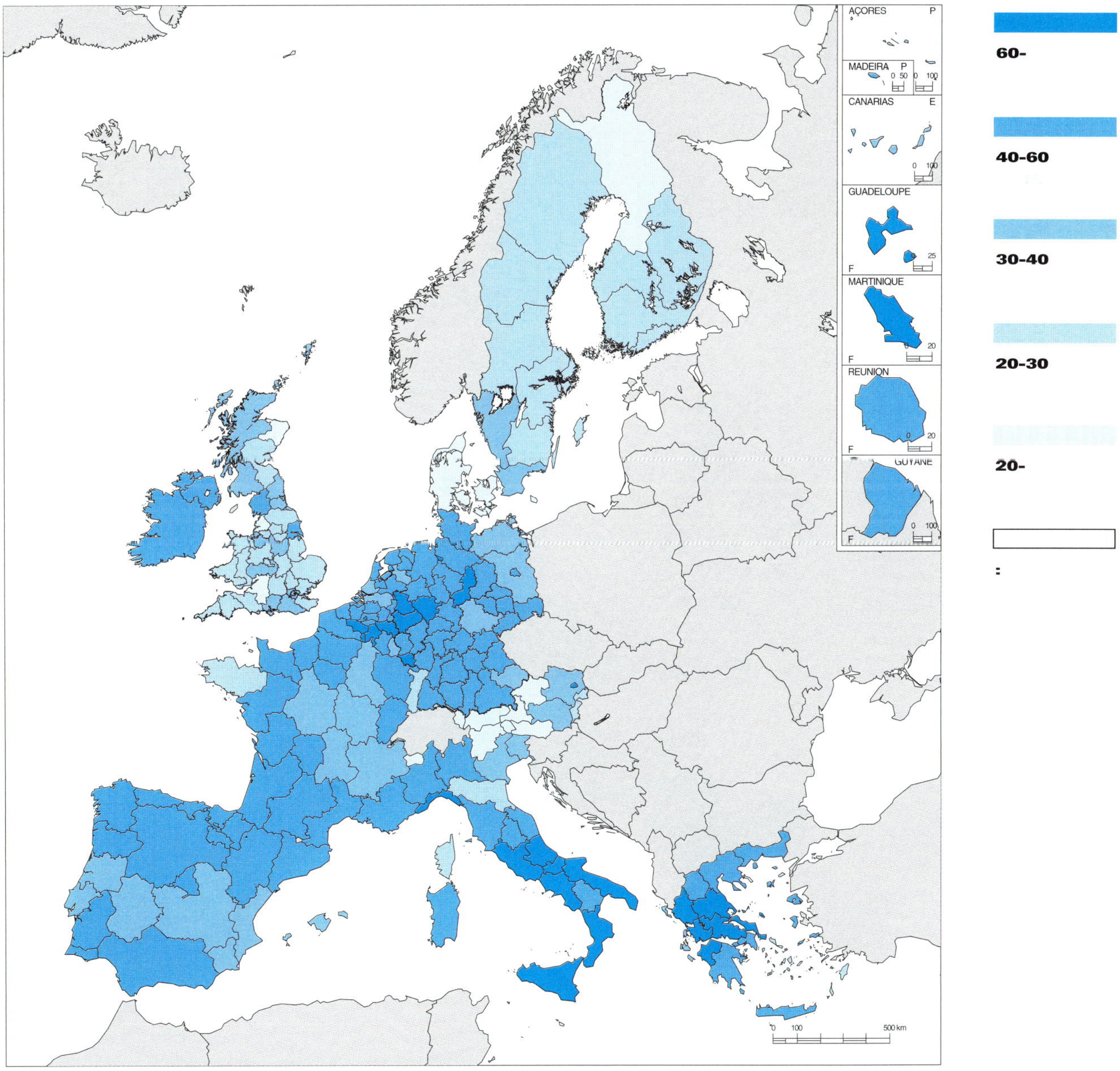

	60-
	40-60
	30-40
	20-30
	20-
	:

AÇORES P

MADEIRA P

CANARIAS E

GUADELOUPE F

MARTINIQUE F

REUNION F

GUYANE F

Further reading: Regions, statistical yearbook, 2000. Eurostat.   NUTS 2. NUTS 1: IRL. IRL: 1997.

Need access to Eurostat's databases? Ask your Data Shop

EUROSTAT YEARBOOK 2001

143

1

Unemployment rate of people aged less than 25. 1999

15-

10-15

5-10

5-

:

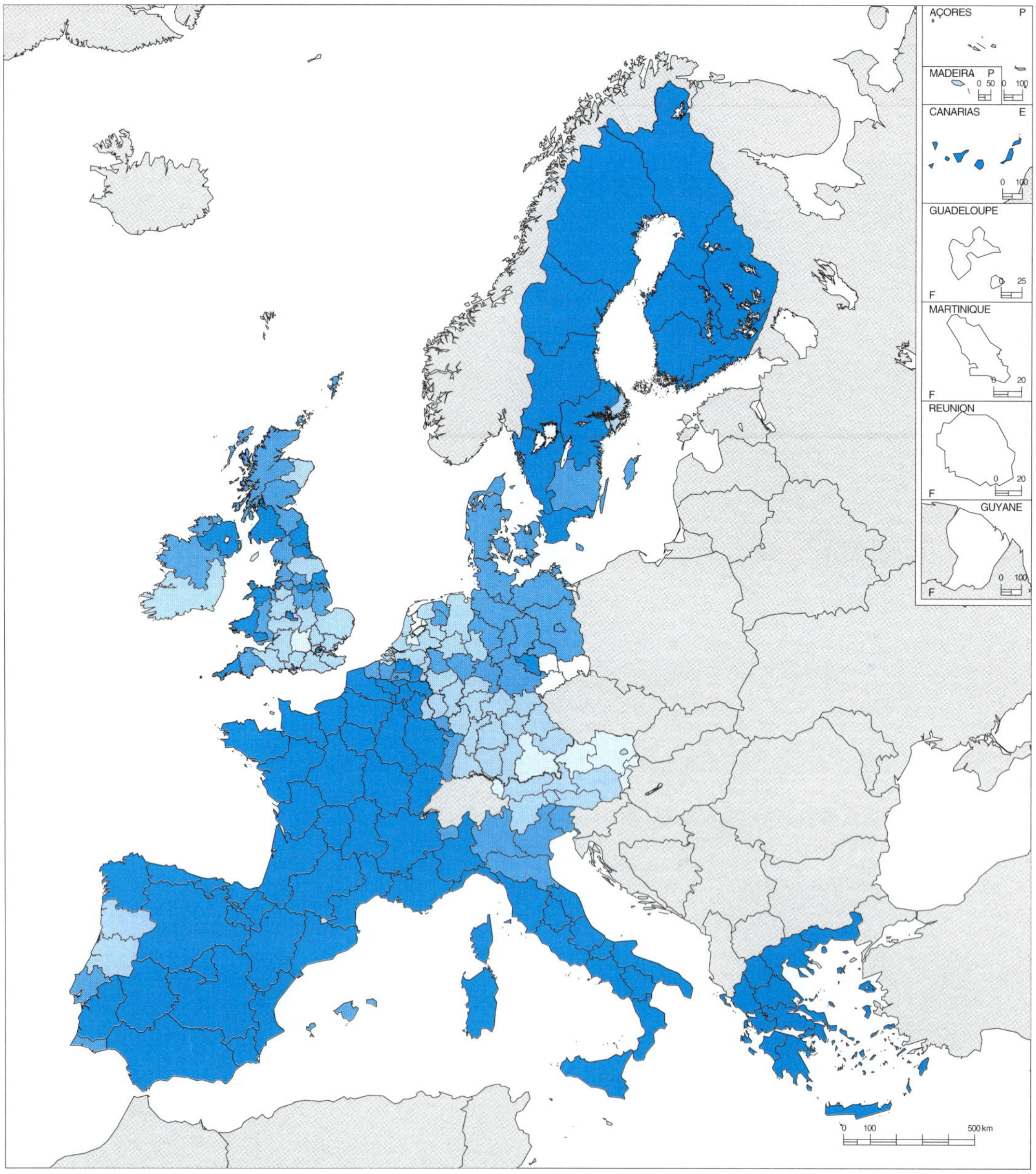

ACORES P

MADEIRA P
0 50 0 100

CANARIAS E
0 100

GUADELOUPE
F 25

MARTINIQUE
F 20

REUNION
0 20
F

GUYANE
0 100
F

7R1IK

0 100   500 km

Further reading: Regions, statistical yearbook, 2000. Eurostat. Statistics in focus —   NUTS 2.
Regions, 2000. Eurostat.

European Union figures on earnings come from two different sources: surveys on the structure of earnings (the last was in 1995, the next one will be in 2002) and the harmonised statistics on earnings (annual data). The statistics on the structure of earnings provide information on annual, monthly and hourly earnings, broken down by age, sex, occupation, level of education and length of service of employees. The 1999 and 2000 editions of the yearbook provided information on earnings from this survey. For the present edition, the data are from the 'Harmonised statistics of earnings' which pro-

vide regular information on average gross earnings for manual and non-manual workers, broken down by sex and economic activity (industry and services). These statistics are based on data from existing sources. Although harmonised, there are significant methodological differences; these make the data more appropriate for depicting and comparing trends rather than comparing levels. Gross earnings cover remuneration in cash paid directly and regularly to the employee, before tax deductions and social security contributions are made by the employer.

Average gross hourly earnings of manual workers in industry. ECU

	1989	1990	1991	1992	1993	1994	1995	1996	1997	1998	1999	
EU-15	:	:	:	:	:	:	:	:	:	:	:	**EU-15**
B	7,51	8,06	8,63	9,40	9,52	10,37	10,24	10,16	10,12	10,47	:	**B**
DK	:	:	:	:	:	:	:	18,73	19,32	20,75		**DK**
D				11,17	12,17	12,48	13,39	13,35	13,26	13,66	14,05	**D**
EL	3,36	3,43	3,64	3,63	3,81	4,03	4,29	4,69	4,98	4,87		**EL**
E	5,49	5,93	6,54	6,47	6,20	6,35	6,62	6,89	6,96	7,14		**E**
F	6,14	6,53	6,77	7,36	7,51	:	:	8,32	9,60	9,93		**F**
IRL	6,69	7,11	7,50	7,95	7,82	8,09	8,17	8,62	9,46	9,34		**IRL**
I	:	:	:	:	:	:	:	:	:	:		**I**
L	8,09	8,41	8,91	9,62	10,28	10,97	11,23	10,99	10,93	11,00	11,55	**L**
NL	7,88	8,31	8,64	9,48	10,00	10,33	13,75	14,10	14,04	14,43	15,12	**NL**
A	:	:	:	:	:	:	1824	1869	1835	1871	1929	**A**
P	1,66	1,83	2,16	2,50	2,28	2,41	2,54	2,80	2,96	2,99		**P**
FIN	:	:	:	:	:	:	:	10,80	10,72	10,98		**FIN**
S	:	:	:	:	8,58	8,99	9,52	11,19	11,43	10,92		**S**
UK	7,49	7,94	8,43	7,82	8,20	7,99	7,96	8,76	10,54	10,70		**UK**
IS	:	:	:	:	:	:	:	:	:	:		**IS**
NO	11,47	11,63	12,14	12,49	12,41	:	:	:	:	:	:	**NO**
EEA											:	**EEA**
CH	11,53	12,47	13,27	13,55	14,58	:	:	18,62	:	18,30	:	**CH**
US	10,18	9,08	9,57	9,31	10,56	10,68	9,97	10,61	12,27	12,79	13,92	**US**
CA	9,30	8,51	9,36	8,77	9,24	8,72	7,99	8,50	9,48	9,08	9,68	**CA**
JP	8,92	7,73	9,11	9,72	12,74	14,11	14,17	12,80	13,23	12,57	15,30	**JP**

Further reading: Earnings in industry and services, hours of work in industry 1996–98.

NL: manual and non-manual workers since 1995. A: monthly earnings. S: manufacturing industry. JP: manual and non-manual workers.

5NA1E

More data on this in Eurostat's database

This domain covers harmonised gross earnings on manual workers (since 1972) and non-manual workers (since 1980) in industry and services. Information is also available on net earnings in manufacturing industries, according to different family situations.

➤➤➤ **DOMAIN EARNING IN DATABASE NEW CRONOS**

Average gross monthly earnings of non-manual workers in industry. ECU

	1989	1990	1991	1992	1993	1994	1995	1996	1997	1998	1999	
EU-15	:	:	:	:	:	:	:	:	:	:	:	**EU-15**
B	1 927	2 065	2 220	2 385	2 437	2 638	2 708	2 682	2 685	2 764	:	**B**
DK	:	:	:	:	:	:	:	3 620	3 658	3 829	:	**DK**
D-W	2 324	2 460	2 627	2 883	3 057	3 122	3 328	3 315	3 293	3 394	:	**D-W**
D-E	:	:	:	:	1 908	2 095	2 355	2 440	2 450	2 525	:	**D-E**
EL	862	896	961	943	1 018	1 065	1 122	1 255	1 340	1 325	:	**EL**
E	1 311	1 415	1 532	1 527	1 465	1 488	1 549	1 623	1 652	1 685	:	**E**
F	1 796	1 900	1 971	2 149	2 203	2 245	2 299	2 358	2 730	2 788	:	**F**
IRL	1 791	1 883	1 981	2 119	2 069	2 181	2 187	2 301	2 554	2 547	:	**IRL**
I	:	:	:	:	:	:	:	:	:	:	:	**I**
L	2 489	2 677	2 825	3 064	3 215	3 313	3 479	3 528	3 428	3 414	3 535	**L**
NL	1 877	1 974	2 048	2 224	2 340	2 419	1 914	1 947	1 931	1 973	2 054	**NL**
A	:	:	:	:	:	:	2 371	2 411	2 401	2 440	2 506	**A**
P	481	537	650	735	732	783	820	900	892	935	:	**P**
FIN	:	:	:	:	:	:	2 283	2 300	2 286	:	:	**FIN**
S	:	:	:	:	:	2 066	2 215	2 576	2 664	2 541	:	**S**
UK	1 896	2 020	2 154	2 024	2 167	2 167	2 114	2 335	2 764	2 834	:	**UK**
IS	:	:	:	:	:	:	:	:	:	:	:	**IS**
NO	2 337	2 391	2 495	2 589	2 596	2 662	2 790	1 952			:	**NO**
EEA	:	:	:	:	:	:	:	:	:	:	:	**EEA**
CH	2 667	2 870	3 041	3 086	3 334	:	:	:	:	:	:	**CH**
US	:	:	:	:	:	:	:	:	:	:	:	**US**
CA												**CA**
JP	1 613	1 375	1 590	1 650	2 110	2 338	2 355	2 146	2 201	2 055	2 498	**JP**

5NA2E

Further reading: Earnings in industry and services, hours of work in industry 1996–98.

NL: manual and non–manual workers since 1996. A: monthly earnings. S: manufacturing industry.

Average gross monthly earnings of employees in industry and services (sections C to K of NACE Rev. 1). Women. ECU

5NA3E

	1989	1990	1991	1992	1993	1994	1995	1996	1997	1998	1999	
B	:	:	:	:	:	:	:	:	:	:	:	B
DK	:	:	:	:	:	:	:	2 616	2 587	2 656	:	DK
D	:	:	:	1 676	1 840	1 908	2 046	2 048	2 051	2 122	2 194	D
D-W	:	:	:	1 740	1 886	1 948	2 080	2 086	2 086	2 158	2 229	D-W
D-E	:	:	:	1 176	1 414	1 533	1 711	1 729	1 736	1 797	1 861	D-E
EL	:	:	:	:	:	:	:	:	:	:	:	EL
E	:	759	836	838	801	819	858	896	915	954	976	E
F	:	:	:	:	:	:	1 653	1 698	1 774	1 820	:	F
IRL	:	:	:	:	:	:	:	:	:	:	:	IRL
I	:	:	:	:	:	:	:	:	:	:	:	I
L	:	:	:	:	:	:	2 285	2 272	2 293	2 305	2 411	L
NL	:	:	:	:	:	:	1 011	1 009	1 008	1 070	:	NL
A	:	:	:	:	:	:	1 427	1 437	1 412	1 429	1 468	A
P	:	:	:	:	:	:	:	:	520	525	:	P
FIN	:	:	:	:	:	:	1 649	1 694	1 667	1 715	:	FIN
S	:	:	:	1 779	1 502	1 561	1 575	1 820	1 873	1 884	:	S
UK	:	:	:	:	:	:	:	1 577	1 937	1 961	2 115	UK
CH	:	:	:	:	:	:	:	:	:	:	:	CH
US	:	:	:	:	:	:	:	:	:	:	:	US
CA	:	:	:	:	:	:	:	:	:	:	:	CA
JP	1 016	852	991	1 041	1 336	1 466	1 465	1 325	1 349	1 264	1 485	JP

Further reading: Earnings in industry and services, hours of work in industry 1996–98.

Average gross monthly earnings of employees in industry and services (sections C to K of NACE Rev. 1). Men. ECU

5NA4E

	1989	1990	1991	1992	1993	1994	1995	1996	1997	1998	1999	
B	:	:	:	:	:	:	:	:	:	:	:	B
DK	:	:	:	:	:	:	:	3 195	3 138	3 256	:	DK
D	:	:	:	2 290	2 457	2 540	2 711	2 692	2 678	2 763	2 847	D
D-W	:	:	:	2 393	2 540	2 622	2 787	2 756	2 739	2 823	2 906	D-W
D-E	:	:	:	1 354	1 628	1 743	1 912	1 978	1 973	2 025	2 091	D-E
EL	:	:	:	:	:	:	:	:	:	:	:	EL
E	:	1 084	1 182	1 182	1 123	1 146	1 186	1 230	1 230	1 253	1 289	E
F	:	:	:	:	:	:	2 368	2 404	2 230	2 282	:	F
IRL	:	:	:	:	:	:	:	:	:	:	:	IRL
I	:	:	:	:	:	:	:	:	:	:	:	I
L	:	:	:	:	:	:	3 602	3 602	3 569	3 562	3 686	L
NL	:	:	:	:	:	:	1 971	1 941	1 950	2 049	:	NL
A	:	:	:	:	:	:	2 072	2 100	2 079	2 118	2 179	A
P	:	:	:	:	:	:	:	:	722	723	:	P
FIN	:	:	:	:	:	:	2 110	2 136	2 117	2 178	:	FIN
S	:	:	:	2 124	1 798	1 855	1 854	2 184	2 266	2 288	:	S
UK	:	:	:	:	:	:	:	2 608	3 155	3 205	2 977	UK
CH	:	:	:	:	:	:	:	:	:	:	:	CH
US	:	:	:	:	:	:	:	:	:	:	:	US
CA	:	:	:	:	:	:	:	:	:	:	:	CA
JP	1 970	1 668	1 922	1 997	2 558	2 805	2 812	2 532	2 581	2 404	2 880	JP

Further reading: Earnings in industry and services, hours of work in industry 1996–98.

Need more data on this topic? Ask your Data Shop

EUROSTAT YEARBOOK 2001

147

1

Average gross monthly earnings of employees in industry and services (sections C to K of NACE Rev. 1). Total. ECU

	1989	1990	1991	1992	1993	1994	1995	1996	1997	1998	1999	
B	:	:	:	:	:	:	:	:	:	:	:	**B**
DK	:	:	:	:	:	:	:	2 993	2 946	3 047	:	**DK**
D	:	:	:	2 121	2 294	2 373	2 537	2 516	2 510	2 593	2 674	**D**
D-W	:	:	:	2 215	2 367	2 444	2 602	2 577	2 566	2 649	2 730	**D-W**
D-E	:	:	:	1 300	1 568	1 686	1 858	1 898	1 897	1 951	2 016	**D-E**
EL	:	:	:	:	:	:	:	:	:	:	:	**EL**
E	:	1 017	1 107	1 101	1 028	1 073	1 115	1 150	1 155	1 179	1 208	**E**
F	:	:	:	:	:	:	:	1 808	2 075	2 127	:	**F**
IRL	:	:	:	:	:	:	:	:	:	:	:	**IRL**
I	:	:	:	:	:	:	:	:	:	:	:	**I**
L	:	:	:	:	:	:	3 085	3 092	3 088	3 092	3 213	**L**
NL	:	:	:	:	:	:	1 661	1 636	1 636	1 719	:	**NL**
A	:	:	:	:	:	:	1 826	1 850	1 827	1 854	1 905	**A**
P	:	:	:	:	:	:	:*	:	643	645	:	**P**
FIN	:	:	:	:	:	:	1 933	1 968	1 949	2 006	:	**FIN**
S	:	:	:	1 951	1 634	1 702	1 715	1 997	2 069	2 086	:	**S**
UK	:	:	:	:	:	:	:	1 947	2 365	2 400	2 723	**UK**
CH	:	:	:	:	:	:	:	3 173	:	3 129	:	**CH**
US	1 315	1 175	1 238	1 214	1 383	1 406	1 306	1 388	1 624	1 709	1 857	**US**
CA	:	:	:	:	:	:	:	:	:	:	:	**CA**
JP	1 619	1 359	1 566	1 629	2 084	2 285	2 289	2 064	2 106	1 966	2 319	**JP**

5NA5E

Further reading: Earnings in industry and services, hours of work in industry 1996–98.

Earnings of women as percentage of men, 1998. Industry and services (sections C to K of NACE Rev. 1)

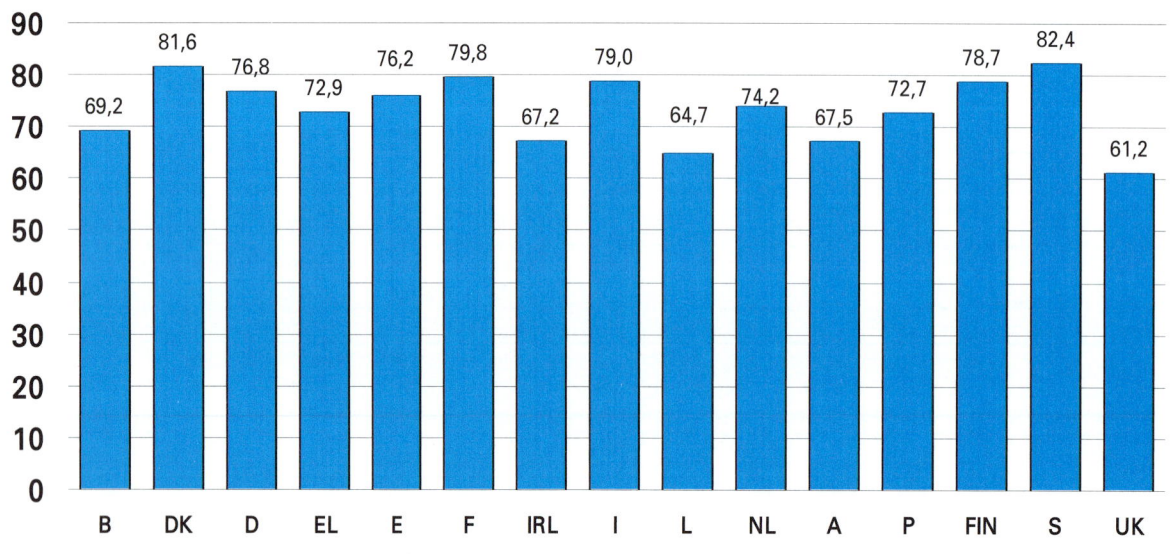

B	DK	D	EL	E	F	IRL	I	L	NL	A	P	FIN	S	UK
69,2	81,6	76,8	72,9	76,2	79,8	67,2	79,0	64,7	74,2	67,5	72,7	78,7	82,4	61,2

5NA6E

Further reading: Earnings in industry and services, hours of work in industry 1996–98.

B: Only non-manual workers for sections C–F + G + J + K of NACE Rev. 1. F: 1995 and 1996 figures are not comparable with 1997 and onwards figures. IRL: Industry (sections C–F of NACE Rev. 1). L: Only non-manual workers. Sections I, K and division 67 of NACE Rev. 1 are excluded. NL: Only full-time workers. S: Sections C–O of NACE Rev. 1. D: Sections H, I and K are excluded.

1J3BA

Monthly net earnings of a couple: manual workers with two average salaries and no children. Manufacturing industries. ECU

	1989	1990	1991	1992	1993	1994	1995	1996	1997	1998	1999	
B	1 771	1 885	1 993	2 146	2 094	2 176	2 137	2 122	2 171	2 231	:	B
DK	2 001	2 100	2 155	2 309	2 307	2 143	2 288	2 278	2 271	2 387	:	DK
D-W	1 935	2 156	2 213	2 345	2 493	2 535	2 680	2 615	2 537	2 599	2 678	D-W
D-E	:	:	:	1 436	1 713	1 823	2 002	2 078	2 038	2 095	2 175	D-E
EL	1 011	1 057	1 099	1 113	1 242	1 302	1 446	1 414	1 515	1 490	:	EL
E	1 441	1 615	1 751	1 730	1 637	1 641	1 698	1 794	1 823	1 885	1 961	E
F	1 520	1 617	1 663	1 784	1 787	1 864	2 098	2 146	2 122	2 217	:	F
IRL	1 523	1 473	1 535	1 792	1 734	1 865	1 941	2 045	2 320	2 591	:	IRL
I	:	:	:	:	:	:	1 594	:	:	:	:	I
L	2 076	2 118	2 365	2 564	2 769	2 978	3 075	3 064	3 042	3 114	3 226	L
NL	1 691	1 852	1 916	2 087	2 228	2 304	:	:	:	:	:	NL
A	:	:	:	:	2 170	2 196	2 389	2 423	2 361	2 398	:	A
P	442	496	576	609	579	611	650	711	726	743	:	P
FIN	:	:	:	:	:	:	2 563	2 617	2 663	2 507	:	FIN
S	:	:	:	:	:	:	:	:	:	:	:	S
UK	1 877	1 784	2 025	2 198	2 012	2 080	2 011	2 102	2 592	2 953	2 987	UK

Further reading: Net earnings of employees in manufacturing industry in the European Union 1980–96. Eurostat. Statistics in focus — net earnings in the European Union 1998, 2000.

A: data on Austria are not fully comparable to data of the other EU countries. Until further notice, results will no longer be compiled for Germany as a whole owing to the difference in the level of earnings between the former Federal territory and the new *Länder* and East Berlin.

1J3BC

Monthly net earnings of a couple: one manual worker's salary with two children. Manufacturing industries. ECU

	1989	1990	1991	1992	1993	1994	1995	1996	1997	1998	1999	
B	1 355	1 434	1 514	1 630	1 588	1 725	1 706	1 679	1 677	1 701	:	B
DK	1 354	1 418	1 446	1 542	1 414	1 558	1 676	1 629	1 635	1 713	:	DK
D-W	1 397	1 537	1 592	1 709	1 803	1 838	1 944	2 003	1 965	2 001	2 116	D-W
D-E	:	:	:	1 024	1 236	1 348	1 529	1 593	1 591	1 626	1 740	D-E
EL	604	633	659	654	787	819	870	893	955	929	:	EL
E	793	881	934	935	840	889	921	974	991	1 030	1 247	E
F	977	1 053	1 085	1 170	1 171	1 210	1 378	1 408	1 382	1 434	:	F
IRL	1 054	1 096	1 200	1 217	1 217	1 285	1 308	1 367	1 538	1 549	:	IRL
I	:	:	:	:	:	:	1 065	:	:	:	:	I
L	1 638	1 667	1 768	1 942	2 133	2 265	2 308	2 306	2 278	2 333	2 495	L
NL	1 139	1 222	1 268	1 379	1 469	1 515	:	:	:	:	:	NL
A	:	:	:	:	1 587	1 597	1 708	1 727	1 676	1 700	:	A
P	297	332	395	444	416	440	465	501	560	573	:	P
FIN	:	:	:	:	:	:	1 481	1 506	1 532	1 502	:	FIN
S	:	:	:	:	:	:	:	:	:	:	:	S
UK	1 256	1 187	1 348	1 554	1 420	1 366	1 310	1 369	1 685	1 916	1 937	UK

Further reading: Net earnings of employees in manufacturing industry in the European Union 1980–96. Eurostat. Statistics in focus — net earnings in the European Union 1998, 2000.

A: data on Austria are not fully comparable to data of the other EU countries. Until further notice, results will no longer be compiled for Germany as a whole owing to the difference in the level of earnings between the former Federal territory and the new *Länder* and East Berlin.

Net earnings are calculated from gross earnings, after deduction of taxes and social security contributions payable by employees and, where appropriate, after addition of family allowances. These, of course, will vary between different fiscal and social protection systems. In order to show the effects of tax scales on income and take into account the possibility of families benefiting from family allowances, the calculation of net earnings from gross earnings is made for a number of standard cases.

Social security as % of gross earnings of a single male manual worker's average salary in manufacturing industry

	1989	1990	1991	1992	1993	1994	1995	1996	1997	1998	1999	
B	13,0	13,0	13,0	14,1	14,1	14,1	14,1	14,1	14,1	14,1	:	**B**
DK	1,9	2,0	2,0	1,9	2,0	2,7	6,4	7,6	8,3	9,3	:	**DK**
D-W	17,9	17,8	18,3	18,4	18,7	19,5	19,7	20,3	21,0	21,0	20,8	**D-W**
D-E	:	:	:	18,3	18,3	19,5	19,6	20,3	21,2	21,2	21,0	**D-E**
EL	15,0	15,0	15,0	16,0	15,4	15,5	15,6	15,1	15,4	15,4	:	**EL**
E	6,1	6,1	6,1	6,1	6,1	6,6	6,4	6,4	6,4	6,4	6,4	**E**
F	18,0	18,0	17,9	18,5	20,2	20,5	18,6	18,9	21,4	20,8	:	**F**
IRL	7,7	7,8	7,8	8,7	8,8	7,7	6,8	6,3	5,6	5,4	:	**IRL**
I	:	:	:	9,6	:	:	9,9	:	:	:	:	**I**
L	12,2	12,2	12,2	12,3	12,3	12,3	12,3	12,2	12,3	12,7	13,2	**L**
NL	25,1	23,6	23,2	23,4	23,6	25,2	:	:	:	:	:	**NL**
A	:	:	:	:	18,1	18,1	18,1	18,1	18,1	18,1	:	**A**
P	11,0	11,0	11,0	11,0	11,0	11,0	11,0	11,0	11,0	11,0	:	**P**
FIN	:	:	:	:	:	:	5,9	5,8	6,0	6,1	:	**FIN**
S	:	:	:	:	:	:	:	:	:	:	:	**S**
UK	7,7	7,7	7,6	7,7	7,6	8,5	8,5	8,5	8,6	8,5	8,1	**UK**

1G7AA

Further reading: Net earnings of employees in manufacturing industry in the European Union 1980–96. Eurostat. Statistics in focus — net earnings in the European Union 1998, 2000.

Data on Austria are not fully comparable to data of the other EU countries. Until further notice, results will no longer be compiled for Germany as a whole owing to the difference in the level of earnings between the former Federal territory and the new *Länder* and East Berlin.

Income tax as % of gross earnings of a single male manual worker's average salary in manufacturing industry

	1989	1990	1991	1992	1993	1994	1995	1996	1997	1998	1999	
B	24,8	25,1	25,4	25,2	25,5	26,5	25,0	25,6	25,8	26,3	:	**B**
DK	44,3	44,2	44,4	44,6	44,4	42,9	42,7	42,7	42,8	42,7	:	**DK**
D-W	23,7	20,3	21,6	22,3	21,4	21,8	22,3	24,1	24,3	24,2	24,4	**D-W**
D-E	:	:	:	13,4	14,3	15,9	18,7	18,6	19,2	19,3	19,2	**D-E**
EL	8,0	8,0	8,0	8,0	2,4	2,8	3,1	3,2	3,5	3,6	:	**EL**
E	10,3	9,1	11,2	11,6	12,3	13,0	13,2	13,5	13,8	13,8	13,3	**E**
F	6,1	6,1	6,2	6,6	6,5	6,4	7,2	7,3	6,7	6,5	:	**F**
IRL	29,3	28,9	28,8	30,2	27,1	26,0	25,7	25,1	24,0	22,6	:	**IRL**
I	:	:	:	15,6	:	:	17,2	:	:	:	:	**I**
L	15,5	14,8	12,5	13,4	14,1	12,1	11,6	12,0	12,3	10,0	10,9	**L**
NL	14,8	12,0	12,8	13,6	13,5	9,0	:	:	:	:	:	**NL**
A	:	:	:	:	9,6	11,8	10,5	11,1	12,2	12,5	:	**A**
P	7,9	7,8	7,0	8,0	8,0	8,0	7,5	6,5	8,5	8,5	:	**P**
FIN	:	:	:	:	:	:	31,5	31,1	29,2	29,0	:	**FIN**
S	:	:	:	:	:	:	:	:	:	:	:	**S**
UK	19,2	19,1	18,9	18,5	18,4	18,4	18,6	17,7	18,0	17,0	16,5	**UK**

1G7AE

Further reading: Net earnings of employees in manufacturing industry in the European Union 1980–96. Eurostat. Statistics in focus — net earnings in the European Union 1998, 2000.

Data on Austria are not fully comparable to data of the other EU countries. Until further notice, results will no longer be compiled for Germany as a whole owing to the difference in the level of earnings between the former Federal territory and the new *Länder* and East Berlin.

National accounts

The national accounts — i.e. the macroeconomic summary of the economy, finances, jobs, etc. — have entered the year 2000 with the following updated features:

– the new national accounts system **ESA 95**, which has been gradually introduced since 1999 as an expanded and fuller version of the earlier ESA 79.

The ESA 95 is compatible with the United Nations' SNA 1993 standard and provides:

– greater **exhaustiveness**: new activities (leasing, stock options, etc.) and inclusion or official acceptance of certain concepts (purchasing power parity, active population, unemployment, balance sheets, etc.);

– **new concepts** (actual final consumption, real disposable national income, holding gains, household subsectors, basic price evaluation, more detailed treatment of trade and transport margins, etc.);

– **new statistical tools** (recording methods and thresholds);

– characteristics relating to the **European institutions**.

As a result of the changeover from ESA 79 to ESA 95, the figures for gross domestic product (GDP) have increased by a few percentage points.

– The new (versions of) related **nomenclatures**: NACE Rev. 1 for economic activities, Coicop (Classification of individual consumption by purpose) for final consumption of households and COFOG (Nomenclature of consumption functions of government) for consumption functions of government.

They improve the breakdown of the economy to provide a better response to the changing needs of statistical users.

In this way national accounts data — including the main component, **gross domestic product (GDP)** which covers all goods and services produced by a country in a given period — will be measured with increasing accuracy and exhaustiveness.

This is a guarantee of quality for all the economic and social analyses that are based on these data.

When we prepared this issue of the Yearbook (Yearbook 2001), only a few Member States and some candidate countries had supplied their consumption data based on ESA 95. Hence, these data under ESA 79 are reproduced in the following chapter.

For Member States, upon comparing ESA 79 with ESA 95 for 1995, the final consumption expenditure shows positive increases from + 0.3 % for Portugal to + 5.1 % for Ireland, with two exceptions: - 2.0 % for Belgium and - 0.4 % for Italy.

Further reading: Statistics in focus Implementation of the new European system of accounts (ESA 95), Eurostat, 1999.

Statistics on private national consumption come from Eurostat national accounts statistics. 'Private' means households, i.e. individuals as well as NPISHs (non-profit–making institutions serving households). 'National' means related to the citizens, wherever they live in the world, while 'domestic' refers to the economic territory of the country. The private consumption is the value of goods and services used for directly meeting human requirements. It is presented in ecus on the first page of the chapter 'Consumption and spending' and hereafter covers actual expenditures on purchases of goods and services, the consumption of own production (such as garden produce) and imputed rent of owner-occupied dwellings.

More data on this in Eurostat's database

Eurostat Database New Cronos

The domain SEC 2 contains disaggregated macroeconomic data harmonised following the ESA 79 standard for 18 European countries, the USA, Japan and several groups of countries (European Union, EFTA, EEA, etc.):

(a) for 25 homogeneous branches of production and their groupings;

(b) for 7 investment products and their groupings;

(c) for 42 consumption functions and their groupings.

➤ ➤ ➤ DOMAIN SEC 2 IN DATABASE NEW CRONOS

Consumption of meat. Volume indices. 1990 = 100

	1989	1990	1991	1992	1993	1994	1995	1996	1997	1998	1999	
EU-15	:	:	:	:	:	:	:	:	:	:	:	**EU-15**
EUR-11	:	:	:	:	:	:	:	:	:	:	:	**EUR-11**
B	97,9 *	100,0 *	101,8 *	101,2 *	97,1 *	102,2 *	102,1 *	96,6 *	91,9 *	:	:	**B**
DK	103,4	100,0	100,3	103,7	107,0	112,8	116,1	116,8	:	:	:	**DK**
D	:	:	:	:	:	:	:	:	:	:	:	**D**
EL	102,0 *	100,0 *	96,0 *	97,2 *	97,9 *	98,8 *	100,8 *	98,4 *	96,8 *	:	:	**EL**
E	:	:	:	:	:	:	:	:	:	:	:	**E**
F	98,7	100,0	101,3	99,9	99,4	98,5	99,5	97,9	98,9	:	:	**F**
IRL	101,0	100,0	101,1	111,9	110,7	114,9	117,5	113,3	112,7	:	:	**IRL**
I	99,9	100,0	100,0	100,1	99,7	99,4	98,0	93,7	95,1	:	:	**I**
L	98,2 *	100,0 *	97,4 *	:	:	:	:	:	:	:	:	**L**
NL	98,3 *	100,0 *	100,8 *	103,3 *	103,3 *	102,9 *	104,3 *	106,2 *	106,3 *	:	:	**NL**
A	98,8 *	100,0 *	102,4 *	105,3 *	102,9 *	100,3 *	99,8 *	98,4 *	97,0 *	:	:	**A**
P	93,8	100,0	98,1	104,7	109,0	113,8	114,5	:	:	:	:	**P**
FIN	101,2	100,0	98,3	94,6	94,2	93,7	97,7	99,6	101,0	:	:	**FIN**
S	98,1 *	100,0 *	101,3 *	108,1 *	112,0 *	113,9 *	120,9 *	123,0 *	:	:	:	**S**
UK	105,2	100,0	99,8	99,1	103,5	105,9	105,7	105,4	:	:	:	**UK**

1J5AB

Further reading: National accounts ESA — detailed tables by branch, 1970–97. Eurostat.

Consumption of fish. Volume indices. 1990 = 100

5A1GC

	1989	1990	1991	1992	1993	1994	1995	1996	1997	1998	1999	
EU-15	:	:	:	:	:	:	:	:	:	:	:	EU-15
EUR-11	:	:	:	:	:	:	:	:	:	:	:	EUR-11
B	88,9 *	100,0 *	99,6 *	102,9 *	101,3 *	108,1 *	116,2 *	115,3 *	127,0 *	:	:	B
DK	100,3	100,0	108,5	124,3	113,2	115,5	118,9	119,6	:	:	:	DK
D	:	:	:	:	:	:	:	:	:	:	:	D
EL	97,9 *	100,0 *	100,7 *	102,3 *	105,4 *	102,3 *	103,4 *	104,7 *	107,1 *	:	:	EL
E	:	:	:	:	:	:	:	:	:	:	:	E
F	95,8	100,0	102,3	103,5	107,9	107,9	111,1	111,1	110,9	:	:	F
IRL	94,5	100,0	102,1	102,7	101,9	99,5	101,3	101,6	101,9	:	:	IRL
I	99,7	100,0	101,9	101,6	100,6	100,5	98,1	98,0	98,3	:	:	I
L	106,7 *	100,0 *	112,5 *	:	:	:	:	:	:	:	:	L
NL	99,0 *	100,0 *	102,9 *	105,8 *	104,9 *	108,7 *	115,5 *	115,5 *	125,2 *	:	:	NL
A	98,8 *	100,0 *	97,2 *	99,8 *	98,3 *	106,8 *	96,6 *	107,3 *	111,8 *	:	:	A
P	97,4	100,0	104,9	108,6	109,5	107,0	108,4	:	:	:	:	P
FIN	98,9	100,0	102,3	103,3	101,3	102,6	106,3	108,9	110,3	:	:	FIN
S	102,6 *	100,0 *	92,2 *	96,1 *	90,8 *	100,5 *	93,3 *	103,0 *	:	:	:	S
UK	105,3	100,0	98,5	97,5	102,4	111,9	114,1	124,3	:	:	:	UK

Further reading: National accounts ESA — detailed tables by branch, 1970–97.
Eurostat.

Consumption of fruits and vegetables. Volume indices. 1990 = 100

5A1GD

	1989	1990	1991	1992	1993	1994	1995	1996	1997	1998	1999	
EU-15	:	:	:	:	:	:	:	:	:	:	:	EU-15
EUR-11	:	:	:	:	:	:	:	:	:	:	:	EUR-11
B	102,0 *	100,0 *	98,9 *	111,0 *	113,7 *	109,8 *	111,1 *	106,9 *	109,5 *	:	:	B
DK	98,5	100,0	104,9	106,7	109,7	107,6	110,8	111,4	:	:	:	DK
D	:	:	:	:	:	:	:	:	:	:	:	D
EL	103,5 *	100,0 *	97,8 *	98,7 *	98,5 *	100,1 *	105,2 *	104,6 *	101,2 *	:	:	EL
E	:	:	:	:	:	:	:	:	:	:	:	E
F	100,2	100,0	96,7	99,5	100,5	101,7	102,1	100,7	100,2	:	:	F
IRL	99,0	100,0	103,7	108,2	117,3	119,5	116,9	131,2	132,9	:	:	IRL
I	99,6	100,0	100,3	100,8	101,0	101,2	100,7	98,7	99,3	:	:	I
L	:	:	:	:	:	:	:	:	:	:	:	L
NL	98,6 *	100,0 *	98,3 *	101,9 *	105,8 *	109,8 *	112,1 *	113,7 *	115,6 *	:	:	NL
A	96,9 *	100,0 *	98,1 *	98,9 *	101,4 *	99,4 *	99,1 *	97,6 *	99,3 *	:	:	A
P	90,2	100,0	98,7	113,4	113,0	117,0	115,7	:	:	:	:	P
FIN	101,2	100,0	105,3	109,2	108,9	115,6	114,1	113,9	118,8	:	:	FIN
S	98,6 *	100,0 *	102,4 *	103,7 *	104,8 *	107,3 *	106,3 *	109,5 *	:	:	:	S
UK	98,5	100,0	102,2	110,2	114,1	114,5	116,6	121,7	:	:	:	UK

Further reading: National accounts ESA — detailed tables by branch, 1970–97.
Eurostat.

Consumption of milk, cheese and eggs. Volume indices. 1990 = 100

	1989	1990	1991	1992	1993	1994	1995	1996	1997	1998	1999	
EU-15	:	:	:	:	:	:	:	:	:	:	:	EU-15
EUR-11	:	:	:	:	:	:	:	:	:	:	:	EUR-11
B	95,1 *	100,0 *	100,2 *	106,7 *	106,8 *	104,5 *	98,8 *	104,3 *	113,4 *	:	:	B
DK	102,1	100,0	104,1	107,8	105,2	113,3	116,6	117,3	:	:	:	DK
D	:	:	:	:	:	:	:	:	:	:	:	D
EL	99,0 *	100,0 *	99,1 *	100,8 *	100,9 *	103,6 *	104,5 *	105,8 *	106,8 *	:	:	EL
E	:	:	:	:	:	:	:	:	:	:	:	E
F	99,7	100,0	100,9	101,9	103,0	104,4	106,4	107,5	109,4	:	:	F
IRL	102,3	100,0	99,4	106,3	108,2	111,3	108,9	110,2	111,2	:	:	IRL
I	100,1	100,0	100,4	101,1	101,2	101,5	102,7	104,1	101,8	:	:	I
L	103,5 *	100,0 *	101,5 *	:	:	:	:	:	:	:	:	L
NL	98,6 *	100,0 *	100,3 *	102,7 *	101,7 *	104,6 *	106,8 *	109,0 *	110,8 *	:	:	NL
A	97,7 *	100,0 *	103,0 *	103,3 *	104,3 *	105,7 *	114,5 *	110,4 *	112,0 *	:	:	A
P	97,2	100,0	104,0	103,8	103,1	105,7	109,8	:	:	:	:	P
FIN	100,3	100,0	97,9	98,3	98,9	98,8	102,2	101,9	100,5	:	:	FIN
S	98,8 *	100,0 *	97,7 *	100,0 *	101,4 *	102,3 *	101,8 *	103,6 *	:	:	:	S
UK	101,6	100,0	100,6	101,5	98,8	94,7	91,2	90,9	:	:	:	UK

1J5AC

Further reading: National accounts ESA — detailed tables by branch, 1970–97.
Eurostat.

Consumption of potatoes, manioc and other tubers. Volume indices. 1990 = 100

	1989	1990	1991	1992	1993	1994	1995	1996	1997	1998	1999	
EU-15	:	:	:	:	:	:	:	:	:	:	:	EU-15
EUR-11	:	:	:	:	:	:	:	:	:	:	:	EUR-11
B	93,6 *	100,0 *	105,0 *	107,8 *	102,9 *	111,0 *	99,0 *	92,0 *	99,6 *	:	:	B
DK	114,7	100,0	94,8	100,8	93,6	118,5	121,9	122,6	:	:	:	DK
D	:	:	:	:	:	:	:	:	:	:	:	D
EL	105,8 *	100,0 *	104,7 *	102,6 *	114,9 *	108,4 *	108,8 *	106,4 *	104,7 *	:	:	EL
E	:	:	:	:	:	:	:	:	:	:	:	E
F	108,3	100,0	101,6	103,3	106,6	101,3	102,6	102,3	101,8	:	:	F
IRL	101,2	100,0	99,7	104,6	108,0	123,1	115,5	121,7	119,7	:	:	IRL
I	100,1	100,0	99,5	99,8	100,0	100,1	96,0	96,8	95,3	:	:	I
L	:	:	:	:	:	:	:	:	:	:	:	L
NL	99,2 *	100,0 *	96,9 *	98,5 *	101,5 *	105,3 *	107,6 *	108,4 *	109,2 *	:	:	NL
A	97,3 *	100,0 *	104,2 *	101,4 *	102,6 *	87,1 *	108,0 *	94,3 *	95,0 *	:	:	A
P	93,9	100,0	100,6	102,6	98,9	98,3	97,8	:	:	:	:	P
FIN	101,7	100,0	98,9	98,2	117,5	115,6	124,0	130,6	128,4	:	:	FIN
S	97,3 *	100,0 *	102,5 *	104,4 *	104,5 *	104,5 *	112,1 *	114,7 *	:	:	:	S
UK	98,0	100,0	101,7	109,0	110,2	105,8	105,0	120,3	:	:	:	UK

5A1GE

Further reading: National accounts ESA — detailed tables by branch, 1970–97.
Eurostat.

Consumption of sugar. Volume indices. 1990 = 100

	1989	1990	1991	1992	1993	1994	1995	1996	1997	1998	1999	
EU-15	:	:	:	:	:	:	:	:	:	:	:	EU-15
EUR-11	:	:	:	:	:	:	:	:	:	:	:	EUR-11
B	95,7 *	100,0 *	99,9 *	94,5 *	92,0 *	94,6 *	88,2 *	94,1 *	100,4 *	:	:	B
DK	96,3	100,0	100,4	100,7	111,8	98,7	101,6	102,2	:	:	:	DK
D	:	:	:	:	:	:	:	:	:	:	:	D
EL	99,1 *	100,0 *	99,9 *	101,4 *	99,5 *	101,5 *	106,5 *	106,5 *	117,1 *	:	:	EL
E	:	:	:	:	:	:	:	:	:	:	:	E
F	102,1	100,0	98,5	103,2	94,9	91,2	90,7	88,0	84,0	:	:	F
IRL	105,3	100,0	96,1	92,0	88,6	76,4	84,6	85,3	85,9	:	:	IRL
I	99,1	100,0	100,2	100,4	100,3	99,8	100,3	97,3	99,5	:	:	I
L	:	:	:	:	:	:	:	:	:	:	:	L
NL	100,0 *	100,0 *	100,0 *	107,1 *	107,1 *	110,7 *	110,7 *	110,7 *	107,1 *	:	:	NL
A	101,2 *	100,0 *	98,9 *	97,6 *	97,7 *	97,5 *	97,4 *	96,1 *	94,1 *	:	:	A
P	103,1	100,0	98,5	95,1	91,1	87,8	88,1	:	:	:	:	P
FIN	107,5	100,0	101,2	109,8	117,3	117,6	118,8	116,1	116,3	:	:	FIN
S	106,1 *	100,0 *	101,2 *	101,8 *	98,0 *	102,4 *	84,1 *	89,7 *	:	:	:	S
UK	107,5	100,0	96,9	89,3	86,5	80,9	75,2	82,8	:	:	:	UK

Further reading: National accounts ESA — detailed tables by branch, 1970–97.
Eurostat.

5A1GF

Consumption of oils and fats. Volume indices. 1990 = 100

	1989	1990	1991	1992	1993	1994	1995	1996	1997	1998	1999	
EU-15	:	:	:	:	:	:	:	:	:	:	:	EU-15
EUR-11	:	:	:	:	:	:	:	:	:	:	:	EUR-11
B	96,3 *	100,0 *	97,2 *	97,4 *	101,4 *	101,8 *	101,2 *	101,6 *	100,0 *	:	:	B
DK	108,9	100,0	106,3	107,5	105,8	97,9	100,8	101,4	:	:	:	DK
D	:	:	:	:	:	:	:	:	:	:	:	D
EL	100,1 *	100,0 *	101,0 *	101,0 *	93,0 *	94,0 *	94,4 *	96,2 *	102,8 *	:	:	EL
E	:	:	:	:	:	:	:	:	:	:	:	E
F	103,0	100,0	98,8	97,7	96,0	95,6	93,3	93,6	95,4	:	:	F
IRL	102,6	100,0	98,1	96,5	94,8	92,6	92,9	93,6	94,3	:	:	IRL
I	100,3	100,0	100,0	100,1	99,4	98,3	96,0	92,1	92,5	:	:	I
L	100,5 *	100,0 *	88,5 *	:	:	:	:	:	:	:	:	L
NL	97,3 *	100,0 *	100,9 *	102,7 *	104,5 *	107,1 *	107,1 *	106,3 *	108,9 *	:	:	NL
A	97,9 *	100,0 *	99,1 *	98,4 *	97,4 *	97,7 *	99,0 *	93,2 *	93,2 *	:	:	A
P	100,2	100,0	102,2	103,2	102,3	103,5	107,6	:	:	:	:	P
FIN	108,9	100,0	105,0	108,0	104,7	97,4	96,7	94,1	93,5	:	:	FIN
S	100,3 *	100,0 *	97,6 *	96,4 *	97,0 *	95,6 *	98,1 *	98,3 *	:	:	:	S
UK	105,6	100,0	97,0	97,3	93,7	91,7	89,3	92,1	:	:	:	UK

Further reading: National accounts ESA — detailed tables by branch, 1970–97.
Eurostat.

5A1GG

The drinks include milk, non–alcoholic and alcoholic beverages, as well as coffee, tea and cocoa when they are consumed in liquid form. Milk is presented together with cheese and eggs.

Milk, coffee, tea and cocoa are sometimes included in the overall food, hence letting only the other beverages (non–alcoholic and alcoholic) as drinks *sensu stricto*.

Consumption of coffee, tea and cocoa. Volume indices. 1990 = 100

	1989	1990	1991	1992	1993	1994	1995	1996	1997	1998	1999	
EU-15	:	:	:	:	:	:	:	:	:	:	:	EU-15
EUR-11	:	:	:	:	:	:	:	:	:	:	:	EUR-11
B	100,1 *	100,0 *	91,8 *	84,7 *	76,6 *	74,6 *	79,2 *	82,6 *	87,0 *	:	:	B
DK	101,4	100,0	106,3	105,5	90,8	83,8	86,2	86,7	:	:	:	DK
D	:	:	:	:	:	:	:	:	:	:	:	D
EL	93,8 *	100,0 *	100,5 *	101,5 *	105,0 *	109,1 *	112,0 *	114,0 *	115,9 *	:	:	EL
E	:	:	:	:	:	:	:	:	:	:	:	E
F	100,8	100,0	99,6	98,9	100,6	100,0	97,8	105,5	105,7	:	:	F
IRL	96,7	100,0	99,8	106,2	103,7	113,5	102,4	115,3	107,4	:	:	IRL
I	99,2	100,0	100,0	99,9	100,1	100,1	100,9	102,8	103,6	:	:	I
L	:	:	:	:	:	:	:	:	:	:	:	L
NL	98,1 *	100,0 *	101,9 *	105,7 *	105,7 *	101,9 *	103,8 *	105,7 *	107,0 *	:	:	NL
A	97,8 *	100,0 *	99,2 *	94,7 *	90,9 *	75,5 *	69,1 *	70,9 *	67,4 *	:	:	A
P	87,4	100,0	101,4	101,4	102,0	108,2	105,1	:	:	:	:	P
FIN	98,6	100,0	98,3	100,0	101,5	95,5	90,7	97,8	93,1	:	:	FIN
S	99,0 *	100,0 *	98,5 *	94,6 *	98,0 *	105,5 *	96,9 *	103,4 *	:	:	:	S
UK	104,1	100,0	101,5	95,1	93,4	89,7	85,4	88,1	:	:	:	UK

5A1GH

Further reading: National accounts ESA — detailed tables by branch, 1970–97. Eurostat.

Consumption of non-alcoholic beverages. Volume indices. 1990 = 100

	1989	1990	1991	1992	1993	1994	1995	1996	1997	1998	1999	
EU-15	:	:	:	:	:	:	:	:	:	:	:	EU-15
EUR-11	:	:	:	:	:	:	:	:	:	:	:	EUR-11
B	91,4	100,0	97,9	103,2	97,6	106,4	111,7	109,2	114,6	:	:	B
DK	102,5	100,0	100,2	113,0	137,1	159,4	167,2	171,0	:	:	:	DK
D	:	:	:	:	:	:	:	:	:	:	:	D
EL	91,5 *	100,0 *	102,3 *	106,4 *	112,2 *	119,5 *	119,4 *	119,3 *	119,9 *	:	:	EL
E	:	:	:	:	:	:	:	:	:	:	:	E
F	89,2	100,0	103,2	102,5	106,4	110,8	118,7	120,9	124,4	:	:	F
IRL	111,2	100,0	91,9	124,8	107,1	110,1	117,2	127,8	133,7	:	:	IRL
I	92,4	100,0	104,6	108,6	111,4	113,3	116,2	116,9	119,1	:	:	I
L	99,9 *	100,0 *	109,0 *	:	:	:	:	:	:	:	:	L
NL	92,0 *	100,0 *	100,6 *	106,3 *	108,0 *	114,2 *	119,3 *	122,2 *	126,1 *	:	:	NL
A	89,5 *	100,0 *	102,5 *	109,4 *	106,8 *	109,2 *	115,8 *	106,5 *	108,3 *	:	:	A
P	95,0	100,0	105,5	103,1	102,8	113,1	121,6	:	:	:	:	P
FIN	101,7	100,0	96,7	100,5	92,5	103,7	117,8	123,7	135,0	:	:	FIN
S	100,3 *	100,0 *	102,8 *	110,1 *	119,4 *	123,0 *	138,6 *	139,1 *	:	:	:	S
UK	96,9	100,0	100,8	101,4	102,2	110,4	112,3	113,6	:	:	:	UK

5A1BJ

Further reading: National accounts ESA — detailed tables by branch, 1970–97. Eurostat. Key data on health, 2000. Eurostat.

The non-alcoholic drinks include among others coffee, tea, cocoa and soft drinks but not milk which is included above in the category milk, cheese and eggs.

Food, drink and tobacco traditionally used to account for the biggest share of consumption. The other main consumption functions are clothing and footwear, dwellings, furniture and household articles, health services, transport and communication, recreation, entertainment, education and other goods and services. Food, drink and tobacco have gradually been overtaken in the majority of the Member States both by spending on dwellings, and by spending on transport and communications.

Consumption of alcoholic drinks and tobacco at current prices as % of total consumption

	1989	1990	1991	1992	1993	1994	1995	1996	1997	1998	1999	
EU-15	:	: |	:	:	:	:	:	:	:	:	:	EU-15
EUR-11	:	: |	:	:	:	:	:	:	:	:	:	EUR-11
B	2,7	2,8	2,7	2,7	2,7	2,7	2,8	2,8	2,8	:	:	B
DK	5,9	5,9	5,7	5,7	5,5	5,1	4,8 *	4,8 *	:	:	:	DK
D	4,5	4,5 |	4,5 *	4,3 *	4,2 *	4,2 *	4,1 *	4,0 *	4,0 *	:	:	D
EL	6,1	6,6	4,0	4,0	4,2	4,4	4,2	4,2	4,3	:	:	EL
E	:	:	:	:	:	:	:	:	:	:	:	E
F	3,1	3,1	3,1	3,1	3,3	3,4	3,4 *	3,4 *	3,5 *	:	:	F
IRL	14,7	14,8	15,0	15,1	14,8	15,0	15,3	15,2	15,0	:	:	IRL
I	2,6	2,5	2,5	2,4	2,7	2,7	2,6	2,7 *	2,6 *	:	:	I
L	6,8	6,9	7,0	:	:	:	:	:	:	:	:	L
NL	3,1	3,1	3,0	3,1	3,1	3,0	3,0	2,9	2,8	:	:	NL
A	4,0	3,8	3,7	3,5	3,4	3,4	3,4	3,3	3,3	:	:	A
P	6,2	6,0	5,5	5,2 *	5,2 *	5,4 *	5,3 *	:	:	:	:	P
FIN	6,6	6,6	7,0	7,0	6,6	6,2	5,9	5,6	5,6	:	:	FIN
S	5,1	5,1	4,9	4,9	4,9	4,8	4,6	4,5	:	:	:	S
UK	8,7	8,9	9,2	9,0	8,8	8,8	8,6	8,6	:	:	:	UK

1J5BD

Further reading: National accounts ESA — detailed tables by branch, 1970–97. Eurostat.

The consumption of alcoholic drinks and of tobacco is shown separately on next page.

Consumption expenditure in restaurants, cafés and hotels. Volume indices. 1990 = 100

	1989	1990	1991	1992	1993	1994	1995	1996	1997	1998	1999	
EU-15	:	: |	:	:	:	:	:	:	:	:	:	EU-15
EUR-11	:	: |	:	:	:	:	:	:	:	:	:	EUR-11
B	95,4 *	100,0 *	101,8 *	106,2 *	103,1 *	105,7 *	107,9 *	110,5 *	114,9 *	:	:	B
DK	101,4	100,0	100,9	105,5	108,0	108,2	107,0	110,8	:	:	:	DK
D	95,8 *	100,0 *|	103,0 *	103,4 *	102,3 *	101,9 *	:	:	:	:	:	D
EL	96,9 *	100,0 *	94,9 *	100,7 *	103,8 *	108,0 *	109,4 *	114,1 *	122,4 *	:	:	EL
E	:	:	:	:	:	:	:	:	:	:	:	E
F	98,0	100,0	101,3	101,0	100,0	100,6	100,4	100,8	102,8	:	:	F
IRL	90,5	100,0	106,4	110,4	116,7	127,4	135,4	143,4	148,0	:	:	IRL
I	97,5	100,0	104,0	102,3	100,9	104,0	108,5	112,7	113,7	:	:	I
L	:	:	:	:	:	:	:	:	:	:	:	L
NL	96,3 *	100,0 *	106,6 *	112,0 *	115,1 *	119,0 *	118,3 *	118,1 *	124,4 *	:	:	NL
A	96,8 *	100,0 *	104,0 *	108,3 *	106,2 *	104,7 *	105,0 *	102,4 *	102,4 *	:	:	A
P	90,5	100,0	106,2	104,1	101,1	103,0	102,6	:	:	:	:	P
FIN	99,7	100,0	91,9	87,0	83,4	86,2	89,3	92,8	98,1	:	:	FIN
S	110,7 *	100,0 *	91,7 *	87,4 *	89,7 *	93,7 *	97,2 *	101,0 *	:	:	:	S
UK	99,0	100,0	92,5	92,7	95,0	95,2	97,7	103,0	:	:	:	UK

1J5EC

Further reading: National accounts ESA — detailed tables by branch, 1970–97. Eurostat.

For Greece, Ireland and the United Kingdom, the expenses of food, beverages and tobacco in restaurants, cafés and hotels are included in other pages of this chapter.

1

Consumption of alcoholic beverages. Volume indices. 1990 = 100

	1989	1990	1991	1992	1993	1994	1995	1996	1997	1998	1999	
EU-15	:	:	:	:	:	:	:	:	:	:	:	EU-15
EUR-11	:	:	:	:	:	:	:	:	:	:	:	EUR-11
B	90,6	100,0	94,1	98,0	99,4	100,0	104,4	109,2	115,8	:	:	B
DK	100,7	100,0	102,6	108,0	105,6	106,2	107,6	111,4	:	:	:	DK
D	92,8 *	100,0 *|	120,4 *	123,0 *	122,9 *	125,4 *	126,4 *	125,9 *	125,1 *	:	:	D
EL	97,2 *	100,0 *	99,0 *	99,8 *	98,3 *	99,8 *	100,1 *	100,5 *	101,4 *	:	:	EL
E	:	:	:	:	:	:	:	:	:	:	:	E
F	99,6	100,0	99,2	99,1	105,8	104,3	105,6	106,0	106,0	:	:	F
IRL	97,1	100,0	101,6	104,6	104,5	109,7	113,8	122,8	126,0	:	:	IRL
I	101,4	100,0	98,8	96,6	93,9	92,3	91,6	91,2	89,6	:	:	I
L	104,2 *	100,0 *	109,1 *	:	:	:	:	:	:	:	:	L
NL	96,7 *	100,0 *	101,0 *	102,1 *	100,6 *	101,3 *	103,3 *	105,8 *	108,1 *	:	:	NL
A	102,0 *	100,0 *	98,6 *	97,3 *	95,9 *	90,8 *	102,2 *	102,1 *	95,6 *	:	:	A
P	94,8	100,0	92,2	88,8	81,9	81,3	82,4	:	:	:	:	P
FIN	99,2	100,0	97,3	92,1	87,2	85,2	85,9	87,6	90,4	:	:	FIN
S	101,7 *	100,0 *	100,6 *	100,9 *	98,8 *	98,9 *	95,8 *	91,0 *	:	:	:	S
UK	100,7	100,0	96,3	92,3	92,0	94,9	92,8	96,3	:	:	:	UK

1J5BA

Further reading: National accounts ESA — detailed tables by branch, 1970–97.
Eurostat.

Consumption of tobacco. Volume indices. 1990 = 100

	1989	1990	1991	1992	1993	1994	1995	1996	1997	1998	1999	
EU-15	:	:	:	:	:	:	:	:	:	:	:	EU-15
EUR-11	:	:	:	:	:	:	:	:	:	:	:	EUR-11
B	104,4	100,0	101,1	98,6	91,7	89,9	94,2	95,7	94,0	:	:	B
DK	96,2	100,0	97,6	96,3	100,4	96,4	90,6	89,6	:	:	:	DK
D	93,8 *	100,0 *|	114,8 *	108,1 *	104,8 *	109,9 *	110,6 *	111,3 *	111,9 *	:	:	D
EL	99,7 *	100,0 *	102,6 *	104,2 *	105,5 *	108,5 *	108,5 *	109,6 *	109,1 *	:	:	EL
E	:	:	:	:	:	:	:	:	:	:	:	E
F	97,9	100,0	102,3	101,7	97,1	94,6	93,1	91,4	88,2	:	:	F
IRL	97,7	100,0	107,9	103,0	98,4	101,5	108,9	103,5	107,2	:	:	IRL
I	103,6	100,0	100,0	95,6	99,9	97,7	96,6	97,0	97,5	:	:	I
L	93,3 *	100,0 *	108,0 *	:	:	:	:	:	:	:	:	L
NL	98,0 *	100,0 *	101,0 *	97,7 *	91,2 *	92,2 *	92,5 *	92,2 *	89,7 *	:	:	NL
A	97,2 *	100,0 *	103,4 *	101,2 *	98,1 *	100,5 *	95,2 *	92,9 *	98,5 *	:	:	A
P	99,0	100,0	101,2	98,6	102,1	113,5	106,7	:	:	:	:	P
FIN	108,3	100,0	97,8	96,2	83,2	79,0	74,0	66,2	69,1	:	:	FIN
S	102,9 *	100,0 *	101,3 *	99,5 *	89,1 *	86,2 *	81,4 *	81,2 *	:	:	:	S
UK	100,9	100,0	97,5	92,1	87,4	85,9	83,5	80,9	:	:	:	UK

1J5BB

Further reading: National accounts ESA — detailed tables by branch, 1970–97.
Eurostat.

Consumption of gross rent and water charges. Volume indices. 1990 = 100

1J5CA

	1989	1990	1991	1992	1993	1994	1995	1996	1997	1998	1999	
EU-15	:	: |	:	:	:	:	:	:	:	:	:	EU-15
EUR-11	:	: |	:	:	:	:	:	:	:	:	:	EUR-11
B	97,6	100,0	102,5	104,0	105,5	106,9	108,6	110,1	111,9	:	:	B
DK	99,2	100,0	100,6	101,0	101,3	101,5	101,8	102,1	:	:	:	DK
D	96,5 *	100,0 *|	106,8 *	110,6 *	114,9 *	119,7 *	124,3 *	129,1 *	133,5 *	:	:	D
EL	97,3 *	100,0 *	102,7 *	103,7 *	104,3 *	102,7 *	103,2 *	105,0 *	106,2 *	:	:	EL
E	:	:	:	:	:	:	:	:	:	:	:	E
F	97,0	100,0	103,2	106,2	108,9	111,8	115,4	119,0	122,1	:	:	F
IRL	97,1	100,0	103,1	106,2	109,2	112,7	116,6	121,9	128,1	:	:	IRL
I	98,0	100,0	102,0	103,2	103,2	106,1	107,0	109,1	109,1	:	:	I
L	101,7 *	100,0 *	107,5 *	:	:	:	:	:	:	:	:	L
NL	95,6 *	100,0 *	103,0 *	105,5 *	108,5 *	111,2 *	114,5 *	117,1 *	120,2 *	:	:	NL
A	97,2 *	100,0 *	101,1 *	103,9 *	105,3 *	110,0 *	113,4 *	115,2 *	117,4 *	:	:	A
P	98,4	100,0	99,6	100,7	100,0	99,5	102,0	:	:	:	:	P
FIN	97,1	100,0	103,2	106,3	111,0	114,3	118,2	120,7	125,0	:	:	FIN
S	99,1 *	100,0 *	101,1 *	102,4 *	103,0 *	103,3 *	103,6 *	103,8 *	:	:	:	S
UK	99,6	100,0	100,1	100,9	103,1	104,4	105,2	106,2	:	:	:	UK

Further reading: National accounts ESA — detailed tables by branch, 1970–97.
Eurostat.

Consumption of fuel and power. Volume indices. 1990 = 100

1J5CB

	1989	1990	1991	1992	1993	1994	1995	1996	1997	1998	1999	
EU-15	:	: |	:	:	:	:	:	:	:	:	:	EU-15
EUR-11	:	: |	:	:	:	:	:	:	:	:	:	EUR-11
B	97,5	100,0	108,6	109,0	110,6	110,4	114,3	124,4	119,5	:	:	B
DK	101,2	100,0	104,1	104,2	110,4	112,8	115,6	121,4	:	:	:	DK
D	96,0 *	100,0 *|	127,0 *	126,9 *	131,6 *	129,6 *	131,9 *	140,4 *	137,0 *	:	:	D
EL	101,8 *	100,0 *	101,6 *	104,5 *	104,1 *	105,5 *	109,3 *	120,2 *	125,1 *	:	:	EL
E	:	:	:	:	:	:	:	:	:	:	:	E
F	98,6	100,0	109,4	109,1	109,3	105,4	109,1	116,3	112,5	:	:	F
IRL	99,7	100,0	106,6	103,3	106,3	116,6	112,5	116,0	120,4	:	:	IRL
I	96,9	100,0	108,1	104,3	104,2	97,8	104,6	106,6	104,7	:	:	I
L	99,3 *	100,0 *	107,6 *	:	:	:	:	:	:	:	:	L
NL	100,5 *	100,0 *	109,7 *	106,0 *	111,3 *	108,3 *	110,8 *	122,8 *	114,9 *	:	:	NL
A	96,7 *	100,0 *	110,2 *	105,8 *	111,4 *	109,7 *	119,1 *	127,0 *	122,9 *	:	:	A
P	94,2	100,0	108,0	116,5	123,1	125,8	129,5	:	:	:	:	P
FIN	92,9	100,0	106,5	105,7	109,6	113,1	105,5	111,2	109,1	:	:	FIN
S	102,1 *	100,0 *	109,4 *	107,9 *	110,6 *	112,7 *	112,5 *	119,7 *	:	:	:	S
UK	100,4	100,0	107,6	105,8	109,1	107,1	105,9	112,1	:	:	:	UK

Further reading: National accounts ESA — detailed tables by branch, 1970–97.
Eurostat.

1

S hare of housing, varying greatly from one country to another, has increased almost everywhere.
Greece and Spain and particularly Ireland have a
low share. However, in Ireland some household
expenditure is covered by the State and is therefore
not included in household consumption.

Consumption of gross rent, fuel and power at current prices as % of total consumption

	1989	1990	1991	1992	1993	1994	1995	1996	1997	1998	1999	
EU-15	17,6	17,5 |	17,9	18,3	19,2	19,5	19,9	20,3 *	20,4 *	:	:	EU-15
EUR-11	16,9	17,0 |	17,1	17,4	18,6	19,0	19,5	19,9 *	20,1 *	:	:	EUR-11
B	18,6	18,5	18,7	18,9	19,7	19,8	20,1	20,4	20,1	:	:	B
DK	27,1	27,9	28,3	28,3	28,8	27,4	27,2	27,0	27,0 *	:	:	DK
D	18,7	18,3 |	17,3	17,8	19,2	19,8	20,3	21,0	21,6	:	:	D
EL	11,4	11,5	17,2	17,2	18,1	17,6	17,7	18,0	17,8	:	:	EL
E	13,5	13,5	13,6	13,5	14,0	14,1	14,2	14,3	14,1	:	:	E
F	18,8	19,0	19,9	20,3	21,1	21,3	21,8	22,3	22,5	:	:	F
IRL	15,4	15,5	15,9	15,6	15,7	15,5	15,1	14,9	14,8	:	:	IRL
I	14,2	14,6	15,4	15,6	16,6	17,0	17,5	18,0	18,1	:	:	I
L	20,5	19,8	19,8	19,8	19,8	19,8	19,8	19,8 *	19,8 *	:	:	L
NL	18,0	18,2	18,6	18,7	19,4	19,8	20,5	21,3	21,3	:	:	NL
A	16,7	16,9	16,8	16,9	17,3	18,1	19,2	20,1	20,5	:	:	A
P	9,6	9,5	10,2	10,4	10,7	10,6	10,7	10,7 *	10,7 *	:	:	P
FIN	17,7	18,7	20,8	22,7	24,8	25,0	24,8	25,1	25,7	:	:	FIN
S	24,7	25,7	29,1	31,3	32,7	32,5	32,4	33,4	33,4 *	:	:	S
UK	19,0	17,9	18,8	19,8	19,9	19,9	19,9	19,7	19,7 *	:	:	UK

1J5CD

Further reading: National accounts ESA — detailed tables by branch, 1970–97.
Eurostat.

Consumption of gross rent, fuel and power. Volume indices. 1990 = 100

	1989	1990	1991	1992	1993	1994	1995	1996	1997	1998	1999	
EU-15	97,7 *	100,0 *|	105,0 *	106,6 *	109,0 *	110,7 *	113,4 *	116,9 *	119,6 *	:	:	EU-15
EUR-11	97,1 *	100,0 *|	106,0 *	108,0 *	110,5 *	112,6 *	115,9 *	119,9 *	121,5 *	:	:	EUR-11
B	97,6	100,0	103,9	105,1	106,7	107,7	109,9	113,4	113,6	:	:	B
DK	99,7	100,0	101,5	101,8	103,5	104,3	105,1	106,8	113,8 *	:	:	DK
D	96,4 *	100,0 *|	110,7 *	113,8 *	118,2 *	121,6 *	125,8 *	131,3 *	134,2 *	:	:	D
EL	98,1 *	100,0 *	102,5 *	103,8 *	104,3 *	103,2 *	104,1 *	107,3 *	109,0 *	:	:	EL
E	98,0 *	100,0 *	102,6 *	104,5 *	105,8 *	107,5 *	109,0 *	111,1 *	112,8 *	:	:	E
F	97,3	100,0	104,4	106,8	109,0	110,6	114,2	118,5	120,2	:	:	F
IRL	97,8	100,0	104,1	105,3	108,3	113,8	115,4	120,2	125,8	:	:	IRL
I	97,7	100,0	103,4	103,5	103,5	104,1	106,4	108,5	108,1	:	:	I
L	100,7 *	100,0 *	107,6 *	110,4 *	116,9 *	122,5 *	128,1 *	132,7 *	137,6 *	:	:	L
NL	96,4 *	100,0 *	104,1 *	105,5 *	108,9 *	110,8 *	113,9 *	117,9 *	119,3 *	:	:	NL
A	97,0 *	100,0 *	103,9 *	104,5 *	107,2 *	109,9 *	115,1 *	118,9 *	119,1 *	:	:	A
P	97,1	100,0	102,1	105,4	107,0	107,4	110,3	113,0	116,4	:	:	P
FIN	96,2	100,0	103,9	106,2	110,7	114,0	115,5	118,7	121,7	:	:	FIN
S	99,7 *	100,0 *	102,7 *	103,5 *	104,4 *	105,0 *	105,2 *	106,6 *	110,1 *	:	:	S
UK	99,7	100,0	101,6	101,9	104,3	104,9	105,4	107,4	114,5 *	:	:	UK

5A1HC

Further reading: National accounts ESA — detailed tables by branch, 1970–97.
Eurostat.

Consumption of clothing and footwear. Volume indices. 1990 = 100

	1989	1990	1991	1992	1993	1994	1995	1996	1997	1998	1999	
EU-15	96,7 *	100,0 *|	105,0 *	105,4 *	102,8 *	103,0 *	104,2 *	104,6 *	107,0 *	:	:	EU-15
EUR-11	96,3 *	100,0 *|	106,0 *	106,2 *	102,5 *	101,7 *	102,4 *	101,6 *	103,0 *	:	:	EUR-11
B	92,4	100,0	100,2	102,3	101,3	100,3	98,0	95,4	98,4	:	:	B
DK	97,3	100,0	100,9	96,3	98,0	106,1	109,5	117,5	125,2 *	:	:	DK
D	90,4 *	100,0 *|	116,6 *	118,4 *	118,5 *	114,6 *	115,0 *	114,9 *	113,5 *	:	:	D
EL	100,1 *	100,0 *	100,9 *	103,5 *	98,8 *	102,8 *	105,3 *	108,6 *	108,6 *	:	:	EL
E	97,3 *	100,0 *	102,8 *	103,8 *	96,3 *	96,6 *	97,0 *	98,0 *	100,9 *	:	:	E
F	98,3	100,0	98,7	97,5	95,1	92,7	90,5	89,9	91,3	:	:	F
IRL	101,3	100,0	103,7	105,8	112,7	124,6	137,5	154,2	183,2	:	:	IRL
I	100,9	100,0	103,4	103,7	95,4	98,1	101,5	98,1	100,7	:	:	I
L	99,5 *	100,0 *	101,9 *	104,6 *	110,8 *	116,1 *	121,4 *	125,7 *	130,4 *	:	:	L
NL	91,9 *	100,0 *	108,5 *	108,4 *	106,8 *	106,9 *	107,0 *	109,2 *	112,4 *	:	:	NL
A	98,0 *	100,0 *	100,2 *	97,8 *	94,2 *	90,6 *	86,0 *	86,6 *	86,0 *	:	:	A
P	96,3	100,0	106,2	106,9	106,0	108,0	109,7	112,5	115,8	:	:	P
FIN	101,2	100,0	93,8	80,7	75,5	75,6	80,6	81,6	84,5	:	:	FIN
S	97,4 *	100,0 *	103,2 *	96,8 *	90,2 *	87,2 *	85,1 *	84,8 *	87,5 *	:	:	S
UK	99,0	100,0	99,7	102,8	108,6	114,3	119,0	127,0	135,4 *	:	:	UK

1J5BC

Further reading: National accounts ESA — detailed tables by branch, 1970–97.
Eurostat.

Consumption of clothing and footwear in current prices as % of total consumption

	1989	1990	1991	1992	1993	1994	1995	1996	1997	1998	1999	
EU-15	7,6	7,6 |	7,5	7,3	7,0	6,8	6,6	6,5 *	6,4 *	:	:	EU-15
EUR-11	7,9	7,9 |	7,8	7,6	7,2	6,9	6,7	6,5 *	6,5 *	:	:	EUR-11
B	7,4	7,7	7,5	7,6	7,5	7,2	7,0	6,6	6,6	:	:	B
DK	5,5	5,5	5,5	5,2	5,2	5,3	5,2	5,4	5,4 *	:	:	DK
D	7,2	7,4 |	7,2	7,0	7,0	6,5	6,3	6,1	6,0	:	:	D
EL	9,3	9,0	11,7	11,5	10,6	10,6	10,8	10,8	10,5	:	:	EL
E	8,2	8,1	8,0	7,8	7,3	7,0	6,8	6,7	6,6	:	:	E
F	6,6	6,6	6,4	6,2	6,0	5,7	5,4	5,2	5,2	:	:	F
IRL	6,6	6,4	6,4	6,2	6,3	6,5	6,7	6,9	7,1	:	:	IRL
I	10,4	10,0	9,9	9,8	9,1	9,1	9,1	8,7	8,7	:	:	I
L	6,4	6,1	5,9	5,7	5,7	5,7	5,7	5,7 *	5,7 *	:	:	L
NL	7,1	7,2	7,3	7,0	6,8	6,5	6,1	6,0	5,9	:	:	NL
A	9,7	9,5	9,3	8,9	8,6	8,3	7,7	7,4	7,2	:	:	A
P	9,3	8,9	9,2	9,0	8,9	8,6	8,5	8,5 *	8,5 *	:	:	P
FIN	5,8	5,7	5,5	4,9	4,6	4,6	4,7	4,6	4,5	:	:	FIN
S	7,4	7,2	6,9	6,5	5,8	5,7	5,5	5,3	5,3 *	:	:	S
UK	6,2	6,2	6,0	5,9	6,0	6,0	6,0	5,9	5,9 *	:	:	UK

1J5BE

Further reading: National accounts ESA — detailed tables by branch, 1970–97.
Eurostat.

Clothing and footwear slowly decrease as a share of consumption. This is partially related to the low-salary textile exporting countries.

Consumption of furniture, furnishings and household equipment, including repairs, current operations and domestic services. Volume indices. 1990 = 100

	1989	1990	1991	1992	1993	1994	1995	1996	1997	1998	1999	
EU-15	97,0 *	100,0 *|	105,7 *	107,0 *	106,7 *	108,8 *	109,5 *	110,3 *	112,3 *	:	:	EU-15
EUR-11	96,1 *	100,0 *|	107,3 *	108,8 *	107,7 *	109,2 *	109,9 *	110,0 *	111,0 *	:	:	EUR-11
B	95,2	100,0	103,5	103,5	99,1	99,8	101,0	103,2	107,3	:	:	B
DK	101,9	100,0	101,4	99,9	104,0	107,9	105,4	111,7	119,1 *	:	:	DK
D	92,4 *	100,0 *|	119,7 *	125,3 *	126,5 *	127,5 *	124,5 *	123,7 *	121,8 *	:	:	D
EL	98,3 *	100,0 *	97,9 *	99,7 *	98,5 *	104,3 *	108,7 *	112,6 *	115,9 *	:	:	EL
E	95,9 *	100,0 *	103,8 *	105,7 *	102,7 *	103,2 *	106,6 *	107,2 *	111,0 *	:	:	E
F	99,4	100,0	99,0	97,7	97,1	97,9	99,2	100,1	101,0	:	:	F
IRL	107,8	100,0	102,7	100,7	107,1	116,6	123,4	132,6	147,2	:	:	IRL
I	97,4	100,0	104,7	104,9	101,1	104,3	106,8	104,8	106,7	:	:	I
L	93,8 *	100,0 *	106,2 *	109,0 *	115,4 *	121,0 *	126,5 *	131,0 *	135,8 *	:	:	L
NL	94,7 *	100,0 *	102,3 *	103,1 *	103,4 *	104,6 *	107,5 *	110,6 *	114,1 *	:	:	NL
A	94,9 *	100,0 *	100,8 *	104,1 *	105,6 *	109,1 *	109,9 *	112,7 *	113,1 *	:	:	A
P	95,3	100,0	106,1	109,4	107,3	108,6	110,0	112,8	116,1	:	:	P
FIN	103,5	100,0	92,4	84,0	79,2	79,8	84,3	89,2	94,4	:	:	FIN
S	98,1 *	100,0 *	99,9 *	92,7 *	89,0 *	89,5 *	90,7 *	88,1 *	90,9 *	:	:	S
UK	101,4	100,0	98,1	99,7	105,4	110,5	111,5	116,5	124,2 *	:	:	UK

Further reading: National accounts ESA — detailed tables by branch, 1970–97.
Eurostat.

1J5CC

Consumption of furniture, furnishings and household equipment, including repairs, current operations and domestic services at current prices as % of total consumption

	1989	1990	1991	1992	1993	1994	1995	1996	1997	1998	1999	
EU-15	8,0	8,0		8,0	7,9	7,8	7,8	7,6	7,5 *	7,4 *	:	:	EU-15
EUR-11	8,4	8,3		8,4	8,3	8,2	8,1	7,9	7,7 *	7,6 *	:	:	EUR-11
B	10,4	10,5	10,5	10,3	9,9	9,7	9,6	9,5	9,5	:	:	B
DK	6,5	6,4	6,4	6,2	6,3	6,1	5,9	6,0	6,0 *	:	:	DK
D	8,3	8,4		8,5	8,5	8,5	8,4	8,0	7,7	7,5	:	:	D
EL	8,4	8,2	7,0	6,8	6,4	6,5	6,5	6,5	6,4	:	:	EL
E	7,0	7,1	7,2	7,1	7,0	6,8	6,8	6,8	6,7	:	:	E
F	8,1	8,0	7,8	7,6	7,5	7,4	7,4	7,3	7,3	:	:	F
IRL	7,2	6,5	6,5	6,1	6,1	6,3	6,4	6,4	6,7	:	:	IRL
I	9,4	9,4	9,5	9,3	9,1	9,2	9,2	8,9	8,8	:	:	I
L	10,6	10,8	10,8	10,8	10,8	10,8	10,8	10,8 *	10,8 *	:	:	L
NL	7,4	7,4	7,3	7,1	7,0	6,8	6,8	6,8	6,7	:	:	NL
A	8,0	8,1	7,9	7,9	8,1	8,3	8,2	8,1	7,9	:	:	A
P	8,4	8,1	8,1	7,9	7,8	7,5	7,5	7,5 *	7,5 *	:	:	P
FIN	7,1	6,8	6,4	6,1	5,8	5,7	5,9	6,0	6,1	:	:	FIN
S	7,6	7,6	7,2	6,8	6,6	6,5	6,6	6,4	6,4 *	:	:	S
UK	6,7	6,6	6,5	6,5	6,6	6,6	6,5	6,5	6,5 *	:	:	UK

Further reading: National accounts ESA — detailed tables by branch, 1970–97.
Eurostat.

1J5CE

Consumption of personal transport equipment and its operations. Volume indices. 1990 = 100

	1989	1990	1991	1992	1993	1994	1995	1996	1997	1998	1999	
EU-15	:	: |	:	:	:	:	:	:	:	:	:	EU-15
EUR-11	:	: |	:	:	:	:	:	:	:	:	:	EUR-11
B	94,0 *	100,0 *	102,0 *	105,0 *	96,9 *	100,2 *	98,8 *	103,3 *	104,7 *	:	:	B
DK	99,5 *	100,0 *	101,6 *	103,4 *	104,3 *	140,2 *	135,8 *	142,1 *	:	:	:	DK
D	90,8 *	100,0 *|	125,7 *	126,0 *	114,3 *	117,3 *	120,4 *	126,1 *	127,3 *	:	:	D
EL	:	:	:	:	:	:	:	:	:	:	:	EL
E	:	:	:	:	:	:	:	:	:	:	:	E
F	98,6 *	100,0 *	97,2 *	99,1 *	94,5 *	99,1 *	101,2 *	104,8 *	101,0 *	:	:	F
IRL	93,0 *	100,0 *	96,0 *	103,2 *	101,5 *	114,4 *	121,0 *	132,6 *	145,0 *	:	:	IRL
I	98,4 *	100,0 *	99,2 *	104,8 *	92,6 *	94,3 *	96,0 *	98,7 *	112,2 *	:	:	I
L	:	:	:	:	:	:	:	:	:	:	:	L
NL	94,8 *	100,0 *	101,0 *	104,5 *	102,6 *	107,0 *	108,6 *	111,9 *	115,3 *	:	:	NL
A	:	:	:	:	:	:	:	:	:	:	:	A
P	:	:	:	:	:	:	:	:	:	:	:	P
FIN	:	:	:	:	:	:	:	:	:	:	:	FIN
S	109,7 *	100,0 *	98,8 *	90,4 *	85,6 *	90,2 *	91,6 *	92,6 *	:	:	:	S
UK	103,1 *	100,0 *	91,3 *	89,0 *	94,4 *	96,5 *	95,9 *	98,5 *	:	:	:	UK

1J5DB

Further reading: National accounts ESA — detailed tables by branch, 1970–97.
Eurostat.

Consumption of purchased transport and communications. Volume indices. 1990 = 100

	1989	1990	1991	1992	1993	1994	1995	1996	1997	1998	1999	
EU-15	:	: |	:	:	:	:	:	:	:	:	:	EU-15
EUR-11	:	: |	:	:	:	:	:	:	:	:	:	EUR-11
B	98,3	100,0	102,3	106,4	108,0	109,3	112,5	114,8	116,1	:	:	B
DK	103,0	100,0	101,8	104,4	105,2	115,0	127,4	119,6	:	:	:	DK
D	95,0 *	100,0 *|	116,8 *	118,8 *	124,8 *	127,4 *	131,6 *	133,6 *	140,3 *	:	:	D
EL	99,1 *	100,0 *	97,8 *	99,7 *	101,3 *	101,6 *	108,7 *	110,3 *	119,9 *	:	:	EL
E	:	:	:	:	:	:	:	:	:	:	:	E
F	96,4	100,0	101,9	104,7	104,4	105,5	105,6	111,7	117,7	:	:	F
IRL	96,2	100,0	103,1	109,3	114,4	126,1	136,0	149,4	165,9	:	:	IRL
I	96,8	100,0	105,8	109,4	113,2	117,7	125,2	132,9	139,3	:	:	I
L	:	:	:	:	:	:	:	:	:	:	:	L
NL	93,7 *	100,0 *	108,3 *	116,5 *	121,5 *	126,7 *	135,3 *	144,1 *	156,0 *	:	:	NL
A	93,5 *	100,0 *	106,6 *	114,0 *	120,5 *	129,1 *	134,6 *	141,0 *	154,4 *	:	:	A
P	95,0 *	100,0 *	106,0 *	108,1	112,0	116,0	120,4	:	:	:	:	P
FIN	97,5	100,0	98,0	98,6	102,0	102,5	114,0	126,5	146,6	:	:	FIN
S	94,7 *	100,0 *	98,8 *	103,9 *	100,1 *	103,9 *	108,0 *	113,5 *	:	:	:	S
UK	97,9	100,0	97,8	100,8	103,9	111,2	118,2	123,1	:	:	:	UK

1J5DC

Further reading: National accounts ESA — detailed tables by branch, 1970–97.
Eurostat.

For Ireland, Sweden and the United Kingdom, the purchased transports also include the package tours.

1

The development of transport and communications went along with price decreases in this field (cheaper air fares, cheaper computer networks, etc.). In the majority of the Member States their share in total consumption is greater than that of food and beverages (due among others to second cars, etc.).

Consumption of transport and communications at current prices as % of total consumption

	1989	1990	1991	1992	1993	1994	1995	1996	1997	1998	1999	
EU-15	15,5	15,4 |	15,4	15,3	14,9	15,2	15,2	15,5 *	15,6 *	:	:	EU-15
EUR-11	14,9	14,9 |	15,0	15,1	14,5	14,8	14,9	15,2 *	15,3 *	:	:	EUR-11
B	12,6	12,9	12,7	12,9	12,3	12,6	12,3	12,7	12,7	:	:	B
DK	15,7	15,4	15,4	15,3	15,0	17,9	18,0	17,9	17,9 *	:	:	DK
D	15,4	15,9 |	17,0	16,5	15,5	15,8	15,8	16,1	16,2	:	:	D
EL	13,3	14,1	12,0	12,6	12,3	10,7	10,6	10,8	10,9	:	:	EL
E	15,0	14,5	14,4	14,9	14,5	14,9	14,6	15,0	15,6	:	:	E
F	17,1	17,0	16,4	16,4	15,8	16,3	16,3	16,7	16,3	:	:	F
IRL	12,8	13,3	12,7	12,7	12,5	13,0	13,2	13,7	14,3	:	:	IRL
I	12,5	12,3	11,9	12,3	11,6	11,9	12,1	12,4	13,3	:	:	I
L	17,3	17,5	19,1	19,9	19,9	19,9	19,9	19,9 *	19,9 *	:	:	L
NL	12,6	12,9	12,8	13,1	12,9	13,3	13,3	13,7	13,8	:	:	NL
A	15,6	15,6	15,9	15,9	15,4	15,2	15,2	16,0	15,7	:	:	A
P	15,4	15,3	15,5	16,0	16,0	16,0	16,3	16,3 *	16,3 *	:	:	P
FIN	18,0	17,2	15,2	14,5	14,4	14,6	15,3	15,7	16,1	:	:	FIN
S	17,5	17,3	16,7	16,0	16,1	16,4	16,6	17,1	17,1 *	:	:	S
UK	18,0	17,9	17,2	16,9	17,1	17,2	17,0	17,1	17,1 *	:	:	UK

1J5DE

Further reading: National accounts ESA — detailed tables by branch, 1970–97.
Eurostat.

Consumption of transport and communications. Volume indices. 1990 = 100

	1989	1990	1991	1992	1993	1994	1995	1996	1997	1998	1999	
EU-15	97,4 *	100,0 *|	104,4 *	106,1 *	102,3 *	105,8 *	108,1 *	112,3 *	116,8 *	:	:	EU-15
EUR-11	96,0 *	100,0 *|	107,2 *	109,8 *	103,8 *	107,0 *	109,4 *	113,9 *	117,8 *	:	:	EUR-11
B	94,7	100,0	102,1	105,2	98,7	101,7	101,0	105,1	106,5	:	:	B
DK	100,5	100,0	101,7	103,8	104,6	133,4	133,9	136,0	145,0 *	:	:	DK
D	91,7 *	100,0 *|	123,6 *	124,3 *	116,6 *	119,6 *	122,9 *	127,7 *	130,2 *	:	:	D
EL	97,1 *	100,0 *	106,6 *	112,2 *	108,7 *	98,6 *	103,1 *	107,1 *	113,1 *	:	:	EL
E	100,6 *	100,0 *	100,0 *	105,3 *	97,7 *	101,9 *	101,2 *	106,9 *	115,6 *	:	:	E
F	98,1	100,0	98,3	100,3	96,8	100,5	102,2	106,4	104,8	:	:	F
IRL	94,1	100,0	98,4	105,2	105,8	118,3	126,0	138,2	152,0	:	:	IRL
I	98,0	100,0	100,7	105,8	97,3	99,6	102,6	106,4	118,3	:	:	I
L	94,1 *	100,0 *	115,6 *	118,7 *	125,7 *	131,7 *	137,7 *	142,6 *	147,9 *	:	:	L
NL	94,5 *	100,0 *	102,9 *	107,5 *	107,4 *	112,0 *	115,4 *	120,1 *	125,9 *	:	:	NL
A	95,0 *	100,0 *	106,6 *	109,6 *	107,2 *	106,0 *	106,8 *	111,5 *	110,6 *	:	:	A
P	95,9	100,0	106,4	114,2	111,2	114,2	116,6	119,5	123,1	:	:	P
FIN	105,8	100,0	87,8	80,7	76,0	79,2	84,8	91,1	99,1	:	:	FIN
S	105,1 *	100,0 *	98,8 *	94,6 *	90,2 *	94,5 *	96,8 *	99,2 *	102,4 *	:	:	S
UK	101,5	100,0	93,2	92,5	97,2	100,9	102,5	105,8	112,8 *	:	:	UK

5A1HB

Further reading: National accounts ESA — detailed tables by branch, 1970–97.
Eurostat.

Medical care consumption has risen slightly in all countries. But the national health services' share of total consumption varies greatly. Denmark, Ireland and the United Kingdom have very low shares due to their public health services. Greece, Spain and Italy have mixed private and public healthcare systems. In other countries, private contributions are the basis of health services.

Consumption of medical care. Volume indices. 1990 = 100

	1989	1990	1991	1992	1993	1994	1995	1996	1997	1998	1999	
EU-15	93,5 *	100,0 *|	106,1 *	114,0 *	116,9 *	118,5 *	122,0 *	126,0 *	130,3 *	:	:	EU-15
EUR-11	93,4 *	100,0 *|	106,2 *	114,4 *	117,3 *	118,7 *	122,3 *	126,4 *	130,7 *	:	:	EUR-11
B	101,7	100,0	106,8	110,0	109,8	109,5	112,6	115,8	115,8	:	:	B
DK	97,4	100,0	96,1	96,8	104,6	106,7	111,1	118,0	125,8 *	:	:	DK
D	92,8 *	100,0 *|	107,5 *	121,3 *	124,8 *	126,3 *	132,2 *	138,1 *	144,5 *	:	:	D
EL	100,3 *	100,0 *	95,5 *	101,2 *	103,7 *	129,6 *	128,7 *	125,1 *	126,1 *	:	:	EL
E	89,6 *	100,0 *	111,7 *	120,9 *	127,8 *	134,2 *	148,4 *	154,7 *	158,0 *	:	:	E
F	92,6	100,0	105,5	109,9	114,2	115,6	116,7	118,4	120,4	:	:	F
IRL	97,7	100,0	103,4	106,9	109,2	111,0	116,9	120,8	127,4	:	:	IRL
I	92,0	100,0	104,0	107,0	106,6	107,2	106,6	110,0	112,5	:	:	I
L	95,1 *	100,0 *	104,5 *	107,2 *	113,6 *	119,0 *	124,4 *	128,9 *	133,6 *	:	:	L
NL	96,8 *	100,0 *	103,6 *	107,7 *	110,0 *	111,7 *	113,1 *	115,9 *	118,8 *	:	:	NL
A	95,2 *	100,0 *	103,5 *	107,6 *	110,7 *	113,2 *	113,7 *	116,6 *	131,2 *	:	:	A
P	96,2	100,0	101,7	105,7	108,8	112,1	113,8	116,6	120,1	:	:	P
FIN	97,3	100,0	101,0	100,4	98,4	97,0	102,1	108,3	114,0	:	:	FIN
S	95,8 *	100,0 *	110,0 *	115,3 *	121,2 *	125,7 *	129,6 *	132,8 *	137,1 *	:	:	S
UK	96,0	100,0	106,3	107,8	107,2	109,4	111,8	111,8	119,2 *	:	:	UK

1J5DA

Further reading: National accounts ESA — detailed tables by branch, 1970–97.
Eurostat.

Consumption of medical care at current prices as % of total consumption

	1989	1990	1991	1992	1993	1994	1995	1996	1997	1998	1999	
EU-15	7,6	7,8		8,2	8,7	9,0	9,2	9,5	9,4 *	9,1 *	:	:	EU-15
EUR-11	9,3	9,5		9,8	10,3	10,7	11,0	11,2	11,2 *	11,1 *	:	:	EUR-11
B	10,7	10,7	11,1	11,5	11,9	11,8	12,3	12,5	12,1	:	:	B
DK	2,1	2,2	2,1	2,1	2,2	2,1	2,1	2,1	2,1 *	:	:	DK
D	14,2	14,2		14,4	15,3	15,3	15,9	16,4	16,8	16,7	:	:	D
EL	3,4	3,4	4,3	4,5	5,0	5,9	5,7	5,5	5,3	:	:	EL
E	3,4	3,6	3,9	4,1	4,3	4,4	4,7	4,8	4,6	:	:	E
F	9,3	9,5	9,7	10,0	10,3	10,3	10,3	10,2	10,3	:	:	F
IRL	3,6	3,7	3,8	4,0	4,1	4,0	4,1	4,0	4,0	:	:	IRL
I	6,3	6,7	6,7	6,8	7,1	6,9	6,5	6,6	6,7	:	:	I
L	7,5	7,5	7,3	7,3	7,3	7,3	7,3	7,3 *	7,3 *	:	:	L
NL	12,9	13,0	13,1	13,3	13,4	13,2	13,1	12,9	12,8	:	:	NL
A	4,3	4,4	4,4	4,7	4,9	5,1	5,2	5,3	5,9	:	:	A
P	4,5	4,4	4,5	4,7	5,0	5,1	5,2	5,2 *	5,2 *	:	:	P
FIN	4,3	4,6	4,9	5,2	5,3	5,3	5,4	5,5	5,7	:	:	FIN
S	1,7	1,7	1,9	2,1	2,3	2,4	2,5	2,6	2,6 *	:	:	S
UK	1,3	1,4	1,6	1,7	1,6	1,7	1,7	1,6	1,6 *	:	:	UK

1J5DD

Further reading: National accounts ESA — detailed tables by branch, 1970–97.
Eurostat.

1

Consumption of education, books and newspapers. Volume indices. 1990 = 100

	1989	1990	1991	1992	1993	1994	1995	1996	1997	1998	1999	
EU-15	:	:	:	:	:	:	:	:	:	:	:	EU-15
EUR-11	:	:	:	:	:	:	:	:	:	:	:	EUR-11
B	:	:	:	:	:	:	:	:	:	:	:	B
DK	98,9 *	100,0 *	98,9 *	97,9 *	96,5 *	98,3 *	104,6 *	111,0 *		:	:	DK
D	:	:	:	:	:	:	:	:	:	:	:	D
EL	104,4 *	100,0 *	97,9 *	99,6 *	98,8 *	105,4 *	108,8 *	111,2 *	101,1 *	:	:	EL
E	:	:	:	:	:	:	:	:	:	:	:	E
F	101,2 *	100,0 *	98,8 *	99,0 *	97,5 *	99,3 *	97,7 *	97,9 *	98,2 *	:	:	F
IRL	97,1 *	100,0 *	103,6 *	112,0 *	117,6 *	120,8 *	130,6 *	137,9 *	144,9 *	:	:	IRL
I	98,9	100,0	99,9	101,6	100,3	100,8	100,3	101,9 *	103,6 *	:	:	I
L	:	:	:	:	:	:	:	:	:	:	:	L
NL	95,8 *	100,0 *	103,0 *	102,6 *	102,3 *	102,4 *	100,6 *	102,6 *	105,3 *	:	:	NL
A	94,2 *	100,0 *	102,3 *	103,5 *	108,2 *	106,0 *	104,0 *	103,3 *	107,2 *	:	:	A
P	92,8 *	100,0 *	113,2 *	130,6 *	132,8 *	142,7 *	152,4 *	:	:	:	:	P
FIN	100,1 *	100,0 *	99,1 *	93,6 *	97,6 *	95,7 *	98,6 *	98,8 *	101,7 *	:	:	FIN
S	101,5 *	100,0 *	98,0 *	96,9 *	89,8 *	86,6 *	83,3 *	78,3 *	:	:	:	S
UK	93,7 *	100,0 *	103,0 *	105,6 *	107,8 *	111,9 *	113,3 *	111,2 *	:	:	:	UK

Further reading: National accounts ESA — detailed tables by branch, 1970–97.
Eurostat.

1J5EA

Consumption of education, books and newspapers at current prices as % of total consumption

	1989	1990	1991	1992	1993	1994	1995	1996	1997	1998	1999	
EU-15	:	:	:	:	:	:	:	:	:	:	:	EU-15
EUR-11	:	:	:	:	:	:	:	:	:	:	:	EUR-11
B	:	:	:	:	:	:	:	:	:	:	:	B
DK	3,2	3,3	3,3	3,3	3,2	3,1	3,3 *	3,4 *	:	:	:	DK
D	:	:	:	:	:	:	:	:	:	:	:	D
EL	1,8	1,8	2,6	2,8	2,8	2,9	3,0	2,9	2,7	:	:	EL
E	:	:	:	:	:	:	:	:	:	:	:	E
F	2,1	2,1	2,0	2,1	2,0	2,0	2,0 *	1,9 *	1,9 *	:	:	F
IRL	5,3	5,4	5,5	5,8	6,0	5,8	6,0	6,0	6,0	:	:	IRL
I	2,5	2,5	2,4	2,4	2,4	2,3	2,3	2,3 *	2,3 *	:	:	I
L	:	:	:	:	:	:	:	:	:	:	:	L
NL	2,7	2,7	2,7	2,6	2,6	2,6	2,5	2,5	2,5	:	:	NL
A	1,3	1,3	1,4	1,3	1,4	1,4	1,4	1,4	1,4	:	:	A
P	1,6	1,6	1,8	2,2 *	2,5 *	2,7 *	3,0 *	:	:	:	:	P
FIN	2,4	2,5	2,6	2,6	2,7	2,5	2,6	2,5	2,5	:	:	FIN
S	1,8	1,8	1,7	1,9	1,8	1,8	1,7	1,6	:	:	:	S
UK	2,1	2,3	2,5	2,6	2,7	2,7	2,7	2,7	:	:	:	UK

Further reading: National accounts ESA — detailed tables by branch, 1970–97.
Eurostat.

1J5ED

Expenditure on recreation, entertainment and education varies considerably from one country to another, due partly to public spending patterns.

The share of hotels, restaurants and tourism in total household consumption has risen in nearly every country.

Consumption of entertainment, recreational and cultural services, excluding hotels and restaurants. Volume indices. 1990 = 100

	1989	1990	1991	1992	1993	1994	1995	1996	1997	1998	1999	
EU-15	:	:	:	:	:	:	:	:	:	:	:	EU-15
EUR-11	:	:	:	:	:	:	:	:	:	:	:	EUR-11
B	95,8	100,0	100,0	99,3	101,1	111,5	112,7	106,3	107,9	:	:	B
DK	94,9	100,0	105,5	112,0	115,7	122,3	127,1	139,5	:	:	:	DK
D	:	:	:	:	:	:	:	:	:	:	:	D
EL	95,5 *	100,0 *	124,5 *	127,3 *	124,3 *	141,8 *	147,6 *	154,6 *	170,9 *	:	:	EL
E	:	:	:	:	:	:	:	:	:	:	:	E
F	97,2	100,0	103,1	114,7	116,5	117,8	119,2	120,9	121,9	:	:	F
IRL	94,4	100,0	108,1	110,7	114,0	116,7	117,9	119,7	124,3	:	:	IRL
I	94,5	100,0	98,6	98,8	102,2	101,6	108,3	108,8	112,3	:	:	I
L	:	:	:	:	:	:	:	:	:	:	:	L
NL	96,6 *	100,0 *	104,1 *	107,3 *	111,9 *	114,6 *	118,1 *	120,9 *	123,3 *	:	:	NL
A	90,8 *	100,0 *	107,8 *	112,2 *	110,9 *	110,5 *	117,3 *	122,4 *	118,0 *	:	:	A
P	90,0	100,0	105,1	116,0	111,3	117,3	117,1	:	:	:	:	P
FIN	94,8	100,0	100,1	98,0	102,9	102,6	105,9	110,1	114,6	:	:	FIN
S	101,1 *	100,0 *	102,3 *	108,7 *	108,6 *	111,0 *	117,9 *	122,1 *	:	:	:	S
UK	99,9	100,0	96,0	92,2	94,8	97,3	111,5	111,2	:	:	:	UK

Further reading: National accounts ESA — detailed tables by branch, 1970–97.
Eurostat.

1J5EB

Consumption of entertainment, recreational and cultural services, excluding hotels, restaurants and cafés, at current prices as % of total consumption

	1989	1990	1991	1992	1993	1994	1995	1996	1997	1998	1999	
EU-15	:	:	:	:	:	:	:	:	:	:	:	EU-15
EUR-11	:	:	:	:	:	:	:	:	:	:	:	EUR-11
B	1,7	1,7	1,7	1,6	1,7	1,8	1,8	1,7	1,7	:	:	B
DK	2,6	2,7	2,8	2,9	3,0	3,0	3,1	3,3	:	:	:	DK
D	:	:	:	:	:	:	:	:	:	:	:	D
EL	1,6	1,6	2,0	1,9	1,7	1,8	1,9	2,0	2,1	:	:	EL
E	:	:	:	:	:	:	:	:	:	:	:	E
F	2,0	2,0	2,0	2,2	2,3	2,3	2,3	2,3	2,4	:	:	F
IRL	2,2	2,3	2,5	2,5	2,5	2,5	2,4	2,3	2,3	:	:	IRL
I	2,4	2,5	2,4	2,6	2,7	2,6	2,6	2,6	2,5	:	:	I
L	:	:	:	:	:	:	:	:	:	:	:	L
NL	3,1	3,1	3,0	3,1	3,2	3,2	3,3	3,3	3,3	:	:	NL
A	3,8	3,9	4,1	4,3	4,3	4,5	4,6	4,7	4,5	:	:	A
P	2,5	2,7	2,7	2,8	2,9	3,0	3,0	:	:	:	:	P
FIN	3,1	3,3	3,3	3,5	3,6	3,5	3,5	3,6	3,6	:	:	FIN
S	3,2	3,2	3,1	3,5	3,4	3,4	3,5	3,6	:	:	:	S
UK	3,3	3,3	3,3	3,2	3,2	3,3	3,7	3,6	:	:	:	UK

Further reading: National accounts ESA — detailed tables by branch, 1970–97.
Eurostat.

1J5EF

Percentage of households living in houses. 1996

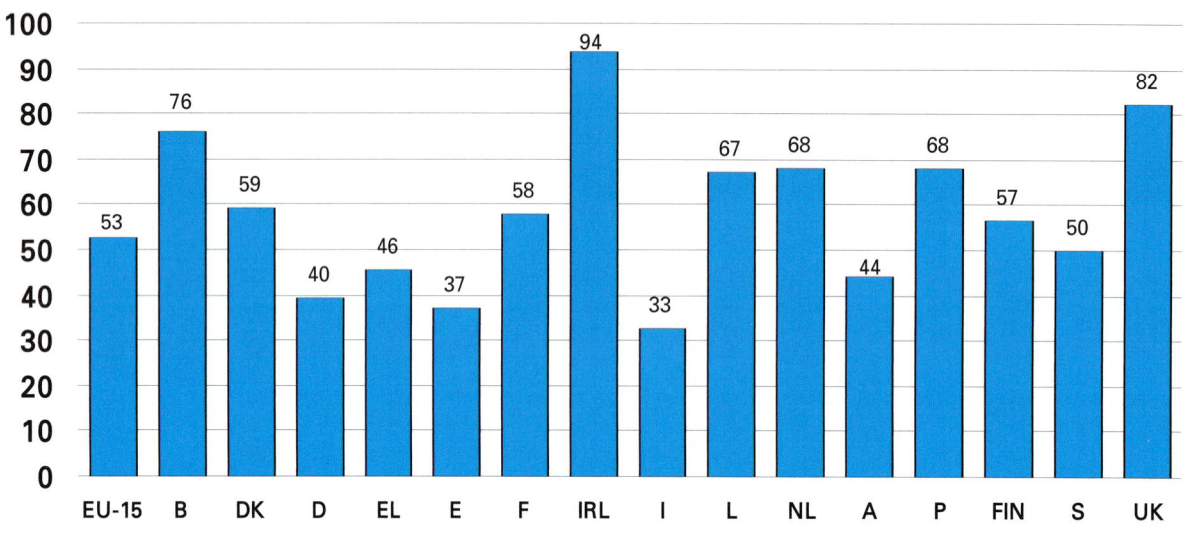

2H1AA

Further reading: Living conditions in Europe, statistical pocket book, 2000 Edition.
New Cronos Theme 3 Housing.

Source: European Community household panel.

Percentage of households owning their accommodation. 1996

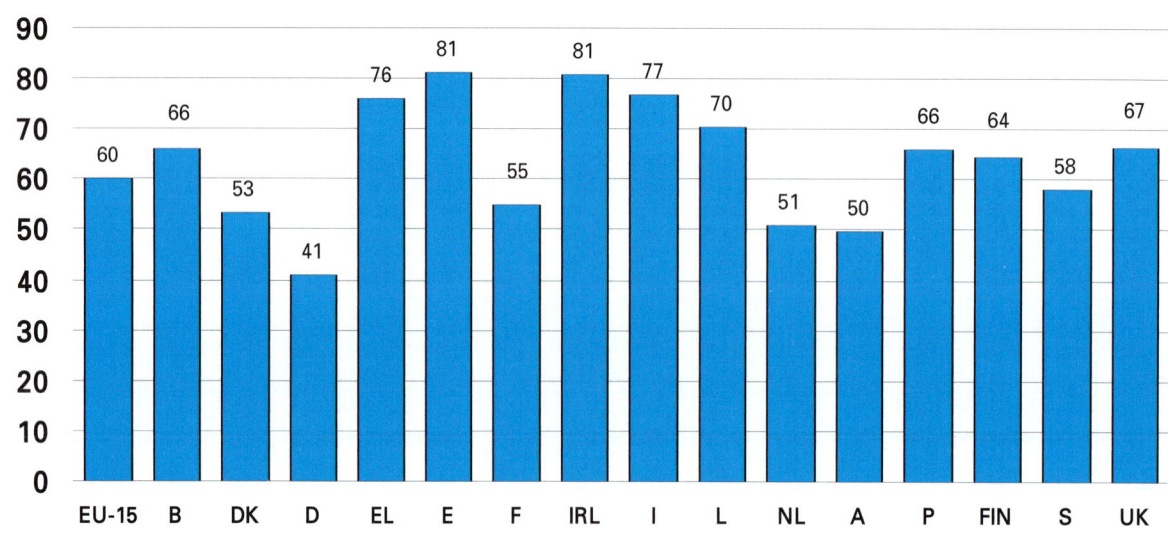

2H1BB

Further reading: Living conditions in Europe, statistical pocket book, 2000 Edition.
New Cronos Theme 3 Housing.

Source: European Community household panel.

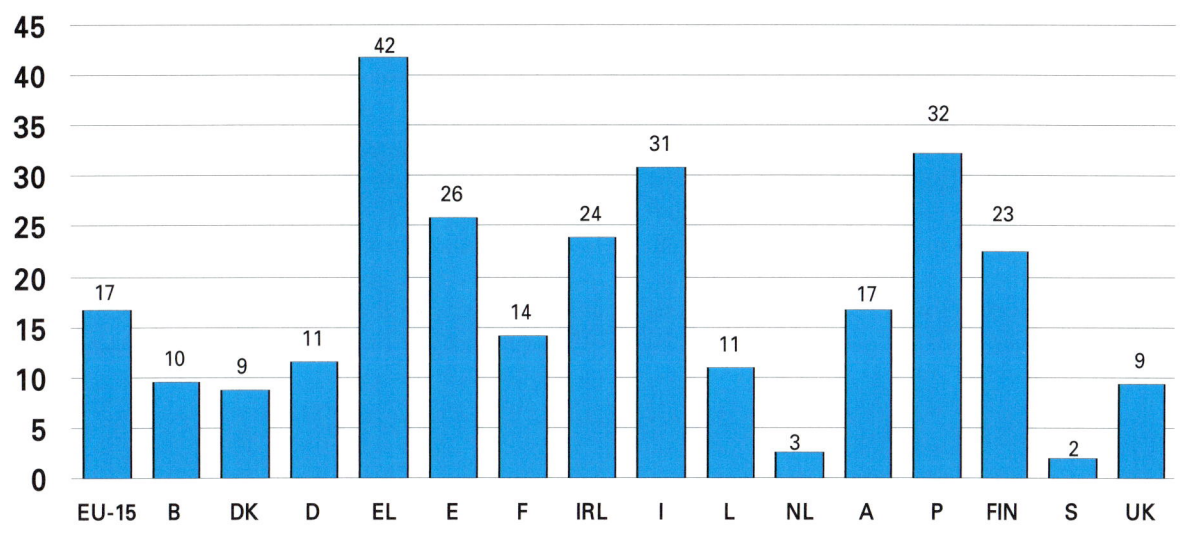

Percentage of the population that is living in overcrowded conditions, i.e. more than one person per room. 1996

Further reading: Living conditions in Europe, statistical pocket book, 2000 Edition. New Cronos Theme 3 Housing.

Source: European Community household panel.

Percentage of households lacking at least one of three basic amenities. 1996

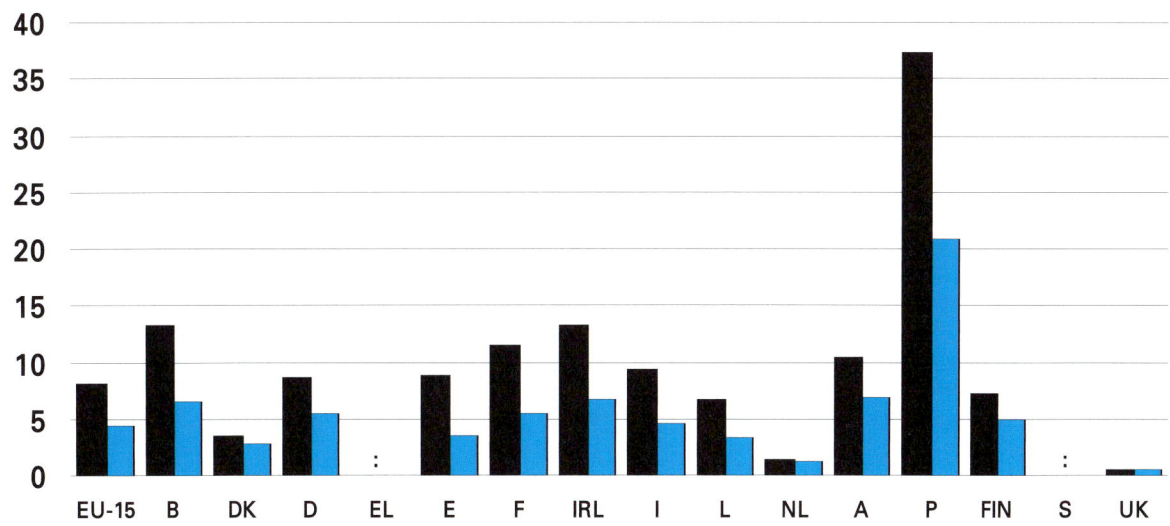

Black: elderly households; colour: all households.

Further reading: Living conditions in Europe, statistical pocket book, 2000 Edition. New Cronos Theme 3 Housing.

The three basic amenities are bath/shower, indoor flushing toilet and hot running water. *Source:* European Community household panel.

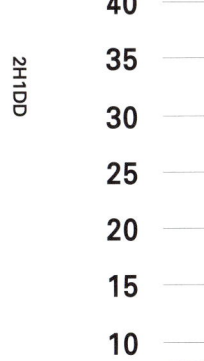

One of the main criteria for describing the well-being of a person is the monetary income available to the household in which the person is living. The income measure refers to the equivalised total net monetary income of households in the reference year. Differences in household size and composition are taken into account by considering equivalised incomes.

The income data are based on the third wave of the European Community household panel (1996) but refer to the year prior to the survey. In order to take account of differences in household size and composition in income levels, the household's total income is divided by its 'equivalent size', computed using the modified OECD equivalence scale.

This scale gives a weight of 1.0 to the first adult, 0.5 to the second and each subsequent adult and 0.3 to children aged less than 14 in the household.

The mean equivalised net annual income was approximately 14 000 PPS in around half of the Member States. A north/south divide remains with income levels in Greece, Spain, Italy and Portugal between 7 700 and 10 100 PPS.

In most countries, around 70 % of equivalised income arises from work (employment and self-employment), around 25–30 % from pensions and other social transfers, and the remainder from capital of other private income.

Mean equivalised net income per person

	EU-15	EUR-11	B	DK	D	EL	E	F
In national currency	:	:	583 809	136 782	30 183	1 986 494	1 227 846	98 170
In PPS	12 343	:	13 857	14 043	14 052	8 400	9 102	13 496

Source: European Community household panel, 1996. Eurostat.

1WP1A

Mean equivalised net income per person

	IRL	I	L	NL	A	P	FIN	S	UK
In national currency	7 699	17 131	897 062	30 182	218 381	1 101 984	:	:	10 023
In PPS	10 949	10 101	21 992	13 414	14 377	7 722	:	:	13 721

I: In national currency = 1 000 ITL.
Source: European Community household panel, 1996. Eurostat.

1WP1A

Equivalised income components. %

	EU-15	EUR-11	B	DK	D	EL	E	F
Income from work	70	:	61	69	68	72	71	:
Private income	4	:	6	3	4	7	3	:
Old-age/survivors pensions	18	:	19	12	20	19	18	:
Other social transfers	8	:	14	17	7	2	7	:

Source: European Community household panel, 1996. Eurostat.

1WP1B

Equivalised income components. %

	IRL	I	L	NL	A	P	FIN	S	UK
Income from work	75	69	69	70	68	76	:	:	72
Private income	2	4	4	2	3	3	:	:	4
Old-age/survivors pensions	10	24	18	15	18	16	:	:	12
Other social transfers	13	3	9	12	11	5	:	:	11

Source: European Community household panel, 1996. Eurostat.

1WP1B

Although social transfers constitute only 26 % of equivalised income, 73 % of EU citizens benefit from such transfers, either directly or indirectly, i.e. through other household members. The percentage varies from only 50 % in Greece and Italy to around 90 % in Belgium, Ireland and Portugal.

EU-wide, 13 % of the population rely on social transfers as their only source of income. The proportion ranges from 4 % in France to 19 % in Belgium.

Income inequality is measured as the share ratio S80/S20. Persons are ranked according to their net equivalised income and then divided into 5 groups of equal size known as quintiles. The share ratio S80/S20 represents the income share available to the top 20 % to that of the bottom 20 %.

At EU-level, the richest 20 % of the population have 5.2 times more income than the 20 % of the population that is least well-off. The differences are smallest in Denmark (2.9) and Austria (4.0).

Percentage of persons in households that receive social transfers

	EU-15	EUR-11	B	DK	D	EL	E	F
Any social transfer	73	:	89	85	78	50	58	79
As main source of income	30	:	36	29	30	25	30	:
As only source of income	13	:	19	14	15	13	12	4

Source: European Community household panel, 1996. Eurostat. Social transfers include old-age/survivors pensions; benefits related to unemployment, family, sickness, invalidity, education and other housing allowances and social assistance.

Percentage of persons in households that receive social transfers

	IRL	I	L	NL	A	P	FIN	S	UK
Any social transfer	90	51	86	81	86	89	:	:	85
As main source of income	33	28	27	30	27	23	:	:	33
As only source of income	16	17	11	15	8	13	:	:	14

Source: European Community household panel, 1996. Eurostat. Social transfers include old-age/survivors pensions; benefits related to unemployment, family, sickness, invalidity, education and other housing allowances and social assistance.

Share ratio S80/S20 — measuring inequality in the income distribution

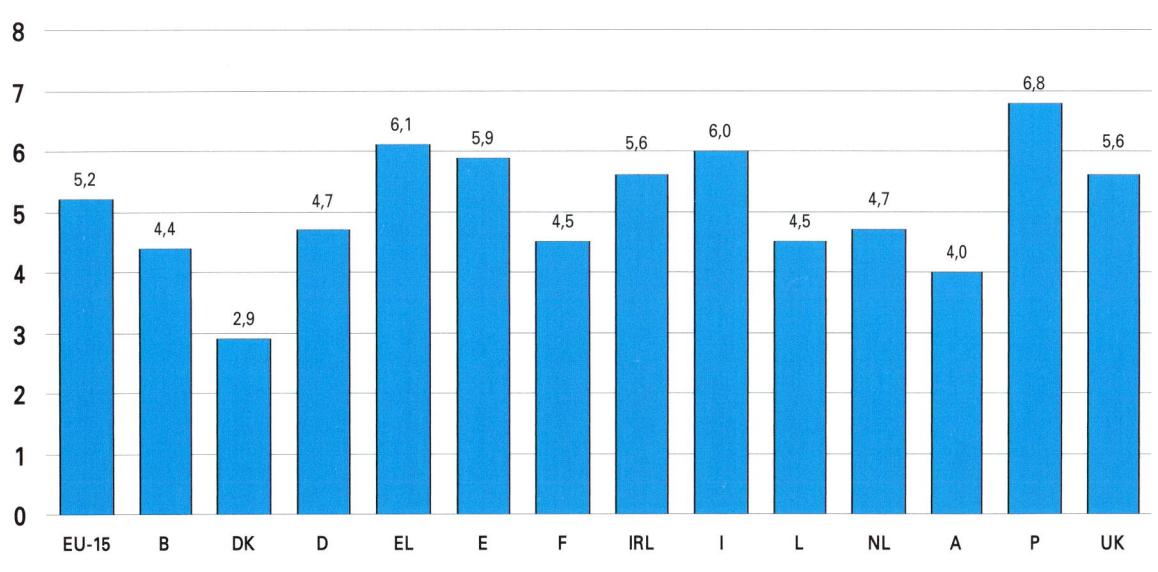

Source: European Community household panel, 1996. Eurostat.

eurostat

Where is your nearest Data Shop? Addresses at the end of the book

171

The extent of low income is measured in terms of the proportion of the population with equivalised income below 60 % of the median equivalised income in each country.

Around 17 % of EU citizens had an equivalised income that was less than 60 % of the median for their country in 1996. The proportion of 'poor' people was relatively high (over 20 %) in Greece and Portugal and lowest in Denmark, Luxembourg, the Netherlands and Austria (11–13 %).

The proportion of children (aged under 16) living in a household with low income is higher (21 %) than for the population as a whole. Children in Spain, Ireland and the United Kingdom seem to be particularly worse off compared with adults. In Denmark they are considerably less likely to live in low-income households.

Percentage of persons living in low-income households

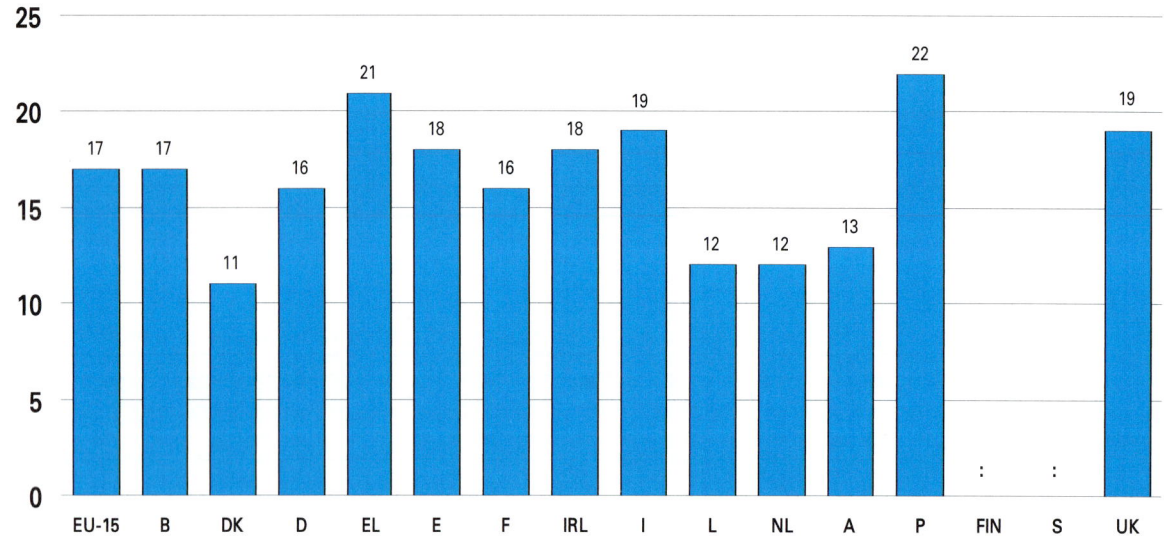

Source: European Community household panel, 1996. Eurostat.

3WP3A

Percentage of children (aged under 16) in low-income households

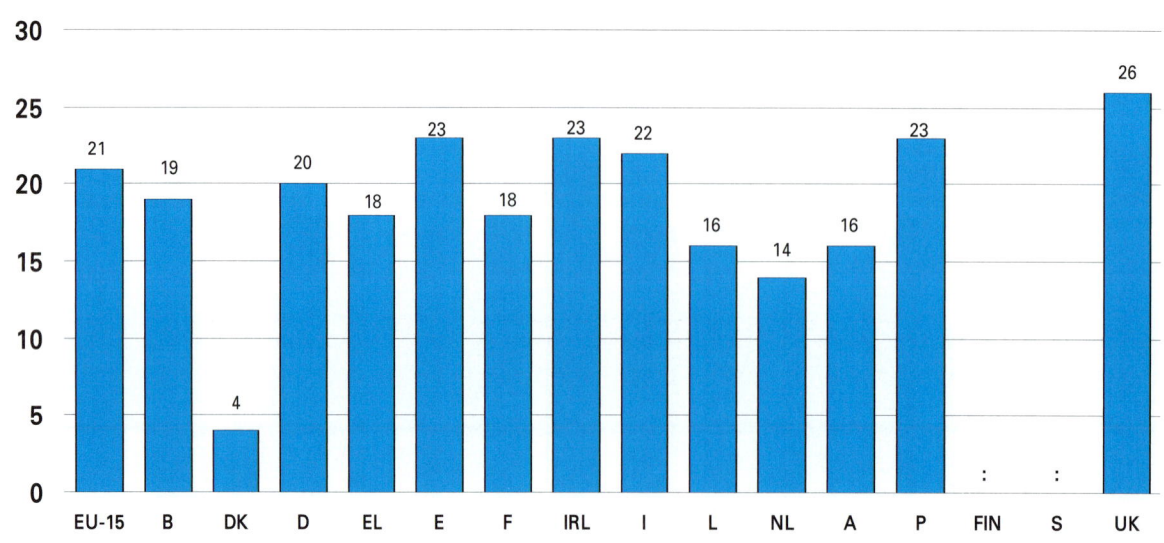

Source: European Community household panel, 1996. Eurostat.

3WP3B

Poverty tends to be more prevalent among 'lone parents with dependent children', 'adults living alone' and 'two adults with three or more dependent children'. Rates for older people are generally higher than their younger counterparts. More than one in three old people living alone in Greece and the United Kingdom (and one in two in Portugal) can be classified as having 'low income'.

Percentage of persons living in low-income households by household type. 1996

	EU-15	EUR-11	B	DK	D	EL	E	F
One adult aged 16–64	22	:	17	22	21	23	17	26
One adult aged 65 +	25	:	28	28	21	36	10	25
Lone parent with dependent children	36	:	27	6	49	25	30	31
Two adults aged 16–64 without dependent children	11	:	12	10	11	16	15	11

Source: European Community household panel, 1996. Eurostat.

4WP4A

Percentage of persons living in low-income households by household type. 1996

	IRL	I	L	NL	A	P	FIN	S	UK
One adult aged 16–64	31	18	12	25	20	40	:	:	23
One adult aged 65 +	28	25	14	9	27	51	:	:	36
Lone parent with dependent children	51	18	:	37	35	32	:	:	52
Two adults aged 16–64 without dependent children	10	9	11	5	8	22	:	:	8

Source: European Community household panel, 1996. Eurostat.

4WP4A

Percentage of persons living in low-income households by household type. 1996

	EU-15	EUR-11	B	DK	D	EL	E	F
Two adults at least one of them aged 65 + without dependent children	16	:	19	21	12	35	19	14
Two adults with one dependent child	12	:	12	4	10	11	15	8
Two adults with three or more dependent children	25	:	24	4	22	16	32	19
Total	17	:	17	11	16	21	18	16

Source: European Community household panel, 1996. Eurostat.

4WP4B

Percentage of persons living in low-income households by household type. 1996

	IRL	I	L	NL	A	P	FIN	S	UK
Two adults at least one of them aged 65 + without dependent children	11	12	12	9	13	37	:	:	22
Two adults with one dependent child	11	15	6	10	10	15	:	:	12
Two adults with three or more dependent children	25	34	22	17	26	36	:	:	25
Total	18	19	12	12	13	22	:	:	19

Source: European Community household panel, 1996. Eurostat.

4WP4B

eurostat

the land and the environment

2

Key features   179

Total area and population density: 179

1 000 sq kms   179

Inhabitants per sq km   179

National area and population compared to EU-15:   179

National area as % of EU-15 area   179

National population as % of EU-15 population   179

Population density. 1997   180

Woodland. 1 000 ha   181

Subsidies received per hectare of agricultural land. Average 1993 to 1997. EUR 1 000 per 1 km². NUTS 2   182

Inland waters as % of total national area. 1996   183

Total inland water abstraction: 184

Million m³ per year   184

m³ per person   184

Groundwater abstraction as % of total water abstraction   184

Wastewater treatment plants: 184

Total number   184

Capacity, 1 000 i.e.   184

Population connected to sewerage, %   184

Wastewater treatment plants with secondary or tertiary treatment: 185

Total number (secondary treatment)   185

Capacity, 1 000 i.e. (secondary treatment)   185

Total number (tertiary treatment)   185

Capacity, 1 000 i.e. (tertiary treatment)   185

Utilised agricultural area. 1 000 ha   186

Breakdown of the utilised agricultural area. 1 000 ha: 186

Arable land   186

Permanent grassland   186

Land under permanent crops   186

Emissions and pollutants   187

Emissions of volatile organic compounds. 1 000 t of HC   187

Emissions of volatile organic compounds. kg of HC per person   187

Emissions of carbon monoxide. 1 000 t of CO   188

Emissions of carbon monoxide. kg of CO per person   188

Emissions of carbon dioxide. Million t of CO_2 189

Emissions of carbon dioxide. Tonnes per person   189

Emissions of sulphur oxides. SO_2, 1 000 t   190

Emissions of sulphur oxides. SO_2, kg per person   190

Emissions of nitrogen oxides. NO_2, 1 000 t   191

Emissions of nitrogen oxides. NO_2, kg per person   191

Fertilisers, pesticides   192

Consumption of commercial fertilisers. 1 000 t   192

Total   192

Phosphate   192

Nitrogen   193

Potash   193

Sales of pesticides   194

Sales of fungicides for use in agriculture in tonnes of active ingredients   194

Sales of herbicides for use in agriculture in tonnes of active ingredients   194

Sales of insecticides for use in agriculture in tonnes of active ingredients   194

Sales of other pesticides for use in agriculture in tonnes of active ingredients   194

Waste and recycling   195

Waste generation by sector. 1 000 t. 1995:   195

Agriculture   195

Mining and quarrying   195

Manufacturing   195

Energy production   195

Municipal waste   195

Other sectors   195

Municipal waste. kg per person   196

Recovery rates. %:   196

Paper and board   196

Glass   196

Total area and population density

	1 000 sq kms	Inhabitants per sq km					
	1999	1985	1990	1995	1998	1999	
EU-15	3 191	112	114	117	118	118	EU-15
B	31	323	327	332	334	335	B
DK	43	119	119	121	123	124	DK
D	357	218	222	229	230	230	D
EL	132	75	77	79	80	80	EL
E	505	76	77	78	78	78	E
F	544	102	104	107	108	109	F
IRL	69	51	51	52	54	55	IRL
I	301	188	188	190	191	191	I
L	3	142	148	158	165	167	L
NL	41	353	364	377	383	385	NL
A	84	90	92	96	96	96	A
P	92	109	108	108	108	109	P
FIN	338	14	15	15	15	15	FIN
S	411	20	21	21	22	22	S
UK	242	234	238	242	245	246	UK
IS	103	2	2	3	3	3	IS
NO	324	13	13	13	14	14	NO
EEA	3 618	100	102	104	105	105	EEA
CH	41	157	163	171	172	173	CH
US	9 373	25	26	28	29	29	US
CA	9 971	3	3	3	3	3	CA
JP	378	320	327	332	334	334	JP

Further reading: European social statistics. Demography. Edition 2000. Eurostat.

D: includes in all years data on the former GDR. F: metropolitan France.

2A2AA

2A2AB

National area and population compared to EU-15

	National area as % of EU-15 area	National population as % of EU-15 population					
	1999	1985	1990	1995	1998	1999	
EU-15	100	100,0	100,0	100,0	100,0	100,0	EU-15
B	1	2,7	2,7	2,7	2,7	2,7	B
DK	1	1,4	1,4	1,4	1,4	1,4	DK
D	11	21,7	21,7	21,9	21,9	21,8	D
EL	4	2,8	2,8	2,8	2,8	2,8	EL
E	16	10,7	10,7	10,5	10,5	10,5	E
F	17	15,4	15,6	15,6	15,7	15,7	F
IRL	2	1,0	1,0	1,0	1,0	1,0	IRL
I	9	15,8	15,6	15,4	15,4	15,3	I
L	0	0,1	0,1	0,1	0,1	0,1	L
NL	1	4,0	4,1	4,2	4,2	4,2	NL
A	3	2,1	2,1	2,2	2,2	2,2	A
P	3	2,8	2,7	2,7	2,7	2,7	P
FIN	11	1,4	1,4	1,4	1,4	1,4	FIN
S	13	2,3	2,3	2,4	2,4	2,4	S
UK	8	15,8	15,8	15,7	15,8	15,8	UK
IS	3	0,1	0,1	0,1	0,1	0,1	IS
NO	10	1,2	1,2	1,2	1,2	1,2	NO
EEA	113	101,2	101,2	101,3	101,3	101,3	EEA
CH	1	1,8	1,8	1,9	1,9	1,9	CH
US	294	66,1	68,2	70,4	71,8	72,7	US
CA	312	7,2	7,6	7,9	8,1	8,2	CA
JP	12	33,8	34,0	33,8	33,7	33,6	JP

2A2AC

2A2AD

Further reading: European social statistics. Demography. Edition 2000. Eurostat.

D: includes in all years data on the former GDR.

Need more data on this topic? Ask your Data Shop

2

EU total land area has changed little over the last 10 years. German unification and land reclamation in the Netherlands are the most important changes. EU-15 population has increased relatively slowly; as a result, overall population density has been very stable. However, there are big differences in population density between the Member States. Overall density ranges from Finland's 15 per km² to 376 per km² in the Netherlands, with even bigger differences between urban and rural areas in Member States.

Population density. 1997

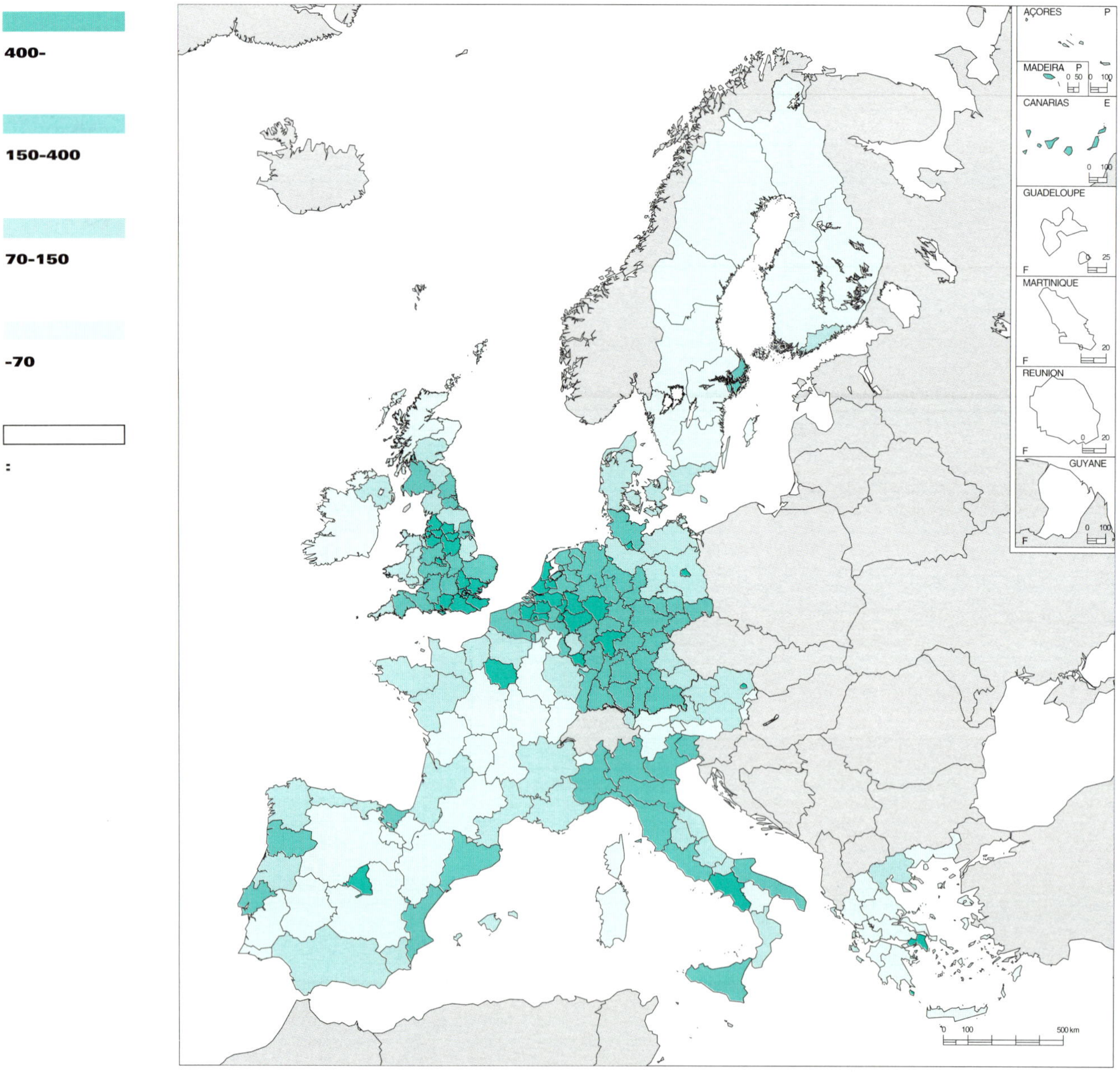

400-

150-400

70-150

-70

:

2A2AE

ACORES   P

MADEIRA   P
0 50   0   100

CANARIAS   E

0   100

GUADELOUPE

F   0   25

MARTINIQUE

F   0   20

REUNION

0   20

GUYANE

F   0   100

0   100   500 km

Further reading: Demographic statistics, 2000. Eurostat. Regions, statistical yearbook, 1999. Eurostat.

NUTS 2. NUTS 1: IRL.

Woodland. 1 000 ha

2B2AA

	1989	1990	1991	1992	1993	1994	1995	1996	1997	1998	1999	
EU-15	:	:	:	:	:	:	:	:	:	:	:	EU-15
EUR-11	:	:	:	:	:	:	:	:	:	:	:	EUR-11
B	617	617	617	617	617	617	617	617	617	:	:	B
DK	493	445	445	445	445	445	445	445	445	445	445	DK
D	:	:	:	:	10 454	:	:	:	10 491	:	:	D
EL	2 951	2 951	2 940	2 940	2 940	2 940	2 940	:	:	:	:	EL
E	12 511	15 807	15 858	15 915	15 915	15 915	15 915	15 915	15 915	15 915	:	E
F	14 790	14 820	14 849	14 870	14 944	15 015	15 042	15 069	15 095	15 123	15 190	F
IRL	:	:	:	:	:	:	327	:	:	:	:	IRL
I	6 420	6 434	:	:	:	:	:	:	:	:	:	I
L	89	89	89	89	89	89	88	88	88	88	88	L
NL	330	330	330	330	330	330	330	330	330	330	330	NL
A	3 191	3 229	3 229	3 229	3 245	3 245	3 289	3 289	3 274	3 274	:	A
P	3 108	3 108	3 108	3 108	3 108	3 108	3 108	3 108	3 108	3 324	3 324	P
FIN	23 186	23 186	23 186	23 186	23 186	23 186	23 186	:	:	:	:	FIN
S	22 535	22 535	22 535	22 323	22 323	22 323	22 323	22 323	22 323	:	:	S
UK	2 297	2 297	2 425	2 438	2 430	:	:	:	:	:	:	UK
IS	:	:	:	:	:	:	:	:	:	:	:	IS
NO	:	:	:	:	:	:	:	:	:	:	:	NO
CH	:	:	:	:	:	:	:	:	:	:	:	CH

Further reading: Agriculture statistics: quarterly bulletin, 2000. Eurostat.

eurostat

Subsidies received per hectare of agricultural land. Average 1993 to 1997. EUR 1 000 per 1 km². NUTS 2

2B2AG

30-78

20-30

12-20

5-12

:

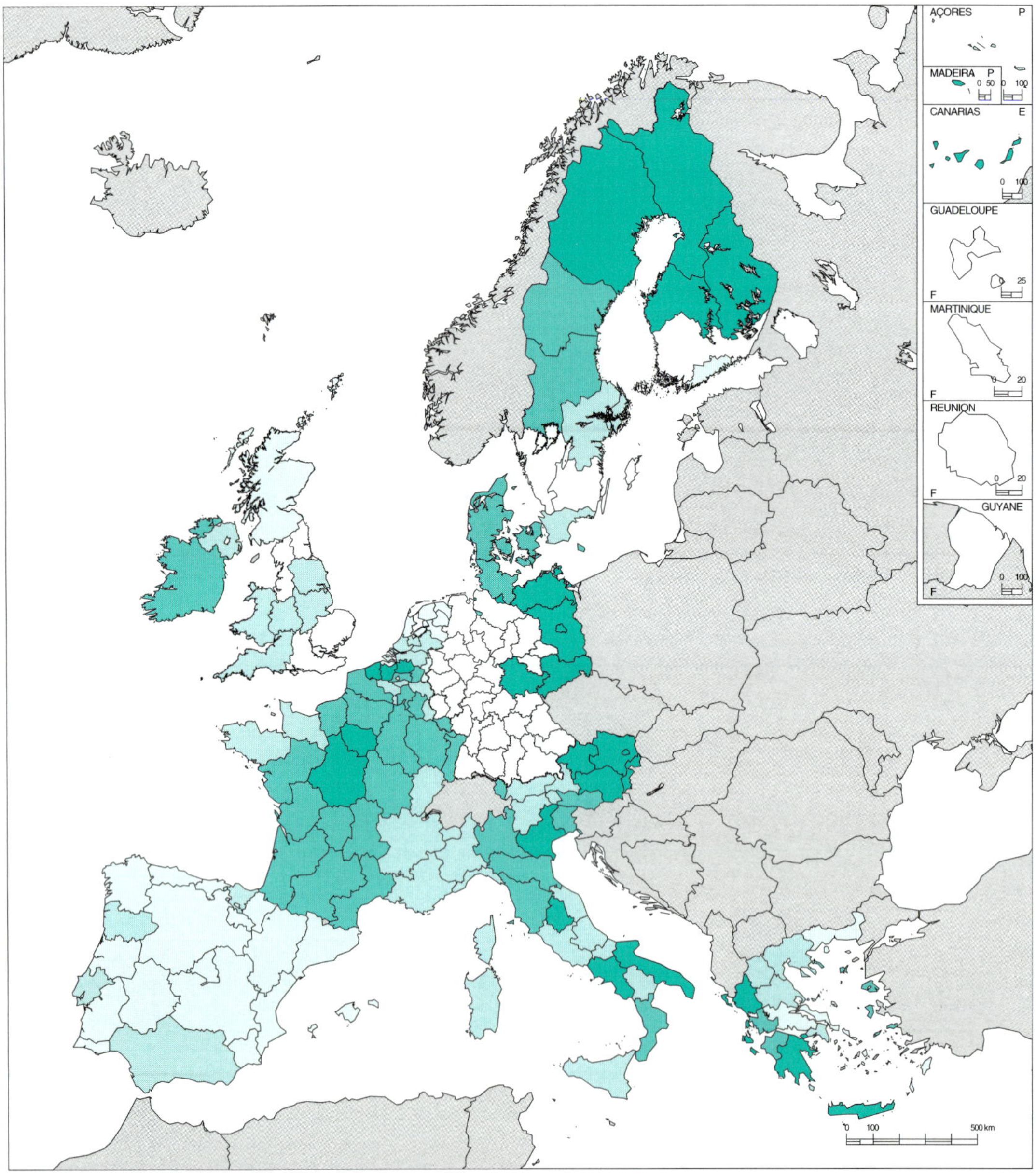

AÇORES P

MADEIRA P
0 50 0 100

CANARIAS E
0 100

GUADELOUPE
F 25

MARTINIQUE
F 20

REUNION
F 20

GUYANE
F 0 100

0 100   500 km

Further reading: Regions, statistical yearbook, 2000. Eurostat.

B, I, FIN: 1992–96. E, UK: 1991–95. NL: 1989–93. EL: 1989–90, 1992–94.
NUTS 2. NUTS 1: D, IRL, UK.

Water resources, abstraction and water supply data are compiled from a mixture of sources. Renewable water resources, according to the OECD definition, are the long-term freshwater balance of a country, calculated as precipitation minus evaporation and transpiration plus inflows of water from neighbouring countries. Abstraction is water removed from any source permanently or temporarily. Mine and drainage water is included. Supply is delivery of water to final users plus net abstraction of water for own final use.

More data on this in Eurostat's database

This domain contains data on air pollution, water, waste and environmental expenditure.

Sectorial indicators are also included (transport, agriculture, forestry). It also presents data on land use, global climate change, wildlife, public opinion and nuclear energy.

➤ ➤ ➤ **DOMAIN MILIEU IN DATABASE NEW CRONOS**

Inland waters as % of total national area. 1996

2B4AB

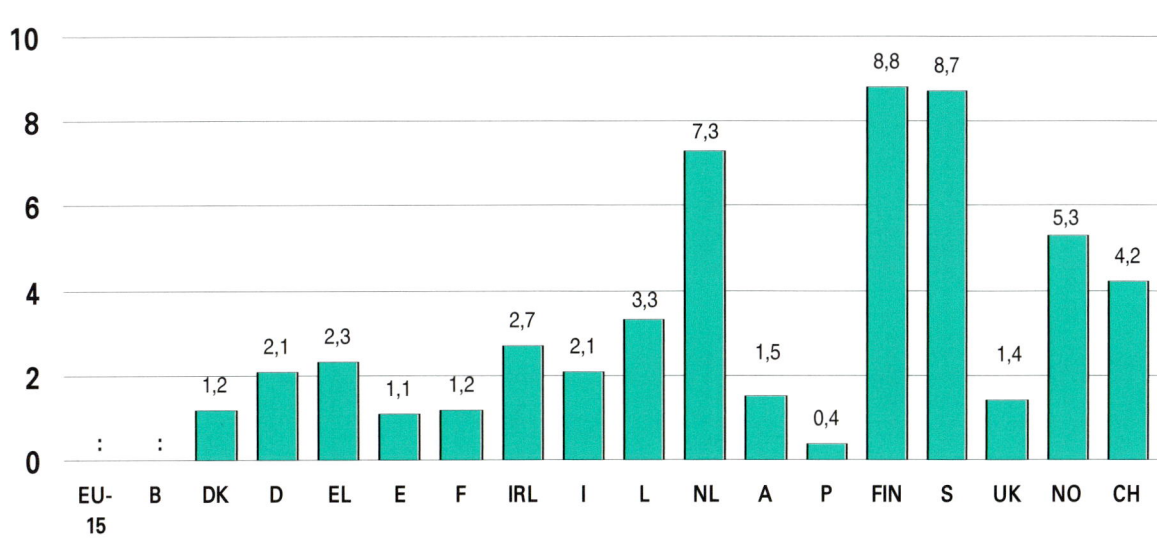

eurostat

Need longer time series? Ask your Data Shop

EUROSTAT YEARBOOK 2001
183

Total inland water abstraction

	Million m³ per year			m³ per person			Groundwater abstraction as % of total water abstraction			
	1985	1990	1995	1985	1990	1995	1985	1990	1995	
EU-15	:	:	:	:	:	:	:	:	:	EU-15
B	:	:	8 148	:	:	804	:	:	8,0	B
DK	1 705	1 200	887	334	234	170	100,0	:	100,0	DK
D	:	:	43 374	:	:	532	:	:	18,0	D
EL	:	:	:	:	:	:	:	:	:	EL
E	46 250	33 289	33 288	1 206	858	850	12,0	17,0	17,0	E
F	34 878	38 287	40 641	632	677	700	18,0	16,0	15,0	F
IRL	:	:	1 176	:	:	327	:	:	19,0	IRL
I	52 000	56 200	:	919	991	:	23,0	:	:	I
L	67	47	57	183	124	140	67,0	46,0	51,0	L
NL	9 348	7 800	:	647	524	:	12,0	13,0	:	NL
A	2 120	2 516	2 250	280	327	280	53,0	66,0	61,0	A
P	:	7 288	:	:	735	:	:	42,0	:	P
FIN	4 000	2 347	2 430	817	472	477	8,0	10,0	10,0	FIN
S	2 970	2 968	2 709	356	348	307	21,0	21,0	23,0	S
UK	12 947	14 237	12 118	229	248	207	20,0	19,0	22,0	UK
IS	103	:	164	:	:	:	93,0	:	96,0	IS
NO	2 025	:	1 100	427	:	614	20,0	:	12,0	NO
EEA	:	:	:	:	:	:	:	:	:	EEA
CH	2 646	2 665	2 596	488	:	253	36,0	35,0	34,0	CH
US	:	:	:	410	399	376	:	:	:	US
CA	:	:	:	:	:	:	:	:	:	CA
JP	:	:	:	:	:	:	:	:	:	JP

UK: England and Wales only.

Wastewater treatment plants

	Total number		Capacity, 1 000 i.e.		Population connected to sewerage, %		
	1990	1995	1990	1995	1990	1995	
EU-15	:	:	:	:	:	:	EU-15
B	:	323	:	5 878	:	60	B
DK	1 948	1 675	13 000	13 100	86	87	DK
D	:	10 273	:	155 311	89	92	D
EL	:	99	:	:	:	55	EL
E	:	1 754	:	:	48	48	E
F	9 936	:	68 400	:	77	81	F
IRL	524	:	:	:	66	:	IRL
I	5 295	:	:	:	:	:	I
L	300	:	789	:	:	88	L
NL	473	423	23 730	24 388	95	98	NL
A	:	1 230	:	17 365	72	77	A
P	324	:	:	:	55	:	P
FIN	475	545	:	:	76	77	FIN
S	1 305	1 273	:	:	94	93	S
UK	6 330	6 197	:	:	97	98	UK
IS	:	25	:	:	90	90	IS
NO	2 145	2 216	4 106	5 227	77	80	NO
EEA	:	:	:	:	:	:	EEA
CH	949	:	13 200	:	90	94	CH
US	:	:	:	:	:	:	US
CA	:	:	:	:	:	91	CA
JP	:	:	:	:	:	:	JP

3B5IC

3B5ID

3B5IE

3B5JA

3B5JB

3B5JD

Wastewater treatment plants cover primary removal of gross solids; secondary removal of organic material by bacteria under aerobic or anaerobic conditions; and tertiary removal of nutrients, phosphorus and nitrogen by chemical or biological treatment. Capacity is measured by biochemical oxygen demand (BOD) or inhabitant equivalents (IE). An inhabitant equivalent corresponds to the amount of daily discharged oxygen-demanding materials of which oxygen consumption in biodegradation equals average oxygen demand of the daily amount of waste water from one inhabitant.

Wastewater treatment plants with secondary or tertiary treatment

	Total number (secondary treatment)		Capacity, 1 000 i.e. (secondary treatment)		Total number (tertiary treatment)		Capacity, 1 000 i.e. (tertiary treatment)		
	1990	1995	1990	1995	1990	1995	1990	1995	
EU-15	:	:	:	:	:	:	:	:	EU-15
B	:	312	:	5 249	:	16	:	731	B
DK	723	538	:	:	236	485	:	:	DK
D	:	5 160	:	19 484	:	3 810	:	129 732	D
EL	73	64	:	:	:	21	:	:	EL
E	:	1 208	:	:	:	29	:	:	E
F	9 328	:	60 900	:	:	:	:	:	F
IRL	289	:	:	:	17	:	:	:	IRL
I	:	:	:	:	:	:	:	:	I
L	68	83	614	835	2	21	130	:	L
NL	410	275	21 196	11 550	48	144	2 386	12 808	NL
A	:	1 168	:	17 108	:	:	:	:	A
P	:	:	:	:	:	:	:	:	P
FIN	:	:	:	:	:	:	:	:	FIN
S	372	361	:	:	914	893	:	:	S
UK	:	4 304	:	:	:	1 133	:	:	UK
IS	:	:	:	:	:	:	:	:	IS
NO	123	125	63	70	937	950	2 842	3 588	NO
EEA	:	:	:	:	:	:	:	:	EEA
CH	440	:	:	:	509	:	:	:	CH
US	:	:	:	:	:	:	:	:	US
CA	A	:	:	:	:	:	:	:	CA
JP	:	:	:	:	:	:	:	:	JP

3B5JE 3B5JF 3B5JG 3B5JH

Utilised agricultural area is all agricultural land in use, whether arable or permanently under grass or crops. Utilised agricultural area tends to decrease because of the urban pressure and forest development. Arable land has gone up (especially cereals and oilseeds) while the permanent crops and grassland (which occupy the land for more than five years) have been reduced. Distinction between permanent grassland, wooded area and heath is rather difficult to make. This explains partly the differences among the sources.

Utilised agricultural area. 1 000 ha

	1989	1990	1991	1992	1993	1994	1995	1996	1997	1998	1999	
EU-15	:	144 304	141 741	140 991	140 619	138 557	138 058	:	:	:	:	EU-15
EUR-11	:	114 473	112 640	111 979	112 133	111 475	111 298	109 758	109 596	109 859	:	EUR-11
B	1 387	1 384	1 375	1 354	1 371	1 370	1 386	1 390	1 383	1 391	1 394	B
DK	2 785	2 788	2 770	2 756	2 722	2 712	2 721	2 732	2 764	2 706	2 684	DK
D	:	17 869	17 136	16 950	17 162	17 308	17 344	17 335	17 327	17 389	17 152	D
EL	5 207	5 180	5 169	5 181	5 162	5 116	5 116	5 109	:	:	:	EL
E	30 633	30 625	30 054	30 000	29 756	29 597	29 864	29 694	29 382	29 361	29 175	E
F	30 706	30 589	30 441	30 317	30 129	30 084	30 092	30 034	30 169	30 150	29 937	F
IRL	4 676	4 536	4 444	4 415	4 406	4 393	4 388	4 341	4 432	4 415	4 418	IRL
I	17 215	17 294	16 946	16 792	17 409	16 795	16 501	15 284	15 256	15 564	:	I
L	126	127	126	126	127	127	127	126	127	127	127	L
NL	2 013	2 012	1 981	1 975	1 977	1 971	1 981	1 975	1 954	1 961	1 962	NL
A	3 503	3 458	3 477	3 469	3 449	3 450	3 430	3 429	3 423	3 497	3 410	A
P	4 029	4 019	4 121	4 053	4 054	4 062	4 024	4 004	3 994	3 812	3 939	P
FIN	2 468	2 560	2 539	2 528	2 293	2 318	2 161	2 144	2 150	2 192	2 201	FIN
S	3 425	3 416	3 358	3 336	3 362	3 370	3 063	3 122	3 109	3 107	3 071	S
UK	18 563	18 447	17 804	17 739	17 240	15 884	15 859	:	:	:	:	UK
IS	:	:	:	:	:	:	:	:	:	:	:	IS
NO	:	:	:	:	:	:	1 026	1 031	1 039	1 046	1 038	NO
CH	:	:	:	:	:	:	:	:	:	:	:	CH

2B5AA

Further reading: Agriculture statistics: quarterly bulletin, 2000. Eurostat.

Breakdown of the utilised agricultural area. 1 000 ha

	Arable land			Permanent grassland			Land under permanent crops			
	1989	1994	1999	1989	1994	1999	1989	1994	1999	
EU-15	77 285	75 732	:	55 185	51 317	:	:	11 144	:	EU-15
EUR-11	62 848	62 243	:	40 792	38 874	37 946	:	10 010	:	EUR-11
B	736	934	854	615	407	515	15	19	21	B
DK	2 555	2 510	2 508	219	194	171	11	8	5	DK
D	11 949	11 805	11 821	5 664	5 271	5 114	:	210	208	D
EL	2 358	2 250	3 870	1 789	1 789	:	1 060	1 077	1 108	EL
E	15 512	13 562	14 006	10 243	11 321	10 315	4 878	4 675	4 812	E
F	17 700	18 056	18 193	11 555	10 612	10 386	1 217	1 195	1 154	F
IRL	802	1 095	1 076	3 872	3 295	3 339	2	2	3	IRL
I	8 917	9 760	:	4 883	3 895	4 419	3 325	3 024	:	I
L	56	57	62	69	68	64	1	1	1	L
NL	903	899	970	1 067	1 012	926	37	33	33	NL
A	1 442	1 403	1 385	1 970	1 952	1 943	74	76	73	A
P	2 381	2 373	2 243	838	888	903	780	772	767	P
FIN	2 451	2 299	2 177	15	16	21	2	3	3	FIN
S	2 853	2 780	2 696	568	587	372	4	3	3	S
UK	6 671	5 949	5 796	11 817	9 873	10 023	59	46	39	UK
IS	:	:	:	:	:	:	:	:	:	IS
NO	:	:	883	:	:	150	:	:	3	NO
CH	:	:	:	:	:	:	:	:	:	CH

2B5AG   2B5AH   2B5AI

Further reading: Agriculture statistics: quarterly bulletin, 2000. Eurostat.

2D4AA

Emissions of volatile organic compounds. 1 000 t of HC

	1989	1990	1991	1992	1993	1994	1995	1996	1997	1998	1999	
EU-15	:	15 384	:	14 506	:	:	:	12 847	:	:	:	EU-15
B	:	338	:	354	345	316	302	324	:	:	:	B
DK	176	160	:	151	142	146	141	136	149		:	DK
D	3 187	3 194	:	2 537	2 311	2 175	1 981	1 877	1 807	:	:	D
EL	:	374	:	379	381	390	398	410	:	:	:	EL
E	1 099	1 133	:	1 210	1 199	1 199	1 162	:	:	:	:	E
F	:	2 911	:	2 820	2 687	2 653	2 574	2 450	:	:	:	F
IRL	:	197	:	199	202	175	179	178	:	:	:	IRL
I	2 518	2 498	:	2 590	:	:	:	:	:	:	:	I
L	:	20	:	:	18	19	18	18	18	:	:	L
NL	479	500	:	436	403	388	367	355	333	:	:	NL
A	482	474	:	420	408	397	391	384	:	:	:	A
P	207	218	:	230	227	223	:	:	:	:	:	P
FIN	:	209	:	171	162	158	152	182	:	:	:	FIN
S	:	527	:	502	:	:	:	447	418	:	:	S
UK	2 686	2 632	:	2 489	2 375	2 331	2 200	2 111	:	:	:	UK
IS	13	13	:	14	14	14	12	12	10	:	:	IS
NO	284	310	:	331	347	358	370	368	359	:	:	NO
EEA	:	:	:	:	:	:	:	:	:	:	:	EEA
CH	298	292	:	256	239	226	211	203	195	:	:	CH

2D4AB

Emissions of volatile organic compounds. kg of HC per person

	1989	1990	1991	1992	1993	1994	1995	1996	1997	1998	1999	
EU-15	:	42	:	40	:	:	:	34	:	:	:	EU-15
B	:	34	:	35	34	31	30	32	:	:	:	B
DK	34	31	:	29	27	28	27	26	28	:	:	DK
D	41	40	:	32	29	27	24	23	22	:	:	D
EL	:	37	:	37	37	37	38	39	:	:	:	EL
E	28	29	:	31	31	31	30	:	:	:	:	E
F	:	51	:	49	47	46	44	42	:	:	:	F
IRL	:	56	:	56	57	49	50	49	:	:	:	IRL
I	44	44	:	46	:	:	:	:	:	:	:	I
L	:	53	:		46	47	44	44	43	:	:	L
NL	32	34	:	29	26	25	24	23	21	:	:	NL
A	63	62	:	53	51	50	49	48	:	:	:	A
P	21	22	:	23	23	23	:	:	:	:	:	P
FIN	:	42	:	34	32	31	30	35	:	:	:	FIN
S		62	:	58	:	:	:	51	47	:	:	S
UK	47	46	:	43	41	40	38	36	:	:	:	UK
IS	50	50	:	54	52	54	45	45	36	:	:	IS
NO	67	73	:	78	81	83	85	84	82	:	:	NO
EEA	:	:	:	:	:	:	:	:	:	:	:	EEA
CH	45	44	:	37	35	32	30	29	28	:	:	CH

Need an update for this indicator? Ask your Data Shop

Emissions of carbon monoxide. 1 000 t of CO

	1989	1990	1991	1992	1993	1994	1995	1996	1997	1998	1999	
EU-15	:	60 307	:	56 127	:	:	:	47 556	:	:	:	EU-15
B	:	1 446	:	1 615	1 539	1 479	1 434	1 434	:	:	:	B
DK	979	705	:	683	638	624	595	598	557	:	:	DK
D	11 481	11 164	:	8 377	7 643	7 183	6 885	6 717	6 374	:	:	D
EL	:	1 338	:	1 304	1 288	1 296	1 317	1 339	:	:	:	EL
E	4 873	4 752	:	4 787	4 802	4 645	4 372	:	:	:	:	E
F	7 575	10 450	:	10 045	9 576	8 887	8 514	8 253	:	:	:	F
IRL	:	431	:	403	416	333	344	297	:	:	:	IRL
I	9 037	8 905	:	9 089	:	:	:	:	:	:	:	I
L		171	:	:	219	145	105	101	82	:	:	L
NL	1 162	1 197	:	978	959	906	909	886	826	:	:	NL
A	1 376	1 286	:	1 185	1 158	1 133	1 055	993	:	:	:	A
P	:	1 086	:	1 151	1 128	1 092	:	:	:	:	:	P
FIN	:	556	:	477	457	443	436	461	:	:	:	FIN
S	:	1 217	:	1 182	1 154	1 148	1 094	1 085	968	:	:	S
UK	16 473	15 602	:	14 632	13 370	12 514	11 524	10 839	:	:	:	UK
IS	57	58	:	61	60	60	49	50	39	:	:	IS
NO	867	856	:	782	781	766	728	695	656	:	:	NO
CH	764	707	:	620	578	579	510	490	469	:	:	CH

2D4AC

B: Wallony only.

Emissions of carbon monoxide. kg of CO per person

	1989	1990	1991	1992	1993	1994	1995	1996	1997	1998	1999	
EU-15	:	166	:	153	:	:	:	128	:	:	:	EU-15
B	:	145	:	161	153	146	142	141	:	:	:	B
DK	191	137	:	132	123	120	114	114	106	:	:	DK
D	146	141	:	104	94	88	84	82	78	:	:	D
EL	:	132	:	127	124	125	126	128	:	:	:	EL
E	126	122	:	123	123	119	112	:	:	:	:	E
F	135	185	:	176	166	154	147	142	:	:	:	F
IRL		123	:	114	117	93	96	82	:	:	:	IRL
I	160	157	:	160	:	:	:	:	:	:	:	I
L	:	451	:	:	554	362	258	245	196	:	:	L
NL	79	80	:	65	63	59	59	57	53	:	:	NL
A	180	167	:	151	145	141	131	123	:	:	:	A
P	:	109	:	117	114	110	:	:	:	:	:	P
FIN	:	112	:	95	90	87	85	90	:	:	:	FIN
S	:	143	:	137	133	131	124	123	109	:	:	S
UK	288	272	:	253	230	215	197	185	:	:	:	UK
IS	226	229	:	234	228	227	185	186	144	:	:	IS
NO	205	2 025	:	183	182	177	167	159	149	:	:	NO
EEA	:	:	:	:	:	:	:	:	:	:	:	EEA
CH	115	106	:	91	84	83	73	59	66	:	:	CH

2D4AD

B: Wallony only.

Non-methane volatile organic compounds (NMVOCs) include all hydrocarbons except methane. NMVOC emissions from industrial processes, solvent use and fuel combustion in motor vehicles are particularly important but the reliability of such estimates is variable.

As statistics on air pollution emissions are based on complex estimation and modelling procedures, results are subject to several sources of uncertainty. However, these statistics still give useful information, particularly on trends for a single country.

Emissions of carbon dioxide. Million t of CO_2

	1989	1990	1991	1992	1993	1994	1995	1996	1997	1998	1999	
EU-15	:	3 078	3 113	3 065	3 014	3 000	3 049	3 135	3 058	:	:	**EU-15**
B	:	105	110	110	107	111	111	117	116	:	:	**B**
DK	:	53	62	57	59	63	60	74	64	:	:	**DK**
D	:	943	919	877	870	857	864	872	831	:	:	**D**
EL	:	71	71	73	73	76	78	82	83	:	:	**EL**
E	:	204	216	225	212	223	228	227	243	:	:	**E**
F	:	354	369	363	350	336	347	365	359	:	:	**F**
IRL	:	30	30	31	31	32	33	35	36	:	:	**IRL**
I	:	391	390	389	386	382	405	401	402	:	:	**I**
L	:	11	11	11	11	11	9	9	9	:	:	**L**
NL	:	153	157	158	164	161	167	178	169	:	:	**NL**
A	:	55	59	54	54	54	57	60	60	:	:	**A**
P	:	39	41	45	44	44	48	46	48	:	:	**P**
FIN	:	52	52	52	55	59	56	60	59	:	:	**FIN**
S	:	51	50	51	51	54	54	58	52	:	:	**S**
UK	:	568	577	569	547	538	532	552	530	:	:	**UK**

Emissions of carbon dioxide. Tonnes per person

	1989	1990	1991	1992	1993	1994	1995	1996	1997	1998	1999	
EU-15	:	8,5	8,5	8,4	8,2	8,1	8,2	8,4	8,2	:	:	**EU-15**
B	:	10,5	11,0	11,0	10,6	11,0	11,0	11,5	11,4	:	:	**B**
DK	:	10,3	12,1	11,0	11,3	12,1	11,5	14,2	12,1	:	:	**DK**
D	:	11,9	11,5	10,9	10,8	10,5	10,6	10,7	10,1	:	:	**D**
EL	:	7,0	7,0	7,0	7,1	7,3	7,5	7,9	7,9	:	:	**EL**
E	:	5,3	5,5	5,8	5,4	5,7	5,8	5,8	6,2	:	:	**E**
F	:	6,3	6,5	6,3	6,1	5,8	6,0	6,3	6,1	:	:	**F**
IRL	:	8,5	8,6	8,7	8,6	9,0	9,2	9,6	9,9	:	:	**IRL**
I	:	6,9	6,9	6,9	6,8	6,7	7,1	7,0	1,8	:	:	**I**
L	:	28,0	29,4	28,5	28,6	26,7	21,4	21,6	20,3	:	:	**L**
NL	:	10,3	10,5	10,4	10,8	10,5	10,8	11,5	10,9	:	:	**NL**
A	:	7,2	7,5	6,8	6,8	6,8	7,1	7,4	7,4	:	:	**A**
P	:	3,9	4,1	4,5	4,4	4,5	4,8	4,6	4,8	:	:	**P**
FIN	:	10,4	10,3	10,3	10,9	11,6	11,0	11,8	11,4	:	:	**FIN**
S	:	5,9	5,8	5,9	5,9	6,2	6,1	6,6	5,8	:	:	**S**
UK	:	9,9	10,0	9,8	9,4	9,2	9,1	9,4	9,0	:	:	**UK**

Emissions of sulphur oxides, SO$_2$. 1 000 t

	1989	1990	1991	1992	1993	1994	1995	1996	1997	1998	1999	
EU-15	16 852	16 470	:	13 641	12 623	11 540	10 341	9 432	:	:	:	**EU-15**
B	325	320	:	310	289	251	245	240	:	:	:	**B**
DK	231	218	:	202	163	161	150	180	109	:	:	**DK**
D	6 150	5 315	:	3 300	2 938	2 466	2 102	1 544	1 468	:	:	**D**
EL	:	509	:	554	550	532	558	544	:	:	:	**EL**
E	2 337	2 266	:	2 195	2 062	2 066	1 927	:	:	:	:	**E**
F	1 334	1 252	:	1 202	1 062	1 010	959	947	:	:	:	**F**
IRL	162	178	:	161	157	177	166	143	:	:	:	**IRL**
I	1 885	1 678	:	1 424	1 490	:	:	:	:	:	:	**I**
L	12	14	:	:	15	13	9	8	6	:	:	**L**
NL	206	202	:	172	163	146	145	135	125	:	:	**NL**
A	85	75	:	55	53	52	48	44		:	:	**A**
P	:	283	:	345	290	258	:	:	:	:	:	**P**
FIN	244	260	:	141	122	115	96	105	100	:	:	**FIN**
S	160	136	:	103	102	97	94	99	91	:	:	**S**
UK	3 720	3 764	:	3 477	3 166	2 705	2 351	2 028	:	:	:	**UK**
IS	8	8	:	8	9	8	8	9	9	:	:	**IS**
NO	58	53	:	36	35	34	34	33	30	:	:	**NO**
CH	50	43	:	38	33	31	34	34	33	:	:	**CH**

2D2AA

Emissions of sulphur oxides, SO$_2$. kg per person

	1989	1990	1991	1992	1993	1994	1995	1996	1997	1998	1999	
EU-15	47	45	:	37	34	31	28	25	:	:	:	**EU-15**
B	33	32	:	31	29	25	24	24	:	:	:	**B**
DK	45	42	:	39	32	31	29	34	21	:	:	**DK**
D	78	67	:	41	36	30	26	19	18	:	:	**D**
EL	:	50	:	54	53	51	53	52	:	:	:	**EL**
E	60	58	:	56	53	53	49		:	:	:	**E**
F	24	22	:	21	18	17	17	16	:	:	:	**F**
IRL	46	51	:	45	44	49	46	40	:	:	:	**IRL**
I	33	30	:	25	26	:	:	:	:	:	:	**I**
L	32	37	:		38	32	22	19	14	:	:	**L**
NL	14	14	:	11	11	10	9	9	8	:	:	**NL**
A	11	10	:	7	7	6	6	5	:	:	:	**A**
P		29	:	35	29	26	:	:	:	:	:	**P**
FIN	49	52	:	28	24	23	19	21	20	:	:	**FIN**
S	19	16	:	12	12	11	11	11	10	:	:	**S**
UK	65	65	:	60	54	46	40	35	:	:	:	**UK**
IS	33	32	:	31	33	30	30	32	32	:	:	**IS**
NO	14	12	:	9	8	8	8	8	7	:	:	**NO**
EEA	:	:	:	:	:	:	:	:	:	:	:	**EEA**
CH	8	6	:	6	5	4	5	5	5	:	:	**CH**

2D2AB

2

2D3AA

Emissions of nitrogen oxides, NO$_2$. 1 000 t

	1989	1990	1991	1992	1993	1994	1995	1996	1997	1998	1999	
EU-15	13 533	13 307	:	12 888	12 256	12 017	11 681	11 543	:	:	:	EU-15
B	357	343	:	354	344	346	341	334	:	:	:	B
DK	285	282	:	275	273	270	252	288	248	:	:	DK
D	2 959	2 676	:	2 296	2 139	2 009	1 945	1 887	1 803	:	:	D
EL	:	343	:	351	349	360	364	380	:	:	:	EL
E	1 154	1 177	:	1 250	1 223	1 240	1 243	:	:	:	:	E
F	1 772	1 886	:	1 879	1 776	1 749	1 729	1 698	:	:	:	F
IRL	127	116	:	125	123	117	116	115	:	:	:	IRL
I	2 019	2 047	:	2 117	1 997	:	:	:	:	:	:	I
L	:	23	:	:	25	23	20	20	20	:	:	L
NL	592	579	:	556	535	510	498	487	454	:	:	NL
A	184	180	:	177	167	176	163	152	:	:	:	A
P	:	217	:	245	238	256	:	:	:	:	:	P
FIN	301	300	:	284	282	282	258	268	260	:	:	FIN
S	418	388	:	382	377	384	354	358	337	:	:	S
UK	2 783	2 752	:	2 572	2 408	2 297	2 145	2 060	:	:	:	UK
IS	25	26	:	28	29	29	28	30	29	:	:	IS
NO	220	218	:	207	215	212	212	220	222	:	:	NO
CH	169	166	:	153	145	134	136	132	129	:	:	CH

2D3AB

Emissions of nitrogen oxides, NO$_2$. kg per person

	1989	1990	1991	1992	1993	1994	1995	1996	1997	1998	1999	
EU-15	37	37	:	35	33	32	31	31	:	:	:	EU-15
B	36	34	:	35	34	34	34	33	:	:	:	B
DK	56	55	:	53	53	52	48	55	47	:	:	DK
D	38	34	:	29	26	25	24	23	22	:	:	D
EL	:	34	:	34	34	35	35	36	:	:	:	EL
E	30	30	:	32	31	32	32	:	:	:	:	E
F	31	33	:	33	31	30	30	29	:	:	:	F
IRL	36	33	:	35	34	33	32	32	:	:	:	IRL
I	36	36	:	37	35	:	:	:	:	:	:	I
L	:	61	:	:	63	57	49	48	48	:	:	L
NL	40	39	:	37	35	33	32	31	29	:	:	NL
A	24	23	:	23	21	22	20	19	:	:	:	A
P	:	22	:	25	24	26	:	:	:	:	:	P
FIN	61	60	:	56	56	55	51	52	51	:	:	FIN
S	49	46	:	44	43	44	40	41	38	:	:	S
UK	49	48	:	44	41	39	37	35	:	:	:	UK
IS	100	104	:	109	112	110	106	111	106	:	:	IS
NO	52	51	:	48	50	49	49	50	51	:	:	NO
EEA	:	:	:	:	:	:	:	:	:	:	:	EEA
CH	26	25	:	22	21	19	19	19	18	:	:	CH

Consumption of commercial fertilisers. 1 000 t

Total

	1990	1995	1996	1997	1998	
EU-15	19 551,2	17 307,3	18 000,3	17 486,7	17 151,5	**EU-15**
B/L	384,0	307,0	314,0	307,0	304,0	**B/L**
DK	633,2	438,0	449,0	436,0	403,0	**DK**
D	3 272,0	2 819,9	2 818,9	2 856,9	2 938,5	**D**
EL	685,1	505,0	560,0	504,0	486,0	**EL**
E	1 975,9	1 868,7	2 171,0	2 061,5	2 106,8	**E**
F	5 683,0	4 914,5	5 065,2	4 988,8	4 831,0	**F**
IRL	692,3	748,0	682,0	695,0	706,0	**IRL**
I	1 944,4	1 865,9	1 883,0	1 769,0	1 742,0	**I**
L	:	:	:	:	:	**L**
NL	558,6	535,0	537,6	494,5	465,0	**NL**
A	303,0	237,0	265,0	253,0	252,0	**A**
P	278,4	244,0	258,0	236,0	248,0	**P**
FIN	443,1	340,0	313,0	311,0	305,0	**FIN**
S	328,3	293,3	307,6	309,1	280,2	**S**
UK	2 370,0	2 191,0	2 376,0	2 265,0	2 084,0	**UK**

2E1AC

EL: land under permanent pasture only. Total commercial fertilisers is the sum of nitrogen, phosphate and potash.

Consumption of commercial fertilisers. 1 000 t

Phosphate

	1990	1995	1996	1997	1998	
EU-15	4 412,4	3 566,0	3 697,9	3 526,3	3 449,1	**EU-15**
B/L	78,0	51,0	46,0	44,0	42,0	**B/L**
DK	88,6	49,0	53,0	50,0	44,0	**DK**
D	609,0	401,7	415,1	409,6	406,8	**D**
EL	187,3	136,0	145,0	132,0	128,0	**EL**
E	534,2	509,9	559,9	540,2	548,3	**E**
F	1 349,0	1 031,4	1 051,9	1 038,8	1 011,0	**F**
IRL	138,5	141,0	128,0	113,0	124,0	**IRL**
I	644,7	542,0	575,0	501,0	490,0	**I**
L	:	:	:	:	:	**L**
NL	74,0	70,0	65,0	60,0	55,0	**NL**
A	74,0	52,0	60,0	57,0	57,0	**A**
P	80,3	71,0	76,0	67,0	73,0	**P**
FIN	117,2	72,0	57,0	56,0	53,0	**FIN**
S	57,8	49,0	50,0	49,7	48,0	**S**
UK	380,0	390,0	416,0	408,0	369,0	**UK**

2E1AB

EL: land under permanent pasture only.

2E1AA

Consumption of commercial fertilisers. 1 000 t

Nitrogen

	1990	1995	1996	1997	1998	
EU-15	10 218,1	9 532,2	10 019,4	9 760,8	9 696,7	**EU-15**
B/L	186,0	165,0	172,0	171,0	172,0	**B/L**
DK	394,9	291,0	288,0	283,0	262,0	**DK**
D	1 788,0	1 769,2	1 758,0	1 788,4	1 903,0	**D**
EL	426,6	315,0	340,0	307,0	298,0	**EL**
E	1 063,1	912,8	1 153,1	1 041,9	1 047,5	**E**
F	2 492,0	2 392,0	2 525,1	2 513,1	2 488,0	**F**
IRL	370,0	425,0	394,0	433,0	433,0	**IRL**
I	879,0	918,9	894,0	855,0	843,0	**I**
L	:	:	:	:	:	**L**
NL	390,0	390,0	400,6	367,8	350,0	**NL**
A	135,0	125,0	133,0	127,0	128,0	**A**
P	150,1	125,0	132,0	121,0	127,0	**P**
FIN	206,8	183,0	174,0	177,0	176,0	**FIN**
S	211,7	192,3	204,6	205,6	179,2	**S**
UK	1 525,0	1 328,0	1 451,0	1 370,0	1 290,0	**UK**

Data for nitrogen refer to the total amounts of each included in both straight and compound fertilisers and are related to the apparent consumption during the fertiliser year (generally 1 July to 30 June) except as noted. *Source:* FAO.

6X1AD

Consumption of commercial fertilisers. 1 000 t

Potash

	1990	1995	1996	1997	1998	
EU-15	4 920,6	4 209,1	4 283,0	4 199,6	4 005,7	**EU-15**
B/L	120,0	91,0	96,0	92,0	90,0	**B/L**
DK	149,7	98,0	108,0	103,0	97,0	**DK**
D	875,0	649,0	645,8	658,9	628,7	**D**
EL	71,3	54,0	75,0	65,0	60,0	**EL**
E	378,6	446,0	458,0	479,4	511,0	**E**
F	1 842,0	1 491,1	1 488,2	1 436,9	1 332,0	**F**
IRL	183,8	182,0	160,0	149,0	149,0	**IRL**
I	420,8	405,0	414,0	413,0	409,0	**I**
L	:	:	:	:	:	**L**
NL	94,6	75,0	72,0	66,7	60,0	**NL**
A	94,0	60,0	72,0	69,0	67,0	**A**
P	48,0	48,0	50,0	48,0	48,0	**P**
FIN	119,1	85,0	82,0	78,0	76,0	**FIN**
S	58,7	52,0	53,0	53,7	53,0	**S**
UK	465,0	473,0	509,0	487,0	425,0	**UK**

Source: FAO.

Pesticide use is, in principle, recorded as amounts of active ingredients, although some countries use formulation weight including diluents and adjuvants. Active ingredients are the substances which cause the desired effect on agriculturally harmful fungi, plants or animals. Pesticide applica- tion varies widely year by year depending on weather and other factors. Since the 1980s, inor- ganic fungicide compounds requiring several tens of kilograms per hectare have been replaced by more biologically active organic compounds requiring a few kilograms per hectare.

Sales of pesticides

Sales of fungicides for use in agriculture in tonnes of active ingredients

	1990	1995	1996	1997	1998
EU-15	:	115 956	123 779	138 318	138 784
B	2 743	2 659	2 402	2 402	2 402
DK	1 396	1 055	631	794	770
D	10 984	9 652	10 404	9 397	10 530
EL	:	3 072	3 248	3 104	4 731
E	12 312	9 021	10 165	11 299	11 984
F	41 514	42 578	48 625	64 050	58 807
IRL	459	850	750	712	516
I	106 121	25 546	25 074	23 745	24 761
L	:	154	181	182	224
NL	4 140	3 990	3 624	4 356	5 127
A	1 683	1 410	1 697	1 688	1 336
P	:	9 078	9 746	9 397	10 475
FIN	163	114	115	154	209
S	643	200	253	262	300
UK	6 689	6 577	6 864	6 776	6 612

Sales of herbicides for use in agriculture in tonnes of active ingredients

	1990	1995	1996	1997	1998	
	:	103 152	116 159	113 503	117 006	EU-15
	5 213	6 240	5 953	5 953	5 953	B
	3 128	3 281	2 915	2 726	2 619	DK
	16 970	16 065	16 541	16 485	17 269	D
	:	2 131	2 717	2 116	2 303	EL
	13 395	6 326	8 652	9 153	9 413	E
	37 429	27 416	36 052	33 576	36 439	F
	985	1 426	1 126	1 137	678	IRL
	26 671	9 248	9 888	9 740	9 555	I
	:	164	148	121	183	L
	3 468	3 070	3 016	2 984	2 921	NL
	1 945	1 607	1 536	1 601	1 583	A
	:	1 660	1 584	1 769	1 914	P
	1 580	791	677	734	844	FIN
	1 631	975	1 236	1 303	1 269	S
	18 360	22 752	24 118	24 105	24 063	UK

6X1AE   6X1AF

Sales of pesticides

Sales of insecticides for use in agriculture in tonnes of active ingredients

	1990	1995	1996	1997	1998
EU-15	:	40 715	36 602	37 981	37 738
B	1 295	1 140	1 199	1 199	1 199
DK	259	163	36	51	55
D	1 638	4 925	3 797	4 696	6 276
EL	:	2 529	2 440	2 436	2 505
E	9 194	9 538	9 758	9 944	10 173
F	11 039	7 091	5 399	6 074	4 672
IRL	149	89	76	74	36
I	34 619	9 651	8 992	8 687	8 390
L	:	12	10	9	11
NL	0	2 871	2 256	1 982	1 577
A	285	123	98	96	85
P	:	667	727	916	1 079
FIN	96	57	55	47	46
S	26	17	13	15	27
UK	2 083	1 842	1 746	1 755	1 607

Sales of other pesticides for use in agriculture in tonnes of active ingredients

	1990	1995	1996	1997	1998	
	:	24 491	28 546	25 368	28 787	EU-15
	1 012	900	849	849	849	B
	867	310	87	104	175	DK
	3 554	3 889	4 343	4 069	4 809	D
	:	793	1 465	1 378	1 940	EL
	4 661	2 967	4 661	3 627	3 500	E
	7 719	6 921	7 813	6 092	7 835	F
	209	274	616	179	80	IRL
	25 097	4 045	4 096	4 064	4 092	I
	:	27	18	20	12	L
	0	992	1 022	1 075	1 097	NL
	333	264	235	304	301	A
	:	413	400	668	914	P
	198	92	86	80	77	FIN
	44	32	27	28	33	S
	2 385	2 572	2 828	2 831	3 073	UK

6X1AG   6X1AH

eurostat

Waste generation and recovery vary markedly between countries. This may be due to both differing definitions and economic factors. Therefore, and because of the non-availability of figures in countries, it is difficult to arrive at a total amount of waste produced for EU-15. However, as a result of economic growth during the last few years, there has been a general increase in the amounts of waste generated from all sources. Most countries have a strong upward trend in municipal waste generation; most of which is still disposed of by landfill, although incineration is an increasing practice in many countries.

Data on recycling, analysed via recycling rates (percentage of apparent consumption), show an overall tendency towards an increase in the amounts of glass and paper recycled. This is already an important step forward in the targets set by Agenda 21 (Rio Conference) and the fifth environmental action programme that recommend an efficient waste reuse and recycling, and to stabilise waste production at 1985 level for the year 2000.

Waste generation by sector. 1 000 t. 1995

	Agriculture	Mining and quarrying	Manufacturing	Energy production	Municipal waste	Other sectors	
	1995	1995	1995	1995	1995	1995	
EU-15	:	:	:	:	:	:	EU-15
B	:	:	:	:	5 006	:	B
DK	:	:	2 563	1 699	2 814	657	DK
D	:	:	:	:	:	:	D
EL	:	3 900	2 905	:	:	:	EL
E	:	:	:	:	:	380	E
F	:	:	101 000	:	34 700	:	F
IRL	31 000	22 000	3 781	353	1 325	:	IRL
I	:	:	:	:	25 780	:	I
L	:	:	:	:	195	:	L
NL	:	266	:	1 392	8 465	:	NL
A	:	:	13 300	:	5 306	:	A
P	:	:	:	:	3 500	:	P
FIN	:	:	:	:	2 100	:	FIN
S	:	:	:	600	3 200	:	S
UK	80 000	82 000	56 000	13 000	29 000	15 000	UK
IS	:	:	9	:	153	21	IS
NO	:	:	3 288	:	2 217	:	NO
EEA	:	:	:	:	:	:	EEA
CH	:	:	796	:	4 235	:	CH

2E4AG
2E4AH
2E4AI
2E4AJ
2E4AK
2E4AL

160 million data in New Cronos, Eurostat's reference database

Municipal waste. kg per person

	1980	1985	1990	1992	1993	1994	1995	1996	1997	
EU-15	:	:	:	:	:	:	:	:	:	EU-15
B	:	:	:	:	:	:	1 582	:	:	B
DK	399	475	:	:	:	519	538	553	559	DK
D	:	339	632	:	536	:	:	:	:	D
EL	261	302	296	311	:	:	:	344	:	EL
E	270	261	315	354	:	355	380	390	:	E
F	:	:	533	471	:	585	597	:	:	F
IRL	:	:	:	:	:	:	:	:	:	IRL
I	:	:	:	:	:	:	265	353	457	I
L	:	:	586	498	505	486	475	461	460	L
NL	:	478	:	:	601	602	584	599	:	NL
A	:	:	619	:	668	:	:	654	:	A
P	:	235	303	332	:	384	:	:	:	P
FIN	:	:	622	:	:	413	:	:	:	FIN
S	302	317	374	:	:	364	:	:	:	S
UK	:	:	:	:	:	:	495	476	:	UK
IS	:	:	:	578	580	571	572	558	556	IS
NO	416	458	472	519	514	546	624	630	619	NO
EEA	:	:	:	:	:	:	:	:	:	EEA
CH	441	516	609	601	600	605	:	:	:	CH
US	:	:	:	:	:	:	:	:	:	US
CA	:	:	:	:	:	:	:	:	:	CA
JP	:	:	:	:	:	:	:	:	:	JP

2E4AA

Recovery rates. %

	Paper and board					Glass					
	1992	1993	1994	1995	1996	1992	1993	1994	1995	1996	
EU-15	:	:	:	:	:	:	:	:	:	:	EU-15
B	34	38	36	37	38	54	55	67	67	66	B
DK	36	46	42	44	52	65	68	63	68	71	DK
D	50	55	59	67	71	65	65	75	75	79	D
EL	30	30	30	31	31	20	20	25	25	25	EL
E	36	37	36	41	41	27	29	31	32	35	E
F	36	42	42	38	41	44	46	48	50	50	F
IRL	12	19	19	17	17	27	21	21	29	29	IRL
I	38	41	78	28	31	53	52	54	53	53	I
L	:	:	:	:	:	:	:	:	:	:	L
NL	59	59	67	69	69	73	76	77	80	81	NL
A	56	68	66	66	71	64	68	76	76	:	A
P	39	38	39	37	39	31	29	32	42	42	P
FIN	38	37	38	38	39	44	46	50	50	63	FIN
S	50	50	60	59	66	58	59	56	61	72	S
UK	32	31	35	35	40	26	29	28	27	27	UK
IS	:	:	:	:	:	:	:	:	:	:	IS
NO	31	38	38	41	44	44	67	72	75	75	NO
EEA	:	:	:	:	:	:	:	:	:	:	EEA
CH	39	49	54	54	58	:	:	:	:	:	CH
US	:	:	:	:	:	:	:	:	:	:	US
CA	:	:	:	:	:	:	:	:	:	:	CA
JP	:	:	:	:	:	:	:	:	:	:	JP

2E4AB

2E4AF

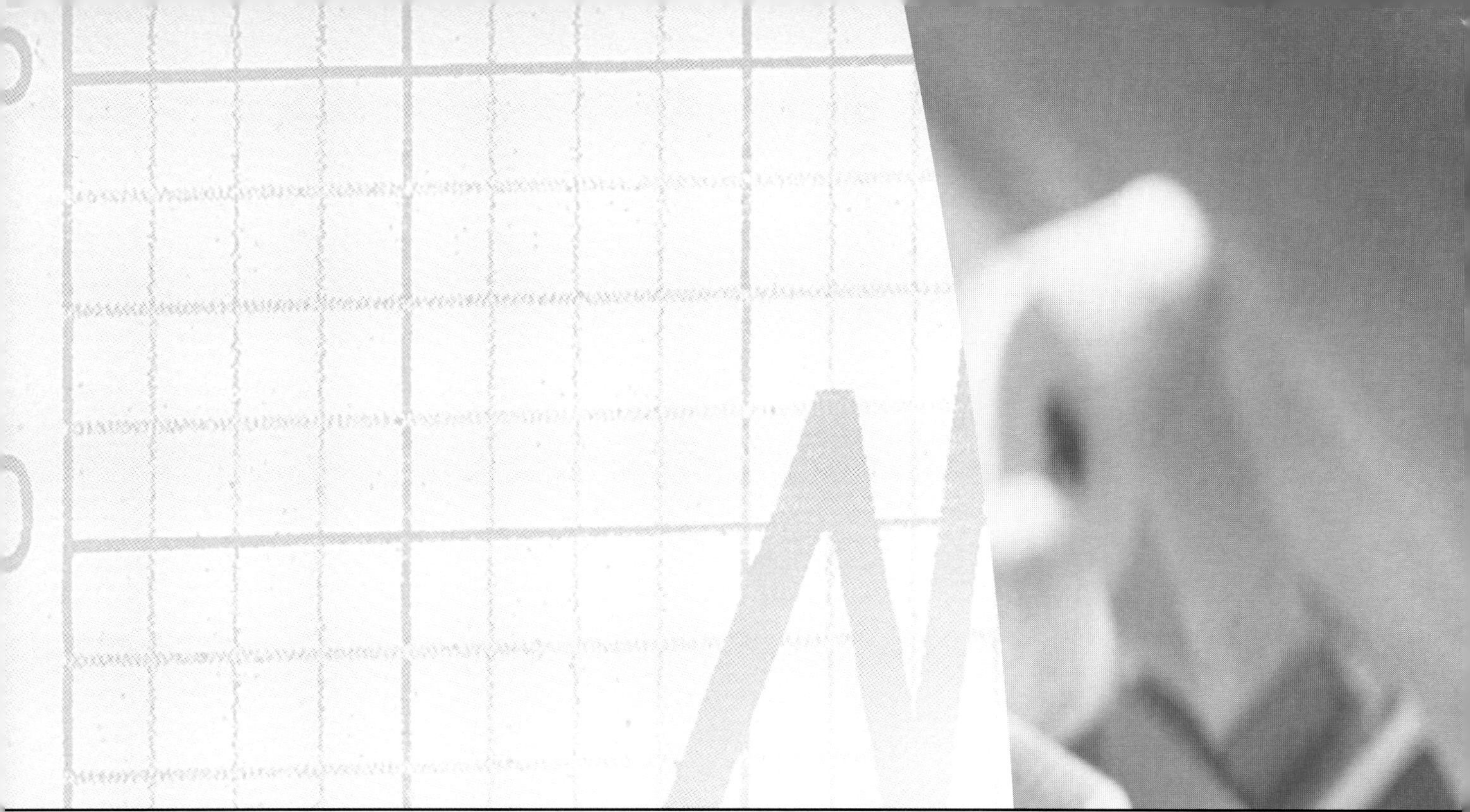

3 national income and expenditure

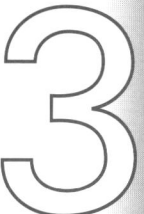

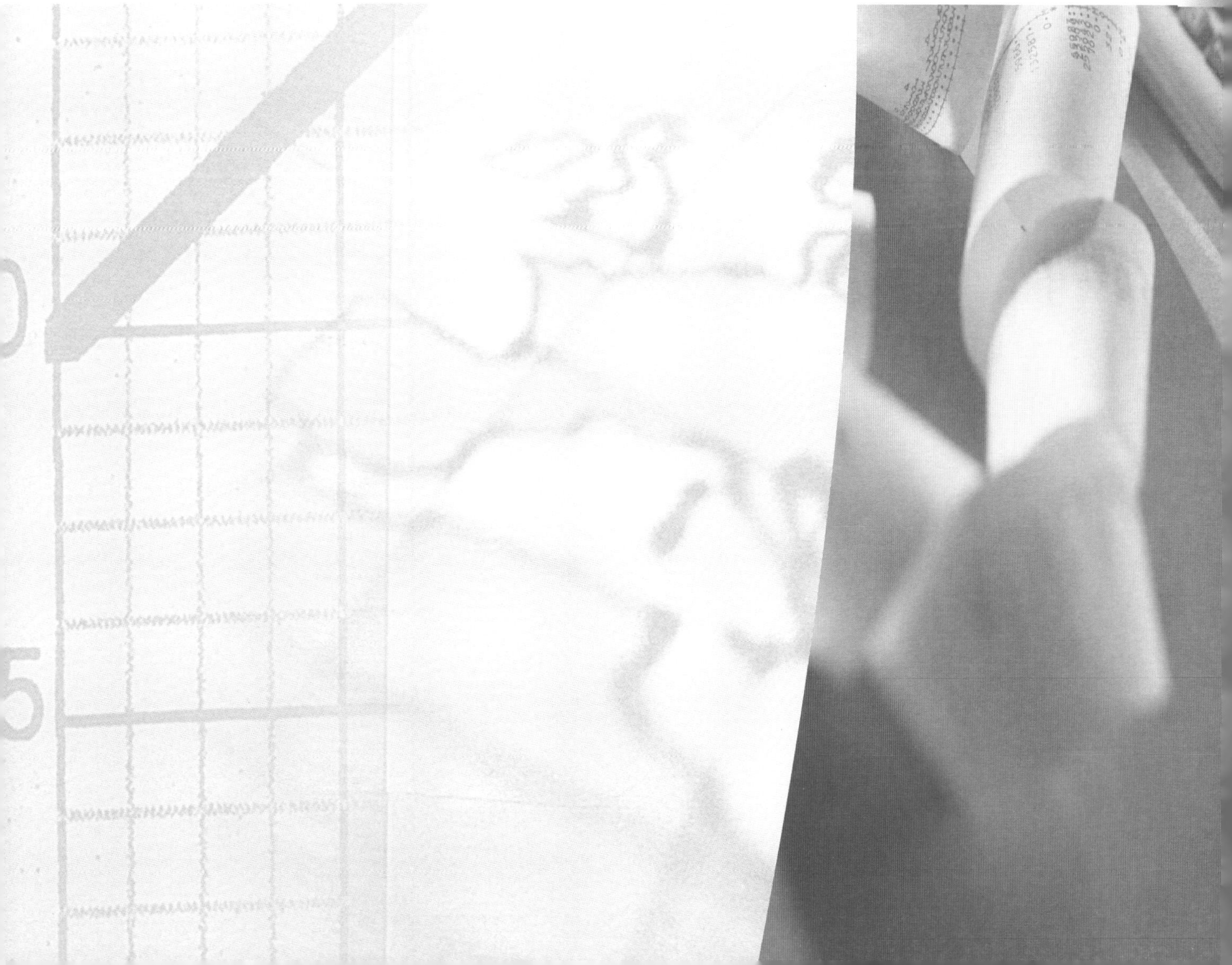

Economic growth	203
Gross domestic product at market prices in purchasing power parities per person. EU-15 = 100. 1997	203
Gross domestic product at market prices. Current series in million ECU/EUR	204
Gross domestic product at market prices. Percentage change on previous period — Constant prices	204
Gross domestic product at market prices at current prices. Million PPS	205
Gross domestic product at market prices. Current series PPS per head	206
Gross value added at basic prices. Current series in million ECU/EUR	207
Gross value added at basic prices. Yearly growth as % of previous year (real growth in volume)	207
Contribution to output by industry	208
Gross value added at market prices of agricultural, forestry and fishery products at current prices and current exchange rates. Million ECU	208
Gross value added at market prices of agricultural, forestry and fishery products at current prices and current exchange rates as % of all branches	208
Gross value added at market prices of fuel and power products at current prices and current exchange rates. Million ECU	209
Gross value added at market prices of fuel and power products at current prices and current exchange rates as % of all branches	209
Gross value added at market prices of manufactured products at current prices and current exchange rates. Million ECU	210
Gross value added at market prices of manufactured products at current prices and current exchange rates as % of all branches	210
Gross value added at market prices of building and construction at current prices and current exchange rates. Million ECU	211
Gross value added at market prices of building and construction at current prices and current exchange rates as % of all branches	211
Gross value added at market prices of market services at current prices and current exchange rates. Million ECU	212
Gross value added at market prices of market services at current prices and current exchange rates as % of all branches	212
Gross value added at market prices of non-market services at current prices and current exchange rates. Million ECU	213
Gross value added at market prices of non-market services at current prices and current exchange rates as % of all branches	213
Consumption and spending	214
Final consumption expenditure of households and NPISH (non-profit institutions serving households). Current series in million ECU/EUR	214
Final consumption expenditure of general government. Current series in million ECU/EUR	215
Final consumption expenditure of households and NPISH (non-profit institutions serving households). Current series in % of GDP	216
Final consumption expenditure of general government. Current series in % of GDP	216
Gross fixed capital formation (investments). Current series in million ECU	217
Consumption of fixed capital. Current series in million ECU	218

Gross fixed capital formation (investments). Current series in % of GDP	218
Changes in inventories. Current series in million ECU	219
Factor incomes	220
Compensation of employees: total industry. Current series in million ECU	220
Compensation of employees. Current series in % of GDP	220
Gross wages and salaries: total industry. Current series in million ECU	221
Gross wages and salaries: total industry. Current series in % of GDP	221
Gross operating surplus and mixed income: total economy. Current series in million ECU	222
Gross operating surplus. Current series in % of GDP	222
External balance of goods and services. Current series in million ECU	223
External balance of goods and services. Current series in % of GDP	223
Government receipts and spending	224
General government output as a % of GDP	224
General government intermediate consumption as a % of GDP	225
General government final consumption expenditure as a % of GDP	226
General government gross fixed capital formation as a % of GDP	227
Taxes on production and imports as a % of GDP	228
Current taxes on income and wealth as a % of GDP	229
Social contributions as a % of GDP	230
Subsidies paid by general government as a % of GDP	231
Social benefits (other than social transfers in kind) paid by general government as a % of GDP	232
Compensation of employees paid by general government as a % of GDP	233
Social protection	234
Total expenditure on social protection at current prices as a % of GDP. 1997	234
Total expenditure on social protection at current prices as a % of GDP	234
Total expenditure on social protection per head of population in ECU. 1997	235
Total expenditure on social protection per head of population in ECU	235
Total expenditure on social protection per head of population at constant prices. 1990 = 100	236
Total expenditure on social protection by type as a % of total expenditure:	236
Social benefits	236
Administration costs	236
Other expenditure	236
Social benefits by function as a % of total benefits:	237
Sickness and health care	237
Disability	237
Old age	237
Survivors	237
Family and children	237
Unemployment	237
Housing	237
Social exclusion	237

3

Social benefits per head of population in current PPS. 1997 | 238
Social benefits per head of population at constant prices. 1990 = 100 | 238
Social benefits per head of population in current PPS: | 239
Sickness and health care | 239
Disability | 239
Old age | 239
Survivors | 239
Family and children | 239
Unemployment | 239
Housing | 239
Social exclusion | 239
Social benefits per head of population at constant prices. 1990 = 100: | 240
Sickness and health care | 240
Disability | 240
Old age | 241
Survivors | 241
Family and children | 242
Unemployment | 242
Housing | 243
Social exclusion | 243
Social protection receipts by type as a % of total receipts. 1997 | 244
Social protection receipts by type as a % of total receipts: | 245
Employers' social contributions | 245
Social contributions by protected persons | 245
General government contributions | 245
Other receipts | 245

Consumer prices and interest rates | 246
Harmonised indices of consumer prices, rate of change (%) | 246
Harmonised indices of consumer prices, index 1996 = 100 | 247
Cost-of-living comparisons in the European Union. Most and least expensive cities for different expenditure groups in 1999. B = 100 | 248
Cost-of-living comparisons in the European Union in 1999. B = 100 | 248

Balance of payments | 249
Balance of the current account at current prices. % of GDP | 249
Average flows of the current account. % of GDP | 249
EU external balances of the current account: current account balance, goods balance, services balance, income balance and current transfers. 1 000 million ECU | 250
Current account balance of EU, US and Japan with the rest of the world. 1 000 million ECU | 250
Balance of international trade in goods and services at current prices. % of GDP | 251
International trade in goods and services, cover rates. % | 251
Balance of international trade in goods and services at current prices of EU, US and Japan with the rest of the world. 1 000 million ECU | 252
International trade in goods and services of the EU, the US and Japan with the rest of the world, cover rates. % | 252
Total trade in goods (exports-fob + imports-fob), % of current account total flows | 253
Total trade in services (exports + imports), % of current account total flows | 253

Trade in goods of EU, US and Japan with the rest of the world, cover rates. % | 254
Services' balance of EU, US and Japan with the rest of the world. 1 000 million ECU | 255
Share of EU, US, JP and the rest of the world in world total transactions in services (exports + imports). %. 1998 | 255
EU direct investment: inward, outward and intra-flows. Million ECU/EUR | 256
Direct investment inflows, the EU, the US, Japan. Million ECU/EUR | 257
Direct investment outflows the EU, the US, Japan. Million ECU/EUR | 257
EU direct investment inflows. Suppliers of direct investment to the EU. Million ECU/EUR | 258
EU direct investment inflows from the Extra EU. Suppliers of direct investment to the EU. Million ECU/EUR | 258
EU direct investment inflows. Recipients of direct investment from the rest of the world. Million ECU/EUR | 259
EU direct investment inflows in percentage of GDP | 259
EU direct investment outflows. Recipients of direct investment. Million ECU/EUR | 260
EU direct investment outflows to the Extra EU. Recipients of direct investment. Million ECU/EUR | 260
EU direct investment outflows. Suppliers of direct investment to the rest of the world. Million ECU/EUR | 261
EU direct investment outflows in percentage of GDP | 261
EU direct investment intra-flows. Suppliers of direct investment. Shares. 1999 | 262
EU direct investment intra-flows. Recipients of direct investment. Shares. 1999 | 262
Suppliers of EU direct investment, intra-flows. Million ECU/EUR | 263
Recipients of EU direct investment, intra-flows. Million ECU/EUR | 263

Trade in services | 264
Exports of transport services as % of services total exports | 264
Imports of transport services as % of services total imports | 264
International freight by air and sea: balance of EU, US and Japan with the rest of the world. 1 000 million ECU | 265
International passenger transport by air and sea: balance of EU, US and Japan with the rest of the world. 1 000 million ECU | 265
Exports of travel services as % of services total exports | 266
Imports of travel services as % of services total imports | 266
EU balance of travel services with the US and Japan. 1 000 million ECU | 267
Extra-EU balance of travel services. 1 000 million ECU. 1998 | 267
International trade in services other than transport and travel, cover rates. % | 268
Average flows in services other than transport and travel as % of GDP | 268
EU international trade in trade earnings, financial, business and construction services, cover rates. % | 269
EU international trade in communications services, advertising, audiovisual, royalties and licence fees, and computer and information services, cover rates. % | 269

Trade in goods | 270
Exports (fob) at current prices. 1 000 million ECU | 270
Imports (cif) at current prices. 1 000 million ECU | 270

Trade balance at current prices. 1 000 million ECU — 271

Exports (fob) at 1995 prices. 1995 = 100 — 272

Imports (cif) at 1995 prices. 1995 = 100 — 272

Volume ratio. 1995 = 100 — 273

Exports of agrifood products at current prices. 1 000 million ECU — 274

Imports of agrifood products at current prices. 1 000 million ECU — 274

Trade balance of agrifood products at current prices. 1 000 million ECU — 275

Exports of mineral fuels, lubricants and related products at current prices. 1 000 million ECU — 276

Imports of mineral fuels, lubricants and related products at current prices. 1 000 million ECU — 276

Trade balance in mineral fuels, lubricants and related products at current prices. 1 000 million ECU — 277

Exports of chemicals and related products at current prices. 1 000 million ECU — 278

Imports of chemicals and related products at current prices. 1 000 million ECU — 278

Trade balance in chemicals and related products, at current prices. 1 000 million ECU — 279

Exports of manufactured products at current prices. 1 000 million ECU — 280

Imports of manufactured products at current prices. 1 000 million ECU — 280

Trade balance in manufactured products at current prices. 1 000 million ECU — 281

Exports of machinery and transport equipment at current prices. 1 000 million ECU — 282

Imports of machinery and transport equipment at current prices. 1 000 million ECU — 282

Trade balance in machinery and transport equipment at current prices. 1 000 million ECU — 283

Key figures on the labour market — 284

Statutory minimum monthly wages (annual averages). ECU/EUR — 284

Minimum monthly wages as a proportion of average earnings — 284

Structure of labour costs (%) in industry in 1998 — 285

Average hourly labour costs (manual and non-manual workers) in total industry. ECU — 285

Hourly labour costs in ECU (current exchange rates), structure of costs as % of total cost. 1998 — 286

Employment rate. 1999 — 288

Unemployment rate. 1999 — 289

Research and development — 290

Research and development expenditure, as % of GDP, all sectors — 290

Research and development expenditure by sectors of economy as % of the GDP. 1999 — 290

Total research and development expenditure as % of GDP. 1997 — 291

Research and development personnel head count as percentage of the labour force all sectors — 292

Research and development personnel head count, by sectors of economy as % of the labour force. 1998 — 292

Total research and development personnel head count by country, as % of the labour force. 1997 — 293

Socio-economic breakdown of government research and development appropriations in the EEA in 1998. % of the total — 294

Government research and development appropriations as % of GDP — 295

Total government research and development appropriations (GBAORD) as % of GDP: comparison of EEA with Japan and the United States of America — 295

European Patent applications per million labour force. 1999 — 296

Total European patent applications per country — 297

European patent applications per million labour force — 297

Employment in high technology sectors as a share of total employment. 1998 — 298

Innovating enterprises and novel innovators, manufacturing sector. 1996 — 299

Distribution of turnover in manufacturing sector, EEA. 1996 — 299

Innovating enterprises as percentage of all enterprises. 1996 — 300

New and improved products as percentage of total turnover. 1996 — 300

Innovating enterprises as percentage of all enterprises. 1996 — 301

New and improved products as percentage of total turnover. 1996 — 301

Innovation expenditure as percentage of total turnover. 1996 — 302

3

In 1997 the average EU gross domestic product per capita in purchasing power standards (PPS) was 19 735 PPS. It varied between 8 225 PPS for the Greek region Ipeiros (42.5 % of the EU average) and 44 928 PPS for inner London in the United Kingdom (232 % of the EU average). About 38 % of all NUTS 2 regions showed higher PPS values per head than the EU average. On the other hand, about one fifth of all NUTS 2 regions were below 75 % of the EU average. The largest differences between the poorest and the wealthiest regions are to be found in Germany and the United Kingdom. Sweden and the Netherlands show the smallest discrepancy between the richest and the poorest regions.

Gross domestic product at market prices in purchasing power parities per person. EU-15 = 100. 1997

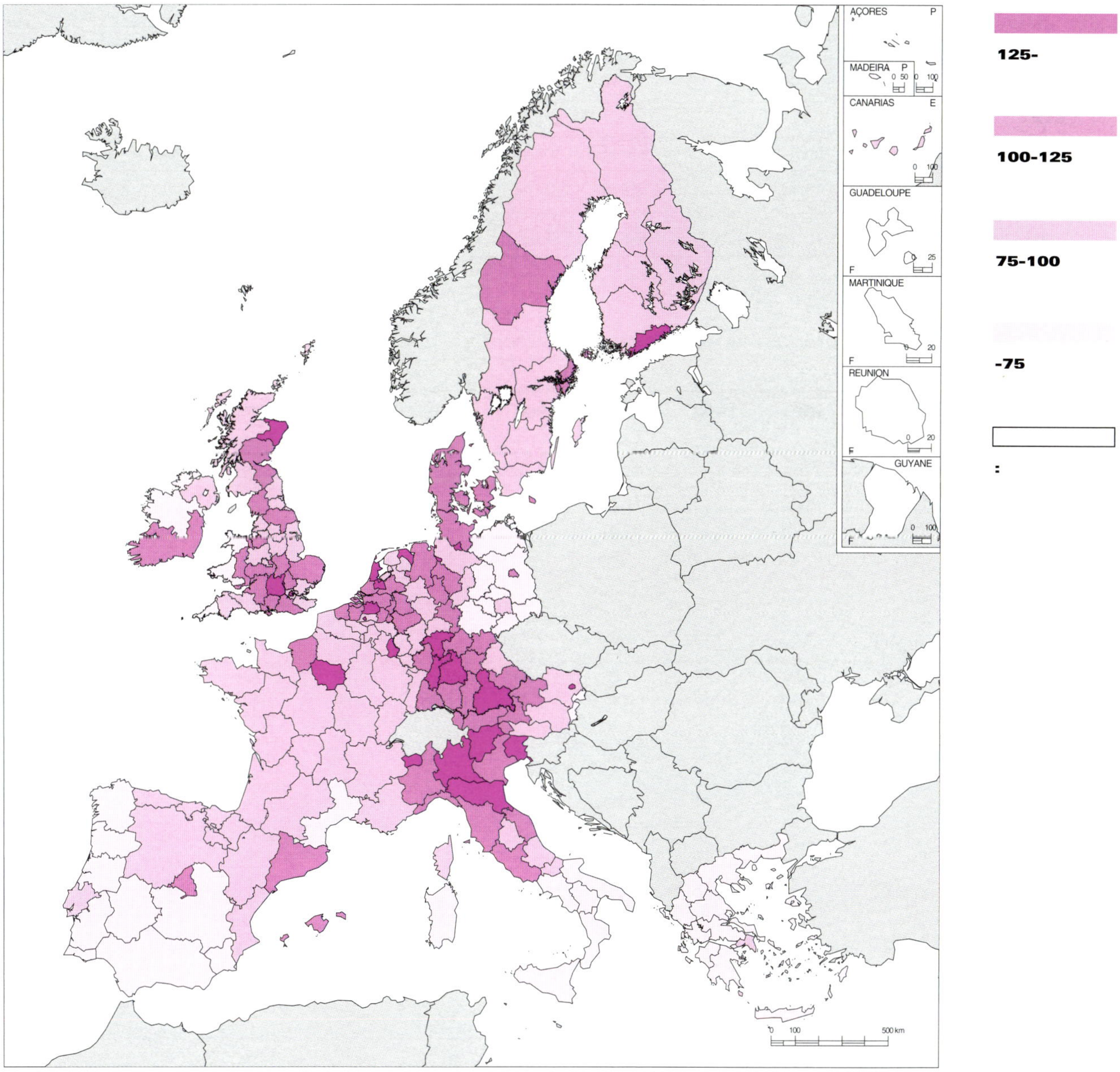

3A1CD

	125-
	100-125
	75-100
	-75
	:

3

Further reading: Regions, statistical yearbook, 2000. Eurostat. Statistics in focus — Regions, 2000/1. Eurostat.

NUTS 2.

Gross domestic product at market prices. Current series in million ECU/EUR

	1989	1990	1991	1992	1993	1994	1995	1996	1997	1998	1999	
EU-15	:	:	5 778 763	6 023 066	6 039 638	6 333 040	6 581 729	6 910 477	7 274 430	7 603 655	7 974 019 *	**EU-15**
EUR-11	:	:	4 563 068	4 809 750	4 857 481	5 073 144	5 308 976	5 533 027	5 646 153	5 868 847	6 116 441 *	**EUR-11**
B	143 644	155 398	163 636	174 865	183 613	196 509	210 857	211 308	214 944	223 749	233 159	**B**
DK	97 971	105 048	108 446	113 694	118 541	128 024	137 793	144 155	148 586	155 191	163 514	**DK**
D	:	:	1 432 638	1 561 740	1 670 845	1 763 760	1 880 187	1 878 200	1 866 496	1 921 866	1 982 381	**D**
EL	:	:	:	:	:	:	89 889	97 972	106 744	108 580	117 401 *	**EL**
E	:	:	:	:	:	:	446 882	479 717	492 999	520 196	559 352	**E**
F	892 712	957 587	987 210	1 040 541	1 089 370	1 139 320	1 188 101	1 224 606	1 241 129	1 293 104	1 344 417	**F**
IRL	:	37 248	38 648	41 447	42 570	46 148	50 776	57 514	70 581	77 052	87 677	**IRL**
I	792 341	867 836	939 613	951 165	849 037	863 369	839 041	971 065	1 028 273	1 063 828	1 099 105	**I**
L	:	:	:	:	:	:	13 967	14 339	15 409	16 389	18 141	**L**
NL	216 232	232 629	244 463	259 112	278 334	296 347	317 324	324 479	332 392	349 675	369 530	**NL**
A	:	:	:	:	:	:	180 178	182 608	182 452	188 453	195 397	**A**
P	:	:	:	:	:	:	82 765	88 668	93 406	99 004	105 579 *	**P**
FIN	105 009	107 732	99 829	83 851	73 565	84 369	98 898	100 523	108 072	115 533	121 703	**FIN**
S	:	:	:	:	164 188	174 216	183 597	206 273	209 582	212 003	223 910	**S**
UK	762 329	779 178	833 846	824 463	819 700	873 298	861 474	929 049	1 163 365	1 259 035	1 352 753	**UK**
IS	:	:	:	5 326	5 191	5 235	5 332	5 746	6 588	7 360	:	**IS**
NO	89 737	90 923	95 224	97 607	99 128	103 600	112 090	124 026	136 703	131 038	143 534	**NO**
EEA	:	:	:	:	:	:	:	:	:	:	:	**EEA**
CH	162 945	180 062	188 248	188 344	202 173	220 482	235 052	233 328	226 028	234 281	243 229	**CH**
US	4 982 122	4 557 196	4 830 880	4 867 832	5 672 359	5 930 383	5 657 888	6 153 332	7 335 177	7 840 728	8 725 236	**US**
CA	495 627	449 834	473 663	438 202	472 210	465 139	442 918	473 730	550 726	533 002	595 512	**CA**
JP	2 632 640	2 341 499	2 752 656	2 868 185	3 652 634	3 950 321	3 928 223	3 623 235	3 717 963	3 404 713	4 081 409	**JP**

6T1AA

Further reading: National accounts — aggregates — annual and quarterly data (ESA 95). Publication: ESA 95 main economic aggregates.

Gross domestic product at market prices. Percentage change on previous period — Constant prices

	1989	1990	1991	1992	1993	1994	1995	1996	1997	1998	1999	
EU-15	:	:	:	1,30	- 0,50	2,80	2,30	1,60	2,40	2,70	2,40 *	**EU-15**
EUR-11	:	:	:	1,60	- 0,80	2,40	2,20	1,40	2,20	2,70	2,40 *	**EUR-11**
B	3,60	2,70	2,00	1,60	- 1,50	3,00	2,50	1,00	3,50	2,70	2,50	**B**
DK	0,20	1,00	1,10	0,60	0,00	5,50	2,80	2,50	3,10	2,50	1,70	**DK**
D	:	:	:	2,20	- 1,10	2,30	1,70	0,80	1,40	2,10	1,60	**D**
EL	:	:	:	:	:	:	:	2,40	3,40	3,70	3,50 *	**EL**
E	:	:	:	:	:	:	2,90	2,30	3,80	4,00	3,70	**E**
F	4,20	2,60	1,00	1,50	- 0,90	2,10	1,70	1,10	1,90	3,10	2,90	**F**
IRL	:	:	1,90	3,30	2,70	5,80	9,70	7,70	10,70	8,60	9,80	**IRL**
I	2,90	2,00	1,40	0,80	- 0,90	2,20	2,90	1,10	1,80	1,50	1,40	**I**
L	:	:	:	:	:	:	:	2,90	7,30	5,00	7,50	**L**
NL	4,70	4,10	2,30	2,00	0,80	3,20	2,30	3,00	3,80	3,70	3,60	**NL**
A	:	:	:	:	:	:	:	2,00	1,20	2,90	2,10	**A**
P	5,40	4,80	2,40	1,90	- 1,40	2,50	3,70	3,60	3,70	3,50	2,90 *	**P**
FIN	5,10	0,00	- 6,30	- 3,30	- 1,10	4,00	3,80	4,00	6,30	5,50	4,00	**FIN**
S	:	:	:	:	:	4,10	3,70	1,10	2,00	3,00	3,80	**S**
UK	2,10	0,70	- 1,50	0,10	2,30	4,40	2,80	2,60	3,50	2,60	2,10	**UK**
IS	:	:	1,20	- 3,30	0,90	3,60	0,60	5,70	5,30	5,10	3,40 *	**IS**
NO	0,90	2,00	3,10	3,30	2,70	5,50	3,80	4,90	4,70	2,00	0,90	**NO**
EEA	:	:	:	:	:	:	:	:	:	:	:	**EEA**
CH	4,30	3,70	- 0,80	- 0,10	- 0,50	0,50	0,50	0,30	1,70	2,10	1,70	**CH**
US	3,50	1,80	- 0,50	3,10	2,70	4,00	2,70	3,60	4,40	4,40	4,20	**US**
CA	2,40	0,20	- 1,90	0,90	2,30	4,70	2,70	1,50	4,40	3,30	4,60	**CA**
JP	4,80	5,10	3,80	1,00	0,30	0,60	1,50	5,10	1,60	- 2,50	0,20	**JP**

6T1AB

Further reading: National accounts — aggregates — annual and quarterly data (ESA 95). Publication: ESA 95 main economic aggregates.

eurostat

Gross domestic product at market prices is the final result of the production activity of resident producer units. It can be defined in three ways: (i) GDP is the sum of gross value added of the various institutional sectors or the various industries plus taxes and less subsidies on products (which are not allocated to sectors and industries). It is also the balancing item in the total economy production account (production approach); (ii) GDP is the sum of final uses of goods and services by resident institutional units (actual final consumption and gross capital formation), plus exports and minus imports of goods and services (expenditure approach); (iii) GDP is the sum of uses in the total economy generation of income account (compensation of employees, taxes on production and imports less subsidies, gross operating surplus and mixed income of the total economy) (income approach) — (ESA, 1995, 8.89).

In these tables, GDP corresponds to the economy's output of goods and services less intermediate consumption, plus VAT on products and net taxes (i.e. taxes less subsidies) linked to imports. Valuation at constant prices means valuing the flows and stocks in an accounting period at the prices of the reference period (ESA, 1995, 1.56).

More data on this in Eurostat's database

NA_AGGR provides the main statistics for national account aggregates on an annual and quarterly basis. The domain offers ESA 95 data as well as the old ESA 79 and/or national concept figures. Aggregates are presented in current and constant prices, national currency, euro and PPS, growth rates, deflators, indices and ratios on main totals. The domain includes also economic and social indicators.

Data refer to eurozone, EU and the individual Member States, the Union's main trading partners and the main economic groupings in the world: G7; NAFTA, etc.

➤ ➤ ➤ DOMAIN NA_AGGR IN DATABASE NEW CRONOS

Gross domestic product at market prices at current prices. Million PPS

	1989	1990	1991	1992	1993	1994	1995	1996	1997	1998	1999	
EU-15	.	.	:	:	:	:	6 581 729	6 910 477	7 274 430	7 603 655	7 974 019 *	**EU-15**
EUR-11	:	:	:	:	:	:	5 200 698	5 430 672	5 677 754	5 932 382	6 216 276 *	**EUR-11**
B	143 674	154 733	166 045	177 879	184 677	194 347	200 738	207 268	218 979	229 635	239 684	**B**
DK	76 850	81 355	87 949	89 713	94 935	103 117	100 054	115 902	122 562	127 385	133 164	**DK**
D	:	:	1 320 841	1 411 495	1 426 197	1 525 388	1 585 874	1 660 583	1 719 954	1 788 408	1 864 376	**D**
EL	:	:	:	:	:	:	121 681	129 262	133 827	140 146	149 380 *	**EL**
E	:	:	:	:	:	:	541 396	575 264	607 195	641 445	682 535	**E**
F	861 530	926 874	995 204	1 026 095	1 019 301	1 053 045	1 088 834	1 122 033	1 149 876	1 203 544	1 265 139	**F**
IRL	:	38 366	41 903	45 674	48 010	53 347	59 197	62 956	73 595	80 962	90 395	**IRL**
I	805 090	860 802	926 902	961 448	944 946	1 002 700	1 046 025	1 096 015	1 136 836	1 176 186	1 219 323	**I**
L	:	:	:	:	:	:	12 568	13 118	14 263	15 249	16 893	**L**
NL	210 776	230 083	243 477	255 068	262 956	280 010	298 068	306 694	340 348	357 296	376 801	**NL**
A	:	:	:	:	:	:	156 927	166 486	174 704	182 365	189 913	**A**
P	:	:	:	:	:	:	123 676	129 876	142 941	151 260	160 469 *	**P**
FIN	72 330	75 862	72 631	70 823	75 039	79 021	87 393	90 378	99 064	106 034	110 747	**FIN**
S	:	:	:	:	141 213	149 976	159 800	165 790	174 455	181 794	191 507	**S**
UK	810 058	855 100	866 349	912 658	929 983	976 100	990 696	1 068 851	1 165 832	1 221 948	1 283 692	**UK**
IS	:	4 079	4 463	4 473	4 637	4 813	5 400	5 803	6 229	6 734	:	**IS**
NO	64 318	68 767	75 414	80 279	87 340	88 472	92 155	99 629	110 790	109 934	118 268	**NO**
EEA	:	:	:	:	:	:	:	:	:	:	:	**EEA**
CH	122 870	133 653	140 753	146 277	152 115	158 446	163 939	163 332	176 181	184 092	194 252	**CH**
US	5 036 611	5 373 330	5 552 106	5 854 349	6 155 716	6 558 235	6 882 361	7 346 689	7 904 710	8 398 057	8 970 026	**US**
CA	451 888	474 985	482 726	496 827	519 913	562 058	596 209	632 192	676 471	697 345	757 156	**CA**
JP	1 850 319	2 038 684	2 223 436	2 332 109	2 405 361	2 461 658	2 553 310	2 751 098	2 850 074	2 818 113	2 896 995	**JP**

6T1AC

Further reading: National accounts — aggregates — annual and quarterly data (ESA 95). Publication: ESA 95 main economic aggregates.

GDP, and in particular the GDP per capita, is one of the main indicators for economic analysis as well as spatial and/or temporal international comparisons.

In order to facilitate these international comparisons, the GDP in national currency of each Member State is converted into a common currency (ECU until 1998, euro starting from 1999), by means of the official exchange rate. However, this does not necessarily reflect the actual purchasing power of each national currency on its economic territory, because the converted GDP is a function, not only of the level of goods and services produced on the economic territory, but also of the general price level. Therefore, the simple use of the GDP converted into a common currency does not provide, in most cases, a correct indication of the 'real' volume of goods and services.

In order to remove the distortions due to price level differences, transitive Purchasing Power Parities (PPPs) are calculated and used as a factor of conversion. These parities are obtained as a weighted average of relative price ratios regarding a homogeneous basket of goods and services, comparable and representative for each Member State.

The 'real' values of GDP obtained in this way are then expressed in terms of purchasing power standards (PPS), a unit that is independent of any national currency.

Gross domestic product at market prices. Current series PPS per head

	1989	1990	1991	1992	1993	1994	1995	1996	1997	1998	1999	
EU-15	:	:	:	:	:	:	17 618	18 446	19 362	20 194	21 131 *	EU-15
EUR-11	:	:	:	:	:	:	17 904	18 644	19 440	20 273	21 200 *	EUR-11
B	14 454	15 523	16 595	17 705	18 310	19 212	19 803	20 410	21 511	22 507	23 446	B
DK	14 978	15 834	17 077	17 366	18 310	19 826	20 845	22 051	23 213	24 021	25 026	DK
D	:	:	16 514	17 513	17 568	18 734	19 420	20 277	20 962	21 802	22 712	D
EL	:	:	:	:	:	:	11 640	12 339	12 747	13 333	14 198 *	EL
E	:	:	:	:	:	:	13 808	14 649	15 441	16 292	17 319 *	E
F	15 269	15 972	17 047	17 470	17 254	17 742	18 262	18 735	19 117	19 925	20 861 *	F
IRL	:	10 944	11 885	12 869	13 473	14 940	16 438	17 362	20 105	21 853	24 133 *	IRL
I	14 206	15 177	16 333	16 909	16 564	17 529	18 255	19 095	19 767	20 424	21 158	I
L	:	:	:	:	:	:	30 446	31 361	33 663	35 528	38 773	L
NL	:	:	:	:	:	:	19 280	19 757	21 810	22 758	23 838	NL
A	:	:	:	:	:	:	19 502	20 657	21 643	22 574	23 484	A
P	:	:	:	:	:	:	12 471	13 083	14 379	15 174	16 065 *	P
FIN	14 571	15 215	14 486	14 047	14 812	15 528	17 109	17 635	19 273	20 577	21 442	FIN
S	:	:	:	:	16 196	17 080	18 104	18 752	19 721	20 539	21 620	S
UK	14 123	14 856	14 987	15 734	15 982	16 715	16 904	18 183	19 753	20 631	21 598	UK
IS	:	16 009	17 302	17 131	17 578	18 093	20 196	21 578	22 991	24 597	:	IS
NO	15 216	16 215	17 695	18 731	20 255	20 399	21 146	22 741	25 151	24 805	26 552 *	NO
EEA	:	:	:	:	:	:	:	:	:	:	:	EEA
CH	18 339	19 948	20 699	21 199	22 046	22 635	23 420	23 004	24 814	25 928	27 196 *	CH
US	20 368	21 505	21 983	22 933	23 859	25 174	26 172	27 682	29 502	31 048	32 867 *	US
CA	16 561	17 147	17 221	17 508	18 113	19 357	20 311	21 306	22 543	23 017	24 769 *	CA
JP	15 031	16 508	17 931	18 747	19 274	19 662	20 345	21 869	22 602	22 295	22 874 *	JP

6T1AD

Further reading: National accounts — aggregates — annual and quarterly data
(ESA 95). Publication: ESA 95 main economic aggregates.

Gross value added is recorded at basic prices. It is the net result of output valued at basic prices less intermediate consumption valued at purchasers' prices (ESA, 1995, 9.23). The basic price is the price receivable by the producers from the purchaser for a unit of a good or service produced as output minus any tax payable on that unit as a consequence of its production or sale (i.e. taxes on products), plus any subsidy receivable on that unit as a consequence of its production or sale (i.e. subsidies on products). It excludes any transport charges invoiced separately by the producer. It includes any transport margins charged by the producer on the same invoice, even when they are included as a separate item on the invoice (ESA, 1995, 3.48).

Gross value added at basic prices. Current series in million ECU/EUR

	1989	1990	1991	1992	1993	1994	1995	1996	1997	1998	1999	
EU-15	:	:	:	:	:	:	6 141 271	6 438 155	:	:	:	EU-15
EUR-11	:	:	:	:	:	:	4 968 499	5 170 964	5 263 896	5 456 110 *	:	EUR-11
B	134 967	145 728	153 894	164 361	172 088	183 348	198 352	198 359	200 473	208 928	217 518	B
DK	87 817	94 688	97 673	102 266	107 397	114 885	123 195	127 871	131 119	136 095	144 137	DK
D	:	:	1 345 632	1 467 181	1 567 704	1 647 129	1 758 735	1 759 769	1 751 706	1 801 579	1 847 103	D
EL	:	:	:	:	:	:	83 063	89 967	97 780	98 925	:	EL
E	:	:	:	:	:	:	431 125	459 378	470 043	492 797	524 940	E
F	833 394	894 663	921 634	975 118	1 020 273	1 060 634	1 100 950	1 129 014	1 143 261	1 189 700	:	F
IRL	:	33 379	34 818	37 043	38 447	41 184	45 144	51 101	61 446	67 124 *	:	IRL
I	761 406	830 644	893 545	905 527	808 582	817 031	789 580	915 068	962 433	987 983	1 015 858	I
L	:	:	:	:	:	:	14 289	14 774	15 535	16 398	18 199	L
NL	:	:	:	:	:	:	295 517	300 233	306 166	321 827	339 794	NL
A	:	:	:	:	:	:	170 970	172 915	171 840	177 287	183 840	A
P	:	:	:	:	:	:	75 409	80 605	85 302	90 296	:	P
FIN	93 123	96 628	89 458	74 544	66 118	75 860	88 428	89 749	95 691	102 192	107 707	FIN
S	:	:	:	:	150 604	158 903	168 974	189 704	:	:	:	S
UK	713 665	729 592	768 843	767 957	760 784	814 703	797 541	859 649	1 070 051	1 157 583	1 241 463	UK
IS	:	:	:	:	:	:	:	:	:	:	:	IS
NO	83 205	84 439	88 170	90 036	90 826	93 544	100 301	110 735	121 852	116 335	128 097	NO
US	:	:	:	:	:	:	:	:	:	:	:	US
CA	439 702	398 393	418 072	385 228	414 158	408 923	389 834	417 649	:	:	:	CA
JP	:	:	:	:	:	:	:	:	:	:	:	JP

Further reading: National accounts — aggregates — annual and quarterly data (ESA 95). Publication: ESA 95 main economic aggregates.

Gross value added at basic prices. Yearly growth as % of previous year (real growth in volume)

	1989	1990	1991	1992	1993	1994	1995	1996	1997	1998	1999	
EU-15	:	:	:	:	:	:	:	1,6	2,5	:	:	EU-15
EUR-11	:	:	:	:	.	.	.	1,4	2,3	:	:	EUR-11
B	3,4	2,7	2,2	1,4	- 1,8	2,5	3,5	0,8	2,9	2,8	2,5	B
DK	0,9	1,1	0,5	- 0,1	- 0,2	4,4	3,0	2,3	2,7	2,3	2,1	DK
D	:	:	:	2,3	- 1,0	2,2	2,1	1,1	1,9	2,5	1,7	D
EL	:	:	:	:	:	:	:	1,8	3,4	3,8	:	EL
E	:	:	:	:	:	:	2,8	1,7	3,6	3,5	3,1	E
F	4,2	2,4	0,9	1,7	- 1,1	1,7	1,4	1,0	1,7	2,9	:	F
IRL	:	:	:	:	:	:	:	:	:	:	:	IRL
I	2,9	1,9	1,1	1,0	- 0,6	2,4	2,6	1,2	1,7	1,6	1,2	I
L	:	:	:	:	:	:	:	2,3	6,2	4,3	6,0	L
NL	:	:	:	:	:	:	:	2,9	3,7	3,6	3,5	NL
A	:	:	:	:	:	:	:	1,9	1,6	3,2	2,1	A
P	:	:	:	:	:	:	:	3,7	5,1	6,5	:	P
FIN	5,4	0,9	- 6,9	- 3,6	0,7	3,9	3,7	4,3	6,3	5,3	4,4	FIN
S	:	:	:	:	:	3,1	4,7	1,4	2,5	2,5	3,7	S
UK	2,3	1,2	- 1,5	0,1	2,2	4,7	2,7	2,7	3,5	3,1	2,1	UK
IS	:	:	:	:	:	:	:	:	:	:	:	IS
NO	1,8	1,7	3,3	3,0	2,1	4,7	3,6	4,0	4,6	1,9	1,1	NO
US	:	:	:	:	:	:	:	:	:	:	:	US
CA	2,1	0,3	- 1,5	0,7	2,3	4,5	2,7	1,5	4,1	2,9	:	CA
JP	:	:	:	:	:	:	:	:	:	:	:	JP

Further reading: National accounts — aggregates — annual and quarterly data (ESA 95). Publication: ESA 95 main economic aggregates.

6T1AE

6T1AH

3

A t the time when we prepared this issue of the Yearbook (Yearbook 2001) only a few Member States and some candidate countries had supplied their value added data based on ESA 95.

Hence these data under ESA 79 are reproduced in the rest of the following chapter.

For Member States, upon comparing ESA 79 with ESA 95 for 1995, the gross domestic product (GDP), which is overwhelmlingly composed of value added at market prices, shows positive increases ranging between + 0.2 % for Ireland and + 6.4 % for Denmark.

Further reading: Statistics in focus Implementation of the New European System of Accounts (ESA 95), Eurostat, 1999.

Gross value added at market prices of agricultural, forestry and fishery products at current prices and current exchange rates. Million ECU

	1989	1990	1991	1992	1993	1994	1995	1996	1997	1998	1999	
EU-15	149 573	153 010 ǀ	149 381	143 233	129 410	133 383	133 283	140 067	141 938 *	:	:	EU-15
EUR-11	121 019	124 419 ǀ	122 385	116 689	104 169	107 282	105 467	111 869	110 207 *	:	:	EUR-11
B	3 065	2 819	2 940	2 877	2 832	2 855	2 503	2 445	2 423	:	:	B
DK	4 008	3 931	3 821	3 834	3 885	3 569	3 855	4 015	4 141	:	:	DK
D	17 478	17 444 ǀ	16 170	16 192	14 974	15 112	15 570	16 337	15 853	:	:	D
EL	8 788	8 688	7 591	6 883	6 651	7 525	7 933	7 687	7 848	:	:	EL
E	17 929	19 257	18 973	16 759	15 561	14 600	13 834	17 026	15 851	:	:	E
F	30 650	32 089	29 355	28 874	25 003	27 020	27 880	28 133	27 742	:	:	F
IRL	2 786	2 573	2 533	2 834	2 761	2 557	2 539	2 422	2 907 *	:	:	IRL
I	27 544	27 683	31 206	29 659	25 042	24 817	23 869	26 934	26 607	:	:	I
L	141	138	110	124	122	126	136	124	115	:	:	L
NL	8 871	9 039	9 290	9 031	8 423	9 443	9 417	9 136	9 032	:	:	NL
A	3 590	3 922	3 672	3 519	3 473	3 726	2 709	2 534	2 524	:	:	A
P	3 020	3 474	3 323	3 123	2 682	2 944	3 170	3 310	3 467 *	:	:	P
FIN	5 945	5 982	4 813	3 697	3 298	4 081	3 840	3 467	3 685	:	:	FIN
S	4 924	4 651	4 173	3 921	3 015	3 155	3 510	3 466	3 478 *	:	:	S
UK	10 833	11 320	11 411	11 905	11 690	11 852	12 518	13 029	16 265 *	:	:	UK

6T1AI

Further reading: National accounts ESA — detailed tables by branch, 1970–97. Eurostat.

Gross value added at market prices of agricultural, forestry and fishery products at current prices and current exchange rates as % of all branches

	1989	1990	1991	1992	1993	1994	1995	1996	1997	1998	1999	
EU-15	3,2	3,0 ǀ	2,8	2,6	2,3	2,3	2,2	2,2	2,1 *	:	:	EU-15
EUR-11	3,3	3,1 ǀ	2,9	2,6	2,3	2,3	2,2	2,2	2,1 *	:	:	EUR-11
B	2,3	1,9	1,9	1,7	1,6	1,5	1,2	1,2	1,2	:	:	B
DK	4,7	4,3	4,1	3,9	3,7	3,2	3,2	3,2	3,2	:	:	DK
D	1,7	1,5 ǀ	1,3	1,2	1,1	1,0	1,0	1,0	1,0	:	:	D
EL	16,3	15,4	11,4	9,9	9,2	9,8	9,7	8,6	8,1	:	:	EL
E	5,0	4,8	4,3	3,6	3,7	3,5	3,1	3,6	3,3	:	:	E
F	3,6	3,5	3,1	2,9	2,4	2,5	2,5	2,4	2,4	:	:	F
IRL	9,1	7,7	7,2	7,4	7,0	5,9	5,3	4,5	4,5 *	:	:	IRL
I	3,6	3,3	3,4	3,2	3,0	2,9	2,9	2,9	2,7	:	:	I
L	1,8	1,6	1,2	1,2	1,1	1,0	1,0	0,9	0,8	:	:	L
NL	4,5	4,3	4,2	3,8	3,3	3,5	3,2	3,1	3,0	:	:	NL
A	3,3	3,3	2,8	2,5	2,3	2,3	1,6	1,5	1,4	:	:	A
P	6,3	6,4	5,3	4,4	3,8	4,1	4,1	4,1	4,1 *	:	:	P
FIN	6,4	6,2	5,4	5,0	5,1	5,5	4,4	3,9	3,9	:	:	FIN
S	3,0	2,7	2,3	2,2	2,0	2,0	2,1	1,8	1,8 *	:	:	S
UK	1,5	1,5	1,5	1,5	1,5	1,4	1,5	1,5	1,5 *	:	:	UK

6T1AJ

Further reading: National accounts ESA — detailed tables by branch, 1970–97. Eurostat.

eurostat

*Gross value added at market prices of fuel and power products
at current prices and current exchange rates. Million ECU*

6T1AK

	1989	1990	1991	1992	1993	1994	1995	1996	1997	1998	1999	
EU-15	210 792 *	223 056 *|	249 208 *	257 871 *	257 957 *	267 188 *	274 224 *	290 792 *	304 884 *	:	:	EU-15
EUR-11	154 836 *	169 299 *|	190 328 *	201 170 *	202 307 *	209 244 *	216 440 *	227 169 *	228 329 *	:	:	EUR-11
B	5 524	6 024	6 350	6 858	7 367	7 939	8 575	9 014	9 108	:	:	B
DK	2 281	2 562	2 720	2 900	2 913	3 056	3 301	3 438	3 546	:	:	DK
D	42 651	44 487 |	48 955	53 092	57 153	60 842	64 183	62 763	61 386	:	:	D
EL	2 088	2 357	2 036	2 191	2 005	2 001	2 184	2 511	2 548	:	:	EL
E	17 941	19 936	23 966	25 204	23 229	22 934	23 377	25 082	25 052	:	:	E
F	32 744	35 219	38 374	39 935	43 231	43 927	45 851	48 115	47 273	:	:	F
IRL	749 *	822 *	882 *	968 *	995 *	1 151 *	1 317 *	1 473 *	1 768 *	:	:	IRL
I	38 096	44 271	50 490	53 824	48 346	50 087	48 677	54 155	56 522	:	:	I
L	121	139	142	152	174	191	204	209	208	:	:	L
NL	8 722	9 906	11 431	10 960	11 252	11 230	12 291	13 891	14 035	:	:	NL
A	4 497	4 656	5 069	5 482	5 916	5 998	6 670	6 797	7 122	:	:	A
P	1 834	1 882	2 457	2 798	2 952	2 961	3 019	3 329	3 487 *	:	:	P
FIN	1 957	1 958	2 211	1 895	1 693	1 984	2 274	2 341	2 369	:	:	FIN
S	5 247	5 675	6 325	6 204	5 351	5 454	5 400	6 275	6 296 *	:	:	S
UK	46 340	43 162	47 799	45 406	45 381	47 432	46 899	51 400	64 164 *	:	:	UK

Further reading: National accounts ESA — detailed tables by branch, 1970–97.
Eurostat.

*Gross value added at market prices of fuel and power products
at current prices and current exchange rates as % of all branches*

6T1AL

	1989	1990	1991	1992	1993	1994	1995	1996	1997	1998	1999	
EU-15	4,5 *	4,4 *|	4,6 *	4,6 *	4,6 *	4,6 *	4,6 *	4,6 *	4,6 *	:	:	EU-15
EUR-11	4,3 *	4,3 *|	4,5 *	4,5 *	4,5 *	4,5 *	4,5 *	4,5 *	4,4 *	:	:	EUR-11
B	4,1	4,1	4,1	4,1	4,2	4,2	4,3	4,4	4,4	:	:	B
DK	2,7	2,8	2,9	2,9	2,8	2,8	2,8	2,8	2,8	:	:	DK
D	4,1	3,9 |	3,9	4,0	4,0	4,1	4,1	4,0	3,9	:	:	D
EL	3,9	4,2	3,1	3,2	2,8	2,6	2,7	2,8	2,6	:	:	EL
E	5,0	5,0	5,4	5,5	5,5	5,5	5,3	5,3	5,2	:	:	E
F	3,9	3,9	4,1	4,1	4,2	4,1	4,1	4,2	4,0	:	:	F
IRL	2,5 *	2,5 *	2,5 *	2,5 *	2,5 *	2,6 *	2,8 *	2,7 *	2,7 *	:	:	IRL
I	4,9	5,2	5,5	5,8	5,8	5,9	5,9	5,8	5,7	:	:	I
L	1,5	1,6	1,5	1,5	1,5	1,5	1,5	1,5	1,4	:	:	L
NL	4,4	4,7	5,1	4,7	4,4	4,2	4,2	4,7	4,6	:	:	NL
A	4,1	3,9	3,9	3,9	3,9	3,8	3,9	3,9	4,1	:	:	A
P	3,9	3,5	3,9	3,9	4,2	4,1	3,9	4,1	4,1 *	:	:	P
FIN	2,1	2,0	2,5	2,6	2,6	2,7	2,6	2,7	2,5	:	:	FIN
S	3,2	3,3	3,5	3,4	3,6	3,4	3,2	3,3	3,3 *	:	:	S
UK	6,2	5,8	6,1	5,8	5,9	5,7	5,7	5,9	5,9 *	:	:	UK

Further reading: National accounts ESA — detailed tables by branch, 1970–97.
Eurostat.

*Gross value added at market prices of manufactured products
at current prices and current exchange rates. Million ECU*

	1989	1990	1991	1992	1993	1994	1995	1996	1997	1998	1999	
EU-15	:	: |	:	:	1 167 674 *	1 216 356 *	1 267 067 *	1 303 295 *	1 381 054 *	:	:	EU-15
EUR-11	:	: |	:	:	951 022 *	982 063 *	1 025 303 *	1 046 909 *	1 078 645 *	:	:	EUR-11
B	30 006	32 137	31 460	32 532	33 346	36 280	39 593	38 350	39 334	:	:	B
DK	15 636	16 860	17 392	18 510	19 629	21 242	22 941	23 891	24 643	:	:	DK
D	310 835	339 606 |	363 148	369 947	354 514	359 712	372 548	364 497	366 405	:	:	D
EL	9 324	9 268	9 928	10 120	10 181	10 050	10 479	12 250	12 668	:	:	EL
E	77 476	82 039	86 024	85 087	75 192	75 098	80 370	83 740	87 117	:	:	E
F	178 623	190 840	190 322	193 812	195 487	203 452	213 429	217 062	222 699	:	:	F
IRL	9 046 *	9 927 *	10 658 *	11 693 *	12 017 *	13 904 *	15 910 *	17 789 *	21 349 *	:	:	IRL
I	185 144	192 921	195 825	192 982	168 599	173 254	171 564	192 893	202 689	:	:	I
L	1 841	1 815	1 719	1 779	1 812	1 936	2 057	2 055	2 077	:	:	L
NL	:	:	:	:	47 141	50 288	54 405	54 940	56 784	:	:	NL
A	25 514	27 853	29 455	30 246	31 127	32 709	34 385	34 591	35 772	:	:	A
P	12 607	13 802	15 347	17 210	16 330	16 906	18 132	19 010	19 910 *	:	:	P
FIN	22 711	22 063	18 271	16 226	15 457	18 523	22 911	21 983	24 509	:	:	FIN
S	36 166	35 095	33 989	32 564	28 087	32 155	37 652	40 183	40 318 *	:	:	S
UK	173 297	166 327	164 024	159 717	158 755	170 846	170 691	180 062	224 779 *	:	:	UK

Further reading: National accounts ESA — detailed tables by branch, 1970–97.
Eurostat.

6T1AM

*Gross value added at market prices of manufactured products
at current prices and current exchange rates as % of all branches*

	1989	1990	1991	1992	1993	1994	1995	1996	1997	1998	1999	
EU-15	:	: |	:	:	21,0 *	20,9 *	21,0 *	20,6 *	20,7 *	:	:	EU-15
EUR-11	:	: |	:	:	21,3 *	21,2 *	21,2 *	20,8 *	20,9 *	:	:	EUR-11
B	22,1	21,8	20,3	19,7	19,1	19,4	19,7	18,9	19,2	:	:	B
DK	18,2	18,3	18,4	18,6	18,7	19,2	19,2	19,2	19,2	:	:	DK
D	29,9	29,8 |	29,2	27,6	25,1	24,4	23,9	23,3	23,4	:	:	D
EL	17,3	16,4	15,0	14,6	14,1	13,1	12,8	13,7	13,0	:	:	EL
E	21,7	20,4	19,3	18,5	17,7	17,9	18,2	17,8	18,2	:	:	E
F	21,2	21,1	20,4	19,7	19,0	18,9	19,0	18,8	19,0	:	:	F
IRL	29,6 *	29,7 *	30,4 *	30,7 *	30,3 *	32,0 *	33,3 *	33,2 *	33,2 *	:	:	IRL
I	23,9	22,7	21,4	20,7	20,2	20,5	20,9	20,5	20,4	:	:	I
L	23,5	21,2	18,4	17,5	16,1	15,0	14,9	14,4	14,2	:	:	L
NL	:	:	:	:	18,5	18,6	18,8	18,5	18,6	:	:	NL
A	23,1	23,1	22,8	21,7	20,6	20,6	20,2	20,0	20,4	:	:	A
P	26,5	25,5	24,4	24,2	23,2	23,5	23,2	23,5	23,5 *	:	:	P
FIN	24,5	23,0	20,6	22,1	23,8	24,8	26,4	25,0	26,1	:	:	FIN
S	21,9	20,7	18,9	18,0	18,8	20,3	22,3	21,1	20,9 *	:	:	S
UK	23,3	22,2	20,9	20,5	20,5	20,6	20,9	20,6	20,6 *	:	:	UK

Further reading: National accounts ESA — detailed tables by branch, 1970–97.
Eurostat.

6T1AN

Building and construction is not divided into sub-branches here. Gross value added and other aggregates based on production are analysed by branch of activity (homogeneous units of production). Aggregates like income, expenditure and finance are analysed by sectors, which are groups of institutional units, i.e. companies, with similar economic behaviour. A unit of homogeneous production can thus be an institutional unit or a part of such a unit. Statistics on branches are therefore different from statistics on sectors.

Gross value added at market prices of building and construction at current prices and current exchange rates. Million ECU

	1989	1990	1991	1992	1993	1994	1995	1996	1997	1998	1999	
EU-15	288 929	313 747	329 066	332 484	317 663	319 639	325 608	330 353	342 576 *	:	:	EU-15
EUR-11	216 198	240 457	257 608	266 577	258 023	257 748	264 280	264 272	264 165 *	:	:	EUR-11
B	7 531	8 214	8 488	9 319	9 359	9 918	10 633	10 340	10 676	:	:	B
DK	5 155	5 267	4 946	5 558	5 473	5 790	6 254	6 513	6 717	:	:	DK
D	56 634	62 750	67 762	76 166	79 318	80 765	81 872	75 538	70 425	:	:	D
EL	3 571	3 916	5 351	5 017	5 668	5 392	5 376	6 078	7 159	:	:	EL
E	29 479	36 099	40 522	38 946	33 965	33 155	35 956	36 766	36 644	:	:	E
F	45 650	48 569	51 269	53 051	53 964	52 000	53 215	51 784	52 546	:	:	F
IRL	1 431	1 698	1 753	1 834	1 886	2 062	2 264	2 693	3 232 *	:	:	IRL
I	44 789	50 347	54 628	54 993	46 500	44 239	41 485	47 504	49 182	:	:	I
L	480	602	667	730	792	861	889	830	800	:	:	L
NL	11 376	12 039	12 429	12 955	13 927	14 427	15 164	15 499	16 055	:	:	NL
A	7 066	7 958	9 020	9 849	10 973	12 208	12 880	13 414	13 639	:	:	A
P	2 861	3 228	3 679	4 249	4 203	4 348	4 961	4 889	5 121 *	:	:	P
FIN	8 900	8 953	7 389	4 484	3 136	3 764	4 963	5 016	5 845	:	:	FIN
S	11 782	12 511	13 175	12 185	8 715	8 151	8 067	9 139	9 169 *	:	:	S
UK	52 223	51 596	47 986	43 146	39 784	42 558	41 632	44 351	55 366 *	:	:	UK

6T1AO

Further reading: National accounts ESA — detailed tables by branch, 1970–97.
Eurostat.

Gross value added at market prices of building and construction at current prices and current exchange rates as % of all branches

	1989	1990	1991	1992	1993	1994	1995	1996	1997	1998	1999	
EU-15	6,2	6,2	6,1	6,0	5,7	5,5	5,4	5,2	5,1 *	:	:	EU-15
EUR-11	5,9	6,1	6,1	6,0	5,8	5,6	5,5	5,2	5,1 *	:	:	EUR-11
B	5,5	5,6	5,5	5,6	5,4	5,3	5,3	5,1	5,2	:	:	B
DK	6,0	5,7	5,2	5,6	5,2	5,2	5,2	5,2	5,2	:	:	DK
D	5,4	5,5	5,5	5,7	5,6	5,5	5,2	4,8	4,5	:	:	D
EL	6,6	6,9	8,1	7,2	7,9	7,0	6,6	6,8	7,4	:	:	EL
E	8,3	9,0	9,1	8,5	8,0	7,9	8,2	7,8	7,7	:	:	E
F	5,4	5,4	5,5	5,4	5,2	4,8	4,7	4,5	4,5	:	:	F
IRL	4,7	5,1	5,0	4,8	4,8	4,7	4,7	5,0	5,0 *	:	:	IRL
I	5,8	5,9	6,0	5,9	5,6	5,2	5,1	5,0	5,0	:	:	I
L	6,1	7,0	7,2	7,2	7,0	6,6	6,5	5,8	5,5	:	:	L
NL	5,8	5,7	5,6	5,5	5,5	5,3	5,2	5,2	5,3	:	:	NL
A	6,4	6,6	7,0	7,1	7,3	7,7	7,6	7,8	7,8	:	:	A
P	6,0	6,0	5,8	6,0	6,0	6,0	6,4	6,0	6,0 *	:	:	P
FIN	9,6	9,3	8,3	6,1	4,8	5,0	5,7	5,7	6,2	:	:	FIN
S	7,1	7,4	7,3	6,7	5,8	5,2	4,8	4,8	4,7 *	:	:	S
UK	7,0	6,9	6,1	5,5	5,1	5,1	5,1	5,1	5,1 *	:	:	UK

6T1AP

Further reading: National accounts ESA — detailed tables by branch, 1970–97.
Eurostat.

Market services include recovery and repair, wholesale and retail trade, lodging and catering, inland, maritime, air and auxiliary transport services, communications and credit and insurance institutions and other market services. They are services produced for sale, usually with the aim of making a profit. From 2000 on, the recycling activity will be taken out of the market services and put among the industrial (manufacturing) activities.

Gross value added at market prices of market services at current prices and current exchange rates. Million ECU

	1989	1990	1991	1992	1993	1994	1995	1996	1997	1998	1999	
EU-15	2 194 809	2 391 978	2 593 807	2 753 627	2 819 383	2 987 371	3 108 552	3 290 089	3 487 170 *	:	:	EU-15
EUR-11	1 719 376	1 895 097	2 052 991	2 200 580	2 260 775	2 373 312	2 488 067	2 621 160	2 693 213 *	:	:	EUR-11
B	71 986	78 871	84 996	91 819	97 135	104 588	111 633	115 320	115 876	:	:	B
DK	39 388	42 696	44 060	46 024	48 920	52 185	56 359	58 693	60 540	:	:	DK
D	470 975	525 747	583 318	648 311	712 045	760 752	815 555	833 979	842 848	:	:	D
EL	20 973	22 328	33 159	36 690	38 974	42 798	45 746	50 691	55 359	:	:	EL
E	169 419	192 721	215 488	228 721	215 645	215 313	226 141	241 009	247 873	:	:	E
F	419 092	451 655	471 083	501 518	528 848	560 671	583 567	598 720	607 776	:	:	F
IRL	12 126	13 587	14 069	14 995	15 950	17 433	19 086	22 012	26 418 *	:	:	IRL
I	375 267	413 998	452 196	470 774	430 558	436 457	428 324	495 377	524 645	:	:	I
L	4 376	4 815	5 556	6 122	6 973	8 292	8 826	9 277	9 640	:	:	L
NL	87 286	94 278	99 991	108 285	119 583	128 450	138 691	144 006	148 774	:	:	NL
A	52 427	57 527	62 084	68 309	74 640	77 824	85 515	87 712	91 680	:	:	A
P	20 553	23 859	28 334	31 910	32 299	32 926	35 630	37 023	38 776 *	:	:	P
FIN	35 868	38 037	35 876	29 815	27 099	30 607	35 099	36 725	38 906	:	:	FIN
S	66 068	68 741	74 815	76 033	65 904	69 074	75 522	83 461	83 743 *	:	:	S
UK	349 004	363 116	388 782	394 299	404 810	450 001	442 858	476 084	594 315 *	:	:	UK

Further reading: National accounts ESA — detailed tables by branch, 1970–97. Eurostat.

Gross value added at market prices of market services at current prices and current exchange rates as % of all branches

	1989	1990	1991	1992	1993	1994	1995	1996	1997	1998	1999	
EU-15	46,9	47,5	48,4	49,3	50,6	51,4	51,6	52,1	52,4 *	:	:	EU-15
EUR-11	47,3	47,8	48,4	49,4	50,6	51,2	51,4	52,0	52,3 *	:	:	EUR-11
B	53,0	53,6	54,9	55,5	55,8	55,8	55,6	56,7	56,5	:	:	B
DK	45,8	46,4	46,7	46,3	46,6	47,1	47,1	47,1	47,1	:	:	DK
D	45,3	46,1	46,9	48,3	50,5	51,5	52,2	53,3	53,9	:	:	D
EL	39,0	39,5	49,9	52,9	54,0	55,8	55,9	56,5	56,9	:	:	EL
E	47,5	47,9	48,5	49,7	50,8	51,3	51,3	51,3	51,8	:	:	E
F	49,7	49,9	50,4	50,9	51,4	52,0	51,8	51,8	51,9	:	:	F
IRL	39,7	40,7	40,1	39,4	40,2	40,1	40,0	41,0	41,0 *	:	:	IRL
I	48,5	48,8	49,5	50,4	51,5	51,7	52,2	52,6	52,8	:	:	I
L	55,8	56,4	59,6	60,3	61,9	64,1	64,1	65,2	65,9	:	:	L
NL	44,3	44,7	45,0	46,1	47,0	47,6	47,8	48,4	48,8	:	:	NL
A	47,6	47,8	48,0	49,0	49,5	49,1	50,3	50,7	52,3	:	:	A
P	43,2	44,1	45,0	44,8	45,8	45,7	45,7	45,7	45,7 *	:	:	P
FIN	38,7	39,7	40,5	40,6	41,7	41,1	40,4	41,8	41,4	:	:	FIN
S	40,0	40,5	41,6	42,0	44,0	43,7	44,7	43,8	43,3 *	:	:	S
UK	46,9	48,5	49,5	50,6	52,2	54,1	54,2	54,5	54,5 *	:	:	UK

Further reading: National accounts ESA — detailed tables by branch, 1970–97. Eurostat.

Non-market services are measured by their cost of production and are mainly government services, as well as public social security. Other examples are private welfare institutions and outside domestic help. Non-market services do not include production of goods and services by households using their unpaid labour for their own consumption; the value added of such activities is presently excluded from conventional macroeconomic aggregates.

Gross value added at market prices of non-market services at current prices and current exchange rates. Million ECU

	1989	1990	1991	1992	1993	1994	1995	1996	1997	1998	1999	
EU-15	712 706	771 606 ǀ	832 644	879 124	876 460	891 066	918 102	968 364	1 003 157 *	:	:	EU-15
EUR-11	530 962	583 883 ǀ	630 263	673 206	690 225	708 607	736 422	771 079	776 568 *	:	:	EUR-11
B	17 815	19 166	20 675	22 132	24 154	25 888	27 752	27 773	27 772	:	:	B
DK	19 441	20 663	21 370	22 565	24 143	24 883	26 873	27 986	28 866	:	:	DK
D	140 936	151 402 ǀ	163 323	178 513	193 355	199 447	211 874	211 990	208 268	:	:	D
EL	9 049	9 972	8 320	8 394	8 712	8 963	10 122	10 455	11 701	:	:	EL
E	44 800	52 219	59 673	65 729	60 995	58 955	61 481	65 916	65 712	:	:	E
F	136 871	146 878	154 417	167 374	182 606	191 636	202 345	212 084	213 622	:	:	F
IRL	4 398	4 797	5 156	5 735	6 088	6 393	6 645	7 256	8 709 *	:	:	IRL
I	103 079	119 798	129 966	131 455	116 316	114 792	105 966	124 605	133 323	:	:	I
L	884	1 035	1 124	1 251	1 395	1 537	1 662	1 741	1 786	:	:	L
NL	41 049	43 483	45 953	49 709	54 346	56 234	59 913	59 960	60 066	:	:	NL
A	17 152	18 496	20 144	22 060	24 636	26 139	27 889	27 964	24 469	:	:	A
P	6 733	7 800	9 809	11 968	11 987	11 988	13 078	13 479	14 117 *	:	:	P
FIN	17 246	18 808	20 024	17 281	14 346	15 599	17 819	18 310	18 724	:	:	FIN
S	41 136	43 150	47 535	50 157	38 559	40 183	42 391	50 093	50 262 *	:	:	S
UK	112 118	113 938	125 156	124 800	114 821	108 431	102 294	108 752	135 759 *	:	:	UK

Further reading: National accounts ESA — detailed tables by branch, 1970–97.
Eurostat.

Gross value added at market prices of non-market services at current prices and current exchange rates as % of all branches

	1989	1990	1991	1992	1993	1994	1995	1996	1997	1998	1999	
EU-15	15,2	15,3 ǀ	15,5	15,7	15,7	15,3	15,2	15,3	15,1 *	:	:	EU-15
EUR-11	14,6	14,7 ǀ	14,9	15,1	15,5	15,3	15,2	15,3	15,1 *	:	:	EUR-11
B	13,1	13,0	13,3	13,4	13,9	13,8	13,8	13,7	13,5	:	:	B
DK	22,6	22,5	22,7	22,7	23,0	22,5	22,5	22,5	22,5	:	:	DK
D	13,6	13,3 ǀ	13,1	13,3	13,7	13,5	13,6	13,5	13,3	:	:	D
EL	16,8	17,6	12,5	12,1	12,1	11,7	12,4	11,7	12,0	:	:	EL
E	12,5	13,0	13,4	14,3	14,4	14,0	13,9	14,0	13,7	:	:	E
F	16,2	16,2	16,5	17,0	17,7	17,8	18,0	18,3	18,2	:	:	F
IRL	14,4	14,4	14,7	15,1	15,3	14,7	13,9	13,5	13,5 *	:	:	IRL
I	13,3	14,1	14,2	14,1	13,9	13,6	12,9	13,2	13,4	:	:	I
L	11,3	12,1	12,1	12,3	12,4	11,9	12,1	12,2	12,2	:	:	L
NL	20,9	20,6	20,7	21,1	21,3	20,8	20,7	20,2	19,7	:	:	NL
A	15,6	15,4	15,6	15,8	16,3	16,5	16,4	16,2	14,0	:	:	A
P	14,1	14,4	15,6	16,8	17,0	16,6	16,8	16,6	16,6 *	:	:	P
FIN	18,6	19,6	22,6	23,5	22,1	20,9	20,5	20,8	19,9	:	:	FIN
S	24,9	25,4	26,4	27,7	25,8	25,4	25,1	26,3	26,0 *	:	:	S
UK	15,1	15,2	15,9	16,0	14,8	13,0	12,5	12,4	12,4 *	:	:	UK

Further reading: National accounts ESA — detailed tables by branch, 1970–97.
Eurostat.

Final consumption expenditure (ESA, 1995, 3.75) consists of expenditure incurred by resident institutional units on goods or services that are used for the direct satisfaction of individual needs or wants or the collective needs of members of the community. The acquisition of these goods and services is financed from disposable income of households. The private final consumption expenditure includes households' and NPISHs' final consumption expenditure. Households consist of employers, employees, recipients of property incomes, recipients of pensions, recipients of other transfer incomes and NPISHs consist of non-profit-making institutions which are separate legal entities, which serve households and which are private non-market producers. Their principal resources, apart from those derived from occasional sales, are derived from voluntary contributions in cash or in kind from households in their capacity as consumers, from payments made by general governments and from property income.

Final consumption expenditure of households and NPISH (non-profit institutions serving households). Current series in million ECU/EUR

	1989	1990	1991	1992	1993	1994	1995	1996	1997	1998	1999	
EU-15	:	:	3 322 698	3 484 911	3 509 334	3 658 184	3 778 080	3 992 600	4 207 324	4 403 029	4 643 980 *	EU-15
EUR-11	:	:	2 585 404	2 740 723	2 771 788	2 876 967	2 998 384	3 143 089	3 196 205	3 319 985	3 470 394 *	EUR-11
B	79 443	86 208	91 530	96 747	101 175	107 944	113 731	114 618	115 235	120 377	124 975	B
DK	48 856	51 539	53 490	56 249	59 281	65 465	69 535	72 454	75 366	79 247	82 505	DK
D	:	:	813 025	884 938	959 953	1 001 426	1 069 438	1 077 463	1 075 303	1 106 033	1 145 877	D
EL	:	:	:	:	:	:	69 108	75 742	81 410	81 407	86 947 *	EL
E	:	:	:	:	:	:	267 205	286 027	292 375	308 195	332 563	E
F	493 318	529 996	547 624	577 172	607 763	633 057	659 533	683 880	682 067	711 385	736 626	F
IRL	:	22 015	23 012	24 604	24 598	26 574	27 663	31 041	36 330	38 661	42 994	IRL
I	463 101	499 236	545 545	563 582	496 269	508 465	492 798	566 307	605 320	627 412	654 474	I
L	:	:	:	:	:	:	6 686	6 965	7 131	7 401	7 870	L
NL	105 454	113 629	120 717	128 557	138 030	146 635	155 639	161 759	164 087	173 194	185 212	NL
A	:	:	:	:	:	:	101 086	104 720	103 711	105 797	110 090	A
P	:	:	:	:	:	:	53 433	57 375	59 625	63 703	68 446 *	P
FIN	53 257	54 293	53 667	46 044	40 192	45 019	51 173	52 933	55 022	57 828	61 269	FIN
S	:	:	:	:	87 097	90 675	92 140	103 837	106 248	106 607	113 175	S
UK	475 981	487 347	526 212	525 931	529 610	560 056	548 914	597 478	748 095	815 783	890 959	UK
IS	:	:	:	3 326	3 132	3 092	3 220	3 506	3 982	4 537	:	IS
NO	44 554	44 927	46 935	49 112	49 538	51 718	55 335	59 824	64 950	65 273	69 591	NO
EEA	:	:	:	:	:	:	:	:	:	:	:	EEA
CH	93 752	101 912	109 129	111 046	119 511	130 257	139 773	140 175	136 194	140 882	146 584	CH
US	3 264 513	3 008 813	3 204 796	3 242 923	3 804 189	3 964 966	3 798 894	4 124 857	4 875 759	5 218 886	5 881 769	US
CA	274 585	254 383	274 779	256 725	277 738	268 931	251 751	271 751	318 556	312 249	344 176	CA
JP	1 532 796	1 357 336	1 572 982	1 658 081	2 141 441	2 358 633	2 361 742	2 167 821	2 231 650	2 081 527	2 528 932	JP

Further reading: National accounts ESA — aggregates, 1970–97. Eurostat.

6T1AU

Government final consumption expenditure (ESA, 1995, 3.79) includes two categories of expenditure: the value of goods and services produced by general government itself other than own-account capital formation, and sales and purchases by general government of goods and services produced by market producers that are supplied to households — without any transformation — as social transfers in kind.

Final consumption expenditure of general government. Current series in million ECU/EUR

	1989	1990	1991	1992	1993	1994	1995	1996	1997	1998	1999	
EU-15	:	:	1 192 358	1 266 171	1 287 164	1 325 336	1 361 560	1 430 098	1 475 034	1 517 477	1 593 718	**EU-15**
EUR-11	:	:	925 257	995 174	1 028 976	1 057 106	1 093 671	1 142 309	1 150 939	1 175 992	1 226 722	**EUR-11**
B	29 442	31 569	34 301	36 740	39 515	42 125	45 264	45 987	45 663	47 184	49 431	**B**
DK	25 414	26 848	27 885	29 344	31 727	33 182	35 521	37 308	38 020	40 020	42 087	**DK**
D	:	:	274 986	308 675	332 046	347 733	372 419	374 593	363 098	366 878	377 349	**D**
EL	:	:	:	:	:	:	13 777	14 230	15 685	16 027	16 792	**EL**
E	:	:	:	:	:	:	80 732	86 269	86 921	90 271	95 697	**E**
F	198 999	213 150	222 491	240 248	266 562	275 027	283 648	296 200	300 465	304 414	318 279	**F**
IRL	:	6 119	6 717	7 360	7 476	8 025	8 350	9 068	10 724	11 191	12 233	**IRL**
I	153 246	175 390	190 551	190 747	169 298	165 163	149 818	175 511	186 871	191 514	199 096	**I**
L	:	:	:	:	:	:	2 468	2 616	2 663	2 748	3 219	**L**
NL	51 537	54 598	57 844	63 203	68 982	71 468	76 250	75 040	76 279	80 299	85 548	**NL**
A	22 467	24 124	26 225	28 781	32 348	34 456	36 718	36 971	36 104	37 279	38 564	**A**
P	:	:	:	:	:	:	15 423	16 783	17 894	19 234	21 170	**P**
FIN	21 183	23 319	24 797	21 334	17 879	19 731	22 582	23 271	24 256	24 979	26 137	**FIN**
S	:	:	:	:	46 587	47 683	48 373	55 911	56 021	56 640	60 490	**S**
UK	148 354	154 962	173 663	175 166	168 481	175 762	170 218	180 340	214 370	228 798	247 628	**UK**
IS	:	:	:	1 077	1 070	1 076	1 111	1 185	1 340	1 556	:	**IS**
NO	18 282	18 884	20 203	21 585	21 655	22 280	23 477	25 226	27 234	28 052	30 386	**NO**
EEA	:	:	:	:	:	:	:	:	:	:	:	**EEA**
CH	23 200	26 355	28 698	29 354	30 906	33 830	35 598	36 127	34 193	34 824	35 647	**CH**
US	819 175	758 348	819 226	806 889	915 565	926 678	866 873	922 861	1 078 711	1 125 800	1 243 882	**US**
CA	106 247	102 024	114 319	107 614	113 278	105 606	96 075	98 783	109 077	105 249	113 257	**CA**
JP	238 748	211 295	248 392	263 437	344 005	377 037	385 478	350 678	361 512	346 115	420 261	**JP**

Further reading: National accounts — aggregates — annual and quarterly data (ESA 95).
Publication: ESA 95 main economic aggregates.

Where is your nearest Data Shop? Addresses at the end of the book

EUROSTAT YEARBOOK 2001
215

*Final consumption expenditure of households and
NPISH (non-profit institutions serving households). Current series in % of GDP*

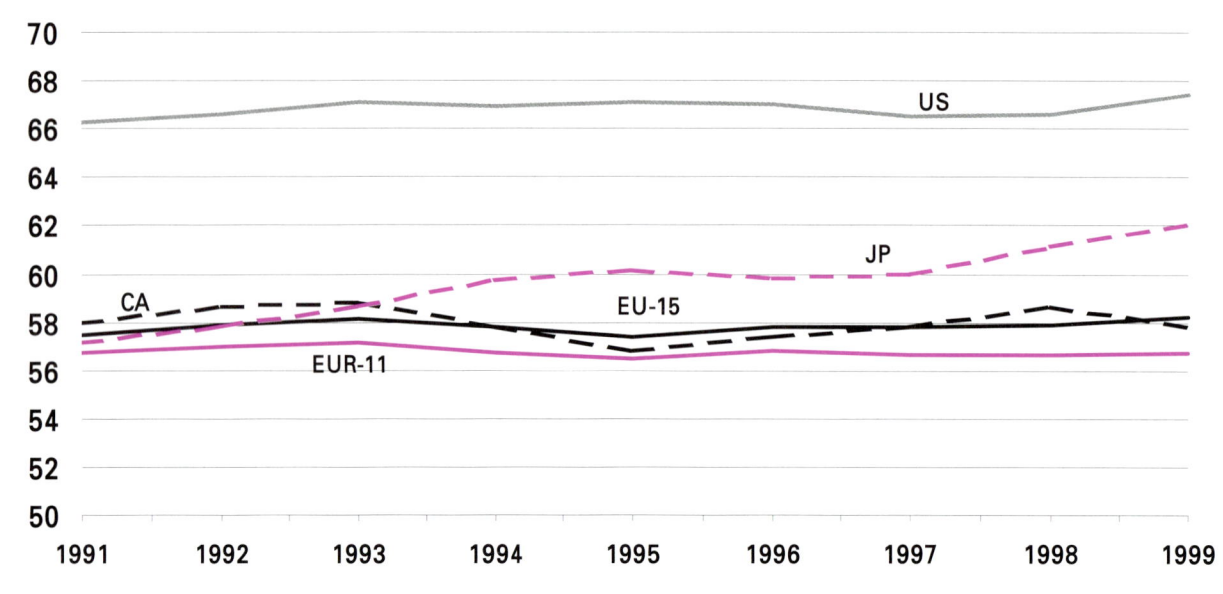

6T1AV

Further reading: National accounts — aggregates — annual and quarterly data (ESA 95).
                    Publication: ESA 95 main economic aggregates.

3

Final consumption expenditure of general government. Current series in % of GDP

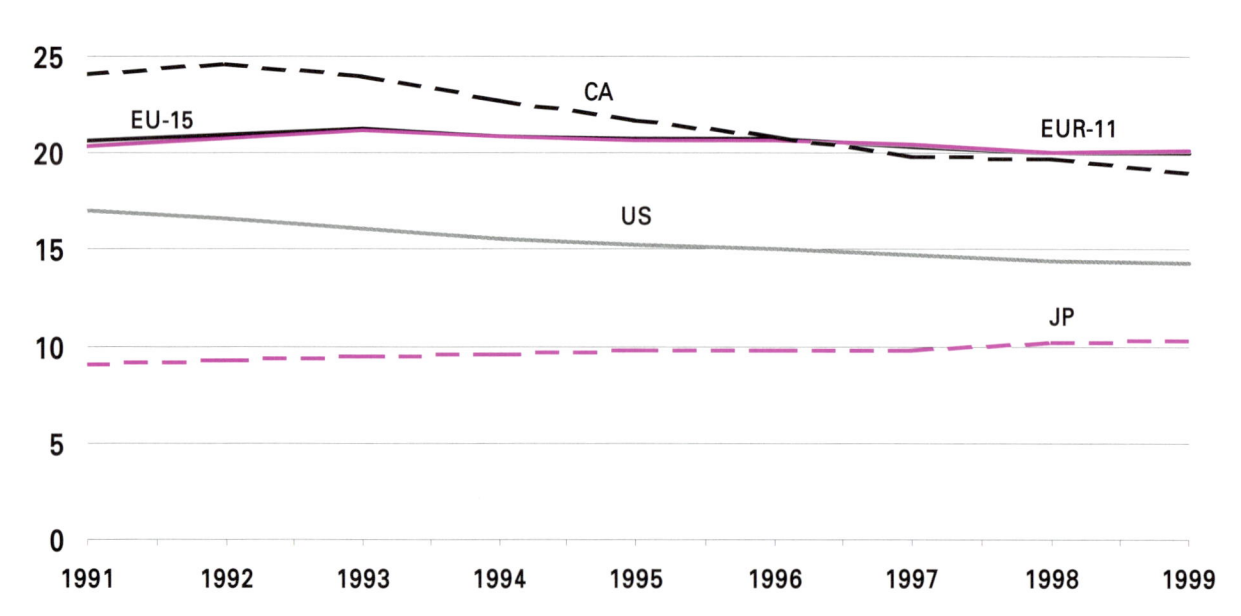

6T1AX

Further reading: National accounts — aggregates — annual and quarterly data (ESA 95).
                    Publication: ESA 95 main economic aggregates.

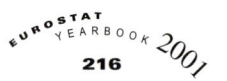

eurostat

Gross fixed capital formation (ESA, 1995, 3.102) consists of resident producers' acquisitions, less disposals, of fixed assets during a given period plus certain additions to the value of non-produced assets realised by the productive activity of produc-er or institutional units. Fixed assets are tangible or intangible assets produced as outputs from process-es of production that are themselves used repeated-ly, or continuously, in processes of production for more than one year.

Gross fixed capital formation (investments). Current series in million ECU

	1989	1990	1991	1992	1993	1994	1995	1996	1997	1998	1999	
EU-15	:	:	:	:	:	:	1 303 614	1 353 924	1 412 341	1 504 704	1 610 087 *	**EU-15**
EUR-11	:	:	:	:	:	:	1 092 446	1 121 230	1 136 064	1 197 002	1 273 235 *	**EUR-11**
B	31 431	35 906	35 228	37 172	37 657	39 279	42 860	42 931	44 829	46 602	49 051	**B**
DK	20 086	20 913	20 705	20 358	20 321	22 137	25 635	26 744	28 869	31 291	32 240	**DK**
D	:	:	340 352	375 437	384 851	407 997	421 919	408 732	399 399	409 770	422 859	**D**
EL	:	:	:	:	:	:	16 720	19 074	22 466	23 981	27 074 *	**EL**
E	:	:	:	:	:	:	98 249	103 733	107 962	118 434	133 600	**E**
F	201 226	216 072	216 714	217 846	211 136	217 336	223 272	226 271	224 831	238 542	256 148 *	**F**
IRL	:	6 970	6 621	6 985	6 596	7 633	8 736	10 807	14 323	16 884	20 494	**IRL**
I	169 109	186 157	197 700	194 709	156 535	155 403	153 911	178 078	186 401	196 102	207 956	**I**
L	:	:	:	:	:	:	3 026	2 908	3 103	3 144	3 565 *	**L**
NL	49 607	51 941	53 205	55 419	56 947	59 307	64 410	68 366	71 272	75 948	82 271	**NL**
A	:	:	:	:	:	:	41 829	42 429	42 135	45 541	47 551	**A**
P	:	:	:	:	:	:	18 122	19 864	22 373	24 466	26 460 *	**P**
FIN	30 972	30 810	24 346	16 690	12 040	13 059	16 111	17 111	19 437	21 568	23 280	**FIN**
S	:	:	:	:	25 133	26 242	28 415	32 446	31 163	33 531	37 120	**S**
UK	164 908	160 137	149 327	135 943	129 784	138 407	140 398	154 430	193 778	218 900	240 418	**UK**
IS	:	:	:	932	810	793	779	1 031	1 228	1 573	:	**IS**
NO	23 022	19 653	19 637	19 441	20 242	21 419	23 235	26 379	31 439	32 711	31 913	**NO**
EEA	:	:	:	:	:	:	:	:	:	:	:	**EEA**
CH	44 694	48 720	47 941	43 255	43 590	48 552	50 231	47 123	44 336	46 530	49 134	**CH**
US	946 586	834 717	823 745	827 881	986 252	1 059 336	1 031 226	1 152 080	1 404 119	1 562 562	1 797 352	**US**
CA	111 689	94 921	91 803	80 991	83 468	85 733	76 513	82 965	106 982	104 550	117 774	**CA**
JP	804 759	743 040	864 886	873 968	1 079 030	1 131 628	1 118 677	1 067 647	1 062 243	912 432	1 064 163	**JP**

6T1AY

Further reading: National accounts — aggregates — annual and quarterly data (ESA 95).
Publication: ESA 95 main economic aggregates.

Consumption of fixed capital. Current series in million ECU

	1989	1990	1991	1992	1993	1994	1995	1996	1997	1998	1999	
EU-15	:	:	:	:	:	:	:	:	:	:	:	EU-15
EUR-11	:	:	:	:	:	:	:	:	:	:	:	EUR-11
B	18 950	21 138	22 003	24 009	24 882	26 456	28 589	30 129	30 936	32 504	34 285	B
DK	15 310	16 414	17 136	18 165	18 894	19 349	20 751	21 578	22 572	22 776	22 913	DK
D	:	:	200 589	223 288	249 201	261 062	278 132	278 742	277 182	283 400	291 534	D
EL	:	:	:	:	:	:	8 149	8 959	10 552	11 264	:	EL
E	:	:	:	:	:	:	:	:	:	:	:	E
F	:	:	:	:	:	:	:	:	:	:	:	F
IRL	:	3 500	3 813	4 057	4 166	4 677	5 068	5 746	6 929	7 767	9 033	IRL
I	106 999	116 407	125 921	129 382	118 955	120 359	115 269	131 651	139 163	144 077	150 187	I
L	:	:	:	:	:	:	2 062	2 121	2 070	2 145	:	L
NL	:	:	:	:	:	:	47 968	49 005	49 489	51 642	54 513	NL
A	:	:	:	:	:	:	23 778	24 167	24 235	25 088	26 169	A
P	:	:	:	:	:	:	12 541	13 124	13 830	14 629	:	P
FIN	17 585	19 135	19 233	16 562	14 652	16 203	17 892	17 684	18 074	18 661	19 644	FIN
S	:	:	:	:	26 040	25 315	25 141	28 123	28 537	29 213	31 489	S
UK	95 009	96 571	106 450	104 729	107 175	109 398	104 635	110 043	136 536	145 466	156 835	UK
IS	:	:	:	:	:	:	:	:	:	:	:	IS
NO	16 201	15 649	15 925	16 383	16 562	17 039	18 136	19 218	20 845	21 341	23 089	NO
EEA	:	:	:	:	:	:	:	:	:	:	:	EEA
CH	:	:	:	:	:	:	:	:	:	:	:	CH
US	567 697	511 620	548 671	549 640	621 555	653 617	609 126	653 792	765 291	:	:	US
CA	56 538	53 656	58 472	55 095	59 961	58 922	56 090	61 270	70 740	69 394	75 820	CA
JP	:	:	:	:	:	:	:	:	:	:	:	JP

6U1AA

Further reading: National accounts — aggregates — annual and quarterly data (ESA 95).
Publication: ESA 95 main economic aggregates.

Gross fixed capital formation (investments). Current series in % of GDP

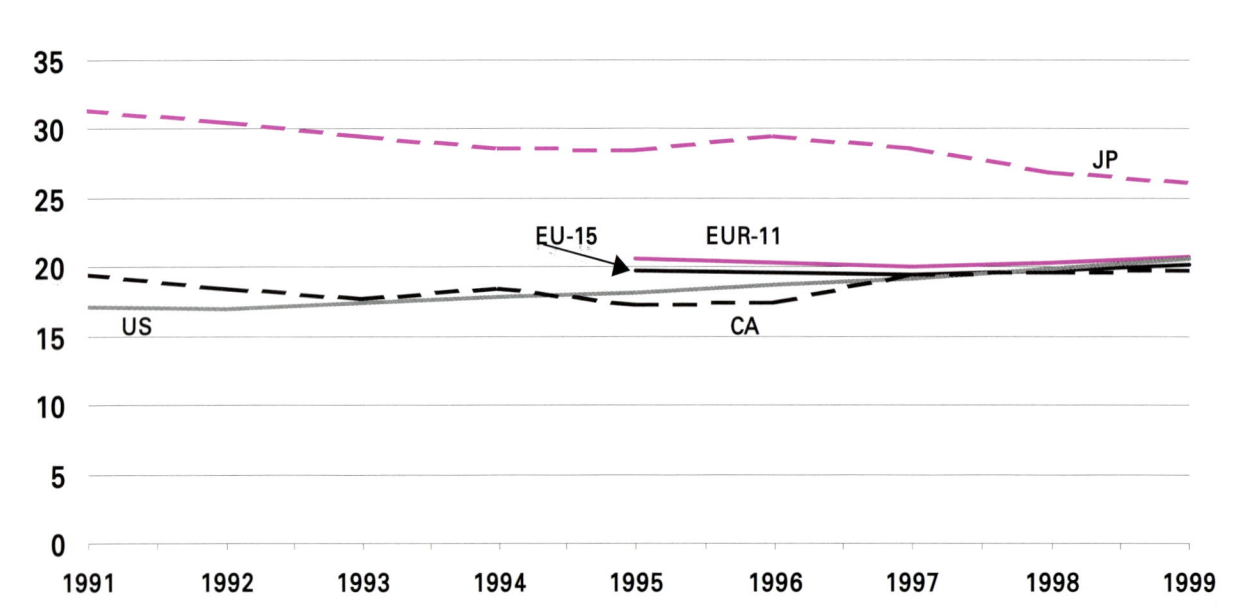

6T1AZ

Further reading: National accounts — aggregates — annual and quarterly data (ESA 95).
Publication: ESA 95 main economic aggregates.

Changes in inventories (ESA, 1995, 3.117) are measured by the value of the entries into inventories less the value of withdrawals and the value of any recurrent losses of goods held in inventories.

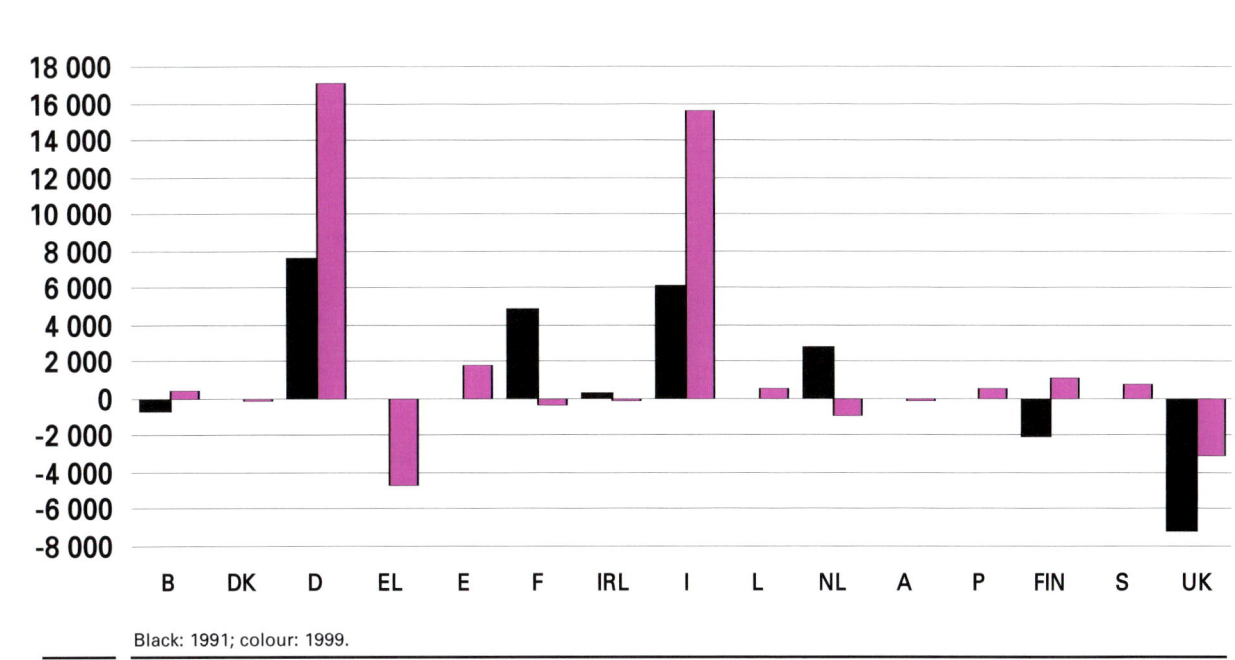

Changes in inventories. Current series in million ECU

Black: 1991; colour: 1999.

Further reading: National accounts — aggregates — annual and quarterly data (ESA 95).
Publication: ESA 95 main economic aggregates.

Compensation of employees (ESA, 1995, 4.02) is defined as the total remuneration, in cash or in kind, payable by an employer to an employee in return for work done by the latter during the accounting period. Compensation of employees is broken down into:

(a) wages and salaries (D.11):
– wages and salaries in cash;
– wages and salaries in kind;

(b) employers' social contributions (D.12):
– employers' actual social contributions (D.121);
– employers' imputed social contributions (D.122).

Compensation of employees: total industry. Current series in million ECU

	1989	1990	1991	1992	1993	1994	1995	1996	1997	1998	1999	
EU-15	:	:	:	:	:	:	3 392 152	3 534 302	3 693 711	3 836 818	4 042 525 *	**EU-15**
EUR-11	:	:	:	:	:	:	2 724 746	2 812 677	2 837 633	2 913 750	3 044 416 *	**EUR-11**
B	72 897	80 835	87 194	93 014	97 921	103 522	109 702	109 232	110 043	114 006	118 893	**B**
DK	54 835	58 345	59 879	62 441	64 815	67 599	72 884	76 186	78 559	82 771	87 856	**DK**
D	:	:	804 979	886 037	946 795	976 704	1 040 641	1 030 551	1 005 546	1 022 625	1 054 412	**D**
EL	:	:	:	:	:	:	28 989	31 273	34 755	35 784	38 382 *	**EL**
E	:	:	:	:	:	:	223 032	237 742	244 977	260 759	279 656	**E**
F	463 239	501 330	519 224	550 301	576 931	593 269	618 831	638 600	644 326	669 828	701 022	**F**
IRL	:	17 239	18 321	19 852	20 334	21 806	22 943	25 493	29 944	32 078	35 993	**IRL**
I	360 718	400 462	434 909	439 355	389 249	382 179	357 079	412 876	439 270	433 136	449 726	**I**
L	:	:	:	:	:	:	7 390	7 624	7 884	8 305	9 078	**L**
NL	:	:	:	:	:	:	162 508	165 547	168 196	176 966	189 241	**NL**
A	:	:	:	:	:	:	96 992	96 091	94 799	98 576	103 172	**A**
P	:	:	:	:	:	:	36 357	38 621	40 203	42 149	45 020 *	**P**
FIN	56 333	59 810	58 229	47 378	38 799	42 732	49 272	50 300	52 444	55 324	58 201	**FIN**
S	:	:	:	:	95 023	98 270	100 521	117 088	118 201	119 977	125 937	**S**
UK	424 456	441 560	476 240	470 462	456 831	476 813	465 012	497 078	624 564	684 537	745 934	**UK**
IS	:	:	:	:	:	:	:	:	:	:	:	**IS**
NO	45 265	44 941	46 655	48 277	47 683	49 647	53 120	57 410	63 553	66 012	71 512	**NO**
EEA	:	:	:	:	:	:	:	:	:	:	:	**EEA**
CH	:	:	:	:	:	:	:	:	:	:	:	**CH**
US	2 860 020	2 631 524	2 788 122	2 807 769	3 257 369	3 376 324	3 212 887	3 461 792	4 101 535	4 445 823	4 972 666	**US**
CA	268 914	248 345	267 000	247 215	261 347	249 227	233 351	247 647	288 747	285 017	314 923	**CA**
JP	:	:	:	:	:	:	:	:	:	:	:	**JP**

Further reading: National accounts — aggregates — annual and quarterly data (ESA 95). Publication: ESA 95 main economic aggregates.

Compensation of employees. Current series in % of GDP

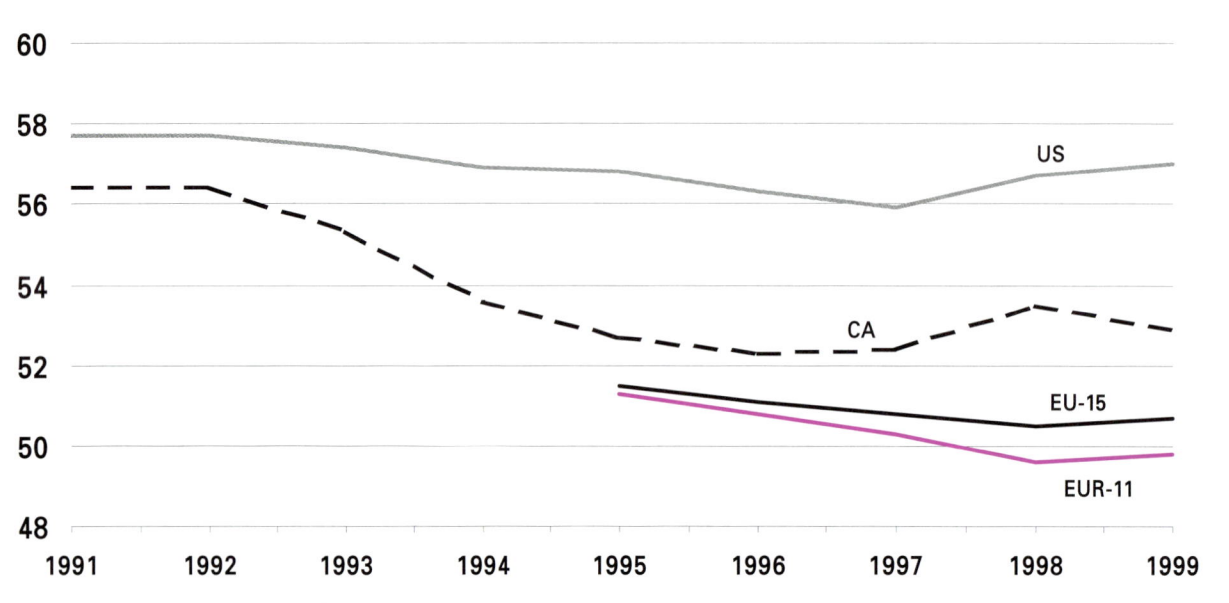

6U1AC

6U1AD

Gross wages and salaries: total industry. Current series in million ECU

	1989	1990	1991	1992	1993	1994	1995	1996	1997	1998	1999	
EU-15	:	:	:	:	:	:	:	:	:	:	:	EU-15
EUR-11	:	:	:	:	:	:	:	:	:	:	:	EUR-11
B	15 397	16 993	17 690	18 146	18 252	19 078	19 923	19 391	19 394	19 749	20 236	B
DK	11 389	12 200	12 371	12 812	13 083	13 432	14 665	14 913	15 138	15 540	16 269	DK
D	:	:	234 391	249 026	251 949	249 864	262 052	256 690	247 799	252 396	256 929	D
EL	:	:	:	:	:	:	5 108	5 487	5 821	5 940	:	EL
E	:	:	:	:	:	:	:	:	:	:	:	E
F	:	:	:	94 170	94 081	96 379	99 418	101 490	:	:	:	F
IRL	:	4 329	4 468	4 723	4 678	5 055	5 283	5 853	6 858	7 100	:	IRL
I	74 050	79 714	85 049	84 024	73 341	73 275	68 797	78 085	82 173	85 308	87 778	I
L	:	:	:	:	:	:	1 155	1 147	1 144	1 155	1 197	L
NL	:	:	:	:	:	:	28 877	28 485	28 311	27 223	28 256	NL
A	:	:	:	:	:	:	19 925	19 390	19 231	19 882	20 538	A
P	:	:	:	:	:	:	6 938	7 228	7 624	7 850	:	P
FIN	11 256	11 627	10 668	8 644	7 200	8 309	10 076	10 343	10 788	11 481	11 863	FIN
S	:	:	:	:	:	:	:	:	:	:	:	S
UK	109 645	112 197	116 466	112 200	106 165	110 685	108 092	111 002	134 640	141 601	161 397	UK

2J4AA

Gross wages and salaries: total industry. Current series in % of GDP

	1989	1990	1991	1992	1993	1994	1995	1996	1997	1998	1999	
EU-15	:	:	:	:	:	:	:	:	:	:	:	EU-15
EUR-11	:	:	:	:	:	:	:	:	:	:	:	EUR-11
B	10,7	10,9	10,8	10,4	9,9	9,7	9,4	9,2	9,0	8,8	8,7	B
DK	11,6	11,6	11,4	11,3	11,0	10,5	10,6	10,3	10,2	10,0	9,9	DK
D	:	:	16,4	15,9	15,1	14,2	13,9	13,7	13,3	13,1	13,0	D
EL	:	:	:	:	:	:	5,7	5,6	5,5	5,5	:	EL
E	:	:	:	:	:	:	:	:	:	:	:	E
F	:	:	:	9,1	8,6	8,5	8,4	8,3	:	:	:	F
IRL	:	11,6	11,6	11,4	11,0	11,0	10,4	10,2	9,7	9,2	:	IRL
I	9,3	9,2	9,1	8,8	8,6	8,5	8,2	8,0	8,0	8,0	8,0	I
L	:	:	:	:	:	:	8,3	8,0	7,4	7,0	6,6	L
NL	:	:	:	:	:	:	9,1	8,8	8,5	7,8	7,6	NL
A	:	:	:	:	:	:	11,1	10,6	10,5	10,5	10,5	A
P	:	:	:	:	:	:	8,4	8,2	8,2	7,9	:	P
FIN	10,7	10,8	10,7	10,3	9,8	9,8	10,2	10,3	10,0	9,9	9,7	FIN
S	:	:	:	:	:	:	:	:	:	:	:	S
UK	14,4	14,4	14,0	13,6	13,0	12,7	12,5	11,9	11,6	11,2	11,9	UK

6U3AA

Gross operating surplus and mixed income: total economy. Current series in million ECU

	1989	1990	1991	1992	1993	1994	1995	1996	1997	1998	1999	
EU-15	:	:	:	:	:	:	2 439 503	2 579 453	2 714 962	2 821 806	:	EU-15
EUR-11	:	:	:	:	:	:	1 994 607	2 099 400	2 158 085	2 244 129	:	EUR-11
B	55 208	58 133	59 337	63 289	65 423	70 282	77 355	77 204	78 907	82 604	85 791	B
DK	29 029	32 319	33 940	36 740	38 353	43 061	46 126	47 763	48 458	48 706	51 326	DK
D	:	:	491 291	522 044	555 545	605 059	654 186	662 395	673 680	705 322	715 410	D
EL	:	:	:	:	:	:	51 322	55 603	59 326	59 321	:	EL
E	:	:	:	:	:	:	185 032	199 551	202 291	209 766	222 826	E
F	310 484	328 872	338 021	356 691	371 509	390 442	403 176	408 974	416 939	434 925	447 512	F
IRL	:	15 920	16 197	16 889	17 805	18 960	22 156	25 598	32 551	36 893	41 744	IRL
I	366 918	389 091	415 600	419 652	372 840	391 220	390 662	456 042	473 401	479 314	494 633	I
L	:	:	:	:	:	:	4 908	5 025	5 637	6 088	6 206	L
NL	:	:	:	:	:	:	122 496	124 766	129 554	135 011	139 344	NL
A	:	:	:	:	:	:	61 304	64 259	63 856	65 768	67 345	A
P	:	:	:	:	:	:	34 681	36 896	39 049	42 419	:	P
FIN	34 894	34 634	29 707	26 843	26 431	31 968	38 651	38 690	42 220	46 018	48 476	FIN
S	:	:	:	:	51 842	58 115	63 994	65 651	65 315	63 513	63 665	S
UK	242 912	241 753	248 464	248 408	258 973	284 937	283 455	311 036	383 778	406 137	420 067	UK
IS	:	:	:	:	:	:	:	:	:	:	:	IS
NO	34 340	36 133	38 273	38 474	40 131	41 411	44 716	50 783	55 264	47 113	53 153	NO
EEA	:	:	:	:	:	:	:	:	:	:	:	EEA
CH	:	:	:	:	:	:	:	:	:	:	:	CH
US	:	:	:	:	:	:	:	:	:	:	:	US
CA	163 613	143 360	143 528	129 916	143 835	151 717	149 266	162 020	188 170	176 847	202 960	CA
JP	:	:	:	:	:	:	:	:	:	:	:	JP

6U1AE

Further reading: National accounts — aggregates — annual and quarterly data (ESA 95). Publication: ESA 95 main economic aggregates.

Gross operating surplus. Current series in % of GDP

	1989	1990	1991	1992	1993	1994	1995	1996	1997	1998	1999	
EU-15	:	:	:	:	:	:	37,1	37,3	37,3	37,1	:	EU-15
EUR-11	:	:	:	:	:	:	37,6	37,9	38,2	38,2	:	EUR-11
B	38,4	37,4	36,3	36,2	35,6	35,8	36,7	36,5	36,7	36,9	36,8	B
DK	29,6	30,8	31,3	32,3	32,4	33,6	33,5	33,1	32,6	31,4	31,4	DK
D	:	:	34,3	33,4	33,2	34,3	34,8	35,3	36,1	36,7	36,1	D
EL	:	:	:	:	:	:	57,1	56,8	55,6	54,6	:	EL
E	:	:	:	:	:	:	41,4	41,6	41,0	40,3	39,8	E
F	34,8	34,3	34,2	34,3	34,1	34,3	33,9	33,4	33,6	33,6	33,3	F
IRL	:	42,7	41,9	40,7	41,8	41,1	43,6	44,5	46,1	47,9	47,6	IRL
I	46,3	44,8	44,2	44,1	43,9	45,3	46,6	47,0	46,0	45,1	45,0	I
L	:	:	:	:	:	:	35,1	35,0	36,6	37,1	34,2	L
NL	:	:	:	:	:	:	38,6	38,5	39,0	38,6	37,7	NL
A	:	:	:	:	:	:	34,0	35,2	35,0	34,9	34,5	A
P	:	:	:	:	:	:	41,9	41,6	41,8	42,8	:	P
FIN	33,2	32,1	29,8	32,0	35,9	37,9	39,1	38,5	39,1	39,8	39,8	FIN
S	:	:	:	:	31,6	33,4	34,9	31,8	31,2	30,0	28,4	S
UK	31,9	31,0	29,8	30,1	31,6	32,6	32,9	33,5	33,0	32,3	31,1	UK

2J9AB

Exxternal balance (ESA, 1995, 8.68). Imports of goods and services are recorded on the resources side of the account and exports of goods and services on the uses side. The difference between resources and uses is the balancing item in the account, called 'external balance of goods and services'. If it is positive, there is a surplus for the rest of the world and a deficit for the total economy and vice versa if it is negative.

6U1AF

External balance of goods and services. Current series in million ECU

	1989	1990	1991	1992	1993	1994	1995	1996	1997	1998	1999	
EU-15	:	:	:	:	:	:	106 401	133 567	161 834	137 819	97 933	EU-15
EUR-11	:	:	:	:	:	:	98 092	125 666	149 671	141 785	110 509	EUR-11
B	3 412	2 925	3 290	4 876	6 563	7 996	8 560	8 507	9 711	8 998	9 311	B
DK	3 033	5 328	6 374	7 513	8 069	6 845	5 637	7 097	5 197	2 969	6 871	DK
D	:	:	- 3 355	- 3 851	2 938	5 601	12 115	19 518	25 520	29 221	19 235	D
EL	:	:	:	:	:	:	- 6 575	- 7 817	- 8 639	- 8 510	- 8 724	EL
E	:	:	:	:	:	:	- 834	2 371	4 713	1 756	- 4 370	E
F	- 8 048	- 9 301	- 4 550	6 017	16 368	15 162	16 295	20 337	37 108	34 532	33 775	F
IRL	:	1 722	1 924	3 161	4 518	4 564	5 815	6 693	8 935	8 784	12 035	IRL
I	- 1 484	354	- 304	- 805	27 536	30 095	34 145	47 892	41 719	35 578	22 018	I
L	:	:	:	:	:	:	1 838	1 868	2 467	3 041	2 914	L
NL	6 879	9 189	9 917	10 072	15 607	17 347	18 848	18 636	20 321	19 593	17 463	NL
A	:	:	:	:	:	:	- 1 440	- 1 956	- 2 636	- 1 009	- 682	A
P	:	:	:	:	:	:	- 5 088	- 5 803	- 7 002	- 8 939	- 11 068	P
FIN	- 2 131	- 1 802	- 878	843	3 601	4 999	7 837	7 605	8 817	10 229	9 877	FIN
S	:	:	:	:	6 322	8 152	12 637	13 767	14 877	13 335	12 396	S
UK	30 903	- 20 588	- 8 205	- 9 999	- 8 585	- 5 881	- 3 389	- 5 147	728	- 11 760	- 23 119	UK
IS	:	:	:	- 2	167	274	195	37	40	- 321	:	IS
NO	3 314	5 963	7 694	6 751	6 534	6 450	6 731	10 667	10 218	572	8 635	NO
EEA	:	:	:	:	:	:	:	:	:	:	:	EEA
CH	- 318	927	2 589	6 588	9 971	9 862	9 419	9 593	9 877	8 916	11 129	CH
US	73 270	- 56 109	- 16 685	- 21 454	- 51 623	- 73 223	- 64 411	- 70 053	- 78 789	- 135 158	- 238 347	US
CA	- 307	282	- 3 103	- 1 968	- 343	5 312	14 073	19 241	9 201	7 286	17 501	CA
JP	36 750	16 596	45 656	63 632	83 398	82 616	57 888	19 393	43 889	66 364	66 595	JP

3

External balance of goods and services. Current series in % of GDP

1J5AA

	1989	1990	1991	1992	1993	1994	1995	1996	1997	1998	1999	
EU-15	:	:	:	:	:	:	1,6	1,9	2,2	1,8	1,2 *	EU-15
EUR-11	:	:	:	:	:	:	1,8	2,3	2,7	2,4	1,8 *	EUR-11
B	2,4	1,9	2,0	2,8	3,6	4,1	4,1	4,0	4,5	4,0	4,0	B
DK	3,1	5,1	5,9	6,6	6,8	5,3	4,1	4,9	3,5	1,9	4,2	DK
D	:	:	- 0,2	- 0,2	0,2	0,3	0,6	1,0	1,4	1,5	1,0	D
EL	:	:	:	:	:	:	- 7,3	- 8,0	- 8,1	- 7,8	- 7,4 *	EL
E	:	:	:	:	:	:	- 0,2	0,5	1,0	0,3	- 0,8	E
F	- 0,9	- 1,0	- 0,5	0,6	1,5	1,3	1,4	1,7	3,0	2,7	2,5	F
IRL	:	4,6	5,0	7,6	10,6	9,9	11,5	11,6	12,7	11,4	13,7	IRL
I	- 0,2	0,0	0,0	- 0,1	3,2	3,5	4,1	4,9	4,1	3,3	2,0	I
L	:	:	:	:	:	:	13,2	13,0	16,0	18,6	16,1	L
NL	3,2	3,9	4,1	3,9	5,6	5,9	5,9	5,7	6,1	5,6	4,7	NL
A	:	:	:	:	:	:	- 0,8	- 1,1	- 1,4	- 0,5	- 0,3	A
P	:	:	:	:	:	:	- 6,1	- 6,5	- 7,5	- 9,0	- 10,5 *	P
FIN	- 2,0	- 1,7	- 0,9	1,0	4,9	5,9	7,9	7,6	8,2	8,9	8,1	FIN
S	:	:	:	:	3,9	4,7	6,9	6,7	7,1	6,3	5,5	S
UK	- 4,1	- 2,6	- 1,0	- 1,2	- 1,0	- 0,7	- 0,4	- 0,6	0,1	- 0,9	- 1,7	UK

Further reading: National accounts ESA — detailed tables by branch, 1970–97. Eurostat.

The general government sector includes all institutional units whose output is intended for individual and collective consumption, and mainly financed by compulsory payments made by units belonging to other sectors, and/or all institutional units principally engaged in the redistribution of national income and wealth.

General government output as a % of GDP

		1995	1996	1997	1998	1999	
EU-15		19,0	19,0	18,7	18,4	18,4	EU-15
EUR-11		17,9	17,9	17,7	17,3	17,3	EUR-11
B		16,5	16,6	16,3	16,3	16,4	B
DK		27,6	27,7	27,4	27,6	27,6	DK
D		14,7	14,5	14,1	13,8	13,6	D
EL		16,7	15,9	16,6	16,9	16,6	EL
E		17,0	16,8	16,5	16,2	16,0	E
F		21,9	22,4	22,5	21,8	21,9	F
IRL		16,6	15,9	15,2	14,6	14,1	IRL
I		17,2	17,5	17,6	17,4	17,6	I
L		16,4	16,6	15,7	15,5	15,0	L
NL		19,8	19,5	19,1	18,9	18,9	NL
A		21,6	21,4	18,2	18,2	18,2	A
P		19,1	19,4	19,7	19,8	20,6	P
FIN		27,5	28,0	26,8	25,7	25,4	FIN
S		29,5	29,9	29,4	29,6	30,0	S
UK		22,6	22,0	20,8	20,5	20,6	UK

1A1GG

General government output as a % of GDP

1B1GG

Intermediate consumption consists of the value of the goods and services consumed as inputs by a process of production, excluding fixed assets whose consumption is recorded as consumption of fixed capital. The goods and services may be either transformed or used up by the production process.

2A1GC

General government intermediate consumption as a % of GDP

	1995	1996	1997	1998	1999	
EU-15	5,9	6,0	6,0	5,9	6,1	**EU-15**
EUR-11	4,8	4,8	4,8	4,6	4,7	**EUR-11**
B	2,8	2,9	2,8	2,9	3,1	**B**
DK	7,7	7,8	7,7	7,8	8,0	**DK**
D	4,1	4,0	3,8	3,8	3,9	**D**
EL	5,3	5,0	4,8	4,9	4,8	**EL**
E	4,2	4,0	4,1	4,0	4,0	**E**
F	5,6	5,8	6,0	5,4	5,6	**F**
IRL	5,6	5,4	5,2	5,1	5,2	**IRL**
I	4,8	4,8	4,7	4,7	4,9	**I**
L	3,6	3,7	3,4	3,4	3,4	**L**
NL	6,3	6,3	6,2	6,2	6,2	**NL**
A	6,4	6,5	5,5	5,7	5,8	**A**
P	3,6	3,9	3,9	3,7	4,1	**P**
FIN	9,5	9,8	9,6	9,3	9,2	**FIN**
S	9,8	9,6	9,3	9,8	10,1	**S**
UK	11,9	11,8	11,2	11,3	11,5	**UK**

General government intermediate consumption as a % of GDP

2B1GC

Final consumption expenditure consists of expenditure incurred by resident institutional units on goods or services that are used for the direct satisfaction of individual needs or wants or the collective needs of members of the community.

General government final consumption expenditure as a % of GDP

	1995	1996	1997	1998	1999	
EU-15	20,7	20,7	20,3	20,0	20,0	EU-15
EUR-11	20,6	20,6	20,4	20,0	20,1	EUR-11
B	21,5	21,8	21,3	21,2	21,4	B
DK	25,8	25,9	25,6	25,8	25,7	DK
D	19,8	19,9	19,5	19,1	19,0	D
EL	15,3	14,5	15,2	15,3	15,0	EL
E	18,1	17,9	17,6	17,5	17,3	E
F	23,9	24,2	24,2	23,5	23,7	F
IRL	16,4	15,8	15,2	14,5	14,0	IRL
I	17,9	18,1	18,2	18,0	18,1	I
L	18,2	18,8	17,8	17,2	17,5	L
NL	24,0	23,1	22,9	22,8	22,8	NL
A	20,4	20,3	19,7	19,6	19,8	A
P	18,6	18,9	19,2	19,3	20,1	P
FIN	22,8	23,2	22,4	21,7	21,5	FIN
S	26,3	27,1	26,7	26,7	27,0	S
UK	19,8	19,4	18,4	18,2	18,5	UK

3A1GF

General government final consumption expenditure as a % of GDP

3B1GF

Gross fixed capital formation (GFCF) consists of resident producers' acquisitions, less disposals, of fixed assets during a given period plus certain additions to the value of non-produced assets realised by the productive activity of producer or institutional units. Fixed assets are tangible or intangible assets produced as outputs from processes of production that are themselves used repeatedly, or continuously, in processes of production for more than one year.

General government gross fixed capital formation as a % of GDP

	1995	1996	1997	1998	1999	
EU-15	2,6	2,4	2,2	2,2	2,3	**EU-15**
EUR-11	2,7	2,6	2,4	2,4	2,5	**EUR-11**
B	1,8	1,6	1,6	1,5	1,8	**B**
DK	1,8	2,0	1,9	1,7	1,6	**DK**
D	2,3	2,1	1,9	1,8	1,8	**D**
EL	3,2	3,2	3,4	3,6	4,1	**EL**
E	3,7	3,1	3,1	3,3	3,3	**E**
F	3,3	3,2	3,0	2,9	2,9	**F**
IRL	2,3	2,4	2,5	2,7	2,6	**IRL**
I	2,1	2,2	2,2	2,4	2,6	**I**
L	4,6	4,7	4,3	4,6	4,5	**L**
NL	3,0	3,1	2,9	3,0	3,0	**NL**
A	3,1	2,8	2,0	1,9	1,8	**A**
P	3,7	4,2	4,4	4,0	4,2	**P**
FIN	2,8	2,9	3,2	2,9	2,8	**FIN**
S	3,4	3,0	2,6	2,7	2,8	**S**
UK	2,0	1,5	1,2	1,2	1,1	**UK**

4A1CF

General government gross fixed capital formation as a % of GDP

4B1CF

Taxes on production and imports consist of compulsory, unrequited payments, in cash or in kind which are levied by general government, or by the institutions of the European Union, in respect of the production and importation of goods and services, the employment of labour, the ownership or use of land, buildings or other assets used in production.

Taxes on production and imports as a % of GDP

	1995	1996	1997	1998	1999	
EU-15	12,7	12,9	13,1	13,7	14,0	EU-15
EUR-11	12,5	12,7	12,8	13,5	13,8	EUR-11
B	12,2	12,7	12,9	12,9	13,3	B
DK	16,9	17,3	17,6	18,1	17,8	DK
D	11,4	11,4	11,4	11,6	12,2	D
EL	13,5	14,0	14,3	14,4	15,2	EL
E	10,2	10,2	10,5	11,1	11,7	E
F	15,4	16,1	16,0	16,0	16,0	F
IRL	13,5	13,7	13,5	13,2	13,1	IRL
I	12,1	11,8	12,5	15,4	15,3	I
L	12,4	12,6	12,8	13,4	14,2	L
NL	10,7	11,2	11,4	11,6	12,2	NL
A	14,2	14,5	15,0	15,0	15,0	A
P	14,3	14,3	14,3	14,6	15,2	P
FIN	13,7	13,5	14,3	14,1	14,0	FIN
S	13,7	14,3	14,8	15,5	17,0	S
UK	13,2	13,3	13,6	13,5	14,0	UK

5A1TP

Taxes on production and imports as a % of GDP

5B1TP

Current taxes on income and wealth cover all compulsory, unrequited payments, in cash or in kind, levied periodically by general government and by the rest of the world on the income and wealth of institutional units, and some periodic taxes which are assessed neither on the income nor the wealth.

Current taxes on income and wealth as a % of GDP

	1995	1996	1997	1998	1999	
EU-15	12,6	13,0	13,2	13,7	14,0	EU-15
EUR-11	11,5	12,0	12,2	12,5	12,9	EUR-11
B	16,7	16,7	17,1	17,6	17,2	B
DK	30,4	30,6	30,5	29,7	30,2	DK
D	11,1	11,5	11,2	11,5	12,0	D
EL	7,4	7,1	7,8	9,5	10,5	EL
E	10,1	10,3	10,5	10,2	10,3	E
F	8,5	8,9	9,5	11,7	12,2	F
IRL	13,6	14,1	14,0	13,9	13,8	IRL
I	14,8	15,4	16,2	14,5	15,2	I
L	17,5	18,4	17,4	17,0	16,4	L
NL	12,4	12,9	12,4	12,1	12,2	NL
A	12,0	13,1	13,5	13,7	13,4	A
P	9,3	9,9	10,1	10,0	10,5	P
FIN	17,4	18,9	18,4	18,8	18,6	FIN
S	20,2	21,6	21,8	22,6	22,4	S
UK	15,0	14,8	15,1	16,5	16,3	UK

Current taxes on income and wealth as a % of GDP

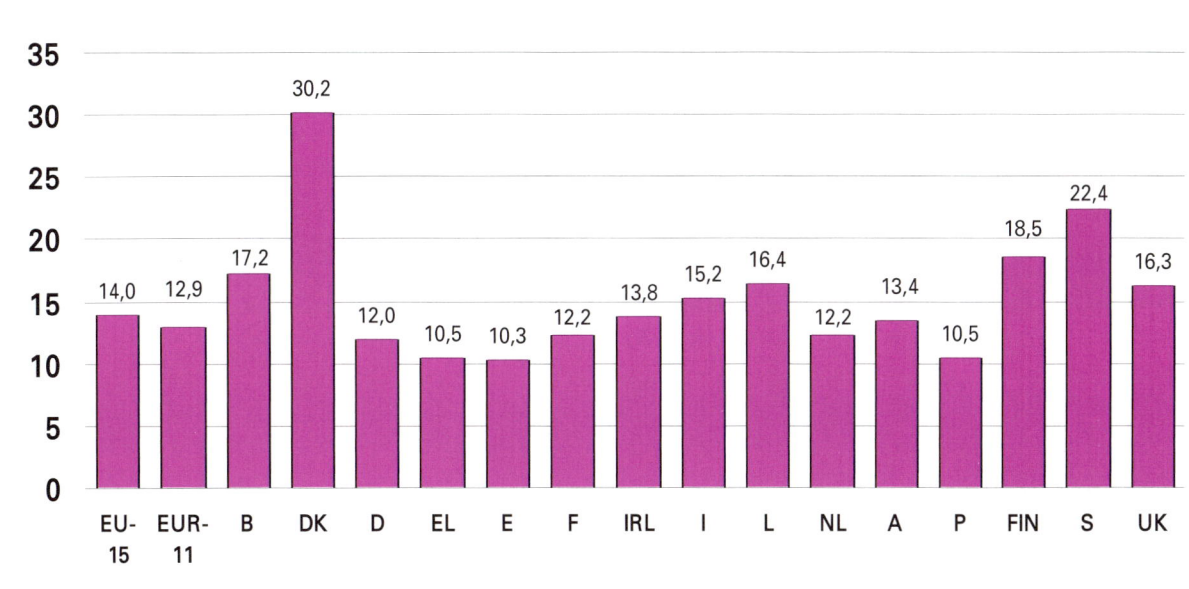

6A1CT

6B1CT

eurostat

Social contributions are paid on a compulsory or a voluntary basis by the employers, the employees and the self- and non-employed persons. They are of two types: actual and imputed.

Social contributions as a % of GDP

	1995	1996	1997	1998	1999	
EU-15	15,7	15,8	15,6	14,7	14,6	**EU-15**
EUR-11	17,4	17,7	17,6	16,5	16,5	**EUR-11**
B	16,8	16,8	16,7	16,5	16,5	**B**
DK	2,6	2,6	2,6	2,6	3,2	**DK**
D	18,8	19,4	19,6	19,2	18,9	**D**
EL	12,6	12,9	13,3	13,5	13,7	**EL**
E	13,0	13,2	13,1	13,1	13,1	**E**
F	20,5	20,7	20,3	18,2	18,4	**F**
IRL	6,8	6,3	6,0	5,7	5,8	**IRL**
I	14,8	15,0	15,4	12,9	12,7	**I**
L	12,4	12,3	11,8	11,6	11,9	**L**
NL	17,2	16,6	16,6	16,5	17,1	**NL**
A	17,4	17,5	17,3	17,2	17,1	**A**
P	10,9	11,0	11,2	11,5	11,7	**P**
FIN	14,9	14,3	13,4	13,0	13,0	**FIN**
S	14,2	15,2	15,0	15,1	14,2	**S**
UK	7,6	7,5	7,5	7,6	7,5	**UK**

7A1SC

Social contributions as a % of GDP

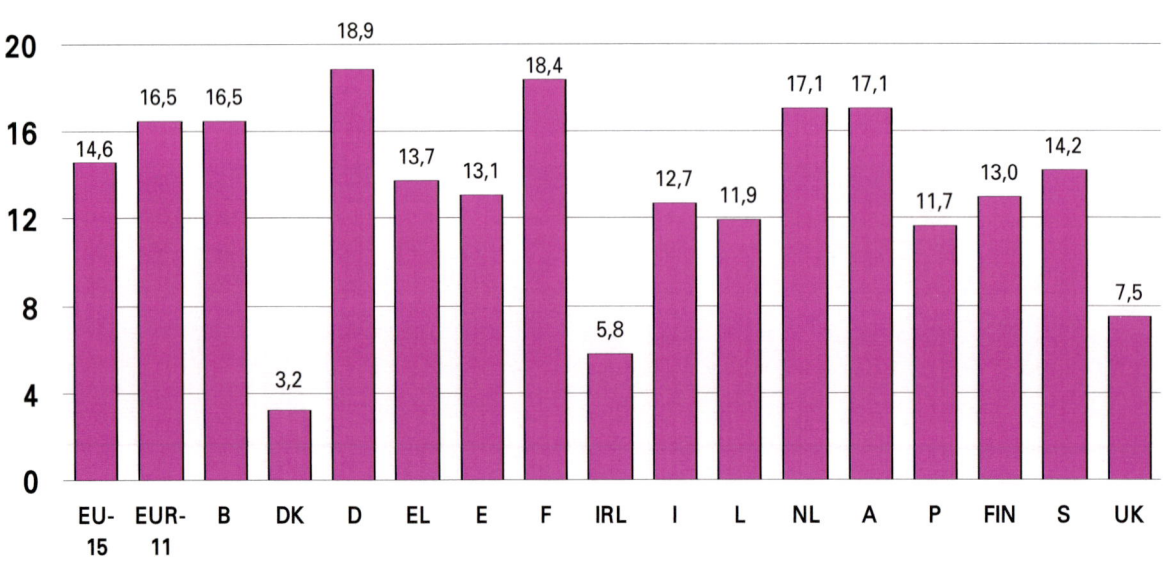

7B1SC

S ubsidies are current unrequited payments which general government or the institutions of the European Union make to resident producers, with the objective of influencing their levels of production, their prices or the remuneration of the factors of production.

8A1PG

Subsidies paid by general government as a % of GDP

	1995	1996	1997	1998	1999	
EU-15	1,6	1,6	1,4	1,4	1,4	EU-15
EUR-11	1,7	1,7	1,5	1,5	1,5	EUR-11
B	1,5	1,6	1,4	1,5	1,5	B
DK	2,5	2,6	2,5	2,3	2,4	DK
D	2,1	2,0	1,8	1,8	1,7	D
EL	0,4	0,5	0,2	0,1	0,2	EL
E	1,1	1,0	0,9	1,1	1,2	E
F	1,5	1,5	1,5	1,4	1,3	F
IRL	1,0	1,0	1,0	0,8	0,7	IRL
I	1,5	1,5	1,2	1,3	1,3	I
L	1,8	2,0	1,8	1,8	1,5	L
NL	1,1	1,2	1,5	1,5	1,6	NL
A	2,9	2,6	2,6	2,8	2,6	A
P	1,4	1,5	1,2	1,1	1,0	P
FIN	2,8	2,1	1,9	1,7	1,6	FIN
S	3,8	3,3	2,7	2,2	2,0	S
UK	0,7	0,8	0,6	0,5	0,6	UK

Subsidies paid by general government as a % of GDP

8B1PG

 Need longer time series? Ask your Data Shop

EUROSTAT YEARBOOK 2001
231

Social benefits (other than social transfers in kind) are those paid to households by social security funds, other government units, NPISH (non-profit institutions serving households), insurance enter- prises, employers administering unfunded social insurance schemes and other institutional units administering private-funded insurance schemes.

Social benefits (other than social transfers in kind) paid by general government as a % of GDP

	1995	1996	1997	1998	1999	
EU-15	17,2	17,4	17,2	16,7	16,5	EU-15
EUR-11	17,3	17,7	17,6	17,2	17,1	EUR-11
B	16,6	16,6	16,3	16,0	15,7	B
DK	20,4	19,8	18,9	18,2	17,7	DK
D	18,1	19,3	19,3	18,9	18,9	D
EL	15,1	15,4	15,6	15,6	15,8	EL
E	13,9	13,8	13,3	12,8	12,4	E
F	18,5	18,7	18,8	18,4	18,4	F
IRL	11,8	11,6	10,9	10,3	10,2	IRL
I	16,7	16,9	17,3	17,0	17,4	I
L	16,5	16,4	15,7	15,4	15,1	L
NL	15,3	14,8	13,9	13,0	12,5	NL
A	19,5	19,5	18,9	18,6	18,6	A
P	11,8	11,8	11,7	11,8	11,9	P
FIN	22,2	21,5	19,9	18,4	17,9	FIN
S	21,3	20,3	19,7	19,5	19,1	S
UK	15,4	14,9	14,4	13,7	13,5	UK

9A1SB

Social benefits (other than social transfers in kind) paid by general government as a % of GDP

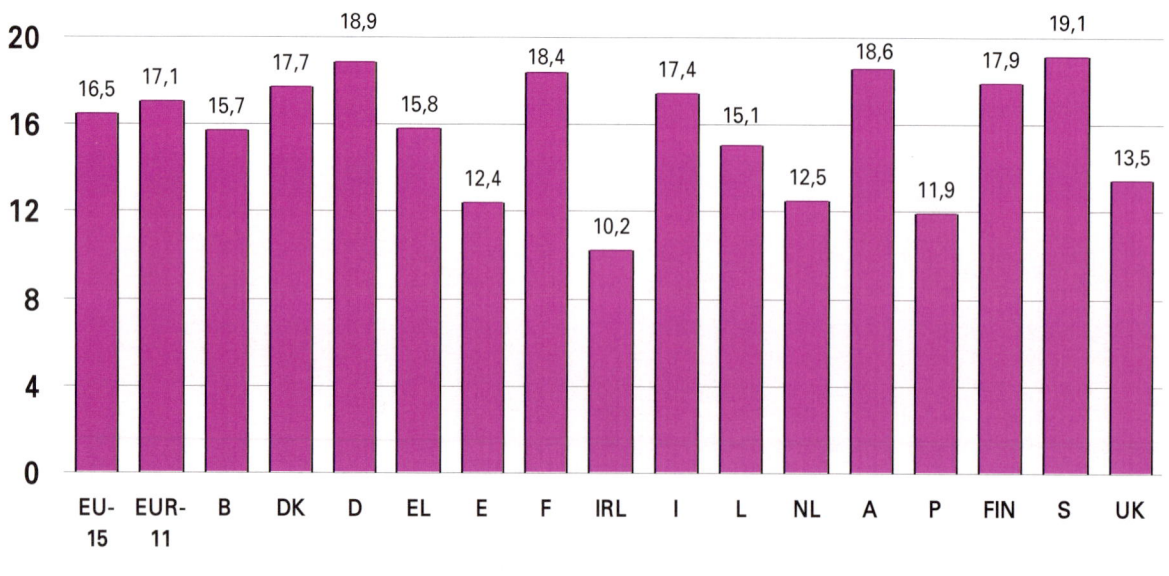

9B1SB

eurostat

Compensation of employees is defined as the total remuneration, in cash or in kind, payable by an employer to an employee in return for work done by the latter during the accounting period.

Compensation of employees paid by general government as a % of GDP

	1995	1996	1997	1998	1999	
EU-15	11,2	11,1	10,8	10,5	10,4	**EU-15**
EUR-11	11,2	11,2	11,0	10,8	10,7	**EUR-11**
B	12,0	11,9	11,8	11,7	11,6	**B**
DK	17,3	17,3	17,2	17,4	17,3	**DK**
D	9,0	8,9	8,7	8,4	8,3	**D**
EL	11,3	10,7	11,6	11,7	11,5	**EL**
E	11,3	11,3	10,9	10,7	10,5	**E**
F	13,7	13,9	13,8	13,7	13,7	**F**
IRL	10,2	9,7	9,2	8,8	8,2	**IRL**
I	11,2	11,5	11,6	10,7	10,7	**I**
L	9,6	9,6	9,3	9,1	8,7	**L**
NL	10,8	10,4	10,2	10,2	10,2	**NL**
A	12,6	12,3	11,5	11,3	11,4	**A**
P	13,7	13,7	13,9	14,2	14,6	**P**
FIN	15,4	15,6	14,6	13,9	13,6	**FIN**
S	17,3	17,8	17,5	16,9	16,7	**S**
UK	8,8	8,3	7,8	7,4	7,5	**UK**

10A1C

Compensation of employees paid by general government as a % of GDP

10B1C

D ata on social protection expenditure and receipts are harmonised according to the European system of integrated social protection statistics (Esspros). Social protection encompasses all action by public or private bodies to relieve house- holds and individuals of the burden of a defined set of risks or needs associated with old age, sickness, childbearing and family, disability, unemployment, etc. Expenditure on education is excluded.

Total expenditure on social protection at current prices as a % of GDP. 1997

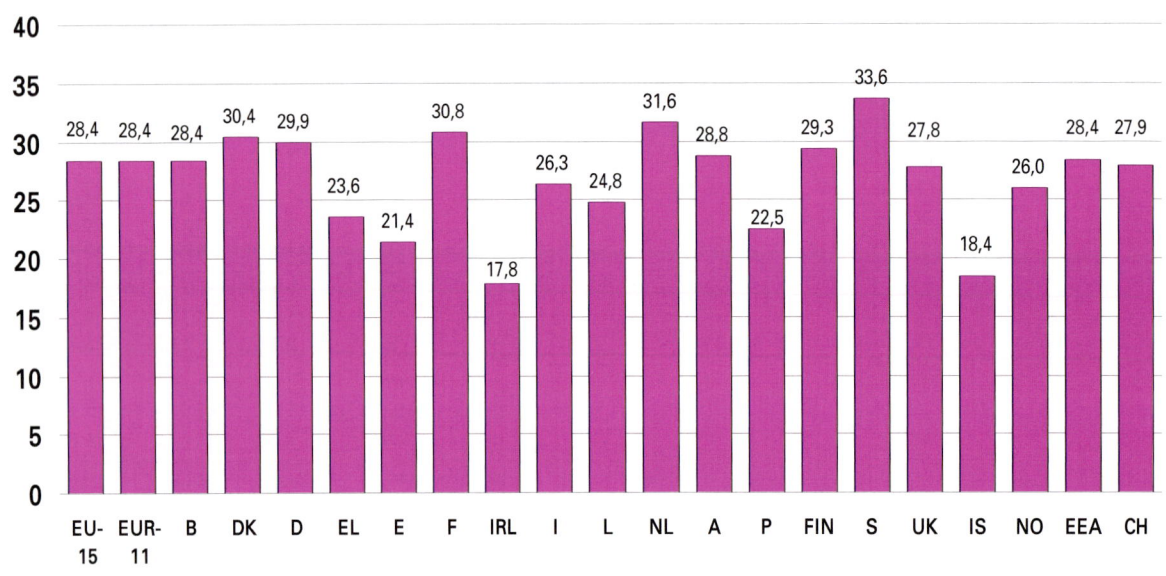

Further reading: Esspros manual, 1996. Eurostat.
Social protection expenditure and receipts, data 1980–97. Eurostat.

Social benefits are recorded without any deduction of taxes or other compulsory levies payable on them by beneficiaries.

Total expenditure on social protection at current prices as a % of GDP

	1989	1990	1991	1992	1993	1994	1995	1996	1997	1998	1999	
EU-15	:	25,4 |	26,6 |	28,0	29,1	28,7	28,7	28,9 *	28,4 *	:	:	EU-15
EUR-11	:	25,4 |	26,4 |	27,6	28,7	28,4	28,5	28,8 *	28,4 *	:	:	EUR-11
B	:	26,6	27,2	27,2	29,3	28,9	28,2	28,8 *	28,4 *	:	:	B
DK	:	28,7	29,7	30,3	31,9	32,9	32,2	31,4	30,4	29,9	:	DK
D	26,0	25,4 |	27,0 |	28,3	29,1	28,9	29,6	30,6 *	29,9 *	:	:	D
EL	:	23,2	21,9	21,5	22,3	22,3	22,6	23,1	23,6	24,5 *	:	EL
E	19,2	19,9	21,2	22,4	24,0	22,8	22,1	21,9 *	21,4 *	:	:	E
F	:	27,7	28,4	29,4	31,0	30,6	30,7	31,0	30,8	:	:	F
IRL	:	19,4	20,5	21,0	21,0	20,4	19,9	18,7	17,8	16,9 *	:	IRL
I	:	24,3	24,8	26,0	26,2	26,0	25,0	25,7	26,3	25,8 *	:	I
L	:	22,6	23,5	23,7	24,5	24,1	24,9	25,2	24,8	:	:	L
NL	:	32,5	32,6	33,2	33,6	32,7	33,1	32,2	31,6 *	:	:	NL
A	:	26,7	27,0	27,6	28,9	29,8	29,7	29,6	28,8	28,4	:	A
P	:	15,6	16,9	18,6	21,0	21,0	20,8	21,6	22,5 *	:	:	P
FIN	23,8	25,1	29,8	33,6	34,6	33,8	31,8	31,6	29,3	27,3 *	:	FIN
S	:	33,1	34,3	37,1	38,6	37,2	35,2	34,5	33,6	33,3 *	:	S
UK	:	23,5	25,8	28,3	29,6	28,8	28,6	28,6	27,8	:	:	UK
IS	:	17,1	17,8	18,4	18,9	18,6	19,0	18,7	18,4	:	:	IS
NO	:	26,4 *	27,6 *	28,6 *	28,8 *	28,1 *	27,2 *	26,2 *	26,0 *	:	:	NO
EEA	:	25,4 *|	: |	28,0 *	29,1 *	28,7 *	28,6 *	28,9 *	28,4 *	:	:	EEA
CH		20,2	21,6	23,6	25,1	25,2	25,8	26,9	27,9 *	28,0 *	:	CH

Further reading: Esspros manual, 1996. Eurostat.
Social protection expenditure and receipts, data 1980–97. Eurostat.

Social benefits are recorded without any deduction of taxes or other compulsory levies payable on them by beneficiaries.

5A1CW

Total expenditure on social protection per head of population in ECU. 1997

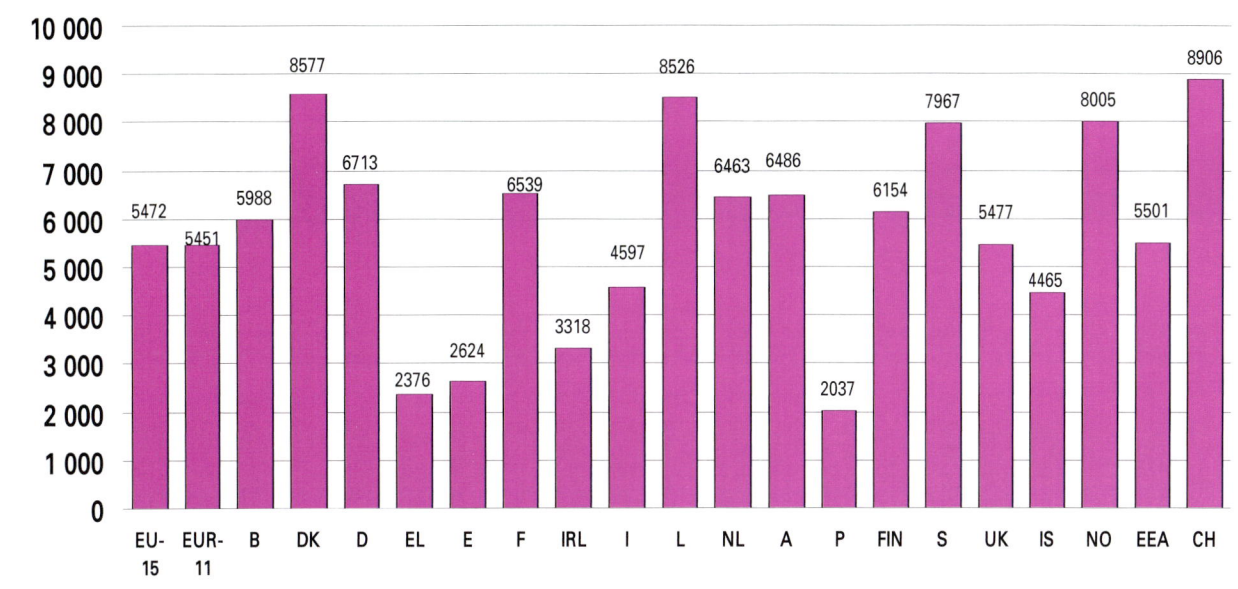

Further reading: Esspros manual, 1996. Eurostat.
Social protection expenditure and receipts, data 1980–97. Eurostat.

Social benefits are recorded without any deduction of taxes or other compulsory levies payable on them by beneficiaries.

3

3C1AC

Total expenditure on social protection per head of population in ECU

	1989	1990	1991	1992	1993	1994	1995	1996	1997	1998	1999	
EU-15	:	3 640 |	4 126	4 493	4 668	4 827	5 005	5 290 *	5 472 *	:	:	**EU-15**
EUR-11	:	3 669 |	4 156	4 544	4 752	4 905	5 144	5 415 *	5 451 *	:	:	**EUR-11**
B	:	4 145	4 455	4 734	5 343	5 611	5 865	5 995 *	5 988 *	:	:	**B**
DK		5 874	6 257	6 666	7 289	8 082	8 494	8 615	8 577	8 850	:	**DK**
D	4 507	4 738 |	4 700	5 358	5 851	6 147	6 668	6 887 *	6 713 *	:	:	**D**
EL	:	1 492	1 537	1 582	1 693	1 783	1 915	2 140	2 376	2 526 *	:	**EL**
E	1 762	2 044	2 396	2 630	2 579	2 443	2 478	2 629 *	2 624 *	:	:	**E**
F	:	4 588	4 834	5 216	5 718	5 903	6 267	6 495	6 539	:	:	**F**
IRL	:	1 984	2 169	2 391	2 445	2 607	2 767	2 933	3 318	3 412 *	:	**IRL**
I	:	3 661	4 039	4 272	3 842	3 865	3 606	4 256	4 597	4 678 *	:	**I**
L	:	5 009	5 604	6 076	6 940	7 510	8 175	8 438	8 526	:	:	**L**
NL	:	4 835	5 068	5 415	5 852	5 988	6 500	6 444	6 463 *	6 634 *	:	**NL**
A	:	4 339	4 652	5 047	5 645	6 129	6 526	6 593	6 486	6 669	:	**A**
P	:	858	1 083	1 378	1 519	1 576	1 686	1 869	2 037 *	:	:	**P**
FIN	4 942	5 426	5 938	5 588	5 024	5 606	6 158	6 203	6 154	6 126 *	:	**FIN**
S	:	6 993	7 702	8 181	7 275	7 385	7 316	8 045	7 967	7 989 *	:	**S**
UK	:	3 177	3 715	4 014	4 157	4 310	4 208	4 522	5 477	:	:	**UK**
IS	:	3 300	3 748	3 749	3 713	3 662	3 797	3 999	4 465	5 012 *	:	**IS**
NO	:	5 652 *	6 162 *	6 524 *	6 612 *	6 707 *	6 984 *	7 411 *	8 005 *	:	:	**NO**
EEA	:	3 663 *|	4 149 *	4 516 *	4 689 *	4 848 *	5 027 *	5 314 *	5 501 *	:	:	**EEA**
CH	:	5 419	5 987	6 471	7 318	7 952	8 622	8 865	8 906 *	9 270 *	:	**CH**

Further reading: Esspros manual, 1996. Eurostat.
Social protection expenditure and receipts, data 1980–97. Eurostat.

Social benefits are recorded without any deduction of taxes or other compulsory levies payable on them by beneficiaries.

eurostat

Need an update for this indicator? Ask your Data Shop

Social protection expenditure includes provision of social benefits, administration costs and other expenditure (for example, interest paid to banks).

Benefits provision represents the core of social protection expenditure. Benefits are classified according to eight social protection 'functions'.

Total expenditure on social protection per head of population at constant prices. 1990 = 100

	1989	1990	1991	1992	1993	1994	1995	1996	1997	1998	1999	
EU-15	:	100 |	108	115	118	119	122	125 *	125 *	:	:	EU-15
EUR-11	:	100 |	109	115	118	118	121	124 *	125 *	:	:	EUR-11
B	:	100	104	106	113	114	114	116 *	118 *	:	:	B
DK	:	100	105	108	113	122	122	122	121	122	:	DK
D	98	100 |	120	130	131	133	138	143 *	141 *	:	:	D
EL	:	100	96	94	96	97	101	105	111	120 *	:	EL
E	93	100	110	117	124	119	119	120 *	121 *	:	:	E
F	:	100	103	107	111	112	116	117	118	:	:	F
IRL	:	100	106	112	119	123	131	133	139	144 *	:	IRL
I	:	100	105	109	109	109	108	113	118	118 *	:	I
L	:	100	108	112	120	125	129	134	138	:	:	L
NL	:	100	101	103	104	102	106	105	106 *	106 *	:	NL
A	:	100	104	107	110	116	117	118	118	121	:	A
P	:	100	112	128	143	148	151	162	176 *	:	:	P
FIN	94	100	108	115	116	119	119	122	121	120 *	:	FIN
S	:	100	100	105	108	108	106	106	106	109 *	:	S
UK	:	100	109	119	128	129	130	134	134	:	:	UK
IS	:	100	105	103	104	106	110	113	118	127 *	:	IS
NO	:	100 *	106 *	110 *	113 *	114 *	115 *	119 *	122 *	:	:	NO
EEA	:	100 *|	108 *	115 *	118 *	119 *	121 *	124 *	125 *	:	:	EEA
CH	:	100	105	112	117	118	120	124	130 *	132 *	:	CH

3C1AB

Further reading: Esspros manual, 1996. Eurostat.
Social protection expenditure and receipts, data 1980–97. Eurostat.

Social benefits are recorded without any deduction of taxes or other compulsory levies payable on them by beneficiaries.

Total expenditure on social protection by type as a % of total expenditure

	Social benefits			Administration costs			Other expenditure			
	1990	1993	1997	1990	1993	1997	1990	1993	1997	
EU-15	: |	96	96 *	: |	4	3 *	: |	1	1 *	EU-15
EUR-11	96 |	95	96 *	4 |	4	3 *	1 |	1	1 *	EUR-11
B	95	94	94 *	3	4	4 *	2	2	2 *	B
DK	97	97	97	3	3	3	:	:	:	DK
D	96 |	96	97 *	4 |	4	3 *	0 |	0	0 *	D
EL	94	96	96	5	3	4	1	1	0	EL
E	98	97	98 *	3	3	2 *	0	0	0 *	E
F	95	95	95	4	4	4	1	2	1	F
IRL	96	96	96	4	4	4	0	0	0	IRL
I	95	95	97	4	3	3	1	2	1	I
L	96	97	96	3	3	3	1	1	1	L
NL	95	95	95 *	4	4	4 *	1	1	1 *	NL
A	97	97	97	2	2	2	1	1	1	A
P	87	87	88 *	5	4	4 *	7	9	8 *	P
FIN	97	97	97	4	3	3	:	:	:	FIN
S	:	99	99	:	1	1	:	0	0	S
UK	96	96	97	4	4	3	0	0	0	UK
IS	98	98	98	2	2	2	:	:	:	IS
NO	98 *	98 *	98 *	2 *	2 *	2 *	:	:	:	NO
EEA	: |	96 *	96 *	: |	3 *	3 *	: |	1 *	1 *	EEA
CH	:	:	:	4	4	4 *	7	6	5 *	CH

5A1CX   5A1CY   5A1CZ

Further reading: Esspros manual, 1996. Eurostat.
Social protection expenditure and receipts, data 1980–97. Eurostat.

Social benefits are recorded without any deduction of taxes or other compulsory levies payable on them by beneficiaries.

5A1DA 5A1DB 5A1DC 5A1DD

Social benefits by function as a % of total benefits

	Sickness and health care		Disability		Old age		Survivors		
	1990	1997	1990	1997	1990	1997	1990	1997	
EU-15	: |	26,3 *	: |	8,3 *	: |	39,8 *	: |	5,6 *	**EU-15**
EUR-11	29,1 |	27,1 *	7,7 |	7,5 *	40,1 |	40,4 *	6,3 |	5,7 *	**EUR-11**
B	26,6	24,0 *	7,5	8,7 *	29,3	31,9 *	11,1	11,1 *	**B**
DK	20,1	18,1	10,0	10,8	36,6	39,3	0,1	0,1	**DK**
D	31,7 |	28,1 *	6,3 |	8,0 *	43,4 |	39,9 *	2,5 |	2,0 *	**D**
EL	24,8	25,2	8,5	6,1	42,5	42,9	9,2	8,5	**EL**
E	28,8	28,8 *	7,7	7,7 *	38,3	41,9 *	4,6	4,3 *	**E**
F	29,4	28,8	6,1	5,2	35,9	37,5	6,8	6,1	**F**
IRL	33,5	35,4	4,5	4,8	23,3	18,7	6,7	5,9	**IRL**
I	26,0	23,1	7,7	6,5	48,9	52,7	10,7	11,2	**I**
L	25,0	24,9	14,1	13,1	31,0	29,7	14,8	13,8	**L**
NL	28,3	25,6 *	16,5	11,6 *	32,0	33,9 *	5,4	5,5 *	**NL**
A	26,0	25,7	7,0	8,3	38,5	38,1	11,6	10,4	**A**
P	30,2	33,3 *	16,5	12,7 *	35,4	35,3 *	7,5	7,5 *	**P**
FIN	28,5	21,9	15,5	14,7	29,6	29,9	4,2	4,0	**FIN**
S	:	22,2	:	11,5	:	37,2	:	2,3	**S**
UK	26,1	24,6	8,9	11,5	38,1	37,6	6,2	6,4	**UK**
IS	42,9	37,6	8,5	12,2	26,7	28,0	2,9	3,0	**IS**
NO	29,0 *	31,4 *	14,7 *	15,5 *	32,7 *	30,6 *	1,7 *	1,4 *	**NO**
EEA	: |	26,4 *	: |	8,5 *	: |	39,7 *	: |	5,5 *	**EEA**
CH	27,7	23,0 *	10,2	11,7 *	45,9	43,9 *	6,2	5,7 *	**CH**

Further reading: Esspros manual, 1996. Eurostat.
Social protection expenditure and receipts, data 1980–97. Eurostat.

Social benefits are recorded without any deduction of taxes or other compulsory levies payable on them by beneficiaries.

5A1DE 5A1DF 5A1DG 5A1DH

Social benefits by function as a % of total benefits (continued)

	Family and children		Unemployment		Housing		Social exclusion		
	1990	1997	1990	1997	1990	1997	1990	1997	
EU-15	: |	8,4 *	: |	7,6 *	: |	2,2 *	: |	1,8 *	**EU-15**
EUR-11	7,2 |	8,1 *	7,1 |	8,1 *	1,1 |	1,2 *	1,4 |	1,9 *	**EUR-11**
B	9,2	8,8 *	13,3	12,7 *	:	:	2,9	2,7 *	**B**
DK	11,9	12,6	15,4	12,6	2,3	2,4	3,6	4,0	**DK**
D	7,6 |	10,1 *	5,9 |	9,1 *	0,6 |	0,6 *	2,1 |	2,3 *	**D**
EL	7,5	8,2	4,1	4,6	2,4	3,3	1,0	1,2	**EL**
E	1,7	2,0 *	18,0	14,1 *	0,6	0,3 *	0,4	0,8 *	**E**
F	9,3	10,0	8,3	7,8	2,9	3,3	1,2	1,3	**F**
IRL	11,2	13,0	15,8	16,9	3,5	3,3	1,6	2,0	**IRL**
I	4,9	3,5	1,7	2,9	0,0	0,0	0,0	0,1	**I**
L	10,8	13,2	2,6	3,7	0,2	0,2	1,5	1,3	**L**
NL	5,6	4,5 *	8,3	8,6 *	1,1	1,5 *	2,8	8,7 *	**NL**
A	10,5	10,5	4,6	5,5	0,5	0,3	1,3	1,1	**A**
P	7,1	5,3 *	3,0	5,0 *	0,0	0,0 *	0,3	0,9 *	**P**
FIN	13,5	12,6	6,1	13,3	0,8	1,2	1,9	2,4	**FIN**
S	:	10,6	:	10,4	:	2,6	:	3,2	**S**
UK	8,7	8,6	5,5	3,8	5,8	6,7	0,7	0,8	**UK**
IS	14,5	13,0	1,9	3,2	0,0	0,6	2,5	2,5	**IS**
NO	10,8 *	13,5 *	6,9 *	4,3 *	0,6 *	0,7 *	3,5 *	2,7 *	**NO**
EEA	: |	8,4 *	: |	7,5 *	: |	2,1 *	: |	1,8 *	**EEA**
CH	6,4	5,3 *	0,8	6,9 *	0,6	0,7 *	2,2	2,8 *	**CH**

Further reading: Esspros manual, 1996. Eurostat.
Social protection expenditure and receipts, data 1980–97. Eurostat.

Social benefits are recorded without any deduction of taxes or other compulsory levies payable on them by beneficiaries.

Social benefits are direct transfers in cash or kind by social protection schemes to households and individuals to relieve them of the burden of distinct risks or needs. Benefits via the fiscal system are excluded. Benefits are classified according to eight social protection 'functions' (1. sickness and health-care; 2. disability; 3. old age; 4. survivors; 5. family and children; 6. unemployment; 7. housing; 8. social exclusion).

Social benefits per head of population in current PPS. 1997

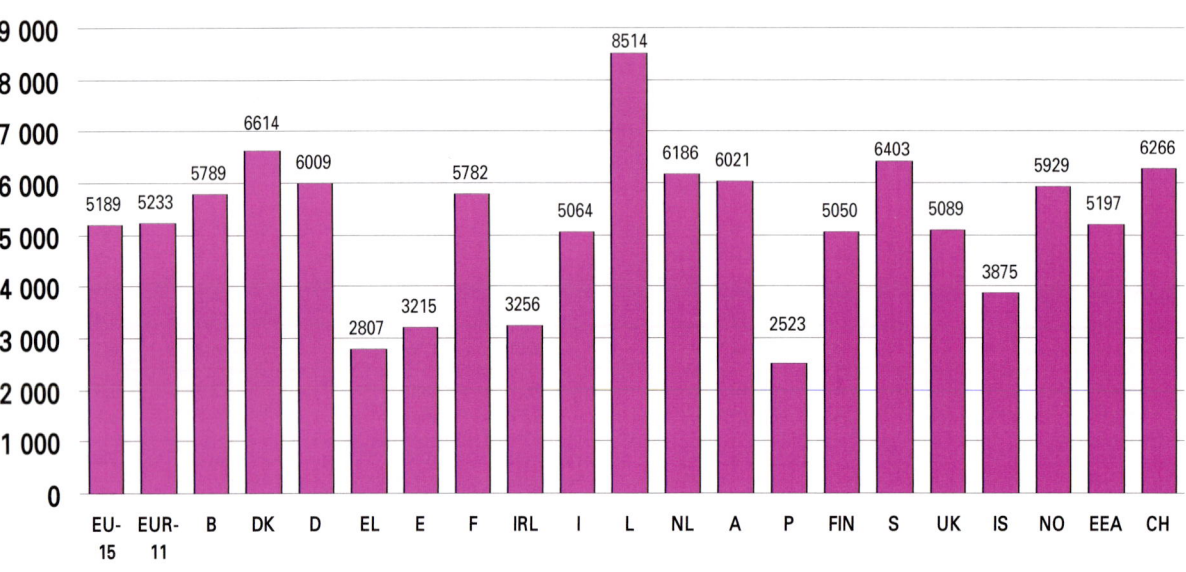

5A1CD

Further reading: Esspros manual, 1996. Eurostat.
Social protection expenditure and receipts, data 1980–97. Eurostat.

Social benefits are recorded without any deduction of taxes or other compulsory levies payable on them by beneficiaries.

Social benefits per head of population at constant prices. 1990 = 100

	1989	1990	1991	1992	1993	1994	1995	1996	1997	1998	1999	
EU-15	:	100 |	:	:	118	119	122	125 *	126 *	:	:	**EU-15**
EUR-11	:	100 |	109	115	117	118	121	124 *	126 *	:	:	**EUR-11**
B	94 *	100	104	107	112	112	114	116 *	117 *	:	:	**B**
DK	98	100	105	108	114	123	123	122	121	122	:	**DK**
D	98	100 |	120	130	131	133	138	143 *	141 *	:	:	**D**
EL	:	100	98	97	98	100	103	107	114	124 *	:	**EL**
E	93	100	109	117	124	120	119	120 *	121 *	:	:	**E**
F	98 *	100	103	106	110	111	115	116	118	:	:	**F**
IRL	96 *	100	106	112	119	123	131	133	140	144 *	:	**IRL**
I	93 *	100	104	109	109	109	109	114	119	120 *	:	**I**
L	96	100	108	112	121	125	130	134	138	:	:	**L**
NL	93 *	100	101	103	103	102	106	104	106 *	105 *	:	**NL**
A	:	100	104	107	110	115	117	118	118	121	:	**A**
P	90 *	100	114	129	142	151	154	165	177 *	:	:	**P**
FIN	94	100	109	116	117	120	120	122	122	120 *	:	**FIN**
S	:	:	:	:	:	:	:	:	:	:	:	**S**
UK	:	100	109	120	129	130	131	136	135	:	:	**UK**
IS	:	100	105	103	104	106	110	113	118	127 *	:	**IS**
NO	:	100 *	106 *	110 *	113 *	114 *	114 *	119 *	122 *	:	:	**NO**
EEA	:	100 *|	:	:	118 *	119 *	122 *	125 *	126 *	:	:	**EEA**
CH	:	100	106	113	119	120	122	127	133 *	135 *	:	**CH**

5A1CE

Further reading: Social protection expenditure and receipts, data 1980–97. Eurostat.
Statistics in focus: social protection in Europe, 2000. Eurostat.

Social benefits are recorded without any deduction of taxes or other compulsory levies payable on them by beneficiaries.

Social benefits per head of population in current PPS

	Sickness and health care		Disability		Old age		Survivors		
	1990	**1997**	**1990**	**1997**	**1990**	**1997**	**1990**	**1997**	
EU-15	:		1 365 *	:		430 *	:		2 085 *	:		301 *	**EU-15**
EUR-11	978		1 413 *	262		393 *	1 356		2 133 *	217		308 *	**EUR-11**
B	1 024	1 392 *	290	506 *	1 130	1 848 *	427	644 *	**B**
DK	844	1 198	419	717	1 539	2 599	3	4	**DK**
D	1 309		1 691 *	259		479 *	1 792		2 395 *	103		117 *	**D**
EL	468	708	160	172	803	1 205	174	238	**EL**
E	620	927 *	166	249 *	824	1 346 *	99	137 *	**E**
F	1 227	1 664	256	301	1 498	2 167	284	354	**F**
IRL	648	1 153	86	156	451	608	130	192	**IRL**
I	912	1 170	269	330	1 713	2 667	374	569	**I**
L	1 239	2 119	700	1 118	1 537	2 532	736	1 178	**L**
NL	1 293	1 586 *	753	720 *	1 466	2 097 *	245	341 *	**NL**
A	1 020	1 545	275	502	1 507	2 294	456	628	**A**
P	369	839 *	201	320 *	432	890 *	92	189 *	**P**
FIN	975	1 107	531	740	1 013	1 509	143	200	**FIN**
S	:	1 422	:	738	:	2 381	:	149	**S**
UK	883	1 253	300	584	1 290	1 913	209	327	**UK**
IS	1 064	1 457	212	471	663	1 083	72	115	**IS**
NO	1 118 *	1 861 *	569 *	918 *	1 260 *	1 814 *	67 *	85 *	**NO**
EEA	:		1 371 *	:		435 *	:		2 081 *	:		298 *	**EEA**
CH	965	1 438 *	353	734 *	1 596	2 754 *	215	358 *	**CH**

Further reading: Esspros manual, 1996. Eurostat.
Social protection expenditure and receipts, data 1980–97. Eurostat.

Social benefits are recorded without any deduction of taxes or other compulsory levies payable on them by beneficiaries.

Social benefits per head of population in current PPS

	Family and children		Unemployment		Housing		Social exclusion		
	1990	**1997**	**1990**	**1997**	**1990**	**1997**	**1990**	**1997**	
EU-15	:		418 *	:		390 *	:		108 *	:		92 *	**EU-15**
EUR-11	239		405 *	241		423 *	38		59 *	44		98 *	**EUR-11**
B	356	508 *	512	733 *	:	:	113	159 *	**B**
DK	498	835	645	834	99	162	152	265	**DK**
D	313		608 *	244		545 *	26		39 *	85		136 *	**D**
EL	142	230	78	128	45	92	19	33	**EL**
E	37	66 *	386	454 *	12	11 *	8	25 *	**E**
F	388	577	346	453	120	191	51	74	**F**
IRL	217	423	306	549	67	109	31	66	**IRL**
I	172	177	60	144	1	1	1	5	**I**
L	537	1 126	129	317	10	13	75	111	**L**
NL	257	280 *	382	533 *	51	90 *	127	540 *	**NL**
A	410	634	179	333	19	19	50	66	**A**
P	87	134 *	36	127 *	1	0 *	4	23 *	**P**
FIN	462	636	208	673	26	60	64	123	**FIN**
S	:	679	:	663	:	169	:	202	**S**
UK	296	439	187	194	196	339	25	40	**UK**
IS	361	505	48	124	1	22	62	98	**IS**
NO	416 *	800 *	267 *	253 *	23 *	39 *	137 *	158 *	**NO**
EEA	:		423 *	:		388 *	:		107 *	:		93 *	**EEA**
CH	224	333 *	29	433 *	22	43 *	75	173 *	**CH**

Further reading: Statistics in focus: social protection in Europe, 2000. Eurostat.

Social benefits are recorded without any deduction of taxes or other compulsory levies payable on them by beneficiaries.

Sickness/healthcare benefits include mainly paid sick leave, medical care and provision of pharmaceutical products. Disability benefits include mainly disability pensions and the provision of goods and services (other than medical care) to the disabled.

More data on this in Eurostat's database

Harmonised data on social protection expenditure (such as pensions, unemployment benefits, health care, family allowances) and receipts (such as social contributions by employers and employees, government contributions) in the 15 Member States of the European Union, Iceland and Norway.

➤ ➤ ➤ **DOMAIN SESPROS IN DATABASE NEW CRONOS**

Social benefits per head of population at constant prices. 1990 = 100

	Sickness and health care					Disability					
	1990	**1995**	**1996**	**1997**	**1998**	**1990**	**1995**	**1996**	**1997**	**1998**	
EU-15	: |	:	:	:	:	: |	:	:	:	:	**EU-15**
EUR-11	100 |	117	118 *	117 *	:	100 |	113	119 *	122 *	:	**EUR-11**
B	100	101	107 *	106 *	:	100	133	134 *	136 *	:	**B**
DK	100	109	108	109	117	100	130	131	132	142	**DK**
D	100 |	134	133 *	126 *	:	100 |	153	168 *	179 *	:	**D**
EL	100	109	109	116	121 *	100	80	80	83	91 *	**EL**
E	100	119	121 *	121 *	:	100	114	120 *	121 *	:	**E**
F	100	114	116	115	:	100	96	100	100	:	**F**
IRL	100	137	135	148	158 *	100	137	146	150	157 *	**IRL**
I	100	98	101	106	108 *	100	100	105	101	96 *	**I**
L	100	127	137	138	:	100	121	124	128	:	**L**
NL	100	102	98	96 *	101 *	100	78	75	75 *	72 *	**NL**
A	100	115	114	116	121	100	129	136	140	148	**A**
P	100	167	180	195 *	:	100	112	116	136 *	:	**P**
FIN	100	88	92	94	96 *	100	116	116	115	111 *	**FIN**
S	:	:	:	:	:	:	:	:	:	:	**S**
UK	100	121	127	128	:	100	176	177	175	:	**UK**
IS	100	97	99	104	113 *	100	150	155	168	179 *	**IS**
NO	100 *	104 *	115 *	132 *	:	100 *	117 *	121 *	128 *	:	**NO**
EEA	: |	:	:	:	:	: |	:	:	:	:	**EEA**
CH	100	103	106	110 *	115 *	100	137	145	153 *	160 *	**CH**

Further reading: Esspros manual, 1996. Eurostat.
Social protection expenditure and receipts, data 1980–97. Eurostat.

Social benefits are recorded without any deduction of taxes or other compulsory levies payable on them by beneficiaries.

5A1CN   5A1CO

eurostat

Old-age benefits include mainly old-age pensions and the provision of goods and services (other than medical care) to the elderly. Survivors' benefits include income maintenance and support in connection with the death of a family member, such as survivors' pensions.

Social benefits per head of population at constant prices. 1990 = 100

	Old age					Survivors					
	1990	**1995**	**1996**	**1997**	**1998**	**1990**	**1995**	**1996**	**1997**	**1998**	
EU-15	: |	:	:	:	:	: |	:	:	:	:	**EU-15**
EUR-11	100 |	121	124 *	127 *	:	100 |	110	113 *	115 *	:	**EUR-11**
B	100	124	125 *	127 *	:	100	113	112 *	118 *	:	**B**
DK	100	126	130	130	127	100	91	86	84	79	**DK**
D	100 |	129	130 *	130 *	:	100 |	114	111 *	111 *	:	**D**
EL	100	103	108	115	128 *	100	92	101	105	117 *	**EL**
E	100	123	128 *	133 *	:	100	111	113 *	113 *	:	**E**
F	100	119	121	123	:	100	104	106	106	:	**F**
IRL	100	111	108	112	117 *	100	116	119	123	129 *	**IRL**
I	100	116	122	129	131 *	100	112	119	126	120 *	**I**
L	100	128	128	133	:	100	123	125	129	:	**L**
NL	100	104	107	112 *	113 *	100	107	110	109 *	98 *	**NL**
A	100	115	117	117	119	100	106	107	106	106	**A**
P	100	156	168	177 *	:	100	150	161	176 *	:	**P**
FIN	100	117	124	123	124 *	100	112	114	116	115 *	**FIN**
S	:	:	:	:	:	:	:	:	:	:	**S**
UK	100	126	131	133	:	100	134	139	141	:	**UK**
IS	100	112	117	124	137 *	100	108	116	121	131 *	**IS**
NO	100 *	112 *	117 *	115 *	:	100 *	99 *	101 *	101 *	:	**NO**
EEA	: |	:	:	:	:	: |	:	:	:	:	**EEA**
CH	100	120	123	127 *	129 *	100	116	120	123 *	123 *	**CH**

5A1CP

5A1CQ

Further reading: Esspros manual, 1996. Eurostat.
    Social protection expenditure and receipts, data 1980–97. Eurostat.

Social benefits are recorded without any deduction of taxes or other compulsory levies payable on them by beneficiaries.

F amily/children benefits include support (except health care) in connection with the costs of pregnancy, childbirth, childbearing and caring for other family members. Unemployment benefits also include vocational training financed by public agencies.

Social benefits per head of population at constant prices. 1990 = 100

	Family and children					Unemployment					
	1990	**1995**	**1996**	**1997**	**1998**	**1990**	**1995**	**1996**	**1997**	**1998**	
EU-15	: |	:	:	:	:	: |	:	:	:	:	**EU-15**
EUR-11	100 |	119	133 *	138 *	:	100 |	147	152 *	145 *	:	**EUR-11**
B	100	108	108 *	111 *	:	100	111	112 *	112 *	:	**B**
DK	100	128	128	129	134	100	117	110	100	93	**DK**
D	100 |	139	181 *	189 *	:	100 |	212	233 *	217 *	:	**D**
EL	100	121	123	124	133 *	100	114	109	127	143 *	**EL**
E	100	122	137 *	145 *	:	100	110	99 *	95 *	:	**E**
F	100	122	122	127	:	100	108	111	111	:	**F**
IRL	100	135	150	162	164 *	100	152	155	149	141 *	**IRL**
I	100	72	81	85	88 *	100	225	212	199	192 *	**I**
L	100	159	164	169	:	100	155	180	197	:	**L**
NL	100	84	80	85 *	85 *	100	122	123	109 *	89 *	**NL**
A	100	127	124	119	116	100	142	149	143	145	**A**
P	100	125	131	133 *	:	100	295	326	301 *	:	**P**
FIN	100	119	113	113	114 *	100	283	281	266	237 *	**FIN**
S	:	:	:	:	:	:	:	:	:	:	**S**
UK	100	130	134	134	:	100	127	113	93	:	**UK**
IS	100	98	105	106	110 *	100	247	212	195	172 *	**IS**
NO	100 *	144 *	152 *	153 *	:	100 *	112 *	97 *	75 *	:	**NO**
EEA	: |	:	:	:	:	: |	:	:	:	:	**EEA**
CH	100	105	108	110 *	110 *	100	814	925	1 121 *	920 *	**CH**

Further reading: Esspros manual, 1996. Eurostat.
Statistics in focus: social protection in Europe, 2000. Eurostat.

Social benefits are recorded without any deduction of taxes or other compulsory levies payable on them by beneficiaries.

5A1CR   5A1CS

Housing benefits include interventions by public authorities to help households meet the cost of housing. Social exclusion benefits include income support, rehabilitation of alcohol and drug abusers and other miscellaneous benefits (except health care).

Social benefits per head of population at constant prices. 1990 = 100

	Housing					Social exclusion					
	1990	1995	1996	1997	1998	1990	1995	1996	1997	1998	
EU-15	: |	:	:	:	:	: |	:	:	:	:	EU-15
EUR-11	100 |	131	128 *	137 *	:	100 |	162	165 *	173 *	:	EUR-11
B	:	:	:	:	:	100	105	106 *	110 *	:	B
DK	100	128	125	126	128	100	148	137	134	125	DK
D	100 |	133	139 *	146 *	:	100 |	152	157 *	155 *	:	D
EL	100	115	126	158	161 *	100	119	134	134	131 *	EL
E	100	127	74 *	73 *	:	100	187	261 *	268 *	:	E
F	100	128	125	135	:	100	114	118	123	:	F
IRL	100	120	126	134	142 *	100	151	165	178	186 *	IRL
I	100	217	234	204	153 *	100	480	547	584	594 *	I
L	100	106	102	104	:	100	113	113	120	:	L
NL	100	128	130	139 *	147 *	100	303	286	331 *	354 *	NL
A	100	76	75	76	80	100	106	111	102	104	A
P	100	79	77	71 *	:	100	200	323	500 *	:	P
FIN	100	239	208	193	229 *	100	134	153	157	140 *	FIN
S	:	:	:	:	:	:	:	:	:	:	S
UK	100	153	158	155	:	100	103	143	142	:	UK
IS	100	1 497	2 213	2 650	3 302 *	100	124	122	120	115 *	IS
NO	100 *	142 *	160 *	135 *	:	100 *	122 *	97 *	92 *	:	NO
EEA	: |	:	:	:	:	: |	:	:	:	:	EEA
CH	100	127	136	147 *	164 *	100	148	156	170 *	175 *	CH

Further reading: Esspros manual, 1996. Eurostat.
Statistics in focus: social protection in Europe, 2000. Eurostat.

Social benefits are recorded without any deduction of taxes or other compulsory levies payable on them by beneficiaries.

Units responsible for providing social protection are financed in different ways. Their receipts comprise social contributions paid by employers and by protected persons, contributions by general government and other receipts. Other receipts come from a variety of sources, for example interest, dividends, rent and claims against third parties.

Social protection receipts by type as a % of total receipts. 1997

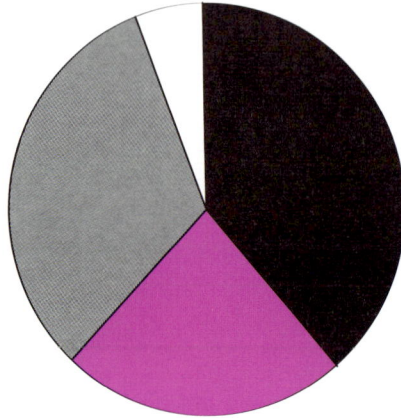

Black: employers' social contributions; colour: social contributions by protected persons; grey: general government contributions; white: other receipts.

Further reading: Esspros manual, 1996 Eurostat.
Social protection expenditure and receipts, data 1980–97. Eurostat.

Protected persons include employees, the self-employed, pensioners and other people.

Social protection receipts by type as a % of total receipts. 1997

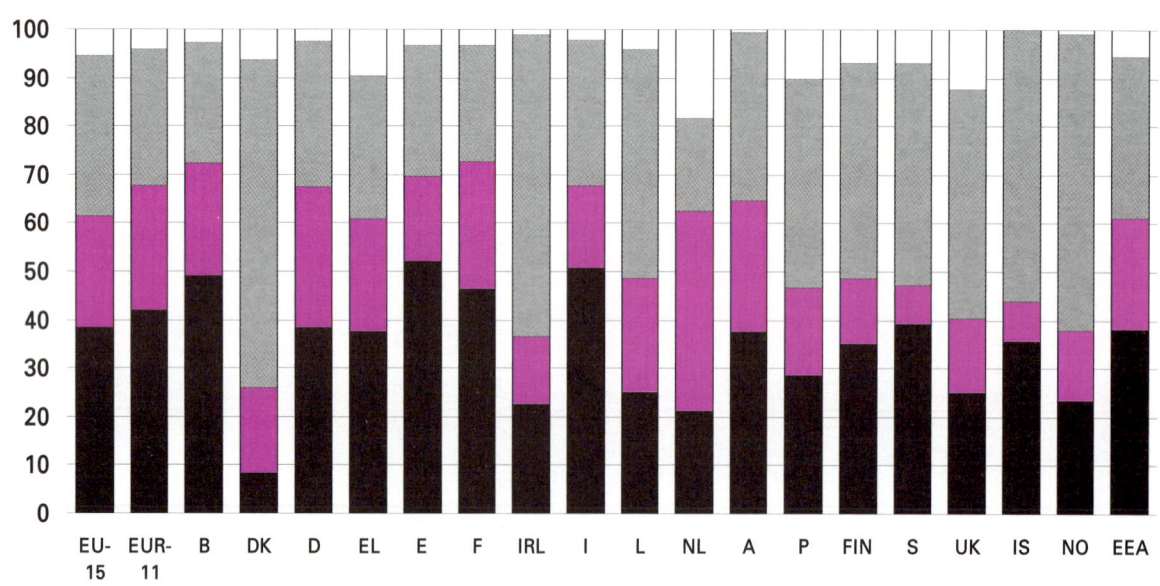

Black: employers' social contributions; colour: social contributions by protected persons; grey: general government contributions; white: other receipts.

Further reading: Esspros manual, 1996. Eurostat.
Social protection expenditure and receipts, data 1980–97. Eurostat.

Protected persons include employees, the self-employed, pensioners and other people.

5A2DJ

5A1DI

Social contributions are paid by employers and by the protected persons. Social contributions by employers are all costs incurred by employers to secure employees' entitlement to social benefits. These include all payments by employers to social protection institutions (actual contributions) and social benefits paid directly by employers to employees (imputed contributions). Social contributions by protected persons comprise contributions paid by employees, by the self-employed and by pensioners and other persons.

Social protection receipts by type as a % of total receipts

	Employers' social contributions					Social contributions by protected persons					
	1990	1995	1996	1997	1998	1990	1995	1996	1997	1998	
EU-15	: |	38,9	38,8 *	38,5 *	:	: |	23,4	23,3 *	23,1 *	:	EU-15
EUR-11	46,0 |	42,5	42,2 *	42,1 *	:	24,8 |	26,1	25,9 *	25,6 *	:	EUR-11
B	40,9	48,9	49,3 *	49,2 *	:	25,2	22,2	22,4 *	23,1 *	:	B
DK	7,8	9,9	10,0	8,5	8,7	5,3	13,4	15,0	17,5	17,9	DK
D	43,6 |	40,5	38,7 *	38,6 *	:	28,4 |	28,6	28,6 *	28,9 *	:	D
EL	39,4	37,4	39,1	37,6	37,6 *	19,6	23,5	23,0	23,2	24,1 *	EL
E	54,4	50,2	51,8 *	52,2 *	:	16,9	17,2	17,6 *	17,5 *	:	E
F	52,0	47,4	46,9	46,4	:	28,8	27,5	28,0	26,4	:	F
IRL	24,5	22,3	22,0	22,8	23,9 *	15,6	14,0	14,2	13,7	13,6 *	IRL
I	52,9	50,4	50,9	50,9	44,7 *	15,0	17,3	17,3	16,9	14,8 *	I
L	28,9	25,3	25,8	25,1	:	22,6	23,4	22,9	23,6	:	L
NL	20,0	21,5	22,0	21,3 *	28,9 *	39,1	40,9	40,4	41,3 *	34,2 *	NL
A	38,1	37,0	37,4	37,7	37,5	25,1	25,9	26,4	27,1	27,1	A
P	37,1	30,0	25,9	28,6 *	:	20,0	18,9	16,8	18,1 *	:	P
FIN	44,1	33,7	34,9	35,3	36,2 *	8,0	13,7	13,4	13,4	13,8 *	FIN
S	:	37,5	39,5	39,4	39,1 *	:	5,3	6,6	7,9	9,3 *	S
UK	27,2	24,2	24,6	25,2	:	16,3	14,2	14,4	15,3	:	UK
IS	24,9	30,7	32,3	35,8	38,9 *	7,3	8,2	8,6	8,3	8,2 *	IS
NO	24,0 *	22,4 *	23,5 *	23,6 *	:	12,4 *	14,3 *	14,3 *	14,4 *	:	NO
EEA	: |	38,7 *	38,6 *	38,2 *	:	: |	23,2 *	23,2 *	23,0 *	:	EEA

5A1DM 5A1DO

Further reading: Esspros manual, 1996. Eurostat.
Social protection expenditure and receipts, data 1980–97. Eurostat.

Protected persons include employees, the self-employed, pensioners and other people.

Social protection receipts by type as a % of total receipts (continued)

	General government contributions					Other receipts					
	1990	1995	1996	1997	1998	1990	1995	1996	1997	1998	
EU-15	: |	32,3	32,4 *	32,9 *	:	: |	5,4	5,4 *	5,5 *	:	EU-15
EUR-11	25,0 |	27,4	27,9 *	28,3 *	:	4,2 |	4,0	4,0 *	3,9 *	:	EUR-11
B	24,7	26,1	25,5 *	24,9 *	:	9,3	2,9	2,8 *	2,8 *	:	B
DK	80,1	70,6	68,9	67,8	67,2	6,8	6,1	6,2	6,2	6,3	DK
D	25,3 |	28,6	30,3 *	30,1 *	:	2,8 |	2,2	2,4 *	2,4 *	:	D
EL	33,0	29,0	28,5	29,6	29,2 *	8,0	10,0	9,5	9,6	9,1 *	EL
E	26,2	29,8	27,7 *	27,1 *	:	2,5	2,7	2,9 *	3,3 *	:	E
F	16,7	21,6	21,9	24,0	:	2,5	3,5	3,2	3,2	:	F
IRL	58,9	62,8	62,9	62,5	61,3 *	1,0	0,8	0,9	1,0	1,2 *	IRL
I	29,0	29,9	29,3	29,9	38,3 *	3,1	2,4	2,5	2,3	2,2 *	I
L	40,6	46,1	46,7	47,2	:	7,9	5,1	4,6	4,1	:	L
NL	25,0	19,0	18,6	19,1 *	18,8 *	15,9	18,7	19,0	18,3 *	18,1 *	NL
A	35,9	36,4	35,7	34,6	34,5	0,9	0,7	0,6	0,6	0,9	A
P	33,7	39,4	42,0	43,3 *	:	9,2	11,7	15,3	10,1 *	:	P
FIN	40,6	45,8	44,4	44,4	43,1 *	7,3	6,9	7,2	6,8	6,8 *	FIN
S	:	49,2	46,6	46,0	45,8 *	:	8,0	7,3	6,8	5,9 *	S
UK	39,9	49,5	48,6	47,3	:	16,6	12,1	12,3	12,3	:	UK
IS	67,8	61,2	59,2	56,0	52,9 *	:	:	:	:	:	IS
NO	63,0 *	62,4 *	61,2 *	61,1 *	:	0,5 *	0,9 *	1,0 *	0,9 *	:	NO
EEA	: |	32,8 *	32,9 *	33,4 *	:	: |	5,3 *	5,3 *	5,4 *	:	EEA

5A1DK 5A1DL

Further reading: Esspros manual, 1996. Eurostat.
Statistics in focus: social protection in Europe, 2000. Eurostat.

3

Following the Treaty on European Union, the maintenance of price stability is the primary objective of the European System of Central Banks (ESCB). The European Central Bank (ECB) defines price stability as a year-on-year increase in the harmonised index of consumer prices for the euro zone of below 2 %.

The annual rate of inflation as measured by the harmonised index of consumer prices for the 15 EU Member States (European index of consumer prices — EICP) shows a significant general downward trend up to February 1999, which reverses from March 1999 to an overall upward trend.

Harmonised indices of consumer prices, rate of change (%)

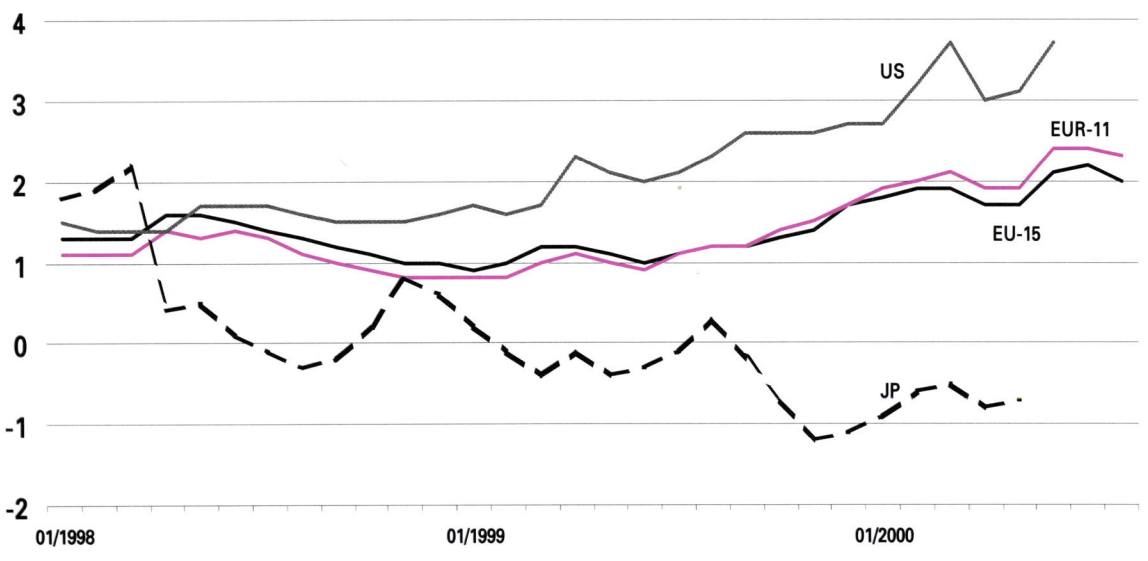

Further reading: Economy and finance, Statistics in focus, monthly publication. Eurostat.

US, JP: data on the national consumer price indices (CPIs) are given, which are not strictly comparable with the harmonised indices of consumer prices (HICPs). EEAICP: European Economic Area index of consumer prices. EICP: European index of consumer prices (EU-15). MUICP: monetary union index of consumer prices (EUR-11).

Harmonised indices of consumer prices, rate of change (%)

	1998	1999	01/2000	02/2000	03/2000	04/2000	05/2000	06/2000	07/2000	08/2000	
EU-15	1,3	1,2	1,8	1,9	1,9	1,7	1,7	2,1	2,2	2,0 *	EU-15
EUR-11	1,1	1,1	1,9	2,0	2,1	1,9	1,9	2,4	2,4	2,3 *	EUR-11
B	0,9	1,1	1,8	2,1	2,5	2,3	2,4	3,0	3,1	3,4	B
DK	1,3	2,1	2,8	2,8	3,0	2,9	2,8	2,9	2,8	2,2	DK
D	0,6	0,6	1,9	2,1	2,1	1,6	1,5	2,0	2,0	1,8	D
EL	4,5	2,1	2,4	2,6	2,8	2,1	2,6	2,2	2,6	2,9	EL
E	1,8	2,2	2,9	3,0	3,0	3,0	3,2	3,5	3,7	3,6	E
F	0,7	0,6	1,7	1,5	1,7	1,4	1,6	1,9	2,0	2,0 *	F
IRL	2,1	2,5	4,4	4,6	5,0	5,0	5,1	5,4	5,9	5,7	IRL
I	2,0	1,7	2,2	2,4	2,6	2,4	2,5	2,7	2,6	2,6	I
L	1,0	1,0	3,5	2,6	3,0	3,2	2,9	4,4	4,7	3,7	L
NL	1,8	2,0	1,6	1,5	1,6	1,7	2,0	2,5	2,8	2,5 *	NL
A	0,8	0,5	1,4	2,0	2,0	1,8	1,6	2,4	2,0	1,9 *	A
P	2,2	2,2	1,9	1,6	1,4	1,9	2,4	2,8	3,3	3,6	P
FIN	1,4	1,3	2,3	2,7	3,2	2,5	2,7	3,1	2,9	2,9	FIN
S	1,0	0,6	1,0	1,4	1,4	1,0	1,3	1,4	1,3	1,4	S
UK	1,6	1,3	0,8	1,0	0,7	0,6	0,5	0,8	1,0	0,6	UK
IS	1,3	2,1	4,6	4,4	4,6	5,1	5,0	4,7	5,1	3,9	IS
NO	2,0	2,1	2,6	2,9	2,6	2,7	2,9	3,5	3,3	3,5	NO
EEA	1,3	1,2	1,8	1,9	1,9	1,7	1,7	2,1	2,2	2,0 *	EEA
CH	0,0	0,8	1,6	1,6	1,5	1,4	1,6	1,9	2,0	1,3	CH
US	1,6	2,2	2,7	3,2	3,7	3,0	3,1	3,7	3,5	3,4	US
CA	:	:	:	:	:	:	:	:	:	:	CA
JP	0,6	- 0,3	- 0,9	- 0,6	- 0,5	- 0,8	- 0,7	- 0,7	- 0,5	:	JP

Further reading: Economy and finance, Statistics in focus, monthly publication. Eurostat.

US, JP: data on the national consumer price indices (CPIs) are given, which are not strictly comparable with the harmonised indices of consumer prices (HICPs). EEAICP: European Economic Area index of consumer prices. EICP: European index of consumer prices (EU-15). MUICP: monetary union index of consumer prices (EUR-11).

3A6AC

3A6AA

The HICP measures the change in consumer price inflation in the European Union. The methodology used ensures comparability between Member States. HICP coverage follows the international classification Coicop (Classification of individual consumption by purpose), adapted to the needs of HICPs. For ease of comparison, they are presented with a common base year 1996 = 100.

The HICP is intended to cover all forms of household expenditure on goods and services ('household final monetary consumption expenditure'). With the index for January 2000, the coverage was brought to virtually 100 % of household final monetary consumption expenditure with the inclusion of further goods and services, mainly in the health, education and social protection sectors and the completion of geographic and population coverage.

The EU aggregate indices, the monetary union index of consumer prices (MUICP), the European index of consumer prices (EICP), and the European Economic Area index of consumer prices (EEAICP) are compiled as annual chain indices. They are calculated as weighted averages of the national price indices of the countries covered,

allowing country weights to change each year. For all indices, the country weights used in 2000 are national accounts data for 1998, updated to December 1999 prices.

For the MUICP, a Member State's weight is its share of household final monetary consumption expenditure in the EMU total. Weights in national currencies are converted into euro using the fixed conversion rates.

For the EICP and the EEAICP, a Member State's weight is its share of household final monetary consumption expenditure in the EU and EEA totals. For those two indices, expenditure in national currencies is converted into purchasing power standards (PPS).

With the launch of the euro in January 1999 the MUICP is used for the monitoring of inflation in the EMU and for assessment of inflation convergence. As price stability is the primary objective of the European System of Central Banks (ESCB), the MUICP is used by the European Central Bank (ECB) as a main indicator for monetary policy management for the euro zone.

3

Harmonised indices of consumer prices, index 1996 = 100

	1998	1999	01/2000	02/2000	03/2000	04/2000	05/2000	06/2000	07/2000	08/2000	
EU-15	103,0	104,3	105,0	105,4	105,8	106,0	106,1	106,5	106,5	106,5 *	**EU-15**
EUR-11	102,7	103,8	104,8	105,2	105,6	105,7	105,8	106,3	106,5	106,5 *	**EUR-11**
B	102,4	103,6	104,7	105,2	105,7	105,9	106,2	106,6	106,9	107,0	**B**
DK	103,3	105,4	106,5	107,0	107,8	108,0	108,4	108,8	108,3	108,0	**DK**
D	102,1	102,8	103,8	104,2	104,4	104,3	104,2	104,9	105,4	105,2	**D**
EL	110,2	112,6	113,2	112,7	115,6	116,3	116,6	115,9	113,9	114,1	**EL**
E	103,7	106,0	107,7	107,9	108,4	108,8	109,0	109,3	110,0	110,4	**E**
F	102,0	102,5	103,3	103,5	104,0	104,0	104,2	104,5	104,3	104,5 *	**F**
IRL	103,4	106,0	108,2	109,1	109,8	110,5	111,3	111,9	111,9	112,5	**IRL**
I	103,9	105,7	106,9	107,3	107,7	107,7	108,1	108,4	108,6	108,6	**I**
L	102,4	103,4	104,3	105,4	105,9	106,6	106,6	108,1	107,0	107,7	**L**
NL	103,7	105,8	105,8	106,4	107,6	108,0	108,3	108,3	108,0	108,4 *	**NL**
A	102,0	102,5	103,5	104,3	104,4	104,2	104,1	104,5	104,2	104,3 *	**A**
P	104,2	106,4	107,3	107,0	107,2	108,4	109,1	109,7	110,2	110,3	**P**
FIN	102,6	103,9	104,8	105,6	106,3	106,5	107,0	107,4	106,9	107,0	**FIN**
S	102,9	103,4	103,5	104,0	104,6	104,4	105,0	105,0	104,4	104,5	**S**
UK	103,4	104,8	104,5	104,9	105,1	105,5	105,7	105,9	105,4	105,4	**UK**
IS	103,2	105,4	108,2	107,8	108,4	109,4	109,8	110,1	110,8	110,0	**IS**
NO	104,6	106,8	108,5	109,0	109,3	109,7	109,8	110,5	110,0	109,7	**NO**
EEA	103,1	104,3	105,0	105,4	105,9	106,0	106,1	106,6	106,6	106,6 *	**EEA**
CH	100,5	101,4	102,2	102,5	102,6	102,6	102,6	103,0	103,2	102,9	**CH**
US	103,9	106,2	107,6	108,2	109,1	109,2	109,3	109,9	109,9	110,2	**US**
CA	:	:	:	:	:	:	:	:	:	:	**CA**
JP	102,4	102,1	101,3	101,2	101,4	101,6	101,7	101,4	101,2	:	**JP**

6Q1AA

Further reading: Economy and finance, Statistics in focus, monthly publication. Eurostat.

US, JP: data on the national consumer price indices (CPIs) are given, which are not strictly comparable with the harmonised indices of consumer prices (HICPs). EEAICP: European Economic Area index of consumer prices. EICP: European index of consumer prices (EU-15). MUICP: monetary union index of consumer prices (EUR-11).

Cost-of-living comparison is carried out by calculation of index numbers (Brussels = 100) based on (a) prices of a basket of over 3 000 goods and services, (b) expenditure patterns of international officials, and (c) exchange rates. All information refers to 1 July 1999. The data come from the work of Eurostat in the field of cost-of-living adjustments to salaries of EU officials. Staff regulations fix indices for Belgium and Luxembourg at 100. Hence, indices are available for all EU capitals except Brussels and Luxembourg. Country codes refer to the capital city.

Cost-of-living comparisons in the European Union. Most and least expensive cities for different expenditure groups in 1999. B = 100

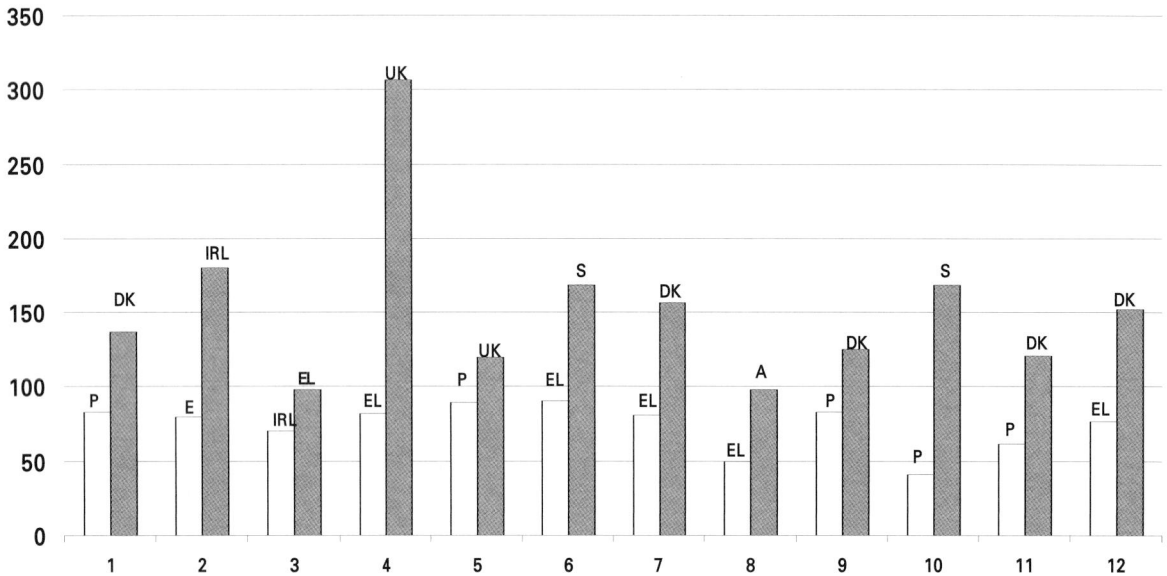

1: food and non-alcoholic beverages; 2: alcoholic beverages and tobacco; 3: clothing and footwear; 4: housing, water, electricity, gas and other fuels; 5: furnishing, household equipment and maintenance of house; 6: health; 7: transport; 8: communications; 9: recreation and culture; 10: education; 11: hotels, cafes and restaurants; 12: miscellaneous goods and services. Grey: most expensive; white: least expensive.

Further reading: Cost-of-living comparisons in the European Union. Eurostat 1995.

Country codes refer to the capital of the countries.

Cost-of-living comparisons in the European Union in 1999. B = 100

	1	2	3	4	5	6	7	8	9	10	11	12	Total	Total (1)	
DK	137	138	85	149	111	126	157	65	125	119	121	152	132	129	DK
D	99	90	92	124	107	146	106	76	103	114	101	112	108	104	D
EL	93	115	98	83	91	91	81	50	99	60	97	77	87	87	EL
E	85	80	83	100	98	110	90	62	105	71	80	107	92	90	E
F	106	107	92	160	116	97	107	69	108	126	105	121	119	107	F
IRL	99	181	70	148	99	108	112	87	91	72	111	86	110	98	IRL
I	104	106	81	114	106	120	93	66	105	72	91	114	101	98	I
NL	95	102	80	172	99	113	115	68	93	109	106	121	114	101	NL
A	103	106	94	134	109	136	106	98	109	117	87	103	110	104	A
P	83	85	78	95	89	104	105	64	83	41	61	79	85	83	P
FIN	113	176	93	124	115	142	122	80	114	90	118	122	118	115	FIN
S	123	174	85	139	110	168	116	82	116	169	104	120	120	116	S
UK	111	179	85	307	119	111	125	95	114	105	120	138	157	116	UK

1: food and non-alcoholic beverages; 2: alcoholic beverages and tobacco; 3: clothing and footwear; 4: housing, water, electricity, gas and other fuels; 5: furnishing, household equipment and maintenance of house; 6: health; 7: transport; 8: communications; 9: recreation and culture; 10: education; 11: hotels, cafes and restaurants; 12: miscellaneous goods and services; total: total; total (1): total excluding rents.

Further reading: Cost-of-living comparisons in the European Union. Eurostat 1995.

Balance of the current account at current prices. % of GDP

	1989	1990	1991	1992	1993	1994	1995	1996	1997	1998	1999	
EU-15	- 0,4	- 0,6	- 1,0 │	- 0,8	- 0,1	0,0	0,3	0,5	0,7	0,2	:	**EU-15**
EUR-11	:	:	:	:	:	:	0,5	0,6	1,0	0,5	:	**EUR-11**
B/L	2,3	2,2	2,3 │	2,7	4,8	5,0	4,9	4,9	5,4	4,5	:	**B/L**
DK	- 1,1	1,0	1,6 │	3,0	2,8	2,2	1,4	2,4	0,5	- 1,3	:	**DK**
D	4,8	3,3 │	- 1,0	- 1,0	- 0,7	- 1,0	- 0,8	- 0,2	- 0,1	- 0,2	:	**D**
EL	0,1	- 2,0	0,5 │	- 1,8	1,3	2,3	- 1,2	- 2,3	- 0,4	- 1,9	:	**EL**
E	- 2,8	- 3,4	- 3,1 │	- 3,6	- 1,2	- 1,3	0,0	0,0	0,4	- 0,2	:	**E**
F	- 0,6	- 1,2	- 0,5 │	0,4	0,7	0,6	0,7	1,3	2,8	2,8	:	**F**
IRL	- 1,4	0,1	3,2 │	1,0	3,7	2,7	2,6	2,8	2,5	0,9	:	**IRL**
I	- 1,4	- 1,6	- 2,1 │	- 2,4	1,0	1,4	2,4	3,3	2,9	1,7	:	**I**
L	:	:	:	:	:	:	:	:	:	:	:	**L**
NL	3,5	3,7	3,2 │	2,3	4,4	5,3	6,0	5,5	7,4	4,9	:	**NL**
A	:	:	: │	- 0,2	- 0,5	- 1,1	- 2,3	- 2,1	- 2,6	- 2,2	:	**A**
P	0,5	- 0,1	- 0,7 │	- 4,5	- 4,7	- 6,2	- 2,9	- 4,2	- 5,4	- 6,7	:	**P**
FIN	:	:	:	- 4,6	- 1,3	1,3	4,2	4,0	5,5	5,9	:	**FIN**
S	:	:	:	- 3,6	- 1,3	- 0,4	2,4	2,6	2,8	2,0	:	**S**
UK	- 5,5	- 4,6	- 2,4 │	- 2,8	- 2,9	- 2,0	- 0,5	- 0,1	0,8	0,0	:	**UK**
US	- 2,3	- 1,8	- 0,1 │	- 1,0	- 1,6	- 2,2	- 2,1	- 1,8	- 1,8	- 2,7	:	**US**
CA	:	:	:	:	:	:	:	:	:	:	:	**CA**
JP	2,0	1,2	2,1 │	3,2	3,1	2,7	2,1	1,4	2,3	3,2	:	**JP**

Further reading: EU international transactions — 1999 edition. Eurostat. International trade in services — EU, 1989–98. Eurostat.

The National Bank of Belgium produces the balance of payments for Belgium and Luxembourg, B/L, as a whole. EU = EU-12 until 1991; EU = EU-15 from 1992 onwards. With the exception of Germany, data until 1991 includes the capital account. Data for Japan includes the capital account until 1994.

3A7AA

3

Average flows of the current account. % of GDP

	1989	1990	1991	1992	1993	1994	1995	1996	1997	1998	1999	
EU-15	15,4	15,0	14,3 │	12,8	13,4	13,6	13,9	14,6	16,0	15,7	:	**EU-15**
EUR-11	:	:	:	:	:	:	18,4	18,8	21,0	21,2	:	**EUR-11**
B/L	99,9	100,8	103,5 │	102,7	99,1	101,0	90,7	88,2	93,2	93,6	:	**B/L**
DK	44,7	44,8	48,4 │	51,1	50,8	52,1	50,9	54,4	51,7	50,6	:	**DK**
D	35,3	35,1 │	32,8	30,6	28,5	28,7	29,8	30,4	33,0	33,8	:	**D**
EL	28,4	27,4	26,7 │	24,6	23,9	24,1	23,0	22,3	23,4	22,8	:	**EL**
E	21,8	20,8	21,6 │	22,8	23,6	25,9	27,6	28,8	31,9	32,9	:	**E**
F	29,5	30,4	31,8 │	31,9	31,8	32,8	27,8	27,8	30,5	31,8	:	**F**
IRL	74,8	71,4	71,7 │	72,8	75,7	79,6	86,4	87,4	92,1	98,7	:	**IRL**
I	23,5	23,6	22,9 │	23,6	26,2	27,0	29,6	29,0	30,8	31,0	:	**I**
L	:	:	:	:	:	:	:	:	:	:	:	**L**
NL	65,1	62,7	62,5 │	63,8	61,7	62,4	66,2	68,1	73,4	71,3	:	**NL**
A	:	:	: │	44,3	43,0	43,4	45,2	47,1	50,6	52,2	:	**A**
P	42,3	42,4	39,2 │	34,4	37,2	38,2	42,0	43,7	45,0	46,0	:	**P**
FIN	:	:	:	30,9	35,2	37,2	39,7	39,8	41,6	41,4	:	**FIN**
S	:	:	:	34,3	38,1	40,7	47,7	46,3	50,4	52,7	:	**S**
UK	40,7	40,6	38,4 │	36,6	38,0	37,9	42,6	46,5	44,3	42,5	:	**UK**
US	13,0	13,1	12,3 │	12,8	12,9	13,7	14,9	15,6	16,4	16,1	:	**US**
CA	:	:	:	:	:	:	:	:	:	:	:	**CA**
JP	13,3	14,4	13,5 │	12,6	11,5	11,4	12,3	14,5	15,7	15,6	:	**JP**

Further reading: EU international transactions — 1999 edition. Eurostat. International trade in services — EU, 1989–98. Eurostat.

The National Bank of Belgium produces the balance of payments for Belgium and Luxembourg, B/L, as a whole. EU = EU-12 until 1991; EU = EU-15 from 1992 onwards. With the exception of Germany, data until 1991 includes the capital account. Data for Japan includes the capital account until 1994.

3A7AB

The balance of payments (BOP) records all economic transactions undertaken between the residents and non-residents of a country during a given period. The balance of payments is divided into two broad sub-balances: the current account and the capital and financial account. The current account covers all transactions (other than those in financial items) that involve economic values. The broadest categorisation of the current account differentiates goods, services, income and current transfers. The balance of each item is calculated as the difference between credits (exports) and debits (imports). The methodological framework is that of the fourth IMF BOP manual until 1991 and of the fifth IMF BOP manual from 1992 onwards. This switch appears as a break in the data series.

EU external balances of the current account: current account balance, goods balance, services balance, income balance and current transfers. 1 000 million ECU

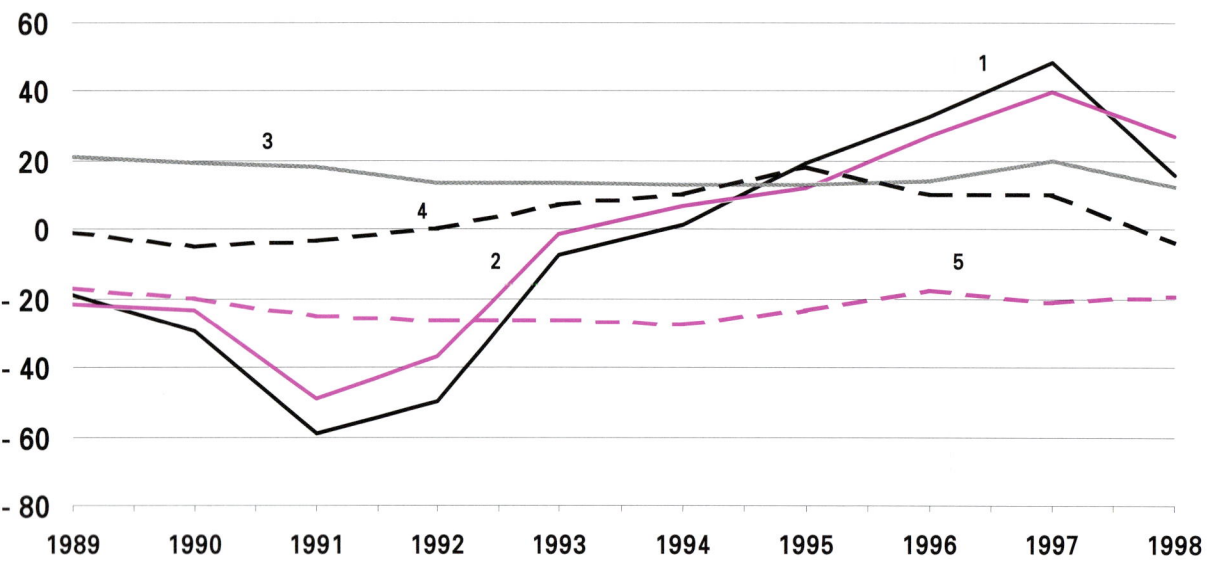

1: current account; 2: goods balance; 3: services balance; 4: income balance; 5: current transfers.

3A7AC

Further reading: EU international transactions — 1999 edition. Eurostat. International trade in services — EU, 1989–98. Eurostat.

Until 1991 data refer to EU-12 and from 1992 onwards data refer to EU-15. Until 1991 current transfers include capital transfers and the current account includes the capital account.

Current account balance of EU, US and Japan with the rest of the world. 1 000 million ECU

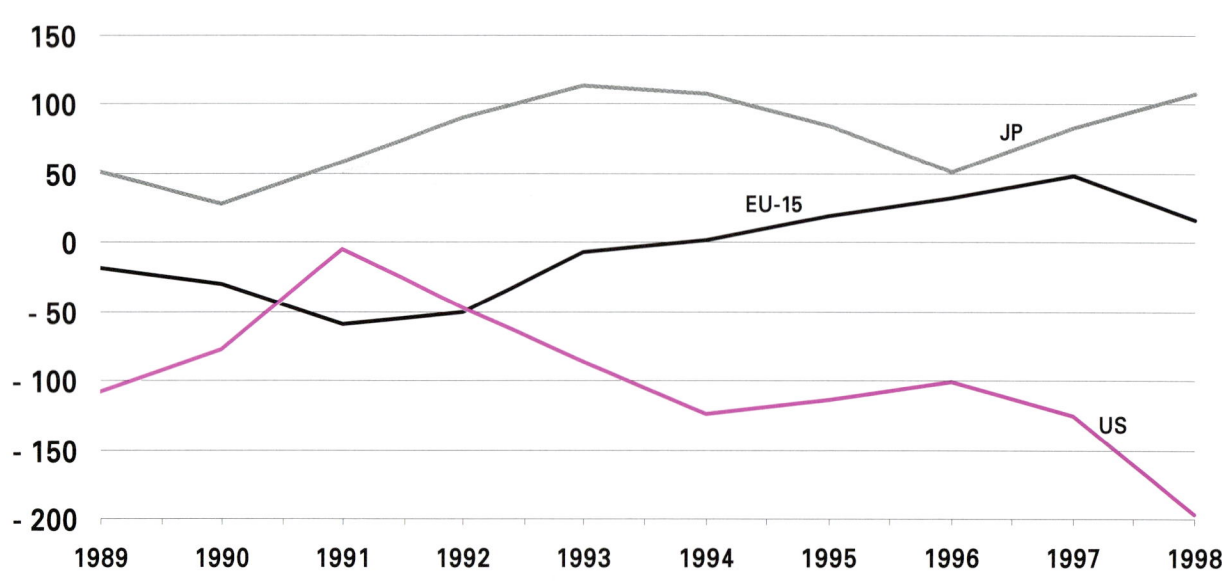

3A7AD

Further reading: EU international transactions — 1999 edition. Eurostat. International trade in services — EU, 1989–98. Eurostat.

Until 1991 data refer to EU-12 and from 1992 onwards data refer to EU-15. Data includes the capital account until 1991 for the EU and the US, until 1994 for Japan.

Balance of international trade in goods and services at current prices. % of GDP

	1989	1990	1991	1992	1993	1994	1995	1996	1997	1998	1999	
EU-15	0,0	- 0,1	- 0,5		- 0,4	0,2	0,3	0,4	0,6	0,8	0,5	:	**EU-15**
EUR-11	:	:	:	:	:	:	1,1	1,3	1,7	1,6	:	**EUR-11**
B/L	2,7	2,8	1,8		2,7	3,9	4,2	4,1	4,1	4,5	3,8	:	**B/L**
DK	3,2	5,8	6,4		7,4	6,8	6,2	4,8	5,9	3,5	1,8	:	**DK**
D	5,3	3,5		- 0,1	- 0,1	0,4	0,6	0,8	1,2	1,5	1,6	:	**D**
EL	- 3,4	- 5,6	- 4,5		- 4,9	- 2,7	- 2,0	- 5,1	- 5,4	- 4,1	- 5,2	:	**EL**
E	- 3,3	- 3,5	- 3,3		- 3,0	- 0,7	0,0	- 0,1	0,6	1,1	0,5	:	**E**
F	0,4	0,2	0,5		1,5	1,9	2,0	1,9	2,0	3,3	3,2	:	**F**
IRL	7,3	6,0	6,5		7,6	10,6	9,5	11,1	11,2	12,5	11,8	:	**IRL**
I	- 0,3	- 0,1	- 0,1		0,0	3,4	3,7	4,2	5,2	4,3	3,4	:	**I**
L	:	:	:	:	:	:	:	:	:	:	:	**L**
NL	3,9	4,5	4,4		3,9	5,7	6,0	6,1	6,0	6,6	5,8	:	**NL**
A	:	:	:	0,8	0,5	- 0,3	- 0,9	- 1,2	- 1,6	- 0,7	:	**A**
P	- 6,9	- 7,8	- 8,6		- 8,8	- 7,9	- 7,7	- 7,0	- 7,3	- 8,5	- 9,9	:	**P**
FIN	:	:	:	1,2	5,1	6,2	8,1	8,0	8,6	9,2	:	**FIN**
S	:	:	:	1,6	3,6	4,3	6,3	6,7	6,9	6,1	:	**S**
UK	- 4,2	- 2,8	- 1,2		- 1,4	- 1,3	- 1,0	- 0,7	- 0,6	0,1	- 1,0	:	**UK**
US	- 1,7	- 1,4	- 0,5		- 0,6	- 1,1	- 1,6	- 1,5	- 1,4	- 1,3	- 2,0	:	**US**
CA	:	:	:	:	:	:	:	:	:	:	:	**CA**
JP	1,3	0,6	1,7		2,3	2,3	2,0	1,4	0,5	1,1	1,9	:	**JP**

3A7BA

Further reading: EU international transactions — 1999 edition. Eurostat. International trade in services — EU, 1989–98. Eurostat.

The National Bank of Belgium produces the balance of payments for Belgium and Luxembourg, B/L, as a whole. EU = EU-12 until 1991; EU = EU-15 from 1992 onwards.

International trade in goods and services, cover rates. %

	1989	1990	1991	1992	1993	1994	1995	1996	1997	1998	1999	
EU-15	100	99	95		96	102	103	104	105	107	104	:	**EU-15**
EUR-11	:	:	:	:	:	:	108	109	111	110	:	**EUR-11**
B/L	104	104	103		104	107	107	107	107	107	106	:	**B/L**
DK	109	117	119		123	123	119	114	118	110	105	:	**DK**
D	119	112		100	100	102	102	103	105	106	106	:	**D**
EL	87	78	81		79	87	90	76	74	81	76	:	**EL**
E	84	82	83		85	96	100	100	103	104	102	:	**E**
F	102	101	102		107	109	109	109	109	114	113	:	**F**
IRL	113	112	113		114	119	116	117	117	119	116	:	**IRL**
I	99	100	100		100	118	118	119	124	119	115	:	**I**
L	:	:	:	:	:	:	:	:	:	:	:	**L**
NL	108	109	109		108	112	112	111	111	111	110	:	**NL**
A	:	:	:	102	101	99	98	97	96	99	:	**A**
P	82	80	76		74	78	79	82	81	79	77	:	**P**
FIN	:	:	:	105	118	121	127	126	127	130	:	**FIN**
S	:	:	:	106	112	113	118	120	118	115	:	**S**
UK	85	90	95		95	95	97	98	98	100	96	:	**UK**
US	85	87	96		94	90	87	88	89	90	85	:	**US**
CA	:	:	:	:	:	:	:	:	:	:	:	**CA**
JP	114	106	120		129	132	127	118	105	111	120	:	**JP**

3A7BB

Further reading: EU international transactions — 1999 edition. Eurostat. International trade in services — EU, 1989–98. Eurostat.

The National Bank of Belgium produces the balance of payments for Belgium and Luxembourg, B/L, as a whole. EU = EU-12 until 1991; EU = EU-15 from 1992 onwards.

The compilation of the EU/euro-zone balance of payments is based on extra-EU/extra-euro-zone transactions: it is obtained by aggregating cross-border transactions of residents vis-à-vis non-residents as reported by the 15/11 participating Member States. In principle, intra transactions should net out and the EU-15/EUR-11 totals could be compiled by adding up the net flows of the countries involved. In practice, bilateral data do not match, thus resulting in significant discrepancies (intra-asymmetries) at the EU-15/EUR-11 levels. Cover rates are calculated as (credits/debits) x 100.

Balance of international trade in goods and services at current prices of EU, US and Japan with the rest of the world. 1 000 million ECU

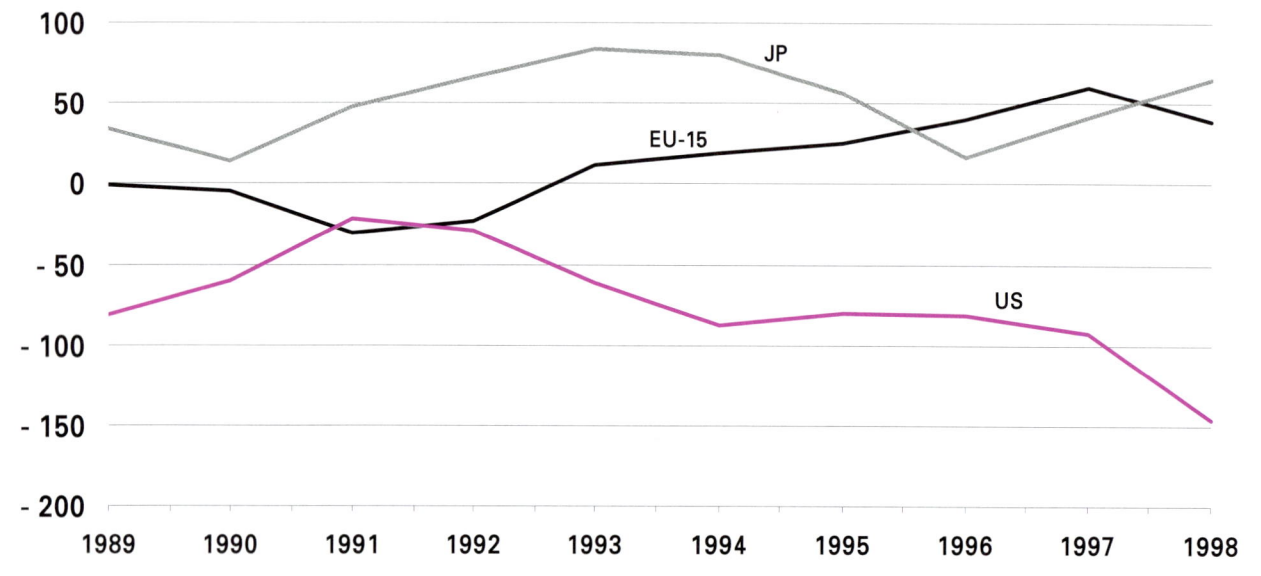

3A7BC

Further reading: EU international transactions — 1999 edition. Eurostat. International trade in services — EU, 1989–98. Eurostat.

Until 1991 data refer to EU-12 and from 1992 onwards data refer to EU-15.

International trade in goods and services of the EU, the US and Japan with the rest of the world, cover rates. %

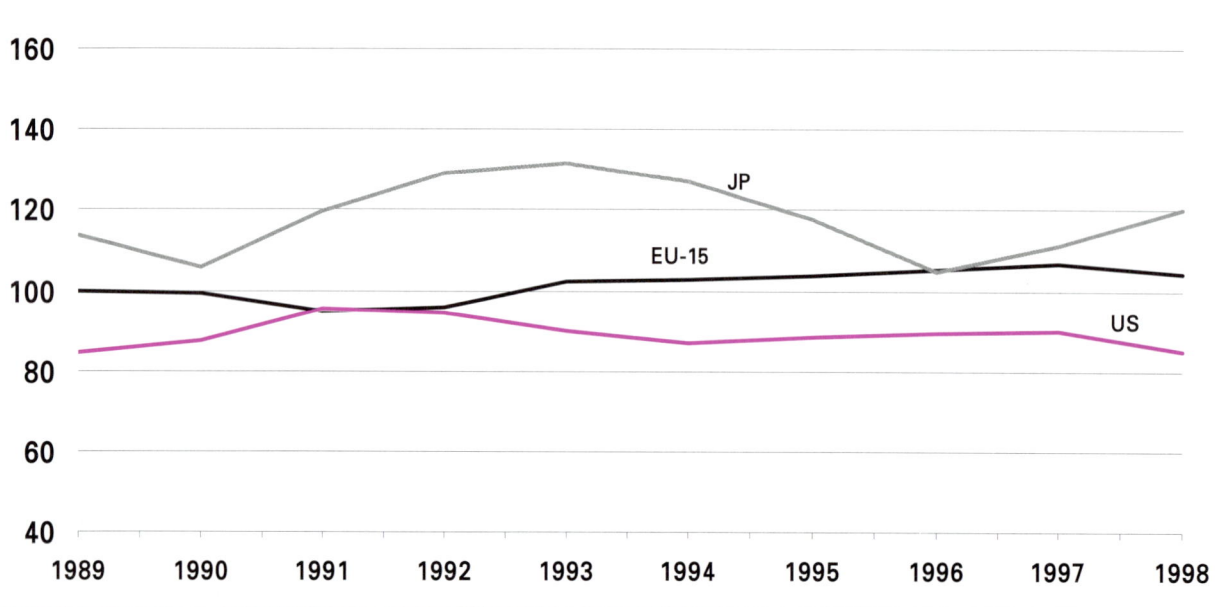

3A7BD

Further reading: EU international transactions — 1999 edition. Eurostat. International trade in services — EU, 1989–98. Eurostat.

Until 1991 data refer to EU-12 and from 1992 onwards data refer to EU-15.

eurostat

Total trade in goods (exports-fob + imports-fob), % of current account total flows

	1989	1990	1991	1992	1993	1994	1995	1996	1997	1998	1999	
EU-15	56,8	55,7	54,4	56,0	56,5	58,4	59,9	58,7	58,6	58,5	:	**EU-15**
EUR-11	:	:	:	:	:	:	59,1	59,4	59,3	59,4	:	**EUR-11**
B/L	55,3	52,9	50,1	48,6	47,4	47,7	56,9	59,7	60,5	59,6	:	**B/L**
DK	58,5	57,8	54,6	51,1	49,5	50,7	53,1	48,6	53,8	53,5	:	**DK**
D	72,5	71,2	69,7	68,9	66,4	68,7	68,5	68,5	68,8	69,6	:	**D**
EL	50,8	50,4	49,6	48,6	46,9	45,6	48,8	49,2	47,1	47,6	:	**EL**
E	65,1	65,2	62,9	60,0	59,7	63,1	64,4	64,3	64,9	63,7	:	**E**
F	62,5	59,6	56,6	53,8	49,4	50,5	64,3	64,4	64,5	63,7	:	**F**
IRL	67,7	65,6	65,0	64,5	66,1	66,5	66,4	65,6	64,8	63,3	:	**IRL**
I	69,2	65,6	64,2	61,2	59,2	63,1	64,9	62,7	61,0	61,8	:	**I**
L	:	:	:	:	:	:	:	:	:	:	:	**L**
NL	65,5	65,9	64,2	64,1	62,1	63,3	66,9	66,5	64,8	65,8	:	**NL**
A	:	:	:	56,8	54,2	56,3	58,4	57,4	58,3	58,2	:	**A**
P	67,5	67,2	65,6	70,6	63,9	67,2	64,8	63,5	65,0	65,0	:	**P**
FIN	:	:	:	67,1	68,5	70,7	68,6	70,5	70,9	71,9	:	**FIN**
S	:	:	:	61,2	64,4	68,3	65,3	65,1	64,8	63,7	:	**S**
UK	51,0	50,3	49,4	52,2	53,7	55,5	53,2	50,5	50,9	49,7	:	**UK**
US	61,3	61,2	64,7	63,1	63,9	63,7	63,1	61,8	61,1	60,7	:	**US**
CA	:	:	:	:	:	:	:	:	:	:	:	**CA**
JP	59,9	57,9	55,5	56,6	57,0	58,0	57,3	53,9	54,3	52,9	:	**JP**

Further reading: EU international transactions — 1999 edition. Eurostat. International trade in services — EU, 1989–98. Eurostat.

The National Bank of Belgium produces the balance of payments for Belgium and Luxembourg, B/L, as a whole. EU = EU-12 until 1991; EU = EU-15 from 1992 onwards.

Total trade in services (exports + imports), % of current account total flows

	1989	1990	1991	1992	1993	1994	1995	1996	1997	1998	1999	
EU-15	18,7	19,2	19,3	20,1	20,3	20,0	19,1	19,4	19,6	19,5	:	**EU-15**
EUR-11	:	:	:	:	:	:	18,3	19,0	19,0	18,7	:	**EUR-11**
B/L	14,7	14,4	13,2	12,9	13,7	14,3	13,0	13,6	13,9	14,2	:	**B/L**
DK	23,0	22,9	22,3	19,9	16,8	17,0	17,2	16,8	16,9	18,1	:	**DK**
D	13,5	13,7	13,4	13,9	14,9	14,6	14,6	15,1	14,9	14,5	:	**D**
EL	32,8	34,0	32,0	34,5	34,0	35,7	31,4	31,6	34,9	34,3	:	**EL**
E	21,7	21,3	20,3	20,3	21,5	20,5	19,6	20,0	19,8	20,6	:	**E**
F	18,7	18,7	18,2	19,4	19,5	18,3	17,7	17,7	17,2	16,9	:	**F**
IRL	11,9	12,1	12,5	14,5	14,2	14,6	14,4	15,2	15,1	15,9	:	**IRL**
I	15,4	19,0	18,2	19,6	19,4	18,8	18,3	19,6	20,3	17,9	:	**I**
L	:	:	:	:	:	:	:	:	:	:	:	**L**
NL	17,0	16,9	18,0	18,9	20,0	20,1	17,9	17,8	18,4	18,6	:	**NL**
A	:	:	:	29,3	31,4	30,6	28,7	29,5	27,9	28,1	:	**A**
P	14,7	15,4	15,7	14,3	19,8	18,0	16,9	15,2	15,2	15,8	:	**P**
FIN	:	:	:	17,7	17,2	16,8	17,4	16,6	15,6	14,1	:	**FIN**
S	:	:	:	20,5	18,1	17,2	14,8	15,2	16,6	16,7	:	**S**
UK	13,8	13,6	13,7	15,1	15,5	15,8	15,1	14,1	14,7	15,4	:	**UK**
US	16,6	18,1	19,9	19,2	19,0	17,9	16,8	16,9	16,6	16,9	:	**US**
CA	:	:	:	:	:	:	:	:	:	:	:	**CA**
JP	16,0	15,5	15,3	16,0	16,4	16,1	14,9	14,8	14,6	14,7	:	**JP**

Further reading: EU international transactions — 1999 edition. Eurostat. International trade in services — EU, 1989–98. Eurostat.

The National Bank of Belgium produces the balance of payments for Belgium and Luxembourg, B/L, as a whole. EU = EU-12 until 1991; EU = EU-15 from 1992 onwards.

The trade balance in goods, according to the balance of payments concept, includes all movable property whose ownership is transferred from a resident to a non-resident or vice versa. These figures should be based on customs data, which are imports at **cif** values (including costs relating to transport and insurance) and exports at **fob** values (excluding transport costs). Imports at cif values are corrected to imports at fob values in order to classify costs relating to transport and insurance as transport services and insurance services. Transactions on goods crossing a border without change of ownership are not regarded as exports; but transactions on goods between residents and non-residents are regarded as exports, even if the goods do not cross a border. This explains why external trade statistics and balance of payments figures for goods are not the same.

Trade in goods of EU, US and Japan with the rest of the world, cover rates. %

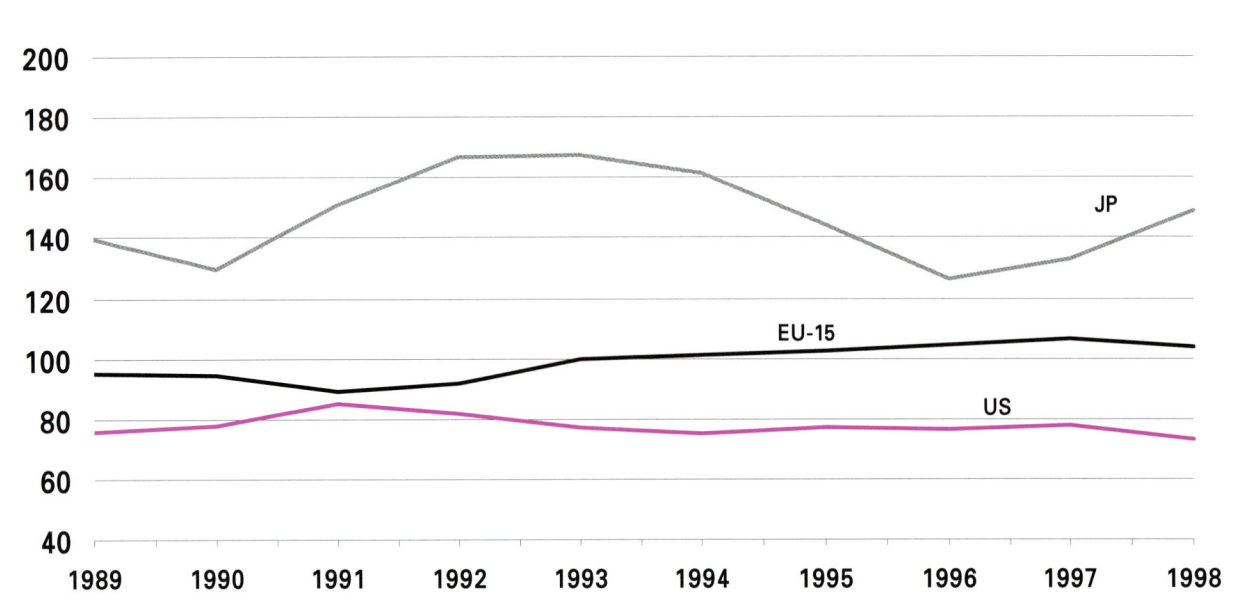

3A7CD

Further reading: EU international transactions — 1999 edition. Eurostat. International trade in services — EU, 1989–98. Eurostat.

Until 1991 data refer to EU-12 and from 1992 onwards data refer to EU-15.

The trade balance in services includes three main sub-balances: transport, tourism and other services. Services flows are recorded as the economic value of services. Due to its intangible nature, international trade in services is much more difficult to record than trade in goods. Three types of problems may arise: difficulty in defining the ser-

vice; value of the service not specified separately but aggregated with the value of other transactions on the same invoice; practical difficulties for identifying gross flows as many services can be paid for by means of an international offsetting mechanism. Therefore underestimates of certain flows are almost inevitable.

Services' balance of EU, US and Japan with the rest of the world. 1 000 million ECU

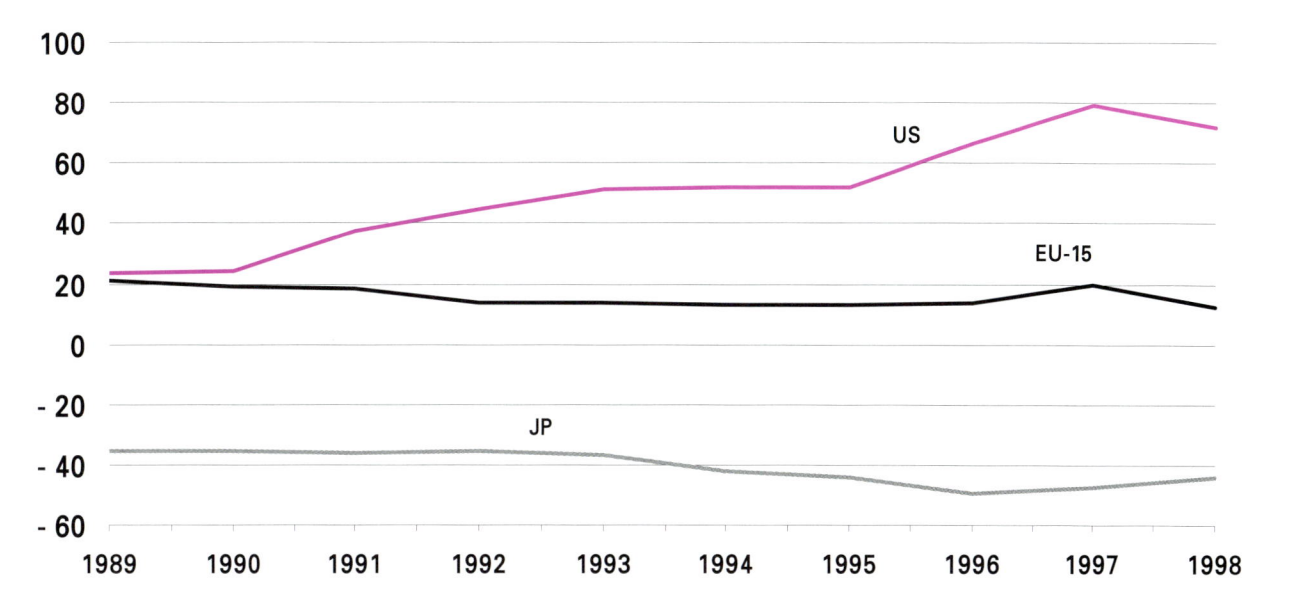

Further reading: EU international transactions — 1999 edition. Eurostat. International trade in services — EU, 1989–98. Eurostat.

Until 1991 data refer to EU-12 and from 1992 onwards data refer to EU-15.

Share of EU, US, JP and the rest of the world in world total transactions in services (exports + imports). %. 1998

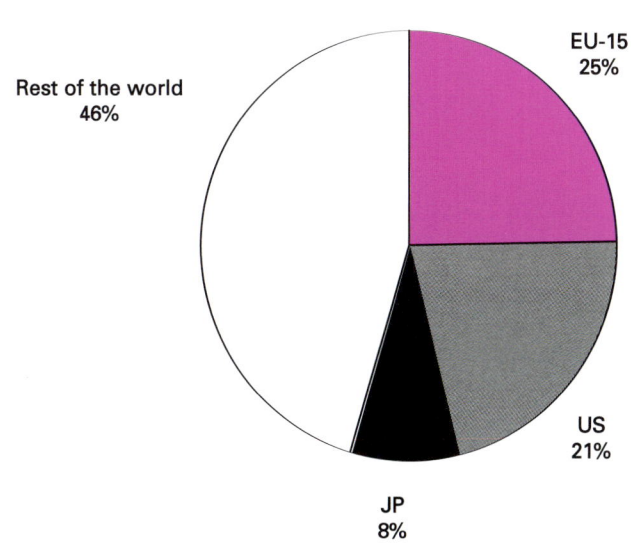

Further reading: EU international transactions — 1999 edition. Eurostat. International trade in services — EU, 1989–98. Eurostat.

The annual European Union direct investment yearbook gives a snapshot of foreign direct investment (FDI) flows and stocks, showing who invests where, in which sectors and the amounts. It also addresses such questions as: who are the main investors? Who are the main receivers? Why invest abroad rather than at home? Why invest now rather than 10 years ago? In manufacturing rather than finance? A firm wishing to sell overseas has a variety of modes to employ. Exporting, licensing and using agents are some examples, with straight-forward exporting up to now being the most common. FDI is an increasingly adopted alternative — producing and selling directly in the chosen country. FDI is of two kinds. First, creation of productive assets by foreigners who build something from scratch — greenfield investment; or second, purchase of existing assets by foreigners — acquisitions, mergers, takeovers, etc. FDI encompasses investments made with the express purpose of ownership and control of companies abroad. The investor's purpose is an effective voice in management and, at the same time, a lasting interest in the enterprise. Direct investment does not include only the initial acquisition of equity capital but also subsequent capital transactions between the foreign investor and domestic and affiliated enterprises.

More data on this in Eurostat's database

Focusing on the European Union, this domain covers quarterly balance of payments statistics, annual current account statistics emphasising international trade in services with detailed geographical breakdown, annual foreign direct investment statistics (flows, income and positions) with geographical and sectoral breakdown, and annual balance of payments statistics of the EU institutions. Annual and quarterly balance of payments data on candidate countries and other related countries are also provided.

➤ ➤ ➤ **DOMAIN BOP IN DATABASE NEW CRONOS**

EU direct investment: inward, outward and intra-flows. Million ECU/EUR

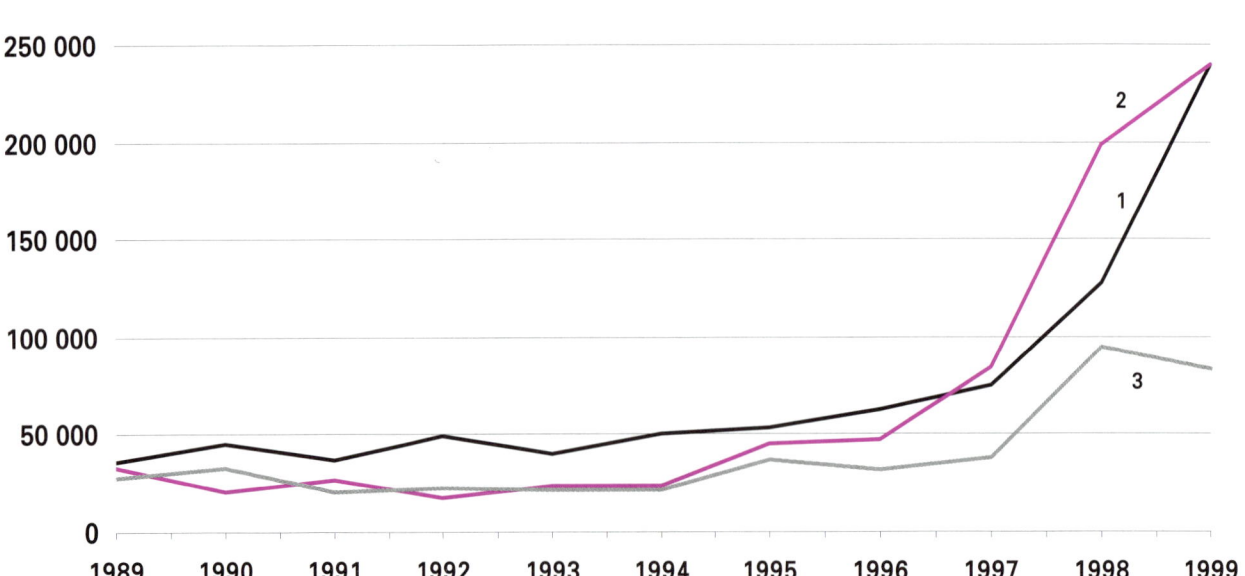

1: intra-EU flows; 2: EU outward flows to non-EU countries; 3: EU inward flows from non-EU countries.

Further reading: European Union direct investment, Yearbook 2000. Eurostat.

EU-12 from 1989 to 1991 and EU-15 from 1992, figures exclude reinvested earnings.

Direct investment inflows, the EU, the US, Japan. Million ECU/EUR

6P2BP

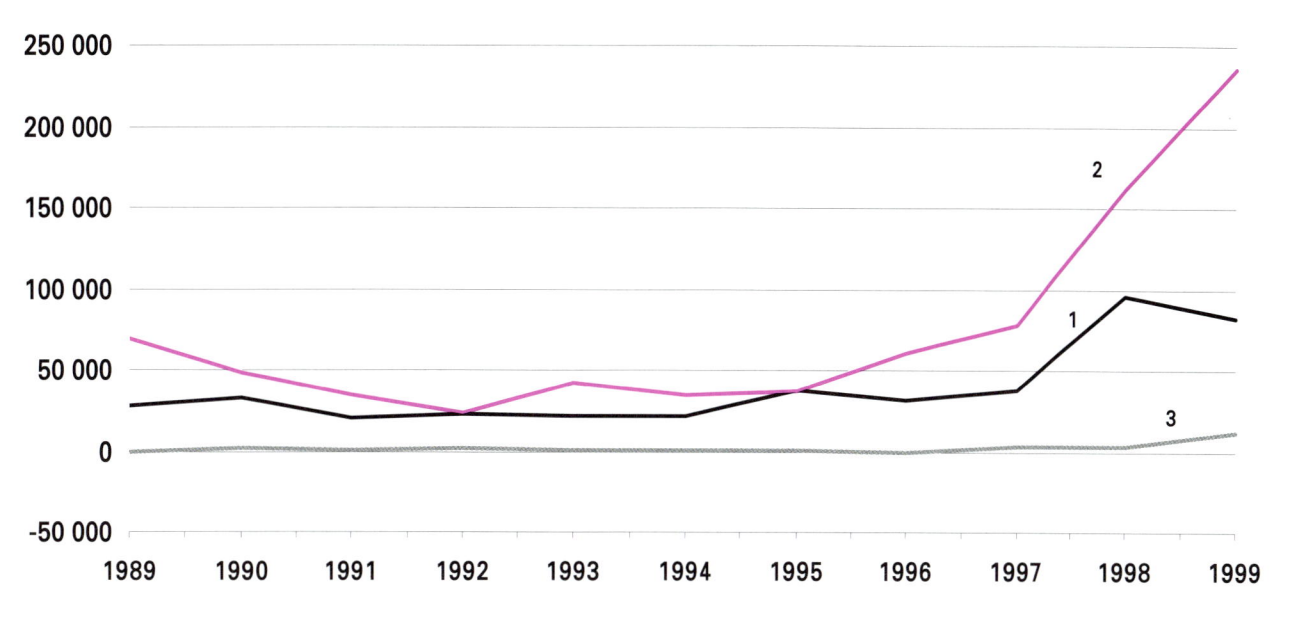

1: EU from Extra EU; 2: US from the rest of the world; 3: Japan from the rest of the world.

Further reading: European Union direct investment, Yearbook 2000. Eurostat.   EU-12 from 1989 to 1991, EU-15 from 1992, figures exclude reinvested earnings.

Direct investment outflows, the EU, the US, Japan. Million ECU/EUR

6P3BP

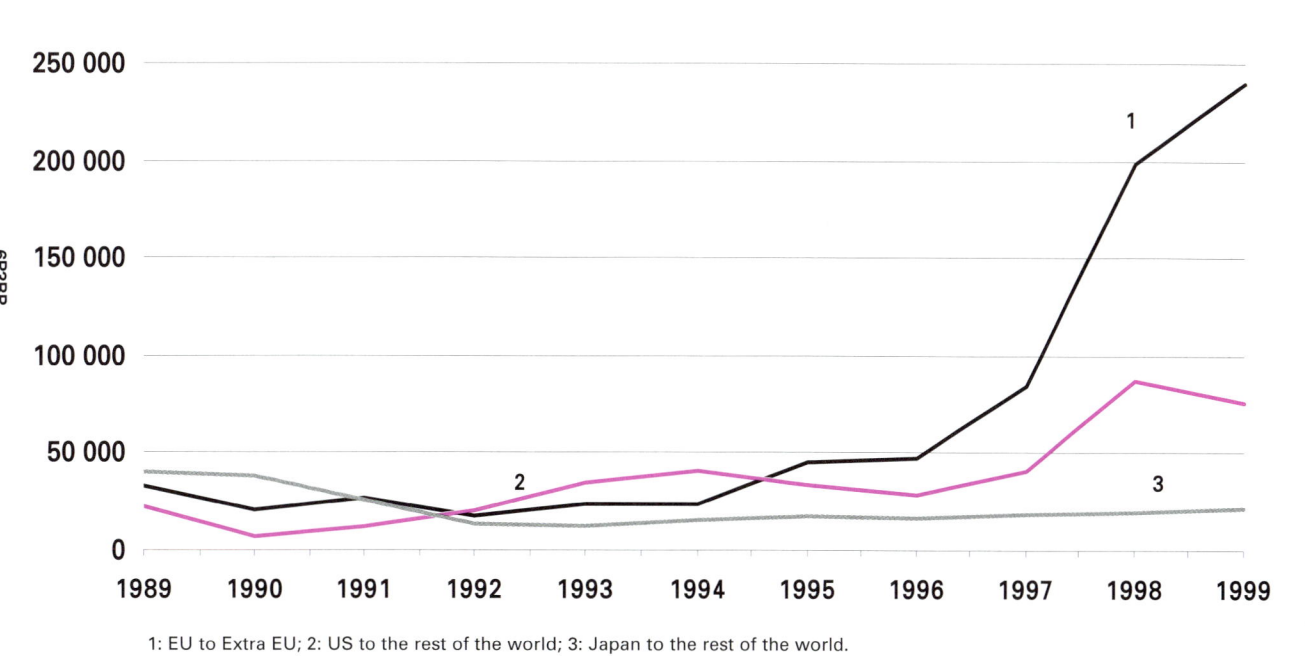

1: EU to Extra EU; 2: US to the rest of the world; 3: Japan to the rest of the world.

Further reading: European Union direct investment, Yearbook 2000. Eurostat.   EU-12 from 1989 to 1991, EU-15 from 1992, figures exclude reinvested earnings.

EU direct investment inflows. Suppliers of direct investment to the EU. Million ECU/EUR

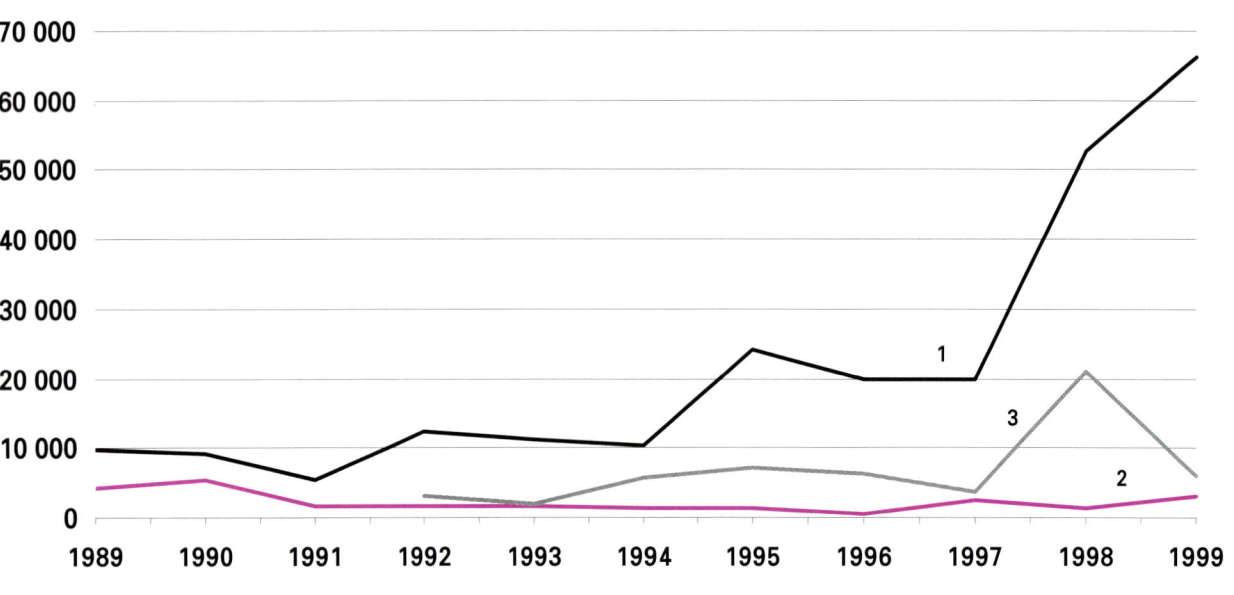

1: US in EU; 2: Japan in EU; 3: EFTA in the EU.

Further reading: European Union direct investment, Yearbook 2000. Eurostat.

EU-12 from 1989 to 1991 and EU-15 from 1992, figures exclude reinvested earnings.

EU direct investment inflows from the extra-EU.
Suppliers of direct investment to the EU. Million ECU/EUR

	1989	1990	1991	1992	1993	1994	1995	1996	1997	1998	1999
US in EU	9 846	9 178	5 411	12 286	11 296	10 347	24 293	19 989	19 990	52 679	66 190
Japan in EU	4 354	5 406	1 682	1 859	1 600	1 454	1 535	468	2 729	1 515	3 272
EFTA in EU	:	:	:	3 303	2 016	5 630	7 064	6 298	3 688	21 084	6 168
Total EU inflows	27 943	32 753	20 933	22 760	21 504	21 814	37 220	31 828	37 793	95 032	83 435

Further reading: European Union direct investment, Yearbook 2000. Eurostat.

EU-12 from 1989 to 1991 and EU-15 from 1992, figures exclude reinvested earnings.

EU direct investment inflows. Recipients of direct investment from the rest of the world.
Million ECU/EUR

	1989	1990	1991	1992	1993	1994	1995	1996	1997	1998	1999	
EU-12/EU-15	53 264	66 345	61 177	55 494	55 893	57 735	80 344	77 759	100 020	202 842	304 309	**EU-12/EU-15**
B/L	7 520	6 269	6 517	8 735	9 201	7 014	8 267	11 078	10 989	18 560	36 288	**B/L**
DK	1 180	950	985	785	1 424	4 130	3 196	605	2 472	5 761	8 016	**DK**
D	2 138	3 082	4 667	2 058	3 181	6 706	11 076	8 750	10 203	19 511	49 238	**D**
EL	:	:	:	:	:	:	:	:	:	:	:	**EL**
E	8 273	10 199	7 207	6 365	8 167	7 819	4 808	5 375	5 638	10 541	8 782	**E**
F	8 957	7 120	8 675	12 308	10 450	13 836	18 659	18 135	19 982	24 577	32 112	**F**
IRL	:	:	:	:	:	:	:	:	5 350	7 663	17 197	**IRL**
I	2 008	4 995	1 980	2 442	3 202	1 883	3 683	2 784	3 263	2 332	3 423	**I**
L	:	:	:	:	:	:	:	:	:	:	:	**L**
NL	4 250	6 995	5 782	5 255	6 259	3 848	8 762	9 439	8 357	29 042	28 139	**NL**
A	:	:	:	727	838	1 109	581	3 032	1 414	3 176	1 260	**A**
P	1 930	1 968	1 421	1 485	1 297	1 057	506	557	1 479	1 988	- 46	**P**
FIN	- 16	759	278	445	719	1 069	358	510	1 256	9 751	1 854	**FIN**
S	5 108	1 608	1 084	700	2 287	4 106	9 208	3 551	8 023	14 390	52 194	**S**
UK	11 219	21 262	22 149	11 767	7 476	3 658	9 935	10 670	21 440	55 252	65 380	**UK**

6P1AC

Further reading: European Union direct investment, Yearbook 2000. Eurostat.

EU-12 from 1989 to 1991 and EU-15 from 1992, figures exclude reinvested earnings. A: data before 1995 only cover equity capital.

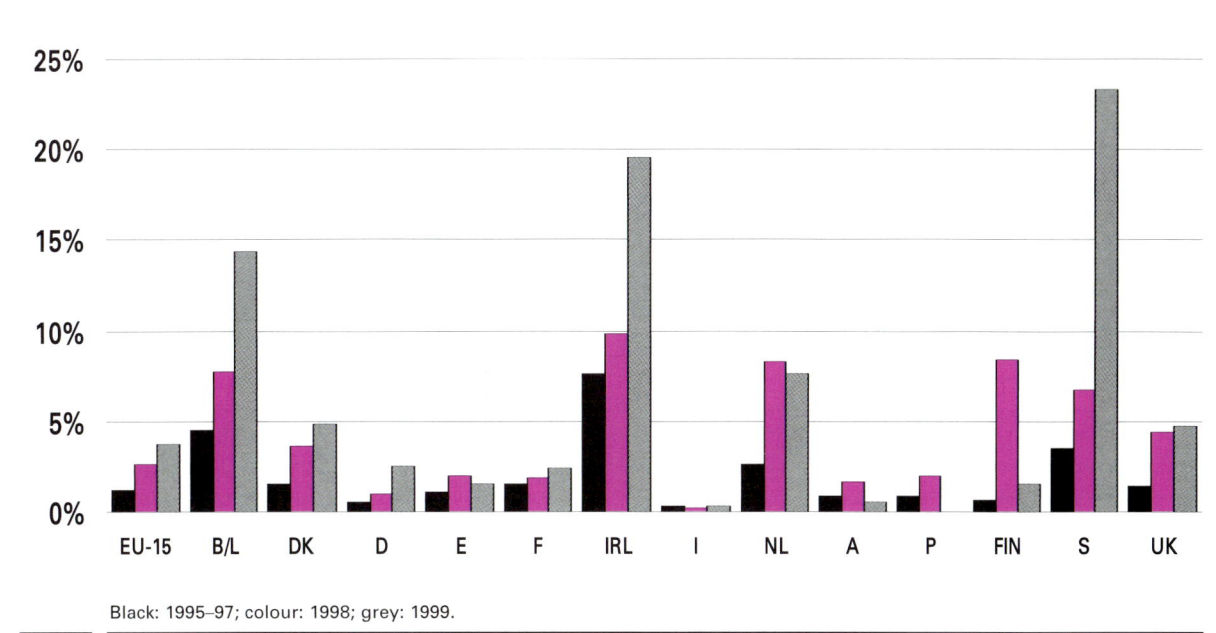

EU direct investment inflows in percentage of GDP

6P1AP

Black: 1995–97; colour: 1998; grey: 1999.

Further reading: European Union direct investment, Yearbook 2000. Eurostat.

Figures exclude reinvested earnings.

EU direct investment outflows. Recipients of direct investment. Million ECU/EUR

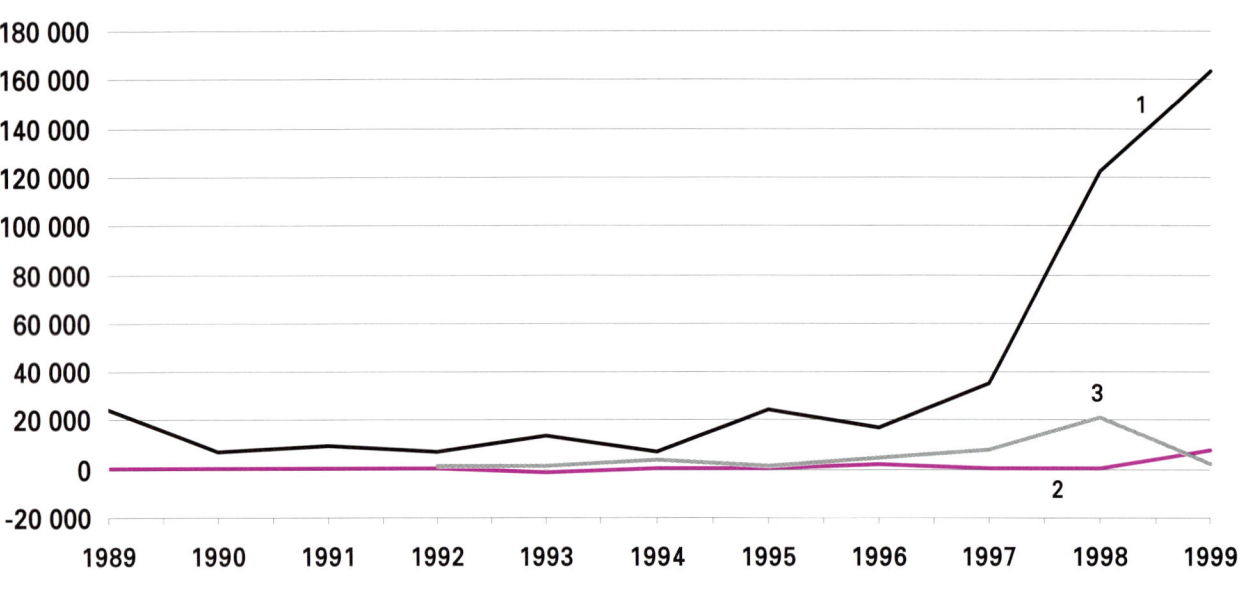

1: EU in US; 2: EU in Japan; 3: EU in EFTA.

Further reading: European Union direct investment, Yearbook 2000. Eurostat.

EU-12 from 1989 to 1991 and EU-15 from 1992, figures exclude reinvested earnings.

EU direct investment outflows to the extra-EU. Recipients of direct investment. Million ECU/EUR

	1989	1990	1991	1992	1993	1994	1995	1996	1997	1998	1999
EU in US	24 053	7 155	9 232	6 941	13 789	7 426	24 534	17 272	35 343	122 045	163 457
EU in Japan	682	911	341	445	- 1 229	272	854	2 159	446	338	8 289
EU in EFTA	:	:	:	1 539	1 758	4 279	1 797	4 368	8 272	21 290	2 195
Total EU outflows	33 282	20 527	26 732	17 828	24 157	24 129	45 580	47 412	84 748	198 267	239 222

Further reading: European Union direct investment, Yearbook 2000. Eurostat.

EU-12 from 1989 to 1991 and EU-15 from 1992, figures exclude reinvested earnings.

EU direct investment outflows. Suppliers of direct investment to the rest of the world.
Million ECU/EUR

	1989	1990	1991	1992	1993	1994	1995	1996	1997	1998	1999	
EU-12/EU-15	- 64 208	- 65 525	- 69 018	- 67 107	- 64 361	- 74 687	- 99 150	- 110 413	- 160 679	- 325 967	- 479 396	EU-12/EU-15
B/L	- 4 852	- 4 849	- 5 819	- 8 030	- 4 008	- 1 017	- 8 956	- 6 354	- 6 833	- 22 792	- 31 949	B/L
DK	- 1 658	- 1 274	- 2 017	- 1 729	- 1 076	- 3 335	- 2 343	- 1 985	- 3 715	- 3 467	- 8 917	DK
D	- 16 239	- 16 434	- 11 365	- 14 353	- 13 853	- 14 488	- 28 216	- 35 241	- 32 801	- 75 114	- 87 770	D
EL	:	:	:	:	:	:	:	:	:	:	:	EL
E	- 2 879	- 2 228	- 1 329	- 961	- 2 708	- 3 466	- 3 180	- 4 406	- 11 074	- 16 921	- 33 240	E
F	- 16 583	- 21 204	- 16 408	- 14 519	- 10 393	- 19 321	- 14 393	- 22 889	- 29 757	- 34 334	- 94 817	F
IRL	:	:	:	:	:	:	:	:	- 2 542	- 3 489	- 5 085	IRL
I	- 5 495	- 5 843	- 1 890	- 4 374	- 6 174	- 4 302	- 4 384	- 5 092	- 9 373	- 10 787	- 3 194	I
L	:	:	:	:	:	:	:	:	:	:	:	L
NL	- 9 810	- 10 332	- 10 483	- 10 781	- 9 818	- 12 137	- 10 754	- 22 375	- 18 953	- 33 948	- 37 297	NL
A	:	:	:	- 1 446	- 1 253	- 1 013	- 948	- 1 297	- 1 366	- 2 108	- 2 254	A
P	- 383	- 130	- 70	- 529	- 83	- 239	- 530	- 629	- 1 493	- 2 385	- 2 382	P
FIN	- 683	- 2 498	- 2 784	- 409	- 2 160	- 3 669	- 1 059	- 2 650	- 3 727	- 19 326	- 3 211	FIN
S	- 5 065	- 10 017	- 7 135	- 733	- 1 323	- 3 074	- 4 613	- 268	- 6 993	- 15 035	- 11 163	S
UK	- 4 760	- 2 639	- 18 439	- 6 868	- 9 124	- 7 724	- 16 621	- 6 298	- 31 866	- 85 909	- 157 643	UK

Further reading: European Union direct investment, Yearbook 2000. Eurostat.

EU-12 from 1989 to 1991 and EU-15 from 1992, figures exclude reinvested earnings. A: data before 1995 only cover equity capital.

EU direct investment outflows in percentage of GDP

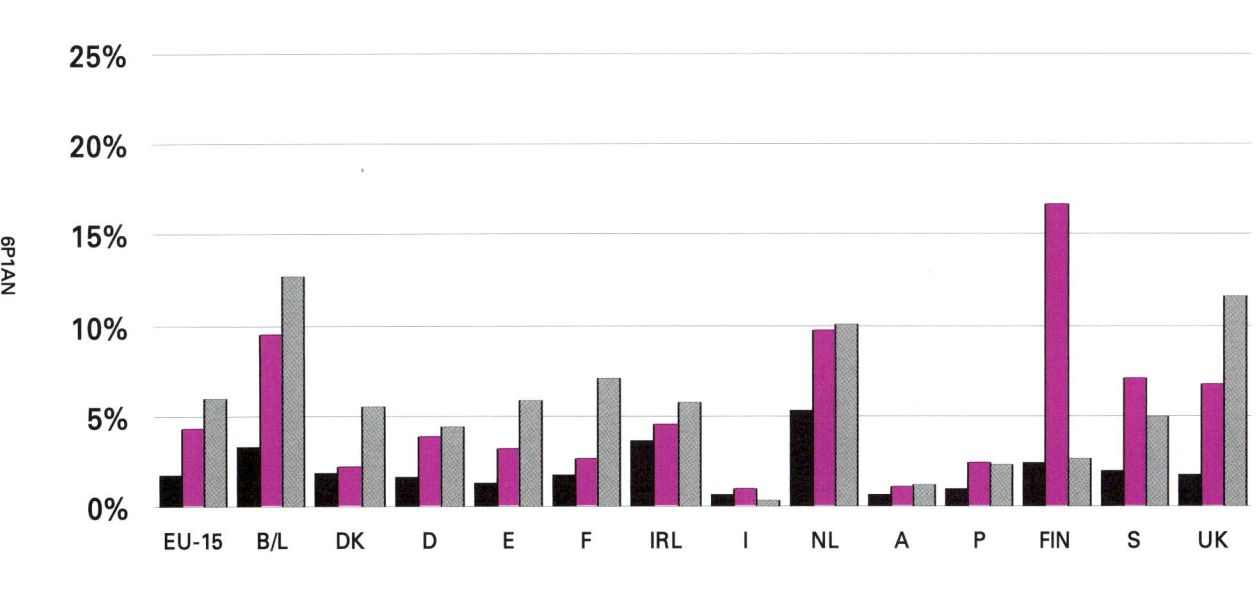

Black: 1995-1997; colour: 1998; grey: 1999.

Further reading: European Union direct investment, Yearbook 2000. Eurostat.

Figures exclude reinvested earnings.

EU direct investment intra-flows. Suppliers of direct investment. Shares. 1999

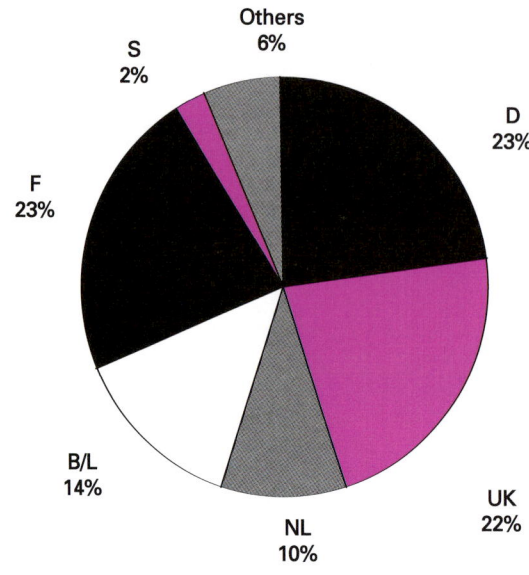

6P1AD

Further reading: European Union direct investment, Yearbook 2000. Eurostat.   Figures exclude reinvested earnings.

EU direct investment intra-flows. Recipients of direct investment. Shares. 1999

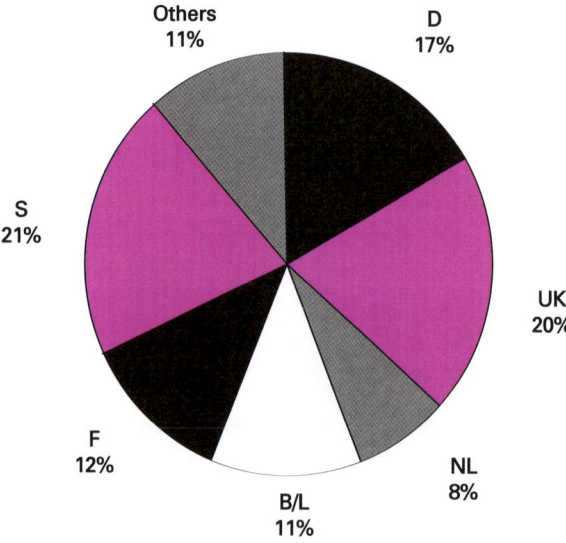

6P1AE

Further reading: European Union direct investment, Yearbook 2000. Eurostat.   Figures exclude reinvested earnings.

Suppliers of EU direct investment, intra-flows. Million ECU/EUR

	1989	1990	1991	1992	1993	1994	1995	1996	1997	1998	1999	
EU-12/EU-15	- 35 736	- 44 998	- 37 477	- 49 279	- 40 204	- 50 320	- 53 564	- 62 554	- 75 497	- 127 549	- 240 201	EU-12/EU-15
B/L	- 4 674	- 3 673	- 4 482	- 7 332	- 2 675	- 866	- 6 671	- 2 347	- 5 930	- 16 778	- 32 539	B/L
DK	- 1 620	- 859	- 823	- 1 460	- 297	- 2 212	- 998	- 1 614	- 2 459	- 3 280	- 5 904	DK
D	- 6 850	- 11 066	- 11 355	- 9 929	- 10 022	- 8 558	- 17 292	- 17 202	- 10 467	- 22 091	- 54 928	D
EL	:	:	:	:	:	:	:	:	:	:	:	EL
E	- 914	- 1 495	- 1 763	- 234	- 1 584	- 474	- 827	- 1 634	- 3 826	- 5 241	- 5 391	E
F	- 10 203	- 14 340	- 8 782	- 11 891	- 6 012	- 10 345	- 9 014	- 11 626	- 15 597	- 15 647	- 55 783	F
IRL									- 1 417	- 1 126	- 1 510	IRL
I	- 2 132	- 4 812	- 1 132	- 2 464	- 4 732	- 3 201	- 3 601	- 3 732	- 5 667	- 5 183	- 1 448	I
L	:	:	:	:	:	:	:	:	:	:	:	L
NL	- 5 301	- 5 836	- 6 631	:	- 6 840	- 9 102	- 5 927	- 11 482	- 8 415	- 17 163	- 23 299	NL
A	- 478	- 536	- 624	- 912	- 484	- 442	- 411	- 437	- 750	- 1 282	- 771	A
P	- 55	- 104	- 324	- 462	- 77	- 163	- 416	- 196	- 686	- 971	1 933	P
FIN	- 949	- 935	- 91	- 87	- 1 983	- 3 418	- 691	- 1 952	- 2 545	- 18 154	- 1 747	FIN
S	- 4 629	- 8 595	- 4 081	69	- 1 192	- 2 655	- 1 214	- 663	- 1 305	- 9 519	- 5 774	S
UK	- 360	- 247	- 1 630	- 6 364	- 4 421	- 5 090	- 5 017	- 9 580	- 16 340	- 10 928	- 52 763	UK

6P1AA

Further reading: European Union direct investment, Yearbook 2000. Eurostat.

EU-12 from 1989 to 1991 and EU-15 from 1992, figures exclude reinvested earnings. A: data before 1995 covers equity capital only.

Recipients of EU direct investment, intra-flows. Million ECU/EUR

	1989	1990	1991	1992	1993	1994	1995	1996	1997	1998	1999	
EU-12/EU-15	33 234	33 592	32 332	32 734	34 389	36 101	43 119	44 509	60 282	105 997	222 980	EU-12/EU-15
B/L	4 649	4 913	5 746	6 737	6 302	5 357	6 489	7 943	7 866	12 229	25 497	B/L
DK	345	383	543	541	843	3 053	2 587	208	1 857	1 320	5 729	DK
D	2 997	895	1 698	1 400	1 093	4 262	5 572	4 634	6 439	16 192	37 113	D
EL	:	:	:	:	:	:	:	:	:	:	:	EL
E	5 080	7 243	6 133	4 300	6 963	5 446	3 784	3 590	4 719	9 493	6 859	E
F	6 575	3 755	4 669	8 212	7 803	9 341	11 646	13 152	14 279	19 959	27 249	F
IRL									2 429	4 382	5 870	IRL
I	1 690	1 975	720	1 501	2 528	1 467	2 567	2 274	2 224	2 117	2 401	I
L	:	:	:	:	:	:	:	:	:	:	:	L
NL	3 078	3 982	1 443	:	5 987	1 616	5 104	2 822	7 058	12 833	17 290	NL
A	486	356	454	570	598	497	387	2 920	1 090	3 471	818	A
P	1 056	1 382	1 410	1 168	1 070	681	390	609	1 137	492	- 95	P
FIN	142	154	154	221	538	826	206	776	1 112	9 508	1 864	FIN
S	157	1 005	4 557	196	1 264	2 378	853	2 205	5 092	12 950	47 242	S
UK	6 459	6 601	5 608	3 011	- 428	1 259	1 344	1 256	4 861	849	44 775	UK

6P1AB

Further reading: European Union direct investment, Yearbook 2000. Eurostat.

EU-12 from 1989 to 1991 and EU-15 from 1992, figures exclude reinvested earnings. A: data before 1995 covers equity capital only.

eurostat

Need more data on this topic? Ask your Data Shop

Exports of transport services as % of services total exports

	1989	1990	1991	1992	1993	1994	1995	1996	1997	1998	1999	
EU-15	29,5	28,0	28,8	28,6	27,4	26,9	26,3	25,2	26,7	25,8	:	**EU-15**
EUR-11	:	:	:	:	:	:	26,2	25,1	26,2	24,8	:	**EUR-11**
B/L	29,0	28,7	29,9	28,4	26,8	25,7	27,8	26,7	27,1	26,0	:	**B/L**
DK	57,6	53,4	56,3	53,5	56,7	55,5	52,7	50,3	65,3	63,2	:	**DK**
D	23,2	23,1	23,6	24,3	24,6	25,1	23,9	23,3	23,3	24,3		**D**
EL	37,5	35,3	36,6	35,6	26,7	26,7	23,4	22,9	26,5	21,4	:	**EL**
E	20,9	20,4	19,6	14,1	14,2	15,1	14,8	15,3	15,5	14,8	:	**E**
F	24,4	22,0	22,5	20,6	20,6	19,3	24,3	24,1	24,1	24,5	:	**F**
IRL	32,0	30,7	28,9	26,9	24,8	22,6	21,2	19,7	18,6	17,6	:	**IRL**
I	27,2	20,1	23,1	20,4	23,5	24,3	24,9	21,6	22,1	15,8	:	**I**
L	:	:	:	:	:	:	:	:	:	:	:	**L**
NL	47,1	45,6	44,0	42,0	40,1	39,1	40,0	40,6	40,5	39,1	:	**NL**
A	:	:	:	8,2	8,3	8,8	11,6	11,8	21,5	22,8	:	**A**
P	16,9	18,0	16,7	18,1	17,2	15,3	18,5	18,1	18,2	17,8	:	**P**
FIN	:	:	:	33,7	36,3	33,1	27,1	28,1	27,3	30,5	:	**FIN**
S	:	:	:	31,9	34,5	32,7	31,5	29,8	31,8	27,5	:	**S**
UK	24,5	24,8	23,6	23,3	23,3	23,8	22,1	20,5	19,4	19,2	:	**UK**
US	24,6	25,3	23,4	22,7	21,8	21,9	22,1	19,7	18,6	17,4	:	**US**
CA	:	:	:	:	:	:	:	:	:	:	:	**CA**
JP	42,0	40,5	40,2	38,3	34,4	35,3	34,5	31,9	31,5	34,1	:	**JP**

3A8AA

Further reading: EU international transactions — 1999 edition. Eurostat. International trade in services — EU, 1989–98. Eurostat.

The National Bank of Belgium produces the balance of payments for Belgium and Luxembourg, B/L, as a whole. EU = EU-12 until 1991; EU = EU-15 from 1992 onwards.

Imports of transport services as % of services total imports

	1989	1990	1991	1992	1993	1994	1995	1996	1997	1998	1999	
EU-15	32,2	30,9	30,4	28,8	27,2	27,4	28,1	27,6	28,5	25,5	:	**EU-15**
EUR-11	:	:	:	:	:	:	27,3	26,5	26,5	23,5	:	**EUR-11**
B/L	29,1	29,3	27,7	26,7	24,4	22,6	23,7	23,0	23,9	21,3	:	**B/L**
DK	45,7	43,3	45,5	41,5	45,3	47,1	45,3	46,6	55,8	50,0	:	**DK**
D	21,1	21,1	21,9	21,0	19,8	19,6	19,3	19,4	19,3	19,5	:	**D**
EL	37,3	36,3	38,8	34,1	27,6	29,9	26,2	29,9	31,2	30,7	:	**EL**
E	33,8	31,8	30,3	23,7	23,4	26,9	28,8	28,4	29,0	27,9	:	**E**
F	30,9	29,7	30,3	27,7	27,3	25,5	32,1	30,7	30,5	30,3	:	**F**
IRL	29,0	29,6	28,8	19,2	19,1	17,3	15,9	14,1	13,3	11,1	:	**IRL**
I	36,6	28,9	30,6	29,4	32,4	36,5	40,1	34,8	35,2	21,6	:	**I**
L	:	:	:	:	:	:	:	:	:	:	:	**L**
NL	37,6	37,1	34,3	32,9	33,0	32,3	30,0	30,0	29,9	31,4	:	**NL**
A	:	:	:	13,6	11,6	12,2	11,8	11,0	19,1	20,0	:	**A**
P	49,3	47,8	45,3	49,9	24,6	26,2	25,7	26,9	27,7	27,1	:	**P**
FIN	:	:	:	23,0	24,6	26,7	22,7	23,0	23,1	26,6	:	**FIN**
S	:	:	:	23,4	28,8	27,9	28,0	25,8	24,8	20,2	:	**S**
UK	30,5	29,9	27,9	28,7	27,6	28,0	26,3	27,1	29,5	28,5	:	**UK**
US	28,6	29,3	28,6	30,1	30,0	30,5	30,6	28,7	28,2	27,8	:	**US**
CA	:	:	:	:	:	:	:	:	:	:	:	**CA**
JP	30,8	29,9	31,1	29,7	30,0	30,0	29,3	25,8	25,2	25,4	:	**JP**

3A8AB

Further reading: EU international transactions — 1999 edition. Eurostat. International trade in services — EU, 1989–98. Eurostat.

The National Bank of Belgium produces the balance of payments for Belgium and Luxembourg, B/L, as a whole. EU = EU-12 until 1991; EU = EU-15 from 1992 onwards.

eurostat

The breakdown of transport services represents a cross-classification, on the one hand, by mode of transportation: sea, air and other transport (like space, rail, road, etc.) and on the other hand by kind of services: transport of passengers, transport of freight and auxiliary services. Auxiliary services cover a range of supporting and auxiliary services provided in ports, airports and other terminal facilities, for example, cargo handling, storage, packing, hiring of vehicles and vessels with crews etc.

International freight by air and sea: balance of EU, US and Japan with the rest of the world. 1 000 million ECU

3A8AC

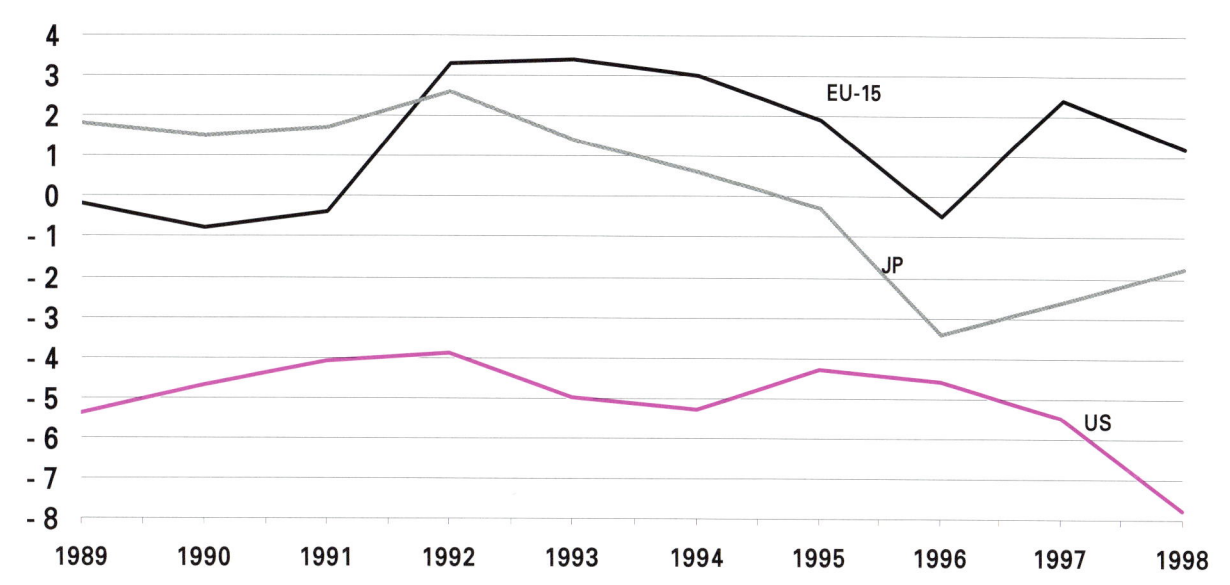

Further reading: EU international transactions — 1999 edition. Eurostat. International trade in services — EU, 1989–98. Eurostat.

Until 1991 data refer to EU-12 and from 1992 onwards data refer to EU-15.

International passenger transport by air and sea: balance of EU, US and Japan with the rest of the world. 1 000 million ECU

3A8AD

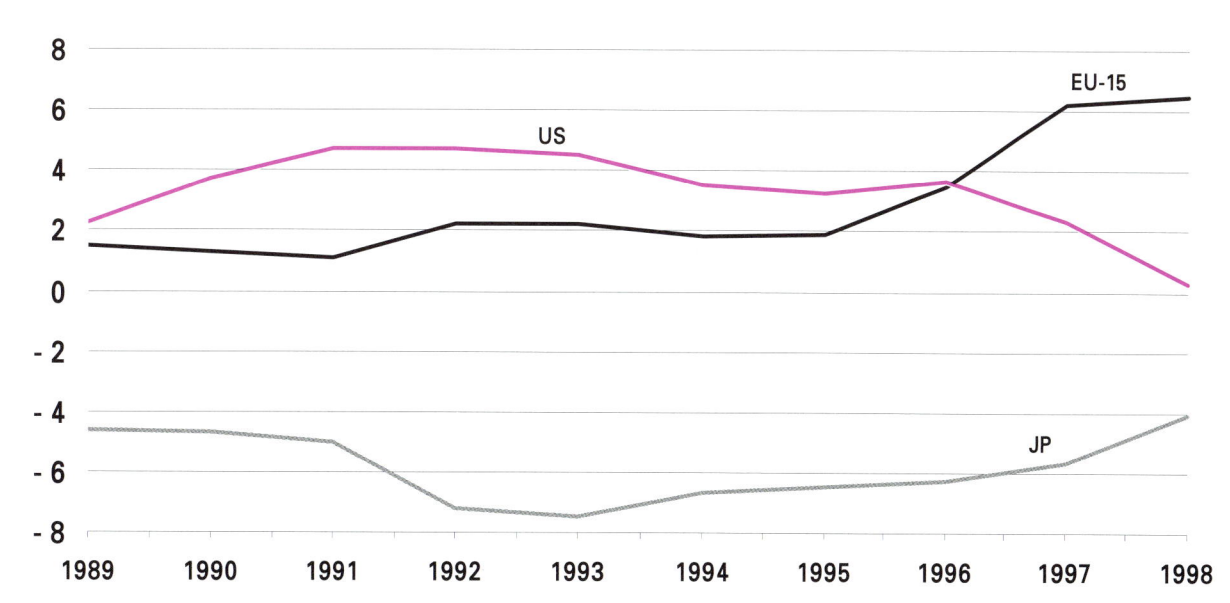

Further reading: EU international transactions — 1999 edition. Eurostat. International trade in services — EU, 1989–98. Eurostat.

Until 1991 data refer to EU-12 and from 1992 onwards data refer to EU-15.

eurostat

Exports of travel services as % of services total exports

	1989	1990	1991	1992	1993	1994	1995	1996	1997	1998	1999	
EU-15	24,2	23,6	23,1	23,5	24,1	24,1	25,3	25,9	25,6	25,8	:	EU-15
EUR-11	:	:	:	:	:	:	27,6	27,8	28,3	28,6	:	EUR-11
B/L	11,8	11,3	12,4	12,6	12,6	13,7	16,5	16,7	14,9	14,8	:	B/L
DK	20,9	23,1	22,1	23,4	27,0	25,7	24,5	20,8	22,0	21,4	:	DK
D	21,6	22,6	23,1	22,5	22,3	21,8	21,4	20,1	19,8	19,4	:	D
EL	47,0	48,5	44,8	47,2	36,9	37,7	37,7	37,2	36,9	42,0	:	EL
E	66,8	65,4	63,3	65,7	64,5	63,9	63,5	62,1	60,9	60,9	:	E
F	26,9	26,9	27,6	27,8	27,7	27,8	32,8	33,9	34,3	34,8	:	F
IRL	41,9	43,4	42,6	40,2	42,5	41,8	44,0	43,0	41,8	38,7	:	IRL
I	38,4	33,9	38,6	41,8	43,7	45,1	45,9	42,8	41,2	44,4	:	I
L	:	:	:	:	:	:	:	:	:	:	:	L
NL	11,9	11,6	12,4	15,3	13,9	12,7	13,6	13,0	12,1	12,9	:	NL
A	:	:	:	50,4	47,7	44,5	41,8	37,7	37,1	34,6	:	A
P	68,9	67,9	69,2	71,0	59,2	61,4	58,6	60,3	60,4	61,9	:	P
FIN	:	:	:	28,6	29,2	25,1	21,9	24,3	26,6	24,1	:	FIN
S	:	:	:	19,1	21,3	21,0	22,3	21,6	20,9	23,0	:	S
UK	23,2	24,4	22,6	22,9	23,9	23,7	24,6	26,0	24,0	24,1	:	UK
US	28,6	29,2	29,7	34,8	35,1	33,9	33,0	34,2	33,1	32,0	:	US
CA	:	:	:	:	:	:	:	:	:	:	:	CA
JP	7,5	8,2	7,2	6,9	6,0	5,7	5,0	6,0	6,2	6,0	:	JP

3A8BA

Further reading: EU international transactions — 1999 edition. Eurostat. International trade in services — EU, 1989–98. Eurostat.

The National Bank of Belgium produces the balance of payments for Belgium and Luxembourg, B/L, as a whole. EU = EU-12 until 1991; EU = EU-15 from 1992 onwards.

Imports of travel services as % of services total imports

	1989	1990	1991	1992	1993	1994	1995	1996	1997	1998	1999	
EU-15	24,0	24,2	23,8	25,3	25,8	25,6	26,4	26,9	26,8	27,9	:	EU-15
EUR-11	:	:	:	:	:	:	25,3	25,1	24,4	24,5	:	EUR-11
B/L	19,4	19,9	20,0	22,2	21,7	22,7	27,1	28,4	26,3	25,8	:	B/L
DK	26,2	28,3	25,6	28,0	30,7	29,9	30,0	28,1	29,7	29,1	:	DK
D	42,6	41,9	41,4	38,3	39,8	41,0	39,9	38,3	36,4	36,0	:	D
EL	22,0	21,9	22,0	23,7	29,2	29,3	32,4	28,5	29,1	34,1	:	EL
E	24,2	25,5	26,0	26,0	24,5	21,6	20,1	20,1	18,1	18,0	:	E
F	21,7	20,6	20,1	19,1	18,6	19,6	24,7	26,4	26,2	26,5	:	F
IRL	25,2	25,4	23,9	19,2	18,2	19,1	18,0	16,4	14,6	11,9	:	IRL
I	21,2	19,8	24,0	31,2	28,8	24,4	21,8	23,2	23,7	27,9	:	I
L	:	:	:	:	:	:	:	:	:	:	:	L
NL	26,2	25,5	24,6	24,7	23,4	22,6	25,4	25,0	22,5	23,1	:	NL
A	:	:	:	42,4	39,5	41,9	39,3	37,6	35,3	31,6	:	A
P	21,8	22,6	24,2	28,1	34,7	31,3	31,7	34,9	34,3	34,4	:	P
FIN	:	:	:	33,9	25,7	23,6	23,8	26,0	26,2	26,4	:	FIN
S	:	:	:	37,0	33,9	33,7	33,0	34,5	34,2	35,1	:	S
UK	35,1	35,1	34,6	37,1	37,8	38,6	37,8	38,0	38,6	41,8	:	UK
US	33,1	32,2	30,3	32,9	33,0	33,3	32,9	32,9	32,2	32,0	:	US
CA	:	:	:	:	:	:	:	:	:	:	:	CA
JP	27,8	28,0	26,0	27,3	26,3	27,5	30,0	28,5	26,7	25,7	:	JP

3A8BB

Further reading: EU international transactions — 1999 edition. Eurostat. International trade in services — EU, 1989–98. Eurostat.

The National Bank of Belgium produces the balance of payments for Belgium and Luxembourg, B/L, as a whole. EU = EU-12 until 1991; EU = EU-15 from 1992 onwards.

Tourism or travel records on the credit side (exports) the **receipts** from all goods and services provided by a resident economy to a non-resident staying less than one year in that economy for whatever reason — leisure, work, health or study.

On the debit side (imports), travel records **expenditure** of the same type spent abroad by residents displaying the same characteristics. The international carriage of travellers, which is covered in transport services, is excluded.

3A8BC

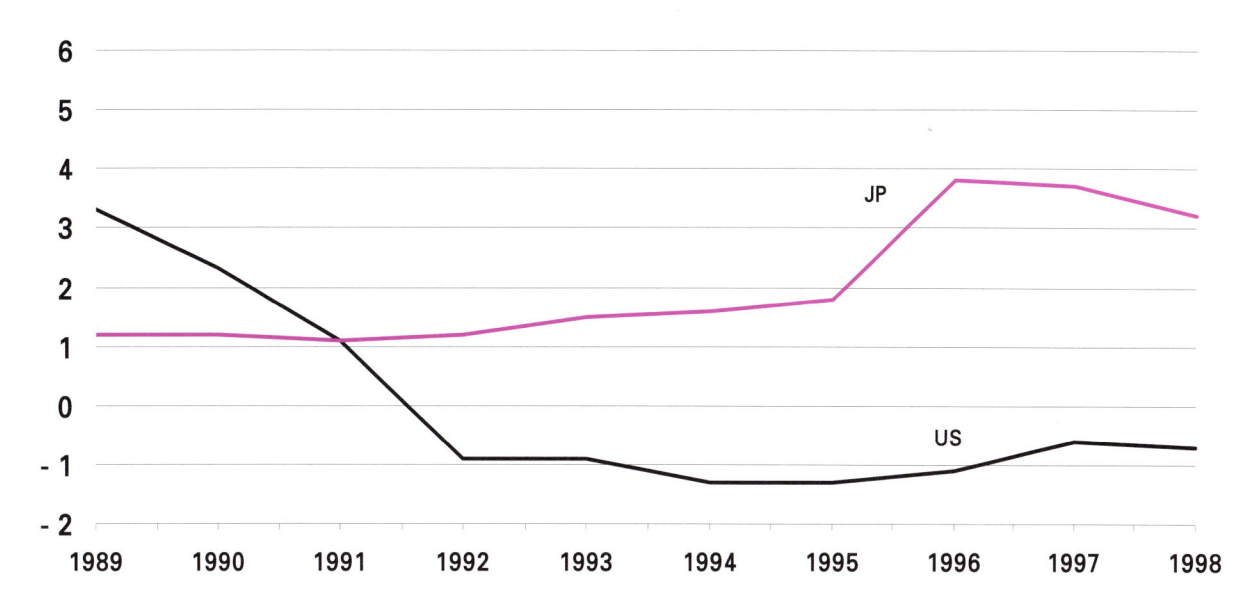

EU balance of travel services with the US and Japan. 1 000 million ECU

Further reading: EU international transactions — 1999 edition. Eurostat. International trade in services — EU, 1989–98. Eurostat.

Until 1991 data refer to EU-12 and from 1992 onwards data refer to EU-15.

3A8BD

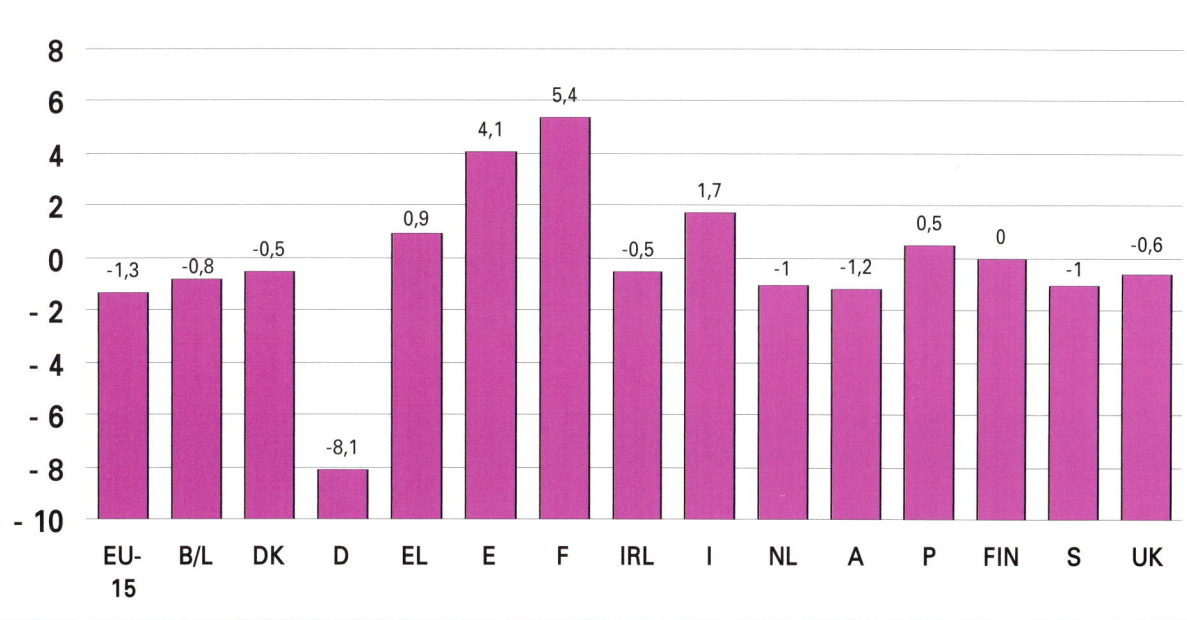

Extra-EU balance of travel services. 1 000 million ECU. 1998

Further reading: EU international transactions — 1999 edition. Eurostat. International trade in services — EU, 1989–98. Eurostat.

Need longer time series? Ask your Data Shop

EUROSTAT YEARBOOK 2001
267

International trade in services other than transport and travel, cover rates.%

	1989	1990	1991	1992	1993	1994	1995	1996	1997	1998	1999	
EU-15	116	117	118	111	110	111	113	115	117	110	:	**EU-15**
EUR-11	:	:	:	:	:	:	98	98	93	90	:	**EUR-11**
B/L	103	113	117	126	124	123	121	127	130	121	:	**B/L**
DK	81	99	96	97	77	92	101	132	90	71	:	**DK**
D	121	115	110	91	87	84	86	88	85	83	:	**D**
EL	91	82	110	96	283	302	291	297	304	279	:	**EL**
E	56	56	66	64	65	72	77	80	79	79	:	**E**
F	95	98	98	101	104	109	115	117	124	121	:	**F**
IRL	37	42	45	30	29	29	23	23	22	19	:	**IRL**
I	81	84	84	83	80	78	77	86	89	82	:	**I**
L	:	:	:	:	:	:	:	:	:	:	:	**L**
NL	110	118	100	102	107	110	109	112	112	117	:	**NL**
A	:	:	:	137	122	135	111	113	94	95	:	**A**
P	66	61	55	63	73	68	67	69	68	64	:	**P**
FIN	:	:	:	57	47	67	75	80	78	84	:	**FIN**
S	:	:	:	105	112	113	108	111	102	92	:	**S**
UK	171	164	160	183	177	176	175	184	226	243	:	**UK**
US	140	137	150	171	173	178	182	187	188	182	:	**US**
CA	:	:	:	:	:	:	:	:	:	:	:	**CA**
JP	57	50	53	51	62	69	79	71	73	69	:	**JP**

3A8CA

Further reading: EU international transactions — 1999 edition. Eurostat. International trade in services — EU, 1989–98. Eurostat.

The National Bank of Belgium produces the balance of payments for Belgium and Luxembourg, B/L, as a whole. EU = EU-12 until 1991; EU = EU-15 from 1992 onwards.

Average flows in services other than transport and travel as % of GDP

	1989	1990	1991	1992	1993	1994	1995	1996	1997	1998	1999	
EU-15	0,9	0,9	0,9	1,2	1,3	1,3	1,2	1,3	1,4	1,4	:	**EU-15**
EUR-11	:	:	:	:	:	:	1,5	1,7	1,9	1,9	:	**EUR-11**
B/L	5,1	5,0	7,5	7,3	7,8	8,4	6,2	6,3	7,0	7,5	:	**B/L**
DK	2,5	2,6	2,7	2,7	1,7	1,8	2,1	2,5	1,2	1,7	:	**DK**
D	2,1	2,1	1,9	2,0	1,9	1,9	2,0	2,2	2,4	2,4	:	**D**
EL	2,1	2,3	2,1	2,1	3,1	3,2	2,9	2,8	3,0	2,8	:	**EL**
E	0,9	0,9	1,0	1,5	1,7	1,7	1,7	1,9	2,2	2,4	:	**E**
F	1,5	1,7	1,7	2,7	2,9	2,8	1,9	2,0	2,2	2,2	:	**F**
IRL	3,4	3,2	3,5	5,4	5,6	6,3	7,0	8,0	8,7	10,8	:	**IRL**
I	1,1	1,3	1,3	1,4	1,5	1,5	1,6	2,0	2,2	2,2	:	**I**
L	:	:	:	:	:	:	:	:	:	:	:	**L**
NL	3,8	3,7	4,2	5,1	5,5	5,9	5,4	5,6	6,4	6,2	:	**NL**
A	:	:	:	5,5	6,2	6,2	6,2	7,1	6,1	6,7	:	**A**
P	0,8	0,8	0,8	0,8	2,3	2,2	2,3	1,9	2,0	2,1	:	**P**
FIN	:	:	:	2,2	2,6	2,9	3,6	3,3	3,2	2,7	:	**FIN**
S	:	:	:	3,1	2,8	3,0	3,0	3,1	3,7	4,1	:	**S**
UK	2,5	2,4	2,4	2,5	2,6	2,6	2,9	2,9	3,0	2,9	:	**UK**
US	0,7	0,7	0,8	1,0	1,0	1,0	1,0	1,1	1,2	1,3	:	**US**
CA	:	:	:	:	:	:	:	:	:	:	:	**CA**
JP	0,2	0,3	0,2	0,2	0,2	0,2	0,9	1,1	1,2	1,2	:	**JP**

3A8CB

Further reading: EU international transactions — 1999 edition. Eurostat. International trade in services — EU, 1989–98. Eurostat.

The National Bank of Belgium produces the balance of payments for Belgium and Luxembourg, B/L, as a whole. EU = EU-12 until 1991; EU = EU-15 from 1992 onwards.

Other services comprise all international service transactions other than tourism and transport. They cover highly varied services such as communications services, construction services, insurance services, financial services, computer and information services, royalties and licence fees, trade earnings, miscellaneous business services, audiovisual and recreational services, and government services. Growth in the volume of trade in certain services is linked to very rapidly changing technologies, for example communications and computer services; this does not appear clearly in value terms due to a sharp fall in prices.

EU international trade in trade earnings, financial, business and construction services, cover rates.%

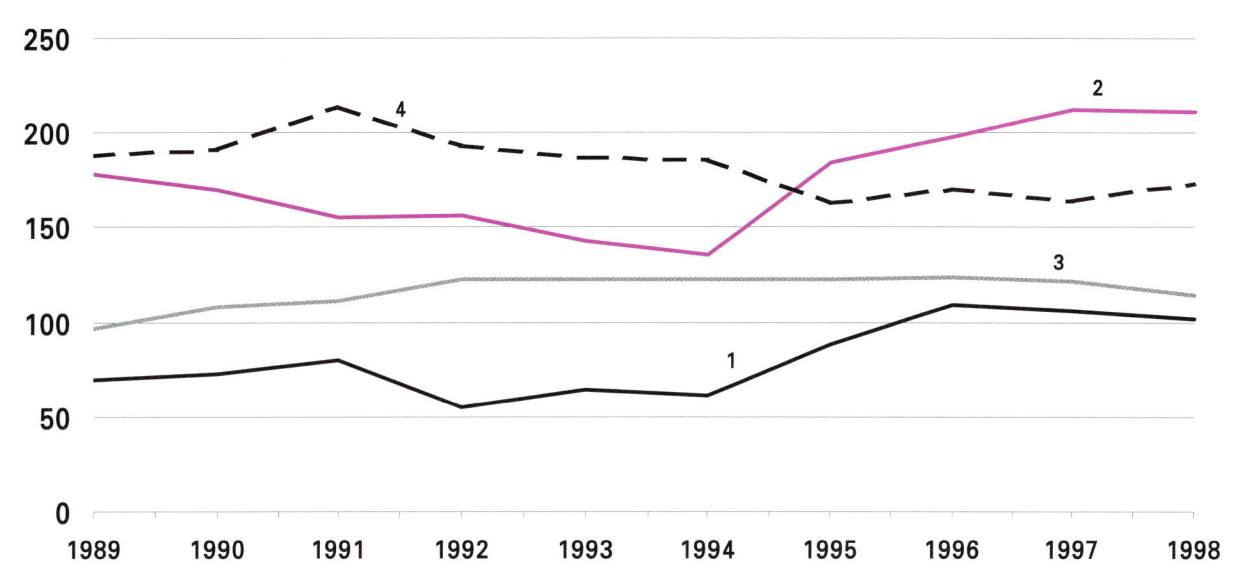

1: trade earnings; 2: financial services; 3: business services; 4: construction services.

Further reading: EU international transactions — 1999 edition. Eurostat. International trade in services — EU, 1989–98. Eurostat.

Until 1991 data refer to EU-12 and from 1992 onwards data refer to EU-15.

EU international trade in communications services, advertising, audiovisual, royalties and licence fees, and computer and information services, cover rates.%

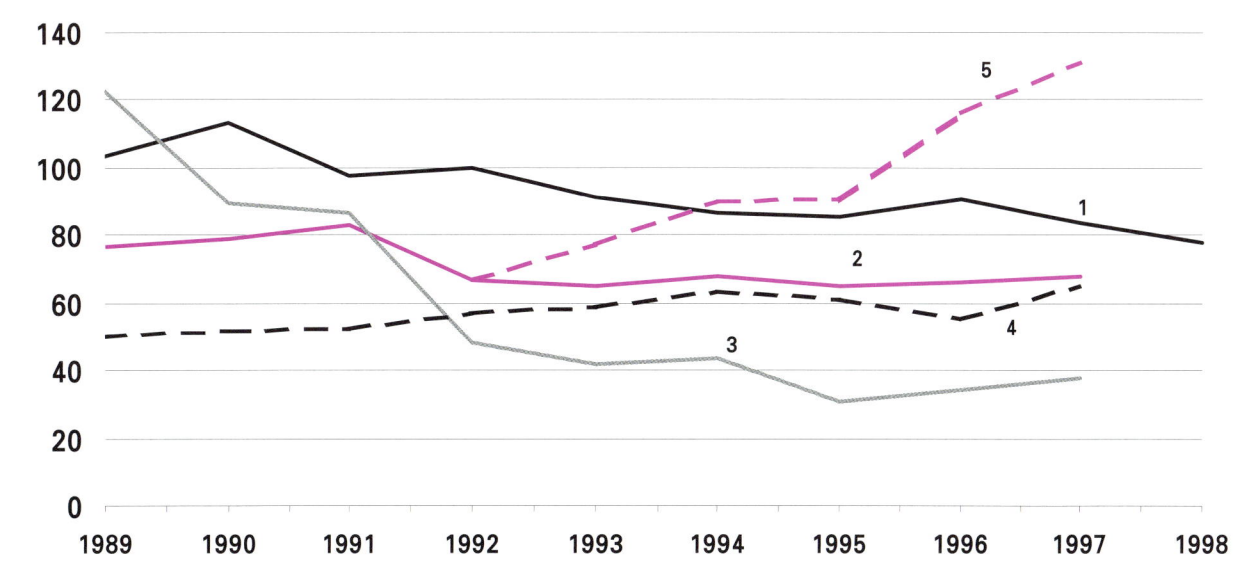

1: communications services; 2: advertising; 3: audiovisual; 4: royalties and licence fees; 5: computer and information services.

Further reading: EU international transactions — 1999 edition. Eurostat. International trade in services — EU, 1989–98. Eurostat.

Until 1991 data refer to EU-12 and from 1992 onwards data refer to EU-15.

Exports (fob) at current prices. 1 000 million ECU

	1989	1990	1991	1992	1993	1994	1995	1996	1997	1998	1999	
EU-15	395,5	395,9 |	403,4	415,3	468,1	523,8	573,3	626,6	721,1	733,3	760,1	**EU-15**
EUR-11	435,4	435,6 |	440,7	456,5	498,5	559,5	622,5	669,3	762,8	796,3	829,8	**EUR-11**
B	90,9	93,0	95,1	95,4	106,7	119,1	131,9	137,8	152,3	162,3 |	164,5	**B**
DK	26,0	27,9	29,5	31,2	32,2	35,6	38,9	40,5	43,4	43,7	47,4	**DK**
D	308,8	312,4 |	323,8	331,3	324,6	358,9	400,2	413,2	452,3	485,0	503,1	**D**
EL	6,8	6,3	7,0	7,6	7,2	7,9	8,5	9,2	10,0	9,7	9,8	**EL**
E	42,3	46,2	51,0	53,0	55,2	64,5	74,8	84,5	88,8	99,9	98,0	**E**
F	168,0	174,7	184,8	192,5	189,3	210,6	230,2	240,3	266,4	286,0	304,3	**F**
IRL	18,8	18,6	19,5	21,8	24,8	28,6	34,2	38,1	47,0	57,4	66,4	**IRL**
I	127,3	133,7	136,8	137,6	144,5	160,9	178,7	198,7	212,0	215,6	216,3	**I**
L	-	-	-	-	-	-	-	-	-	-	7,7	**L**
NL	104,3	106,3	107,8	108,6	106,3	128,9	140,2	164,6	183,3	190,9	205,1	**NL**
A	29,5	32,9	33,2	34,2	34,3	37,9	44,1	45,9	52,7	57,2	62,0	**A**
P	11,6	12,8	13,2	14,2	13,2	15,1	17,4	19,4	21,1	22,1	22,4	**P**
FIN	21,1	21,0	18,6	18,5	20,1	25,0	31,0	32,4	36,6	39,0	39,6	**FIN**
S	46,8	45,1	44,5	43,2	42,6	51,5	61,5	66,9	73,0	75,2	79,6	**S**
UK	138,1	143,6	147,3	144,6	154,9	172,4	181,9	203,6	247,3	244,4	255,2	**UK**
IS	1,3	1,2	1,3	1,2	1,2	1,4	1,4	1,5	1,6	1,7	1,7	**IS**
NO	24,5	26,8	27,5	27,1	27,2	29,2	31,9	38,6	42,8	36,0	42,3	**NO**
EEA	386,8	387,1 |	394,2	406,1	459,1	513,5	562,2	614,6	706,7	714,9	746,2	**EEA**
CH	46,8	50,1	49,7	50,6	54,0	59,1	62,4	63,7	67,2	70,3	78,2	**CH**
US	330,1	308,5	340,2	344,6	396,9	430,7	445,7	490,5	606,3	606,9	650,0	**US**
CA	105,3	99,7	102,3	103,6	123,5	139,8	146,1	159,3	190,5	191,4	224,0	**CA**
JP	249,8	225,3	253,8	261,7	308,2	332,6	338,6	323,6	371,2	346,2	391,4	**JP**

3A9BA

Further reading: External trade, statistical yearbooks. Eurostat. Comext on CD-ROM.   B: includes L up to 1998.
Eurostat.

Imports (cif) at current prices. 1 000 million ECU

	1989	1990	1991	1992	1993	1994	1995	1996	1997	1998	1999	
EU-15	431,9	442,5 |	471,6	465,4	464,7	514,3	545,3	581,1	672,6	710,5	776,7	**EU-15**
EUR-11	425,1	445,4 |	482,1	478,0	462,6	519,4	562,7	594,0	674,2	711,0	775,9	**EUR-11**
B	93,0	98,6	102,5	101,9	98,3	107,1	121,1	128,9	140,6	150,7 |	149,8	**B**
DK	24,7	25,5	26,8	26,8	26,7	30,8	35,1	35,7	39,6	41,8	43,2	**DK**
D	244,8	268,4 |	314,0	315,6	292,6	320,6	354,6	361,6	393,0	420,5	436,2	**D**
EL	14,6	15,6	17,4	18,4	18,8	18,1	19,8	22,2	23,7	27,0	26,3	**EL**
E	61,6	66,2	72,5	74,9	66,2	74,7	86,8	95,5	102,0	121,9	127,0	**E**
F	182,8	191,8	200,1	199,4	185,6	206,8	221,2	231,0	251,3	274,5	294,2	**F**
IRL	15,7	16,3	16,8	16,8	18,1	21,5	24,7	27,0	33,3	38,5	43,2	**IRL**
I	138,5	142,9	147,3	145,6	126,5	142,2	157,5	164,0	185,3	192,5	203,6	**I**
L	-	-	-	-	-	-	-	-	-	-	10,5	**L**
NL	101,4	106,6	110,7	113,5	95,7	120,1	126,6	150,4	168,2	174,5	193,4	**NL**
A	35,3	39,3	40,9	41,7	41,5	46,5	50,6	54,0	58,0	62,0	66,9	**A**
P	17,3	19,3	21,3	23,4	20,7	22,7	24,9	27,7	30,9	33,9	36,2	**P**
FIN	22,3	21,3	17,6	16,3	15,4	19,6	22,5	24,7	27,9	29,4	30,1	**FIN**
S	44,4	42,9	40,2	38,4	36,4	43,5	49,7	52,7	57,8	60,7	64,3	**S**
UK	180,1	175,6	169,5	171,3	178,8	196,8	204,3	226,3	271,2	286,5	304,7	**UK**
IS	1,3	1,3	1,4	1,3	1,2	1,2	1,3	1,6	1,8	2,2	2,0	**IS**
NO	21,5	21,1	20,6	20,1	20,5	22,9	25,0	27,0	31,5	33,4	31,7	**NO**
EEA	420,4	428,6 |	456,3	450,4	449,8	497,2	526,0	560,1	647,8	692,0	755,7	**EEA**
CH	52,8	54,7	53,7	50,6	51,9	57,2	61,3	62,4	67,0	71,4	77,8	**CH**
US	447,5	406,4	410,7	426,4	515,1	579,3	589,3	643,9	791,9	842,3	986,2	**US**
CA	103,4	91,5	95,3	94,3	112,2	124,6	125,7	134,4	173,7	179,6	202,3	**CA**
JP	191,4	184,4	191,0	179,5	205,5	231,0	257,0	275,0	298,8	250,3	290,8	**JP**

3A9BB

Further reading: External trade, statistical yearbooks. Eurostat. Comext on CD-ROM.   B: includes L up to 1998.
Eurostat.

Exports and imports measured at current prices are not fully comparable from country to country because some include exports from and imports to customs warehouses (general trade system) while others do not (special trade system). Imports include costs of freight and insurance (except Cana-da); exports do not. EU-15, EUR-11 and EEA aggregates are calculated as total trade less intra-EU-15 trade, intra-EUR-11 trade and intra-EEA trade respectively. Figures do not include the former GDR before 1991.

3A9BC

Trade balance at current prices. 1 000 million ECU

	1989	1990	1991	1992	1993	1994	1995	1996	1997	1998	1999	
EU-15	- 36,4	- 46,6 I	- 68,2	- 50,1	3,4	9,4	28,0	45,6	48,6	22,7	- 16,6	EU-15
EUR-11	10,3	- 9,8 I	- 41,4	- 21,5	35,9	40,2	59,7	75,4	88,6	85,3	53,9	EUR-11
B	- 2,2	- 5,6	- 7,4	- 6,5	8,3	12,0	10,8	8,9	11,7	11,5 I	14,7	B
DK	1,2	2,4	2,6	4,4	5,5	4,8	3,8	4,8	3,9	1,9	4,2	DK
D	64,0	44,1 I	9,8	15,7	32,0	38,3	45,6	51,6	59,2	64,5	67,0	D
EL	- 7,8	- 9,3	- 10,4	- 10,8	- 11,6	- 10,2	- 11,3	- 13,0	- 13,8	- 17,3	- 16,5	EL
E	- 19,3	- 20,0	- 21,4	- 21,8	- 11,0	- 10,2	- 12,0	- 11,0	- 13,2	- 22,0	- 29,0	E
F	- 14,8	- 17,2	- 15,3	- 6,9	3,6	3,8	9,0	9,3	15,1	11,5	10,1	F
IRL	3,1	2,4	2,7	5,0	6,7	7,0	9,5	11,0	13,8	18,9	23,2	IRL
I	- 11,2	- 9,2	- 10,4	- 8,0	18,0	18,7	21,2	34,7	26,7	23,1	12,7	I
L	-	-	-	-	-	-	-	-	-	-	- 2,8	L
NL	2,9	- 0,3	- 2,9	- 4,9	10,5	8,8	13,6	14,2	15,1	16,4	11,7	NL
A	- 5,8	- 6,4	- 7,8	- 7,5	- 7,2	- 8,6	- 6,5	- 8,1	- 5,3	- 4,8	- 4,9	A
P	- 5,7	- 6,5	- 8,1	- 9,2	- 7,5	- 7,6	- 7,5	- 8,3	- 9,8	- 11,9	- 13,8	P
FIN	- 1,2	- 0,3	1,0	2,1	4,7	5,4	8,4	7,6	8,7	9,6	9,5	FIN
S	2,4	2,3	4,3	4,7	6,2	8,0	11,8	14,2	15,1	14,5	15,3	S
UK	- 42,1	- 31,9	- 22,2	- 26,7	- 23,9	- 24,4	- 22,4	- 22,7	- 23,9	- 42,2	- 49,5	UK
IS	0,0	- 0,1	- 0,1	- 0,1	0,0	0,1	0,0	- 0,1	- 0,1	- 0,5	- 0,3	IS
NO	3,1	5,6	6,9	7,0	6,7	6,3	6,9	11,5	11,3	2,6	10,5	NO
EEA	- 33,6	- 41,5 I	- 62,1	- 44,3	9,3	16,3	36,1	54,5	59,0	22,9	- 9,5	EEA
CH	- 6,1	- 4,6	- 4,0	- 0,1	2,0	2,0	1,1	1,2	0,2	- 1,1	0,4	CH
US	- 117,4	- 97,9	- 70,5	- 81,8	- 118,2	- 148,5	- 143,6	- 153,4	- 185,6	- 235,4	- 336,2	US
CA	1,9	8,2	7,0	9,3	11,4	15,2	20,4	24,9	16,8	11,8	21,8	CA
JP	58,4	41,0	62,8	82,1	102,7	101,6	81,7	48,6	72,5	95,9	100,6	JP

Further reading: External trade, statistical yearbooks. Eurostat. Comext on CD-ROM. Eurostat.   B: includes L up to 1998.

Need an update for this indicator? Ask your Data Shop

EUROSTAT YEARBOOK 2001
271

Exports (fob) at 1995 prices. 1995 = 100

	1989	1990	1991	1992	1993	1994	1995	1996	1997	1998	1999	
EU-15	82,2	81,4 |	80,2	81,3	88,4	94,9	100,0	105,5	114,1	117,6	118,2	EU-15
EUR-11	79,2	78,6 |	79,4	80,3	87,1	94,3 |	100,0	105,2	113,8	119,6	121,5	EUR-11
B/L	79,4	80,3	81,7	81,6	86,2	95,8	100,0	100,8	110,2	119,6 |	127,8	B/L
DK	81,0	85,2	88,6	93,4	89,7	95,4	100,0	104,2	113,3	114,5	119,9	DK
D	99,9	99,3 |	100,7	98,9	91,4	96,8	100,0	102,9	115,4	121,7	125,0	D
EL	89,6	81,0	87,6	101,6	95,8	57,5	100,0	97,9	105,1	97,2	94,3	EL
E	65,8	69,3	72,9	76,1	80,1	93,4	100,0	110,3	117,7	124,6	126,4	E
F	88,7	90,4	94,2	95,9	90,9	95,8	100,0	100,4	113,5	123,1	129,3	F
IRL	65,4	68,2	71,8	82,1	88,1	91,9	100,0	104,3	130,4	168,0	194,3	IRL
I	83,0	83,0	81,2	81,6	84,9	92,4	100,0	100,8	106,1	108,5	107,9	I
L	-	-	-	-	-	-	-	-	-	-	-	L
NL	86,4	86,8	87,2	87,9	84,2	103,1	100,0	97,7	122,1	134,7	139,8	NL
A	:	:	:	:	:	:	100,0	102,3	122,1	134,4	146,5	A
P	72,4	80,1	79,7	84,8	81,0	84,7	100,0	109,1	118,2	125,1	127,8	P
FIN	:	:	:	:	:	:	100,0	103,0	118,0	129,4	133,1	FIN
S	:	:	:	:	:	:	100,0	100,1	110,0	122,4	124,3	S
UK	89,9	92,7	90,4	90,1	90,5	97,5	100,0	102,6	113,0	109,6	106,9	UK

3A9CA

Further reading: External trade, statistical yearbooks. Eurostat. Comext on CD-ROM. B: includes L.
Eurostat.

3

Imports (cif) at 1995 prices. 1995 = 100

	1989	1990	1991	1992	1993	1994	1995	1996	1997	1998	1999	
EU-15	82,2	87,6 |	93,2	93,6	88,6	94,7 |	100,0	102,9	109,6	124,9	130,3	EU-15
EUR-11	80,6	86,7 |	94,6	94,5	87,7	94,9 |	100,0	102,3	109,3	125,2	132,1	EUR-11
B/L	91,3	96,0	98,8	98,4	88,3	95,9	100,0	105,3	108,0	119,5 |	124,0	B/L
DK	86,2	89,1	91,9	92,7	85,3	94,6	100,0	108,5	114,9	121,1	122,0	DK
D	81,9	90,1 |	104,0	103,7	93,2	98,2	100,0	106,3	109,7	120,3	124,0	D
EL	84,8	90,7	98,7	104,7	104,6	68,1	100,0	104,8	101,9	111,6	101,4	EL
E	82,9	87,0	93,9	99,2	86,4	93,7	100,0	109,9	113,0	127,6	140,4	E
F	97,5	100,6	103,3	103,0	92,9	97,9	100,0	102,7	108,6	118,9	125,5	F
IRL	76,2	80,8	83,3	80,8	84,1	91,9	100,0	101,2	111,4	131,5	145,9	IRL
I	92,1	95,5	98,5	98,8	86,9	93,7	100,0	99,7	109,2	119,9	126,2	I
L	-	-	-	-	-	-	-	-	-	-	-	L
NL	90,2	94,3	96,9	98,5	81,4	101,3	100,0	106,2	122,6	137,5	142,0	NL
A	:	:	:	:	:	:	100,0	105,1	108,2	116,1	122,7	A
P	74,6	84,6	88,8	98,8	89,8	91,9	100,0	108,6	113,1	128,4	139,3	P
FIN	:	:	:	:	:	:	100,0	112,1	123,1	137,1	136,6	FIN
S	:	:	:	:	:	:	100,0	99,4	106,2	114,7	115,0	S
UK	103,2	101,6	94,1	97,2	95,4	100,5	100,0	104,5	109,8	115,4	114,5	UK

3A9CB

Further reading: External trade, statistical yearbooks. Eurostat. Comext on CD-ROM. B: includes L.
Eurostat.

The indices which are linked from year to year, relate to EU-12 up to 1995 and to EU-15 thereafter. Imports and exports are not fully comparable because imports include costs of freight and insurance.

Volume ratio. 1995 = 100

	1989	1990	1991	1992	1993	1994	1995	1996	1997	1998	1999	
EU-15	100,0	92,9	86,1	86,9	99,8	100,2	100,0	102,5	104,1	94,2	90,7	**EU-15**
EUR-11	98,3	90,7	83,9	85,0	99,3	99,4	100,0	102,8	104,1	95,5	92,0	**EUR-11**
B/L	87,0	83,6	82,7	82,9	97,6	99,9	100,0	95,7	102,0	100,1	103,1	**B/L**
DK	94,0	95,6	96,4	100,8	105,2	100,8	100,0	96,0	98,6	94,5	98,3	**DK**
D	122,0	110,2	96,8	95,4	98,1	98,6	100,0	96,8	105,2	101,2	100,8	**D**
EL	105,7	89,3	88,8	97,0	91,6	84,4	100,0	93,4	103,1	87,1	93,0	**EL**
E	79,4	79,7	77,6	76,7	92,7	99,7	100,0	100,4	104,2	97,6	90,0	**E**
F	91,0	89,9	91,2	93,1	97,8	97,9	100,0	97,8	104,5	103,5	103,0	**F**
IRL	85,8	84,4	86,2	101,6	104,8	100,0	100,0	103,1	117,1	127,8	133,2	**IRL**
I	90,1	86,9	82,4	82,6	97,7	98,6	100,0	101,1	97,2	90,5	85,5	**I**
L	-	-	-	-	-	-	-	-	-	-	-	**L**
NL	95,8	92,0	90,0	89,2	103,4	101,8	100,0	92,0	99,6	98,0	98,5	**NL**
A	:	:	:	:	:	:	100,0	97,3	112,8	115,8	119,4	**A**
P	97,1	94,7	89,8	85,8	90,2	92,2	100,0	100,5	104,5	97,4	91,7	**P**
FIN	:	:	:	:	:	:	100,0	91,9	95,9	94,4	97,4	**FIN**
S	:	:	:	:	:	:	100,0	100,7	103,6	106,7	108,1	**S**
UK	87,1	91,2	96,1	92,7	94,9	97,0	100,0	98,2	102,9	95,0	93,4	**UK**

3A9CC

Further reading: External trade, statistical yearbooks. Eurostat. Comext on CD-ROM. Eurostat.

Volume ratio: exports at 1995 prices divided by imports at 1995 prices. B: includes L.

Exports of agrifood products at current prices. 1 000 million ECU

	1989	1990	1991	1992	1993	1994	1995	1996	1997	1998	1999	
EU-15	30,3 I	29,8	30,1	32,4	34,9	37,3	39,0	40,9	45,9	43,9	43,6	**EU-15**
EUR-11	35,4 I	35,0	35,7	38,6	40,4	43,9	46,8	49,2	53,5	53,9	54,3	**EUR-11**
B	8,3	8,4	9,4	9,9	11,3	12,5	13,9	14,4	15,2	16,0 I	15,8	**B**
DK	6,8	7,2	7,7	7,8	8,1	8,9	9,2	9,2	10,1	9,6	9,9	**DK**
D	14,2 I	14,0	16,2	17,0	16,7	18,0	18,8	20,4	20,8	22,2	20,4	**D**
EL	1,8	1,6	2,0	2,1	1,9	2,0	2,0	2,1	2,3	2,3	2,2	**EL**
E	6,0	6,2	6,9	7,6	8,1	9,4	10,6	11,9	12,8	14,0	13,3	**E**
F	23,9	24,8	25,2	26,8	27,7	28,4	30,1	30,5	32,5	32,6	33,5	**F**
IRL	4,5	4,1	4,4	5,3	5,5	6,0	6,6	5,9	5,6	5,7	6,3	**IRL**
I	7,5	7,9	8,9	9,1	9,5	10,3	11,0	12,1	12,7	13,1	13,5	**I**
L	-	-	-	-	-	-	-	-	-	-	0,5	**L**
NL	20,4	20,4	21,0	22,2	21,8	25,1	25,7	29,4	29,3	29,9	30,8	**NL**
A	1,0	1,1	1,1	1,1	1,2	1,4	1,8	2,0	2,4	2,6	3,1	**A**
P	0,8	0,8	1,0	1,0	0,9	1,0	1,1	1,3	1,4	1,4	1,5	**P**
FIN	0,4	0,5	0,5	0,5	0,6	0,8	0,7	0,9	1,0	0,9	0,7	**FIN**
S	0,8	0,9	0,8	0,8	0,8	1,0	1,3	1,6	1,9	1,8	1,9	**S**
UK	9,4	9,9	11,0	11,7	11,3	11,8	11,8	12,6	15,9	15,1	15,1	**UK**
IS	0,9	1,0	1,1	1,0	0,9	1,1	1,0	1,1	1,2	1,2	:	**IS**
NO	1,6	1,8	2,0	2,1	2,2	2,6	2,6	3,0	3,3	3,5	:	**NO**
EEA	30,4 I	29,9	30,3	32,4	35,1	37,5	39,3	41,4	46,5	44,4	:	**EEA**
CH	1,3	1,4	1,4	1,5	1,6	1,8	1,8	1,8	1,9	1,8	2,0	**CH**
US	32,5	29,3	30,1	31,5	34,5	36,5	38,4	42,4	43,5	41,2	:	**US**
CA	7,6	7,8	8,5	9,0	9,1	9,3	9,6	11,5	13,8	12,8	13,8	**CA**
JP	1,5	1,3	1,4	1,5	1,7	1,7	1,6	1,5	1,9	1,8	2,0	**JP**

3A9DB

Further reading: External trade, statistical yearbooks. Eurostat. Comext on CD-ROM. Eurostat.   B: includes L up to 1998.

Imports of agrifood products at current prices. 1 000 million ECU

	1989	1990	1991	1992	1993	1994	1995	1996	1997	1998	1999	
EU-15	37,6	37,4 I	40,0	39,5	38,1	43,4	43,2	44,9	48,5	49,9	50,1	**EU-15**
EUR-11	37,5	37,8 I	41,6	41,6	39,7	45,2	46,0	46,6	50,1	51,0	50,7	**EUR-11**
B	8,4	8,8	9,8	10,1	10,3	11,4	12,9	13,2	13,7	14,5 I	13,8	**B**
DK	2,9	2,9	3,1	3,3	3,5	3,9	4,2	4,4	4,8	5,0	5,2	**DK**
D	23,4	25,3 I	29,2	30,4	27,3	30,6	32,5	33,2	33,6	34,6	31,3	**D**
EL	2,2	2,2	2,2	2,6	2,5	2,7	3,0	3,1	3,3	3,5	3,4	**EL**
E	5,8	6,4	7,8	8,3	8,6	9,6	10,3	10,3	10,9	12,5	12,1	**E**
F	16,9	17,2	18,6	18,8	18,8	20,7	21,0	21,0	22,2	23,3	23,5	**F**
IRL	1,7	1,7	1,8	1,9	1,8	2,0	2,1	2,2	2,6	2,7	3,0	**IRL**
I	16,6	15,8	17,5	17,0	15,4	16,1	16,6	17,3	18,3	18,7	18,6	**I**
L	-	-	-	-	-	-	-	-	-	-	1,1	**L**
NL	12,2	12,2	12,4	13,6	12,0	14,7	14,8	17,0	17,5	17,5	18,9	**NL**
A	1,8	2,0	2,0	2,0	2,1	2,4	2,9	3,2	3,5	3,7	3,9	**A**
P	1,7	1,9	2,4	2,6	2,5	2,9	3,0	3,3	3,5	3,9	4,1	**P**
FIN	1,1	1,0	1,0	1,0	1,0	1,3	1,2	1,5	1,7	1,8	1,8	**FIN**
S	2,6	2,5	2,7	2,7	2,7	3,3	3,0	3,5	3,8	3,9	4,2	**S**
UK	16,9	17,2	17,5	18,0	17,1	18,6	18,8	21,0	24,5	25,3	26,5	**UK**
IS	0,1	0,1	0,1	0,1	0,1	0,1	0,2	0,2	0,2	0,2	:	**IS**
NO	1,2	1,1	1,2	1,3	1,3	1,5	1,6	1,7	1,8	2,0	:	**NO**
EEA	36,3	35,8 I	38,2	37,6	36,4	41,6	41,5	43,1	46,6	47,7	:	**EEA**
CH	3,3	3,3	3,5	3,3	3,4	3,8	3,8	4,0	4,1	4,2	4,6	**CH**
US	24,7	22,8	23,4	23,4	26,4	27,8	26,8	30,1	37,6	39,3	:	**US**
CA	5,7	5,4	5,9	5,8	6,7	7,2	6,9	7,5	9,1	9,6	10,3	**CA**
JP	28,1	24,8	27,8	28,7	33,5	39,2	38,9	39,9	40,6	36,9	41,5	**JP**

3A9DC

Further reading: External trade, statistical yearbooks. Eurostat. Comext on CD-ROM. Eurostat.   B: includes L up to 1998.

Agrifood products are food products obtained from agriculture. They are determined according to sections 0 and 1 of the standard international trade classification (SITC) revision 3. Comparability is incomplete because of the use of different trade systems — general or special. Figures do not include the former GDR before 1991.

Trade balance of agrifood products at current prices. 1 000 million ECU

	1989	1990	1991	1992	1993	1994	1995	1996	1997	1998	1999	
EU-15	- 7,4	- 7,6 |	- 9,8	- 7,1	- 3,2	- 6,2	- 4,2	- 4,0	- 2,6	- 6,1	- 6,5	**EU-15**
EUR-11	- 2,1	- 2,8 |	- 6,0	- 3,0	0,7	- 1,4	0,8	2,6	3,4	2,8	3,6	**EUR-11**
B	- 0,1	- 0,5	- 0,5	- 0,2	1,1	1,1	1,0	1,3	1,5	1,6 |	2,0	**B**
DK	4,0	4,3	4,5	4,6	4,6	5,0	5,0	4,8	5,3	4,5	4,8	**DK**
D	- 9,2	- 11,2 |	- 13,1	- 13,5	- 10,6	- 12,6	- 13,6	- 12,7	- 12,8	- 12,4	- 10,9	**D**
EL	- 0,5	- 0,6	- 0,3	- 0,4	- 0,6	- 0,7	- 1,0	- 1,0	- 1,0	- 1,1	- 1,2	**EL**
E	0,3	- 0,3	- 0,8	- 0,8	- 0,5	- 0,2	0,3	1,6	1,9	1,5	1,2	**E**
F	7,0	7,6	6,6	8,0	8,9	7,7	9,2	9,6	10,4	9,3	10,0	**F**
IRL	2,9	2,5	2,6	3,4	3,7	4,0	4,5	3,6	3,0	2,9	3,2	**IRL**
I	- 9,0	- 7,9	- 8,6	- 7,8	- 5,9	- 5,9	- 5,6	- 5,2	- 5,6	- 5,6	- 5,1	**I**
L	-	-	-	-	-	-	-	-	-	-	- 0,6	**L**
NL	8,2	8,2	8,5	8,6	9,8	10,3	10,9	12,3	11,8	12,4	11,9	**NL**
A	- 0,8	- 0,9	- 1,0	- 0,9	- 1,0	- 1,1	- 1,1	- 1,1	- 1,2	- 1,1	- 0,8	**A**
P	- 0,9	- 1,0	- 1,4	- 1,6	- 1,6	- 1,9	- 1,8	- 2,1	- 2,1	- 2,5	- 2,7	**P**
FIN	- 0,7	- 0,5	- 0,5	- 0,5	- 0,3	- 0,5	- 0,5	- 0,7	- 0,7	- 0,9	- 1,0	**FIN**
S	- 1,7	- 1,6	- 1,9	- 2,0	- 1,9	- 2,2	- 1,7	- 1,9	- 1,9	- 2,1	- 2,3	**S**
UK	- 7,5	- 7,3	- 6,5	- 6,3	- 5,8	- 6,8	- 6,9	- 8,4	- 8,6	- 10,2	- 11,3	**UK**
IS	0,8	0,9	0,9	0,8	0,8	0,9	0,9	0,9	1,0	1,0	:	**IS**
NO	0,4	0,7	0,8	0,8	0,9	1,1	1,1	1,3	1,4	1,6	:	**NO**
EEA	- 6,0	- 5,9 |	- 8,0	- 5,2	- 1,4	- 4,1	- 2,2	- 1,7	- 0,1	- 3,3	:	**EEA**
CH	- 2,0	- 2,0	- 2,0	- 1,8	- 1,9	- 2,0	- 2,0	- 2,1	- 2,2	- 2,4	- 2,6	**CH**
US	7,8	6,5	6,7	8,1	8,2	8,7	11,6	12,3	5,9	1,8	:	**US**
CA	1,8	2,4	2,6	3,2	2,3	2,1	2,7	4,0	4,7	3,3	3,5	**CA**
JP	- 26,6	- 23,5	- 26,3	- 27,2	- 31,8	- 37,5	- 37,3	- 38,4	- 38,7	- 35,1	- 39,5	**JP**

3A9DA

Further reading: External trade, statistical yearbooks. Eurostat. Comext on CD-ROM. Eurostat.

B: includes L up to 1998.

Exports of mineral fuels, lubricants and related products at current prices.
1 000 million ECU

	1989	1990	1991	1992	1993	1994	1995	1996	1997	1998	1999	
EU-15	12,5	14,2		14,0	13,3	14,2	15,3	13,3	15,4	17,1	14,0	16,5	EU-15
EUR-11	10,4	11,6		11,8	11,2	12,1	12,4	11,1	13,1	14,4	12,6	13,5	EUR-11
B	3,1	3,2	3,7	3,3	3,5	3,5	3,0	3,8	4,5	3,8		4,8	B
DK	0,8	0,9	1,0	1,1	1,1	1,1	1,0	1,7	1,6	1,2	1,8	DK
D	3,8	4,0		4,1	4,1	3,9	4,0	3,8	5,2	5,3	4,7	4,8	D
EL	0,4	0,5	0,6	0,4	0,6	0,8	0,5	0,8	0,9	0,7	0,9	EL
E	1,9	2,0	1,8	1,5	1,6	1,5	1,6	2,2	2,5	2,2	2,5	E
F	3,4	4,0	4,4	4,2	4,7	4,8	5,1	5,7	6,2	5,6	5,9	F
IRL	0,1	0,1	0,1	0,1	0,1	0,1	0,1	0,1	0,2	0,2	0,2	IRL
I	2,4	3,0	3,1	2,9	3,0	2,6	2,4	2,9	3,5	2,9	3,1	I
L	-	-	-	-	-	-	-	-	-	-	0,0	L
NL	10,0	10,4	10,7	9,3	9,6	11,1	10,7	11,8	12,4	10,1	13,2	NL
A	0,4	0,3	0,3	0,4	0,4	0,5	0,4	0,6	0,6	0,6	0,7	A
P	0,4	0,5	0,4	0,4	0,4	0,6	0,6	0,4	0,5	0,3	0,4	P
FIN	0,2	0,3	0,6	0,6	0,5	0,6	0,6	1,0	0,8	0,7	0,9	FIN
S	1,3	1,4	1,4	1,4	1,4	1,3	1,3	1,8	1,9	1,1	1,9	S
UK	9,0	10,9	10,1	9,3	10,3	11,2	10,8	12,7	15,0	10,4	14,3	UK
IS	0,0	0,0	0,0	0,0	0,0	0,0	0,0	0,0	0,0	0,0	:	IS
NO	10,4	12,8	13,4	13,5	14,0	14,5	15,1	21,1	23,0	15,6	:	NO
EEA	13,0	15,2		14,8	14,4	15,4	16,8	15,1	18,1	20,1	15,8	:	EEA
CH	0,0	0,0	0,1	0,1	0,1	0,1	0,1	0,1	0,2	0,1	0,2	CH
US	9,0	9,7	9,9	8,6	8,4	7,5	8,0	9,6	11,1	9,0	:	US
CA	9,7	10,0	11,0	10,7	13,0	13,5	13,3	16,7	19,4	15,8	19,0	CA
JP	0,9	1,0	1,1	1,2	1,7	1,9	1,9	1,5	1,7	1,1	1,1	JP

3A9UX

B: includes L up to 1998.

Imports of mineral fuels, lubricants and related products at current prices.
1 000 million ECU

	1989	1990	1991	1992	1993	1994	1995	1996	1997	1998	1999	
EU-15	69,4	79,1		81,4	73,3	68,1	68,9	64,8	76,0	85,2	61,7	77,9	EU-15
EUR-11	64,3	73,5		75,7	68,0	63,0	65,2	62,1	71,6	81,3	58,5	77,5	EUR-11
B	6,9	7,6	8,2	7,4	7,1	7,2	7,2	8,7	9,6	7,6		8,9	B
DK	1,8	1,7	1,8	1,6	1,3	1,5	1,5	1,7	1,5	1,4	1,4	DK
D	18,5	22,2		26,1	23,5	23,2	22,4	22,0	27,6	29,5	23,5	24,8	D
EL	0,9	1,2	1,7	1,8	2,0	1,8	1,4	2,3	1,8	2,0	1,5	EL
E	7,1	7,7	7,7	7,4	6,9	6,8	7,0	8,6	9,5	7,8	9,0	E
F	15,3	17,6	18,0	15,9	15,2	14,8	14,0	14,9	19,2	14,9	17,7	F
IRL	0,9	1,0	1,0	0,9	0,9	0,8	0,8	1,0	1,2	1,0	1,2	IRL
I	13,3	14,9	13,8	12,3	11,7	11,4	11,4	13,7	14,6	10,7	13,3	I
L	-	-	-	-	-	-	-	-	-	-	0,4	L
NL	11,3	12,2	11,8	10,6	9,2	12,3	10,5	11,8	12,7	5,2	14,3	NL
A	2,0	2,5	2,4	2,1	2,1	2,0	2,2	2,5	3,0	2,6	2,9	A
P	1,8	2,1	1,9	1,9	1,8	1,9	2,1	2,1	2,4	1,8	2,5	P
FIN	2,2	2,5	2,3	2,1	2,0	2,3	1,9	2,3	2,6	2,1	2,5	FIN
S	3,4	3,9	3,6	3,4	3,4	3,2	3,1	4,3	4,5	2,8	3,9	S
UK	8,9	10,8	10,6	9,4	9,1	7,5	7,0	8,6	9,4	7,0	8,0	UK
IS	0,1	0,1	0,1	0,1	0,1	0,1	0,1	0,1	0,1	0,1	:	IS
NO	0,8	0,9	0,9	0,7	0,7	0,8	0,7	1,2	1,0	0,8	:	NO
EEA	61,6	69,6		71,2	63,9	57,2	56,7	52,4	63,3	67,7	50,5	:	EEA
CH	2,1	2,5	2,5	2,2	2,0	1,9	1,8	2,2	3,0	2,1	2,3	CH
US	50,9	54,0	47,0	45,2	50,6	50,5	48,2	60,7	72,8	55,4	:	US
CA	4,9	5,7	4,6	4,1	4,5	4,3	4,5	5,8	7,6	6,0	6,7	CA
JP	39,8	45,1	44,5	40,9	42,1	40,5	41,2	47,9	55,4	38,6	46,8	JP

3A9EB

B: includes L up to 1998.

Trade in fuel products refers to products determined according to section 3 of the standard international trade classification (SITC) revision 3.

Comparability is incomplete because of the use of different trade systems — general or special. Figures do not include the former GDR before 1991.

3

Trade balance in mineral fuels, lubricants and related products at current prices.
1 000 million ECU

	1989	1990	1991	1992	1993	1994	1995	1996	1997	1998	1999	
EU-15	- 57,0	- 64,9 |	- 67,4	- 60,0	- 53,9	- 53,6	- 51,4	- 60,5	- 68,1	- 47,7	- 61,5	EU-15
EUR-11	- 54,0	- 61,9 |	- 63,9	- 56,8	- 50,9	- 52,8	- 51,0	- 58,6	- 66,8	- 45,9	- 64,0	EUR-11
B	- 3,8	- 4,4	- 4,5	- 4,1	- 3,6	- 3,7	- 4,1	- 5,0	- 5,1	- 3,8 |	- 4,2	B
DK	- 1,0	- 0,8	- 0,8	- 0,6	- 0,2	- 0,4	- 0,4	- 0,1	0,1	- 0,2	0,4	DK
D	- 14,7	- 18,2 |	- 22,1	- 19,4	- 19,3	- 18,4	- 18,2	- 22,3	- 24,2	- 18,8	- 20,0	D
EL	- 0,6	- 0,7	- 1,0	- 1,4	- 1,4	- 0,9	- 0,9	- 1,5	- 0,9	- 1,3	- 0,6	EL
E	- 5,3	- 5,6	- 5,8	- 5,8	- 5,3	- 5,3	- 5,4	- 6,4	- 7,1	- 5,5	- 6,4	E
F	- 11,9	- 13,5	- 13,6	- 11,7	- 10,5	- 10,0	- 8,9	- 9,3	- 13,0	- 9,3	- 11,8	F
IRL	- 0,8	- 0,9	- 0,8	- 0,8	- 0,7	- 0,7	- 0,7	- 0,9	- 1,0	- 0,8	- 1,0	IRL
I	- 10,8	- 11,9	- 10,7	- 9,4	- 8,7	- 8,8	- 9,0	- 10,8	- 11,1	- 7,9	- 10,2	I
L	-	-	-	-	-	-	-	-	-	-	- 0,4	L
NL	- 1,4	- 1,7	- 1,1	- 1,3	0,4	- 1,2	0,2	0,0	- 0,4	4,8	- 1,1	NL
A	- 1,6	- 2,1	- 2,1	- 1,8	- 1,7	- 1,6	- 1,8	- 1,9	- 2,4	- 2,0	- 2,2	A
P	- 1,4	- 1,6	- 1,6	- 1,5	- 1,4	- 1,3	- 1,5	- 1,7	- 1,9	- 1,5	- 2,1	P
FIN	- 2,0	- 2,2	- 1,8	- 1,5	- 1,4	- 1,7	- 1,3	- 1,3	- 1,8	- 1,4	- 1,6	FIN
S	- 2,1	- 2,5	- 2,1	- 2,0	- 1,9	- 1,9	- 1,8	- 2,5	- 2,6	- 1,7	- 2,0	S
UK	0,1	0,1	- 0,6	- 0,1	1,2	3,7	3,8	4,2	5,7	3,4	6,4	UK
IS	- 0,1	- 0,1	- 0,1	- 0,1	- 0,1	- 0,1	- 0,1	- 0,1	- 0,1	- 0,1	:	IS
NO	9,6	11,9	12,5	12,8	13,3	13,7	14,4	19,9	22,0	14,7	:	NO
EEA	- 48,6	- 54,4 |	- 56,4	- 49,4	- 41,8	- 39,9	- 37,3	- 45,1	- 47,6	- 34,7	:	EEA
CH	- 2,1	- 2,4	- 2,4	- 2,1	- 2,0	- 1,8	- 1,7	- 2,1	- 2,9	- 2,0	- 2,2	CH
US	- 41,9	- 44,3	- 37,1	- 36,6	- 42,2	- 43,0	- 40,2	- 51,1	- 61,7	- 46,5	:	US
CA	4,8	4,2	6,4	6,6	8,5	9,2	8,8	10,9	11,8	9,8	12,3	CA
JP	- 38,9	- 44,1	- 43,5	- 39,6	- 40,4	- 38,5	- 39,3	- 46,4	- 53,7	- 37,5	- 45,6	JP

Further reading: External trade, statistical yearbooks. Eurostat. Comext on CD-ROM. Eurostat.

B: includes L up to 1998.

3A9EA

Exports of chemicals and related products at current prices. 1 000 million ECU

	1989	1990	1991	1992	1993	1994	1995	1996	1997	1998	1999	
EU-15	51,9	51,5 |	54,5	57,0	60,2	68,1	73,5	79,1	93,3	95,9	106,5	EU-15
EUR-11	55,7	54,4 |	56,7	58,9	62,3	72,0	79,5	85,5	99,6	104,4	113,6	EUR-11
B	12,5	13,0	13,4	14,0	16,7	19,9	23,7	24,4	28,2	31,6 |	34,0	B
DK	2,4	2,4	2,5	2,8	3,0	3,3	3,8	2,7	4,3	4,5	5,4	DK
D	40,1	39,7 |	41,2	41,7	41,6	48,1	52,9	53,9	59,7	62,4	62,9	D
EL	0,3	0,2	0,3	0,3	0,3	0,3	0,4	0,5	0,6	0,6	0,7	EL
E	3,9	4,0	4,3	4,5	4,8	5,6	6,9	7,0	7,3	8,5	8,8	E
F	21,6	22,1	23,1	24,1	25,1	28,4	32,1	33,5	37,1	39,1	42,2	F
IRL	2,7	2,9	3,4	4,2	4,8	5,9	6,4	8,5	11,9	18,4	21,1	IRL
I	9,0	8,8	9,2	10,0	10,7	12,2	14,2	15,6	17,5	18,0	19,5	I
L	-	-	-	-	-	-	-	-	-	-	0,5	L
NL	16,6	16,1	15,8	17,3	16,8	22,2	24,8	26,8	28,7	26,7	26,8	NL
A	2,7	2,8	2,9	3,0	3,1	3,5	4,1	3,9	5,1	5,3	5,8	A
P	0,6	0,7	0,6	0,6	0,6	0,7	0,9	0,9	1,0	1,1	1,1	P
FIN	1,3	1,3	1,3	1,2	1,3	1,7	1,8	1,3	2,3	2,4	2,5	FIN
S	3,4	3,4	3,8	4,0	4,2	4,8	5,3	5,6	6,3	5,9	7,3	S
UK	15,4	18,4	19,6	20,3	22,1	24,3	25,2	27,3	31,7	33,0	35,4	UK
IS	0,0	0,0	0,0	0,0	0,0	0,0	0,0	0,0	0,0	0,0	:	IS
NO	1,7	1,8	1,7	1,7	1,7	1,9	1,0	1,1	1,3	1,3	:	NO
EEA	51,1	50,7 |	53,6	56,0	59,1	67,0	71,8	77,5	91,5	93,9	:	EEA
CH	10,2	10,8	11,2	12,1	13,5	15,1	16,2	17,3	18,6	20,0	22,7	CH
US	33,5	31,0	35,0	34,5	39,2	44,1	47,2	49,6	62,5	61,8	:	US
CA	5,6	5,2	5,5	5,5	6,4	7,6	8,5	9,0	11,2	10,9	12,1	CA
JP	13,3	12,4	14,0	14,7	17,2	19,8	23,0	22,7	26,4	24,3	28,8	JP

3A9FB

Further reading: External trade, statistical yearbooks. Eurostat. Comext on CD-ROM. Eurostat.   B: includes L up to 1998.

Imports of chemicals and related products at current prices. 1 000 million ECU

	1989	1990	1991	1992	1993	1994	1995	1996	1997	1998	1999	
EU-15	30,1	30,2 |	31,9	32,7	32,1	37,5	43,1	44,3	51,6	55,6	58,6	EU-15
EUR-11	35,1	36,0 |	38,6	40,0	39,3	46,4	52,1	54,1	62,5	68,0	70,6	EUR-11
B	11,2	11,8	12,2	12,5	13,1	14,4	17,5	18,1	21,2	25,1 |	24,9	B
DK	2,8	2,9	2,9	3,0	3,1	3,5	4,0	3,7	4,1	4,2	4,5	DK
D	23,0	24,2 |	26,4	27,0	24,2	28,6	32,4	31,9	34,8	40,5	38,9	D
EL	1,6	1,6	1,8	1,9	2,1	2,3	2,6	2,8	3,0	3,3	3,3	EL
E	6,3	6,7	7,4	7,8	7,3	8,8	10,7	11,2	11,9	14,3	13,9	E
F	18,7	19,6	19,7	20,4	19,8	23,4	26,3	26,7	29,2	31,9	33,6	F
IRL	2,0	2,0	2,2	2,2	2,3	2,8	3,2	3,5	4,3	4,3	4,9	IRL
I	15,6	15,9	16,2	16,8	15,7	18,2	20,3	21,3	24,1	24,8	26,4	I
L	-	-	-	-	-	-	-	-	-	-	1,0	L
NL	11,1	11,1	11,3	12,0	10,7	14,7	16,4	18,1	20,0	20,3	20,5	NL
A	3,6	3,9	4,0	4,1	4,3	4,8	5,4	5,6	6,1	6,6	6,9	A
P	1,6	1,8	1,9	2,1	2,0	2,3	2,6	2,8	3,1	3,3	3,5	P
FIN	2,3	2,3	2,0	2,0	2,1	2,5	2,7	2,6	3,2	3,2	3,3	FIN
S	4,3	4,1	4,1	4,1	4,2	4,8	5,3	5,4	5,8	5,9	6,6	S
UK	14,3	15,1	15,6	15,7	16,4	18,6	21,1	22,3	25,9	26,8	29,4	UK
IS	0,1	0,1	0,1	0,1	0,1	0,1	0,1	0,1	0,2	0,2	:	IS
NO	1,7	1,7	1,8	1,9	1,9	2,2	2,4	2,5	2,7	2,8	:	NO
EEA	29,1	29,2 |	30,9	31,7	31,1	36,6	41,9	43,2	50,2	54,1	:	EEA
CH	6,2	6,4	6,4	6,6	7,2	8,2	9,0	9,2	10,7	11,5	13,1	CH
US	19,8	18,6	20,4	22,3	26,0	29,8	32,2	36,7	46,0	50,3	:	US
CA	6,5	6,1	6,6	6,9	8,6	9,8	10,1	11,3	14,2	15,1	17,2	CA
JP	13,7	12,0	13,6	13,0	15,1	16,6	18,4	18,0	20,2	18,3	21,4	JP

3A9FC

Further reading: External trade, statistical yearbooks. Eurostat. Comext on CD-ROM. Eurostat.   B: includes L up to 1998.

3

Trade in chemicals refers to products deter-mined according to section 5 of the standard international trade classification (SITC) revision 3.

Comparability is incomplete because of the use of different trade systems — general or special. Figures do not include the former GDR before 1991.

Trade balance in chemicals and related products, at current prices. 1 000 million ECU

	1989	1990	1991	1992	1993	1994	1995	1996	1997	1998	1999	
EU-15	21,9	21,3	22,6	24,3	28,1	30,6	30,4	34,8	41,7	40,4	47,9	**EU-15**
EUR-11	20,6	18,5	18,0	18,9	22,9	25,6	27,4	31,4	37,1	36,4	43,0	**EUR-11**
B	1,2	1,2	1,2	1,5	3,6	5,6	6,2	6,3	7,0	6,4	9,0	**B**
DK	- 0,4	- 0,5	- 0,4	- 0,2	- 0,1	- 0,1	- 0,2	- 1,0	0,2	0,2	0,8	**DK**
D	17,0	15,5	14,8	14,8	17,4	19,5	20,5	22,0	24,9	21,9	23,9	**D**
EL	- 1,3	- 1,4	- 1,5	- 1,7	- 1,7	- 2,0	- 2,2	- 2,3	- 2,5	- 2,7	- 2,6	**EL**
E	- 2,4	- 2,7	- 3,1	- 3,3	- 2,6	- 3,3	- 3,8	- 4,2	- 4,6	- 5,8	- 5,1	**E**
F	2,9	2,6	3,4	3,7	5,3	5,1	5,8	6,8	7,9	7,2	8,6	**F**
IRL	0,7	0,9	1,2	2,0	2,4	3,1	3,2	5,0	7,6	14,1	16,2	**IRL**
I	- 6,6	- 7,2	- 7,1	- 6,8	- 5,0	- 6,0	- 6,1	- 5,7	- 6,6	- 6,8	- 6,9	**I**
L	-	-	-	-	-	-	-	-	-	-	- 0,5	**L**
NL	5,5	5,0	4,5	5,2	6,1	7,5	8,4	8,7	8,7	6,4	6,3	**NL**
A	- 0,8	- 1,1	- 1,0	- 1,1	- 1,2	- 1,4	- 1,4	- 1,6	- 1,0	- 1,3	- 1,1	**A**
P	- 0,9	- 1,1	- 1,3	- 1,5	- 1,4	- 1,5	- 1,7	- 2,0	- 2,1	- 2,2	- 2,4	**P**
FIN	- 1,0	- 1,0	- 0,8	- 0,8	- 0,7	- 0,9	- 0,9	- 1,4	- 0,9	- 0,8	- 0,8	**FIN**
S	- 0,9	- 0,7	- 0,3	- 0,1	0,1	- 0,1	- 0,1	0,2	0,5	0,0	0,6	**S**
UK	1,1	3,2	4,0	4,6	5,7	5,7	4,1	5,0	5,9	6,2	6,0	**UK**
IS	- 0,1	- 0,1	- 0,1	- 0,1	- 0,1	- 0,1	- 0,1	- 0,1	- 0,1	- 0,2	:	**IS**
NO	0,0	0,0	- 0,1	- 0,2	- 0,2	- 0,3	- 1,4	- 1,3	- 1,4	- 1,5	:	**NO**
EEA	22,0	21,5	22,7	24,3	28,0	30,5	29,9	34,3	41,3	39,8	:	**EEA**
CH	4,0	4,4	4,8	5,5	6,2	6,9	7,3	8,1	7,9	8,5	9,7	**CH**
US	13,8	12,4	14,7	12,2	13,1	14,3	14,9	12,9	16,5	11,5	:	**US**
CA	- 1,0	- 0,9	- 1,1	- 1,4	- 2,2	- 2,2	- 1,6	- 2,3	- 3,0	- 4,2	- 5,1	**CA**
JP	- 0,3	0,4	0,4	1,6	2,1	3,2	4,6	4,7	6,1	6,0	7,4	**JP**

Further reading: External trade, statistical yearbooks. Eurostat. Comext on CD-ROM.   B: includes L up to 1998.
Eurostat.

3A9FA

Exports of manufactured products at current prices. 1 000 million ECU

	1989	1990	1991	1992	1993	1994	1995	1996	1997	1998	1999	
EU-15	128,7	124,8 ǀ	123,3	124,4	138,0	154,3	167,6	182,1	203,9	202,6	206,1	**EU-15**
EUR-11	143,4	139,6 ǀ	138,0	140,1	149,0	166,8	182,7	195,3	217,6	221,7	224,2	**EUR-11**
B	36,7	36,5	36,2	35,6	38,6	41,7	47,2	47,8	52,3	56,3 ǀ	55,6	**B**
DK	6,6	7,2	7,7	8,2	8,7	9,5	10,8	10,7	11,5	12,0	12,6	**DK**
D	89,8	89,8 ǀ	91,0	91,8	87,3	95,4	105,2	105,0	113,7	121,9	118,9	**D**
EL	3,2	3,0	3,1	3,5	3,2	3,3	3,7	3,7	4,3	4,1	3,8	**EL**
E	13,4	14,2	14,9	15,4	16,3	18,8	21,9	24,2	24,9	27,7	26,6	**E**
F	44,9	46,8	47,0	48,6	47,2	52,7	58,0	59,6	63,6	66,8	68,2	**F**
IRL	4,0	4,2	4,5	5,0	4,9	5,8	6,9	7,5	8,2	8,5	9,2	**IRL**
I	57,7	60,1	60,8	61,5	65,0	73,2	79,8	87,1	92,8	92,3	90,7	**I**
L	-	-	-	-	-	-	-	-	-	-	4,3	**L**
NL	23,1	23,5	24,4	26,2	24,2	28,9	31,7	37,4	41,7	42,4	43,8	**NL**
A	13,5	14,6	14,6	15,0	14,9	16,1	18,4	17,4	21,1	22,9	23,5	**A**
P	6,3	7,1	7,6	8,1	7,6	8,5	8,9	9,7	10,5	10,9	10,7	**P**
FIN	10,5	10,2	9,4	9,1	9,5	11,5	13,7	12,5	14,8	15,5	15,3	**FIN**
S	16,6	15,5	15,5	15,0	14,2	16,9	19,2	20,5	21,8	21,2	21,8	**S**
UK	39,4	41,5	41,1	40,2	40,5	47,2	48,8	54,1	62,6	61,5	61,3	**UK**
IS	0,3	0,2	0,2	0,2	0,2	0,2	0,2	0,2	0,3	0,3	:	**IS**
NO	6,3	5,7	5,4	5,0	5,0	5,7	5,8	6,0	6,7	6,7	:	**NO**
EEA	124,6	120,2 ǀ	118,1	119,4	133,6	149,4	161,9	176,1	197,2	195,1	:	**EEA**
CH	20,0	21,4	20,7	20,8	22,4	23,9	23,6	23,5	24,7	25,5	28,4	**CH**
US	57,9	60,3	68,2	68,9	79,9	87,1	90,9	100,4	124,7	126,2	:	**US**
CA	21,5	19,6	20,4	21,0	25,0	28,3	32,1	34,7	41,0	43,1	48,6	**CA**
JP	52,9	46,1	51,5	51,1	58,4	61,2	64,3	62,3	71,5	65,9	74,9	**JP**

3A9GB

Further reading: External trade, statistical yearbooks. Eurostat. Comext on CD-ROM.   B: includes L up to 1998.
Eurostat.

Imports of manufactured products at current prices. 1 000 million ECU

	1989	1990	1991	1992	1993	1994	1995	1996	1997	1998	1999	
EU-15	118,4	121,2 ǀ	132,4	134,7	137,8	154,0	164,9	169,5	196,8	211,4	223,6	**EU-15**
EUR-11	116,2	121,8 ǀ	134,3	136,6	133,5	150,2	163,7	167,0	189,3	202,0	209,3	**EUR-11**
B	31,6	33,0	33,4	33,4	32,8	35,6	39,8	41,7	45,8	49,0 ǀ	48,7	**B**
DK	8,0	8,2	8,7	9,0	8,8	10,2	11,7	11,4	12,7	13,7 *	13,6	**DK**
D	81,2	88,4 ǀ	102,1	103,7	93,2	103,7	111,9	109,4	115,1	124,0	116,6	**D**
EL	4,5	4,8	5,0	5,2	5,0	5,4	6,5	6,6	7,5	8,0	7,5	**EL**
E	13,3	15,4	17,8	19,0	16,0	18,0	21,6	22,9	25,0	30,8	30,3	**E**
F	55,1	57,9	58,3	58,4	54,2	59,7	65,3	65,4	70,6	76,5	79,1	**F**
IRL	4,4	4,7	5,0	5,2	4,6	5,3	5,9	6,6	7,7	8,1	8,6	**IRL**
I	34,2	34,6	35,0	35,6	30,7	36,8	42,3	42,2	48,5	51,7	52,5	**I**
L	-	-	-	-	-	-	-	-	-	-	3,1	**L**
NL	30,0	32,2	33,5	34,1	27,8	33,6	35,4	42,3	46,5	49,3	51,0	**NL**
A	12,8	14,1	14,6	15,1	15,6	17,5	18,6	19,3	20,5	21,6	22,9	**A**
P	4,6	5,2	6,1	6,8	5,9	6,5	7,4	8,1	9,2	10,3	10,5	**P**
FIN	6,5	6,1	5,1	4,6	4,1	5,2	5,7	5,8	6,7	6,9	6,8	**FIN**
S	14,1	14,0	13,3	12,8	11,7	13,8	14,2	14,4	15,6	16,2	16,8	**S**
UK	57,8	56,3	54,3	53,9	51,8	58,9	60,6	65,5	79,5	83,8	86,6	**UK**
IS	0,4	0,4	0,5	0,4	0,4	0,4	0,5	0,5	0,6	0,7	:	**IS**
NO	6,8	6,9	7,2	7,2	7,1	8,2	8,7	8,8	10,1	10,7	:	**NO**
EEA	114,7	117,9 ǀ	129,4	132,3	135,8	151,5	161,4	166,2	193,4	207,9	:	**EEA**
CH	22,9	23,4	22,7	21,4	22,4	23,9	24,4	24,6	26,4	27,9	29,1	**CH**
US	132,1	116,6	119,1	125,5	152,8	170,0	170,7	183,4	229,5	255,7	:	**US**
CA	25,3	22,5	23,4	23,6	28,1	31,1	31,0	31,8	41,6	44,9	49,8	**CA**
JP	50,0	46,0	47,2	42,6	51,0	59,9	68,0	71,5	76,1	63,7	73,0	**JP**

3A9GC

Further reading: External trade, statistical yearbooks. Eurostat. Comext on CD-ROM.   B: includes L up to 1998.
Eurostat.

Trade in manufactured products refers to products determined according to sections 6 and 8 of the standard international trade classification (SITC) revision 3. Comparability is incomplete because of the use of different trade systems — general or special. Figures do not include the former GDR before 1991.

Trade balance in manufactured products at current prices. 1 000 million ECU

	1989	1990	1991	1992	1993	1994	1995	1996	1997	1998	1999	
EU-15	10,3 |	3,6	- 9,2	- 10,4	0,2	0,3	2,7	12,6	7,1	- 8,7	- 17,5	**EU-15**
EUR-11	27,1 |	17,9	3,7	3,5	15,5	16,6	19,0	28,3	28,3	19,7	14,9	**EUR-11**
B	5,1	3,5	2,8	2,2	5,8	6,0	7,3	6,1	6,6	7,3 |	6,8	**B**
DK	- 1,4	- 1,0	- 1,0	- 0,8	- 0,2	- 0,7	- 0,9	- 0,7	- 1,2	- 1,7	- 1,0	**DK**
D	8,7 |	1,4	- 11,1	- 12,0	- 5,9	- 8,2	- 6,6	- 4,4	- 1,4	- 2,0	2,3	**D**
EL	- 1,3	- 1,8	- 1,9	- 1,7	- 1,8	- 2,1	- 2,9	- 2,9	- 3,2	- 3,9	- 3,7	**EL**
E	0,2	- 1,2	- 2,9	- 3,7	0,3	0,8	0,3	1,2	0,0	- 3,0	- 3,7	**E**
F	- 10,2	- 11,1	- 11,3	- 9,8	- 7,0	- 7,0	- 7,3	- 5,8	- 7,0	- 9,7	- 10,9	**F**
IRL	- 0,4	- 0,6	- 0,5	- 0,2	0,3	0,5	1,1	0,9	0,5	0,4	0,6	**IRL**
I	23,5	25,6	25,8	26,0	34,3	36,5	37,5	44,9	44,2	40,6	38,2	**I**
L	-	-	-	-	-	-	-	-	-	-	1,2	**L**
NL	- 6,9	- 8,7	- 9,1	- 7,9	- 3,6	- 4,7	- 3,7	- 4,9	- 4,8	- 6,9	- 7,2	**NL**
A	0,8	0,5	0,0	- 0,1	- 0,7	- 1,3	- 0,2	- 2,0	0,6	1,3	0,6	**A**
P	1,7	1,9	1,5	1,3	1,8	2,0	1,6	1,6	1,2	0,6	0,2	**P**
FIN	4,0	4,1	4,3	4,5	5,4	6,3	8,0	6,7	8,1	8,7	8,6	**FIN**
S	2,5	1,5	2,2	2,2	2,5	3,1	5,1	6,1	6,1	5,0	5,0	**S**
UK	- 18,4	- 14,9	- 13,3	- 13,7	- 11,3	- 11,7	- 11,7	- 11,4	- 16,8	- 22,3	- 25,3	**UK**
IS	- 0,2	- 0,2	- 0,3	- 0,3	- 0,2	- 0,2	- 0,2	- 0,3	- 0,3	- 0,3	:	**IS**
NO	- 0,4	- 1,2	- 1,8	- 2,3	- 2,1	- 2,4	- 2,9	- 2,8	- 3,4	- 4,0	:	**NO**
EEA	9,9 |	2,3	- 11,4	- 12,8	- 2,2	- 2,1	0,5	9,9	3,8	- 12,8	:	**EEA**
CH	- 2,9	- 2,0	- 2,0	- 0,6	0,1	0,0	- 0,8	- 1,1	- 1,7	- 2,5	- 0,7	**CH**
US	- 74,1	- 56,3	- 50,9	- 56,6	- 72,9	- 82,9	- 79,8	- 83,0	- 104,8	- 129,5	:	**US**
CA	- 3,7	- 2,9	- 3,0	- 2,6	- 3,1	- 2,9	1,1	2,9	- 0,6	- 1,7	- 1,2	**CA**
JP	2,8	0,1	4,3	8,5	7,4	1,4	- 3,7	- 9,3	- 4,6	2,2	2,0	**JP**

Further reading: External trade, statistical yearbooks. Eurostat. Comext on CD-ROM. Eurostat.   B: includes L up to 1998.

3A9GA

Exports of machinery and transport equipment at current prices. 1 000 million ECU

	1989	1990	1991	1992	1993	1994	1995	1996	1997	1998	1999	
EU-15	161,6	169,2	175,3	179,9	202,8	228,9	255,9	283,0	331,4	345,5	352,1	**EU-15**
EUR-11	174,6	179,8	181,5	190,1	210,8	239,9	271,3	295,8	343,8	371,1	383,0	**EUR-11**
B	23,0	25,4	25,7	25,8	29,2	33,9	36,0	38,9	42,9	48,6	48,9	**B**
DK	6,6	7,5	7,6	8,4	8,0	8,9	10,1	10,5	11,7	12,2	13,2	**DK**
D	150,3	154,4	158,7	164,7	156,8	175,9	195,8	203,6	227,0	252,0	258,2	**D**
EL	0,2	0,3	0,3	0,4	0,5	0,5	0,7	0,7	0,9	1,0	1,0	**EL**
E	15,0	17,5	20,5	22,1	22,5	26,5	30,8	35,4	36,6	42,7	42,5	**E**
F	66,6	70,3	78,9	82,9	79,2	90,2	98,4	104,3	120,4	135,0	144,2	**F**
IRL	6,0	5,8	5,7	5,9	7,1	8,8	11,9	13,5	17,8	21,2	26,0	**IRL**
I	46,9	50,2	51,5	50,6	53,1	59,0	67,0	76,2	80,1	84,4	84,1	**I**
L	-	-	-	-	-	-	-	-	-	-	2,3	**L**
NL	22,8	25,1	25,1	25,9	26,4	32,2	38,1	47,5	58,4	64,0	72,0	**NL**
A	10,1	12,3	12,7	13,3	13,4	14,8	17,3	18,4	21,4	23,6	26,6	**A**
P	2,2	2,5	2,6	3,1	2,8	3,3	4,7	6,1	6,6	7,3	7,7	**P**
FIN	6,1	6,5	5,1	5,4	6,3	8,0	11,1	12,6	14,4	16,5	17,1	**FIN**
S	19,9	19,5	19,1	18,4	18,4	23,2	27,7	31,6	34,8	34,8	37,7	**S**
UK	53,7	57,1	60,3	57,8	60,1	70,4	77,6	89,2	114,4	116,5	121,4	**UK**
IS	0,0	0,0	0,0	0,0	0,0	0,1	0,1	0,1	0,1	0,1	:	**IS**
NO	3,3	3,7	4,1	4,0	3,5	3,6	4,3	4,3	5,2	5,6	:	**NO**
EEA	158,3	166,0	172,5	176,6	199,0	224,0	250,7	276,6	323,1	335,7	:	**EEA**
CH	14,6	15,8	15,6	15,5	15,7	17,5	19,6	20,2	21,0	22,1	23,9	**CH**
US	143,0	143,4	161,5	165,6	192,0	212,1	215,2	241,1	311,0	319,5	:	**US**
CA	40,5	37,1	38,3	38,8	48,7	56,0	56,3	61,0	74,2	78,0	95,4	**CA**
JP	175,8	159,4	180,0	187,3	222,0	239,3	238,1	225,1	256,7	239,5	268,8	**JP**

3A9HB

Further reading: External trade, statistical yearbooks. Eurostat. Comext on CD-ROM. B: includes L up to 1998.
Eurostat.

Imports of machinery and transport equipment at current prices. 1 000 million ECU

	1989	1990	1991	1992	1993	1994	1995	1996	1997	1998	1999	
EU-15	128,2	132,5	146,1	143,8	143,9	160,4	173,4	189,0	230,0	267,2	304,0	**EU-15**
EUR-11	123,5	133,0	151,3	149,8	141,3	160,4	177,4	193,5	230,0	270,1	304,0	**EUR-11**
B	23,1	25,8	27,5	27,1	25,0	27,0	31,2	35,9	41,6	47,0	46,5	**B**
DK	7,5	8,1	8,5	8,1	8,0	9,7	11,7	12,1	13,3	14,6	15,6	**DK**
D	74,6	86,8	110,1	109,1	96,8	108,6	118,9	124,3	135,7	157,5	165,5	**D**
EL	4,5	4,8	5,7	6,2	6,6	5,2	5,4	6,6	7,2	9,4	9,9	**EL**
E	24,0	25,4	27,4	28,0	23,6	26,4	31,1	36,2	37,8	49,4	55,0	**E**
F	67,6	71,2	77,6	78,3	70,9	80,0	85,5	91,2	101,4	118,8	130,0	**F**
IRL	5,8	5,9	5,9	5,6	6,6	8,2	10,3	11,0	14,4	18,9	22,0	**IRL**
I	39,6	43,0	45,7	46,5	35,9	40,2	46,1	49,4	57,3	64,9	71,8	**I**
L	-	-	-	-	-	-	-	-	-	-	4,2	**L**
NL	29,5	32,1	35,1	36,2	30,3	37,0	41,2	52,2	61,6	71,6	78,5	**NL**
A	13,1	14,9	16,0	16,5	15,6	17,7	18,6	20,2	22,0	24,6	27,5	**A**
P	6,4	7,1	7,8	8,9	7,4	7,8	8,4	9,8	11,1	13,0	14,1	**P**
FIN	9,0	8,2	6,1	5,4	5,2	7,1	8,9	9,9	11,2	13,0	13,2	**FIN**
S	17,8	16,5	14,9	13,8	13,1	16,5	19,8	21,3	23,9	25,8	27,3	**S**
UK	67,9	64,8	60,2	62,5	66,5	79,0	82,8	93,2	118,0	126,6	137,6	**UK**
IS	0,4	0,5	0,5	0,4	0,3	0,4	0,4	0,6	0,7	0,9	:	**IS**
NO	9,2	8,7	7,9	7,6	8,0	8,5	9,4	10,6	13,4	14,7	:	**NO**
EEA	131,2	134,7	147,5	145,0	145,4	161,6	173,9	189,7	231,8	269,2	:	**EEA**
CH	16,6	17,3	17,1	15,6	15,4	17,6	20,5	20,9	21,1	22,9	26,9	**CH**
US	191,3	168,1	174,6	182,6	226,8	264,5	273,6	290,8	355,2	385,0	:	**US**
CA	54,2	46,0	48,6	47,7	56,9	64,2	64,8	68,5	90,1	93,9	107,8	**CA**
JP	25,5	28,3	30,3	29,0	34,9	44,3	58,0	67,1	73,7	66,8	80,0	**JP**

3A9HC

Further reading: External trade, statistical yearbooks. Eurostat. Comext on CD-ROM. B: includes L up to 1998.
Eurostat.

eurostat

Trade in machinery and transport equipment refers to products determined according to section 7 of the standard international trade classification (SITC) revision 3. Comparability is incomplete because of the use of different trade systems — general or special. Figures do not include the former GDR before 1991.

3A9HA

Trade balance in machinery and transport equipment at current prices. 1 000 million ECU

	1989	1990	1991	1992	1993	1994	1995	1996	1997	1998	1999	
EU-15	33,3	36,7	29,2	36,1	59,0	68,5	82,6	94,0	101,5	78,3	48,1	EU-15
EUR-11	51,1	46,9	30,2	40,3	69,5	79,5	94,0	102,2	113,8	101,0	79,1	EUR-11
B	0,0	- 0,4	- 1,8	- 1,3	4,2	6,9	4,8	2,9	1,3	1,7	2,4	B
DK	- 0,9	- 0,6	- 0,9	0,3	0,0	- 0,8	- 1,5	- 1,5	- 1,7	- 2,4	- 2,4	DK
D	75,7	67,6	48,6	55,5	59,9	67,3	76,9	79,3	91,3	94,5	92,7	D
EL	- 4,3	- 4,6	- 5,4	- 5,9	- 6,2	- 4,7	- 4,8	- 5,9	- 6,3	- 8,3	- 8,9	EL
E	- 9,1	- 8,0	- 6,9	- 5,9	- 1,2	0,1	- 0,3	- 0,8	- 1,2	- 6,7	- 12,5	E
F	- 1,1	- 0,9	1,3	4,6	8,3	10,3	12,9	13,1	19,0	16,2	14,1	F
IRL	0,1	0,0	- 0,2	0,3	0,6	0,6	1,6	2,5	3,3	2,3	4,0	IRL
I	7,3	7,2	5,8	4,1	17,2	18,9	20,9	26,7	22,9	19,5	12,3	I
L	-	-	-	-	-	-	-	-	-	-	- 2,0	L
NL	- 6,6	- 7,0	- 10,0	- 10,3	- 3,8	- 4,8	- 3,0	- 4,7	- 3,2	- 7,5	- 6,4	NL
A	- 3,0	- 2,6	- 3,3	- 3,2	- 2,3	- 2,9	- 1,4	- 1,8	- 0,6	- 1,0	- 0,9	A
P	- 4,2	- 4,6	- 5,2	- 5,8	- 4,6	- 4,5	- 3,7	- 3,7	- 4,4	- 5,6	- 6,4	P
FIN	- 2,9	- 1,7	- 1,0	0,0	1,1	0,9	2,1	2,8	3,2	3,5	3,9	FIN
S	2,1	3,0	4,2	4,6	5,3	6,8	8,0	10,3	10,9	9,0	10,5	S
UK	- 14,1	- 7,7	0,1	- 4,7	- 6,4	- 8,6	- 5,2	- 4,0	- 3,5	- 10,1	- 16,2	UK
IS	- 0,4	- 0,4	- 0,5	- 0,4	- 0,3	- 0,3	- 0,4	- 0,5	- 0,6	- 0,8	:	IS
NO	- 5,9	- 4,9	- 3,8	- 3,6	- 4,4	- 4,9	- 5,2	- 6,3	- 8,2	- 9,1	:	NO
EEA	27,1	31,3	25,0	31,7	53,6	62,5	76,8	86,9	91,3	66,5	:	EEA
CH	- 2,0	- 1,5	- 1,4	- 0,1	0,3	- 0,1	- 0,9	- 0,6	- 0,2	- 0,8	- 3,0	CH
US	- 48,3	- 24,7	- 13,1	- 17,0	- 34,8	- 52,4	- 58,4	- 49,7	- 44,2	- 65,5	:	US
CA	- 13,7	- 8,9	- 10,4	- 8,8	- 8,1	- 8,3	- 8,5	- 7,5	- 15,9	- 16,0	- 12,3	CA
JP	150,3	131,1	149,7	158,3	187,1	195,0	180,2	158,0	182,9	172,7	188,8	JP

Further reading: External trade, statistical yearbooks. Eurostat. Comext on CD-ROM. Eurostat.   B: includes L up to 1998.

In general, in the European Union, private sector salaries are negotiated by the social partners by means of collective bargaining. In addition the possibility exists in some countries to apply a national minimum wage through legal means. At present, nine Member States of the European Union apply such a national minimum wage: Belgium, Greece, Spain, France, Ireland (since 1 April 2000), Luxembourg, the Netherlands, Portugal and the United Kingdom.

Statutory minimum monthly wages (annual averages). ECU/EUR

	1990	1991	1992	1993	1994	1995	1996	1997	1998	1999	2000	
EU-15	:	:	:	:	:	:	:	:	:	:	:	EU-15
B	853	895	942	999	1 032	1 081	1 074	1 061	1 067	1 074	1 096	B
DK	:	:	:	:	:	:	:	:	:	:	:	DK
D	:	:	:	:	:	:	:	:	:	:	:	D
EL	335	338	343	353	371	386	412	440	434	458	461	EL
E	451	484	495	458	445	449	471	472	475	486	496	E
F	753	783	828	878	904	939	978	993	1 019	1 036	1 066	F
IRL	:	:	:	:	:	:	:	:	:	:	983	IRL
I	:	:	:	:	:	:	:	:	:	:	:	I
L	762	839	894	985	1 040	1 125	1 113	1 139	1 139	1 174	1 221	L
NL	877	903	948	992	1 001	1 030	1 026	1 018	1 018	1 064	1 092	NL
A	:	:	:	:	:	:	:	:	:	:	:	A
P	225	262	297	294	292	309	325	338	341	357	371	P
FIN	:	:	:	:	:	:	:	:	:	:	:	FIN
S	:	:	:	:	:	:	:	:	:	:	:	S
UK	:	:	:	:	:	:	:	:	:	920	1 036	UK

5A1AL

Further reading: Minimum wages. A comparative study. 1997. Eurostat. Statistics in focus: minimum wages in the European Union. 1999. Eurostat. Statistics in focus: minimum wages in the European Union, 2000. Eurostat.

EL: for unmarried non-manual employees in their first job. These data have been adjusted to take into account annual supplementary pay (for example 13th and 14th months).

Minimum monthly wages as a proportion of average earnings

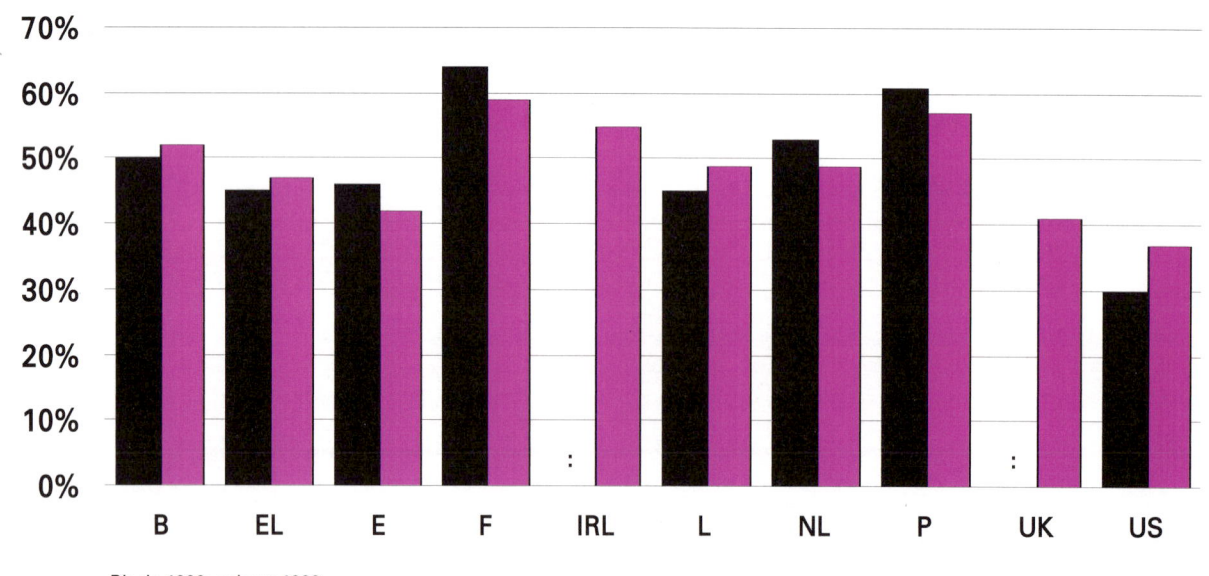

Black: 1990; colour: 1999.

5A1AM

Further reading: Minimum wages. A comparative study. 1997. Eurostat. Statistics in focus: minimum wages in the European Union, 2000. Eurostat.

Single male manual workers in manufacturing industry. EL: data are for non-manual employees. UK: 1999. IRL: 2000.

Surveys of labour costs have been carried out since 1966 and at present take place every four years, the latest being for 1996. Data for intervening years are estimated by each Member State using a methodology proposed by Eurostat. The term 'labour costs' is taken to mean expenditure incurred by employers in order to employ workers. These costs can be subdivided into two main categories: direct and indirect. Direct costs are all earnings including earnings in kind. Indirect costs are mainly social contributions, whether statutory, conventional or voluntary.

Structure of labour costs (%) in industry in 1998

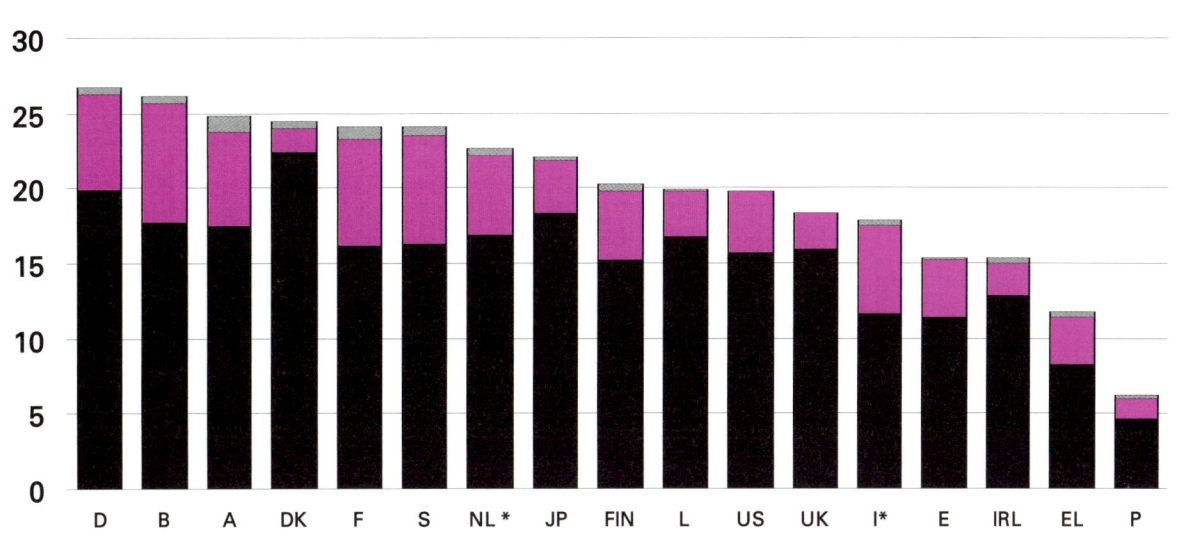

Black: direct costs; colour: employer's social security contributions; white: other costs.

Further reading: Labour costs 1996, principal results. Eurostat. Statistics in focus Labour costs, 1996, 1999. Eurostat, Statistics in focus Labour costs, 1998, Eurostat.

NL, I: Eurostat estimates.

Average hourly labour costs (manual and non-manual workers) in total industry. ECU

	1989	1990	1991	1992	1993	1994	1995	1996	1997	1998	1999	
EUR-11	:	:	:	17,68 *	18,33 *	19,05 *	19,47 *	20,10 *	20,97 *	21,45 *	:	**EUR-11**
B	17,75	19,30	20,53	21,27	22,81	24,26	25,13	25,81	25,63	26,17	:	**B**
DK	15,96	17,19	18,07	19,28	:	:	:	22,99	23,45 *	24,45 *	25,67 *	**DK**
D	:	:	:	:	:	:	26,12	26,50	26,33	26,77	27,52	**D**
EL	:	:	:	6,97	7,33	7,64	8,15	9,60	12,20	11,76	:	**EL**
E	10,30	11,30	12,38	15,11	14,38	14,13	14,42	14,86	15,03	15,41	15,77	**E**
F	:	:	:	19,12	20,27	20,90	21,59	23,11	23,35	24,10	:	**F**
IRL	11,01	11,64	12,29	12,80	12,98	13,23	13,17	13,90	15,18 *	:	:	**IRL**
I	:	:	:	18,74	17,03 *	16,93 *	15,67 *	17,21 *	18,23	17,90 *	:	**I**
L	14,48	15,32	:	17,26	18,31	19,30	19,65	19,92	19,68	19,92	20,90	**L**
NL	16,58	17,44	18,08	19,27	:	:	:	22,59	:	:	:	**NL**
A	:	:	:	:	:	:	:	24,56	24,33	24,88	25,94	**A**
P	3,21	3,57	4,20	5,55	5,41	5,45	5,75	6,06	6,18	6,28	:	**P**
FIN	:	:	:	:	:	:	19,39	19,65	19,76	20,24	20,90	**FIN**
S	:	:	:	:	:	:	:	23,11	23,88	24,10	25,47	**S**
UK	11,61	12,20	13,57	13,11	12,80	13,75	13,43	13,93	:	:	:	**UK**
IS	:	:	:	9,67	9,26	8,95	9,18	:	:	:	:	**IS**
NO	:	:	:	19,37	19,01	19,42	20,53	21,66	:	:	:	**NO**
EEA	:	:	:	:	:	:	:	:	:	:	:	**EEA**
CH	:	:	:	:	:	:	:	:	:	:	:	**CH**
US	15,62	13,78	14,91	14,93	17,27	17,53	15,86	16,75	19,28	19,86	21,45	**US**
CA												**CA**
JP	:	:	16,26	:	:	:	24,85	:	:	22,12	:	**JP**

Further reading: Labour costs 1992 — detailed results updating 1993–95 (diskette version). Results of the Labour costs 1996 and updating 1997–99. Statistics in focus: labour costs, 1996. 1999. Eurostat.

US data concern mining, manufacturing and construction. Labour costs exclude vocational training costs, other expenditures, and taxes and subsidies. Year-to-year changes may be affected by sample replacements. Particularly true for 1994–95. JP: 1991 instead of 1992; regular employees, including part-time in establishments with 30 or more regular employees. NO: 1995 and 1996 data from National Accounts.

eurostat

Hourly labour costs in ECU (current exchange rates), structure of costs as % of total cost. 1998

Industry and services (sections C–K)	EU-15	EUR-11	B	DK	D	EL	E	F	IRL
Hourly labour cost (ECU)	:	:	:	:	26,1	:	14,8	23,0	:
Direct cost (%)	:	:	:	:	74,4	:	:	67,4	:
Direct remuneration (%)	:	:	:	:	62,9	:	:	:	:
Indirect cost (%)	:	:	:	:	25,6	:	:	32,6	:
Social security (%)	:	:	:	:	23,4	:	:	:	:
Industry (sections C–F)									
Hourly labour cost (ECU)	:	:	26,2	24,5	26,8	11,8	15,4	24,1	:
Direct cost (%)	:	:	67,8	:	74,2	69,8	:	66,4	:
Direct remuneration (%)	:	:	55,4	:	62,7	:	:	:	:
Indirect cost (%)	:	:	32,2	:	25,8	30,2	:	33,6	:
Social security (%)	:	:	30,1	:	23,8	27,1	:	:	:
Manufacturing industry (section D)									
Hourly labour cost (ECU)	:	:	26,5	:	27,7	9,9	15,7	23,4	:
Direct cost (%)	:	:	69,1	:	74,8	68,4	:	:	:
Direct remuneration (%)	:	:	56,4	:	63,3	:	:	:	:
Indirect cost (%)	:	:	30,9	:	25,2	31,6	:	:	:
Social security (%)	:	:	28,9	:	23,4	29,1	:	:	:
Electricity, gas and water supply (section E)									
Hourly labour cost (ECU)	:	:	43,2	:	34,0	16,5	25,8	:	:
Direct cost (%)	:	:	61,5	:	67,5	72,2	:	:	:
Direct remuneration (%)	:	:	52,2	:	56,7	:	:	:	:
Indirect cost (%)	:	:	38,5	:	32,5	27,8	:	:	:
Social security (%)	:	:	34,4	:	29,7	25,6	:	:	:
Construction (section F)									
Hourly labour cost (ECU)	:	:	22,8	:	21,1	:	12,8	20,0	:
Direct cost (%)	:	:	63,2	:	73,9	:	:	:	:
Direct remuneration (%)	:	:	51,1	:	62,5	:	:	:	:
Indirect cost (%)	:	:	36,8	:	26,1	:	:	:	:
Social security (%)	:	:	35,4	:	23,3	:	:	:	:
Services (sections G–K)									
Hourly labour cost (ECU)	:	:	:	:	24,6	:	14,4	:	:
Direct cost (%)	:	:	:	:	74,8	71,8	:	:	:
Direct remuneration (%)	:	:	:	:	63,4	:	:	:	:
Indirect cost (%)	:	:	:	:	25,2	28,2	:	:	:
Social security (%)	:	:	:	:	22,3	25,2	:	:	:
Wholesale and retail trade (section G), hotels and restaurants (section H)									
Hourly labour cost (ECU)	:	:	:	:	21,6	8,9	13,4	19,6	:
Direct cost (%)	:	:	:	:	76,9	72,5	:	:	:
Direct remuneration (%)	:	:	:	:	65,4	:	:	:	:
Indirect cost (%)	:	:	:	:	23,1	27,5	:	:	:
Social security (%)	:	:	:	:	20,8	25,4	:	:	:
Financial intermediation (section J) and real estate, renting and business activities (section K)									
Hourly labour cost (ECU)	:	:	:	:	33,0	15,3	15,0	26,7	:
Direct cost (%)	:	:	:	:	70,9	70,9	:	:	:
Direct remuneration (%)	:	:	:	:	59,8	:	:	:	:
Indirect cost (%)	:	:	:	:	29,1	29,1	:	:	:
Social security (%)	:	:	:	:	25,1	27,2	:	:	:

Further reading: Labour costs 1996, principal results. Eurostat. Statistics in focus: labour costs 1996, 1999. Eurostat. Statistics in focus: labour costs 1998, 2000. Eurostat.

Direct remunerations include irregular bonuses. F: 'C–F' does not include F. D: The aggregate C_K only includes C, G, J; the aggregate G_K only includes G, J.

602CC

Hourly labour costs in ECU (current exchange rates), structure of costs as % of total cost.
1998

	I	L	NL	A	P	FIN	S	UK	
									Industry and services (sections C–K)
	19,2	21,7	:	:	7,0	20,1	24,2	:	Hourly labour cost (ECU)
	65,5	83,9	:	:	76,2	75,8	67,8	:	Direct cost (%)
	60,7	62,7	:	:	69,9	64,4	60,7	:	Direct remuneration (%)
	34,5	16,0	:	:	23,8	24,2	32,2	:	Indirect cost (%)
	32,7	14,6	:	:	20,4	21,9	29,5	:	Social security (%)
									Industry (sections C–F)
	18,2	19,9	:	24,9	6,3	20,2	24,1	:	Hourly labour cost (ECU)
	65,0	84,3	:	70,6	75,3	75,3	67,8	:	Direct cost (%)
	59,3	66,0	:	61,4	69,1	58,9	60,7	:	Direct remuneration (%)
	35,0	15,8	:	29,4	24,8	24,7	32,3	:	Indirect cost (%)
	32,8	15,1	:	25,1	20,8	22,4	29,6	:	Social security (%)
									Manufacturing industry (section D)
	17,8	21,8	:	24,0	6,2	20,3	24,3	:	Hourly labour cost (ECU)
	65,2	84,5	:	71,5	75,5	75,4	67,6	:	Direct cost (%)
	59,2	65,5	:	62,3	69,4	64,1	60,7	:	Direct remuneration (%)
	34,8	15,5	:	28,5	24,5	24,6	32,4	:	Indirect cost (%)
	32,6	14,8	:	24,0	20,5	22,4	29,7	:	Social security (%)
									Electricity, gas and water supply (section E)
	29,8	35,9	:	37,2	12,8	:	26,3	:	Hourly labour cost (ECU)
	62,6	76,8	:	62,1	68,3	:	66,0	:	Direct cost (%)
	61,1	55,9	:	53,4	61,8	:	59,5	:	Direct remuneration (%)
	37,4	23,1	:	38,0	31,8	:	34,0	:	Indirect cost (%)
	35,4	21,3	:	34,3	26,2	:	29,3	:	Social security (%)
									Construction (section F)
	17,2	15,6	:	:	5,8	18,8	22,1	:	Hourly labour cost (ECU)
	65,0	84,3	:	:	76,9	76,2	69,3	:	Direct cost (%)
	59,3	68,6	:	:	70,7	64,3	61,1	:	Direct remuneration (%)
	35,0	15,7	:	:	23,1	23,8	30,7	:	Indirect cost (%)
	33,2	15,4	:	:	20,0	22,4	29,2	:	Social security (%)
									Services (sections G–K)
	21,2	23,7	:	:	8,3	19,8	24,4	:	Hourly labour cost (ECU)
	66,4	83,4	:	:	77,6	:	67,9	:	Direct cost (%)
	63,5	59,7	:	:	71,1	:	60,8	:	Direct remuneration (%)
	33,6	16,6	:	:	22,4	:	32,1	:	Indirect cost (%)
	32,5	14,4	:	:	19,9	:	29,4	:	Social security (%)
									Wholesale and retail trade (section G), hotels and restaurants (section H)
	15,6	15,4	:	:	6,5	18,1	22,2	:	Hourly labour cost (ECU)
	66,3	85,7	:	:	:	76,7	68,7	:	Direct cost (%)
	61,2	68,6	:	:	:	66,4	:	:	Direct remuneration (%)
	33,7	14,3	:	:	:	23,3	31,3	:	Indirect cost (%)
	32,2	13,3	:	:	:	21,0	29,1	:	Social security (%)
									Financial intermediation (section J) and real estate, renting and business activities (section K)
	26,5	35,4	:	:	13,5	22,2	26,9	:	Hourly labour cost (ECU)
	66,4	81,8	:	:	:	76,0	67,1	:	Direct cost (%)
	64,7	52,5	:	:	:	64,2	:	:	Direct remuneration (%)
	33,6	18,1	:	:	:	24,1	32,9	:	Indirect cost (%)
	32,6	15,5	:	:	:	21,1	29,6	:	Social security (%)

Further reading: Labour costs 1996, principal results. Eurostat. Statistics in focus: labour costs 1996, 1999. Eurostat. Statistics in focus: labour costs 1998, 2000. Eurostat.

Direct remunerations include irregular bonuses. FIN: 'C–F' does not include F. I: 1997.

603CC

The employment rate expresses the share of the employed persons on the total population of working age. In 1999, more than half of all NUTS 2 regions had higher employment rates than the EU average of 50.6 %. The lowest employment rates are registered for Spain having all regions below the EU average. On the contrary, the Netherlands, Austria and Sweden only have regions with employ-

ment rates above the EU average. Austria and the Netherlands have the smallest differences between the highest and the lowest employment rates, with 6.7 % for Austria, and 9.7 % for the Netherlands. France and Italy are the countries with the largest discrepancy between the highest and the lowest employment rate in terms of percentage points.

Employment rate. 1999

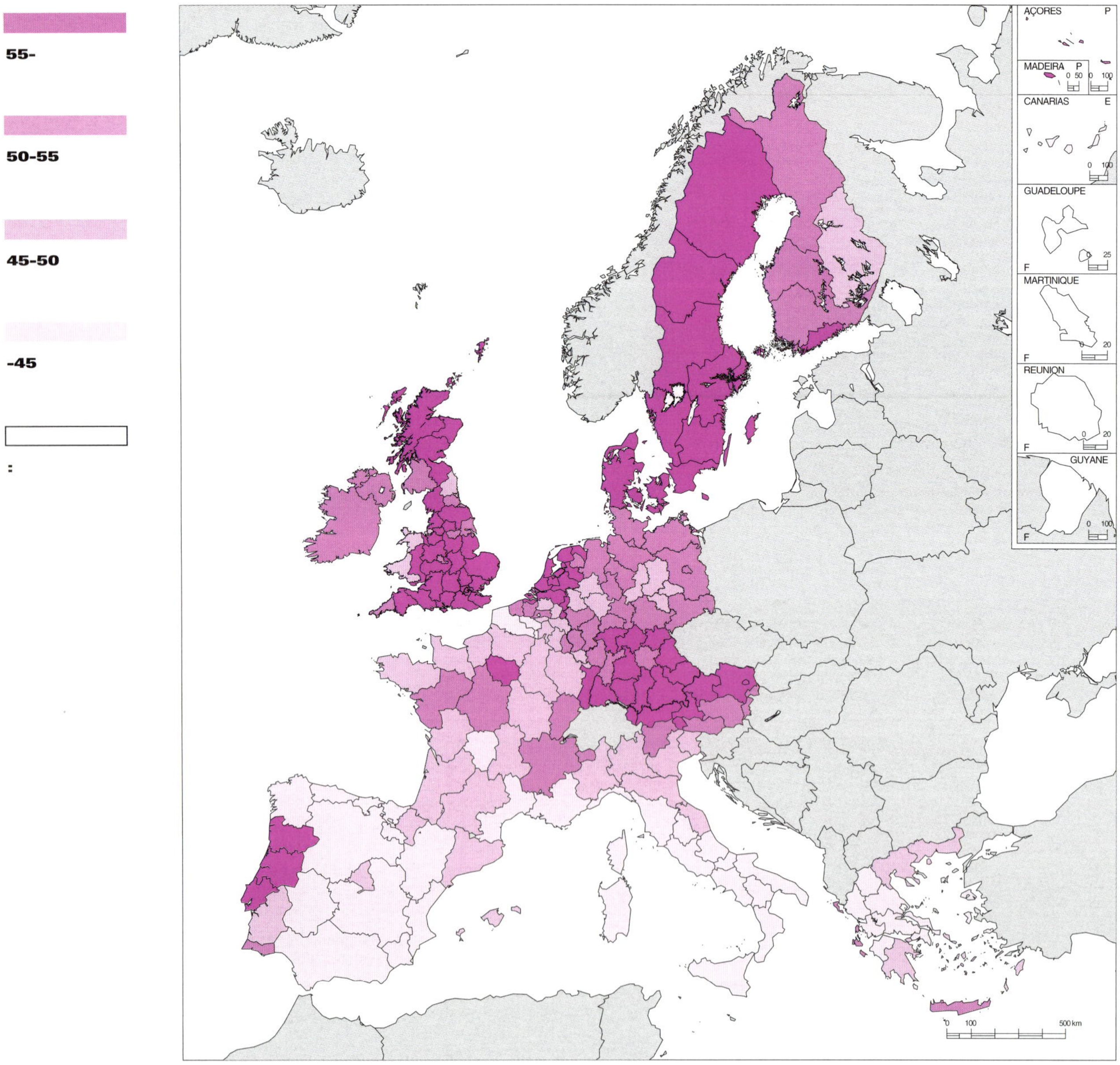

3

55-

50-55

45-50

-45

:

6E1AA

ACORES P

MADEIRA P 0 50 100

CANARIAS E 0 100

GUADELOUPE F 25

MARTINIQUE F 20

REUNION F 20

GUYANE F 0 100

0 100 500 km

NUTS 2. NUTS 1: DED (D Saxony), IRL.

eurostat

More data on this in Eurostat's database

REGIO is the domain of New Cronos relating to the main aspects of economic life in the European Union at regional level. Created in 1975, REGIO is subdivided into eight statistical domains: demography; economic accounts; unemployment; labour force sample survey; energy statistics; transport; agriculture and statistics concerning research and development. The regions are classified in line with a specific system called NUTS (nomenclature of territorial units for statistics).

➤ ➤ ➤ **DOMAIN REGIO IN DATABASE NEW CRONOS**

Unemployment rate. 1999

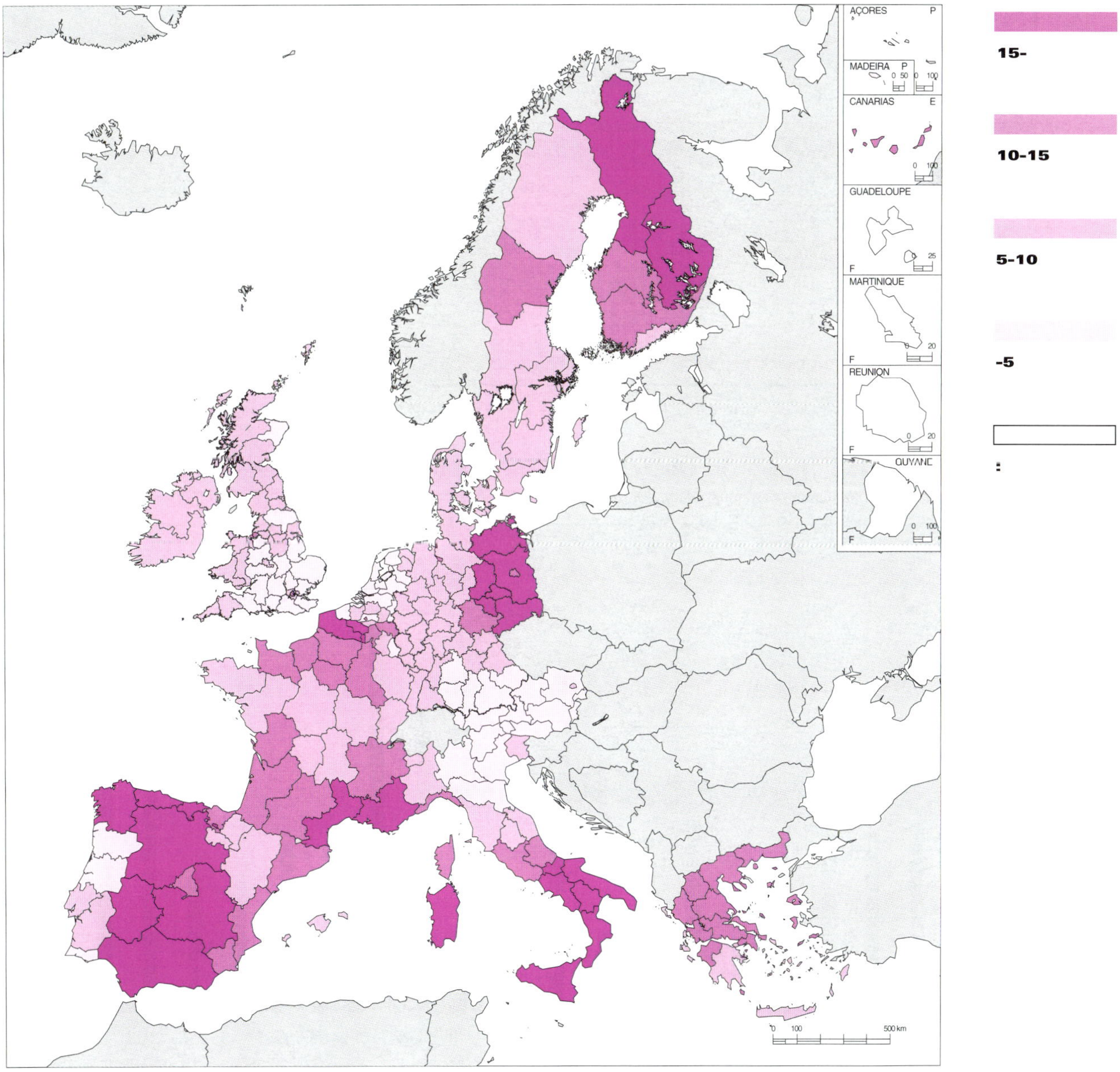

117DC

	15-
	10-15
	5-10
	-5

AÇORES P
MADEIRA P
CANARIAS E
GUADELOUPE F
MARTINIQUE F
REUNION F
GUYANE F

500 km

Further reading: Regions, statistical yearbook, 2000. Eurostat. Statistics in focus — Regions, 2000. Eurostat.

NUTS 2. NUTS 1: DED (D Saxony).

Research and development (R & D) — creative work undertaken on a systematic basis to increase the stock of knowledge, including that of people, culture and society; and the use of this to devise new applications — is an engine of growth.

EU R & D expenditure as a share of GDP has been decreasing in the 1990s, whilst USA and Japan have a much higher R & D intensity. However, Nordic countries show comparable R & D intensity such as those of the United States and Japan.

Research and development expenditure, as % of GDP, all sectors

	1989	1990	1991	1992	1993	1994	1995	1996	1997	1998	1999	
EU-15	2,02 *	2,02 *	1,98 *	1,96 *	1,98 *	1,95 *	1,90 *	1,89 *	1,86 *	1,86 *	1,85 *	EU-15
EUR-11	1,98 *	1,98 *	1,95 *	1,92 *	1,95 *	1,90 *	1,86 *	1,84 *	1,82 *	1,82 *	1,81 *	EUR-11
B	1,67 |	:	1,64	:	1,79 *	1,78 *	1,74 *	1,82 *	1,84 *	:	:	B
DK	1,56	1,63 *	1,70	1,74 *	1,80	:	1,84	1,85 *	1,94	1,93 *	1,99 *	DK
D	2,84	2,67 |	2,57 |	2,45 |	2,40	2,31 |	2,26 |	2,26 *	2,29	2,29 *	:	D
EL	0,38 |	:	0,37	:	0,48	:	0,49	:	0,51	:	:	EL
E	0,73	0,83	0,85 |	0,89 |	0,89	0,82	0,81	0,83 *	0,82	0,90	0,90 *	E
F	2,33	2,42	2,41 |	2,43 |	2,47	2,39	2,31	2,30	2,21	2,19 *	:	F
IRL	0,81	0,86	0,97	1,01	1,18 *	1,31 *	1,37 *	1,42	1,40	:	:	IRL
I	1,25	1,30 |	1,24 |	1,20	1,14	1,07	1,00	1,01	0,99	1,02 *	1,04 *	I
L	:	:	:	:	:	:	:	:	:	:	:	L
NL	2,12	2,16 |	2,05	1,99	2,01 |	2,05	1,99	2,03	2,04	:	:	NL
A	1,37	1,41 *	1,49 *	1,47 *	1,49	1,56 *	1,55 *	1,60 *	1,68 *	1,80 *	1,82 *	A
P	:	0,53	:	0,63	:	:	0,57	:	0,63	:	:	P
FIN	1,83	1,91	2,07	2,18	2,23	2,34	2,29	2,54	2,72	2,89	3,09 *	FIN
S	2,93	:	2,87	:	3,19	:	3,47	:	3,70	3,77 *	3,71 *	S
UK	2,21	2,21	2,12	2,11	2,15	2,10	1,98	1,93	1,84	1,82	:	UK
IS	1,02	0,99	1,16	1,34	1,34	1,39	1,54	1,51 *	1,87	2,02 *	1,82 *	IS
NO	1,69	:	1,65	:	1,73	:	1,71	:	1,66	:	:	NO
EEA	2,02 *	2,01 *	1,97 *	1,96 *	1,98 *	1,94 *	1,89 *	1,88 *	1,86 *	1,86 *	1,85 *	EEA
US	2,73	2,78	2,81	2,74 |	2,62	2,52	2,61	2,66	2,71	2,74 *	2,84 *	US
CA	:	:	:	:	:	:	:	:	:	:	:	CA
JP	2,77	2,85	2,82	2,76	2,68	2,63	2,77 |	2,80	2,89	3,03	:	JP

Further reading: Statistics on science and technology in Europe. 2000. Eurostat.

F: overseas departments: business enterprise sector not surveyed. D, I, NO: data do not exist for private non-profit sector. FIN: data do not exist for private non-profit sector after 1995. US, JP: *Source:* OECD.

Research and development expenditure by sectors of economy as % of the GDP. 1999

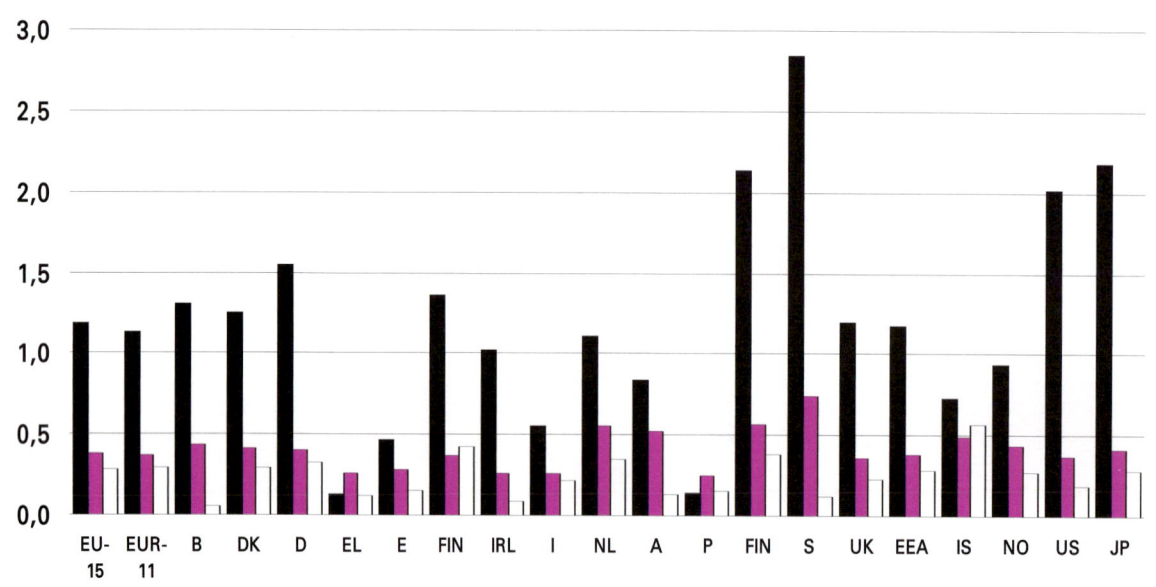

Black: business enterprise sector; colour: higher education sector; white: government sector.

Further reading: Statistics on science and technology in Europe, Panorama, 2000. Eurostat.

D, F, S, UK, JP: 1998 data, B, EL, IRL, NL, P, NO: 1997 data, A: 1993 data. EU-15, EUR-11, DK, D, E, I, FIN, EEA are estimates. JP, US: *Source:* OECD.

611AB

611CC

Among R & D input statistics, R & D expenditure is one of the 'first priority indicators' necessary to give a representation of the effort devoted to R & D. The basic measure is 'intramural expenditures', i.e. all expenditures for R & D performed within a statistical unit or sector of the economy, whatever the source of funds. Top leading R & D regions are mainly located in Germany where R & D expenditure can be over 4 % of their GDP.

611AI

Total research and development expenditure as % of GDP. 1997

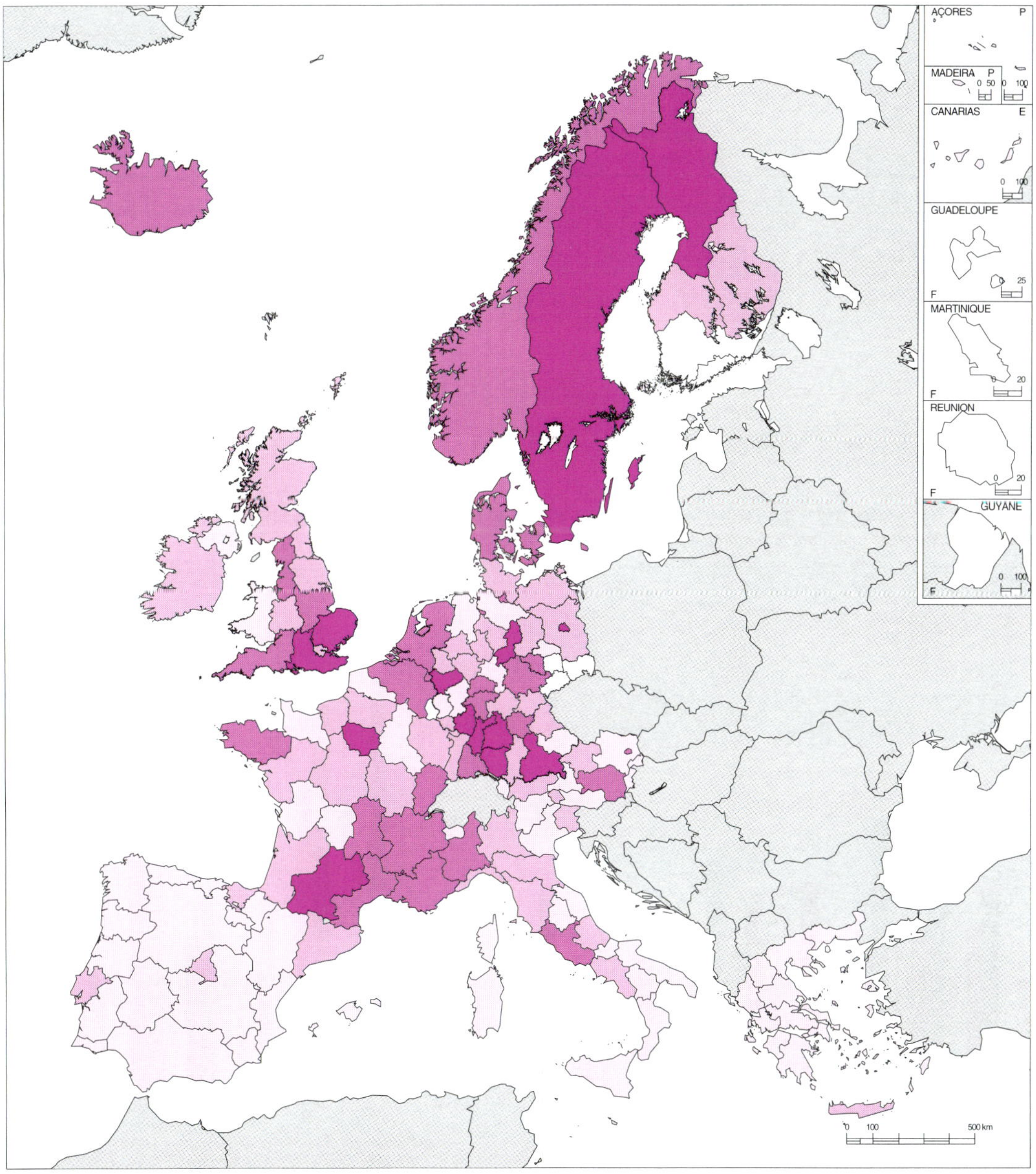

 AÇORES P

MADEIRA P 0 50 0 100

CANARIAS E

0 100

GUADELOUPE

F 0 25

MARTINIQUE

F 0 20

REUNION

F 0 20

GUYANE

F 0 100

2-

1,5-2

0,75-1,5

-0-0,75

:

3

0 100 500 km

Further reading: Statistics on science and technology in Europe, Panorama, 2000. Eurostat.

NUTS 2. B, NL: NUTS 0. IRL, S, UK, NO: NUTS 1. A: 1993. UK: 1995. I, NL: 1996.

Research and development personnel head count as percentage of the labour force all sectors

	1989	1990	1991	1992	1993	1994	1995	1996	1997	1998	1999	
EU-15	1,23 *	1,27 *	1,24 *	1,25 *	1,25 *	1,26 *	1,26 *	1,26 *	1,25 *	1,27 *	1,28 *	**EU-15**
EUR-11	1,23 *	1,29 *	1,25 *	1,25 *	1,24 *	1,24 *	1,25 *	1,25 *	1,25 *	1,26 *	1,27 *	**EUR-11**
B	1,40 *	:	1,37 *	:	: |	1,20 *	1,22 *	:	:	:	:	**B**
DK	1,49	1,46 *	1,43	1,47 *	1,53	:	1,81	1,84 *	1,85	1,99 *	:	**DK**
D	1,88 *	: |	1,70 *	:	1,57 *	:	1,50 *	1,47 *	1,49 *	1,48 *	:	**D**
EL	0,46 *	:	0,56	:	0,75	:	0,87	:	1,02	:	:	**EL**
E	0,68	0,72	0,77	0,79	0,80	0,87 *	0,94	0,98 *	0,97	1,02 *	:	**E**
F	1,37	1,39	1,40 |	1,45	1,44	1,45	1,46	1,46	1,51	:	:	**F**
IRL	0,68 *	0,73 *	0,83 *	0,89 *	1,06 *	1,05 *	1,17 *	:	:	:	:	**IRL**
I	0,76	0,76	0,75	0,79	0,79	0,81	0,81	0,81	0,81 *	:	:	**I**
L	:	:	:	:	:	:	:	:	:	:	:	**L**
NL	1,34 *|	1,50 *	1,45 *	1,44 *	1,45 *|	1,48 *	1,44 *	1,45 *	1,44 *	:	:	**NL**
A	1,16 *	:	:	:	1,16 *	:	:	:	:	:	:	**A**
P	:	0,39	:	0,44 *	:	:	0,53	: |	0,61 *	:	:	**P**
FIN	1,50	:	1,80	:	1,69	1,71 *	1,97	:	2,23	2,43	:	**FIN**
S	1,62 *	:	1,56 *	:	1,84	:	2,18	:	2,34	2,35 *	2,36 *	**S**
UK	1,28 *	1,25 *	1,20 *	1,24 *	1,28 *	:	:	:	:	:	:	**UK**
IS	:	:	:	:	:	:	:	1,80 *	2,47	2,50	2,56	**IS**
NO	1,48	: |	1,47 *	:	1,59	:	1,87	:	1,91	:	:	**NO**
EEA	1,24 *	1,27 *	1,24 *	1,25 *	1,26 *	1,27 *	1,26 *	1,26 *	1,26 *	1,28 *	1,29 *	**EEA**
JP	:	:	:	:	:	:	: |	:	:	:	:	**JP**

Further reading: Statistics on science and technology in Europe, Panorama, 2000. Eurostat.

6I1AC

3

Research and development personnel head count, by sectors of economy as % of the labour force. 1998

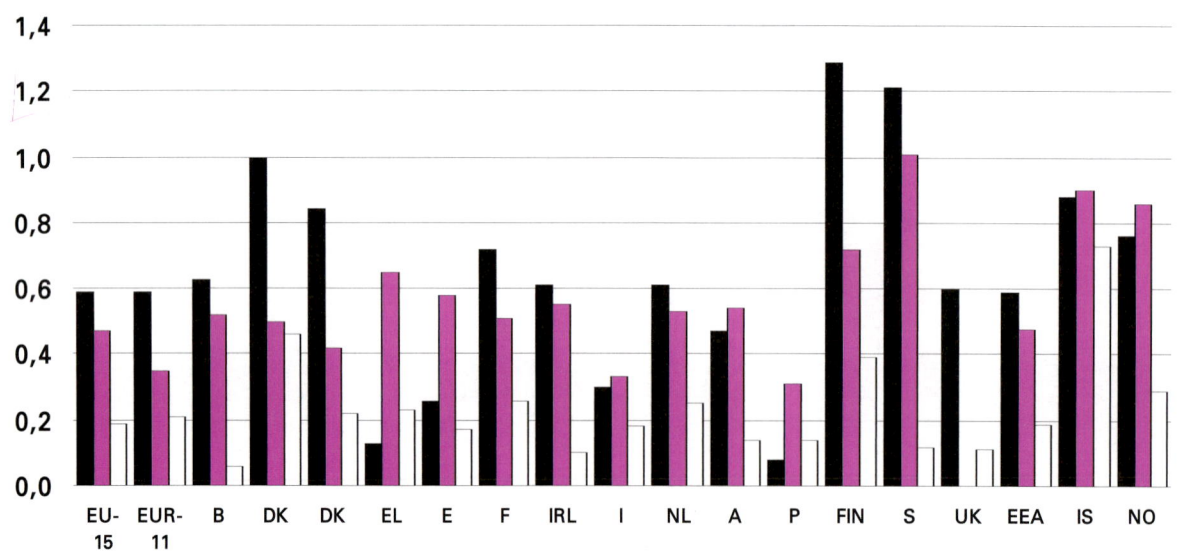

Black: business enterprise sector; colour: higher education sector; white: government sector.

Further reading: Statistics on science and technology in Europe, Panorama, 2000. Eurostat.

D, EL, F, I, NL,P,S,NO: 1997 data. B, IRL: 1995 data. A, UK (higher education sector): 1993 data. EU-15, EUR-11, EEA: data are estimates.

8A1AB

Another main R & D input indicator, also available for most countries down to the NUTS 2 regional level and measured on an annual basis, is R & D personnel. These data on scientific and technical personnel, together with R & D expenditure, provide for useful international comparisons of resources devoted to R & D. For statistical purposes, indicators on R & D personnel are compiled both in terms of physical persons (head count) and in full-time equivalent (FTE) or person–years.

Total research and development personnel head count by country, as % of the labour force. 1997

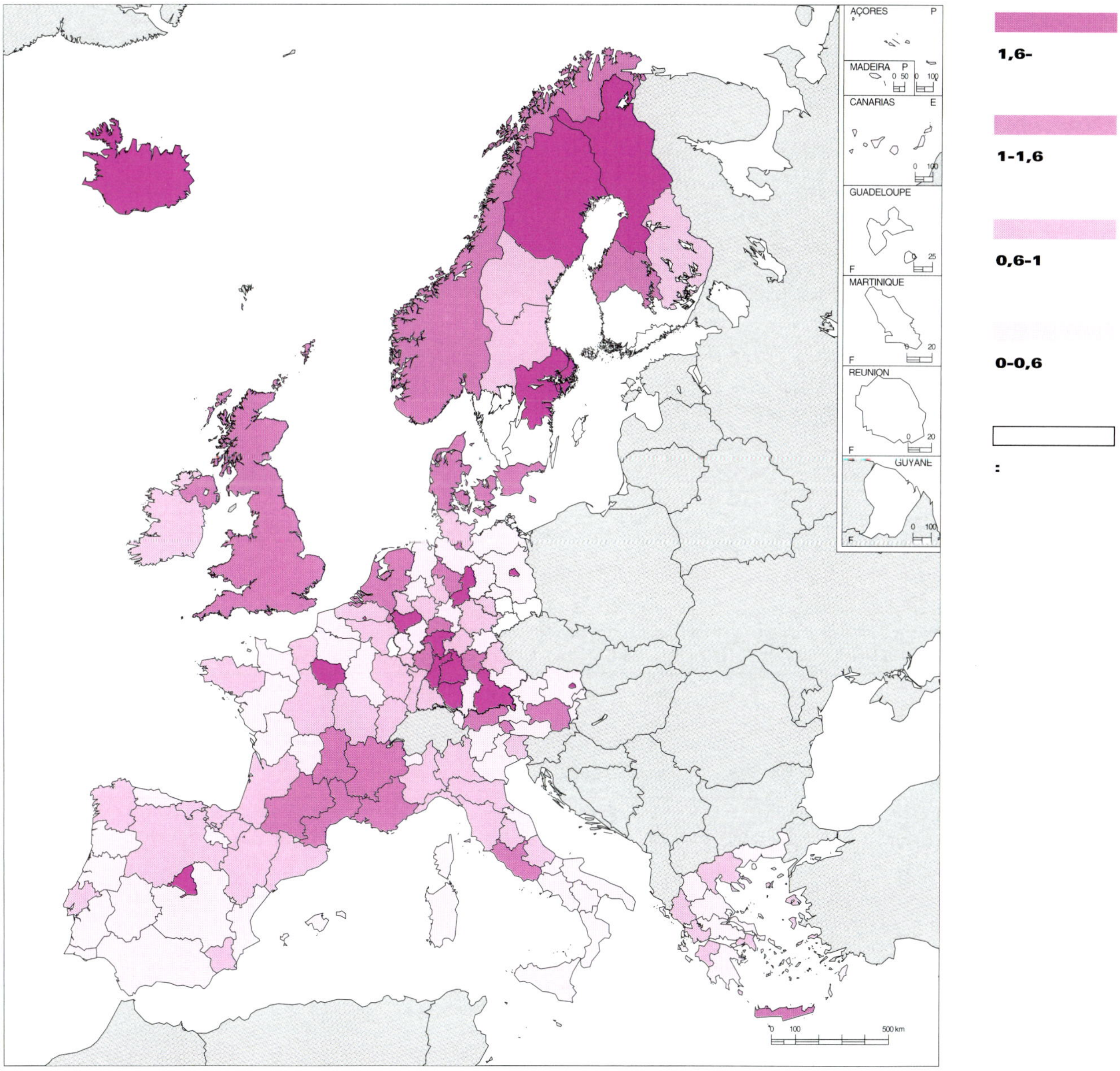

611AX

1,6-

1-1,6

0,6-1

0-0,6

:

Further reading: Statistics on science and technology in Europe, Panorama, 2000. Eurostat.

NUTS 2. NL, UK: NUTS 0. B, IRL, NO: NUTS 1. A, UK: 1993.
B, IRL: 1995. I, NL: 1996. Labour force A: 1995.

Socioeconomic breakdown of government research and development appropriations in the EEA in 1998.% of the total

	EU-15	EUR-11	CEC	B	DK	D	EL	E	F	IRL
Earth/exploration/exploitation	1,4 *	1,4 *	2,1	0,7	1,2	1,8	4,3	1,9	0,9 *	0,5
General planning of land-use	1,6 *	1,4 *	5,3	1,0	1,4	1,7	3,8	0,6	0,7 *	2,9
Environment: control/care	2,9 *	3,0 *	6,0	1,9	3,7	3,5	3,3	2,6	2,3 *	1,7
Human health: protection	5,9 *	4,4 *	7,8	1,6	1,8	3,2	4,9	4,6	5,7 *	3,1
Energy: production/utilisation	3,5 *	4,1 *	11,0	2,8	2,0	3,7	1,8	3,5	5,3 *	0,1
Agricultural production	3,6 *	3,4 *	6,1	3,3	8,4	2,7	8,8	4,1	4,0 *	20,7
Industrial production/technology	9,2 *	10,9 *	38,0	22,6	10,0	12,5	8,1	15,2	5,9 *	29,5
Social structures and relationships	2,7 *	2,4 *	2,6	4,4	9,4	2,6	3,9	0,6	1,2 *	6,5
Space: exploration/exploitation	6,0 *	6,9 *	2,1	12,8	2,6	4,7	1,0	5,3	11,3 *	:
General university funds	32,3 *	33,3 *	:	19,9	58,8	38,8	51,8	24,6	17,6 *	24,1
Non-oriented research	14,7 *	15,7 *	8,8	23,4	:	15,8	7,0	7,0	21,1 *	11,0
Other civil research	1,0 *	1,1 *	10,3	5,0	:	0,3	0,3	1,2	1,8 *	:
Defence	15,2 *	11,9 *	:	0,5	0,6	8,8	1,3	29,0	22,4 *	:
Total	100,0 *	100,0 *	100,0	100,0	100,0	100,0	100,0	100,0	100,0 *	100,0

Further reading: Statistics on science and technology in Europe, Panorama, 2000. Eurostat.

3

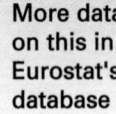

More data on this in Eurostat's database

These figures cover both initial and final budgets for the 15 EU countries plus Norway and Iceland. The data breakdown is by NABS.

➤ ➤ ➤ **DOMAIN ZRD 1 IN DATABASE NEW CRONOS**

Socio-economic breakdown of government research and development appropriations in the EEA in 1998.% of the total

	I	NL	A	P	FIN	S	UK	EEA	NO
Earth/exploration/exploitation	1,6	0,9	1,8	2,7	1,3	1,2 *	1,4	1,5 *	2,3
General planning of land-use	0,6	4,2	2,0	2,8	2,9	5,9 *	1,8	1,6 *	2,3
Environment: control/care	3,4	4,1	2,2	4,3	2,2	0,9 *	2,5	2,9 *	3,0
Human health: protection	5,6	3,7	2,6	5,2	7,6	0,9 *	15,0	5,9 *	6,8
Energy: production/utilisation	5,0	2,5	0,6	1,4	6,4	4,3 *	0,5	3,5 *	2,4
Agricultural production	1,9	2,9	3,2	12,9	6,3	1,8 *	4,5	3,7 *	8,7
Industrial production/technology	8,1	13,1	5,8	15,1	26,8	5,0 *	1,1	9,3 *	13,0
Social structures and relationships	3,6	2,7	2,2	4,2	5,5	6,9 *	2,7	2,9 *	6,9
Space: exploration/exploitation	8,3	3,3	0,0	0,3	1,9	2,4 *	2,5	5,9 *	2,7
General university funds	48,0	44,0	65,8	38,5	25,9	50,1 *	19,0	32,4 *	38,9
Non-oriented research	11,1	11,1	13,8	7,3	11,9	13,2 *	11,9	14,5 *	7,7
Other civil research	:	4,1	0,2	4,2	:	:	0,5	1,0 *	:
Defence	2,7	3,4	0,0	1,3	1,4	7,3 *	36,8	15,0 *	5,5
Total	100,0	100,0	100,0	100,0	100,0	100,0 *	100,0	100,0 *	100,0

Further reading: Statistics on science and technology in Europe, Panorama, 2000. Eurostat.   EEA: Iceland and Liechtenstein are not included.

Government budget appropriations or outlays for research and development (GBAORD is the amount governments allocate towards R & D activities. Comparisons of GBAORD across countries give an impression of the relative importance attached to State-funded R & D.

GBAORD statistics complement the *ex post* figures on 'government financed' gross expenditure on research and development (GERD) and, when broken down by socio economic objective, underline the domains governments believe to be important for current and future policy action.

Government research and development appropriations as % of GDP

	1989	1990	1991	1992	1993	1994	1995	1996	1997	1998	1999	
EU-15	0,94	0,93	0,93	0,92	0,90	0,85	0,83 *	0,81 *	0,79 *	0,75 *	:	EU-15
EUR-11	0,95	0,94	0,94	0,93	0,91	0,86	0,84 *	0,82 *	0,80 *	0,77 *	:	EUR-11
B	0,55	0,52	0,53	0,51	0,54	0,53	0,53	0,55	0,57	0,58	:	B
DK	0,80	0,76	0,75	0,70	0,66	0,68	0,73	0,74 *	0,75	0,76	:	DK
D	1,06	1,04	1,03	1,01	0,99	0,93	0,92	0,91	0,86	0,83	:	D
EL	0,26	0,23	0,21	0,19	0,20	0,21	0,29	0,30	0,31	0,29	:	EL
E	0,50	0,54	0,53	0,51	0,49	0,48	0,49	0,48	0,51	0,58	:	E
F	1,37	1,39	1,38	1,30	1,27	1,22	1,14	1,10	1,05	0,97 *	:	F
IRL	0,31	0,29	0,31	0,32	0,33	0,29	0,34	0,34	0,30	0,28	:	IRL
I	0,73	0,74	0,75	0,80	0,69	0,63	0,62 *	0,59	0,62	0,58	:	I
L	:	:	:	:	:	:	:	:	:	:	:	L
NL	0,91	0,92	0,86	0,85	0,83	0,80	0,79	0,80	0,82	0,83	:	NL
A	0,58	0,55	0,62	0,63	0,67	0,71	0,68	0,64	0,62	0,63	:	A
P	0,29	0,37	0,40	0,49	0,50	0,47	0,46	0,52	0,53	0,56	:	P
FIN	0,77	0,82	0,97	1,05	1,09	1,03	1,01	0,97	1,13	1,11	:	FIN
S	1,18	1,21	1,27	1,28	1,30	1,21	1,19	1,16 *	:	0,85 *	:	S
UK	0,94	0,91	0,87	0,85	0,86	0,78	0,80	0,78	0,75	0,69	:	UK
IS	:	:	0,57	0,47	0,74	0,78	0,83	0,78	0,70	:	:	IS
NO	0,83	0,86	0,87	0,95	0,92	0,87	0,81	0,78	0,76	0,79	:	NO
EEA	0,94	0,93	0,93	0,92	0,90	0,85	0,83 *	0,81 *	0,79 *	0,76 *	:	EEA
US	1,18	1,15	1,15	1,13	1,10	1,02	0,98	0,93	0,91	0,89	0,86 *	US
JP	0,45	0,45	0,44	0,45	0,48	0,49	0,52	0,56	0,59	0,61	0,63	JP

6I1AE

Further reading: Statistics on science and technology in Europe, Panorama, 2000. Eurostat.

Total government research and development appropriations (GBAORD) as % of GDP: comparison of EEA with Japan and the United States of America

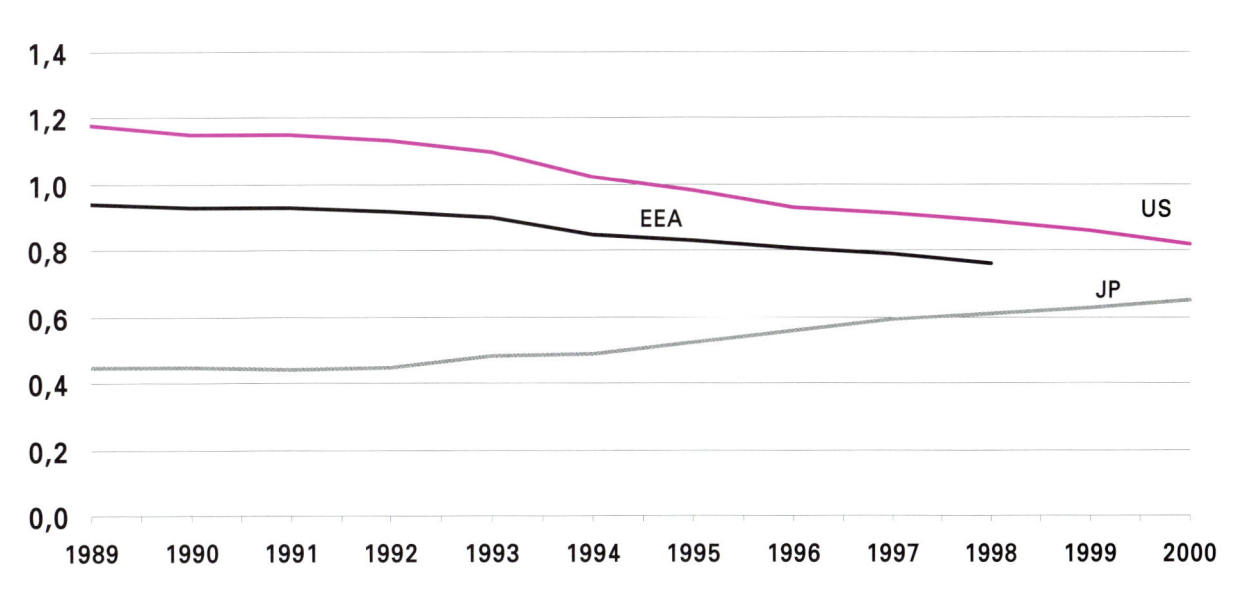

6I1AA

Further reading: Statistics on science and technology in Europe, Panorama, 2000. Eurostat.

EEA: Luxembourg and Liechtenstein not included. IS: not included before 1990. JP, US: *Source:* OECD. 2000: data are provisional. 1999 data for US, EEA are provisional.

Patents are often linked to R & D and are considered as indicators of R & D output, especially for application-oriented R & D. Patents give an indication of the structure and evolution of innovative activities in countries, regions, or industries. Although not all applications are granted, each one still represents technical effort by the inventor and so is regarded as an appropriate indicator of innovative potential. Patent data published here refer to applications filed under the European Patent Convention or under the Patent Convention Treaty and registered by the European Patent Office. For example, for R & D intensity, German regions have the highest patenting activities when measured relative to their labour force. Some regions from France, the United Kingdom and Sweden are present in the top 15 leading regions.

European patent applications per million labour force. 1999

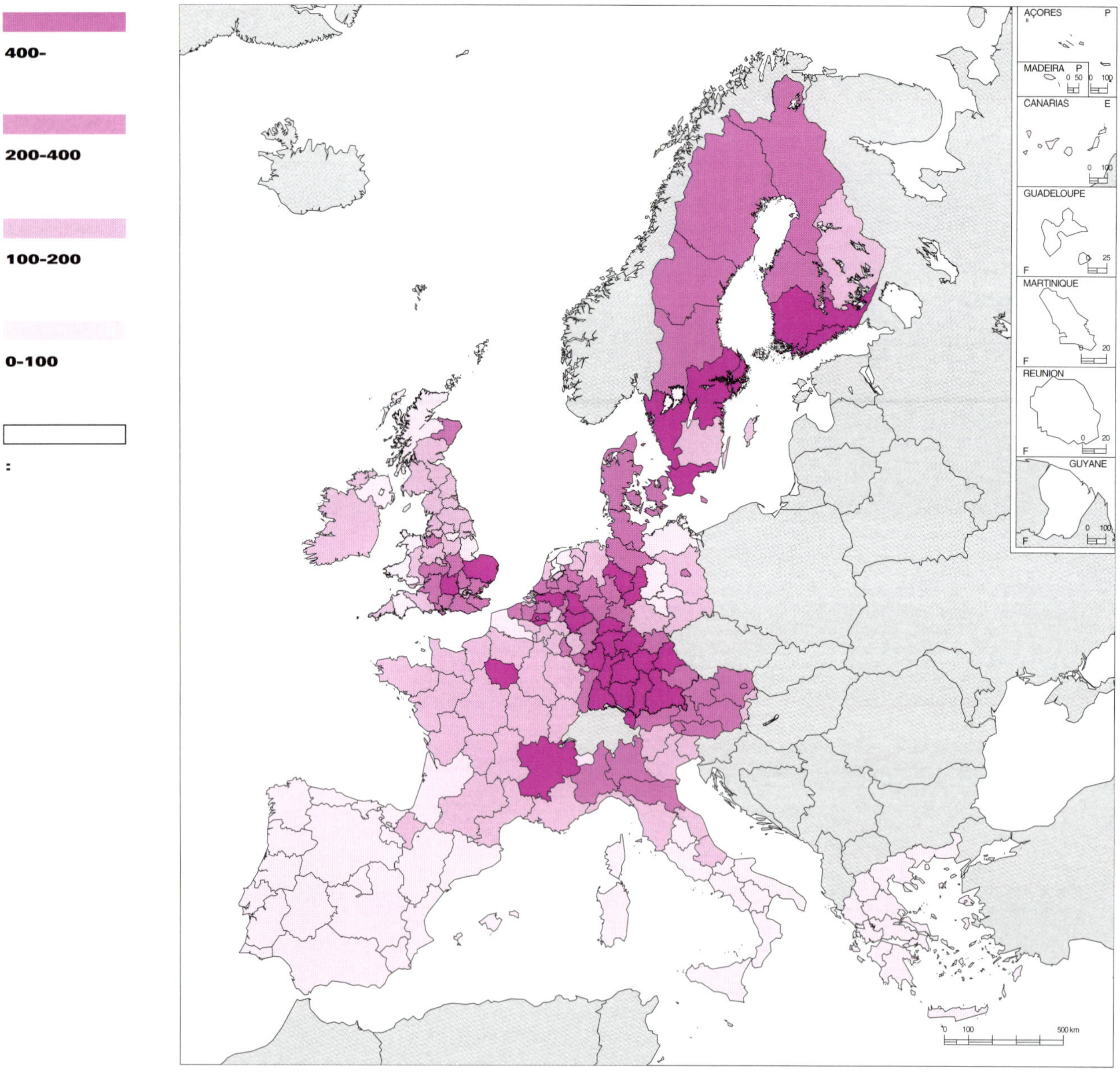

400-

200-400

100-200

0-100

:

8A1AE

Further reading: Statistics on science and technology in Europe, Panorama, 2000. Eurostat.   NUTS 2. NUTS 1: DED (D Saxony), IRL. 1999 data are provisional.

Total European patent applications per country

	1989	1990	1991	1992	1993	1994	1995	1996	1997	1998	1999	
EU-15	29 898	32 310	29 142	30 730	31 733	32 117	34 447	36 469	40 664	48 671	44 767 *	EU-15
EUR-11	23 808	25 898	23 054	24 667	25 457	25 556	27 409	28 984	32 184	39 173	36 374 *	EUR-11
B	606	698	612	747	887	910	952	956	1 144	1 427	1 196 *	B
DK	405	424	463	472	536	591	626	683	761	740	716 *	DK
D	12 964	13 715	11 549	12 421	13 331	12 954	14 075	14 848	16 101 *	20 317	19 521 *	D
EL	22	29	34	44	45	35	43	48	55	75	66 *	EL
E	224	281	332	356	376	462	476	511	657	828	696 *	E
F	5 019	5 501	5 252	5 464	5 159	5 260	5 585	5 773	6 417	7 325	6 665 *	F
IRL	50	78	68	88	111	93	133	142	159	204	210 *	IRL
I	2 130	2 518	2 275	2 626	2 448	2 539	2 635	2 904	3 266	3 707	3 347 *	I
L	33	33	40	35	24	42	29	42	58	61	67 *	L
NL	1 663	1 838	1 624	1 647	1 672	1 732	1 809	2 109	2 568	2 791	2 454 *	NL
A	714	728	707	724	705	755	807	793	898	1 149	988 *	A
P	10	5	9	13	16	22	16	15	27	24	30 *	P
FIN	396	503	585	547	729	789	893	891	890 *	1 339	1 202 *	FIN
S	1 118	1 233	1 211	1 239	1 325	1 451	1 761	1 926	2 339	2 716	2 096 *	S
UK	4 544	4 725	4 381	4 309	4 370	4 486	4 609	4 829	5 325	5 967	5 514 *	UK

8A1AC

Further reading: Statistics on science and technology in Europe, Panorama, 2000. Eurostat.

More data on this in Eurostat's database

The data concern European patent applications registered by the EPO (European Patent Office) and give an indication of the structure and evolution of innovative activities in a country or region.

➤ ➤ ➤ **DOMAIN PATENT IN DATABASE NEW CRONOS**

European patent applications per million labour force

	1989	1990	1991	1992	1993	1994	1995	1996	1997	1998	1999	
EU-15	194,0	206,5	175,6	186,6	193,7	195,6	209,3	218,0	241,7	286,7	261,1 *	EU-15
EUR-11	208,7	222,8	182,9	197,5	204,9	204,9	220,0	227,5	251,2	302,5	278,0 *	EUR-11
B	155,0	178,7	153,1	184,8	217,7	219,3	227,5	228,3	271,3	335,6	273,9 *	B
DK	141,5	146,2	159,8	162,7	186,6	214,1	223,8	242,6	269,1	262,2	250,9 *	DK
D	446,1	449,8	295,5	318,5	347,0	338,2	370,7	379,9	411,1 *	515,8	493,0 *	D
EL	5,6	7,2	8,6	11,0	11,0	8,4	10,2	11,1	13,0	16,7	14,8 *	EL
E	15,2	18,7	22,1	23,5	24,6	29,8	30,6	32,2	40,9	51,1	42,6 *	E
F	208,6	228,7	215,7	222,7	208,7	211,5	223,1	227,8	253,0	286,5	257,5 *	F
IRL	38,4	59,0	50,6	65,0	81,1	66,1	92,5	96,1	104,3	125,9	124,1 *	IRL
I	91,0	107,0	95,0	115,3	108,1	112,4	116,6	127,5	142,9	160,0	143,4 *	I
L	212,4	205,4	243,7	208,9	143,4	243,3	176,1	243,7	334,4	346,6	369,7 *	L
NL	251,6	270,2	234,5	235,2	236,0	239,7	247,7	284,7	294,2	360,5	311,0 *	NL
A	206,7	206,1	196,0	196,9	188,7	194,5	210,1	207,7	221,0	299,4	256,0 *	A
P	2,0	1,1	1,7	2,8	3,3	4,7	3,4	3,2	5,0	4,8	5,9 *	P
FIN	153,4	195,3	228,6	216,3	290,6	315,3	367,6	364,5	357,1 *	533,4	455,0 *	FIN
S	249,9	272,6	268,7	279,7	306,7	339,9	391,4	436,8	458,3	626,8	477,6 *	S
UK	158,4	164,1	152,9	150,9	153,8	158,0	162,3	169,4	165,3	208,2	190,9 *	UK

8A1AD

Further reading: Statistics on science and technology in Europe, Panorama, 2000. Eurostat.

eurostat

This regional indicator based on the measure-ment of 'employment in high technology sectors' differs from traditional R & D personnel measurement. It includes the part of total employ-ment which is employed in sectors of the economy considered as R & D intensive (i.e. with a high level of R & D spending as a proportion of value added or GDP). The regional distribution of high tech-nology sectors (for both manufacturing and ser-vices) at NUTS 2 level is shown in map. Stuttgart, Karlsruhe and Rheinhessen-Pfalz are the three top 'high-tech' regions in Europe with more than 20 % of their employment working in high-tech sectors.

Employment in high technology sectors as a share of total employment. 1999

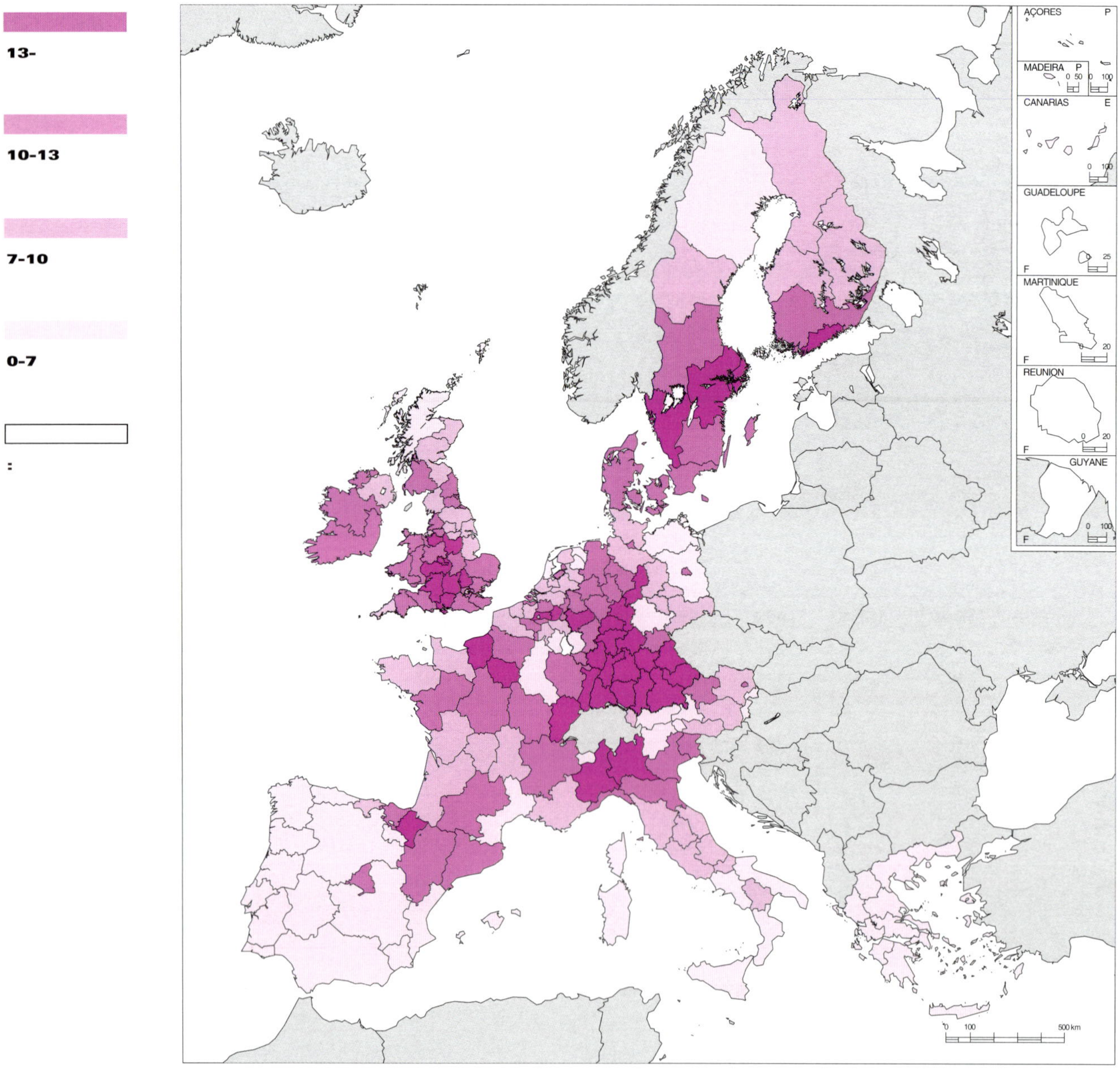

13-

10-13

7-10

0-7

:

8A1SP

Further reading: Statistics on science and technology in Europe, Panorama, 2000. Eurostat.   NUTS 2. NUTS 1: DED (D Saxony). EL: 1998.

The second Community Innovation Survey (CIS2) gives information on technological innovation in the business enterprise sector. Technological innovations comprise implemented new or significantly improved products and processes. It requires an objective improvement in the performance of a product or in the way in which it is produced or delivered. An innovation has been implemented, if it has been introduced on the market (product innovation) or used within a production process (process innovation). The product or process should be new to the enterprise, but does not necessarily have to be new to the enterprise's market.

Innovating enterprises and novel innovators, manufacturing sector. 1996

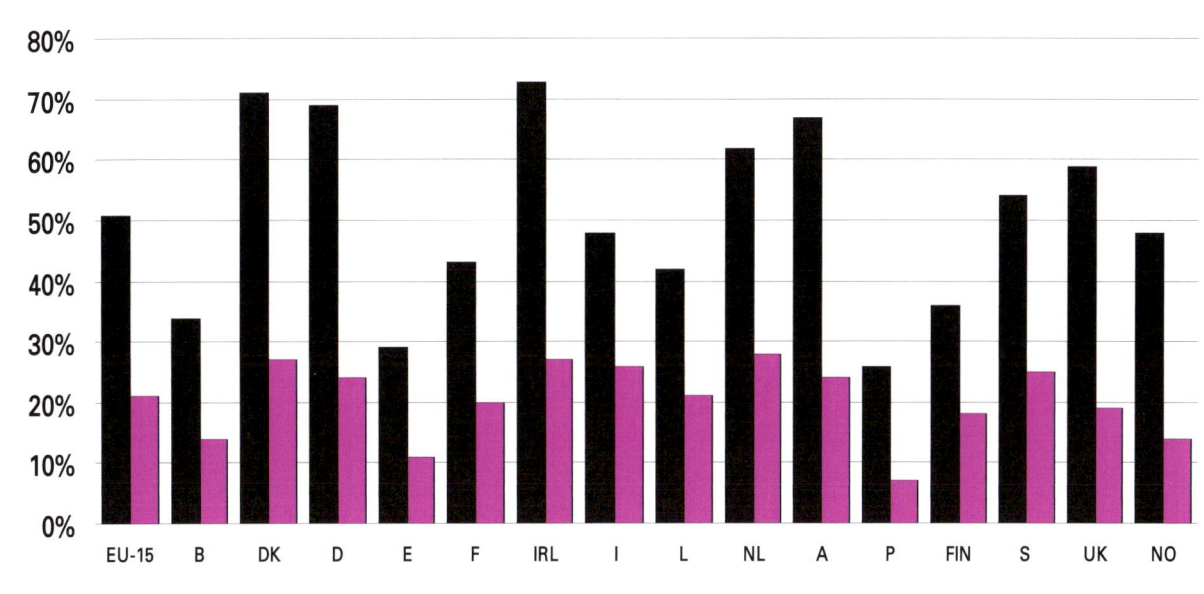

Black: innovating enterprises; colour: novel innovators.

Further reading: Statistics on innovation in Europe, Panorama, 2000. Eurostat.   P, NO: 1997. EU-15 without EL; EEA except EL, IS and LI.

Distribution of turnover in manufacturing sector, EEA. 1996

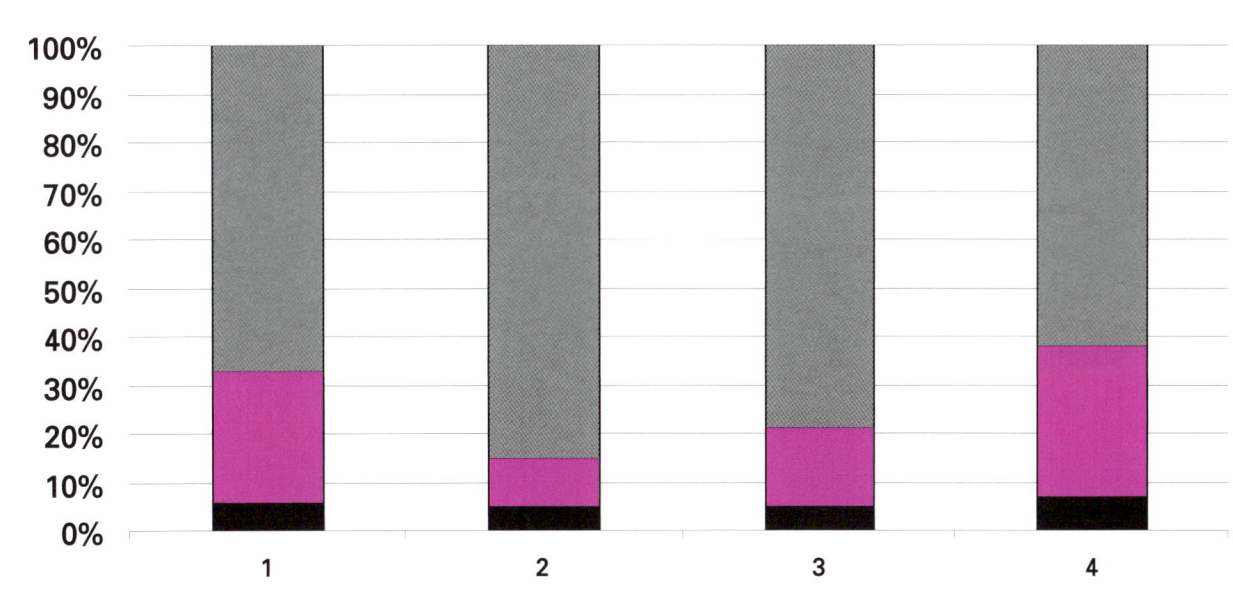

Black: products new to the market. Colour: Products new to the firm only. Grey: Unchanged products. 1. All enterprises. 2. Small. 3. Medium-sized. 4. Large.

Further reading: Statistics on innovation in Europe, Panorama, 2000. Eurostat.   (Products new to the market) without EL, L, IS and LI.

Need more data on this topic? Ask your Data Shop

An innovating enterprise is an enterprise that has introduced new or improved products on the market or new or improved processes. Enterprises can have innovation activity without introducing an innovation on the market (it may either have unsuccessful projects or not yet completed projects to develop or introduce). Novel innovators are innovating enterprises having introduced new or improved products also for the market.

Innovating enterprises as percentage of all enterprises. 1996

	EU-15	B	DK	D	EL	E	F	IRL	I	L
Total manufacturing	51	34	71	69	:	29	43	73	48	42
Small	44	33	64	63	:	21	34	68	44	21
Medium-sized	58	34	76	70	:	43	48	78	57	52
Large	79	51	91	85	:	76	75	85	73	85
15-16: Manuf. of food prod.; beverages, tobacco	50	27	73	68	:	22	45	65	59	15
17-19: Manuf. of textiles, leather	35	28	55	62	:	18	30	58	32	:
20-22: Manuf. of wood, pulp, paper, publishing	45	30	70	59	:	21	32	68	45	43
23-24: Manuf. of coke, chemicals	70	46	93	75	:	62	68	79	61	53
25-26: Manuf. of rubber, plastic, other non-metallic minerals	51	34	63	67	:	31	49	79	44	51
27-28: Manuf. of basic metals and fabricated prod.	48	39	58	59	:	25	31	68	54	44
29: Manuf. of machinery and equipment n.e.c.	68	44	80	84	:	46	63	89	61	70
30-33: Manuf. of electrical and optical equipment	69	51	88	78	:	55	61	88	56	50
34-35: Manuf. of transport equipment	57	41	85	72	:	46	49	88	47	-
36-37: Manufacturing n.e.c.	48	25	60	69	:	23	38	71	53	:
Total services	40	13	30	46	:	:	31	58	:	48
Small	37	11	24	41	:	:	25	60	:	45
Medium-sized	49	21	45	60	:	:	33	49	:	55
Large	73	55	71	83	:	:	73	87	:	83
51: Wholesale trade and commission trade	34	10	27	39	:	:	:	52	:	37
60-62: Transport	24	9	13	26	:	:	11	33	:	57
64.2: Telecommunications	65	27	100	100	:	:	52	86	:	:
65-67: Financial intermediation	54	13	48	69	:	:	45	67	:	43
72: Computer and related activities	68	41	89	71	:	:	52	73	:	88
74.2: Engineering services	55	43	36	61	:	:	39	78	:	76
40-41: Water, gas and electricity	36	58	48	38	:	37	24	:	36	:

Further reading: Statistics on innovation in Europe, Panorama, 2000. Eurostat. EU-15 without EL for manufacturing; without EL, E and I for services.

6R2LA

New and improved products as percentage of total turnover. 1996

	EU-15	B	DK	D	EL	E	F	IRL	I	L
Total manufacturing	33	14	21	45	:	27	21	32	27	:
Small	15	11	18	30	:	9	8	21	15	:
Medium-sized	21	12	18	31	:	16	14	26	20	:
Large	38	16	22	48	:	37	25	43	38	:
15-16: Manuf. of food prod.; beverages, tobacco	17	10	7	25	:	15	8	10	19	:
17-19: Manuf. of textiles, leather	18	18	7	32	:	14	11	34	16	:
20-22: Manuf. of wood, pulp, paper, publishing	15	7	13	16	:	13	12	20	16	:
23-24: Manuf. of coke, chemicals	27	15	20	34	:	29	20	22	44	:
25-26: Manuf. of rubber, plastic, other non-metallic minerals	27	13	13	41	:	20	20	28	19	:
27-28: Manuf. of basic metals and fabricated prod.	16	10	18	15	:	17	13	26	15	:
29: Manuf. of machinery and equipment n.e.c.	37	23	31	42	:	40	28	40	32	:
30-33: Manuf. of electrical and optical equipment	52	35	56	55	:	43	41	71	37	:
34-35: Manuf. of transport equipment	54	12	52	69	:	49	29	20	43	:
36-37: Manufacturing n.e.c.	29	7	33	46	:	21	23	27	24	:

Further reading: Statistics on innovation in Europe, Panorama, 2000. Eurostat. EU-15 without EL and L.

6R3LA

 eurostat

3

The main indicators, in addition to the number of innovating enterprises and novel innovators, are the sale of new and improved products (both sfor the firm and for the market) and innovation expenditure. These indicators are presented as a percentage of the total turnover.

Innovating enterprises as percentage of all enterprises. 1996

NL	A	P	FIN	S	UK	EEA	IS	NO	
62	67	26	36	54	59	51	:	48	Total manufacturing
54	59	22	26	43	54	44	:	39	Small
71	73	30	40	61	59	58	:	56	Medium-sized
84	88	52	77	79	81	79	:	77	Large
58	67	25	25	38	58	50	:	47	15-16: Manuf. of food prod.; beverages, tobacco
49	55	19	37	45	56	35	:	45	17-19: Manuf. of textiles, leather
53	62	23	30	45	51	45	:	36	20-22: Manuf. of wood, pulp, paper, publishing
85	71	77	61	61	81	70	:	76	23-24: Manuf. of coke, chemicals
67	45	36	44	57	53	51	:	54	25-26: Manuf. of rubber, plastic, other non-metallic minerals
53	68	19	31	41	56	48	:	43	27-28: Manuf. of basic metals and fabricated prod.
80	80	36	41	73	63	68	:	64	29: Manuf. of machinery and equipment n.e.c.
74	87	80	51	75	76	69	:	65	30-33: Manuf. of electrical and optical equipment
60	78	19	36	58	63	56	:	44	34-35: Manuf. of transport equipment
57	82	17	22	59	44	48	:	51	36-37: Manufacturing n.e.c.
36	55	28	24	32	40	40	:	22	Total services
32	54	28	22	29	40	36	:	20	Small
45	58	27	30	48	37	48	:	26	Medium-sized
71	74	52	43	45	55	73	:	50	Large
36	58	26	15	29	33	34	:	18	51: Wholesale trade and commission trade
21	54	28	16	19	34	24	:	5	60-62: Transport
74	81	45	79	51	60	65	:	56	64.2: Telecommunications
40	55	43	28	56	49	54	:	44	65-67: Financial intermediation
68	69	53	63	55	81	68	:	50	72: Computer and related activities
52	20	30	31	47	38	55	:	38	74.2: Engineering services
58	22	36	19	23	64	35	:	24	40-41: Water, gas and electricity

Further reading: Statistics on innovation in Europe, Panorama, 2000. Eurostat.

P, NO: 1997. EEA without EL, IS and LI for manufacturing; without EL, E, I, IS and LI for services.

New and improved products as percentage of total turnover. 1996

NL	A	P	FIN	S	UK	EEA	IS	NO	
25	31	14	25	31	23	32	:	20	Total manufacturing
15	29	4	6	11	14	15	:	9	Small
20	20	9	13	22	21	21	:	16	Medium-sized
28	37	20	28	34	25	38	:	26	Large
20	24	4	11	16	16	17	:	14	15-16: Manuf. of food prod.; beverages, tobacco
16	19	7	9	16	18	18	:	15	17-19: Manuf. of textiles, leather
15	26	12	10	16	18	15	:	6	20-22: Manuf. of wood, pulp, paper, publishing
31	22	5	19	19	20	27	:	30	23-24: Manuf. of coke, chemicals
23	27	6	19	19	17	27	:	11	25-26: Manuf. of rubber, plastic, other non-metallic minerals
14	28	6	12	19	22	16	:	23	27-28: Manuf. of basic metals and fabricated prod.
32	34	30	42	38	26	36	:	32	29: Manuf. of machinery and equipment n.e.c.
46	57	29	64	65	55	52	:	42	30-33: Manuf. of electrical and optical equipment
30	43	51	31	40	19	54	:	24	34-35: Manuf. of transport equipment
22	33	7	13	17	19	29	:	11	36-37: Manufacturing n.e.c.

Further reading: Statistics on innovation in Europe, Panorama, 2000. Eurostat.

P, NO: 1997. EEA without El, L, IS and LI.

Innovation expenditure as percentage of total turnover. 1996

	EU-15	B	DK	D	EL	E	F	IRL	I	L
Total manufacturing	3,7	2,1	4,8	4,1	:	1,8	3,9	3,3	2,6	:
Small	2,5	2,1	10,4	3,3	:	1,0	1,4	2,8	2,4	:
Medium-sized	2,3	1,4	3,5	2,4	:	1,6	2,2	3,2	2,2	:
Large	4,2	2,3	4,5	4,4	:	2,2	4,9	3,7	3,1	:
15-16: Manuf. of food prod.; beverages, tobacco	1,6	0,7	1,9	2,1	:	0,9	0,9	1,1	1,9	:
17-19: Manuf. of textiles, leather	1,6	0,6	3,0	1,7	:	1,0	1,2	3,2	1,3	:
20-22: Manuf. of wood, pulp, paper, publishing	2,5	3,8	3,0	1,7	:	1,4	0,9	2,2	1,9	:
23-24: Manuf. of coke, chemicals	4,0	2,5	9,3	7,4	:	1,8	3,4	5,3	2,5	:
25-26: Manuf. of rubber, plastic, other non-metallic minerals	2,7	2,6	8,1	2,5	:	1,5	2,9	2,9	2,4	:
27-28: Manuf. of basic metals and fabricated prod.	2,1	2,8	2,4	2,2	:	1,4	1,6	4,6	2,1	:
29: Manuf. of machinery and equipment n.e.c.	3,7	1,9	6,0	3,9	:	2,0	3,7	3,8	2,6	:
30-33: Manuf. of electrical and optical equipment	8,2	7,1	13,2	7,6	:	3,8	11,7	5,0	5,4	:
34-35: Manuf. of transport equipment	4,3	1,1	6,7	4,0	:	2,9	6,7	5,8	4,7	:
36-37: Manufacturing n.e.c.	2,3	1,4	6,1	2,2	:	1,7	1,9	3,9	2,4	:
Total services	2,8	1,2	4,7	3,0	:	:	1,2	2,1	:	:
Small	2,9	0,9	2,6	3,1	:	:	0,8	6,0	:	:
Medium-sized	2,4	2,7	1,5	2,5	:	:	1,0	1,2	:	:
Large	2,8	1,1	6,3	3,0	:	:	1,5	2,9	:	:
60-62: Transport	1,8	0,7	5,5	1,7	:	:	0,9	2,7	:	:
72: Computer and related activities	4,4	2,2	3,9	5,1	:	:	2,0	1,7	:	:
40-41: Water, gas and electricity	0,8	0,9	0,1	0,4	:	0,8	1,5	:	1,9	:

Further reading: Statistics on innovation in Europe, Panorama, 2000. Eurostat.

EU–15 without EL and L for manufacturing; without EL, E, I and L for services.

6R5LA

Innovation expenditure as percentage of total turnover. 1996

	NL	A	P	FIN	S	UK	EEA	IS	NO
Total manufacturing	3,8	3,5	1,7	4,3	7,0	3,2	3,7	:	2,7
Small	3,0	4,4	1,8	1,6	2,6	3,3	2,5	:	2,2
Medium-sized	1,8	3,1	1,9	1,6	2,7	2,9	2,3	:	2,8
Large	4,6	3,5	1,6	5,1	8,2	3,2	4,2	:	2,8
15-16: Manuf. of food prod.; beverages, tobacco	1,2	1,3	1,0	1,0	1,2	2,2	1,6	:	1,2
17-19: Manuf. of textiles, leather	1,1	2,2	2,1	1,1	1,0	3,2	1,6	:	1,7
20-22: Manuf. of wood, pulp, paper, publishing	3,2	2,3	:c	:c	3,7	3,6	2,5	:	2,5
23-24: Manuf. of coke, chemicals	4,7	6,3	0,5	3,0	7,3	2,8	4,0	:	5,6
25-26: Manuf. of rubber, plastic, other non-metallic minerals	3,4	4,2	2,0	1,8	2,4	3,1	2,7	:	1,9
27-28: Manuf. of basic metals and fabricated prod.	1,7	2,8	0,5	1,3	1,8	2,5	2,1	:	2,4
29: Manuf. of machinery and equipment n.e.c.	3,3	4,0	1,6	3,0	5,3	4,2	3,7	:	2,2
30-33: Manuf. of electrical and optical equipment	:	7,1	:c	10,6	16,1	7,3	8,2	:	6,8
34-35: Manuf. of transport equipment	:	4,1	3,2	:	10,5	1,7	4,3	:	2,7
36-37: Manufacturing n.e.c.	2,4	2,4	2,0	1,0	4,8	2,4	2,3	:	1,8
Total services	1,6	3,0	1,1	2,4	3,8	4,0	2,8	:	3,5
Small	2,4	2,8	2,1	3,6	1,1	6,9	2,9	:	2,2
Medium-sized	2,4	3,9	1,6	3,0	6,1	2,7	2,3	:	1,2
Large	1,3	2,7	0,7	1,8	5,0	3,7	2,9	:	5,4
60-62: Transport	1,2	2,1	1,0	1,7	1,9	3,4	1,8	:	2,8
72: Computer and related activities	1,9	4,9	2,0	4,4	8,1	5,3	4,4	:	5,9
40-41: Water, gas and electricity	2,6	0,4	0,1	1,5	0,9	0,4	0,8	:	0,3

Further reading: Statistics on innovation in Europe, Panorama, 2000. Eurostat.

P, NO: 1997. EEA without EL, L, IS and LI for manufacturing; except EL, E, I, L, IS and LI for services.

7L3RD

enterprises and activities in Europe

4

Agriculture 309
Holdings by size classes of the agricultural area.
(1 000 holdings) 309
Distribution of holdings by size classes of the agricultural
area (% of total holdings) 310
Distribution of the agricultural area by size classes of the
agricultural area (% of total area) 311
Holdings with mixed livestock: *1 000 holdings* 312
Holdings with mixed cropping: *1 000 holdings* 312
Holdings with combined livestock cropping: *1 000 holdings* 312
Holdings with mixed farming: *1 000 holdings* 312
Holdings with specialised farming: *1 000 holdings* 313
Holdings specialising in field crops: *1 000 holdings* 313
Holdings specialising in horticulture: *1 000 holdings* 313
Holdings specialising in permanent crops: *1 000 holdings* 313
Holdings specialising in grazing livestock: *1 000 holdings* 314
Holdings specialising in pigs and/or poultry (granivores):
1 000 holdings 314
Number of female farm managers as % of all farm managers 314
Farm labour force: 315
1 000 persons 315
Number of persons per 100 ha of agricultural land 315
Farm labour input: 315
1 000 annual work units 315
1990 = 100 315
Employment in agriculture as % of total employment. 1997 316
Family labour in annual work units. 1 000s 317
Family labour as % of total farm labour input 317
Age of managers as % of total managers 318
Production of cereals. 1 000 t: 319
Total (without rice) 319
of which wheat 319
Cereal yields. 100 kg per ha. EU-15 319
Production of fruit and vegetables. 1 000 t. 320
Tomatoes 320
Apples 320
Production of wine. 1 000 hl 320
Collection of cow's milk (cumulated monthly data): *1 000 t* 321
Production of cheese: *1 000 t* 321
Production of butter: *1 000 t* 322
Production of milk powder: *1 000 t* 322
Yearly yield of dairy cows. 1 000 kg milk per cow 323
EU-15 production of milk powder, butter and cheese
(1 000 t) 323
Gross value added at market prices in EUR 1 000 per
person employed in agriculture. 1997. NUTS 2 324
Production of meat: 325
Pork: slaughtering in 1 000 t 325
Poultry: slaughtering in 1 000 t 325
Production of meat: 325
Veal and beef: slaughtering in 1 000 t 325
Sheep and goats: slaughtering in 1 000 t 325
Meat production: gross indigenous production in 1 000 t 326
Producer price indices, nominal; total agricultural produc-
tion. 1990 = 100 327
Producer price indices, deflated; total agricultural production.
1990 = 100 328
Purchase price indices, nominal; total means of agricultural
production. 1990 = 100 328
Purchase price indices, deflated; total means of agricultural
production. 1990 = 100 328

Producer price indices, nominal; crop products. 1990 = 100 329
Producer price indices, nominal; animals and animal
products. 1990 = 100 329
Producer price indices, deflated; crop products. 1990 = 100 330
Producer price indices, deflated; animals and animal
products. 1990 = 100 330
Crop output. Million ECU/EUR 331
Animal output. Million ECU/EUR 331
Crop and animal output as % of agricultural output. 1999 332
Principal agricultural output. Million ECU/EUR. EU-15 332
Gross value added at basic prices. Million ECU/EUR 333
Net value added at basic prices. Million ECU/EUR 333

Forestry 334
Total roundwood production. 1 000 m³ 334
Roundwood: degree of self-sufficiency. % 334
Coniferous roundwood production. 1 000 m³ 335
Non-coniferous roundwood production. 1 000 m³ 335
Privately owned forests as % of total wooded area. 1999 336
Fellings as % of net annual increment of growing stock. 1999 336

Fisheries 337
Annual catches in all regions. 1 000 t live weight 337
Total aquaculture production. 1 000 t live weight 337
Annual catches in all regions as % of total world catches 338
Annual catches in the north-east Atlantic. 1 000 t live weight 338
Annual catches in the north-west Atlantic. 1 000 t live weight 339
Annual catches in the Mediterranean. 1 000 t live weight 339
Annual catches in the east central Atlantic. 1 000 t live
weight 340
Catches of fish, crustaceans and molluscs. Million tonnes
live weight. 1998 340
Fishing fleet: 341
Total tonnage, GT 341
Total power, kW 341
Number of vessels in tonnage classes as % of total 341

Key figures on businesses 344
Turnover. Million ECU. 1997 344
Value added at factor cost. Million ECU. 1997 346
Personnel costs. Million ECU. 1997 346
Number of persons employed. 1997 348
Share of small and medium-sized enterprises (with less than
250 employees) in total employment. %. 1997 349
Number of persons employed. 1997 349

Industry and construction 350
Share of main industries in EU-15 manufacturing in terms of
value added at factor cost. %. 1999 estimates 350
Share of main industries in EU-15 manufacturing in terms of
employment. %. 1999 estimates 350
Evolution of labour productivity. 1 000 ECU. EU-15 estimates
1991–99 350
Wage-adjusted labour productivity. %. EU-15 estimates 1997 351
Share of gross operating surplus in value-added. %. EU-15
estimates 1997 352
Share of value added in production. %. EU-15 estimates 1997 352
EU-15 and EUR-11 production indices, total industry (exclud-
ing construction) 353
Production, total industry (excluding construction), year on
year growth rates, working day adjusted 354

Employment index in the EU, seasonally adjusted.
1995 = 100 — 355

Employment, total industry (excluding construction), year on
year growth rates, seasonally adjusted — 356

Industrial producer prices, total industry (excl. construction),
growth rates. Gross — 357

Producer prices, total industry (excl. construction), year on
year growth rates. Gross — 357

Industrial production index: main industrial groupings, working days adjusted series. 1995 = 100 — 358

Relative specialisation index in the countries' three main
areas of specialisation. 1997: — 360
Global specialisation index — 360
First activity of specialisation — 360
Second activity of specialisation — 360
Third activity of specialisation — 360
Weight of activities 1, 2 and 3 in total value added (%) — 360

Annual growth rate of value added in high and low technology industries between 1990 and 1997. % — 361

Annual growth rate of employment in high and low technology industries between 1990 and 1997. % — 361

Share of high technology industries' employment in total
manufacturing. %. 1997 — 362

Share of low technology industries' employment in total
manufacturing. %. 1997 — 363

Construction: breakdown by activity. EU-15 estimates. 1997: — 364
Share of activity in construction total employment (%) — 364
Value-added in production (%) — 364
Share of gross operating surplus in value added (%) — 364
Wage-adjusted labour productivity (%) — 364
Share of employees in persons employed (%) — 364
Construction sector. Employment index. 1995 = 100 — 364

EU-15 production indices, total construction, seasonally
adjusted. 1995 = 100 — 365

Building permits: dwellings authorised. 1 000s — 365

Distributive trades — 366

Share of motor, wholesale and retail trades in EU-15 total
distributive trades in terms of turnover. %. 1996 estimates — 366

Share of motor, wholesale and retail trades in EU-15 total distributive trades in terms of employment. %. 1996 estimates — 366

Average size of enterprises in terms of turnover. 1 000 ECU.
EU-15 estimates. 1997 — 366

Share of vehicle sales in motor trade in terms of turnover
and employment. %. 1997 — 367

Share of wholesales on a fee or contract basis in wholesales
trade in terms of turnover and employment. %. 1997 — 368

Share of non-specialised stores in retail trade in terms of
turnover and employment. %. 1997 — 368

Retail Trade, volume of sales in the EU. 1995 = 100 — 369

Retail trade, volume of sales, year on year growth rate, working day adjusted — 369

Share of retail sale of food in total retail trade in terms of
turnover and employment. %. 1997 — 370

Breakdown of turnover in retail sale of food between specialised and non-specialised stores. %. 1997 — 370

Services including financial sector — 371

Turnover per persons employed in services. 1 000 ECU.
EU-15 estimates. 1997 — 371

Unit personnel cost in services. 1 000 ECU. EU-15
estimates. 1997 — 372

Number of persons employed in services. 1997 — 372

Breakdown of high technology services in terms of employment.
%. 1997 — 373

Unit personnel cost in transport activities 1 000 ECU. EU-15
estimates. 1997 — 374

Breakdown of turnover in rail, road, water and air transport.
%. 1997 — 374

Credit institutions — 375

Credit institutions: evolution in the total number of
enterprises. 1994/98 — 375

Credit institutions: local units and employment. 1998: — 375
Automatic teller machines (units) — 375
Number of local units (units) — 375
Number of persons employed (units) — 375
Average number of persons employed per enterprise
(units) — 375
Average number of persons employed per local unit (units) — 375
Personnel costs. Million ECU — 375

Credit institutions: financial indicators. 1998: — 376
Interest receivable and similar income. Million ECU — 376
Interest payable and similar charges. Million ECU — 376
Commissions receivable. Million ECU — 376
Commissions payable. Million ECU — 376
Net interest/net commission income (%) — 376
Net interest income/balance sheet total (%) — 376

Credit institutions: balance sheet data. 1998
Loans and advances to customers. Million ECU — 376
Loans and advances to customers as a % of balance sheet
total — 376
Amounts owed to customers. Million ECU — 376
Amounts owed to customers as a % of balance sheet total — 376
Total of capital and reserves. Million ECU — 376
Total of capital and reserves as a % of balance sheet total — 376
Balance sheet total. Million ECU — 376

Insurance services — 377

Insurance: evolution in the total number of enterprises. 1990,
1992–98 — 377

Insurance: financial indicators and employment. 1998: — 377
Gross premiums written. Million ECU — 377
Gross claims incurred. Million ECU — 377
Total investments. Million ECU — 377
Total capital and reserves. Million ECU — 377
Technical provisions. Million ECU — 377
Total persons employed (units) — 377

Insurance: gross premiums written, by type of insurance
enterprises. % — 378

Non-life insurance: gross direct premiums written broken
down by product, %. 1998: — 378
Accident and health — 378
Motor vehicle — 378
Marine, aviation and transport — 378
Fire and other damage to property — 378
General liability — 378
Credit and suretyship — 378
Assistance, legal expenses and miscellaneous financial loss — 378
Other non-life insurance — 378

4

Information society
Number of main telephone lines	379
Main telephone lines per 100 inhabitants	379
Number of mobile phone subscribers (1 000s)	380
Mobile phone subscribers per 100 inhabitants	380
Number of personal computers (1 000s)	381
Personal computers per 100 inhabitants	381
Internet hosts per 100 inhabitants	382
Number of Internet hosts (1 000s)	383
Internet hosts per 100 inhabitants. 1999	383

Energy
Total production of primary energy. Million toe	384
Net imports of primary energy. Million toe	384
Total production of primary energy, as % of gross inland consumption	385
Net imports of primary energy, as % of gross inland consumption	385
Production of coal and lignite, as % of total production of primary energy	386
Production of crude oil, as % of total production of primary energy	386
Production of natural gas, as % of total production of primary energy	387
Production of renewable energy, as % of total production of primary energy	388
Primary production of nuclear energy, as % of total production of primary energy	389
Gross inland consumption of primary energy per person. Toe per capita	390
Gross inland consumption of primary energy. Million toe	390
Gross inland consumption of primary energy per person. 1985 = 100%	391
Energy transformed (input) by power stations and refineries. Million toe. EU-15	391
Electricity generation by origin, as % of total electricity production	392
Solld fuels: coal and brown coal	392
Petroleum products	392
Natural and derived gases	392
Nuclear	392
Hydroelectricity	392
Geothermal, wind, photovoltaic	392
Electricity production. 1 000 GWh	393
Consumption of electricity by industry, transport activities and households. 1 000 GWh. EU-15	393
Final energy consumption. Million toe	394
Contribution of major energy sources as % of total final energy consumption:	394
Petroleum products	394
Electricity	394
Gas	394
Final energy consumption per person. Toe per capita	395
Final energy consumption. Million toe	395
Consumption by industry, as % of final energy consumption	396
Consumption by transport, as % of final energy consumption	396

Natural gas prices for large industrial standard consumers: 418 600 GJ per year, euro per GJ. 1 January 2000	397
Electricity prices for large industrial standard consumers: 24 GWh per year, euro per 100 kWh. 1 January 2000	397
Consumption by households, trades, services, etc., as % of final energy consumption	398
Consumption of electricity in households per person. kWh per capita	398
Natural gas prices for small standard consumers: 16.74 GJ per year, euro per GJ. 1 January 2000	399
Electricity prices for small standard consumers: 1 200 kWh per year, euro per 100 kWh. 1 January 2000	399
Final consumption of petroleum products by households, trades, services, etc., as % of final consumption of petroleum products	400
Final consumption of petroleum products by transport, as % of final consumption of petroleum products	400
Prices of premium unleaded gasoline 95 Ron, euro per 1 000 l. 1 January 2000	401
Final consumption of petroleum products by transport. Million toe. 1998	401

Tourism
Tourism	402
Tourist accommodation: hotels and similar establishments	402
Tourist accommodation: other collective accommodation establishments	402
Average number of hotels and similar establishments per 100 000 inhabitants	403
Average number of travel agencies per 100 000 inhabitants. 1998	404
Tourist accommodation: number of bed places in hotels and similar establishments. 1 000s	405
Average number of bed places per hotel and similar establishments	405
Bed places in hotels and similar establishments per 100 000 inhabitants. 1998	406
Nights spent by residents in collective tourist accommodation per 100 000 inhabitants	407
Nights spent by non-residents in collective tourist accommodation per 100 000 inhabitants	407
Total nights spent in collective tourist accommodation per 100 000 inhabitants. 1999	408
Nights spent by residents in collective tourist accommodation per 100 000 inhabitants	409
Nights spent by non-residents in collective tourist accommodation per 100 000 inhabitants	409
Utilisation of bed places in hotels and similar establishments. 1999. %	410

Transport
Transport	412
Total length of motorways in km	412
Total length of railway lines in km	412
Total inland transport per mode: EEA and Switzerland	413
Passenger cars per 1 000 inhabitants	414
Goods transport by road (million tonne-kilometres)	414
Goods transport by rail (million tonne-kilometres)	415

4

Goods transport by inland waterways (million tonne-kilometres) 415

Goods transport by oil pipelines (million tonne-kilometres) 415

Inland goods transport (1 000 million tonne-kilometres). EEA and Switzerland 416

Worldwide commercial space launches 416

Sea transport of goods. Million tonnes 417

Air transport of goods. 1 000 tonnes 417

EEA sea transport of goods per country. 1998 417

EEA air transport of passengers per country. 1998 417

Passenger transport (1 000 million passenger kilometres). EEA and Switzerland 418

Air transport of passengers. Million 418

Bus transport of passengers. Million passenger kilometres 418

Passenger car transport. Million passenger kilometres 419

Rail transport of passengers. Million passenger kilometres 419

Road freight traffic: 1996 420

Trucks per day 420

4

eurostat

Holdings by size classes of the agricultural area (1 000 holdings)

	Less than 5 ha			5 to 20 ha			20 to 50 ha			
	1990	**1995**	**1997**	**1990**	**1995**	**1997**	**1990**	**1995**	**1997**	
EU-15	:	4 193,6	3 901,7	:	1742,29	1 686,9	:	848,4	802,0	**EU-15**
B	32,1	23,7	21,6	29,44	22,98	21,0	18,6	18,3	17,8	**B**
DK	2,2	2,1	2,2	32,2	26,29	23,8	31,3	23,3	19,6	**DK**
D	218,6	179,2	168,1	225,63	183,99	168,2	153,1	132,2	122,4	**D**
EL	645,2	603,3	626,8	183,05	173,95	169,9	18,0	21,8	21,6	**EL**
E	971,4	706,4	647,1	410,38	358,84	347,1	124,9	115,3	115,3	**E**
F	248,8	200,9	182,4	235,53	158,19	136,8	259,7	177,3	158,9	**F**
IRL	19,2	14,8	11,1	72,4	61,16	58,5	59,4	57,2	57,4	**IRL**
I	2 099,1	1 938,3	1 753,6	439,48	398,28	424,1	87,7	105,3	96,0	**I**
L	1,0	0,8	0,7	0,77	0,53	0,5	1,1	0,7	0,6	**L**
NL	40,3	37,4	34,5	46,89	38,83	36,5	31,6	29,8	29,2	**NL**
A	:	87,3	79,6	:	90,69	86,2	:	35,8	35,8	**A**
P	492,4	345,6	317,1	83,51	80,15	75,2	13,6	15,1	14,8	**P**
FIN	:	10,6	7,9	:	48,26	41,9	:	35,2	33,7	**FIN**
S	:	11,0	12,8	:	34,53	34,1	:	24,7	23,6	**S**
UK	33,5	32,3	36,2	67,88	65,58	63,1	60,7	56,5	55,4	**UK**
IS	:	:	:	:	:	:	:	:	:	**IS**
NO	33,3	23,9	20,8	49,9	44,8	43,2	11,5	13,3	14,0	**NO**

3B1AA   3B1AB   3B1AC

Further reading: Agriculture, statistical yearbook, 1999. Eurostat. Farm structure, 1997 survey. Eurostat. Farm structure historical results. Surveys from 1966/67 to 1997. Eurostat.

4

Holdings by size classes of the agricultural area (1 000 holdings)

	50 to 100 ha			100 ha or more			Total			
	1990	**1995**	**1997**	**1990**	**1995**	**1997**	**1990**	**1995**	**1997**	
EU-15	:	370,9	372,2	:	214,8	226,3	:	7 370,0	6 989,1	**EU-15**
B	4,1	5,1	5,6	0,8	0,9	1,1	85,0	71,0	67,2	**B**
DK	12,2	12,1	12,0	3,4	5,0	5,6	81,3	68,8	63,2	**DK**
D	44,4	51,6	53,3	11,9	19,9	22,3	653,6	566,9	534,4	**D**
EL	2,9	2,7	2,7	1,0	0,7	0,5	850,1	802,4	821,4	**EL**
E	48,8	51,7	51,5	38,2	45,4	47,3	1 593,6	1 277,6	1 208,3	**E**
F	131,2	128,2	125,7	48,3	70,3	76,1	923,6	734,8	679,8	**F**
IRL	15,7	16,1	16,6	3,9	4,1	4,2	170,6	153,4	147,8	**IRL**
I	24,7	26,9	27,4	13,7	13,4	14,1	2 664,6	2 482,1	2 315,2	**I**
L	1,0	1,0	0,9	0,1	0,2	0,2	4,0	3,2	3,0	**L**
NL	5,3	6,2	6,6	0,7	0,9	1,1	124,8	113,2	107,9	**NL**
A	:	5,2	5,7	:	2,8	2,8	:	221,8	210,1	**A**
P	3,9	4,4	4,2	5,4	5,4	5,4	598,7	450,6	416,7	**P**
FIN	:	6,0	7,0	:	0,8	1,1	:	101,0	91,4	**FIN**
S	:	13,0	13,1	:	5,6	6,0	:	88,8	89,6	**S**
UK	42,5	40,9	39,9	38,5	39,3	38,6	243,1	234,5	233,2	**UK**
IS	:	:	:	:	:	:	:	:	:	**IS**
NO	0,9	1,1	1,2	0,1	0,1	0,1	95,6	83,2	79,3	**NO**

3B1AD   3B1AE   3B1AF

Further reading: Agriculture, statistical yearbook, 1999. Eurostat. Farm structure, 1997 survey. Eurostat. Farm structure, historical results. Surveys from 1966/67 to 1997. Eurostat.

eurostat

EUROSTAT YEARBOOK 2001
309

Distribution of holdings by size classes of the agricultural area (% of total holdings)

	Less than 5 ha				5 to 20 ha				20 to 50 ha				
	1990	**1993**	**1995**	**1997**	**1990**	**1993**	**1995**	**1997**	**1990**	**1993**	**1995**	**1997**	
EU-15	:	:	56,9	55,8	:	:	23,6	24,1	:	:	11,5	11,5	**EU-15**
B	37,7	35,0	33,3	32,2	34,6	33,5	32,4	31,3	21,9	24,5	25,8	26,5	**B**
DK	2,7	2,6	3,0	3,5	39,6	39,0	38,2	37,7	38,5	36,1	33,8	31,0	**DK**
D	33,4	31,6	31,6	31,5	34,5	34,1	32,5	31,5	23,4	23,4	23,3	22,9	**D**
EL	75,9	75,7	75,2	76,3	21,5	21,5	21,7	20,7	2,1	2,4	2,7	2,6	**EL**
E	61,0	58,1	55,3	53,6	25,8	26,9	28,1	28,7	7,8	8,3	9,0	9,5	**E**
F	26,9	27,6	27,3	26,8	25,5	22,6	21,5	20,1	28,1	25,6	24,1	23,4	**F**
IRL	11,2	10,4	9,7	7,5	42,4	42,1	39,9	39,6	34,8	35,6	37,3	38,8	**IRL**
I	78,8	77,5	78,1	75,7	16,5	17,1	16,0	18,3	3,3	3,8	4,2	4,1	**I**
L	25,8	26,5	25,2	24,2	19,5	16,8	16,7	16,4	26,8	22,6	20,8	19,5	**L**
NL	32,3	34,1	33,1	32,0	37,6	34,9	34,3	33,8	25,3	25,4	26,3	27,0	**NL**
A	:	:	39,4	37,9	:	:	40,9	41,0	:	:	16,1	17,0	**A**
P	82,2	78,1	76,7	76,1	13,9	16,9	17,8	18,0	2,3	3,0	3,3	3,6	**P**
FIN	:	:	10,5	8,6	:	:	47,8	45,8	:	:	34,9	36,8	**FIN**
S	:	:	12,3	14,3	:	:	38,9	38,1	:	:	27,8	26,4	**S**
UK	13,8	15,2	13,8	15,5	27,9	27,7	28,0	27,1	25,0	24,2	24,1	23,8	**UK**
IS	:	:	:	:	:	:	:	:	:	:	:	:	**IS**
NO	34,9	:	28,7	26,3	52,2	:	53,9	54,5	12,0	:	16,0	17,6	**NO**

3B1BA

3B1BB

3B1BC

Further reading: Agriculture, statistical yearbook, 1999. Eurostat. Farm structure, 1997 survey. Eurostat. Farm structure, historical results. Surveys from 1966/67 to 1997. Eurostat.

4

Distribution of holdings by size classes of the agricultural area (% of total holdings)

	50 to 100 ha					100 ha or more				
	1990	**1993**	**1995**	**1997**		**1990**	**1993**	**1995**	**1997**	
EU-15	:	:	5,0	5,3		:	:	2,9	3,2	**EU-15**
B	4,8	5,9	7,1	8,4		0,9	1,1	1,3	1,7	**B**
DK	15,0	16,4	17,7	19,0		4,2	5,8	7,3	8,8	**DK**
D	6,8	8,1	9,1	10,0		1,8	2,7	3,5	4,2	**D**
EL	0,3	0,3	0,3	0,3		0,1	0,1	0,1	0,1	**EL**
E	3,1	3,6	4,0	4,3		2,4	3,1	3,6	3,9	**E**
F	14,2	16,5	17,4	18,5		5,2	7,6	9,6	11,2	**F**
IRL	9,2	9,6	10,5	11,2		2,3	2,3	2,7	2,8	**IRL**
I	0,9	1,1	1,1	1,2		0,5	0,6	0,5	0,6	**I**
L	25,1	28,8	30,8	31,5		2,5	5,3	6,6	8,1	**L**
NL	4,3	5,0	5,5	6,1		0,6	0,7	0,8	1,0	**NL**
A	:	:	2,3	2,7		:	:	1,3	1,3	**A**
P	0,6	0,8	1,0	1,0		0,9	1,1	1,2	1,3	**P**
FIN	:	:	6,0	7,6		:	:	0,8	1,2	**FIN**
S	:	:	14,6	14,6		:	:	6,3	6,7	**S**
UK	17,5	16,9	17,4	17,1		15,8	15,9	16,7	16,5	**UK**
IS	:	:	:	:		:	:	:	:	**IS**
NO	0,9	:	1,4	1,5		0,1	:	0,1	0,1	**NO**

3B1BD

3B1BE

Further reading: Agriculture, statistical yearbook, 1999. Eurostat. Farm structure, 1997 survey. Eurostat. Farm structure, historical results. Surveys from 1966/67 to 1997. Eurostat.

eurostat

Distribution of the agricultural area by size classes of the agricultural area (% of total area)

	Less than 5 ha				5 to 20 ha				20 to 50 ha				
	1990	1993	1995	1997	1990	1993	1995	1997	1990	1993	1995	1997	
EU-15	:	:	5,7	5,4	:	:	13,8	13,4	:	:	20,9	19,8	EU-15
B	4,4	3,8	3,4	3,0	24,9	21,6	19,1	17,1	42,4	43,2	42,5	41,1	B
DK	0,2	0,1	0,1	0,2	13,7	12,1	11,0	10,1	36,2	31,4	27,7	23,8	DK
D	2,8	2,5	2,3	2,2	14,9	13,6	12,0	10,9	28,2	26,4	24,6	22,9	D
EL	31,3	32,3	30,8	31,7	44,4	44,1	43,3	43,7	14,0	15,9	17,5	17,7	EL
E	7,6	6,3	5,6	5,1	16,2	14,7	13,8	13,3	15,7	14,3	14,0	13,9	E
F	1,7	1,6	1,4	1,3	9,6	7,3	6,3	5,4	30,2	24,2	21,0	18,9	F
IRL	1,3	1,2	1,0	0,8	19,9	19,4	17,4	16,8	41,4	41,7	41,6	41,6	IRL
I	21,0	19,6	19,7	19,0	27,4	27,2	25,2	26,8	17,6	19,0	21,6	19,6	I
L	1,6	1,4	1,2	1,1	6,9	5,0	4,6	4,2	30,0	21,7	18,5	16,4	L
NL	4,0	4,1	3,9	3,6	25,9	23,0	21,5	20,1	47,9	46,6	46,5	45,7	NL
A	:	:	5,9	5,6	:	:	29,5	28,2	:	:	30,8	31,1	A
P	18,9	16,4	15,2	14,3	19,0	19,4	19,1	18,3	10,2	11,3	11,6	11,7	P
FIN	:	:	1,5	1,1	:	:	26,3	23,6	:	:	49,2	47,8	FIN
S	:	:	1,1	1,1	:	:	12,3	12,0	:	:	26,0	24,5	S
UK	0,5	0,5	0,5	0,5	4,6	4,6	4,5	4,4	12,1	11,9	11,3	11,3	UK
IS	:	:	:	:	:	:	:	:	:	:	:	:	IS
NO	8,7	:	5,7	5,0	52,8	:	48,0	45,6	32,0	:	37,9	40,1	NO

Further reading: Agriculture, statistical yearbook, 1999. Eurostat. Farm structure, 1997 survey. Eurostat. Farm structure, historical results. Surveys from 1966/67 to 1997. Eurostat.

3B1BF
3B1BG
3B1BH

4

Distribution of the agricultural area by size classes of the agricultural area (% of total area)

	50 to 100 ha					100 ha or more				
	1990	1993	1995	1997		1990	1993	1995	1997	
EU-15	:	:	19,9	20,0		:	:	39,7	41,3	EU-15
B	20,2	22,2	24,7	27,2		8,1	9,2	10,2	11,6	B
DK	29,4	30,1	30,7	31,0		20,5	26,2	30,5	34,9	DK
D	17,3	19,5	20,4	21,3		36,8	38,0	40,7	42,7	D
EL	5,1	4,8	4,8	5,0		5,2	2,9	3,6	2,0	EL
E	13,7	13,9	14,2	13,9		46,8	50,7	52,3	53,8	E
F	31,8	32,6	31,7	31,3		26,7	34,3	39,5	43,1	F
IRL	23,6	24,0	25,0	25,6		13,8	13,6	15,0	15,2	IRL
I	11,3	12,4	12,5	12,6		22,7	21,7	21,0	22,1	I
L	52,0	53,6	54,0	52,4		9,4	18,4	21,8	25,9	L
NL	17,0	19,0	20,1	21,3		5,2	7,2	8,0	9,3	NL
A	:	:	9,8	10,9		:	:	24,0	24,2	A
P	6,7	7,3	7,6	7,5		45,2	45,5	46,5	48,1	P
FIN	:	:	17,8	20,8		:	:	5,1	6,7	FIN
S	:	:	29,3	29,0		:	:	31,3	33,5	S
UK	18,2	17,8	17,6	17,5		64,5	65,2	66,1	66,3	UK
IS	:	:	:	:		:	:	:	:	IS
NO	5,5	:	7,2	7,9		0,9	:	1,2	1,4	NO

Further reading: Agriculture, statistical yearbook, 1999. Eurostat. Farm structure, 1997 survey. Eurostat. Farm structure, historical results. Surveys from 1966/67 to 1997. Eurostat.

3B1BI
3B1BJ

eurostat

There are eight main categories in Community farm typology. Specialised farms generate more than two thirds of their total standard gross margin from the main categories of field crops, horticulture, permanent crops, grazing livestock or granivores (pigs and poultry). Non-specialised farms or holdings with mixed farming generate less than two thirds of their total standard gross margin from one of the main categories. Standard gross margin (SGM) was introduced to allow different agricultural products to be measured on a common basis. It is basically the difference between the production value and certain costs of production, and is measured for each type of crop or animal production.

Holdings with mixed livestock

1 000 holdings

	1990	1993	1995	1997
EU-15	:	:	249,8	193,4
B	5,5	5,0	4,3	3,8
DK	3,2	3,1	2,3	1,8
D	33,1	45,6	33,8	24,2
EL	24,6	19,0	15,0	15,3
E	59,0	42,6	46,1	34,8
F	57,7	46,4	40,2	35,1
IRL	0,4	0,4	0,4	0,4
I	55,9	39,5	37,8	23,8
L	0,2	0,2	0,2	0,1
NL	6,1	5,6	4,6	4,3
A	:	:	10,8	10,5
P	63,7	46,7	49,0	33,9
FIN	:	:	1,1	1,0
S	:	:	1,6	1,2
UK	2,7	3,2	2,7	3,1

Holdings with mixed cropping

1 000 holdings

	1990	1993	1995	1997	
EU-15	:	:	627,3	597,7	**EU-15**
B	2,7	2,1	1,9	1,8	**B**
DK	2,8	3,1	2,3	2,1	**DK**
D	25,0	26,8	23,9	22,7	**D**
EL	97,0	93,2	74,7	75,1	**EL**
E	143,2	102,9	101,1	103,1	**E**
F	59,1	47,7	42,0	36,7	**F**
IRL	0,2	0,2	0,2	0,1	**IRL**
I	317,2	280,8	262,6	246,4	**I**
L	0,1	0,0	0,0	0,0	**L**
NL	2,8	2,7	2,5	2,4	**NL**
A	:	:	8,3	7,3	**A**
P	153,6	129,3	99,7	94,0	**P**
FIN	:	:	2,5	1,9	**FIN**
S	:	:	2,2	1,8	**S**
UK	4,2	3,5	3,2	2,9	**UK**

3B1DG 3B1FA

Further reading: Agriculture, statistical yearbook, 1999. Eurostat. Farm structure, 1997 survey. Eurostat. Farm structure, historical results. Surveys from 1966/67 to 1997. Eurostat.

4

Holdings with combined livestock cropping

1 000 holdings

	1990	1993	1995	1997
EU-15	:	:	559,0	491,7
B	11,9	9,2	8,6	8,2
DK	15,2	13,1	12,1	11,6
D	109,0	100,3	92,4	86,8
EL	60,1	45,9	48,0	46,5
E	93,8	68,7	65,5	56,5
F	102,7	85,8	78,9	72,6
IRL	4,3	4,3	4,0	3,6
I	147,6	120,5	121,0	96,4
L	0,5	0,3	0,4	0,4
NL	5,8	5,1	4,8	4,9
A	:	:	19,5	17,2
P	93,9	67,8	62,6	50,3
FIN	:	:	11,7	5,8
S	:	:	15,5	16,9
UK	15,6	14,1	14,0	14,0

Holdings with mixed farming

1 000 holdings

	1990	1993	1995	1997	
EU-15	:	:	1 436,1	1 283,0	**EU-15**
B	20,1	16,3	14,8	13,8	**B**
DK	21,1	19,3	16,7	15,5	**DK**
D	167,1	172,6	150,1	133,8	**D**
EL	181,6	158,1	137,8	136,9	**EL**
E	295,9	214,3	212,6	194,4	**E**
F	219,5	179,8	161,1	144,4	**F**
IRL	4,9	4,9	4,7	4,1	**IRL**
I	520,7	440,8	421,4	366,6	**I**
L	0,7	0,5	0,5	0,5	**L**
NL	14,7	13,4	11,8	11,6	**NL**
A	:	:	38,6	35,0	**A**
P	311,2	243,8	211,3	178,2	**P**
FIN	:	:	15,3	8,6	**FIN**
S	:	:	19,4	19,9	**S**
UK	22,5	20,8	19,8	19,9	**UK**

3B1FC 3B1CD

Further reading: Agriculture, statistical yearbook, 1999. Eurostat. Farm structure, 1997 survey. Eurostat. Farm structure, historical results. Surveys from 1966/67 to 1997. Eurostat.

Holdings with specialised farming

1 000 holdings

Holdings specialising in field crops

1 000 holdings

	1990	1993	1995	1997		1990	1993	1995	1997	
EU-15	:	:	5 888,7	5 671,1		:	:	1 604,9	1 535,7	**EU-15**
B	64,7	59,8	56,0	53,2		9,3	8,5	8,3	8,8	**B**
DK	60,2	54,5	52,1	47,7		37,7	31,9	30,0	29,1	**DK**
D	464,7 |	433,3	416,6	402,2		137,5 |	124,1	116,4	117,5	**D**
EL	668,4	661,0	664,4	684,5		221,3	201,9	208,6	210,5	**EL**
E	1 285,1	1 157,3	1 052,7	1 007,9		284,6	225,8	214,1	206,3	**E**
F	703,8	621,2	573,4	535,1		169,7	151,6	140,2	136,9	**F**
IRL	165,6	154,3	148,5	143,7		5,0	4,4	4,3	3,7	**IRL**
I	2 118,4	2 013,5	2 030,4	1 922,1		685,4	601,8	664,2	609,3	**I**
L	3,2	2,9	2,6	2,5		0,3	0,2	0,2	0,2	**L**
NL	110,1	106,3	101,3	96,3		16,3	14,6	14,9	14,7	**NL**
A	:	:	182,7	174,9		:	:	34,3	32,2	**A**
P	287,4	245,1	239,2	238,2		69,2	50,4	47,4	43,0	**P**
FIN	:	:	85,6	82,8		0,0	:	39,5	37,5	**FIN**
S	:	:	69,4	68,1		:	:	39,6	40,5	**S**
UK	219,6	220,5	213,7	211,8		43,2	42,2	43,0	45,5	**UK**

3B1CA
3B1DA

Further reading: Agriculture, statistical yearbook, 1999. Eurostat. Farm structure, 1997 survey. Eurostat. Farm structure, historical results. Surveys from 1966/67 to 1997. Eurostat.

4

Holdings specialising in horticulture

1 000 holdings

Holdings specialising in permanent crops

1 000 holdings

	1990	1993	1995	1997		1990	1993	1995	1997	
EU-15	:	:	202,5	190,8		:	:	2 259,6	2 296,7	**EU-15**
B	7,1	6,1	5,7	5,2		2,9	2,8	2,6	2,6	**B**
DK	1,7	1,5	1,6	1,2		0,8	0,8	0,7	0,6	**DK**
D	13,0 |	13,9	11,3	12,1		51,8 |	48,6	45,5	43,0	**D**
EL	16,7	14,7	16,6	16,6		363,7	395,6	382,9	407,4	**EL**
E	74,4	70,5	59,1	52,3		572,1	554,9	539,7	530,9	**E**
F	30,2	23,0	20,7	18,2		138,0	128,4	115,0	107,0	**F**
IRL	0,6	0,5	0,7	0,2		0,3	0,1	0,2	0,0	**IRL**
I	45,2	32,4	45,1	46,0		1 105,9	1 088,3	1 018,4	1 045,6	**I**
L	0,1	0,0	0,0	0,0		0,7	0,6	0,6	0,5	**L**
NL	18,0	16,8	15,9	14,8		5,8	5,9	5,8	5,6	**NL**
A	:	:	1,7	1,7		:	:	24,9	22,1	**A**
P	14,7	13,9	12,3	12,0		139,4	132,6	119,4	127,2	**P**
FIN	:	:	4,5	4,0		:	:	0,5	0,5	**FIN**
S	:	:	1,9	1,7		:	:	0,7	0,6	**S**
UK	8,3	6,2	5,5	4,9		3,2	3,6	2,9	3,2	**UK**

3B1DC
3B1EA

Further reading: Agriculture, statistical yearbook, 1999. Eurostat. Farm structure, 1997 survey. Eurostat. Farm structure, historical results. Surveys from 1966/67 to 1997. Eurostat.

eurostat

160 million data in New Cronos, Eurostat's reference database

Holdings specialising in grazing livestock

1 000 holdings

Holdings specialising in pigs and/or poultry (granivores)

1 000 holdings

	1990	1993	1995	1997		1990	1993	1995	1997	
EU-15	:	:	1 711,3	1 557,2		:	:	110,5	90,7	EU-15
B	40,5	36,9	34,5	32,0		4,9	5,6	5,0	4,7	B
DK	16,3	15,1	15,0	12,9		3,6	5,2	4,7	3,8	DK
D	253,9	226,1	230,4	221,2		8,5	20,6	13,0	8,4	D
EL	63,2	46,3	53,6	46,3		3,5	2,5	2,9	3,8	EL
E	332,1	287,3	222,2	203,3		21,8	18,9	17,6	15,1	E
F	352,0	305,4	286,3	263,5		13,9	12,8	11,2	9,5	F
IRL	158,9	148,7	142,6	139,1		0,8	0,7	0,7	0,7	IRL
I	269,6	280,0	288,9	212,4		12,3	11,0	13,8	8,8	I
L	2,2	2,0	1,8	1,7		0,0	0,1	0,0	0,0	L
NL	58,3	58,0	54,6	51,2		11,8	11,1	10,2	10,0	NL
A	:	:	115,1	110,6		:	:	6,7	8,3	A
P	51,4	40,0	52,2	50,5		12,8	8,2	7,9	5,6	P
FIN	:	:	36,8	37,1		:	:	4,4	3,8	FIN
S	:	:	26,0	24,2		:	:	1,3	1,2	S
UK	158,1	161,1	151,1	151,4		6,8	7,4	11,2	6,8	UK

3B1EC 3B1EG

Further reading: Agriculture, statistical yearbook, 1999. Eurostat. Farm structure, 1997 survey. Eurostat. Farm structure, historical results. Surveys from 1966/67 to 1997. Eurostat.

4

Number of female farm managers as % of all farm managers

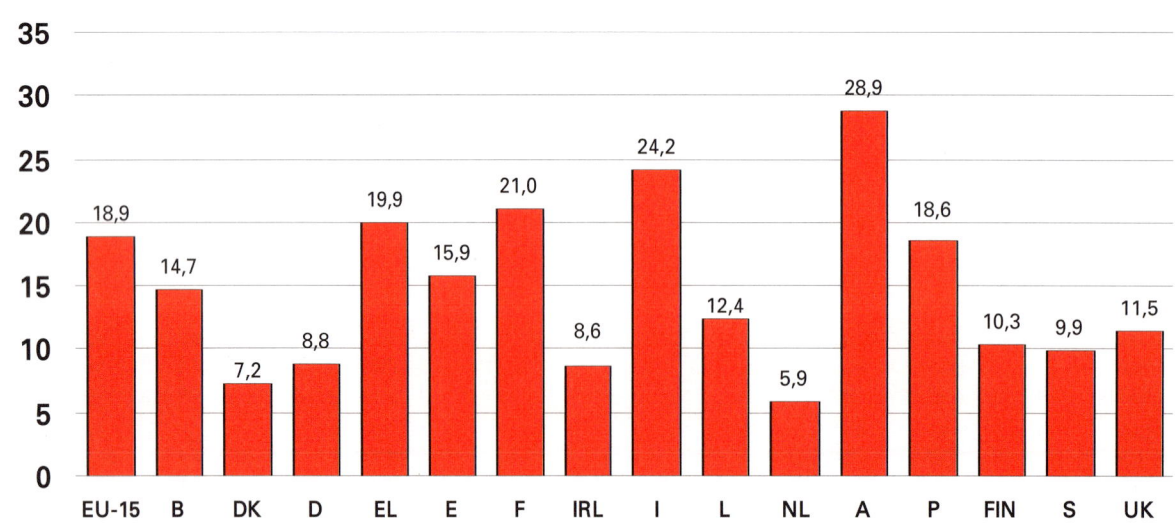

3B1HQ

Further reading: Agriculture, statistical yearbook, 1999. Eurostat. Farm structure, 1997 survey. Eurostat. Farm structure, historical results. Surveys from 1966/67 to 1997. Eurostat.

Farm labour force

	1 000 persons					Number of persons per 100 ha of agricultural land				
	1990	**1993**	**1995**	**1997**		**1990**	**1993**	**1995**	**1997**	
EU-15	:	:	15 243,6	14 757,3		:	:	11,9	11,5	**EU-15**
B	141,0	131,8	122,0	116,7		10,5	9,8	9,0	8,4	**B**
DK	139,1	142,3	141,1	130,2		5,0	5,2	5,2	4,8	**DK**
D	1 775,9	1 478,0	1 325,2	1 230,7		10,4	8,7	7,7	7,2	**D**
EL	1 543,5	1 773,5	1 566,7	1 595,6		42,2	50,1	43,8	45,6	**EL**
E	2 838,7	2 570,8	2 543,1	2 496,5		11,6	10,4	10,1	9,7	**E**
F	1 859,0	1 610,2	1 507,4	1 404,3		6,6	5,7	5,3	5,0	**F**
IRL	312,7	320,0	293,3	281,9		7,0	7,5	6,8	6,5	**IRL**
I	5 287,4	4 761,8	4 773,2	4 601,1		35,4	32,3	32,5	31,0	**I**
L	9,3	7,9	7,3	6,8		7,4	6,2	5,7	5,4	**L**
NL	289,2	289,7	276,2	282,5		14,4	14,4	13,8	14,1	**NL**
A	:	:	547,3	512,6		:	:	16,0	15,0	**A**
P	1 561,0	1 263,5	1 172,8	1 070,3		39,0	32,0	29,9	28,0	**P**
FIN	:	:	232,1	223,7		:	:	10,6	10,3	**FIN**
S	:	:	164,2	168,6		:	:	5,4	5,4	**S**
UK	659,1	651,1	571,7	636,0		4,0	4,0	3,5	3,9	**UK**

3B1GA

3B1GB

Further reading: Agriculture, statistical yearbook, 1999. Eurostat. Farm structure, 1997 survey. Eurostat. Farm structure, historical results. Surveys from 1966/67 to 1997. Eurostat.

FIN, S: per 100 ha of arable land.

Farm labour input

	1 000 annual work units					1990 = 100				
	1990	**1993**	**1995**	**1997**		**1990**	**1993**	**1995**	**1997**	
EU-15	:	:	7 263,5	7 023,2		:	:	:	:	**EU-15**
B	93,5	85,2	78,9	79,1		100	91	84	85	**B**
DK	95,2	104,8	105,0	97,9		100	110	110	103	**DK**
D	1 029,7	804,2	711,0	656,8		100	78	69	64	**D**
EL	680,3	702,2	637,9	597,3		100	103	94	88	**EL**
E	1 143,4	1 112,1	1 089,6	1 099,0		100	97	95	96	**E**
F	1 256,5	1 081,1	1 015,4	958,1		100	86	81	76	**F**
IRL	249,7	239,5	218,5	202,3		100	96	88	81	**IRL**
I	1 924,0	1 836,7	1 818,0	1 798,1		100	95	94	93	**I**
L	6,3	5,8	5,3	5,1		100	92	85	80	**L**
NL	225,0	224,4	210,0	208,7		100	100	93	93	**NL**
A	:	:	187,4	177,6		:	:	:	:	**A**
P	846,9	604,7	583,6	519,8		100	71	69	61	**P**
FIN	:	:	131,4	125,7		:	:	:	:	**FIN**
S	:	:	87,7	81,8		:	:	:	:	**S**
UK	473,7	433,9	384,0	416,0		100	92	81	88	**UK**

3B1GC

3B1GG

Further reading: Agriculture, statistical yearbook, 1999. Eurostat. Farm structure, 1997 survey. Eurostat. Farm structure, historical results. Surveys from 1966/67 to 1997. Eurostat.

4

Farm labour is measured in two ways. According to the survey on the structure of agriculture, the labour force includes total employment in agricultural holdings. According to the European system of integrated economic accounts (ESA) farm labour is employment in agricultural activities. An annual work unit (AWU) is the time worked by one person employed full time over a whole year. Figures on the structure of agriculture and the labour force come from surveys of agricultural holdings. The surveys are carried out approximately every two years, the latest from which figures are available having been conducted in 1997.

Employment in agriculture as % of total employment. 1997

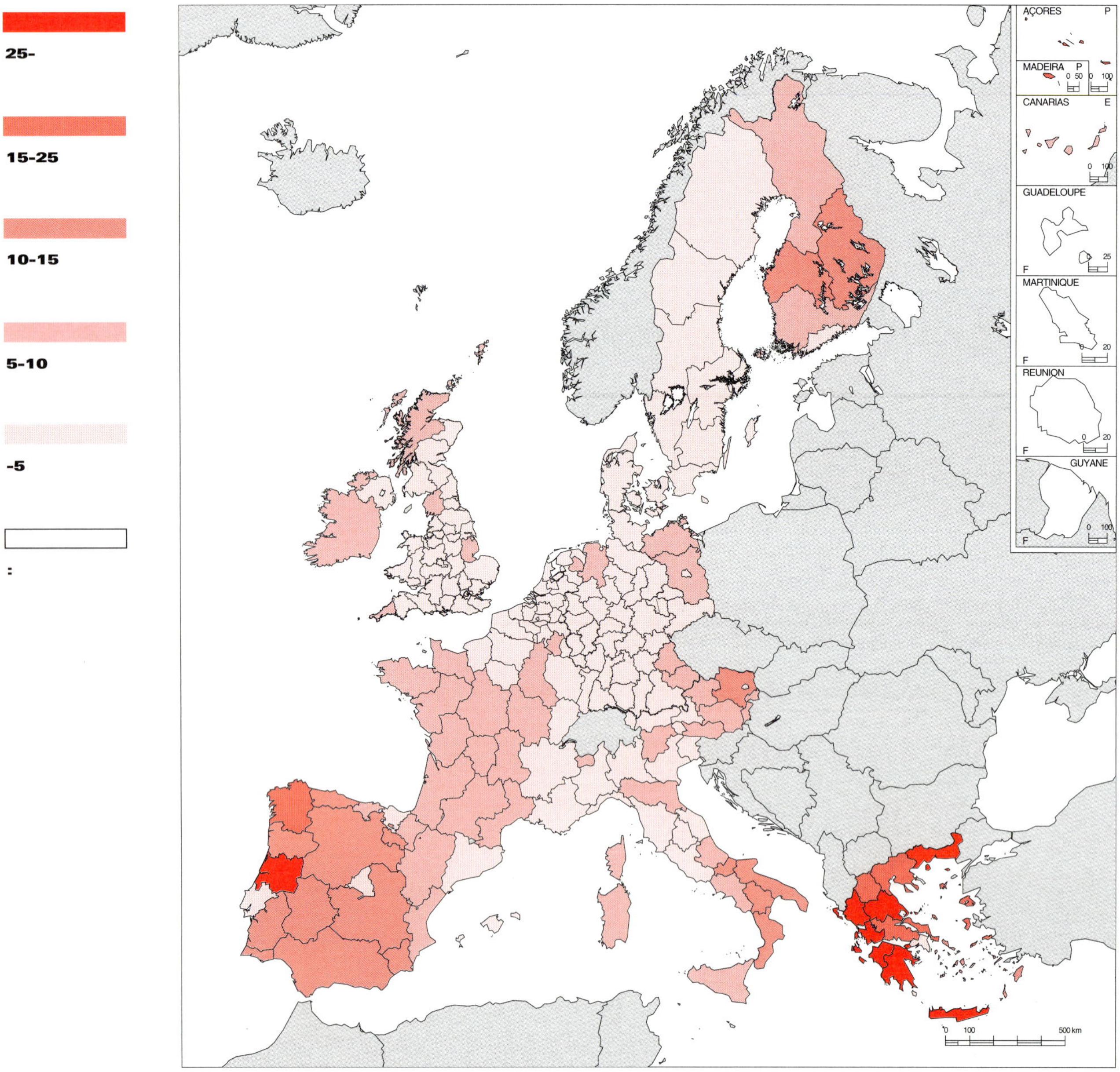

25-

15-25

10-15

5-10

-5

:

3B1GE

NUTS 2. NUTS 1: DED (D Saxony), IRL.

Further reading: Regions, statistical yearbook, 1999. Eurostat.

3B1HF

Family labour in annual work units. 1 000s

	1990	1993	1995	1997	
EU-15	:	:	5 848,3	5 560,7	EU-15
B	86,7	77,4	70,2	69,2	B
DK	71,4	77,1	66,6	59,2	DK
D	650,6	597,8	534,6	472,9	D
EL	625,5	623,1	555,9	523,4	EL
E	852,7	841,0	801,8	778,6	E
F	1 037,5	870,8	800,5	737,5	F
IRL	234,2	223,4	201,7	188,3	IRL
I	1 598,3	1 572,9	1 559,7	1 541,2	I
L	5,7	5,1	4,7	4,4	L
NL	173,6	167,6	152,1	153,8	NL
A	:	:	171,0	161,4	A
P	720,9	509,4	488,8	429,8	P
FIN	:	:	126,4	119,4	FIN
S	:	:	65,1	62,8	S
UK	289,0	267,7	249,4	258,9	UK

Further reading: Agriculture, statistical yearbook, 1999. Eurostat. Farm structure, 1997
survey. Eurostat. Farm structure, historical results. Surveys from
1966/67 to 1997. Eurostat.

4

3B1HB

Family labour as % of total farm labour input

	1990	1993	1995	1997	
EU-15	:	:	80,5	79,2	EU-15
B	92,7	90,9	89,0	87,5	B
DK	75,0	73,6	63,5	60,4	DK
D	63,2	74,3	75,2	72,0	D
EL	91,9	88,7	87,1	87,6	EL
E	74,6	75,6	73,6	70,8	E
F	82,6	80,5	78,8	77,0	F
IRL	93,8	93,3	92,3	93,1	IRL
I	83,1	85,6	85,8	85,7	I
L	90,1	88,1	87,2	86,5	L
NL	77,1	74,7	72,4	73,7	NL
A	:	:	91,3	90,9	A
P	85,1	84,2	83,8	82,7	P
FIN	:	:	96,2	95,0	FIN
S	:	:	74,2	76,8	S
UK	61,0	61,7	64,9	62,2	UK

Further reading: Agriculture, statistical yearbook, 1999. Eurostat. Farm structure, 1997
survey. Eurostat. Farm structure, historical results. Surveys from
1966/67 to 1997. Eurostat.

Family labour measured according to the survey on the structure of agricultural holdings includes work by the farmer and his family in agriculture.

More data on this in Eurostat's database

Summarises the main data in the Eurofarm database and contains the results of Community surveys on the structure of agricultural holdings. This domain also contains the main indicators on the structure of agricultural holdings by region.

▶ ▶ ▶ **DOMAIN EUROFARM IN DATABASE NEW CRONOS**

Age of managers as % of total managers

	Aged under 35			Aged 35 to 54			Aged 55 to 64			Aged 65 or over			
	1990	**1995**	**1997**	**1990**	**1995**	**1997**	**1990**	**1995**	**1997**	**1990**	**1995**	**1997**	
EU-15	:	8,5	8,2	:	37,9	38,7	:	27,2	26,2	:	26,4	26,8	**EU-15**
B	11,8	15,9	14,1	37,9	42,0	44,4	30,0	25,3	23,3	20,3	16,8	18,2	**B**
DK	10,9	11,7	11,5	43,4	43,0	45,1	25,8	23,5	22,7	19,8	21,9	20,7	**DK**
D	16,5	18,0	17,0	49,4	48,0	50,3	27,5	27,0	25,3	6,6	7,1	7,4	**D**
EL	8,7	6,1	5,5	37,4	34,6	33,9	28,6	28,3	26,5	25,3	30,9	34,1	**EL**
E	8,4	7,7	7,7	39,4	37,6	38,1	31,0	29,1	27,1	21,2	25,6	27,1	**E**
F	13,4	12,9	12,0	42,7	47,8	51,3	30,2	24,1	21,0	13,7	15,2	15,7	**F**
IRL	14,3	14,8	13,0	42,2	42,4	43,8	22,0	22,5	22,2	21,5	20,3	20,9	**IRL**
I	5,4	4,8	5,4	34,6	30,8	31,3	28,9	28,4	28,7	31,1	36,0	34,7	**I**
L	13,4	15,7	15,4	45,6	47,5	50,0	26,8	20,4	17,8	13,9	16,7	16,4	**L**
NL	11,0	12,1	7,1	48,0	47,4	45,9	27,1	25,8	28,0	14,0	14,7	19,0	**NL**
A	:	19,7	18,2	:	51,7	53,3	:	20,0	19,4	:	8,6	9,0	**A**
P	7,0	4,4	3,9	36,1	31,9	30,7	28,7	29,0	28,3	28,2	34,6	37,1	**P**
FIN	:	16,0	14,5	:	59,2	62,0	:	17,9	17,7	:	6,9	5,8	**FIN**
S	:	9,5	8,3	:	48,7	49,0	:	21,0	22,7	:	20,9	20,1	**S**
UK	10,5	8,9	8,6	45,6	46,7	48,3	24,9	24,6	24,4	19,0	19,9	18,8	**UK**
IS	:	:	:	:	:	:	:	:	:	:	:	:	**IS**
NO	15,2	13,9	12,9	50,5	54,7	55,3	20,2	19,5	19,8	14,0	11,9	12,1	**NO**

3B1IG 3B1IH 3B1II 3B1IJ

Further reading: Agriculture, statistical yearbook, 1999. Eurostat. Farm structure, 1997 survey. Eurostat. Farm structure, historical results. Surveys from 1966/67 to 1997. Eurostat.

Cereals are the main Community agricultural production in volume. Wheat, barley and grain maize represent more than 85 % of the total. The yields are higher in Europe than in the other big producers, because of an intensive way of growing.

Having achieved self-sufficiency, the EU exports a large part of its cereal harvest. From 1993, the new common agricultural policy has been bringing the supply into line with the demand, combining subsidies to cereal farmers with a compulsory set-aside scheme.

Production of cereals. 1 000 t

	Total (without rice)						of which wheat					
	1989	**1991**	**1994**	**1997**	**1999**		**1989**	**1991**	**1994**	**1997**	**1999**	
EU-15	:	:	174 321	205 741	201 457		:	93 978	85 698	94 877	97 582	**EU-15**
EUR-11	:	:	136 853	162 159	161 343		:	71 325	64 614	70 771	74 565	**EUR-11**
B	2 242	2 068	2 091	2 394	2 407		1 444	1 399	1 425	1 661	1 528	**B**
DK	8 795	9 231	7 825	9 530	8 775		3 224	3 670	3 725	4 965	4 471	**DK**
D	:	39 268	36 329	45 486	44 452		:	16 612	16 481	19 827	19 615	**D**
EL	5 722	6 056	5 318	4 533	4 288		2 763	3 138	2 698	2 067	2 021	**EL**
E	19 358	18 885	14 833	18 563	17 161		5 469	5 468	4 303	4 676	5 084	**E**
F	57 486	60 221	53 284	63 322	64 668		31 823	34 345	30 501	33 858	37 005	**F**
IRL	1 920	1 964	1 609	1 943	2 011		461	673	572	725	597	**IRL**
I	15 887	17 984	17 826	18 464	19 763		7 413	9 416	8 251	6 758	7 760	**I**
L	144	156	134	162	154		39	44	45	57	46	**L**
NL	1 365	1 249	1 406	1 623	1 416		1 047	944	981	1 063	851	**NL**
A	:	5 045	4 436	5 009	4 806		1 419	1 375	1 255	1 352	1 416	**A**
P	1 687	1 620	1 513	1 395	1 636		616	619	463	330	407	**P**
FIN	:	:	3 391	3 799	2 868		507	431	337	464	254	**FIN**
S	:	5 207	4 370	5 986	4 931		1 750	1 481	1 345	2 056	1 659	**S**
UK	22 729	22 641	19 955	23 533	22 119		14 033	14 364	13 316	15 018	14 866	**UK**
IS	:	:	:	3	:		:	:	:	:	:	**IS**
NO	:	:	1 015	1 288	1 303		:	:	195	:	:	**NO**
CH	:	:	:	:	:		:	:	:	:	:	**CH**

6A1AA
6A1AB

Further reading: Agriculture statistics: quarterly bulletin, 2000. Eurostat.

Cereal yields. 100 kg per ha. EU-15

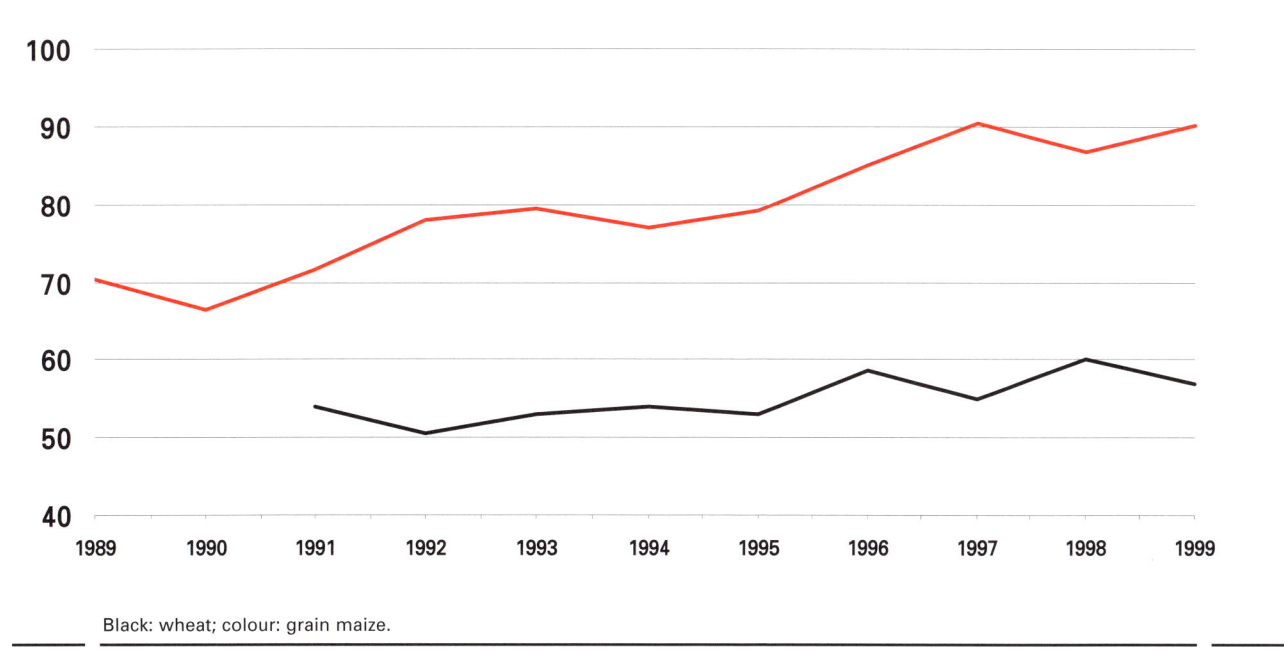

6A1AD

Black: wheat; colour: grain maize.

Further reading: Agriculture statistics: quarterly bulletin, 2000. Eurostat.

Fruit and vegetables are widely grown in the EU and represent a large part of the food exchanges amongst the Member States. Tomatoes are the main vegetables produced in Europe, especially in the southern countries. Apples count for one half of the total fruit tree production.

The EU is the world's leading wine producer with more than one half of total world production. The main part of the production is consumed in Europe, although exchanges with the other continents (particularly America and Asia) are increasing.

Production of fruit and vegetables. 1 000 t

	Tomatoes						Apples					
	1989	1991	1994	1997	1999		1989	1991	1994	1997	1999	
EU-15	:	13 036	13 427	13 642	:		:	6 178	8 766	8 000	:	EU-15
EUR-11	:	11 027	11 319	11 589	:		:	:	:	:	:	EUR-11
B	225	314	309	303	292		315	137	502	367	550	B
DK	17	18	20	19	:		52	32	38	33	:	DK
D	:	32	25	36	42		:	781	880	765	1 036	D
EL	2 052	1 840	1 961	1 900	1 888		312	186	330	292	336	EL
E	2 964	2 665	3 109	3 360	3 865		810	517	774	984	922	E
F	802	831	800	805	921		2 330	1 672	2 683	2 486	2 643	F
IRL	11	9	12	7	:		12	12	12	10	:	IRL
I	5 730	5 798	5 575	5 574	7 561		1 924	1 830	2 233	1 966	2 344	I
L	0	0	0	0	0		7	2	9	4	12	L
NL	621	636	561	510	525		417	223	530	420	570	NL
A	18	14	15	18	20		108	128	147	188	188	A
P	865	698	879	942	1 387		266	263	212	286	:	P
FIN	30	30	35	33	36		2	2	2	3	2	FIN
S	16	18	19	20	:		:	17	18	19	:	S
UK	130	133	109	115	117		446	376	399	177	352	UK
IS	1	1	:	1	:		:	:	:	:	:	IS
NO	10	10	10	10	:		:	:	:	:	:	NO
CH	:	:	:	:	:		:	:	:	:	:	CH

3B1LC

3B1LD

Further reading: Agriculture statistics: quarterly bulletin, 2000. Eurostat.

Production of wine. 1 000 hl

	1989	1990	1991	1992	1993	1994	1995	1996	1997	1998	1999	
EU-15	:	:	184 579	159 408	193 566	160 847	155 916	152 817	169 324	157 777	162 562	EU-15
EUR-11	:	:	:	:	:	:	:	:	:	:	:	EUR-11
B	2	2	2	1	2	2	2	2	2	2	2	B
DK	0	0	0	0	0	0	0	0	0	0	0	DK
D	:	:	9 505	10 699	13 482	9 920	10 406	8 361	8 678	8 394	10 727	D
EL	4 345	4 531	3 525	4 021	4 050	3 378	3 051	3 875	4 105	3 980	3 826	EL
E	22 252	31 276	38 658	30 796	34 032	26 495	20 995	20 876	31 000	33 218	31 173	E
F	57 170	60 508	63 940	41 438	63 256	52 059	53 325	54 354	57 240	53 612	53 071	F
IRL	0	0	0	0	0	0	0	0	0	0	0	IRL
I	60 360	59 727	54 266	59 238	68 086	62 068	58 776	55 702	56 322	50 563	57 140	I
L	142	232	151	86	271	170	175	150	128	75	159	L
NL	0	0	0	0	0	0	0	0	0	0	0	NL
A	3 502	2 581	3 166	3 093	2 590	1 866	2 647	2 229	2 110	1 802	2 703	A
P	3 938	7 901	11 351	10 021	7 771	4 871	6 521	7 255	9 712	6 124	3 750	P
FIN	0	0	0	0	0	0	0	0	0	0	0	FIN
S	0	0	0	0	0	0	0	0	0	0	0	S
UK	6	21	15	15	26	18	18	13	27	7	11	UK
IS	:	:	:	:	:	:	:	:	:	:	:	IS
NO	:	:	:	:	:	:	:	:	:	:	:	NO
CH	:	:	:	:	:	:	:	:	:	:	:	CH

3B1MD

Further reading: Agriculture statistics: quarterly bulletin, 2000. Eurostat.

4

The year 1999 was marked by a clear resumption of milk collection within the EU. After several years of stability, it has risen by 1.3 % compared to 1998. This increase is more pronounced in the southern countries (Spain, Portugal, Italy). It is less so in the principal producer countries (Germany, France).

Collection of cow's milk (cumulated monthly data)

1 000 t

	1988	1991	1994	1997	1998	1999	
EU-15	:	:	:	113 155	113 243	114 725	**EU-15**
EUR-11	:	:	:	90 674	90 885	91 988	**EUR-11**
B	3 118	3 084	2 948	2 908	3 287	3 264	**B**
DK	4 539	4 440	4 442	4 432	4 468	4 455	**DK**
D	:	26 409	25 862	26 986	26 752	26 783	**D**
EL	486	534	584	549	550	527	**EL**
E	4 377	5 829	4 926	5 488	5 378	5 662	**E**
F	24 092	23 379	23 224	22 922	22 969	23 121	**F**
IRL	5 196	5 019	5 272	5 256	5 091	5 121	**IRL**
I	8 554	9 894	9 540	9 877	10 130	10 371	**I**
L	269	253	251	255	255	258	**L**
NL	11 048	10 570	10 468	10 519	10 541	10 683	**NL**
A	:	:	:	2 420	2 430	2 535	**A**
P	1 232	1 535	1 476	1 673	1 689	1 797	**P**
FIN	:	:	:	2 370	2 363	2 394	**FIN**
S	:	:	:	3 240	3 278	3 299	**S**
UK	14 582	14 130	14 333	14 261	14 063	14 456	**UK**
IS	:	:	:	106	109	111	**IS**
NO	:	:	:	1 731	1 713	1 682	**NO**

Further reading: Agriculture statistical yearbook, 2000. Eurostat.

3B1PF

4

Production of cheese

1 000 t

	1988	1991	1994	1997	1998	1999	
EU-15	:	:	:	5 901	5 972	:	**EU-15**
EUR-11	:	:	:	5 114	5 190	:	**EUR-11**
B	59	64	70	71	70	60	**B**
DK	260	285	288	291	292	290	**DK**
D	:	1 245	1 399	1 590	1 602	1 594	**D**
EL	15	13	12	10	8	9	**EL**
E	74	84	64	97	77	118	**E**
F	1 284	1 396	1 475	1 521	1 550	1 553	**F**
IRL	75	73	93	96	92	105	**IRL**
I	649	765	767	799	900	918	**I**
L	4	4	4	3	3	:	**L**
NL	565	613	663	705	649	652	**NL**
A	:	:	:	97	107	105	**A**
P	33	40	44	47	48	52	**P**
FIN	:	:	:	88	93	92	**FIN**
S	:	:	:	119	125	127	**S**
UK	299	285	334	368	357	361	**UK**
IS	:	:	:	5	5	5	**IS**
NO	:	:	:	67	71	64	**NO**

6B2BO

Further reading: Agriculture statistical yearbook, 2000. Eurostat.

With an increase of 4 %, butter production also diplays a clear resumption. With more than 1 800 000 tonnes, it has reached a level higher than that of 1996, while over this period it has been showing a regular decrease.

Production of butter

1 000 t

	1988	1991	1994	1997	1998	1999	
EU-15	:	:	:	1 779	1 742	:	EU-15
EUR-11	:	:	:	1 531	1 517	:	EUR-11
B	51	49	28	97	104	113	B
DK	94	70	59	50	49	48	DK
D	:	553	461	442	426	427	D
EL	1	1	1	1	1	1	EL
E	24	37	19	30	22	36	E
F	513	478	439	467	463	448	F
IRL	124	140	137	148	140	143	IRL
I	79	102	92	92	94	104	I
L	6	4	3	3	3	:	L
NL	170	163	128	131	149	179	NL
A	:	:	:	40	38	36	A
P	9	15	16	21	19	25	P
FIN	:	:	:	59	58	60	FIN
S	:	:	:	58	39	48	S
UK	140	129	148	139	137	141	UK
IS	:	:	:	1	1	2	IS
NO	:	:	:	18	27	20	NO

6A1AK

Further reading: Agriculture statistical yearbook, 2000. Eurostat.

4

Production of milk powder

1 000 t

	1988	1991	1994	1997	1998	1999	
EU-15	:	:	:	864	:	:	EU-15
EUR-11	:	:	:	658	701	:	EUR-11
B	52	47	66	72	78	60	B
DK	97	109	114	104	107	98	DK
D	:	237	202	201	203	200	D
EL	0	0	0	0	:	:	EL
E	14	21	10	5	13	7	E
F	237	302	280	251	259	259	F
IRL	0	0	0	0	0	0	IRL
I	2	3	0	0	0	:	I
L	0	0	0	0	13	0	L
NL	183	175	135	112	116	105	NL
A	:	:	:	5	7	6	A
P	5	8	8	8	8	8	P
FIN	:	:	:	4	4	3	FIN
S	:	:	:	6	:	:	S
UK	104	73	83	96	97	102	UK
IS	:	:	:	0	0	0	IS
NO	:	:	:	2	2	3	NO

6A1AO

Further reading: Agriculture statistical yearbook, 2000. Eurostat.

Cheese production continues to show a regular increase (+ 1.2 % between 1998 and 1999). This movement confirms the change in consumer eating habits which turns more to this type of product.

The production of milk powder shows a fall of almost 6 % in 1999. This variation cancels out the two increases in 1997 and 1998.

Yearly yield of dairy cows. 1 000 kg milk per cow

6A1AM

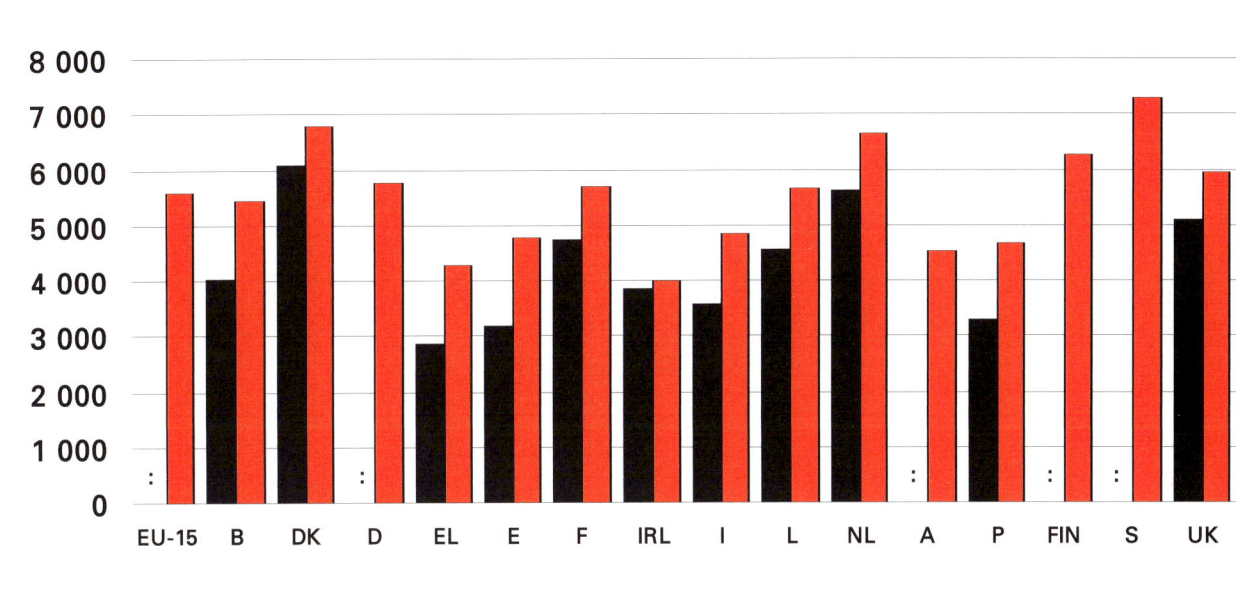

Black: 1988; colour: 1999.

Further reading: Agriculture statistical yearbook, 1998. Eurostat.   Eurostat estimation including confidential data.

EU-15 production of milk powder, butter and cheese (1 000 t)

6A1AN

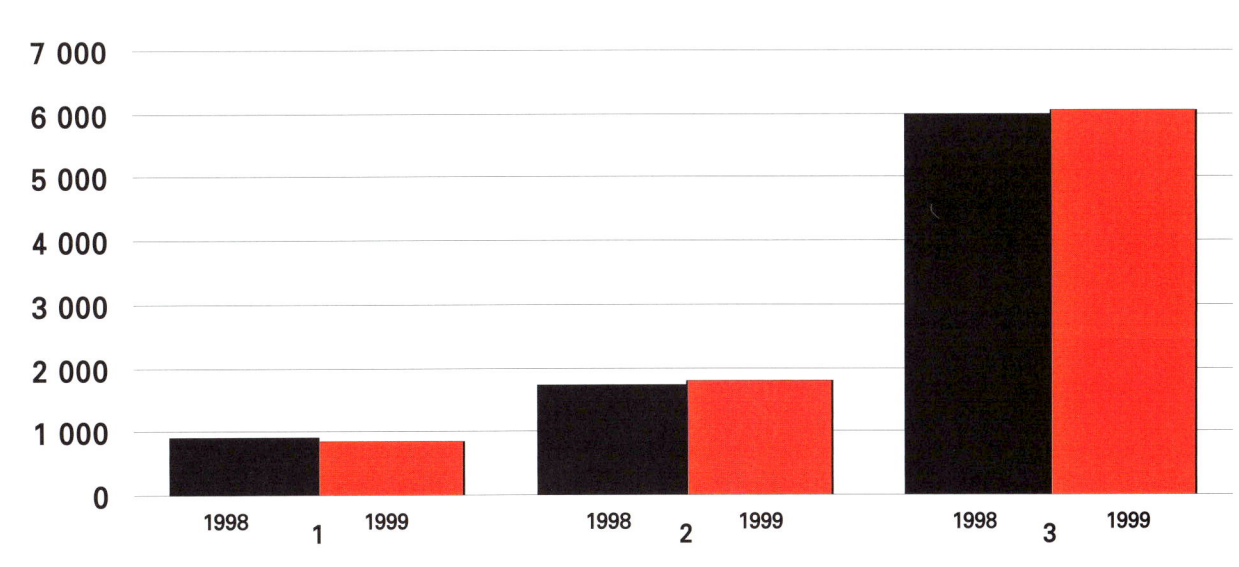

1: milk powder; 2: butter and other yellow fat dairy products; 3: cheese.

Further reading: Agriculture statistical yearbook, 1999. Eurostat.   Eurostat estimation including confidential data.

Gross value added at market prices in EUR 1 000 per person employed in agriculture. 1997. NUTS 2

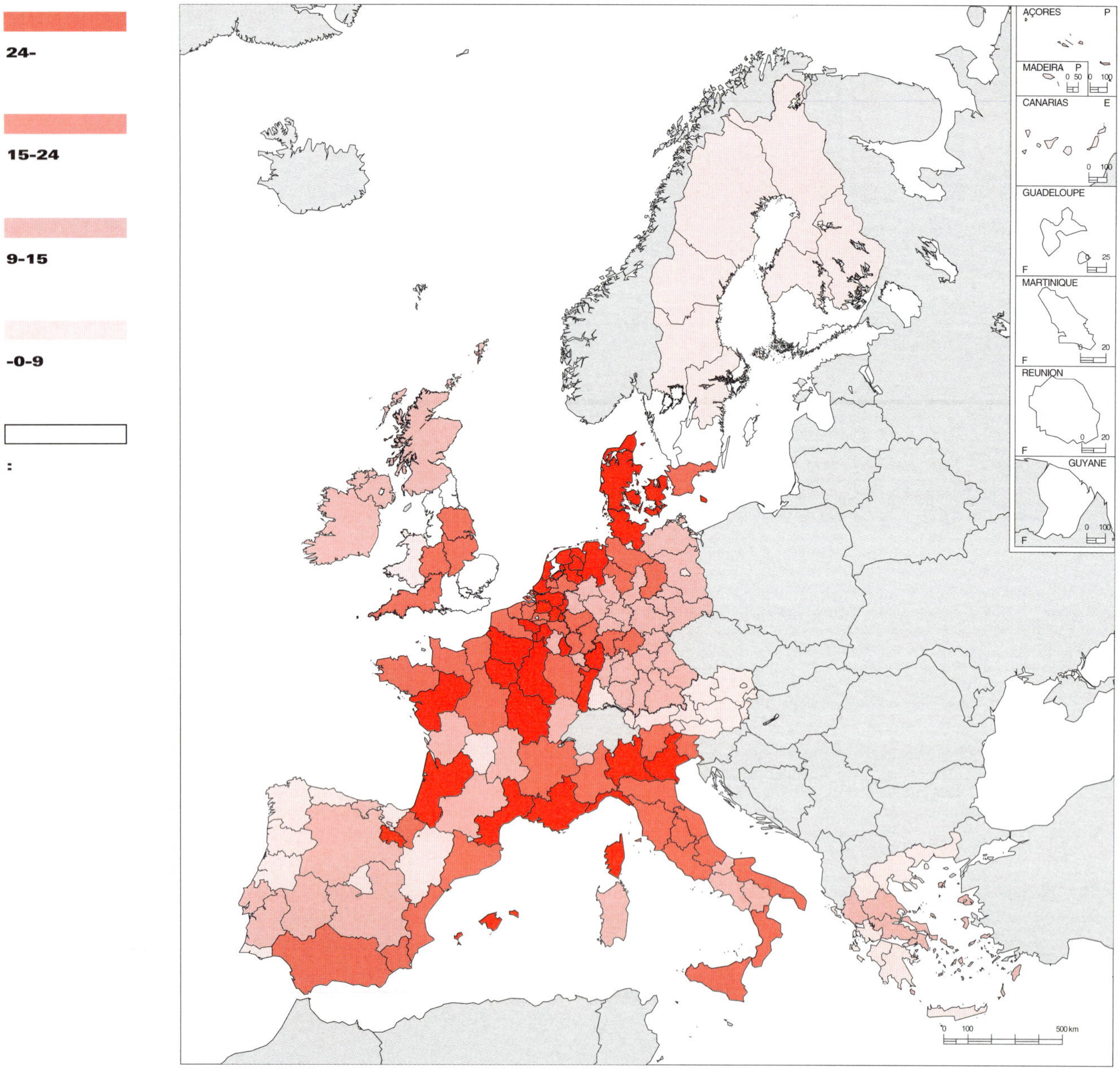

24-

15-24

9-15

-0-9

4

:

7R3BD

Further reading: Regions, statistical yearbook, 2000. Eurostat.

B, I, FIN: 1992–96. E, UK: 1991–95. NL: 1989–93. EL: 1989–90, 1992–94.
NUTS 2. DED (D Saxony), IRL, UK: NUTS 1.

Production of meat

Pork: slaughtering in 1 000 t   Poultry: slaughtering in 1 000 t

	1989	1992	1995	1998	1999		1989	1992	1995	1998	1999	
EU-15	:	:	15 976	17 635	18 020		:	:	8 042	8 821	:	EU-15
B	825	944	1 035	1 077	993		154	194	270	346	325	B
DK	1 163	1 372	1 475	1 631	1 642		128	160	184	194	205	DK
D	:	3 684	3 602	3 834	4 113		:	604	664	790	807	D
EL	151	153	142	143	138		153	175	161	149	:	EL
E	1 694	1 912	2 175	2 744	2 892		828	858	1 008	999	:	E
F	1 754	1 903	2 144	2 313	2 377		1 557	1 865	2 079	2 319	:	F
IRL	144	202	211	239	251		69	90	112	122	:	IRL
I	1 295	1 328	1 346	1 412	1 472		1 094	1 095	1 098	1 148	1 131	I
L	8	7	8	9	12		:	:	:	:	:	L
NL	1 606	1 585	1 622	1 725	1 711		498	574	610	674	:	NL
A	:	:	466	508	520		:	:	99	107	104	A
P	210	237	282	330	344		183	217	231	298	287	P
FIN	:	:	166	184	182		:	:	43	61	66	FIN
S	:	:	309	330	325		:	:	80	88	92	S
UK	939	971	992	1 155	1 047		1 117	1 229	1 404	1 526	1 502	UK

6A1AS   6A1AT

Further reading: Agriculture statistical yearbook, 2000. Eurostat.   D: includes since 1991 data on the former GDR.

More data on this in Eurostat's database

The data concern agricultural production:
- the means of production: land use; livestock (number and structure); annual data;
- crop production (area, yield, production); annual data;
- animal production (production and trade); monthly and annual data;
- summary data (balance sheets); annual data.

➤ ➤ ➤ **DOMAIN ZPA1 IN DATABASE NEW CRONOS**

4

Production of meat

Veal and beef: slaughtering in 1 000 t   Sheep and goats: slaughtering in 1 000 t

	1989	1992	1995	1998	1999		1989	1992	1995	1998	1999	
EU-15	:	:	7 964	7 646	7 681		:	:	1 136	1 124	1 116	EU-15
B	298	352	349	296	273		10	6	5	4	2	B
DK	204	217	185	163	157		1	2	2	1	1	DK
D	:	1 829	1 408	1 366	1 374		:	44	42	44	44	D
EL	81	80	70	68	65		131	132	128	126	126	EL
E	453	535	508	651	678		220	247	242	249	239	E
F	1 673	1 877	1 683	1 630	1 604		161	172	148	144	140	F
IRL	432	565	480	590	640		63	95	90	83	86	IRL
I	1 147	1 218	1 181	1 113	1 164		79	86	76	73	73	I
L	7	7	7	8	9		0	0	0	0	0	L
NL	486	635	580	534	508		14	17	16	16	17	NL
A	:	:	196	198	203		:	:	6	8	8	A
P	129	123	104	90	96		15	14	14	13	12	P
FIN	:	:	96	93	90		:	:	1	1	1	FIN
S	:	:	143	142	144		:	:	3	3	4	S
UK	978	960	974	705	678		366	357	365	356	362	UK

6A1AU   6A1AV

Further reading: Agriculture statistical yearbook, 2000. Eurostat.   D: includes since 1991 data on the former GDR.

From 1996 to 1999, the overall development of the meat markets in the European Union was characterised by turbulent trends. In 1996, the BSE crisis in the beef sector caused major problems, whilst the other sectors were able to derive benefits from it. Beef production recovered again in 1997. The market prices which had fallen in 1996 rose constantly in 1997/98 to reach pre-crisis level again at the beginning of 1999. The beef market regained its balance, thanks to the measures introduced by the European Commission and the restoration of consumer confidence.

The pigmeat market is going through a period of major turbulence. In 1996 it derived benefits from the BSE crisis but in 1997 it underwent a serious production crisis following the outbreak of classical swine fever. In the Netherlands, there was a 33 % decline in production in 1997 compared with 1996 and Germany and Spain recorded appreciable declines in specific areas. In the regions not affected by the disease, however, pig producers reacted quickly by expanding their herds in order to profit from the high prices. The EU as a whole therefore recorded hardly any decline in pig production at the end of 1997 compared with 1996. These extra production capacities and the resumption of production in the Netherlands caused pig production in the EU to rise by 7.5 % in 1998 compared with 1997. This over-supply, exacerbated by a marketing crisis in third countries (Russia, Asia) led to a sharp fall in prices starting in the second half of 1998. Producers reacted to this situation with restraint and a fall in production, and thus a stabilisation of the market, was not expected until the last quarter of 1999.

In the wake of the BSE crisis, the supply of sheepmeat rose sharply in 1996. The wet summer of 1997 led to a fall in production, but rising prices kept demand down. In 1998 production recovered but the rise in supplies was accompanied by marketing problems (weak demand in Europe, export problems in third countries) leading to low prices in late 1998. The level of production at the end of 1998 was about the same as at the end of 1996. The long-term trend over the past seven years shows an average fall in production of 1.4 % per year.

Production of poultrymeat exceeded that of beef in 1996. Poultrymeat now takes second place in meat production and consumption in the EU after pigmeat. Increases in production of over 2 % per year were recorded for 1997 compared with 1996 and 1998 compared with 1997.

Overall meat production in the EU amounts to about 38.5 million tonnes carcass weight. Of this, some 45 % is accounted for by pigmeat, 23 % by poultrymeat, 20 % by beef and veal and 3 % by sheep and goatmeat.

4

Meat production: gross indigenous production in 1 000 t

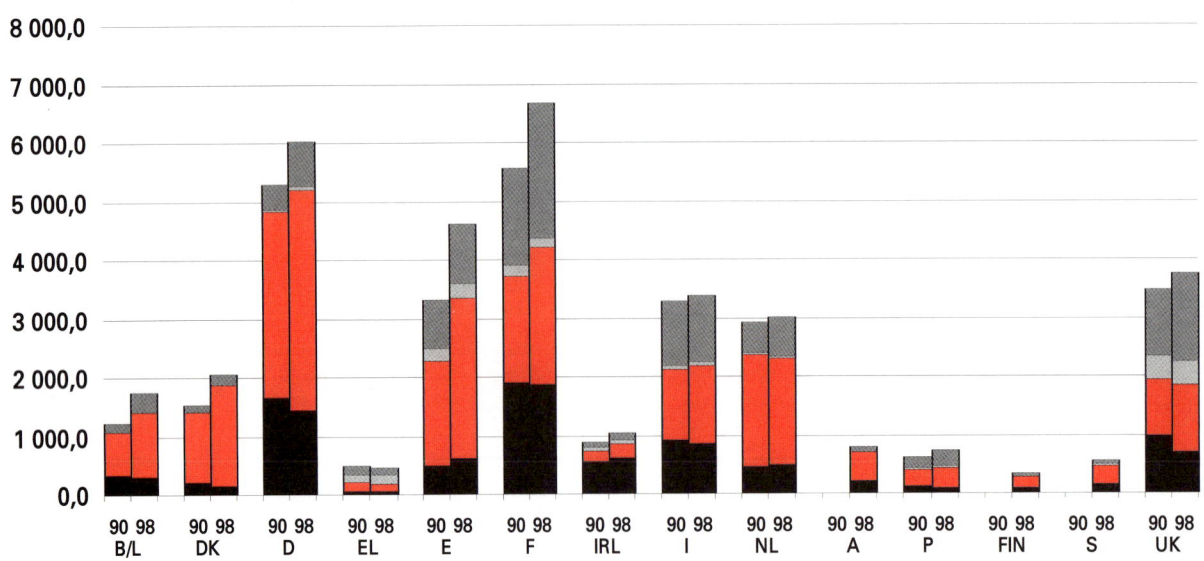

Black: beef and veal; colour: pork; light grey: sheep and goats; grey: poultry.

Further reading: Agriculture statistical yearbook, 2000. Eurostat.   D: includes since 1991 data on the former GDR.

Producer price indices, nominal; total agricultural production. 1990 = 100

	1989	1990	1991	1992	1993	1994	1995	1996	1997	1998	1999	
EU-15	:	100	103	99	97	101	105	105	104	101	98	EU-15
EUR-11	:	100	102	97	95	98	101	101	100	98	95	EUR-11
B	107	100	101	98	91	94	90	91	93	88	82	B
DK	108	100	98	97	85	86	86	87	87	78	75	DK
D	:	100	99	98	90	91	92	91	92	87	82	D
EL	84	100	120	125	134	154	168	180	186	186	187	EL
E	100	100	101	94	99	109	121	121	115	113	112	E
F	100	100	101	95	90	90	90	89	90	90	87	F
IRL	113	100	96	98	104	106	108	103	96	95	91	IRL
I	96	100	109	100	103	106	116	118	118	118	114	I
L	102	100	92	87	86	86	84	83	84	83	82	L
NL	105	100	105	99	92	95	98	100	105	100	93	NL
A	:	100	100	99	97	98	74	75	77	72	70	A
P	96	100	97	90	90	92	102	102	95	101	97	P
FIN	:	100	96	96	96	96	72	61	60	60	59	FIN
S	:	100	100	97	93	98	98	94	91	92	90	S
UK	99	100	99	101	105	107	116	114	99	90	87	UK

Further reading: Agricultural prices, price indices and absolute prices, 1989–98. Eurostat. Agriculture, statistical yearbook, 1999. Eurostat.   D: includes since 1991 data on the former GDR.

More data on this in Eurostat's database

The domain PRAG contains monthly and annual data on agricultural price indices and absolute prices. The price indices comprise the EU index of producer prices of agricultural products and the EU index of purchase prices of the means of agricultural production. The absolute prices comprise selling prices of crop products and animal products, purchase prices of the means of agricultural production, agricultural land prices and rents.

➤ ➤ ➤ **DOMAIN PRAG IN DATABASE NEW CRONOS**

Producer price indices, deflated; total agricultural production. 1990 = 100

	1989	1990	1991	1992	1993	1994	1995	1996	1997	1998	1999	
EU-15	:	100	97	89	85	85	85	83	80	77	73	EU-15
EUR-11	:	100	98	89	84	84	84	82	80	78	74	EUR-11
B	110	100	98	92	84	85	79	79	79	75	68	B
DK	111	100	96	93	80	79	78	77	76	67	63	DK
D	:	100	95	91	81	79	79	77	76	71	67	D
EL	101	100	101	90	84	87	88	87	85	81	79	EL
E	107	100	95	83	84	89	94	91	85	82	79	E
F	103	100	98	90	84	82	80	79	78	78	75	F
IRL	117	100	93	92	97	96	96	89	82	80	75	IRL
I	103	100	103	90	88	87	91	89	87	85	81	I
L	106	100	90	82	78	76	74	71	71	70	68	L
NL	108	100	101	92	83	84	85	85	87	82	74	NL
A	1	100	97	92	87	86	63	63	63	59	57	A
P	109	100	87	74	70	68	72	70	64	67	62	P
FIN	:	100	93	90	88	87	64	54	53	52	50	FIN
S	:	100	92	86	79	82	80	76	74	75	72	S
UK	108	100	94	92	95	93	98	94	79	70	66	UK

Further reading: Agricultural prices, price indices and absolute prices, 1989–98. Eurostat. Agriculture, statistical yearbook, 1999. Eurostat.   D: includes since 1991 data on the former GDR.

Producer price indices cover sales of products (output) from agriculture to the rest of the economy. Purchase price indices cover purchases of means of agricultural production (input). Indices are calculated from farm-gate prices excluding VAT. Deflation is calculated by using the consumer price index.

Purchase price indices, nominal; total means of agricultural production. 1990 = 100

	1989	1990	1991	1992	1993	1994	1995	1996	1997	1998	1999	
EU-15	:	100	103	106	108	109	113	117	118	116	115	**EU-15**
EUR-11	:	100	103	105	106	108	110	114	116	114	113	**EUR-11**
B	103	100	101	101	100	100	101	105	107	103	102	**B**
DK	101	100	100	99	100	98	99	102	105	103	103	**DK**
D	:	100	103	105	105	106	106	109	111	107	107	**D**
EL	76	100	121	136	152	169	181	196	201	204	205	**EL**
E	98	100	102	103	107	110	114	119	122	122	120	**E**
F	100	100	101	102	103	103	105	109	111	108	107	**F**
IRL	99	100	101	101	102	104	106	110	109	108	109	**IRL**
I	95	100	104	108	115	117	126	131	132	130	130	**I**
L	74	100	103	106	105	106	107	110	111	110	111	**L**
NL	101	100	102	104	103	101	104	108	109	107	106	**NL**
A	:	100	103	106	108	107	107	111	114	112	112	**A**
P	96	100	105	110	106	112	113	114	111	109	109	**P**
FIN	:	100	106	108	110	108	87	88	90	89	88	**FIN**
S	:	100	105	105	106	109	115	121	123	122	122	**S**
UK	97	100	104	107	112	112	115	122	118	111	110	**UK**

3B2EA

Further reading: Agricultural prices, price indices and absolute prices, 1989–98. Eurostat. Agriculture, statistical yearbook, 1999. Eurostat.

D: includes since 1991 data on the former GDR.

Purchase price indices, deflated; total means of agricultural production. 1990 = 100

	1989	1990	1991	1992	1993	1994	1995	1996	1997	1998	1999	
EU-15	:	100	98	96	95	93	93	94	93	90	88	**EU-15**
EUR-11	:	100	98	96	94	93	92	93	93	90	88	**EUR-11**
B	107	100	97	95	92	90	89	91	91	87	85	**B**
DK	104	100	97	95	94	91	90	91	91	88	86	**DK**
D	:	100	99	97	94	92	91	92	92	88	87	**D**
EL	91	100	101	98	96	96	94	94	91	88	87	**EL**
E	105	100	96	92	91	90	89	90	90	88	85	**E**
F	103	100	98	97	95	94	94	96	96	93	92	**F**
IRL	103	100	98	95	95	94	94	95	93	91	89	**IRL**
I	102	100	98	97	98	97	99	99	97	94	92	**I**
L	76	100	100	99	96	94	94	95	94	93	92	**L**
NL	103	100	98	97	93	89	90	92	90	87	84	**NL**
A	:	100	100	98	97	94	91	93	94	92	91	**A**
P	108	100	95	91	82	83	80	78	75	72	70	**P**
FIN	:	100	101	100	100	97	77	79	79	77	75	**FIN**
S	:	100	96	94	90	91	94	98	100	99	98	**S**
UK	106	100	98	98	100	98	98	101	94	86	84	**UK**

3B2ED

Further reading: Agricultural prices, price indices and absolute prices, 1989–98. Eurostat. Agriculture, statistical yearbook, 1999. Eurostat.

D: includes since 1991 data on the former GDR.

3B2DB

Producer price indices, nominal; crop products. 1990 = 100

	1989	1990	1991	1992	1993	1994	1995	1996	1997	1998	1999	
EU-15	:	100	107	97	95	101	110	110	107	109	106	EU-15
EUR-11	:	100	106	94	93	98	106	105	102	105	102	EUR-11
B	101	100	109	96	91	102	96	96	93	99	94	B
DK	107	100	101	97	85	87	88	85	84	82	79	DK
D	:	100	102	95	87	92	96	91	88	87	84	D
EL	83	100	124	126	133	154	172	188	195	193	191	EL
E	95	100	102	91	97	109	128	124	112	115	117	E
F	96	100	105	92	86	86	87	88	86	88	86	F
IRL	107	100	104	101	105	105	113	99	91	104	102	IRL
I	93	100	114	99	99	104	117	120	121	122	118	I
L	99	100	100	74	77	81	78	88	92	94	94	L
NL	100	100	110	97	94	102	110	111	118	121	115	NL
A	:	100	99	93	94	97	72	74	75	73	72	A
P	93	100	98	85	85	90	111	107	95	115	109	P
FIN	:	100	93	94	94	93	62	57	57	58	57	FIN
S	:	100	104	92	80	93	104	97	89	93	102	S
UK	96	100	101	97	96	98	112	103	86	87	84	UK

Further reading: Agricultural prices, price indices and absolute prices, 1989–98.   D: includes since 1991 data on the former GDR.
Eurostat. Agriculture, statistical yearbook, 1999. Eurostat.

4

3B2DC

Producer price indices, nominal; animals and animal products. 1990 = 100

	1989	1990	1991	1992	1993	1994	1995	1996	1997	1998	1999	
EU-15	:	100	99	100	99	100	100	101	101	94	90	EU-15
EUR-11	:	100	98	99	96	97	96	97	99	93	88	EUR-11
B	110	100	97	99	91	90	86	89	93	82	75	B
DK	110	100	97	97	85	85	84	88	89	76	73	DK
D	:	100	97	100	91	91	90	91	94	86	82	D
EL	85	100	111	124	136	153	159	160	165	171	177	EL
E	108	100	98	99	101	109	111	116	120	110	103	E
F	104	100	97	98	94	94	93	92	94	92	88	F
IRL	114	100	95	97	104	106	108	103	97	94	90	IRL
I	101	100	103	103	108	110	114	116	114	111	108	I
L	103	100	91	90	88	87	86	82	83	80	79	L
NL	109	100	101	100	90	90	89	92	96	85	77	NL
A	:	100	101	101	98	98	75	75	77	71	69	A
P	99	100	96	94	94	93	93	96	95	88	84	P
FIN	:	100	98	97	97	97	76	63	62	61	60	FIN
S	:	100	99	98	97	99	96	93	92	92	85	S
UK	101	100	98	104	112	112	119	122	108	92	88	UK

Further reading: Agricultural prices, price indices and absolute prices, 1989–98.   D: includes since 1991 data on the former GDR.
Eurostat. Agriculture, statistical yearbook, 1999. Eurostat.

The producer price indices cover sales of crop and animal products from agriculture to the rest of the economy. The share of crop and animal products in total agricultural sales differs between Member States. Indices are calculated from farm-gate prices excluding VAT. Deflation is calculated by using the consumer price index.

Producer price indices, deflated; crop products. 1990 = 100

	1989	1990	1991	1992	1993	1994	1995	1996	1997	1998	1999	
EU-15	:	100	101	87	82	84	88	84	80	80	77	EU-15
EUR-11	:	100	101	86	82	84	87	84	81	81	78	EUR-11
B	104	100	105	90	84	92	85	83	79	84	79	B
DK	109	100	99	92	80	81	80	76	73	70	66	DK
D	:	100	98	88	78	80	82	77	73	71	69	D
EL	100	100	104	91	84	88	90	90	89	84	81	EL
E	102	100	96	81	83	89	99	93	83	83	83	E
F	99	100	101	87	80	79	78	77	75	76	73	F
IRL	111	100	101	95	98	95	100	86	78	87	83	IRL
I	100	100	107	89	85	85	92	91	89	89	84	I
L	103	100	97	70	69	72	68	75	78	79	78	L
NL	102	100	106	91	85	90	96	94	98	99	92	NL
A	:	100	95	86	84	85	61	62	62	60	59	A
P	106	100	88	71	66	67	79	74	64	75	70	P
FIN	:	100	89	88	86	84	56	50	50	50	49	FIN
S	:	100	95	82	69	78	85	79	72	75	82	S
UK	105	100	95	88	86	86	95	85	69	68	64	UK

3B2DE

Further reading: Agricultural prices, price indices and absolute prices, 1989–98. Eurostat. Agriculture, statistical yearbook, 1999. Eurostat.

D: includes since 1991 data on the former GDR.

Producer price indices, deflated; animals and animal products. 1990 = 100

	1989	1990	1991	1992	1993	1994	1995	1996	1997	1998	1999	
EU-15	:	100	94	92	87	86	83	82	80	73	69	EU-15
EUR-11	:	100	94	92	86	84	81	80	80	74	69	EUR-11
B	114	100	94	93	84	81	76	77	79	70	63	B
DK	112	100	95	93	80	79	76	78	78	65	61	DK
D	:	100	94	93	82	79	77	77	78	71	66	D
EL	103	100	93	89	86	87	83	77	75	74	75	EL
E	116	100	92	88	86	88	86	87	88	79	73	E
F	107	100	94	92	88	86	83	80	82	79	76	F
IRL	118	100	92	91	97	96	95	90	83	79	73	IRL
I	108	100	97	92	92	90	90	87	84	81	77	I
L	106	100	88	85	80	77	75	70	70	68	66	L
NL	112	100	97	93	82	80	77	78	79	69	61	NL
A	:	100	98	94	88	86	64	63	64	58	56	A
P	112	100	86	78	73	69	66	66	64	58	54	P
FIN	:	100	94	90	88	88	67	56	54	53	51	FIN
S	:	100	90	88	83	83	78	75	74	75	69	S
UK	110	100	93	94	100	98	101	101	86	71	68	UK

3B2DF

Further reading: Agricultural prices, price indices and absolute prices, 1989–98. Eurostat. Agriculture, statistical yearbook, 1999. Eurostat.

D: includes since 1991 data on the former GDR.

4

Under the new methodology of the Economic Accounts for Agriculture (EAA 97), crop output includes sales between agricultural holdings as well as intra-unit consumption of crop products used in animal feed (excluded under the old methodology which was based on the concept of the national farm). The EAA 97 constitute a satellite account of the European System of Accounts (ESA 95).

More data on this in Eurostat's database

COSA contains six collections: economic accounts for agriculture; economic accounts for forestry; income of the agricultural household sector (IAHS statistics, formerly TIAH) per socioprofessional group; agricultural labour input; gross domestic product data; exchange rates (EUR, PPS) which have been used in the calculation of the derived series.

➤ ➤ ➤ **DOMAIN COSA IN DATABASE NEW CRONOS**

Crop output. Million ECU/EUR

3B2FD

	1989	1990	1991	1992	1993	1994	1995	1996	1997	1998	1999	
EU-15	:	:	:	:	:	:	:	:	:	:	:	EU-15
EUR-11	:	:	:	:	:	:	:	:	:	:	:	EUR-11
B	:	:	:	:	:	:	2 751	2 669	2 593	2 770	:	B
DK	:	3 355	3 238	2 730	3 194	3 165	3 511	3 483	3 404	3 313	3 207	DK
D	:	:	19 786	19 420	21 041	23 257	23 459	23 367	22 943	22 693	21 866	D
EL	:	:	:	:	:	:	8 070	8 202	8 496	8 177	:	EL
E	:	19 175	19 234	16 847	16 260	17 132	17 797	19 842	20 585	21 049	:	E
F	31 367	32 690	30 935	31 539	30 210	32 654	34 886	35 886	35 854	37 101	36 854	F
IRL	:	:	:	:	:	:	:	:	:	:	:	IRL
I	:	26 819	30 540	28 648	24 178	23 613	23 179	26 455	27 110	26 938	:	I
L	80	77	70	91	82	81	87	86	71	86	90	L
NL	:	:	:	:	:	:	9 037	8 915	9 146	9 210	9 357	NL
A	:	:	:	:	:	:	2 700	2 471	2 608	2 539	2 464	A
P	:	:	:	:	:	:	3 091	3 186	2 825	2 853	:	P
FIN	:	2 952	2 365	1 891	1 822	1 880	1 605	1 565	1 573	1 406	:	FIN
S	2 307	2 478	2 199	1 928	1 581	1 559	1 893	2 121	2 050	1 875	:	S
UK	7 889	7 879	8 336	8 046	8 063	8 330	9 222	9 261	9 163	9 142	9 375	UK

Further reading: Manual on the Economic Accounts for Agriculture and Forestry EAA/EAF 97 (Rev. 1.1). Eurostat. Agriculture, statistical yearbook, 2000. Eurostat.

Animal output. Million ECU/EUR

3B2FE

	1989	1990	1991	1992	1993	1994	1995	1996	1997	1998	1999	
EU-15	:	:	:	:	:	:	:	:	:	:	:	EU-15
EUR-11	:	:	:	:	:	:	:	:	:	:	:	EUR-11
B	:	:	:	:	:	:	3 951	4 157	4 190	3 640	:	B
DK	:	4 479	4 349	4 673	4 435	4 490	4 785	4 970	5 022	4 362	4 220	DK
D	:	:	20 204	20 557	19 752	19 570	20 274	20 322	20 252	18 585	18 425	D
EL	:	:	:	:	:	:	2 655	2 422	2 563	2 558	:	EL
E	:	11 068	11 432	11 002	10 011	10 627	10 712	12 013	11 959	11 398	:	E
F	21 481	22 064	21 308	22 309	22 470	22 941	23 418	23 776	23 885	23 370	22 647	F
IRL	:	:	:	:	:	:	:	:	:	:	:	IRL
I	:	14 097	14 170	14 010	12 685	12 505	11 874	13 565	13 451	12 861	:	I
L	151	156	140	142	152	150	164	156	148	149	147	L
NL	:	:	:	:	:	:	9 346	9 367	8 311	8 201	7 633	NL
A	:	:	:	:	:	:	2 517	2 505	2 437	2 351	2 190	A
P	:	:	:	:	:	:	2 119	2 327	2 288	2 190	:	P
FIN	:	3 669	3 304	2 761	2 428	2 662	2 395	2 125	2 109	1 891	:	FIN
S	3 439	3 195	2 955	2 954	2 547	2 551	2 341	2 480	2 451	2 299	:	S
UK	13 336	12 529	12 769	12 801	13 362	13 706	13 182	13 714	15 151	13 324	12 876	UK

Further reading: Manual on the Economic Accounts for Agriculture and Forestry EAA/EAF 97 (Rev. 1.1). Eurostat. Agriculture, statistical yearbook, 2000. Eurostat.

4

Agricultural output comprises all (agricultural) output sold by agricultural units, held in stock on the farms, or used for further processing by agricultural producers. Furthermore, it includes the intra–unit consumption of crop products used in animal feed, as well as output accounted for by own-account production of fixed capital goods and own final consumption (of agricultural units).

Crop and animal output as % of agricultural output. 1999

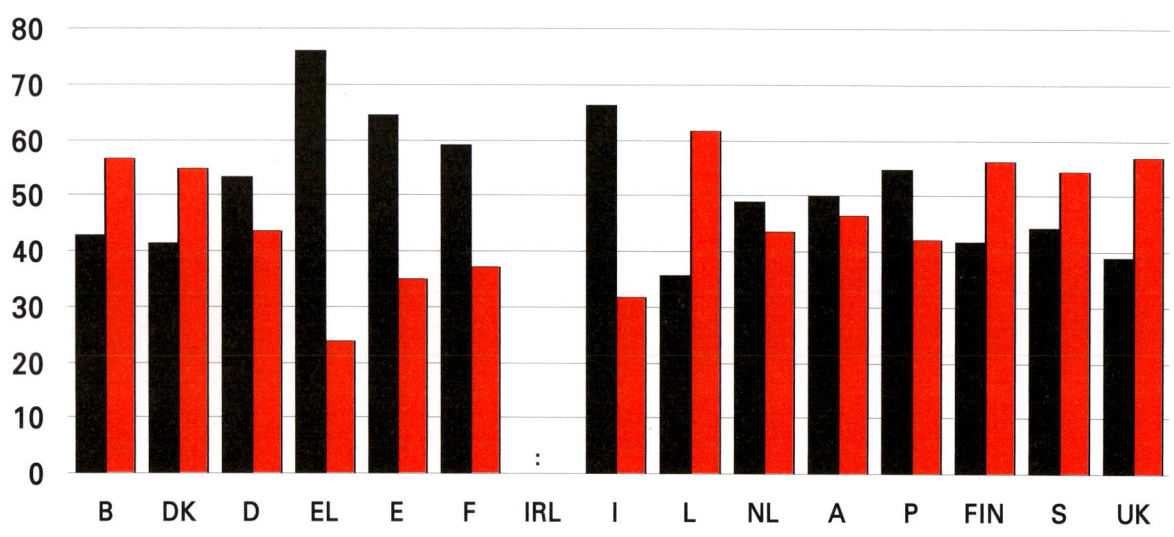

6C1AA

Black: crop production; colour: animal production.

Further reading: Manual on the Economic Accounts for Agriculture and Forestry EAA/EAF 97 (Rev. 1.1). Eurostat. Agriculture, statistical yearbook, 2000. Eurostat.

Principal agricultural output. Million ECU/EUR. EU-15

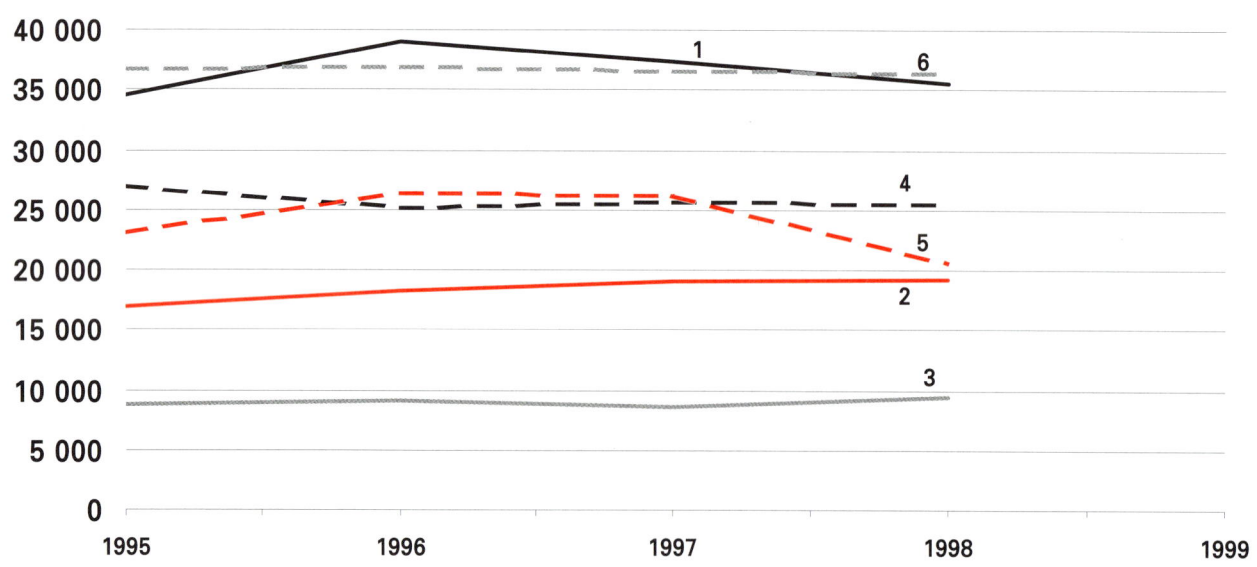

6C1AB

1: cereal output; 2: fresh vegetables output; 3: fresh fruit output; 4: cattle output; 5: pig output; 6: milk output.

Further reading: Manual on the Economic Accounts for Agriculture and Forestry EAA/EAF 97 (Rev. 1.1). Eurostat. Agriculture, statistical yearbook, 2000. Eurostat.

IRL: data not available.

Gross value added at basic prices is calculated by deducting intermediate consumption from the output of the agricultural industry (which includes, besides agricultural output, the output of non-agricultural secondary activities which are inseparable from the principal agricultural activity). Output is valued at the basic price which is defined as the price received by the producer, after deducting all taxes on products but including all subsidies on products. Intermediate consumption is valued at the purchaser price which includes taxes less subsidies on products.

Gross value added at basic prices. Million ECU/EUR

3B2GA

	1989	1990	1991	1992	1993	1994	1995	1996	1997	1998	1999	
EU-15	:	:	:	:	:	:	:	:	:	:	:	**EU-15**
EUR-11	:	:	:	:	:	:	:	:	:	:	:	**EUR-11**
B	:	:	:	:	:	:	2 770	2 867	2 883	2 657	:	**B**
DK	:	3 550	3 409	3 170	3 239	3 439	3 993	4 064	3 914	3 240	3 143	**DK**
D	:	:	15 380	16 125	16 645	16 169	18 328	18 596	18 348	16 414	17 062	**D**
EL	:	:	:	:	:	:	8 392	8 168	8 556	8 400	:	**EL**
E	:	19 777	19 847	17 544	17 466	18 883	18 543	21 575	22 110	21 869	:	**E**
F	27 325	29 034	26 207	27 654	27 148	29 572	30 910	30 890	31 059	32 287	31 338	**F**
IRL	:	:	:	:	:	:	:	:	:	:	:	**IRL**
I	:	26 272	29 195	28 304	24 228	24 470	24 021	27 478	28 458	28 060	:	**I**
L	122	120	97	115	122	121	135	123	110	122	122	**L**
NL	:	:	:	:	:	:	9 667	9 385	8 835	8 885	8 459	**NL**
A	:	:	:	:	:	:	2 721	2 497	2 416	2 412	2 304	**A**
P	:	:	:	:	:	:	2 862	2 961	2 801	2 836	:	**P**
FIN	:	3 136	2 583	1 862	1 679	1 959	1 529	1 356	1 307	1 021	:	**FIN**
S	2 262	2 261	1 987	1 886	1 723	1 601	1 663	1 642	1 578	1 420	:	**S**
UK	10 517	10 129	10 374	10 597	11 519	11 841	12 187	12 056	12 056	11 046	10 898	**UK**

Further reading: Manual on the Economic Accounts for Agriculture and Forestry EAA/EAF 97 (Rev. 1.1). Eurostat. Agriculture, statistical yearbook, 2000. Eurostat.

Net value added at basic prices. Million ECU/EUR

3B6UE

	1989	1990	1991	1992	1993	1994	1995	1996	1997	1998	1999	
EU-15	:	:	:	:	:	:	:	:	:	:	:	**EU-15**
EUR-11	:	:	:	:	:	:	:	:	:	:	:	**EUR-11**
B	:	:	:	:	:	:	2 152	2 299	2 267	2 055	:	**B**
DK	:	2 642	2 512	2 269	2 307	2 494	2 981	3 019	2 855	2 169	2 063	**DK**
D	:	:	8 987	9 277	9 416	8 911	10 790	11 174	11 165	9 292	9 913	**D**
EL	:	:	:	:	:	:	7 781	7 527	7 913	7 768	:	**EL**
E	:	17 254	17 248	15 083	15 244	16 673	16 218	19 096	19 584	19 368	:	**E**
F	20 861	22 423	19 423	20 704	20 090	22 444	23 797	23 635	23 805	24 896	23 677	**F**
IRL	:	:	:	:	:	:	:	:	:	:	:	**IRL**
I	:	19 624	22 008	21 049	17 624	17 802	17 630	20 343	21 113	20 690	:	**I**
L	97	92	64	80	86	83	97	85	73	84	83	**L**
NL	:	:	:	:	:	:	7 380	7 131	6 641	6 662	6 356	**NL**
A	:	:	:	:	:	:	1 483	1 269	1 208	1 187	1 076	**A**
P	:	:	:	:	:	:	2 706	2 814	2 660	2 711	:	**P**
FIN	:	1 954	1 451	915	862	1 094	743	613	590	318	:	**FIN**
S	1 482	1 480	1 196	1 125	1 090	965	1 019	942	888	750	:	**S**
UK	7 354	7 049	7 214	7 690	8 393	8 689	9 198	8 986	8 353	7 423	7 291	**UK**

Further reading: Manual on the Economic Accounts for Agriculture and Forestry EAA/EAF 97 (Rev. 1.1). Eurostat. Agriculture, statistical yearbook, 2000. Eurostat.

eurostat

Need more data on this topic? Ask your Data Shop

Total roundwood production. 1 000 m³

	1989	1990	1991	1992	1993	1994	1995	1996	1997	1998	1999	
EU-15	267 124	297 273	232 310	226 734	226 283	248 647	263 928	247 749	259 930	261 510	262 138	EU-15
EUR-11	200 275	233 305	169 683	162 561	161 648	181 581	189 667	180 263	188 648	190 420	192 196	EUR-11
B	4 669	5 363	4 360	3 868	3 938	3 930	4 340	4 185	4 470 *	4 435 *	4 435 *	B
DK	2 101	2 255	2 309	1 915	1 777	1 853	1 926	1 876	1 817	1 538	1 530	DK
D	48 126	84 707	33 618	27 759	27 958	34 618	39 343	37 011	38 207	39 053	37 634	D
EL	2 491	2 492	2 546	2 193	2 096	2 091	1 961	2 117	1 783	1 692	2 215	EL
E	17 891	15 590	15 188	13 822	13 756	15 305	16 074	15 631	15 631 *	14 875	14 875 *	E
F	44 076	44 713	43 554	42 418	39 363	42 240	43 371	40 472	41 962	42 527	43 380	F
IRL	1 500	1 625	1 670	1 960	1 861	2 018	2 204	2 291	2 180	2 266	2 520	IRL
I	8 780	7 972	8 327	9 067	9 042	9 452	9 730	9 018	9 146	9 550	11 138	I
L	327	707	599	372	302	411	477 *	443 *	450 *	450 *	259	L
NL	1 325	1 420	1 123	1 086	1 045	1 018	1 079	951	1 109	1 023	1 044	NL
A	16 255	16 773	15 572	12 249	12 256	14 360	13 805	15 011	14 725	14 033	14 083	A
P	10 205	11 205	10 809	10 278	10 207	9 819	9 350	8 978	8 970	8 548	8 978	P
FIN	47 121	43 230	34 863	39 682	41 920	48 410	49 894	46 272	51 798	53 660	53 850	FIN
S	55 830	52 871	51 400	53 520	54 000	55 900	62 900	56 400	60 200	60 600	58 700	S
UK	6 427	6 350	6 372	6 545	6 762	7 222	7 474	7 093	7 482	7 260	7 497	UK
IS	-	-	-	0	0	0	0	0	326	326	326	IS
NO	11 508	11 819	11 279	10 134	9 710	8 744	9 365	8 485	8 346	8 172	8 432	NO
EEA	278 632	309 092	243 589	229 872	229 310	249 511	273 293	256 234	268 602	270 008	270 896	EEA
CH	4 612	6 332	4 607	4 483	4 337	4 609	4 678	3 996	2 690	3 260	5 000	CH
US	513 000	510 100	478 600	493 400	488 792	498 438	499 310	478 830	479 547	485 996	500 745	US
CA	188 254	162 127	160 168	169 895	176 193	183 224	188 432	189 778	191 178	:	:	CA
JP	30 619	29 403	28 106	27 276	25 708	24 594	23 035	23 218	22 294	:	:	JP

Further reading: Eurostat forestry statistics, 1995–98. Eurostat.

Roundwood: degree of self-sufficiency. %

	1989	1990	1991	1992	1993	1994	1995	1996	1997	1998	1999	
EU-15	95	97	97	96	96	95	92	94	92	91	:	EU-15
EUR-11	98	98	100	99	99	98	91	93	93	91	:	EUR-11
B/L	72	74	75	80	77	69	67	73	72	71 *	97 *	B/L
DK	115	105	109	104	99	91	84	86	71	75	75	DK
D	104	103	124	119	113	106	109	105	107	107	104	D
EL	90	90	89	97	98	102	102	99	87	86	89	EL
E	93	94	94	86	91	93	90	90	94	81	84 *	E
F	129	113	121	105	102	102	101	102	102	103	103	F
IRL	112	113	128	119	108	103	113	112	109	99	111	IRL
I	60	55	56	61	65	60	66	66	66	64	68	I
L	.	.	.	.	.	.	.	.	.	.	.	L
NL	86	86	88	91	92	91	86	99	89	84	71	NL
A	84	85	76	73	74	76	77	79	76	76	68	A
P	97	97	99	100	100	95	92	94	90	85	91	P
FIN	90	90	89	89	90	90	86	89	89	86	85	FIN
S	91	95	94	93	94	91	91	94	90	89	87	S
UK	101	100	103	98	97	96	92	90	94	98	99	UK
IS	:	:	:	:	:	:	:	:	:	:	:	IS
NO	91	95	96	96	95	80	74	80	81	73	77	NO
EEA	:	:	:	:	:	:	:	93	93		:	EEA
CH	99	107	113	118	119	116	120	123	149	128	128	CH
US	106	106	106	105	104	104	104	104	103	:	:	US
CA	100	101	100	99	99	98	97	98	97	:	:	CA
JP	39	38	37	37	36	35	32	32	32	:	:	JP

Further reading: Eurostat forestry statistics, 1995–98. Eurostat.

Coniferous roundwood production. 1 000 m³

	1989	1990	1991	1992	1993	1994	1995	1996	1997	1998	1999	
EU-15	187 918	222 272	161 396	156 805	158 857	180 231	192 059	178 297	190 733	189 230	187 301	EU-15
EUR-11	133 284	169 161	109 610	102 562	103 540	121 146	126 201	119 517	127 578	126 773	126 256	EUR-11
B	3 282	3 960	3 170	2 617	2 626	2 625	2 870	2 730	2 874 *	2 851 *	2 851 *	B
DK	1 395	1 498	1 514	1 202	1 080	1 153	1 220	1 195	1 169 *	1 006	990	DK
D	35 201	70 928	23 608	21 306	21 710	27 594	30 440	28 323	31 062	29 570	27 911	D
EL	644	620	642	513	600	629	521	522	440	442	592	EL
E	10 627	10 246	9 099	7 509	7 283	8 509	8 653	8 154	8 154 *	7 851	7 851 *	E
F	22 894	23 481	22 595	19 390	18 074	20 105	21 032	19 326	20 249	20 608	21 280	F
IRL	1 410	1 535	1 560	1 850	1 776	1 976	2 163	2 250	2 129	2 208	2 485	IRL
I	1 712	1 413	1 281	1 182	1 522	1 603	1 732	1 386	1 385	1 397	1 512	I
L	164	460	204	153	144	245	280 *	270 *	270 *	270 *	121	L
NL	900	980	718	656	605	576	668	583	694	647	651	NL
A	13 780	14 408	13 316	10 056	10 155	12 218	11 786	13 017	12 638	11 951	11 967	A
P	5 833	6 684	5 726	5 311	5 283	5 107	5 117	4 760	4 575	4 384	4 380	P
FIN	37 481	35 066	28 333	32 532	34 362	40 588	41 460	38 718	43 548	45 036	45 247	FIN
S	47 388	45 738	44 420	46 670	47 500	50 800	57 400	50 660	54 810	54 386	52 570	S
UK	5 207	5 255	5 210	5 858	6 137	6 503	6 717	6 403	6 736	6 623	6 893	UK
IS	-	-	-	0	0	0	0	0	198	198	198	IS
NO	10 451	10 722	10 220	9 113	9 026	8 166	8 669	7 794	7 955	7 638	7 809	NO
EEA	198 369	232 994	171 616	158 922	161 200	180 517	200 728	186 091	198 886	197 066	195 308	EEA
CH	3 435	5 125	3 521	3 303	3 173	3 449	3 456	2 797	2 257	2 282	3 600	CH
US	333 900	326 700	290 900	303 600	279 824	286 255	286 621	276 662	276 897	281 915	295 113	US
CA	171 575	142 087	139 526	147 933	151 775	155 263	158 310	159 656	161 056	:	:	CA
JP	20 078	19 549	19 037	18 900	18 772	19 090	18 067	17 993	17 315	:	:	JP

4C6AA

Further reading: Eurostat forestry statistics, 1995–98. Eurostat.

Non-coniferous roundwood production. 1 000 m³

	1989	1990	1991	1992	1993	1994	1995	1996	1997	1998	1999	
EU-15	79 206	75 001	70 914	69 929	67 426	68 416	71 869	69 452	69 197	72 280	74 837	EU-15
EUR-11	66 991	64 144	60 073	59 999	58 108	60 435	63 466	60 746	61 070	63 647	65 940	EUR-11
B	1 387	1 403	1 190	1 251	1 312	1 305	1 470	1 455	1 596 *	1 584 *	1 584 *	B
DK	706	757	795	713	697	700	706	681	648	532	540	DK
D	12 925	13 779	10 010	6 453	6 248	7 024	8 903	8 688	7 145	9 483	9 723	D
EL	1 847	1 872	1 904	1 680	1 496	1 462	1 440	1 595	1 343	1 250	1 623	EL
E	7 264	5 344	6 089	6 313	6 473	6 796	7 421	7 477	7 477 *	7 024	7 024 *	E
F	21 182	21 232	20 959	23 028	21 289	22 135	22 339	21 146	21 713	21 919	22 100	F
IRL	90	90	110	110	85	42	41	41	51	58	35	IRL
I	7 068	6 559	7 046	7 885	7 520	7 849	7 998	7 632	7 761	8 153	9 626	I
L	163	247	395	219	158	166	197 *	173 *	180 *	180 *	138	L
NL	425	440	405	430	440	442	411	368	415	376	393	NL
A	2 475	2 365	2 256	2 193	2 101	2 142	2 019	1 994	2 087	2 082	2 116	A
P	4 372	4 521	5 083	4 967	4 924	4 712	4 233	4 218	4 395	4 164	4 598	P
FIN	9 640	8 164	6 530	7 150	7 558	7 822	8 434	7 554	8 250	8 624	8 603	FIN
S	8 442	7 133	6 980	6 850	6 500	5 100	5 500	5 740	5 390	6 214	6 130	S
UK	1 220	1 095	1 162	687	625	719	757	690	746	637	604	UK
IS	-	-	-	0	0	0	0	0	128	128	128	IS
NO	1 057	1 097	1 059	1 021	684	578	696	691	391	534	623	NO
EEA	80 263	76 098	71 973	70 950	68 110	68 994	72 565	70 143	69 716	72 942	75 588	EEA
CH	1 177	1 207	1 086	1 180	1 164	1 160	1 222	1 199	433	978	1 400	CH
US	179 100	183 400	187 700	189 800	208 968	212 183	212 689	202 168	202 554	203 985	205 632	US
CA	16 679	20 040	20 642	21 962	24 418	27 961	30 122	30 122	30 122	:	:	CA
JP	10 541	9 854	9 069	8 376	6 936	5 504	4 968	5 225	4 979	:	:	JP

5A1DS

Further reading: Eurostat forestry statistics, 1995–98. Eurostat.

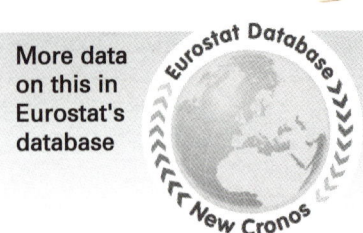

More data on this in Eurostat's database

This domain affords a statistical insight into the forestry sector of the European Union in the first half of the 1990s. Besides the present EU of the 15 Member States, this domain sets out the basic forestry statistics for Iceland, Liechtenstein, Norway and Switzerland.

➤ ➤ ➤ **DOMAIN FOREST IN DATABASE NEW CRONOS**

Privately owned forests as % of total wooded area. 1999

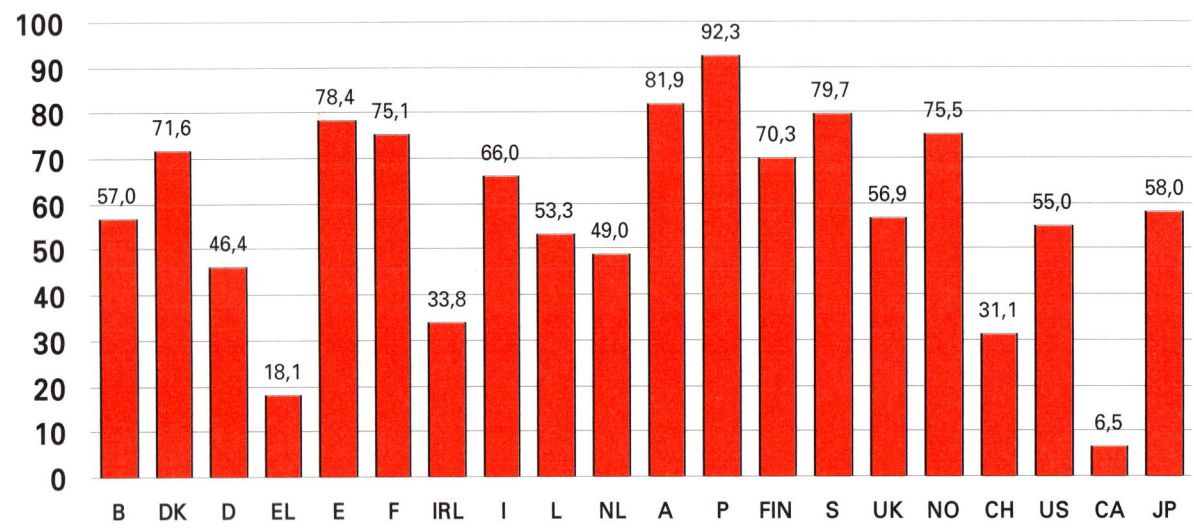

Further reading: Eurostat forestry statistics, 1995–98. Eurostat.

4

Fellings as % of net annual increment of growing stock. 1999

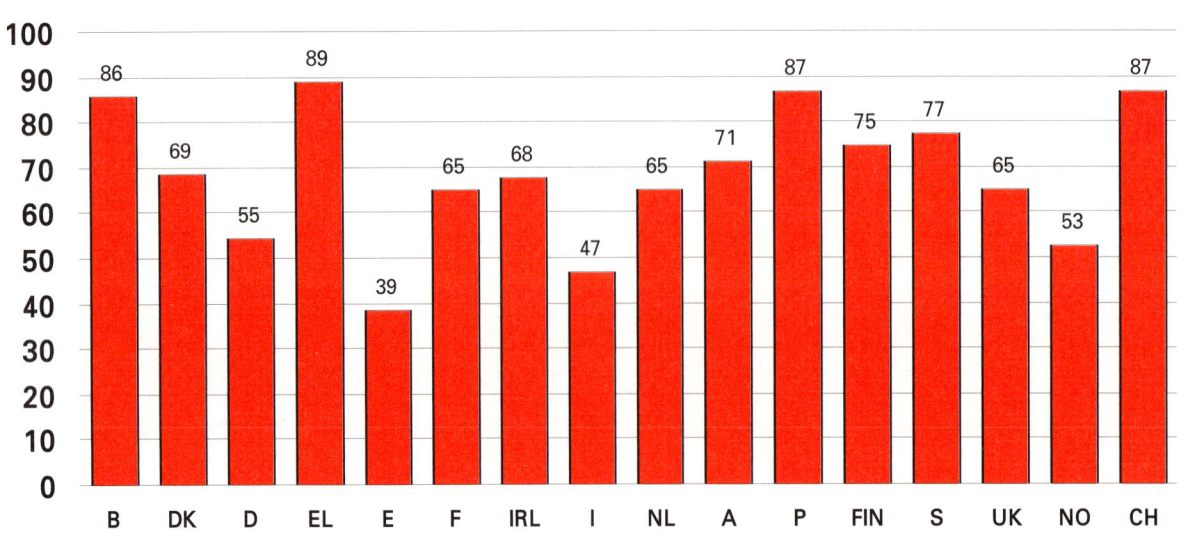

Further reading: Eurostat forestry statistics, 1995–98. Eurostat.

Annual catches in all regions. 1 000 t live weight

3B3AA

	1989	1990	1991	1992	1993	1994	1995	1996	1997	1998	1999	
EU-15	7 147	6 338	6 552	6 868	6 654	6 981	7 405	6 798	6 912	6 736	:	EU-15
EUR-11	3 999	3 699	3 621	3 625	3 783	3 676	3 920	3 713	3 657	3 714	:	EUR-11
B	40	42	40	38	36	34	36	31	31	31	30	B
DK	1 896	1 476	1 751	1 954	1 492	1 844	1 999	1 681	1 827	1 557	:	DK
D	364	347	235	219	257	233	248	237	259	267	:	D
EL	135	137	144	159	167	191	165	162	170	128	:	EL
E	1 368	1 161	1 138	1 152	1 159	1 164	1 229	1 206	1 250	1 215	:	E
F	649	629	653	662	700	651	675	636	580	583	:	F
IRL	261	264	286	281	328	335	437	371	333	363	:	IRL
I	420	384	408	396	396	398	396	368	343	318	:	I
L	0	0	0	0	0	0	0	0	0	0	:	L
NL	421	416	421	449	478	440	458	427	471	540	:	NL
A	1	1	1	0	0	0	0	0	0	0	:	A
P	335	326	326	294	293	267	264	263	223	229	:	P
FIN	141	128	114	133	136	152	156	165	166	168	:	FIN
S	250	251	237	308	342	387	405	371	357	411	:	S
UK	867	775	799	822	870	883	916	870	900	925	:	UK
IS	1 519	1 522	1 058	1 584	1 728	1 574	1 629	2 083	2 231	1 710	1 736	IS
NO	1 979	1 807	2 210	2 627	2 595	2 559	2 717	2 812	3 048	3 030	:	NO
EEA	10 645	9 667	9 820	11 078	10 977	11 114	11 751	11 692	12 191	11 476	:	EEA
CH	3	3	4	3	2	1	2	2	2	2	:	CH
US	5 459	5 496	5 248	5 308	5 607	5 698	5 326	5 020	4 976	4 752	:	US
CA	1 634	1 627	1 471	1 317	1 161	1 052	876	926	992	1 023	:	CA
JP	10 598	9 755	8 652	7 896	7 418	6 758	6 117	6 089	6 065	5 374	:	JP

Further reading: Fisheries, yearly statistics, 2000. Eurostat.　　　　D: for all years, includes data on the former GDR.

Total aquaculture production. 1 000 t live weight

4

3B3AB

	1989	1990	1991	1992	1993	1994	1995	1996	1997	1998	1999	
EU-15	905	944	946	917	922	1 042	1 115	1 171	1 193	1 340	:	EU-15
EUR-11	810	833	823	789	771	873	936	971	968	1 094	:	EUR-11
B	1	1	1	1	1	1	1	1	1	1	:	B
DK	33	42	42	43	43	43	45	41	39	42	:	DK
D	67	64	68	90	63	42	58	75	59	67	:	D
EL	5	10	13	20	33	33	33	40	49	60	:	EL
E	223	203	225	169	126	178	224	232	240	316	:	E
F	225	257	245	250	277	281	281	285	287	274	:	F
IRL	21	27	28	27	30	29	27	35	37	40	:	IRL
I	134	154	175	170	176	206	236	216	219	250	:	I
L	0	0	0	0	0	0	0	0	0	0	:	L
NL	109	101	52	54	71	109	84	100	98	120	:	NL
A	4	3	3	3	3	3	3	3	3	3	:	A
P	9	5	6	6	6	7	5	6	8	8	:	P
FIN	19	19	19	18	18	17	17	18	16	16	:	FIN
S	8	9	8	7	6	7	8	8	7	6	:	S
UK	49	50	61	57	69	86	94	110	130	138	:	UK
IS	2	3	3	3	3	3	3	4	4	4	:	IS
NO	114	150	161	138	173	218	278	322	367	409	:	NO
EEA	1 021	1 097	1 110	1 057	1 098	1 264	1 396	1 496	1 564	1 752	:	EEA
CH	1	1	1	1	1	1	1	1	1	1	:	CH
US	369	315	364	414	417	391	413	393	438	445	:	US
CA	30	37	44	45	51	54	66	71	83	91	:	CA
JP	1 370	1 370	1 359	1 397	1 359	1 420	1 390	1 349	1 340	1 290	:	JP

Further reading: Fisheries, yearly statistics, 2000. Eurostat.　　　　D: for all years, includes data on the former GDR.

Annual catches in all regions as % of total world catches

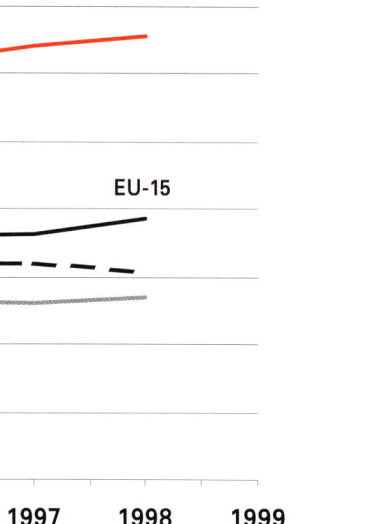

3B3AD

Further reading: Fisheries, yearly statistics, 2000. Eurostat.

4

Annual catches in the north-east Atlantic. 1 000 t live weight

	1989	1990	1991	1992	1993	1994	1995	1996	1997	1998	1999	
EU-15	5 155	4 617	4 843	5 210	5 001	5 284	5 700	5 087	5 272	5 163	:	EU-15
EUR-11	2 163	2 123	2 063	2 133	2 302	2 175	2 383	2 168	2 191	2 273	:	EUR-11
B	40	41	40	37	36	34	36	31	31	31	29	B
DK	1 894	1 475	1 749	1 950	1 491	1 843	1 998	1 681	1 826	1 557	1 404	DK
D	273	276	211	205	246	222	225	202	207	220	:	D
EL	-	-	-	-	-	-	-	-	-	-	-	EL
E	398	393	395	422	448	428	460	442	548	520	:	E
F	462	428	441	437	462	412	448	429	400	410	:	F
IRL	254	261	283	278	325	332	433	367	329	359	:	IRL
I	0	0	0	0	0	0	0	0	0	0	0	I
L	-	-	-	-	-	-	-	-	-	-	-	L
NL	413	414	411	447	477	438	453	378	368	414	388	NL
A	-	-	-	-	-	-	-	-	-	-	-	A
P	231	230	217	225	225	207	220	202	189	198	177	P
FIN	92	79	65	82	85	104	107	117	119	120	108	FIN
S	248	249	235	305	340	385	403	369	355	410	:	S
UK	850	771	796	821	868	881	916	869	900	924	835	UK
IS	1 519	1 521	1 057	1 583	1 724	1 570	1 620	2 062	2 223	1 702	1 727	IS
NO	1 968	1 774	2 184	2 611	2 561	2 532	2 698	2 804	3 043	3 026	2 615	NO
EEA	8 642	7 913	8 085	9 403	9 287	9 386	10 018	9 952	10 538	9 891	:	EEA
CH	-	-	-	-	-	-	-	-	-	-	-	CH
US	0	0	0	0	0	0	0	0	0	0	0	US
CA	0	0	0	0	0	0	0	0	0	0	0	CA
JP	2	7	5	5	5	7	7	4	3	2	:	JP

3B3BA

Further reading: Fisheries, yearly statistics, 2000. Eurostat.   D: for all years, includes data on the former GDR.

eurostat

Annual catches in the north-west Atlantic. 1 000 t live weight

3B3BF

	1989	1990	1991	1992	1993	1994	1995	1996	1997	1998	1999	
EU-15	162	121	135	100	84	85	33	31	38	42	55	EU-15
EUR-11	156	119	133	97	83	85	33	31	37	41	54	EUR-11
B	-	-	-	-	-	-	-	-	-	-	-	B
DK	2	1	2	3	1	0	0	0	0	1	0	DK
D	37	23	15	5	0	0	0	0	0	0	1	D
EL	-	-	-	-	-	-	-	-	-	-	-	EL
E	64	29	36	55	47	54	20	21	28	31	37	E
F	0	0	0	0	0	0	0	0	0	0	0	F
IRL	0	0	0	0	0	0	0	0	0	0	0	IRL
I	0	0	0	0	0	0	0	0	0	0	0	I
L	-	-	-	-	-	-	-	-	-	-	-	L
NL	5	0	6	0	0	0	0	0	0	0	0	NL
A	-	-	-	-	-	-	-	-	-	-	-	A
P	50	67	75	36	36	30	13	9	9	10	17	P
FIN	-	-	-	-	-	-	-	-	-	-	-	FIN
S	-	-	-	-	-	-	-	-	-	-	-	S
UK	4	2	0	0	0	0	0	0	0	0	0	UK
IS	0	0	0	0	2	2	8	21	7	7	9	IS
NO	7	27	11	3	10	12	12	8	4	3	4	NO
EEA	169	148	146	103	96	99	53	59	49	51	68	EEA
CH	-	-	-	-	-	-	-	-	-	-	-	CH
US	1 220	1 263	1 342	1 315	1 239	1 109	1 227	1 188	1 103	1 046	1 015	US
CA	1 299	1 283	1 109	979	832	700	615	650	712	770	741	CA
JP	13	12	8	11	6	4	5	4	3	3	3	JP

Further reading: Fisheries, yearly statistics, 2000. Eurostat.   D: for all years, includes data on the former GDR.

Annual catches in the Mediterranean. 1 000 t live weight

4

3B3BD

	1989	1990	1991	1992	1993	1994	1995	1996	1997	1998	1999	
EU-15	628	610	641	652	662	687	702	673	644	562	:	EU-15
EUR-11	518	499	520	516	520	518	563	535	495	461	:	EUR-11
B	-	-	-	-	-	-	-	-	-	-	-	B
DK	-	-	-	-	-	-	-	-	-	-	-	DK
D	-	-	-	-	-	-	-	-	-	-	-	D
EL	110	111	121	136	141	168	139	138	149	101	:	EL
E	142	143	144	145	146	148	149	150	133	121	:	E
F	45	42	43	51	46	40	38	28	33	33	:	F
IRL	-	-	-	-	-	-	-	-	-	-	-	IRL
I	331	314	332	319	328	330	376	356	328	307	:	I
L	-	-	-	-	-	-	-	-	-	-	-	L
NL	-	-	-	-	-	-	-	-	-	-	-	NL
A	-	-	-	-	-	-	-	-	-	-	-	A
P	0	0	0	0	0	0	0	0	0	0	:	P
FIN	-	-	-	-	-	-	-	-	-	-	-	FIN
S	-	-	-	-	-	-	-	-	-	-	-	S
UK	-	-	-	-	-	-	-	-	-	-	-	UK
IS	-	-	-	-	-	-	-	-	-	-	-	IS
NO	-	-	-	-	-	-	-	-	-	-	-	NO
EEA	628	610	641	652	662	687	702	673	644	562	:	EEA
CH	-	-	-	-	-	-	-	-	-	-	-	CH
US	-	-	-	-	-	-	-	-	-	-	-	US
CA	-	-	-	-	-	-	-	-	-	-	-	CA
JP	0	0	0	0	1	1	1	1	0	0	:	JP

Further reading: Fisheries, yearly statistics, 2000. Eurostat.

Annual catches in the east central Atlantic. 1 000 t live weight

	1989	1990	1991	1992	1993	1994	1995	1996	1997	1998	1999	
EU-15	494	493	526	476	499	493	450	534	543	603	:	**EU-15**
EUR-11	480	482	515	462	484	483	442	526	538	597	:	**EUR-11**
B	-	-	-	-	-	-	-	-	-	-	-	**B**
DK	-	-	-	-	-	-	-	-	-	-	-	**DK**
D	1	13	0	0	0	0	0	11	29	23	:	**D**
EL	14	11	12	14	15	9	9	8	5	6	:	**EL**
E	357	338	368	308	318	327	335	344	315	358	:	**E**
F	53	76	78	72	93	88	76	80	63	67	:	**F**
IRL	-	-	-	-	-	-	-	-	-	-	-	**IRL**
I	52	34	40	51	43	44	8	3	7	6	:	**I**
L	-	-	-	-	-	-	-	-	-	-	-	**L**
NL	0	0	0	0	0	0	0	48	101	124	:	**NL**
A	-	-	-	-	-	-	-	-	-	-	-	**A**
P	18	21	29	30	30	25	23	39	23	18	:	**P**
FIN	-	-	-	-	-	-	-	-	-	-	-	**FIN**
S	-	-	-	-	-	-	-	-	-	-	-	**S**
UK	-	-	-	-	-	-	-	-	-	-	-	**UK**
IS	:	:	:	:	:	:	:	:	:	:	:	**IS**
NO	2	2	0	0	0	0	0	0	0	0	:	**NO**
EEA	496	495	526	476	499	493	450	534	543	603	:	**EEA**
CH	-	-	-	-	-	-	-	-	-	-	-	**CH**
US	:	:	:	:	:	:	:	:	:	:	:	**US**
CA	:	:	:	:	:	:	:	:	:	:	:	**CA**
JP	28	26	15	14	23	20	24	25	15	16	:	**JP**

3B3BB

Further reading: Fisheries, yearly statistics, 2000. Eurostat.   D: for all years, includes data on the former GDR.

4

Catches of fish, crustaceans and molluscs. Million tonnes live weight. 1998

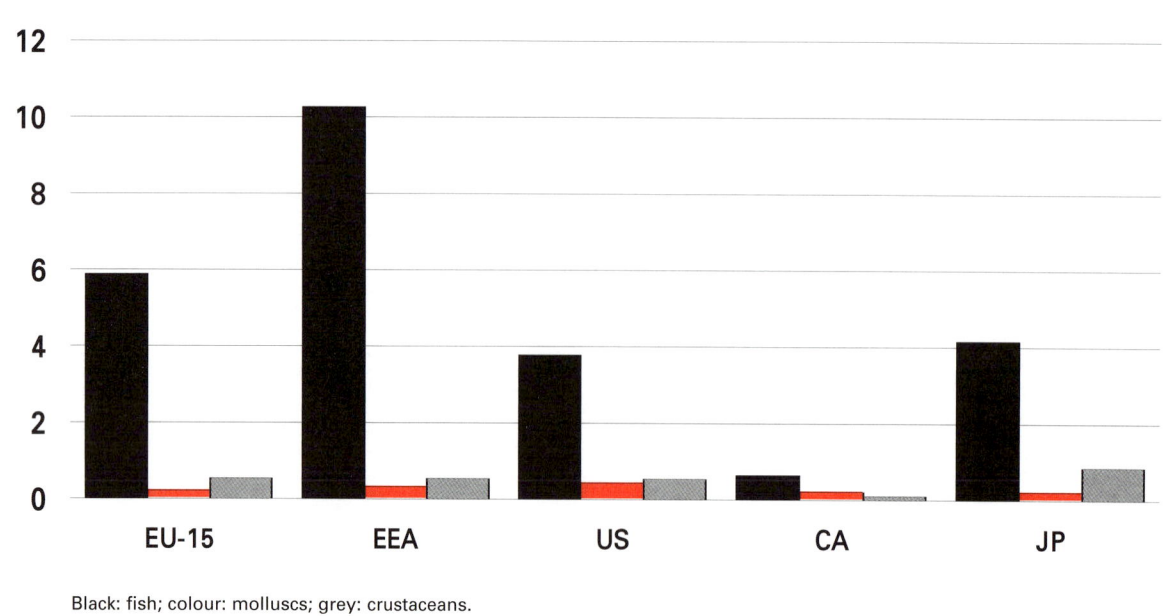

3D1AE

Black: fish; colour: molluscs; grey: crustaceans.

Further reading: Fisheries, yearly statistics, 2000. Eurostat.

Fishing fleet

	Total tonnage, GT						Total power, kW					
	1995	**1996**	**1997**	**1998**	**1999**		**1995**	**1996**	**1997**	**1998**	**1999**	
EU-15	2 107 293	2 065 735	2 010 346	1 986 234	:		8 140 679	7 921 283	7 942 347	7 813 369	:	**EU-15**
EUR-11	1 588 090	1 554 534	1 503 680	1 478 853	:		5 699 040	5 568 673	5 636 423	5 541 263	:	**EUR-11**
B	23 101	22 557	23 051	22 787	:		65 965	63 540	64 896	64 352	:	**B**
DK	96 856	97 553	97 738	97 664	:		404 981	392 392	376 409	369 967	:	**DK**
D	76 772	73 058	68 631	67 748	:		169 182	167 967	161 486	159 720	:	**D**
EL	116 400	113 048	107 080	104 931	:		655 290	654 607	653 065	643 830	:	**EL**
E	658 166	614 374	574 900	553 265	:		1 631 379	1 537 271	1 467 993	1 405 668	:	**E**
F	178 399	197 741	209 816	210 780	:		990 509	986 287	1 144 135	1 125 613	:	**F**
IRL	62 091	61 128	60 914	58 263	:		197 846	190 941	195 730	189 487	:	**IRL**
I	260 198	260 603	247 352	247 332	:		1 515 842	1 513 677	1 508 639	1 519 029	:	**I**
L	-	-	-	-	-		-	-	-	-		**L**
NL	179 593	177 820	173 942	177 309	:		506 990	497 555	480 101	474 740	:	**NL**
A	-	-	-	-	-		-	-	-	-		**A**
P	125 430	123 406	120 853	118 814	:		396 943	392 157	393 102	391 630	:	**P**
FIN	24 340	23 847	24 221	22 555	:		224 384	219 278	220 341	211 024	:	**FIN**
S	51 134	48 840	48 539	47 779	:		266 205	256 542	244 644	236 509	:	**S**
UK	254 813	251 760	253 309	257 007	:		1 115 163	1 049 069	1 031 806	1 021 800	:	**UK**

Further reading: Fisheries, yearly statistics, 2000. Eurostat.

6D1AF
6D1AG

Number of vessels in tonnage classes as % of total

	Less than 25 GT						25–100 GT					
	1995	**1996**	**1997**	**1998**	**1999**		**1995**	**1996**	**1997**	**1998**	**1999**	
EU-15	85	85	87	87	:		9	9	8	8	:	**EU-15**
EUR-11	84	84	86	86	:		11	11	10	10	:	**EUR-11**
B	5	3	3	2	:		44	45	44	44	:	**B**
DK	88	89	89	88	:		7	7	7	7	:	**DK**
D	84	84	84	84	:		11	12	12	12	:	**D**
EL	94	95	96	96	:		3	3	3	3	:	**EL**
E	81	81	82	82	:		10	10	10	10	:	**E**
F	78	78	84	83	:		17	17	13	13	:	**F**
IRL	67	67	65	65	:		24	22	21	20	:	**IRL**
I	84	84	87	87	:		13	13	11	11	:	**I**
L	-	-	-	-	-		-	-	-	-		**L**
NL	31	36	37	40	:		32	29	29	28	:	**NL**
A	-	-	-	-	-		-	-	-	-		**A**
P	95	94	94	94	:		3	3	3	3	:	**P**
FIN	96	96	96	96	:		4	4	4	3	:	**FIN**
S	56	56	81	82	:		9	9	9	9	:	**S**
UK	81	81	81	82	:		11	11	11	10	:	**UK**

6D1AH
6D1AI

Further reading: Fisheries, yearly statistics, 2000. Eurostat.

Need an update for this indicator? Ask your Data Shop

EUROSTAT YEARBOOK 2001
341

These fishing fleet statistics have been compiled from Eurostat's statistical register of EU fishing vessels which is updated from the administrative file maintained by the Fisheries DG. Data relate to the situation on 31 December of the reference year. It should be noted that data might not be comparable from year to year, particularly with regard to tonnage measures and coverage of smaller vessels. From its establishment in 1990, overall coverage has been extended and is now virtually complete. No comparable data are available for non-EU countries.

More data on this in Eurostat's database

This database contains data on annual catches by fishing regions, annual data on aquaculture production, monthly data on the quantities and values of fishery products, annual data on the EU fishing fleets, annual data on the number of fishermen and summary annual data on foreign trade in fishery products.

➤ ➤ ➤ **DOMAIN FISH IN DATABASE NEW CRONOS**

Number of vessels in tonnage classes as % of total (continued)

	100–500 GT					500 GT or more						
	1995	1996	1997	1998	1999	1995	1996	1997	1998	1999		
EU-15	4	4	4	4	:	0	0	0	0	:	**EU-15**	6D1AL
EUR-11	5	5	4	4	:	1	1	0	0	:	**EUR-11**	
B	52	53	53	54	:	-	-	-	-	-	**B**	6D1AM
DK	4	4	4	4	:	0	0	0	0	:	**DK**	
D	4	4	4	4	:	1	1	1	1	:	**D**	
EL	0	0	0	0	:	0	0	0	0	:	**EL**	
E	8	8	7	7	:	1	1	1	1	:	**E**	
F	3	3	3	3	:	1	1	1	1	:	**F**	
IRL	8	10	10	11	:	1	1	1	1	:	**IRL**	
I	3	3	2	2	:	0	0	0	0	:	**I**	
L	-	-	-	-	-	-	-	-	-	-	**L**	
NL	32	30	30	28	:	5	5	5	5	:	**NL**	
A	-	-	-	-	-	-	-	-	-	-	**A**	
P	2	2	2	2	:	0	0	0	0	:	**P**	
FIN	1	1	1	1	:	0	0	0	0	:	**FIN**	
S	5	5	5	5	:	0	0	0	0	:	**S**	
UK	7	7	7	7	:	0	0	1	1	:	**UK**	

Further reading: Fisheries, yearly statistics, 2000. Eurostat.

The following chapters give an overview of and specific insights into the performances of businesses engaged in market activities. The data presented here are extracted from Eurostat's SBS database named after the Council Regulation on Structural Business Statistics.

This Regulation provides a harmonised framework for the annual collection of structural data from businesses in the European Union. It defines the nomenclatures (NACE Rev. 1, NUTS) and the statistical units to be used, the coverage (without size threshold), common deadlines and quality criteria to be fulfilled.

Data collection is carried out by the National Statistical Institutes, and the aggregated data are transmitted to Eurostat, which takes on the work of calculating the European totals.

EU totals (levels) are only calculated when all countries are available and their comparability is assessed. In 1997, EU totals cannot be calculated for the population including all enterprises as two or more countries are missing depending on the activity. This situation results from the fact that the SBS Regulation is still in a transition period during which Member States were granted derogations for them to adapt their system to the harmonised requirements.

The year 1999 will be the first reference year for which all countries have to comply to the Regulation, and thus for which a consistent EU data set will be available.

EU averages or ratios, that are of special interest for structural analysis, have been estimated when the available data allowed to calculate them with sufficient accuracy.

The regulation covers all market activities (excluding agriculture) normally included in the sectors of industry, construction, distributive trades and services (Sections C to K of NACE Rev. 1).

Among a number of variables describing the input and output sides of businesses activity, a selection of basic indicators is presented for all industries available in industry, construction, distributive trades and services.

Turnover corresponds to the total of all sales (excluding VAT) of goods and services carried out by the enterprises of a sector during the reference year.

More data on this in Eurostat's database

All business structural data from 1995 onwards on the legal basis of the SBS regulation as well as some long-time series (NACE Rev. 1 G to K from 1990, NACE Rev. 1 C to F from 1985). It also includes historical services data in NACE 70 (1980–94) and annual regional statistics.

► ► ► **DOMAIN SBS IN DATABASE NEW CRONOS**

4

Turnover. Million ECU. 1997

	B	DK	D	EL	E	F	IRL	I
Manufacturing	149 805,5	62 091,4	1 122 585,9	:	299 593,6	750 234,0	58 025,9 *	692 315,3
Food products, beverages and tobacco	26 660,8	17 612,4	133 575,8	:	62 681,5	136 805,9	16 216,8 *	88 070,7
Manuf. of textiles	8 895,4	1 828,3	27 138,6	:	15 065,5	27 999,0	1 117,5 *	63 468,6
Manuf. of leather	307,1	319,0	3 617,2	:	6 144,7	4 346,1	87,2 *	22 971,0
Manuf. of wood	2 196,6	1 652,4	15 669,0	:	6 367,0	9 988,1	642,1 *	13 794,2
Manuf. of paper, publishing and printing	8 481,0	5 449,1	65 514,0	:	19 388,7	48 157,6	5 746,8 *	36 481,9
Coke, refined petroleum and nuclear fuel	10 855,4	69,6	56 529,1	:	14 291,1	45 530,9	..	39 046,3
Manuf. of chemicals and man-made fibres	23 542,7	5 234,1	119 477,6	:	27 897,6	89 546,8	11 256,0 *	59 111,2
Manuf. of rubber and plastic products	5 580,7	2 269,0	46 956,8	:	11 393,1	27 291,9	1 103,6 *	27 060,0
Manuf. of other non-metallic mineral products	6 581,1	2 303,6	35 744,6	:	15 973,4	21 476,6	1 242,3 *	28 375,7
Manuf. of basic metals	19 332,5	5 496,1	119 549,9	:	33 910,1	73 669,2	1 529,6 *	91 282,3
Machinery and equipment n.e.c.	7 933,6	8 336,7	135 350,6	:	15 340,4	46 734,4	1 619,0 *	81 452,3
Electrical and optical equipment	8 949,1	5 430,2	141 573,0	:	19 547,8	83 649,0	15 270,1 *	56 991,5
Transport equipment	15 606,0	2 465,2	193 844,7	:	42 631,7	114 345,5	830,3 *	54 579,2
Electricity, gas and water supply	20 865,8	8 611,5	114 377,2	:	22 239,5	51 320,7	..	42 909,3
Construction	21 850,3	15 494,7	123 926,8	:	:	116 065,8	:	104 227,0
Sale and repair of motor vehicles	35 536,5	:	:	:	:	98 439,3	8 378,4	108 329,3
Wholesale trade and commission trade	123 450,8	:	:	:	:	419 811,3	18 732,2	287 914,2
Retail trade	41 875,7	24 916,4	:	:	114 763,4	255 996,6	13 339,5	179 024,2
Hotels and restaurants	6 218,3	:	41 430,4	:	:	39 186,2	:	37 749,7
Transport, storage and communication	32 280,1	:	:	:	:	141 513,4	7 936,2	101 346,9
Real estate, renting and business activities	32 291,1	:	385 932,3	:	:	227 484,4	5 914,6	101 563,4

Further reading: Panorama of European business, 1999. Enterprises in Europe, sixth report.

D: enterprises with 20 persons or more employed in industry and construction. Since additional information is not available, it is not possible to calculate the EU-15 total. IRL: enterprises with three persons or more employed in industry.

eurostat

Gross value added at factor cost corresponds to the difference between the value of what is produced and intermediate consumption entering the production, corrected for subsidies on production and costs and assimilated taxes and levies. It can be interpreted as the wealth created by the enterprises of a sector and which is used to remunerate the production factors, capital in the form of the gross operating surplus, and labour in the form of the personnel costs.

Personnel costs are defined as the total amounts paid by the enterprises of a sector to remunerate the work of the enterprise's employees during the reference year. They cover wages and salaries and the social contributions paid by the employer.

The number of persons employed is defined as the total number of persons who work for the enterprises of the sector, whether they are paid or not. This total however excludes borrowed staff and agency workers.

Eurostat's SBS database presents the data in absolute values and in the form of some basic ratios. Providing such raw information allows the user to make use of the data in many different ways:

– calculate specific aggregates not foreseen by the nomenclature: e.g. in 1997, the Dutch turnover for the textile and leather industries amounts to ECU 4 183 million,

– compare levels between countries: in the textile and leather industries the Dutch turnover represents approximately 1/3 of the Portuguese turnover (ECU 11 669 million)

– calculate the share of an industry in a total: the textile and leather industry represents 2.4 % of the Dutch manufacturing industry whereas it accounts for 18 % of the Portuguese manufacturing industry.

Other types of analysis of the data, especially using economic ratios are presented in the sectoral chapters.

Turnover. Million ECU. 1997

L	NL	A	P	FIN	S	UK	NO	
6 753,8 *	186 450,2 *	89 828,9	63 408,1	75 669,7	136 966,5	682 094,4	49 762,0	Manufacturing
596,4 *	46 809,6 *	12 411,0	11 645,2	8 289,6	14 067,0	123 078,7	12 913,2	Food products, beverages and tobacco
388,2 *	3 771,9 *	3 565,2	8 888,1	1 264,2	1 429,0	26 258,9	727,1	Manuf. of textiles
0,0 *	410,7 *	810,8	2 780,9	237,6	172,5	3 024,0	68,3	Manuf. of leather
90,1 *	2 272,0 *	4 425,2	3 152,2	4 434,4	6 867,9	8 303,2	2 104,0	Manuf. of wood
297,4 *	16 255,2 *	7 664,5	4 169,9	16 900,1	17 482,5	58 095,4	5 630,1	Manuf. of paper, publishing and printing
0,0 *	11 103,0 *	..	4 045,3	4 412,6	707,5	50 655,9	0,0	Coke, refined petroleum and nuclear fuel
548,6 *	30 289,1 *	6 098,5	3 914,2	4 467,6	9 795,1	66 841,1	3 591,0	Manuf. of chemicals and man-made fibres
906,4 *	5 191,6 *	3 506,8	1 474,2	1 676,5	3 319,4	28 812,4	869,2	Manuf. of rubber and plastic products
510,5 *	5 629,9 *	5 037,5	4 052,8	1 924,8	2 473,9	16 628,4	1 450,9	Manuf. of other non-metallic mineral products
2 602,7 *	17 204,6 *	10 910,5	4 497,9	7 790,3	15 935,5	60 557,2	7 135,4	Manuf. of basic metals
522,0 *	12 492,2 *	9 084,5	2 413,4	8 559,7	16 717,3	52 541,9	3 487,5	Machinery and equipment n.e.c.
162,2 *	20 548,6 *	11 836,0	4 087,9	11 730,4	21 180,5	84 380,0	3 365,3	Electrical and optical equipment
28,7 *	9 812,5 *	6 881,2	5 798,3	2 506,5	23 672,7	81 633,5	6 737,0	Transport equipment
673,9 *	16 901,9	10 298,8	6 219,0	6 895,3	16 400,6	:	:	Electricity, gas and water supply
1 719,4 *	45 568,8	22 513,4	21 800,3	10 358,4	21 418,3	126 669,5	14 340,0	Construction
:	45 677,6	17 839,1	21 971,9	10 577,3	23 846,7	172 327,5	17 767,4	Sale and repair of motor vehicles
:	:	71 474,6	50 570,6	38 928,9	82 414,8	:	52 289,4	Wholesale trade and commission trade
:	61 578,0	32 245,8	28 715,6	18 985,0	36 379,3	:	24 197,5	Retail trade
707,3 *	10 961,7	8 295,7	5 907,9	3 442,6	5 863,6	68 884,5	:	Hotels and restaurants
:	40 862,6	23 497,3	13 143,3	15 470,1	38 592,1	:	:	Transport, storage and communication
2 277,3 *	:	21 796,2	14 141,3	10 723,6	46 814,8	250 622,6	:	Real estate, renting and business activities

Further reading: Panorama of European business, 1999. Enterprises in Europe, sixth report.

0D2MN

Value added at factor cost. Million ECU. 1997

	B	DK	D	EL	E	F	IRL	I
Manufacturing	38 586,3	21 596,7	337 524,0	:	80 166,1	184 852,0	19 998,2 *	185 122,8
Food products, beverages and tobacco	5 024,1	4 231,6	26 631,1	:	12 620,7	24 564,4	3 722,3 *	16 289,4
Manuf. of textiles	2 394,5	588,7	7 817,0	:	4 482,1	7 773,5	386,5 *	18 601,0
Manuf. of leather	92,0	71,0	981,9	:	1 253,8	1 438,2	24,1 *	5 485,8
Manuf. of wood	563,7	624,1	4 977,6	:	1 856,7	2 904,6	185,1 *	4 014,6
Manuf. of paper, publishing and printing	2 797,6	2 302,8	24 289,2	:	6 919,0	15 004,9	2 044,9 *	11 130,7
Coke, refined petroleum and nuclear fuel	1 178,1	21,6	2 940,7	:	1 556,0	4 220,6	..	2 424,8
Manuf. of chemicals and man-made fibres	6 797,9	2 137,2	36 371,0	:	7 856,1	22 787,0	6 330,1 *	14 869,8
Manuf. of rubber and plastic products	1 614,8	932,2	16 884,9	:	3 674,2	8 799,3	429,4 *	8 336,4
Manuf. of other non-metallic mineral products	2 203,3	980,4	13 355,7	:	5 908,6	7 038,1	554,0 *	9 598,2
Manuf. of basic metals	5 665,6	2 220,5	41 073,3	:	10 668,8	23 503,1	506,8 *	29 925,9
Machinery and equipment n.e.c.	2 413,0	3 355,0	51 456,0	:	5 147,7	14 031,6	628,2 *	25 007,0
Electrical and optical equipment	3 352,7	1 988,9	48 085,0	:	5 811,0	24 910,6	4 326,1 *	18 205,7
Transport equipment	3 365,0	875,2	52 900,4	:	9 344,6	21 668,4	298,5 *	13 139,8
Electricity, gas and water supply	5 760,5	2 471,1	34 697,2	:	10 505,7	20 866,3	..	19 068,8
Construction	7 045,5	6 027,6	47 628,0	:	:	40 055,1	:	35 107,1
Sale and repair of motor vehicles	2 599,1	:	:	:	:	13 049,1	865,3	10 620,1
Wholesale trade and commission trade	11 288,1	:	:	:	:	43 429,1	2 516,6	36 741,4
Retail trade	6 573,7	4 628,7	:	:	23 578,8	43 913,4	2 419,1	29 186,1
Hotels and restaurants	2 445,3	:	:	:	:	16 635,2	:	14 408,1
Transport, storage and communication	13 965,2	:	:	:	:	58 211,7	3 181,0	47 687,8
Real estate, renting and business activities	13 611,8	:	:	:	:	89 629,8	3 145,4	49 062,4

Further reading: Panorama of European business, 1999. Enterprises in Europe, sixth report.

D: enterprises with 20 persons or more employed in industry and construction. Since additional information is not available, it is not possible to calculate the EU-15 total. IRL: enterprises with three persons or more employed in industry.

OD3MN

4

Personnel costs. Million ECU. 1997

	B	DK	D	EL	E	F	IRL	I
Manufacturing	24 604,1	14 698,5	263 209,9	:	47 067,8	134 071,2	6 193,5 *	111 120,4
Food products, beverages and tobacco	2 936,2	2 574,8	17 680,7	:	6 758,8	16 381,7	1 251,0 *	9 117,8
Manuf. of textiles	1 568,8	426,5	6 157,8	:	3 127,2	6 164,8	291,1 *	11 456,8
Manuf. of leather	70,8	43,6	764,1	:	862,0	1 134,1	16,3 *	3 544,3
Manuf. of wood	375,1	450,0	3 909,2	:	1 216,3	2 214,7	98,2 *	2 025,6
Manuf. of paper, publishing and printing	1 830,4	1 675,3	17 501,2	:	3 947,6	11 516,0	684,7 *	6 750,8
Coke, refined petroleum and nuclear fuel	429,6	11,4	1 483,6	:	390,4	2 043,8	..	1 090,5
Manuf. of chemicals and man-made fibres	3 538,1	1 158,3	26 339,6	:	3 943,2	13 356,7	733,2 *	8 499,2
Manuf. of rubber and plastic products	1 019,8	643,1	12 471,5	:	2 257,6	6 625,6	237,9 *	4 884,3
Manuf. of other non-metallic mineral products	1 394,4	590,2	9 570,6	:	3 257,7	5 156,9	275,6 *	5 752,8
Manuf. of basic metals	4 047,9	1 628,5	32 720,6	:	6 669,3	18 300,5	334,0 *	16 793,5
Machinery and equipment n.e.c.	1 697,9	2 528,0	42 258,4	:	3 518,4	11 020,6	359,1 *	15 735,2
Electrical and optical equipment	2 318,9	1 395,7	39 966,0	:	3 464,5	19 740,6	1 457,8 *	11 523,1
Transport equipment	2 621,8	662,8	44 560,3	:	5 494,0	15 615,9	202,7 *	9 150,2
Electricity, gas and water supply	2 224,5	780,7	16 186,0	:	2 385,2	10 230,7	..	7 318,4
Construction	4 973,6	4 379,0	41 104,5	:	:	34 760,8	:	16 989,5
Sale and repair of motor vehicles	1 586,0	:	:	:	:	10 601,7	:	4 859,8
Wholesale trade and commission trade	6 764,7	:	:	:	:	32 889,9	:	14 803,9
Retail trade	3 801,9	3 124,2	:	:	10 701,5	30 488,5	:	12 926,3
Hotels and restaurants	1 363,9	:	:	:	:	12 183,0	:	7 555,6
Transport, storage and communication	9 850,6	:	:	:	:	46 450,0	:	31 070,7
Real estate, renting and business activities	8 136,0	:	:	:	:	65 422,3	:	19 448,6

Further reading: Panorama of European business, 1999. Enterprises in Europe, sixth report.

D: enterprises with 20 persons or more employed in industry and construction. Since additional information is not available, it is not possible to calculate the EU-15 total. IRL: enterprises with three persons or more employed in industry.

OD5MN

Value added at factor cost. Million ECU. 1997

L	NL	A	P	FIN	S	UK	NO	
2 045,0 *	49 359,6 *	29 865,3	16 507,1	23 268,1	43 858,3	205 451,8	14 346,3	Manufacturing
174,5 *	9 189,1 *	3 324,6	2 043,5	2 095,0	3 442,7	27 965,8	2 514,1	Food products, beverages and tobacco
164,1 *	1 064,1 *	1 267,3	2 682,0	486,6	501,4	10 132,6	2 514,2	Manuf. of textiles
0,0 *	123,2 *	234,3	780,8	89,3	57,1	1 091,4	254,2	Manuf. of leather
13,9 *	720,1 *	1 483,4	726,3	1 316,6	1 916,9	2 861,5	582,1	Manuf. of wood
123,0 *	6 403,4 *	2 824,2	1 516,2	5 253,1	6 120,2	23 421,0	2 221,9	Manuf. of paper, publishing and printing
0,0 *	1 200,4 *	..	433,4	287,5	246,0	2 908,6	0,0	Coke, refined petroleum and nuclear fuel
150,2 *	7 446,8 *	1 900,2	1 077,3	1 441,9	3 475,8	21 031,1	1 189,3	Manuf. of chemicals and man-made fibres
285,2 *	1 750,0 *	1 313,1	446,7	671,2	1 208,1	10 933,7	282,3	Manuf. of rubber and plastic products
227,5 *	2 103,1 *	2 112,5	1 574,0	729,2	889,6	6 931,9	510,3	Manuf. of other non-metallic mineral products
629,9 *	6 007,7 *	4 040,0	1 392,3	2 680,5	5 622,0	22 076,7	1 933,5	Manuf. of basic metals
164,8 *	4 155,8 *	3 338,0	829,7	2 866,7	5 775,6	19 284,9	1 190,3	Machinery and equipment n.e.c.
69,6 *	5 265,0 *	3 733,1	1 155,5	4 005,7	8 623,8	25 743,8	1 210,0	Electrical and optical equipment
10,9 *	2 406,8 *	1 858,3	1 158,5	802,6	4 931,3	22 968,1	1 847,0	Transport equipment
198,6 *	5 202,6	4 775,2	2 395,0	2 272,8	5 079,6	22 730,7	:	Electricity, gas and water supply
766,3 *	14 658,4	10 250,1	4 943,8	3 463,4	7 268,1	42 192,5	4 695,9	Construction
:	4 421,4	2 677,1	2 031,4	1 315,3	2 756,1	:	2 031,8	Sale and repair of motor vehicles
:	:	9 698,8	5 474,5	4 559,5	10 263,3	:	6 053,3	Wholesale trade and commission trade
:	12 325,7	6 511,5	4 061,0	3 309,9	6 347,7	:	4 097,6	Retail trade
312,0 *	4 773,7	3 959,4	1 769,6	1 243,2	2 259,0	:	:	Hotels and restaurants
:	21 241,5	11 044,6	5 285,1	6 793,0	12 740,4	:	:	Transport, storage and communication
1 194,6 *	:	10 575,0	4 432,7	5 416,6	22 818,2	:	:	Real estate, renting and business activities

Further reading: Panorama of European business, 1999. Enterprises in Europe, sixth
report.

4

Personnel costs. Million ECU. 1997

L	NL	A	P	FIN	S	UK	NO	
1 235,3 *	28 119,2 *	21 070,4	9 684,0	12 956,4	27 554,0	120 220,0	10 355,9	Manufacturing
98,7 *	4 564,1 *	2 345,2	1 147,9	1 315,5	2 242,4	13 187,1	1 769,3	Food products, beverages and tobacco
63,4 ^	714,9 ^	926,7	1 860,9	324,2	393,8	6 594,4	199,6	Manuf. of textiles
0,0 *	80,3 *	176,1	551,8	60,4	41,4	676,1	19,7	Manuf. of leather
11,7 *	504,5 *	1 001,0	437,1	726,1	1 193,7	1 801,7	453,3	Manuf. of wood
79,5 *	3 717,6 *	1 748,2	760,7	2 690,8	3 823,1	14 795,6	1 587,2	Manuf. of paper, publishing and printing
0,0 *	409,0 *	..	113,5	193,8	126,5	1 156,4	0,0	Coke, refined petroleum and nuclear fuel
53,3 *	3 357,8 *	1 172,7	529,6	652,8	1 782,8	10 009,8	636,1	Manuf. of chemicals and man-made fibres
170,7 *	1 044,8 *	908,4	237,4	394,4	803,5	6 657,6	213,4	Manuf. of rubber and plastic products
96,1 *	1 089,1 *	1 386,1	777,4	420,3	616,8	3 989,1	326,5	Manuf. of other non-metallic mineral products
446,6 *	3 875,5 *	2 940,2	903,1	1 563,6	4 056,1	14 375,0	1 248,6	Manuf. of basic metals
136,5 *	2 779,7 *	2 665,5	545,0	1 937,9	4 003,5	12 274,4	954,6	Machinery and equipment n.e.c.
53,8 *	3 443,2 *	3 012,1	774,5	1 767,5	4 041,0	15 586,9	891,8	Electrical and optical equipment
6,7 *	1 581,2 *	1 223,8	580,4	539,0	3 601,3	14 046,8	1 599,7	Transport equipment
79,2 *	1 547,5	2 145,0	523,8	690,6	1 357,2	:	:	Electricity, gas and water supply
600,9 *	11 709,3	8 026,1	2 864,0	2 412,4	5 555,7	27 135,2	3 600,0	Construction
:	2 803,2	1 835,6	1 286,7	774,7	1 834,1	10 372,6	1 391,3	Sale and repair of motor vehicles
:	:	6 374,9	2 972,6	2 622,5	7 036,4	:	4 093,2	Wholesale trade and commission trade
:	7 037,6	4 623,9	2 503,3	2 023,1	4 753,9	:	2 991,9	Retail trade
193,9 *	2 734,9	2 587,9	1 297,8	885,0	1 706,2	13 478,2	:	Hotels and restaurants
:	11 616,0	7 259,2	2 986,2	3 887,0	9 101,9	:	:	Transport, storage and communication
740,9 *	:	5 304,8	2 490,3	3 357,2	12 039,8	72 413,3	:	Real estate, renting and business activities

Further reading: Panorama of European business, 1999. Enterprises in Europe, sixth
report.

From the four indicators presented in the 'key figures on businesses' chapter, one can deduct a number of basic elements on the structure of the market economy in European countries. Focusing on those countries for which data is available for all activities, it appears that the relative importance of industry, construction, distributive trades and market services differs from country to country.

Among the seven countries available for all sectors (B, F, NL, A, P, FIN, S), Finland is the country in which industry holds the largest share in market activities (excluding financial services) as it represents 50 % of value added and 41 % of employment. On the other hand, industry only represents around 40 % of value added and less than 35 % of employment in other countries.

In other sectors similar discrepancies can be observed. In terms of value added, the share of construction in total market activities ranges from 7 % in Finland to 11 % in Austria, distributive trades' share varies from 18 % in Finland to 24 % in Portugal and market services (excluding financial services) vary from 24 % in Portugal to 33 % in Sweden.

The SBS data also provide a breakdown by size-classes that can for instance be useful to the analysis of small and medium-size enterprises (SMEs). The European Commission defines SMEs as enterprises with less than 250 persons employed. In the European Union, they represent 66 % of total employment in market activities (see definition in the footnote to the graph).

The importance of SMEs varies greatly from sector to sector. The higher the share of the SMEs in total employment of the sector, the less the sector is concentrated.

In financial services SMEs only employ 27 % of the persons employed in the sector, whereas in construction, 89 % of the workforce is employed in an enterprise employing less than 250 persons. The two other sectors in which SMEs play an important role are the distributive trades and Horeca sector (76 % of total employment) and other services (excluding transport and communications and financial services) where SMEs employ 77 % of the workforce.

The SBS database also includes regional figures, an example of which is presented in the 'industry and construction' chapter.

Number of persons employed. 1997

	B	DK	D	EL	E	F	IRL	I
Manufacturing	654 555	496 394	6 370 617	:	2 317 217	3 988 954	241 170 *	4 816 500
Food products, beverages and tobacco	100 564	89 125	600 074	:	370 608	628 538	47 552 *	430 926
Manuf. of textiles	59 367	16 795	211 908	:	230 425	257 774	18 130 *	671 342
Manuf. of leather	2 838	1 740	26 660	:	69 503	50 680	1 132 *	226 269
Manuf. of wood	14 450	16 972	116 770	:	92 039	90 942	5 084 *	170 179
Manuf. of paper, publishing and printing	50 839	50 122	418 703	:	177 930	311 744	22 585 *	255 701
Coke, refined petroleum and nuclear fuel	5 802	268	20 938	:	8 923	31 285	..	24 158
Manuf. of chemicals and man-made fibres	63 596	30 654	509 188	:	128 901	282 648	20 953 *	213 207
Manuf. of rubber and plastic products	25 726	21 711	347 709	:	100 545	213 393	10 037 *	201 845
Manuf. of other non-metallic mineral products	37 407	20 505	255 829	:	161 951	154 554	9 723 *	242 486
Manuf. of basic metals	104 095	59 725	847 197	:	328 364	564 027	14 244 *	763 394
Machinery and equipment n.e.c.	42 341	82 320	982 556	:	152 849	316 700	15 178 *	568 495
Electrical and optical equipment	53 141	46 866	900 086	:	140 326	495 685	57 411 *	453 772
Transport equipment	61 954	22 850	896 247	:	204 094	401 996	7 509 *	293 845
Electricity, gas and water supply	27 435	20 037	320 860	:	66 072	199 770	..	160 456
Construction	228 008	172 558	1 259 715	:	:	1 370 797	:	1 297 884
Sale and repair of motor vehicles	75 355	:	:	:	:	420 169	30 089	431 115
Wholesale trade and commission trade	216 516	:	:	:	:	941 434	50 157	980 846
Retail trade	272 815	194 594	:	:	1 400 159	1 465 262	132 013	1 534 294
Hotels and restaurants	137 034	:	1 160 600	:	:	669 951	:	718 401
Transport, storage and communication	255 533	:	:	:	:	1 388 055	65 539	1 087 830
Real estate, renting and business activities	350 200	:	:	:	:	2 061 140	91 862	1 574 839

Further reading: Panorama of European business, 1999. Enterprises in Europe, sixth report.

D: enterprises with 20 persons or more employed in industry and construction. Since additional information is not available, it is not possible to calculate the EU-15 total. IRL: enterprises with three persons or more employed in industry.

OD8MN

0D7MN

Share of small and medium-sized enterprises (with less than 250 employees) in total employment. %. 1997

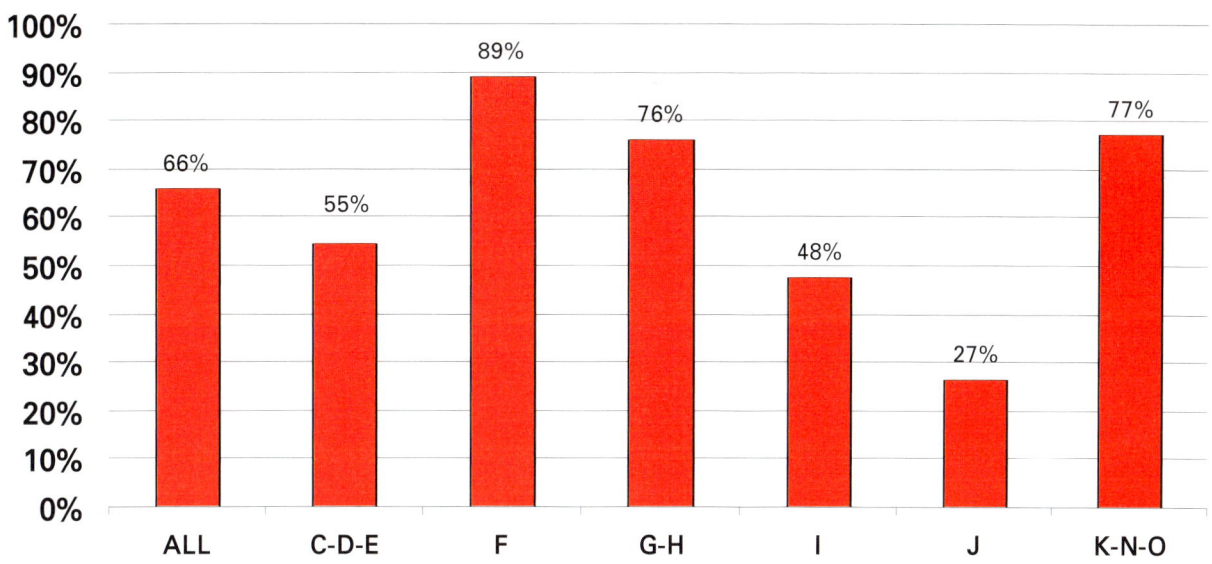

ALL: industry, construction, distributive trades and market services. C-D-E: mining and quarrying, manufacturing, electricity, gas and water supply. F: construction. G-H: distributive trades and hotels and restaurants. I: transport and communications services. J: financial services. K-N-O: other services.

Further reading: Panorama of European business, 1999. Enterprises in Europe, sixth report.

K-N-O: other services exclude public administration, education, activities of membership organisations, private households, extra-territorial organisations.

4

Number of persons employed. 1997

0D9MN

	L	NL	A	P	FIN	S	UK	NO	
	33 001 *	:	628 488	1 018 334	410 499	774 262	4 299 289	287 198	Manufacturing
	4 093 *	:	82 625	122 271	44 629	68 803	494 294	54 981	Food products, beverages and tobacco
	1 211 *	.	36 758	271 978	14 970	16 877	364 356	7 384	Manuf. of textiles
	0 *	3 184	7 373	80 030	2 937	1 804	36 018	774	Manuf. of leather
	439 *	20 092	39 552	60 627	27 378	41 158	91 086	15 091	Manuf. of wood
	2 204 *	119 481	44 565	55 262	72 679	104 928	470 642	46 721	Manuf. of paper, publishing and printing
	0 *	9 331	..	3 145	4 593	2 809	25 555	0	Coke, refined petroleum and nuclear fuel
	1 423 *	70 846	25 912	26 034	18 389	38 863	269 178	14 035	Manuf. of chemicals and man-made fibres
	3 921 *	33 525	26 662	21 101	13 573	24 876	265 677	6 088	Manuf. of rubber and plastic products
	2 913 *	:	35 136	72 745	13 778	19 026	154 715	8 953	Manuf. of other non-metallic mineral products
	10 536 *	:	95 928	96 707	50 967	127 600	538 818	32 935	Manuf. of basic metals
	3 179 *	88 174	71 202	47 248	56 419	106 172	404 658	24 545	Machinery and equipment n.e.c.
	1 992 *	97 730	74 573	54 704	56 253	97 510	544 131	20 178	Electrical and optical equipment
	282 *	50 547	30 927	37 214	17 980	90 628	414 591	40 515	Transport equipment
	1 463 *	40 078	37 677	19 354	19 505	29 915	136 156	:	Electricity, gas and water supply
	24 590 *	431 103	248 264	323 561	95 108	213 800	1 019 023	122 697	Construction
	:	133 388	74 433	144 881	31 236	72 124	:	50 455	Sale and repair of motor vehicles
	:	415 554	193 064	257 926	79 613	209 556	:	105 576	Wholesale trade and commission trade
	:	644 343	257 990	386 838	100 444	233 908	:	175 039	Retail trade
	10 762 *	235 419 *	191 510	234 475	45 189	93 756	:	:	Hotels and restaurants
	:	411 010 *	243 962	169 731	144 876	286 094	:	:	Transport, storage and communication
	25 667 *	1 089 900 *	206 304	243 991	131 093	417 819	:	:	Real estate, renting and business activities

Further reading: Panorama of European business, 1999. Enterprises in Europe, sixth report.

eurostat

Industry and construction indicators: Business Statistics are most complete in the industry and construction sectors as National Statistical Institutes have a long tradition for collecting data in these areas. At European level, reliable series could be calculated for EU-15 back to 1985, but only for enterprises with 20 persons employed or more.

Industry is defined as mining and quarrying, manufacturing and the production and distribution of water and energy. The chapter first presents a variety of structural and short-term indicators on manufacturing industry where the data set is most complete and some information on the construction industry.

Structural indicators in the manufacturing industry: One of the basic information provided by structural business statistics is on the relative size of industries. This size is generally measured in terms of value added or in terms of employment.

Value added measures the relative contribution of an activity to the wealth created in, for instance, manufacturing industry. Employment shares indicate which industries provide most jobs.

The two pie charts below present the shares of the seven (out of 14 NACE Rev. 1 subsections) largest manufacturing industries in Europe. They represent approximately 75 % of the European manufacturing industry. It can be noted that industries contributing most to the creation of wealth are not necessarily those providing most jobs. In this respect, a capital intensive industry such as the chemical industry represents 11 % of value added and only 7 % of EU's employment in manufacturing. On the contrary, in labour-intensive industries, the relationship between the two indicators is opposite. The textile and leather industries, for instance, represent 5 % of value added and 9 % of employment of EU's manufacturing.

Share of main industries in EU-15 manufacturing in terms of value added at factor cost. %. 1999 estimates

Share of main industries in EU-15 manufacturing in terms of employment. %. 1999 estimates

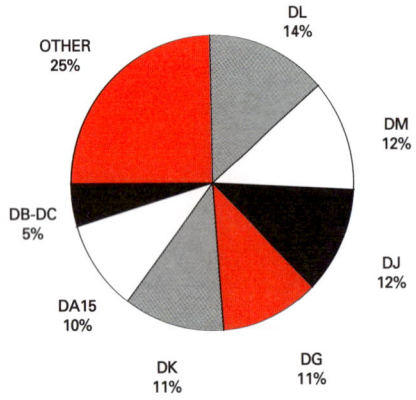

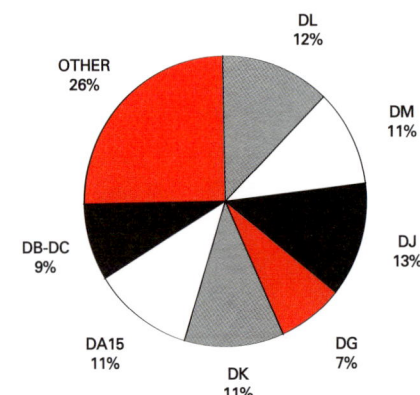

DL: Electrical and optical equipment. DM: Transport equipment. DJ: Basic metals and fabricated metal products. DG: Chemical industry. DK: Machinery and equipment. DA15: Food and beverages. DB-DC: Textile and leather. OTHER: Other manufacturing industries.

Further reading: Panorama of European Business, 1999. Enterprises in Europe, sixth report.

Enterprises with 20 persons or more employed.

Evolution of labour productivity. 1 000 ECU. EU-15 estimates 1991–99

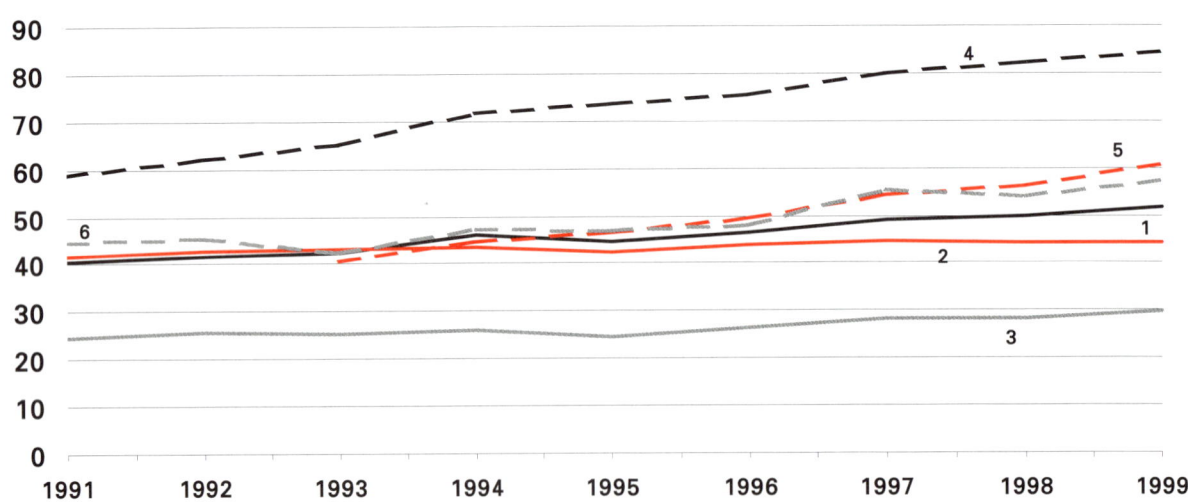

1. Manufacturing; 2. Food products and beverages; 3. Textiles and textile products; 4. Chemicals and man-made fibres; 5. Electrical and optical equipment; 6. Transport equipment.

Enterprises with 20 persons or more employed. Labour productivity is defined here as the ratio of value added at constant prices to the number of persons employed.

Manufacturing: labour productivity

Structural information is also given in the form of basic economic ratios. One of the most used for economic analysis is the labour productivity which aims at measuring the amount of wealth created within an industry by a given amount of labour. Different ratios are used depending on which variables are used to measure 'wealth' on the one hand and 'labour' on the other hand. The most simple one is given by apparent labour productivity that relates value added at factor costs to the number of persons employed. In this ratio the amount of labour is roughly approximated by the number of persons employed which, for instance, doesn't take into account the number of hours actually worked. In order to present an evolution of the ratio over a decade, value added has been corrected for the effects of price inflation. The evolution of apparent labour productivity is presented here for a choice of large industries in the EU including manufacturing industry as whole.

Depending on the activity, apparent labour productivity stands at rather different levels. It is highest in the capital-intensive chemical industry and lowest in the labour-intensive textile industry.

A steady growth of productivity is observed in all sectors from 1991 to 1999, but it has been fastest in the chemical, the transport equipment and especially the electrical equipment industries, including computer industry. High technology industries are described later on in this chapter.

Wage adjusted labour productivity is another ratio commonly used to measure productivity. It relates value added at factor costs to personnel costs, which partly takes account of the skill levels of the workforce. In addition this ratio is corrected by the share of employees in total employment to take account of the work done by unpaid persons employed. In the chart below several statistical measures are presented. The EU-15 estimate of the ratio is a weighted average of the ratios of the countries available (if the number of countries is sufficient to obtain a reliable estimate). The minimum and maximum values correspond to the two countries that recorded respectively the lowest and highest ratio for the sector. The median is the middle of a distribution: half of the countries are above the median and half are below the median. The median is less sensitive to extreme scores than the average.

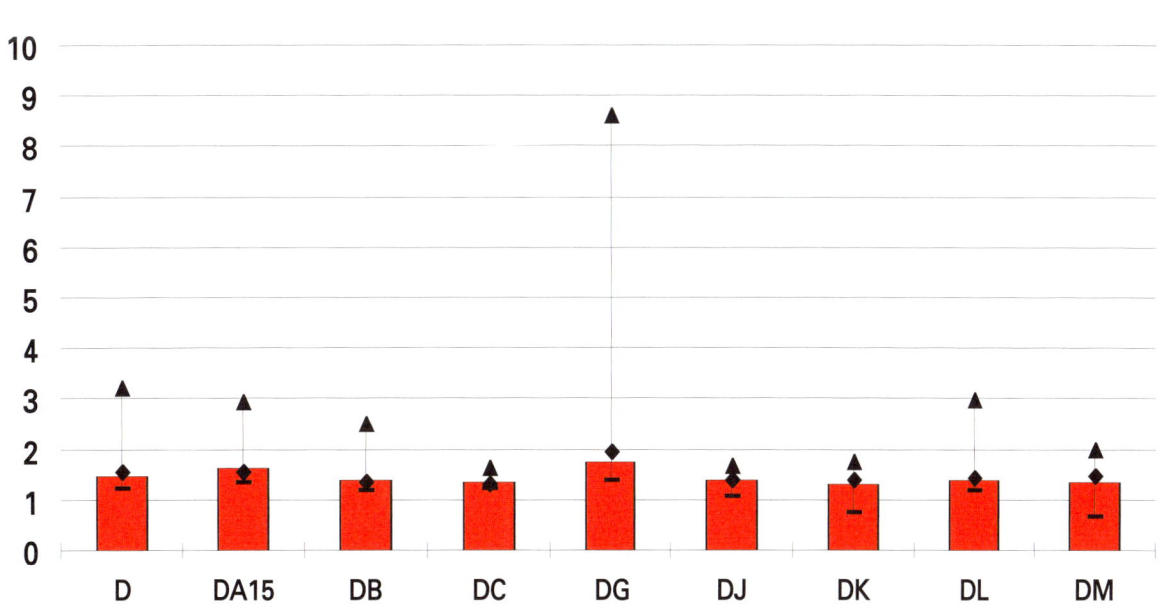

Wage adjusted labour productivity. %. EU-15 estimates 1997

Column: EU-15 average; ◆ : median; ▲ : maximum; ▬ : minimum.

D: Manufacturing industry; DA15: Food and beverages; DB: Textile; DC: Leather; DG: Chemical industry; DJ: Basic metals and fabricated metal products; DK: Machinery and equipment; DL: Electrical and optical equipment; DM: Transport equipment.

Further reading: Panorama of European business, 1999. Enterprises in Europe, sixth report.

Enterprises with 20 persons or more employed. Wage adjusted labour productivity is defined here as the ratio of value added to personnel costs corrected by the share of employees in total employment.

Share of the gross operating surplus in value added

Value added is used to remunerate the production factors, capital in the form of the gross operating surplus (GOS), and labour in the form of the personnel costs. The relative share of the GOS varies greatly from sector to sector. It is close to 45 % in the chemical industry, and smaller than 30 % in labour intensive industries such as the textile industry.

Value added in production

The ratio presented here relates value added to the value of production. It is an indicator of the degree of integration of the enterprises of the sector, i.e. of the importance of the transformations that they carry out on products during the production process. Structurally, a high ratio reflects the existence of a production process comprising an important share of transformation of the products in the manufacturing channel. This ratio is very stable over time but varies much from one activity to the other.

Share of gross operating surplus in value added. %. EU-15 estimates 1997

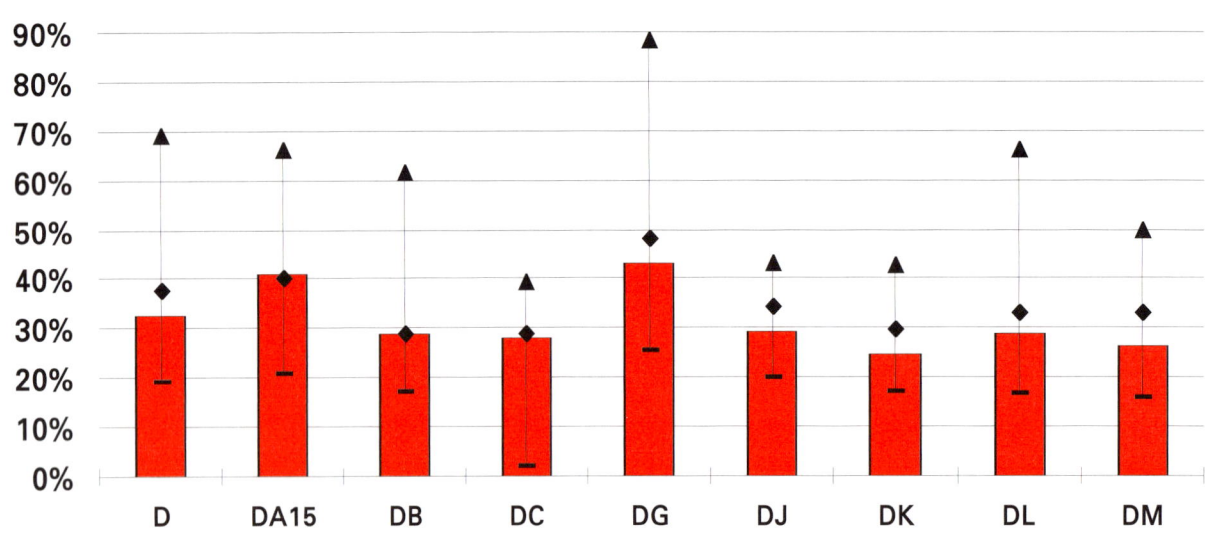

Column: EU-15 average; ◆ : median; ▲ : maximum; ▬ : minimum.
D: Manufacturing industry; DA15: Food and beverages; DB: Textile; DC: Leather; DG: Chemical industry; DJ: Basic metals and fabricated metal products; DK: Machinery and equipment; DL: Electrical and optical equipment; DM: Transport equipment.

Further reading: Panorama of European Business, 1999. Enterprises in Europe, sixth report.

Enterprises with 20 persons or more employed.

Share of value added in production. %. EU-15 estimates 1997

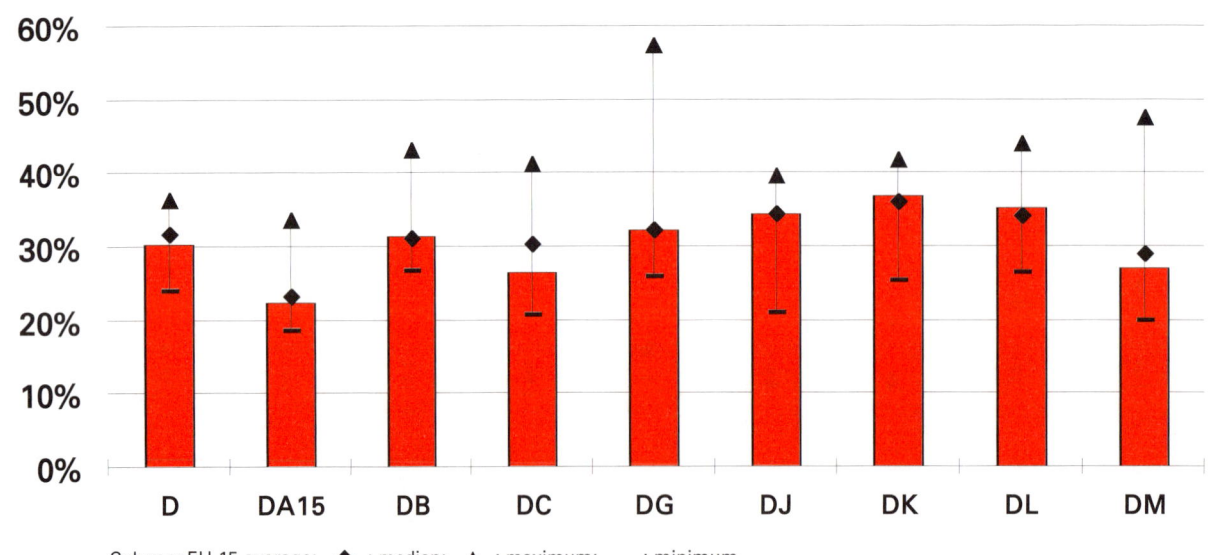

Column: EU-15 average; ◆ : median; ▲ : maximum; ▬ : minimum.
D: Manufacturing industry; DA15: Food and beverages; DB: Textile; DC: Leather; DG: Chemical industry; DJ: Basic metals and fabricated metal products; DK: Machinery and equipment; DL: Electrical and optical equipment; DM: Transport equipment.

Further reading: Panorama of European Business, 1999. Enterprises in Europe, sixth report.

Enterprises with 20 persons or more employed.

The production index for industry (excluding construction) is a key indicator for the monthly monitoring of economic activity. Its objective is to show the evolution of value added at factor cost at constant prices. However, the production index is only measured accurately at longer intervals. On a short-term basis, it is approximated by practical measures, such as the continuation with deflated gross production value, continuation with volumes, or continuation with deflated turnover. Income and expenditure classified as financial or extraordinary in company accounts is excluded from value added.

It is calculated 'gross' as value adjustments (such as depreciation) are not subtracted.

The index is available for all Member States of the European Union on a quite detailed level. European estimates for production are calculated on a monthly basis by Eurostat about 50 to 55 days after the reference period. The index exhibits strong working day and seasonal effects. For this reason, seasonally adjusted figures are used for monthly growth rates. Yearly growth rates are calculated on a working day adjusted basis.

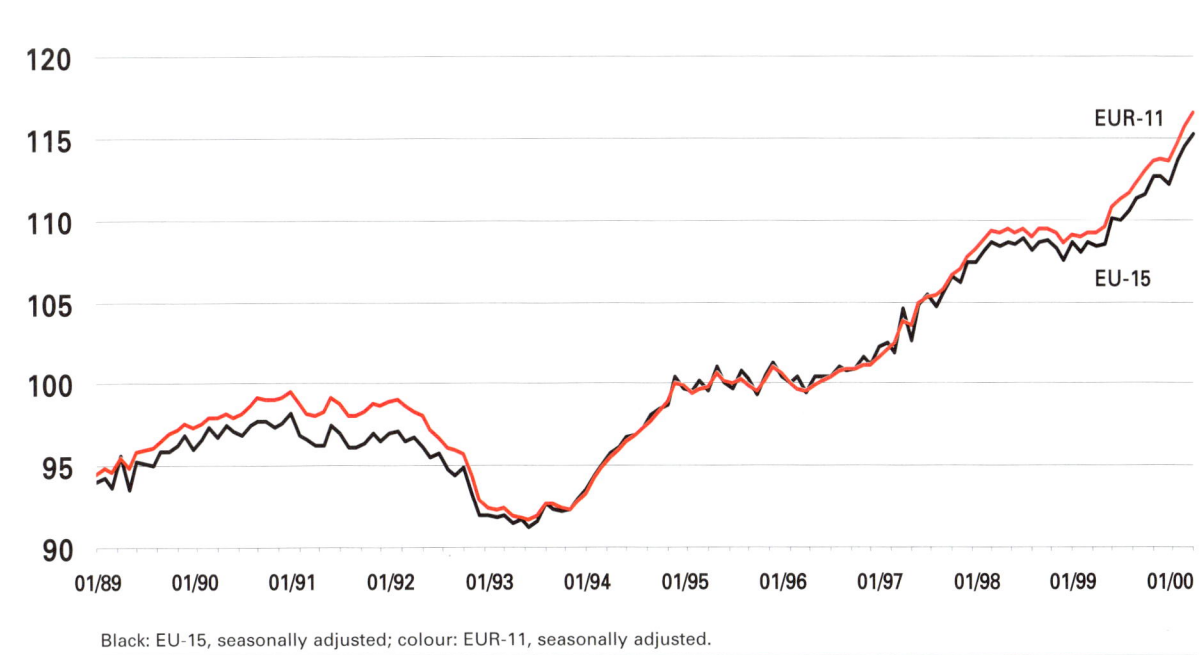

EU-15 and EUR-11 production indices, total industry (excluding construction)

Black: EU-15, seasonally adjusted; colour: EUR-11, seasonally adjusted.

Further reading: Monthly Panorama of European industry. Eurostat.

Recent trends in the index development in Europe reflect the economic recovery by exhibiting a fairly strong growth after being almost stable in 1998 until well into 1999. The recent growth has been particularly pronounced in the durable consumer goods and, to a lesser extent, in capital goods. The production in intermediate goods industry developed in line with the industry as a whole, while the growth rates were lower than average for non-durable consumer goods.

Production, total industry (excluding construction), year on year growth rates, working day adjusted

	1989	1990	1991	1992	1993	1994	1995	1996	1997	1998	1999	
EU-15	4,3	2,1	- 0,5	- 1,4	- 3,5	5,2	3,4	0,4	3,9	3,7	1,6	**EU-15**
EUR-11	4,7	2,5	0,2	- 1,7	- 4,7	4,7	3,5	0,3	4,3	4,2	1,8	**EUR-11**
B	3,5	7,0	- 1,9	- 0,4	- 5,1	2,1	6,5	0,5	4,7	3,4	0,9	**B**
DK	2,2	0,8	0,2	3,0	- 2,7	10,7	4,2	1,6	5,3	2,2	1,8	**DK**
D	5,3	5,0	1,4	- 2,3	- 7,6	3,6	1,2	0,6	3,5	4,2	1,5	**D**
EL	1,6	- 2,3	- 1,4	- 0,9	- 3,0	1,0	1,8	1,0	1,8	8,3	3,4	**EL**
E	4,6	- 0,1	- 0,8	- 4,0	- 4,7	7,7	4,8	- 1,3	6,9	5,5	2,6	**E**
F	3,9	- 0,3	- 0,2	- 1,4	- 3,4	4,1	2,4	0,6	3,9	5,2	2,1	**F**
IRL	11,6	4,7	3,2	9,2	5,6	11,9	20,5	7,6	14,7	15,3	:	**IRL**
I	3,9	- 0,7	- 0,9	- 1,3	- 2,1	6,2	6,1	- 1,9	3,8	1,1	0,0	**I**
L	7,8	- 0,7	0,3	- 0,7	- 4,4	5,9	0,4	0,2	5,8	7,6	3,5	**L**
NL	:	:	:	:	:	:	:	2,5	3,1	1,4	0,5	**NL**
A	6,0	7,6	1,6	- 1,1	- 2,1	4,6	9,0	1,0	6,4	8,2	5,5	**A**
P	6,7	9,1	1,3	- 1,6	- 4,4	- 0,3	5,0	5,3	2,8	5,2	2,9	**P**
FIN	3,3	- 0,5	- 8,7	1,1	5,1	11,0	6,2	3,7	9,2	7,8	5,5	**FIN**
S	3,7	6,8	- 5,0	- 2,3	- 0,9	10,9	10,6	1,7	7,1	4,1	1,0	**S**
UK	2,6	- 0,1	- 3,4	0,1	2,4	6,5	1,8	0,6	1,3	0,8	0,6	**UK**
NO	9,3	2,5	2,5	5,6	3,6	7,0	5,9	5,4	3,4	- 0,6	- 0,2	**NO**
US	1,9	- 0,2	- 2,1	3,2	3,4	5,5	4,8	4,4	6,4	4,1	3,5	**US**
JP	6,1	4,1	1,9	- 6,0	- 3,3	1,3	3,4	2,1	3,7	- 6,6	0,8	**JP**

0B2BX

Further reading: Monthly Panorama of European industry. Eurostat.

The employment index shows the evolution in the number of persons employed in industry (excluding construction).

This includes working proprietors, partners working regularly in the unit and unpaid family workers, as well as persons, such as sales representatives, delivery personnel, repair and maintenance teams, who work outside the observation units but are paid by them. It also includes persons absent for a short period (e.g. sick leave, paid leave or special leave), and also those on strike, but not those absent for an indefinite period. Employment is not restricted to full-time employment. It also covers part-time employees who are regarded as such under the laws of the country concerned and who are on the payroll, as well as seasonal workers, apprentices and home workers on the payroll. Also covered are unpaid family workers.

The number of persons employed, however, excludes manpower from other enterprises, such as persons carrying out repair and maintenance work on behalf of other enterprises, as well as those on compulsory military service.

Ideally, the index would be normalised to full-time equivalents. However, this meets practical problems and is not carried out in the current index calculation.

The Member States of the European Union have the option to approximate, for a limited period, the index of the number of persons employed by number of employees, which is less comprehensive: for example, it does not cover unpaid family workers.

Employment index in the EU, seasonally adjusted. 1995 = 100

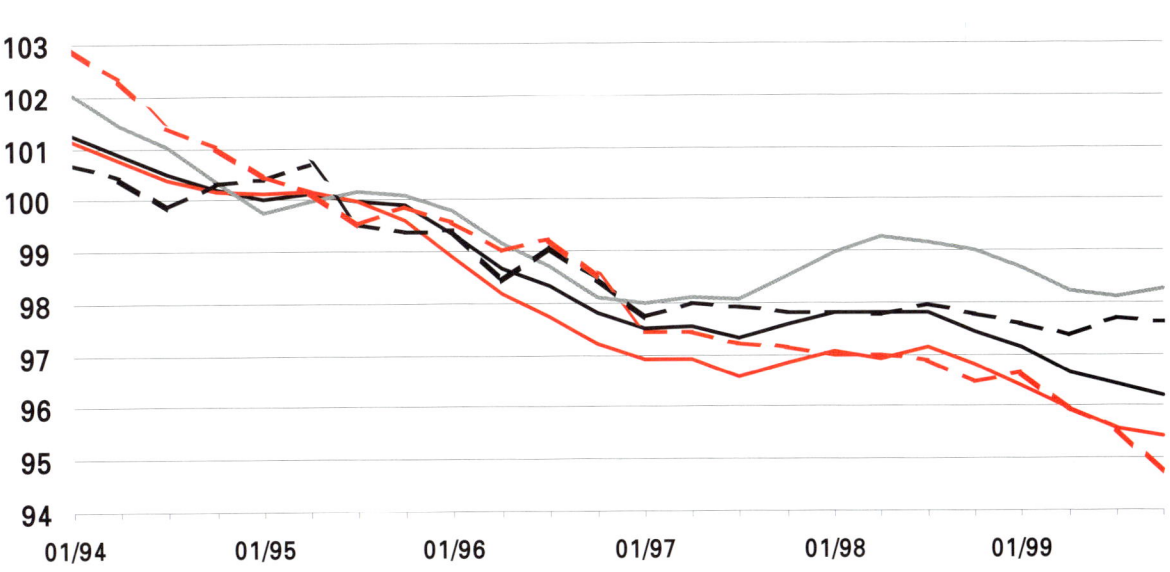

Black: total industry; colour: intermediate goods; grey: capital goods; dotted black: consumer durables; dotted colour: consumer non-durables.

Further reading: Monthly Panorama of European industry. Eurostat.

0E5EX

eurostat

More data on this in Eurostat's database

Monthly and quarterly short-term statistics (industry, construction, retail trade and other services).

➤ ➤ ➤ **DOMAIN EBT IN DATABASE NEW CRONOS**

4

Employment, total industry (excluding construction), year on year growth rates, seasonally adjusted

	1989	1990	1991	1992	1993	1994	1995	1996	1997	1998	1999	
EU-15	-	-	-	-	-	-	- 0,6	- 1,5	- 1,0	0,4	- 0,9	**EU-15**
EUR-11	-	-	- 0,9	- 6,2	- 7,0	- 3,7	- 1,3	- 2,1	- 1,4	0,4	- 0,4	**EUR-11**
B	2,0	0,7	- 0,9	- 3,6	- 5,5	- 0,2	1,8	- 1,4	- 1,2	0,8	- 1,6	**B**
DK	-	-	-	-	-	-	1,9	- 1,0	1,5	0,9	- 1,1	**DK**
D	2,3	2,8	1,4	- 10,2	- 8,7	- 6,5	- 3,5	- 4,1	- 3,5	- 0,3	- 0,7	**D**
EL	-	-	- 7,5	- 4,8	- 4,8	- 1,6	- 1,9	- 2,6	- 2,7	- 0,5	-	**EL**
E	3,4	2,8	- 3,0	- 3,0	- 9,4	- 2,6	0,5	0,6	3,2	5,0	2,8	**E**
F	-	-	- 1,8	- 3,3	- 4,5	- 2,2	0,2	- 1,3	- 1,0	0,2	0,1	**F**
IRL	1,4	2,1	0,7	- 0,1	- 0,1	2,4	5,3	4,1	6,0	2,2	-	**IRL**
I	0,0	- 1,7	- 2,8	- 5,5	- 6,0	- 2,9	- 1,6	- 1,5	- 2,3	- 2,0	- 3,1	**I**
L	0,1	- 1,9	- 0,9	- 0,8	- 5,1	- 3,2	- 0,7	- 0,3	- 0,3	1,2	1,5	**L**
NL	2,2	1,7	- 0,8	- 0,8	- 3,7	- 2,8	- 0,4	- 0,7	1,3	1,2	0,5	**NL**
A	-	-	0,1	- 2,9	- 6,1	- 2,9	- 1,1	- 4,3	- 2,0	1,7	- 1,6	**A**
P	1,3	- 1,5	- 1,7	- 3,1	- 6,5	- 0,5	- 2,3	- 1,5	- 1,7	- 1,2	- 2,9	**P**
FIN	-	- 1,2	- 9,2	- 9,7	- 6,5	0,3	6,7	0,9	0,5	2,4	2,7	**FIN**
S	-	-	- 6,2	- 8,2	- 8,9	1,6	4,2	1,0	- 0,6	1,4	0,0	**S**
UK	- 0,6	- 3,1	- 8,2	- 6,6	- 4,3	- 0,4	2,0	1,4	1,0	0,4	- 3,1	**UK**
US	0,4	- 1,6	- 3,5	- 1,6	- 0,2	1,4	1,1	- 0,2	0,9	0,3	-	**US**
JP	2,3	2,6	2,5	0,7	- 0,7	- 2,2	- 1,8	- 2,2	- 0,9	- 1,4	- 2,6	**JP**

0A2BB

Further reading: Monthly Panorama of European industry. Eurostat.

The producer price (also called output price) measures the average price development of industrial goods and related services. It is an indicator of the future evolution of consumer prices, although the range of goods and services covered are only indirectly linked to the goods and services covered by the consumer price index.

The producer price index (total industry, excluding construction) is calculated as weighted average of the relevant product price indices. According to the destination of goods, producer prices are distinguished in those for the domestic market and those for the non-domestic markets. The indices shown here are covering the domestic market.

All price-determining characteristics of the products are taken into account. For example: quantity of units sold, transport provided, rebates, service conditions, guarantee conditions and destination.

After falling from the beginning of 1998 until well into 1999, the producer prices have grown again. This has been fuelled by strong growth in the prices of petrol products. This increase is first visible in the intermediate goods industry.

0B1AA

Industrial producer prices, total industry (excl. construction), growth rates. Gross

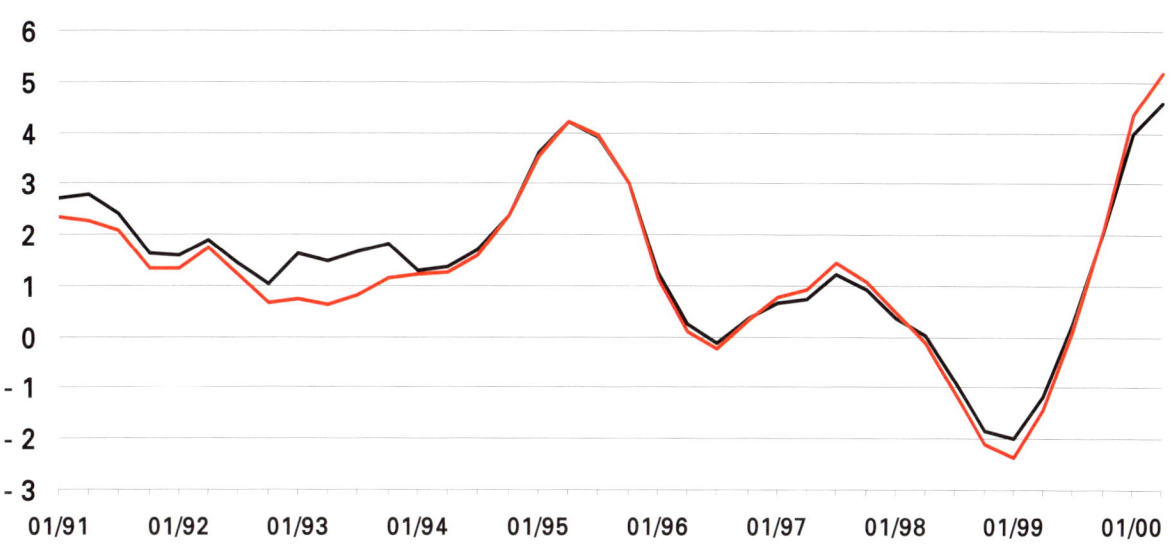

Black: EU-15 annual % change on a quarterly basis; colour: EUR-11 annual % change on a quarterly basis.

Further reading: Monthly Panorama of European Industry. Eurostat

0C3DD

Producer prices, total industry (excl. construction), year on year growth rates. Gross

	1989	1990	1991	1992	1993	1994	1995	1996	1997	1998	1999	
EU-15	:	:	2,3	1,4	1,5	1,7	3,6	0,4	0,9	-0,6	-0,2	EU-15
EUR-11	:	:	1,9	1,2	0,8	1,6	3,6	0,3	1,0	-0,8	-0,4	EUR-11
B	5,7	0,6	-1,1	0,2	-1,0	1,4	2,2	0,6	1,7	-1,2	-0,5	B
DK	6,3	1,6	1,1	-1,0	-1,1	0,7	3,8	1,5	1,8	-0,4	1,2	DK
D	3,1	1,7	2,4	1,4	0,2	0,6	1,7	-1,2	1,2	-0,4	-1,0	D
EL	12,9	23,4	13,1	11,8	8,9	8,0	9,2	6,2	4,0	2,6	3,3	EL
E	4,2	2,2	1,5	1,4	2,4	4,3	6,4	1,7	1,0	-0,7	0,7	E
F	4,2	1,7	1,0	0,6	-1,0	0,3	2,2	0,2	0,1	-1,7	-0,2	F
IRL	5,0	0,3	1,1	2,1	2,3	2,0	3,7	1,8	0,1	0,0	0,9	IRL
I	5,9	4,1	3,3	1,9	3,8	3,7	7,9	1,9	1,3	0,1	-0,3	I
L	7,6	-2,1	1,5	2,6	0,9	2,0	3,4	-4,3	2,9	2,7	-2,1	L
NL	2,9	1,6	2,2	-0,4	-1,6	0,7	3,0	1,6	2,7	-1,2	-0,3	NL
A	:	:	:	:	:	:	:	:	:	:	:	A
P	:	:	3,9	1,5	3,6	2,8	3,8	3,8	2,2	-3,7	1,4	P
FIN	5,7	3,2	-0,3	1,3	2,8	1,9	1,8	-0,9	1,3	-1,4	-1,2	FIN
S			2,3	-0,3	2,0	4,3	8,0	0,6	1,1	-0,4	0,1	S
UK	4,8	4,7	4,2	3,0	5,9	1,5	2,8	0,6	-0,3	-0,1	0,3	UK
US	4,9	3,6	0,2	0,6	1,5	1,3	3,6	2,3	-0,1	-2,5	0,8	US
JP	2,1	1,6	1,1	-0,9	-1,6	-1,8	-0,7	-1,8	0,7	-1,4	-1,5	JP

Further reading: Monthly Panorama of European industry. Eurostat.

*Industrial production index: main industrial groupings, working days adjusted series.
1995 = 100*

0C3CX

EU-15

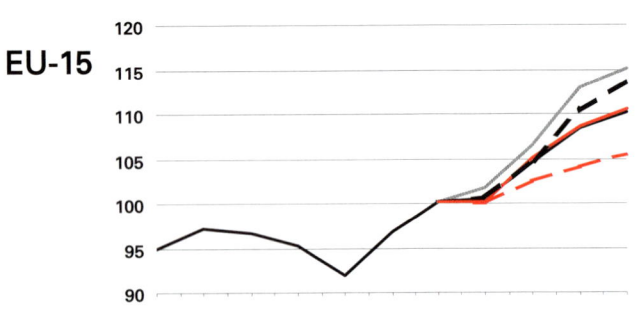

B

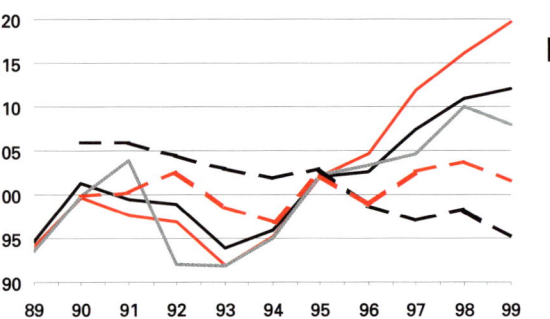

DK

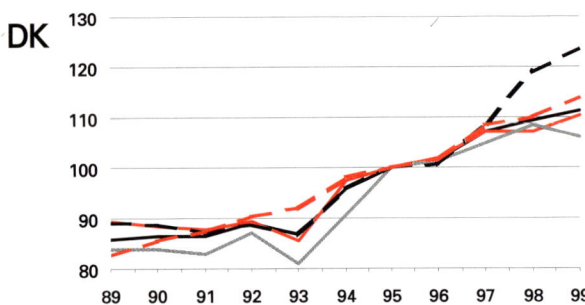

D

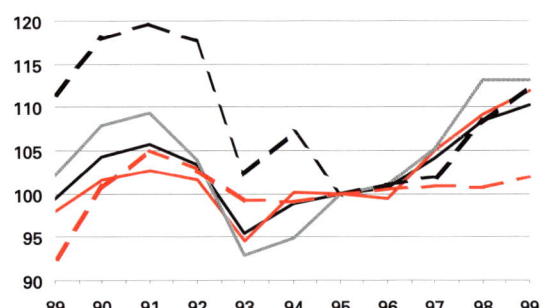

EL

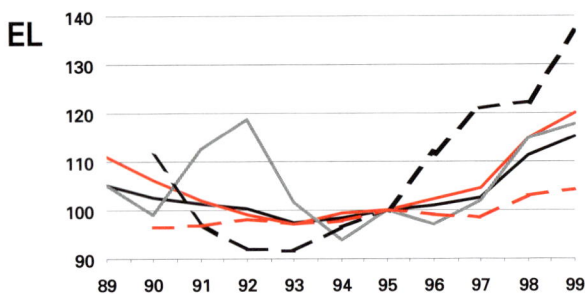

E

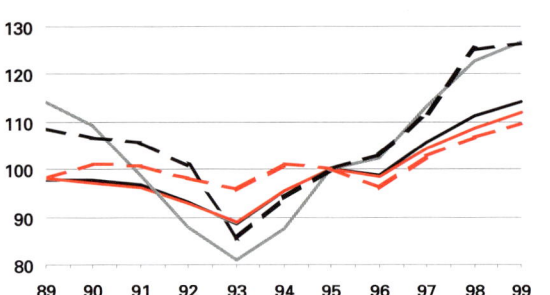

F

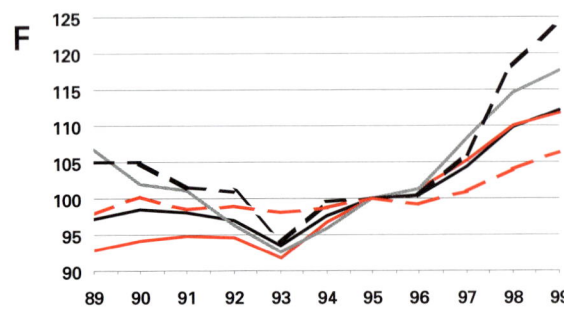

IRL

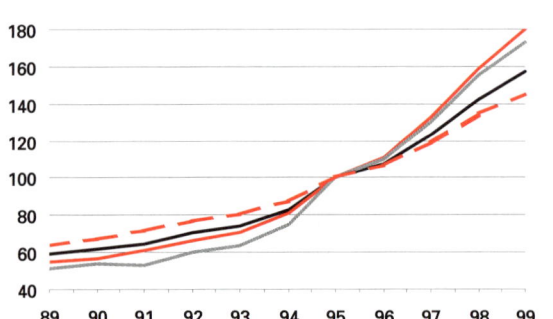

Black: total industry; colour: intermediate goods; grey: capital goods; dotted black: consumer durables;
dotted colour: consumer non-durables.

Further reading: Monthly Panorama of European industry. Eurostat.   The scales for each country may be different.

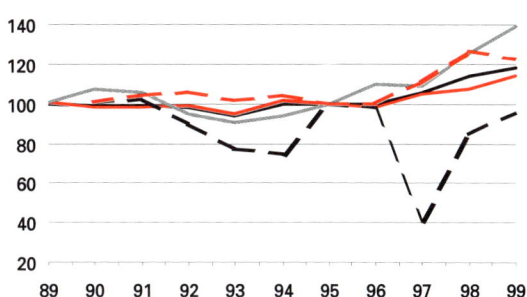

Industrial production index: main industrial groupings, working days adjusted series.
1995 = 100

0D4DX

I

L

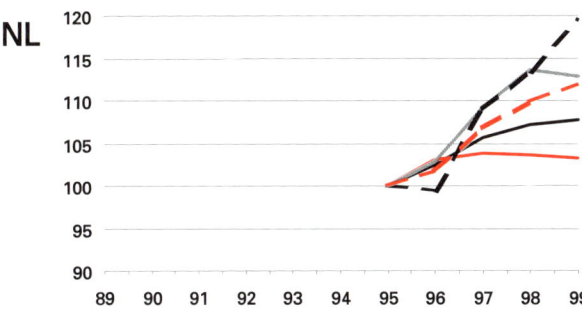

NL

A

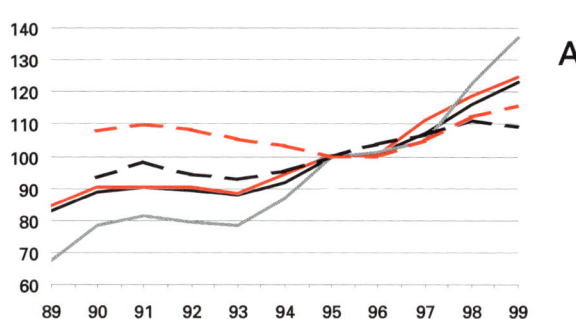

P

FIN

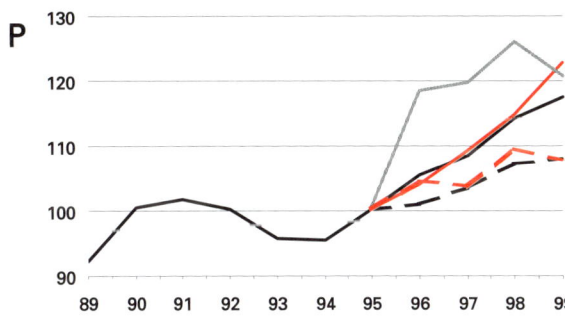
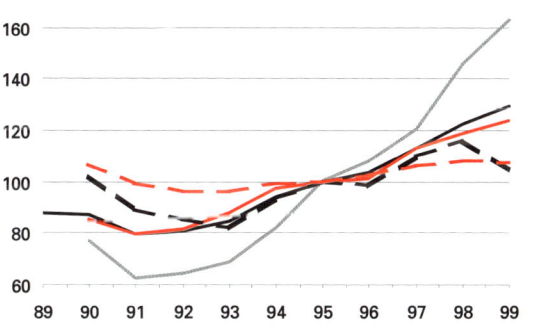

S

UK

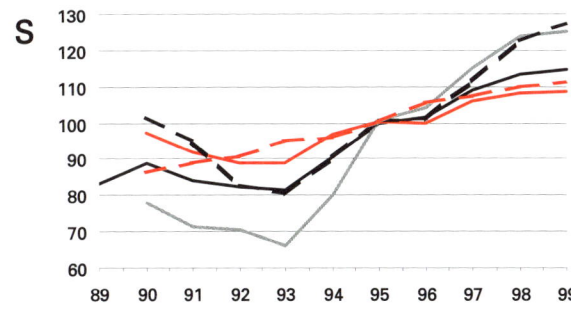
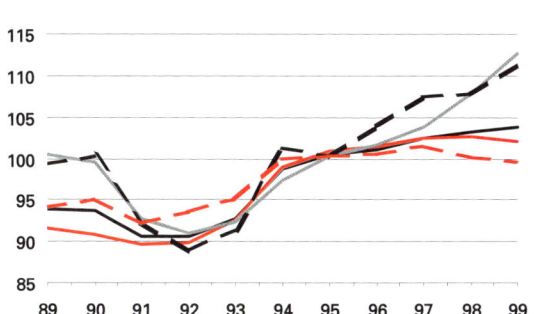

Black: total industry; colour: intermediate goods; grey: capital goods; dotted black: consumer durables;
dotted colour: consumer non-durables.

Further reading: Monthly Panorama of European industry. Eurostat.   The scales for each country may be different.

eurostat

Specialisation in manufacturing industry

The global specialisation index indicates the degree of homogeneity of the distribution of value added in the activities of a sector. The higher the index, the more the industry is concentrated in a small number of activities; the lower the index, the more diversified it is. The global index allows countries to be classified by the degree of specialisation of their manufacturing industry, although it does not show whether this specialisation is in the same activities as in the EU or not. By convention, the index is standardised to give the EU an index equal to zero.

Small countries (Luxembourg, Denmark) are often more specialised than large ones. Ireland appears to be the most specialised country, whereas Austria and Portugal are more diversified than France and Italy, that are as diversified as the EU as a whole.

The rate of a specific country's relative specialisation S_i in an activity i is calculated with reference to the structure of European industry. The relative share of an activity in a country's total for manufacturing industry is related to the same share of this activity for European industry. This specialisation rate is negative if the activity is under-represented in a country compared with the EU as a whole, and it is nil if the share is the same as the EU figure. Highest rates of specialisation occur in the industries, which figure prominently in a country's economy. The table below shows that Ireland is specialised in the information technologies sectors and in the chemical industry that represent together 46 % of the Irish manufacturing industry. France and the United Kingdom specialise in activities that have little significance either at national or European level, the relative share of most of their largest industries being the same as in the European Union.

Germany is specialised in car industry and machinery and equipment while Italy is specialised in textiles and clothing.

Relative specialisation index in the countries' three main areas of specialisation. 1997

	Global specialisation index	1. First activity of specialisation		2. Second activity of specialisation		3. Third activity of specialisation		Weight of activities 1, 2 and 3 in total value added (%)
IRL	1,25	Office machinery and computers	1,7	Chemical industry	1,0	Radio, television & communication equipment	0,6	46%
L	0,60	Manufacture of basic metals	1,5	Recycling	1,2	Rubber and plastic products	1,1	34%
DK	0,43	Furniture; manufacturing n.e.c.	0,6	Food products and beverages	..	Tobacco	..	26%
NL	0,29	Tobacco	1,5	Coke, refined petroleum & nuclear fuel	0,5	Publishing, printing, recorded media	0,5	15%
EL	0,28	Tobacco	1,3	Coke, refined petroleum & nuclear fuel	1,2	Clothing and furs	1,2	12%
S	0,21	Radio, television & communication equipment	1,3	Pulp, paper & paper products	1,0	Manufacture of wood	0,9	27%
D	0,21	Electrical machinery	0,4	Motor vehicles	0,4	Machinery & equipment	0,3	37%
FIN	0,20	Pulp, paper & paper products	1,6	Manufacture of wood	1,2	Radio, television & communication equipment	1,0	32%
B	0,19	Recycling	1,3	Coke, refined petroleum & nuclear fuel	0,6	Textile industry	0,6	9%
E	0,06	Leather and footwear	0,6	Other non-metallic mineral products	0,5	Clothing and furs	0,4	12%
JP	0,03	Radio, television & communication equipment	0,8	Office machinery and computers	0,7	Manufacture of basic metals	0,1	17%
UK	0,01	Manufacture of other transport equipment	0,5	Office machinery and computers	0,5	Tobacco	0,4	8%
I	-0,01	Leather and footwear	1,1	Textile industry	0,8	Clothing and furs	0,7	11%
F	-0,01	Recycling	0,7	Coke, refined petroleum & nuclear fuel	0,5	Manufacture of other transport equipment	0,4	7%
US	-0,04	Radio, television & communication equipment	0,8	Office machinery and computers	0,8	Tobacco	0,8	13%
P	-0,06	Leather and footwear	1,7	Clothing and furs	1,6	Textile industry	1,1	21%
A	-0,06	Manufacture of wood	0,9	Radio, television & communication equipment	0,6	Coke, refined petroleum & nuclear fuel	..	..

Further reading: Panorama of European business, 1999. Enterprises in Europe, sixth report.

The data relates to enterprises with 20 persons employed or more. Reading note: the manufacture of office machinery and computers is the main activity in which Ireland is specialised, with a relative specialisation index reaching 1.7. The three activities in which Ireland is most specialised represent 46 % of Ireland's manufacturing industry.

0E8MN   0E9MN   0E10N   0E11N   0E12N

eurostat

Progress of high technology industries

The technological level of an industry is defined by the weight of Research & Development in the turnover of the industry. This ratio is a proxy of the efforts made by the industry towards innovation and technological progress. The dawn of the so-called 'information society', a society whose wealth and growth is based on its ability to efficiently handle information, influences more and more enterprises, strategies. Thus, it boosts the high technologies

industries such as computers, telecommunications and other IT industries.

Between 1990 and 1997, high technology industries have grown very fast in Ireland, Sweden, Finland and Portugal. In almost every country, it has been superior to the growth of the low technologies industries. In Ireland and Finland, the growth of high technologies employment has been superior to 5 % per year.

Annual growth rate of value added in high and low technology industries between 1990 and 1997. %

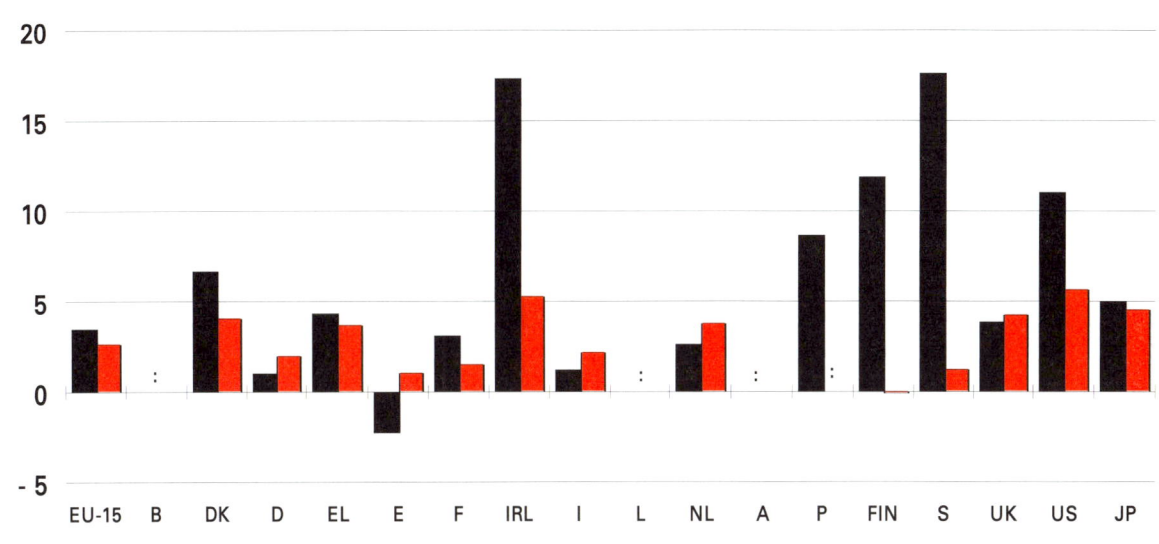

Black: high technology industries; colour: low technology industries.

Further reading: Panorama of European Business, 1999. Enterprises in Europe, sixth report.

High technology industries include the manufacture of aircraft and spacecraft; office machinery and computers; radio, television and communication equipment; and pharmaceuticals. Low technology industries include food, beverages and tobacco; textile and leather; paper and printing industries; and wood products. The data relates to enterprises with 20 persons or more employed.

Annual growth rate of employment in high and low technology industries between 1990 and 1997. %

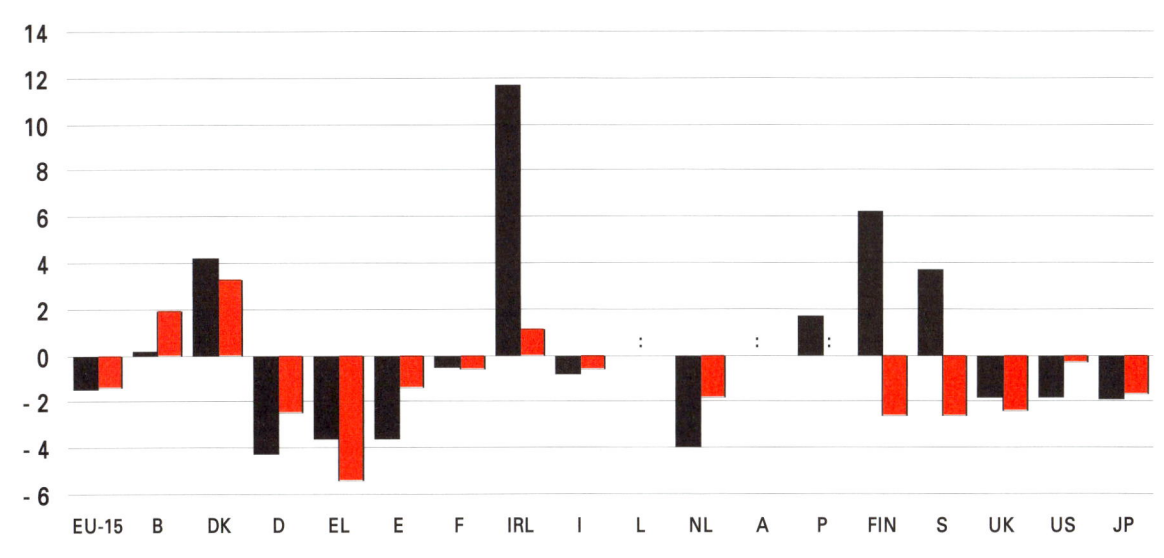

Black: high technology industries; colour: low technology industries.

Further reading: Panorama of European Business, 1999. Enterprises in Europe, sixth report.

High technology industries include the manufacture of aircraft and spacecraft; office machinery and computers; radio, television and communication equipment; and pharmaceuticals. Low technology industries include food, beverages and tobacco; textile and leather; paper and printing industries; and wood products. The data relates to enterprises with 20 persons or more employed.

High technology: employment by region

The map below presents the share of high technology industries (defined in the table's footnote) in total manufacturing employment. The weight of high technology industries in manufacturing is highest in northern Europe and in the vicinity of large cities (Frankfurt, Hamburg, Rome, Paris, Stockholm, etc.). The position of Ireland as a whole among the regions where high technology employment is relatively strong relates to the fact that this country is specialised in high technology industries (see previous page). Some specific regions also appear where it is known that high-tech areas have developed combining active universities, research centres and large high-tech industries: for instance, in the Pohjois-Suomi region in northern Finland, one finds the Oulu valley where many knowledge intensive activities developed with in the wake the firm NOKIA and in the 'Midi-Pyrénées', in southern France the Aerospace industry have developed in the area of Toulouse.

Please note that due to data availability at the regional level, the definition of high-tech industries also includes other transport industries such as ship building and not aerospace industries only.

Share of high technology industries' employment in total manufacturing. %. 1997

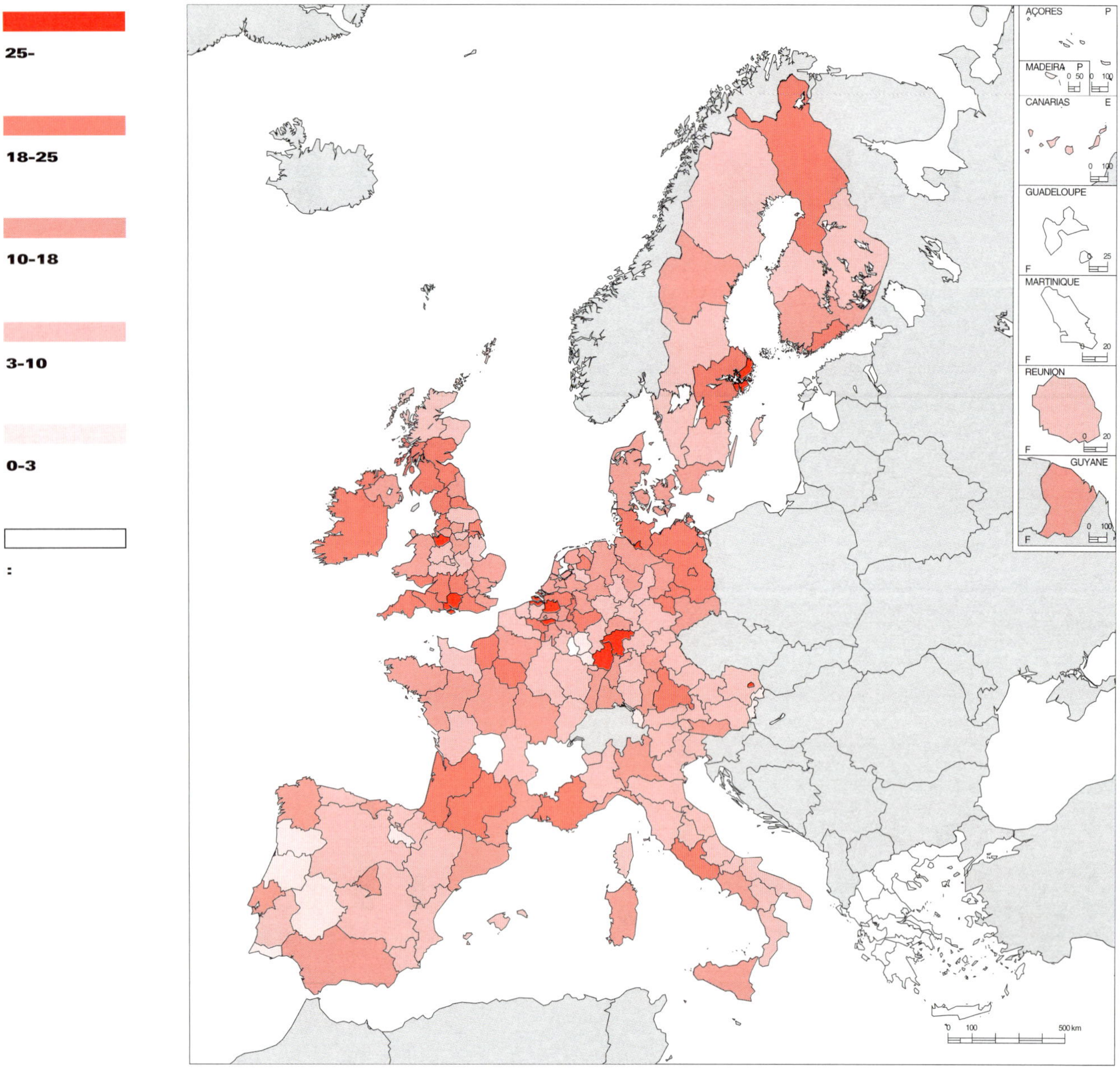

25-

18-25

10-18

3-10

0-3

:

Further reading: Panorama of European business, 1999. Enterprises in Europe, sixth report.

NUTS 2. NUTS 95. High technology industries include the manufacture of other transport equipment (aircraft, railways, ships and motorcycles); office machinery and computers; radio, television and communication equipment; and chemicals (including pharmaceuticals). The data relate to local units belonging to enterprises with 20 persons or more employed.

Low technology: employment by region

The map below presents the share of low technology industries (defined in the table's footnote) in total manufacturing employment.

Low technologies industries provide the largest employment shares in southern Europe. In agricultural areas where agro-food industries play a large role, agro-food represents 31 % of manufacturing employment in Alentejo and 39 % in Algarve (PT),

29 % in Andalucia, 40 % in Extremadura and 30 % in Murcia (ES), 25 % in Languedoc-Roussillon, 47 % in Corsica and 38 % in Brittany (FR). The textile and leather industry is also dominant in some of the southern European regions such as the northern part of Portugal and in Italy.

In Finland the wood and paper industry represents no less than 35 % of employment in the Itä-Suomi region.

Share of low technology industries' employment in total manufacturing. %. 1997

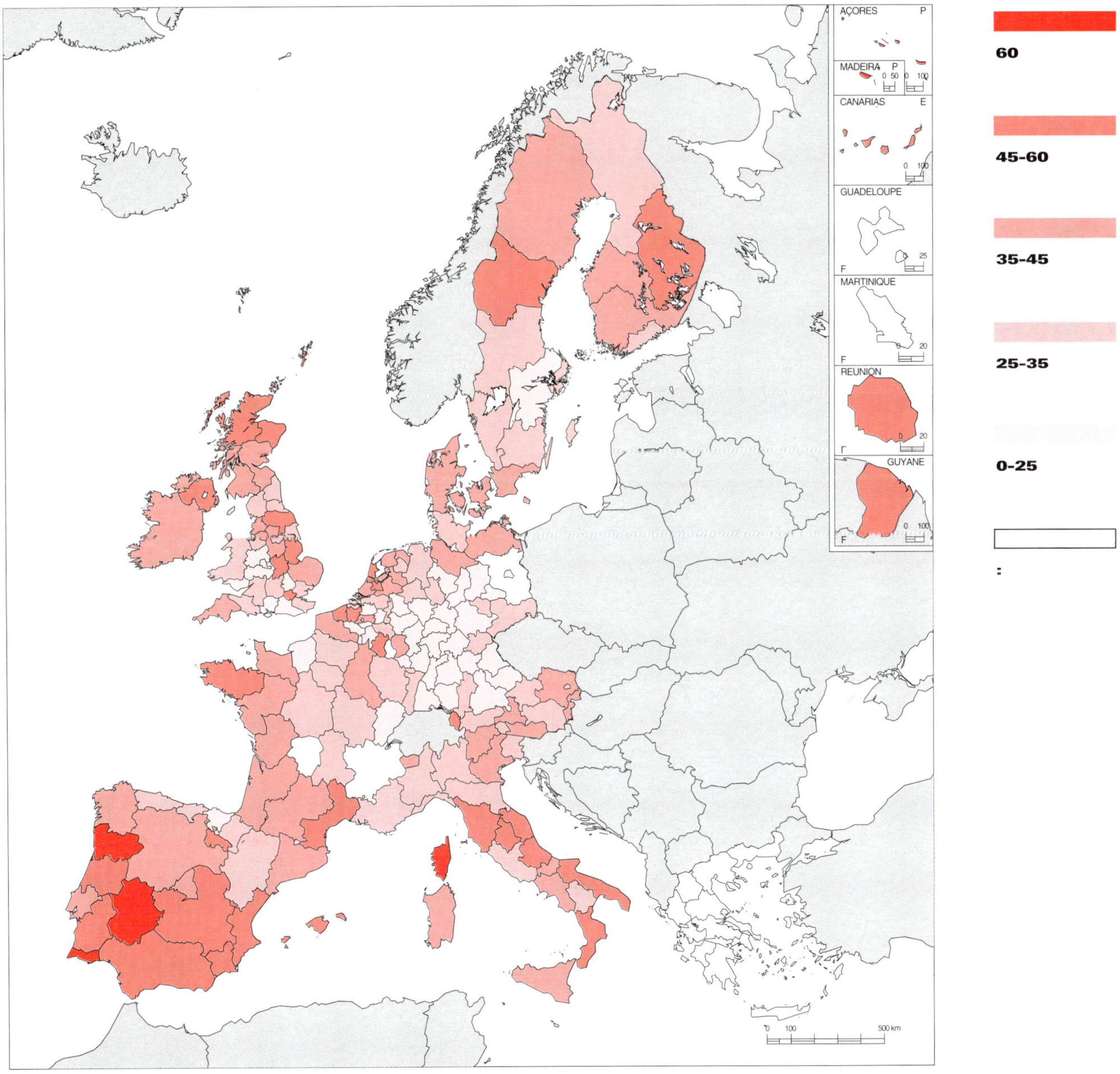

0E16N

■	**60**
■	**45-60**
■	**35-45**
■	**25-35**
□	**0-25**
□	:

Further reading: Panorama of European business, 1999. Enterprises in Europe, sixth report.

NUTS 2. NUTS 95. Low technology industries include food, beverages and tobacco; textile and leather; paper and printing industries; and wood products. The data relate to local units belonging to enterprises with 20 persons or more employed.

The construction industry accounts for about 14 % of total production in the European Union, while the percentage of people it employs is slightly higher.

Construction activities can be broken down into four main types: house-building, non-residential building, civil engineering, and repair and maintenance; this last one represents about one quarter of the total activity.

Whilst the civil engineering activities registered a higher growth until the mid-1990s, in the second half of the decade the predominant growth was observed in the building construction sector. Recent trends in the construction industry in the EU-15 show that, further to a strong growth in the late 1980s and beginning of the 1990s, there was an overall contraction of activity which attained its peak in 1993 and 1996, followed by a gradual recovering from 1996 onwards and attaining its highest level in the beginning of 2000.

Construction: breakdown by activity. EU-15 estimates. 1997

	Share of activity in construction total employment (%)	Value added in production (%)	Share of gross operating surplus in value added (%)	Wage adjusted labour productivity (%)	Share of employees in persons employed (%)
Construction	100	36	34	118	79
Site preparation	3	35	32	119	81
Building of complete constructions and civil engineering	54	34	36	130	83
Building installation	24	40	27	107	78
Building completion	18	43	32	97	66
Renting of construction equipment with operator	1	54	47	152	81

Further reading: Panorama of European Business, 1999. Enterprises in Europe, sixth report.

Construction sector. Employment index. 1995 = 100

	1989	1990	1991	1992	1993	1994	1995	1996	1997	1998	1999	
EU-15	:	:	108,6	104,1	98,7	98,2	100,0	99,0	99,6	100,9	103,8	**EU-15**
EUR-11	:	:	105,6	102,7	98,5	98,2	100,0	98,5	98,2	98,5	101,4	**EUR-11**
B	92,5	97,3	101,9	102,4	99,4	97,9	100,0	99,2	99,4	102,4	109,0	**B**
DK	:	123,6	117,8	118,6	92,0	97,3	100,0	101,3	105,8	106,9	106,0	**DK**
D	:	:	90,8	92,2	95,1	99,5	100,0	92,9	86,5	79,8	78,6	**D**
EL	:	:	:	:	:	:	:	:	:	:	:	**EL**
E	99,9	107,6	112,2	105,4	96,1	93,3	100,0	103,6	109,5	115,2	:	**E**
F	110,7	112,7	111,9	107,9	101,8	100,2	100,0	96,7	94,9	94,9	96,5	**F**
IRL	95,8	104,9	101,5	99,4	93,4	95,8	100,0	108,2	118,2	128,6	137,0	**IRL**
I	115,1	119,1	125,8	118,5	107,4	103,2	100,0	99,7	99,5	98,2	:	**I**
L	97,4	104,0	107,8	108,4	107,8	102,6	100,0	99,2	99,3	101,3	103,6	**L**
NL	98,6	100,5	100,1	99,5	98,3	97,5	100,0	103,2	106,6	108,3	110,6	**NL**
A	:	:	:	:	:	:	:	105,4	104,6	113,0	108,2	**A**
P	:	:	:	:	:	:	:	:	:	:	:	**P**
FIN	170,8	173,9	152,4	127,2	105,6	94,1	100,0	102,3	112,6	120,2	129,2	**FIN**
S	:	138,8	142,3	119,9	103,0	95,8	100,0	100,6	96,8	97,6	102,7	**S**
UK	129,9	130,7	119,9	108,5	99,7	99,6	100,0	102,2	113,9	126,0	127,3	**UK**
NO	:	110,0	103,5	97,5	92,7	95,0	100,0	104,6	112,7	118,1	121,4	**NO**

Further reading: Monthly Panorama of European industry. Eurostat.

0018A

EU-15 production indices, total construction, seasonally adjusted. 1995 = 100

Black: total construction; colour: building; grey: civil engineering.

Further reading: Monthly Panorama of European industry. Eurostat.

0018B

Building permits: dwellings authorised. 1000s

	1989	1990	1991	1992	1993	1994	1995	1996	1997	1998	1999	
EU-15	:	:	:	:	:	:	:	:	:	:	:	EU-15
EUR-11	:	:	:	:	:	:	:	:	:	:	:	EUR-11
B	50 966	52 228	47 723	51 277	56 436	56 631	44 956	48 707	50 847	40 048	46 918	B
DK	26 408	19 121	15 002	15 269	13 025	13 093	11 552	15 809	16 711	16 349	16 133	DK
D	279 792	396 693	406 090	485 366	606 612	712 798	639 101	576 376	530 263	477 707	437 584	D
EL	117 327	120 240	100 339	85 095	79 150	80 607	70 865	86 741	89 553	97 259	:	EL
E	242 601	233 431	215 387	227 292	222 804	237 214	282 530	265 956	304 763	364 086	404 832	E
F	:	:	:	:	:	357 944	308 298	301 589	299 828	376 752	333 699	F
IRL	20 400	22 074	20 517	21 302	24 035	25 735	28 837	34 864	37 060	47 389	49 945	IRL
I	187 386	210 495	212 217	211 526	172 979	179 792	173 608	160 553	145 435	118 987	132 729	I
L	2 983	3 796	4 452	4 316	4 022	2 744	2 676	2 797	3 411	3 215	3 739	L
NL	102 626	89 747	82 160	87 034	89 358	106 503	98 404	102 119	101 501	87 673	84 201	NL
A	37 800	36 200	42 000	51 900	58 320	60 980	53 117	52 163	44 917	40 540	:	A
P	:	:	:	:	:	:	76 946	84 609	94 786	109 734	117 830	P
FIN	76 167	57 961	46 921	32 716	28 570	23 855	18 840	25 122	31 117	32 468	37 563	FIN
S	:	:	:	:	:	:	:	10 314	11 822	12 530	13 498	S
UK	201 200	164 100	163 800	156 600	185 500	201 100	167 700	173 300	188 900	176 700	179 300	UK
IS	:	:	:	:	:	:	:	:	:	:	:	IS
NO	:	17 731	15 072	14 012	12 402	23 166	21 493	20 713	24 252	22 017	:	NO
US	1 376 100	1 192 600	1 014 000	1 199 600	1 287 600	1 457 000	1 354 200	1 476 900	1 474 000	1 617 000	1 666 500	US
JP	1 662 600	1 707 100	1 370 300	1 402 500	1 485 700	1 570 400	1 470 300	1 643 200	1 387 000	1 198 200	1 214 700	JP

Further reading: Monthly Panorama of European industry. Eurostat.

D: data refer to Germany as constituted after 3.10.1990. Data prior to 1991 have been estimated by Eurostat. UK, US and JP: dwellings started.

Need access to Eurostat's databases? Ask your Data Shop

Distributive trades indicators

Since 1995, Structural Business Statistics have been collected in the area of distributive trades according to the SBS regulation harmonised framework. Short-term indicators have been collected at EU level in this area since reference year 1998.

Structural indicators in the distributive trades

One of the basic information provided by structural business statistics is on the relative size of industries.

This size is measured here in terms of turnover and in terms of employment. Turnover represents the sales of an activity. Employment shares indicate which industries provide most jobs.

The two pie charts below present the relative shares of the three areas of distributive trades: motor trade, wholesale and retail trades. While retail trade provides more than half of the jobs in distributive trades it accounts for slightly less than one third of turnover. The opposite situation is found in the highly concentrated activity of wholesale trade. Motor trade represents 14 % of the total distributive trades turnover and employment.

Share of motor, wholesale and retail trades in EU-15 total distributive trades in terms of turnover. %. 1996 estimates

Share of motor, wholesale and retail trades in EU-15 total distributive trades in terms of employment %. 1996 estimates

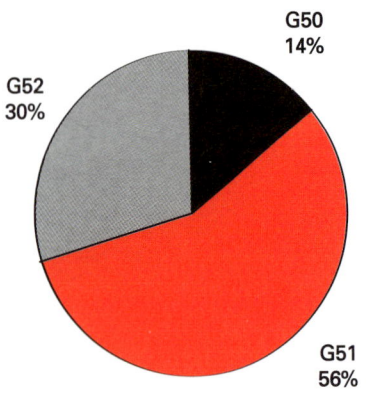

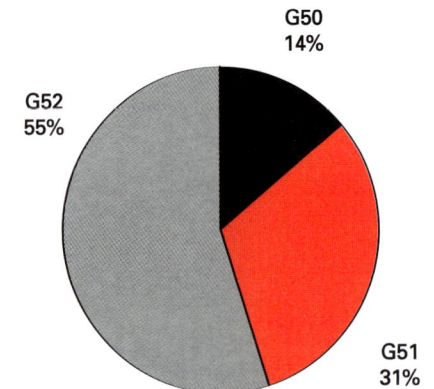

0D10N

0D11N

G50: Motor trade. G51: Wholesale trade except motor trade. G52: Retail trade except motor trade.

Further reading: Panorama of European business, 1999. Enterprises in Europe, sixth report. Distributive trades in Europe.

Average size of enterprises in terms of turnover. 1 000 ECU. EU-15 estimates. 1997

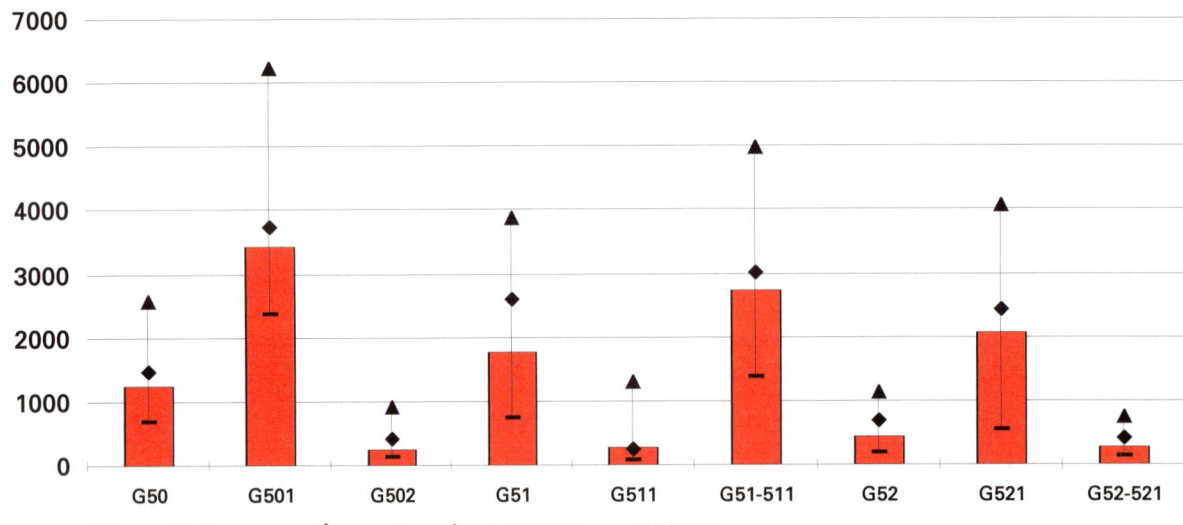

0D12N

Column: EU-15 average; ◆ : median; ▲ : maximum; ▬ : minimum.

G50: Motor trade. G501: Sale of motor vehicles. G502: Maintenance and repair of motor vehicles. G51: Wholesale trade except motor trade. G511: Wholesale on a fee or contract basis. G51-511: Wholesale trade without fee or contract basis. G52: Retail trade except motor trade. G521: Retail sale in non-specialised stores. G52-521: Retail sale in specialised stores.

Further reading: Panorama of European business, 1999. Enterprises in Europe, sixth report. Distributive trades in Europe.

Motor trade

Motor trade includes the sale, maintenance and repair of motor vehicles and retail sale of automotive fuel. The main activity in the sector is the sale of motor vehicles as it is approaching 70 % of total turnover and around 50 % of employment.

These shares range from 50 % of turnover and less than 20 % of employment in Italy to close to 75 % of turnover and more than 60 % of employment in the Netherlands. These variations might partly result from the different ways enterprises are organised. Car sales in Italy might partly be carried out by car producers or by garages and thus be accounted for as industrial turnover or as maintenance and repair of motor vehicles in the SBS statistics.

Wholesale trade

Wholesale trade includes the sale without transformation of new and used goods to professional users as well as the usual manipulations involved in wholesale. Apart from wholesale on own account, wholesale trade includes the activities of commission agents and all other wholesalers who trade on behalf of others.

The share of wholesale on a fee or contract basis in total wholesale turnover varies from country to country, it is highest in France where it reaches 12 % of wholesale turnover and lowest in Ireland where it doesn't reach 1 %. In terms of employment, it reaches 30 % in Italy and is lowest in Austria and Ireland where it is below 5 %.

Retail trade

This division includes the sale without transformation of new and used goods to the general public for personal or household consumption, as well as the repair of household goods and retail sale by commission agents.

The retail distribution networks vary greatly from country to country with regards to the type of store — specialised or non-specialised — dominating the sector. In Portugal, only 25 % of all retail sales is realised in supermarket type of stores, whereas, this share reaches 60 % in Finland.

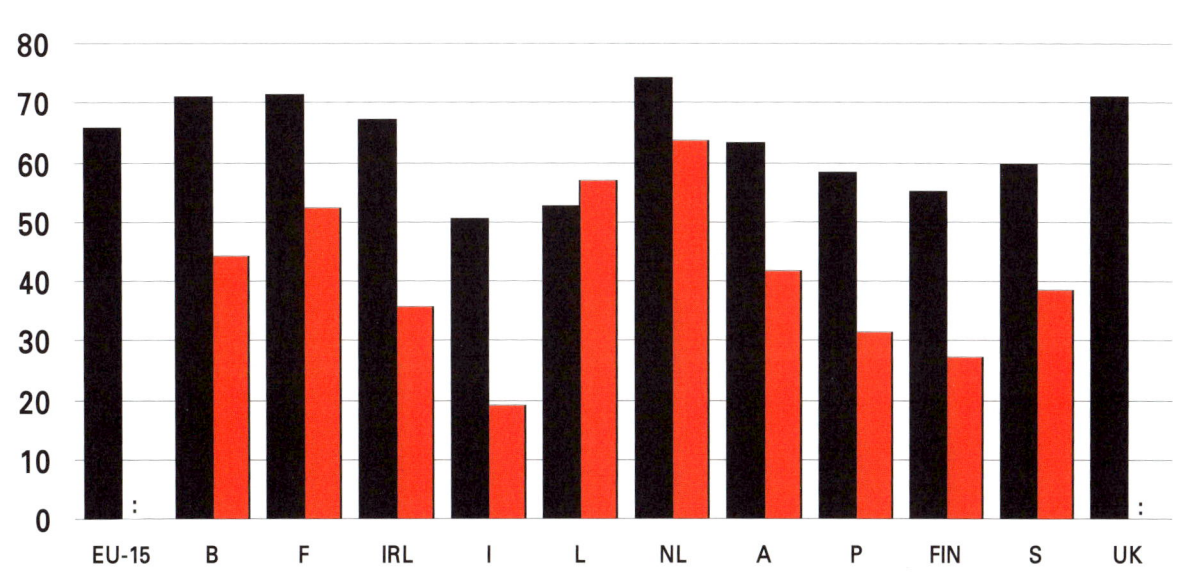

Share of vehicle sales in motor trade in terms of turnover and employment. %. 1997

Black: turnover; colour: employment.

Further reading: Panorama of European business, 1999. Enterprises in Europe, sixth report. Distributive trades in Europe.

EU-15: estimate.

Share of wholesales on a fee or contract basis in wholesales trade in terms of turnover and employment. %. 1997

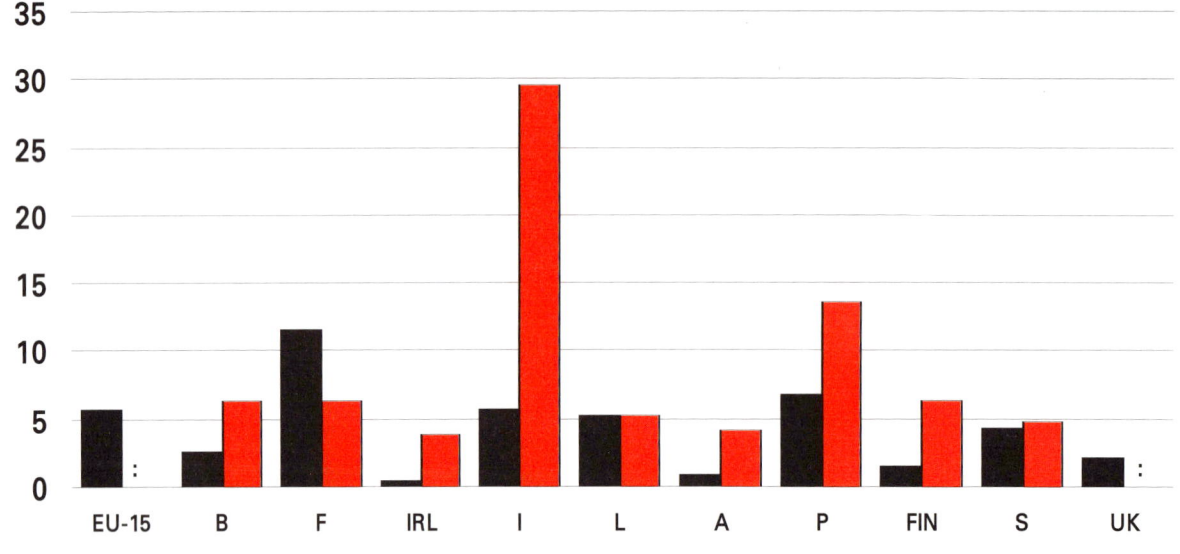

Black: turnover; colour: employment.

Further reading: Panorama of European business, 1999. Enterprises in Europe, sixth report. Distributive trades in Europe.

EU-15: estimate.

0D14N

Share of non-specialised stores in retail trade in terms of turnover and employment. %. 1997

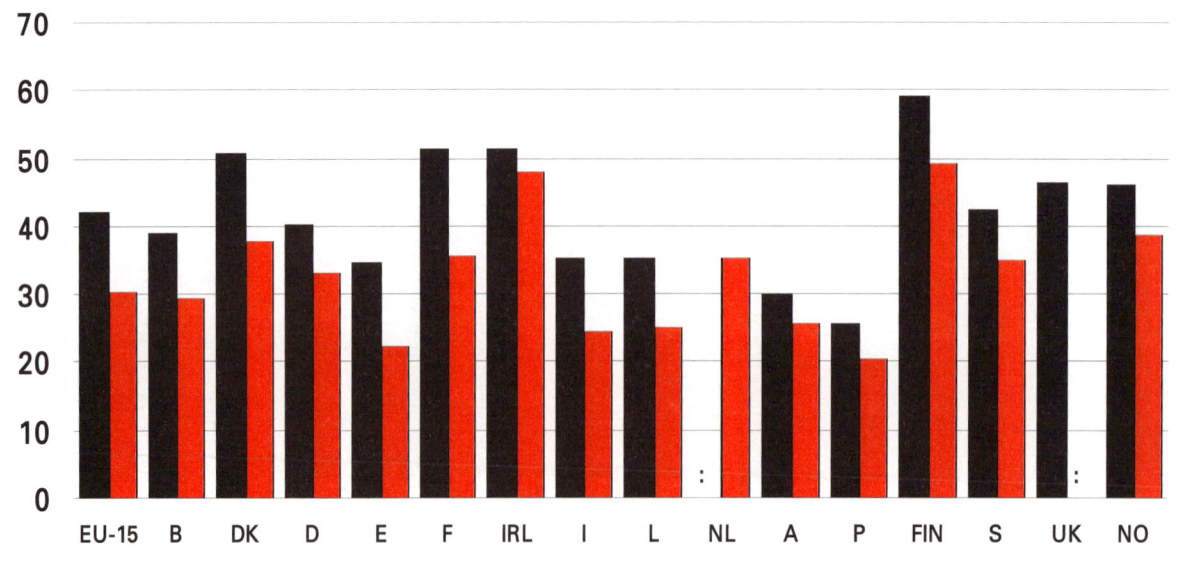

Black: turnover; colour: employment.

Further reading: Panorama of European business, 1999. Enterprises in Europe, sixth report. Distributive trades in Europe.

EU-15: estimate.

0D15N

The retail trade index is an important indicator of demand and consumer confidence. The retail trade index measures turnover of retail enterprises. For better transparency of the index evolution, the turnover is deflated in order to show the evolution at constant prices.

The retail trade growth accelerated recently, showing a more positive general economic climate that is also visible in other indicators. Growth was particularly strong in household goods followed by food products, but less pronounced in textile products.

Retail trade, volume of sales in the EU. 1995 = 100

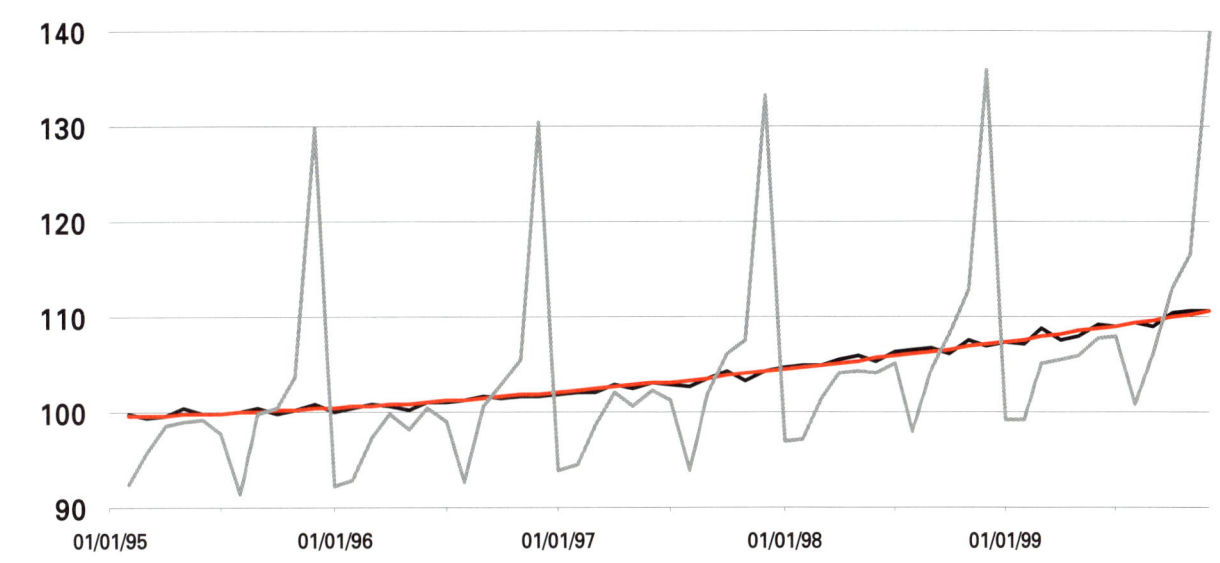

Black: seasonally adjusted; colour: trend; grey: working day adjusted.

Further reading: Monthly Panorama of European industry. Eurostat.

Retail trade, volume of sales, year on year growth rate, working day adjusted

	1989	1990	1991	1992	1993	1994	1995	1996	1997	1998	1999	
EU-15	:	:	:	:	:	:	:	1,0	1,9	3,0	2,8	EU-15
EUR-11	:	:	:	:	:	:	:	0,5	1,2	3,0	2,6	EUR-11
B	:	:	:	0,8	- 1,6	0,6	0,5	1,2	3,0	4,6	2,0	B
DK	- 0,1	0,3	2,2	- 1,2	0,8	5,3	0,9	1,2	2,1	2,1	1,1	DK
D	:	:	:	:	:	:	0,6	- 1,0	- 1,7	0,7	0,9	D
EL		- 2,3	- 6,4	- 0,2	- 3,4	0,6	- 1,4	4,0	3,7	2,3	2,0	EL
E	:	:	:	:	:	:	:	- 1,8	2,2	6,0	3,3	E
F	3,4	1,8	0,5	0,3	1,5	1,4	1,6	1,2	2,9	4,3	4,9	F
IRL	4,8	2,8	- 0,3	3,0	1,7	4,3	2,5	6,7	7,7	8,9	4,8	IRL
I	:	:	- 1,4	- 0,7	- 1,3	- 1,5	0,4	1,3	1,2	1,0	0,8	I
L	:	:	:	:	:	:	:	- 0,5	6,8	2,5	2,8	L
NL	:	:	:	:	:	:	1,6	2,8	4,2	4,1	3,4	NL
A	:	:	2,2	0,7	- 0,7	1,4	0,2	1,3	1,2	2,4	3,9	A
P	:	:	:	:	:	:	:	4,0	3,3	10,0	5,2	P
FIN	:	:	:	:	:	:	:	4,0	4,1	5,5	3,7	FIN
S			3,5	- 4,0	- 3,1	- 0,3	0,5	0,7	2,2	3,8	5,8	S
UK	2,0	0,3	- 1,2	0,6	3,1	3,5	1,3	3,3	5,0	3,1	3,4	UK
IS	:	:	:	:	:	:	:	:	:	:	:	IS
NO	:	:	0,8	1,5	2,0	4,5	3,2	2,4	4,9	4,8	:	NO
US	:	:	:	:	:	:	:	:	:	:	:	US
JP	:	:	:	:	:	:	:	:	:	:	:	JP

Further reading: Monthly Panorama of European industry. Eurostat.

Need more data on this topic? Ask your Data Shop

EUROSTAT YEARBOOK 2001
369

Retail sale of food

In all EU countries, the retail sale of food products constitutes a large share of total retail trade activities both in terms of total sales (turnover) and in terms of number of persons employed. This share ranges from approximately one third in Denmark, Austria and Portugal to close to one half in France and Ireland.

The retail sale of food is either carried out in specialised or non-specialised stores. In the EU as a whole more than 80 % of food products are sold in non-specialised stores such as supermarkets. This turnover share is lowest in Spain (~ 60 %) and highest in Finland (more than 90 %).

Share of retail sale of food in total retail trade in terms of turnover and employment. %. 1997

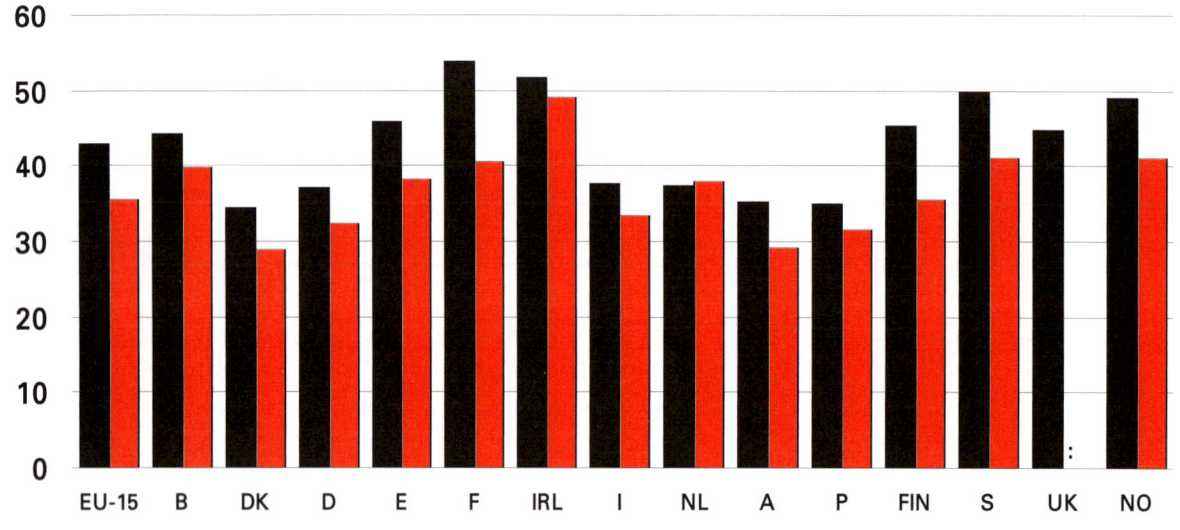

Black: turnover; colour: employment.

Further reading: Panorama of European business, 1999. Enterprises in Europe, sixth report. Distributive trades in Europe.

EU–15: estimate.

Breakdown of turnover in retail sale of food between specialised and non-specialised stores. %. 1997

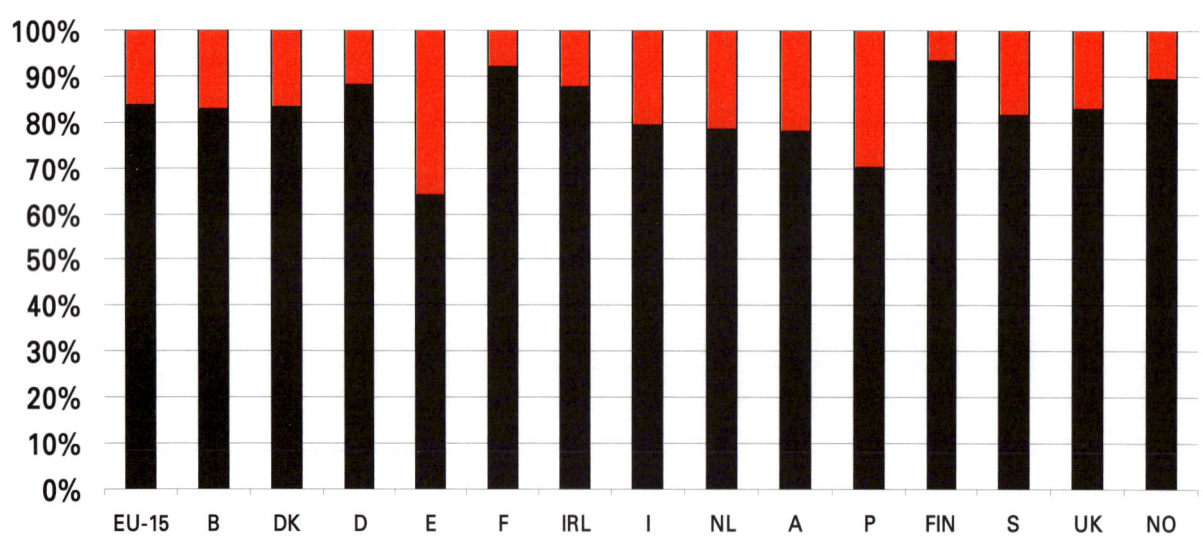

Black: retail sale of food in non-specialised stores; colour: retail sale of food in specialised stores.

Further reading: Panorama of European business, 1999. Enterprises in Europe, sixth report. Distributive trades in Europe.

EU–15: estimate.

0D16N

0D17N

Services

Structural Business Statistics cover market services activities in sections H to K of NACE Rev. 1. These sections group the following activities: hotels and restaurants (section H), transport, storage and communication (section I), financial intermediation (section J), and real estate, renting and business activities (section K). Financial intermediation activities are treated separately at the end of this chapter as specific statistics are collected in this sector.

In the chart below several statistical measures are presented. The EU-15 estimate of the ratio is a weighted average of the countries available (if there are enough countries to obtain a reliable estimate). The minimum and maximum values correspond to the two countries that recorded respectively the lowest and highest ratio for the sector. The median is the middle of a distribution: half of the countries are above the median and half are below the median. The median is less sensitive to extreme scores than the average.

Turnover on employment

The ratio of turnover on employment varies greatly from activity to activity. The EU-15 estimated average is lower than ECU 50 000 in labour-intensive activities such as industrial cleaning, labour recruitment and the hotels and restaurants and reaches more than ECU 150 000 in the renting activities and advertising.

Unit labour costs

Unit labour costs that relate personnel costs (including social charges) to the number of employees also vary greatly from activity to activity. It is lowest in activities employing less-qualified personnel (industrial cleaning, labour recruitment and the hotels and restaurants) and highest in activities employing highly qualified personnel: the computer-related activities, research and development and legal, accounting, bookkeeping and auditing activities. It is also in these activities that labour unit costs show the greatest variations from country to country.

High technology services

High technology services are defined here as telecommunications, computer-related activities and research and development activities.

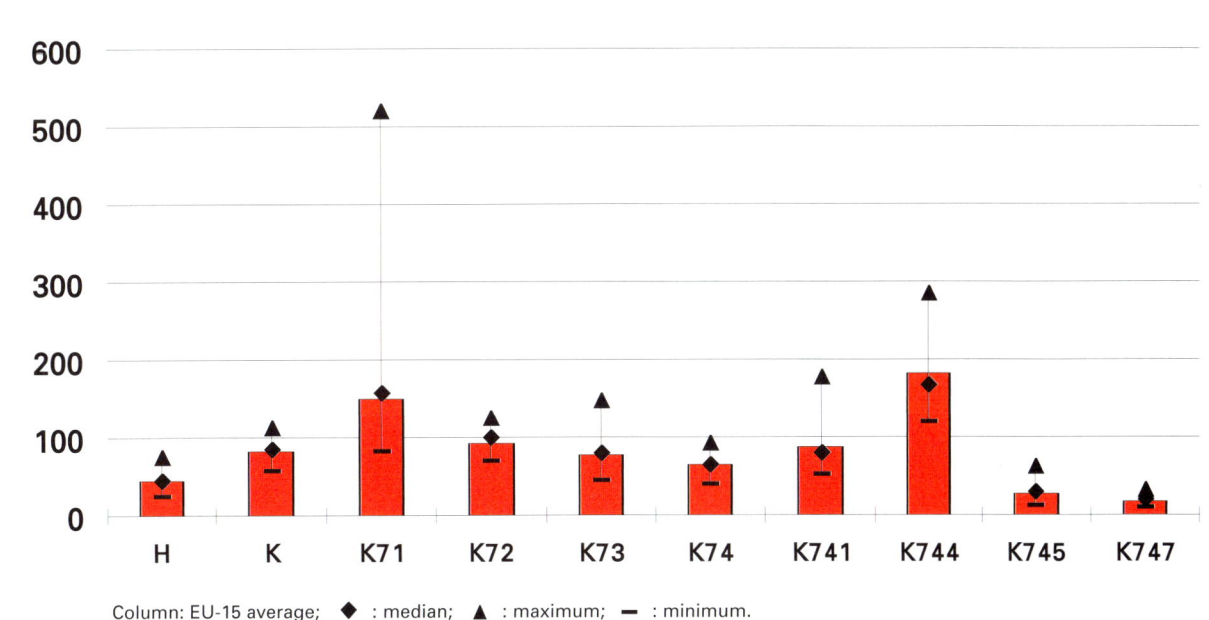

Turnover per persons employed in services. 1 000 ECU. EU-15 estimates. 1997

Column: EU-15 average; ◆ : median; ▲ : maximum; ▬ : minimum.

H: Hotels and restaurants; K: Real estate, renting and business activities; K71: Renting of machinery without operator; K72: Computer and related activities; K73: Research and development; K74: Other business activities; K741: Legal, accounting and other consultancy activities; K744: Advertising; K745: Labour recruitment and provision of personnel; K747: Industrial cleaning.

Further reading: Panorama of European business, 1999. Enterprises in Europe, sixth report.

Unit personnel cost in services. 1 000 ECU. EU-15 estimates. 1997

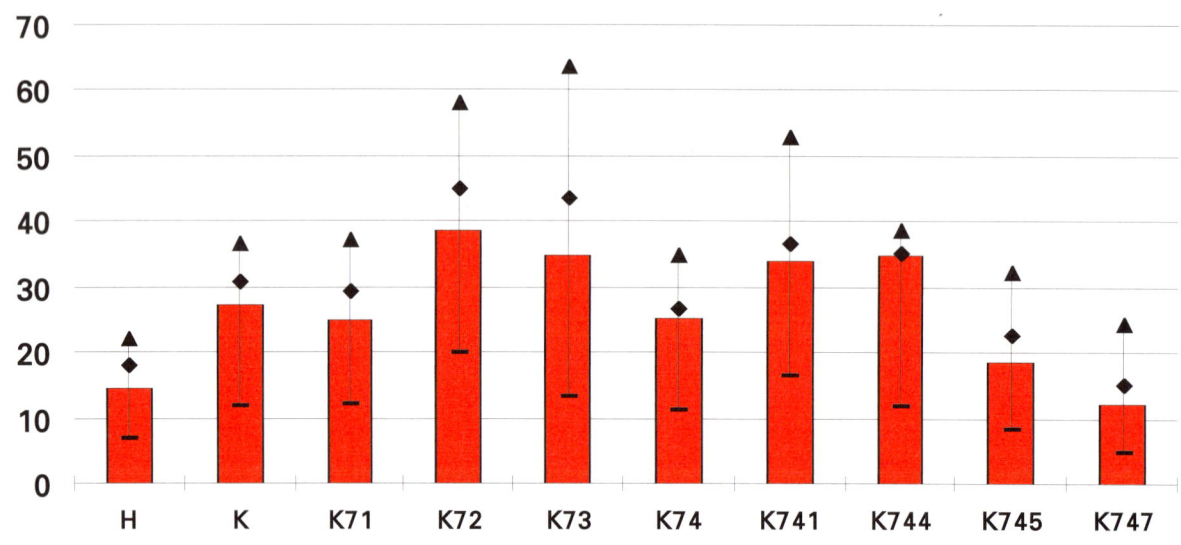

Column: EU-15 average; ◆ : median; ▲ : maximum; ▬ : minimum.

H: Hotels and restaurants; K: Real estate, renting and business activities; K71: Renting of machinery without operator; K72: Computer and related activities; K73: Research and development; K74: Other business activities; K741: Legal, accounting and other consultancy activities; K744: Advertising; K745: Labour recruitment and provision of personnel; K747: Industrial cleaning.

Further reading: Panorama of European business, 1999. Enterprises in Europe, sixth report.

Number of persons employed in services. 1997

	B	DK	D	EL	E	F	IRL	I
Hotels and restaurants	137 034	:	1 160 600	:	:	669 951	:	:
Hotels and other accommodation	20 277	:	329 000	:	:	194 131	:	:
Restaurants, bars, canteens and catering	116 757	:	831 600	:	:	475 820	81 070	
Transport, storage and communication	255 533	:	:	:	:	1 388 055	65 539	:
Land transport; transport via pipelines	122 165	:	:	:	:	637 697	21 520	:
Water transport	2 248	:	:	:	:	15 408	1 666	:
Air transport	12 040	9 853	46 600	:	31 682	59 683	6 215	:
Supporting and auxiliary transport activities	39 462	:	:	:	:	226 232	12 013	:
Post and telecommunications	79 618	52 176	:	:	:	449 035	24 125	:
Real estate, renting and business activities	350 200	:	:	:	:	2 061 140	91 862	:
Real estate activities	19 867	:	:	:	:	302 529	6 890	:
Renting of machinery without operator	8 803	:	:	:	:	65 265	5 698	:
Computer and related activities	26 504	:	:	:	:	200 011	9 688	:
Research and development	3 599	:	:	:	:	21 890	385	:
Other business activities	291 427	:	:	:	:	1 471 445	69 201	:
Legal, accounting and other consultancy activities	71 311	:	:	:	:	302 157	29 597	:
Architectural and engineering activities	33 049	:	:	:	151 398	189 284	9 226	:
Advertising	12 294	:	:	:	:	93 904	4 009	:
Labour recruitment and provision of personnel	106 927	:	:	:	:	406 905	3 879	:
Investigation and security activities	9 302	:	:	:	:	96 179	5 592	:
Industrial cleaning	38 254	:	:	:	:	225 460	9 337	:
Miscellaneous business activities n.e.c.	20 290	:	:	:	:	157 556	7 561	:

Further reading: Panorama of European business, 1999. Enterprises in Europe, sixth report.

0D20N

Breakdown of high technology services in terms of employment. %. 1997

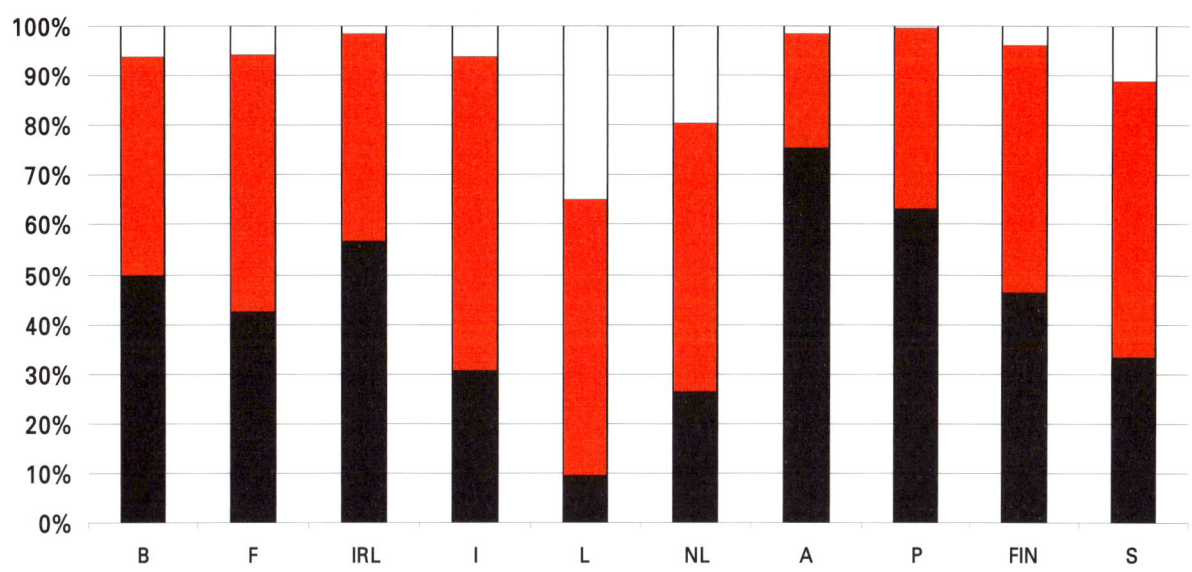

Black: telecommunications; colour: computer and related activities; white: research and development.

Further reading: Panorama of European business, 1999. Enterprises in Europe, sixth report.

Sweden: breakdown in terms of employees instead of persons employed.

4

0D22N

Number of persons employed in services. 1997

L	NL	A	P	FIN	S	UK	NO	
10 762 *	235 419 *	191 510	234 475	45 189	93 756	:	:	Hotels and restaurants
3 068 *	47 027 *	102 528	45 281	11 774	27 235	:	:	Hotels and other accommodation
7 694 *	188 392 *	88 982	189 194	33 415	66 521	:	:	Restaurants, bars, canteens and catering
:	411 010 *	243 962	169 731	144 876	286 094	:	:	Transport, storage and communication
:	..	139 110	94 184	62 961	119 218	:	:	Land transport; transport via pipelines
:	15 198 *	258	2 138	..	14 454	:	:	Water transport
:	..	6 807	9 723	..	12 793	:	:	Air transport
:	74 273 *	32 078	26 887	20 099	48 671	:	:	Supporting and auxiliary transport activities
:	..	65 709	36 799	44 570	90 958	:	:	Post and telecommunications
25 667 *	1 089 900 *	206 304	243 991	131 093	417 819	:	:	Real estate, renting and business activities
1 554 *	57 671 *	20 810	23 559	22 329	72 566	:	:	Real estate activities
499 *	22 827 *	5 879	9 006	2 565	11 828	:	5 295	Renting of machinery without operator
..	79 015 *	19 846	11 825	18 139	60 985	:	19 869	Computer and related activities
..	28 542 *	1 323	125	1 410	12 077	:	6 677	Research and development
19 397 *	901 845 *	158 446	199 476	86 650	260 363	:	:	Other business activities
5 738 *	222 406 *	48 553	43 461	20 986	83 260	:	:	Legal, accounting and other consultancy activities
2 357 *	97 860 *	33 150	22 654	23 565	69 851	:	31 487	Architectural and engineering activities
604 *	37 078 *	10 261	16 032	5 465	25 400	:	6 759	Advertising
4 788 *	340 660 *	15 489	21 008	4 515	777	:	:	Labour recruitment and provision of personnel
..	15 098 *	5 873	16 171	3 877	13 714	:	4 723	Investigation and security activities
..	136 992 *	34 399	41 409	20 035	32 881	:	18 674	Industrial cleaning
..	51 751 *	10 722	38 741	8 207	34 480	:	15 711	Miscellaneous business activities n.e.c.

Further reading: Panorama of European business, 1999. Enterprises in Europe, sixth report.

Transport services

Transport activities are covered by divisions 60 to 63 of the NACE Rev. 1 classification. It includes activities related to providing passenger or freight transport, whether scheduled or not, by rail, pipeline, road, water or air as well as supporting activities and renting of transport equipment with driver or operator.

In EU-15 as a whole freight transport by road is the largest transport activity with close to 45 % of the turnover in the sector, ahead of air transport (around 20 %) and water, railways and other land passenger transport (slightly more than 10 % each). However the situation varies greatly from country to country as the graph below shows.

In the EU, unit personnel costs are highest in air and rail transport and lowest in road and other land transport.

Unit personnel cost in transport activities 1 000 ECU. EU-15 estimates. 1997

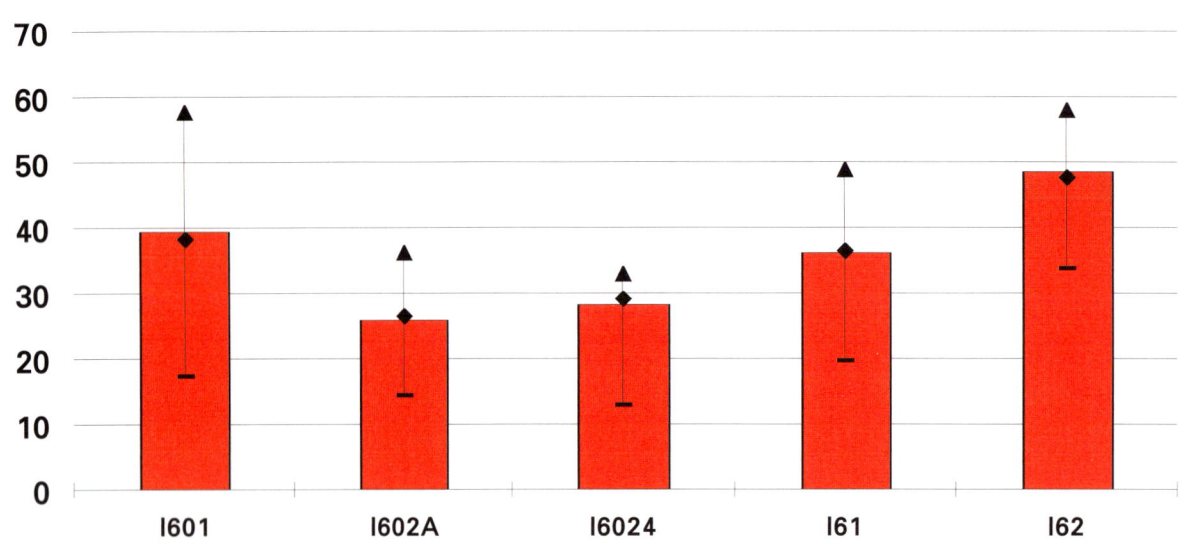

Column: EU-15 average; ◆ : median; ▲ : maximum; ▬ : minimum.
I601: transport via railways; I602A: passenger transport by road; I6024: freight transport by road; I61: water transport; I62: air transport.

Further reading: Panorama of European business, 1999. Enterprises in Europe, sixth report.

Breakdown of turnover in rail, road, water and air transport. %. 1997

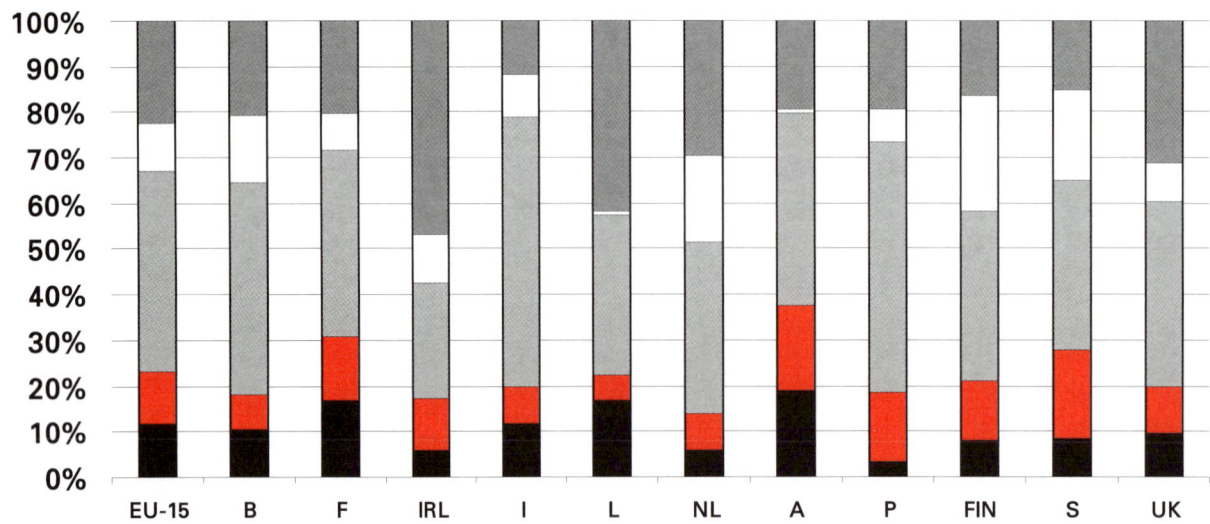

Black: transport via railways; colour: passenger transport by road; light grey: freight transport by road; white: water transport; dark grey: air transport.

Further reading: Panorama of European business, 1999. Enterprises in Europe, sixth report.

EU-15: estimate.

In the following tables, basic structural data for credit institutions are presented. On the basis of this data, it can be observed that large structural changes of credit institutions took place over the recent years and will probably continue for the time being. This is, in particular, reflected in the diminishing number of banks, their higher level of concentration (measured on the balance-sheet total) and a changing structure of income.

Credit institutions: evolution in the total number of enterprises. 1994/98

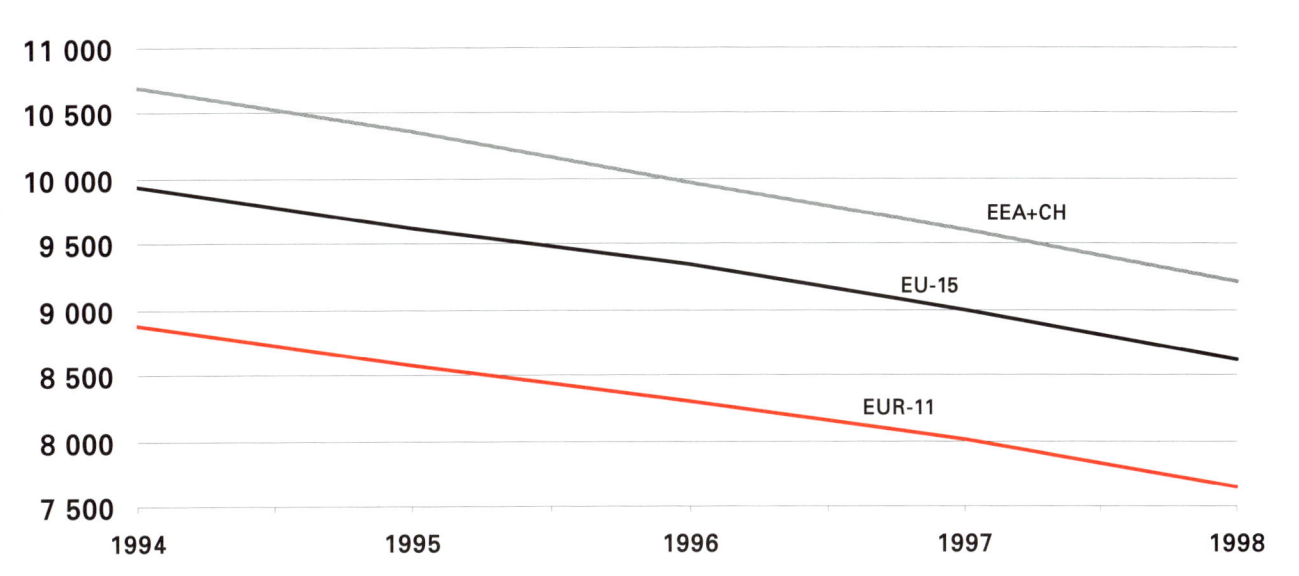

Further reading: Detailed tables: special feature on banking, 2000. Eurostat (pdf-publication). Statistics in focus: statistics on credit institutions. Less enterprises but stable employment, 4–9/2000. Eurostat.

EEA+CH does not include LI.

Credit institutions: local units and employment. 1998

	Automatic teller machines (units)	Number of local units (units)	Number of persons employed (units)	Average number of persons employed per enterprise (units)	Average number of persons employed per local unit (units)	Personnel costs. Million ECU	
EU-15	:	:	:	:	:	:	**EU-15**
EUR-11	:	:	:	:	:	:	**EUR-11**
B	5 712	5 932	77 410	815	13	4 665	**B**
DK	2 549	2 185	47 536	236	22	2 378	**DK**
D	45 615	63 208	751 517	228	12	36 891	**D**
EL	2 168	2 401	54 787	1 274	23	1 722	**EL**
E	37 599	39 039	247 679	613	6	10 852	**E**
F	16 704	26 192	366 372	352	14	22 748	**F**
IRL	:	:	:	-	-	:	**IRL**
I	27 794	26 260	345 651	375	13	20 219	**I**
L	:	533	19 814	95	37	1 275	**L**
NL	6 568	6 854	121 000 *	747	18	5 105	**NL**
A	2 424	5 498	73 814	80	13	4 182	**A**
P	7 081	5 056	61 004	270	12	1 872	**P**
FIN	2 725	1 964	26 279	73	13	899	**FIN**
S	-	2 197	:	:	:	2 670	**S**
UK	25 658	15 873	463 923	884	29	16 840	**UK**

Further reading: Detailed tables: special feature on banking, 2000. Eurostat (pdf-publication). Statistics in focus: statistics on credit institutions. Less enterprises but stable employment, 4–9/2000. Eurostat.

B: including foreign branches of Belgian credit institutions and excluding EEA branches in Belgium. S: local units only refer to licensed banks. UK: personnel costs include NACE Rev. 1 class 65.11.

eurostat

Credit institutions: financial indicators. 1998

	Interest receivable and similar income. Million ECU	Interest payable and similar charges. Million ECU	Commissions receivable. Million ECU	Commissions payable. Million ECU	Net interest/net commission income (%)	Net interest income/balance sheet total (%)	
EU-15	:	:	:	:	:	:	EU-15
EUR-11	:	:	:	:	:	:	EUR-11
B	55 264	47 022	2 689	1 105	5,2	0,2	B
DK	20 819	15 679	1 660	333	3,9	0,4	DK
D	300 660	235 259	24 005	4 617	3,4	0,3	D
EL	9 861	7 431	928	137	3,1	0,7	EL
E	38 765	28 434	7 159	1 268	1,8	0,7	E
F	177 188	151 956	17 848	4 242	1,9	0,5	F
IRL	:	:	:	:	-	-	IRL
I	77 541	40 656	18 923	1 434	2,1	1,1	I
L	37 129	34 300	2 718	753	1,4	0,4	L
NL	43 255	31 820	3 760	:	3,0	0,5	NL
A	22 511	16 243	2 890	612	2,8	0,5	A
P	12 110	8 103	1 096	168	4,3	0,3	P
FIN	5 764	3 396	964	151	2,9	0,7	FIN
S	26 049	20 551	2 423	453	2,8	0,4	S
UK	251 767	212 841	23 287	6 472	2,3	0,4	UK

Further reading: Detailed tables: special feature on banking, 2000. Eurostat (pdf-publication). Statistics in focus: statistics on credit institutions. Less enterprises but stable employment, 4–9/2000. Eurostat.

Data are delivered according to either the home or the host country principle.

Credit institutions: balance sheet data. 1998

	Loans and advances to customers. Million ECU	Loans and advances to customers as a % of balance sheet total	Amounts owed to customers. Million ECU	Amounts owed to customers as a % of balance sheet total	Total of capital and reserves. Million ECU	Total of capital and reserves as a % of balance sheet total	Balance sheet total. Million ECU	
EU-15	10 312 043	53,9	9 294 657	48,6	981 462	5,1	19 142 329	EU-15
EUR-11	6 479 493	45,7	5 509 518	38,9	688 912	4,9	14 171 484	EUR-11
B	235 664	34,7	274 713	40,4	22 130	3,3	680 045	B
DK	218 462	61,1	94 354	26,4	21 377	6,0	357 841	DK
D	2 943 973	49,9	2 315 487	39,2	181 178	3,1	5 906 088	D
EL	42 207	38,8	81 567	74,9	6 078	5,6	108 841	EL
E	464 813	51,4	466 527	51,6	76 456	8,5	904 262	E
F	1 018 735	36,9	929 165	33,7	116 353	4,2	2 760 194	F
IRL	66 577	49,6	63 684	47,5	9 980	7,4	134 112	IRL
I	762 475	47,5	570 117	35,5	159 649	10,0	1 604 178	I
L	97 542	18,2	190 148	35,4	12 897	2,4	537 148	L
NL	459 329	59,9	356 128	46,5	54 807	7,2	766 543	NL
A	233 495	49,5	154 109	32,6	32 056	6,8	472 078	A
P	110 640	38,8	132 245	46,4	15 890	5,6	284 862	P
FIN	86 250	70,7	57 195	46,9	7 516	6,2	121 974	FIN
S	248 715	55,4	112 488	25,1	37 392	8,3	448 754	S
UK	3 323 166	81,9	3 496 730	86,2	227 703	5,6	4 055 409	UK

Further reading: Detailed tables: special feature on banking, 2000. Eurostat (pdf-publication). Statistics in focus: statistics on credit institutions. Less enterprises but stable employment, 4–9/2000. Eurostat.

Data are delivered according to either the home or the host country principle. IRL: 1997.

In the following tables, basic structural data for insurance enterprises are presented. These are collected in the frame of Council Regulation (EC) No 410/98, amending the basic regulation on structural business statistics (Council Regulation (EC) No 58/97). As was the case with banks, insur-ance enterprises also faced large structural changes in the recent years. This is mainly due to the open-ing-up of the internal market for insurance, which leads to higher competition, decreasing prices and a larger variety of products in Europe.

Insurance: evolution in the total number of enterprises. 1990, 1992–98

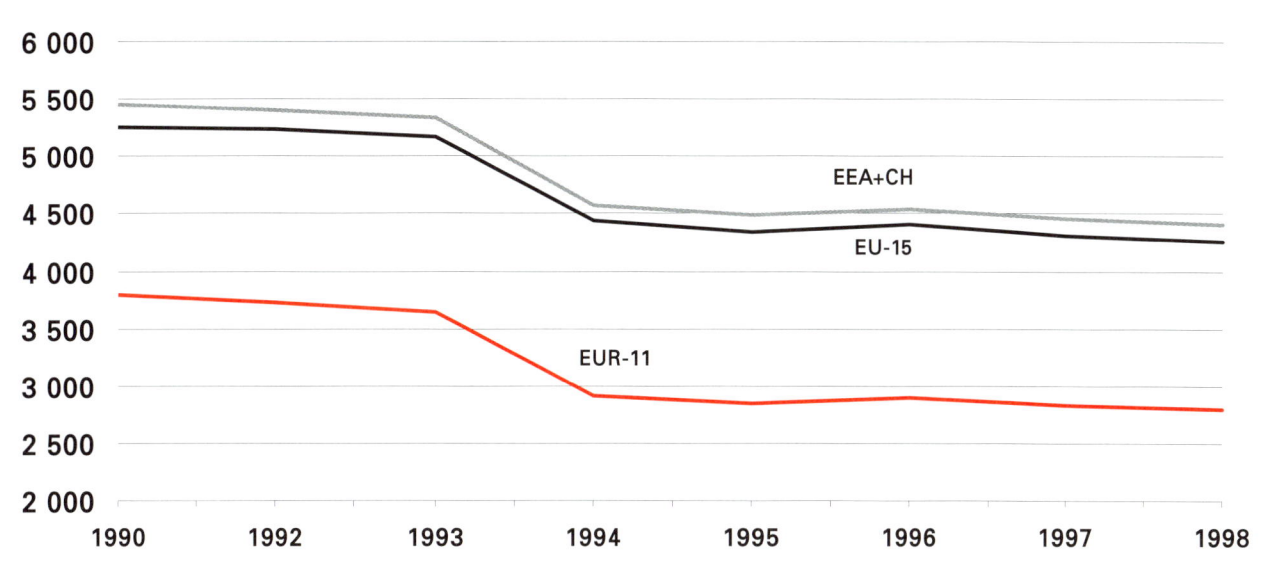

Further reading: Detailed tables: special feature on insurance and pension funds, 2000. Eurostat (pdf-publication). Statistics in focus: insurance services statis-tics. Life and non-life insurance: investments, capital and reserves and gross technical provisions, 1/2000. Eurostat. Statistics in focus: insur-ance services statistics. Slow progress for insurance in the single mar-ket, 4–18/1999. Eurostat.

Before 1994 including Spanish social benefit institutions. EEA +CH does not cover LI.

Insurance: financial indicators and employment. 1998

	Gross premiums written. Million ECU	Gross claims incurred. Million ECU	Total investments. Million ECU	Total capital and reserves. Million ECU	Technical provisions. Million ECU	Total persons employed (units)	
EU-15	678 051	:	:	:	:	:	**EU-15**
EUR-11	438 877	:	:	:	:	:	**EUR-11**
B	16 578	9 803	16 108	8 545	67 976	26 861	**B**
DK	11 465	7 433	105 143	18 359	90 440	15 082	**DK**
D	156 485	107 588	773 634	64 804	675 409	214 352	**D**
EL	1 433	:	:	:	:	:	**EL**
E	26 535	18 070	65 825	9 367	65 455	43 007	**E**
F	114 100	76 316	633 776	49 107	619 480	:	**F**
IRL	6 287	:	29 011	1 426	26 430	:	**IRL**
I	56 202	31 428	172 052	32 983	213 270	43 002	**I**
L	7 262	4 026	24 190	1 907	24 080	1 760	**L**
NL	33 790	20 036	221 171	37 938	176 931	:	**NL**
A	11 592	8 334	43 168	4 523	40 842	26 121	**A**
P	5 361	2 697	15 629	3 061	13 763	13 170	**P**
FIN	4 684	2 791	18 158	2 449	17 183	9 500	**FIN**
S	13 485	7 687	161 904	7 736	90 169	16 530	**S**
UK	212 791	174 858	1 382 980	105 181	880 834	:	**UK**

Further reading: Detailed tables: special feature on insurance and pension funds, 2000. Eurostat (pdf-publication). Statistics in focus: insurance services statis-tics. life and non-life insurance: Investments, capital and reserves and gross technical provisions, 1/2000. Eurostat. Statistics in focus: insur-ance services statistics. Slow progress for insurance in the single mar-ket, 4–18/1999. Eurostat.

Includes life insurance, non-life insurance, composite insurance and specialist reinsurance. Total invesments: valuation rules can differ. EL, IRL: 1997.

eurostat

Insurance: gross premiums written, by type of insurance enterprises. %

1995

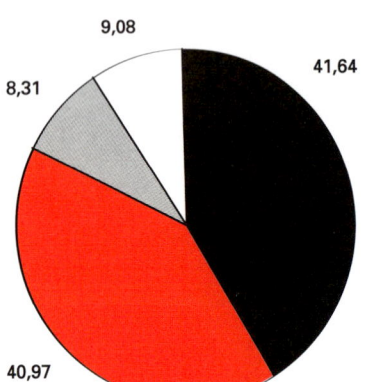

9,08

8,31

41,64

40,97

1998

6,22

29,98

36,88

26,92

Black: life insurance; colour: non-life insurance; grey: composite insurance; white: specialist reinsurance.

Further reading: Detailed tables: special feature on insurance and pension funds, 2000. Eurostat (pdf-publication). Statistics in focus: insurance services statistics. Life and non-life insurance: investments, capital and reserves and gross technical provisions, 1/2000. Eurostat. Statistics in focus: insurance services statistics. Slow progress for insurance in the single market, 4–18/1999. Eurostat.

Includes 1997 figures for Greece. UK: provisional figures.

Non-life insurance: gross direct premiums written broken down by product. %. 1998

	Accident and health	Motor vehicle	Marine, aviation and transport	Fire and other damage to property	General liability	Credit and suretyship	Assistance, legal expenses and misc. financial loss	Other non-life insurance	
EU-15	:	:	:	:	:	:	:	:	EU-15
EUR-11	26,3	33,9	2,6	18,3	8,2	1,7	4,0	4,9	EUR-11
B	20,7	12,2	1,9	31,3	21,6	1,8	10,6	0,0	B
DK	21,7	29,8	3,0	40,9	3,5	1,1	0,0	0,0	DK
D	35,3	27,9	2,1	16,9	9,0	1,4	5,0	2,5	D
EL	4,4	64,3	6,5	14,7	1,5	0,7	0,0	8,0	EL
E	22,7	39,9	2,1	4,1	4,3	2,2	1,4	23,2	E
F	17,3	38,5	3,4	27,6	6,6	1,9	4,8	0,0	F
IRL	4,9	48,4	2,0	22,4	18,2	1,1	3,2	0,0	IRL
I	13,8	57,1	2,9	13,5	7,6	3,1	0,7	1,3	I
L	3,4	27,7	35,8	15,5	6,1	0,0	11,6	0,0	L
NL	44,7	22,9	3,7	17,7	0,0	0,0	0,0	11,0	NL
A	28,3	35,2	1,6	21,5	7,0	1,0	4,4	1,0	A
P	27,0	51,4	2,2	15,3	1,6	1,2	1,3	0,0	P
FIN	30,5	31,1	4,5	22,8	5,2	2,3	1,1	2,4	FIN
S	19,7	32,3	4,2	33,3	5,5	1,7	1,0	2,3	S
UK	:	:	:	:	:	:	:	:	UK

Further reading: Detailed tables: special feature on insurance and pension funds, 2000. Eurostat (pdf-publication). Statistics in focus: insurance services statistics. Life and non-life insurance: investments, capital and reserves and gross technical provisions, 1/2000. Eurostat. Statistics in focus: insurance services statistics. Slow progress for insurance in the single market, 4–18/1999. Eurostat.

Including business of composite enterprises. EL: 1997.

A 'main line' is a telephone line connecting the subscribers' terminal equipment to a dedicated port in the telephone exchange equipment. Several telephone sets can be connected to a telephone line. In 1996, 94 % of EU households had a telephone. The growth of the number of fixed telephone lines has slowed down considerably in the recent past, as a result of market saturation and the rapid expansion of the use of mobile phones. The last two decades have brought a switch from analogue to digital technology: in 1998 over 96 % of main lines in the EU were digital.

Number of main telephone lines

	1980	1985	1990	1995	1996	1997	1998	1999	
EU-15	96 580 780	123 774 782	153 438 629	182 567 787	188 197 433	193 339 494	197 871 750	201 051 400	**EU-15**
B	2 463 000	3 060 663	3 912 629	4 632 091	4 725 496	4 938 641	5 073 010	5 100 000	**B**
DK	2 225 774	2 543 291	2 911 198	3 202 525	3 251 124	3 340 501	3 495 860	3 628 000	**DK**
D	20 535 000	25 391 800	32 000 000	42 000 000	44 100 000	45 200 000	46 500 000	48 300 000	**D**
EL	2 270 406	3 116 798	3 948 654	5 162 772	5 328 794	5 430 855	5 535 520	5 610 900	**EL**
E	7 229 000	9 340 458	12 602 600	15 095 300	15 412 785	15 854 400	16 288 610	16 480 400	**E**
F	15 898 000	23 030 564	28 084 922	32 400 000	33 000 000	33 700 000	34 000 000	34 100 000	**F**
IRL	483 000	703 000	983 000	1 310 000	1 390 000	1 500 000	1 600 000	1 770 000	**IRL**
I	13 017 000	17 396 113	22 350 000	24 845 000	25 259 000	25 698 000	25 986 120	26 502 000	**I**
L	132 000	154 152	183 700	230 512	244 205	279 700	293 080	310 900	**L**
NL	4 892 100	5 823 000	6 940 000	8 120 000	8 431 000	8 860 000	9 337 000	9 610 000	**NL**
A	2 191 030	2 729 389	3 223 161	3 749 087	3 778 993	3 969 400	3 996 600	3 862 400	**A**
P	989 470	1 400 418	2 379 265	3 586 089	3 724 281	3 818 997	4 116 950	4 229 800	**P**
FIN	1 739 000	2 189 000	2 670 000	2 810 000	2 842 000	2 861 000	2 855 000	2 856 000	**FIN**
S	4 820 000	5 242 497	5 849 500	6 013 000	6 032 000	6 010 000	5 965 000	5 889 000	**S**
UK	17 696 000	21 653 639	25 400 000	29 411 411	30 677 755	31 878 000	32 829 000	33 750 000	**UK**
IS	84 800	102 657	130 500	148 675	153 551	155 316	178 430	188 800	**IS**
NO	1 197 287	1 757 656	2 132 290	2 431 271	2 440 185	2 325 010	2 935 000	3 165 000	**NO**
EEA	1 282 087	1 860 313	2 262 790	2 579 946	2 593 736	2 480 326	3 113 430	3 353 800	**EEA**
CH	2 839 000	3 277 026	3 942 701	4 480 000	4 571 000	4 688 000	4 803 000	4 992 000	**CH**
US	:	:	136 114 000	159 735 000	165 047 000	172 452 000	179 822 000	179 822 100	**US**
JP	:	:	54 528 000	61 106 000	63 126 000	63 471 000	62 550 000	62 490 000	**JP**

Source: International Telecommunication Union for 1998 and 1999.

Main telephone lines per 100 inhabitants

	1980	1985	1990	1995	1996	1997	1998	1999	
EU-15	27,2	34,5	42,2	49,1	50,5	51,7	52,8	53,6	**EU-15**
B	25,0	31,0	39,3	45,7	46,6	48,6	49,8	49,7	**B**
DK	43,5	49,8	56,7	61,4	61,9	63,3	66,0	68,3	**DK**
D	26,3	32,7	40,4	51,5	53,9	55,1	56,7	58,9	**D**
EL	23,7	31,4	39,0	49,4	50,9	51,8	52,7	53,3	**EL**
E	19,4	24,4	32,5	38,5	39,3	40,3	41,4	41,8	**E**
F	29,6	41,8	49,6	55,8	56,6	57,6	57,9	57,8	**F**
IRL	14,2	19,8	28,0	36,4	38,4	41,1	43,3	47,4	**IRL**
I	23,1	30,7	39,4	43,4	44,1	44,7	45,1	46,0	**I**
L	36,3	42,1	48,4	56,7	59,2	66,9	69,2	72,4	**L**
NL	34,7	40,3	46,6	52,6	54,4	56,9	59,6	61,0	**NL**
A	29,0	36,0	41,9	46,6	46,9	49,2	49,5	47,8	**A**
P	10,2	14,0	24,0	36,2	37,5	38,4	41,3	42,4	**P**
FIN	36,4	44,7	53,7	55,1	55,5	55,7	55,5	55,4	**FIN**
S	58,1	62,8	68,6	68,2	68,3	68,0	67,4	66,5	**S**
UK	31,4	38,3	44,2	50,3	52,3	54,1	55,6	55,4	**UK**
IS	37,4	42,7	51,4	55,7	57,3	57,6	65,5	68,5	**IS**
NO	29,4	42,4	50,4	55,9	55,8	52,9	66,4	71,2	**NO**
EEA	27,3	34,6	42,3	49,2	50,6	51,8	53,0	53,8	**EEA**
CH	45,0	50,8	59,1	63,8	64,7	66,2	67,7	70,1	**CH**
US	:	:	54,9	61,0	62,5	64,7	66,8	66,2	**US**
JP	:	:	44,1	48,7	50,3	50,9	50,4	49,4	**JP**

7Z1AA

7Z2AB

4

The statistics available refer to the number of cellular mobile telephone subscriptions, the number of mobile phone sets roughly corresponding to the number of subscriptions. Mobile phones were first introduced in Europe in the early 1980s. Constrained by weight and power requirements they were at the beginning mainly confined to cars. As mobile phones became lighter, cheaper and technically more advanced the market started to take off, especially in the second half of the 1990s. In 1999 the number of mobile phone subscribers in the EU increased by over 60 %. As with main telephone lines there has been a switch from analogue to digital technology: in 1998, digital mobile phones represented already over 90 % of the market.

Number of mobile phone subscribers (1 000s) / *Mobile phone subscribers per 100 inhabitants*

	1990	1995	1996	1997	1998	1999	1990	1995	1996	1997	1998	1999	
EU-15	3 114	21 160	33 476	52 663	90 145	146 579	0,9	5,7	9,0	14,1	24,1	39,1	EU-15
B	45	235	478	974	1 756	3 193	0,4	2,3	4,7	9,6	17,2	31,3	B
DK	148	822	1 317	1 444	1 931	2 650	2,9	15,8	25,1	27,4	36,5	49,9	DK
D	273	3 750	5 790	8 170	13 925	23 470	0,3	4,6	7,1	10,0	17,0	28,6	D
EL	:	273	550	938	2 057	3 300	:	2,6	5,3	8,9	19,6	31,4	EL
E	55	944	2 997	4 338	7 051	12 300	0,1	2,4	7,6	11,0	17,9	31,2	E
F	283	1 024	2 463	5 817	11 210	21 434	0,5	1,8	4,2	9,9	19,1	36,3	F
IRL	25	158	289	533	946	1 400	0,7	4,4	8,0	14,6	25,6	37,5	IRL
I	266	3 925	6 413	11 734	20 489	30 296	0,5	6,9	11,2	20,4	35,6	52,6	I
L	1	27	45	67	131	209	0,2	6,6	10,9	16,1	30,8	48,7	L
NL	79	513	804	1 717	3 351	6 900	0,5	3,3	5,2	11,0	21,4	43,8	NL
A	72	347	563	1 160	2 293	4 242	0,9	4,3	7,0	14,4	28,4	52,5	A
P	7	341	664	1 507	3 076	4 672	0,1	3,4	6,7	15,2	30,9	46,8	P
FIN	258	1 039	1 502	2 162	2 947	3 445	5,2	20,4	29,4	42,1	57,3	66,8	FIN
S	463	2 025	2 492	3 169	4 108	5 125	5,4	23,0	28,2	35,8	46,4	57,9	S
UK	1 140	5 736	7 109	8 933	14 874	23 944	2,0	9,8	12,1	15,2	25,2	40,4	UK
IS	10	31	46	66	91	173	3,9	11,6	17,3	24,4	33,6	62,6	IS
NO	197	981	1 261	1 677	2 107	2 745	4,6	22,6	28,9	38,2	47,7	61,7	NO
EEA	207	1 012	1 308	1 743	2 198	2 917	0,9	5,9	9,2	14,4	24,3	39,3	EEA
CH	125	447	663	1 044	1 672	3 000	1,9	6,4	9,4	14,7	23,6	42,1	CH
US	5 283	33 786	44 043	55 312	69 209	86 047	2,1	12,9	16,7	20,8	25,7	31,7	US
JP	868	11 712	26 907	38 254	47 285	56 849	0,7	9,3	21,4	30,7	37,5	45,0	JP

Source: International Telecommunication Union for 1998 and 1999.

Mobile phone subscribers per 100 inhabitants

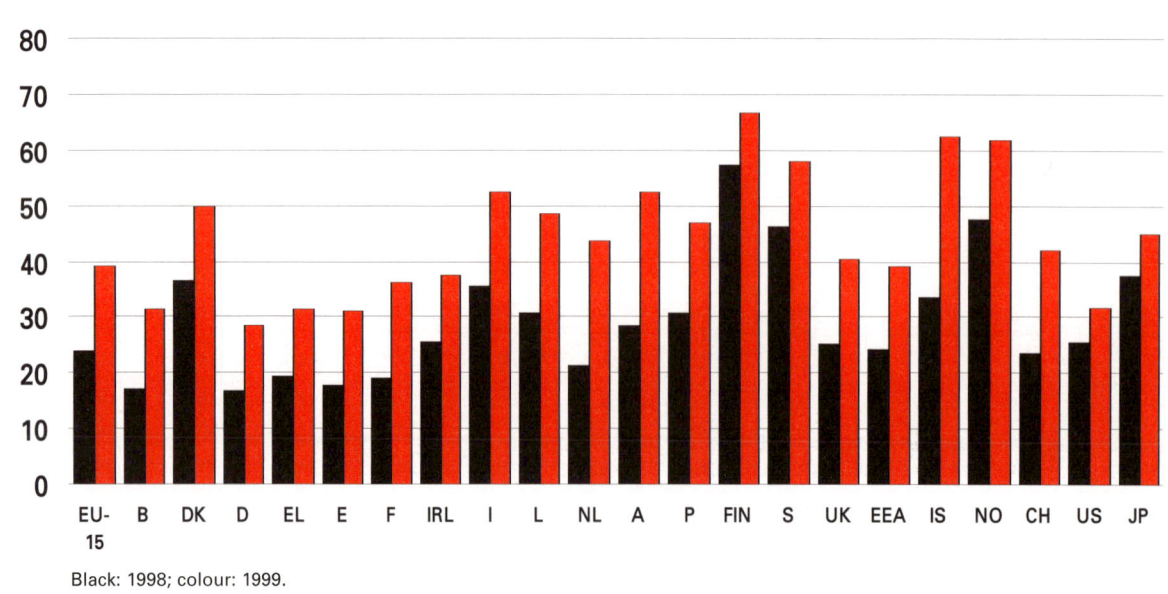

Black: 1998; colour: 1999.

The data on the number of PCs in the table include PCs at home and PCs used at work. In 1998, 31 % of the EU population (15 years and older), or 95 million persons, used a PC at home, whilst 40 % used a PC at work. The number of PC users is higher than the number of PCs because a computer can be used by several persons and it can be used at home and for the purpose of work at the same time. In 1998 21 million computers (of which 15 % portable and 85 % desktop) were sold in the EU. The number of personal computers in the EU increased by 14 million in the same year. The large number of old computers being dismantled reflects Moore's law — the doubling of the processing power of computers every 18 months.

	Number of personal computers (1 000s)						*Personal computers per 100 inhabitants*		
	1990	**1995**	**1996**	**1997**	**1998**	**1999**	**1998**	**1999**	
EU-15	25 520	56 210	64 755	73 550	84 725	93 200 *	22,6	24,8 *	**EU-15**
B	880	1 800	2 200	2 500	2 900	3 200 *	28,5	31,3 *	**B**
DK	590	1 410	1 600	1 900	2 000	2 200 *	37,8	41,4 *	**DK**
D	6 550	15 600	19 100	21 000	22 900	24 400 *	27,9	29,7 *	**D**
EL	180	350	370	470	550	640 *	5,2	6,1 *	**EL**
E	1 100	3 500	4 100	4 200	4 300	4 800 *	10,9	12,2 *	**E**
F	4 000	7 800	8 800	10 200	12 400	13 000 *	21,1	22,0 *	**F**
IRL	300	660	760	880	1 000	1 200 *	27,1	32,1 *	**IRL**
I	2 100	4 800	5 300	6 500	10 000	11 000 *	17,4	19,1 *	**I**
L	60	140	155	160	165	170 *	38,9	39,6 *	**L**
NL	1 400	3 100	3 600	4 400	5 000	5 700 *	31,9	36,2 *	**NL**
A	500	1 300	1 400	1 700	1 900	2 100 *	23,5	26,0 *	**A**
P	260	550	670	740	810	930 *	8,1	9,3 *	**P**
FIN	500	1 200	1 400	1 600	1 800	1 860 *	35,0	36,0 *	**FIN**
S	900	2 200	2 600	3 000	3 500	4 000 *	39,6	45,2 *	**S**
UK	6 200	11 800	12 700	14 300	15 500	18 000 *	26,2	30,4 *	**UK**
IS	10	60	70	80	90	100 *	33,0	36,3 *	**IS**
NO	:	1 190	1 390	1 590	1 660	2 000 *	37,6	45,0 *	**NO**
EEA	10	1 250	1 460	1 670	1 750	2 100 *	22,8	25,1 *	**EEA**
CH	6 000	2 000	2 400	2 800	3 000	3 300 *	42,3	46,3 *	**CH**
US	54 200	86 300	96 600	109 000	124 000	141 000 *	46,1	51,9 *	**US**
JP	7 400	15 100	20 400	25 500	30 000	36 300 *	23,8	28,7 *	**JP**

Source: International Telecommunication Union.

Personal computers per 100 inhabitants

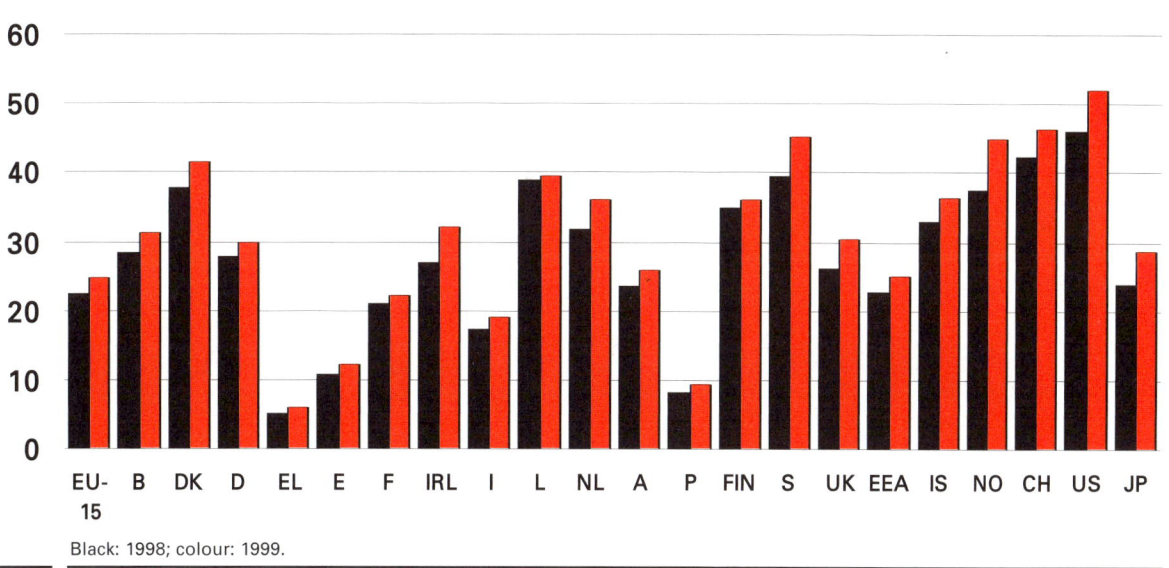

Black: 1998; colour: 1999.

More information on the Eurostat web site: www.europa.eu.int/comm/eurostat

8X1CC

8X2DD

8X3EE

There are different approaches to measure the growth of the use of the Internet. Computer-based automated host counts are counting the computers connected to the Internet only. On a country level these counts are furthermore in some statistics restricted to country code top level domains (domain names like .de, .uk or .fr). This is also the case for the figures produced by RIPE NCC, which are shown on this page. Based on registrations, some statistics also attribute generic domain codes (examples are .com and .org) to countries. This results in higher figures than the counting of the country code top level domains only: in 1999, for example, 11 million hosts in the EU versus less than 7 million of country code top level domains are considered only.

Household surveys provide a more complete overview on the number of Internet users. Because of the costs involved they are, however, carried out less frequently, they are less standardised and they are not available for all countries. Figures published often represent estimations and projections.

The number of Internet users is several times higher than the number of Internet host computers (in 1999 it was 4 times higher, the factor declines over time). In 1999 there were, according to the Euro-barometer survey, 42 million Internet users (population over 15) in the EU.

Internet hosts per 100 inhabitants

	1995	1996	1997	1998	1999	
EU-15	0,5	0,8	1,2	1,7	2,3	EU-15
B	0,3	0,6	1,1	2,0	3,3	B
DK	1,0	2,0	3,2	5,6	6,4	DK
D	0,6	0,8	1,4	1,8	2,0	D
EL	0,1	0,2	0,3	0,5	0,7	EL
E	0,1	0,3	0,5	0,8	1,2	E
F	0,3	0,4	0,6	0,9	2,1	F
IRL	0,4	0,7	1,1	1,5	1,7	IRL
I	0,1	0,3	0,4	0,7	0,5	I
L	0,5	0,9	1,1	1,8	2,2	L
NL	1,1	1,7	2,5	4,0	6,1	NL
A	0,7	1,1	1,3	2,1	3,2	A
P	0,1	0,2	0,4	0,6	0,8	P
FIN	4,2	6,1	9,5	8,9	8,9	FIN
S	1,6	2,7	3,9	4,3	5,9	S
UK	0,8	1,2	1,7	2,5	2,9	UK
IS	3,1	4,3	6,9	9,1	10,8	IS
NO	1,9	3,4	6,7	7,2	9,9	NO
EEA	0,5	0,9	1,3	1,8	2,4	EEA
CH	1,1	1,9	2,7	3,5	3,8	CH
US	2,3	3,8	7,7	11,3	19,6	US
JP	0,2	0,6	0,9	1,3	2,1	JP

8X5GG

8X4FF

Number of Internet hosts (1 000s)

	1990	1995	1996	1997	1998	1999	
EU-15	33	1 894	3 063	4 652	6 417	8 489	EU-15
B	0	31	65	107	209	339	B
DK	1	51	107	169	298	338	DK
D	8	474	692	1 132	1 450	1 635	D
EL	0	8	17	28	50	75	EL
E	0	51	113	196	307	470	E
F	4	151	237	355	511	1 233	F
IRL	0	13	27	40	56	64	IRL
I	1	75	148	254	387	302	I
L	0	2	4	5	8	10	L
NL	5	172	271	391	626	959	NL
A	1	53	89	108	173	263	A
P	0	12	23	42	56	78	P
FIN	4	216	314	487	460	462	FIN
S	8	145	238	3 486	379	523	S
UK	1	440	719	988	1 449	1 739	UK
IS	0	8	12	19	25	30	IS
NO	3	84	150	292	319	439	NO
EEA	3	93	162	311	344	469	EEA
CH	7	80	133	189	245	270	CH
US	:	6 055	10 113	20 624	30 489	53 176	US
JP	:	269	734	1 169	1 688	2 637	JP

Source: International Telecommunication Union.

4

7T1BA

Internet hosts per 100 inhabitants. 1999

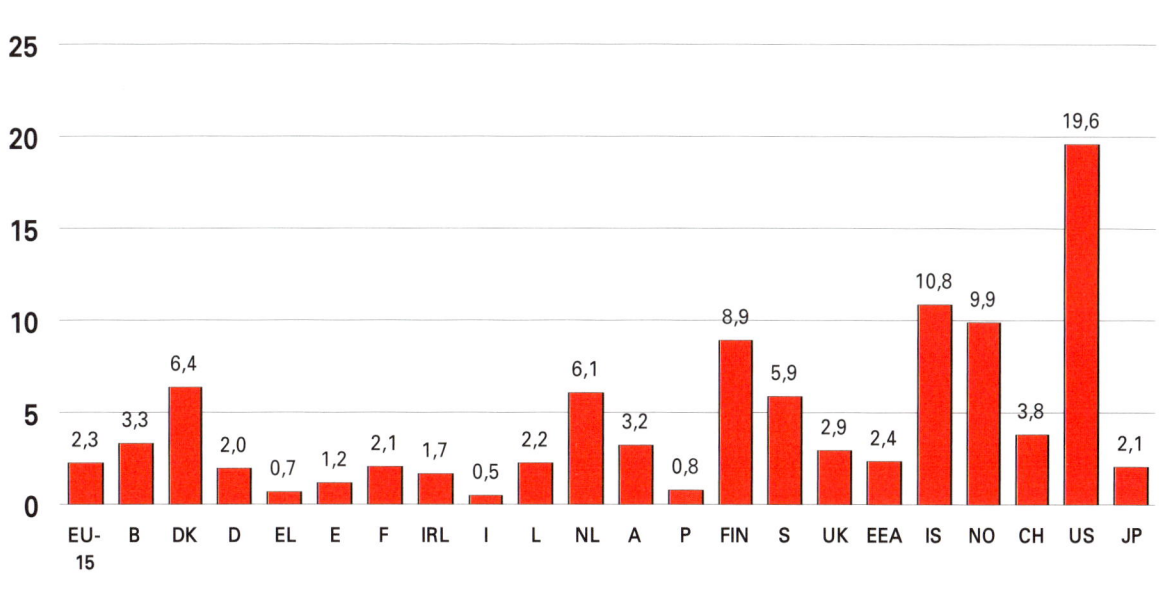

Total production of primary energy. Million toe

	1989	1990	1991	1992	1993	1994	1995	1996	1997	1998	1999	
EU-15	722,1	705,1 |	707,8	702,3	709,6	722,7	737,1	762,6	759,6	751,2 *	:	**EU-15**
EUR-11	466,3	453,5 |	445,4	441,4	439,5	429,1	430,7	442,1	436,1	421,7 *	:	**EUR-11**
B	12,2	12,0	11,8	11,5	11,0	10,8	11,0	11,4	12,6	12,1 *	:	**B**
DK	9,2	9,9	11,8	12,8	13,6	14,9	15,5	17,5	20,3	20,2 *	:	**DK**
D	200,2	185,8 |	164,9	159,7	148,1	141,3	140,2	138,2	138,2	131,7	:	**D**
EL	9,3	9,2	9,1	9,0	8,8	9,1	9,7	10,1	9,9	10,1	:	**EL**
E	34,3	33,4	33,3	32,6	32,5	32,2	31,4	32,2	30,9	31,3 *	:	**E**
F	106,0	108,1	114,6	115,0	121,4	119,1	122,5	125,4	123,8	120,7	:	**F**
IRL	3,4	3,5	3,3	3,1	3,5	3,6	4,3	3,6	2,8	2,5 *	:	**IRL**
I	27,1	27,2	27,8	28,8	30,0	31,2	30,7	31,5	34,7	34,5	:	**I**
L	0,0	0,0	0,0	0,0	0,0	0,1	0,0	0,0	0,0	0,1	:	**L**
NL	59,8	60,3	67,1	67,1	68,2	66,1	65,9	73,7	65,5	62,7	:	**NL**
A	8,8	8,7	8,6	8,9	9,0	8,4	8,7	9,0	9,1	9,4 *	:	**A**
P	2,5	2,8	2,8	2,5	3,0	3,1	2,8	3,6	3,6	3,6 *	:	**P**
FIN	12,0	11,7	11,2	12,1	12,8	13,1	13,2	13,4	14,7	13,1	:	**FIN**
S	28,9	29,6	31,4	29,1	29,0	30,8	31,1	31,3	31,7	30,2	:	**S**
UK	208,5	202,9	210,2	210,1	218,7	238,7	250,2	261,6	261,6	269,1	:	**UK**
IS	1,6	1,5	1,4	1,4	1,4	1,4	1,4	1,4	1,5	1,7	:	**IS**
NO	113,7	119,6	130,0	145,9	153,4	169,8	181,4	207,2	211,6	205,9	:	**NO**
EEA	837,4	826,2 |	839,2	849,6	864,4	893,8	920,0	971,2	972,8	958,9	:	**EEA**
CH	9,4	9,7	9,8	10,0	10,4	11,1	11,0	10,5	11,0	11,2	:	**CH**
US	1 615,3	1 648,8	1 637,0	1 643,2	1 596,9	1 663,6	1 663,6	1 688,5	1 686,0	1 695,4	:	**US**
CA	274,0	273,7	285,1	294,0	315,7	338,2	349,0	358,5	364,7	365,7	:	**CA**
JP	71,5	75,6	79,5	80,5	88,1	91,1	99,1	102,5	107,0	110,0	:	**JP**

3B5AA

Further reading: Energy, yearly statistics, 1998. Eurostat. Energy balance sheets
1997–98. Eurostat.

4

Net imports of primary energy. Million toe

	1989	1990	1991	1992	1993	1994	1995	1996	1997	1998	1999	
EU-15	622,1	643,7 |	668,0	679,3	651,0	631,6	651,2	678,9	692,6	722,9	:	**EU-15**
EUR-11	571,6	594,1 |	615,4	628,0	608,5	619,0	642,1	666,2	683,2	716,3	:	**EUR-11**
B	37,8	38,9	41,5	42,7	41,0	42,7	43,7	47,0	47,1	50,0	:	**B**
DK	10,4	9,1	8,4	7,8	6,1	6,2	7,9	6,0	4,2	1,8	:	**DK**
D	157,4	165,3 |	180,1	186,6	188,5	191,4	195,2	207,8	208,3	212,8	:	**D**
EL	14,2	15,4	15,6	17,7	17,2	15,8	18,2	18,8	19,2	21,1	:	**EL**
E	57,2	59,9	63,6	67,0	63,3	68,4	75,4	73,9	80,2	87,2	:	**E**
F	114,9	119,8	126,1	123,1	115,2	109,6	115,3	124,3	122,1	131,1	:	**F**
IRL	6,3	7,1	6,9	6,7	6,8	7,0	7,6	8,3	9,5	10,6	:	**IRL**
I	130,5	132,0	129,1	134,2	127,2	125,8	134,7	134,5	134,2	140,4	:	**I**
L	3,3	3,5	3,7	3,8	3,8	3,7	3,3	3,4	3,3	3,3	:	**L**
NL	16,1	17,4	14,4	14,1	13,3	17,2	16,3	14,0	22,7	23,5	:	**NL**
A	15,4	17,3	17,9	17,5	17,0	16,8	17,4	19,2	18,9	19,8	:	**A**
P	14,5	15,2	15,1	16,6	15,9	16,0	17,9	16,7	18,4	19,4	:	**P**
FIN	18,1	18,0	17,0	15,8	16,5	20,4	15,4	17,2	18,4	18,3	:	**FIN**
S	17,6	17,8	17,3	17,3	18,2	19,7	19,1	21,1	20,0	20,0	:	**S**
UK	8,2	7,3	11,3	8,4	1,0	- 29,2	- 36,1	- 33,2	- 34,0	- 36,4	:	**UK**
IS	0,7	0,8	0,7	0,8	0,8	0,8	0,8	0,9	0,9	1,0	:	**IS**
NO	- 92,0	- 96,2	- 108,3	- 122,9	- 128,9	- 145,7	- 156,8	- 182,1	- 186,9	- 180,1	:	**NO**
EEA	530,7	548,3 |	560,4	557,2	522,8	486,7	495,3	497,7	506,5	543,7	:	**EEA**
CH	14,1	15,2	15,3	15,2	13,8	14,0	13,9	15,2	15,0	15,6	:	**CH**
US	346,0	344,7	325,2	359,5	421,5	453,2	438,6	470,4	509,8	547,2	:	**US**
CA	- 57,3	- 59,7	- 76,5	- 83,9	- 93,9	- 106,8	- 119,7	- 120,6	- 121,8	- 128,4	:	**CA**
JP	355,3	369,4	376,5	381,7	381,4	402,8	405,2	416,3	419,3	401,0	:	**JP**

3B5AE

Further reading: Energy, yearly statistics, 1998. Eurostat. Energy balance sheets
1997–98. Eurostat.

Production of primary energy comprises energy extracted from natural sources: coal, lignite, crude oil and natural gas. Geothermal energy, hydroelectricity and nuclear energy are also considered primary energy sources. Nuclear energy is defined as energy from heat released during fission of uranium fuel in a nuclear reactor. Net imports of energy (imports minus exports) as a percentage of gross inland consumption show national energy dependence — excluding fuel consumed by maritime bunkers.

Total production of primary energy, as % of gross inland consumption

3B5AC

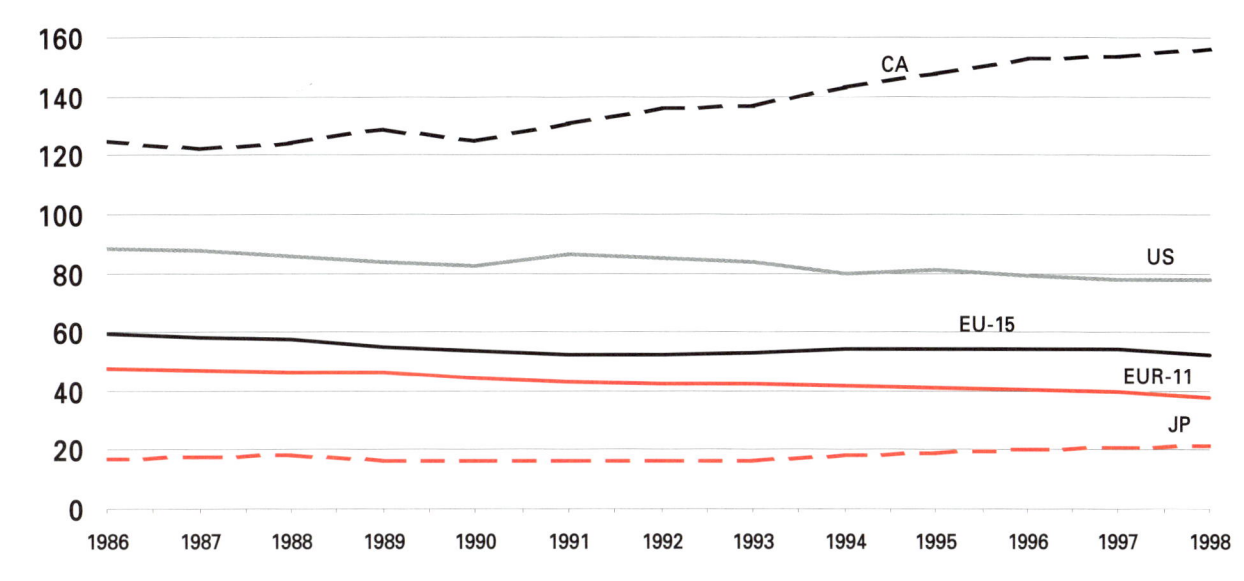

Further reading: Energy, yearly statistics, 1998. Eurostat. Energy balance sheets
1997–98. Eurostat.

Net imports of primary energy, as % of gross inland consumption

3B5AD

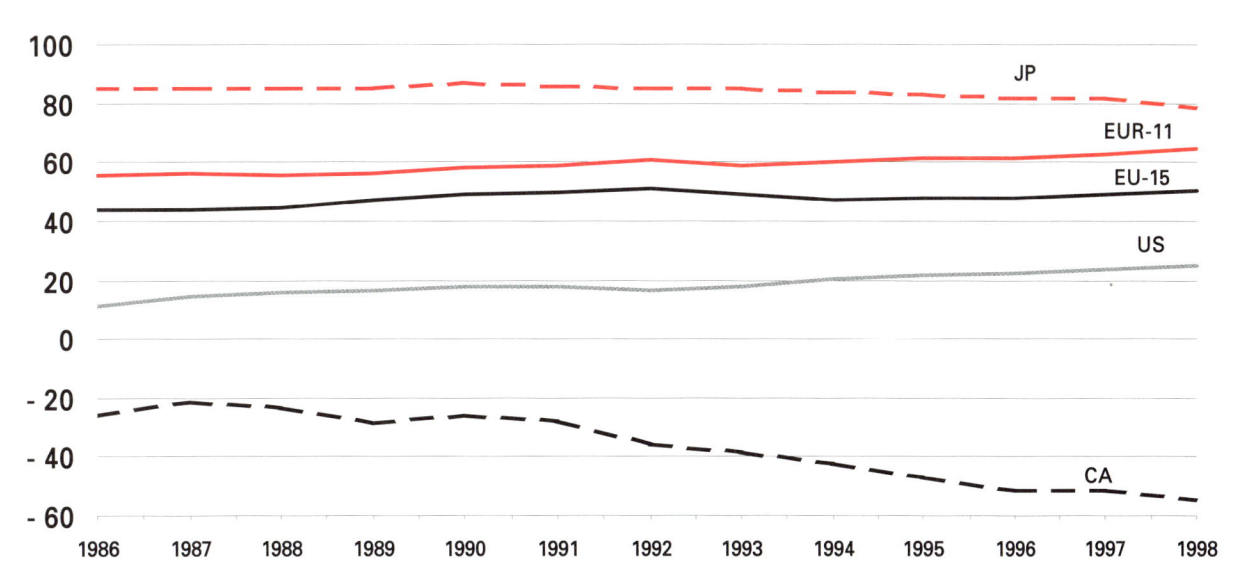

Further reading: Energy, yearly statistics, 1998. Eurostat. Energy balance sheets
1997–98. Eurostat.

Energy dependence. EU-15: data sets for periods before and after the year 1990 are not fully comparable as they refer to Germany before and after unification.

eurostat

EUROSTAT YEARBOOK 2001
385

Production of coal and lignite, as % of total production of primary energy

	1989	1990	1991	1992	1993	1994	1995	1996	1997	1998	1999	
EU-15	31,3	29,5	26,6	24,9	21,8	18,9	18,5	17,1	16,5	15,1 *	:	EU-15
EUR-11	34,5	32,8	28,6	27,0	24,7	23,4	22,7	20,9	20,2	18,9 *	:	EUR-11
B	9,6	5,1	3,2	1,1	-	-	-	-	-	0,0	:	B
DK	-	-								0,0	:	DK
D	68,0	67,3	64,4	61,2	59,3	57,3	56,2	53,4	51,1	49,9	:	D
EL	76,7	77,3	75,7	78,0	79,2	80,5	81,5	80,8	81,1	83,0	:	EL
E	34,4	34,9	32,6	34,9	34,0	32,6	32,3	31,0	32,0	29,7 *	:	E
F	7,5	6,8	6,1	5,6	4,9	4,4	3,9	3,8	3,1	2,7	:	F
IRL	40,9	41,0	36,5	33,1	33,2	32,8	41,9	34,9	26,0	32,8 *	:	IRL
I	1,2	1,2	0,9	0,9	0,6	0,2	0,3	0,2	0,1	0,0	:	I
L	-	-	-	-	-	-	-	-	-	0,0	:	L
NL	-	-	-	-	-	-	-	-	-	0,0	:	NL
A	6,1	7,4	6,4	5,2	4,8	4,0	3,5	2,9	2,9	2,9 *	:	A
P	4,3	4,2	4,0	3,6	2,7	2,0	-	-	-	0,0	:	P
FIN	12,4	12,4	7,2	13,6	14,0	16,5	15,6	16,8	18,1	3,3	:	FIN
S	0,7	0,9	1,1	1,1	1,0	0,9	1,0	1,2	0,9	1,1	:	S
UK	27,6	25,7	25,5	23,1	17,9	12,0	12,2	11,2	11,0	9,3	:	UK
IS	-	-	-	-	-	-	-	-	-	0,0	:	IS
NO	0,2	0,2	0,2	0,2	0,1	0,1	0,1	0,1	0,1	0,1	:	NO
EEA	27,0	25,2	22,4	20,6	17,9	15,3	14,9	13,4	12,9	11,9	:	EEA
CH	-	-	-	-	-	-	-	-	-	-	:	CH
US	30,9	31,9	32,7	31,2	31,2	29,9	32,4	32,4	33,3	33,6	:	US
CA	13,4	14,2	13,8	13,8	11,9	11,9	11,7	11,6	11,8	11,2	:	CA
JP	10,0	8,9	6,6	6,1	5,7	4,8	4,2	3,5	2,2	1,8	:	JP

3B5BA

Further reading: Energy, yearly statistics, 1998. Eurostat. Energy balance sheets
1997–98. Eurostat.

4

Production of crude oil, as % of total production of primary energy

	1989	1990	1991	1992	1993	1994	1995	1996	1997	1998	1999	
EU-15	16,0	16,3	16,4	16,9	17,5	21,2	21,1	20,2	20,2	21,0 *	:	EU-15
EUR-11	3,8	3,8	3,8	3,7	3,6	4,0	3,7	3,4	3,5	3,5 *	:	EUR-11
B	-	-	-	-	-	-	-	-	-	-	:	B
DK	60,9	60,9	60,0	61,7	61,2	61,8	60,2	58,8	57,2	57,7 *	:	DK
D	1,9	2,0	2,1	2,1	2,1	2,1	2,1	2,1	2,1	2,2	:	D
EL	9,9	9,1	9,2	7,7	6,4	5,8	4,7	5,1	4,7	3,1	:	EL
E	3,0	2,4	3,2	3,3	2,7	2,9	2,5	1,6	1,2	1,7 *	:	E
F	3,1	2,8	2,6	2,5	2,3	2,3	2,1	1,7	1,7	1,6	:	F
IRL	-	-	-	-	-	-	-	-	-	-	:	IRL
I	17,1	17,3	15,7	15,7	15,6	15,8	17,2	17,5	17,3	16,4	:	I
L	-	-	-	-	-	-	-	-	-	-	:	L
NL	6,4	6,6	5,6	5,1	4,8	6,6	5,3	4,3	4,5	4,3	:	NL
A	13,5	13,6	15,3	13,5	13,0	13,5	12,1	10,7	10,7	10,6 *	:	A
P	0,0	0,0	0,0	0,0	0,0	0,0	0,0	0,0	0,0	0,0	:	P
FIN	-	-	-	-	-	-	-	-	-	-	:	FIN
S	0,0	0,0	0,0	0,0	-	-	-	-	-	-	:	S
UK	43,8	44,7	43,3	44,7	45,6	52,9	51,8	49,1	48,3	48,6	:	UK
IS	-	-	-	-	-	-	-	-	-	-	:	IS
NO	66,9	70,4	73,7	74,9	76,4	77,5	78,0	77,5	75,7	74,5	:	NO
EEA	22,9	24,1	25,2	26,9	28,0	31,8	32,3	32,4	32,3	32,4	:	EEA
CH	-	-	-	-	-	-	-	-	-	-	:	CH
US	29,0	27,2	25,7	25,5	25,0	25,0	23,9	23,6	23,5	22,7	:	US
CA	35,3	34,3	34,4	33,0	33,4	32,9	32,1	32,6	33,5	34,2	:	CA
JP	1,1	1,1	0,9	1,1	1,4	1,0	0,9	0,8	0,7	0,7	:	JP

3B5BB

Further reading: Energy, yearly statistics, 1998. Eurostat. Energy balance sheets
1997–98. Eurostat.

Coal is the main solid fuel produced in most EU countries. But in Greece the main solid fuel produced is lignite, which has a lower net calorific value than coal. German unification created a break in the statistical series of primary production of lig-

nite, as the former GDR is an important producer. In Luxembourg and Portugal the importance of renewable energy in primary production results from a lack of other primary energy sources.

4

Production of natural gas, as % of total production of primary energy

	1989	1990	1991	1992	1993	1994	1995	1996	1997	1998	1999	
EU-15	17,9	18,8	20,6	20,9	22,3	22,1	22,6	24,7	24,0	24,2 *	:	**EU-15**
EUR-11	19,2	19,6	21,7	22,1	22,6	22,7	22,8	24,2	22,4	22,2 *	:	**EUR-11**
B	0,1	0,1	0,1	0,0	0,0	0,0	0,0	0,0	0,0	0,0	:	**B**
DK	27,2	27,5	29,3	28,1	29,0	28,7	30,1	32,2	34,3	33,5 *	:	**DK**
D	7,2	7,4	8,2	8,7	9,3	10,2	10,6	11,7	11,6	11,9	:	**D**
EL	1,5	1,5	1,5	1,4	1,1	0,5	0,5	0,5	0,5	0,4	:	**EL**
E	4,0	3,8	3,6	3,3	1,8	0,6	1,2	1,3	0,5	0,3 *	:	**E**
F	2,5	2,2	2,5	2,4	2,4	2,4	2,3	1,9	1,7	1,5	:	**F**
IRL	54,8	54,2	58,2	61,6	62,1	60,5	52,8	60,0	67,0	56,8 *	:	**IRL**
I	50,8	51,5	50,8	51,2	52,3	53,0	53,3	51,9	45,4	45,1	:	**I**
L	-	-	-	-	-	-	-	-	-	-	:	**L**
NL	90,7	90,6	92,0	92,4	92,5	90,6	91,7	92,7	92,5	91,9	:	**NL**
A	12,9	12,7	13,2	13,8	14,0	13,7	14,4	14,1	13,3	14,3 *	:	**A**
P	-	-	-	-	-	-	-	-	-	-	:	**P**
FIN	-	-	-	-	-	-	-	-	-	-	:	**FIN**
S	-	-	-	-	-	-	-	-	-	-	:	**S**
UK	17,8	20,2	21,7	21,7	24,9	24,4	25,4	29,0	29,5	30,2	:	**UK**
IS	-	-	-	-	-	-	-	-	-	-	:	**IS**
NO	23,5	20,2	18,4	17,7	16,4	16,2	15,7	17,7	19,4	20,1	:	**NO**
EEA	18,6	19,0	20,2	20,3	21,2	21,0	21,2	23,2	22,9	23,2	:	**EEA**
CH	-	-	-	-	-	-	-	-	-	-	:	**CH**
US	24,8	25,3	25,4	25,0	25,3	26,7	26,7	26,1	26,2	25,9	:	**US**
CA	30,2	31,6	32,5	33,0	35,4	35,7	36,7	37,8	37,8	38,9	:	**CA**
JP	3,0	2,8	2,6	2,6	2,6	2,3	2,2	1,9	1,9	1,8	:	**JP**

Further reading: Energy, yearly statistics, 1998. Eurostat. Energy balance sheets 1997–98. Eurostat.

3B5BC

More data on this in Eurostat's database

This gives structural, social and economic data on the sector and data on the main energy sources: hydrocarbons, gas and electricity. This domain also covers internal flows and external trade. Prices of the main energy sources by type of consumer (industrial or domestic).

► ► ► DOMAIN SIRENE IN DATABASE NEW CRONOS

4

Production of renewable energy, as % of total production of primary energy

	1989	1990	1991	1992	1993	1994	1995	1996	1997	1998	1999	
EU-15	9,0	9,3	9,7	10,1	10,2	10,1	10,0	10,0	10,8	11,3 *	:	EU-15
EUR-11	10,8	11,2	12,2	12,4	12,7	13,2	13,0	13,5	14,5	15,6 *	:	EUR-11
B	5,3	5,4	5,6	5,7	5,4	5,3	6,2	5,9	5,2	5,5 *	:	B
DK	11,9	11,6	10,7	10,2	9,8	9,5	9,7	9,0	8,5	8,8 *	:	DK
D	2,9	3,1	3,4	3,7	4,0	4,3	4,5	4,7	5,4	6,5	:	D
EL	11,9	12,1	13,6	12,9	13,4	13,2	13,3	13,6	13,7	13,5	:	EL
E	16,5	17,9	18,5	16,8	18,3	19,6	18,5	22,6	22,5	22,3 *	:	E
F	14,1	14,6	16,0	16,2	14,8	15,0	14,7	14,3	13,4	14,0	:	F
IRL	4,3	4,8	5,2	5,3	4,6	6,7	5,3	5,2	7,0	10,5 *	:	IRL
I	30,9	30,0	32,6	32,2	31,6	31,1	29,2	30,4	37,2	38,5	:	I
L	100,0	100,0	100,0	100,0	100,0	100,0	100,0	100,0	100,0	100,0	:	L
NL	1,2	1,3	1,2	1,2	1,2	1,3	1,4	1,6	2,1	2,3	:	NL
A	67,5	66,3	65,2	67,5	68,1	68,8	70,0	72,4	73,0	72,3 *	:	A
P	95,7	95,8	96,0	96,4	97,3	98,0	100,0	100,0	100,0	100,0 *	:	P
FIN	46,1	44,9	47,2	45,0	45,4	45,2	46,8	45,7	45,3	55,3	:	FIN
S	40,1	39,1	35,1	41,9	43,8	37,8	41,0	37,5	42,3	45,4	:	S
UK	0,5	0,5	0,5	0,7	0,6	0,8	0,8	0,7	0,8	0,8	:	UK
IS	100,0	100,0	100,0	100,0	100,0	100,0	100,0	99,3	100,0	100,0	:	IS
NO	9,4	9,2	7,7	7,3	7,1	6,2	6,2	4,7	4,8	5,4	:	NO
EEA	9,2	9,5	9,6	9,7	9,8	9,4	9,3	9,0	9,6	10,2	:	EEA
CH	30,3	30,3	29,6	31,7	31,6	33,1	42,8	37,3	39,7	39,5	:	CH
US	2,6	2,6	6,0	7,4	6,8	7,4	6,4	6,9	6,7	6,8	:	US
CA	12,3	12,3	12,4	12,3	12,3	11,6	11,1	11,3	11,0	10,6	:	CA
JP	14,0	14,0	13,3	13,6	13,8	14,0	16,1	17,0	17,4	16,9	:	JP

3B5BE

Further reading: Energy, yearly statistics, 1998. Eurostat. Energy balance sheets 1997–98. Eurostat.

Renewable energy: hydro, wind, geothermal energy and biomass.

4

3B5BD

Primary production of nuclear energy, as % of total production of primary energy

	1989	1990	1991	1992	1993	1994	1995	1996	1997	1998	1999	
EU-15	25,3	25,7 |	26,4	26,8	27,8	27,3	27,3	27,4	28,0	27,9 *	:	**EU-15**
EUR-11	31,7	32,4 |	33,6	34,7	36,3	36,6	37,6	37,9	39,3	39,8 *	:	**EUR-11**
B	85,0	89,4	91,2	93,1	94,6	94,7	93,8	94,1	94,8	94,5 *	:	**B**
DK	-	-	-	-	-	-	-	-	-	*	:	**DK**
D	20,0	20,3 |	21,9	24,4	25,4	26,1	26,6	28,2	29,8	29,5	:	**D**
EL	-	-	-	-	-	-	-	-	-	-	:	**EL**
E	42,0	41,1	42,1	41,7	43,2	44,3	45,5	43,5	43,8	46,0 *	:	**E**
F	72,4	73,2	72,4	72,8	75,2	75,4	76,7	78,0	79,7	80,0	:	**F**
IRL	-	-	-	-	-	-	-	-	-	-	:	**IRL**
I	-	-	-	-	-	-	-	-	-	-	:	**I**
L	-	-	-	-	-	-	-	-	-	-	:	**L**
NL	1,7	1,5	1,2	1,3	1,4	1,5	1,6	1,4	0,9	1,5	:	**NL**
A	-	-	-	-	-	-	-	-	-	-	:	**A**
P	-	-	-	-	-	-	-	-	-	-	:	**P**
FIN	41,6	42,7	45,6	41,4	40,5	38,3	37,6	37,5	36,6	40,9	:	**FIN**
S	59,1	60,0	63,8	57,0	55,1	61,3	57,9	61,3	56,9	53,5	:	**S**
UK	8,5	8,2	8,2	8,9	10,1	8,9	8,5	8,5	8,9	9,6	:	**UK**
IS	-	-	-	-	-	-	-	-	-	-	:	**IS**
NO	-	-	-	-	-	-	-	-	-	-	:	**NO**
EEA	21,8	22,0 |	22,3	22,2	22,9	22,1	21,9	21,5	21,9	21,9	:	**EEA**
CH	59,4	66,1	61,6	59,8	61,1	60,0	57,2	62,7	60,4	60,5	:	**CH**
US	9,0	9,1	9,7	10,2	10,3	10,4	10,7	11,0	10,3	11,0	:	**US**
CA	7,9	7,6	6,9	7,7	7,1	7,9	8,4	6,8	5,9	5,1	:	**CA**
JP	72,8	73,3	76,4	76,2	76,5	77,5	79,6	76,9	77,7	78,8	:	**JP**

Further reading: Energy, yearly statistics, 1998. Eurostat. Energy balance sheets
1997–98. Eurostat.

Gross inland consumption of primary energy per person. Toe per capita

	1989	1990	1991	1992	1993	1994	1995	1996	1997	1998	1999	
EU-15	3,8	3,7 ǀ	3,7	3,6	3,6	3,6	3,7	3,8	3,8	3,8 *	:	EU-15
EUR-11	3,8	3,7 ǀ	3,7	3,6	3,6	3,6	3,6	3,7	3,7	3,8 *	:	EUR-11
B	4,7	4,7	4,9	5,0	4,8	4,9	5,0	5,3	5,4	5,5 *	:	B
DK	3,5	3,5	3,9	3,7	3,8	3,9	3,9	4,4	4,1	4,0 *	:	DK
D	5,8	4,8 ǀ	4,3	4,2	4,2	4,1	4,1	4,2	4,2	4,2	:	D
EL	2,2	2,2	2,2	2,2	2,2	2,3	2,3	2,4	2,4	2,6	:	EL
E	2,3	2,3	2,4	2,4	2,3	2,5	2,6	2,6	2,7	2,8 *	:	E
F	3,9	3,9	4,1	4,1	4,1	3,9	4,0	4,3	4,1	4,3	:	F
IRL	2,7	2,9	2,9	2,9	2,9	3,1	3,1	3,2	3,3	3,5 *	:	IRL
I	2,7	2,7	2,8	2,8	2,7	2,7	2,8	2,8	2,9	3,0	:	I
L	9,0	9,3	9,7	9,6	9,7	9,3	8,1	8,2	8,0	8,2	:	L
NL	4,4	4,5	4,6	4,6	4,6	4,6	4,7	4,9	4,8	4,8	:	NL
A	3,2	3,3	3,5	3,3	3,2	3,2	3,3	3,5	3,5	3,6 *	:	A
P	1,7	1,7	1,7	1,9	1,9	1,9	2,0	2,0	2,1	2,3 *	:	P
FIN	5,9	5,7	5,8	5,6	5,8	6,0	5,7	6,0	6,3	6,4	:	FIN
S	5,6	5,5	5,6	5,3	5,3	5,6	5,7	5,9	5,7	5,4	:	S
UK	3,7	3,7	3,7	3,7	3,8	3,8	3,7	3,9	3,8	3,9	:	UK
IS	8,9	8,7	7,9	8,0	8,2	8,0	8,0	8,4	8,6	9,7	:	IS
NO	5,0	5,0	5,1	5,1	5,4	5,3	5,4	5,2	5,6	5,7 *	:	NO
EEA	3,8	3,7 ǀ	3,7	3,7	3,6	3,6	3,7	3,8	3,8	3,9	:	EEA
CH	3,6	3,5	3,7	3,7	3,7	3,6	3,6	3,6	3,7	3,7	:	CH
US	7,8	7,9	7,7	7,8	7,8	7,9	7,8	8,1	8,1	8,1	:	US
CA	7,9	8,0	7,6	7,5	7,5	7,7	7,8	7,9	7,9	7,7	:	CA
JP	3,2	3,3	3,5	3,6	3,6	3,7	3,9	4,1	4,1	4,0	:	JP

3B5CA

Further reading: Energy, yearly statistics, 1998. Eurostat.

4

Gross inland consumption of primary energy. Million toe

	1989	1990	1991	1992	1993	1994	1995	1996	1997	1998	1999	
EU-15	1 311,8	1 318,1 ǀ	1 346,4	1 336,3	1 335,8	1 335,7	1 363,5	1 412,7	1 409,5	1 435,6 *	:	EU-15
EUR-11	1 011,6	1 019,8 ǀ	1 039,9	1 033,4	1 028,8	1 023,4	1 049,6	1 084,2	1 089,2	1 109,0 *	:	EUR-11
B	46,4	47,3	49,5	50,3	48,9	49,7	50,5	54,0	55,1	56,2 *	:	B
DK	17,9	18,2	19,9	19,3	19,6	20,3	20,6	23,2	21,6	21,1 *	:	DK
D	358,0	354,0 ǀ	346,6	339,8	338,3	335,2	336,2	347,7	344,1	343,2	:	D
EL	22,1	22,2	22,4	23,0	22,6	23,6	24,1	25,4	25,6	26,9	:	EL
E	87,3	89,1	94,1	95,5	91,7	97,4	102,3	100,9	106,1	110,7 *	:	E
F	218,2	223,2	235,8	233,0	235,3	226,4	235,4	249,0	243,1	250,3	:	F
IRL	9,5	10,2	10,2	10,2	10,3	11,0	11,0	11,7	12,3	13,0 *	:	IRL
I	153,3	154,8	156,7	158,7	156,2	154,1	162,7	162,4	168,1	172,6	:	I
L	3,4	3,6	3,8	3,8	3,8	3,8	3,3	3,4	3,4	3,3	:	L
NL	65,3	66,8	69,9	69,5	70,8	70,6	73,3	76,1	74,8	74,7	:	NL
A	24,4	25,7	27,0	25,7	25,6	25,7	26,3	28,0	28,5	29,1 *	:	A
P	16,5	16,9	17,2	18,6	18,4	18,8	19,8	20,0	21,3	22,8 *	:	P
FIN	29,1	28,5	28,9	28,4	29,5	30,7	28,9	30,9	32,5	33,2	:	FIN
S	47,4	46,9	48,6	46,2	46,5	49,0	49,9	51,7	50,3	48,1	:	S
UK	212,8	210,9	215,6	214,4	218,2	219,4	219,2	228,1	222,7	230,5	:	UK
IS	2,3	2,2	2,0	2,1	2,2	2,1	2,1	2,3	2,3	2,6	:	IS
NO	21,3	21,2	21,6	22,0	23,1	23,2	23,5	22,8	24,8	25,4 *	:	NO
EEA	1 335,3	1 341,5 ǀ	1 370,0	1 360,4	1 361,0	1 360,9	1 389,1	1 437,8	1 436,7	1 463,6	:	EEA
CH	23,3	25,0	25,2	25,5	25,0	25,5	25,2	25,6	26,2	26,6	:	CH
US	1 961,8	1 925,6	1 938,4	1 975,5	2 021,3	2 058,5	2 089,7	2 140,1	2 162,2	2 181,8	:	US
CA	218,0	209,1	208,8	213,9	220,8	228,6	231,9	235,0	238,0	234,3	:	CA
JP	417,1	438,8	448,7	457,0	461,3	483,5	497,0	510,4	514,9	510,1	:	JP

3B5AB

Further reading: Energy, yearly statistics, 1998. Eurostat.

Gross inland consumption is defined as primary production plus imports, recovered products and change in stocks, less exports and fuel supply to maritime bunkers (for seagoing ships of all flags). It therefore reflects the energy necessary to satisfy inland consumption within strict limits of national territory. The energy-producing sector itself is a substantial energy consumer. Most primary energy sources are converted into energy products or transformed into electricity for final use in industry, transport and households. Gross inland consumption of energy per person varies from country to country due to structural differences in their final energy consumption and the degree of industrialisation.

Gross inland consumption of primary energy per person. 1985 = 100 %

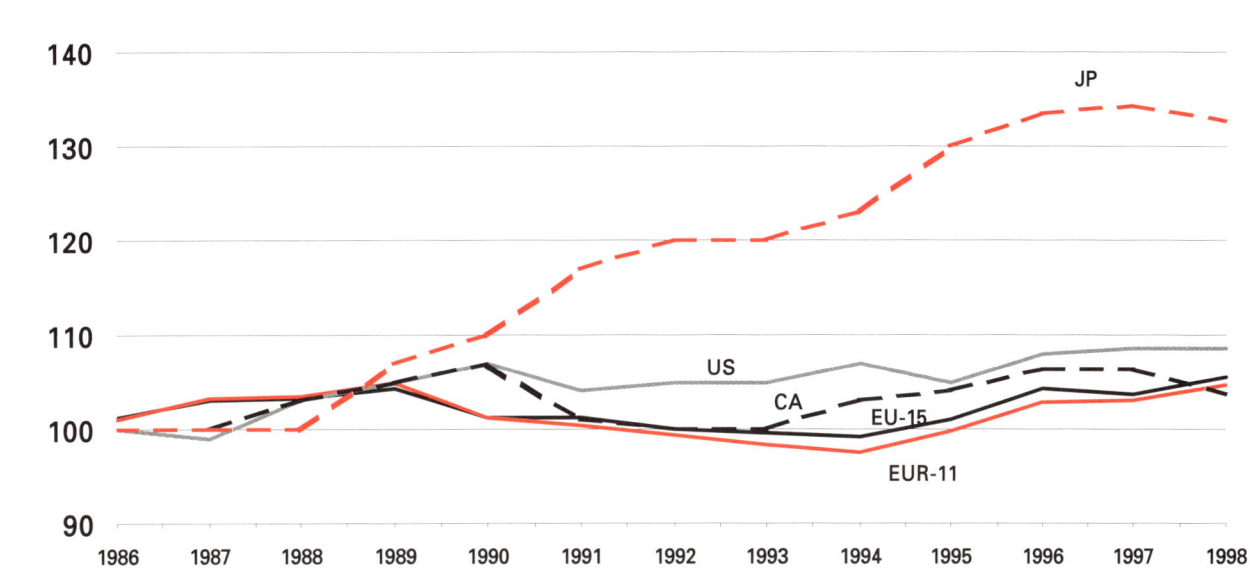

3B5CC

Further reading: Energy, yearly statistics, 1998. Eurostat.

Energy transformed (input) by power stations and refineries. Million toe. EU-15

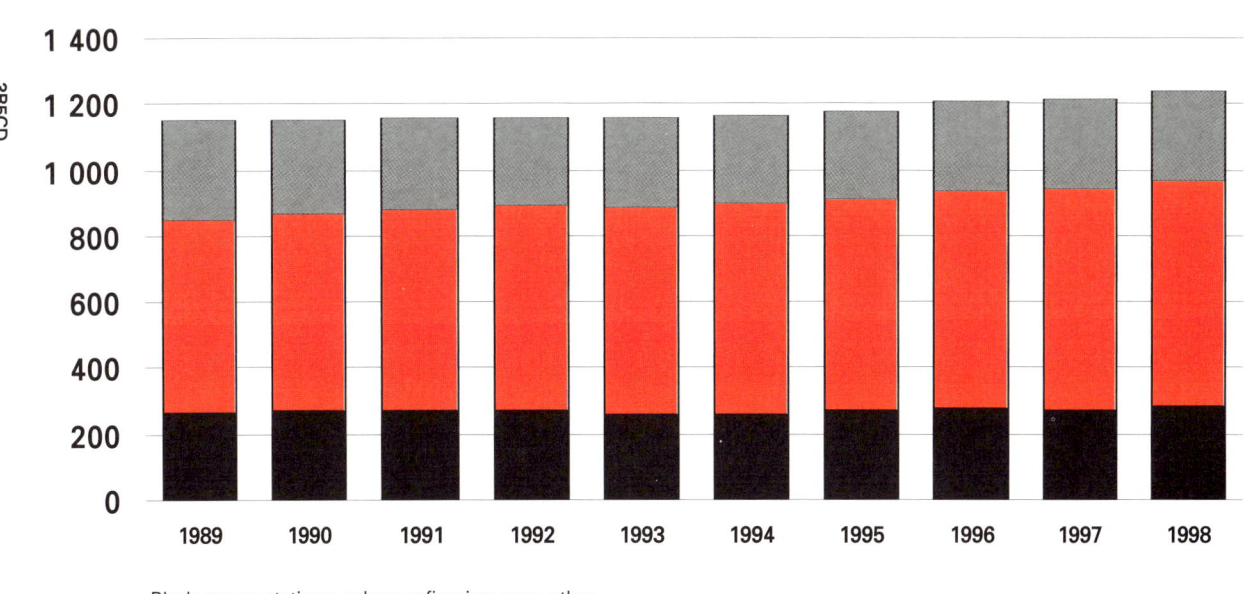

3B5CD

Black: power stations; colour: refineries; grey: other.

Further reading: Energy, yearly statistics, 1998. Eurostat.

Electricity generation by origin, as % of total electricity production

	Solid fuels: coal and brown coal			Petroleum products			Natural and derived gases			
	1987	1992	1998	1987	1992	1998	1987	1992	1998	
EU-15	33,8	33,3	26,8	8,8	10,1	7,7	7,4	7,6	15,8	EU-15
EUR-11	27,4	29,0	25,8	9,4	10,5	8,9	9,8	9,5	14,0	EUR-11
B	19,9	22,2	17,0	3,3	2,1	3,1	7,2	12,7	21,3	B
DK	94,7	89,4	57,6	4,2	3,6	12,1	0,4	2,5	19,9	DK
D	49,5	55,2	52,6	3,1	2,5	1,1	8,5	7,8	11,0	D
EL	68,1	71,1	70,0	21,9	21,9	17,4	0,2	0,2	3,7	EL
E	41,1	40,5	31,4	4,7	9,0	8,9	1,8	1,7	9,1	E
F	7,0	7,4	6,6	1,4	2,1	2,3	1,8	1,4	1,7	F
IRL	52,6	55,2	39,9	20,6	15,4	22,9	18,2	22,8	30,4	IRL
I	14,9	9,4	9,0	44,8	51,4	41,4	17,1	17,1	29,1	I
L	·	·	·	3,1	4,6	0,0	39,1	41,6	15,6	L
NL	24,8	29,3	26,6	5,3	4,2	3,9	63,7	59,6	60,6	NL
A	9,5	10,0	7,2	5,0	5,0	5,4	10,6	12,7	17,0	A
P	25,1	33,8	30,7	25,8	46,1	27,4	0,2	0,3	5,4	P
FIN	30,6	20,5	18,5	2,8	2,4	1,5	4,0	9,0	13,5	FIN
S	1,4	1,8	1,3	1,7	1,8	2,1	0,1	0,4	1,0	S
UK	70,1	60,1	34,3	8,5	10,5	1,6	1,1	2,2	33,0	UK

3B5DA 3B5DB 3B5DC

Further reading: Energy, yearly statistics, 1998. Eurostat.

Breakdown of the total electricity production by source of energy.

Electricity generation by origin, as % of total electricity production

	Nuclear			Hydroelectricity			Geothermal, wind, photovoltaic			
	1987	1992	1998	1987	1992	1998	1987	1992	1998	
EU-15	33,1	34,1	34,3	16,2	13,7	13,1	0,2	0,2	0,7	EU-15
EUR-11	36,3	36,6	36,1	16,2	13,0	12,8	0,2	0,2	0,7	EUR-11
B	66,3	60,1	55,5	2,3	1,6	1,8	0,0	0,0	0,0	B
DK	·	·	·	0,1	0,1	0,1	0,6	2,9	6,8	DK
D	32,9	29,6	29,0	5,2	3,9	3,9	0,0	0,1	0,8	D
EL	·	·	·	9,8	6,4	8,3	·	0,0	0,2	EL
E	30,9	35,2	30,1	21,1	13,2	18,3	·	0,1	1,1	E
F	70,2	73,1	76,0	19,3	15,8	13,0	·	0,0	0,0	F
IRL	·	·	·	8,6	6,6	5,6	·	0,0	0,8	IRL
I	0,1	0,0	0,0	21,1	20,3	18,3	1,5	1,5	1,7	I
L	·	·	·	53,9	50,3	80,1	·	·	0,8	L
NL	5,2	4,9	4,2	·	0,2	0,1	0,0	0,2	0,7	NL
A	·	·	·	71,5	67,8	67,3	·	·	0,1	A
P	·	·	·	45,6	16,9	33,5	0,0	0,0	0,4	P
FIN	36,8	33,4	31,1	25,8	26,2	21,4	·	0,0	0,0	FIN
S	46,0	43,3	46,5	49,4	51,0	47,0	0,0	0,0	0,2	S
UK	18,3	24,2	28,0	2,1	2,5	1,9	0,0	0,0	0,2	UK
IS	·	·	·	94,0	94,8	89,5	5,9	5,1	10,4	IS
NO	·	·	·	99,5	99,6	99,4	·	·	0,0	NO
EEA	31,4	32,4	32,7	20,4	18,0	17,2	0,2	0,2	0,7	EEA
CH	38,8	42,4	41,9	59,6	55,5	54,2	0,0	0,0	0,0	CH
US	15,5	19,1	18,8	11,4	9,0	7,7	0,4	0,6	0,5	US
CA	12,8	17,6	12,7	67,4	61,6	59,1	0,0	0,0	0,0	CA
JP	23,7	29,7	32,1	13,7	11,2	8,9	0,2	0,2	0,3	JP

3B5DD 3B5DE 3B5DF

Further reading: Energy, yearly statistics, 1998. Eurostat.

Breakdown of the total electricity production by source of energy.

Since the electricity supply industry is capital-intensive and characterised by long construction periods, industry structure changes slowly over a decade. In the case of multi-fired power stations, electricity generation by fuel type (petroleum products, coal and lignite, and natural and derived gas) is estimated pro rata on the basis of fuel consumption.

Electricity production. 1 000 GWh

3B5DG

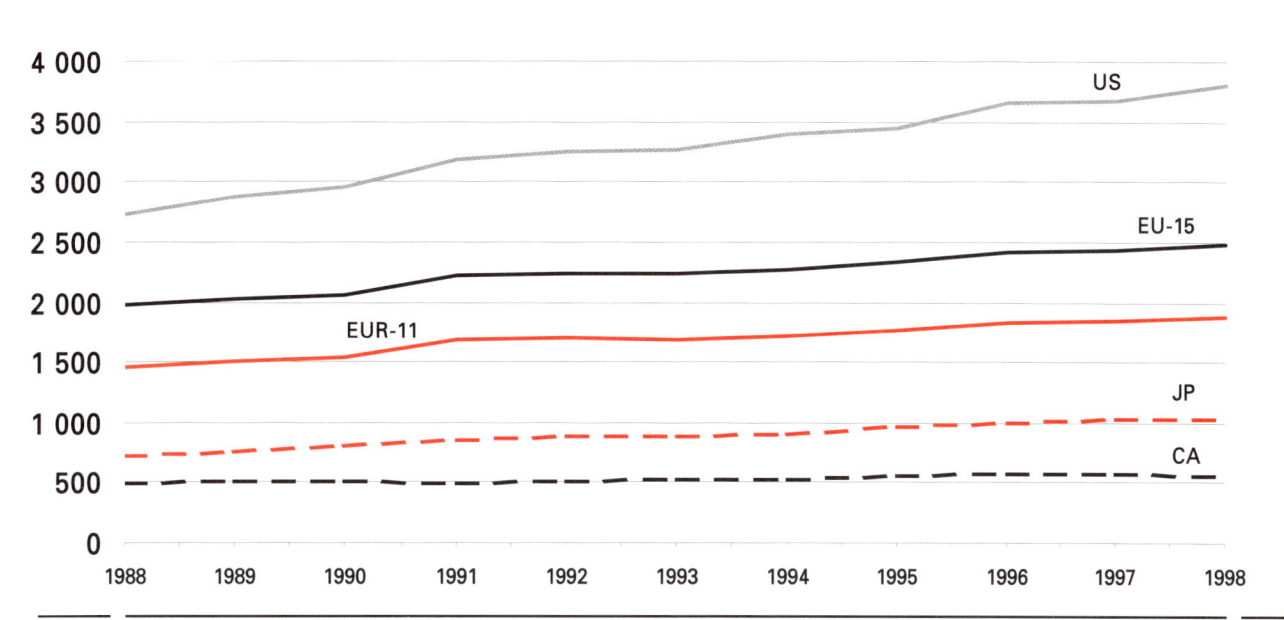

Further reading: Energy, yearly statistics, 1998. Eurostat.

Electricity production. EU-15 and EUR-11: data sets for periods before and after the year 1990 are not fully comparable as they refer to Germany before and after unification.

4

Consumption of electricity by industry, transport activities and households. 1 000 GWh. EU-15

3B5DH

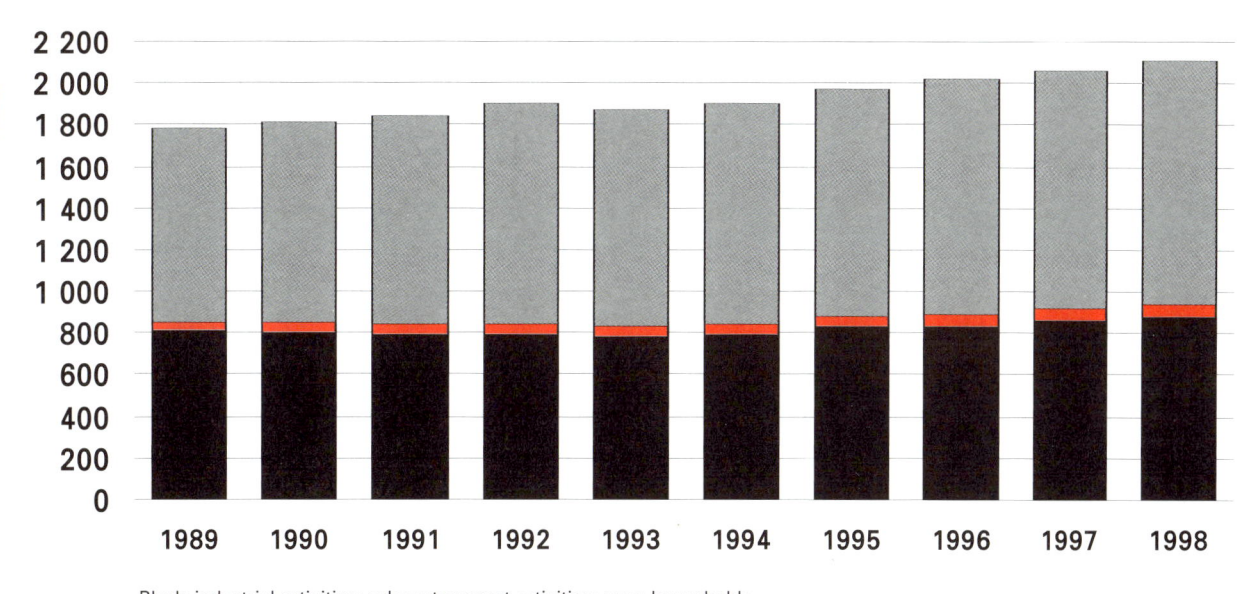

Black: industrial activities; colour: transport activities; grey: households.

Further reading: Energy, yearly statistics, 1998. Eurostat.

eurostat

Where is your nearest Data Shop? Addresses at the end of the book

EUROSTAT YEARBOOK 2001
393

Final energy consumption. Million toe

	1989	1990	1991	1992	1993	1994	1995	1996	1997	1998	1999	
EU-15	855,6	862,2|	882,8	882,3	884,6	879,4	897,5	935,2	931,0	945,5 *	:	EU-15
EUR-11	659,9	666,5	681,8	680,7	681,4	674,0	691,6	717,5	717,6	729,7 *	:	EUR-11
B	30,8	30,8	32,5	33,2	32,6	33,4	34,2	36,4	36,5	37,4 *	:	B
DK	14,0	14,3	14,5	14,2	14,5	14,8	15,0	15,6	15,1	15,1 *	:	DK
D	228,7	227,3	224,3	221,5	220,0	216,3	221,3	228,6	223,9	223,6 *	:	D
EL	14,3	14,5	14,8	15,0	15,2	15,4	15,8	16,9	17,3	18,2	:	EL
E	54,4	56,5	60,1	59,9	59,2	62,3	62,9	65,2	67,7	71,2 *	:	E
F	134,6	136,1	142,6	143,2	143,8	137,9	141,6	148,7	146,5	150,3	:	F
IRL	6,9	7,1	7,0	7,1	7,1	7,6	7,8	8,2	8,7	9,2 *	:	IRL
I	109,4	110,4	113,3	113,4	113,6	111,8	116,6	117,3	121,2	123,5	:	I
L	3,2	3,3	3,6	3,6	3,6	3,6	3,1	3,2	3,2	3,2	:	L
NL	41,3	43,0	45,2	44,8	46,4	45,7	47,4	51,3	49,1	49,2	:	NL
A	19,3	19,9	21,0	20,5	20,7	20,3	21,2	22,2	22,9	22,8 *	:	A
P	10,7	11,2	11,7	12,3	12,5	13,0	13,5	14,2	15,0	15,6 *	:	P
FIN	20,5	20,9	20,6	21,1	21,8	22,1	22,0	22,1	22,9	23,6	:	FIN
S	30,9	30,4	30,6	30,6	32,2	33,2	33,7	34,1	33,4	33,6	:	S
UK	136,5	136,4	141,0	141,8	141,3	142,1	141,3	151,1	147,6	148,9	:	UK
IS	1,6	1,6	1,6	1,6	1,7	1,7	1,7	1,9	1,9	2,0	:	IS
NO	15,7	15,7	15,4	15,3	15,8	16,3	16,5	17,3	17,0	18,3	:	NO
EEA	872,9	879,5	899,8	899,2	902,1	897,4	915,6	954,4	949,9	965,8	:	EEA
CH	19,0	19,6	20,4	20,6	19,9	19,7	20,1	20,6	20,2	21,0	:	CH
US	1339,7	1306,3	1306,5	1308,6	1336,4	1367,5	1390,5	1433,8	1438,2	1429,7	:	US
CA	165,2	161,3	159,1	162,4	166,6	172,5	176,1	182,8	185,1	182,5	:	CA
JP	283,7	294,5	303,3	307,3	308,5	319,9	330,1	336,8	340,1	336,5	:	JP

3B5EA

Further reading: Energy, yearly statistics, 1998. Eurostat.

Contribution of major energy sources as % of total final energy consumption

	Petroleum products			Electricity			Gas			
	1987	1992	1998	1987	1992	1998	1987	1992	1998	
EU-15	45,7	46,8	46,1 *	17,0	18,6	19,2 *	20,3	21,9	23,6 *	EU-15
EUR-11	46,3	47,5	46,9 *	16,4	18,2	18,8 *	19,5	21,4	23,0 *	EUR-11
B	48,1	48,6	48,0 *	14,7	16,2	17,0 *	23,5	22,4	24,6 *	B
DK	59,7	52,2	48,6 *	16,6	18,2	18,2 *	8,3	9,3	12,3 *	DK
D	41,5	47,1	46,9 *	15,8	18,3	17,9 *	18,2	20,6	24,1 *	D
EL	67,9	68,8	69,7	16,4	17,7	18,6	0,1	0,1	0,8	EL
E	59,5	60,4	59,9 *	19,0	18,8	20,0 *	6,4	9,3	12,8 *	E
F	50,2	48,1	48,0	17,7	19,8	21,0	17,4	18,5	20,1	F
IRL	51,7	56,2	62,3 *	13,6	16,0	16,5 *	5,6	9,7	10,4 *	IRL
I	53,0	48,0	44,1	15,8	16,9	17,7	23,8	28,0	29,6	I
L	44,1	53,2	62,5	11,6	10,3	14,3	18,9	17,0	18,6	L
NL	30,5	31,0	32,5	12,9	14,9	16,2	51,2	49,4	43,6	NL
A	40,9	41,6	40,6 *	17,2	18,7	18,4 *	14,7	15,9	17,7 *	A
P	56,0	60,5	61,6 *	16,7	18,0	18,6 *	0,8	0,8	2,1 *	P
FIN	39,9	36,7	31,5	22,7	24,4	26,5	4,5	7,9	7,3	FIN
S	41,7	38,8	36,6	32,3	33,8	31,6	1,4	1,9	1,8	S
UK	39,9	42,1	41,4	16,7	17,1	18,2	32,0	32,2	34,9	UK
IS	36,5	38,4	40,9	20,8	20,5	23,7	0,0	0,0	0,0	IS
NO	40,0	36,1	37,2	49,2	55,7	51,3	0,2	0,1	0,1	NO
EEA	45,5	46,6	45,9	17,6	19,2	19,8	19,9	21,5	23,1	EEA
CH	75,8	66,1	63,3	18,7	20,2	20,4	6,8	8,5	10,3	CH
US	57,4	51,3	54,4	15,2	16,5	19,6	22,3	22,8	21,5	US
CA	47,7	44,0	43,8	20,8	22,4	21,5	25,0	25,3	27,3	CA
JP	65,7	58,9	63,1	20,2	22,0	23,7	4,7	5,0	6,3	JP

3B5EB 3B5EC 3B5ED

Further reading: Energy, yearly statistics, 1998. Eurostat.

4

Final energy consumption is measured net of energy losses and energy sector consumption. It also excludes consumption for non-energy purposes such as feedstocks in the petrochemical industry.

Final use of petroleum products involves only refined products — for example, motor spirit, gas oil, domestic fuel, kerosene and jet fuels. Final use of gas is mainly in the form of natural gas.

Final energy consumption per person. Toe per capita

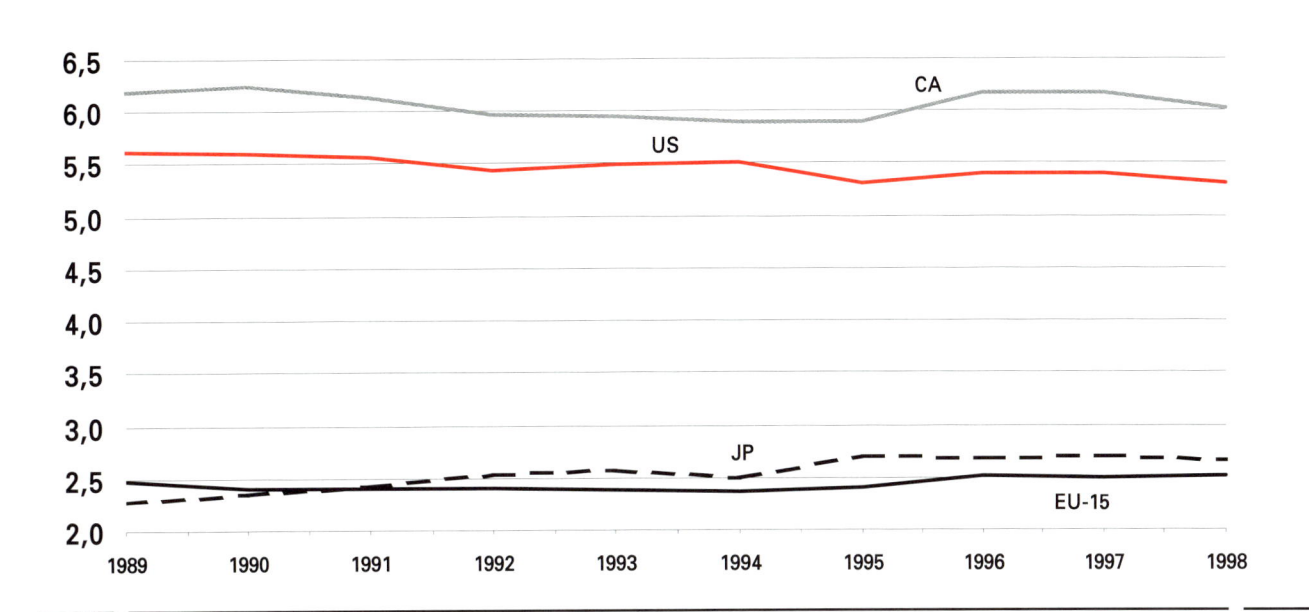

Further reading: Energy, yearly statistics, 1998. Eurostat.

Final energy consumption. Million toe

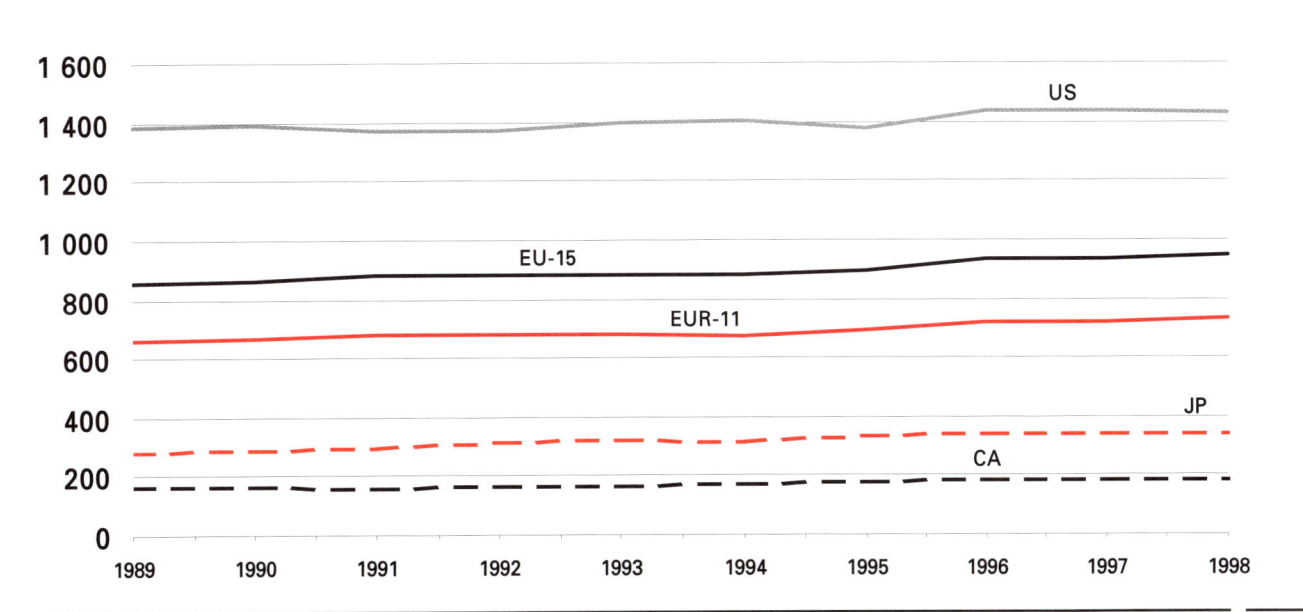

Further reading: Energy, yearly statistics, 1998. Eurostat.

Consumption by industry, as % of final energy consumption

	1989	1990	1991	1992	1993	1994	1995	1996	1997	1998	1999	
EU-15	31,7	30,8 |	29,0	28,6	27,9	28,5	28,7	27,8	28,2	27,8 *	:	EU-15
EUR-11	33,0	31,9 |	29,9	29,4	28,8	29,2	29,5	28,3	28,8	28,3 *	:	EUR-11
B	36,3	37,2	35,9	35,4	33,9	34,9	34,4	31,8	34,3	34,9 *	:	B
DK	19,0	20,1	20,3	18,9	19,0	19,8	19,7	19,4	19,9	20,0 *	:	DK
D	34,2	31,5 |	28,9	27,6	26,4	27,2	28,0	26,5	26,0	25,7 *	:	D
EL	29,1	27,1	25,3	25,5	24,4	24,3	25,9	25,5	25,1	24,3	:	EL
E	35,5	34,9	33,6	32,4	32,4	31,8	31,6	30,2	31,9	30,9 *	:	E
F	28,3	27,2	25,7	25,8	25,4	25,3	26,5	25,2	25,7	25,2	:	F
IRL	27,6	28,1	28,7	27,3	22,9	22,7	22,9	21,8	21,4	20,8 *	:	IRL
I	33,5	33,4	31,8	31,8	30,8	32,1	31,8	31,1	30,9	29,7	:	I
L	54,9	51,8	47,4	45,1	45,6	43,7	37,5	35,5	31,9	27,1	:	L
NL	29,3	30,8	27,4	28,0	28,5	27,3	26,7	25,7	26,9	26,6	:	NL
A	29,9	28,9	27,0	26,4	26,1	27,6	27,7	27,1	30,8	30,7 *	:	A
P	37,0	36,9	36,4	35,6	35,0	35,1	32,0	33,3	35,5	35,2 *	:	P
FIN	43,3	42,3	41,0	42,3	45,2	44,5	45,2	45,1	46,2	46,2	:	FIN
S	38,6	38,9	37,9	36,9	36,6	37,1	37,5	36,4	37,8	37,7	:	S
UK	25,6	25,1	24,3	24,4	22,8	24,7	24,0	24,6	24,5	24,2	:	UK
IS	23,4	23,5	22,3	21,9	22,4	23,7	23,9	25,9	27,5	28,8	:	IS
NO	37,7	36,3	34,2	33,2	33,4	34,5	34,9	33,5	32,9	36,4	:	NO
EEA	31,8	30,8 |	29,1	28,7	28,0	28,6	28,8	27,9	28,3	27,9	:	EEA
CH	18,1	17,7	17,4	16,8	16,8	16,5	18,5	18,0	18,5	18,0	:	CH
US	30,0	30,1	30,4	30,8	29,1	28,9	25,8	24,9	24,6	24,4	:	US
CA	38,1	37,0	36,7	35,7	35,7	35,6	35,7	36,0	36,0	36,7	:	CA
JP	45,5	45,9	46,4	44,4	44,7	44,5	42,8	39,7	39,8	38,8	:	JP

3B5FA

Further reading: Energy, yearly statistics, 1998. Eurostat.

4

Consumption by transport, as % of final energy consumption

	1989	1990	1991	1992	1993	1994	1995	1996	1997	1998	1999	
EU-15	28,6	29,4 |	29,1	30,1	30,7	30,9	30,7	30,3	31,0	31,6 *	:	EU-15
EUR-11	27,8	28,6 |	28,6	29,6	30,3	30,7	30,4	30,1	30,7	31,4 *	:	EUR-11
B	24,7	25,0	24,1	24,9	25,6	25,4	24,8	24,5	25,2	25,6 *	:	B
DK	30,3	31,4	30,5	31,2	30,2	31,0	30,8	30,3	31,4	31,4 *	:	DK
D	24,4	25,9 |	26,4	27,7	28,5	28,6	28,4	27,4	28,4	28,9 *	:	D
EL	37,6	40,0	40,3	41,1	42,4	42,0	40,7	38,9	38,9	40,1	:	EL
E	39,3	39,5	40,2	41,5	41,5	41,3	41,4	42,6	41,4	42,8	:	E
F	29,8	30,8	29,1	29,7	31,0	31,6	31,1	30,9	32,0	32,3	:	F
IRL	27,6	27,9	28,7	28,7	29,2	30,2	28,2	32,8	33,7	35,7 *	:	IRL
I	29,9	30,3	30,3	31,6	32,2	32,8	32,3	32,4	31,9	33,1	:	I
L	26,4	30,3	33,2	35,9	35,7	37,7	41,5	41,9	45,4	48,9	:	L
NL	24,5	24,0	23,3	24,9	24,8	25,7	26,1	25,5	27,5	27,6	:	NL
A	27,3	27,1	28,4	29,2	29,4	30,0	29,4	28,8	27,8	27,1 *	:	A
P	32,8	33,3	34,0	35,1	35,7	36,0	35,9	36,0	35,1	36,5 *	:	P
FIN	20,3	20,4	20,1	19,4	18,5	18,8	18,7	18,2	18,5	18,2	:	FIN
S	24,9	23,8	23,3	24,3	22,7	22,8	22,8	22,3	23,0	23,1	:	S
UK	32,5	33,3	31,7	32,1	33,1	33,0	33,2	32,3	33,5	33,5	:	UK
IS	17,5	17,7	17,8	17,3	16,6	17,5	16,4	17,3	15,9	16,7	:	IS
NO	25,7	26,3	25,0	26,2	26,6	25,8	25,5	26,1	27,1	25,9	:	NO
EEA	28,6	29,4 |	29,0	30,0	30,6	30,8	30,6	30,2	30,9	31,4	:	EEA
CH	18,1	17,7	31,8	31,3	31,9	31,1	32,9	31,6	33,3	32,7	:	CH
US	35,1	35,1	35,4	34,9	36,7	36,5	38,8	38,9	39,6	40,7	:	US
CA	26,0	25,8	25,9	26,8	27,2	27,0	27,6	27,4	27,9	29,0	:	CA
JP	23,7	24,4	25,7	26,6	26,5	26,6	25,1	26,7	27,1	27,5	:	JP

3B5FB

Further reading: Energy, yearly statistics, 1998. Eurostat.

Large energy-consuming industries are those where energy is a basic part of the production process, such as the iron and steel, chemical, glass, ceramics and building materials industries. Mechanical energy and space heating are a relatively minor part of total industrial consumption. This has to be taken into account when comparing countries with similar industrial activity. Gas and electricity prices have been collected since 1991 on the basis of standard consumers and locations defined by Council Directive 90/377/EEC on Community procedure to improve transparency of gas and electricity prices charged to industrial end-users.

Natural gas prices for large industrial standard consumers: 418 600 GJ per year, euro per GJ. 1 January 2000

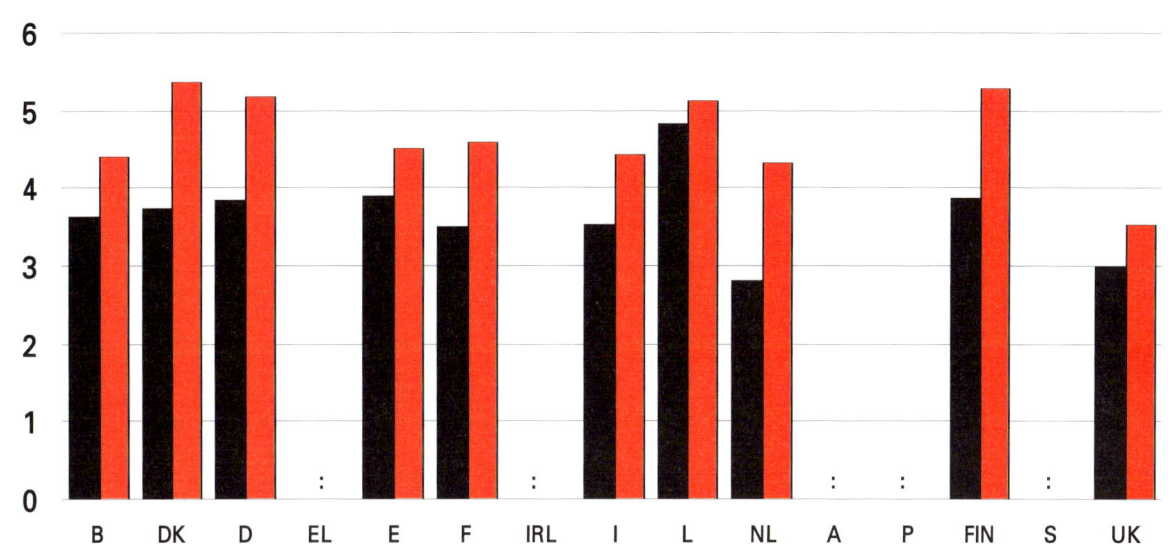

Black: without taxes; colour: taxes included.

Further reading: Gas prices, 1990–2000. Eurostat. Statistics in focus: gas prices. Eurostat.

Half-yearly data. EL, IRL, A, P, S: data not available. Data relate to national average or regional prices depending on country.

Electricity prices for large industrial standard consumers: 24 GWh per year, euro per 100 kWh. 1 January 2000

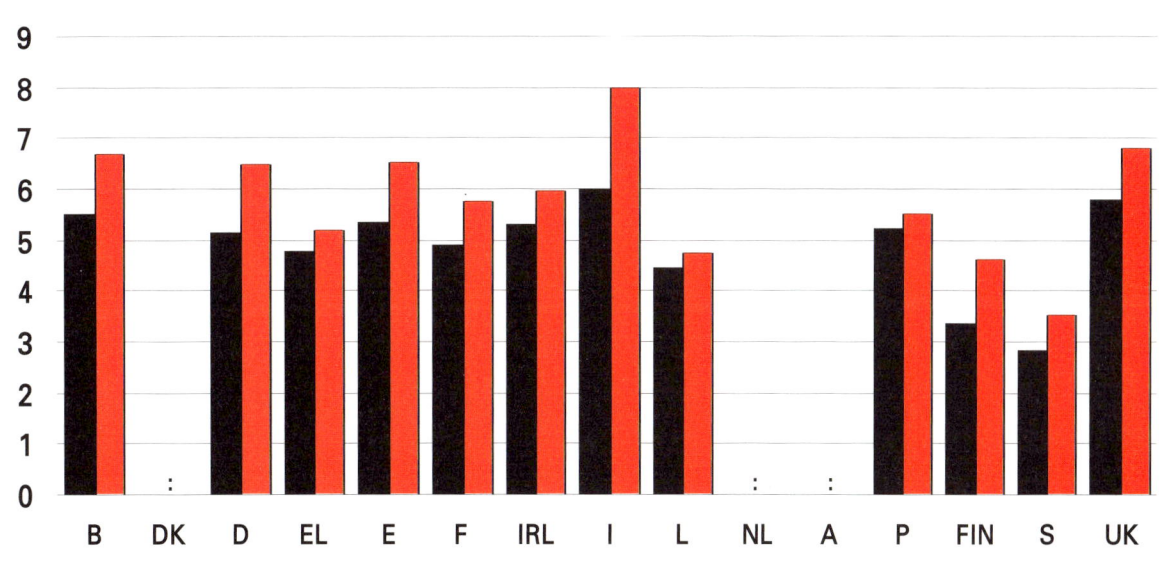

Black: without taxes; colour: taxes included.

Further reading: Electricity prices, 1990–2000. Eurostat. Statistics in focus: electricity prices. Eurostat.

Half-yearly data. L: 50 % power reduction. DK, NL, A: data not available. Data relate to national average or regional prices according to country.

eurostat

Consumption by households, trades, services, etc., as % of final energy consumption

	1989	1990	1991	1992	1993	1994	1995	1996	1997	1998	1999	
EU-15	39,6	39,8	41,8	41,3	41,5	40,5	40,6	41,9	40,8	40,7 *	:	**EU-15**
EUR-11	39,2	39,5	41,5	41,0	41,0	40,1	40,1	41,7	40,5	40,4 *	:	**EUR-11**
B	39,0	37,9	39,9	39,7	40,5	39,7	40,8	43,8	40,5	39,5 *	:	**B**
DK	50,6	48,5	49,2	49,9	50,9	49,2	49,5	50,3	48,7	48,5 *	:	**DK**
D	41,4	42,7	44,7	44,7	45,1	44,2	43,6	46,1	45,5	45,4	:	**D**
EL	33,3	32,9	34,4	33,4	33,2	33,7	33,5	35,7	36,0	35,6	:	**EL**
E	25,1	25,6	26,1	26,1	26,1	26,9	27,0	27,2	26,7	26,3 *	:	**E**
F	41,9	42,0	45,2	44,5	43,6	43,1	42,5	43,9	42,3	42,4	:	**F**
IRL	44,8	44,0	42,6	44,0	47,9	47,1	48,9	45,4	44,9	43,5 *	:	**IRL**
I	36,7	36,3	37,9	36,6	37,0	35,1	35,9	36,5	37,2	37,2	:	**I**
L	18,7	17,9	19,4	18,9	18,8	18,6	21,0	22,7	22,7	24,0	:	**L**
NL	46,2	45,2	49,4	47,0	46,6	47,0	47,1	48,8	45,6	45,7	:	**NL**
A	42,8	44,0	44,7	44,4	44,4	42,5	42,9	44,1	41,4	42,2 *	:	**A**
P	30,2	29,8	29,6	29,2	29,3	28,9	32,1	30,7	29,4	28,3 *	:	**P**
FIN	36,4	37,3	38,9	38,3	36,3	36,6	36,2	36,7	35,3	35,6	:	**FIN**
S	36,6	37,4	38,8	38,8	40,7	40,1	39,7	41,3	39,2	39,1	:	**S**
UK	41,9	41,6	44,0	43,5	44,1	42,3	42,9	43,2	42,0	42,3	:	**UK**
IS	59,1	58,7	59,9	60,7	61,0	58,8	59,7	53,0	52,4	49,5	:	**IS**
NO	36,6	37,4	40,7	40,6	39,9	39,7	39,5	40,4	40,0	37,7	:	**NO**
EEA	39,6	39,8	41,8	41,3	41,5	40,5	40,6	41,9	40,8	40,6	:	**EEA**
CH	50,2	50,0	49,0	49,8	49,6	50,5	46,6	48,6	46,4	47,4	:	**CH**
US	30,8	30,9	29,7	30,4	30,0	30,4	30,9	31,8	31,4	30,6	:	**US**
CA	32,5	33,8	34,3	33,6	33,9	34,0	33,4	33,2	32,6	31,0	:	**CA**
JP	27,1	26,3	24,5	25,1	26,0	26,1	29,0	30,6	30,0	30,6	:	**JP**

3B5GA

Further reading: Energy, yearly statistics, 1998. Eurostat. Energy consumption in households. Eurostat.

4

Consumption of electricity in households per person. kWh per capita

	1989	1990	1991	1992	1993	1994	1995	1996	1997	1998	1999	
EU-15	1 454	1 447	1 502	1 515	1 542	1 554	1 565	1 642	1 621	1 655	:	**EU-15**
EUR-11	1 338	1 331	1 375	1 391	1 417	1 427	1 438	1 513	1 503	1 530	:	**EUR-11**
B	1 519	1 847	1 989	2 015	2 091	2 111	2 181	2 287	2 253	2 292	:	**B**
DK	1 750	1 771	1 849	1 848	2 025	1 977	2 005	2 069	1 951	1 931	:	**DK**
D	1 857	1 596	1 527	1 523	1 553	1 544	1 574	1 634	1 594	1 595	:	**D**
EL	906	893	977	1 028	1 010	1 049	1 101	1 169	1 183	1 216	:	**EL**
E	761	778	794	805	828	888	918	955	1 020	1 059	:	**E**
F	1 647	1 708	1 872	1 910	1 933	1 921	1 872	2 064	2 032	2 093	:	**F**
IRL	1 234	1 304	1 359	1 427	1 445	1 483	1 516	1 584	1 453	1 490	:	**IRL**
I	900	930	963	980	989	997	999	1 010	1 017	1 030	:	**I**
L	1 672	1 702	1 770	1 794	1 804	1 819	1 798	1 808	1 812	1 889	:	**L**
NL	1 078	1 104	1 135	1 153	1 170	1 201	1 274	1 288	1 307	1 324	:	**NL**
A	1 425	1 452	1 523	1 510	1 542	1 514	1 581	1 649	1 604	1 610	:	**A**
P	571	598	669	689	721	747	793	850	847	881	:	**P**
FIN	2 719	2 928	3 119	3 145	3 220	3 338	3 182	3 363	3 389	3 520	:	**FIN**
S	4 473	4 451	4 780	4 664	4 799	4 841	4 803	4 900	4 813	4 783	:	**S**
UK	1 609	1 629	1 697	1 715	1 726	1 740	1 747	1 831	1 770	1 854	:	**UK**
IS	2 229	2 255	2 004	2 077	2 117	2 090	2 094	2 153	2 153	2 153	:	**IS**
NO	6 828	7 144	7 652	7 618	7 605	7 843	7 944	8 055	7 714	7 759	:	**NO**
EEA	1 519	1 515	1 573	1 586	1 613	1 627	1 639	1 716	1 692	1 726	:	**EEA**
CH	1 901	1 921	2 037	2 050	2 060	2 042	2 089	2 155	2 099	2 126	:	**CH**
US	3 622	3 637	3 752	3 782	3 662	3 857	3 869	4 076	4 032	4 177	:	**US**
CA	4 649	4 949	5 015	4 775	4 609	4 616	4 470	4 605	4 484	4 275	:	**CA**
JP	1 318	1 393	1 508	1 554	1 601	1 641	1 819	1 907	1 931	1 990	:	**JP**

3B5GB

Further reading: Energy, yearly statistics, 1998. Eurostat. Energy consumption in households. Eurostat.

Final consumption of households varies greatly from country to country according to climatic conditions and standard of living. Household consumption of electricity per person excludes consumption by the commercial and services sectors. Gas and electricity prices paid by domestic consumers are collected on the basis of a definition of standard consumers and locations.

Natural gas prices for small standard consumers: 16.74 GJ per year, euro per GJ.
1 January 2000

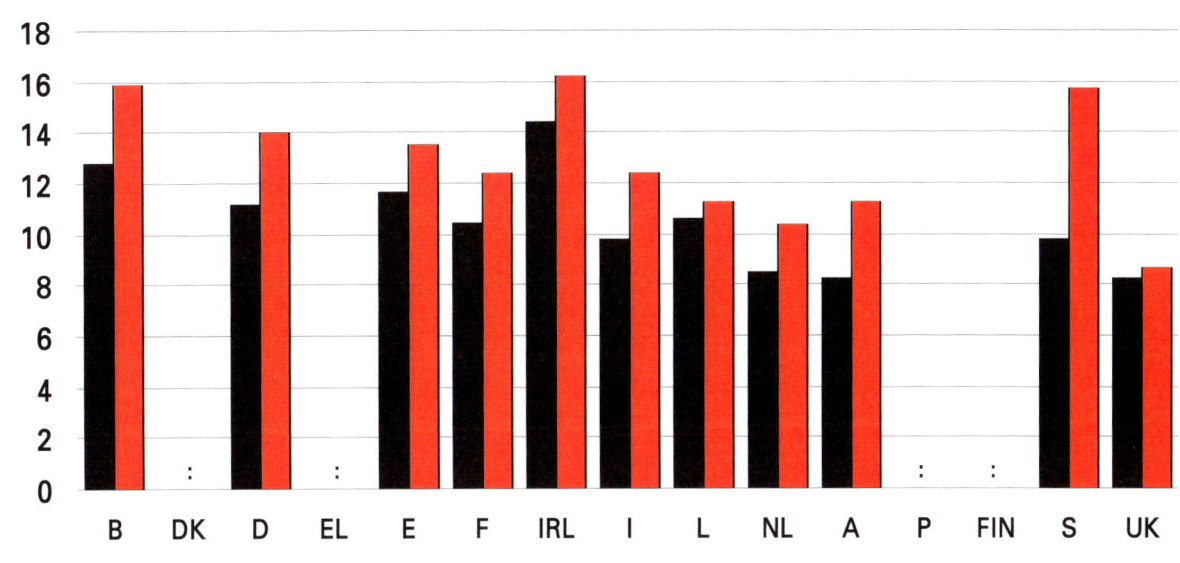

Black: without taxes; colour: taxes included.

Further reading: Gas prices, 1990–2000. Eurostat. Statistics in focus: gas prices. Eurostat.

Half-yearly data. DK, EL, P, FIN: data not available. Data relate to national average or regional prices according to country.

Electricity prices for small standard consumers: 1 200 kWh per year, euro per 100 kWh.
1 January 2000

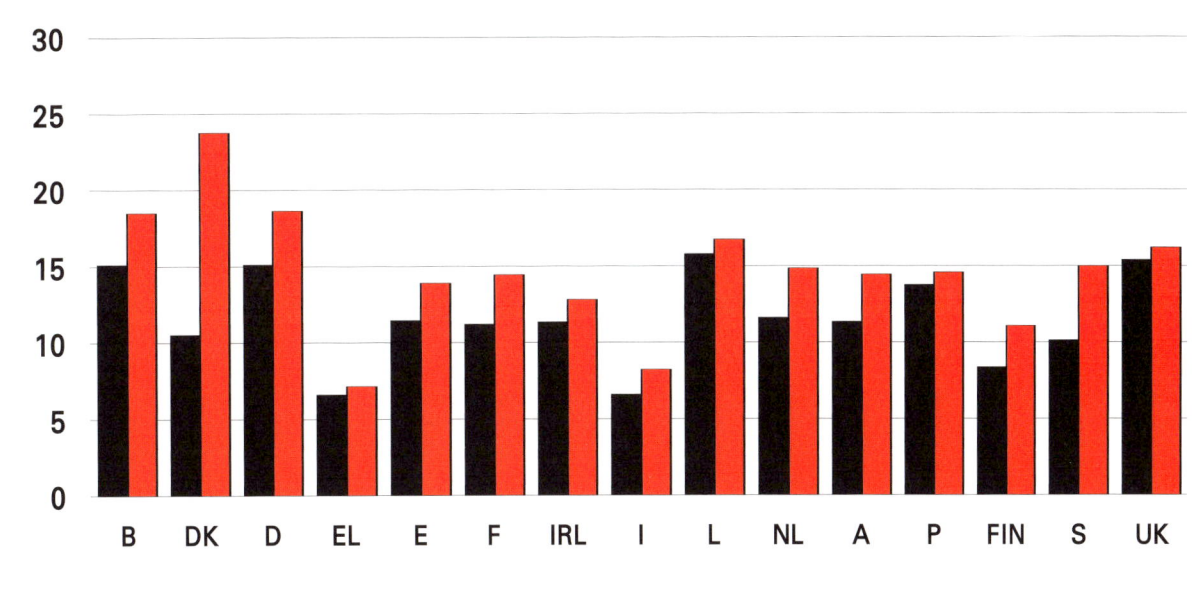

Black: without taxes; colour: taxes included.

Further reading: Electricity prices, 1990–2000. Eurostat. Statistics in focus: electricity prices. Eurostat.

Half-yearly data. Data relate to national average or regional prices according to country.

eurostat

Final consumption of petroleum products by households, trades, services, etc., as % of final consumption of petroleum products

	1989	1990	1991	1992	1993	1994	1995	1996	1997	1998	1999	
EU-15	25,0	24,8 |	26,3	25,3	24,9	24,0	23,9	24,8	23,6	22,9	:	EU-15
EUR-11	27,2	27,1 |	28,7	27,5	27,0	26,1	25,9	27,1	25,8	25,0	:	EUR-11
B	36,0	36,0	36,0	36,4	35,2	36,4	38,3	41,3	38,4	35,6	:	B
DK	32,1	26,9	28,4	28,4	29,1	27,2	27,1	27,9	26,3	25,9	:	DK
D	31,1	31,9 |	35,0	33,7	34,4	33,9	32,7	35,6	34,1	32,9	:	D
EL	26,4	25,5	27,1	24,6	23,9	24,0	23,5	26,8	26,8	26,3	:	EL
E	17,4	18,0	18,9	17,9	17,3	17,6	17,6	17,7	16,5	15,8	:	E
F	28,9	28,3	30,0	29,1	26,8	25,9	25,7	26,2	25,0	25,7	:	F
IRL	24,3	24,1	24,9	24,5	32,0	32,7	37,1	31,4	31,8	29,9	:	IRL
I	26,3	24,8	24,7	22,7	22,0	19,3	20,2	19,9	18,7	17,2	:	I
L	20,4	19,4	20,4	18,7	17,9	17,0	17,6	18,8	18,4	18,2	:	L
NL	13,4	12,3	13,3	11,6	11,1	10,2	9,2	9,3	9,1	8,8	:	NL
A	23,9	26,1	27,7	24,6	25,7	23,8	24,1	25,1	25,8	28,3	:	A
P	17,6	17,6	17,2	17,4	17,5	16,8	17,3	19,7	17,8	16,1	:	P
FIN	32,8	33,4	33,6	34,8	31,4	31,7	31,0	29,8	30,9	30,9	:	FIN
S	26,3	27,1	27,0	27,0	25,6	25,5	25,2	26,5	24,8	23,9	:	S
UK	12,0	11,7	12,9	12,6	12,8	12,3	12,1	11,1	10,3	10,1	:	UK
IS	36,6	37,1	39,8	39,9	40,9	40,5	41,1	36,3	35,4	33,3	:	IS
NO	17,5	16,7	21,8	20,8	19,8	19,3	19,8	20,7	20,1	18,3	:	NO
EEA	24,9	24,7 |	26,3	25,2	24,8	24,0	23,8	24,7	23,5	22,9	:	EEA
CH	46,0	45,8	43,9	44,8	43,8	45,5	39,7	41,5	38,7	40,4	:	CH
US	11,0	10,6	8,6	8,7	8,8	8,9	8,4	8,4	8,0	7,3	:	US
CA	15,1	16,0	15,6	14,5	15,3	15,2	15,0	14,4	14,4	13,2	:	CA
JP	25,6	24,2	20,7	21,4	22,1	21,5	22,5	22,2	21,2	21,0	:	JP

3B5HA

Further reading: Energy, yearly statistics, 1998. Eurostat.

4

Final consumption of petroleum products by transport, as % of final consumption of petroleum products

	1989	1990	1991	1992	1993	1994	1995	1996	1997	1998	1999	
EU-15	61,7	62,9 |	61,9	63,2	63,9	64,3	64,7	64,7	66,0	67,3	:	EU-15
EUR-11	59,7	60,7 |	59,8	61,2	61,9	62,6	62,9	63,0	64,2	65,7	:	EUR-11
B	51,8	53,2	50,0	50,6	52,4	52,7	52,3	51,1	52,4	52,7	:	B
DK	55,5	59,1	57,8	59,6	59,2	60,9	61,8	61,4	64,0	64,3	:	DK
D	59,2	59,5 |	56,2	57,5	57,4	58,0	59,0	57,3	59,1	60,4	:	D
EL	54,9	57,8	58,3	59,6	61,7	61,5	59,4	55,9	55,8	57,4	:	EL
E	65,4	65,6	65,9	67,7	67,1	65,0	66,0	68,8	68,5	70,7	:	E
F	58,6	60,9	60,4	60,6	62,6	63,7	63,0	63,4	65,5	66,0	:	F
IRL	53,5	51,9	51,6	51,0	51,6	50,2	46,4	54,4	54,7	57,3	:	IRL
I	57,3	59,7	61,5	64,3	66,4	68,6	67,9	68,8	69,3	73,3	:	I
L	58,4	63,6	63,7	67,3	67,9	70,0	74,2	74,0	76,5	77,8	:	L
NL	78,9	77,4	79,1	79,5	79,4	80,3	83,6	83,4	84,2	84,1	:	NL
A	64,3	63,4	64,2	66,8	65,5	67,6	67,2	67,4	66,2	64,6	:	A
P	55,6	55,4	56,2	57,7	59,0	57,8	59,5	58,2	56,5	58,9	:	P
FIN	51,5	52,5	51,8	52,3	51,9	53,2	52,5	54,4	57,8	57,1	:	FIN
S	58,9	58,5	59,5	60,7	60,8	59,7	60,0	58,0	60,6	61,3	:	S
UK	75,0	76,5	74,6	75,6	76,5	75,5	76,7	77,6	79,5	80,0	:	UK
IS	48,1	47,4	48,0	45,2	43,8	45,3	43,6	40,0	38,0	40,7	:	IS
NO	64,2	67,9	66,9	70,3	71,3	68,4	69,2	65,0	69,7	67,3	:	NO
EEA	61,8	63,0 |	61,9	63,2	64,0	64,4	64,7	64,7	66,0	67,3	:	EEA
CH	42,6	43,5	46,2	45,6	46,3	45,8	50,0	48,6	51,2	50,0	:	CH
US	67,3	68,3	68,9	69,9	69,5	70,0	70,2	70,7	71,2	72,7	:	US
CA	58,7	58,2	58,7	59,0	58,1	57,5	58,9	58,1	58,1	58,9	:	CA
JP	38,4	39,8	42,7	43,0	42,8	42,7	41,1	41,2	42,0	42,7	:	JP

3B5HB

Further reading: Energy, yearly statistics, 1998. Eurostat.

Petroleum products predominate in the consumption of the transport sector, excluding rail, as there is no practical alternative. But petroleum products, electricity and gas are interchangeable in satisfying household energy needs. In the Netherlands and the United Kingdom household heating is mainly gas.

Prices of premium unleaded gasoline 95 Ron, euro per 1 000 litres. 1 January 2000

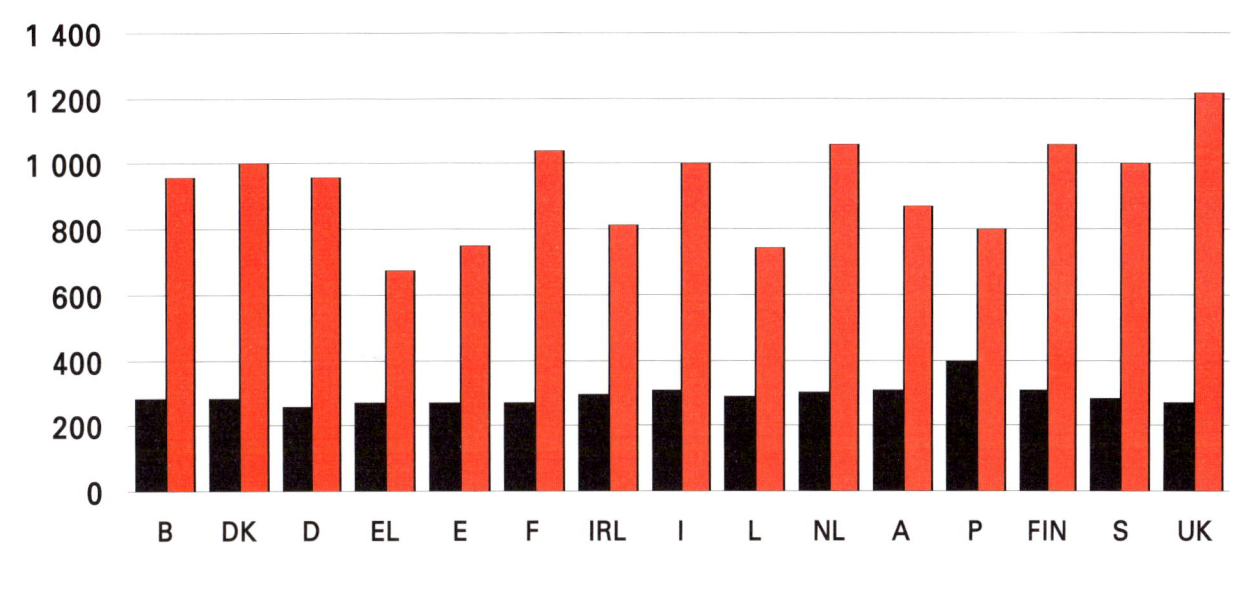

Black: without taxes; colour: taxes included.

Further reading: Energy prices, 1985–99. Eurostat.   Average monthly data.

Final consumption of petroleum products by transport. Million toe. 1998

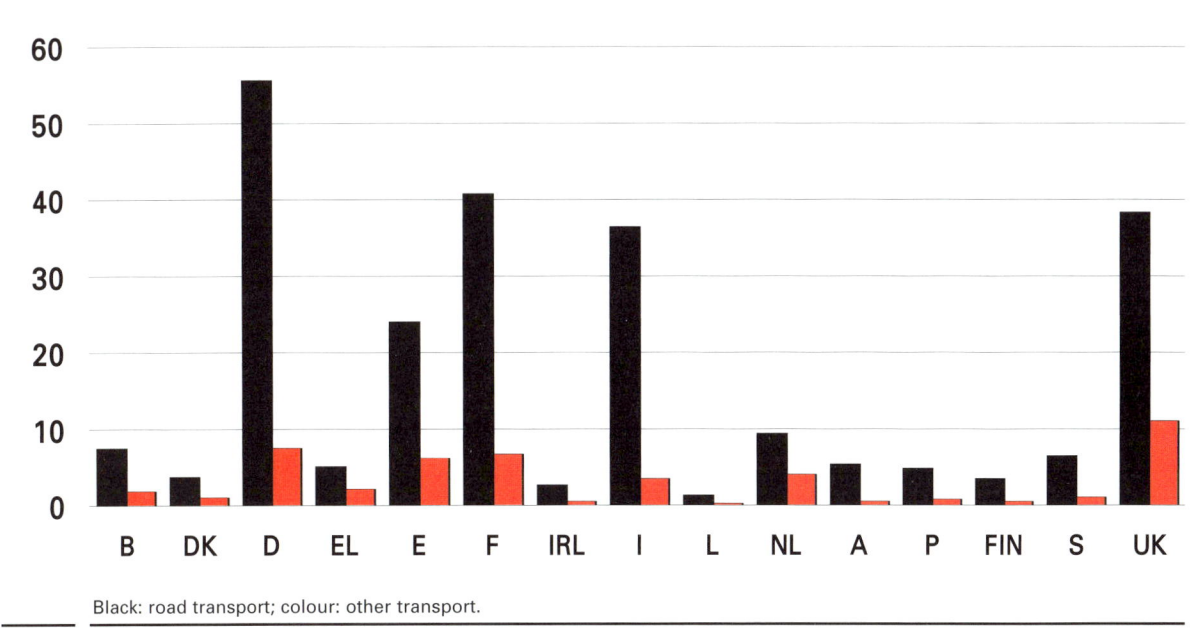

Black: road transport; colour: other transport.

Further reading: Energy, yearly statistics, 1998. Eurostat.

Need access to Eurostat's databases? Ask your Data Shop

EUROSTAT YEARBOOK 2001

401

Tourist accommodation: hotels and similar establishments

	1989	1990	1991	1992	1993	1994	1995	1996	1997	1998	1999	
EU-15	183 906	197 001	196 403	195 434	191 514	188 413	189 389	189 577	186 852	186 484	198 271	EU-15
EUR-11	135 419	133 562	134 398	133 419	132 141	131 723	133 021	133 111	130 375	128 648	136 663	EUR-11
B	2 148	2 123	1 957	1 914	1 888	1 946	2 038	2 062	2 000	1 998	2 015	B
DK	531	539	545	555	576	565	564	478	470	467	464	DK
D	37 873	37 423	38 393	37 162	36 646	37 307	38 172	38 565	38 971	38 914	38 914	D
EL	6 555	6 713	6 991	7 185	7 510	7 604	7 754	7 916	7 850	7 946	7 946	EL
E	9 883	9 436	9 603	9 792	9 734	10 063	10 422	9 482	7 520	7 539	16 229	E
F	20 239	20 472	20 602	20 998	20 654	19 645	20 147	20 849	20 273	19 555	19 379	F
IRL	3 448	3 478	3 956	4 427	4 832	5 034	5 039	5 274	5 164	5 460	5 460	IRL
I	37 162	36 423	35 792	35 371	34 870	34 549	34 296	34 080	33 828	33 540	33 379	I
L	398	401	398	401	390	372	369	368	344	342	325	L
NL	1 544	1 546	1 531	1 525	1 698	1 726	1 749	1 739	1 857	2 788	2 826	NL
A	19 992	19 406	19 257	18 955	18 693	18 402	18 120	17 990	17 692	15 780	15 378	A
P	1 701	1 758	1 785	1 777	1 777	1 728	1 733	1 744	1 768	1 754	1 754	P
FIN	1 031	1 096	1 124	1 097	959	951	936	958	958	978	1 004	FIN
S	1 687	1 723	1 784	1 744	1 716	1 855	1 829	1 851	1 905	1 891	1 898	S
UK	39 714	54 464	52 685	52 531	49 571	46 666	46 221	46 221	46 252	47 532	51 300	UK
IS	121	122	131	140	142	157	211	216	231	253	253	IS
NO	1 101	1 135	1 168	1 183	1 184	1 195	1 179	1 186	1 198	1 176	1 176	NO
EEA	185 180	198 310	197 754	196 809	192 892	189 817	190 834	191 031	188 333	187 965	199 752	EEA
CH	6 800	6 634	6 468	6 327	6 223	6 165	6 081	6 004	5 952	5 890	5 890	CH
US	:	:	:	:	:	:	:	:	:	:	:	US
CA	:	:	:	:	:	:	:	:	:	:	:	CA
JP	:	:	:	:	:	:	:	:	:	:	:	JP

5A1GI

Further reading: Tourism — annual statistics, Eurostat. Tourism in Europe — trends 1995–98, Eurostat. Tourism in Europe — key figures 1997–98, Eurostat. Statistics in focus (theme 4): tourism, Eurostat. Community methodology on tourism statistics, Eurostat.

Hotels and similar establishments include: hotels, apartment hotels, motels, roadside inns, beach hotels, residential clubs, rooming and boarding houses, tourist residences and similar accommodation.

Tourist accommodation: other collective accommodation establishments

	1989	1990	1991	1992	1993	1994	1995	1996	1997	1998	1999	
EU-15	:	:	:	:	:	206 027	:	:	:	:	:	EU-15
EUR-11	:	:	:	:	:	180 947	192 415	:	:	:	:	EUR-11
B	1 337	1 293	1 239	1 442	1 487	1 638	1 667	1 714	1 689	1 655	1 646	B
DK	491	493	499	507	521	524	623	635	633	627	621	DK
D	10 112	10 436	14 204	14 507	14 312	14 936	14 545	15 242	16 001	16 486	16 697	D
EL	313	332	346	329	330	319	320	334	335	340	340	EL
E	100 715	118 601	123 949	119 452	124 179	124 757	131 659	:	:	:	:	E
F	:	:	60 414	60 199	64 579	9 361	9 721	9 211	9 226	9 169	9 140	F
IRL	:	:	:	1 794	1 863	2 370	2 375	2 375	2 375	2 525	2 525	IRL
I	30 133	25 430	22 678	18 551	17 570	21 900	26 450	33 736	31 842	35 991	36 822	I
L	139	139	139	135	301	303	298	315	313	320	297	L
NL	2 089	2 099	2 083	2 028	1 943	1 901	1 947	1 973	2 212	3 502	3 595	NL
A	2 929	2 888	2 942	2 809	2 963	2 991	2 985	2 949	3 026	5 207	5 290	A
P	207	215	225	228	228	224	223	225	234	233	233	P
FIN	:	:	:	:	:	566	545	548	538	537	524	FIN
S	1 367	1 402	1 411	1 331	1 584	1 615	1 612	1 602	1 617	1 601	1 602	S
UK	22 622	22 622	22 622	22 622	22 622	22 622	:	:	9 432	11 214	11 214	UK
IS	:	248	274	306	308	391	421	:	296	294	294	IS
NO	:	:	:	:	:	:	:	:	:	1 235	1 235	NO
EEA	:	:	:	:	:	:	:	:	:	:	:	EEA
CH	93 998	93 958	93 913	93 885	93 895	:	:	3 837	93 945	94 073	94 073	CH
US	:	:	:	:	:	:	:	:	:	:	:	US
CA	:	:	:	:	:	:	:	:	:	:	:	CA
JP	:	:	:	:	:	:	:	:	:	:	:	JP

5A1GJ

Further reading: Tourism — annual statistics, Eurostat. Tourism in Europe — trends 1995–98, Eurostat. Tourism in Europe — key figures 1997–98, Eurostat. Statistics in focus (theme 4): tourism, Eurostat. Community methodology on tourism statistics, Eurostat.

Other collective establishments include holiday dwellings, tourist campsites, youth hostels, tourist dormitories, group accommodation, school dormitories and other similar accommodation.

Tourism demand can be measured from different aspects; the number of tourists signifies visitors who stay at least one night in a collective or private accommodation in the place/country visited; the number of tourism trips means overnight trips made by tourists. In terms of the purpose of a trip, there is only one main purpose, in the absence of which the trip would not have taken place. There are two main reasons to travel: business and professional; holidays, recreation or leisure. The latter include also visits to friends and relatives.

The principal mode of transport used is the means of transport used for the longest part of the trip. Tourism expenditure for tourist trips is the total consumption expenditure made by a visitor or on behalf of a visitor for and during his/her trip and stay at his/her destination. Tourism expenditure encompasses a wide variety of items, ranging from the purchase of consumer goods and services inherent in travel and stays to the purchase of small durable goods for personal use.

Average number of hotels and similar establishments per 100 000 inhabitants

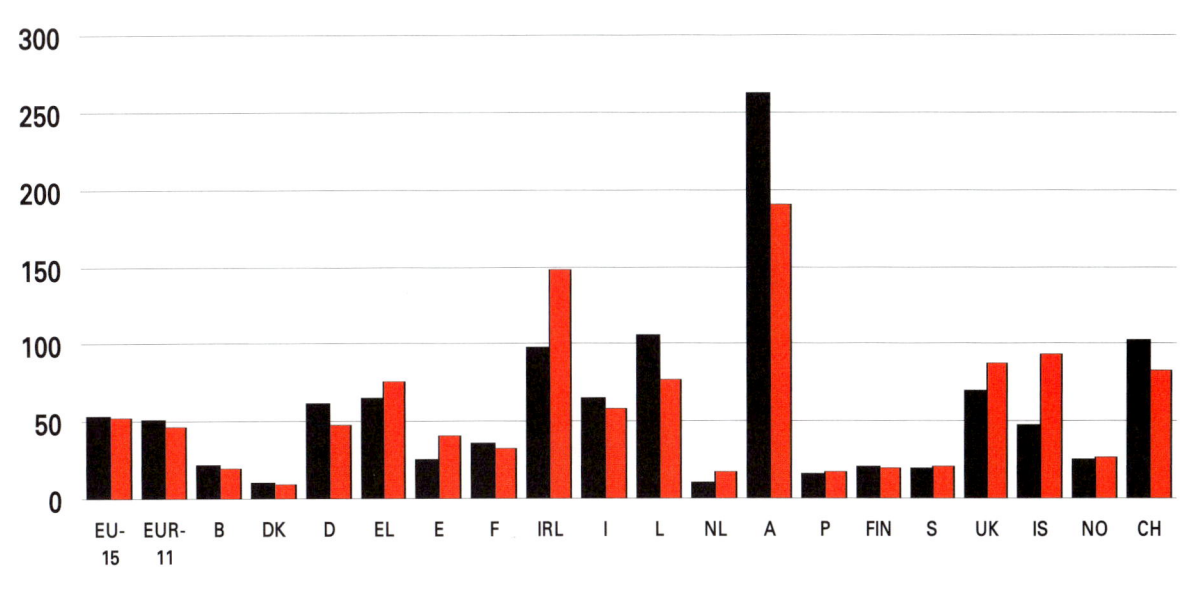

Black: 1989; colour: 1999.

Further reading: Tourism — annual statistics, Eurostat. Tourism in Europe — trends 1995–98, Eurostat. Tourism in Europe — key figures 1997–98, Eurostat. Statistics in focus (theme 4): tourism, Eurostat. Community methodology on tourism statistics, Eurostat.

Tourist accommodation, i.e. the supply of tourism services, is measured by the number of tourist accommodation establishments and the number of bed places in an establishment. The latter represents the number of people who can stay overnight in permanent beds, discounting any extra beds set up at the customers' request. The term 'bed place' applies to a single bed; a double bed is counted as two bed places. Data from 1996 and onwards are harmonised and comparable in the frame of the Council Directive 95/57/EC on tourism statistics. Data before 1996 are not fully comparable between countries because the statistical unit (local unit or enterprise) and coverage vary, but the trend over time can be compared.

4

3B9AD

Average number of travel agencies per 100 000 inhabitants. 1998

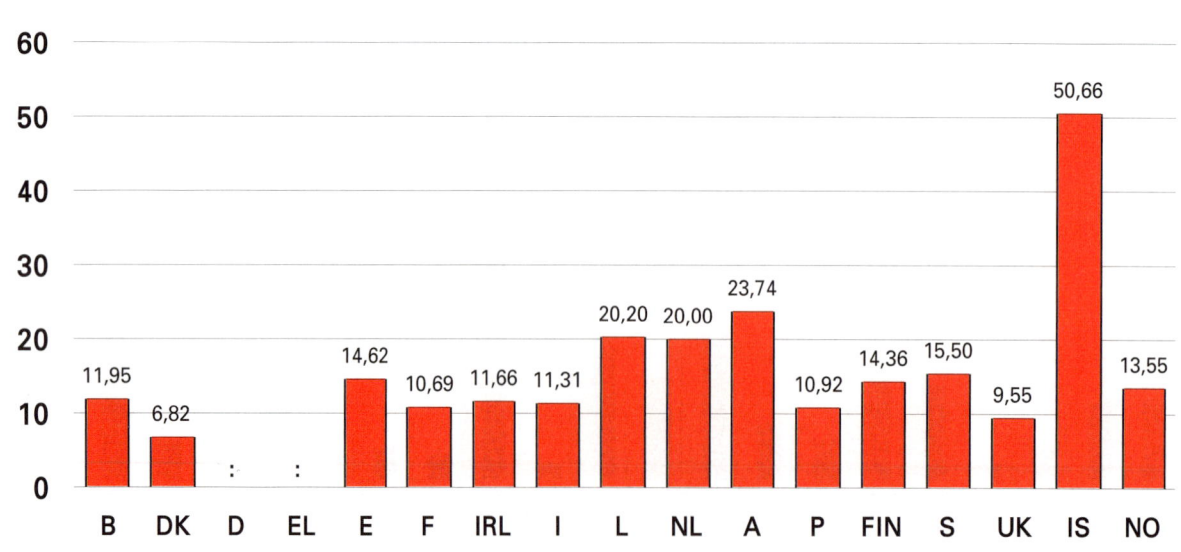

Further reading: Tourism — annual statistics, Eurostat. Tourism in Europe — trends 1995–98, Eurostat. Tourism in Europe — key figures 1997–98, Eurostat. Statistics in focus (theme 4): tourism, Eurostat. Community methodology on tourism statistics, Eurostat.

E, NO: 1994. A, I: 1995. NL, IS: 1998.

Tourist accommodation: number of bed places in hotels and similar establishments.

1 000s

	1989	1990	1991	1992	1993	1994	1995	1996	1997	1998	1999	
EU-15	7 648 *	7 819	8 055 *	8 335 *	8 570 *	8 685	8 613	8 939	8 960	9 013	9 462 *	EU-15
EUR-11	6 012 *	6 044	6 226 *	6 561 *	6 770 *	6 859	6 733	7 079	7 089	7 087	7 455 *	EUR-11
B	93	94	86	102	108	109	115	117	118	116	119	B
DK	85	88	93	96	97	99	99	60	59	60	61	DK
D	1 145	1 136	1 140	1 166	1 321	1 381	1 447	1 491	1 527	1 547	1 547 *	D
EL	424	438	459	476	500	508	557	572	577	585	585 *	EL
E	919	930	972	1 003	1 009	1 053	1 032	1 025	973	979	1 299	E
F	1 082	1 088	1 174	1 409	1 411	1 380	1 193	1 472	1 467	1 451	1 486	F
IRL	70	70	77	81	90	100	97	97	107	117	117 *	IRL
I	1 670	1 679	1 708	1 723	1 725	1 724	1 740	1 765	1 772	1 782	1 795	I
L	15 *	15 *	15 *	15 *	15 *	15	15	15	15	15	14	L
NL	109	111	113	116	133	138	143	143	158	169	170	NL
A	657	651	654	654	651	650	646	640	634	585	577	A
P	168	179	189	191	199	202	204	208	211	216	216 *	P
FIN	84	92	97	101	107	106	103	106	107	110	115	FIN
S	156	162	169	166	163	174	174	178	183	185	185	S
UK	971	1 086	1 108	1 036	1 040	1 045	1 050	1 050	1 052	1 096	1 176	UK
IS	6	6	7	7	8	8	10	10	11	12	12 *	IS
NO	105	113	117	120	123	129	131	134	136	137	137 *	NO
EEA	7 761 *	7 939 *	8 180 *	8 464 *	8 702 *	8 823	8 755	9 083	9 108	9 163	9 612 *	EEA
CH	271	270	267	266	265	265	265	262	261	260	260 *	CH
US	:	:	:	:	:	:	:	:	:	:	:	US
CA	:	:	:	:	:	:	:	:	:	:	:	CA
JP	:	:	:	:	:	:	:	:	:	:	:	JP

3B9AA

Further reading: Tourism — annual statistics, Eurostat. Tourism in Europe — trends 1995–98, Eurostat. Tourism in Europe — key figures 1997–98, Eurostat. Statistics in focus (theme 4): tourism, Eurostat. Community methodology on tourism statistics, Eurostat.

Average number of bed places per hotel and similar establishments

	1989	1990	1991	1992	1993	1994	1995	1996	1997	1998	1999	
EU-15	41,6 *	39,7 *	41,0 *	42,7 *	44,7 *	46,1	45,5	47,2	48,0	48,4	47,8 *	EU-15
EUR-11	44,4 *	45,3 *	46,3 *	49,2 *	51,2 *	52,1	50,6	53,2	54,4	55,2	54,7 *	EUR-11
B	43,1	44,1	44,2	53,2	57,3	55,9	56,4	56,9	58,8	58,2	59,2	B
DK	160,1	164,1	169,8	173,0	168,5	175,7	175,5	125,7	126,3	128,0	130,4	DK
D	30,2	30,3	29,7	31,4	36,1	37,0	37,9	38,7	39,2	39,8	39,8 *	D
EL	64,7	65,3	65,7	66,2	66,5	66,9	71,9	72,2	73,5	73,6	73,6	EL
E	93,0	98,5	101,2	102,5	103,7	104,7	99,0	108,1	129,4	129,9	80,0	E
F	53,5	53,1	57,0	67,1	68,3	70,2	59,2	70,6	72,4	74,2	76,7	F
IRL	20,3	20,2	19,6	18,3	18,6	19,9	19,2	18,4	20,8	22,7	22,7 *	IRL
I	45,0	46,1	47,7	48,7	49,5	49,9	50,7	51,8	52,4	53,1	53,8	I
L	37,7 *	36,9	37,7 *	37,4 *	38,5 *	39,5	40,0	40,1	43,0	43,0	44,5	L
NL	70,7	72,0	73,5	76,0	78,3	80,0	81,5	82,1	85,0	60,6	60,1	NL
A	32,9	33,5	34,0	34,5	34,8	35,3	35,7	35,6	35,8	37,1	37,5	A
P	99,0	102,0	105,6	107,4	111,9	117,2	117,7	119,4	119,5	122,9	123,1 *	P
FIN	81,4	84,0	86,7	91,9	111,6	111,9	109,5	110,6	111,6	112,3	114,4	FIN
S	92,7	93,9	94,5	95,3	95,2	93,5	95,0	96,0	95,9	97,6	97,5	S
UK	24,5	19,9	21,0	19,7	21,0	22,4	22,7	22,7	22,7	23,1	22,9	UK
IS	51,4	52,4	54,2	50,6	55,6	51,8	46,2	47,3	46,4	47,5	47,4 *	IS
NO	95,6	99,3	100,1	101,8	104,0	108,1	111,3	112,6	113,2	116,7	116,5 *	NO
EEA	41,9 *	40,0	41,4 *	43,0 *	45,1 *	46,5	45,9	47,6	48,4	48,8	48,2 *	EEA
CH	39,9	40,7	41,3	42,1	42,6	43,0	43,6	43,7	43,9	44,2	44,1 *	CH
US	:	:	:	:	:	:	:	:	:	:	:	US
CA	:	:	:	:	:	:	:	:	:	:	:	CA
JP	:	:	:	:	:	:	:	:	:	:	:	JP

3B9AB

Further reading: Tourism — annual statistics, Eurostat. Tourism in Europe — trends 1995–98, Eurostat. Tourism in Europe — key figures 1997–98, Eurostat. Statistics in focus (theme 4): tourism, Eurostat. Community methodology on tourism statistics, Eurostat.

4

Need more data on this topic? Ask your Data Shop

Bed places in hotels and similar establishments per 100 000 inhabitants. 1998

10000–

3000–10000

1500–3000

–1500

:

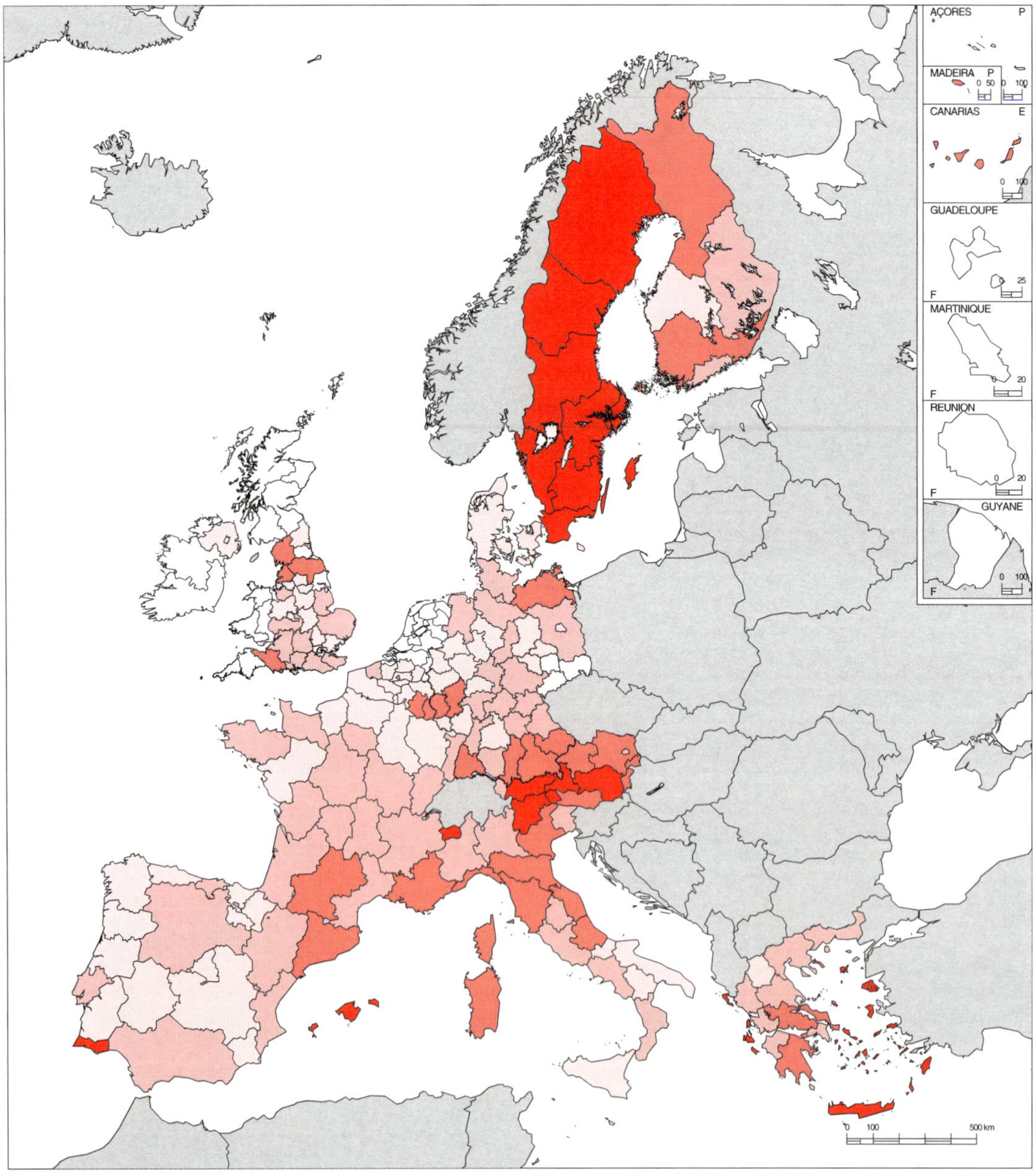

5A1GK

Further reading: Tourism — annual statistics, Eurostat. Tourism in Europe — trends 1995–98, Eurostat. Tourism in Europe — key figures 1997–98, Eurostat. Statistics in focus (theme 4): tourism, Eurostat. Community methodology on tourism statistics, Eurostat.

NUTS 2.

Nights spent by residents in collective tourist accommodation per 100 000 inhabitants

3B9BA

	1989	1990	1991	1992	1993	1994	1995	1996	1997	1998	1999	
EU-15	:	275 *	284 *	294 *	284 *	273 *	267 *	265	267	268	283	EU-15
EUR-11	:	258 *	268 *	276 *	272 *	274 *	262 *	258	259	268	279	EUR-11
B	240	241	221	146	142	140	140	141	135	129	129	B
DK	247	260	261	272	268	276	239	283	286	281	288	DK
D	268	279	311	349	341	343	295	292	285	288	300	D
EL	119	118	117	121	120	118	119 *	121	134	138	138 *	EL
E	158	172	184	170	176	181	185	183	188	203	206	E
F	271	273	268	272	271	271	267	259	266	270	292	F
IRL	:	228 *	227 *	226 *	224 *	223 *	284	221	237	243	244 *	IRL
I	282	295	304	306	295	304	303	302	303	310	318	I
L	77	79	94	87	97	83	56	52	58	62	60	L
NL	248	264	261	268	256	249	273	273	278	331	357	NL
A	301	302	314	312	305	303	304	291	291	302	315	A
P	126	133	136	139	142	139	141	146	148	154	151 *	P
FIN	204	206	195	185	193	199	208	210	220	226	229	FIN
S	339	318	270	275	281	322	334	326	331	333	354	S
UK	774	384	394	416	378	285	308	309	316	280	319	UK
IS	144	145	151	138	131	152	170	171	185	186	186	IS
NO	455	471	487	483	497	504	283	286	295	374	374	NO
EEA	:	277 *	286 *	296 *	287 *	275 *	267 *	265	267	269	287	EEA
CH	601	584	590	573	552	544	190	183	492	501	498	CH
US	:	:	:	:	:	:	:	:	:	:	:	US
CA	:	:	:	:	:	:	:	:	:	:	:	CA
JP	:	:	:	:	:	:	:	:	:	:	:	JP

Further reading: Tourism — annual statistics, Eurostat. Tourism in Europe — trends 1995–98, Eurostat. Tourism in Europe — key figures 1997–98, Eurostat. Statistics in focus (theme 4): tourism, Eurostat. Community methodology on tourism statistics, Eurostat.

Collective tourist accommodation refers to hotels and similar establishments, campsites, holiday dwellings and other collective accommodation.

Nights spent by non-residents in collective tourist accommodation per 100 000 inhabitants

3B9BB

	1989	1990	1991	1992	1993	1994	1995	1996	1997	1998	1999	
EU-15	:	:	:	:	:	176	166	165	172	179	194	EU-15
EUR-11	:	:	:	:	:	164	167	167	173	182	203	EUR-11
B	123	130	122	127	130	132	137	142	145	146	151	B
DK	167	182	203	225	203	205	185	206	207	194	188	DK
D	43	44	47	48	43	43	43	43	44	45	47	D
EL	343	365	301	365	359	396	366	344	391	412	414	EL
E	214	195	203	208	226	266	275	271	288	308	406	E
F	146	151	150	161	158	164	151	144	159	169	185	F
IRL	:	:	:	:	:	367	400	472	477	462	463	IRL
I	153	149	153	147	150	177	197	206	206	211	222	I
L	659	641	664	599	642	584	572	522	549	542	574	L
NL	97	111	115	119	113	117	128	123	138	157	176	NL
A	919	919	940	931	886	839	794	775	748	783	790	A
P	183	195	222	203	184	209	224	219	228	254	254	P
FIN	57	57	52	51	58	67	65	64	71	72	73	FIN
S	90	77	65	67	70	78	89	87	87	91	97	S
UK	:	:	:	289	295	204	131	134	135	134	128	UK
IS	233	260	263	257	259	269	304	311	329	363	368	IS
NO	:	:	:	:	:	167	168	166	165	178	175	NO
EEA	:	:	:	:	:	176	166	166	172	179	194	EEA
CH	543	553	549	541	532	520	267	249	442	454	447	CH
US	:	:	:	:	:	:	:	:	:	:	:	US
CA	:	:	:	:	:	:	:	:	:	:	:	CA
JP	:	:	:	:	:	:	:	:	:	:	:	JP

Further reading: Tourism — annual statistics, Eurostat. Tourism in Europe — trends 1995–98, Eurostat. Tourism in Europe — key figures 1997–98, Eurostat. Statistics in focus (theme 4): tourism, Eurostat. Community methodology on tourism statistics, Eurostat.

Collective tourist accommodation refers to hotels and similar establishments, campsites, holiday dwellings and other collective accommodation. UK 1995–99: without holiday dwellings.

Total nights spent in collective tourist accommodation per 100 000 inhabitants. 1999

600-

300-600

200-300

-200

:

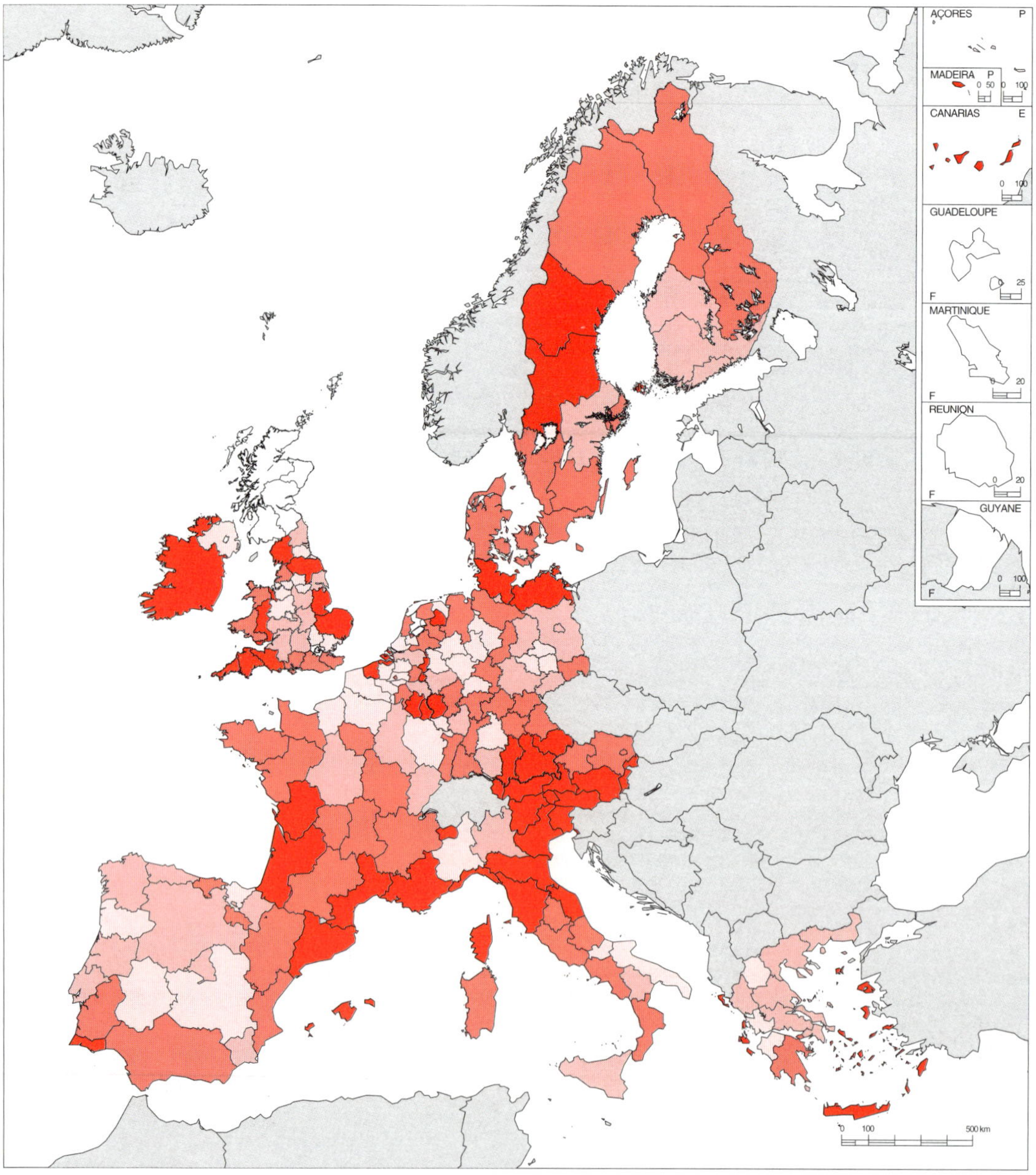

5A1GL

AÇORES P

MADEIRA P
0 50 100

CANARIAS E
0 100

GUADELOUPE
F 0 25

MARTINIQUE
F 0 20

REUNION
F 0 20

GUYANE
F 0 100

0 100 500 km

Further reading: Tourism — annual statistics, Eurostat. Tourism in Europe — trends 1995–98, Eurostat. Tourism in Europe — key figures 1997–98, Eurostat. Statistics in focus (theme 4): tourism, Eurostat. Community methodology on tourism statistics, Eurostat.

NUTS 2. NUTS 1: IRL.

eurostat

Demand for accommodation by tourists includes all types of accommodation: hotels and similar establishments, camping sites, holiday dwellings, youth hostels and other collective accommodation. Data from 1996 and onwards are harmonised and comparable in the frame of the Council Directive 95/57/EC on tourism statistics. Data before 1996 are not fully comparable between countries because the statistical unit (local unit or enterprise) and coverage vary, but the trend over time can be compared.

Nights spent by residents in collective tourist accommodation per 100 000 inhabitants

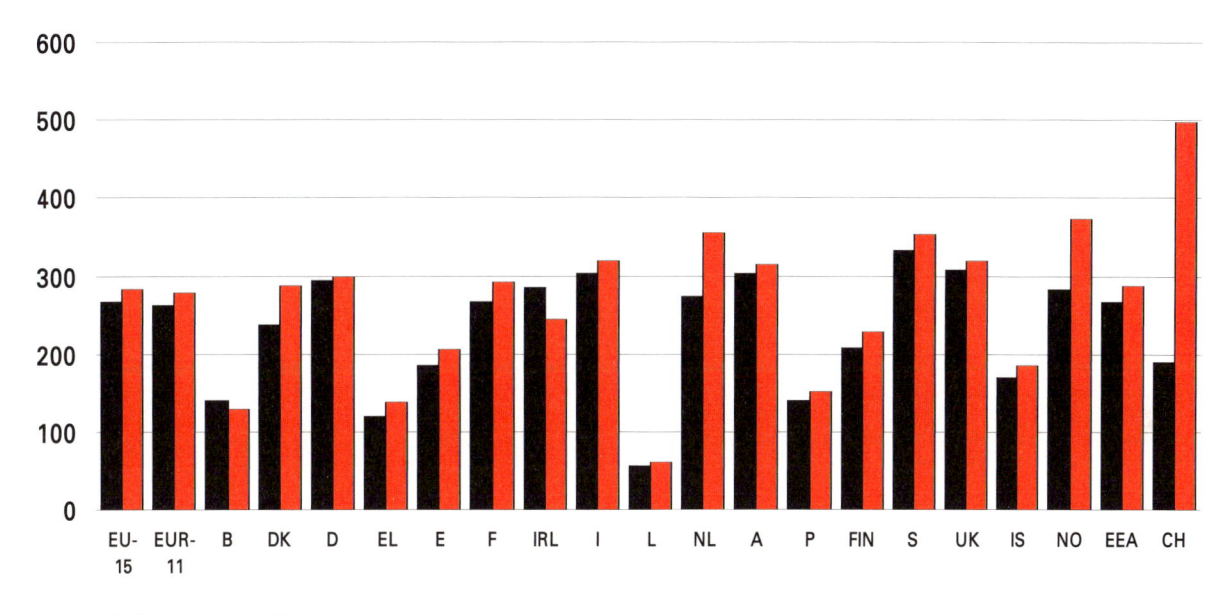

Black: 1995; colour: 1999.

Further reading: Tourism — annual statistics, Eurostat. Tourism in Europe — trends 1995–98, Eurostat. Tourism in Europe — key figures 1997–98, Eurostat. Statistics in focus (theme 4): tourism, Eurostat. Community methodology on tourism statistics, Eurostat.

Collective tourist accommodation refers to hotels and similar establishments, campsites, holiday dwellings and other collective accommodation.

Nights spent by non-residents in collective tourist accommodation per 100 000 inhabitants

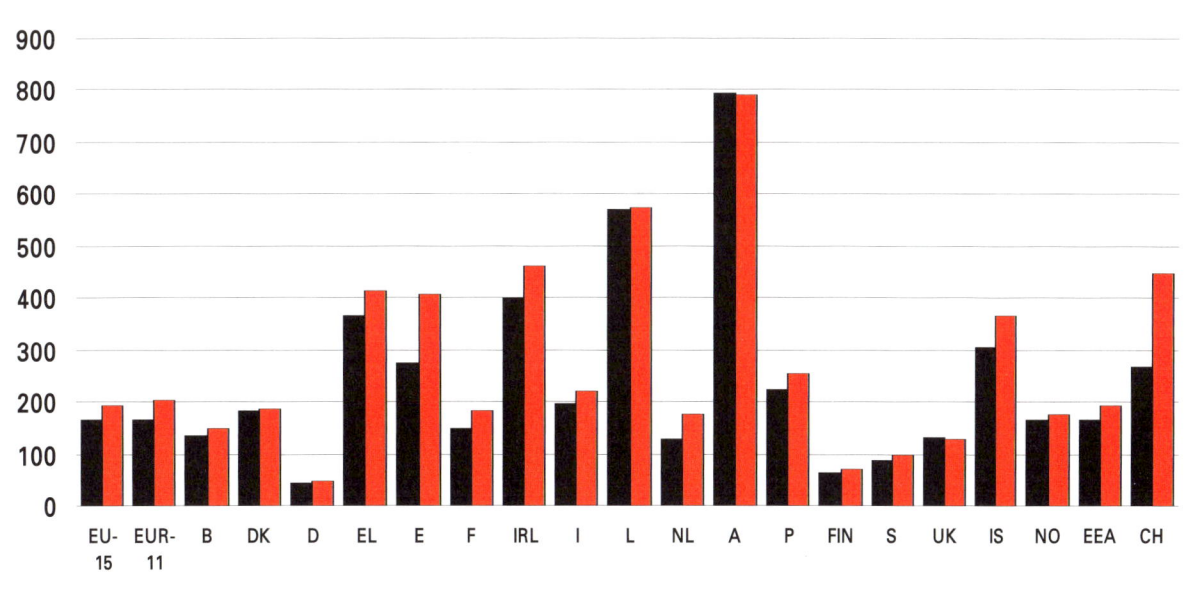

Black: 1995; colour: 1999.

Further reading: Tourism — annual statistics, Eurostat. Tourism in Europe — trends 1995–98, Eurostat. Tourism in Europe — key figures 1997–98, Eurostat. Statistics in focus (theme 4): tourism, Eurostat. Community methodology on tourism statistics, Eurostat.

Collective tourist accommodation refers to hotels and similar establishments, campsites, holiday dwellings and other collective accommodation.

eurostat

Need longer time series? Ask your Data Shop

EUROSTAT YEARBOOK 2001

409

Utilisation of bed places in hotels and similar establishments. 1999. %

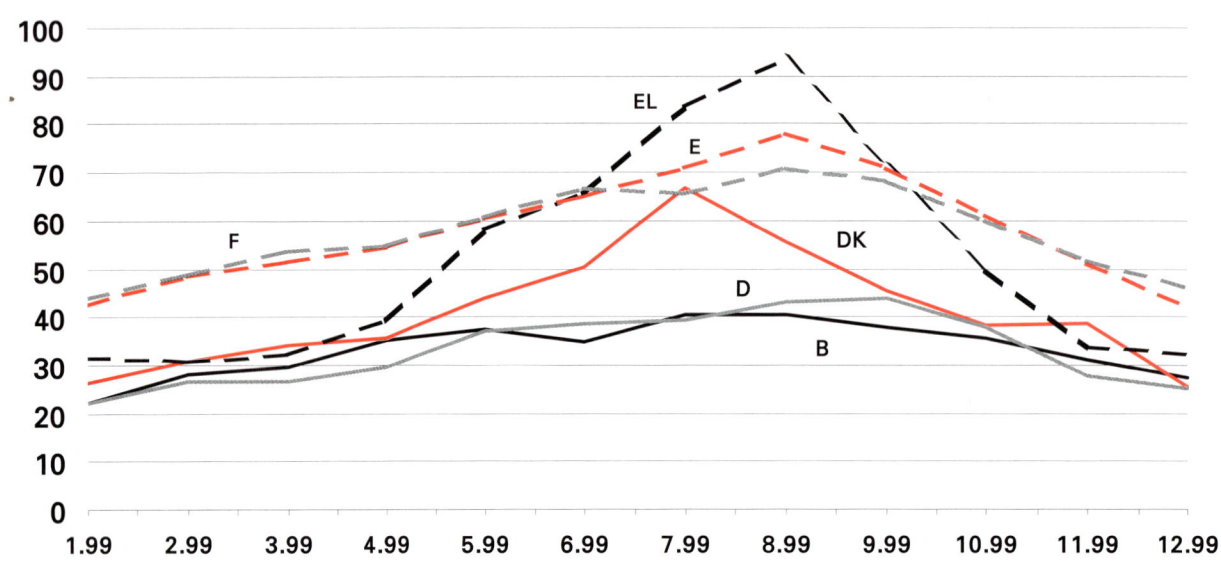

5A1GN

Further reading: Tourism — annual statistics, Eurostat. Tourism in Europe — trends
1995–98, Eurostat. Tourism in Europe — key figures 1997–98, Eurostat. Statistics in focus (theme 4): tourism, Eurostat. Community
methodology on tourism statistics, Eurostat.

Utilisation of bed places in hotels and similar establishments. 1999. %

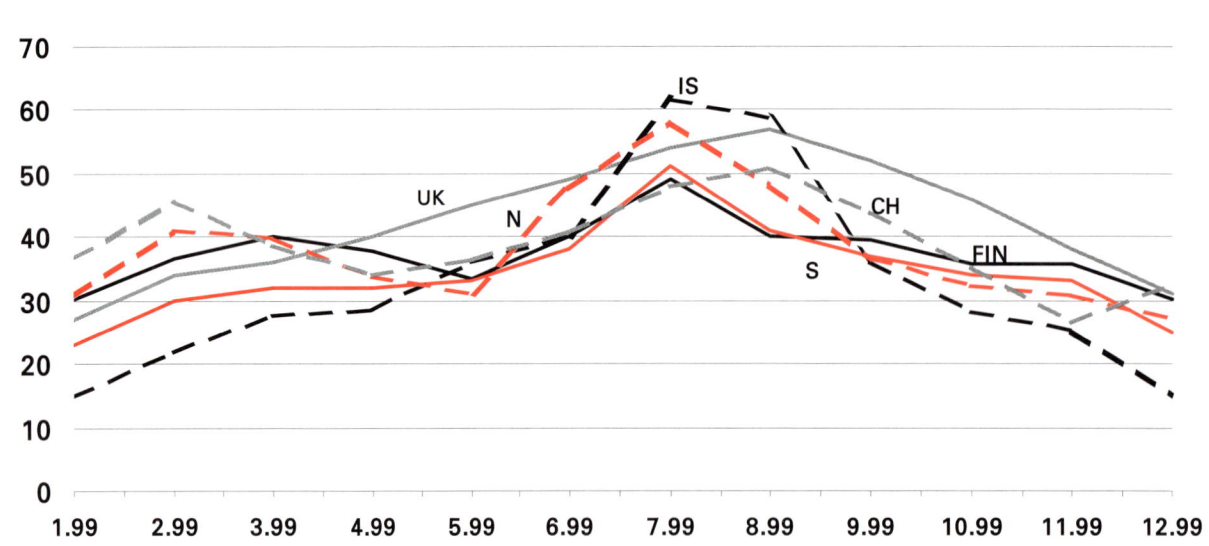

5A1XX

Further reading: Tourism — annual statistics, Eurostat. Tourism in Europe — trends
1995–98, Eurostat. Tourism in Europe — key figures 1997–98, Eurostat. Statistics in focus (theme 4): tourism, Eurostat. Community
methodology on tourism statistics, Eurostat.

More data on this in Eurostat's database

Available statistics include variables on capacity of tourist accommodation establishments, occupancy in these establishments and data on residents' tourism demand.

➤ ➤ ➤ **DOMAIN TOUR IN DATABASE NEW CRONOS**

Utilisation of bed places in hotels and similar establishments. 1999. %

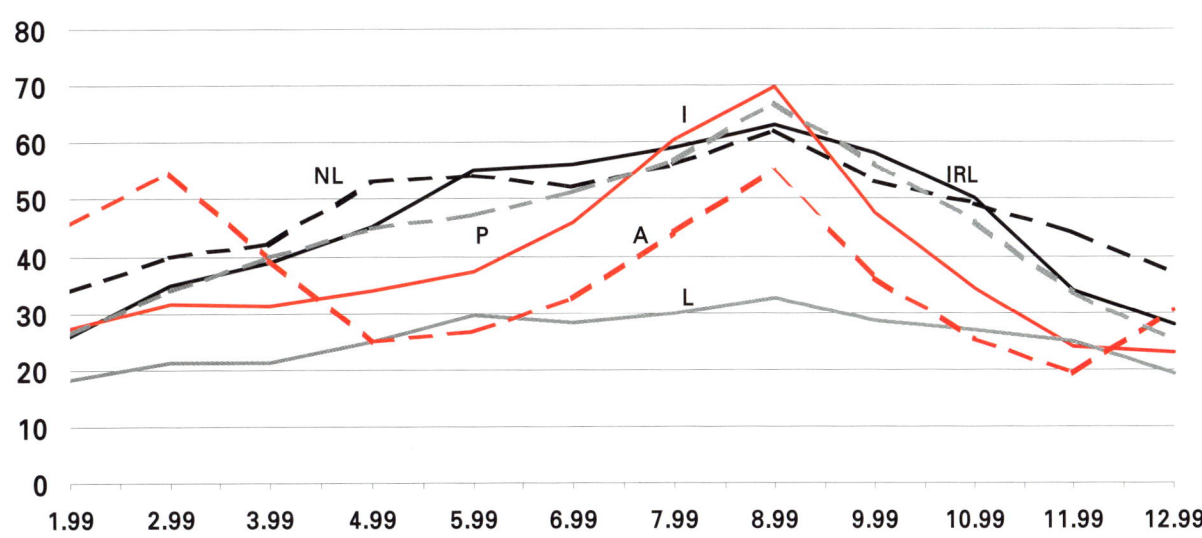

5A1YY

Further reading: Tourism — annual statistics, Eurostat. Tourism in Europe — trends 1995–98, Eurostat. Tourism in Europe — key figures 1997–98, Eurostat. Statistics in focus (theme 4): tourism, Eurostat. Community methodology on tourism statistics, Eurostat.

Total length of motorways in km

	1989	1990	1991	1992	1993	1994	1995	1996	1997	1998	1999	
EU-15	37 728	39 303	40 761	42 743	43 504	44 151	45 330	46 333	:	:	:	**EU-15**
B	1 631	1 666	1 650	1 667	1 686	1 665	1 666	1 674	1 679	1 682	:	**B**
DK	601	601	653	696	737	786	830	880	855	861	:	**DK**
D	10 672	10 809	10 955	11 013	11 080	11 143	11 190	11 300	11 309	11 427	:	**D**
EL	120	190	225	280	330	380	420	470	500	500	:	**EL**
E	3 785	4 693	5 235	6 486	6 577	6 485	6 962	7 293	7 750	8 257	:	**E**
F	6 680	6 824	7 080	7 408	7 614	7 956	8 275	8 300	8 864	9 303	:	**F**
IRL	8	26	32	32	50	56	70	80	94	94	:	**IRL**
I	6 193	6 193	6 301	6 289	6 401	6 401	6 401	6 439	6 445	6 453	:	**I**
L	78	78	78	95	100	121	123	115	115	115	:	**L**
NL	2 061	2 092	2 118	2 134	2 150	2 167	2 300	2 360	2 360	2 360	:	**NL**
A	1 406	1 470	1 532	1 554	1 567	1 589	1 596	1 607	1 613	1 613	:	**A**
P	256	316	474	520	579	587	687	710	797	1 252	:	**P**
FIN	215	225	249	318	337	388	394	431	444	467	:	**FIN**
S	929	939	968	1 005	1 044	1 141	1 231	1 330	1 423	1 428	:	**S**
UK	3 093	3 181	3 211	3 246	3 252	3 286	3 308	3 344	3 412	3 421	:	**UK**
IS	-	-	-	-	-	-	-	-	-	-	:	**IS**
NO	336	355	379	395	437	437	512	527	560	570	:	**NO**
CH	1 495	1 495	1 502	1 515	1 530	1 533	1 540	1 594	1 613	1 638	:	**CH**
US	:	84 862	85 258	86 818	87 447	87 814	88 035	88 588	89 203	:	:	**US**
CA	:	14 985	15 516	:	:	:	16 571	:	:	:	:	**CA**
JP	:	:	:	5 054	5 410	5 568	5 700	5 900	:	:	:	**JP**

2A5AB

Further reading: EU transport in figures, latest issue. DG TREN and Eurostat. Panorama of transport, latest issue. Eurostat.

JP: not including motorways constructed by local authorities.

Total length of railway lines in km

	1989	1990	1991	1992	1993	1994	1995	1996	1997	1998	1999	
EU-15	159 111	159 531	159 521	157 912	155 876	156 764	156 147	155 363	152 826	153 640	:	**EU-15**
B	3 513	3 479	3 466	3 432	3 410	3 396	3 368	3 380	3 422	3 410	:	**B**
DK	2 344	2 344	2 344	2 344	2 349	2 349	2 349	2 349	2 232	2 232	:	**DK**
D	41 080	40 981	41 113	40 815	40 397	41 401	41 719	40 826	38 385	38 126	:	**D**
EL	2 479	2 484	2 484	2 484	2 474	2 474	2 474	2 474	2 503	2 503	:	**EL**
E	12 565	12 560	12 570	13 041	12 601	12 646	12 280	12 284	12 294	12 303	:	**E**
F	34 469	34 260	33 990	33 555	32 579	32 275	31 939	31 852	31 821	31 727	:	**F**
IRL	1 944	1 944	1 944	1 944	1 944	1 944	1 947	1 945	1 908	1 909	:	**IRL**
I	16 030	16 086	16 066	16 112	15 942	16 002	15 998	16 014	16 030	16 041	:	**I**
L	272	271	271	275	275	275	275	275	275	274	:	**L**
NL	2 810	2 780	2 780	2 753	2 757	2 757	2 739	2 739	2 805	2 808	:	**NL**
A	5 641	5 624	5 623	5 605	5 600	5 636	5 672	5 672	5 672	5 643	:	**A**
P	3 126	3 126	3 117	3 054	3 063	3 070	2 850	2 850	2 856	2 794	:	**P**
FIN	5 884	5 867	5 874	5 874	5 885	5 880	5 880	5 881	5 865	5 867	:	**FIN**
S	10 022	10 801	10 970	9 781	9 746	9 661	9 782	9 821	9 759	11 156	:	**S**
UK	16 932	16 924	16 909	16 843	16 854	16 998	16 875	17 001	16 999	16 847	:	**UK**
IS	-	-	-	-	-	-	-	-	-	-	:	**IS**
LI	19	19	19	19	19	19	19	19	19	19	:	**LI**
NO	4 044	4 044	4 027	4 027	4 023	4 023	4 023	4 021	4 021	4 021	:	**NO**
CH	2 994	2 978	2 982	2 985	2 983	2 983	2 987	2 989	:	:	:	**CH**
US	:	192 732	187 691	:	177 712	175 953	174 234	170 235	164 359	:	:	**US**
CA	:	:	85 563	85 191	84 648	83 351	80 326	:	:	:	:	**CA**
JP	:	:	:	30 201	30 190	30 178	30 178	:	:	:	:	**JP**

2A5AC

Further reading: EU transport in figures, latest issue. DG TREN and Eurostat. Panorama of transport, latest issue. Eurostat.

'Victory is the beautiful bright coloured flower. Transport is the stem without which it could never have blossomed'. Winston S. Churchill

Even though Mr Churchill was referring to a military victory, the phrase could apply to the success achieved in increasing the standard of living in Europe and one of the major reasons behind this success: transport.

At the beginning of the 20th century, goods transport in Europe was dominated by waterways and by railways. The railway network was larger then, than it is today — which is impressive considering that the first railway was not opened until 1822. For passenger transport, water and rail were also dominant for long journeys, whereas for short journeys, walking and horse transport were predominant.

During the last 100 years, the shares between the modes of transport have changed and the volumes increased tremendously. Waterways and railways still play an important role, roughly 15 % of all tonnage transported, but the dominating mode of transport today is definitely road transport with its flexibility and individualism. About 80 % of all tonnage transported (44 % of all tonne-kilometres) and of all passenger-kilometres are by road. The number of passenger cars has increased to more than 170 million. The downside of this is that even though fatalities are decreasing, more than 40 000 people are killed in road accidents each year. Air transport is also increasing fast, and today more passenger-kilometres are by air than by rail. In the future we can wonder if environmental and safety issues will change the transport market and if 'virtual transport' will partly replace 'factual transport'.

More data on this in Eurostat's database

This domain presents aggregated data from the common questionnaire (Eurostat — UNECE — ECMT) as well as detailed annual and monthly freight transport data from Council Directive 80/1177/EEC of 4 December 1980.

➤ ➤ ➤ **DOMAIN RAIL IN DATABASE NEW CRONOS**

Total inland transport per mode: EEA and Switzerland

1980

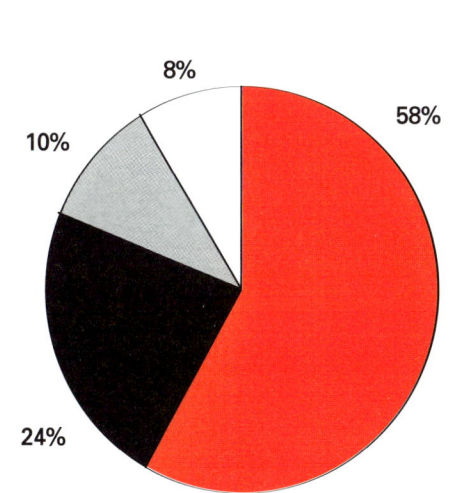

1998

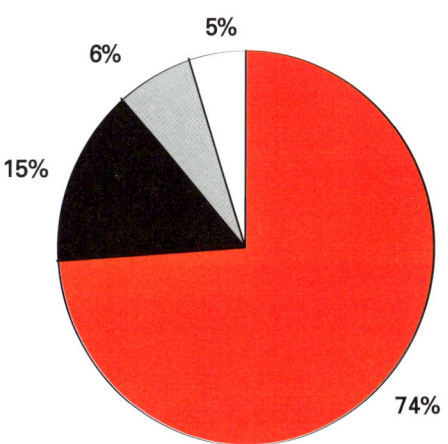

Black: rail; colour: road; grey: inland waterways; white: oil pipelines.

Further reading: EU transport in figures, latest issue. DG TREN and Eurostat. Panorama of transport, latest issue. Eurostat.

Need an update for this indicator? Ask your Data Shop

413

Passenger cars per 1 000 inhabitants

	1989	1990	1991	1992	1993	1994	1995	1996	1997	1998	1999	
EU-15	390	402	410	410	418	423	432	437	447	454	:	**EU-15**
B	376	388	397	400	408	423	428	435	434	440	:	**B**
DK	311	309	309	310	312	310	320	330	337	343	:	**DK**
D	479	485	489	447	478	488	495	500	504	508	:	**D**
EL	159	171	173	177	189	199	211	224	238	254	:	**EL**
E	296	309	322	336	344	351	362	378	389	408	:	**E**
F	408	415	417	419	423	430	478	477	445	456	:	**F**
IRL	222	227	237	242	249	262	264	270	310	309	:	**IRL**
I	463	483	503	518	521	540	553	571	535	545	:	**I**
L	485	503	519	532	523	540	559	559	562	572	:	**L**
NL	356	368	370	373	376	383	381	370	372	376	:	**NL**
A	379	387	397	410	421	433	447	460	469	481	:	**A**
P	236	258	281	309	334	357	378	401	297	321	:	**P**
FIN	385	389	384	384	370	368	372	379	379	392	:	**FIN**
S	421	421	420	414	409	409	411	413	419	428	:	**S**
UK	359	375	383	382	371	376	382	385	398	404	:	**UK**
IS	490	468	467	458	439	436	445	463	487	510	:	**IS**
LI	572	582	590	593	586	596	609	620	636	639	:	**LI**
NO	382	380	379	378	379	381	387	379	399	402	:	**NO**
CH	436	445	450	450	448	453	459	462	468	475	:	**CH**
US	:	:	:	511	508	505	503	506	:	:	:	**US**
CA	:	:	:	:	:	:	445	:	:	:	:	**CA**
JP	:	:	:	313	327	341	356	375	:	:	:	**JP**

5A1FK

Further reading: EU transport in figures, latest issue. DG TREN and Eurostat. Panorama of transport, latest issue. Eurostat.   UK: GB only.

4

Goods transport by road (million tonne-kilometres)

	1989	1990	1991	1992	1993	1994	1995	1996	1997	1998	1999	
EU-15	909 900	929 200	1 007 300	1 021 100	1 020 400	1 091 600	1 142 600	1 148 000	1 200 600	1 254 900	:	**EU-15**
B	23 900	25 000	27 000	28 500	29 700	32 900	34 600	31 400	34 100	35 000	:	**B**
DK	13 400	13 700	13 900	14 100	13 300	14 500	14 700	14 500	14 700	15 300	:	**DK**
D	181 200	182 800	250 200	252 400	251 500	272 500	279 700	280 700	301 800	315 900	:	**D**
EL	10 100	10 900	11 400	11 900	12 900	12 800	14 800	15 900	16 500	17 000	:	**EL**
E	76 200	78 900	82 600	85 900	88 000	92 200	94 600	92 500	96 200	103 000	:	**E**
F	187 600	190 500	195 100	198 700	191 200	210 700	232 800	229 200	237 200	245 400	:	**F**
IRL	5 400	5 100	5 100	5 200	5 100	5 300	5 400	5 500	5 700	5 900	:	**IRL**
I	174 300	177 900	180 200	184 900	179 400	187 200	194 800	198 300	207 200	219 800	:	**I**
L	1 200	1 300	1 500	1 700	1 800	1 700	1 900	1 900	2 000	2 100	:	**L**
NL	30 100	31 800	35 400	39 600	39 500	40 700	42 200	43 900	45 000	46 500	:	**NL**
A	13 200	13 300	13 500	13 700	14 200	14 700	14 900	15 500	15 700	16 100	:	**A**
P	11 800	12 200	12 200	12 100	11 400	13 000	13 000	13 200	13 500	14 200	:	**P**
FIN	24 900	26 300	26 000	24 700	25 000	25 700	23 200	24 100	25 400	26 500	:	**FIN**
S	24 600	26 500	25 000	24 300	25 900	27 000	29 300	31 200	33 100	32 700	:	**S**
UK	132 000	133 000	128 200	123 400	131 500	140 700	146 700	150 200	152 500	159 500	:	**UK**
IS	:	:	:	:	:	:	:	:	:	:	:	**IS**
NO	:	:	:	:	:	:	:	13 100	14 700	15 347	:	**NO**
CH	:	:	:	:	:	:	:	:	:	:	:	**CH**
US	:	:	:	:	1 257 100	1 325 700	1 344 700	1 419 100	1 534 500	:	:	**US**
CA	:	:	:	:	:	101 870	110 011	121 133	:	:	:	**CA**
JP	:	:	:	:	:	:	:	272 000	:	:	:	**JP**

5A1GB

Further reading: EU transport in figures, latest issue. DG TREN and Eurostat. Panorama of transport, latest issue. Eurostat.

 eurostat

Goods transport by rail (million tonne-kilometres)

	1989	1990	1991	1992	1993	1994	1995	1996	1997	1998	1999	
EU-15	216 046	215 227		233 007	219 332	205 030	218 123	219 892	220 325	237 294	239 711	:	EU-15
B	8 066	8 370	8 150	8 070	7 570	8 099	7 300	7 265	7 465	7 600	:	B
DK	1 689	1 742	1 872	1 883	1 814	2 040	1 900	1 770	1 619	2 066	:	DK
D	62 064	61 900		80 300	69 800	64 900	69 100	68 800	67 700	72 700	73 600	:	D
EL	640	609	560	527	503	324	324	337	317	322	:	EL
E	11 704	11 149	10 316	9 600	8 100	8 928	10 419	10 219	11 490	11 800	:	E
F	52 449	50 667	51 480	49 536	45 033	48 750	47 900	49 512	53 855	53 965	:	F
IRL	556	589	600	633	575	569	569	570	522	466	:	IRL
I	18 702	19 476	19 654	19 934	18 427	20 500	22 200	21 270	23 000	22 450	:	I
L	607	615	600	597	607	645	529	570	566	561	:	L
NL	3 108	3 070	3 000	2 760	2 680	2 830	3 097	3 123	3 400	3 778	:	NL
A	11 969	12 797	12 975	12 325	12 000	13 164	13 900	13 380	14 195	14 714	:	A
P	1 579	1 459	1 760	1 767	1 666	1 635	2 019	1 859	2 247	2 048	:	P
FIN	7 957	8 357	7 630	7 850	9 260	9 948	9 293	8 806	9 856	9 855	:	FIN
S	18 214	18 441	18 810	18 542	18 130	18 591	18 542	18 800	19 113	19 086	:	S
UK	16 742	15 986	15 300	15 508	13 765	13 000	13 100	15 144	16 949	17 400	:	UK
IS	.	.	.	.	.	.	.	.	.	.	:	IS
NO	:	:	:	:	:	2 678	2 715	2 636	2 399	2 421	:	NO
CH	:	8 958	8 826	8 316	7 964	8 725	8 796	7 957	8 166	:	:	CH
US	:	:	:	:	:	:	1 906 300	1 979 719	1 969 428	:	:	US
CA	:	:	:	:	:	256 337	248 377	238 590	:	:	:	CA
JP	:	:	:	:	25 433	24 493	25 101	24 968	:	:	:	JP

Further reading: EU transport in figures, latest issue. DG TREN and Eurostat. Panorama of transport, latest issue. Eurostat.

5A1FL

Goods transport by inland waterways (million tonne-kilometres)

Goods transport by oil pipelines (million tonne-kilometres)

	1994	1995	1996	1997	1998	1994	1995	1996	1997	1998	
EU-15	111 340	113 904	111 171	118 270	120 897	84 996	84 897	84 800	85 500	87 220	EU-15
B	5 575	5 806	5 794	6 120	6 300	1 370	1 370	1 500	1 500	1 570	B
DK	-	-	-	-	-	3 106	2 890	3 500	3 800	3 900	DK
D	61 800	64 000	61 300	62 150	64 270	16 800	16 600	14 500	13 200	14 850	D
EL	-	-	-	-	-	-	-	-	-	-	EL
E	-	-	-	-	-	5 479	5 887	6 100	6 500	6 900	E
F	5 610	5 864	5 740	5 682	6 207	22 187	22 200	21 900	22 100	21 600	F
IRL	-	-	-	-	-	-	-	-	-	-	IRL
I	108	135	125	201	126	12 500	12 800	12 600	13 200	13 000	I
L	310	305	320	320	300	-	-	-	-	-	L
NL	36 038	35 501	35 520	41 020	40 714	5 621	5 280	6 000	6 000	6 000	NL
A	1 820	2 046	2 101	2 087	2 280	6 990	6 770	7 100	8 000	8 200	A
P	-	-	-	-	-	-	-	-	-	-	P
FIN	:	604	571	500	500	-	-	-	-	-	FIN
S	-	-	-	-	-	-	-	-	-	-	S
UK	200	200	190	190	200	10 943	11 100	11 600	11 200	11 200	UK
IS	-	-	-	-	-	-	-	-	-	-	IS
NO	-	-	-	-	-	6 209	:	:	:	:	NO
CH	49	:	:	:	:	1 211	1 249	1 203	:	:	CH
US	1 189 759	1 179 280	1 116 440	:	:	863 442	904 030	877 604	:	:	US
CA	:	34 000	:	:	:	:	150 000	:	:	:	CA
JP	-	-	-	-	-	:	:	:	:	:	JP

5A1FM

5A1FN

Further reading: EU transport in figures, latest issue. DG TREN and Eurostat. Carriage of goods: inland waterways, latest edition. Eurostat. Panorama of transport, latest issue. Eurostat.

Only the countries with an international or transit transport exceeding one million tonnes report their data to Eurostat. EL, IRL, L, P, FIN, S, IS: report to Eurostat as not having oil pipelines.

4

Inland goods transport (1 000 million tonne-kilometres). EEA and Switzerland

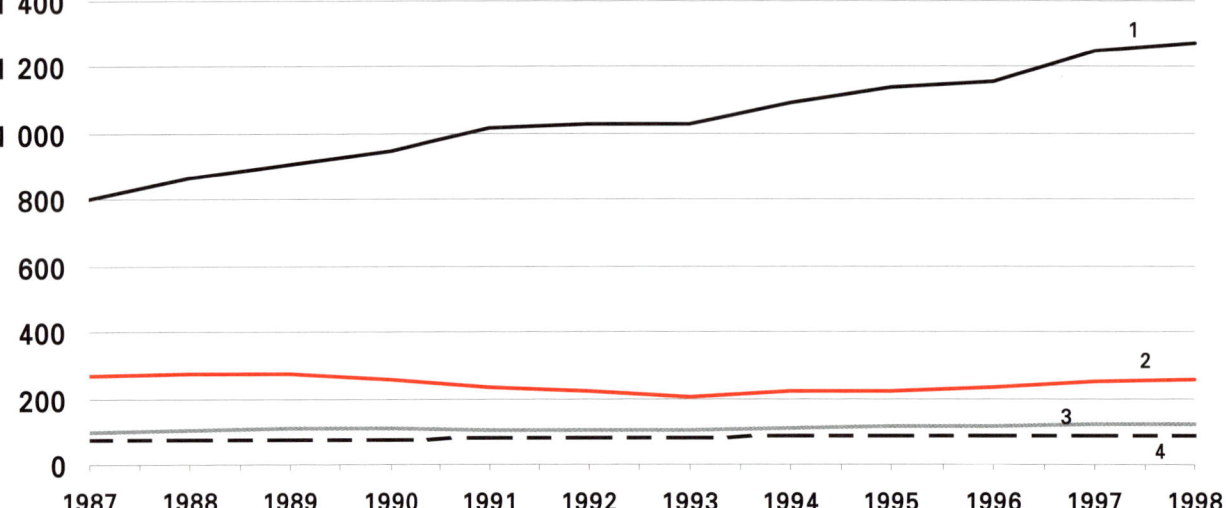

1. Rail; 2. Road; 3. Inland waterways; 4. Oil pipelines.

Further reading: EU transport in figures, latest issue. DG TREN and Eurostat. Panorama of transport, latest issue. Eurostat.

More data on this in Eurostat's database

This domain gives information on aggregated data from the common questionnaire (Eurostat — UNECE — ECMT) and detailed annual, quarterly and monthly freight transport data from Council Directive 80/1119/EEC of 17 November 1980.

➤ ➤ ➤ DOMAIN INLANDWW IN DATABASE NEW CRONOS

Worldwide commercial space launches

	1990	1991	1992	1993	1994	1995	1996	1997	1998
Space launches total	13	12	14	9	14	19	21	37	36
USA	7	6	6	3	4	8	8	16	17
Europe (ESA)	5	6	6	6	8	8	9	11	9
Russia	0	0	0	0	0	0	2	7	5
China	1	0	2	0	2	3	2	3	4
Ukraine	0	0	0	0	0	0	0	0	1

The data in this chart apply only to commercial, international competed (non-captive), satellite launches in the medium-to-large vehicle class. ESA (European Space Agency): Members: EEA (except EL, L, LI and IS) and CH. *Source:* US Department of Transportation.

5A1FQ

5A1FR

	Sea transport of goods. Million tonnes					Air transport of goods. 1 000 tonnes					
	1994	**1995**	**1996**	**1997**	**1998**	**1994**	**1995**	**1996**	**1997**	**1998**	
EU-15	2 479	2 541	2 515	:	:	:	:	:	:	:	**EU-15**
B	166	164	156	159	168	375	430	451	530	590	**B**
DK	54	58	61	64 *	:	:	:	:	:	:	**DK**
D	193	198	201	213	217	1 722	1 808	1 877	2 019	2 000	**D**
EL	60	68	73	:	:	82	:	:	106	101	**EL**
E	249	278	270	283 *	:	174	244	281	309	309	**E**
F	303	297	295	305	319	1 006	1 034	1 103	1 029	1 069	**F**
IRL	30	32	32	29	31	43	58	39	70	59	**IRL**
I	250	252	231	:	:	438	459	475	454	446	**I**
L	-	-	-	-	-	242 *	287 *	281 *	340 *	382	**L**
NL	375	380	382	402	405	842	983	1 084	1 163	1 174	**NL**
A	-	-	-	-	-	85	96	98	109	111	**A**
P	51	54	49	55	58	94	102	103	105 *	:	**P**
FIN	83	82	82	86 *	:	:	:	:	92	94	**FIN**
S	127	131	130	150	156	152 *	169 *	200 *	227 *	:	**S**
UK	538	548	554	559	569	1 486	1 584	1 657	1 847	1 990	**UK**
IS	:	5	5	5 *	:	17 *	19 *	23 *	26 *	:	**IS**
NO	:	238	257	270 *	:	:	:	:	44	47	**NO**
CH	:	:	:	:	:	366	382	390	360	357	**CH**

Further reading: International transport by air, latest issue. Eurostat. EU transport in figures, latest issue. DG TREN and Eurostat. Panorama of transport, latest issue. Eurostat.

5A1FS

5A1FT

EEA sea transport of goods per country. 1998

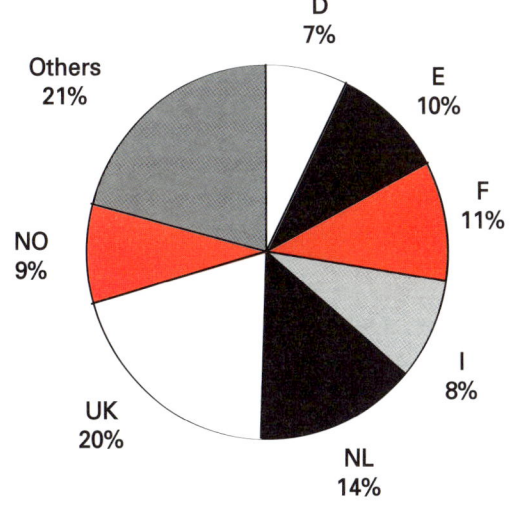

EEA air transport of passengers per country. 1998

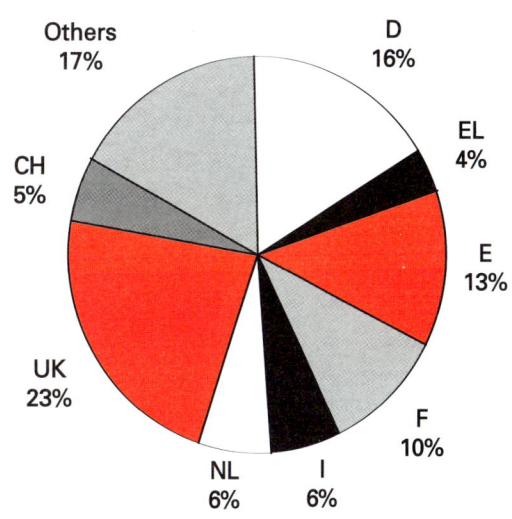

Further reading: International transport by air, latest issue. Eurostat. EU transport in figures, latest issue. DG TREN and Eurostat. Panorama of transport, latest issue. Eurostat.

Passenger transport (1 000 million passenger kilometres). EEA and Switzerland

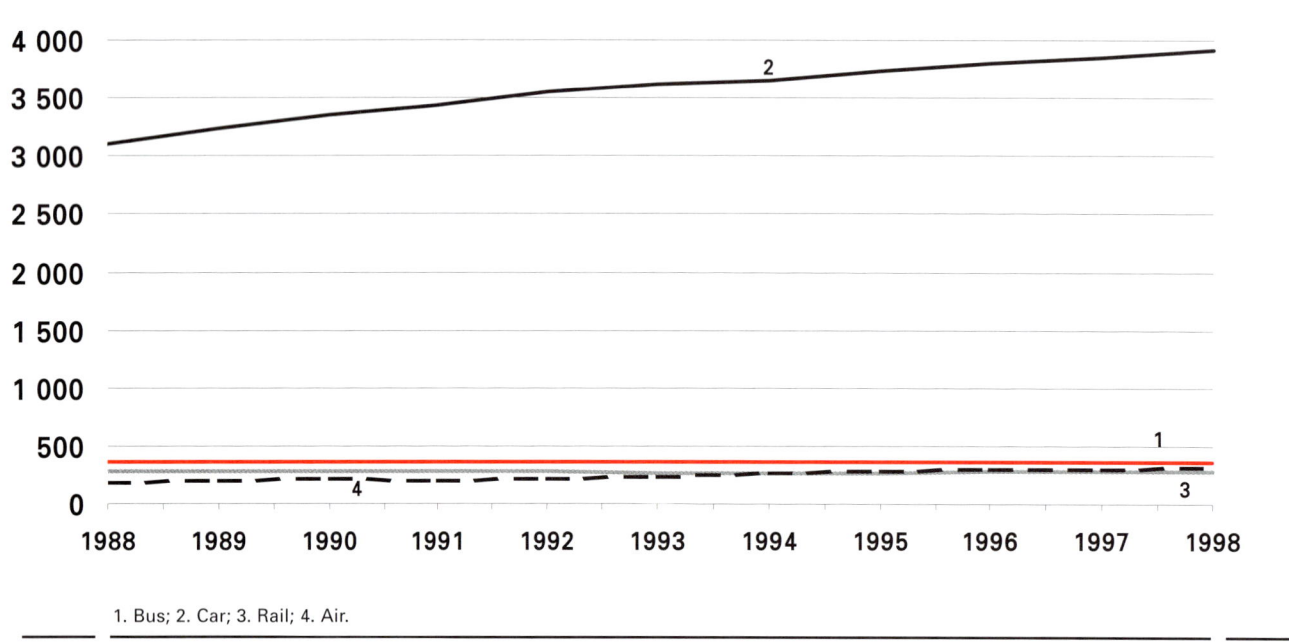

1. Bus; 2. Car; 3. Rail; 4. Air.

5A1FU

Further reading: EU transport in figures, latest issue. DG TREN and Eurostat. Panorama of transport, latest issue. Eurostat.

4

Air transport of passengers. Million

Bus transport of passengers. Million passenger kilometres

	1994	1995	1996	1997	1998	1994	1995	1996	1997	1998	
EU-15	:	:	:	478	517	390 262	401 053	404 000	409 700	415 385	**EU-15**
B	11	13	13	16	18	12 000 *	12 500	11 400	11 900	12 000 *	**B**
DK	11	12	13	14	15 *	9 500	10 600	11 400	11 400	11 135	**DK**
D	68	73	76	82	85	68 600	68 500	68 200	68 000	69 400	**D**
EL	20	19	19	19	20	19 600 *	20 200	20 400	20 700	21 200	**EL**
E	51	55	57	62	69	38 130	40 200	38 100	44 000	45 900	**E**
F	44	45	49	51	55	58 892	58 253	58 700 *	58 900 *	58 800 *	**F**
IRL	8	9	9	12	13	5 000	5 200	5 300	5 500	5 700	**IRL**
I	27	29	31	34	35	79 300	85 900	88 100	88 100	89 150	**I**
L	1	1	1	1	1	490 *	500 *	500 *	500 *	400 *	**L**
NL	24	25	28	32	35	13 900	14 500	14 400	14 500	14 500	**NL**
A	9	10	10	12	13	10 800	10 500	12 500	12 500	12 700	**A**
P	9	10	10	10	12	12 550	13 100	13 500	13 100	14 000	**P**
FIN	:	:	:	6	7	8 000	8 000	8 000	8 000	7 800	**FIN**
S	7	11	12	13	14	9 200	8 800	9 300	9 400	9 500	**S**
UK	96	101	105	114	125	44 300	44 300	44 200	43 200	43 200	**UK**
IS	1 *	1 *	1	1	1	:	:	:	:	:	**IS**
NO	:	:	:	4	4	:	3 752	4 117	4 248	4 248	**NO**
CH	20	21	22	24	26	:	:	:	:	:	**CH**

5A1FV

5A1FW

Further reading: EU transport in figures, latest issue. DG TREN and Eurostat. International transport by air, latest issue. Eurostat. Panorama of transport, latest issue. Eurostat.

5A1FX

Passenger car transport. Million passenger kilometres

	1989	1990	1991	1992	1993	1994	1995	1996	1997	1998	1999	
EU-15	3 060 792	3 165 768 |	3 331 210 |	3 455 008	3 499 270 |	3 533 656	3 607 691	3 673 155	3 731 209	3 775 806	:	EU-15
B	75 646	80 748	82 940	84 550	86 850	89 480	91 200	92 400	94 030	95 660	:	B
DK	52 300	53 700	55 300	56 600	57 400	59 100	61 500	63 500	65 500	58 046	:	DK
D	582 300 *	601 800 |	713 500	731 500	740 800	731 200	741 200	745 600	740 500	740 300	:	D
EL	48 000	49 000	50 000	50 608	53 480	55 976	58 791	61 655	64 379	68 000	:	EL
E	274 000	282 000	293 400	305 200	311 800	318 600	328 300	339 300	350 000	351 800	:	E
F	576 100	586 000	599 000	618 000	634 600	651 200	664 300	674 300	685 100	708 400	:	F
IRL	17 600	18 100	19 200	19 800	20 600	21 800	23 200	25 100	27 100	28 500	:	IRL
I	480 615	522 593	538 270	602 210	603 090	600 300	614 500	625 600	633 200	647 100	:	I
L	3 431	3 527	3 700 |	4 300	4 500	4 600	4 700	4 700	4 800	5 000	:	L
NL	136 700	136 200	136 700	138 640	140 450	146 900	146 800	145 900	151 200	150 600	:	NL
A	60 600	62 400	70 400	69 300	67 900	68 200	68 100	65 700	67 000	68 500	:	A
P	38 600	40 500	44 800	49 100	53 400	57 700	62 000	66 300	70 800	75 600	:	P
FIN	45 800	51 200	50 600	50 500	49 700	49 600	50 100	50 400	51 500	53 300	:	FIN
S	88 100	90 000	91 400	91 700	90 700 |	84 000	87 000	92 700	93 600	95 000	:	S
UK	581 000	588 000	582 000	583 000	584 000	595 000	606 000	620 000	632 500	630 000	:	UK
IS	:	:	:	:	:	:	:	:	:	:	:	IS
NO	42 500	42 500	42 000	41 500	42 000	43 659	45 217	44 934	46 514	45 780	:	NO
CH	72 500	73 500	74 500	75 000	76 000	:	:	:	:	:	:	CH

Further reading: EU transport in figures, latest issue. DG TREN and Eurostat. Panorama of transport, latest issue. Eurostat.

5A1FY

Rail transport of passengers. Million passenger kilometres

	1989	1990	1991	1992	1993	1994	1995	1996	1997	1998	1999	
EU-15	252 572	256 557 |	271 772	274 514	267 554	268 931	270 521	279 600 |	282 158	289 781	:	EU-15
B	6 400	6 539	6 770	6 798	6 694	6 638	6 757	6 800	6 984	7 097	:	B
DK	4 929	5 057	4 912	4 802	4 798	5 080	5 000	4 900	4 988	5 558	:	DK
D	42 433	44 588 |	57 500	57 200	58 700	60 700	63 600	65 300	64 000	66 500	:	D
EL	2 020	1 977	2 000	2 004	1 726	1 400	1 568	1 800 |	1 884	1 816	:	EL
E	15 999	16 733	16 357	17 625	16 490	16 143	16 600	16 600	17 326	18 875	:	E
F	64 490	63 761	62 300	62 647	58 164	58 900	55 600	59 800	61 800	64 500	:	F
IRL	1 220	1 226	1 290	1 226	1 274	1 260	1 290	1 300	1 387	1 420	:	IRL
I	47 197	48 293	49 199	51 146	49 901	51 700	52 400	52 800	52 100	50 289	:	I
L	224	208	230	255	262	289	286	300	295	295	:	L
NL	10 162	11 060	15 120	15 350	15 200	14 439	13 977	14 100	14 425	14 760	:	NL
A	8 614	8 731	9 380	9 731	9 522	9 384	9 800	9 900	8 320	8 150	:	A
P	5 908	5 664	5 690	5 694	5 397	5 110	4 809	4 500	4 563	4 600	:	P
FIN	3 208	3 331	3 230	3 057	3 007	3 037	3 184	3 300	3 376	3 377	:	FIN
S	6 362	6 189	5 794	5 479	5 900	6 051	6 350	6 200	6 286	7 144	:	S
UK	33 406	33 200	32 000	31 500	30 519	28 800	29 300	32 000	34 424	35 400	:	UK
IS	-	-	-	-	-	-	-	-	-	-	:	IS
NO	:	2 104	2 150	2 256	2 316	2 398	2 381	2 449	2 561	2 597	:	NO
CH	:	11 061	12 383	11 504	11 670	12 085	11 712	11 622	12 386	12 412	:	CH

Further reading: EU transport in figures, latest issue. DG TREN and Eurostat. Panorama of transport, latest issue. Eurostat.

Road freight traffic. 1996

Trucks per day

N 25 000-70 000

N 14 000-25 000

N 8 000-14 000

N 3 000-8 000

N -3 000

N No assignment

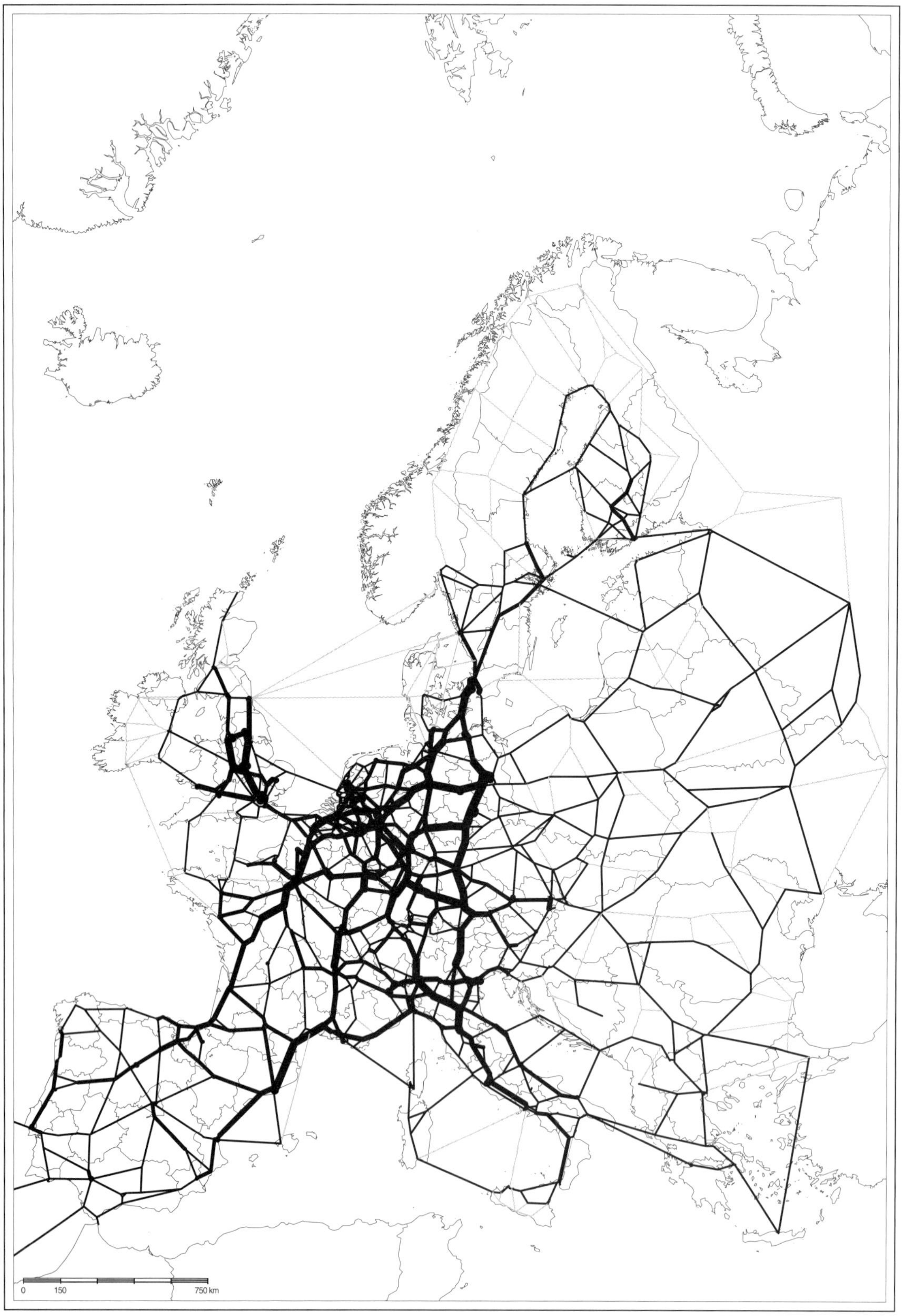

5A2HS

Further reading: EU transport in figures, latest issue. DG TREN and Eurostat. Panorama of transport, latest issue. Eurostat.

the European Union

5

Consumer prices, interest and exchange rates 425

Exchange rates. 1 unit of national currency = USD.
1995 = 100 425

ECU/EUR exchange rates. Annual average. ECU/EUR 1 = ... 425

Short-term interest rates: three-month interbank rates. % 426

Short-term interest rates: day-to-day money rates. % 426

Index of share prices. 1995 = 100 427

Index of share prices. 1995 = 100 427

EMU convergence criteria: 428

Deficit (-) or surplus of general government as % of GDP 428

Gross debt of general government as % of GDP 428

Change in the purchasing power of the ECU/EUR: harmonised indices of consumer prices adjusted for ECU/EUR
exchange rates. 1996 = 100 429

EMU convergence criteria: long-term interest rates 430

Yield on 10-year government bonds, secondary market 430

ECU/EUR exchange rates. 1996 = 100 430

Foreign official reserves as a percentage of total world
reserves (excluding gold) 432

Foreign official reserves, end of year, as % of EU total foreign official reserves (including gold) 432

Stock of euro-denominated securities issued by euro zone
residents and non-euro zone residents. 1 000 million EUR 433

Euro-denominated securities issues and redemption by residency of the issuers. 1 000 million EUR 433

EU budget 434

Allocation of 1999 operating expenditure by sector and
Member State (million EUR) 434

Own resources payments by Member State in 1999
(million EUR) 434

Internal economy 436

All-energy balance sheet, as % of gross inland consumption.
EU-15 436

Energy intensity: gross inland consumption per unit of GDP
in 1990 prices. kgoe per EUR 1 000 436

Gross inland consumption of energy and population. World
share. 1998 437

Energy intensity: gross inland consumption per unit of GDP
in 1990 prices. kgoe per EUR 1 000 437

Hard-coal balance sheet, as % of gross inland consumption.
EU-15 438

Brown-coal balance sheet, as % of gross inland consumption. EU-15 438

Years of remaining coal production at 1998 rate: reserves of
hard coal measured as a multiple of production in 1998 439

Reserves of hard coal, as % of world reserves 439

Crude oil and petroleum products balance sheet, as % of
gross inland consumption. EU-15 440

Net imports of crude oil and petroleum products, as % of
gross inland consumption of energy 440

Years of remaining oil production at 1998 rate: reserves of
crude oil measured as a multiple of production in 1998 441

Reserves of crude oil, as % of world reserves 441

Natural and derived gases balance sheet, as % of gross
inland consumption. EU-15 442

Net imports of natural gas, as % of gross inland consumption of energy 442

Years of remaining gas at 1998 rate: reserves of gas measured as a multiple of production in 1998 443

Reserves of natural gas, as % of world reserves 443

Electricity balance sheet, as % of consumption of internal
market. EU-15 444

Production of electricity per person. 1 000 kWh per capita 444

Renewable energy primary production: biomass, hydro,
geothermal and wind-solar. Million toe. EU-15 445

Production of electricity per person. 1 000 kWh per capita 445

Production of crude steel. 1 000 t 446

Production of hot-rolled steel products. 1 000 t 446

World production of pig-iron. Million t. 1994 and 1999 447

World production of crude steel. Million t. 1994 and 1999 447

Capacity and actual production of crude steel as % of
EU total. 1999 448

Total production of hot-rolled steel products. Million t. 1999 448

Final consumption of ECSC crude steel per person. kg 449

Employment in the iron and steel industry, situation at end
of year in 1 000s 449

Imports of ECSC steel by country of origin as % of EU total
imports 450

Exports of ECSC steel by country of destination as % of EU
total exports 450

Exports of ECSC steel to third countries, of which plate and
sheet and coils. Million t 451

Imports of ECSC steel from third countries, of which plate
and sheet and coils. Million t 451

Hard coal primary production. 1990 = 100 % 452

Hard coal primary production. Million t 452

Hard coal industry: production, imports and underground
employment. 1990 = 100 %. EU-15 453

Hard-coal deliveries to major consumers: public and pithead
power stations, coking plants and other consumers. Million t.
EU-15 453

The European market 454

Exports to EU countries as % of total national exports (fob) 454

Imports from EU countries as % of total national Imports (cif) 454

Exports to EU countries at current prices. 1 000 million ECU 455

Imports from EU countries at current prices. 1 000 million
ECU 455

Intra-EU exports of agricultural products at current prices.
1 000 million ECU 456

Intra-EU exports of mineral fuels, lubricants and related
products at current prices. 1 000 million ECU 456

Intra-EU exports of chemicals at current prices. 1 000
million ECU 457

Intra-EU exports of manufactured products at current prices.
1 000 million ECU 457

Intra-EU exports of machinery and transport equipment at
current prices. 1 000 million ECU 457

International trade balance in goods and services with EU as
a partner. 1 000 million ECU 458

International trade in goods and services with EU as a
partner. Cover rates. % 458

EU current account with the US, Japan and EFTA. Cover
rates. % 459

EU current account balance with ACP, OPEC, CEEC, CIS and
former State-trading countries. Cover rates. % 459

5

EU trade in goods and services by geographical and economic zone, exports as % of EU total exports — 460

EU trade in goods and services by geographical and economic zone, imports as % of EU total imports — 460

EU trade in goods and services with the US, Japan and EFTA. Cover rates. % — 461

EU trade in goods and services with ACP, OPEC, CEEC, CIS and former State-trading countries. Cover rates. % — 461

EU trade in goods by geographical and economic zone, exports as % of EU total exports — 462

EU trade in goods by geographical and economic zone, imports as % of EU total imports — 462

EU trade in goods with the US, Japan and EFTA. Cover rates. % — 463

EU trade in goods with ACP, OPEC, CEEC, CIS and former State-trading countries. Cover rates. % — 463

EU trade in services by geographical and economic zone, exports as % of EU total exports — 464

EU trade in services by geographical and economic zones, imports as % of EU total imports — 464

EU trade in services with the US, Japan and EFTA. Cover rates. % — 465

EU trade in services with ACP, OPEC, CEEC, CIS and former State-trading countries. Cover rates. % — 465

Extra-EU exports by main trading partners. 1 000 million ECU — 466

Extra-EU imports by main trading partners. 1 000 million ECU — 466

Extra-EU trade balance by main trading partners. 1 000 million ECU — 467

Extra-EU exports of agrifood products by main trading partners. 1 000 million ECU — 468

Extra-EU imports of agrifood products by main trading partners. 1 000 million ECU — 468

Extra-EU trade balance in agrifood products by main trading partners. 1 000 million ECU — 469

Extra-EU exports of mineral fuels, lubricants and related products by main trading partners. 1 000 million ECU — 470

Extra-EU imports of mineral fuels, lubricants and related products. 1 000 million ECU — 470

Extra-EU trade balance in mineral fuels, lubricants and related products by main trading partners. 1 000 million ECU — 471

Extra-EU exports of chemicals and related products by main trading partners. 1 000 million ECU — 472

Extra-EU imports of chemicals and related products by main trading partners. 1 000 million ECU — 472

Extra-EU trade balance in chemicals and related products by main trading partners. 1 000 million ECU — 473

Extra-EU exports of manufactured goods. 1 000 million ECU — 474

Extra-EU imports of manufactured goods by main trading partners. 1 000 million ECU — 474

Extra-EU trade balance in manufactured goods by main trading partners. 1 000 million ECU — 475

Extra-EU exports of machinery and transport equipment by main trading partners. 1 000 million ECU — 476

Extra-EU imports of machinery and transport equipment by main trading partners. 1 000 million ECU — 476

Extra-EU trade balance in machinery and transport equipment by main trading partners. 1 000 million ECU — 477

5

eurostat

Exchange rates. 1 unit of national currency = USD. 1995 = 100

3A6BC

Further reading: Money, finance and the euro: statistics (monthly).

ECU/EURO exchange rates. Annual average. ECU/EUR 1 =...

3A6BA

	1989	1990	1991	1992	1993	1994	1995	1996	1997	1998	1999	
B/L	43,38	42,43	42,22	41,59	40,47	39,66	38,55	39,30	40,53	40,62	40,34	B/L
DK	8,05	7,86	7,91	7,81	7,59	7,54	7,33	7,36	7,48	7,50	7,44	DK
D	2,07	2,05	2,05	2,02	1,94	1,92	1,87	1,91	1,96	1,97	1,96	D
EL	178,84	201,41	225,22	247,03	268,57	288,03	302,99	305,55	309,36	330,73	325,76	EL
E	130,41	129,41	128,47	132,53	149,12	158,92	163,00	160,75	165,89	167,18	166,39	E
F	7,02	6,91	6,97	6,85	6,63	6,58	6,53	6,49	6,61	6,60	6,56	F
IRL	0,78	0,77	0,77	0,76	0,80	0,79	0,82	0,79	0,75	0,79	0,79	IRL
I	1 510,47	1 521,98	1 533,24	1 595,52	1 841,23	1 915,06	2 130,14	1 958,96	1 929,30	1 943,65	1 936,27	I
L	.	.	.	.	.	.	.	.	.	.	.	L
NL	2,34	2,31	2,31	2,27	2,18	2,16	2,10	2,14	2,21	2,22	2,20	NL
A	14,57	14,44	14,43	14,22	13,62	13,54	13,18	13,43	13,82	13,85	13,76	A
P	173,41	181,11	178,61	174,71	188,37	196,90	196,11	195,76	198,59	201,70	200,48	P
FIN	4,72	4,85	5,00	5,81	6,70	6,19	5,71	5,83	5,88	5,98	5,95	FIN
S	7,10	7,52	7,48	7,53	9,12	9,16	9,33	8,51	8,65	8,92	8,81	S
UK	0,67	0,71	0,70	0,74	0,78	0,78	0,83	0,81	0,69	0,68	0,66	UK
IS	:	:	:	74,66	79,25	83,11	84,69	84,66	80,44	79,70	77,18	IS
NO	7,60	7,95	8,02	8,04	8,31	8,37	8,29	8,20	8,02	8,47	8,31	NO
EEA	:	:	:	:	:	:	:	:	:	:	:	EEA
CH	1,80	1,76	1,77	1,82	1,73	1,62	1,55	1,57	1,64	1,62	1,60	CH
US	1,10	1,27	1,24	1,30	1,17	1,19	1,31	1,27	1,13	1,12	1,07	US
CA	1,30	1,49	1,42	1,57	1,51	1,62	1,79	1,73	1,57	1,67	1,58	CA
JP	151,94	183,66	166,49	164,22	130,15	121,32	123,01	138,08	137,08	146,42	121,32	JP

Further reading: Money, finance and the euro: statistics (monthly).

Very short-term interest rates can vary considerably each day, depending on central bank operations in the money market (to manage liquidity and for monetary policy) and on the financial sector's supply of and demand for funds. The table shows day-to-day money rates; these usually denote the rates at which banks lend and borrow among themselves overnight on the interbank market. Very short-term interest rates averaged over a year are a good indicator of the state of monetary policy in that year.

Short-term interest rates: three-month interbank rates. %

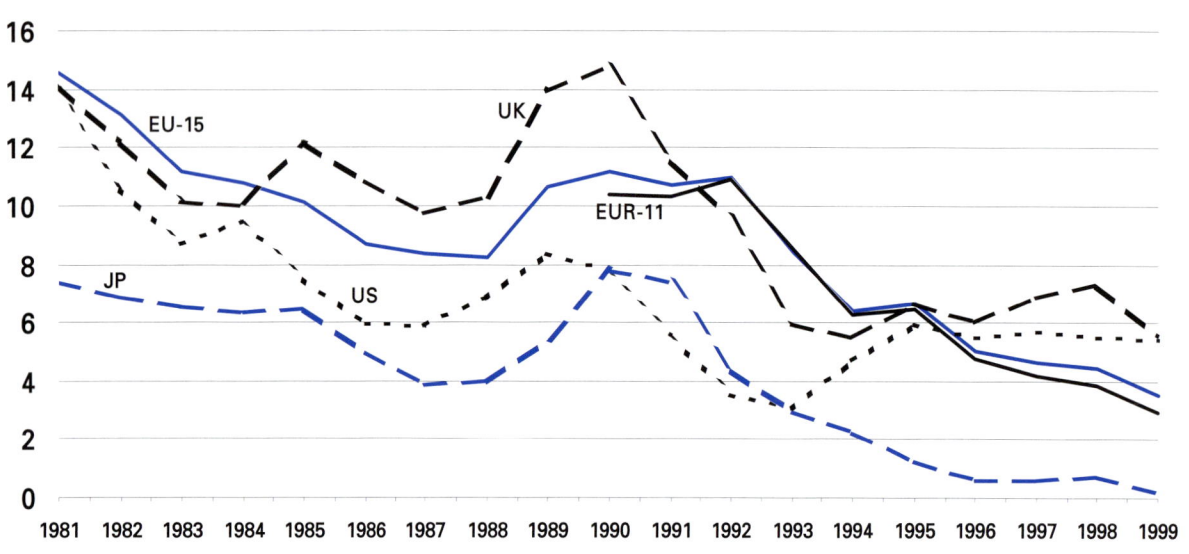

3A6BD

Further reading: Money, finance and the euro: statistics (monthly).

Short-term interest rates: day-to-day money rates. %

	1989	1990	1991	1992	1993	1994	1995	1996	1997	1998	1999	
EU-15	:	:	:	:	:	:	:	:	:	:	3,3	EU-15
EUR-11	:	:	:	:	:	5,2	5,6	4,0	4,0	3,1	2,7	EUR-11
B	7,0	8,3	:	:	8,7	5,5	4,6	3,2	3,4	3,5	:	B
DK	:	:	9,5	11,0	12,0	5,8	6,0	3,9	3,5	4,1	3,1	DK
D	6,6	7,9	8,8	9,4	7,5	5,3	4,5	3,3	3,2	3,4	:	D
EL	20,2	21,5	22,7	23,5	23,5	23,8	15,8	13,3	12,9	12,6	10,4	EL
E	14,4	14,8	13,2	13,0	12,2	7,8	9,0	7,6	5,5	4,3	:	E
F	9,1	10,0	9,5	10,4	8,7	5,7	6,4	3,7	3,2	3,4	:	F
IRL	9,3	11,5	10,5	15,6	15,0	5,3	5,6	5,2	6,1	5,8	:	IRL
I	12,0	10,9	11,8	14,4	10,3	8,2	10,1	9,1	7,0	5,2	:	I
L	:	:	:	:	:	:	:	:	:	:	:	L
NL	7,0	8,3	9,0	9,3	7,1	5,1	4,2	2,9	3,1	3,2	:	NL
A	7,5	8,5	9,1	9,3	7,2	5,0	4,4	3,2	3,3	3,4	:	A
P	12,9	13,7	15,8	17,5	13,3	10,9	8,9	7,4	5,8	4,3	:	P
FIN	10,3	10,6	14,9	13,3	7,7	4,4	5,2	3,6	2,9	3,3	:	FIN
S	11,6	13,4	11,8	16,5	9,1	7,4	8,6	6,3	4,2	4,2	3,1	S
UK	13,4	14,7	11,8	9,6	5,9	5,0	6,3	5,9	6,5	7,2	5,3	UK
IS	:	:	:	:	:	:	:	:	:	7,5	7,9	IS
NO	11,3	11,4	10,6	14,1	7,7	5,5	5,6	5,1	3,7	5,8	7,0	NO
EEA	:	:	:	:	:	:	:	:	:	:	:	EEA
CH	6,8	8,2	7,7	7,7	5,0	3,9	2,8	1,7	1,2	1,2	1,0	CH
US	9,2	8,1	5,7	3,5	3,0	4,2	5,8	5,3	5,5	5,4	5,0	US
CA	:	:	:	:	:	:	6,9	4,5	3,3	4,9	4,8	CA
JP	4,9	7,3	7,5	4,7	3,1	2,2	1,2	0,5	0,5	0,4	0,1	JP

3A6BB

Further reading: Money, finance and the euro: statistics (monthly).

eurostat

Index of share prices. 1995 = 100

5A1AA

300

250   EU-15

200   EUR-11

150   UK

100   JP

50   US

0
1992   1993   1994   1995   1996   1997   1998   1999

Further reading: Money, finance and the euro: statistics (monthly).

Index of share prices. 1995 = 100

3A6CB

	1992	1993	1994	1995	1996	1997	1998	1999	
EU-15	77,8	89,0	100,0	100,0	117,8	161,7	208,0	237,9	**EU-15**
EUR-11	78,2	90,1	102,2	100,0	116,2	159,1	214,4	249,4	**EUR-11**
B	81,0	90,2	102,0	100,0	122,2	161,2	218,4	225,7	**B**
DK	88,7	92,3	104,3	100,0	119,8	175,1	224,1	218,9	**DK**
D	76,5	84,6	99,2	100,0	120,1	174,0	234,8	249,8	**D**
EL	87,7	92,0	102,4	100,1	106,2	167,4	253,7	423,3	**EL**
E	76,3	90,6	105,2	100,0	126,4	194,5	284,4	309,7	**E**
F	99,0	108,1	110,1	100,0	111,2	147,6	197,5	243,4	**F**
IRL	64,7	79,2	92,2	100,0	124,5	168,4	237,5	248,8	**IRL**
I	:	100,7	109,5	100,0	100,3	137,4	220,0	245,0	**I**
L	55,9	77,0	110,7	100,0	117,5	152,9	192,6	25,7	**L**
NL	67,0	76,8	93,7	100,0	126,6	189,9	249,0	283,3	**NL**
A	89,7	91,4	110,9	100,0	108,4	130,8	134,9	118,9	**A**
P	:	76,6	103,7	100,0	115,6	188,4	305,3	280,5	**P**
FIN	40,2	64,6	96,3	100,0	105,9	167,2	236,0	406,6	**FIN**
S	53,1	70,8	89,6	100,0	121,6	177,9	202,9	235,5	**S**
UK	76,4	88,4	93,7	100,0	114,2	140,1	168,0	187,5	**UK**
NO	56,9	73,3	92,1	100,0	120,6	174,3	169,0	166,4	**NO**
CH	65,5	84,0	95,8	100,0	127,8	184,6	250,4	251,7	**CH**
US	73,1	78,4	84,4	100,0	127,7	165,7	192,0	233,5	**US**
JP	104,5	110,2	115,0	100,0	121,7	106,2	88,6	97,0	**JP**

Further reading: Money, finance and the euro: statistics (monthly).

On 1 January 1999, the third stage of the monetary union began. The participating countries are: Belgium; Germany; Spain; France; Ireland; Italy; Luxembourg; the Netherlands; Austria; Portugal and Finland. These have been joined by Greece on 1 January 2001.

The Treaty on European Union sets out convergence criteria (see glossary) for deciding which Member States are eligible for monetary union. Two of the criteria relate to government deficit and debt data as notified to the European Commission by Member States under the excessive deficit procedure.

For the EUR-11, the Stability and Growth Pact came into force in 1999, aimed at strengthening economic surveillance and budgetary discipline (see glossary).

EMU convergence criteria

Deficit (-) or surplus of general government as % of GDP

	1991	1992	1993	1994	1995	1996	1997	1998	1999	
EU-15	- 4,2	- 5,1	- 6,1	- 5,4	- 5,0	- 4,2	- 2,4	- 1,5	- 0,7	EU-15
EUR-11	- 4,6	- 4,7	- 5,5	- 5,0	- 4,8	- 4,2	- 2,6	- 2,1	- 1,3	EUR-11
B	- 6,5	- 7,1	- 7,1	- 4,9	- 3,8	- 3,8	- 1,9	- 0,9	- 0,7	B
DK	- 2,1	- 2,2	- 2,8	- 2,4	- 2,4	- 1,0	0,5	1,2	2,8	DK
D	- 3,1	- 2,6	- 3,2	- 2,4	- 3,3	- 3,4	- 2,7	- 2,1	- 1,4	D
EL	- 11,1	- 12,3	- 13,8	- 10,0	- 10,3	- 7,4	- 4,0	- 2,5	- 1,8	EL
E	- 4,5	- 4,1	- 7,0	- 6,3	- 7,1	- 5,0	- 3,2	- 2,6	- 1,1	E
F	- 2,2	- 3,8	- 5,8	- 5,8	- 4,9	- 4,1	- 3,0	- 2,7	- 1,8	F
IRL	- 2,2	- 2,5	- 2,4	- 1,7	- 2,1	- 0,2	0,7	2,1	1,9	IRL
I	- 10,2	- 9,7	- 9,6	- 9,2	- 7,7	- 7,1	- 2,7	- 2,8	- 1,9	I
L	1,9	0,8	1,7	2,8	1,8	2,6	3,4	3,7	4,4	L
NL	- 2,9	- 3,9	- 3,2	- 3,8	- 4,1	- 1,8	- 1,1	- 0,7	1,0	NL
A	- 2,6	- 1,9	- 4,2	- 5,0	- 5,1	- 3,8	- 1,7	- 2,3	- 2,1	A
P	- 6,3	- 3,6	- 6,1	- 6,0	- 5,7	- 4,0	- 2,6	- 2,3	- 2,0	P
FIN	- 1,5	- 5,9	- 8,0	- 6,4	- 4,6	- 3,2	- 1,5	1,3	1,9	FIN
S	- 1,1	- 7,7	- 12,2	- 10,3	- 6,9	- 3,4	- 2,0	1,9	1,9	S
UK	- 2,6	- 6,3	- 7,9	- 6,8	- 5,7	- 4,4	- 2,0	0,4	1,3	UK

4A1BC

Further reading: Money, finance and the euro: statistics (monthly).

Data before 1996 are compiled with ESA 79. Data after 1996 are compiled with ESA 95.

EMU convergence criteria

Gross debt of general government as % of GDP

	1991	1992	1993	1994	1995	1996	1997	1998	1999	
EU-15	55,8	58,3	65,3	67,3	71,2	72,6	71,0	68,9	68,1	EU-15
EUR-11	59,1	61,0	66,5	69,1	73,4	74,5	74,2	73,5	72,2	EUR-11
B	127,7	129,2	135,1	133,3	132,0	130,9	125,4	119,6	116,1	B
DK	65,5	68,6	80,7	76,5	72,1	65,1	61,4	55,8	52,6	DK
D	41,5	44,1	48,0	50,2	58,3	59,8	60,9	60,7	61,1	D
EL	83,3	89,0	111,6	109,3	110,1	111,3	108,3	105,5	104,6	EL
E	45,6	48,1	60,1	62,6	64,2	68,2	66,9	65,1	63,7	E
F	35,9	39,7	45,3	48,5	52,8	57,1	59,3	59,7	58,9	F
IRL	96,0	92,3	96,3	88,2	78,4	74,3	65,1	55,0	50,1	IRL
I	101,4	108,7	119,1	124,9	125,3	122,1	119,8	116,2	115,1	I
L	4,2	5,1	6,1	5,7	5,8	6,2	6,0	6,4	6,0	L
NL	79,0	80,0	81,2	77,9	77,9	75,2	70,0	66,6	62,9	NL
A	58,1	58,0	62,7	65,4	69,4	69,1	64,5	64,0	65,2	A
P	69,3	63,0	63,1	63,8	65,9	62,7	59,4	55,7	55,8	P
FIN	23,0	41,5	58,0	59,6	58,1	57,1	54,1	48,7	46,6	FIN
S	52,8	66,8	75,8	79,0	77,6	76,0	75,0	72,4	65,7	S
UK	35,6	41,8	48,5	50,3	52,5	52,7	51,1	48,0	45,7	UK

4A1BD

Further reading: Money, finance and the euro: statistics (monthly).

Data reported by Member States for September 2000 notification. Data before 1996 are compiled with ESA 79. Data after 1996 are compiled with ESA 95.

Another criterion relates to price stability (see glossary), as measured by the harmonised indices of consumer prices.

More data on this in Eurostat's database

The collections and tables of this domain describe the main elements required for understanding monetary and financial developments: exchange rates (United States dollar, euro, other currencies); stock market and bond market data; interest rates (short- and long-term); purchasing power of the euro; external position; monetary aggregates; official reserves; and public deficit and debt.

➤ ➤ ➤ **DOMAIN MNY IN DATABASE NEW CRONOS**

Change in the purchasing power of the ECU/EUR: harmonised indices of consumer prices adjusted for ECU/EUR exchange rates. 1996 = 100

	1997	1998	1999	12/99	01/00	02/00	03/00	04/00	05/00	06/00	07/00	
EU-15	103,0	104,2	106,4	108,2	108,4	108,9	109,4	110,0	110,0	109,6	109,8	**EU-15**
EUR-11	99,9	100,7	102,3	103,2	103,3	103,7	104,1	104,2	104,3	104,8	105,0	**EUR-11**
B	98,4	99,1	100,8	101,7	101,9	102,4	102,9	103,1	103,4	103,8	104,0	**B**
DK	100,3	101,4	104,3	105,4	105,3	105,8	106,5	106,7	107,0	107,3	106,9	**DK**
D	98,7	99,0	100,3	100,9	101,3	101,6	101,8	101,7	101,6	102,3	102,8	**D**
EL	104,1	101,8	105,6	106,3	104,5	103,3	105,8	106,0	105,8	105,2	103,3	**EL**
E	98,7	99,7	102,3	103,6	103,9	104,1	104,6	105,0	105,2	105,5	106,2	**E**
F	99,4	100,3	101,4	102,3	102,2	102,4	102,9	102,9	103,1	103,4	103,2	**F**
IRL	107,4	104,3	106,6	109,2	108,9	109,8	110,5	111,2	112,0	112,6	112,6	**IRL**
I	103,4	104,7	106,7	107,8	108,0	108,4	108,8	108,8	109,2	109,5	109,7	**I**
L	98,3	99,0	100,6	102,1	101,5	102,6	103,1	103,8	103,8	105,2	104,1	**L**
NL	98,6	99,9	102,6	102,9	102,6	103,2	104,4	104,8	105,0	105,0	104,8	**NL**
A	98,3	98,9	100,0	101,4	101,0	101,7	101,8	101,6	101,6	101,9	101,6	**A**
P	100,5	101,1	103,8	104,9	104,7	104,4	104,6	105,7	106,4	107,0	107,5	**P**
FIN	100,3	99,9	101,8	102,7	102,6	103,4	104,1	104,3	104,8	105,2	104,7	**FIN**
S	100,2	98,4	100,0	103,2	102,5	104,0	106,1	107,5	108,5	107,5	105,7	**S**
UK	119,6	124,3	129,4	136,9	137,4	138,7	139,9	143,4	142,9	136,8	137,5	**UK**

Further reading: Money, finance and the euro: statistics (monthly).

The two other criteria relate to long-term interest rates and exchange rates (see glossary). Interest rates refer to yields on government bonds with around 10 years to maturity. Data concerning exchange rates show ECU exchange rates as an index based on 1996 = 100. On 1 January 1999 the ECU was replaced by the euro at the rate of 1:1.

EMU convergence criteria: long-term interest rates

Yield on 10-year government bonds, secondary market

	1989	1990	1991	1992	1993	1994	1995	1996	1997	1998	1999	
EU-15	:	11,1	10,2	9,8	8,3	8,4	8,8	7,5	6,3	4,9	4,7	EU-15
EUR-11	:	10,9	10,2	9,8	8,1	8,2	8,7	7,2	6,0	4,7	4,7	EUR-11
B	:	10,0	9,3	8,7	7,2	7,8	7,5	6,5	5,8	4,8	4,8	B
DK	9,9	10,7	9,2	8,9	7,3	7,8	8,3	7,2	6,3	4,9	4,9	DK
D	:	8,7	8,5	7,9	6,5	6,9	6,9	6,2	5,6	4,6	4,5	D
EL	:	:	:	24,1	23,3	20,8	17,3	14,4	9,9	8,5	6,3	EL
E	:	14,6	12,3	11,7	10,2	10,0	11,3	8,7	6,4	4,8	4,7	E
F	8,8	9,9	9,0	8,6	6,8	7,2	7,5	6,3	5,6	4,6	4,6	F
IRL	:	10,1	9,3	9,3	7,7	7,9	8,3	7,3	6,3	4,8	4,7	IRL
I	:	12,1	13,1	13,3	11,2	10,5	12,2	9,4	6,9	4,9	4,7	I
L	:	8,6	8,1	7,9	6,9	7,2	7,2	6,3	5,6	4,7	4,7	L
NL	7,2	8,9	8,7	8,1	6,4	6,9	6,9	6,2	5,6	4,6	4,6	NL
A	7,1	8,7	8,6	8,3	6,7	7,0	7,1	6,3	5,7	4,7	4,7	A
P	:	15,1	14,2	11,7	11,2	10,5	11,5	8,6	6,4	4,9	4,8	P
FIN	:	:	11,3	12,0	8,8	9,0	8,8	7,1	6,0	4,8	4,7	FIN
S	11,2	13,2	10,8	10,0	8,5	9,7	10,2	8,0	6,6	5,0	5,0	S
UK	10,2	11,0	9,9	9,1	7,6	8,2	8,3	7,9	7,1	5,6	5,0	UK
NO	10,8	10,7	10,0	9,6	6,9	7,4	7,5	6,8	5,9	5,4	5,5	NO
CH	:	:	6,2	6,4	4,6	5,1	4,7	4,2	3,5	3,1	3,3	CH

4A1BB

Further reading: Money, finance and the euro: statistics (monthly).

ECU/EUR exchange rates. 1996 = 100

	1989	1990	1991	1992	1993	1994	1995	1996	1997	1998	1999	
EU-15	:	:	:	:	:	:	:	:	:	:	:	EU-15
B/L	91	93	93	95	97	99	102	100	97	97	97	B/L
DK	91	94	93	94	97	98	100	100	98	98	99	DK
D	92	93	93	95	99	99	102	100	97	97	98	D
EL	171	152	136	124	114	106	101	100	99	92	94	EL
E	123	124	125	121	108	101	99	100	97	96	97	E
F	92	94	93	95	98	99	100	100	98	98	99	F
IRL	102	103	103	104	99	100	97	100	106	101	101	IRL
I	130	129	128	123	106	102	92	100	101	101	101	I
L	.	.	.	.	.	.	.	.	.	.	.	L
NL	92	93	93	94	98	99	102	100	97	96	97	NL
A	92	93	93	95	99	99	102	100	97	97	98	A
P	113	108	110	112	104	99	100	100	99	97	98	P
FIN	123	120	117	101	87	94	102	100	99	97	98	FIN
S	120	113	114	113	93	93	91	100	98	96	97	S
UK	121	114	116	111	104	105	98	100	118	120	124	UK

4A2AB

Further reading: Money, finance and the euro: statistics (monthly).   1 unit of national currency = ECU/EUR.

The third stage of European monetary union began on 1 January 1999 with the introduction of the euro, the European single currency. Since that date the national currencies of the 11 Member States of the euro zone (Belgium, Germany, Spain, France, Ireland, Italy, Luxembourg, the Netherlands, Austria, Portugal and Finland) were fixed to the euro at irrevocable conversion rates (see table below). Their national currency became therefore a non-decimal subdivision. The ECU was replaced by the euro on a 1:1 basis.

The euro will exist until the end of the year 2001 only as book money (cheque, transfer, payment by card) and its use is voluntary (no compulsion — no prohibition). The coins and notes will be introduced on 1 January 2002, when the use of the euro will become compulsory. The euro coins and notes will circulate during six months in parallel with the national currencies that will be withdrawn gradually.

The national units will no longer be legal tender on 1 July 2002 and the euro will become the single monetary unit of the euro zone.

Fixed conversion rates:

40.3399	BEF
1.95583	DEM
166.386	ESP
6.55957	FRF
0.787564	IEP
1936.27	ITL
40.3399	LUF
2.20371	NLG
13.7603	ATS
200.482	PTE
5.94573	FIM
= 1	EUR

Greece joined the euro zone on 1 January 2001, with a fixed conversion rate of GRD 340.75 = 1 EUR.

The conversion rules of the national currencies to the euro and vice versa are very strict.

The official conversion rate with six significant figures has to be used for each conversion without rounding or truncation. To convert into euro the amount has to be divided by the conversion rate and for the opposite operation the amount has to be multiplied by the rate.

Official external reserves are those held by national monetary authorities for financing balance of payments deficits or influencing their currencies' external value. They are made up of monetary gold, foreign currencies, special drawing rights (SDRs) of the International Monetary Fund (IMF) and reserves held with the IMF. Variations in the level of reserves normally reflect changes in foreign currency assets rather than in other reserve components.

Foreign official reserves as a percentage of total world reserves (excluding gold)

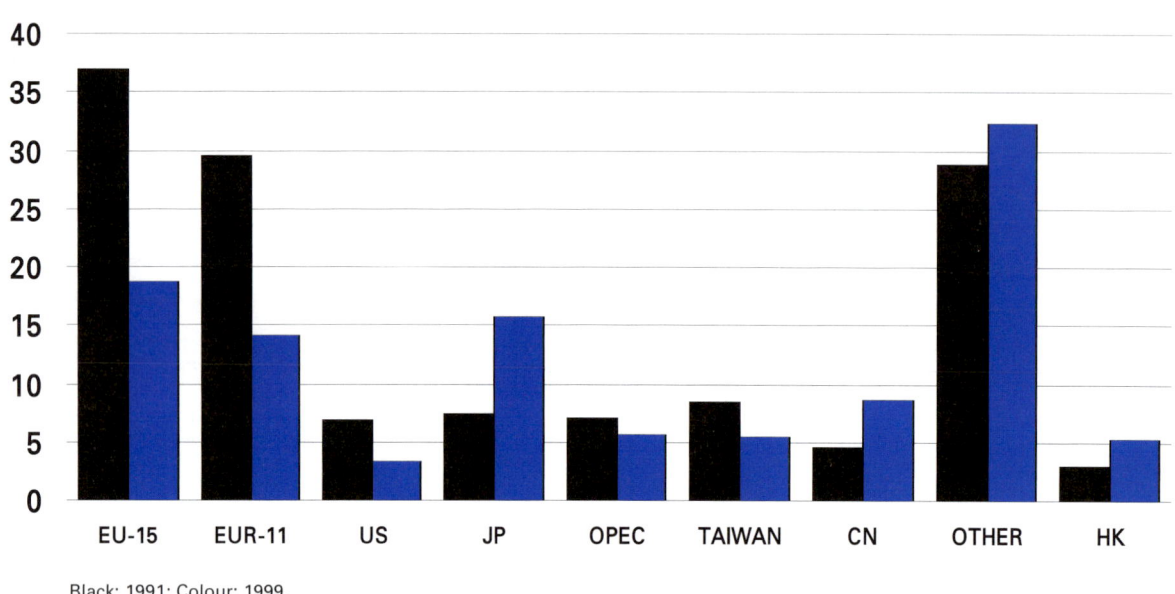

Black: 1991; Colour: 1999.

Further reading: Money, finance and the euro: statistics (monthly).

OPEC: Organisation of petroleum exporting countries. OTHER: rest of the world. HK: Hong Kong.

Foreign official reserves, end of year, as % of EU total foreign official reserves (including gold)

	1989	1990	1991	1992	1993	1994	1995	1996	1997	1998	1999	
EU-15	:	:	:	:	:	:	:	:	:	:	:	EU-15
B/L	5,2	4,7	4,7	4,7	4,5	4,7	4,7	4,3	4,2	4,2	2,9	B/L
DK	1,6	2,2	1,6	2,4	2,3	1,9	2,3	2,8	3,9	3,1	4,9	DK
D	22,3	20,5	19,4	25,9	24,0	22,3	23,4	22,0	20,9	21,5	19,8	D
EL	1,0	0,9	1,3	1,3	1,9	3,1	3,1	3,5	2,7	3,7	4,1	EL
E	10,8	11,2	14,3	10,7	9,9	9,3	7,8	11,8	14,5	12,1	8,1	E
F	12,9	13,4	12,1	11,4	11,4	11,3	11,2	10,6	10,9	14,6	14,3	F
IRL	0,9	1,1	1,2	0,8	1,3	1,2	1,7	1,6	1,3	1,9	1,2	IRL
I	16,5	17,4	14,5	10,5	11,2	11,3	11,7	13,1	14,9	10,7	9,5	I
L	:	:	:	:	:	:	:	:	:	:	:	L
NL	7,7	6,7	6,7	7,7	9,4	9,4	9,1	7,4	6,5	6,2	4,1	NL
A	3,8	3,4	3,5	4,0	4,6	4,7	4,5	5,0	4,4	5,0	4,0	A
P	3,7	4,0	5,3	5,2	4,6	4,2	4,2	4,0	4,0	4,3	3,1	P
FIN	1,3	2,0	1,7	1,2	1,3	2,2	2,0	1,4	1,8	2,0	1,8	FIN
S	2,7	4,0	4,1	5,2	4,5	5,0	5,0	3,9	2,4	3,1	3,6	S
UK	9,5	8,5	9,8	9,0	9,2	9,4	9,4	8,7	7,5	7,7	7,6	UK

Further reading: Money, finance and the euro: statistics (monthly).

Stock of euro-denominated securities issued by euro zone residents and non-euro zone residents. 1 000 million EUR

6M1AE

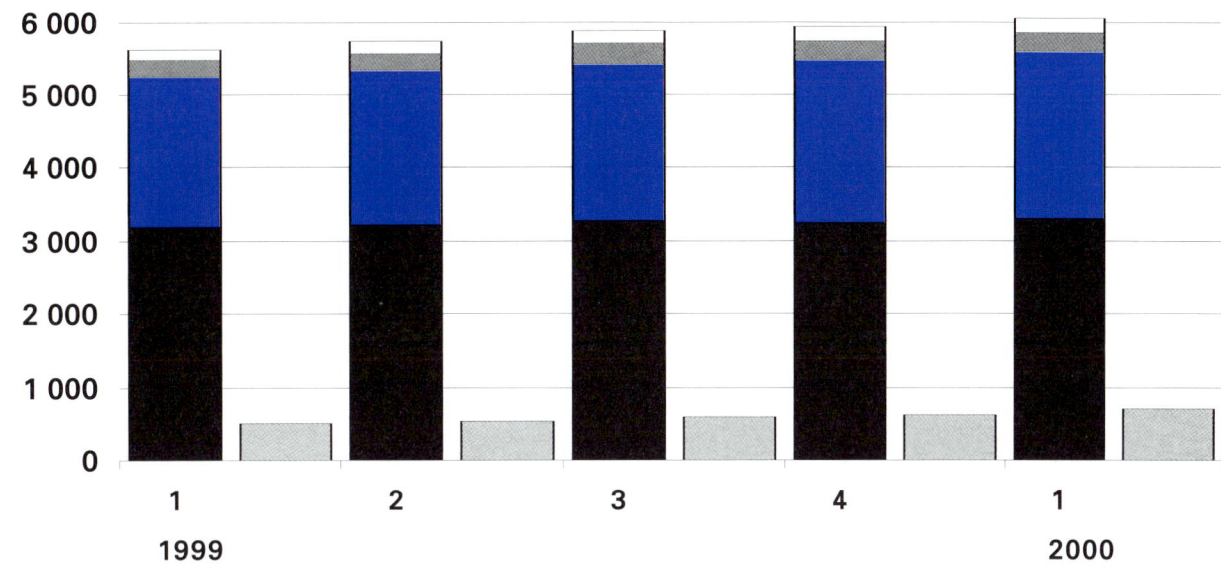

Black: central government; colour: monetary and financial institutions; grey: non-monetary and financial corporations; white: non-financial corporations; light grey: non-residents.

Further reading: Money, finance and the euro (monthly).

Euro-denominated securities issues and redemption by residency of the issuers. 1 000 million EUR

4A2BC

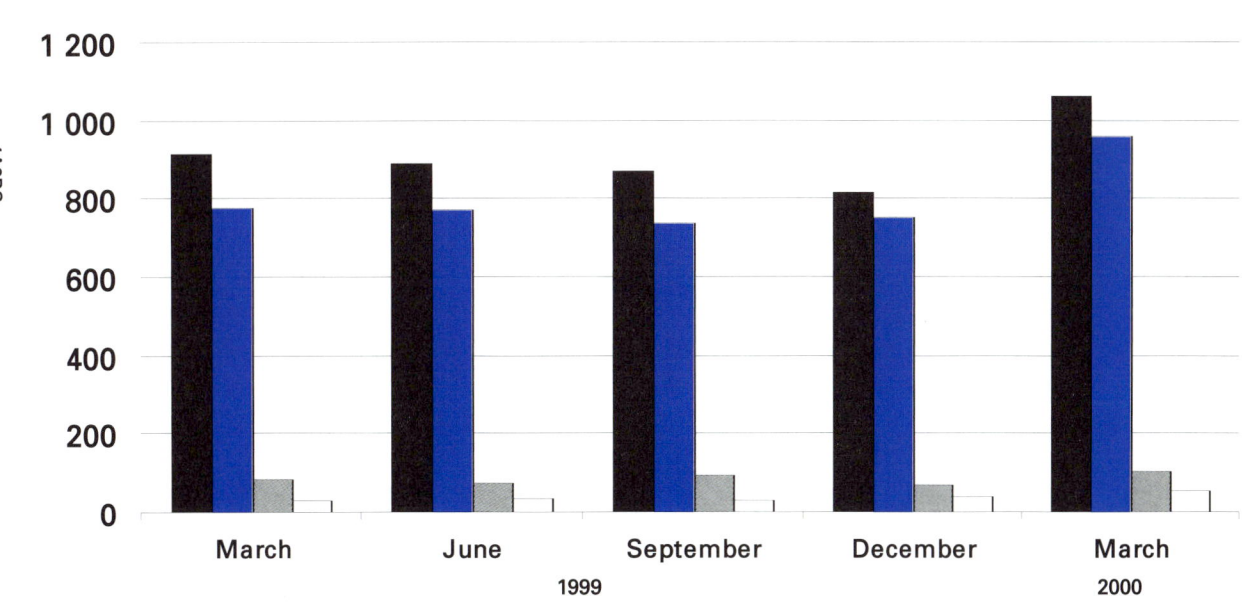

Black: euro zone residents-issues; colour: euro zone residents-redemptions; grey: non-euro zone residents-issues; white: non-euro zone residents-redemptions.

Further reading: Money, finance and the euro (monthly).

Where is your nearest Data Shop? Addresses at the end of the book

EUROSTAT YEARBOOK 2001
433

Allocation of 1999 operating expenditure by sector and Member State (million EUR)

	B	DK	D	EL	E	F	IRL	I
1. Agriculture	1 004,0	1 258,3	5 793,8	2 573,3	5 243,0	9 445,9	1 723,5	4 675,1
2. Structural operations	410,3	126,2	3 316,2	2 296,1	7 405,0	2 864,2	1 080,7	3 759,9
of which								
EAGGF Guidance Section	52,5	46,9	572,6	408,6	1 271,3	711,5	113,6	393,6
Regional Fund	140,0	5,5	1 190,4	1 081,8	2 732,8	1 006,8	459,4	2 222,5
Social Fund	150,7	63,9	1 187,3	422,8	1 869,4	932,2	231,2	830,6
Cohesion Fund	0,0	0,1	0,0	249,7	942,6	0,0	190,4	0,2
other structural actions	67,1	9,9	365,9	133,1	588,9	213,6	86,0	313,0
3. Internal policies	417,2	132,3	742,7	139,3	284,9	544,6	82,2	537,7
of which								
training youth and other social actions	77,5	12,9	86,7	33,9	62,3	95,2	27,0	67,9
energy	15,1	24,0	17,7	7,7	13,1	16,8	2,8	9,9
internal market, industry, networks	133,3	32,9	103,3	23,7	49,6	81,5	5,3	72,2
research and technological development	184,0	58,7	512,8	66,1	124,9	338,0	31,3	362,4
other	7,3	3,9	22,1	7,8	35,0	13,2	15,9	25,3
Total	1 831,5	1 516,8	9 852,7	5 008,6	12 932,9	12 854,7	2 886,3	8 972,8

Further reading: Budget DG: allocation of 1999 EU operating expenditure by Member State. http://europa.eu.int/comm/budget.

Export refunds are allocated to the Member State from which the goods leave the Union. This convention might overestimate payments to Member States with major ports such as Belgium and the Netherlands to the extent that the recipient of the refund is not a local trader. Belgium and Luxembourg benefit from the large number of multinational consultancies or ad-hoc companies based in these countries. Payments made by the Commission to these companies might ultimately be paid to subsidiaries or parent companies located outside Belgium and Luxembourg. It is extremely difficult to identify where the final beneficiary of these payments is located.

Own resources payments by Member State in 1999 (million EUR)

	B	DK	D	EL	E	F	IRL	I
1. Traditional own resources	1 103,0	296,4	3 188,0	187,8	818,8	1 486,3	174,9	1 278,5
of which								
agricultural duties	38,1	8,4	167,8	10,9	57,3	60,5	2,0	81,0
sugar levies	72,3	42,0	347,9	11,9	47,3	334,8	12,1	126,5
customs duties	1 115,1	278,9	3 026,6	185,9	805,1	1 256,1	180,1	1 213,0
collection costs retained by MS	-122,6	-32,9	-354,2	-20,9	-91,0	-165,1	-19,4	-142,1
2. VAT	828,0	543,5	7 864,3	523,1	2 462,2	5 457,1	406,8	3 689,5
of which								
payments relating to 1999	817,1	547,4	8 232,2	505,9	2 300,2	5 428,2	312,0	3 576,9
payments relating to previous years [1]	10,9	-4,0	-367,9	17,2	162,0	28,9	94,9	112,6
3. GNP	1 124,2	723,8	9 329,2	567,4	2 630,0	6 249,2	434,6	5 147,6
of which								
payments relating to 1999	1 117,7	733,9	9 364,6	559,9	2 539,9	6 352,8	344,5	5 155,0
payments relating to previous years [2]	6,5	-10,1	-35,4	7,5	90,1	-103,6	90,1	-7,4
4. Correction of budgetary imbalances	141,0	92,6	687,4	70,6	320,4	801,3	43,5	650,2
Total	3 196,2	1 656,2	21 069,0	1 348,8	6 231,3	13 993,8	1 059,7	10 765,8

Further reading: Budget DG: allocation of 1999 EU operating expenditure by Member State. http://europa.eu.int/comm/budget.

[1] Balances of VAT own resources for previous years (1982 to 1998).
[2] Balances of GNP own resources for previous years (1988 to 1998) including the refunds to Spain and Portugal on the basis of Articles 187 and 374 of their Acts of Accession.

Allocation of 1999 operating expenditure by sector and Member State (million EUR)

L	NL	A	P	FIN	S	UK	Total	
24,8	1 301,5	844,4	653,9	560,0	734,8	3 933,7	39 769,9	1. Agriculture
14,8	166,8	296,3	3 104,7	252,7	287,4	1 277,9	26 659,1	2. Structural operations of which
6,6	10,5	118,2	431,0	58,4	40,1	110,5	4 345,9	EAGGF Guidance Section
0,0	45,8	56,7	1 603,7	48,2	58,1	475,6	11 127,3	Regional Fund
6,8	84,2	104,4	581,5	118,3	155,1	507,4	7 245,8	Social Fund
0,1	0,0	0,0	332,4	0,0	0,0	0,5	1 716,0	Cohesion Fund
1,3	26,4	17,0	156,1	27,8	34,1	183,9	2 224,2	other structural actions
53,7	272,4	85,4	169,1	102,4	124,4	588,6	4 277,0	3. Internal policies of which
7,2	28,8	22,9	26,0	16,6	18,5	67,1	650,5	training youth and other social actions
3,4	6,8	4,9	4,4	6,2	5,7	18,8	157,2	energy
34,3	41,6	14,1	93,3	33,3	17,0	88,3	823,8	internal market, industry, networks
8,1	179,9	39,3	35,0	43,3	80,2	387,5	2 451,5	research and technological development
0,7	15,3	4,2	10,5	3,0	3,0	26,9	194,0	other
93,3	1 740,8	1 226,1	3 927,7	915,1	1 146,6	5 800,2	70 706,0	Total

Further reading: Budget DG: allocation of 1999 EU operating expenditure by Member State. http://europa.eu.int/comm/budget.

Export refunds are allocated to the Member State from which the goods leave the Union. This convention might overestimate payments to Member States with major ports such as Belgium and the Netherlands to the extent that the recipient of the refund is not a local trader. Belgium and Luxembourg benefit from the large number of multinational consultancies or ad-hoc companies based in theses countries. Payments made by the Commission to these companies might ultimately be paid to subsidiaries or parent companies located outside Belgium and Luxembourg. It is extremely difficult to identify where the final beneficiary of these payments is located.

Own resources payments by Member State in 1999 (million EUR)

L	NL	A	P	FIN	S	UK	Total	
20,3	1 612,2	244,6	184,7	128,2	355,6	2 778,3	13 857,6	1. Traditional own resources of which
0,6	192,9	13,8	43,3	7,1	19,8	483,5	1 187,3	agricultural duties
0,0	67,5	34,3	3,2	8,5	22,4	72,7	1 203,6	sugar levies
22,0	1 530,8	223,7	158,6	126,9	352,9	2 530,8	13 006,5	customs duties
-2,3	-179,1	-27,2	-20,5	-14,2	-39,5	-308,7	-1 539,7	collection costs retained by MS
76,1	1 566,8	775,6	469,5	448,2	831,6	5 389,0	31 331,2	2. VAT of which
78,1	1 524,1	818,8	443,3	426,5	807,7	5 562,2	31 380,5	payments relating to 1999
-2,0	42,7	-43,2	26,3	21,7	23,9	-173,2	-49,3	payments relating to previous years [1]
86,9	1 700,2	914,6	511,7	564,8	1 041,5	6 484,0	37 509,8	3. GNP of which
86,2	1 682,9	942,4	489,5	550,7	962,4	6 128,4	37 010,9	payments relating to 1999
0,7	17,3	-27,8	22,2	14,1	79,2	355,6	498,9	payments relating to previous years [2]
10,9	212,3	118,9	61,7	69,5	120,1	-3 567,8	-167,8	4. Correction of budgetary imbalances
194,2	5 091,4	2 053,7	1 227,6	1 210,7	2 348,8	11 083,5	82 530,8	Total

Further reading: Budget DG: allocation of 1999 EU operating expenditure by Member State. http://europa.eu.int/comm/budget.

[1] Balances of VAT own resources for previous years (1982 to 1998).
[2] Balances of GNP own resources for previous years (1988 to 1998) including the refunds to Spain and Portugal on the basis of Articles 187 and 374 of their Acts of Accession.

eurostat

All-energy balance sheet, as % of gross inland consumption. EU-15

	1989	1990	1991	1992	1993	1994	1995	1996	1997	1998
Primary production	55,0	53,5|	52,6	52,6	53,1	54,1	54,1	54,0	53,9	52,3 *
Imports	68,5	70,9|	71,1	73,3	72,3	72,4	71,7	72,3	73,8	75,1 *
Stock change	-0,2	0,1|	0,2	-0,9	0,7	1,1	0,6	0,4	-0,3	0,1 *
Exports	21,1	22,1|	21,5	22,4	23,5	25,2	23,9	24,3	24,6	24,7 *
Gross inland consumption	100,0	100|	100,0	100,0	100,0	100,0	100,0	100,0	100,0	100,0 *
Transformation input	87,8	87,6|	85,9	86,9	86,7	87,3	86,3	85,5	86,1	86,2 *
of power stations	20,1	20,5|	20,4	20,2	19,4	19,6	20,0	19,7	19,4	19,7 *
refineries	44,7	45,1|	44,9	46,6	47,1	47,8	46,6	46,4	47,3	47,7 *
Transformation output	65,6	65,4|	64,0	65,0	65,3	65,9	64,6	64,2	65,2	65,4 *
of power stations	12,5	12,6|	12,8	12,8	12,8	13,0	13,8	14,0	14,0	14,1 *
refineries	44,3	44,7|	44,6	46,3	46,9	47,5	46,3	46,0	47,0	47,3 *
Available for final energy consumption	71,9	71,9|	72,3	72,3	72,9	72,9	72,6	72,8	73,4	73,1 *
Final non-energy consumption	6,5	6,5|	6,5	6,7	6,4	7,0	7,0	6,6	7,0	6,6 *
Final energy consumption	65,2	65,4|	65,6	66,0	66,2	65,8	65,8	66,2	66,1	65,9 *
of industry	20,7	20,1|	19,0	18,9	18,5	18,8	18,9	18,4	18,6	18,3 *
transport	18,7	19,3|	19,1	19,9	20,3	20,4	20,2	20,1	20,5	20,8 *
of air	2,0	2,1|	2,1	2,2	2,2	2,3	2,4	2,4	2,6	2,7 *
road	15,7	16,1|	16,0	16,6	17,0	17,0	16,8	16,6	16,9	17,1 *
rail	0,5	0,5|	0,5	0,5	0,5	0,5	0,5	0,5	0,5	0,5 *
Households	25,8	26,0|	27,4	27,3	27,5	26,7	26,7	27,8	26,9	26,8 *

Further reading: Energy, yearly statistics, 1998. Eurostat. Energy balance sheets
1997–98. Eurostat.

4B2AA

Energy intensity: gross inland consumption per unit of GDP in 1990 prices. kgoe per EUR 1 000

	1989	1990	1991	1992	1993	1994	1995	1996	1997	1998	1999	
EU-15	255,5	253,5		250,5	246,3	247,7	240,6	239,9	244,5	237,7	235,3 *	:	EU-15
EUR-11	251,0	249,4		243,1	238,5	239,9	232,5	233,3	237,3	232,6	230,0 *	:	EUR-11
B	309,8	305,9	315,3	315,5	311,4	309,0	306,2	323,4	320,4	317,6 *	:	B
DK	178,0	179,2	193,1	184,9	186,3	182,2	179,2	196,1	176,4	168,2 *	:	DK
D	298,3	299,5		259,0	248,4	250,3	241,4	239,2	244,3	236,6	229,5	:	D
EL	339,3	340,9	333,2	340,1	339,2	347,2	347,7	357,5	349,2	353,8	:	EL
E	227,2	223,7	231,1	232,8	226,2	235,1	240,3	231,8	235,8	236,9 *	:	E
F	237,3	237,4	249,0	243,8	249,8	234,1	238,5	248,8	237,7	237,2	:	F
IRL	287,5	284,2	278,7	264,0	257,1	253,8	228,9	223,8	212,0	201,7 *	:	IRL
I	181,9	179,7	180,0	181,2	180,5	174,2	178,7	177,2	180,6	182,9	:	I
L	410,5	419,7	426,3	412,9	402,3	378,6	325,8	323,8	306,5	282,8	:	L
NL	305,7	300,1	307,2	299,4	302,4	292,3	296,7	298,8	283,3	272,8	:	NL
A	203,3	204,3	207,9	195,5	193,8	189,2	190,2	199,3	197,6	195,0 *	:	A
P	316,8	310,3	309,3	326,1	325,8	327,1	334,6	328,5	337,6	347,8 *	:	P
FIN	273,7	268,1	293,3	298,7	313,6	312,4	279,7	289,2	286,7	278,0	:	FIN
S	265,8	259,6	271,6	261,8	269,8	275,1	269,7	276,0	263,9	245,2	:	S
UK	280,0	276,3	288,2	288,2	287,3	276,8	269,2	274,2	258,7	261,7	:	UK
IS	415,0	426,5	399,7	419,8	428,1	416,9	420,6	422,4	415,3	444,3	:	IS
NO	238,6	232,7	230,3	227,4	232,4	220,7	215,6	198,8	208,5	209,2	:	NO
EEA	260,1	258,0		254,9	250,8	252,4	245,1	244,4	243,8	237,3	234,9	:	EEA
CH	141,7	134,2	139,6	140,6	142,0	141,1	143,1	142,8	143,7	142,9	:	CH
US	457,4	454,6	440,9	452,6	445,6	444,2	430,5	433,0	422,5	410,3	:	US
CA	:	:	:	:	:	:	:	:	:	:	:	CA
JP	187,0	184,3	184,8	182,0	184,2	185,7	195,3	195,2	195,3	199,3	:	JP

Further reading: Energy, yearly statistics, 1998. Eurostat.

Unit of GDP in 1990 prices and exchange rates to the euro.

4B2AB

5

eurostat

All-energy balance sheets form a uniform quantitative system that records energy availability and its use. Gross inland consumption is the key aggregate of an energy balance sheet. Ratios of other aggregates to gross inland consumption reflect their importance in the overall energy balances. Energy intensity is defined as the ratio between gross inland consumption and GDP in kgoe/EUR 1 000.

Gross inland consumption of energy and population. World share. 1998

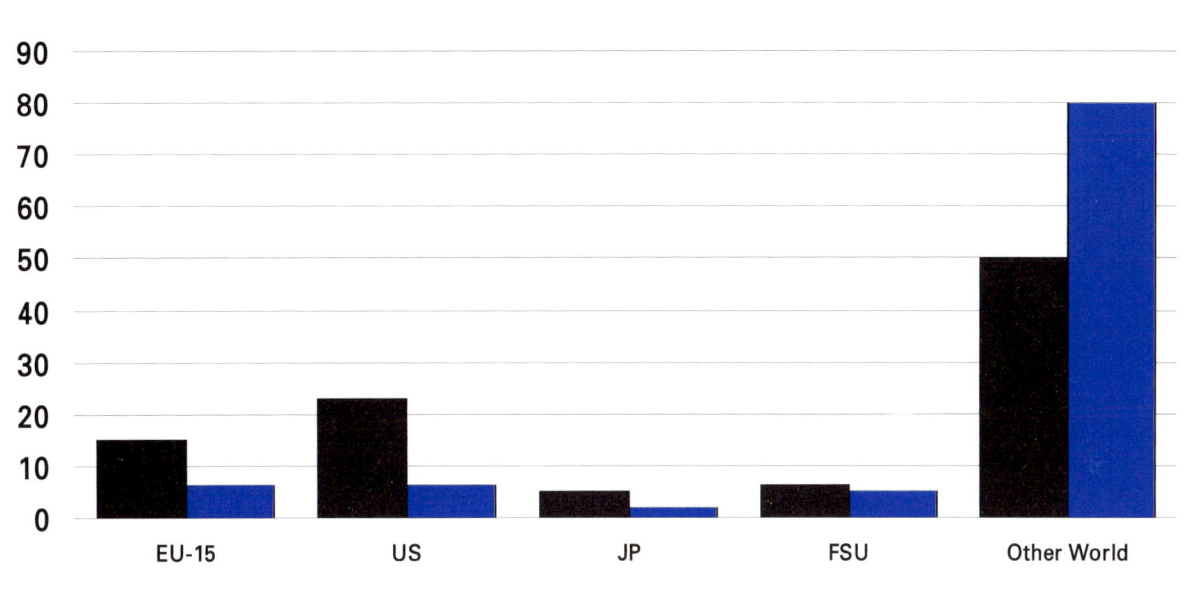

Black: gross inland consumption; colour: population. FSU: former Soviet Union; Other World: other countries of the world.

Further reading: Energy, yearly statistics, 1998. Eurostat.

Energy intensity: gross inland consumption per unit of GDP in 1990 prices. kgoe per EUR 1 000

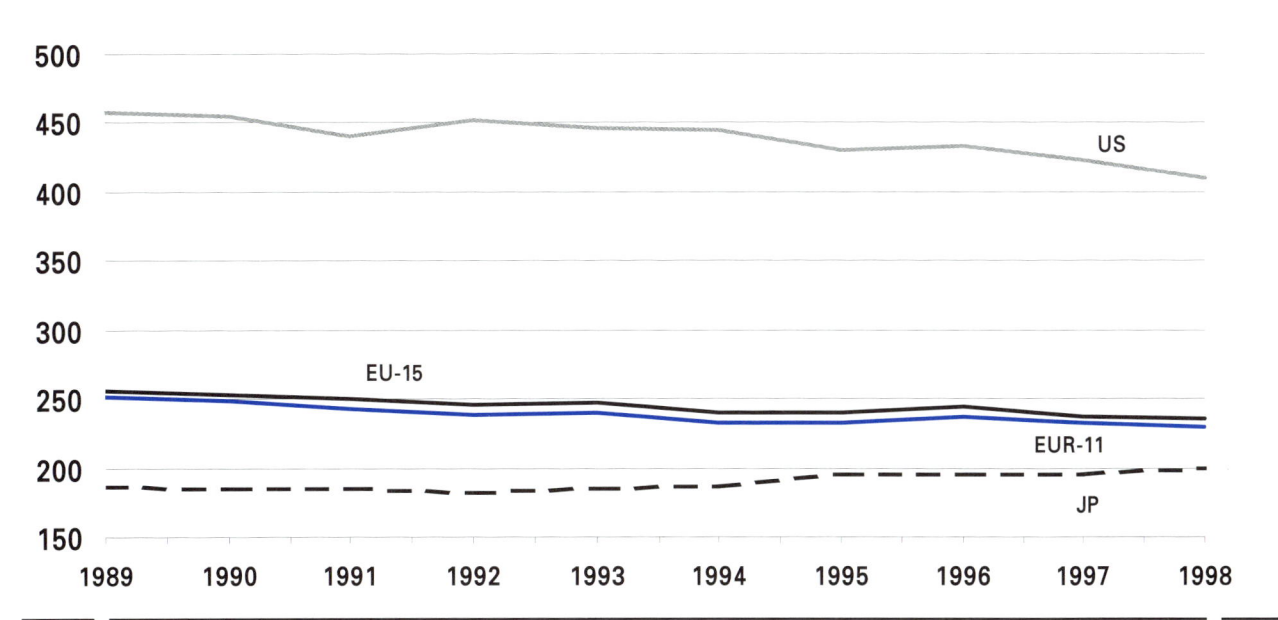

Further reading: Energy, yearly statistics, 1998. Eurostat.

Hard-coal balance sheet, as % of gross inland consumption. EU-15

	1988	1989	1990	1991	1992	1993	1994	1995	1996	1997	1998
Primary production	63,4	61,7	56,9	55,2	55,3	51,8	44,0	45,8	43,4	44,3	39,4
Imports	39,2	41,4	45,4	47,6	50,2	47,7	48,7	52,8	53,7	58,8	60,7
Stock change	0,4	-0,2	0,7	-0,6	-4,0	2,2	9,8	3,0	4,5	-1,0	3,4
Exports	3,9	3,7	3,8	3,1	2,1	2,2	3,0	2,5	2,3	2,8	4,2
Gross inland consumption	100,0	100,0	100,0	100,0	100,0	100,0	100,0	100,0	100,0	100,0	100,0
Transformation input	85,0	86,0	86,4	86,5	86,4	85,6	86,0	86,9	86,3	85,3	87,2
of power stations	57,3	58,9	60,9	62,8	63,1	62,7	63,9	64,6	64,6	62,4	64,6
refineries	-	-	-	-	-	-	-	-	-	-	-
Transformation output	-	-	-	-	-	-	-	-	-	-	-
of power stations	-	-	-	-	-	-	-	-	-	-	-
refineries	-	-	-	-	-	-	-	-	-	-	-
Available for final energy consumption	14,8	13,8	13,5	13,4	13,5	14,3	14,0	13,0	13,6	14,6	12,8
Final non-energy consumption	0,0	0,0	0,0	0,0	0,1	0,1	0,1	0,1	0,1	0,1	0,1
Final energy consumption	14,7	14,0	13,4	13,7	14,2	13,5	13,0	12,4	11,9	13,0	11,1
of industry	9,8	9,7	9,8	9,9	10,8	9,9	9,9	9,8	9,2	10,1	9,0
transport	0,0	0,0	0,0	0,0	0,0	0,0	0,0	0,0	0,0	0,0	0,0
of air	-	-	-	-	-	-	-	-	-	-	-
road	-	-	-	-	-	-	-	-	-	-	-
rail	0,0	0,0	0,0	0,0	0,0	0,0	0,0	0,0	0,0	0,0	0,0
Households	4,9	4,3	3,6	3,8	3,4	3,6	3,1	2,6	2,7	2,9	2,2

4B2BA

Further reading: Energy, yearly statistics, 1998. Eurostat.

Brown-coal balance sheet, as % of gross inland consumption. EU-15

	1988	1989	1990	1991	1992	1993	1994	1995	1996	1997	1998
Primary production	99,6	99,8	98,8	97,2	97,6	97,8	99,3	100,2	98,2	98,9	95,1
Imports	0,7	0,8	0,9	1,5	1,8	1,6	1,6	1,4	1,4	1,5	1,4
Stock change	-0,2	-0,4	0,5	1,3	0,8	0,7	-0,7	-1,6	0,4	-0,3	3,6
Exports	0,1	0,1	0,2	0,1	0,2	0,2	0,2	0,0	0,0	0,0	0,0
Gross inland consumption	100,0	100,0	100,0	100,0	100,0	100,0	100,0	100,0	100,0	100,0	100,0
Transformation input	89,7	90,1	91,2	93,0	93,7	94,8	95,8	96,8	94,8	95,7	99,5
of power stations	55,5	56,8	59,8	69,8	75,2	78,3	81,8	85,1	85,9	88,1	93,3
refineries	-	-	-	-	-	-	-	-	-	-	-
Transformation output	-	-	-	-	-	-	-	-	-	-	-
of power stations	-	-	-	-	-	-	-	-	-	-	-
refineries	-	-	-	-	-	-	-	-	-	-	-
Available for final energy consumption	9,8	9,4	8,3	6,2	5,7	4,6	3,3	2,8	5,0	3,9	-0,1
Final non-energy consumption	-	-	0,1	0,1	0,0	0,0	0,0	-	-	0,0	0,0
Final energy consumption	9,8	9,4	8,2	6,1	5,6	4,7	3,5	3,0	2,8	2,4	2,8
of industry	6,5	6,4	5,5	4,3	3,8	3,3	2,2	1,7	1,8	1,5	1,9
transport	0,0	0,0	0,0	0,0	0,0	0,0	0,0	0,0	0,0	-	-
of air	-	-	-	-	-	-	-	-	-	-	-
road	-	-	-	-	-	-	-	-	-	-	-
rail	0,0	0,0	0,0	0,0	0,0	0,0	0,0	0,0	0,0	-	-
Households	3,3	3,1	2,7	1,8	1,8	1,4	1,3	1,3	1,0	0,9	0,9

4B2BB

Further reading: Energy, yearly statistics, 1998. Eurostat.

Balance sheets for coal and lignite show that these fuels are mainly transformed into electricity in thermal power stations. The remainder is generally used by industry. Coal reserves are rela- tively widespread all over the world. The European continent has one third of all reserves, although the breakdown of individual fuels shows a less even distribution.

Years of remaining coal production at 1998 rate: reserves of hard coal measured as a multiple of production in 1998

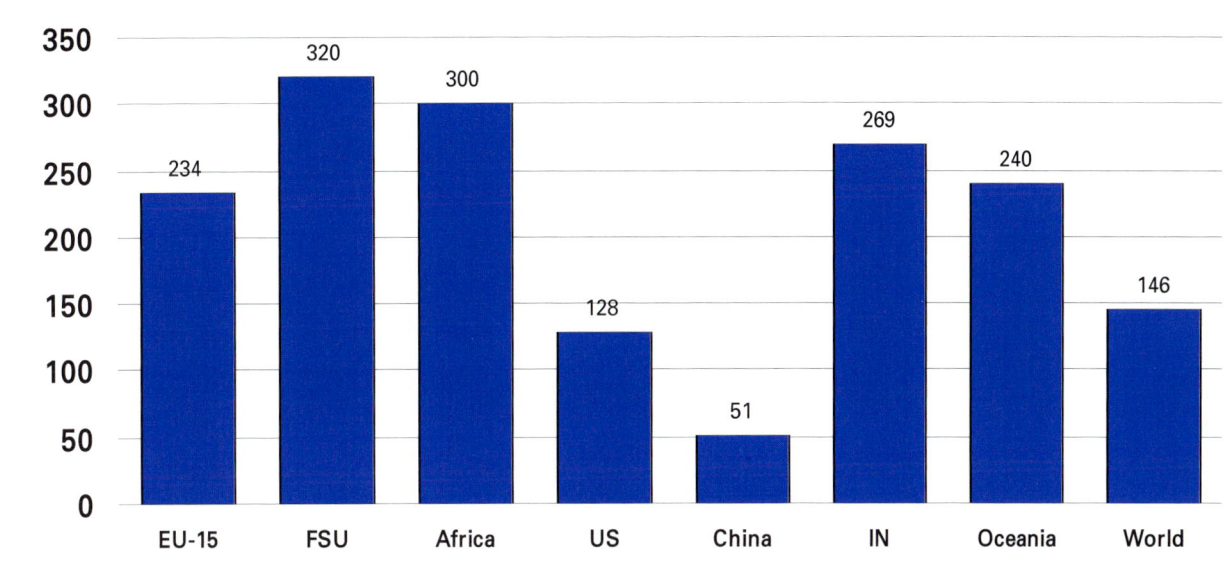

FSU: former Soviet Union; IN: India.

Further reading: Energy, yearly statistics, 1998. Eurostat.

Reserves of hard coal, as % of world reserves

	1989	1990	1991	1992	1993	1994	1995	1996	1997	1998	1999
Europe	34	34	34	34	32	31	31	31	31	27	:
EU-15	12	12	12	12	5	5	5	5	5	5	:
Former Soviet Union	17	17	17	17	20	20	20	20	20	19	:
America	21	21	21	21	24	23	23	23	23	24	:
US	19	19	19	19	22	21	21	21	21	22	:
Canada	1	1	1	1	1	1	1	1	1	1	:
Africa	10	10	10	10	11	12	12	12	12	12	:
China	16	16	16	16	12	12	12	12	12	12	:
India	10	10	10	10	12	13	13	13	13	14	:
Oceania	7	7	7	7	9	9	9	9	9	9	:
World %	100	100	100	100	100	100	100	100	100	100	:

Further reading: Energy, yearly statistics, 1998. Eurostat.

Crude oil and petroleum products balance sheet, as % of gross inland consumption. EU-15

	1988	1989	1990	1991	1992	1993	1994	1995	1996	1997	1998
Primary production	26,8	22,2	21,4 |	21,0	21,2	22,5	27,5	27,7	27,0	26,9	26,9
Imports	123,3	125,4	128,2 |	126,5	127,8	128,9	128,0	124,8	126,9	128,7	130,3
Stock change	0,7	-0,3	0,3 |	0,4	0,1	0,8	-0,2	0,8	0,0	0,1	-1,4
Exports	44,9	41,4	43,7 |	41,9	43,1	46,1	49,4	47,3	47,7	48,8	49,0
Gross inland consumption	100,0	100,0	100,0 |	100,0	100,0	100,0	100,0	100,0	100,0	100,0	100,0
Transformation input	115,6	116,7	117,3 |	115,8	117,5	119,4	120,1	118,2	118,9	120,4	120,6
of power stations	6,8	7,8	7,8 |	7,9	8,1	7,5	7,1	7,6	7,1	6,5	6,5
refineries	108,2	108,3	108,9 |	107,2	108,8	111,4	112,4	110,3	111,5	113,4	113,8
Transformation output	107,3	107,6	108,2 |	106,7	108,2	110,9	111,8	109,6	110,5	112,6	113,0
of power stations	-	-	- |	-	-	-	-	-	-	-	-
refineries	107,3	107,6	108,2 |	106,7	108,2	110,9	111,8	109,6	110,5	112,6	113,0
Available for final energy consumption	86,0	85,2	85,3 |	85,5	85,2	86,3	86,4	86,1	86,1	86,8	86,2
Final non-energy consumption	12,8	12,6	12,7 |	13,0	13,5	12,9	13,9	14,2	13,8	14,6	13,6
Final energy consumption	73,6	72,3	72,8 |	72,5	72,2	73,9	73,2	72,6	73,2	73,1	72,5
of industry	10,4	9,6	9,0 |	8,6	8,3	8,3	8,5	8,3	7,7	7,6	7,1
transport	43,0	44,6	45,8 |	44,9	45,6	47,2	47,1	47,0	47,3	48,2	48,8
of air	4,7	5,0	5,1 |	5,0	5,0	5,3	5,5	5,6	5,8	6,1	6,5
road	36,8	38,0	38,9 |	38,2	38,8	40,2	39,9	39,7	39,9	40,5	40,8
rail	0,6	0,6	0,5 |	0,5	0,5	0,5	0,5	0,5	0,5	0,5	0,4
Households	20,2	18,0	18,0 |	19,1	18,2	18,4	17,6	17,3	18,1	17,2	16,6

Further reading: Energy, yearly statistics, 1998. Eurostat.

4B2CA

Net imports of crude oil and petroleum products, as % of gross inland consumption of energy

	1989	1990	1991	1992	1993	1994	1995	1996	1997	1998	1999	
EU-15	34,6	35,0 |	35,4	36,2	35,0	33,4	32,8	32,9	33,3	34,1 *	:	EU-15
EUR-11	42,6	42,9 |	43,5	44,7	43,8	44,5	43,9	43,9	44,3	45,3 *	:	EUR-11
B	47,3	45,4	48,2	48,3	48,2	48,8	46,7	49,6	49,8	51,4 *	:	B
DK	21,8	17,4	10,1	7,8	5,6	6,2	8,9	6,1	- 1,8	- 0,2 *	:	DK
D	32,5	33,9 |	37,3	39,1	39,0	39,4	38,9	39,0	39,4	40,6	:	D
EL	60,5	64,4	65,3	70,7	72,0	62,6	71,3	69,0	70,7	72,2	:	EL
E	54,8	55,2	53,9	55,1	54,5	55,6	57,1	57,1	58,3	59,7 *	:	E
F	39,4	38,8	38,7	37,5	36,7	35,9	36,3	36,1	36,5	37,3	:	F
IRL	43,1	49,1	47,4	46,8	48,0	50,3	51,6	52,1	54,5	56,7 *	:	IRL
I	58,8	58,1	54,1	57,2	56,0	56,8	55,3	55,0	52,5	52,4	:	I
L	42,9	45,6	49,0	51,5	49,6	51,4	52,7	54,7	57,1	62,7	:	L
NL	46,7	46,2	46,7	49,1	46,3	48,0	44,8	46,2	48,8	48,8	:	NL
A	36,7	37,9	37,6	38,9	38,4	39,3	36,7	37,3	37,5	39,8 *	:	A
P	73,9	73,4	71,7	73,3	70,1	67,5	70,8	65,9	67,9	67,9 *	:	P
FIN	39,3	36,8	35,5	33,4	31,5	38,5	28,4	31,0	31,3	33,2	:	FIN
S	31,1	32,2	30,3	32,0	33,0	33,7	31,9	33,8	33,8	37,3	:	S
UK	- 4,4	- 4,3	- 3,4	- 5,0	- 7,2	- 19,0	- 22,1	- 20,5	- 21,4	- 21,8	:	UK
IS	29,5	32,6	30,2	35,2	33,2	34,1	34,6	35,7	35,6	33,5	:	IS
NO	- 312,8	- 346,5	- 401,2	- 455,3	- 463,8	- 530,2	- 563,0	- 656,2	- 608,9	- 568,5 *	:	NO
EEA	29,0	28,9 |	28,5	28,3	26,5	23,8	22,7	22,0	22,2	23,6	:	EEA
CH	53,6	53,6	53,8	53,3	53,4	49,4	50,3	49,8	50,5	51,4	:	CH
US	17,8	18,9	19,2	17,6	18,6	19,8	20,9	21,2	22,5	23,7	:	US
CA	- 9,9	- 6,2	- 7,2	- 10,1	- 11,7	- 12,1	- 12,7	- 15,8	- 15,6	- 18,1	:	CA
JP	58,6	60,8	60,0	58,9	58,6	57,6	57,5	55,0	54,5	51,1	:	JP

Further reading: Energy, yearly statistics, 1998. Eurostat.

4B2CB

5

Balance sheets for crude oil and petroleum products indicate that all crude oil is converted into refined petroleum products. The highest consumption of petroleum products is in the transport sector, which accounts for half of overall availability. The ratio of net imports of crude oil to gross consumption of energy gives the external oil dependence of the energy economy of each Member State. Net exporting Member States have negative percentages. Reserves of crude oil are concentrated in the Middle East.

4B2CD

Years of remaining oil production at 1998 rate: reserves of crude oil measured as a multiple of production in 1998

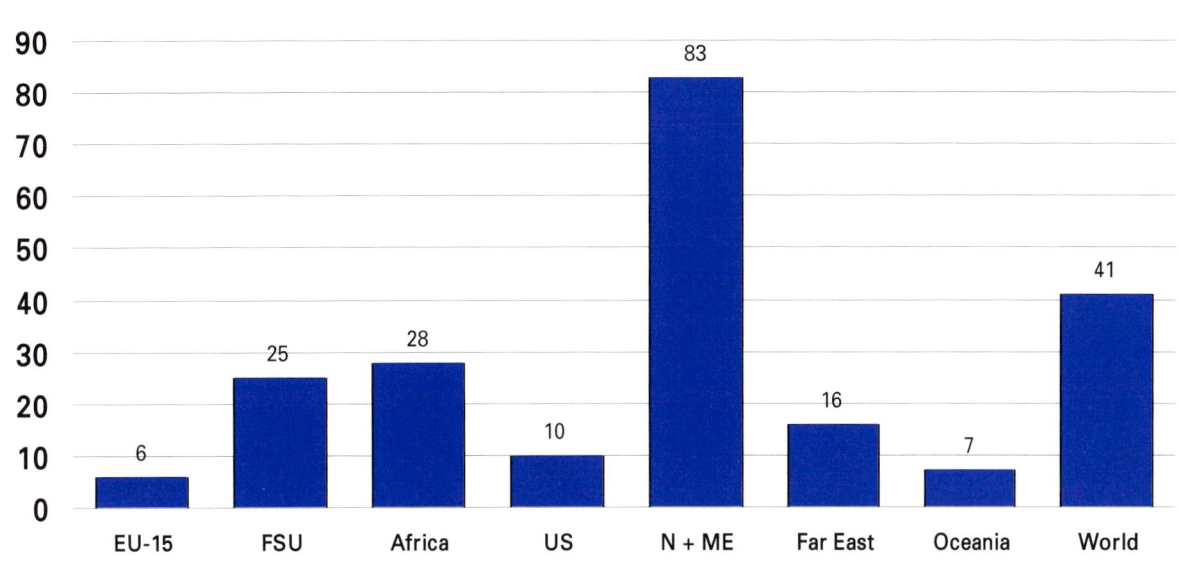

FSU: former Soviet Union; N+ME: Near and Middle East.

Further reading: Energy, yearly statistics, 1998. Eurostat.

More data on this in Eurostat's database

Eurostat Database New Cronos

This gives structural, social and economic data on the sector and data on the main energy sources: hydrocarbons, gas and electricity. This domain also covers internal flows and external trade. Prices of the main energy sources by type of consumer (industrial or domestic).

► ► ► **DOMAIN SIRENE IN DATABASE NEW CRONOS**

4B2CC

Reserves of crude oil, as % of world reserves

	1989	1990	1991	1992	1993	1994	1995	1996	1997	1998	1999
Europe	8	7	8	8	8	7	7	8	8	8	:
EU-15	1	1	1	1	1	1	1	1	1	1	:
Former Soviet Union	6	6	6	6	6	6	6	6	7	6	:
America	16	16	16	16	17	16	17	16	16	17	:
US	3	3	3	3	3	2	3	3	3	3	:
Mexico	0	0	0	5	5	5	5	5	4	5	:
Venezuela	6	6	6	6	7	6	7	6	7	7	:
Africa	6	6	6	6	6	6	7	7	7	7	:
Near and Middle East	66	66	66	66	66	66	65	65	65	64	:
Saudi Arabia	25	26	26	26	26	26	26	25	25	25	:
Far East	5	5	4	4	4	4	4	4	4	4	:
World %	100	100	100	100	100	100	100	100	100	100	:

Further reading: Energy, yearly statistics, 1998. Eurostat.

eurostat

Need access to Eurostat's databases? Ask your Data Shop

EUROSTAT YEARBOOK 2001
441

5

Natural and derived gases balance sheet, as % of gross inland consumption. EU-15

	1988	1989	1990	1991	1992	1993	1994	1995	1996	1997	1998
Primary production	60,4	59,9	59,8	60,8	61,9	62,6	63,0	60,9	61,8	60,2	57,5
Imports	51,1	53,8	54,2	52,7	54,7	51,7	52,4	52,4	52,4	54,0	53,4
Stock change	-0,3	-1,1	-1,4	-0,1	-2,1	-0,2	-1,4	-0,7	-0,6	-1,2	0,8
Exports	11,2	12,6	12,6	13,3	14,6	14,1	14,0	12,6	13,6	12,9	11,7
Gross inland consumption	100,0	100,0	100,0	100,0	100,0	100,0	100,0	100,0	100,0	100,0	100,0
Transformation input	18,0	18,8	18,9	17,6	17,6	18,7	20,4	22,4	22,6	24,0	24,4 *
of power stations	15,2	16,2	16,5	15,3	15,5	16,8	18,5	20,2	21,0	23,4	23,7 *
refineries	-	-	-	-	-	-	-	-	-	-	-
Transformation output	13,4	13,1	11,8	9,9	9,1	8,2	7,9	7,3	6,4	6,5	6,0 *
of power stations	-	-	-	-	-	-	-	-	-	-	-
refineries	-	-	-	-	-	-	-	-	-	-	-
Available for final energy consumption	88,6	87,6	86,5	86,2	85,8	84,4	82,3	79,8	78,5	77,3	76,7 *
Final non-energy consumption	6,4	6,2	5,6	5,0	4,1	4,1	4,4	4,2	3,4	3,7	3,6 *
Final energy consumption	82,1	81,4	80,3	80,8	81,4	78,7	77,0	75,3	74,6	71,6	70,6 *
of industry	35,0	35,5	34,7	31,9	32,6	30,6	30,8	30,0	28,9	28,8	28,3 *
transport	0,1	0,1	0,1	0,1	0,1	0,1	0,1	0,1	0,1	0,1	0,1
of air	-	-	-	-	-	-	-	-	-	-	-
road	0,1	0,1	0,1	0,1	0,1	0,1	0,1	0,1	0,1	0,1	0,1
rail	-	-	-	-	-	-	-	-	-	-	-
Households	47,1	45,8	45,4	48,8	48,8	47,9	46,2	45,2	45,6	42,7	42,2 *

4B2DA

Further reading: Energy, yearly statistics, 1998. Eurostat.

Net imports of natural gas, as % of gross inland consumption of energy

	1989	1990	1991	1992	1993	1994	1995	1996	1997	1998	1999	
EU-15	6,8	7,0	7,0	7,1	7,1	7,3	8,0	8,4	8,8	9,2 *	:	EU-15
EUR-11	8,0	8,5	8,6	8,8	9,0	9,4	10,4	11,0	11,6	12,1 *	:	EUR-11
B	17,6	17,4	17,5	18,2	19,4	19,7	20,6	22,0	20,5	22,1 *	:	B
DK	- 4,6	- 5,1	- 6,3	- 7,1	- 7,3	- 7,4	- 7,3	- 7,3	- 12,9	- 11,9 *	:	DK
D	11,6	11,8	12,6	13,1	14,0	14,7	15,7	17,3	16,9	16,3	:	D
EL	-	-	-	-	-	-	-	0,0	0,5	2,6	:	EL
E	3,5	4,1	4,7	5,1	5,6	6,7	7,4	8,2	10,9	10,9 *	:	E
F	9,9	10,8	10,7	11,1	10,6	11,3	11,4	11,9	12,1	12,0	:	F
IRL	0,0	0,0	0,0	0,0	0,0	0,0	0,8	4,1	7,1	10,7 *	:	IRL
I	15,3	16,4	17,6	17,8	17,1	15,7	17,5	18,7	19,0	20,2	:	I
L	11,9	12,1	11,8	12,3	12,6	13,0	16,7	18,0	18,7	19,4	:	L
NL	- 35,2	- 35,6	- 39,0	- 41,2	- 40,8	- 37,6	- 36,0	- 40,6	- 33,8	- 30,4 *	:	NL
A	14,1	17,5	16,1	16,9	17,9	16,5	20,6	19,9	18,0	18,2 *	:	A
P	-	-	-	-	-	-	-	-	0,5	3,1 *	:	P
FIN	6,4	7,9	8,3	8,7	8,7	9,3	9,8	9,6	8,9	10,0	:	FIN
S	0,9	1,1	1,1	1,4	1,5	1,3	1,4	1,4	1,4	1,5	:	S
UK	4,1	2,9	2,6	2,2	1,5	0,8	0,3	0,2	- 0,3	- 0,7	:	UK
IS	-	-	-	-	-	-	-	-	-	-	:	IS
NO	- 117,1	- 104,8	- 101,8	- 102,3	- 93,9	- 102,1	- 105,5	- 147,8	- 149,7	- 146,0 *	:	NO
EEA	4,8	5,2	5,3	5,3	5,4	5,4	6,0	5,9	6,1	6,5	:	EEA
CH	6,5	7,2	7,2	7,3	7,6	8,2	7,8	9,3	8,7	8,9	:	CH
US	1,5	1,6	2,8	2,0	2,2	2,5	2,8	3,0	3,0	3,2	:	US
CA	- 13,8	- 14,1	- 15,5	- 18,3	- 21,9	- 23,0	- 26,3	- 27,5	- 27,7	- 30,8	:	CA
JP	9,3	9,7	9,8	10,2	10,0	10,0	10,2	10,6	10,7	11,3	:	JP

4B2DB

Further reading: Energy, yearly statistics, 1998. Eurostat.

Balance sheets for gas (natural and manufactured) show that domestic production is still important. Consumption is stable in the two largest sectors, households and industry. Natural gas reserves are located mainly in Russia and the Middle East.

Years of remaining production at current extraction rates are calculated by dividing proven reserves by current annual production.

Years of remaining gas at 1998 rate: reserves of gas measured as a multiple of production in 1998

4B2DD

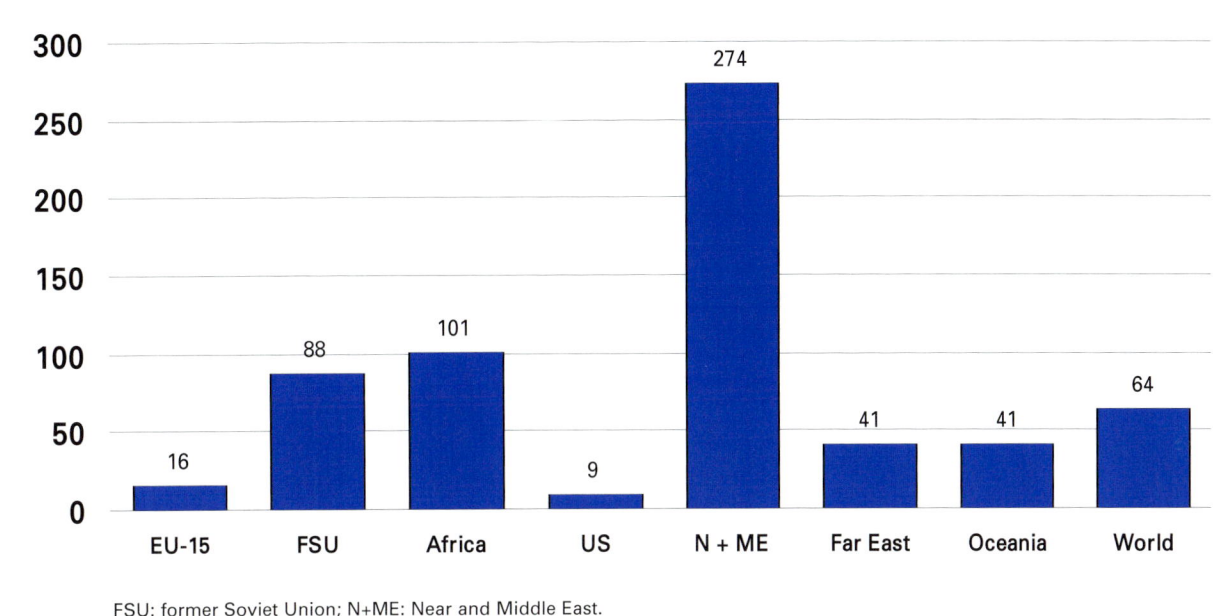

FSU: former Soviet Union; N+ME: Near and Middle East.

Further reading: Energy, yearly statistics, 1998. Eurostat.

Reserves of natural gas, as % of world reserves

4B2DC

	1989	1990	1991	1992	1993	1994	1995	1996	1997	1998	1999
Europe	45	45	43	43	43	43	44	43	43	42	:
EU-15	2	3	2	2	2	2	2	2	2	2	:
Former Soviet Union	40	40	39	38	39	39	40	40	39	39	:
America	11	11	11	10	10	10	10	10	10	10	:
US	4	4	3	3	3	3	3	3	3	3	:
Mexico	2	2	1	1	1	1	1	1	1	1	:
Venezuela	:	:	2	2	2	2	3	3	:	:	:
Africa	6	7	7	7	7	7	7	6	7	7	:
Near and Middle East	29	29	30	31	32	32	32	32	34	34	:
Far East	6	6	7	7	7	7	6	6	6	6	:
Oceania	2	2	2	2	2	2	2	2	2	1	:
World %	100	100	100	100	100	100	100	100	100	100	:

Further reading: Energy, yearly statistics, 1998. Eurostat.

Electricity balance sheet, as % of consumption of internal market. EU-15

	1988	1989	1990	1991	1992	1993	1994	1995	1996	1997	1998
Primary production	0,2	0,2	0,2	0,2	0,2	0,2	0,2	0,2	0,2	0,2	0,2
Imports	7,4	8,0	8,5	7,5	7,8	8,3	8,0	8,3	8,4	8,4	8,0
Exports	6,0	6,5	7,0	6,8	6,8	7,1	7,0	7,4	8,5	8,0	7,4
Gross inland consumption	1,4	1,5	1,5	0,8	1,0	1,2	0,9	0,9	-0,1	0,4	0,6
Transformation input	-	-	-	-	-	-	-	-	-	-	-
Transformation output	100,9	103,8	103,6	104,5	100,8	102,5	102,2	102,3	103,7	102,1	101,9
of public thermal power stations	51,6	53,6	54,3	54,6	51,8	50,6	51,1	51,3	51,9	50,0	50,9
autoproducing thermal power stations	9,9	9,7	9,6	9,5	9,1	9,6	9,5	9,8	9,6	10,3	10,6
nuclear power stations	39,4	40,5	39,7	40,5	39,9	42,4	41,6	41,1	42,1	41,8	40,5
Consumption of the energy branch	11,9	11,4	11,5	11,5	11,1	11,0	10,6	10,6	10,5	10,4	10,3
Distribution losses	7,7	7,4	7,4	7,6	7,1	7,4	7,6	7,5	7,6	6,9	7,3
Available for final energy consumption	100,6	100,5	100,5	100,8	98,7	100,9	100,8	100,0	100,0	100,0	100,0
Final non-energy consumption	-	-	-	-	-	-	-	-	-	-	-
Final energy consumption	100,0	100,0	100,0	100,0	100,0	100,0	100,0	100,0	100,0	100,0	100,0
of industry	45,2	45,3	44,4	42,9	41,4	41,6	41,5	42,1	41,3	41,9	41,9
of iron and steel industry	5,7	5,6	5,3	5,1	4,8	4,8	5,1	5,1	4,9	5,0	4,9
chemical industry	10,5	10,3	10,3	9,6	9,0	9,0	8,6	8,4	8,2	8,2	8,2
transport	2,4	2,4	2,6	2,7	2,6	2,8	2,8	2,8	2,8	2,8	2,6
of air	-	-	-	-	-	-	-	-	-	-	-
road	-	-	-	-	-	-	-	-	-	-	-
rail	2,4	2,4	2,6	2,7	2,6	2,8	2,8	2,8	2,8	2,8	2,6
Households, commerce, public authorities	52,4	52,3	53,0	54,4	56,0	55,7	55,6	55,1	56,0	55,3	55,5
of households	28,6	28,1	28,6	29,8	29,3	30,4	30,3	29,5	30,3	29,5	29,4

Further reading: Energy, yearly statistics, 1998. Eurostat.

4B2EA

Production of electricity per person. 1 000 kWh per capita

	1989	1990	1991	1992	1993	1994	1995	1996	1997	1998	1999	
EU-15	5,8	5,7	6,1	6,1	6,0	6,1	6,3	6,5	6,5	6,6	:	EU-15
EUR-11	5,7	5,5	5,9	5,9	5,9	6,0	6,1	6,3	6,3	6,5	:	EUR-11
B	6,8	7,1	7,2	7,2	7,0	7,1	7,3	7,5	7,7	8,2	:	B
DK	4,4	5,0	7,1	6,0	6,5	7,7	7,0	10,2	8,4	7,7	:	DK
D	7,3	6,2	6,7	6,7	6,5	6,5	6,6	6,8	6,7	6,8	:	D
EL	3,4	3,4	3,5	3,6	3,7	3,9	4,0	4,1	4,1	4,4	:	EL
E	3,8	3,9	4,0	4,1	4,0	4,1	4,3	4,4	4,8	5,0	:	E
F	7,2	7,4	8,0	8,1	8,2	8,2	8,5	8,8	8,6	8,7	:	F
IRL	3,9	4,1	4,3	4,5	4,6	4,8	5,0	5,3	5,5	5,7	:	IRL
I	3,7	3,8	3,9	4,0	3,9	4,0	4,2	4,3	4,4	4,5	:	I
L	3,7	3,6	3,6	3,1	2,7	2,9	3,0	3,2	3,0	3,3	:	L
NL	4,9	4,8	4,9	5,1	5,0	5,2	5,2	5,5	5,6	5,8	:	NL
A	6,7	6,7	6,8	6,7	6,7	6,8	7,0	6,8	7,0	7,1	:	A
P	2,6	2,9	3,0	3,1	3,2	3,2	3,4	3,5	3,4	3,9	:	P
FIN	10,3	10,3	12,4	11,5	12,1	12,9	12,5	13,5	13,5	13,6	:	FIN
S	16,9	17,2	17,2	16,9	16,8	16,3	16,8	15,9	16,9	17,9	:	S
UK	5,5	5,5	5,6	5,6	5,6	5,6	5,7	5,9	5,9	6,1	:	UK
IS	18,4	18,0	17,6	17,5	18,2	17,7	18,4	19,0	20,7	23,3	:	IS
NO	28,2	28,7	26,0	27,4	27,9	26,1	28,2	23,9	25,3	26,4	:	NO
EEA	6,1	6,0	6,3	6,3	6,3	6,3	6,5	6,7	6,7	6,9	:	EEA
CH	8,9	8,0	8,4	8,4	8,6	8,8	9,3	7,9	8,7	8,7	:	CH
US	11,7	11,9	12,9	12,9	12,9	13,2	13,2	13,7	13,8	14,1	:	US
CA	19,5	19,0	18,6	18,9	18,3	18,3	18,9	19,3	19,1	18,5	:	CA
JP	6,1	6,4	6,9	7,1	7,2	7,3	7,6	7,9	8,1	8,2	:	JP

Further reading: Energy, yearly statistics, 1998. Eurostat.

4B2EB

5

The presentation of electricity balance sheets is slightly different because electricity is a derived form of energy. Relative importance of each consuming sector is calculated using the quantity of electricity available for final consumption. Gross production of electricity represents total generation of electricity.

Renewable energy primary production: biomass, hydro, geothermal and wind-solar. Million toe. EU-15

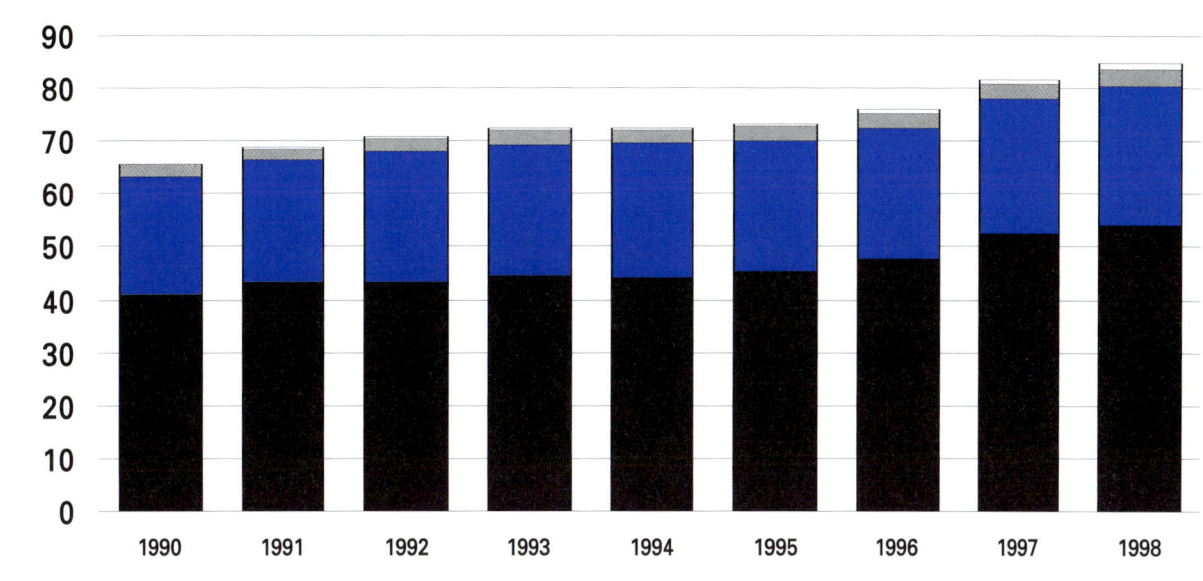

Black: biomass; colour: hydro; grey: geothermal; white: wind-solar.

Further reading: Energy, yearly statistics, 1998. Eurostat.

Production of electricity per person. 1 000 kWh per capita

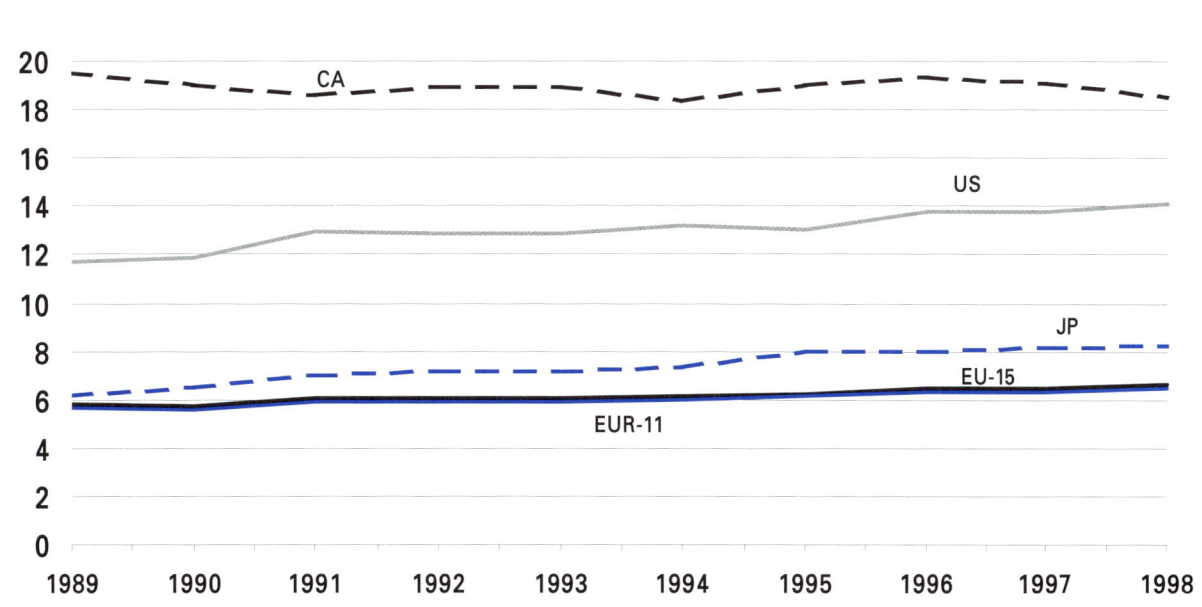

Further reading: Energy, yearly statistics, 1998. Eurostat.

EU-15 and EUR-11: data sets for periods before and after the year 1990 are not fully comparable as they refer to Germany before and after unification.

Need more data on this topic? Ask your Data Shop

EUROSTAT YEARBOOK 2001
445

Production of crude steel. 1 000 t

	1989	1990	1991	1992	1993	1994	1995	1996	1997	1998	1999	
EU-15	152 563	148 369 |	148 746	143 537	144 246	151 750	155 741	146 595	159 815	159 470	155 099	**EU-15**
EUR-11	:	:	:	:	:	:	131 595	122 041	134 364	135 501	132 034	**EUR-11**
B	10 974	11 453	11 348	10 331	10 178	11 331	11 557	10 772	10 738	11 423	10 931	**B**
DK	624	610	633	591	604	722	654	738	786	792	730	**DK**
D	41 073	38 343 |	42 169	39 711	37 625	40 837	42 051	39 792	45 007	44 046	42 061	**D**
EL	957	999	980	924	980	848	939	846	1 015	1 108	951	**EL**
E	12 765	12 936	12 798	12 243	12 960	13 445	13 802	12 154	13 683	14 828	14 884	**E**
F	19 340	19 016	18 442	17 977	17 110	18 025	18 106	17 641	19 773	20 153	20 225	**F**
IRL	324	326	293	257	326	283	309	340	336	359	337	**IRL**
I	25 213	25 467	25 112	24 835	25 720	26 151	27 766	23 910	25 798	25 677	24 738	**I**
L	3 721	3 560	3 379	3 068	3 293	3 073	2 613	2 501	2 580	2 476	2 600	**L**
NL	5 681	5 412	5 171	5 439	6 000	6 171	6 409	6 326	6 641	6 378	6 075	**NL**
A	4 718	4 291	4 187	3 953	4 149	4 399	5 003	4 454	5 194	5 298	5 211	**A**
P	762	746	573	769	775	748	827	869	904	936	1 038	**P**
FIN	2 921	2 860	2 890	3 077	3 256	3 420	3 152	3 281	3 711	3 928	3 934	**FIN**
S	4 692	4 455	4 252	4 358	4 591	4 955	4 898	4 888	5 105	5 122	5 005	**S**
UK	18 798	17 895	16 519	16 004	16 679	17 342	17 655	18 082	18 545	16 947	16 379	**UK**

4B4AB

Further reading: Iron and steel, yearly statistics, 2000. Eurostat.

Production of hot-rolled steel products. 1 000 t

	1989	1990	1991	1992	1993	1994	1995	1996	1997	1998	1999	
EU-15	:	: |	:	124 851	121 989	131 041	134 700	128 270	140 600	139 781	140 806	**EU-15**
EUR-11	:	:	:	:	:	:	112 913	106 416	117 841	118 318	119 830	**EUR-11**
B	8 535	8 934	8 755	10 335	9 750	10 980	11 035	10 963	12 045	12 194	12 779	**B**
DK	619	550	518	541	529	638	630	622	706	661	689	**DK**
D	31 702	29 729,0 |	32 742	33 042	31 138	33 873	34 315	32 889	37 075	36 593	35 879	**D**
EL	1 892	1 948	1 879	1 569	1 354	1 296	1 434	1 246	1 382	1 195	1 368	**EL**
E	10 989	11 067	11 129	10 780	11 563	12 103	12 772	10 972	12 422	13 260	13 847	**E**
F	16 382	15 605	15 387	15 204	14 046	15 278	15 110	15 178	16 588	16 823	17 293	**F**
IRL	296	305	264	243	306	242	275	310	306	325	322	**IRL**
I	22 534	22 356	23 168	22 615	21 760	22 850	24 075	21 245	23 146	22 569	22 917	**I**
L	3 299	3 223	3 050	2 563	2 607	2 645	2 413	2 314	2 465	2 516	2 775	**L**
NL	3 612	3 602	3 669	4 185	4 119	4 555	4 702	4 756	5 174	4 964	4 786	**NL**
A	:	:	:	3 435	3 446	3 820	4 211	3 837	4 515	4 641	4 656	**A**
P	885	846	720	678	718	701	704	660	790	750	800	**P**
FIN	:	:	:	2 819	2 989	3 121	3 301	3 292	3 315	3 683	3 776	**FIN**
S	:	:	:	3 510	3 905	4 501	4 460	4 368	4 542	4 485	4 575	**S**
UK	15 030	14 315	13 702	13 332	13 759	14 438	15 262	15 618	16 129	15 122	14 344	**UK**

4B4AC

Further reading: Iron and steel, yearly statistics, 2000. Eurostat.

The steel industry encompasses all stages of production from raw material processing to finished steel products. There are two main ways of making steel: via pig-iron made in blast furnaces from iron ore and other raw materials (61.8 % of EU-15 crude steel production in 1999); and by recycling steel scrap in electric furnaces (38.2 % of EU-15 production). Most finished products are made by hot rolling. The two main primary product classes are long products, such as rod and wire (38.0 % of EU-15 hot-rolled production in 1999), and flat products, such as sheet and plate (62.0 % of EU-15 production). There are various qualities of steel — ordinary, special and alloy — and nowadays a growing proportion of finished products are coated.

World production of pig-iron. Million t. 1994 and 1999

4B4AD

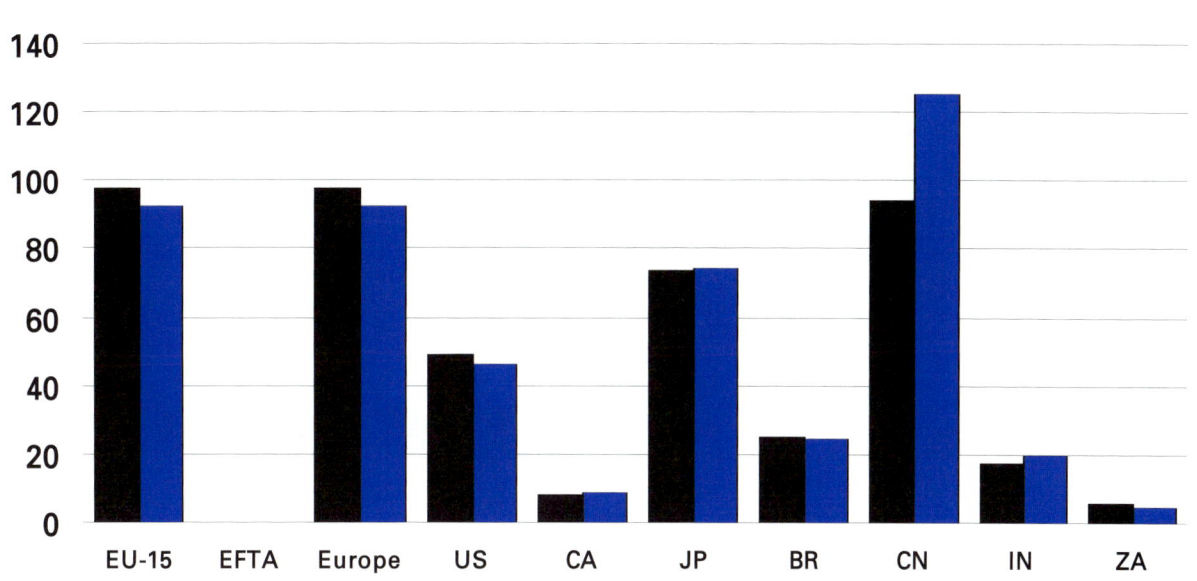

Black: 1994; colour: 1999; EFTA: EFTA; Europe: EU-15 + EFTA; BR: Brazil; ZA: South Africa; CN: China; IN: India; JP: Japan; US: United States; CA: Canada.

Further reading: Iron and steel, yearly statistics, 2000. Eurostat.

World production of crude steel. Million t. 1994 and 1999

4B4AE

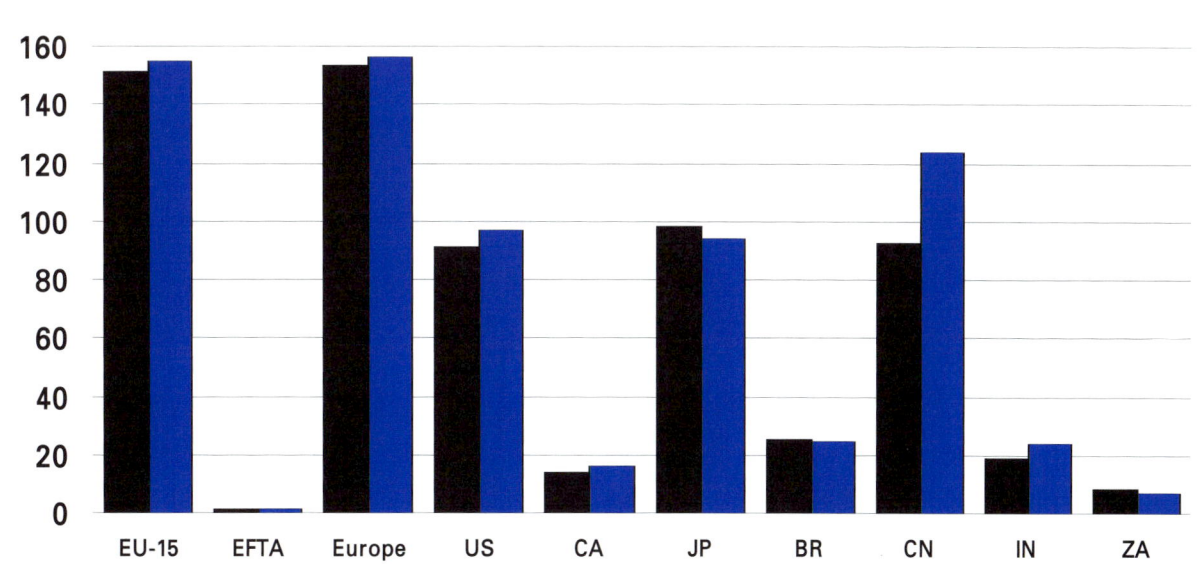

Black: 1994; colour: 1999. EFTA: EFTA; Europe: EU-15 + EFTA; BR: Brazil; ZA: South Africa; CN: China; IN: India; JP: Japan; US: United States; CA: Canada.

Further reading: Iron and steel, yearly statistics, 2000. Eurostat.

Between the mid-1970s and 1987 the steel industry in industrialised countries suffered serious setbacks. Restructuring after 1980 led to significant productivity gains by reducing capacity and cutting the labour force. In 1988 and 1989 there was a major recovery in steel production and consumption. However, new problems arose in the 1990s. There was a recovery in production back to 1989 levels in 1994 and 1995. After a setback in 1996, EU-15 crude steel output rose to nearly 160 million tonnes in 1997, remained nearly unchanged in 1998 and went slightly down to 155 million tonnes in 1999.

Capacity and actual production of crude steel as % of EU total. 1999

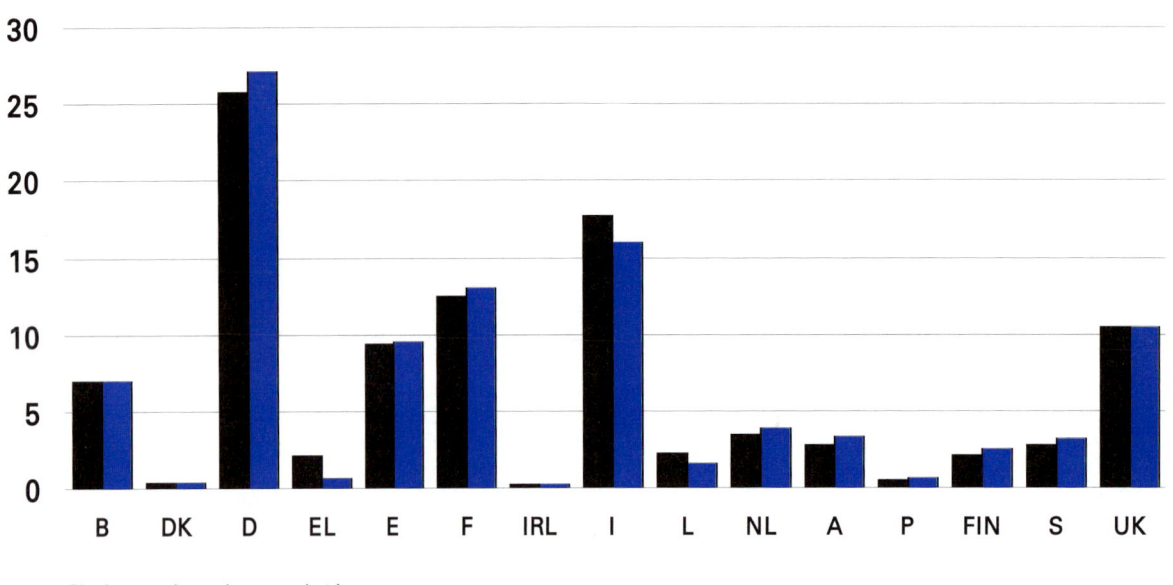

Black: capacity; colour: production.

Further reading: Iron and steel, yearly statistics, 2000. Eurostat. ECSC investments, 1999, European Commission.

Total production of hot-rolled steel products. Million t. 1999

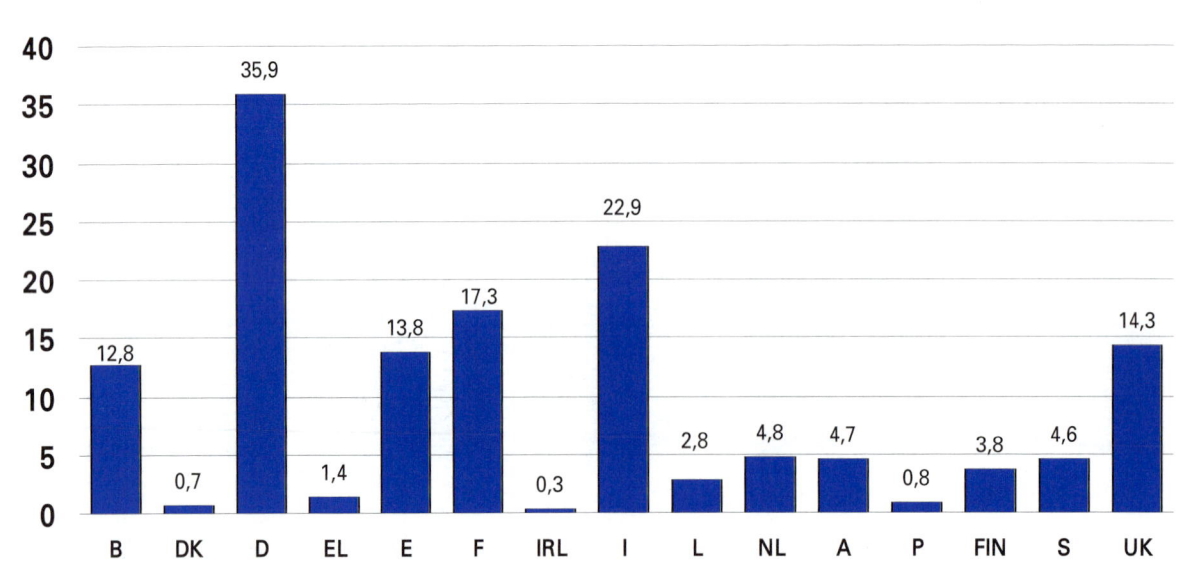

Further reading: Iron and steel, yearly statistics, 2000. Eurostat.

Final consumption of ECSC crude steel per person. kg

4B4CB

	1989	1990	1991	1992	1993	1994	1995	1996	1997	1998	1999	
EU-15	:	:	:	:	:	:	318	333	362	400	401	EU-15
B	438	436	442	483	382	487	347	497	424	559	510	B
DK	367	316	302	275	260	356	357	301	342	365	371	DK
D	472	502	444	472	390	432	423	407	443	498	464	D
EL	216	276	276	227	237	237	366	423	411	436	407	EL
E	287	297	279	275	248	287	379	309	363	430	478	E
F	312	310	299	288	239	275	267	251	264	293	305	F
IRL	218	234	205	219	187	230	304	259	299	329	330	IRL
I	433	417	393	406	286	342	304	322	415	436	460	I
L	:	:	:	:	:	:	:	:	:	:	884	L
NL	348	379	312	325	312	272	369	383	403	320	398	NL
A	:	:	:	:	:	:	377	447	394	355	215	A
P	197	235	229	223	250	209	372	276	314	350	396	P
FIN	:	:	:	:	:	:	329	309	240	474	473	FIN
S	:	:	:	:	:	:	422	404	425	434	320	S
UK	326	287	239	233	251	291	267	266	277	311	307	UK

Further reading: Iron and steel, yearly statistics, 2000. Eurostat.

B: includes L up to 1998.

Employment in the iron and steel industry, situation at end of year in 1 000s

4B4CC

	1989	1990	1991	1992	1993	1994	1995	1996	1997	1998	1999	
EU-15	454,2	434,0	439,6	404,1	365,0	337,9	313,7	297,5	291,1	286,5	277,5	EU-15
EUR-11	368,4	352,4	366,0	337,0	300,8	275,2	258,0	244,3	239,0	237,5	232,6	EUR-11
B	27,7	26,3	26,2	25,4	24,1	23,5	23,3	22,6	20,4	20,3	19,6	B
DK	1,5	1,5	1,3	1,3	1,1	1,1	1,1	1,1	1,2	1,2	1,3	DK
D	130,1	125,2	147,5	132,1	110,3	96,0	89,1	85,1	81,3	79,7	77,5	D
EL	3,4	3,4	3,2	3,0	2,9	2,5	2,5	2,0	2,1	2,0	1,9	EL
E	39,0	36,4	35,6	33,3	27,3	25,8	24,6	22,9	22,8	22,5	22,0	E
F	49,3	46,4	44,5	42,8	40,5	39,3	38,6	38,1	38,3	38,0	37,6	F
IRL	0,7	0,7	0,7	0,6	0,6	0,4	0,4	0,3	0,3	0,3	0,3	IRL
I	57,7	56,0	55,5	50,0	49,3	43,9	40,9	36,2	38,0	38,5	38,7	I
L	9,9	9,3	8,8	7,6	7,1	6,7	5,9	5,2	4,3	4,3	4,2	L
NL	17,7	17,0	16,6	15,9	13,5	12,8	12,5	12,2	12,0	11,9	11,7	NL
A	22,0	21,0	18,0	17,0	16,0	15,0	13,2	12,6	12,5	12,2	11,8	A
P	4,3	4,1	3,6	3,3	3,1	2,8	2,5	2,2	2,0	1,8	1,6	P
FIN	10,0	10,0	9,0	9,0	9,0	9,0	7,0	6,9	7,1	8,0	7,6	FIN
S	28,0	26,0	24,0	22,0	21,0	21,0	14,2	13,6	13,6	13,3	12,8	S
UK	52,9	50,7	45,1	40,8	39,2	38,1	37,9	36,5	35,2	32,5	28,9	UK

Further reading: Iron and steel, yearly statistics, 2000. Eurostat.

Imports of ECSC steel by country of origin as % of EU total imports

	1994	1995	1996	1997	1998	1999
Europe	89	72	71	80	63	69
EFTA of which:	44	7	8	7	5	6
CH	4	3	3	4	2	3
NO	2	3	4	3	3	3
Eastern Europe of which:	43	61	57	62	46	51
PL	:	:	:	10	7	7
CZ	:	:	:	8	5	7
Africa of which:	4	5	5	5	4	5
ZA	2	2	4	2	3	2
America of which:	5	16	17	9	1	1
US	1	5	5	2	1	1
Asia of which:	2	6	6	5	21	13
JP	2	1	1	1	1	2

Further reading: Iron and steel, yearly statistics, 2000. Eurostat.

EFTA: European Free Trade Association (IS, LI, NO, CH); ZA: South Africa; CH: Switzerland; NO: Norway.

4B4DA

Exports of ECSC steel by country of destination as % of EU total exports

	1994	1995	1996	1997	1998	1999
Europe	24	25	19	24	31	32
EFTA of which:	18	13	9	11	13	13
CH	6	8	5	7	9	9
NO	3	5	4	4	4	4
Eastern Europe	3	6	4	6	10	12
America of which:	41	32	36	36	33	32
US	29	21	26	25	28	28
Africa	9	9	9	8	10	8
Asia of which:	26	31	33	27	17	19
CN	4	2	2	2	1	1
IN	4	4	5	4	2	2

Further reading: Iron and steel, yearly statistics, 2000. Eurostat.

EFTA: European Free Trade Association (IS, LI, NO, CH); CH: Switzerland; NO: Norway.

4B4DB

The EU is the world's largest steel producer, followed by China, the United States and Japan. It is also the largest steel exporter. Major markets for EU steel are the United States, Asia (including Japan), and the EFTA countries. Collapse of domestic demand in eastern Europe in the early 1990s had a significant impact on EU steel. Exports to the region fell significantly, whilst imports from eastern Europe rose. There was also intense competition from the region in third markets. More recently, the downturn in the Asian economies starting in the second half of 1997 directly and indirectly affected the EU trade balance in steel products, with the result that for the first time the EU became a net importer of steel products in 1998. The deficit continued in 1999.

Exports of ECSC steel to third countries, of which plate and sheet and coils. Million t

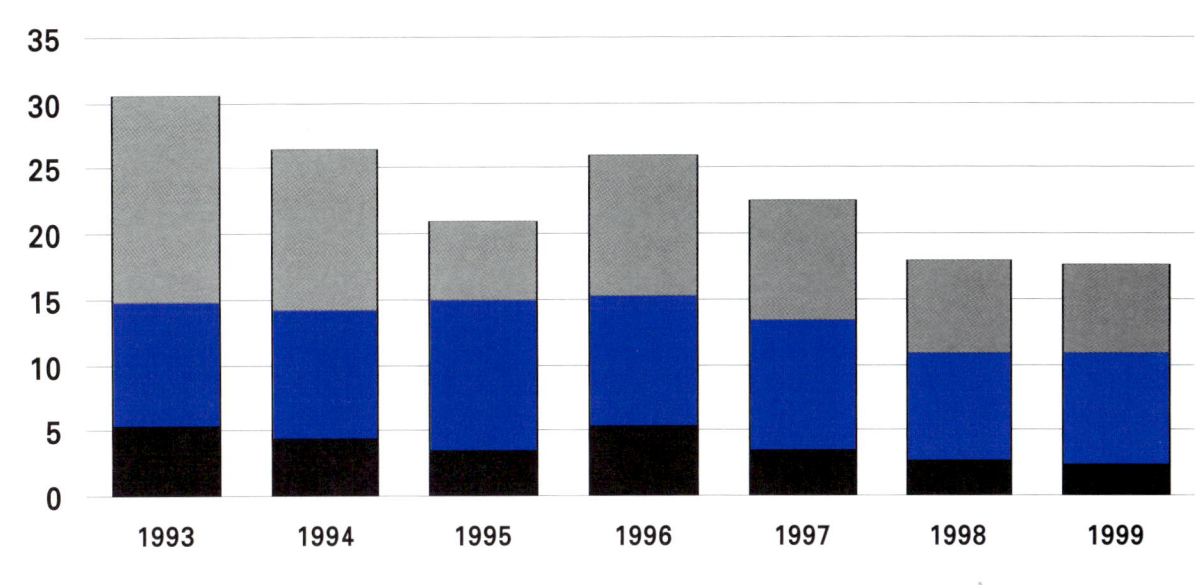

Black: coils; colour: plate and sheet; grey: other.

Further reading: Iron and steel, yearly statistics, 2000. Eurostat.

Imports of ECSC steel from third countries, of which plate and sheet and coils. Million t

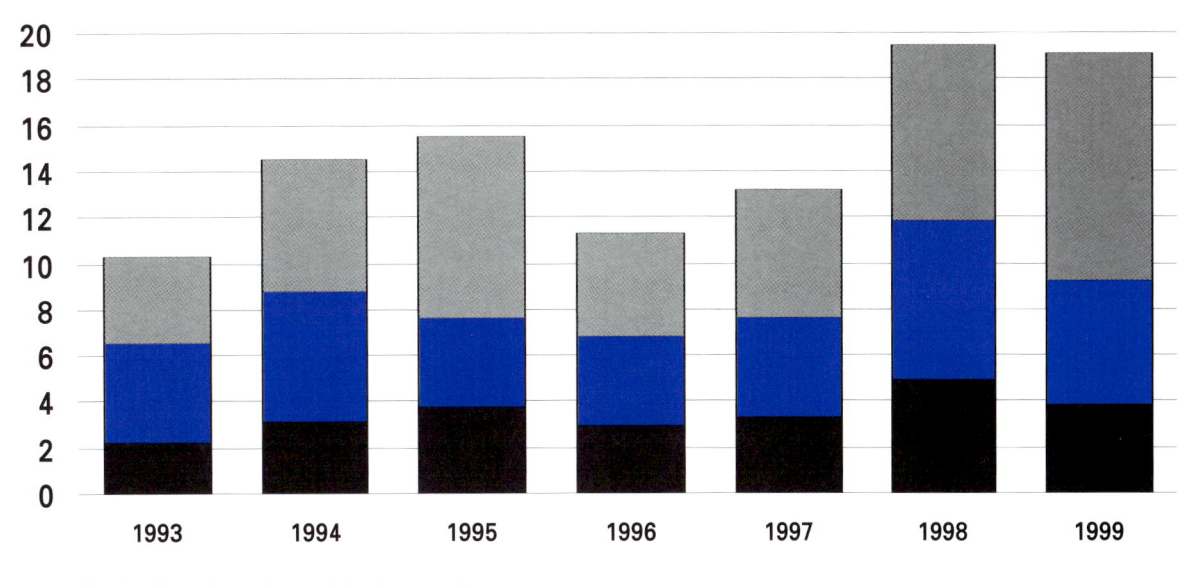

Black: coils; colour: plate and sheet; grey: other.

Further reading: Iron and steel, yearly statistics, 2000. Eurostat.

Hard coal primary production. 1990 = 100. %

	1989	1990	1991	1992	1993	1994	1995	1996	1997	1998	1999	
EU-15	105,8	100,0 |	98,6	93,7	80,5	67,2	69,0	64,2	61,8	54,9	:	EU-15
EUR-11	102,3	100,0 |	94,3	93,4	84,7	77,4	77,4	72,4	69,4	63,3	:	EUR-11
B	182,7	100,0	61,2	21,0	-	-	-	-	-	-	:	B
DK	-	-	-	-	-	-	-	-	-	-	:	DK
D	101,2	100,0 |	95,0	94,3	83,8	75,3	76,9	69,4	66,9	61,7	:	D
EL	-	-	-	-	-	-	-	-	-	-	:	EL
E	98,6	100,0	92,2	95,4	94,7	93,6	90,7	91,0	92,0	83,4	:	E
F	109,4	100,0	96,6	90,4	81,8	71,9	66,9	69,7	55,1	46,4	:	F
IRL	95,6	100,0	13,3	2,2	2,2	2,2	-	-	-	-	:	IRL
I	127,6	100,0	36,2	191,4	17,2	-	-	-	-	-	:	I
L	-	-	-	-	-	-	-	-	-	-	:	L
NL	-	-	-	-	-	-	-	-	-	-	:	NL
A	-	-	-	-	-	-	-	-	-	-	:	A
P	91,8	100,0	96,1	78,6	70,1	52,3	-	-	-	-	:	P
FIN	-	-	-	-	-	-	-	-	-	-	:	FIN
S	-	100,0	254,5	336,4	36,4	-	-	-	-	-	:	S
UK	110,1	100,0	103,8	94,0	75,5	54,8	58,9	54,4	52,6	44,8	:	UK

4B4EC

Further reading: Energy, yearly statistics, 1998. Eurostat.

Hard coal primary production. Million t

	1989	1990	1991	1992	1993	1994	1995	1996	1997	1998	1999	
EU-15	208,7	197,2 |	194,5	184,8	158,8	132,5	136,1	126,7	121,9	108,3	:	EU-15
EUR-11	110,4	107,9 |	101,7	100,7	91,4	83,5	83,5	78,2	74,9	68,3	:	EUR-11
B	1,9	1,0	0,6	0,2	-	-	-	-	-	-	:	B
DK	-	-	-	-	-	-	-	-	-	-	:	DK
D	77,5	76,6 |	72,7	72,2	64,2	57,6	58,9	53,2	51,2	47,2	:	D
EL	-	-	-	-	-	-	-	-	-	-	:	EL
E	19,2	19,4	17,9	18,6	18,4	18,2	17,6	17,7	17,9	16,2	:	E
F	11,5	10,5	10,1	9,5	8,6	7,5	7,0	7,3	5,8	4,9	:	F
IRL	0,0	0,0	0,0	0,0	0,0	0,0	-	-	-	-	:	IRL
I	0,1	0,1	0,0	0,1	0,0	-	-	-	-	-	:	I
L	-	-	-	-	-	-	-	-	-	-	:	L
NL	-	-	-	-	-	-	-	-	-	-	:	NL
A	-	-	-	-	-	-	-	-	-	-	:	A
P	0,3	0,3	0,3	0,2	0,2	0,1	-	-	-	-	:	P
FIN	-	-	-	-	-	-	-	-	-	-	:	FIN
S	0,0	0,0	0,0	0,0	0,0	-	-	-	-	-	:	S
UK	98,3	89,3	92,7	84,0	67,5	49,0	52,6	48,5	47,0	40,0	:	UK

4B4EB

Further reading: Energy, yearly statistics, 1998. Eurostat.

5

eurostat

Despite continued decline in solid fuels produc-tion, they still account for approximately one sixth of EU primary energy production. The contri-bution of lignite to overall production was stable until 1991 when the addition of production from the former GDR almost doubled EU lignite output.

Hard coal industry: production, imports and underground employment.
1990 = 100 %. EU-15

4B4ED

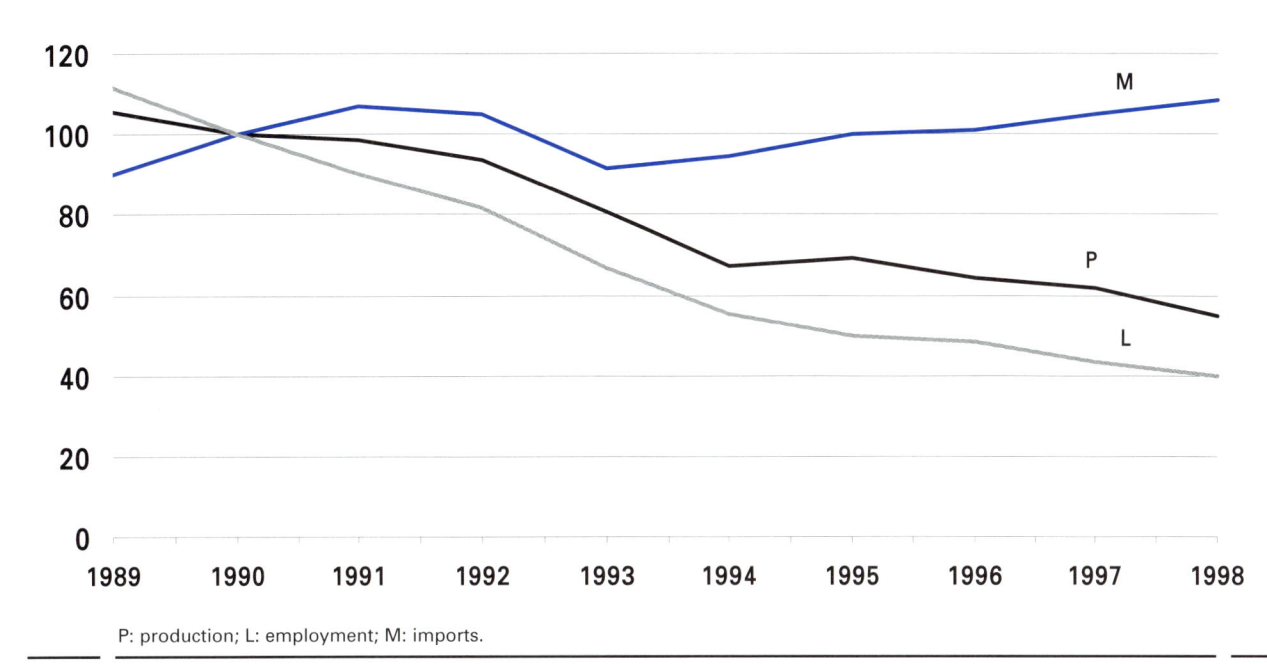

P: production; L: employment; M: imports.

Further reading: Energy, yearly statistics, 1998. Eurostat.

Hard coal deliveries to major consumers: public and pithead power stations, coking plants
and other consumers. Million t. EU-15

4B4EE

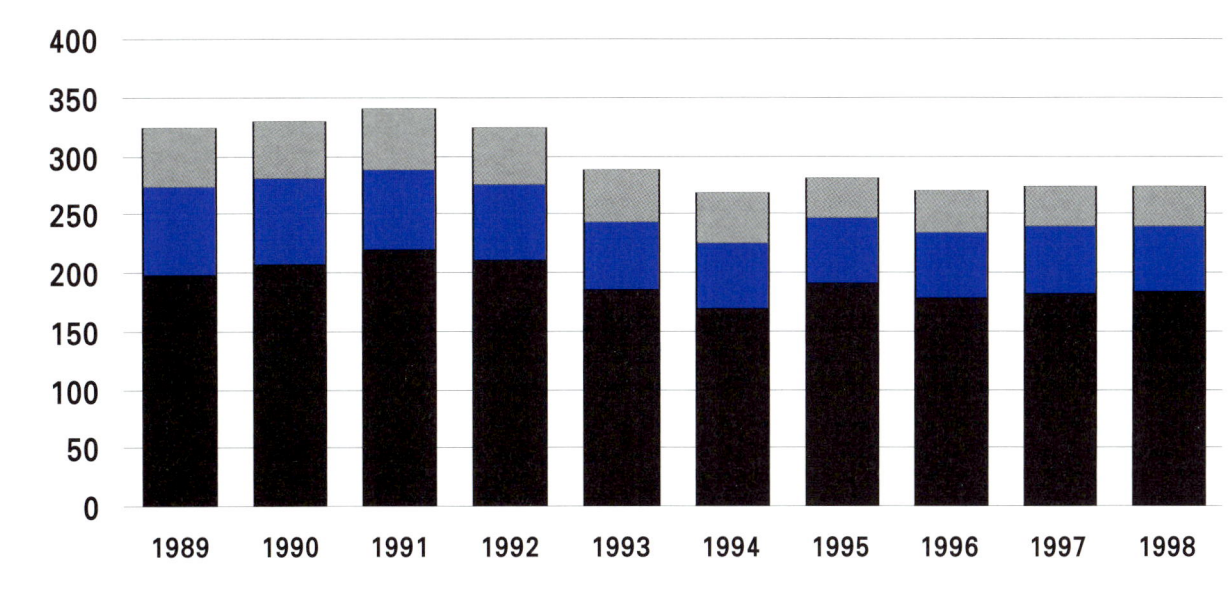

Black: public and pithead power stations; colour: coking plants; grey: other consumers.

Further reading: Energy, yearly statistics, 1998. Eurostat.

EU-15: data sets for periods before and after the year 1990 are not fully comparable as they refer to Germany before and after unifica-tion.

eurostat

Need an update for this indicator? Ask your Data Shop

EUROSTAT YEARBOOK 2001
453

Exports to EU countries as % of total national exports (fob)

	1989	1990	1991	1992	1993	1994	1995	1996	1997	1998	1999	
EU-15	65,5	66,6	67,1	66,8	63,2	63,3	64,0	63,0	61,8	63,1	63,5	EU-15
B	77,7	79,3	79,3	79,2	76,8	75,8	77,1	76,7	74,6	76,2	76,0	B
DK	66,6	68,4	68,8	68,0	66,0	64,9	66,6	66,6	66,4	66,4	66,9	DK
D	64,5	63,9	63,1	63,2	58,5	58,0	58,2	57,4	55,5	56,5	56,9	D
EL	68,7	67,9	67,2	68,7	58,9	57,1	60,1	53,9	50,9	53,8	51,6	EL
E	63,6	66,8	68,9	68,3	64,3	66,6	67,9	67,8	68,3	71,7	71,2	E
F	64,3	65,3	65,8	65,3	62,2	63,4	63,0	62,3	62,0	62,4	62,4	F
IRL	77,2	77,9	77,3	77,0	72,4	73,5	73,9	71,2	68,9	69,3	66,0	IRL
I	60,8	62,5	63,1	61,6	57,1	57,5	57,3	55,4	55,0	56,2	57,3	I
L	-	-	-	-	-	-	-	-	-		85,4	L
NL	79,4	80,8	81,3	80,4	77,7	78,3	79,9	79,7	79,0	78,9	79,5	NL
A	66,6	67,9	68,0	68,1	65,5	64,8	65,8	64,1	62,0	64,2	62,9	A
P	77,8	80,3	81,4	80,6	79,9	80,0	80,1	80,6	80,8	82,0	82,8	P
FIN	58,1	60,2	64,7	65,5	57,3	56,8	57,5	54,5	53,2	56,1	57,7	FIN
S	61,6	62,1	62,0	62,3	59,0	55,5	59,6	57,1	55,6	58,0	58,4	S
UK	54,2	56,9	60,0	59,3	56,7	57,6	58,2	57,6	55,5	58,0	58,6	UK
IS	59,8	70,7	68,9	71,2	61,8	61,6	62,7	62,1	60,6	65,0	62,6	IS
NO	80,1	79,5	80,0	78,8	78,3	77,8	77,2	76,9	76,0	76,9	73,8	NO
EEA	66,0	67,3	68,3	67,8	64,3	64,1	65,1	63,3	62,1	63,4	63,7	EEA
CH	62,7	63,9	64,7	63,2	62,4	60,6	62,3	60,7	59,8	62,4	59,0	CH
US	25,2	26,3	25,7	24,1	21,8	21,0	21,2	20,5	20,6	22,0	22,0	US
CA	9,0	8,5	8,4	7,4	5,9	5,4	6,4	7,0	5,2	5,1	5,0	CA
JP	19,2	20,4	20,4	19,8	16,7	15,5	15,9	15,4	15,6	18,5	16,6	JP

4B7AA

Further reading: External trade, statistical yearbooks. Eurostat. Comext on CD-ROM.   B: includes L up to 1998.
Eurostat.

Imports from EU countries as % of total national imports (cif)

	1989	1990	1991	1992	1993	1994	1995	1996	1997	1998	1999	
EU-15	63,3	64,0	63,7	64,3	62,4	62,8	64,1	63,8	62,2	62,9	61,7	EU-15
B	72,3	74,1	74,0	74,5	72,6	73,4	72,8	73,1	71,3	71,1	71,0	B
DK	68,4	69,4	68,8	69,8	69,3	69,2	71,8	70,6	70,2	70,4	69,8	DK
D	61,1	62,0	62,0	62,3	59,0	59,2	60,4	60,3	58,7	59,0	56,9	D
EL	66,4	67,6	63,9	66,5	63,0	67,9	70,1	64,4	65,0	65,6	66,2	EL
E	60,4	62,3	62,8	63,2	65,0	66,4	68,5	69,3	66,0	70,6	68,7	E
F	68,0	67,9	67,3	68,6	66,9	68,0	68,5	67,8	65,9	67,6	66,6	F
IRL	72,4	73,3	71,6	74,4	67,1	66,0	64,6	66,6	64,0	61,6	62,1	IRL
I	61,0	61,7	61,8	63,0	59,6	60,7	60,9	61,1	61,0	61,6	60,8	I
L	-	-	-	-	-	-	-	-	-		81,7	L
NL	63,9	63,7	62,6	62,7	64,3	61,6	63,2	61,4	58,6	58,1	55,1	NL
A	70,4	71,1	70,2	70,4	69,3	68,4	75,9	74,4	73,4	73,7	72,3	A
P	70,9	72,0	74,8	76,6	74,5	73,5	73,9	76,3	76,3	77,9	77,4	P
FIN	59,0	60,1	58,8	58,9	56,9	54,7	65,0	65,3	64,4	65,7	65,4	FIN
S	63,0	63,1	63,1	62,9	62,5	62,2	68,6	68,5	67,7	69,2	67,6	S
UK	56,1	56,1	54,7	55,3	53,3	54,5	54,6	54,2	53,7	53,4	53,2	UK
IS	62,1	59,8	62,5	57,8	58,0	58,3	59,8	56,4	58,1	56,2	56,8	IS
NO	62,2	66,2	67,9	69,0	67,2	68,9	71,4	70,8	68,0	67,7	68,6	NO
EEA	63,3	64,1	63,7	64,4	63,2	63,4	65,1	64,0	62,3	63,0	61,8	EEA
CH	77,3	78,1	76,6	78,4	78,8	79,2	79,8	79,0	77,1	76,7	74,8	CH
US	19,6	20,0	18,9	18,9	18,1	18,0	17,7	18,0	18,1	19,3	19,0	US
CA	12,3	12,7	11,8	10,7	9,6	9,7	10,0	10,1	9,9	9,5	9,9	CA
JP	14,4	16,0	14,5	14,5	13,7	14,1	14,5	14,1	13,3	13,9	13,2	JP

4B7AB

Further reading: External trade, statistical yearbooks. Eurostat. Comext on CD-ROM.   B: includes L up to 1998.
Eurostat.

5

EU Member States' trade with other EU countries is called intra-EU trade. Comparison of 1993 figures with those before is difficult because of the single market. This resulted in a new way of measuring trade between the EU countries. Before 1993, intra-EU trade was registered by customs authorities. Since 1993, intra-EU trade statistics are compiled directly from questionnaires filled in by EU firms.

Exports to EU countries at current prices. 1 000 million ECU

	1989	1990	1991	1992	1993	1994	1995	1996	1997	1998	1999	
EU-15	749,6	787,7	824,0	833,9	803,3	904,1	1 019,8	1 067,8	1 166,0	1 255,4	1 321,2	**EU-15**
B	73,5	77,3	79,6	79,9	83,7	93,7	105,0	107,2	114,8	123,7	125,1	**B**
DK	17,3	19,1	20,3	21,2	21,3	23,1	25,9	27,0	28,8	29,1	31,7	**DK**
D	200,1	200,4	205,0	210,3	190,0	208,2	232,7	237,1	250,5	274,1	286,1	**D**
EL	4,7	4,2	4,7	5,2	4,2	4,5	5,1	5,0	5,1	5,2	5,1	**EL**
E	26,9	30,9	35,2	36,2	35,5	43,0	50,8	57,3	60,7	71,0	69,8	**E**
F	108,0	114,1	121,5	125,6	117,7	133,6	145,0	149,7	165,3	178,4	189,8	**F**
IRL	14,5	14,5	15,1	16,8	17,9	21,0	25,3	27,1	32,4	39,8	43,8	**IRL**
I	77,4	83,6	86,3	84,7	82,6	92,5	102,4	110,2	116,5	121,2	124,0	**I**
L	-	-	-	-	-	-	-	-	-	-	6,6	**L**
NL	82,7	88,7	94,9	94,4	93,1	105,8	124,2	129,3	144,9	150,7	163,0	**NL**
A	19,6	22,3	22,6	23,3	22,5	24,6	29,0	29,4	32,7	36,7	39,0	**A**
P	9,0	10,3	10,7	11,4	10,5	12,1	14,0	15,6	17,1	18,1	18,6	**P**
FIN	12,3	12,7	12,0	12,1	11,5	14,2	17,8	17,7	19,5	21,9	22,9	**FIN**
S	28,8	28,0	27,6	26,9	25,1	28,6	36,6	38,2	40,5	43,8	46,5	**S**
UK	74,8	81,7	88,5	85,7	87,9	99,2	105,9	117,3	137,2	141,8	149,4	**UK**

4B7AC

Further reading: External trade, statistical yearbooks. Eurostat. Comext on CD-ROM. Eurostat.

B: includes L up to 1998.

Imports from EU countries at current prices. 1 000 million ECU

	1989	1990	1991	1992	1993	1994	1995	1996	1997	1998	1999	
EU-15	744,8	787,6	825,9	838,6	771,1	868,0	974,4	1 023,4	1 108,1	1 204,4	1 252,9	**EU-15**
B	67,2	73,1	75,9	75,9	73,2	82,1	91,8	96,6	101,8	107,2	106,4	**B**
DK	16,9	17,7	18,5	18,7	18,5	21,4	25,2	25,2	27,8	29,4	30,2	**DK**
D	149,5	166,5	194,8	196,7	172,7	190,0	214,1	218,1	228,3	248,1	248,3	**D**
EL	9,7	10,5	11,1	12,2	11,8	12,3	13,9	14,3	15,4	17,7	17,4	**EL**
E	37,2	41,2	45,5	47,3	43,1	49,6	59,5	66,1	67,3	86,1	87,2	**E**
F	124,3	130,4	134,7	136,7	124,1	140,7	151,5	156,7	165,7	185,5	196,0	**F**
IRL	11,4	11,9	12,1	12,5	12,1	14,2	16,0	18,0	21,3	23,7	26,8	**IRL**
I	84,5	88,2	91,0	91,7	75,3	86,3	95,8	100,2	113,1	118,5	123,8	**I**
L	-	-	-	-	-	-	-	-	-	-	8,6	**L**
NL	64,7	67,9	69,2	71,1	69,3	77,9	89,5	92,0	98,5	101,4	106,7	**NL**
A	24,9	27,9	28,7	29,3	28,7	31,8	38,4	40,1	42,6	45,7	48,4	**A**
P	12,3	13,9	16,0	17,9	15,4	16,7	18,4	21,2	23,6	26,4	28,0	**P**
FIN	13,2	12,8	10,3	9,6	8,8	10,7	14,6	16,2	17,9	19,3	19,7	**FIN**
S	28,0	27,0	25,4	24,2	22,8	27,1	34,1	36,1	39,2	42,2	43,5	**S**
UK	101,0	98,6	92,8	94,7	95,3	107,3	111,5	122,7	145,7	153,0	162,0	**UK**

4B7AD

Further reading: External trade, statistical yearbooks. Eurostat. Comext on CD-ROM. Eurostat.

B: includes L up to 1998.

Intra-EU trade by product is based on standard international trade classification (SITC) revision 3. Introduction of Intrastat in 1993 — due to the single market — resulted in important changes in methodology used to measure intra–EU trade.

Intra-EU exports of agricultural products at current prices. 1 000 million ECU

	1989	1990	1991	1992	1993	1994	1995	1996	1997	1998	1999	
EU-15	75,8	78,0	85,8	90,5	90,4	99,4	105,5	113,2	118,0	123,4	124,9	EU-15
B	7,6	7,4	8,1	8,6	9,9	10,6	11,7	12,4	12,8	13,9	14,1	B
DK	4,4	4,8	5,2	5,4	5,4	5,9	6,2	6,2	6,7	6,5	6,8	DK
D	10,5	10,3	11,9	12,4	11,8	12,5	13,1	14,4	14,6	16,2	14,7	D
EL	1,3	1,1	1,4	1,4	1,1	1,2	1,2	1,2	1,3	1,4	1,3	EL
E	4,0	4,2	4,9	5,4	5,7	6,7	7,7	8,9	9,8	11,0	10,2	E
F	16,6	17,7	18,4	19,4	19,9	20,6	21,9	21,9	23,2	23,4	24,1	F
IRL	3,3	3,1	3,5	4,3	4,3	4,6	5,0	4,3	4,1	4,2	4,5	IRL
I	5,2	5,7	6,4	6,4	6,6	7,2	7,6	8,3	8,6	8,9	9,3	I
L	-	-	-	-	-	-	-	-	-	-	0,5	L
NL	15,7	16,1	17,3	18,2	17,2	20,4	20,3	24,1	23,5	24,2	25,1	NL
A	0,6	0,6	0,5	0,6	0,6	0,6	1,1	1,3	1,6	1,8	2,3	A
P	0,5	0,6	0,7	0,7	0,6	0,7	0,8	0,9	1,0	1,1	1,1	P
FIN	0,2	0,2	0,2	0,2	0,2	0,2	0,3	0,3	0,3	0,3	0,3	FIN
S	0,4	0,4	0,4	0,4	0,4	0,4	0,7	0,9	1,1	1,1	1,2	S
UK	5,5	5,7	6,9	7,4	6,6	7,7	7,9	8,1	9,3	9,4	9,3	UK

Further reading: External trade, statistical yearbooks. Eurostat. Comext on CD-ROM. Eurostat.

B: includes L up to 1998.

4B7EA

Intra-EU exports of mineral fuels, lubricants and related products at current prices. 1 000 million ECU

	1989	1990	1991	1992	1993	1994	1995	1996	1997	1998	1999	
EU-15	24,6	27,3	28,3	25,6	27,1	28,5	28,6	35,3	38,7	30,4	38,9	EU-15
B	2,1	2,2	2,5	2,2	2,6	2,5	2,5	3,1	3,1	2,5	3,7	B
DK	0,6	0,8	0,9	0,9	0,9	0,9	0,9	1,3	1,4	1,0	1,6	DK
D	2,1	2,1	2,0	2,0	2,2	2,4	2,3	3,6	3,4	3,3	3,1	D
EL	0,2	0,2	0,2	0,1	0,1	0,1	0,1	0,1	0,1	0,1	0,1	EL
E	0,8	0,9	1,0	0,8	0,6	0,7	0,7	0,9	1,3	1,1	1,3	E
F	2,3	2,6	2,9	2,8	2,9	3,0	3,4	3,5	3,8	3,3	3,8	F
IRL	0,1	0,1	0,1	0,1	0,1	0,1	0,1	0,1	0,2	0,1	0,1	IRL
I	0,9	1,3	1,2	1,1	0,6	0,5	0,5	0,6	1,0	0,8	1,0	I
L	-	-	-	-	-	-	-	-	-	-	0,0	L
NL	8,7	9,0	9,4	8,1	8,2	9,2	9,2	10,5	10,9	8,7	12,0	NL
A	0,3	0,2	0,2	0,3	0,3	0,3	0,2	0,3	0,3	0,3	0,3	A
P	0,2	0,2	0,2	0,2	0,3	0,3	0,3	0,2	0,2	0,1	0,1	P
FIN	0,2	0,3	0,4	0,4	0,4	0,3	0,3	0,6	0,4	0,5	0,6	FIN
S	1,0	1,1	1,1	1,1	1,1	1,0	1,0	1,3	1,1	0,8	1,3	S
UK	5,3	6,4	6,2	5,5	6,7	6,9	7,2	9,3	11,5	7,8	9,8	UK

B: includes L up to 1998.

4B7BR

5

Intra-EU exports of chemicals at current prices. 1 000 million ECU

	1989	1990	1991	1992	1993	1994	1995	1996	1997	1998	1999	
EU-15	80,5	84,3	87,0	90,9	94,7	112,9	128,9	132,8	148,5	161,5	167,3	**EU-15**
B	9,7	10,3	10,5	10,8	12,9	15,2	18,1	18,2	20,6	23,2	24,8	**B**
DK	1,0	1,0	1,1	1,3	1,7	1,8	2,2	1,7	2,5	2,6	3,1	**DK**
D	22,1	22,2	22,7	22,9	23,4	27,5	30,8	30,5	32,3	34,4	32,6	**D**
EL	0,1	0,1	0,1	0,1	0,1	0,1	0,2	0,2	0,2	0,2	0,3	**EL**
E	2,0	2,2	2,3	2,4	2,5	3,3	4,2	4,1	4,6	5,5	5,7	**E**
F	13,4	14,1	14,7	15,3	15,3	17,5	20,2	20,7	22,6	24,8	26,6	**F**
IRL	1,7	2,0	2,3	2,7	2,9	3,8	4,4	5,6	7,6	12,4	12,6	**IRL**
I	5,1	5,1	5,4	5,9	5,9	7,0	8,0	8,8	10,0	10,3	11,3	**I**
L	-	-	-	-	-	-	-	-	-	-	0,4	**L**
NL	12,4	12,2	11,7	13,0	12,0	16,5	18,5	20,2	21,5	20,2	20,3	**NL**
A	1,6	1,7	1,8	1,8	1,8	2,0	2,4	2,3	2,7	2,9	3,0	**A**
P	0,5	0,5	0,5	0,5	0,4	0,6	0,7	0,7	0,8	0,8	0,8	**P**
FIN	0,6	0,6	0,6	0,6	0,6	0,8	1,1	0,6	1,2	1,3	1,4	**FIN**
S	2,2	2,1	2,4	2,5	2,6	2,5	3,2	3,5	3,8	3,5	4,4	**S**
UK	8,1	10,3	10,8	11,0	12,5	14,3	14,9	15,8	18,0	19,3	20,0	**UK**

Further reading: External trade, statistical yearbooks. Eurostat. Comext on CD-ROM. Eurostat. B: includes L up to 1998.

Intra-EU exports of manufactured products at current prices. 1 000 million ECU

	1989	1990	1991	1992	1993	1994	1995	1996	1997	1998	1999	
EU-15	237,1	249,4	254,6	258,8	244,0	275,3	306,7	315,1	340,0	361,4	360,2	**EU-15**
B	26,0	27,0	26,7	26,3	27,2	29,1	34,1	34,1	36,6	41,3	39,2	**B**
DK	4,5	5,1	5,5	5,9	6,3	6,9	8,0	7,8	8,1	8,5	8,9	**DK**
D	59,4	59,9	59,7	60,2	53,5	57,8	63,0	61,3	64,7	71,2	67,2	**D**
EL	2,3	2,1	2,4	2,7	2,2	2,3	2,4	2,2	2,4	2,5	2,2	**EL**
E	7,5	8,4	8,8	9,1	9,0	11,0	13,6	14,9	15,7	18,4	17,6	**E**
F	28,1	29,8	31,1	32,2	29,9	34,0	37,8	38,2	41,0	43,8	44,9	**F**
IRL	3,4	3,6	3,9	4,3	3,9	4,7	5,6	5,9	6,1	6,2	6,5	**IRL**
I	35,4	38,4	39,6	39,4	39,5	43,9	47,4	49,5	51,8	52,2	51,5	**I**
L	-	-	-	-	-	-	-	-	-	-	3,6	**L**
NL	18,7	19,2	19,6	21,6	18,9	22,9	25,5	30,7	33,7	34,6	35,4	**NL**
A	8,9	9,9	9,9	10,2	9,8	10,6	12,4	11,5	13,8	15,5	15,7	**A**
P	5,1	5,9	6,4	6,7	6,3	7,0	7,3	7,9	8,6	9,0	8,9	**P**
FIN	6,7	6,9	6,7	6,5	6,2	7,4	8,9	7,9	9,3	10,0	10,1	**FIN**
S	10,6	10,4	10,4	10,0	9,1	10,8	12,5	13,1	13,6	13,3	13,6	**S**
UK	20,6	22,8	24,0	23,6	22,2	26,9	28,2	30,1	34,5	34,9	34,9	**UK**

Further reading: External trade, statistical yearbooks. Eurostat. Comext on CD-ROM. Eurostat. B: includes L up to 1998.

Intra-EU exports of machinery and transport equipment at current prices. 1 000 million ECU

	1989	1990	1991	1992	1993	1994	1995	1996	1997	1998	1999	
EU-15	268,0	285,0	298,4	304,5	281,0	326,8	371,2	405,6	455,8	514,5	550,9	**EU-15**
B	18,9	21,0	21,6	21,6	23,5	26,5	28,5	31,6	33,5	38,1	39,2	**B**
DK	4,1	4,6	4,7	5,0	4,5	4,9	5,9	6,4	7,2	7,6	8,5	**DK**
D	94,2	94,4	96,6	100,5	84,8	94,9	105,9	107,6	117,0	135,0	139,0	**D**
EL	0,1	0,1	0,2	0,2	0,2	0,2	0,3	0,3	0,3	0,4	0,3	**EL**
E	11,3	13,6	16,3	17,2	16,3	19,5	22,6	25,9	26,7	32,1	32,5	**E**
F	41,6	44,4	49,4	51,2	45,6	53,7	56,7	60,5	69,5	77,9	84,6	**F**
IRL	4,9	4,7	4,4	4,4	4,7	6,3	8,3	9,2	11,8	14,2	17,4	**IRL**
I	28,9	31,0	31,8	30,1	28,3	32,1	36,6	40,6	42,6	46,5	48,3	**I**
L	-	-	-	-	-	-	-	-	-	-	1,9	**L**
NL	16,1	17,7	17,2	18,4	17,6	23,1	28,6	36,7	45,4	49,0	55,8	**NL**
A	7,1	8,7	8,9	9,4	9,0	9,7	11,3	11,6	12,9	14,6	16,2	**A**
P	1,8	2,1	2,2	2,6	2,3	2,7	4,0	5,2	5,6	6,3	6,8	**P**
FIN	2,8	3,2	2,8	3,1	2,9	3,7	4,9	5,4	6,0	7,6	8,2	**FIN**
S	11,0	10,6	10,3	10,0	9,2	10,7	13,7	15,0	16,0	17,5	19,4	**S**
UK	25,3	28,8	31,9	30,9	32,2	38,8	43,9	49,5	61,3	67,7	72,9	**UK**

Further reading: External trade, statistical yearbooks. Eurostat. Comext on CD-ROM. Eurostat. B: includes L up to 1998.

4B7EB   6Y1AY   4B7CA

International trade balance in goods and services with EU as a partner. 1 000 million ECU

	1989	1990	1991	1992	1993	1994	1995	1996	1997	1998	1999	
EU-15	:	:	:	:	:	:	:	:	:	:	:	EU-15
B/L	6,0	6,5	6,4	8,0	9,2	10,7	10,7	10,4	9,5	10,7	:	B/L
DK	0,2	1,3	2,1	4,0	5,5	5,3	4,5	5,8	1,5	0,0	:	DK
D	37,6	22,7	2,3	6,6	8,5	10,3	12,1	11,8	10,5	2,7	:	D
EL	- 1,7	- 2,5	- 2,5	- 3,0	- 2,1	- 2,2	- 4,0	- 4,5	- 3,7	- 3,8	:	EL
E	- 1,4	- 2,2	- 1,1	- 2,2	4,4	6,6	6,8	8,7	11,4	9,6	:	E
F	- 2,2	- 0,6	5,0	13,5	12,0	12,7	7,3	10,7	21,5	19,8	:	F
IRL	:	:	:	2,2	3,1	3,1	3,9	12,9	16,4	17,3	:	IRL
I	- 4,7	- 2,1	- 1,8	- 3,4	13,9	13,9	13,8	18,4	13,9	20,2	:	I
L	:	:	:	:	:	:	:	:	:	:	:	L
NL	15,7	18,5	18,6	14,8	19,9	22,6	28,5	31,3	35,5	38,1	:	NL
A	:	:	:	0,7	- 0,7	- 1,8	- 5,7	- 6,8	- 7,9	- 7,2	:	A
P	- 2,2	- 2,6	- 3,7	- 3,8	- 3,5	- 3,0	- 3,1	- 3,9	- 5,1	- 6,3	:	P
FIN	:	:	:	0,5	2,6	3,7	3,9	2,8	3,1	4,9	:	FIN
S	:	:	:	2,0	4,1	5,2	8,3	9,8	10,3	7,0	:	S
UK	- 21,3	- 13,2	- 2,1	- 9,0	- 8,7	- 10,6	- 7,1	- 6,7	- 7,0	- 9,5	:	UK

4B7BA

Further reading: EU International transactions — 1999 edition. Eurostat. International trade in services — EU, 1989–98. Eurostat.

The National Bank of Belgium produces the balance of payments for Belgium and Luxembourg, B/L, as a whole. EU = EU-12 until 1991; EU = EU-15 from 1992 onwards. The sum of the trade balance in goods and services of the 15 Member States with EU as a partner corresponds to the intra-EU asymmetry.

International trade in goods and services with EU as a partner. Cover rates. %

	1989	1990	1991	1992	1993	1994	1995	1996	1997	1998	1999	
EU-15	:	:	:	:	:	:	:	:	:	:	:	EU-15
B/L	108,5	108,7	108,4	109,9	111,4	111,9	110,9	110,2	108,7	109,4	:	B/L
DK	101,2	108,0	112,4	121,3	124,0	120,5	115,5	119,5	104,6	100,1	:	DK
D	125,1	113,5	101,2	102,9	104,0	104,5	104,8	104,6	103,8	100,9	:	D
EL	80,7	73,8	75,1	73,0	79,0	79,9	67,7	65,7	73,6	73,4	:	EL
E	96,6	95,2	97,9	96,2	108,7	111,4	110,1	111,7	113,7	110,5	:	E
F	98,2	99,6	103,7	109,7	109,1	108,7	104,6	106,8	112,5	110,6	:	F
IRL	:	:	:	115,4	120,3	117,2	118,5	175,5	177,6	166,5	:	IRL
I	94,9	97,9	98,3	97,0	115,0	113,4	112,4	115,4	110,5	115,1	:	I
L	:	:	:	:	:	:	:	:	:	:	:	L
NL	123,1	126,0	124,9	117,1	122,8	123,5	126,6	128,4	130,5	131,7	:	NL
A	:	:	:	101,8	98,3	95,7	88,9	87,4	85,8	88,2	:	A
P	82,4	82,1	77,0	78,8	80,8	84,7	86,3	84,2	81,5	79,5	:	P
FIN	:	:	:	104,3	123,0	127,4	122,2	115,7	115,9	124,4	:	FIN
S	:	:	:	106,4	114,9	116,0	120,4	122,1	120,8	113,2	:	S
UK	77,5	85,6	97,6	92,1	92,4	91,8	94,8	95,4	96,0	94,8	:	UK

4B7BB

Further reading: EU International transactions — 1999 edition. Eurostat. International trade in services — EU, 1989–98. Eurostat.

The National Bank of Belgium produces the balance of payments for Belgium and Luxembourg, B/L, as a whole. EU = EU-12 until 1991; EU = EU-15 from 1992 onwards.

5

Allocating the EU current account balance to the appropriate geographic or economic zone is done according to the residence of that partner. However, precise information on residence is not always available, neither are criteria for identifying the final trade partner. In this case, the currency in which transactions are recorded might be used to determine the origin or destination of the flows. Therefore, comparison between countries should be cautious. It is better to pay attention to structures than to amounts, to trends rather than to absolute values and to cover ratios rather than balances.

EU current account with the US, Japan and EFTA. Cover rates. %

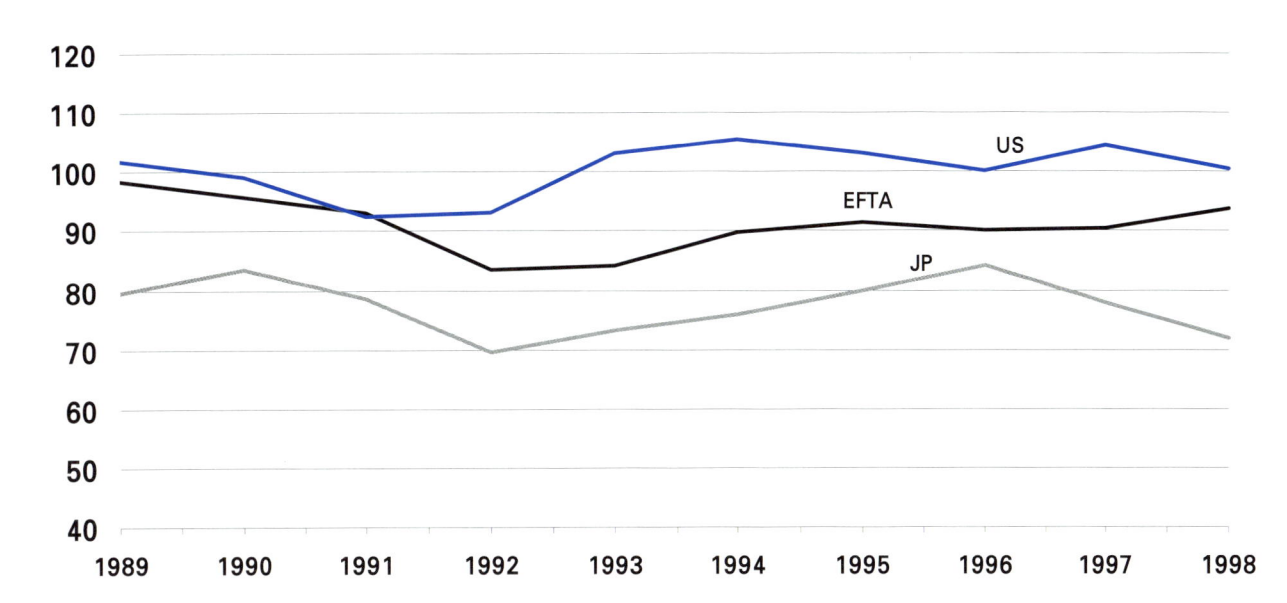

4C1AC

Further reading: EU international transactions — 1999 edition. Eurostat. Geographical breakdown of the EU current account, 1995–98. Eurostat.

From 1985 to 1991: EFTA (A, FIN, IS, LI, NO, S, CH). From 1992 onwards: EFTA (IS, LI, NO, CH). Until 1991 data refer to EU-12 and from 1992 onwards data refer to EU-15.

EU current account with ACP, OPEC, CEEC, CIS and former State-trading countries. Cover rates. %

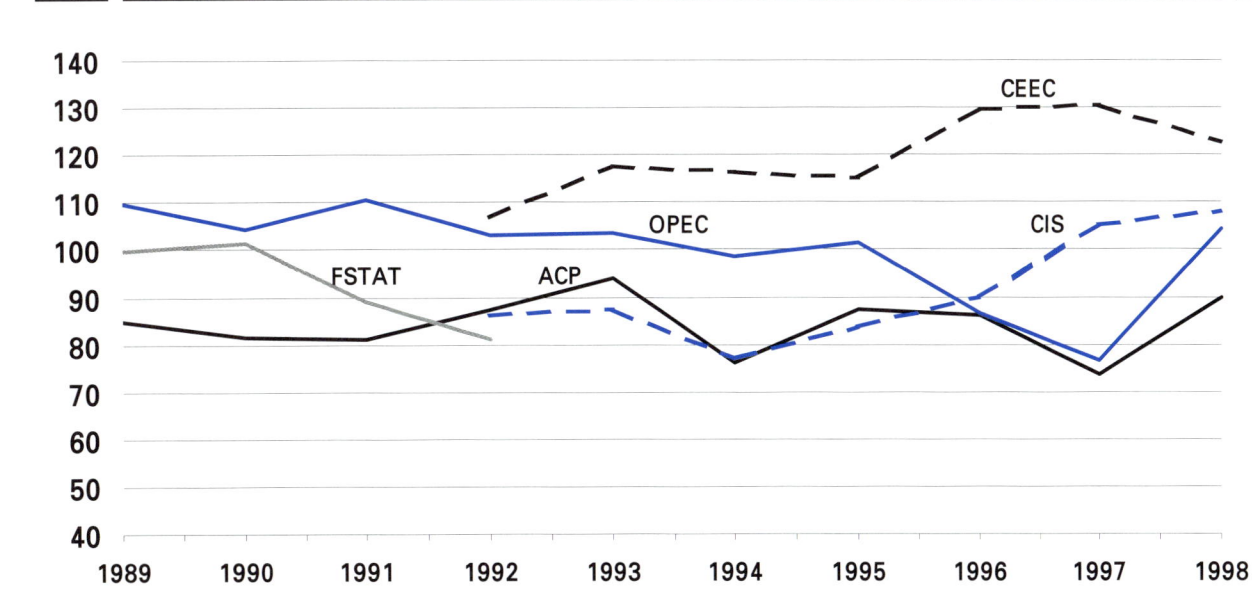

4C1AD

ACP: African, Caribbean and Pacific countries which signed the Lomé agreements; OPEC: Organisation of Petroleum Exporting Countries; FSTAT: former State-trading countries. CEEC: countries from central and eastern Europe; CIS: Commonwealth of Independent States.

Further reading: EU international transactions — 1999 edition. Eurostat. Geographical breakdown of the EU current account, 1995–98. Eurostat.

Until 1991 data refer to EU-12 and from 1992 onwards data refer to EU-15.

eurostat

EU trade in goods and services by geographical and economic zone, exports as % of EU total exports

	1989	1990	1991	1992	1993	1994	1995	1996	1997	1998	1999
World	100,0	100,0	100,0	100,0	100,0	100,0	100,0	100,0	100,0	100,0	:
Intra-EU-15	55,6	56,4	57,8	63,3	61,4	61,8	62,2	61,4	59,9	61,0	:
Extra-EU-15	44,4	43,6	42,2	36,0	38,4	38,1	37,2	38,2	39,7	38,6	:
EFTA	11,0	10,9	10,5	5,3	5,2	5,2	5,1	4,9	4,8	4,8	:
Other Europe	:	:	:	4,7	5,2	5,1	5,6	6,3	6,8	6,9	:
CZ	:	:	:	0,6	0,6	0,6	0,7	0,8	0,8	0,8	:
HU	:	:	:	0,5	0,5	0,6	0,5	0,6	0,6	0,8	:
PL	:	:	:	0,7	0,8	0,8	0,8	1,0	1,1	1,2	:
RU	:	:	:	1,0	1,0	0,9	1,0	1,1	1,2	1,0	:
Africa	:	:	:	3,1	3,1	2,8	2,9	2,8	2,7	2,9	:
America	:	:	:	12,0	12,8	12,8	11,8	12,0	13,3	13,7	:
US	10,3	9,8	9,2	9,1	9,7	9,6	8,7	8,8	9,8	10,0	:
Asia	:	:	:	9,8	10,9	11,0	10,7	11,0	11,0	9,2	:
JP	2,3	2,4	2,2	2,0	2,1	2,2	2,1	2,2	2,1	1,8	:
Australia, Oceania	1,0	0,8	0,7	0,8	0,8	0,8	0,8	0,8	0,9	0,8	:
OECD	:	:	:	82,8	81,3	81,6	80,0	80,2	82,4	83,7	:
CEEC	:	:	:	2,5	2,9	3,1	3,3	3,8	4,1	4,4	:
NAFTA	:	:	:	10,4	10,9	10,8	9,7	9,9	11,0	11,3	:
ACP	1,6	1,5	1,5	1,3	1,4	1,1	1,2	1,2	1,0	1,1	:
OPEC	3,4	3,3	3,5	3,3	3,1	2,6	2,5	2,4	2,2	2,2	:
ASEAN	:	:	:	1,6	1,9	2,1	2,2	2,2	2,2	1,5	:
CIS	:	:	:	1,2	1,2	1,2	1,2	1,3	1,5	1,3	:
Mercosur	:	:	:	0,6	0,8	1,0	1,1	1,1	1,2	1,2	:

4C1BA

Further reading: EU International transactions — 1999 edition. Eurostat. Geographical breakdown of the EU current account, 1995–98. Eurostat.

OECD: Organisation for Economic Cooperation and Development; CEEC: Countries from central and eastern Europe; NAFTA: North American Free Trade Association; ACP: African Caribbean and Pacific countries which signed the Lomé agreements; OPEC: Organisation of Petroleum Exporting Countries; ASEAN: Association of South-East Asian Nations; CIS: Commonwealth of Independent States; Mercosur: Countries of the South Cone common market. Until 1991 data refer to EU-12 and from 1992 onwards data refer to EU-15.

EU trade in goods and services by geographical and economic zone, imports as % of EU total imports

	1989	1990	1991	1992	1993	1994	1995	1996	1997	1998	1999
World	100,0	100,0	100,0	100,0	100,0	100,0	100,0	100,0	100,0	100,0	:
Intra-EU-15	54,6	55,3	55,9	61,8	60,2	60,9	61,8	60,8	59,6	60,4	:
Extra-EU-15	45,4	44,7	44,1	37,6	39,5	39,0	38,1	38,8	40,0	39,2	:
EFTA	10,4	10,5	10,2	5,3	5,5	5,3	5,1	5,3	5,0	4,8	:
Other Europe	:	:	:	4,4	4,7	5,0	5,3	5,3	5,6	6,0	:
CZ	:	:	:	0,5	0,5	0,5	0,6	0,6	0,6	0,7	:
HU	:	:	:	0,4	0,4	0,4	0,5	0,6	0,6	0,7	:
PL	:	:	:	0,6	0,6	0,7	0,7	0,7	0,7	0,9	:
RU	:	:	:	1,2	1,3	1,4	1,3	1,3	1,3	1,0	:
Africa	:	:	:	3,4	3,3	3,2	3,1	3,2	3,2	2,7	:
America	:	:	:	12,2	12,8	12,5	12,1	12,4	13,1	13,2	:
US	9,9	9,7	9,7	9,4	9,9	9,6	9,2	9,4	9,9	10,1	:
Asia	:	:	:	11,5	12,4	12,1	11,7	11,7	12,2	11,7	:
JP	4,1	3,8	4,1	3,9	3,9	3,6	3,5	3,1	3,2	3,1	:
Australia, Oceania	0,7	0,6	0,5	0,6	0,6	0,6	0,5	0,5	0,6	0,6	:
OECD	:	:	:	82,7	81,7	81,8	80,9	80,5	82,3	83,6	:
CEEC	:	:	:	2,2	2,4	2,6	2,9	3,0	3,2	3,7	:
NAFTA	:	:	:	10,4	10,9	10,5	10,2	10,4	11,0	11,1	:
ACP	1,6	1,7	1,6	1,4	1,3	1,4	1,3	1,5	1,5	1,3	:
OPEC	2,8	2,9	3,0	3,0	3,0	2,7	2,5	3,0	3,1	2,2	:
ASEAN	:	:	:	1,8	2,1	2,2	2,1	2,3	2,4	2,3	:
CIS	:	:	:	1,4	1,5	1,6	1,6	1,6	1,6	1,3	:
Mercosur	:	:	:	0,9	0,9	1,0	0,9	0,9	0,9	1,0	:

4C1BB

5

Further reading: EU International transactions — 1999 edition. Eurostat. Geographical breakdown of the EU current account, 1995–98. Eurostat.

OECD: Organisation for Economic Cooperation and Development; CEEC: Countries from central and eastern Europe; NAFTA: North American Free Trade Association; ACP: African Caribbean and Pacific countries which signed the Lomé agreements; OPEC: Organisation of Petroleum Exporting Countries; ASEAN: Association of South-East Asian Nations; CIS: Commonwealth of Independent States; Mercosur: Countries of the South Cone common market. Until 1991 data refer to EU-12 and from 1992 onwards data refer to EU-15.

eurostat

EU trade in goods and services with the US, Japan and EFTA. Cover rates. %

4C1BC

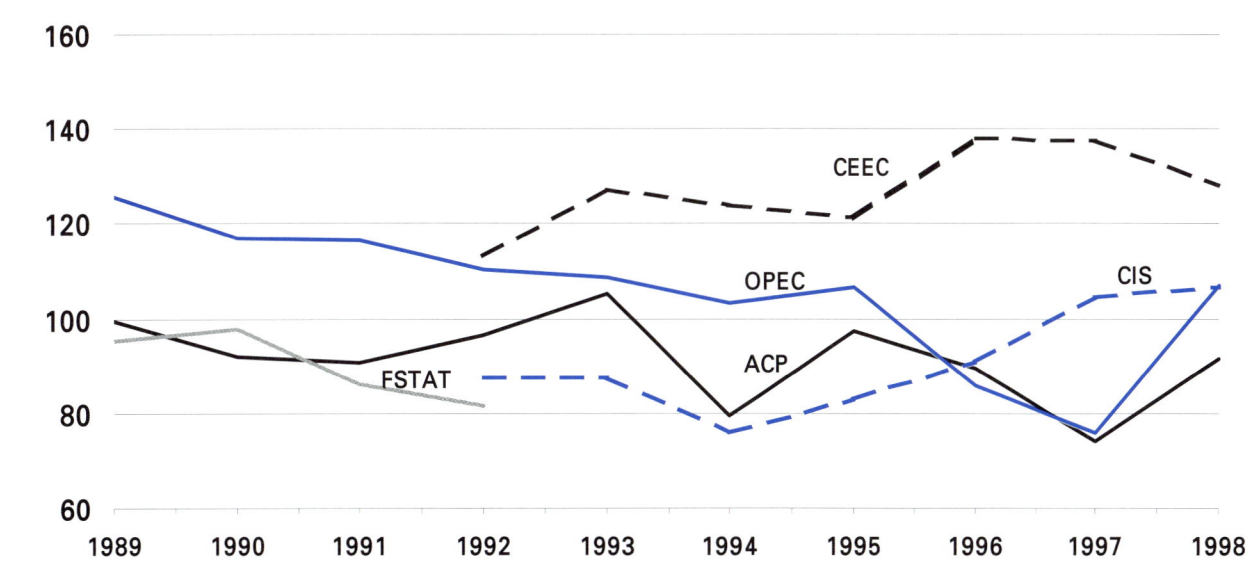

Further reading: EU International transactions — 1999 edition. Eurostat. Geographical breakdown of the EU current account, 1995–98. Eurostat.

From 1985 to 1991: EFTA (A, FIN, IS, LI, NO, S, CH). From 1992 onwards: EFTA (IS, LI, NO, CH). Until 1991 data refer to EU-12 and from 1992 onwards data refer to EU-15.

EU trade in goods and services with ACP, OPEC, CEEC, CIS and former State-trading countries. Cover rates. %

4C1BD

ACP: African, Caribbean and Pacific countries which signed the Lomé agreements; OPEC: Organisation of Petroleum Exporting Countries; FSTAT: former State-trading countries. CEEC: countries from central and eastern Europe; CIS: Commonwealth of Independent States.

Further reading: EU International transactions — 1999 edition. Eurostat. Geographical breakdown of the EU current account, 1995–98. Eurostat.

Until 1991 data refer to EU-12 and from 1992 onwards data refer to EU-15.

EU trade in goods by geographical and economic zone, exports as % of EU total exports

	1989	1990	1991	1992	1993	1994	1995	1996	1997	1998	1999
World	100,0	100,0	100,0	100,0	100,0	100,0	100,0	100,0	100,0	100,0	:
Intra-EU-15	58,4	59,2	60,9	66,2	63,5	63,9	64,1	63,3	62,0	63,0	:
Extra-EU-15	41,6	40,8	39,1	33,6	36,5	36,3	35,3	36,2	37,7	36,7	:
EFTA	11,1	10,8	10,3	4,6	4,6	4,5	4,4	4,3	4,1	4,2	:
Other Europe	:	:	:	5,1	5,8	5,7	6,1	6,9	7,5	7,6	:
CZ	:	:	:	0,7	0,6	0,7	0,8	0,8	0,9	0,9	:
HU	:	:	:	0,5	0,5	0,6	0,6	0,6	0,7	0,9	:
PL	:	:	:	0,8	0,9	0,9	1,0	1,2	1,3	1,4	:
RU	:	:	:	1,1	1,1	1,1	1,0	1,1	1,3	1,0	:
Africa	:	:	:	3,2	3,2	2,9	2,8	2,8	2,8	2,9	:
America	:	:	:	9,8	10,7	10,9	10,1	10,3	11,5	12,2	:
US	8,0	7,4	6,7	7,0	7,6	7,7	7,1	7,3	8,0	8,6	:
Asia	:	:	:	10,2	11,4	11,5	11,0	11,2	11,1	9,1	:
JP	2,1	2,1	2,0	1,8	1,9	2,0	2,0	2,0	1,8	1,5	:
Australia, Oceania	0,9	0,8	0,7	0,7	0,7	0,8	0,8	0,8	0,8	0,7	:
OECD	:	:	:	82,3	80,7	81,1	79,7	79,9	82,1	83,8	:
CEEC	:	:	:	2,8	3,2	3,5	3,7	4,2	4,5	5,0	:
NAFTA	:	:	:	8,2	8,8	8,9	8,1	8,2	9,1	9,8	:
ACP	1,4	1,4	1,3	1,4	1,4	1,1	1,1	1,1	1,0	1,1	:
OPEC	3,5	3,5	3,7	3,8	3,5	2,8	2,5	2,3	2,4	2,2	:
ASEAN	:	:	:	1,7	2,0	2,2	2,3	2,3	2,3	1,5	:
CIS	:	:	:	1,3	1,4	1,4	1,3	1,4	1,7	1,4	:
Mercosur	:	:	:	0,7	0,9	1,0	1,1	1,1	1,3	1,3	:

4C1CA

Further reading: EU International transactions — 1999 edition. Eurostat. Geographical breakdown of the EU current account, 1995–98. Eurostat.

OECD: Organisation for Economic Cooperation and Development; CEEC: Countries from central and eastern Europe; NAFTA: North American Free Trade Association; ACP: African Caribbean and Pacific countries which signed the Lomé agreements; OPEC: Organisation of Petroleum Exporting Countries; ASEAN: Association of South-East Asian Nations; CIS: Commonwealth of Independent States; Mercosur: Countries of the South Cone common market. Until 1991 data refer to EU-12 and from 1992 onwards data refer to EU-15.

EU trade in goods by geographical and economic zone, imports as % of EU total imports

	1989	1990	1991	1992	1993	1994	1995	1996	1997	1998	1999
World	100,0	100,0	100,0	100,0	100,0	100,0	100,0	100,0	100,0	100,0	:
Intra-EU-15	56,1	56,9	57,3	63,2	61,3	62,1	62,9	62,1	61,0	62,0	:
Extra-EU-15	43,9	43,1	42,7	36,4	38,7	38,1	37,0	37,5	38,6	37,7	:
EFTA	10,3	10,2	9,9	4,8	5,1	5,0	4,8	4,8	4,6	4,4	:
Other Europe	:	:	:	4,5	4,8	5,2	5,4	5,5	5,7	6,2	:
CZ	:	:	:	0,6	0,5	0,6	0,6	0,6	0,7	0,8	:
HU	:	:	:	0,4	0,4	0,5	0,5	0,6	0,7	0,8	:
PL	:	:	:	0,6	0,7	0,7	0,8	0,7	0,8	0,9	:
RU	:	:	:	1,3	1,4	1,5	1,5	1,5	1,4	1,1	:
Africa	:	:	:	3,4	3,3	3,2	3,0	3,2	3,2	2,5	:
America	:	:	:	10,4	10,9	10,8	10,6	10,7	11,3	11,4	:
US	8,2	7,8	7,8	7,6	8,1	7,8	7,7	7,9	8,4	8,6	:
Asia	:	:	:	12,6	13,9	13,2	12,6	12,6	13,2	12,6	:
JP	4,7	4,4	4,7	4,5	4,5	4,2	3,9	3,6	3,6	3,5	:
Australia, Oceania	0,6	0,6	0,5	0,5	0,5	0,5	0,5	0,5	0,5	0,5	:
OECD	:	:	:	82,4	81,2	81,5	80,4	80,0	82,2	83,6	:
CEEC	:	:	:	2,4	2,5	2,9	3,1	3,1	3,3	4,0	:
NAFTA	:	:	:	8,6	9,0	8,8	8,6	8,8	9,4	9,5	:
ACP	1,5	1,5	1,4	1,4	1,3	1,4	1,3	1,4	1,4	1,2	:
OPEC	3,0	3,2	3,3	3,3	3,4	2,9	2,7	3,2	3,3	2,3	:
ASEAN	:	:	:	1,9	2,2	2,3	2,2	2,4	2,5	2,4	:
CIS	:	:	:	1,5	1,6	1,8	1,7	1,7	1,7	1,3	:
Mercosur	:	:	:	1,0	1,1	1,1	1,0	0,9	1,0	1,0	:

4C1CB

Further reading: EU International transactions — 1999 edition. Eurostat. Geographical breakdown of the EU current account, 1995–98. Eurostat.

OECD: Organisation for Economic Cooperation and Development; CEEC: Countries from central and eastern Europe; NAFTA: North American Free Trade Association; ACP: African Caribbean and Pacific countries which signed the Lomé agreements; OPEC: Organisation of Petroleum Exporting Countries; ASEAN: Association of South-East Asian Nations; CIS: Commonwealth of Independent States; Mercosur: Countries of the South Cone common market. Until 1991 data refer to EU-12 and from 1992 onwards data refer to EU-15.

EU trade in goods by geographical zone (according to the balance of payments concept) is allocated by country of final destination for exports and country of origin for imports. This comes very close to allocation by residence of the trade partner. Sometimes this information is not available, for example because goods are delivered to a warehouse. If so, flows might be allocated to the country of immediate destination or consignment, where payments are exchanged, or by currency in which flows are recorded.

Concerning intra-EU imports of goods, the Member States are changing the principle of allocation from the country of origin to the country of consignment. EU external imports of goods are expected to decrease and the corresponding balances are expected to increase.

EU trade in goods with the US, Japan and EFTA. Cover rates. %

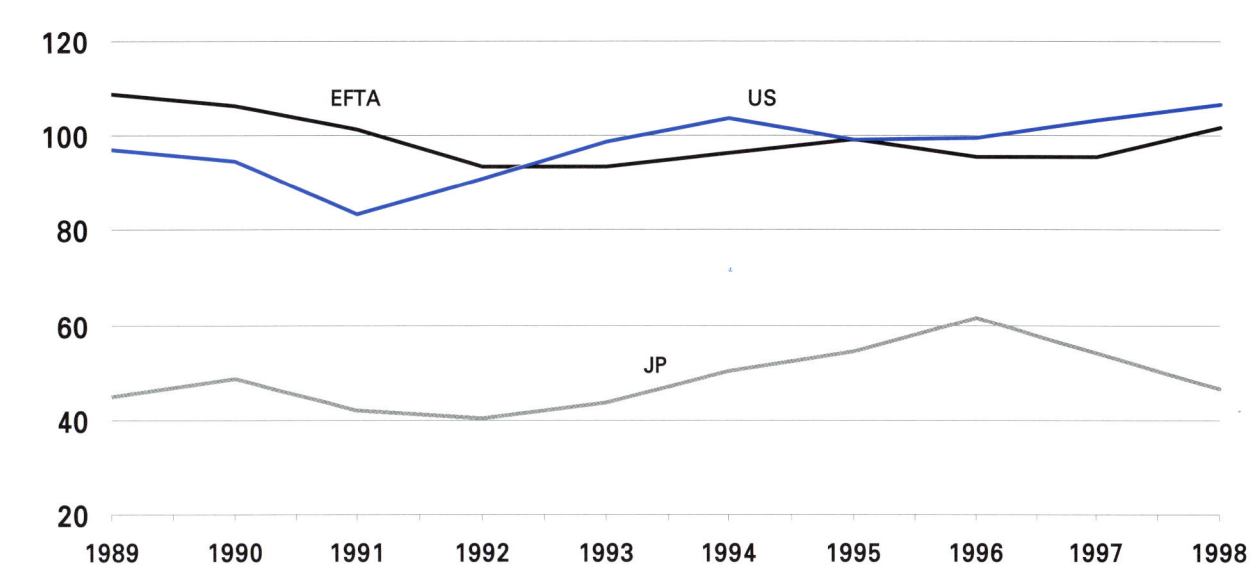

Further reading: EU International transactions — 1999 edition. Eurostat. Geographical breakdown of the EU current account, 1995–98. Eurostat.

From 1985 to 1991: EFTA (A, FIN, IS, LI, NO, S, CH). From 1992 onwards: EFTA (IS, LI, NO, CH). Until 1991 data refer to EU-12 and from 1992 onwards data refer to EU-15.

EU trade in goods with ACP, OPEC, CEEC, CIS and former State-trading countries. Cover rates. %

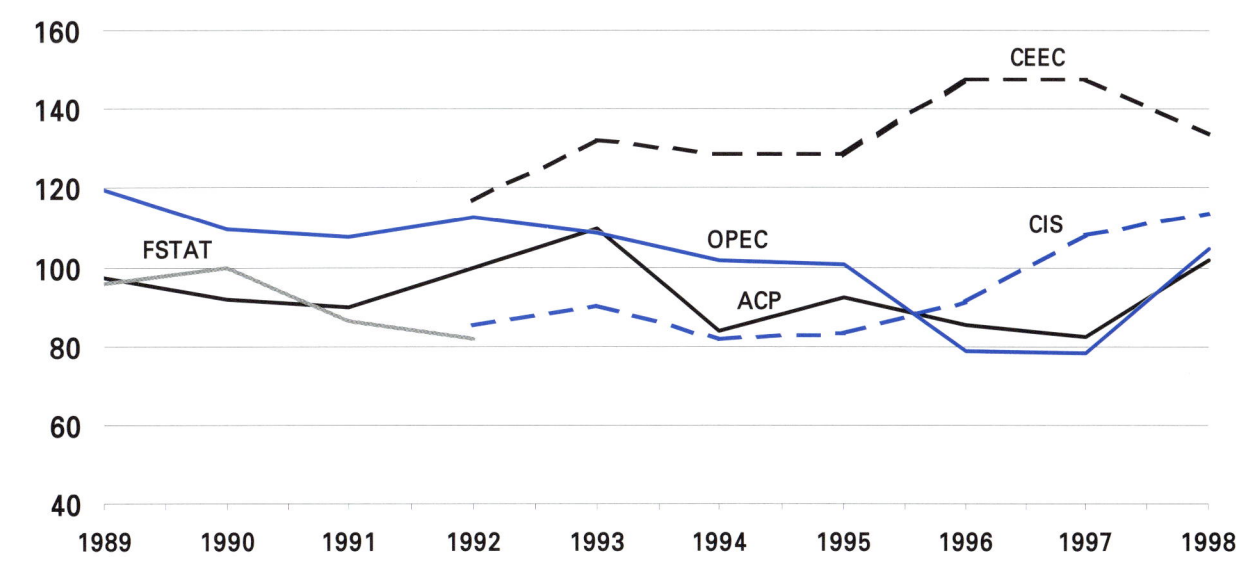

ACP: African, Caribbean and Pacific countries which signed the Lomé agreements; OPEC: Organisation of Petroleum Exporting Countries; FSTAT: former State-trading countries. CEEC: countries from central and eastern Europe; CIS: Commonwealth of Independent States.

Further reading: EU International transactions — 1999 edition. Eurostat. Geographical breakdown of the EU current account, 1995–98. Eurostat.

Until 1991 data refer to EU-12 and from 1992 onwards data refer to EU-15.

EU trade in services by geographical and economic zone, exports as % of EU total exports

	1989	1990	1991	1992	1993	1994	1995	1996	1997	1998	1999
World	100,0	100,0	100,0	100,0	100,0	100,0	100,0	100,0	100,0	100,0	:
Intra-EU-15	45,8	46,6	47,1	53,4	54,4	54,7	55,0	54,2	52,3	53,7	:
Extra-EU-15	54,2	53,4	52,6	43,9	44,5	44,0	44,5	45,5	47,3	45,8	:
EFTA	10,7	11,3	11,4	7,7	7,5	7,5	7,6	7,4	7,3	6,9	:
Other Europe	:	:	:	3,2	3,2	3,1	3,5	4,0	4,2	4,2	:
CZ	:	:	:	0,5	0,4	0,4	0,4	0,4	0,4	0,4	:
HU	:	:	:	0,4	0,4	0,4	0,3	0,4	0,4	0,4	:
PL	:	:	:	0,4	0,4	0,4	0,4	0,5	0,6	0,7	:
RU	:	:	:	0,8	0,5	0,3	0,8	0,8	0,9	0,7	:
Africa	:	:	:	2,7	2,8	2,4	3,1	3,1	2,5	2,7	:
America	:	:	:	19,6	19,5	19,3	18,1	18,2	20,3	19,4	:
US	18,9	18,0	17,6	16,5	16,4	16,3	15,0	14,8	16,4	15,4	:
Asia	:	:	:	8,3	9,0	9,5	9,7	10,1	10,3	9,7	:
JP	3,0	3,1	2,7	2,7	2,8	2,7	2,7	3,1	3,0	2,7	:
Australia, Oceania	1,3	1,1	1,0	1,0	0,9	1,0	1,0	1,1	1,2	1,0	:
OECD	:	:	:	84,6	83,4	83,3	81,5	81,5	83,7	83,4	:
CEEC	:	:	:	1,7	1,8	1,9	1,8	2,3	2,3	2,5	:
NAFTA	:	:	:	17,9	17,8	17,5	16,2	16,0	17,8	16,8	:
ACP	2,2	2,1	2,1	1,2	1,3	1,0	1,7	1,7	0,9	1,0	:
OPEC	3,0	2,7	2,9	1,8	2,1	1,9	2,5	2,6	1,5	2,2	:
ASEAN	:	:	:	1,1	1,4	1,7	1,9	1,8	2,0	1,5	:
CIS	:	:	:	0,8	0,7	0,5	1,0	1,0	1,1	1,0	:
Mercosur	:	:	:	0,5	0,6	0,7	0,8	1,0	1,1	1,0	:

4C1DA

Further reading: EU International transactions — 1999 edition. Eurostat. Geographical breakdown of the EU current account, 1995–98. Eurostat.

OECD: Organisation for Economic Cooperation and Development; CEEC: Countries from central and eastern Europe; NAFTA: North American Free Trade Association; ACP: African Caribbean and Pacific countries which signed the Lomé agreements; OPEC: Organisation of Petroleum Exporting Countries; ASEAN: Association of South-East Asian Nations; CIS: Commonwealth of Independent States; Mercosur: Countries of the South Cone common market. Until 1991 data refer to EU-12 and from 1992 onwards data refer to EU-15.

EU trade in services by geographical and economic zones, imports as % of EU total imports

	1989	1990	1991	1992	1993	1994	1995	1996	1997	1998	1999
World	100,0	100,0	100,0	100,0	100,0	100,0	100,0	100,0	100,0	100,0	:
Intra-EU-15	48,8	49,4	50,5	56,8	56,7	57,0	57,7	56,3	54,7	54,9	:
Extra-EU-15	51,2	50,6	49,3	41,4	42,3	42,0	41,9	43,4	45,0	44,6	:
EFTA	11,1	11,6	11,3	6,8	6,8	6,4	6,4	7,0	6,4	6,3	:
Other Europe	:	:	:	4,0	4,2	4,4	4,8	4,8	5,0	5,1	:
CZ	:	:	:	0,4	0,4	0,4	0,4	0,4	0,4	0,5	:
HU	:	:	:	0,4	0,4	0,4	0,4	0,5	0,5	0,5	:
PL	:	:	:	0,5	0,5	0,5	0,5	0,5	0,6	0,6	:
RU	:	:	:	0,7	0,8	0,9	0,9	0,8	0,7	0,8	:
Africa	:	:	:	3,3	3,3	3,1	3,2	3,3	3,4	3,2	:
America	:	:	:	18,4	18,6	18,4	17,8	18,4	19,4	19,7	:
US	16,6	16,6	16,4	15,6	15,7	15,3	14,6	14,7	15,3	15,5	:
Asia	:	:	:	7,6	7,9	8,3	8,4	8,2	8,8	8,4	:
JP	1,7	1,8	1,6	1,7	1,8	1,7	1,8	1,7	1,6	1,7	:
Australia, Oceania	0,9	0,9	0,7	0,7	0,7	0,7	0,7	0,7	0,9	0,8	:
OECD	:	:	:	83,5	83,2	82,8	82,7	82,4	82,7	83,3	:
CEEC	:	:	:	1,8	1,8	1,9	2,2	2,4	2,6	2,7	:
NAFTA	:	:	:	16,6	16,8	16,4	15,8	15,9	16,7	16,9	:
ACP	2,3	2,4	2,4	1,5	1,5	1,5	1,5	1,7	1,8	1,6	:
OPEC	2,1	1,8	1,7	2,0	2,0	1,8	1,8	2,2	2,4	2,0	:
ASEAN	:	:	:	1,5	1,7	2,0	1,9	1,8	2,0	1,9	:
CIS	:	:	:	0,9	1,0	1,2	1,2	1,2	1,3	1,2	:
Mercosur	:	:	:	0,5	0,5	0,6	0,7	0,7	0,8	0,9	:

4C1DB

5

Further reading: EU International transactions — 1999 edition. Eurostat. Geographical breakdown of the EU current account, 1995–98. Eurostat.

OECD: Organisation for Economic Cooperation and Development; CEEC: Countries from central and eastern Europe; NAFTA: North American Free Trade Association; ACP: African Caribbean and Pacific countries which signed the Lomé agreements; OPEC: Organisation of Petroleum Exporting Countries; ASEAN: Association of South-East Asian Nations; CIS: Commonwealth of Independent States; Mercosur: Countries of the South Cone common market. Until 1991 data refer to EU-12 and from 1992 onwards data refer to EU-15.

eurostat

E U trade in services by geographical zone is allocated by residence of trade partners. When this information is not available, flows might be allocated to the country of payment or by currency in which flows are recorded.

EU trade in services with the US, Japan and EFTA. Cover rates. %

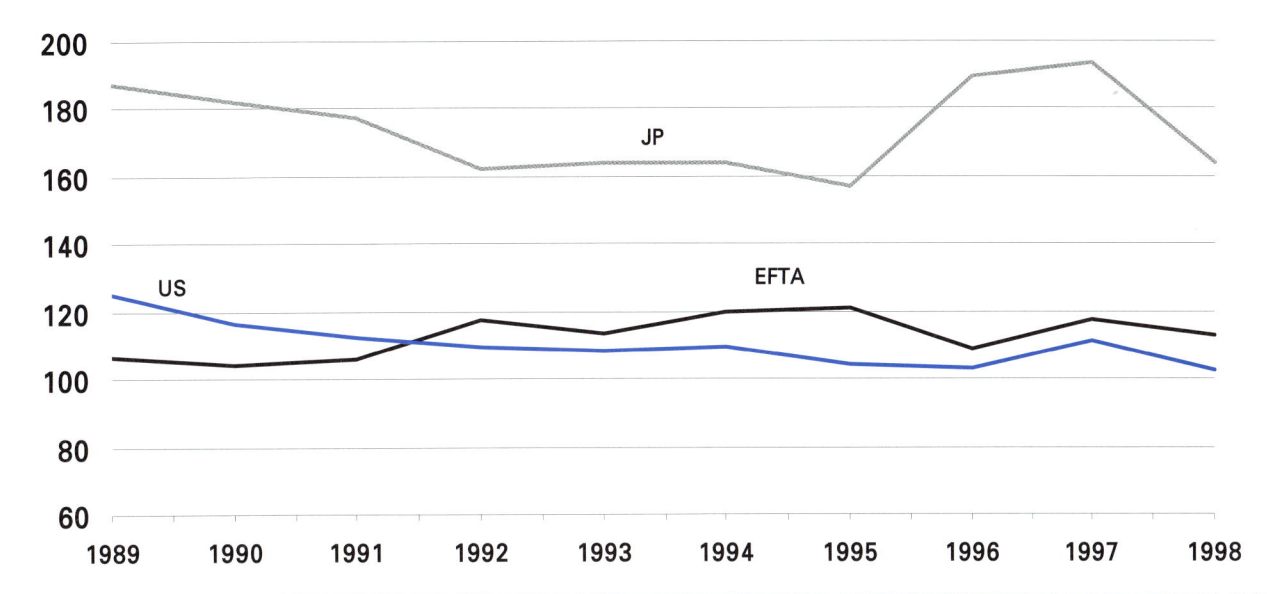

4C1DC

Further reading: EU International transactions — 1999 edition. Eurostat. Geographical breakdown of the EU current account, 1995–98. Eurostat.

From 1985 to 1991: EFTA (A, FIN, IS, LI, NO, S, CH). From 1992 onwards: EFTA (IS, LI, NO, CH). Until 1991 data refer to EU-12 and from 1992 onwards data refer to EU-15.

EU trade in services with ACP, OPEC, CEEC, CIS and former State-trading countries. Cover rates. %

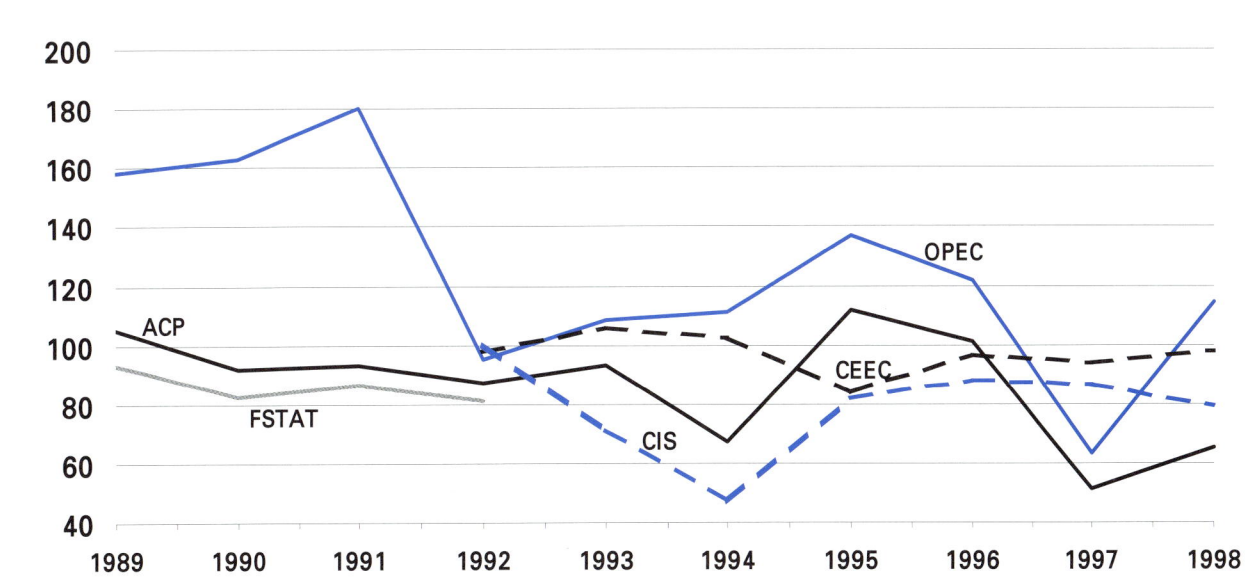

4C1DD

ACP: African, Caribbean and Pacific countries which signed the Lomé agreements; OPEC: Organisation of Petroleum Exporting Countries; FSTAT: former State-trading countries. CEEC: countries from central and eastern Europe; CIS: Commonwealth of Independent States.

Further reading: EU International transactions — 1999 edition. Eurostat. Geographical breakdown of the EU current account, 1995–98. Eurostat.

Until 1991 data refer to EU-12 and from 1992 onwards data refer to EU-15.

Extra-EU exports by main trading partners. 1 000 million ECU

	1989	1990	1991	1992	1993	1994	1995	1996	1997	1998	1999
Extra EU-15	395,5	395,9	403,4	415,3	468,1	523,8	573,3	626,6	721,1	733,3	760,1
US	84,8	82,7	76,8	79,3	91,4	103,4	103,3	114,9	141,4	161,2	182,9
CH	43,6	45,0	43,6	41,9	42,7	46,7	51,0	51,5	53,0	57,2	62,5
JP	22,9	24,5	23,9	22,2	24,7	29,0	32,9	35,8	36,1	31,6	35,5
CN	6,8	5,8	6,3	7,6	12,4	14,0	14,7	14,8	16,5	17,4	19,4
NO	13,2	13,9	14,2	14,3	14,4	16,4	17,5	19,8	23,4	25,1	23,2
PL	4,6	5,0	8,9	9,2	11,1	12,3	15,3	20,0	25,1	28,2	29,0
RU	-	-	-	7,1	13,2	14,4	16,1	19,1	25,5	21,1	14,8
HU	3,8	3,8	4,7	5,4	6,4	8,1	8,7	10,0	13,6	16,9	18,6
TR	6,0	8,2	8,6	8,8	12,4	9,3	13,4	18,3	22,4	22,2	20,6
CZ	-	-	-	-	7,1	9,2	11,7	14,0	15,9	17,2	18,4
CAND	-	-	-	-	51,5	56,5	70,7	86,0	105,0	116,8	118,6
Med. Basin	43,4	48,5	48,4	45,5	56,6	58,2	64,6	73,2	83,8	87,2	88,0
DAE	29,9	31,5	35,3	37,3	46,9	56,9	65,6	70,2	77,7	60,1	61,9
OPEC	36,0	36,6	41,0	43,2	42,1	37,8	39,0	41,9	51,1	47,1	43,9
L. America	16,8	16,9	19,4	21,8	25,4	30,6	32,4	35,6	45,2	49,7	45,7
ACP	23,9	23,2	22,6	23,5	23,1	22,9	26,3	27,5	30,2	33,1	31,6

Further reading: External trade, statistical yearbooks. Eurostat. Comext on CD-ROM. Eurostat.

CN: China; PL: Poland; RU: Russia; TR: Turkey; CZ: Czech Republic; HU: Hungary; CAND: Candidate countries; Med. Basin: countries and territories that make up the Med. Basin; DAE: Dynamic Asian Economies; OPEC: Organisation of Petroleum Exporting countries; L. America: Latin America; ACP: African, Caribbean and Pacific countries which signed the Lomé agreements.

4C2AA

Extra-EU imports by main trading partners. 1 000 million ECU

	1989	1990	1991	1992	1993	1994	1995	1996	1997	1998	1999
Extra EU-15	431,9	442,5	471,6	465,4	464,7	514,3	545,3	581,1	672,6	710,5	776,7
US	91,3	91,5	97,0	92,8	90,6	99,9	103,7	113,1	137,8	152,0	160,0
CH	34,7	37,1	37,3	37,7	38,5	41,8	43,2	42,7	45,1	49,5	53,0
JP	52,4	51,4	56,9	56,3	52,2	53,8	54,3	52,6	59,9	66,0	70,5
CN	9,8	11,4	16,0	18,0	21,1	24,6	26,3	30,0	37,5	42,0	49,6
NO	19,1	20,5	21,4	20,6	21,1	23,7	25,5	27,9	33,7	28,1	29,5
PL	4,7	6,0	7,1	8,0	8,4	10,1	12,3	12,2	14,2	16,2	17,6
RU	-	-	-	10,9	17,6	21,4	21,5	23,4	27,0	23,2	25,9
HU	3,3	3,8	4,6	5,0	4,9	6,1	7,6	8,8	11,7	14,7	17,4
TR	5,8	6,2	6,5	6,9	6,8	7,9	9,2	10,2	11,9	13,6	15,0
CZ	-	-	-	-	5,6	7,4	9,0	9,8	11,8	14,7	16,8
CAND	-	-	-	-	36,6	45,6	55,5	58,8	69,9	82,7	92,5
Med. Basin	38,9	44,3	45,1	39,9	40,8	44,5	45,0	49,6	57,3	57,4	63,1
DAE	36,7	37,1	43,2	43,0	46,0	50,6	54,4	57,9	68,1	77,9	84,9
OPEC	40,7	45,2	46,9	42,8	41,5	41,5	38,4	44,0	51,3	40,5	48,3
L. America	28,3	27,1	27,6	25,9	23,3	28,7	30,4	30,2	34,7	35,6	37,1
ACP	28,4	28,5	28,5	27,9	24,4	26,1	27,6	30,3	32,1	31,2	32,5

Further reading: External trade, statistical yearbooks. Eurostat. Comext on CD-ROM. Eurostat.

CN: China; PL: Poland; RU: Russia; TR: Turkey; CZ: Czech Republic; HU: Hungary; CAND: Candidate countries; Med. Basin: countries and territories that make up the Med. Basin; DAE: Dynamic Asian Economies; OPEC: Organisation of Petroleum Exporting countries; L. America: Latin America; ACP: African, Caribbean and Pacific countries which signed the Lomé agreements.

4C2AB

5

eurostat

Main trading partners of EU-15 are ranked by the total of imports and exports in 1999. EU-15 includes the former GDR from reunification.

Extra-EU trade balance by main trading partners. 1 000 million ECU

	1989	1990	1991	1992	1993	1994	1995	1996	1997	1998	1999
Extra EU-15	- 36,4	- 46,6	- 68,2	- 50,1	3,4	9,4	28,0	45,6	48,6	22,7	- 16,6
US	- 6,4	- 8,9	- 20,2	- 13,4	0,8	3,5	- 0,4	1,7	3,5	9,1	22,9
CH	8,9	7,9	6,3	4,2	4,2	4,9	7,8	8,7	7,9	7,7	9,5
JP	- 29,5	- 26,9	- 33,0	- 34,1	- 27,5	- 24,8	- 21,4	- 16,8	- 23,8	- 34,5	- 35,1
CN	- 3,0	- 5,6	- 9,7	- 10,4	- 8,8	- 10,6	- 11,7	- 15,3	- 21,0	- 24,6	- 30,2
NO	- 5,9	- 6,7	- 7,2	- 6,3	- 6,6	- 7,3	- 8,0	- 8,1	- 10,4	- 3,0	- 6,3
PL	- 0,1	- 1,0	1,8	1,2	2,7	2,2	3,1	7,7	10,9	12,0	11,4
RU	-	-	-	- 3,7	- 4,5	- 7,0	- 5,4	- 4,3	- 1,5	- 2,1	- 11,1
HU	0,4	0,0	0,1	0,4	1,6	2,0	1,1	1,2	1,9	2,2	1,2
TR	0,1	1,9	2,1	1,9	5,6	1,4	4,1	8,1	10,5	8,6	5,5
CZ	-	-	-	-	1,5	1,8	2,7	4,2	4,2	2,5	1,6
CAND	-	-	-	-	14,9	10,8	15,2	27,2	35,1	34,1	26,1
Med. Basin	4,5	4,2	3,3	5,6	15,8	13,7	19,6	23,5	26,5	29,8	24,9
DAE	- 6,7	- 5,7	- 8,0	- 5,7	0,9	6,3	11,2	12,3	9,5	- 17,9	- 22,9
OPEC	- 4,8	- 8,6	- 5,9	0,4	0,5	- 3,6	0,6	- 2,0	- 0,2	6,6	- 4,4
L. America	- 11,4	- 10,2	- 8,2	- 4,1	2,1	2,0	2,0	5,4	10,5	14,2	8,6
ACP	- 4,5	- 5,3	- 5,9	- 4,4	- 1,2	- 3,2	- 1,4	- 2,7	- 1,9	1,9	- 0,9

CN: China; PL: Poland; RU: Russia; TR: Turkey; CZ: Czech Republic; HU: Hungary; CAND: Candidate countries; Med. Basin: countries and territories that make up the Med. Basin; DAE: Dynamic Asian Economies; OPEC: Organisation of Petroleum Exporting countries; L. America: Latin America; ACP: African, Caribbean and Pacific countries which signed the Lomé agreements.

4C2AV

Extra-EU exports of agrifood products by main trading partners. 1 000 million ECU

	1989	1990	1991	1992	1993	1994	1995	1996	1997	1998	1999
Extra EU-15	30,3	29,8	30,1	32,4	34,9	37,3	39,0	40,9	45,9	43,9	43,6
US	4,5	4,4	4,1	4,2	4,4	4,8	4,4	5,0	6,3	6,8	7,8
BR	0,3	0,2	0,3	0,1	0,2	0,4	0,7	0,5	0,5	0,5	0,4
CH	2,2	2,2	2,3	2,3	2,3	2,5	2,5	2,6	2,6	2,7	2,9
JP	2,2	2,2	2,3	2,3	2,4	2,7	2,8	2,9	3,2	3,3	3,5
NO	0,7	0,6	0,6	0,7	0,7	0,8	0,9	0,9	1,0	1,0	1,1
AR	0,0	0,0	0,1	0,1	0,1	0,2	0,2	0,2	0,2	0,2	0,2
RU	-	-	-	1,3	3,1	3,2	3,4	4,0	5,2	3,7	2,4
PL	0,8	0,6	1,0	0,9	1,0	1,0	1,1	1,2	1,3	1,4	1,3
CA	0,8	0,8	0,8	0,8	0,8	0,8	0,8	0,8	1,0	1,1	1,1
TR	0,3	0,4	0,2	0,2	0,3	0,2	0,5	0,6	0,5	0,5	0,4
L. America	1,4	1,3	1,4	1,5	1,7	2,0	2,2	2,0	2,4	2,5	2,1
ACP	2,6	2,4	2,4	2,5	2,4	2,3	2,5	2,5	3,1	3,3	3,2
Med. Basin	4,3	4,7	4,0	3,9	4,9	5,1	5,6	5,4	6,0	6,3	5,9
CAND	-	-	-	-	3,7	3,9	4,5	4,8	5,1	5,3	4,7
OPEC	4,7	4,1	4,0	3,9	4,1	4,1	4,0	3,9	4,5	4,5	4,9
DAE	1,5	1,6	2,0	2,2	2,5	2,6	2,9	3,2	3,8	2,7	3,0

4C2BA

Further reading: External trade, statistical yearbooks. Eurostat. Comext on CD-ROM. Eurostat.

BR: Brazil, RU: Russia; AR: Argentina; PL: Poland; TR: Turkey; L. America: Latin America; ACP: African, Caribbean and Pacific countries; Med. Basin: countries and territories that make up the Med. Basin; CAND: candidate countries; OPEC: Organisation of Petroleum Exporting countries; DAE: Dynamic Asian Economies.

Extra-EU imports of agrifood products by main trading partners. 1 000 million ECU

	1989	1990	1991	1992	1993	1994	1995	1996	1997	1998	1999
Extra EU-15	37,6	37,4	40,0	39,5	38,1	43,4	43,2	44,9	48,5	49,9	50,1
US	4,5	4,4	4,6	4,7	4,5	4,8	4,9	5,2	5,5	5,6	5,3
BR	4,1	3,4	3,4	3,5	3,4	4,2	3,7	3,8	4,5	4,2	4,2
CH	0,8	0,9	0,9	1,0	1,0	1,2	1,0	1,0	1,0	1,0	1,1
JP	0,2	0,1	0,1	0,1	0,1	0,1	0,1	0,1	0,1	0,1	0,1
NO	1,2	1,3	1,5	1,7	1,6	1,7	1,7	1,8	1,9	2,2	2,3
AR	1,7	1,8	2,1	2,1	1,9	2,2	2,0	2,4	2,6	2,6	3,0
RU	-	-	-	0,2	0,3	0,3	0,3	0,4	0,4	0,5	0,5
PL	0,8	1,0	1,1	0,9	0,8	0,9	0,9	0,9	1,0	1,0	1,1
CA	0,8	0,8	0,8	0,8	0,7	0,8	0,9	0,9	1,0	1,0	1,1
TR	0,9	1,0	1,1	1,1	1,1	1,5	1,4	1,5	1,8	1,7	1,8
L. America	10,1	9,5	10,4	10,1	9,7	12,0	11,8	11,9	14,0	13,6	13,4
ACP	6,2	5,7	5,9	5,8	5,5	6,6	7,2	7,4	8,3	8,9	8,7
Med. Basin	3,3	3,5	3,7	3,1	3,0	3,4	3,4	3,7	3,9	4,0	4,1
CAND	-	-	-	-	3,5	4,1	4,0	4,2	4,6	4,7	4,8
OPEC	1,1	1,1	1,2	1,1	1,1	1,2	1,2	1,3	1,5	1,4	1,5
DAE	1,8	2,1	2,1	2,1	2,0	2,1	1,7	1,8	1,9	2,1	2,0

5

4C2BB

Further reading: External trade, statistical yearbooks. Eurostat. Comext on CD-ROM. Eurostat.

BR: Brazil, RU: Russia; AR: Argentina; PL: Poland; TR: Turkey; L. America: Latin America; ACP: African, Caribbean and Pacific countries; Med. Basin: countries and territories that make up the Med. Basin; CAND: candidate countries; OPEC: Organisation of Petroleum Exporting countries; DAE: Dynamic Asian Economies.

Main trading partners of EU-15 in agrifood products are ranked by the total of agrifood imports and exports in 1999. Agrifood products are defined according to sections 0 and 1 of the standard international trade classification (SITC) revision 3. EU-15 includes the former GDR from reunification.

Extra-EU trade balance in agrifood products by main trading partners. 1 000 million ECU

	1989	1990	1991	1992	1993	1994	1995	1996	1997	1998	1999
Extra EU-15	- 7,4	- 7,6	- 9,8	- 7,1	- 3,2	- 6,2	- 4,2	- 4,0	- 2,6	- 6,1	- 6,5
US	0,0	0,0	- 0,4	- 0,5	- 0,1	0,0	- 0,5	- 0,2	0,8	1,2	2,5
BR	- 3,8	- 3,2	- 3,2	- 3,4	- 3,2	- 3,8	- 3,0	- 3,3	- 4,0	- 3,7	- 3,8
CH	1,3	1,4	1,4	1,3	1,3	1,3	1,5	1,6	1,6	1,7	1,8
JP	2,1	2,0	2,1	2,2	2,3	2,6	2,7	2,9	3,1	3,2	3,4
NO	- 0,5	- 0,6	- 0,8	- 1,0	- 0,8	- 0,9	- 0,8	- 0,8	- 0,9	- 1,2	- 1,2
AR	- 1,7	- 1,8	- 2,0	- 2,0	- 1,8	- 2,0	- 1,9	- 2,2	- 2,4	- 2,4	- 2,8
RU	-	-	-	1,1	2,8	2,9	3,1	3,6	4,8	3,2	2,0
PL	- 0,1	- 0,4	0,0	0,0	0,2	0,1	0,2	0,3	0,3	0,3	0,1
CA	0,0	0,0	0,0	- 0,1	0,1	0,0	- 0,1	- 0,1	0,0	0,0	0,0
TR	- 0,6	- 0,5	- 0,9	- 0,9	- 0,8	- 1,3	- 0,9	- 0,9	- 1,2	- 1,2	- 1,4
L. America	- 8,7	- 8,2	- 9,0	- 8,7	- 8,0	- 10,0	- 9,6	- 9,9	- 11,6	- 11,1	- 11,3
ACP	- 3,6	- 3,3	- 3,5	- 3,2	- 3,1	- 4,3	- 4,7	- 4,9	- 5,2	- 5,6	- 5,5
Med. Basin	1,0	1,3	0,3	0,7	1,8	1,6	2,1	1,7	2,2	2,2	1,8
CAND	-	-	-	-	0,2	- 0,2	0,5	0,6	0,5	0,6	- 0,1
OPEC	3,5	3,0	2,8	2,8	2,9	2,9	2,8	2,5	3,0	3,0	3,4
DAE	- 0,4	- 0,4	- 0,1	0,1	0,6	0,6	1,2	1,4	2,0	0,6	1,0

4C2BQ

BR: Brazil, RU: Russia; AR: Argentina; PL: Poland; TR: Turkey; L. America: Latin America; ACP: African, Caribbean and Pacific countries; Med. Basin: countries and territories that make up the Med. Basin; CAND: candidate countries; OPEC: Organisation of Petroleum Exporting countries; DAE: Dynamic Asian Economies.

Extra-EU exports of mineral fuels, lubricants and related products by main trading partners. 1 000 million ECU

	1989	1990	1991	1992	1993	1994	1995	1996	1997	1998	1999
Extra EU-15	12,5	14,2	14,0	13,3	14,2	15,3	13,3	15,4	17,1	14,0	16,5
NO	0,5	0,5	0,5	0,4	0,5	0,6	0,5	0,7	0,8	0,6	0,8
RU	-	-	-	0,1	0,1	0,1	0,1	0,1	0,1	0,1	0,1
LY	0,2	0,2	0,2	0,2	0,2	0,1	0,2	0,1	0,1	0,1	0,1
SA	0,0	0,0	0,0	0,0	0,1	0,0	0,0	0,0	0,0	0,0	0,0
US	3,2	3,6	2,6	2,8	3,6	4,3	3,1	3,5	3,6	2,9	4,7
DZ	0,1	0,0	0,1	0,1	0,1	0,0	0,0	0,0	0,0	0,0	0,0
IR	0,1	0,1	0,2	0,2	0,1	0,0	0,0	0,0	0,0	0,0	0,0
IQ	0,0	0,0	0,0	0,0	0,0	0,0	0,0	0,0	0,0	0,0	0,0
CH	1,6	2,0	2,0	2,0	1,9	2,1	2,1	2,4	2,4	2,3	2,2
NG	0,1	0,1	0,1	0,1	0,1	0,1	0,1	0,2	0,1	0,1	0,2
OPEC	0,5	0,5	0,7	0,6	0,8	0,6	0,5	0,5	0,4	0,4	0,5
Med. Basin	0,9	1,1	1,5	1,1	1,7	1,9	1,8	2,3	2,6	2,1	2,7
ACP	0,4	0,4	0,4	0,3	0,4	0,6	0,7	0,7	0,7	0,7	0,6
CAND	-	-	-	-	1,4	1,5	1,5	2,0	2,4	2,0	2,3
L. America	0,2	0,1	0,1	0,1	0,2	0,2	0,5	0,4	0,5	0,6	0,5
DAE	0,1	0,2	0,1	0,2	0,4	0,4	0,4	0,2	0,2	0,2	0,3

RU: Russia; SA: Saudi Arabia; LY: Libya; DZ: Algeria; IR: Iran; NG: Nigeria; IQ: Iraq; OPEC: Organisation of Petroleum Exporting countries; Med. Basin: countries and territories that make up the Med. Basin; ACP: African, Caribbean and Pacific countries; CAND: candidate countries; L. America: Latin America; DAE: Dynamic Asian Economies.

4C2FY

Extra-EU imports of minerals fuels, lubricants and related products. 1 000 million ECU

	1989	1990	1991	1992	1993	1994	1995	1996	1997	1998	1999
Extra EU-15	69,4	79,1	81,4	73,3	68,1	68,9	64,8	76,0	85,2	61,7	77,9
NO	8,1	9,8	10,5	9,6	11,1	12,3	12,5	12,9	17,7	11,3	12,8
RU	-	-	-	5,4	8,5	9,3	7,7	9,8	11,4	8,2	11,7
LY	6,2	7,8	7,9	6,9	6,1	5,9	5,6	6,9	7,4	5,4	6,7
SA	5,6	7,2	10,1	8,9	8,6	8,0	7,3	7,9	9,1	4,8	6,6
US	3,0	3,2	4,0	3,1	2,2	2,2	2,4	2,5	2,4	2,0	1,6
DZ	4,9	6,2	6,5	5,2	5,3	5,0	4,5	4,7	6,3	4,8	5,7
IR	4,9	5,4	6,0	4,8	5,2	4,5	4,4	4,9	4,2	2,9	3,8
IQ	3,3	2,1	0,0	0,0	0,0	0,0	0,0	0,0	1,4	1,9	3,7
CH	0,3	0,3	0,5	0,3	0,4	0,4	0,3	0,3	0,4	0,4	0,4
NG	3,1	4,2	4,5	3,9	3,1	3,8	2,9	4,4	3,8	2,3	2,3
OPEC	33,0	37,3	37,8	32,5	31,4	30,2	27,3	31,4	34,9	23,7	31,3
Med. Basin	14,5	17,7	17,9	15,6	14,9	14,7	13,2	15,7	17,2	12,8	15,9
ACP	5,5	7,7	8,0	7,0	5,2	6,0	5,1	6,7	6,2	4,7	4,6
CAND	-	-	-	-	2,4	2,8	2,5	2,7	2,6	2,3	2,2
L. America	2,9	3,2	3,2	3,0	2,2	2,2	2,0	1,9	2,2	1,9	2,3
DAE	0,0	0,0	0,0	0,0	0,0	0,0	0,0	0,0	0,0	0,0	0,0

Further reading: External trade, statistical yearbooks. Eurostat. Comext on CD-ROM. Eurostat.

RU: Russia; SA: Saudi Arabia; LY: Libya; DZ: Algeria; IR: Iran; NG: Nigeria; IQ: Iraq; OPEC: Organisation of Petroleum Exporting countries; Med. Basin: countries and territories that make up the Med. Basin; ACP: African, Caribbean and Pacific countries; CAND: Candidate countries; L. America: Latin America; DAE: Dynamic Asian Economies.

4C2FA

5

Main trading partners of EU-15 in fuel products are ranked by the total of fuel imports and exports in 1999. Fuel products are defined according to section 3 of the standard international trade classification (SITC) revision 3. EU-15 includes the former GDR from reunification.

Extra-EU trade balance in mineral fuels, lubricants and related products by main trading partners. 1 000 million ECU

	1989	1990	1991	1992	1993	1994	1995	1996	1997	1998	1999
Extra EU-15	- 57,0	- 64,9	- 67,4	- 60,0	- 53,9	- 53,6	- 51,4	- 60,5	- 68,1	- 47,7	- 61,5
NO	- 7,6	- 9,3	- 9,9	- 9,2	- 10,6	- 11,7	- 11,9	- 12,2	- 16,9	- 10,7	- 12,1
RU	-	-	-	- 5,3	- 8,4	- 9,2	- 7,6	- 9,7	- 11,3	- 8,1	- 11,7
LY	- 6,0	- 7,6	- 7,7	- 6,8	- 6,0	- 5,8	- 5,4	- 6,8	- 7,2	- 5,3	- 6,5
SA	- 5,6	- 7,2	- 10,1	- 8,9	- 8,5	- 7,9	- 7,3	- 7,8	- 9,0	- 4,8	- 6,6
US	0,2	0,4	- 1,3	- 0,2	1,4	2,1	0,7	1,0	1,1	0,9	3,1
DZ	- 4,9	- 6,1	- 6,5	- 5,1	- 5,2	- 5,0	- 4,5	- 4,6	- 6,3	- 4,7	- 5,6
IR	- 4,8	- 5,3	- 5,8	- 4,6	- 5,1	- 4,5	- 4,4	- 4,8	- 4,2	- 2,8	- 3,8
IQ	- 3,3	- 2,1	0,0	0,0	0,0	0,0	0,0	0,0	- 1,4	- 1,9	- 3,7
CH	1,3	1,7	1,6	1,6	1,6	1,7	1,8	2,0	2,0	2,0	1,8
NG	- 3,0	- 4,1	- 4,5	- 3,9	- 3,0	- 3,7	- 2,8	- 4,2	- 3,8	- 2,1	- 2,1
OPEC	- 32,5	- 36,9	- 37,1	- 31,9	- 30,6	- 29,5	- 26,8	- 30,9	- 34,5	- 23,3	- 30,8
Med. Basin	- 13,6	- 16,7	- 16,4	- 14,5	- 13,2	- 12,8	- 11,4	- 13,5	- 14,6	- 10,6	- 13,2
ACP	- 5,1	- 7,4	- 7,7	- 6,7	- 4,7	- 5,4	- 4,4	- 6,0	- 5,5	- 4,0	- 4,0
CAND	-	-	-	-	- 1,0	- 1,3	- 1,0	- 0,7	- 0,2	- 0,3	0,1
L. America	- 2,7	- 3,1	- 3,1	- 2,8	- 2,0	- 1,9	- 1,5	- 1,5	- 1,7	- 1,2	- 1,9
DAE	0,1	0,1	0,1	0,2	0,4	0,4	0,3	0,2	0,2	0,1	0,3

4C2FZ

RU: Russia; SA: Saudi Arabia; LY: Libya; DZ: Algeria; IR: Iran; NG: Nigeria; IQ: Iraq; OPEC: Organisation of Petroleum Exporting countries; Med. Basin: countries and territories that make up the Med. Basin; ACP: African, Caribbean and Pacific countries; CAND: Candidate countries; L. America: Latin America; DAE: Dynamic Asian Economies.

eurostat

Extra-EU exports of chemicals and related products by main trading partners.
1 000 million ECU

	1989	1990	1991	1992	1993	1994	1995	1996	1997	1998	1999
Extra EU-15	51,9	51,5	54,5	57,0	60,2	68,1	73,5	79,1	93,3	95,9	106,5
US	7,3	7,2	7,8	8,7	10,0	11,4	11,6	13,8	17,8	21,5	27,1
CH	5,1	5,3	5,3	5,6	6,2	6,7	7,4	7,6	8,4	9,1	9,9
JP	3,6	3,5	3,9	4,1	4,7	5,2	5,5	5,4	5,8	5,4	6,6
PL	0,7	0,5	1,0	1,2	1,5	1,7	2,1	2,7	3,5	3,8	4,2
NO	1,2	1,2	1,3	1,4	1,5	1,6	1,8	1,8	2,1	2,2	2,2
TR	0,9	1,1	1,1	1,2	1,6	1,4	2,0	2,4	3,2	3,2	3,5
CN	0,6	0,6	0,8	0,7	0,7	0,8	1,0	1,2	1,4	1,4	1,7
RU	-	-	-	0,5	1,0	1,2	1,3	1,9	2,8	2,3	1,7
AU	1,0	1,0	1,0	1,2	1,3	1,5	1,5	1,8	2,1	2,3	2,7
CZ	-	-	-	-	0,8	1,1	1,4	1,6	1,9	2,1	2,2
CAND	-	-	-	-	5,9	6,8	8,8	10,3	12,9	14,0	14,9
Med. Basin	5,2	5,4	5,4	5,2	6,3	6,7	7,9	8,3	10,1	10,7	11,2
DAE	3,6	4,1	4,5	4,8	5,6	6,7	7,2	7,7	8,5	7,0	8,3
L. America	2,6	2,6	3,1	3,3	4,1	4,7	5,0	5,7	6,9	7,3	7,3
OPEC	4,1	4,3	4,3	4,5	4,8	4,8	4,9	4,9	5,8	5,7	5,8
ACP	3,0	2,9	2,9	3,0	3,0	3,1	3,3	3,5	4,0	4,0	4,0

Further reading: External trade, statistical yearbooks. Eurostat. Comext on CD-ROM. Eurostat.

PL: Poland; RU: Russia; TR: Turkey; CN: China; CZ: Czech Republic; AU: Australia; CAND: Candidate countries; Med. Basin: countries and territories that make up the Med. Basin; DAE: Dynamic Asian Economies; L. America: Latin America; OPEC: Organisation of Petroleum Exporting countries; ACP: African, Caribbean and Pacific countries.

4C2DC

Extra-EU imports of chemicals and related products by main trading partners.
1 000 million ECU

	1989	1990	1991	1992	1993	1994	1995	1996	1997	1998	1999
Extra EU-15	30,1	30,2	31,9	32,7	32,1	37,5	43,1	44,3	51,6	55,6	58,6
US	8,9	9,0	9,8	10,1	10,0	11,2	12,3	14,1	17,1	19,3	20,1
CH	6,5	7,0	7,4	7,9	8,3	9,3	10,1	10,5	11,0	11,7	12,5
JP	2,3	2,3	2,6	2,8	2,9	3,2	3,5	3,6	4,0	4,2	4,5
PL	0,3	0,5	0,6	0,6	0,4	0,5	0,7	0,7	0,7	0,8	0,7
NO	1,2	1,2	1,2	1,2	1,2	1,3	1,5	1,5	1,8	1,8	1,9
TR	0,2	0,2	0,2	0,2	0,2	0,2	0,2	0,2	0,3	0,3	0,3
CN	0,7	0,7	0,8	0,8	0,9	1,1	1,5	1,5	1,9	2,0	2,1
RU	-	-	-	0,5	1,0	1,5	1,6	1,3	1,5	1,5	1,5
AU	0,1	0,1	0,1	0,1	0,1	0,2	0,2	0,2	0,2	0,3	0,4
CZ	-	-	-	-	0,4	0,6	0,7	0,7	0,8	0,8	0,8
CAND	-	-	-	-	1,9	2,5	3,3	3,2	3,5	3,6	3,4
Med. Basin	2,1	2,1	1,9	1,6	1,7	2,1	2,5	2,3	2,9	2,9	3,0
DAE	0,5	0,6	0,8	0,9	1,0	1,2	1,6	1,6	2,0	2,6	3,1
L. America	0,9	1,0	1,0	0,9	0,8	0,9	1,1	1,1	1,3	1,4	1,4
OPEC	1,0	0,9	0,8	0,6	0,6	0,8	0,9	0,9	1,1	1,3	1,1
ACP	0,8	0,6	0,5	0,5	0,4	0,5	0,6	0,4	0,6	0,8	0,7

5

Further reading: External trade, statistical yearbooks. Eurostat. Comext on CD-ROM. Eurostat.

PL: Poland; RU: Russia; TR: Turkey; CN: China; CZ: Czech Republic; AU: Australia; CAND: Candidate countries; Med. Basin: countries and territories that make up the Med. Basin; DAE: Dynamic Asian Economies; L. America: Latin America; OPEC: Organisation of Petroleum Exporting countries; ACP: African, Caribbean and Pacific countries.

4C2EC

 eurostat

Main trading partners of EU-15 in chemical products are ranked by the total of chemical imports and exports in 1999. Chemical products are defined according to section 5 of the standard international trade classification (SITC) revision 3. EU-15 includes the former GDR from reunification.

Extra-EU trade balance in chemicals and related products by main trading partners.
1 000 million ECU

	1989	1990	1991	1992	1993	1994	1995	1996	1997	1998	1999
Extra EU-15	21,9	21,3	22,6	24,3	28,1	30,6	30,4	34,8	41,7	40,4	47,9
US	- 1,6	- 1,8	- 2,0	- 1,4	0,0	0,2	- 0,6	- 0,3	0,7	2,2	7,0
CH	- 1,4	- 1,7	- 2,2	- 2,3	- 2,1	- 2,7	- 2,7	- 2,9	- 2,6	- 2,6	- 2,6
JP	1,3	1,2	1,3	1,4	1,9	2,0	2,0	1,9	1,8	1,2	2,1
PL	0,3	0,0	0,4	0,6	1,1	1,2	1,4	2,0	2,7	3,0	3,5
NO	0,0	0,0	0,1	0,2	0,2	0,3	0,3	0,3	0,3	0,4	0,3
TR	0,7	0,9	0,9	1,1	1,4	1,2	1,8	2,2	2,9	2,9	3,2
CN	- 0,1	- 0,1	0,1	- 0,1	- 0,1	- 0,3	- 0,5	- 0,3	- 0,5	- 0,6	- 0,4
RU	-	-	-	0,0	0,0	- 0,3	- 0,3	0,6	1,3	0,9	0,2
AU	0,9	0,9	0,9	1,1	1,2	1,3	1,3	1,6	1,9	2,0	2,4
CZ	-	-	-	-	0,4	0,5	0,7	1,0	1,2	1,3	1,4
CAND	-	-	-	-	4,0	4,3	5,4	7,1	9,4	10,4	11,5
Med. Basin	3,0	3,4	3,5	3,6	4,6	4,5	5,4	5,9	7,2	7,8	8,2
DAE	3,1	3,5	3,7	3,9	4,6	5,6	5,6	6,1	6,5	4,3	5,2
L. America	1,7	1,6	2,1	2,4	3,3	3,9	3,8	4,6	5,5	6,0	5,9
OPEC	3,2	3,4	3,5	3,8	4,3	4,0	4,0	4,0	4,6	4,4	4,7
ACP	2,2	2,3	2,3	2,5	2,6	2,6	2,7	3,0	3,4	3,3	3,4

4C2FW

5

PL: Poland; RU: Russia; TR: Turkey; CN: China; CZ: Czech Republic; AU: Australia; CAND: candidate countries; Med. Basin: countries and territories that make up the Med. Basin; DAE: Dynamic Asian Economies; L. America: Latin America; OPEC: Organisation of Petroleum Exporting countries; ACP: African, Caribbean and Pacific countries.

eurostat

Extra-EU exports of manufactured goods. 1 000 million ECU

	1989	1990	1991	1992	1993	1994	1995	1996	1997	1998	1999
Extra EU-15	128,7	124,8	123,3	124,4	138,0	154,3	167,6	182,1	203,9	202,6	206,1
US	27,5	25,3	23,2	22,8	26,6	30,0	29,5	31,9	38,4	41,7	45,5
CH	17,9	18,5	17,3	16,4	16,5	18,2	19,5	19,0	19,6	20,1	20,4
CN	1,2	0,8	0,9	1,1	2,1	1,7	1,7	2,1	2,5	2,7	3,0
JP	8,3	8,7	7,9	7,1	7,4	8,8	10,0	10,7	10,4	9,1	9,6
PL	1,2	1,5	2,5	2,9	3,6	4,3	5,3	6,4	8,0	9,2	9,4
NO	5,3	5,4	6,0	5,7	5,3	5,9	6,4	6,7	7,6	8,3	7,7
TR	1,5	1,9	2,0	2,2	3,1	2,2	3,2	4,2	5,2	5,0	4,4
CZ	-	-	-	-	2,3	3,1	3,9	4,4	5,1	5,5	5,9
HK	3,3	3,1	3,3	3,9	5,0	5,9	6,2	6,9	7,4	5,7	5,8
IN	3,8	2,8	2,6	2,4	3,1	3,3	4,0	4,0	4,7	4,2	5,1
CAND	-	-	-	-	15,9	18,1	22,8	26,7	32,5	35,9	36,3
Med. Basin	14,1	15,4	15,3	14,7	17,9	18,5	20,8	23,3	26,4	26,9	26,7
DAE	8,6	9,0	9,9	10,6	13,7	16,5	18,0	19,8	20,3	14,2	15,6
OPEC	9,2	9,0	9,9	10,5	10,3	9,5	9,6	10,4	12,0	11,2	10,3
L. America	3,3	3,4	4,2	4,6	5,6	6,4	6,9	7,5	9,9	10,9	9,7
ACP	5,5	5,4	5,3	5,4	5,1	5,1	5,7	6,1	6,7	6,8	6,4

4C2DB

Further reading: External trade, statistical yearbooks. Eurostat. Comext on CD-ROM. Eurostat.

CN: China; PL: Poland; TR: Turkey; IN: India; CZ: Czech Republic; HK: Hong Kong; CAND: Candidate countries; Med. Basin: countries and territories that make up the Med. Basin; DAE: Dynamic Asian Economies; OPEC: Organisation of Petroleum Exporting countries; L. America: Latin America; ACP: African, Pacific and Caribbean countries.

Extra-EU imports of manufactured goods by main trading partners. 1 000 million ECU

	1989	1990	1991	1992	1993	1994	1995	1996	1997	1998	1999
Extra EU-15	118,4	121,2	132,4	134,7	137,8	154,0	164,9	169,5	196,8	211,4	223,6
US	17,7	18,2	19,6	19,4	19,2	21,0	22,0	23,8	28,4	30,9	31,5
CH	11,9	12,7	12,5	12,5	12,6	13,5	14,0	16,0	16,2	17,0	18,8
CN	5,9	7,4	11,0	12,4	14,6	16,2	16,3	18,7	23,1	24,9	28,8
JP	9,4	9,4	10,5	10,5	9,3	9,5	9,4	9,2	10,5	11,7	11,7
PL	1,6	2,2	3,0	3,8	4,1	5,3	6,6	6,4	7,2	8,2	8,7
NO	5,0	4,6	4,4	4,1	3,8	4,6	5,5	5,2	5,7	6,1	6,2
TR	3,5	3,9	4,0	4,4	4,4	4,8	5,7	6,1	7,3	8,3	8,9
CZ	-	-	-	-	2,8	3,6	4,3	4,4	5,1	5,9	6,6
HK	5,0	4,6	5,0	4,8	5,2	5,1	4,8	4,7	5,3	5,5	6,0
IN	3,1	3,4	3,5	3,6	4,4	5,1	5,5	5,7	6,2	6,6	6,6
CAND	-	-	-	-	18,8	23,6	28,5	29,1	33,9	38,7	41,3
Med. Basin	12,2	13,7	13,9	12,1	13,5	15,5	17,1	18,3	21,4	23,4	24,4
DAE	17,6	16,9	19,7	18,7	18,1	17,8	17,0	17,0	19,3	20,8	22,0
OPEC	2,1	2,7	3,5	4,0	4,4	5,0	5,2	5,5	6,7	6,9	7,0
L. America	6,1	5,7	5,3	4,6	4,2	5,2	6,3	5,7	6,4	6,4	6,1
ACP	7,2	6,4	5,7	5,2	3,5	5,0	5,9	6,3	7,2	7,0	7,9

5

4C2EB

Further reading: External trade, statistical yearbooks. Eurostat. Comext on CD-ROM. Eurostat.

CN: China; PL: Poland; TR: Turkey; IN: India; CZ: Czech Republic; HK: Hong Kong; CAND: Candidate countries; Med. Basin: countries and territories that make up the Med. Basin; DAE: Dynamic Asian Economies; OPEC: Organisation of Petroleum Exporting countries; L. America: Latin America; ACP: African, Pacific and Caribbean countries.

eurostat

Main trading partners of EU-15 in manufactured goods are ranked by the total of imports and exports of manufactured goods in 1999. Manufactured goods are defined according to sections 6 and 8 of the standard international trade classification (SITC) revision. EU-15 includes the former GDR from reunification.

Extra-EU trade balance in manufactured goods by main trading partners.
1 000 million ECU

	1989	1990	1991	1992	1993	1994	1995	1996	1997	1998	1999
Extra EU-15	10,3	3,6	- 9,2	- 10,4	0,2	0,3	2,7	12,6	7,1	- 8,7	- 17,5
US	9,7	7,1	3,6	3,4	7,4	9,0	7,5	8,1	10,0	10,8	14,1
CH	6,1	5,8	4,8	3,9	3,8	4,7	5,5	3,0	3,3	3,1	1,7
CN	- 4,7	- 6,5	- 10,0	- 11,3	- 12,4	- 14,4	- 14,6	- 16,6	- 20,6	- 22,3	- 25,8
JP	- 1,1	- 0,7	- 2,6	- 3,4	- 2,0	- 0,6	0,6	1,5	- 0,2	- 2,6	- 2,1
PL	- 0,4	- 0,8	- 0,6	- 0,8	- 0,5	- 1,1	- 1,3	0,0	0,8	0,9	0,7
NO	0,4	0,8	1,5	1,6	1,5	1,3	0,9	1,5	1,8	2,2	1,4
TR	- 2,0	- 2,0	- 2,1	- 2,2	- 1,3	- 2,6	- 2,4	- 1,8	- 2,1	- 3,3	- 4,5
CZ	-	-	-	-	- 0,4	- 0,5	- 0,4	0,0	0,0	- 0,4	- 0,6
HK	- 1,7	- 1,5	- 1,8	- 0,9	- 0,2	0,9	1,4	2,1	2,1	0,2	- 0,2
IN	0,7	- 0,6	- 1,0	- 1,2	- 1,3	- 1,9	- 1,5	- 1,7	- 1,6	- 2,4	- 1,5
CAND	-	-	-	-	- 2,9	- 5,5	- 5,7	- 2,4	- 1,4	- 2,8	- 5,1
Med. Basin	2,0	1,7	1,5	2,6	4,4	3,0	3,7	5,0	5,0	3,5	2,3
DAE	- 8,9	- 8,0	- 9,8	- 8,1	- 4,4	- 1,3	1,0	2,8	1,0	- 6,6	- 6,3
OPEC	7,0	6,3	6,3	6,5	5,9	4,5	4,4	4,9	5,3	4,3	3,3
L. America	- 2,8	- 2,2	- 1,1	- 0,1	1,4	1,2	0,6	1,8	3,5	4,4	3,5
ACP	- 1,7	- 1,0	- 0,4	0,1	1,5	0,1	- 0,2	- 0,3	- 0,5	- 0,1	- 1,5

CN: China; PL: Poland; TR: Turkey; IN: India; CZ: Czech Republic; HK: Hong Kong; CAND: Candidate countries; Med. Basin: countries and territories that make up the Med. Basin; DAE: Dynamic Asian Economies; OPEC: Organisation of Petroleum Exporting countries; L. America: Latin America; ACP: African, Pacific and Caribbean countries.

4C2EW

Extra-EU exports of machinery and transport equipment by main trading partners.
1 000 million ECU

	1989	1990	1991	1992	1993	1994	1995	1996	1997	1998	1999
Extra EU-15	161,6	169,2	175,3	179,9	202,8	228,9	255,9	283,0	331,4	345,5	352,1
US	37,4	37,6	34,7	36,1	42,6	48,7	50,9	55,0	70,2	83,1	92,4
JP	7,1	8,8	8,4	7,2	8,6	10,4	12,8	14,4	14,2	11,8	13,1
CH	13,6	14,2	13,5	13,0	12,9	14,3	16,7	16,5	16,9	19,8	23,5
CN	4,0	3,6	3,6	5,0	8,7	10,3	10,7	10,3	11,2	12,0	12,7
HU	1,4	1,5	1,8	2,1	2,6	3,4	3,7	4,6	6,9	9,3	10,6
TW	3,0	2,7	2,7	3,2	3,8	4,5	4,9	4,5	6,0	6,6	6,0
KR	2,4	3,0	3,6	3,1	3,7	5,2	6,0	7,0	6,9	4,2	4,8
PL	1,5	1,9	3,5	3,1	3,9	4,2	5,6	8,0	10,3	11,9	12,3
SG	2,7	3,0	3,2	3,3	4,1	5,0	5,7	6,9	7,6	6,5	6,9
CZ	-	-	-	-	3,2	4,0	5,0	6,3	7,2	7,8	8,3
DAE	12,5	14,1	15,9	16,6	21,6	27,1	33,5	34,9	39,2	31,8	30,0
CAND	-	-	-	-	21,4	22,8	28,5	36,8	46,3	53,6	54,4
Med. Basin	15,6	18,4	18,4	17,7	22,4	22,4	24,1	28,9	33,3	35,9	36,1
L. America	8,0	8,4	9,4	11,1	12,8	16,0	16,6	18,1	23,5	26,4	24,1
OPEC	13,1	14,9	18,4	20,0	19,5	16,7	17,3	17,8	25,2	22,6	20,1
ACP	10,8	10,9	10,3	11,0	11,1	10,7	13,0	13,3	14,3	16,8	15,8

4C2DA

Further reading: External trade, statistical yearbooks. Eurostat. Comext on CD-ROM. Eurostat.

CN: China; TW: Taiwan; HU: Hungary; PL: Poland; SG: Singapore; KR: South Korea; CZ: Czech Republic; DAE: Dynamic Asian Economies; CAND: Candidate countries; Med. Basin: countries and territories that make up the Med. Basin; L. America: Latin America; OPEC: Organisation of Petroleum Exporting countries; ACP: African, Caribbean and Pacific countries.

Extra-EU imports of machinery and transport equipment by main trading partners.
1 000 million ECU

	1989	1990	1991	1992	1993	1994	1995	1996	1997	1998	1999
Extra EU-15	128,2	132,5	146,1	143,8	143,9	160,4	173,4	189,0	230,0	267,2	304,0
US	43,9	43,8	47,4	43,2	44,2	48,8	49,7	53,7	71,8	81,4	90,7
JP	39,5	38,7	42,9	42,1	39,2	40,2	40,5	38,8	44,4	48,9	53,2
CH	9,3	10,6	10,7	10,7	9,8	10,6	11,8	11,9	12,5	14,5	16,0
CN	1,1	1,7	2,3	2,9	3,9	5,1	6,3	7,6	10,1	12,3	15,8
HU	0,4	0,5	0,8	1,0	1,1	1,7	2,7	3,7	6,1	8,5	10,9
TW	5,0	5,4	6,4	6,4	6,5	6,8	7,2	8,6	10,1	11,8	13,4
KR	3,1	3,0	3,7	3,7	4,6	5,7	7,4	7,5	9,0	10,6	13,0
PL	0,5	0,6	0,7	1,0	1,5	1,6	2,3	2,8	3,5	4,3	5,3
SG	3,1	3,7	4,1	4,5	5,4	6,6	6,8	7,5	9,2	9,5	9,6
CZ	-	-	-	-	1,3	1,8	2,5	3,2	4,4	6,5	7,8
DAE	14,4	15,6	18,6	19,3	22,8	27,1	31,1	34,3	41,1	47,3	53,1
CAND	-	-	-	-	7,0	9,1	12,8	15,6	20,5	28,7	35,2
Med. Basin	3,2	3,9	4,3	3,9	4,6	5,6	6,2	6,5	7,4	9,7	10,8
L. America	2,1	2,0	2,0	2,0	1,7	2,1	2,4	2,4	3,0	4,4	5,8
OPEC	0,7	0,8	1,0	1,5	1,6	1,6	1,8	1,8	2,9	3,1	3,0
ACP	0,9	1,0	0,8	1,2	1,4	1,4	1,5	2,1	2,3	2,6	3,5

4C2EA

5

Further reading: External trade, statistical yearbooks. Eurostat. Comext on CD-ROM. Eurostat.

CN: China; TW: Taiwan; HU: Hungary; PL: Poland; SG: Singapore; KR: South Korea; CZ: Czech Republic; DAE: Dynamic Asian Economies; CAND: Candidate countries; Med. Basin: countries and territories that make up the Med. Basin; L. America: Latin America; OPEC: Organisation of Petroleum Exporting countries; ACP: African, Caribbean and Pacific countries.

Main trading partners of EU-15 in machinery and transport equipment are ranked by the total of imports and exports of machines and vehicles in 1999. Machinery and transport equipment are defined according to section 7 of the standard international trade classification (SITC) revision 3. EU-15 includes the former GDR from reunification.

Extra-EU trade balance in machinery and transport equipment by main trading partners.
1 000 million ECU

	1989	1990	1991	1992	1993	1994	1995	1996	1997	1998	1999
Extra EU-15	33,3	36,7	29,2	36,1	59,0	68,5	82,6	94,0	101,5	78,3	48,1
US	- 6,6	- 6,2	- 12,7	- 7,1	- 1,6	- 0,1	1,3	1,3	- 1,6	1,7	1,8
JP	- 32,3	- 29,9	- 34,6	- 34,9	- 30,6	- 29,9	- 27,7	- 24,4	- 30,1	- 37,1	- 40,1
CH	4,3	3,5	2,8	2,3	3,1	3,7	4,8	4,6	4,5	5,2	7,5
CN	2,9	1,9	1,3	2,1	4,9	5,2	4,4	2,7	1,2	- 0,3	- 3,2
HU	1,1	0,9	1,0	1,1	1,4	1,6	1,0	0,9	0,8	0,8	- 0,3
TW	- 1,9	- 2,7	- 3,6	- 3,2	- 2,7	- 2,3	- 2,3	- 4,1	- 4,1	- 5,3	- 7,4
KR	- 0,7	0,0	- 0,1	- 0,6	- 0,9	- 0,5	- 1,4	- 0,6	- 2,1	- 6,4	- 8,2
PL	1,0	1,2	2,8	2,1	2,4	2,6	3,3	5,2	6,8	7,6	6,9
SG	- 0,4	- 0,7	- 0,9	- 1,3	- 1,3	- 1,6	- 1,1	- 0,6	- 1,6	- 3,0	- 2,7
CZ	-	-	-	-	1,8	2,2	2,5	3,1	2,8	1,3	0,5
DAE	- 1,9	- 1,5	- 2,7	- 2,7	- 1,2	0,0	2,4	0,6	- 1,8	- 15,4	- 23,1
CAND	-	-	-	-	14,4	13,7	15,7	21,2	25,8	24,9	19,2
Med. Basin	12,4	14,5	14,1	13,7	17,8	16,8	17,8	22,4	26,0	26,2	25,3
L. America	5,9	6,4	7,4	9,1	11,1	13,9	14,2	15,7	20,5	22,0	18,3
OPEC	12,3	14,1	17,4	18,5	17,8	15,1	15,5	16,1	22,3	19,4	17,1
ACP	9,9	9,9	9,5	9,7	9,7	9,3	11,4	11,2	11,9	14,2	12,3

CN: China; TW: Taiwan; HU: Hungary; PL: Poland; SG: Singapore; KR: South Korea; CZ: Czech Republic; DAE: Dynamic Asian Economies; CAND: Candidate countries; Med. Basin: countries and territories that make up the Med. Basin; L. America: Latin America; OPEC: Organisation of Petroleum Exporting countries; ACP: African, Caribbean and Pacific countries.

eurostat

EUROSTAT YEARBOOK 2001
477

6

the candidate countries

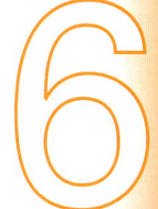

Population | 483

Density of the population. Persons per 1 km². 1999 | 483
Population (average). 1 000s | 484
Total area in km². 1999 | 484

Education | 485

Enrolment in education by level. 1997–98. 1 000s | 485
Basic data on education. 1997–98: | 485
Participation rate in pre-primary education | 485
Duration of compulsory schooling (age) | 485
Average number of foreign languages learnt per pupil in primary and secondary general education. 1997–98 | 486
Percentage of pupils in upper secondary education enrolled in vocational stream. By gender. 1997–98 | 486
Participation rates in education at all levels. By age. 1997–98 | 487
Women among students in tertiary education. 1997–98. % | 487
Percentage of the population aged 25 to 59 having completed at least upper secondary education. Women and men. 1999 | 488
Percentage of the population aged 25 to 59 having completed at least upper secondary education. Women. 1999 | 488
Unemployment rates for men and women aged 25 to 59. By educational level. 1999 | 489

Gross domestic product | 490

Gross domestic product at constant prices. Change over the previous year. % | 490
Change of gross domestic product. 1993 = 100 | 490
Change of gross domestic product. 1993 = 100 | 491
Change of gross domestic product. 1993 = 100 | 491
Gross domestic product at current prices. 1 000 million ECU | 492
Gross domestic product per capita at current prices. ECU | 492

Interest rates | 493

Short-term interest rates: day-to-day money rates. % | 493
ECU/EUR exchange rates: annual averages. EUR 1 =… | 493

Consumer price index | 494

Consumer price index % change over the previous year | 494
Consumer price index % change over the previous year | 494

Imports, exports, trade balance | 495

Imports. Million ECU/EUR | 495
Exports. Million ECU/EUR | 495
Trade balance for 1999. Million EUR | 496

Balance of payments | 496

Balance of the current account at current prices. % of GDP | 496
Average flows of the current account. % of GDP | 496
Balance of international trade in goods and services at current prices. % of GDP | 497
International trade in goods and services. Cover rates. % | 497
Total trade in goods (exports and imports). % of current account total flows | 497
Total trade in services (exports and imports). % of current account total flows | 498
Exports of transport services as % of services total exports | 498

Imports of transport services as % of services total imports | 498
Exports of travel services as % of services total exports | 499
Imports of travel services as % of services total imports | 499
International trade in services other than transport and travel. Cover rates. % | 499

Unemployment | 500

Unemployment rate (Labour force survey). % of labour force |
Unemployment rate (Labour force survey). % of labour force | 500
Unemployment rate by age group. % of labour force (Labour force survey). 1999 | 500
| 501

Labour cost |

Earnings of women as % of men in sections C to K NACE Rev. 1 | 503
Average gross hourly earnings in industry in sections C to F of NACE Rev. 1. ECU. Manual workers | 503
Average gross monthly earnings of all employees in sections C to K of NACE Rev. 1. ECU | 503
Hourly labour costs in industry. ECU. All employees | 503
Hourly labour costs in industry and services. ECU. All employees | 504
Structure of labour costs in %. Total labour costs = 100. Total industry. All employees: | 504
Direct costs. % | 505
Indirect costs. % | 505
Social security. % | 505
Structure of labour costs in %. Total labour costs = 100. Industry and services in sections C to K of NACE Rev. 1. All employees: | 505
Direct costs. % | 506
Indirect costs. % | 506
Social security. % | 506
| 506

Research and development |

Research and development expenditure, as % of GDP, all sectors | 507
Distribution of research and development expenditure by sectors of economy. 1998 | 507
| 507

Industry and agriculture |

Industrial production volume indices. Previous year = 100 | 508
Gross agricultural production volume indices. Previous year = 100 | 508
Structure of gross value added for 1999. % of total: | 508
Agriculture | 509
Industry | 509
Construction | 509
Services | 509
Agriculture as percentage of total gross value added. 1999 | 509
| 509

Agriculture |

Areas (1 000 ha): | 510
Utilised agricultural area (1 000 ha) | 510
Arable land (1 000 ha) | 510
Crops production (1 000 t) | 510
| 510

Production of fruit and vegetables:	511
Apples (including cider apples). 1 000 t	511
Tomatoes. 1 000 t	511
Compared production 1998. EU-15/candidate countries.	
1 000 t	511
Information society	512
Number of personal computers	512
Personal computers per 100 inhabitants	512
Personal computers per 100 inhabitants. 1999	512
Number of Internet hosts	513

Internet hosts per 100 inhabitants	513
Internet hosts per 100 inhabitants. 1999	513
Number of mobile phone subscribers	514
Mobile phone subscribers per 100 inhabitants	514
Mobile phone subscribers per 100 inhabitants. 1999	514
Number of main telephone lines	515
Main telephone lines per 100 inhabitants	515
Transport	516
Railway network, in km per 1 000 km²	516
Length of motorways, in km	516

6

eurostat

Thirteen countries — Bulgaria, Cyprus, Czech Republic, Estonia, Hungary, Latvia, Lithuania, Malta, Poland, Romania, Slovak Republic, Slovenia and Turkey have applied for EU membership. Preparations for enlargement involve extensive negotiations and require comprehensive, comparable and timely statistical information. Since 1989, the Statistical Office of the European Communities (Eurostat) has established a close cooperation with the applicant countries and supports the accession process. Since 1999, Eurostat has published a comprehensive Yearbook with statistics on candidate countries. The latest edition of this publication was published under the title 'Statistical Yearbook on

candidate and south-east European countries' in June 2000 in English only (ISBN 92-828-9150-X, Catalogue No KS-27-00-621-EN-C).

The selected indicators presented in this chapter cover 1994–99 and show the main changes of the national economies during this period of time. In general, data is comparable between the countries. Definitions of most of the indicators correspond to the definitions of the same indicators provided by the Member States. Data is collected from the different countries' national statistical institutes and assembled by Eurostat.

More data on this in Eurostat's database

The CEC domain contains annual and short-term key indicators on central European countries (including the 13 applicant countries).

➤➤➤ **DOMAIN CEC IN DATABASE NEW CRONOS**

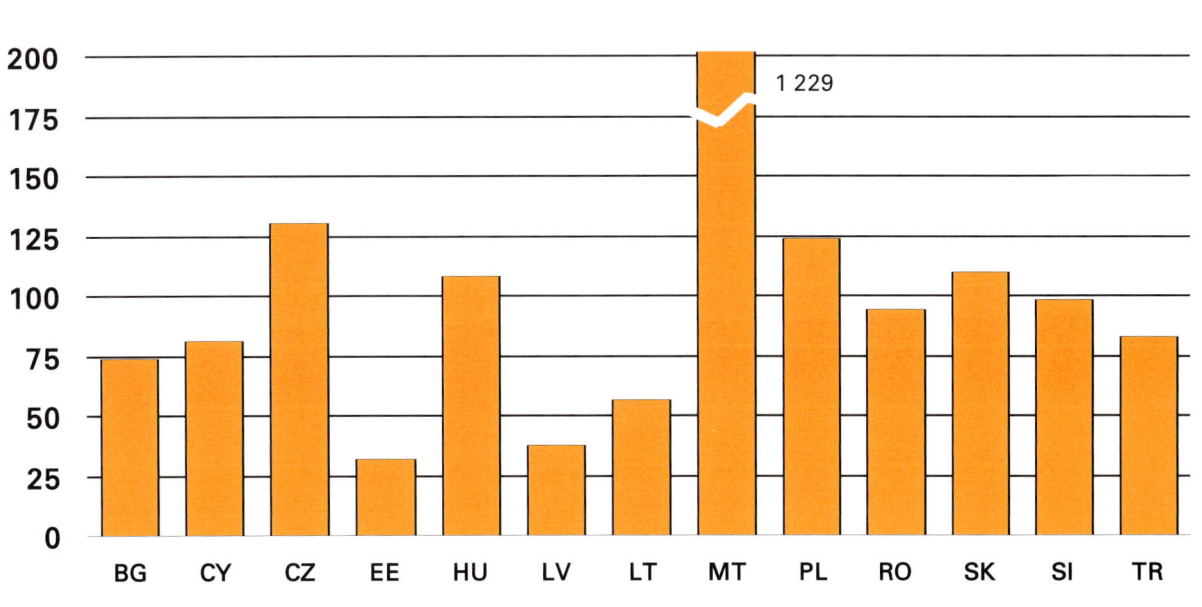

Density of the population. Persons per 1 km². 1999

1 229 (MT)

BG CY CZ EE HU LV LT MT PL RO SK SI TR

CY: density is calculated for the whole of Cyprus. All other indicators, except surface area, refer to the government-controlled area only.

Need more data on this topic? Ask your Data Shop

Population (average). 1 000s

		1995	1996	1997	1998	1999	
BG		8 406	8 363	8 312	8 257	8 211	**BG**
CY		645	652	658	663	667	**CY**
CZ		10 331	10 315	10 304	10 295	10 283	**CZ**
EE		1 484	1 469	1 458	1 450	1 442	**EE**
HU		10 229	10 193	10 155	10 114	10 068	**HU**
LV		2 516	2 491	2 469	2 449	2 432	**LV**
LT		3 715	3 710	3 706	3 702	3 700	**LT**
MT		378	381	384	386	388	**MT**
PL		38 588	38 618	38 650	38 666	38 654	**PL**
RO		22 681	22 608	22 546	22 503	22 458	**RO**
SK		5 364	5 374	5 383	5 391	5 395	**SK**
SI		1 988	1 991	1 987	1 983	1 986	**SI**
TR		60 500	61 450	62 405	63 365	64 330	**TR**

8Z3BB

CY: population data for government-controlled area only. End of year.
PL: Mid-year.

Total area in km². 1999

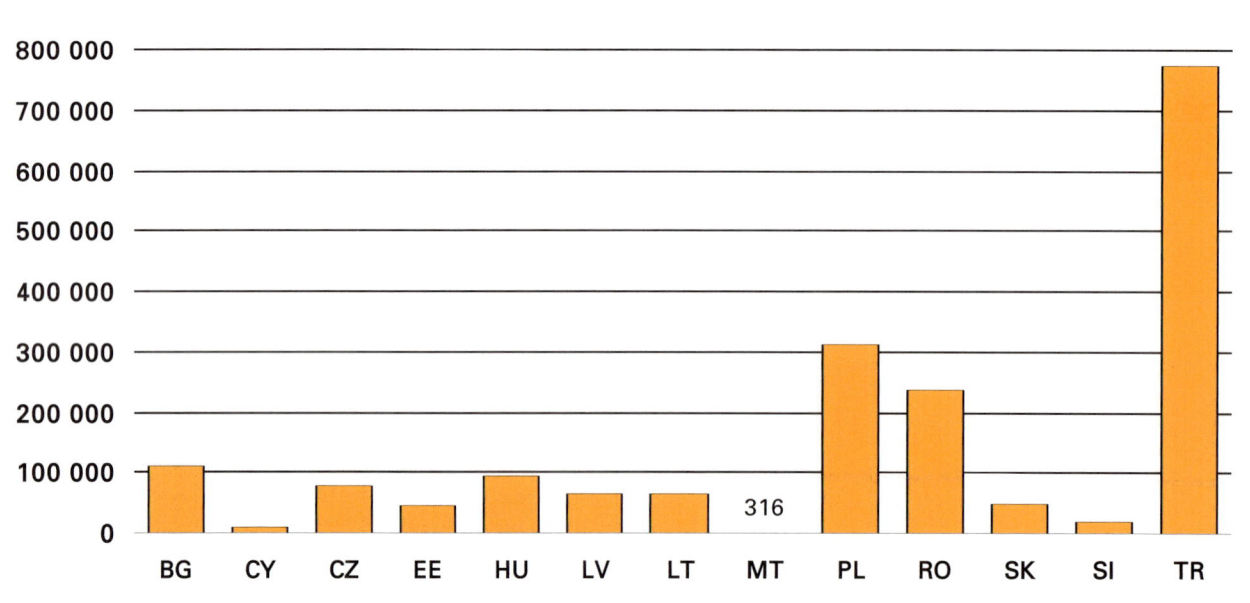

8Z3BB

CY: surface area of the whole of Cyprus.

6

8P1AA

Enrolment in education by level. 1997–98. 1 000s

	Total	Pre-primary	Primary	Lower secondary	Upper secondary	Post-secondary not tertiary	Tertiary	
BG	1 624	220	425	371	341	6	261	**BG**
CY	156	18	65	33	29	-	11	**CY**
CZ	2 230	316	663	528	428	80	215	**CZ**
EE	345	55	128	58	58	3	43	**EE**
HU	2 240	385	504	505	512	79	255	**HU**
LV	531	60	147	162	86	6	70	**LV**
LT	804	91	222	264	126	5	96	**LT**
MT	89	11	35	29	7	1	6	**MT**
PL	9 846	980	4 905		2 596	174	1 191	**PL**
RO	4 643	623	1 373	1 187	1 013	86	361	**RO**
SK	1 293	170	324	359	322	5	113	**SK**
SI	433	48	96	104	116	1	68	**SI**
TR	:	:	:	:	:	:	:	**TR**

Further reading: Education across Europe: statistics and indicators, 1999. Eurostat. Key data on education in Europe, 1999–2000. European Commission.

CY, MT: national sources. PL: ISCED 2 is included in ISCED 1. RO, SI: without ISCED 6.

Basic data on education. 1997–98

8P2AA

8M2AA

	Participation rate in pre-primary education			Duration of compulsory schooling (age)		
	3-year-olds	4-year-olds	5-year-olds	From	To	
EU-15	66	90	92	:	:	**EU-15**
BG	51	61	66	7	15	**BG**
CY	19	52	87	6	14	**CY**
CZ	44	77	92	6	15	**CZ**
EE	80	76	73	7	15	**EE**
HU	68	88	97	6	15	**HU**
LV	47	53	56	7	15	**LV**
LT	38	44	46	7	15	**LT**
MT	85	100	24	5	16	**MT**
PL	21	30	39	7	15	**PL**
RO	35	56	73	7	15	**RO**
SK	:	:	:	6	15	**SK**
SI	:	:	50	6	15	**SI**
TR	:	:	:	:	:	**TR**

Further reading: Education across Europe: statistics and indicators, 1999. Eurostat. Key data on education in Europe, 1999–2000. European Commission.

CY, MT: national sources. SI: 3–5 years.

Average number of foreign languages learnt per pupil in primary and secondary general education. 1997–98

	Primary	Lower secondary general	Upper secondary general	
BG	0,2	1,1	1,8	BG
CY	0,5	2,0	2,0	CY
CZ	0,4	1,1	1,7	CZ
EE	0,8	1,7	2,0	EE
HU	:	1,4	1,6	HU
LV	0,4	1,5	1,5	LV
LT	0,3	1,7	1,7	LT
MT	:	:	:	MT
PL	:	:	1,7	PL
RO	0,7	1,0	1,0	RO
SK	0,1	1,3	1,9	SK
SI	0,2	1,0	1,4	SI
TR	:	:	:	TR

8P5AA

Further reading: Education across Europe: statistics and indicators, 1999. Eurostat. Key data on education in Europe, 1999–2000. European Commission.

SI: ISCED 3 general and vocational. CZ: full-time only.

Percentage of pupils in upper secondary education enrolled in vocational stream. By gender. 1997–98

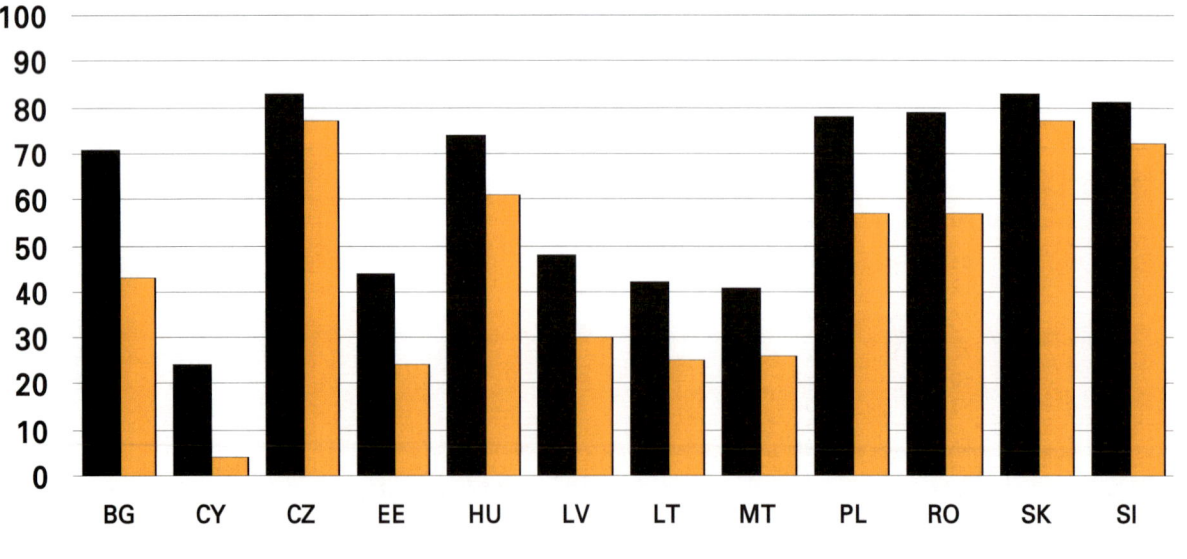

Black: boys; colour: girls.

8M3AA

Further reading: Education across Europe: statistics and indicators, 1999. Eurostat. Key data on education in Europe, 1999–2000. European Commission.

CY, MT: national sources.

6

8M4AA

Participation rates in education at all levels. By age. 1997–98

	16 years	18 years	20 years	22 years	24 years	18–24 years	18–24 years: only tertiary education	
EU-15	90	72	48	34	19	42	23	**EU-15**
BG	79	48	29	26	17	28	22	**BG**
CY	89	29	23	9	3	16	14	**CY**
CZ	96	64	24	20	14	28	14	**CZ**
EE	94	62	39	23	13	34	23	**EE**
HU	98	62	37	20	12	30	15	**HU**
LV	89	61	35	23	18	32	22	**LV**
LT	88	64	37	18	8	31	22	**LT**
MT	60	49	23	11	6	9	12	**MT**
PL	93	73	48	30	17	41	19	**PL**
RO	74	37	26	13	9	21	11	**RO**
SK	:	:	:	:	:	:	:	**SK**
SI	97	67	38	27	16	37	25	**SI**
TR	:	:	:	:	:	:	:	**TR**

Further reading: Education across Europe: statistics and indicators, 1999. Eurostat. Key data on education in Europe, 1999–2000. European Commission.

Horizontal axis: Age of students in years. CY, MT: national sources.

Women among students in tertiary education. 1997–98. %

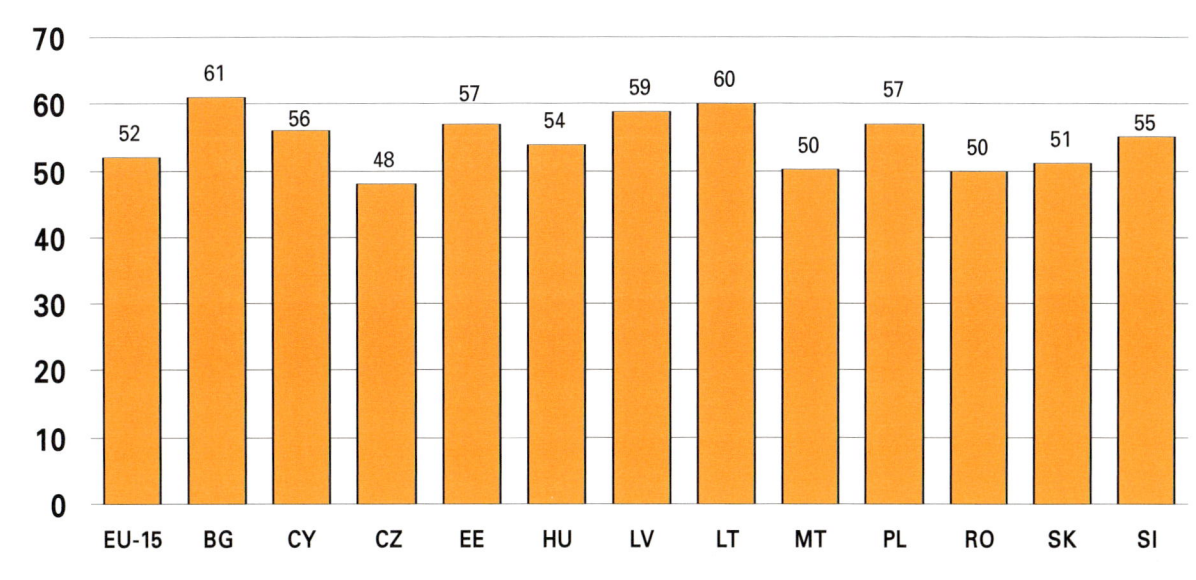

8M5AA

Further reading: Education across Europe: statistics and indicators, 1999. Eurostat. Key data on education in Europe, 1999–2000. European Commission.

CY, MT: national sources.

eurostat

These two indicators are similar to those with the same titles in the education section in Chapter 1.

Percentage of the population aged 25 to 59 having completed at least upper secondary education. Women and men. 1999

	ISCED 3–6	25–59	25–29	30–34	35–39	40–44	45–49	50–54	55–59	
BG		:	:	:	:	:	:	:	:	BG
CY		:	:	:	:	:	:	:	:	CY
CZ		87,4	93,8	91,2	91,5	87,1	84,2	85,2	77,3	CZ
EE		87,6	90,5	91,8	94,0	91,5	86,5	82,2	72,1	EE
HU		75,7	81,6	81,6	80,3	77,2	75,8	73,1	58,0	HU
LV		86,8	90,1	92,6	92,9	91,2	87,5	80,0	69,2	LV
LT		83,8	87,5	90,7	89,9	89,6	84,9	77,7	57,7	LT
MT		:	:	:	:	:	:	:	:	MT
PL		-	-	-	-	-	-	-	-	PL
RO		72,3	86,9	88,0	82,2	75,6	64,9	55,3	37,3	RO
SK		82,6	92,6	89,8	89,0	82,1	80,8	74,9	58,2	SK
SI		76,0	87,6	81,8	81,1	73,5	72,3	68,4	63,1	SI
TR		:	:	:	:	:	:	:	:	TR

8P1LF

Source: European Union labour force survey.
SK: 1998 data.

Percentage of the population aged 25 to 59 having completed at least upper secondary education. Women. 1999

	ISCED 3–6	25–59	25–29	30–34	35–39	40–44	45–49	50–54	55–59	
BG		:	:	:	:	:	:	:	:	BG
CY		:	:	:	:	:	:	:	:	CY
CZ		83,1	93,6	90,3	89,7	82,3	78,6	78,7	68,1	CZ
EE		89,4	93,9	93,4	96,9	92,4	88,8	83,8	73,3	EE
HU		70,2	80,2	79,5	77,6	71,8	69,5	65,1	46,6	HU
LV		88,7	92,2	94,8	94,0	94,1	91,3	80,8	71,3	LV
LT		86,0	90,4	92,4	94,9	92,5	87,8	79,5	58,2	LT
MT		:	:	:	:	:	:	:	:	MT
PL		-	-	-	-	-	-	-	-	PL
RO		66,3	86,1	86,3	78,6	69,2	55,2	44,4	28,6	RO
SK		77,8	92,5	89,3	86,1	78,1	74,3	65,8	47,0	SK
SI		71,5	88,6	82,7	79,1	68,4	65,6	59,9	51,3	SI
TR		:	:	:	:	:	:	:	:	TR

8P2LF

Source: European Union labour force survey.
SK: 1998 data.

6

This indicator is similar to a table and a graph in the education section in Chapter 1.

Unemployment rates for men and women aged 25 to 59. By educational level. 1999

	ISCED 0–2			ISCED 3–4			ISCED 5–6			
	Men	Women	Men and women	Men	Women	Men and women	Men	Women	Men and women	
BG	:	:	:	:	:	:	:	:	:	**BG**
CY	:	:	:	:	:	:	:	:	:	**CY**
CZ	19,9	17,8	18,6	4,9	8,3	6,4	2,3	3,1	2,6	**CZ**
EE	19,2	17,7	18,6	13,1	10,6	12,0	5,7	6,4	6,1	**EE**
HU	14,5	10,3	12,2	6,1	5,5	5,9	1,4	0,9	1,2	**HU**
LV	17,3	17,1	17,2	13,1	15,4	14,2	7,4	4,7	5,9	**LV**
LT	14,2	10,2	12,7	11,7	10,3	11,1	6,2	6,6	6,5	**LT**
MT	:	:	:	:	:	:	:	:	:	**MT**
PL	-	-	-	-	-	-	-	-	-	**PL**
RO	5,1	2,7	3,7	6,6	6,7	6,7	2,3	2,4	2,4	**RO**
SK	-	-	-	-	-	-	-	-	-	**SK**
SI	9,2	8,5	8,8	6,1	6,0	6,1	3,1	2,8	3,0	**SI**
TR	:	:	:	:	:	:	:	:	:	**TR**

Source: European Union labour force survey.
SK: 1998 data.
ISCED 0–2: pre-primary, primary and lower secondary education;
ISCED 3–4: upper secondary and post-secondary education;
ISCED 5–6: higher education.

8P3LF

Gross domestic product at constant prices. Change over the previous year. %

		1994	1995	1996	1997	1998	1999	
BG		1,8	2,9	- 10,1	- 7,0	3,5	2,4	**BG**
CY		5,9	6,1	1,9	2,4	5,0	4,5	**CY**
CZ		5,1	5,9	4,8	- 1,0	- 2,2	- 0,2	**CZ**
EE		- 2,0	4,3	3,9	10,6	4,7	- 1,1	**EE**
HU		2,9	1,5	1,3	4,6	4,9	4,5	**HU**
LV		0,6	- 0,8	3,3	8,6	3,9	0,1	**LV**
LT		- 9,8	3,3	4,7	7,3	5,1	- 4,2	**LT**
MT		5,7	6,2	4,0	4,9	3,4	4,0	**MT**
PL		5,2	7,0	6,0	6,8	4,8	4,2	**PL**
RO		3,9	7,1	3,9	- 6,1	- 5,4	- 3,2	**RO**
SK		4,9	6,7	6,2	6,2	4,1	1,9	**SK**
SI		5,3	4,1	3,5	4,6	3,8	5,0	**SI**
TR		- 5,5	7,2	7,0	7,5	3,1	- 5,0	**TR**

8V1AA

TR: 1998 and 1999 are from national source.

Change of gross domestic product. 1993 = 100

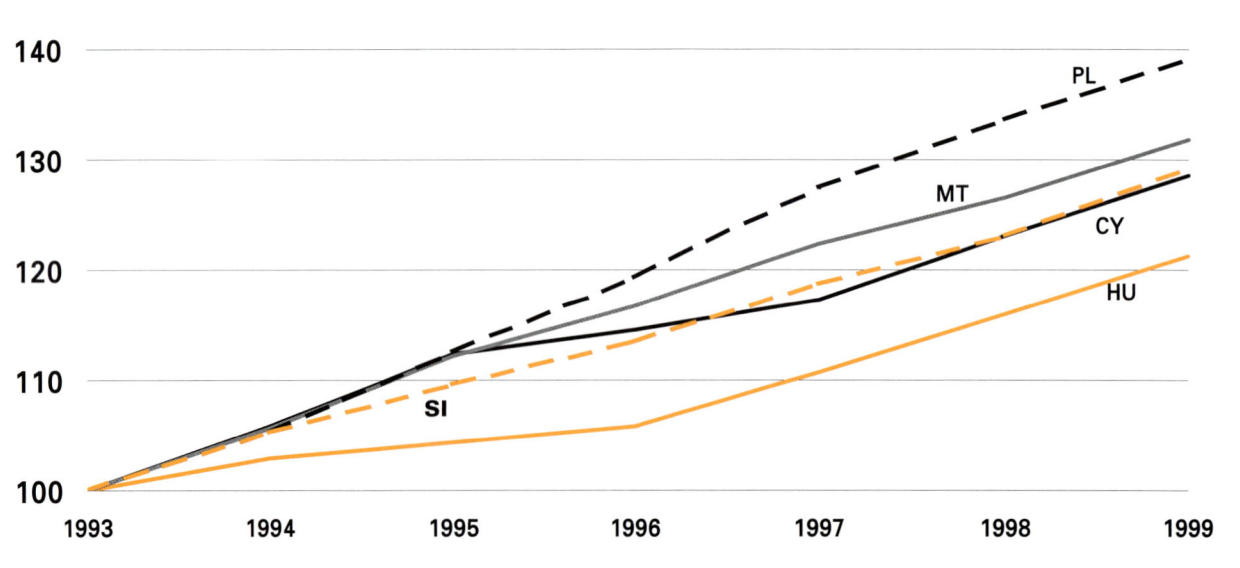

8V2AB

Calculated by Eurostat.

8V3AC

Change of gross domestic product. 1993 = 100

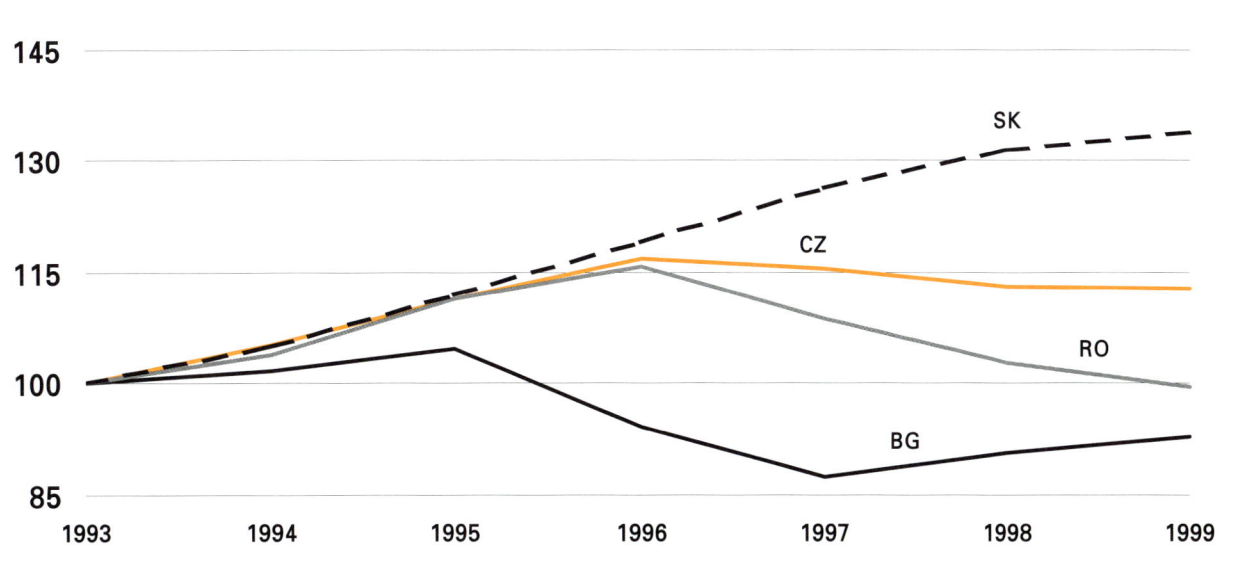

Calculated by Eurostat.

8V4AD

Change of gross domestic product. 1993 = 100

Calculated by Eurostat.

eurostat

Need an update for this indicator? Ask your Data Shop

Gross domestic product at current prices. 1 000 million ECU

	1994	1995	1996	1997	1998	1999	
BG	8,2	10,0	7,8	9,0	11,0	11,6	**BG**
CY	6,3	6,8	7,0	7,5	8,1	8,5	**CY**
CZ	34,5	39,8	45,6	46,4	49,5	49,8	**CZ**
EE	1,9	2,7	3,4	4,1	4,7	4,8	**EE**
HU	34,9	34,1	35,6	40,4	41,9	45,2	**HU**
LV	3,1	3,4	4,0	5,0	5,4	5,9	**LV**
LT	3,6	4,6	6,2	8,5	9,6	10,0	**LT**
MT	2,3	2,5	2,6	2,9	3,1	3,4	**MT**
PL	82,9	97,2	113,3	127,1	141,3	146,0	**PL**
RO	25,3	27,1	27,8	31,2	36,9	31,9	**RO**
SK	11,6	14,0	15,6	18,0	19,0	18,5	**SK**
SI	12,1	14,3	14,9	16,1	17,5	18,7	**SI**
TR	108,9	129,6	143,1	167,8	177,8	173,0	**TR**

8X1XA

Note that BG rebased the national currency in July 1999, dividing it by 1 000. It is now called New Bulgarian Lev. TR: 1998 and 1999 are from national source.

Gross domestic product per capita at current prices. ECU

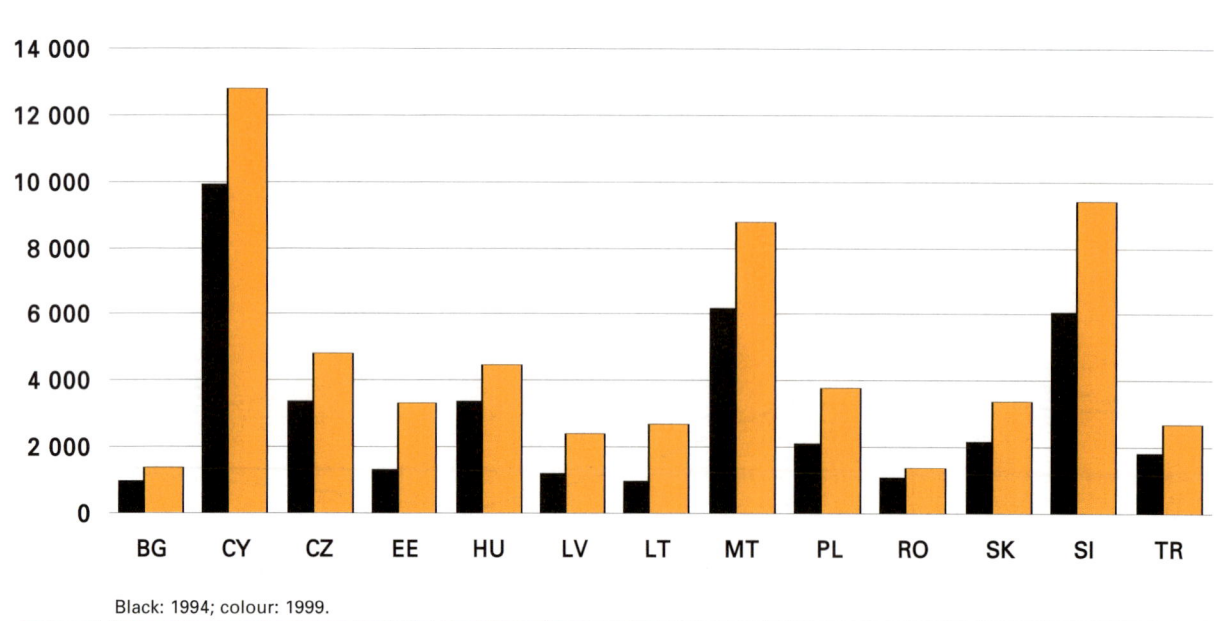

Black: 1994; colour: 1999.

8X1XB

Figures have been calculated using the population figures from national accounts, which may differ from those used in demographic statistics. Note that BG rebased the national currency in July 1999, dividing it by 1 000. It is now called New Bulgarian Lev. TR: 1998 and 1999 are from national source.

3OD1C

Short-term interest rates: day-to-day money rates. %

	1992	1993	1994	1995	1996	1997	1998	1999	
EU-15	:	:	:	:	:	:	:	3,3	EU-15
EUR-11	:	:	5,2	5,6	4,0	4,0	3,1	2,7	EUR-11
BG	:	:	97,4	69,6	287,7	134,8	2,4	2,6	BG
CY	:	:	:	:	:	:	:	:	CY
CZ	:	9,6	7,9	10,6	11,6	19,0	13,6	6,8	CZ
EE	:	:	5,7	4,9	3,5	6,5	11,6	3,3	EE
HU	:	15,5	25,6	31,3	23,8	20,8	18,0	14,8	HU
LV	:	51,4	37,1	22,4	13,1	3,7	4,4	4,7	LV
LT	:	:	:	26,8	18,9	10,7	6,1	6,3	LT
MT	:	:	:	:	:	5,2	5,5	5,0	MT
PL	:	17,5	18,7	26,4	21,2	22,7	21,1	14,1	PL
RO	:	:	:	48,5	53,4	85,9	80,7	94,7	RO
SK	:	:	13,1	5,7	11,6	24,7	14,5	12,6	SK
SI	:	:	29,1	12,1	14,0	9,7	7,4	6,9	SI
TR	:	:	:	:	:	:	:	:	TR

3OD2C

ECU/EUR exchange rates: annual averages. EUR 1 =...

	1989	1990	1991	1992	1993	1994	1995	1996	1997	1998	1999	
BG	0,00	0,00	0,03	0,05	0,03	0,06	0,09	0,23	1,90	1,97	1,96	BG
CY	:	0,58	0,57	0,58	0,58	0,58	0,59	0,59	0,58	0,58	0,58	CY
CZ	:	:	:	:	34,17	34,15	34,70	34,46	35,93	36,32	36,89	CZ
EE	:	:	:	:	15,49	15,40	14,99	15,28	15,72	15,75	15,65	EE
HU	78,99	130,52	142,20	172,78	107,61	125,03	164,55	193,74	211,65	240,57	252,77	HU
LV	:	:	:	:	0,79	0,66	0,69	0,70	0,66	0,66	0,62	LV
LT	:	:	:	:	5,09	4,73	5,23	5,08	4,54	4,48	4,26	LT
MT	:	0,40	0,40	0,41	0,45	0,45	0,46	0,46	0,44	0,43	0,43	MT
PL	0,19	1,96	2,02	2,97	2,12	2,70	3,17	3,42	3,72	3,92	4,23	PL
RO	19,93	46,26	145,37	673,71	885,83	1 971,56	2 661,81	3 922,19	8 111,50	9 984,88	16 345,20	RO
SK	:	:	:	:	36,03	38,12	38,86	38,92	38,11	39,54	44,12	SK
SI	:	:	:	:	132,49	152,77	154,88	171,78	181,00	185,96	194,47	SI
TR	:	3 329,06	5 153,29	8 930,95	12 879,30	35 535,30	59 912,10	103 214,00	171 848,00	293 736,00	447 230,00	TR

Consumer price index. % change over the previous year

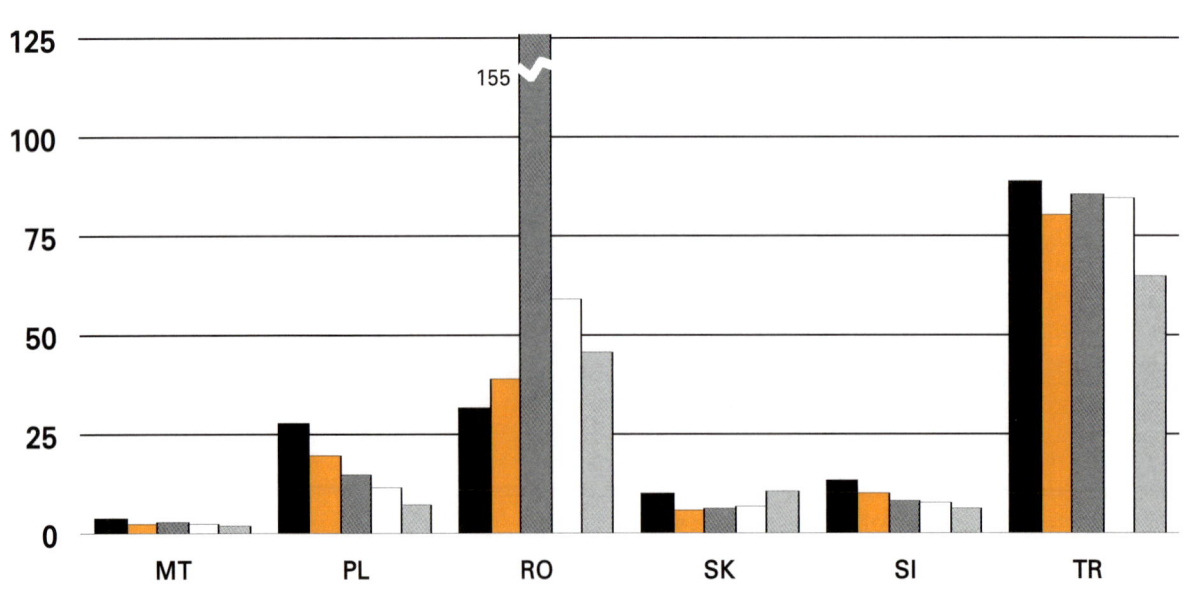

Black: 1995; colour: 1996; dark grey: 1997; white: 1998; grey: 1999.

Most candidate countries changed their methodology towards the Harmonised Indices of Consumer Prices (HICP) in the past years. Proxy HICPs are used in CZ, EE, HU, RO, SK and SI since 1996, BG and PL since 1997, LV since 1999. CY is in accordance with HICP since 1998. LT and TR calculate national indices.

Consumer price index. % change over the previous year

Black: 1995; colour: 1996; dark grey: 1997; white: 1998; grey: 1999.

Most candidate countries changed their methodology towards the Harmonised Indices of Consumer Prices (HICP) in the past years. Proxy HICPs are used in CZ, EE, HU, RO, SK and SI since 1996, BG and PL since 1997, LV since 1999. CY is in accordance with HICP since 1998. LT and TR calculate national indices.

8T1AA

Imports. Million ECU/EUR

	1994	1995	1996	1997	1998	1999	
BG	3 525,0	4 325,0	3 962,2	4 348,2	4 483,0	5 098,0	BG
CY	2 074,0	2 268,3	2 474,9	2 545,0	2 737,0	2 814,8	CY
CZ	14 650,0	19 316,0	21 827,9	23 955,9	25 679,5	27 081,6	CZ
EE	1 400,0	1 830,9	2 287,0	3 113,1	3 505,6	3 223,0	EE
HU	12 235,2	11 824,1	14 289,4	18 724,2	22 929,5	26 279,3	HU
LV	1 043,0	1 392,0	1 827,0	2 400,0	2 849,0	2 764,0	LV
LT	1 978,0	2 789,5	3 589,9	4 977,1	5 167,2	4 536,6	LT
MT	2 047,0	2 248,0	2 199,0	2 250,0	2 379,0	2 667,0	MT
PL	18 133,0	22 224,9	29 252,9	37 348,0	42 020,6	43 112,5	PL
RO	5 976,0	7 955,0	9 097,0	10 077,0	10 583,0	9 875,0	RO
SK	5 557,7	6 704,8	8 760,8	9 092,3	11 661,0	10 602,6	SK
SI	6 140,0	7 244,0	7 437,0	8 262,0	9 014,0	9 322,0	SI
TR	19 280,0	27 777,0	34 860,0	43 303,0	40 485,0	38 597,0	TR

Calculated using ECB exchange rates. CZ, SK: Imports: fob.

8T1AC

Exports. Million ECU/EUR

	1994	1995	1996	1997	1998	1999	
BG	3 357,1	4 093,0	3 818,8	4 355,0	3 847,0	3 697,0	BG
CY	375,0	403,4	385,8	376,8	383,1	372,0	CY
CZ	13 624,0	16 557,0	17 253,0	20 085,7	23 504,8	25 188,1	CZ
EE	1 104,0	1 270,3	1 393,1	1 882,6	2 236,2	2 203,0	EE
HU	8 996,1	9 837,1	12 367,8	16 842,4	20 520,2	23 468,3	HU
LV	832,0	998,0	1 136,0	1 474,0	1 619,0	1 616,0	LV
LT	1 706,0	2 067,9	2 642,6	3 404,3	3 309,9	2 818,3	LT
MT	1 320,0	1 463,0	1 362,0	1 438,0	1 637,0	1 858,0	MT
PL	14 493,0	17 516,0	19 251,5	22 732,1	25 209,3	25 708,7	PL
RO	5 171,0	6 091,0	6 364,0	7 481,0	7 381,0	8 071,0	RO
SK	5 625,0	6 558,8	6 954,9	7 277,5	9 562,1	9 567,6	SK
SI	5 740,0	6 353,0	6 553,0	7 389,0	8 065,0	8 002,0	SI
TR	15 539,0	16 962,0	18 773,0	23 784,0	24 140,0	25 292,0	TR

Calculated using ECB exchange rates.

6

eurostat

Trade balance for 1999. Million EUR

8T1AB

Calculated using ECB exchange rates. BG: Provisional. CZ, SK:
Imports: fob.

Balance of the current account at current prices. % of GDP

	1993	1994	1995	1996	1997	1998	1999	
BG	- 10,1	- 0,3	- 0,2	0,2	4,2	- 0,5	:	BG
CY	:	:	- 1,9	- 5,3	- 4,0	- 6,6	- 2,6	CY
CZ	1,3	- 1,9	- 2,6	- 7,4	- 6,1	- 1,9	:	CZ
EE	1,3	- 7,2	- 4,4	- 9,2	- 12,1	- 9,2	- 6,2	EE
HU	- 11,2	- 9,8	- 5,3	- 3,7	- 2,1	- 4,9	- 4,3	HU
LV	19,7	5,5	- 0,4	- 5,5	- 6,1	- 11,6	:	LV
LT	- 3,1	- 2,1	- 10,2	- 9,2	- 10,2	- 12,1	- 11,2	LT
MT	:	:	- 11,2	- 12,2	- 5,9	- 6,2	- 4,4	MT
PL	:	1,0	0,7	- 2,3	- 4,0	- 4,4	:	PL
RO	- 4,4	- 1,4	- 5,0	- 7,3	- 6,0	- 7,2	:	RO
SK	:	4,8	2,2	- 11,2	- 10,1	- 10,4	- 6,2	SK
SI	:	4,2	- 0,1	0,2	0,2	0,0	:	SI
TR	- 3,6	2,0	- 1,4	- 1,3	- 1,4	0,9	- 0,7	TR

1C1SP

Average flows of the current account. % of GDP

	1993	1994	1995	1996	1997	1998	1999	
BG	53,8	58,2	54,9	67,5	64,4	53,6	:	BG
CY	:	:	52,9	55,0	54,8	52,9	53,0	CY
CZ	55,8	54,9	59,0	58,4	64,3	65,8	:	CZ
EE	:	86,5	80,2	76,9	89,6	90,4	85,3	EE
HU	42,3	39,5	46,2	49,7	60,5	62,4	61,9	HU
LV	67,2	48,3	50,4	58,3	58,8	61,0	:	LV
LT	89,0	60,8	60,8	60,5	62,9	56,6	48,1	LT
MT	:		109,2	103,3	100,7	106,6	128,8	MT
PL	:	27,7	30,7	30,3	32,6	33,4	:	PL
RO	24,8	26,2	30,6	33,1	33,8	29,4	:	RO
SK	:	:	:	:	70,1	- 5,2	- 3,1	SK
SI	:	61,7	59,0	58,8	60,7	60,5	:	SI
TR	:	24,6	25,8	29,0	31,6	31,1	:	TR

1C0SP

6

Balance of international trade in goods and services at current prices. % of GDP

	1993	1994	1995	1996	1997	1998	1999	
BG	- 8,7	- 0,1	2,1	3,1	5,4	- 0,1	:	BG
CY	:	:	- 2,9	- 5,2	- 4,2	- 6,7	- 3,1	CY
CZ	1,4	- 2,2	- 3,5	- 6,8	- 5,3	- 1,4	:	CZ
EE	- 4,3	- 11,0	- 8,1	- 11,5	- 11,5	- 10,5	- 5,7	EE
HU	- 10,0	- 8,6	- 1,7	- 0,4	0,7	- 1,2	- 1,6	HU
LV	15,8	1,6	- 2,4	- 8,1	- 8,5	- 13,9	:	LV
LT	- 7,8	- 6,0	- 11,8	- 9,8	- 10,6	- 11,9	- 10,3	LT
MT	:	:	- 13,2	- 13,4	- 7,9	- 6,0	- 5,3	MT
PL	:	2,3	1,5	- 2,7	- 4,6	- 5,5	:	PL
RO	- 4,7	- 1,9	- 5,4	- 8,1	- 6,8	- 7,9	:	RO
SK	:	5,2	1,8	- 12,0	- 10,3	- 11,5	- 5,6	SK
SI	:	2,3	- 1,7	- 0,9	- 1,0	- 1,3	:	SI
TR	- 4,1	2,2	- 2,1	- 2,2	- 2,4	- 0,4	- 1,6	TR

1C2SP

International trade in goods and services. Cover rates. %

	1993	1994	1995	1996	1997	1998	1999	
BG	83,9	99,9	104,2	105,2	109,5	99,9	:	BG
CY	:	:	94,2	90,1	91,9	86,9	93,7	CY
CZ	102,6	95,9	93,9	88,3	91,5	97,8	:	CZ
EE	94,2	87,4	90,0	85,3	87,1	88,4	93,1	EE
HU	74,0	75,2	96,1	99,1	101,4	97,9	97,2	HU
LV	127,9	103,7	95,1	86,3	85,7	78,3	:	LV
LT	91,4	90,2	81,8	84,4	83,8	79,9	79,4	LT
MT	:	:	87,5	86,4	91,4	93,5	94,4	MT
PL	:	109,9	105,6	90,6	85,7	83,4	:	PL
RO	82,1	92,5	83,2	77,2	80,6	74,4	:	RO
SK	:	- 108,7	- 102,9	- 82,8	- 85,5	- 84,9	- 92,0	SK
SI	:	104,1	97,0	98,3	98,3	97,7	:	SI
TR	77,9	110,6	91,0	92,0	92,1	98,4	- 93,8	TR

1C3SP

Total trade in goods (exports and imports). % of current account total flows

	1993	1994	1995	1996	1997	1998	1999	
BG	71,6	69,8	73,4	72,0	72,5	66,6	:	BG
CY	:	:	48,5	50,7	49,0	47,6	44,6	CY
CZ	74,3	73,7	75,8	72,9	74,1	75,3	:	CZ
EE	:	70,8	71,2	69,3	68,9	68,9	66,1	EE
HU	62,4	58,2	68,6	69,3	74,8	74,8	76,7	HU
LV	71,4	66,4	73,9	63,1	68,3	69,4	:	LV
LT	87,7	82,6	83,4	80,9	79,0	77,6	75,2	LT
MT	:	:	65,2	62,6	59,2	56,7	49,3	MT
PL	:	68,3	66,6	71,9	76,2	73,9	:	PL
RO	83,0	80,8	80,2	79,7	78,8	79,1	:	RO
SK	:	:	:	:	- 7,6	110,8	95,2	SK
SI	:	78,6	79,7	79,3	79,5	79,9	:	SI
TR	:	64,3	65,3	71,5	67,0	62,0	:	TR

1C4SP

6

Total trade in services (exports and imports). % of current account total flows

	1993	1994	1995	1996	1997	1998	1999	
BG	20,6	22,2	18,8	19,6	19,2	24,3	:	BG
CY	:	:	43,5	41,1	42,4	42,8	45,0	CY
CZ	21,6	21,8	18,9	21,4	18,6	18,0	:	CZ
EE	:	23,3	24,1	25,4	24,7	25,3	27,4	EE
HU	16,7	18,6	21,2	21,2	16,7	17,2	16,6	HU
LV	24,9	27,0	21,5	31,2	25,6	24,3	:	LV
LT	9,5	13,5	13,4	15,4	16,0	16,2	18,3	LT
MT	:		25,3	26,5	27,3	26,5	22,0	MT
PL	:	19,3	22,9	18,7	15,8	16,8	:	PL
RO	13,0	14,4	15,3	15,0	14,5	12,7	:	RO
SK	:	:	:	:	0,3	- 0,9	- 4,3	SK
SI	:	16,5	15,4	16,0	15,8	15,1	:	SI
TR	:	22,9	22,4	18,5	23,2	26,8	:	TR

1C5SP

Exports of transport services as % of services total exports

	1993	1994	1995	1996	1997	1998	1999	
BG	36,9	29,9	34,5	32,1	33,6	25,3	:	BG
CY	:	:	13,0	13,7	13,0	12,5	9,4	CY
CZ	26,3	24,1	21,7	16,3	18,3	18,5	:	CZ
EE	66,7	65,7	42,7	39,8	49,9	47,9	46,8	EE
HU	2,6	1,8	8,6	7,0	8,8	10,9	10,1	HU
LV	79,6	91,4	91,6	62,7	69,3	63,4	:	LV
LT	83,5	64,5	59,3	44,9	42,9	39,1	36,6	LT
MT	:	:	24,9	24,1	24,9	26,7	27,4	MT
PL	:	36,4	28,5	28,0	34,6	26,3	:	PL
RO	36,4	36,5	31,5	36,6	38,6	41,4	:	RO
SK	:	23,9	25,9	31,1	34,1	32,5	35,7	SK
SI	:	26,9	25,0	22,6	22,8	26,2	:	SI
TR	11,6	11,3	11,7	13,5	11,3	13,4	17,7	TR

1C6SP

Imports of transport services as % of services total imports

	1993	1994	1995	1996	1997	1998	1999	
BG	41,1	37,4	41,6	39,0	43,2	37,4	:	BG
CY	:	:	52,1	51,8	47,9	49,3	47,3	CY
CZ	19,8	18,3	16,4	11,2	11,7	12,4	:	CZ
EE	48,0	45,0	44,7	45,3	46,8	45,1	41,0	EE
HU	6,9	7,9	10,4	9,0	12,3	10,9	10,6	HU
LV	63,4	45,8	62,2	23,3	30,4	29,1	:	LV
LT	63,1	52,3	58,7	44,2	40,1	30,6	27,1	LT
MT	:	:	49,0	48,3	47,9	47,0	49,4	MT
PL	:	35,4	24,8	26,3	27,3	24,8	:	PL
RO	37,3	33,2	33,2	35,5	29,2	33,8	:	RO
SK	:	10,1	16,7	19,4	16,3	19,0	20,1	SK
SI	:	37,0	31,3	28,4	25,1	26,4	:	SI
TR	30,2	25,2	28,1	27,2	22,1	26,4	25,8	TR

1C7SP

6

Exports of travel services as % of services total exports

	1993	1994	1995	1996	1997	1998	1999	
BG	26,2	28,8	33,0	28,4	27,6	54,0	:	BG
CY	:	:	60,9	58,5	58,6	58,0	59,7	CY
CZ	33,0	43,2	42,8	49,8	50,9	49,6	:	CZ
EE	14,9	17,5	40,6	43,7	36,0	36,4	37,0	EE
HU	42,1	46,0	51,1	53,9	60,5	59,5	60,1	HU
LV	2,9	2,7	2,8	19,1	18,6	17,5	:	LV
LT	11,2	21,3	15,9	39,6	34,8	41,4	50,4	LT
MT	:		63,1	59,3	58,1	55,5	55,8	MT
PL	:	34,7	21,6	32,1	25,6	39,3	:	PL
RO	24,7	39,7	39,5	33,8	34,5	21,4	:	RO
SK	:	25,2	26,2	32,5	25,1	23,4	26,0	SK
SI	:	50,5	53,5	57,8	58,1	54,5	:	SI
TR	37,2	40,0	33,9	43,3	36,1	30,8	31,7	TR

1C8SP

Imports of travel services as % of services total imports

	1993	1994	1995	1996	1997	1998	1999	
BG	20,9	19,6	15,3	15,9	18,9	36,7	:	BG
CY	:	:	29,3	31,6	34,5	35,9	37,2	CY
CZ	14,2	33,9	33,5	47,2	44,1	32,8	:	CZ
EE	9,8	11,6	18,1	17,1	16,6	17,0	23,8	EE
HU	28,6	31,6	29,5	27,2	26,8	27,0	28,0	HU
LV	14,4	10,3	9,9	50,3	49,2	40,2	:	LV
LT	4,6	13,4	21,3	39,3	30,9	33,6	43,4	LT
MT	:	:	28,5	29,0	26,5	24,1	24,0	MT
PL	:	8,3	5,7	9,1	10,1	11,5	:	PL
RO	21,3	37,0	38,3	34,2	35,1	24,5	:	RO
SK	:	17,7	17,5	23,8	20,9	23,0	20,2	SK
SI	:	33,1	37,6	38,1	37,5	37,5	:	SI
TR	23,7	22,9	18,1	19,7	20,2	17,8	16,4	TR

1C9SP

International trade in services other than transport and travel. Cover rates. %

	1993	1994	1995	1996	1997	1998	1999	
BG	92,4	96,8	84,2	95,9	117,1	100,8	:	BG
CY	:	:	369,4	415,4	409,5	517,0	549,5	CY
CZ	78,5	75,5	97,5	106,4	92,1	76,3	:	CZ
EE	56,3	48,5	79,0	82,5	70,0	67,6	75,9	EE
HU	93,3	90,9	98,1	104,5	84,0	68,2	64,3	HU
LV	205,9	29,7	59,6	104,5	91,9	85,2	:	LV
LT	12,9	35,4	121,2	110,4	88,4	69,5	61,2	LT
MT	:	:	74,8	103,2	103,1	90,9	92,0	MT
PL	:	89,1	107,4	94,4	98,4	88,0	:	PL
RO	82,3	68,6	83,6	78,3	59,2	58,1	:	RO
SK	:	- 99,6	- 94,1	- 65,2	- 67,3	- 76,6	- 65,9	SK
SI	:	120,8	100,7	:	:	71,0	:	SI
TR	299,5	267,9	293,9	165,3	207,3	236,6	- 160,4	TR

1C10P

6

Unemployment rate (Labour force survey). % of labour force

	1994	1995	1996	1997	1998	1999	
BG	20,5	14,7	13,7	15,0	16,0	17,0	BG
CY	2,7	2,6	3,1	3,4	3,4	3,6	CY
CZ	4,3	4,0	3,9	4,8	6,5	8,7	CZ
EE	7,6	9,7	10,0	9,7	9,9	11,7	EE
HU	10,7	10,2	9,9	8,7	7,8	7,0	HU
LV	:	18,9	18,3	14,4	13,8	14,5	LV
LT	17,4	17,1	16,4	14,1	13,3	14,1	LT
MT	4,1	3,7	4,4	5,0	5,1	5,3	MT
PL	14,4	13,3	12,3	11,3	10,6	15,3	PL
RO	8,2	8,0	6,7	6,0	6,3	6,8	RO
SK	13,7	13,1	11,3	11,8	12,5	16,2	SK
SI	9,0	7,4	7,3	7,4	7,9	7,6	SI
TR	8,1	6,9	6,0	6,7	6,8	7,6	TR

8S2AA

EE 1999: Second quarter. PL 1999: Fourth quarter (permanent survey with quarterly reporting). LT: in % of total population aged 14 +. RO 1994 and 1995: In % of total population aged 14 +. TR: average of April and October 1997,1998,1999 Household LFS revised results. Ongoing studies on 1995 and 1996 data.

Unemployment rate (Labour force survey). % of labour force

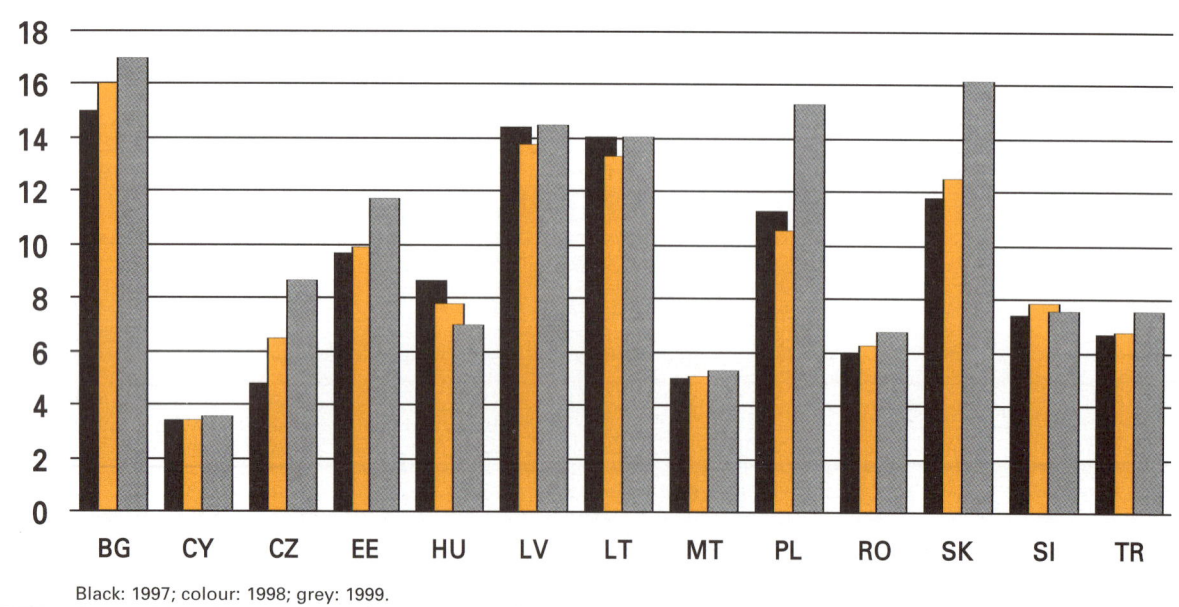

Black: 1997; colour: 1998; grey: 1999.

8S3AA

EE 1999: Second quarter. PL 1999: Fourth quarter (permanent survey with quarterly reporting). LT: In % of total population aged 14 +. TR: average of April and October 1997,1998,1999 Household LFS revised results.

Unemployment rate by age group. % of labour force (Labour force survey). 1999

8V5AE

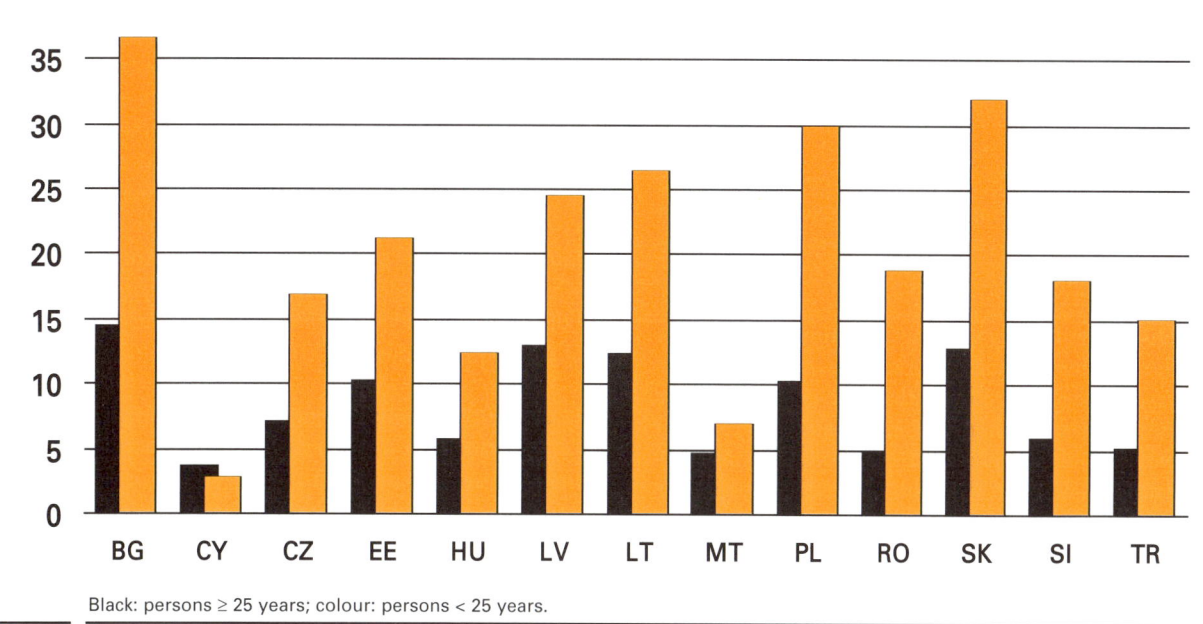

Black: persons ≥ 25 years; colour: persons < 25 years.

EE, PL: Second quarter.

6

Figures on gross earnings and labour costs are in principle collected using the Community recommendations.

– Gross earnings cover remuneration in cash paid directly and regularly to the employee, before tax deductions and social security contributions are made by the employer. For most EU countries, these statistics cover enterprises with 10 or more employees.

– The term 'labour costs' is taken to mean expenditure incurred by employers in order to employ workers. These costs can be subdivided into two main categories: direct and indirect. Direct costs are all earnings including earnings in kind. Indirect costs are mainly social contributions, whether statutory, conventional or voluntary. Community surveys on labour costs are carried out every four years and cover enterprises with 10 or more employees.

The following notes were included by the candidate countries to complete the figures on gross earnings and labour costs.

Bulgaria: Data on gross earnings come from the 'Annual employment and earnings survey'. Data on labour costs are not available.

Cyprus: The data on both earnings and labour costs come from the annual survey on wages and salaries.

Czech Republic: Figures on gross monthly earnings for 1995 and 1996 (Table 2) covered enterprises with 25 or more employees except in industry, trade, hotels and restaurants where enterprises with more than 100 employees are covered and in financial intermediation — one or more employees. Since 1997 enterprises with 20 or more employees are covered irrespective of their activities with the exception of financial intermediation (one or more employees). The non-business sphere is covered in all years irrespective of the number of employees.

Estonia: Hourly earnings (Table 1) are calculated for hours actually worked. All enterprises with more than 19 employees are covered. Data on monthly earnings covers all size-classes in enterprises.

Hungary: Hourly earnings are estimated figures, as the number of hours worked has only been surveyed since 1999. Before that date only the labour costs survey contained information on hours worked by all employees. Earnings and labour costs data are calculated from the updated data of labour costs survey in 1996.

Latvia: All figures contain data on manual and non-manual workers together. Data on earnings are derived from regular surveys. Data on labour costs and structure of labour costs are derived from

labour cost surveys and relate to:
1997 — D by NACE Rev. 1, enterprises with 20 or more employees;
1998 — E, F, G by NACE Rev. 1 — enterprises with 10 or more employees;
1999 — C, H, I, J, K by NACE Rev. 1.

Lithuania: Data on earnings cover units with one or more employees and labour cost data cover units with 10 or more employees.

Malta: Hourly and monthly earnings and labour costs are based on data compiled by the Department of Labour and the Central Office of Statistics. Data on earnings for women were compiled from the Labour force survey 2000.

Poland: Data on average gross hourly earnings in industry (sections C–F) concern manual workers for 1996 and manual and non-manual (all employees) for 1997–99. Hourly labour costs per hour worked and data on the structure of labour costs for 1997–99 are based on estimates.

Slovak Republic: Statistics on earnings cover units with 20 or more employees (until 1997 with 25 or more employees). Statistics on labour costs cover units with one or more employees.

Slovenia: The source of data on earnings is the 'Monthly report on earnings and persons in paid employment in companies, enterprises and organisations' and covers all enterprises with three or more employees.
Data on labour costs are collected every four years with the labour cost survey and do not cover persons working part-time. For the years 1996, 1997 and 1998, data are estimated. The source of the data in Table 7 is the annual survey 'Earnings by level of professional skills'. The data include all activities.

Turkey: Data on gross earnings and labour costs are compiled by 'Annual manufacturing industry survey', 'Annual small-sized manufacturing industry survey', 'Annual mining and quarrying statistics survey', 'Construction and installation establishments survey', 'Annual electricity distribution survey', 'Annual electricity generation survey', 'Annual municipality water statistics survey', 'Annual natural gas distributions survey'. These surveys cover the local units in the industrial activities.

Data on hourly earnings do not include electricity, gas distribution and construction because the following data are not available:
– man-hours worked per year in construction and gas distribution;
– annual payments to operatives in gas distribution;
– annual payments to operatives;
– annual payments to administrative and other workers separately in electricity.

Earnings of women as percentage of men in sections C to K NACE Rev. 1

4AN7A

	1995	1996	1997	1998	1999	
BG	:	:	:	:	:	BG
CY	69,5	70,0	70,2	68,7	69,3	CY
CZ	:	75,8	:	:	:	CZ
EE	73,3	72,6	72,0	74,2	:	EE
HU	80,3	79,0	77,6	81,4	81,3	HU
LV	:	78,4	:	:	:	LV
LT	:	:	:	74,2	:	LT
MT	:	:	:	:	76,4	MT
PL	77,7	77,8	80,2	83,2	82,6	PL
RO	78,0	77,8	74,3	77,5	81,9	RO
SK	:	75,2	75,0	77,5	76,9	SK
SI	85,0	85,4	86,9	88,9	:	SI
TR	:	:	:	:	:	TR

CZ: Full-time employees, Sections A to O of NACE Rev. 1. EE: Hourly earnings, all activities. LV: Data from short-term statistics, bonuses included. PL: *Source:* the representative survey in September of 1995 to 1997 or as of October 1998–99. RO: Only for non-agricultural sectors; bonuses included. *Source:* Annual survey on earnings by occupations for the month of October 1998. SI: All activities; if only industry: 80.6 (1998).

Average gross hourly earnings in industry in sections C to F of NACE Rev. 1. ECU. Manual workers

4AN1A

	1995	1996	1997	1998	1999	
BG	:	70,57	80,38	105,66	:	BG
CY	5,22	5,44	5,94	6,20	6,36	CY
CZ	1,45	1,69	1,73	1,89	1,92	CZ
EE	0,97	1,12	1,28	1,42	:	EE
HU	1,36	1,61	1,83	1,85	2,03	HU
LV	:	:	1,26	1,35	1,46	LV
LT	0,74	0,71	0,98	1,20	1,27	LT
MT	3,92	4,35	4,38	4,45	4,69	MT
PL	:	1,67	2,08	2,28	2,87	PL
RO	105,56	110,96	104,95	125,60	:	RO
SK	:	1,30	1,35	1,40	1,53	SK
SI	:	:	3,88	4,18	4,37	SI
TR	1,41	1,43	1,67 *	:	:	TR

* Provisional figures. BG, RO: monthly earnings. CZ: excluding construction.

Average gross monthly earnings of all employees in sections C to K of NACE Rev. 1. ECU

4AN2A

	1995	1996	1997	1998	1999	
BG	:	67,22	75,72	100,17	:	BG
CY	1 104,00	1 152,00	1 181,00	1 240,00	1 342,00	CY
CZ	243,27	288,67	309,27	339,34	358,73	CZ
EE	170,84	209,34	242,33	276,18	291,10	EE
HU	239,60	248,05	277,07	288,55	317,94	HU
LV	138,51	152,66	197,53	220,73	226,33	LV
LT	100,40	132,62	182,29	212,09	240,06 *	LT
MT	637,94	689,43	759,14	763,55	836,24	MT
PL	224,73	262,68	294,17	322,41	415,18 *	PL
RO	109,54	116,52	111,31	136,49	:	RO
SK	:	231,31	269,02	280,15	271,13	SK
SI	681,21	700,78	736,73	790,48	824,91	SI
TR	342,20	342,40	404,20 *	:	:	TR

* Provisional figures. TR: only industry.

Hourly labour costs in industry. ECU. All employees

	1995	1996	1997	1998	1999	
BG	:	:	:	:	:	BG
CY	6,90	7,10	7,74	8,05	8,21	CY
CZ	2,36	2,72	2,88	3,14	:	CZ
EE	1,59	1,94	:	:	:	EE
HU	:	2,83	3,09	3,14	3,33	HU
LV	:	:	1,77	1,98	:	LV
LT	:	1,37	:	:	:	LT
MT	4,14	4,46	4,97	4,97	5,38	MT
PL	:	2,97	3,36	3,69	4,66	PL
RO	157,4	163,1	158,1	197,8	:	RO
SK	:	2,26	2,53	2,86	2,48	SK
SI	6,62	6.69*	7.05*	7.63*	:	SI
TR	:	:	:	:	:	TR

4AN3A

★ Provisional figures. RO: monthly labour costs.

Hourly labour costs in industry and services. ECU. All employees

	1995	1996	1997	1998	1999	
BG	:	:	:	:	:	BG
CY	6,63	7,25	7,88	8,14	8,31	CY
CZ	2,39	2,82	2,97	3,24	:	CZ
EE	1,90	:	:	:	:	EE
HU	2,86	2,86	3,14	3,26	3,43	HU
LV	:	:	1,77	1,58	2,32	LV
LT	:	1,32	:	:	:	LT
MT	4,69	5,07	5,58	5,62	6,16	MT
PL	2,95	3,38	3,73	:	4,84	PL
RO	153,99	161,11	160,16	201,97	:	RO
SK	2,32	2,53	2,49	2,91	2,45	SK
SI	7,03	7,24 *	7,58 *	7,83 *	:	SI
TR	:	:	:	:	:	TR

4AN5A

★ Provisional figures. BU, RO: monthly labour costs.

Structure of labour costs in %. Total labour costs = 100. Total industry. All employees

Direct costs. %

	1995	1996	1997	1998	1999	
BG	:	:	:	:	:	BG
CY	83,3	83,6	83,1	83,4	83,2	CY
CZ	70,6	70,9	71,0	71,1	:	CZ
EE	72,0	72,1	:	:	:	EE
HU	:	62,2	:	:	64,4	HU
LV	:	:	75,7	76,3	:	LV
LT	:	74,6	:	:	:	LT
MT	75,0	72,5	73,5	73,0	73,0	MT
PL	:	62,2	61,9	61,7	61,6	PL
RO	72,6	73,8	72,9	70,6	:	RO
SK	:	71,0	69,3	69,1	70,1	SK
SI	72,7	73.3*	73.7*	73.6*	:	SI
TR	85,6	84,9	84,2*	:	:	TR

★ Provisional figures.

Structure of labour costs in %. Total labour costs = 100. Total industry. All employees

Indirect costs. %

	1995	1996	1997	1998	1999	
BG	:	:	:	:	:	BG
CY	16,7	16,4	16,9	16,6	16,84	CY
CZ	29,4	29,1	29,0	28,9	:	CZ
EE	28,0	27,9	:	:	:	EE
HU	:	37,8	:	:	35,6	HU
LV	:	:	24,3	23,7	:	LV
LT	:	25,4	:	:	:	LT
MT	25,0	27,5	26,5	27,0	27	MT
PL	:	37,8	38,1	38,3	38,4	PL
RO	27,4	26,2	27,1	29,4	:	RO
SK	:	29,0	30,7	30,9	29,9	SK
SI	27,3	26,8 *	26,2 *	26,4*	:	SI
TR	14,4	15,1	15,8 *	:	:	TR

★ Provisional figures.

Structure of labour costs in %. Total Labour costs = 100. Total industry. All employees

Social security. %

	1995	1996	1997	1998	1999	
BG	:	:	:	:	:	BG
CY	16,7	16,4	16,9	16,6	16,8	CY
CZ	24,9	24,7	24,7	24,7	:	CZ
EE	:	:	:	:	:	EE
HU	:	31,4	:	:	25,7	HU
LV	:	:	23,6	23,3	:	LV
LT	:	22,6	:	:	:	LT
MT	10,0	10,0	10,0	10,0	10,0	MT
PL	:	26,9	:	:	:	PL
RO	22,9	21,7	21,7	19,6	:	RO
SK	:	26,2	26,5	24,8	24,4	SK
SI	17,8	17,1 *	16,7 *	16,9 *	:	SI
TR	8,8	9,9	10,5 *	:	:	TR

★ Provisional figures.

4AN4A

4AN4B

4AN4C

Structure of labour costs in %. Total labour costs = 100. Industry and services in sections C to K of NACE Rev. 1. All employees

Direct costs. %

	1995	1996	1997	1998	1999	
BG	:	:	:	:	:	BG
CY	86,5	86,5	86,1	86,0	85,9	CY
CZ	70,7	70,7	71,0	71,1	:	CZ
EE	:	:	:	:	:	EE
HU	:	62,1	:	:	64,0	HU
LV	75,0	72,5	73,5	73,0	73,0	LV
LT	:	:	75,7	76,9	76,8	LT
MT	:	74,6	:	:	:	MT
PL	:	61,5	61,1	60,8	60,6	PL
RO	72,9	73,7	71,1	69,5	:	RO
SK	:	72,4	70,1	69,5	70,3	SK
SI	72,9	73,7 *	74,0 *	73,6 *	:	SI
TR	:	:	:	:	:	TR

4AN6A

* Provisional figures.

Structure of labour costs in %. Total labour costs = 100. Industry and services in sections C to K of NACE Rev. 1. All employees

Indirect costs. %

	1995	1996	1997	1998	1999	
BG	:	:	:	:	:	BG
CY	13,5	13,5	13,9	14,0	14,1	CY
CZ	29,3	29,3	29,0	28,9	:	CZ
EE	:	:	:	:	:	EE
HU	:	37,9	:	:	36,0	HU
LV	25,0	27,5	26,5	27,0	27,0	LV
LT	:	:	24,3	23,1	23,2	LT
MT	:	25,4	:	:	:	MT
PL	:	38,5	38,9	39,2	39,4	PL
RO	27,1	26,3	28,9	30,5	:	RO
SK	:	27,6	29,9	30,5	29,7	SK
SI	27,1	26,3 *	26,0 *	26,4 *	:	SI
TR	:	:	:	:	:	TR

4AN6B

* Provisional figures.

Structure of labour costs in %. Total labour costs = 100. Industry and services in sections C to K of NACE Rev. 1. All employees

Social security. %

	1995	1996	1997	1998	1999	
BG	:	:	:	:	:	BG
CY	13,5	13,5	13,9	14,0	14,1	CY
CZ	24,8	24,7	24,7	24,6	:	CZ
EE	:	:	:	:	:	EE
HU	:	34,8	:	:	25,5	HU
LV	10,0	10,0	10,0	10,0	10,0	LV
LT	:	:	23,6	22,7	21,6	LT
MT	:	22,5	:	:	:	MT
PL	:	26,9	:	:	:	PL
RO	21,3	21,2	21,1	19,0	:	RO
SK	:	23,6	25,0	24,6	24,0	SK
SI	17,4	16,5*	16,4*	16,6*	:	SI
TR	:	:	:	:	:	TR

4AN6C

* Provisional figures.

6

7L4RD

Research and development expenditure, as % of GDP, all sectors

	1990	1991	1992	1993	1994	1995	1996	1997	
BG	2,38	1,53	1,64	1,18	0,88	0,62	0,52	0,52	BG
CY	:	0,18	0,18	:	:	:	:	:	CY
CZ	2,19	2,12	1,83	1,35	1,25	1,15	:	1,16	CZ
EE	:	:	:	:	:	:	:	:	EE
HU	1,60	1,07	1,05	0,98	0,89	0,74	0,66	0,73	HU
LV	:	:	0,58	0,48	0,42	0,52	0,46	0,43	LV
LT	:	:	:	:	0,52	0,48	0,52	0,57	LT
MT	:	:	:	:	:	:	:	:	MT
PL	0,96	0,81	0,83	0,83	0,77	0,70	0,72	0,72	PL
RO	:	:	:	0,91	0,77	0,80	0,71	0,58	RO
SK	:	:	:	-	1,02	1,04	1,02	1,18	SK
SI	1,80	1,04	1,91	1,60	1,77	1,71	1,44	1,42	SI
TR	:	:	:	:	:	:	:	:	TR

Further reading: R & D and innovation statistics in candidate countries and the Russian Federation. Eurostat. 2000.

CZ: 1991–94 data include non R & D activities. HU: 1990–93 data are not in line with Frascati Manual. RO: 1991–94 data include only current expenditure. SI: 1993–95 data overestimated.

Distribution of research and development expenditure by sectors of economy. 1998

7L5RD

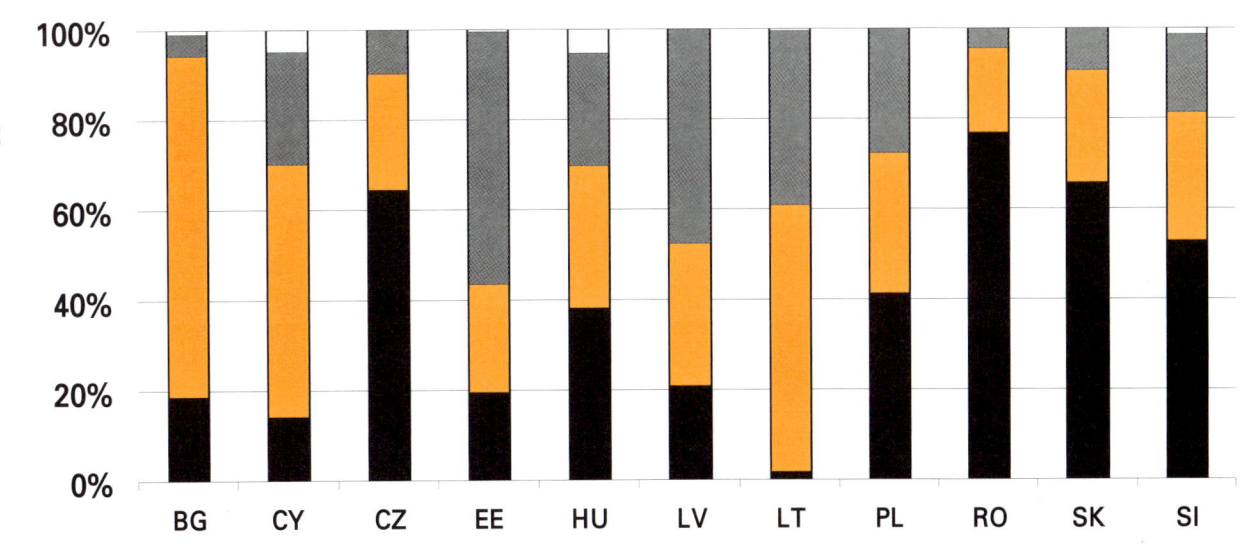

Black: business enterprise sector; colour: government sector; grey: higher education sector; white: private non-profit sector.

Further reading: R & D and innovation statistics in candidate countries and the Russian Federation. Eurostat. 2000.

Hungarian PNP: Eurostat estimate. SI: 1997 data.

Where is your nearest Data Shop? Addresses at the end of the book

507

Industrial production volume indices. Previous year = 100

	1994	1995	1996	1997	1998	1999	
BG	:	:	105,1	90,0	92,1	87,7	**BG**
CY	103,7	101,5	96,9	99,8	102,8	101,7	**CY**
CZ	102,1	109,2	102,0	104,5	101,6	96,9	**CZ**
EE	97,0	101,9	102,9	114,6	104,1	92,3	**EE**
HU	109,6	104,6	103,4	111,1	112,5	110,7	**HU**
LV	90,1	96,3	105,5	113,8	103,1	91,2	**LV**
LT	73,4	105,3	105,0	103,3	108,2	90,1	**LT**
MT	:	110,9	95,3	89,1	114,0	107,1	**MT**
PL	113,1	110,2	109,0	111,2	104,8	104,4	**PL**
RO	103,3	109,4	106,3	92,8	86,2	88,8	**RO**
SK	104,9	108,3	102,5	102,7	103,6	96,6	**SK**
SI	106,4	102,0	101,0	101,0	103,7	99,5	**SI**
TR	:	114,3	122,9	137,0	139,4	134,7	**TR**

8R1AA

LV: Sales of industrial production volume indices. MT: index based on ISIC. A new index based on NACE is being compiled. SK: 1995–98: calculated from goods production; 1999: industrial production index (IPI).

Gross agricultural production volume indices. Previous year = 100

	1994	1995	1996	1997	1998	1999	
BG	107,1	116,0	88,7	112,4	100,2	99,4	**BG**
CY	91,7	116,0	99,6	88,8	109,1	108,4	**CY**
CZ	94,0	105,0	98,6	94,9	100,7	100,6	**CZ**
EE	87,1	100,2	93,7	98,5	95,0	91,8	**EE**
HU	103,2	102,6	106,3	96,2	97,9	100,1	**HU**
LV	80,0	93,0	94,0	100,2	89,0	87,0	**LV**
LT	80,0	108,0	109,0	106,0	97,0	88,0	**LT**
MT	:	107,0	102,6	113,1	101,0	99,5	**MT**
PL	90,7	110,7	100,7	99,8	105,9	94,6	**PL**
RO	100,2	104,5	101,3	103,4	92,5	105,2	**RO**
SK	102,6	102,3	102,0	99,0	94,1	97,5	**SK**
SI	120,0	99,9	100,7	98,8	102,5	97,6	**SI**
TR	:	:	:	:	:	:	**TR**

8R1BB

LV: In 1993 prices. SK: 1996–99: comparable 1995 prices.

6

Structure of gross value added for 1999. % of total

	Agriculture	Industry	Construction	Services	
BG	17,3	23,1	3,7	55,9	**BG**
CY	4,2	13,4	7,7	74,7	**CY**
CZ	3,7	34,3	7,5	54,5	**CZ**
EE	5,7	19,9	5,4	69,0	**EE**
HU	4,9	28,0	4,6	62,6	**HU**
LV	4,0	20,0	7,6	68,4	**LV**
LT	8,8	23,3	7,8	60,1	**LT**
MT	2,5	24,8	2,3	70,4	**MT**
PL	3,8	27,7	8,9	59,6	**PL**
RO	15,5	30,9	5,4	48,2	**RO**
SK	4,5	29,3	5,8	60,4	**SK**
SI	3,6	31,4	6,1	58,9	**SI**
TR	14,3	21,8	5,3	58,6	**TR**

BG, CZ, EE, HU, LV, LT, PL, RO, SK, SI: GVA includes FISIM.
RO 1996 and 1997, and HU: services include statistical discrepancies.
HU: 1998 data.

Agriculture as percentage of total gross value added. 1999

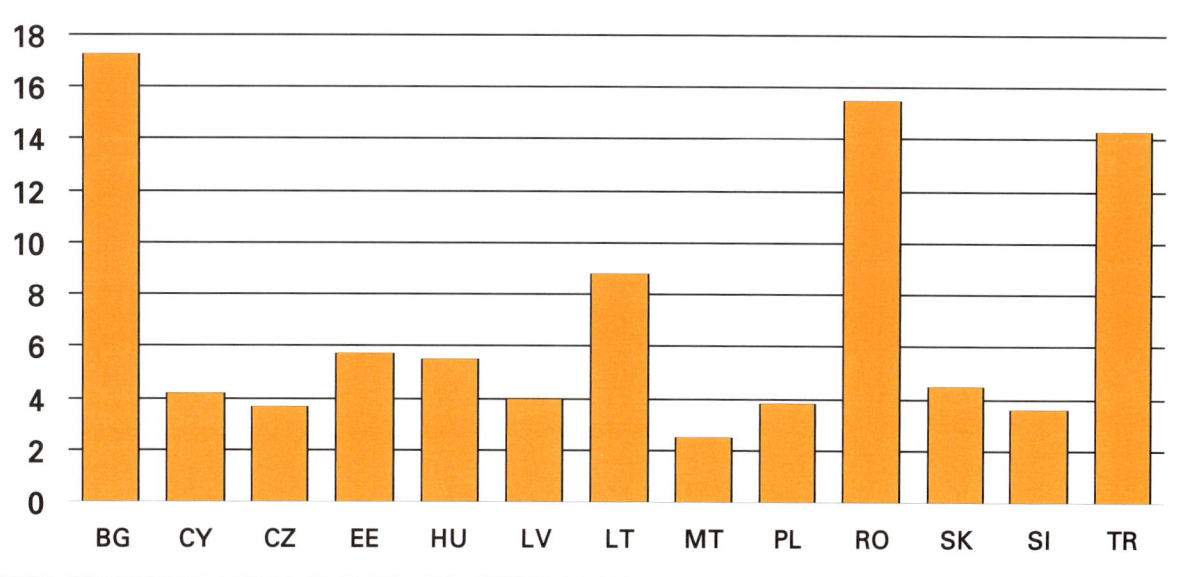

BG, CZ, EE, HU, LV, LT, PL, RO, SK, SI: GVA includes FISIM.
HU: 1998 data.

The candidate countries begin to be fully integrated as data providers of the crop products current statistics. The database includes most of them. Many candidate countries prepare themselves to implement the EU legislation. Consequently, the methodologies used for gathering the statistical information are not yet fully harmonised and, therefore, not yet assessed by the European Commission.

Areas (1 000 ha)

	Utilised agricultural area (1 000 ha)					Arable land (1 000 ha)					
	1994	1995	1996	1997	1998	1994	1995	1996	1997	1998	
BG	6 159	6 164	6 164	6 203	6 203	4 001	3 998	4 203	4 298	4 287	BG
CY	133	134	136	133	134	91	92	93	90	92	CY
CZ	4 281	4 280	4 279	4 280	4 272	3 158	3 143	3 098	3 091	3 090	CZ
EE	1 101	991	1 005	1 024	1 043	949	874	884	889	886	EE
HU	6 122	6 179	6 184	6 195	6 193	4 714	4 716	4 713	4 711	4 710	HU
LV	2 052	2 540	2 541	2 521	2 508	1 225	1 710	1 713	:	1 800	LV
LT	3 513	3 507	3 504	3 502	3 497	2 958	2 947	2 940	2 946	2 945	LT
MT	:	:	:	:	:	:	:	:	:	:	MT
PL	18 450	18 412	18 275	18 266	18 229	14 300	14 286	14 087	14 059	14 114	PL
RO	14 798	14 797	14 787	14 787	14 784	9 336	9 335	9 336	9 352	9 333	RO
SK	2 446	2 446	2 446	2 444	2 445	1 483	1 483	1 479	1 476	1 472	SK
SI	522	538	524	494	491	196	196	191	173	172	SI

7C1SR

7C2SR

Crops production (1 000 t)

	Total wheat		Total barley		Total potatoes		
	1997	1998	1997	1998	1997	1998	
BG	3 575	3 171	810	718	463	479	BG
CY	12	12	36	53	:	:	CY
CZ	3 640	3 845	2 485	2 093	1 402	1 520	CZ
EE	111	118	312	273	438	317	EE
HU	5 258	4 895	1 330	1 305	1 111	1 148	HU
LV	395	385	360	322	946	694	LV
LT	1 127	1 031	1 194	1 104	1 830	1 849	LT
MT	:	:	:	:	34	31	MT
PL	8 193	9 537	3 866	3 612	20 776	25 949	PL
RO	7 157	5 182	1 891	1 238	3 206	3 319	RO
SK	1 886	1 789	869	875	504	412	SK
SI	139	169	39	43	188	196	SI

7C3SR

Production of fruit and vegetables

	Apples (including cider apples). 1 000 t					Tomatoes. 1 000 t					
	1994	**1995**	**1996**	**1997**	**1998**	**1994**	**1995**	**1996**	**1997**	**1998**	
BG	76	149	204	161	:	477	530	324	227	:	**BG**
CY	8	9	10	10	11	30	38	36	34	37	**CY**
CZ	244	226	251	291	283	36	38	28	23	30	**CZ**
EE	14	31	9	20	9	0	0	3	3	2	**EE**
HU	657	353	552	500	482	224	231	263	220	330	**HU**
LV	49	121	81	254	110	3	2	8	10	9	**LV**
LT	19	63	16	86	14	:	:	:	0	1	**LT**
MT	0	0	0	0	0	19	19	20	21	22	**MT**
PL	1 441	1 288	1 952	2 098	1 687	375	401	231	219	356	**PL**
RO	363	457	660	664	365	716	731	689	463	678	**RO**
SK	57	38	79	80	83	75	67	71	84	72	**SK**
SI	77	73	73	55	68	15	15	14	:	:	**SI**

Compared production 1998. EU-15/candidate countries. 1 000 t

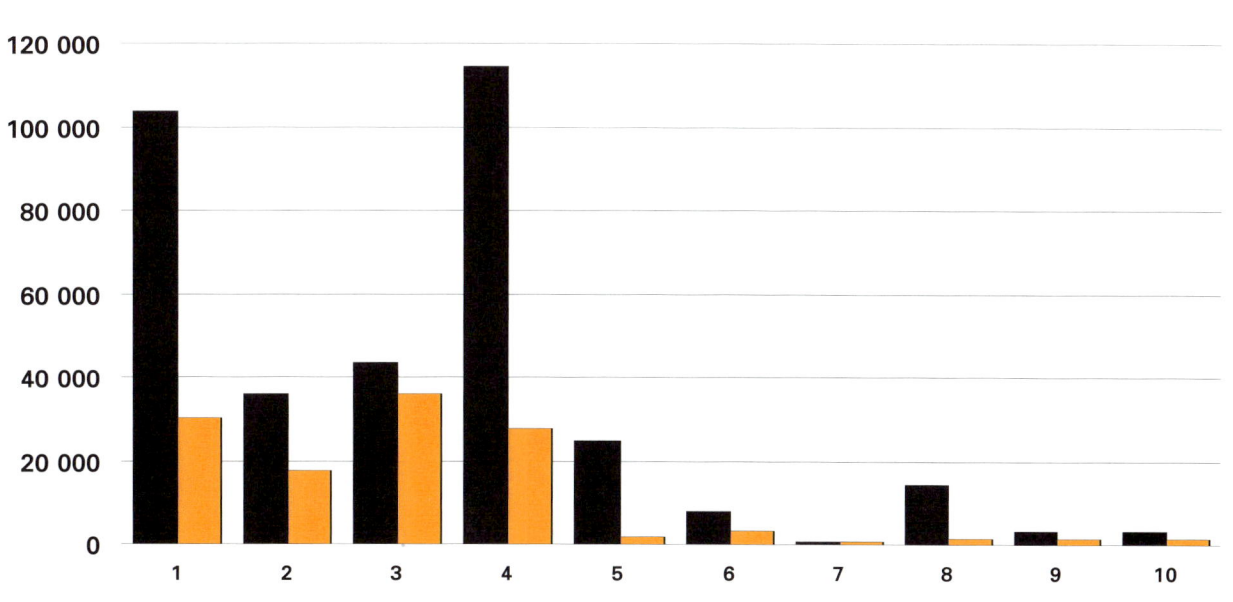

Black: EU-15; colour: aggregate of all candidate countries. 1: wheat; 2: maize; 3: potatoes; 4: sugar beet; 5: grapes; 6: apples; 7: plums; 8: tomatoes; 9: carrots; 10: onions.

eurostat

Want to be alerted on new publications?: www.europa.eu.int/comm/eurostat

Number of personal computers

	1994	1995	1996	1997	1998	1999	
EU-15	45 750 000	56 210 000	64 755 000	73 550 000	84 425 000	93 200 000	**EU-15**
BG	150 000	160 000	170 000	180 000	200 000	220 000	**BG**
CY	25 000	30 000	50 000	70 000	90 000	130 000	**CY**
CZ	450 000	550 000	700 000	850 000	1 000 000	1 100 000	**CZ**
EE	3 800	10 000	15 000	22 000	165 000	195 000	**EE**
HU	350 000	400 000	450 000	500 000	660 000	750 000	**HU**
LV	8 000	20 000	50 000	100 000	150 000	200 000	**LV**
LT	20 000	24 000	95 000	123 000	200 600	220 000	**LT**
MT	25 000	30 000	40 000	50 000	60 000	70 000	**MT**
PL	850 000	1 100 000	1 200 000	1 400 000	1 900 000	2 400 000	**PL**
RO	100 000	120 000	170 000	200 000	480 000	600 000	**RO**
SK	150 000	220 000	250 000	300 000	350 000	400 000	**SK**
SI	150 000	200 000	250 000	375 000	420 200	500 000	**SI**
TR	790 000	920 000	1 100 000	1 300 000	1 700 000	2 200 000	**TR**

7T2BC

Source: International Telecommunication Union.

Personal computers per 100 inhabitants

	1994	1995	1996	1997	1998	1999	
EU-15	12,4	15,1	17,4	19,7	22,5	24,8	**EU-15**
BG	1,8	3,0	:	:	2,4	2,7	**BG**
CY	3,5	4,1	:	:	12,1	17,3	**CY**
CZ	4,4	5,3	6,8	8,2	9,7	10,7	**CZ**
EE	0,3	0,7	1,0	1,5	11,3	13,5	**EE**
HU	3,4	3,9	4,4	4,9	6,5	7,4	**HU**
LV	0,3	0,8	:	:	6,1	8,2	**LV**
LT	0,5	0,6	:	:	5,4	5,9	**LT**
MT	6,8	8,1	:	:	15,9	18,5	**MT**
PL	2,2	2,9	3,1	3,6	4,9	6,2	**PL**
RO	0,4	0,5	0,8	0,9	2,1	2,7	**RO**
SK	2,8	4,1	4,7	5,6	6,5	7,4	**SK**
SI	7,5	10,1	12,6	18,9	21,2	25,3	**SI**
TR	1,3	1,5	1,7	2,1	2,5	3,2	**TR**

7T5BF

Personal computers per 100 inhabitants. 1999

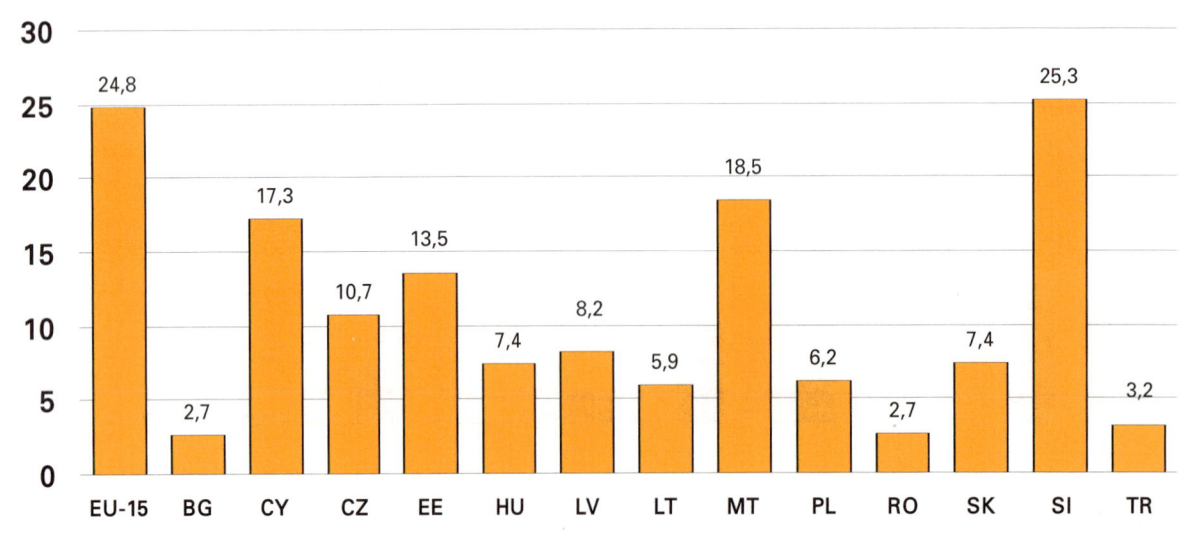

7T4BE

Number of Internet hosts

	1994	1995	1996	1997	1998	1999	
EU-15	869 328	1 893 830	3 062 880	4 652 110	6 417 190	8 488 684	**EU-15**
BG	100	1 100	3 300	6 800	10 300	16 832	**BG**
CY	:	390	1 456	3 014	5 491	6 225	**CY**
CZ	10 397	21 856	40 846	56 869	86 482	122 253	**CZ**
EE	1 154	3 578	7 980	15 831	24 158	30 103	**EE**
HU	7 000	16 000	30 000	68 000	96 000	119 642	**HU**
LV	524	1 321	5 780	7 088	14 332	18 877	**LV**
LT	127	458	1 730	4 045	9 802	14 193	**LT**
MT	:	86	493	821	1 838	6 005	**MT**
PL	11 000	23 000	53 000	88 000	131 000	171 217	**PL**
RO	520	1 740	7 820	13 570	23 510	36 249	**RO**
SK	1 400	2 900	7 900	14 500	22 100	28 183	**SK**
SI	1 600	5 600	13 800	19 500	22 900	23 559	**SI**
TR	1 883	5 549	17 507	35 027	48 873	78 878	**TR**

Source: International Telecommunication Union.

8L1AA

Internet hosts per 100 inhabitants

	1994	1995	1996	1997	1998	1999	
EU-15	0,2	0,5	0,8	1,2	1,7	2,3	**EU-15**
BG	0,0	0,0	0,0	0,1	0,1	0,2	**BG**
CY	:	0,1	0,2	0,4	0,7	0,8	**CY**
CZ	0,1	0,2	0,4	0,6	0,8	1,2	**CZ**
EE	0,1	0,2	0,5	1,1	1,7	2,1	**EE**
HU	0,1	0,2	0,3	0,7	0,9	1,2	**HU**
LV	0,0	0,1	0,2	0,3	0,6	0,8	**LV**
LT	0,0	0,0	0,0	0,1	0,3	0,4	**LT**
MT	:	0,0	0,1	0,2	0,5	1,6	**MT**
PL	0,0	0,1	0,1	0,2	0,3	0,4	**PL**
RO	0,0	0,0	0,0	0,1	0,1	0,2	**RO**
SK	0,0	0,1	0,1	0,3	0,4	0,5	**SK**
SI	0,1	0,3	0,7	1,0	1,2	1,2	**SI**
TR	0,0	0,0	0,0	0,1	0,1	0,1	**TR**

8L2BB

Internet hosts per 100 inhabitants. 1999

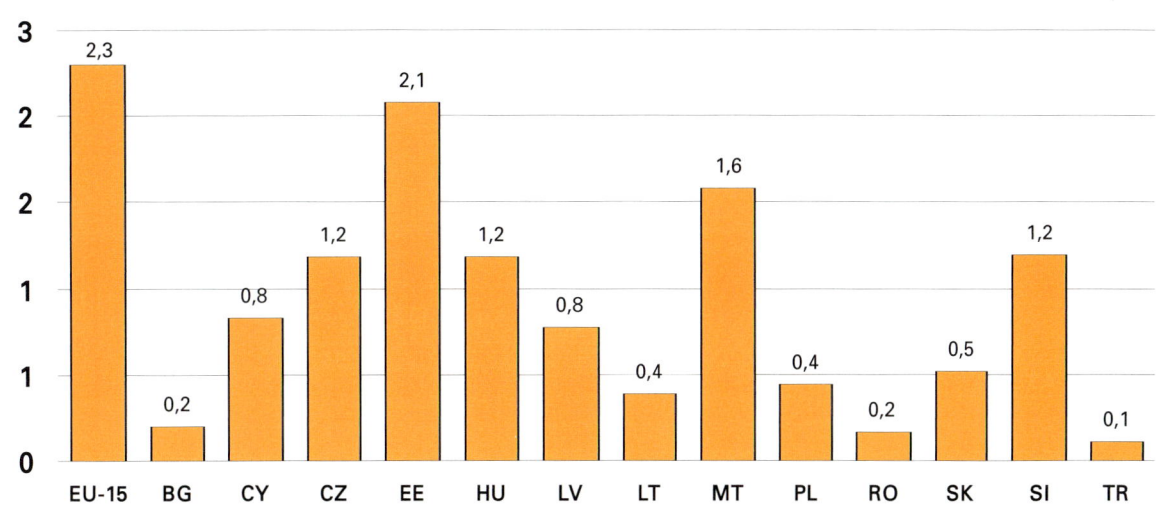

8L3CC

Number of mobile phone subscribers

	1994	1995	1996	1997	1998	1999	
EU-15	13 536 253	21 159 720	33 476 166	52 662 819	90 144 730	146 578 800	**EU-15**
BG	6 500	20 920	26 588	70 000	127 000	350 000	**BG**
CY	22 938	44 453	70 781	91 968	116 429	148 200	**CY**
CZ	30 429	48 900	200 315	526 339	965 476	1 944 600	**CZ**
EE	13 774	30 452	69 500	144 200	247 000	387 000	**EE**
HU	143 000	265 000	473 000	706 000	1 070 000	1 628 200	**HU**
LV	8 364	15 003	28 500	77 100	167 460	274 300	**LV**
LT	4 512	14 795	50 973	165 337	267 615	332 000	**LT**
MT	7 500	10 791	12 500	17 691	22 531	37 500	**MT**
PL	39 000	75 000	217 000	812 000	1 928 000	3 956 000	**PL**
RO	2 775	9 068	17 000	201 000	643 000	1 400 000	**RO**
SK	5 946	12 315	28 658	200 140	465 364	918 000	**SK**
SI	16 332	27 301	41 205	93 611	161 606	161 606	**SI**
TR	32 000	437 000	806 000	1 610 000	3 506 000	8 000 000	**TR**

8L4DD

Source: International Telecommunication Union.

Mobile phone subscribers per 100 inhabitants

	1994	1995	1996	1997	1998	1999	
EU-15	3,7	5,7	9,0	14,1	24,1	39,1	**EU-15**
BG	0,1	0,2	0,3	0,8	1,5	4,3	**BG**
CY	3,2	6,1	9,6	12,4	15,6	19,7	**CY**
CZ	0,3	0,5	1,9	5,1	9,4	18,9	**CZ**
EE	0,9	2,0	4,7	9,9	17,0	26,8	**EE**
HU	1,4	2,6	4,6	6,9	10,6	16,1	**HU**
LV	0,3	0,6	1,1	3,1	6,8	11,2	**LV**
LT	0,1	0,4	1,4	4,5	7,2	9,0	**LT**
MT	2,0	2,9	3,4	4,7	6,0	9,9	**MT**
PL	0,1	0,2	0,6	2,1	5,0	10,2	**PL**
RO	0,0	0,0	0,1	0,9	2,9	6,2	**RO**
SK	0,1	0,2	0,5	3,7	8,6	17,0	**SK**
SI	0,8	1,4	2,1	4,7	8,1	8,2	**SI**
TR	0,1	0,7	1,3	2,6	5,3	11,7	**TR**

8L5EE

Mobile phone subscribers per 100 inhabitants. 1999

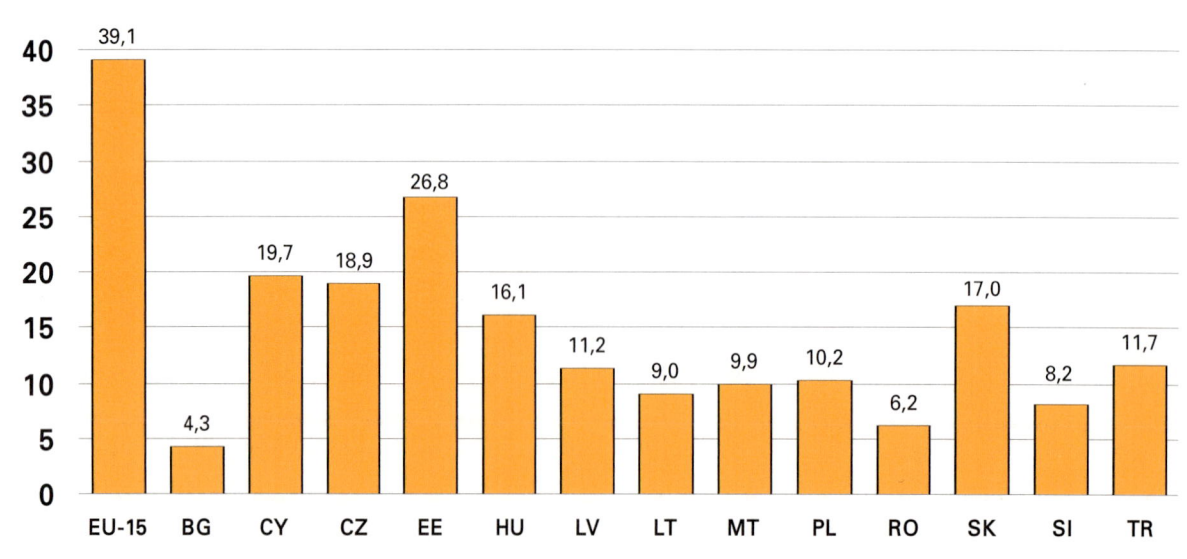

8L6FF

6

8D1MZ

Number of main telephone lines

	1994	1995	1996	1997	1998	1999	
EU-15	176 896 122	182 567 787	188 197 433	193 339 494	197 871 750	201 051 400	EU-15
BG	2 175 000	2 563 000	2 647 000	2 681 000	2 742 000	2 833 400	BG
CY	245 941	347 343	366 363	386 013	404 710	424 100	CY
CZ	1 624 000	2 444 000	2 817 000	3 280 000	3 741 000	3 806 100	CZ
EE	320 000	411 678	438 811	468 593	498 556	510 000	EE
HU	996 000	2 157 000	2 651 000	3 095 000	3 423 000	4 108 600	HU
LV	620 000	704 504	739 200	748 000	741 358	732 000	LV
LT	781 000	941 000	993 000	1 048 000	1 110 000	1 161 000	LT
MT	128 249	170 717	180 608	186 993	191 548	197 800	MT
PL	3 293 000	5 728 000	6 532 000	7 510 000	8 812 000	10 068 000	PL
RO	2 366 000	2 968 000	3 176 000	3 456 000	3 649 000	3 743 000	RO
SK	711 000	1 118 000	1 246 000	1 392 000	1 539 000	1 655 400	SK
SI	421 803	614 796	665 291	710 044	727 645	759 213	SI
TR	6 861 000	13 228 000	14 286 000	15 744 000	16 960 000	18 054 000	TR

Source: International Telecommunication Union.

8D2MZ

Main telephone lines per 100 inhabitants

	1994	1995	1996	1997	1998	1999	
EU-15	48,6	49,1	50,5	51,7	52,8	53,6	EU-15
BG	24,8	30,4	31,6	32,1	33,1	34,4	BG
CY	36,4	47,6	49,8	52,1	54,2	56,4	CY
CZ	15,7	23,7	27,3	31,8	36,3	37,0	CZ
EE	20,4	27,6	29,7	32,0	34,3	35,3	EE
HU	9,6	21,1	26,0	30,4	33,8	40,7	HU
LV	23,2	27,9	29,5	30,2	30,2	30,0	LV
LT	21,1	25,3	26,8	28,3	30,0	31,4	LT
MT	36,4	46,2	48,7	50,0	50,9	52,3	MT
PL	8,7	14,8	16,9	19,4	22,8	26,0	PL
RO	10,2	13,1	14,0	15,3	16,2	16,6	RO
SK	13,4	20,9	23,2	25,9	28,6	30,7	SK
SI	21,1	30,9	33,3	36,4	38,1	:	SI
TR	12,1	21,2	22,4	25,0	25,4	26,5	TR

Need access to Eurostat's databases? Ask your Data Shop

EUROSTAT YEARBOOK 2001

515

Railway network, in km per 1 000 km²

	1994	1995	1996	1997	1998	1999	
BG	:	39	39	39	39	39	BG
CY	0	0	0	0	0	0	CY
CZ	119	120	120	120	120	120	CZ
EE	23	23	23	23	23	21	EE
HU	83	83	83	83	83	83	HU
LV	37	37	37	37	37	37	LV
LT	41	41	40	40	40	38	LT
MT	0	0	0	0	0	0	MT
PL	78	77	75	75	74	73	PL
RO	48	48	48	48	46	46	RO
SK	75	75	75	75	75	75	SK
SI	59	59	59	59	59	59	SI
TR	11	11	11	11	11	11	TR

TR: Calculated by Eurostat.

8R3CC

Length of motorways, in km

	1994	1995	1996	1997	1998	1999	
BG	:	314	314	314	319	324	BG
CY	158	168	194	199	204	216	CY
CZ	392	414	423	485	498	498	CZ
EE	:	64	66	68	74	87	EE
HU	293	335	365	381	448	448	HU
LV	0	0	0	0	0	0	LV
LT	394	394	404	410	417	417	LT
MT	:	:	:	157	157	157	MT
PL	:	246	258	264	268	268	PL
RO	113	113	113	113	113	113	RO
SK	:	198	215	219	288	295	SK
SI	206	293	310	330	369	399	SI
TR	1 167	1 246	1 405	1 528	1 726	1 749	TR

EE, MT: Semi-motorways.

8R3BB

6

annexes

ACP
African, Caribbean and Pacific States party to the Lomé Convention.

Activity rate
People in the labour force as a percentage of all people of 15 years and over.

Agricultural area - utilised
All agricultural land in use, whether arable or permanently under grass or crops.

Agricultural holding
Defined by a number of characteristics laid down by the European Commission in order to obtain the highest possible degree of comparability within the Union. These characteristics comprise a list of agricultural products, definition of management and production means including labour.

Agrifood
Food products from agriculture, determined according to the standard international trade classification (SITC).

Annual work unit (AWU)
Time worked by one person employed full-time over a whole year.

Asylum-seekers
People awaiting a decision on applications for refugee status.

Balance of payments
This aims at identifying and recording transactions between residents of a country and non-residents. It is divided into the current account and capital account.

Balance of trade in merchandise
Component of the balance of payments which differs from the balance drawn up on the basis of international trade statistics because of methodological differences. It includes all movable property whose ownership is transferred from a resident to a non-resident or vice versa. These figures should be based on customs data which are imports at cif values (including costs relating to transport and insurance) and exports at fob values (excluding transport costs). Imports at cif values are corrected to imports at fob values in order to classify costs relating to transport and insurance as transport services and insurance services. Transactions involving goods crossing a border without change of ownership are not regarded as exports, but transactions in goods between residents and non-residents are regarded as exports, even if the goods do not cross a border.

Balance of trade in services
This includes three main sub-balances: transport, tourism and other services. Service flows are recorded as the economic value of services. Some of these flows are under evaluated, either because of compensation mechanisms or because they are collected on a net basis.

Bonds
Securities issued by governments, companies, banks and other institutions. They are normally interest bearing and have a fixed redemption value on a given date.

Business services
These include technical services such as engineering, architecture and technical studies; computer services such as software design and database management; and other professional services such as legal, accounting, consultancy and management services.

CAP
Common agricultural policy which was established to increase agricultural productivity, to ensure a fair standard of living for the agricultural community, to stabilise markets, to guarantee the availability of supplies and to ensure reasonable consumer prices. It includes milk quotas and set-aside programmes, and encourages farmers to take early retirement.

Capital transfers
Unrequited transfers which are designed to finance gross capital formation, other forms of accumulation, or long-term expenditure of the recipient, and made out of wealth or savings of the donor, or which are non-recurrent (quite irregular) for either party to the transaction. Capital transfers do not themselves redistribute income but redistribute savings or wealth among different sectors of the national economy, or among national sectors and the rest of the world.

Causes of death
Here, these are based on the underlying cause of death, as indicated in Section (b) of the death certificate. Causes of death are defined on the basis of the World Health Organisation's international classification of diseases, adopted by most countries. Although definitions are harmonised, the statistics may not be fully comparable as classifications may vary when the cause of death is multiple or difficult to evaluate and because of different notification procedures.

Central government
All administrative departments of the State and other central agencies whose responsibilities extend over the whole economic territory, except for the administration of the social security funds.

cif values
Market values of goods or merchandise (at the customs' border of a country), including insurance and freight to an agreed port of destination but excluding unloading costs. The United States and Canada do not use cif values for their imports but fob values. The UN recommends imports measured in cif values.

CNE
Coefficient of non-erasure.

Collective households
Boarding houses, halls of residence and hospitals.

Comext
The Eurostat database on extra- and intra-EU trade. It has monthly, quarterly and annual data on the Member States and on some non-member countries.

Communications services
Postal and telecommunications services provided by public, semi-public and private companies.

Compensation of employees
All payments in cash and kind by employers in remuneration for the work done by their employees during the relevant period. The payments cover gross wages and salaries, employers' actual social contributions and imputed social contributions.

Consumption of fixed capital
Value, at current replacement costs, of the reproducible fixed assets used up during an accounting period as a result of normal wear and tear, foreseeable obsolescence and a normal rate of accidental damage. Unforeseen obsolescence, major catastrophes and depletion of natural resources are not included.

Convergence criteria
Monetary union can be summarised as follows:

Price stability: Member States should have a price performance that is sustainable and an average rate of inflation, observed over the period of one year before the examination, that does not exceed by more than 1.5 percentage points that of, at most, the three best-performing Member States in terms of price stability.

Government budgetary position: Member States are to avoid situations of 'excessive government deficits', that is to say that their ratio of planned or actual government deficit to GDP should be no more than 3 %, and that their ratio of (general) government debt to GDP should be no more than 60 %, unless the excess over the reference value is only exceptional or temporary or the ratios have declined substantially and continuously.
Exchange rates: Member States should have respected the normal fluctuation margins of the ERM (exchange rate mechanism) without severe tensions for at least the two years before the examination. In particular, the Member State shall not have devalued its currency's bilateral central rate against any other Member State's currency on its own initiative over the same period.
Long-term interest rates: Member States should have had an average nominal long-term interest rate over a period of one year before the examination that does not exceed by more than 2 percentage points that of, at most, the three best-performing Member States in terms of price stability.

Cover ratio
Exports divided by imports.

Crude steel equivalent
The weight of iron and steel products converted into the corresponding crude steel weight by special coefficients appropriate to each product and quality of steel.

Current account transactions
Exports (credits) and imports (debits) of goods and services, income from abroad from investment and labour, and unrequited transfers.

Current balance
Balance of current account: credits minus debits.

Day-to-day money rate
This usually denotes the rate at which banks lend and borrow among themselves overnight on the interbank market. This rate is a good indicator of the general level of short-term market interest rates since it reacts very quickly to changes in market conditions and is a determinant of other short-term interest rates. The day-to-day money rate is largely determined by the level of central bank interest rates, the most important of which is often the repo rate. The various central bank interest rates normally refer to the rates at which, under certain conditions, a central bank will lend to or take deposits from financial institutions.

Death rate, crude
Deaths per 100 000 inhabitants.

Deaths in road accidents
People killed outright or who died within 30 days as a result of the accident; this is calculated as a standard death rate (SDR).

Direct investment
Capital flows between foreign investors and domestic enterprises in which they have a lasting interest, for example, usually ownership of a large part of the equity capital. Direct investment also measures flows between domestic investors and their foreign affiliates. The figures include purchases and sales of equity capital and credits of all kinds granted by one enterprise to another. However, contrary to the definition recommended by the IMF, they do not include undistributed profits, due to lack of data from some EU countries. According to the IMF definition, a direct investment link is established when a resident enterprise owns 10 % or more of the shares of a resident enterprise in another economy. But also other thresholds or subjective criteria are used. The direct investment item includes not only the initial transaction (of lasting interest) but also all flows thereafter between the direct investor and its foreign affiliates.

Distributive trades

Wholesale businesses, sales agents, retail trade and repair of consumer goods and vehicles.

Dwelling

A room or a suite of rooms and its accessories, lobbies and corridors in a permanent building or structurally separated part thereof which, by the way it has been built, rebuilt or converted, is designed for habitation by one private household all the year. A dwelling is either a one-family dwelling in a house or an apartment in a block of flats.

Earnings in industry

All industries are included: manufacturing, energy, building and civil engineering.

Earnings, gross

Remuneration in cash paid directly and regularly by the employer at the time of each wage payment, before tax deductions and social security contributions.

Earnings, net

Calculated from gross earnings after deduction of social security contributions and taxes payable by employees and, where appropriate, after addition of family allowances. The calculations relate to the average earnings of manual workers in manufacturing establishments with 10 or more employees in October each year.

Economic territory

The economic territory of a country consists of the geographical territory administered by a government; within the territory, people, goods and capital circulate freely.

ECU

The former European currency unit may be considered as the cornerstone of the European Monetary System. It was composed of a basket of currencies (see below). In addition to its official use in the EMS, a private market for the ecu developed, allowing its use in monetary transactions and for denominating financial instruments including bonds. The ecu has been replaced by the euro, the new European single currency on 1 January 1999 at a ratio of one to one.

ECU basket

It was defined by specific amounts of 12 currencies of the Member States of the EU. At its inception on 13 March 1979, the ecu was made up of a basket of fixed amounts of the then nine currencies, which was identical at the outset to the European unit of account (EUA). The ecu was redefined twice: in September 1984 when the Greek drachma entered into the basket, and in September 1989 when the Spanish peseta and the Portuguese escudo were introduced. These redefinitions did not affect its external value. The currency composition of the ECU basket was frozen from

November 1993 until the single currency was introduced. The currencies of Austria, Finland and Sweden did not take part in the composition of the ECU basket because they were only members of the EU from January 1995.

EEA countries

In 1989, Jacques Delors, then President of the Commission, proposed a new form of partnership, which was to become the EEA Agreement. The EFTA States, at that time Austria, Finland, Iceland, Liechtenstein, Norway, Sweden and Switzerland, welcomed the ideas with enthusiasm; formal negotiations began in June 1990 and the Agreement was signed on 2 May 1992 in Oporto. The Agreement entered into force on 1 January 1994 and covered EU and all EFTA countries except for Liechtenstein and Switzerland. Since 1 January 1995, Austria, Finland and Sweden have participated in the EEA as EU Member States. Liechtenstein became a full participant in the EEA on 1 May 1995.

EFTA countries

The members of the European Free Trade Association (EFTA) are Iceland, Liechtenstein, Norway and Switzerland.

Emigrants

People travelling abroad with the intention of residing there for a certain minimum period, for example 12 months for Dutch emigrants leaving the Netherlands. Germans are emigrants when they leave their occupied residence. A Briton is an emigrant when intending to live abroad for more than 12 months, having been resident in the UK for the previous 12 months. An Irish person is an emigrant when he or she is already resident abroad, having been resident in Ireland one year previously. In 1976, the United Nations drew up recommendations on international migration statistics. Unfortunately, few countries follow them.

Employees

People attached to enterprises by a contract of employment guaranteeing them remuneration for the work rendered.

Employment rate

Persons in employment as a percentage of the population aged 15 or more.

EMS (European Monetary System)

Formally introduced on 13 March 1979, it was operational until 31 December 1998. Its purpose was 'to create a zone of monetary stability in Europe through the implementation of certain exchange rate, credit and resource transfer policies'. The EMS had three components: the ecu, the exchange rate mechanism (ERM) and the credit mechanism. At the end of its existence the currencies of all EU Member States except Sweden and the United Kingdom were members of the ERM.

EMU (economic and monetary union)
Union of, at first, 11 countries which will have a single currency, the euro. These countries are officially considered to have fulfilled the convergence criteria. The third stage of EMU began on 1 January 1999, when the member currencies were permanently fixed to the euro. The 11 countries have been joined by Greece on 1 January 2001. National currencies will be withdrawn during a maximum period of six months, and they will no longer be legal tender from 1 July 2002.

Energy balance sheets
These make up a uniform quantitative system that records energy availability on the one hand and its uses on the other. Gross inland consumption is the key aggregate of the balance sheets. The ratios of the other aggregates to gross inland consumption give their relative importance in the overall energy balances.

Energy consumption
Energy supplied to the consumers' door for all energy uses. It is measured net of energy losses and consumption of the energy sector. It also excludes consumption for non-energy purposes (among which is petrochemical production). Final use of petroleum products involves only refined products (for example motor spirit, gas oil, domestic fuel, kerosene and jet fuels), whereas final use of gas is mainly in the form of natural gas, which does not undergo a refining process.

Energy consumption, gross
Total primary energy produced, stocked and imported, net of exports. Gross inland consumption is gross consumption less fuel supply to maritime bunkers (for seagoing ships of all flags). It therefore reflects the energy necessary to satisfy inland consumption within the strict limits of the national territory.

Energy dependence, national
Dependence on the rest of the world is measured as net imports of energy (imports minus exports) as a percentage of gross consumption.

Energy intensity
Gross inland consumption divided by gross domestic product. Measured in toe per ecu.

Energy, primary, production of
Energy extracted from a natural source: coal, lignite, crude oil, natural gas and geothermal energy. Hydroelectric energy and nuclear energy are also considered as primary production. Nuclear energy is computed as primary production in the form of the heat released during the fission of uranium in the reactor.

Enterprise density
Number of enterprises per 1 000 inhabitants.

ERM (exchange rate mechanism)
Part of the European Monetary System aimed at achieving greater exchange rate stability. It had two elements: a parity grid of bilateral central rates and fluctuation bands, and the divergence indicator, which measured the extent to which each currency was deviating from its ecu central rate. It ceased to exist at the start of Stage III of monetary union.

ERM 2
On 1 January 1999 the ERM was replaced by the new exchange rate mechanism, ERM 2. It is aimed at preparing 'pre-in' countries for participation in the monetary union, while helping to ensure exchange rate discipline in the EU. The central currency in the system is the euro. At the end of 2000, the currencies of two countries were participating in ERM 2, with fluctuation margins of ± 2.25 % for Denmark and ± 15 % for Greece. Since Greece joined the euro zone on 1 January 2001, Denmark is currently the sole country in the system.

ESA
European system of integrated economic accounts. The new national accounts system ESA 95 has been gradually introduced since 1999 as an expanded and fuller version of the earlier ESA 79. In this way national accounts data — including the main component, gross domestic product (GDP) which covers all goods and services produced by a country in a given period — will be measured with increasing accuracy and exhaustiveness. When we prepared this issue of the Yearbook, only a few Member States and some candidate countries had supplied their consumption data based on ESA 95. Hence, these data under ESA 79 are reproduced in the publication.

Esspros
The European system of integrated social protection statistics. The Esspros methodology was revised by Eurostat in 1996 (Esspros Manual 1996).

Eurobarometer
Eurobarometer public opinion surveys have been conducted on behalf of the Directorate-General for Education and Culture of the European Commission each spring and autumn since autumn 1973. Besides general public opinion surveys, the Survey Research Unit of the Directorate-General for Education and Culture organises specific target groups, as well as qualitative (group discussion, in-depth interview) surveys in all Member States of the EU and, occasionally, in non-member countries.

European Union (EU)
Established on 1 November 1993 when the Maastricht Treaty came into force. On 31 December 1994 the EU had 12 Member States: Belgium, Denmark, Germany, Greece, Spain, France, Ireland, Italy, Luxembourg, the Netherlands, Portugal and the United Kingdom. From January 1995 the EU had three new Member States: Austria, Finland and Sweden.

EUR-11

Countries initially participating in monetary union in January 1999: Belgium, Germany, Spain, France, Ireland, Italy, Luxembourg, the Netherlands, Austria, Portugal and Finland.

Euro

The third stage of European monetary union began on 1 January 1999 with the introduction of the euro, the European single currency. Since that date the national currencies of the 11 Member States of the euro zone (Belgium, Germany, Spain, France, Ireland, Italy, Luxembourg, the Netherlands, Austria, Portugal and Finland) were fixed to the euro at irrevocable conversion rates (see table below). Their national currency became therefore a non-decimal subdivision. The ecu was replaced by the euro on a 1:1 basis.

The euro will exist until the end of the year 2001 only as book money (cheque, transfer, payment by card) and its use is voluntary (no compulsion — no prohibition). The coins and notes will be introduced on 1 January 2002, when the use of the euro will become compulsory. National currencies will be withdrawn during a maximum period of six months, and they will no longer be legal tender on 1 July 2002.

Fixed conversion rates (EUR 1 =)

40.3399	BEF
1.95583	DEM
166.386	ESP
6.55957	FRF
0.787564	IEP
1936.27	ITL
40.3399	LUF
2.20371	NLG
13.7603	ATS
200.482	PTE
5.94573	FIM

Greece joined the euro zone on 1 January 2001, with a fixed conversion rate of
GRD 340.75 = EUR 1.
The conversion rules of the national currencies to the euro and vice versa are very strict.
The official conversion rate with six significant figures has to be used for each conversion without rounding or truncation. To convert in euro the amount has to be divided by the conversion rate and for the opposite operation the amount has to be multiplied by the rate.
The conversion of a national currency of the euro zone to another currency of the euro zone has to be done via the euro using the conversion rates.
A conversion in another currency has to be done also via the euro but using the prevailing exchange rate of this currency to the euro.

Exchange rate

The price at which one currency is exchanged for another.

Extra-EU flows

All transactions between EU countries and countries outside the EU.

Family benefits

Social protection benefits which: (1) provide financial support to households bearing the burden of bringing up children; (2) provide financial assistance to people who support relatives other than children; and (3) provide social services specifically designed to assist and protect the family and, in particular, children.

Farm labour force

People employed in agricultural holdings including their work in areas other than agriculture.

Farm labour input

Employment in agricultural activities. According to the European system of integrated economic accounts (ESA), farm labour input does not include, for example, farmers' work in areas other than agriculture.

Farm structure

Surveys carried out every two years, the latest being in 1997.

Final agricultural output

Output net of intra-branch consumption of agricultural products, for example seeds and animal feedingstuffs produced by the agricultural branch and used directly by it. Data on income and productivity are based on the economic account for agriculture which form part of the European system of integrated economic accounts (ESA).

Financial sector

This sector comprises financial intermediation, insurance, except compulsory social security and auxiliary financial activities. The figures cover only some activities; for example, they do not include financial leasing, credit card companies and auxiliary activities.

Fixed capital formation

Under ESA 79 this represents the value of durable goods intended for non-military purposes and acquired by resident producer units to be used for a period of more than one year in their process of production, including the value of any services embodied in the fixed capital goods acquired. Fixed capital formation can be recorded as gross fixed capital formation (including consumption of fixed capital) or net fixed capital formation (excluding consumption of fixed capital).

Under ESA 95 the coverage of fixed capital formation has been EXTENDED to include matters previously considered as intermediate consumption:

– intangible elements (software, databases, literary and artistic originals particularly in the audiovisual domain)
– expenditure on mineral prospection (oil, ore), whether successful or not
– civil equipment used by the military (hospitals, (air)ports, lorries, educational establishments...)
– expenditure on items of value.

This change of definition results in significant increases in fixed capital formation between ESA 79 and ESA 95, e.g. for the year 1995:
– from + 3.8 % for Portugal
– up to + 17.1 % for Denmark, and
– + 7.2 % for both EUR-11 and EU-15.

fob values
Market values (at the customs' border of a country) of goods or merchandise, including transport and handling costs to an agreed port of loading.

GATT
General Agreement on Tariffs and Trade; a multilateral agreement signed in 1947 which covers all major trading countries. It remained a treaty until 1994, when it became the new 'World Trade Organisation' (WTO).

General government
Central government, local government and social security funds. General government units are engaged mainly in production of non-market services for collective consumption and/or in redistribution of national income and wealth. Their main resources come — directly or indirectly — from compulsory payments from resident households and enterprises outside general government.

General government debt
Total gross debt at nominal value outstanding at the end of the year and consolidated between and within the subsectors of general government.

General government revenue sources
Current taxes on income and wealth, taxes linked to production and imports, and capital taxes. Revenue from current taxes on income and wealth comes from taxes on personal income and on the profits of companies and other corporate bodies. Income from taxes linked to production and imports comes from VAT and other general turnover taxes. The resident sectors formed by taxpayers pay contributions not only to general government but also to other resident sectors, such as private insurance enterprises, and to non-resident sectors. Contributions paid by resident sectors, therefore, usually differ from general government revenue.

Government bonds
Official debt instruments issued by governments in order to fund budget deficits and to cover debt which is being redeemed. Government bond yields usually refer to secondary market yields, i.e. derived from the market where securities which are already in circulation are traded.

Greenhouse gases (GHGs)
Emissions from many sources; they may include some volatile compounds. The main GHGs are CO_2 and CH_4.

Gross domestic product at market prices (GDPmp)
Final result of the production activity of resident producer units. It corresponds to the economy's total output of goods and services, less intermediate consumption. Measured at market prices, it includes VAT on production and net taxes on imports.

Gross domestic product in purchasing power parities (PPPs)
Gross domestic product converted into the EU unit of purchasing power parity, based on relative prices and used to make volume comparisons.

Gross national product (GNP)
Gross domestic product plus net entrepreneurial and property income and labour income received from abroad. National disposable income, compiled as GNP plus net current distributive transactions with the rest of the world and net operating subsidies from EU institutions, shows the income available for national use. Net income from abroad covers, for example, property and entrepreneurial income from the rest of the world, accident insurance transactions and unrequited current transfers.

Gross value added at market prices
Final output minus intermediate consumption, plus subsidies minus taxes linked to production.

Harmonised Indices of Consumer Prices
Harmonised Indices of Consumer Prices (HICPs) are designed for international comparisons of consumer price inflation. The HICPs are the result of the collaboration between Eurostat and National Statistical Institutes (NSIs) of Member States on harmonizing the different methods used to compile price indices. The harmonisation process has resulted in an improved quality of the indices. HICPs are not intended to replace national Consumer Price Indices (CPIs).
HICPs are used by, among others, the European Commission and the European Central Bank (ECB) for monitoring of inflation in the Monetary and Economic Union (EMU) and the assessment of inflation convergence. The Monetary Union Index of Consumer Prices (MUICP) is used by the ECB as a main indicator for monetary policy management for the euro-zone.

Household
According to the household budget surveys, household should be defined in terms of having a shared residence and common arrangements. A household comprises either one person living

alone or a group of people, not necessarily related, living at the same address with common housekeeping, i.e. sharing at least one meal a day or sharing a living or sitting room.

Household consumption

The value of goods and services used for directly meeting household needs. It covers actual expenditure on purchases of goods and services, own consumption such as products from kitchen gardens, and the imputed rent of owner-occupied dwellings.

IMF

International Monetary Fund.

Immigrants

Either non-nationals arriving from abroad or nationals returning from abroad with the intention of residing in the country for a certain period. This period varies from one month for a Dutch person returning to the Netherlands to 12 months for any person entering the United Kingdom.

Implicit price index, GDP

Indicator of trends in the general level of prices of all goods and services in the economy as defined by GDP.

Inactive

People not in the labour force. They are neither employed nor unemployed. Apart from retired and disabled people, they include young people still in education and people working without earning an income, whether they do housework or charity work.

Income from patents

Transactions involving trade in technical knowhow and trade marks protected by licences and patents.

Indirect steel trade

Trade in non-ECSC steel products. Indirect foreign trade entails imports and exports of products containing steel by the processing industries.

Inflation

Here measured by the consumer price index.

Inland waters

Rivers, lakes, artificial water, impoundments and coastal lagoons, but excluding estuaries and water lying on the landward side of the 'normal baseline' along the coast.

Interest

Under the terms of the financial instrument agreed between a debtor and a creditor, interest is the amount that the debtor becomes liable to pay to the creditor over a given period of time without reducing the amount of principal outstanding.

Interpol

International Criminal Police Organisation (ICPO).

Insurance services

All types of insurance and reinsurance. Basically, the credits contain net profits (premiums received from abroad minus claims paid abroad) made by European insurance companies. The debits contain net costs (premiums paid minus claims received) of insurance taken out with foreign companies.

Intra-EU flows

All transactions declared by EU countries with other Member States.

Intrastat

The system applied since 1993 and based on a close link with the system of VAT declarations for collecting statistics relating to the trading of goods between EU Member States. Information on intra-EU trade is collected directly from the operators. The application of thresholds has meant that many are either exempt from formalities or have fewer data to transmit than previously.

ISCED

International standard classification of education, set up by Unesco in 1976.

ISCED 97

International Standard Classification of Education (ISCED) is an instrument suitable for compiling statistics of education internationally. It covers two cross-classification variables: levels and fields of education. Current version of ISCED dates from 1997 (see: http://unescostat.unesco.org/en/pub/pub0.htm).

ISCED 97 levels

Empirically, ISCED assumes that there exist several criteria which can help allocate educational programmes to levels of education. Depending on the level and type of education concerned, there is a need to establish a hierarchical ranking system between main and subsidiary criteria (typical entrance qualification, minimum entrance requirement, minimum age, staff qualification, etc.).

0: Pre-primary education
Initial stage of organised instruction, preceding primary education. In some countries, it may be compulsory.

1: Primary education
This level begins between four and seven years of age, is compulsory in all countries and generally lasts from five to six years.

2: Lower secondary education
It continues the basic programmes of the primary level, although teaching is typically more subject-focused. Usually the end of this level coincides with the end of compulsory education.

3: Upper secondary education
This level generally begins at the end of compulsory education. The entrance age is typically 15 or 16 years. Entrance qualifications (end of compulsory education) and other minimum entry requirements are usually needed. Instruction is

often more subject-oriented than at ISCED 2. The typical duration of ISCED 3 varies from two to five years.

4: Post-secondary non-tertiary education
These programmes straddle the boundary between upper-secondary and post-secondary education from an international point of view. They serve to broaden the knowledge of ISCED 3 graduates. Typical examples are programmes designed to pre-pare students for studies at level 5 while other pro-grammes prepare students for direct labour market entry.

5: Tertiary programmes
Entry to these programmes normally requires the successful completion of ISCED 3 or 4. On the basis of the type of subsequent education this level includes the following sub-levels:

5A: Tertiary programmes with academic orienta-tion. These are largely theoretically based.

5B: Tertiary programmes with occupation ori-entation. These are typically shorter than pro-grammes at level 5A and focus on occupationally specific skills geared for entry into the labour market.

6: Second stage of tertiary education
These programmes lead to an advanced research qualification and typically include the submission of a thesis or dissertation.

ISCED 97 fields
The classification comprises 25 fields of education (at 2-digit level) which can be further refined into 3-digit level. The following nine broad groups (at 1-digit level) can be distinguished:

0 – General programmes
1 – Education
2 – Humanities and arts
3 – Social sciences, business and law
4 – Science, mathematics and computing
5 – Engineering, manufacturing and construction
6 – Agriculture and veterinary
7 – Health and welfare
8 – Services

IUCN
International Union for the Conservation of Nature and Natural Resources. Protected areas on the IUCN list are classified according to their level of protection, characteristics and purposes. The list includes only areas over 1 000 ha (except for some islands), which have been designated and are man-aged by the highest competent authority, usually the national government.

Labour costs, direct
All expenditure including direct remuneration of employees, other bonuses and ex-gratia payments, payments for days not worked and benefits in kind, except canteen expenditure.

Labour costs, indirect
Mainly social contributions, whether statutory, contractual or voluntary, together with other social expenditure, vocational training costs and taxes.

Labour force
People in the labour market, i.e. employed and unemployed people.

Labour force survey (LFS)
This survey of the EU is conducted each spring. It covers the entire population living in private households and excludes those in collective house-holds such as boarding houses, halls of residence and hospitals. The definitions used are common to all EU countries and are based on international recommendations by the International Labour Office (ILO).

Life expectancy
Average number of years still to live for people of a given age under the prevailing conditions of mortality at successive ages of a given population.

Local government
All kinds of public administration bodies (except local agencies of social security funds) where responsibilities extend to only part of the economic territory. Social security funds, in particular, include autonomous pension funds and other insurance institutions which have premiums fixed without reference to the individual risks of the insured. Receipts of central and local government and of social security funds include transfers received from each other. Local government receipts include, for example, a large proportion of revenue from taxes collected by central govern-ment.

Long-term interest rates
Here measured as the yield to redemption on gov-ernment bonds.

Manufacturing industry
All activities included within Section D of NACE Rev. 1 (Statistical Classification of Economic Activities in the European Community). Both cottage industry (crafts) and large-scale activity are included. It should be noted that the use of heavy plant or machinery is not exclusive to Section D. It covers industries such as manufacture of non-metallic mineral products; chemicals; man-made fibres; manufacture of metal articles; food, drink and tobacco; textiles; leather and leather goods; timber and wooden furniture; manufacture of paper and paper prod-ucts, including printing and publishing; and pro-cessing of rubber and plastics. Not included are mining and extraction and building and civil engi-neering.

Market services
Recovery and repair, wholesale and retail trade, accommodation and catering, inland, maritime, air and auxiliary transport services, communications, and credit and insurance institutions and other market services. They are services produced for sale, normally with the aim of making a profit.

Maternity and family benefits
Support to households bringing up children and caring for relatives other than children. Benefits are in cash or in kind.

Migration, net
Immigrants minus emigrants.

Mortality rate, crude
Deaths per 100 000 inhabitants.

Mortality, infant
Deaths per 100 000 children aged less than one year.

Mortality, perinatal
Deaths per 100 000 live born children aged less than seven days.

NACE 70
General industrial classification of economic activities within the European Union (with regard to data from 1970 to 1990).

NACE Rev. 1
This is a revision of the general industrial classification of economic activities (with regard to data from 1991 onwards, see annex 'Classification of economic activities' at the end of this publication).

National citizens
Citizens with citizenship of the country in which they are actually living.

Net operating surplus
Gross domestic product at market prices minus compensation of employees paid by resident employers, taxes net of subsidies on production and imports levied by general government and by the rest of the world including EU institutions, and consumption of fixed capital. Net operating surplus comprises total property and entrepreneurial income from production.

Non-market services
These are measured by their cost of production and are mainly general government services. Other examples are private welfare institutions and outside domestic help. Non-market services do not include the production of goods and services by households using their unpaid labour for producing their own consumption. The value added generated by such activities is excluded from conventional macroeconomic aggregates.

Non-national citizens
Citizens without citizenship of the country in which they are actually living.

NUTS
This nomenclature of territorial units for statistics was drawn up jointly by Eurostat and the other Commission departments in order to provide a single and coherent territorial breakdown for the compilation of EU regional statistics. The current NUTS nomenclature subdivides the territory of the European Union into 78 NUTS 1 regions, 211 NUTS 2 regions and 1 093 NUTS 3 regions.

Official external reserves
These reserves are held by countries' monetary authorities for the purpose of financing balance-of-payments deficits or for influencing their currency's external value. They are made up of monetary gold, foreign currencies, special drawing rights (SDRs) of the International Monetary Fund (IMF), and reserves held with the IMF. Variations in the level of reserves normally reflect changes in foreign currency assets rather than in the other reserve components.

Other services
Services other than tourism and transport. They cover highly varied services such as insurance; trade earnings, banking, advertising, business, construction and communications services, fees and royalties from films and television, income from patents, and miscellaneous services.

Passenger-kilometre
Unit of measurement representing the transport of one passenger over one kilometre.

Permanently utilised land
Land under permanent crops and grassland. Permanent crops occupy the land for more than five years. They include fruit trees, soft-fruit bushes, olive trees, citrus plantations and vineyards, but exclude trees grown for wood or timber. Permanent grassland comprises meadows and pastures in constant use — five years or more — for herbaceous forage crops either cultivated or growing wild. The distinction between permanent grassland and wooded area is rather unclear, especially in cases where scattered trees and bushes are mixed with grasses used occasionally for grazing.

Population density
Number of inhabitants per square kilometre.

Population increase, natural
Births minus deaths.

PPPs
See Purchasing power parities.

PPS
See Purchasing power standards.

Purchasing power parities (PPPs)
They aim at improving comparisons of data on, for example, production of goods and services between countries when data converted at market exchange rates do not give a true comparison of different countries' price levels.

Purchasing power standards — PPS conversion rates specific to household consumption
These conversion rates indicate the national currency units needed, in the various countries, to purchase the same basket of goods and services. If national currency values are converted using these rates, this gives values that are directly comparable in terms of the purchasing power of households.

eurostat

Purchasing power of the ECU/euro
Calculated by multiplying the national consumer price index by the average monthly movement of the national currency against the ECU/euro. It measures the purchasing power of ECU 1/EUR 1 in the country concerned.

Real values
Calculated by deflating each EU country's nominal figures at current prices by the GDP implicit price index.

Refugee
Someone with a well-founded fear of being persecuted for reasons of race, religion, nationality, membership of a particular social group or political opinion; according to Article 1 of the United Nations Convention on Refugees 1951.

Renewable water resources
Long-term freshwater balance for a country, calculated as precipitation minus evaporation and transpiration plus inflows of water from neighbouring countries; according to the OECD definition of 1993.

Research and development (R & D)
Research and development (R & D) comprises creative work undertaken on a systematic basis in order to increase the stock of knowledge of man, culture and society and the use of this stock of knowledge to devise new applications.

Resident producer units
Units engaged in production on the domestic territory of a country.

Room
It should be big enough to hold an adult bed according to the national family budget surveys. This definition includes normal bedrooms, dining rooms, living rooms, habitable cellars and attics, kitchens and other separate spaces used or intended for habitation.

Roundwood production
Wood as raw material. It refers to all wood in the rough, whether destined for industrial use or as fuel. It comprises wood in its natural state as felled or otherwise harvested, with or without bark, and all wood obtained from removals.

Services
The terms service industry(ies), service sector(s) or simply service(s) are generally used to refer to economic activities covered by Sections G to K and M to O of NACE Rev. 1, and the units that carry out those activities.

Share yield
Annual dividends paid divided by market share prices, in percentage terms.

SITC
Standard international trade classification produced by the United Nations Organisation. Revision 3 was introduced in 1988. It is not possible to produce figures prior to 1988 according to SITC Rev. 3 except as estimates (see also NACE and the annex 'Classification of commodities' at the end of this publication.)

SMEs
Small and medium-sized enterprises employing less than 250 people. (According to the definition of the Directorate-General for Enterprise of the European Commission: very small enterprises: 1–9 employees; small enterprises: 10–49 employees; medium-sized enterprises: 50–249 employees; large enterprises: 250 or more employees.) SMEs form the backbone of the EU-15 enterprise culture where over 99 % of businesses employ fewer than 250 people.

Social contributions, actual
All payments made by insured people or their employers to institutions providing social benefits in order to acquire and/or preserve the right to these benefits. They may be voluntary or compulsory.

Social contributions, employers
Costs incurred by employers in order to secure entitlement to social benefits for their employees.

Social contributions, protected people
Payments made by individuals and households to social protection schemes in order to obtain or keep entitlement to social benefits.

Social protection
Social protection encompasses all interventions from public or private bodies intended to relieve households and individuals of the burden of a defined set of risks or needs, provided that there is neither a simultaneous reciprocal or an individual arrangement involved (definition from Esspros Manual 1996).

Social protection, benefits
Transfers in kind or in cash by social protection schemes to households and individuals to relieve them of the burden of a number of distinct risks or needs. The list of risks or needs that may give rise to social protection is fixed by convention in the Esspros Manual 1996 as follows:

(1) sickness/healthcare, (2) disability, (3) old age, (4) survivors, (5) family/children, (6) unemployment, (7) housing, (8) social exclusion not elsewhere classified.

Social protection, expenditure
Social protection expenditure comprises social protection benefits, administration costs and other expenditure. Administration costs are the costs charged to social protection schemes for their management and administration. Other expenditure consists of miscellaneous expenditure by social protection schemes such as interest payable by the scheme to banks and other creditors in respect of loans taken up and payment of taxes on income or wealth.

Social protection, receipts

Social contributions by employers and protected people, contributions by general government and other receipts. Social contributions by employers are all costs incurred by employers to secure entitlement to social benefits for their employees. They include all payments made by employers to the social protection institutions as well as social benefits paid directly by employers to employees (imputed contributions). General government contributions relate to the financing of social protection expenditure by central, State, regional or local governments in their role as public authorities rather than as employers. Other receipts come from a variety of sources, for example interest, rent and claims against third parties.

Social security funds

Central, State and local institutional units whose principal activity is to provide social benefits, and which fulfil each of the following criteria: (1) by law or regulation except regulations concerning government employees certain groups of the population are obliged to participate in the scheme or to pay contributions; (2) general government is responsible for the management of the institution in respect of settlement or approval of the contributions and benefits independently of its role as a supervisory body or employer; (3) general government guarantees the payment of the benefits.

SPACE

Statistique Pénale Annuelle du Conseil de l'Europe embraces annual statistics on Member States' penal policy collected since 1983 by the Council of Europe.

Standard death rate (SDR)

Death rate of a population of a standard age distribution. As most causes of death vary significantly with people's age and sex, the use of standard death rates improves comparability over time and between countries, as they aim at measuring death rates independently of different age structures of populations. The standard death rates used here are calculated by the WHO on the basis of a standard European population.

Stocks

All goods other than fixed capital goods held at a given moment by resident producer units.

Subsidies

Current transfers which general government or the institutions of the European Communities make as a matter of economic or social policy to producing or importing units with the objective of influencing their prices and/or costs.

Taxes linked to production and imports

Compulsory payments levied by general government, or by the institutions of the EU, on producer units in respect of production and import of goods and services or use of factors of production.

Producers are liable to pay them irrespective of whether they operate at a profit.

tkm (tonne-kilometre)

Unit of measurement of goods transport which represents the transport of one tonne of goods over one kilometre taking into account the distance actually travelled.

toe (tonne of oil equivalent)

Conventional standardised unit defined on the basis of a tonne of oil with a net calorific value of 41 868 joules per kilogram.

Tourism accommodation, demand for

This includes all types of accommodation: in hotels and similar establishments, camping sites, holiday dwellings, youth hostels, etc.

Tourist accommodation, supply of

This refers to the number of bed places in an establishment where people can stay overnight in permanent beds, discounting any extra beds set up at the customers' request.

Tourism and travel

On the debit side there is expenditure by residents living abroad for less than a year for whatever reason: leisure, work, health or study. The credit side includes the same activities by foreign travellers on the national territory.

Trade balance in merchandise

Difference between exports/dispatches and imports/arrivals calculated for international trade statistics on a cif-fob basis or fob-fob basis. Generally, the cif-fob basis is used except for the United States and Canada, which use fob-fob.

Trade in services

Payments in connection with trade in goods. They group the items 'merchanting' and 'trade commissions'. International merchanting comprises the balance on transactions involving purchase and resale of merchandises on behalf of the third parties. The merchanting item generally shows a surplus since it relates to profits by resident dealers.

Trade system, general

This covers trade according to the special trade system plus warehouse traffic. Goods in transit are not included. This trade system is at present used by for example, Norway and Canada.

Trade system, special

This covers flows of: (1) imports of goods released for free circulation and/or domestic use on arrival in, or departure from, warehouses, imports for inward processing and imports after outward processing; (2) exports of goods originating in a country or in free circulation there, exports after inward processing and exports for outward processing. Goods in transit and warehouse traffic are not included. The EU trade statistics are reported under this trade system.

Transport, international
Transport between two places (a place of loading/embarkment and a place of unloading/disembarkment) in two different countries, irrespective of the country in which the transport equipment is registered. It may involve transit through one or more additional countries.

Transport, national
Transport between two places (a place of loading/embarkment and a place of unloading/disembarkment) in the same country irrespective of the country in which the transport equipment is registered. It may involve transit through one or more additional countries.

Transport services
These comprise three main categories: freight transport, passenger transport and auxiliary services. Auxiliary services include all types of port services, for example handling and storage and the hiring of vehicles and vessels, together with crews.

Turnover
Turnover comprises the totals invoiced by the observation unit during the reference period, and this corresponds to market sales of goods or services supplied to third parties. Turnover includes all duties and taxes on the goods or services invoiced by the unit with the exception of the VAT invoiced by the unit vis-à-vis its customer and other similar deductible taxes directly linked to turnover. It also includes all other charges (transport, packaging, etc.) passed on to the customer, even if these charges are listed separately in the invoice. Reduction in prices, rebates and discounts as well as the value of returned packing must be deducted. Income classified as other operating income, financial income and extra-ordinary income in company accounts is excluded from turnover. Operating subsidies received from public authorities or the institutions of the European Union are also excluded. For NACE Rev. 1 classes 66.01 and 66.03, the corresponding title of this characteristic is 'Gross premiums written'.

Unemployed person
Person out of work who is available to start work within two weeks and is actively seeking a job; according to the internationally accepted definition.

Unemployment rate
The unemployed as a percentage of people in the labour force.

Unrequited current transfers
Transactions in which one sector provides goods and services to other national sectors or to the rest of the world without receiving any good or service in return, except for taxes linked to production and imports, and subsidies. Current transfers are different from capital transfers because capital transfers involve the acquisition or disposal of financial or non-financial assets.

Unrequited transfers
Transfers of private funds (e.g. by emigrant workers to their country of origin, or migrants to their country of destination) and official unrequited transfers, for example contributions to international organisations, public development aid, gifts and pension payments.

VOCs (volatile organic compounds)
Emissions of all hydrocarbons and hydrocarbons where hydrogen atoms are partly or fully replaced by other atoms. Methane (CH_4) may be included, whereas CO and CO_2 as well as CFCs should be calculated separately.

Waste water treatment plants
Primary treatment: removal of gross solids; secondary treatment: removal of organic material by bacteria under aerobic or anaerobic conditions; tertiary treatment: removal of nutrients, phosphorus and nitrogen by chemical or biological treatment. Capacity is measured by biochemical oxygen demand (BOD) or inhabitant-equivalents (IEs). An inhabitant-equivalent corresponds to the amount of daily discharged oxygen-demanding materials of which the oxygen consumption in biodegradation equals the average oxygen demand of the daily amount of wastewater from one inhabitant.

Woodland
Forests and other wooded areas according to the FAO definition. It embraces land under natural or planted stands of trees, whether productive or not, and also land from which forests have been cleared but which will be reforested in the foreseeable future. Shrubland, savannah, etc. may have been reported with forest and woodland or with permanent meadows and pastures.

EFTA: European Free Trade Association

Iceland, Norway, Liechtenstein, Switzerland.

ACP: African, Caribbean and Pacific countries, signatories to the Partnership Agreement

Sudan, Mauritania, Mali, Burkina Faso, Niger, Chad, Cape Verde, Senegal, Gambia, Guinea-Bissau, Guinea, Sierra Leone, Liberia, Côte d'Ivoire, Ghana, Togo, Benin, Nigeria, Cameroon, Central African Republic, Equatorial Guinea, Sao Tomé and Principe, Gabon, Congo, Congo (Democratic Republic of the), Rwanda, Burundi, Angola, Ethiopia, Eritrea, Djibouti, Somalia, Kenya, Uganda, Tanzania (United Republic of), Seychelles, Mozambique, Madagascar, Mauritius, Comoros, Zambia, Zimbabwe, Malawi, South Africa, Namibia, Botswana, Swaziland, Lesotho, Belize St Kitts and Nevis, Haiti, Bahamas, Dominican Republic, Antigua and Barbuda, Dominica, Jamaica, St Lucia, St Vincent and the Grenadines, Barbados, Trinidad and Tobago, Grenada, Guyana, Suriname, Papua New Guinea, Solomon Islands, Tuvalu, Kiribati, Fiji Islands, Vanuatu, Tonga, Samoa.

Mediterranean basin countries

Ceuta, Melilla, Gibraltar, Malta, Turkey, Albania, Slovenia, Croatia, Bosnia-Herzegovina, Yugoslavia, Former Yugoslav Republic of Macedonia, Morocco, Algeria, Tunisia, Libyan Arab Jamahiriya, Egypt, Cyprus, Lebanon, Syrian Arab Republic, Israel, West Bank/Gaza, Jordan.

OPEC: Organisation of Petroleum Exporting Countries

Algeria, Libyan Arab Jamahiriya, Nigeria, Venezuela, Iraq, Iran (Islamic Republic of), Saudi Arabia, Kuwait, Qatar, United Arab Emirates, Indonesia.

ASEAN: Association of South-East Asian Nations

Myanmar, Thailand, Lao People's Democratic Republic of, Vietnam, Cambodia, Indonesia, Malaysia, Brunei Darussalam, Singapore, Philippines, Latin American countries, Mexico, Guatemala, Honduras, El Salvador, Nicaragua, Costa Rica, Panama, Cuba, Haïti, Dominican Republic, Colombia, Venezuela, Ecuador, Peru, Brazil, Chile, Bolivia, Paraguay, Uruguay, Argentina.

SAARC: South Asian Association for Regional Cooperation

Pakistan, India, Bangladesh, Maldives, Sri Lanka, Nepal, Bhutan.

European Union (15)

France, Netherlands, Germany, Italy, United Kingdom, Ireland, Denmark, Greece, Portugal, Spain, Belgium, Luxembourg, Sweden, Finland, Austria.

EEA: European Economic Area

Iceland, Norway, Liechtenstein, EU.

Further reading: Ramon 'Nomenclature server'
http://europa.eu.int/comm/eurostat/ramon

CEEC: central and east European countries

Estonia, Latvia, Lithuania, Poland, Czech Republic, Slovakia, Hungary, Romania, Bulgaria, Albania, Slovenia, Croatia, Bosnia-Herzegovina, Yugoslavia, Former Yugoslav Republic of Macedonia.

Candidate countries

Malta, Turkey, Estonia, Latvia, Lithuania, Poland, Czech Republic, Slovakia, Hungary, Romania, Bulgaria, Slovenia, Cyprus.

NAFTA: North American Free Trade Agreement

United States, Canada, Mexico.

Mercosur: South American Common Market

Brazil, Paraguay, Uruguay, Argentina.

NICs: Newly-industrialised Asian countries

Singapore, Korea (Republic of), Taiwan, Hong Kong.

DAEs: dynamic Asian economies

Thailand, Malaysia, Singapore, Korea (Republic of), Taiwan, Hong Kong.

APEC: Asia Pacific Economic Cooperation

Russian Federation, United States, Canada, Mexico, Peru, Chile, Thailand, Vietnam, Indonesia, Malaysia, Brunei Darussalam, Singapore, Philippines, China, Korea (Republic of), Japan, Taiwan, Hong Kong, Australia, Papua New Guinea, New Zealand.

Extra-European Union 15

Other European countries, Africa, America, Asia, Oceania and Polar region, miscellaneous (countries not specified) extra.

CIS: Commonwealth of Independent States

Ukraine, Belarus, Moldova (Republic of), Russian Federation, Georgia, Armenia, Azerbaijan, Kazakhstan, Turkmenistan, Uzbekistan, Tajikistan, Kyrgyzistan.

OECD excluding EU

Organisation for Economic Cooperation and Development, excluding EU, Iceland, Norway, Switzerland, Turkey, Poland, Czech Republic, Hungary, United States, Canada, Mexico, Korea (Republic of), Japan, Australia, Australian Oceania, New Zealand, New Zealand Oceania.

Further reading: Ramon 'Nomenclature server'
http://europa.eu.int/comm/eurostat/ramon

eurostat

A.   Agriculture, hunting and forestry

B.   Fishing

C.   Mining and quarrying

CA.   Mining and quarrying of energy producing materials

CB.   Mining and quarrying, except of energy producing materials

D.   Manufacturing

DA.   Food products, beverages and tobacco

DB.   Manufacture of textiles and textile products

DC.   Manufacture of leather and leather products

DD.   Manufacture of wood and wood products

DE.   Manufacture of pulp, paper and paper products; publishing and printing

DF.   Manufacture of coke, refined petroleum products and nuclear fuel

DG.   Manufacture of chemicals, chemical products and man-made fibres

DH.   Manufacture of rubber and plastic products

DI.   Manufacture of other non-metallic mineral products

DJ.   Manufacture of basic metals and fabricated metal products

DK.   Manufacture of machinery and equipment n.e.c.

DL.   Manufacture of electrical and optical equipment

DM.   Manufacture of transport equipment

DN.   Manufacturing n.e.c.

E.   Electricity, gas and water supply

F.   Construction

G.   Wholesale and retail trade

50.   Sale, maintenance and repair of motor and cycle vehicles; retail sale of automotive fuel

51.   Wholesale and commission trade, except motor vehicles and motorcycles

52   Retail trade except of motor vehicles and cycles, repair of personal and household goods

H.   Hotels and restaurants

I.   Transport, storage and communication

60.   Land transport and transport via pipelines

61.   Water transport

62.   Air transport

63.   Supporting and auxiliary transport activities

64.   Post and telecommunications

J.   Financial intermediation

65.   Financial intermediation, except insurance and pension funding

66.   Insurance and pension funding, except compulsory social security

67.   Activities auxiliary to financial intermediation

K.   Real estate, renting and business activities

70.   Real estate activities with own property

71.   Renting of machinery and equipment without operator and of personal and household goods

72.   Computer and related activities

73.   Research and development

74.   Other business activities

L.   Public administration and defence; compulsory social security

M.   Education

N.   Health and social work

O.   Other community, social and personal service activities

90.   Sewage and refuse disposal, sanitation and similar activities

91.   Activities of membership organisations n.e.c.

92.   Recreational, cultural and sporting activities

93.   Other service activities

P.   Private households with employed persons

Q.   Extra-territorial organisations and bodies

0. Food and live animals

00. Live animals other than animals of Division 03
01. Meat and meat preparations
02. Dairy products and birds' eggs
03. Fish (not marine mammals), crustaceans, molluscs and aquatic invertebrates and preparations thereof
04. Cereals and cereal preparations
05. Vegetables and fruit
06. Sugars, sugar preparations and honey
07. Coffee, tea, cocoa, spices and manufactures thereof
08. Feedingstuffs for animals (not including unmilled cereals)
09. Miscellaneous edible products and preparations

1. Beverages and tobacco

11. Beverages
12. Tobacco and tobacco manufactures

2. Crude materials, inedible, except fuels

21. Hides, skins and fur skins, raw
22. Oilseeds and oleaginous fruits
23. Crude rubber (including synthetic and reclaimed)
24. Cork and wood
25. Pulp and waste paper
26. Textile fibres (other than wool tops and other combed wool), and their wastes (not manufactured into yarn or fabric)
27. Crude fertilisers, other than those of division 56, and crude minerals (excluding coal, petroleum and precious stones)
28. Metalliferous ores and metal scrap
29. Crude animal and vegetable materials, n.e.s.

3. Mineral fuels, lubricants and related materials

32. Coal, coke and briquettes
33. Petroleum, petroleum products and related materials
34. Gas, natural and manufactured
35. Electric current

4. Animal and vegetable oils, fats and waxes

41. Animal oils and fats
42. Fixed vegetable fats and oils, crude, refined or fractionated
43. Animal or vegetable fats and oils, processed; waxes of animal or vegetable origin; inedible mixtures or preparations of animal or vegetable fats and oils, n.e.s.

5. Chemicals and related products, n.e.s.

51. Organic chemicals
52. Inorganic chemicals
53. Dyeing, tanning and colouring materials
54. Medical and pharmaceutical products
55. Essential oils and resinoids and perfume materials; toilet, polishing and cleaning preparations
56. Fertilisers (other than those of Group 27)
57. Plastics in primary forms
58. Plastics in non-primary forms
59. Chemical materials and products, n.e.s.

6. Manufactured goods classified chiefly by material

60. Complete industrial plant appropriate to Section 6
61. Leather, leather manufacture, n.e.s., and dressed fur skins
62. Rubber manufacture
63. Cork and wood manufacture (excluding furniture)
64. Paper, paperboard and articles of paper pulp, of paper or of paperboard
65. Textile yarn, fabrics, made-up articles, n.e.s., and related products
66. Non-metallic mineral manufactures, n.e.s.
67. Iron and steel
68. Non-ferrous metals
69. Manufacture of metals, n.e.s.

7. Machinery and transport equipment

70. Complete industrial plant appropriate to Section 7
71. Power-generating machinery and equipment
72. Machinery specialised for particular industries
73. Metalworking machinery
74. General industrial machinery and equipment, n.e.s., and machine parts, n.e.s.
75. Office machines and automatic data-processing machines
76. Telecommunications and sound-recording and reproducing apparatus and equipment
77. Electrical machinery, apparatus and appliances, n.e.s. and electrical parts thereof (including non-electrical counterparts, n.e.s. of electrical household-type equipment)
78. Road vehicles (including air-cushion vehicles)
79. Other transport equipment

8. Miscellaneous manufactured articles

80. Complete industrial plant appropriate to Section 8
81. Prefabricated buildings; sanitary plumbing, heating and lighting fixtures and fittings, n.e.s.
82. Furniture and parts thereof; bedding, mattresses, mattress supports, cushions and similar stuffed furnishings
83. Travel goods, handbags and similar containers
84. Articles of apparel and clothing accessories
85. Footwear
87. Professional, scientific and controlling instruments and apparatus, n.e.s.
88. Photographic apparatus, equipment and supplies and optical goods, n.e.s.; watches and clocks
89. Miscellaneous manufactured articles, n.e.s.

9. Commodities and transactions not classified elsewhere in SITC

91. Postal packages not classified according to kind
93. Special transactions and commodities not classified according to kind
94. Complete industrial plant, n.e.s.
96. Coin (other than gold coin) not being legal tender
97. Gold, non-monetary (excluding gold, ores and concentrates)

European Commission

Eurostat Yearbook 2001

Sixth edition

Luxembourg: Office for Official Publications
of the European Communities, 2001

2001 — 535 pp.— 21 x 29.7 cm (printed version), also
availaible as an electronic version on CD-ROM

Theme 1: General statistics
Collection: Panorama of the EU
ISBN 92-894-0462-0 (printed version, Danish)
ISBN 92-894-0464-7 (printed version, English)
ISBN 92-894-0465-5 (printed version, French)
ISBN 92-894-0463-9 (printed version, German)
ISBN 92-828-8653-0 (electronic version: 1 CD-ROM con-
tains all 11 official languages of the European Union)
Price (excluding VAT) in Luxembourg: EUR 40 (printed ver-
sion)
Price (excluding VAT) in Luxembourg: EUR 40 (CD-ROM)

The book/CD-ROM has six chapters of statistics (tables,
graphs, maps) and comments followed by annexes including a
glossary, geographical nomenclature and classifications of economic activities and commodities.

The six chapters are:

1. The people, with figures on: age, sex and population
increase, life and life risks, family life, international migration,
non-national citizens, education, people in and outside the
labour market, earnings and working hours, social protection,
consumption and spending, housing.

2. The land and the environment, with figures on: population density and use of land, emissions and pollutants, fertilisers
and pesticides, waste and recycling.

3. National income and expenditure, with figures on: economic growth, contribution to output by industry, consumption and spending, factor incomes, government receipts and
spending, consumer prices and interest rates, balance of payments, trade in services, trade in goods, key figures on the
labour market, research and development.

4. Enterprises and activities in Europe, with figures on:
agriculture, forestry, fishing, industry, manufacturing, construction, energy, water, services, transport, tourism, telephone, computer and Internet penetration.

5. The European Union, with figures on: institutions and
budgets, the ecu, the internal economy, the European market,
and external trade.

6. The candidate countries, with figures on: population,
total area, gross domestic product, imports, exports and trade
balance, economic activity rate, unemployment, railways and
motorways, industrial and agricultural production, inflation
rates, labour cost, research and development, agriculture, education, telephone, computer and Internet penetration.

.... Eurostat Data Shops

BELGIQUE/BELGIË

Eurostat Data Shop
Bruxelles/Brussel
Planistat Belgique
Rue du Commerce 124
Handelsstraat 124
B-1000 Bruxelles/Brussel
Tél. (32-2) 234 67 50
Fax (32-2) 234 67 51
E-mail: datashop@planistat.be

DANMARK

DANMARKS STATISTIK
Bibliotek og Information
Eurostat Data Shop
Sejrøgade 11
DK-2100 København Ø
Tlf. (45) 39 17 30 30
Fax (45) 39 17 30 03
E-mail: bib@dst.dk

DEUTSCHLAND

Statistisches Bundesamt
Eurostat Data Shop Berlin
Otto-Braun-Straße 70-72
(Eingang: Karl-Marx-Allee)
D-10178 Berlin
Tel. (49) 1888-644 94 27/28
Fax (49) 1888-644 94 30
E-Mail:
datashop@statistik-bund.de

ESPAÑA

INE
Eurostat Data Shop
Paseo de la Castellana, 183
Oficina 009
Entrada por Estébanez
Calderón
E-28046 Madrid
Tel. (34) 91 583 91 67
Fax (34) 91 579 71 20
E-mail:
datashop.eurostat@ine.es
Member of the MIDAS Net

FRANCE

INSEE Info service
Eurostat Data Shop
195, rue de Bercy
Tour Gamma A
F-75582 Paris Cedex 12
Tél. (33) 1 53 17 88 44
Fax (33) 1 53 17 88 22
E-mail: datashop@insee.fr
Member of the MIDAS Net

ITALIA - ROMA

ISTAT
Centro di informazione
statistica — Sede di Roma
Eurostat Data Shop
Via Cesare Balbo, 11a
I-00184 Roma
Tel. (39) 06 46 73 31 02/06
Fax (39) 06 46 73 31 01/07
E-mail: dipdiff@istat.it
Member of the MIDAS Net

ITALIA - MILANO

ISTAT
Ufficio regionale per la
Lombardia
Eurostat Data Shop
Via Fieno, 3
I-20123 Milano
Tel. (39) 02 80 61 32 460
Fax (39) 02 80 61 32 304
E-mail: mileuro@tin.it
Member of the MIDAS Net

LUXEMBOURG

Eurostat Data Shop Luxembourg
BP 453
L-2014 Luxembourg
4, rue Alphonse Weicker
L-2721 Luxembourg
Tél. (352) 43 35-2251
Fax (352) 43 35-22221
E-mail:
dslux@eurostat.datashop.lu
Member of the MIDAS Net

NEDERLAND

STATISTICS NETHERLANDS
Eurostat Data Shop — Voorburg
Postbus 4000
2270 JM Voorburg
Nederland
Tel. (31-70) 337 49 00
Fax (31-70) 337 59 84
E-mail: datashop@cbs.nl

PORTUGAL

Eurostat Data Shop Lisboa
INE/Serviço de Difusão
Av. António José de Almeida, 2
P-1000-043 Lisboa
Tel. (351) 21 842 61 00
Fax (351) 21 842 63 64
E-mail: data.shop@ine.pt

SUOMI/FINLAND

STATISTICS FINLAND
Eurostat DataShop Helsinki
Tilastokirjasto
PL 2B
FIN-00022 Tilastokeskus
Työpajakatu 13 B, 2. Kerros,
Helsinki
P. (358-9) 17 34 22 21
F. (358-9) 17 34 22 79
Sähköposti:
datashop.tilastokeskus@
tilastokeskus.fi
URL:
http://www.tilastokeskus.fi/tk/k
k/datashop.html

SVERIGE

STATISTICS SWEDEN
Information service
Eurostat Data Shop
Karlavägen 100
Box 24 300
S-104 51 Stockholm
Tfn (46-8) 50 69 48 01
Fax (46-8) 50 69 48 99
E-post: infoservice@scb.se
Internet:
http://www.scb.se/info/
datashop/eudatashop.asp

UNITED KINGDOM

Eurostat Data Shop
Enquiries & advice and
publications
Office for National Statistics
Customers & Electronic
Services Unit B1/05
1 Drummond Gate
London SW1V 2QQ
United Kingdom
Tel. (44-20) 75 33 56 76
Fax (44-1633) 81 27 62
E-mail:
eurostat.datashop@ons.gov.uk
Member of the MIDAS Net

Eurostat Data Shop
Electronic Data Extractions,
enquiries & advice r.cade
1L Mountjoy Research Centre
University of Durham
Durham DH1 3SW
United Kingdom
Tel. (44-191) 374 73 50
Fax (44-191) 384 49 71
E-mail: r-cade@dur.ac.uk
Internet:
http://www-rcade.dur.ac.uk

NORWAY

Statistics Norway
Library and Information Centre
Eurostat Data Shop
Kongens gate 6
Boks 8131 Dep.
N-0033 Oslo
Tel. (47) 21 09 46 42/43
Fax (47) 21 09 45 04
E-mail: Datashop@ssb.no

SCHWEIZ/SUISSE/SVIZZERA

Statistisches Amt des Kantons
Zürich
Eurostat Data Shop
Bleicherweg 5
CH-8090 Zürich
Tel. (41-1) 225 12 12
Fax (41-1) 225 12 99
E-mail: datashop@statistik.zh.ch
Internet:
http://www.zh.ch/statistik

USA

HAVER ANALYTICS
Eurostat Data Shop
60 East 42nd Street
Suite 3310
New York, NY 10165
Tel. (1-212) 986 93 00
Fax (1-212) 986 69 81
E-mail: eurodata@haver.com

EUROSTAT HOME PAGE
www.europa.eu.int/comm/eurostat/

MEDIA SUPPORT
EUROSTAT
(only for professional journalists)
Postal address:
Jean Monnet building
L-2920 Luxembourg
Office: BECH A3/48 —
5, rue Alphonse Weicker
L-2721 Luxembourg
Tel. (352) 43 01-33408
Fax (352) 43 01-32649
E-mail:
Eurostat-mediasupport@cec.eu.int